North Carolina Rules of Court

Volume I – State

2016

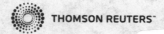

THOMSON REUTERS™

Mat #41608546

This publication was created to provide you with accurate and authoritative information concerning the subject matter covered; however, this publication was not necessarily prepared by persons licensed to practice law in a particular jurisdiction. The publisher is not engaged in rendering legal or other professional advice and this publication is not a substitute for the advice of an attorney. If you require legal or other expert advice, you should seek the services of a competent attorney or other professional.

ISBN: 978–0–314–67428–9

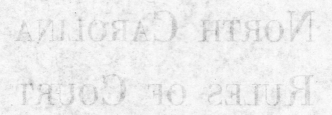

PREFACE

Designed for use in the office or courtroom, this pamphlet contains the North Carolina state rules.

WHAT'S NEW

North Carolina Rules of Court, Volume I – State, 2016, includes rules and associated material governing practice before the North Carolina state courts. It is current with amendments received through September 1, 2015.

CONTACT US

For additional information or research assistance, call the West reference attorneys at 1-800-REF-ATTY (1-800-733-2889). Contact our U.S. legal editorial department directly with your questions and suggestions by e-mail at editors.us-legal@thomsonreuters.com.

Thank you for subscribing to this product. Should you have any questions regarding this product please contact Customer Service at 1-800-328-4880 or by fax at 1-800-340-9378. If you would like to inquire about related publications, or to place an order, please contact us at 1-800-344-5009 or visit us online.

THE PUBLISHER

October, 2015

TABLE OF CONTENTS

RULES OF CIVIL PROCEDURE

(G.S. § 1A–1)
Adopted Pursuant to G.S. § 7A–34, Effective July 1, 1970

§ 1A–1. Rules of Civil Procedure

The Rules of Civil Procedure are as follows:

ARTICLE 1
Scope of Rules — One Form of Action

Rule 1. Scope of Rules

These rules shall govern the procedure in the superior and district courts of the State of North Carolina in all actions and proceedings of a civil nature except when a differing procedure is prescribed by statute. They shall also govern the procedure in tort actions brought before the Industrial Commission except when a differing procedure is prescribed by statute.

Added by Laws 1967, c. 954, § 1. Amended by Laws 1971, c. 818.

Comment

This rule gives literal expression to the scope of intended application, but that scope can be appreciated only by a consideration of the rules themselves and the new jurisdiction statute (G.S. 1–75.1 et seq.), the statutes left undisturbed by Session Laws 1967, c. 954, the statutes amended in s. 3 of c. 954, and those statutes repealed in s. 4 of c. 954. In general it can be said that to the extent a specialized procedure has heretofore governed, it will continue to do so.

Rule 2. One form of action

There shall be in this State but one form of action for the enforcement or protection of private rights or the redress of private wrongs, which shall be denominated a civil action.

Added by Laws 1967, c. 954, § 1.

Comment

This rule, drawn substantially without change from North Carolina Const., Art. IV, § 1, and from former § 1–9, preserves the fundamental reform of 1868, providing for the abolition of the forms of action and for the fusion of law and equity.

ARTICLE 2
Commencement of Action; Service of Process, Pleadings, Motions, and Orders

Rule 3. Commencement of action

(a) A civil action is commenced by filing a complaint with the court. The clerk shall enter the date of filing on the original complaint, and such entry shall be prima facie evidence of the date of filing.

A civil action may also be commenced by the issuance of a summons when

(1) A person makes application to the court stating the nature and purpose of his action and requesting permission to file his complaint within 20 days and

(2) The court makes an order stating the nature and purpose of the action and granting the requested permission.

The summons and the court's order shall be served in accordance with the provisions of Rule 4. When the complaint is filed it shall be served in accordance with the provisions of Rule 4 or by registered mail if the plaintiff so elects. If the complaint is not filed within the period specified in the clerk's order, the action shall abate.

(b) The clerk shall maintain as prescribed by the Administrative Office of the Courts a separate index of all medical malpractice actions, as defined in G.S. 90–21.11. Upon the commencement of a medical malpractice action, the clerk shall provide a current copy of the index to the senior regular resident judge of the district in which the action is pending.

Added by Laws 1967, c. 954, § 1. Amended by Laws 1987, c. 859, § 2.

Comment

Any system of procedure must provide an easily identifiable moment in time when it is possible definitely to say that an action has been "commenced." Under prior practice, former §§ 1–14 and 1–88 combined to say that in most cases an action was commenced with the issuance of summons. The exceptions related to actions in which service of summons was made by publication or was made outside the State pursuant to former § 1–98 and 1–104. In those cases, actions were deemed commenced when the affidavit required by these sections was filed. Under the federal rules, an action is commenced with the filing of a complaint with the court.

As can be seen, the General Statutes Commission preferred for the usual case the federal rule. The commission did so because it wished to take away the special consideration then accorded out-of-state defendants. But more importantly the Commission wished to remove a potential trap for an unwary plaintiff in a North Carolina federal court. A recent case in the Eastern District is illustrative. A plaintiff filed a complaint in the federal court for wrongful death five days before the statute of limitations had run. Because of a failure to post the required bond, summons was not issued until over a month later. The defendant moved to dismiss, relying on the statute. The plaintiff, of course, was relying on the federal rule as he was plainly in time if that rule applied. But the federal court quite properly held that the federal rule did not apply and that North Carolina practice as to when an action was commenced would govern. Thus the action was dismissed. Rios v. Drennan, 209 F. Supp. 927 (E.D.N.C. 1962). The court was faithfully following the United States Supreme Court's decision in Erie R.R. v. Tompkins, 304 U.S. 64, 58 S. Ct. 817, 82 L. Ed. 1188, 114 A.L.R. 1487 (1938), and its progeny, particularly Ragan v. Merchants Transf. & Whse. Co., 337 U.S. 530, 69 S. Ct. 1233, 93 L. Ed. 1520 (1949). The basic notion of the Rios and Ragan cases is that a federal court, irrespective of the federal rules, cannot give to a claim in a diversity action a "longer life ... than it would have had in the state court..." While one may sympathize with the plaintiff in the Rios case in his reliance on the federal rule, still it is clear that his reliance was misplaced. The trap which ensnared him would exist so long as the federal and State practices varied. The Commission believed this variance should be eliminated.

The Commission was not unmindful of the fact that there may be emergencies in which there is no time to prepare a complaint. To take care of these situations, the Commission incorporated in the second paragraph the essence of the first part of former § 1–121, allowing the commencement of an action by the issuance of a summons on application for permission to delay filing of a complaint and an appropriate order by the clerk.

It will be observed that the Commission did not at this point make any provision for discovery prior to filing a complaint. That problem is dealt with in Rule 27 (b) which provides in appropriate cases for discovery without action.

The second sentence of the first paragraph provides the same method formerly provided by § 1–88.1 for making a prima facie case in respect to the date of filing of the complaint. Rule 4(a) makes that method available also in respect to the date of issuance of a summons.

Rule 4. Process

(a) Summons — Issuance; who may serve. — Upon the filing of the complaint, summons shall be issued forthwith, and in any event within five days. The complaint and summons shall be delivered to some proper person for service. In this State, such proper person shall be the sheriff of the county where service is to be made or some other person duly authorized by law to serve summons. Outside this State, such proper person shall be anyone who is not a party and is not less than 21 years of age or anyone duly authorized to serve summons by the law of the place where service is to be made. Upon request of the plaintiff separate or additional summons shall be issued against any defendants. A summons is issued when, after being filled out and dated, it is signed by the officer having authority to do so. The date the summons bears shall be prima facie evidence of the date of issue.

(b) Summons — Contents. — The summons shall run in the name of the State and be dated and signed by the clerk, assistant clerk, or deputy clerk of the court in the county in which the action is commenced. It shall contain the title of the cause and the name of the court and county wherein the action has been commenced. It shall be directed to the defendant or defendants and shall notify each defendant to appear and answer within 30 days after its service upon him and further that if he fails so to appear, the plaintiff will apply to the court for the relief demanded in the complaint. It shall set forth the name and address of plaintiff's attorney, or if there be none, the name and address of plaintiff. If a request for admission is served with the summons, the summons shall so state.

(c) Summons — Return. — Personal service or substituted personal service of summons as prescribed by Rules 4(j) and (j1) must be made within 60 days after the date of the issuance of summons. When a summons has been served upon every party named in the summons, it shall be returned immediately to the clerk who issued it, with notation thereon of its service.

Failure to make service within the time allowed or failure to return a summons to the clerk after it has been served on every party named in the summons shall not invalidate the summons. If the summons is not served within the time allowed upon every party named in the summons, it shall be returned immediately upon the expiration of such time by the officer to the clerk of the court who issued it with notation thereon of its nonservice and the reasons therefor as to every such party not served, but failure to comply with this requirement shall not invalidate the summons.

(d) Summons — Extension; endorsement, alias and pluries. — When any defendant in a civil action is not served within the time allowed for service, the action may be continued in existence as to such defendant by either of the following methods of extension:

(1) The plaintiff may secure an endorsement upon the original summons for an extension of time within which to complete service of process. Return of the summons so endorsed shall be in the same manner as the original process. Such endorsement may be secured within 90 days after the issuance of summons or the date of the last prior endorsement, or

(2) The plaintiff may sue out an alias or pluries summons returnable in the same manner as the original process. Such alias or pluries summons may be sued out at any time within 90 days after the date of issue of the last preceding summons in the chain of summonses or within 90 days of the last prior endorsement.

Provided, in tax and assessment foreclosures under G.S. 47–108.25 and G.S. 105–374, the first endorsement may be made at any time within two years after the issuance of the original summons, and subsequent endorsements may thereafter be made as in other actions; or an alias or pluries summons may be sued out at any time within two years after the issuance of the original summons, and after the issuance of such alias or pluries summons, the chain of summonses may be kept up as in any other action.

Provided, for service upon a defendant in a place not within the United States, the first endorsement may be made at any time within two years after the issuance of the original summons, and subsequent endorsements may thereafter be made at least once every two years; or an alias or pluries summons may be sued out at any time within two years after the issuance of the original summons, and after the issuance of such alias or pluries summons, the chain of summonses may be kept up as in any other action if sued out within two years of the last preceding summons in the chain of summonses or within two years of the last prior endorsement.

Provided, further, the methods of extension may be used interchangeably in any case and regardless of the form of the preceding extension.

(e) Summons — Discontinuance. — When there is neither endorsement by the clerk nor issuance of alias or pluries summons within the time specified in Rule 4(d), the action is discontinued as to any defendant not theretofore served with summons within the time allowed. Thereafter, alias or pluries summons may issue, or an extension be endorsed by the clerk, but, as to such defendant, the action shall be deemed to have commenced on the date of such issuance or endorsement.

(f) Summons — Date of multiple summonses. — If the plaintiff shall cause separate or additional summonses to be issued as provided in Rule 4(a), the date of issuance of such separate or additional summonses shall be considered the same as that of the original summons for purposes of endorsement or alias summons under Rule 4(d).

(g) Summons — Docketing by clerk. — The clerk shall keep a record in which he shall note the day and hour of issuance of every summons, whether original, alias, pluries, or endorsement thereon. When the summons is returned, the clerk shall note on the record the date of the return and the fact as to service or non-service.

(h) Summons — When proper officer not available. — If at any time there is not in a county a proper officer, capable of executing process, to whom summons or other process can be delivered for service, or if a proper officer refuses or neglects to execute such process, or if such officer is a party to or otherwise interested in the action or proceeding, the clerk of the issuing court, upon the facts being verified before him by written affidavit of the plaintiff or his agent or attorney, shall appoint some suitable person who, after he accepts such process for service, shall execute such process in the same manner, with like effect, and subject to the same liabilities, as if such person were a proper officer regularly serving process in that county.

(h1) Summons — When process returned unexecuted. — If a proper officer returns a summons or other process unexecuted, the plaintiff or his agent or attorney may cause service to be made by anyone who is not less than 21 years of age, who is not a party to the action, and who is not related by blood or marriage to a party to the action or to a person upon whom service is to be made. This subsection shall not apply to executions pursuant to Article 28 of Chapter 1 or summary ejectment pursuant to Article 3 of Chapter 42 of the General Statutes.

(i) Summons — Amendment. — At any time, before or after judgment, in its discretion and upon such terms as it deems just, the court may allow any process or proof of service thereof to be amended, unless it clearly appears that material prejudice would result to substantial rights of the party against whom the process issued.

(j) Process — Manner of service to exercise personal jurisdiction. — In any action commenced in a court of this State having jurisdiction of the subject matter and grounds for personal jurisdiction as provided in G.S. 1–75.4, the manner of service of process within or without the State shall be as follows:

(1) Natural Person. — Except as provided in subdivision (2) below, upon a natural person by one of the following:

a. By delivering a copy of the summons and of the complaint to the natural person or by leaving copies thereof at the defendant's dwelling house or usual place of abode with some person of suitable age and discretion then residing therein.

b. By delivering a copy of the summons and of the complaint to an agent authorized by appointment or by law to be served or to accept service of process or by serving process upon such agent or the party in a manner specified by any statute.

c. By mailing a copy of the summons and of the complaint, registered or certified mail, return receipt requested, addressed to the party to be served, and delivering to the addressee.

d. By depositing with a designated delivery service authorized pursuant to 26 U.S.C. § 7502(f)(2) a copy of the summons and complaint, addressed to the party to be served, delivering to the addressee, and obtaining a delivery receipt. As used in this sub-subdivision, "delivery receipt" includes an electronic or facsimile receipt.

e. By mailing a copy of the summons and of the complaint by signature confirmation as provided by the United States Postal Service, addressed to the party to be served, and delivering to the addressee.

(2) Natural Person under Disability. — Upon a natural person under disability by serving process in any manner prescribed in this section (j) for service upon a natural person and, in addition, where required by paragraph a or b below, upon a person therein designated.

a. Where the person under disability is a minor, process shall be served separately in any manner prescribed for service upon a natural person upon a parent or guardian having custody of the child, or if there be none, upon any other person having the care and control of the child. If there is no parent, guardian, or other person having care and control of the child when service is made upon the child, then service of process must also be made upon a guardian ad litem who has been appointed pursuant to Rule 17.

b. If the plaintiff actually knows that a person under disability is under guardianship of any kind, process shall be served separately upon his guardian in any manner applicable and appropriate under this section (j). If the plaintiff does not actually know that a guardian has been appointed when service is made upon a person known to him to be incompetent to have charge of his affairs, then service of process must be made upon a guardian ad litem who has been appointed pursuant to Rule 17.

(3) The State. — Upon the State by personally delivering a copy of the summons and of the complaint to the Attorney General or to a deputy or assistant attorney general; by mailing a copy of the summons and of the complaint, registered or certified mail, return receipt requested, addressed to the Attorney General or to a deputy or assistant attorney general; or by depositing with a designated delivery service authorized pursuant to 26 U.S.C. § 7502(f)(2) a copy of the summons and complaint, addressed to the Attorney General or to a deputy or assistant attorney general, delivering to the addressee, and obtaining a delivery receipt. As used in this subdivision, "delivery receipt" includes an electronic or facsimile receipt.

(4) An Agency of the State. —

a. Upon an agency of the State by personally delivering a copy of the summons and of the complaint to the process agent appointed by the agency in the manner hereinafter provided; by mailing a copy of the summons and of the complaint, registered or certified mail, return receipt requested, addressed to said process agent; or by depositing with a designated delivery service authorized pursuant to 26 U.S.C. § 7502(f)(2) a copy of the summons and complaint, addressed to the process agent, delivering to the addressee, and obtaining a delivery receipt. As used in this sub-subdivision, "delivery receipt" includes an electronic or facsimile receipt.

b. Every agency of the State shall appoint a process agent by filing with the Attorney General the name and address of an agent upon whom process may be served.

c. If any agency of the State fails to comply with paragraph b above, then service upon such agency may be made by personally delivering a copy of the summons and of the complaint to the Attorney General or to a deputy or assistant attorney general; by mailing a copy of the summons and of the complaint, registered or certified mail, return receipt requested, addressed to the Attorney General, or to a deputy or assistant attorney general; or by depositing with a designated delivery service authorized pursuant to 26 U.S.C. § 7502(f)(2) a copy of the summons and complaint, addressed to the Attorney General or to a deputy or assistant attorney general, delivering to the addressee, and obtaining a delivery receipt. As used in this sub-subdivision, "delivery receipt" includes an electronic or facsimile receipt.

d. For purposes of this rule, the term "agency of the State" includes every agency, institution, board, commission, bureau, department, division, council, member of Council of State, or officer of the State government of the State of North Carolina, but does not include counties, cities, towns, villages, other municipal corporations or political subdivisions of the State, county or city boards of education, other local public districts, units, or bodies of any kind, or private corporations created by act of the General Assembly.

(5) Counties, Cities, Towns, Villages and Other Local Public Bodies. —

a. Upon a city, town, or village by personally delivering a copy of the summons and of the complaint to its mayor, city manager or clerk; by mailing a copy of the summons and of the complaint, registered or certified mail, return receipt requested, addressed to its mayor, city manager or clerk; or by depositing with a designated delivery service authorized pursuant to 26 U.S.C. § 7502(f)(2) a copy of the summons and complaint, addressed to the mayor, city manager, or clerk, delivering to the addressee, and obtaining a delivery receipt. As used in this sub-subdivision, "delivery receipt" includes an electronic or facsimile receipt.

b. Upon a county by personally delivering a copy of the summons and of the complaint to its county manager or to the chairman, clerk or any member of the board of commissioners for such county; by mailing a copy of the summons and of the complaint, registered or certified mail, return receipt requested, addressed to its county manager or to the chairman, clerk, or any member of this board of commissioners for such county; or by depositing with a designated delivery service authorized pursuant to 26 U.S.C. § 7502(f)(2) a copy of the summons and complaint, addressed to the county manager or to the chairman, clerk, or any member of the board of commissioners of that county, delivering to the addressee, and obtaining a delivery receipt. As used in this sub-subdivision, "delivery receipt" includes an electronic or facsimile receipt.

c. Upon any other political subdivision of the State, any county or city board of education, or other local public district, unit, or body of any kind (i) by personally delivering a copy of the summons and of the complaint to an officer or director thereof, (ii) by personally delivering a copy of the summons and of the complaint to an agent or attorney-in-fact authorized by appointment or by statute to be served or to accept service in its behalf, (iii) by mailing a copy of the summons and of the complaint, registered or certified mail, return receipt requested, addressed to the officer, director, agent, or attorney-in-fact as specified in (i) and (ii), or (iv) by depositing with a designated delivery service authorized pursuant to 26 U.S.C. § 7502(f)(2) a copy of the summons and complaint, addressed to the officer, director, agent, or attorney-in-fact as specified in (i) and (ii), delivering to the addressee, and obtaining a delivery receipt. As used in this sub-subdivision, "delivery receipt" includes an electronic or facsimile receipt.

d. In any case where none of the officials, officers or directors specified in paragraphs a, b and c can, after due diligence, be found in the State, and that fact appears by affidavit to the satisfaction of the court, or a judge thereof, such court or judge may grant an order that service upon the party sought to be served may be made by personally delivering a copy of the summons and of the complaint to the Attorney General or any deputy or assistant attorney general of the State of North Carolina; by mailing a copy of the summons and of the complaint, registered or certified mail, return receipt requested, addressed to the Attorney General or any deputy or assistant attorney general of the State of North Carolina; or by depositing with a designated delivery service authorized pursuant to 26 U.S.C. § 7502(f)(2) a copy of the summons and complaint, addressed to the Attorney General or any deputy or assistant attorney general of the State of North Carolina, delivering to the addressee, and obtaining a delivery receipt. As used in this sub-subdivision, "delivery receipt" includes an electronic or facsimile receipt.

(6) Domestic or Foreign Corporation. — Upon a domestic or foreign corporation by one of the following:

a. By delivering a copy of the summons and of the complaint to an officer, director, or managing agent of the corporation or by leaving copies thereof in the office of such officer, director, or managing agent with the person who is apparently in charge of the office.

b. By delivering a copy of the summons and of the complaint to an agent authorized by appointment or by law to be served or to accept service of process or by serving process upon such agent or the party in a manner specified by any statute.

c. By mailing a copy of the summons and of the complaint, registered or certified mail, return receipt requested, addressed to the officer, director or agent to be served as specified in paragraphs a and b.

d. By depositing with a designated delivery service authorized pursuant to 26 U.S.C. § 7502(f)(2) a copy of the summons and complaint, addressed to the officer, director, or agent to be served as specified in paragraphs a. and b., delivering to the addressee, and obtaining a delivery receipt. As used in this sub-subdivision, "delivery receipt" includes an electronic or facsimile receipt.

(7) Partnerships. — Upon a general or limited partnership:

a. By delivering a copy of the summons and of the complaint to any general partner, or to any attorney-in-fact or agent authorized by appointment or by law to be served or to accept service of process in its behalf; by mailing a copy of the summons and of the complaint, registered or certified mail, return receipt requested, addressed to any general partner, or to any attorney-in-fact or agent authorized by appointment or by law to be served or to accept service of process in its behalf; or by depositing with a designated delivery service authorized pursuant to 26 U.S.C. § 7502(f)(2) a copy of the summons and complaint, addressed to any general partner or to any attorney-in-fact or agent authorized by appointment or by law to be served or to accept service of process in its behalf, delivering to the addressee, and obtaining a delivery receipt; or by leaving copies thereof in the office of such general partner, attorney-in-fact or agent with the person who is apparently in charge of the office.

As used in this sub-subdivision, "delivery receipt" includes an electronic or facsimile receipt.

b. If relief is sought against a partner specifically, a copy of the summons and of the complaint must be served on such partner as provided in this section (j).

(8) Other Unincorporated Associations and Their Officers. — Upon any unincorporated association, organization, or society other than a partnership by one of the following:

a. By delivering a copy of the summons and of the complaint to an officer, director, managing agent or member of the governing body of the unincorporated association, organization or society, or by leaving copies thereof in the office of such officer, director, managing agent or member of the governing body with the person who is apparently in charge of the office.

b. By delivering a copy of the summons and of the complaint to an agent authorized by appointment or by law to be served or to accept service of process or by serving process upon such agent or the party in a manner specified by any statute.

c. By mailing a copy of the summons and of the complaint, registered or certified mail, return receipt requested, addressed to the officer, director, agent or member of the governing body to be served as specified in paragraphs a and b.

d. By depositing with a designated delivery service authorized pursuant to 26 U.S.C. § 7502(f)(2) a copy of the summons and complaint, addressed to the officer, director, agent, or member of the governing body to be served as specified in paragraphs a. and b., delivering to the addressee, and obtaining a delivery receipt. As used in this sub-subdivision, "delivery receipt" includes an electronic or facsimile receipt.

(9) Foreign States and Their Political Subdivisions, Agencies, and Instrumentalities. — Upon a foreign state or a political subdivision, agency, or instrumentality thereof, pursuant to 28 U.S.C. § 1608.

(j1) Service by publication on party that cannot otherwise be served. — A party that cannot with due diligence be served by personal delivery, registered or certified mail, or by a designated delivery service authorized pursuant to 26 U.S.C. § 7502(f)(2) may be served by publication. Except in actions involving jurisdiction in rem or quasi in rem as provided in section (k), service of process by publication shall consist of publishing a notice of service of process by publication once a week for three successive weeks in a newspaper that is qualified for legal advertising in accordance with G.S. 1–597 and G.S. 1–598 and circulated in the area where the party to be served is believed by the serving party to be located, or if there is no reliable information concerning the location of the party then in a newspaper circulated in the county where the action is pending. If the party's post-office address is known or can with reasonable diligence be ascertained, there shall be mailed to the party at or immediately prior to the first publication a copy of the notice of service of process by publication. The mailing may be omitted if the post-office address cannot be ascertained with reasonable diligence. Upon completion of such service there shall be filed with the court an affidavit showing the publication and mailing in accordance with the requirements of G.S. 1–75.10(a)(2), the circumstances warranting the use of service by publication, and information, if any, regarding the location of the party served.

The notice of service of process by publication shall (i) designate the court in which the action has been commenced and the title of the action, which title may be indicated sufficiently by the name of the first plaintiff and the first defendant; (ii) be directed to the defendant sought to be served; (iii) state either that a pleading seeking relief against the person to be served has been filed or has been required to be filed therein not later than a date specified in the notice; (iv) state the nature of the relief being sought; (v) require the defendant being so served to make defense to such pleading within 40 days after a date stated in the notice, exclusive of such date, which date so stated shall be the date of the first publication of notice, or the date when the complaint is required to be filed, whichever is later, and notify the defendant that upon his failure to do so the party seeking service of process by publication will apply to the court for the relief sought; (vi) in cases of attachment, state the information required by G.S. 1–440.14; (vii) be subscribed by the party seeking service or his attorney and give the post-office address of such party or his attorney; and (viii) be substantially in the following form:

NOTICE OF SERVICE OF PROCESS
BY PUBLICATION

STATE OF NORTH CAROLINA
________ COUNTY

In the ________ Court

[Title of action or special proceeding] [To Person to be served]:

Take notice that a pleading seeking relief against you (has been filed) (is required to be filed not later than ________, ____) in the above-entitled (action) (special proceeding). The nature of the relief being sought is as follows:

(State nature.)

You are required to make defense to such pleading not later than (________, ____) and upon your failure to do so the party seeking service against you will apply to the court for the relief sought.

This, the ____ day of ________, ____

(Attorney)(Party)

(Address)

(j2) Proof of service. — Proof of service of process shall be as follows:

(1) Personal Service. — Before judgment by default may be had on personal service, proof of service must be provided in accordance with the requirements of G.S. 1–75.10(a)(1).

(2) Registered or Certified Mail, Signature Confirmation, or Designated Delivery Service. — Before judgment by default may be had on service by registered or certified mail, signature confirmation, or by a designated delivery service authorized pursuant to 26 U.S.C. § 7502(f)(2) with delivery receipt, the serving party shall file an affidavit with the court showing proof of such service in accordance with the requirements of G.S. 1–75.10(a)(4), 1–75.10(a)(5), or 1–75.10(a)(6), as appropriate. This affidavit together with the return receipt, copy of the proof of delivery provided by the United States Postal Service, or delivery receipt, signed by the person who received the mail or delivery if not the addressee raises a presumption that the person who received the mail or delivery and signed the receipt was an agent of the addressee authorized by appointment or by law to be served or to accept service of process or was a person of suitable age and discretion residing in the addressee's dwelling house or usual place of abode. In the event the presumption described in the preceding sentence is rebutted by proof that the person who received the receipt at the addressee's dwelling house or usual place of abode was not a person of suitable age and discretion residing therein, the statute of limitation may not be pleaded as a defense if the action was initially commenced within the period of limitation and service of process is completed within 60 days from the date the service is declared invalid. Service shall be complete on the day the summons and complaint are delivered to the address. As used in this subdivision, "delivery receipt" includes an electronic or facsimile receipt provided by a designated delivery service.

(3) Publication. — Before judgment by default may be had on service by publication, the serving party shall file an affidavit with the court showing the circumstances warranting the use of service by publication, information, if any, regarding the location of the party served which was used in determining the area in which service by publication was printed and proof of service in accordance with G.S. 1–75.10(a)(2).

(j3) Service in a foreign country. — Unless otherwise provided by federal law, service upon a defendant, other than an infant or an incompetent person, may be effected in a place not within the United States:

(1) By any internationally agreed means reasonably calculated to give notice, such as those means authorized by the Hague Convention on the Service Abroad of Judicial and Extrajudicial Documents; or

(2) If there is no internationally agreed means of service or the applicable international agreement allows other means of service, provided that service is reasonably calculated to give notice:

a. In the manner prescribed by the law of the foreign country for service in that country in an action in any of its courts of general jurisdiction;

b. As directed by the foreign authority in response to a letter rogatory or letter of request; or

c. Unless prohibited by the law of the foreign country, by

1. Delivery to the individual personally of a copy of the summons and the complaint and, upon a corporation, partnership, association or other such entity, by delivery to an officer or a managing or general agent;

2. Any form of mail requiring a signed receipt, to be addressed and dispatched by the clerk of the court to the party to be served; or

(3) By other means not prohibited by international agreement as may be directed by the court.

Service under subdivision (2)c.1. or (3) of this subsection may be made by any person authorized by subsection (a) of this Rule or who is designated by order of the court or by the foreign court.

On request, the clerk shall deliver the summons to the plaintiff for transmission to the person or the foreign court or officer who will make the service. Proof of service may be made as prescribed in G.S. 1–75.10, by the order of the court, or by the law of the foreign country.

Proof of service by mail shall include an affidavit or certificate of addressing and mailing by the clerk of court.

(j4) Process or judgment by default not to be attacked on certain grounds. — No party may attack service of process or a judgment of default on the basis that service should or could have been effected by personal service rather than service by registered or certified mail. No party that receives timely actual notice may attack a judgment by default on the basis that the statutory requirement of due diligence as a condition precedent to service by publication was not met.

(j5) Personal jurisdiction by acceptance of service. — Any party personally, or through the persons provided in Rule 4(j), may accept service of process by notation of acceptance of service together with the signature of the party accepting service and the date thereof on an original or copy of a summons, and such acceptance shall have the same force and effect as would exist had the process been served by delivery of copy and summons and complaint to the person signing said acceptance.

(j6) Service by electronic mailing not authorized. — Nothing in subsection (j) of this section authorizes the use of electronic mailing for service on the party to be served.

(k) Process — Manner of service to exercise jurisdiction in rem or quasi in rem. — In any action commenced in a court of this State having jurisdiction of the subject matter and grounds for the exercise of jurisdiction in rem or quasi in rem as provided in G.S. 1-75.8, the manner of service of process shall be as follows:

(1) Defendant Known. — If the defendant is known, he may be served in the appropriate manner prescribed for service of process in section (j), or, if otherwise appropriate section (j1); except that the requirement for service by publication in (j1) shall be satisfied if made in the county where the action is pending and proof of service is made in accordance with section (j2).

(2) Defendant Unknown. — If the defendant is unknown, he may be designated by description and process may be served by publication in the manner provided in section (j1), except that the requirement for service by publication in (j1) shall be satisfied if made in the county where the action is pending and proof of service is made in accordance with section (j2).

Added by Laws 1967, c. 954, § 1. Amended by Laws 1969, c. 895, §§ 1-4; Laws 1971, c. 962; Laws 1971, c. 1156, § 2; Laws 1975, c. 408; Laws 1975, c. 609; Laws 1977, c. 910, §§ 1-3; Laws 1981, c. 384, § 3; Laws 1981, c. 540, §§ 1-8; Laws 1983, c. 679, § 1, 2; Laws 1989, c. 330; Laws 1989, c. 575, §§ 1, 2; Laws 1995, c. 275, § 1; Laws 1995, c. 389, §§ 2, 3; Laws 1995, c. 509, § 135.1(e), (f); S.L. 1997-469, § 1; S.L. 1999-456, § 59, eff. Jan. 1, 2000; S.L. 2001-379, §§ 1 to 2.2, eff. Oct. 1, 2001; S.L. 2005-221, §§ 1, 2, eff. Oct. 1, 2005; S.L. 2008-36, §§ 1-3, 5, eff. Oct. 1, 2008; S.L. 2011-332, § 3.1, eff. Oct. 1, 2011.

Comment

Comment to Original Rule. — Preliminarily, it should be remarked that this rule is complementary to the jurisdiction statute (G.S. 1-75.1 et seq.) which the General Statutes Commission proposed for consideration contemporaneously with these rules. Both the statute and this rule are designed to take full advantage of the fairly recent developments in the law of jurisdiction. Generally, the statute prescribes the occasions on which North Carolina courts may exercise jurisdiction or, in other words, the grounds of jurisdiction. This rule, on the other hand, deals with the manner in which jurisdiction is exercised or asserted.

Section (a). — This section contemplates a continuance of the present practice of ordinarily having summons issue simultaneously with the filing of the complaint. The five-day period was inserted to mark the outer limits of tolerance in respect to delay in issuing the summons.

The first two sentences avoid any suggestion that the clerk shall personally deliver the summons to a process officer. North Carolina has operated successfully heretofore under language similar to that in the section and presumably will continue to be able to do so. The words "be issued" are inserted in lieu of the word "issue" for consistency.

Since under section (b) the summons is to be directed to the defendant rather than to a process officer, it is incumbent on the plaintiff to select the appropriate process officer. It will further be observed that no change is made as to who is a process officer in North Carolina.

For service outside the State, it seemed that the Commission might safely rely on the law of the place where service is attempted. Thus, in New York, where private service of process is permissible, a North Carolina plaintiff could employ a private person to serve process.

It should be noticed that no formalities of any kind are necessary to authorize service anywhere, in or out of the State.

Section (b). — The Commission has mentioned already the principal change in the content of the summons; that is, that it shall be directed to the defendant rather than to a process officer. This makes it possible for one version of the summons to suffice wherever it is served, whether in this State or beyond its bounds. Service, however, must still be made by a proper person as defined by section (a).

Other changes are minor. The Commission abandoned the requirement contained in former § 1-89 that summons operative outside the county of issuance bear the seal of the issuing court. The Commission added specific requirements that summons bear the title of the action, the name of the issuing court, and the name and address of the plaintiff's attorney or, if there is no attorney, the name and address of the plaintiff.

Section (c). — The provisions for the return of summons are the same as those now prescribed except that the Commission extended the time in which a summons may be served to thirty (30) days [Now 60 days] whereas former § 1-89 prescribed a period of only twenty (20) days. The Commission entertained some question of whether or not the period for service might be still further enlarged but in any event it agreed that it would serve the interest of convenience for the summons to retain its full effectiveness for at least thirty (30) days. Thereby, the unnecessary exertion of securing an alias or pluries summons can frequently be avoided.

Section (d). — This section preserves unchanged the essence of former § 1-95. Alternative methods, either endorsement or the issuance of alias or pluries summons, are provided for continuing the life of an action after the time for service of summons has expired. The same time limits for securing the endorsement or alias or pluries summons are prescribed and the special treatment accorded tax suits is retained.

Section (e). — This section is similar to former § 1–96. Accordingly, an action will be discontinued under the new rules just as formerly. It will be observed that while under Rule 3 the commencement of an action is ordinarily tied to the filing of a complaint, the discontinuance of an action is tied to the failure in apt time to secure an endorsement or an alias or pluries summons. Further, it will be observed that in the special case of an action in which endorsement or the issuance of an alias or pluries summons is secured after the ninety (90) day period, in that case the action will be deemed commenced with the endorsement or the issuance of summons rather than with the filing of a complaint.

Section (f). — Self-explanatory.

Section (g). — Self-explanatory.

Section (h). — This section deals with the problem of the proper person to make service when for stated reasons action by the sheriff in a particular county may not be satisfactory. Formerly, § 1–91 provided for service by the sheriff of an adjoining county when there was not in the county where service was expected to be made a "proper officer" for service or in the case where a sheriff "neglects or refuses" to make service. Section 152–8 empowers the coroner when there is no person "qualified to act as sheriff" to execute all process. While the Commission proposed to leave § 152–8 in effect (§ 1–91 is repealed) it believed that the problem could be taken care of generally by the simple provisions of this section. The procedure outlined by the section does not differ in kind from that prescribed by § 152–8 when the coroner is interested in any action.

Section (i). — This section, in terms, does not provide for any greater liberality of amendment than did former § 1–163, which authorized the court to "amend any ... process ... by correcting a mistake in the name of a party, or a mistake in any other respect..." But it does direct attention to what in the Commission's judgment should be the controlling factor: Is there material prejudice to substantial rights?

Section (j). — Some substantial changes were proposed in respect to the manner of service to exercise personal jurisdiction and they cannot be fully understood without considering the jurisdiction statute (G.S. 1–75.1 et seq.) and the ideas advanced in the commentary thereto. But it perhaps bears emphasis that in the vast majority of cases service is accomplished just as it then was; that is, by a sheriff or his deputy personally delivering a copy of the summons to the defendant and to an officer, director, managing agent or process agent when a partnership or corporation is the defendant.

Subsection (1)a. — This deals with natural persons except those under a disability. As indicated above, the normal procedure, when service is made within this State, will be delivery of summons and complaint to the defendant personally by the sheriff or other proper person as defined in section (a). When service is made outside the State, then service will be accomplished on delivery to the defendant personally of a copy of the summons and complaint by one authorized to serve process under the law of the place of service. Thus, if grounds exist under the jurisdiction statute (G.S. 1–75.1 et seq.) for the exercise or jurisdiction by a court of this State and if the defendant is in New York, since New York permits service by anyone over 18 years of age, the summons and complaint can be effectively served in New York by such a person. In the familiar case of the nonresident motorist, for example, the plaintiff's lawyer would simply place the summons and complaint in the hands of a New York process server. No special prayer for permission to make service in this manner is required nor is there any requirement that service be made on any functionary in North Carolina.

Subsection (1)b. — Here there is limited authorization for substituted service. While no permission of the court is required for resort to this type of service, it cannot be overemphasized that this type of service is available only when service cannot "with reasonable diligence" be made under paragraph a. A party would thus, if at all possible, prefer to effect service under paragraph a. If he does not, he faces the hazard in those cases where the defendant makes no appearance that a court will later find that service could "with reasonable diligence" have been made under paragraph a and the voiding of any judgment obtained. But although a party is faced with some uncertainty when he resorts to paragraph b, he surely would prefer this uncertainty to not being able to sue at all. Nor, in the absence of the defendant, is it possible altogether to relieve the uncertainty.

Subsection (1)c. — This is a continuation of the basic theme of giving the best notice to a defendant consistent with "reasonable diligence." If service may not be had under either paragraph a or paragraph b, then resort may be had to publication and mailing. Again, it is not necessary to have the court's permission for such service, but there must be filed with the court an affidavit that the defendant cannot be served under paragraphs a or b.

It will be observed that the defendant has until forty days after publication of the notice to answer. This will be the controlling time regulation, irrespective of Rule 12(a). The action will have commenced, of course, with the filing of the complaint.

Subsection (1)d. — Self-explanatory.

Subsection (2). — This subsection attempts to insure that a person under disability and anyone who may have custody of such person shall both be served except in the case of a minor 14 years of age and older. Paragraph b is an attempt to alleviate the situation where there is an unknown guardian. This section requires of the plaintiff what current decisions of the Supreme Court of the United States do. See Covey v. Town of Somers, 351 U.S. 141, 76 S. Ct. 724, 100 L. Ed. 1021 (1956).

Subsection (3). — Self-explanatory.

Subsection (4). — The Commission here proposed that State agencies be required to appoint process agents. The utility of this requirement is obvious. The definition of the term "agency of the State" gave the Commission some difficulty but the Commission believes the definition arrived at is a workable one.

Subsection (5). — Only paragraph d would seem to require comment. Isolated cases had been reported to the Commission where such a provision would be useful.

Subsection (6). — It should be emphasized that this subsection, along with the rest of this rule, is to be read in conjunction with the jurisdiction statute (G.S. 1–75.1 et seq.). Here we are dealing only with the manner of asserting jurisdiction. Service of a corporate officer within this State or elsewhere will not suffice to give jurisdiction unless there is a ground for jurisdiction as specified by the jurisdiction statute.

Paragraphs c and d in essence make available all present methods of obtaining service.

Subsection (7). — Self-explanatory.

Subsection (8). — It perhaps should be said here that this subsection does not deal in any way with the problem of capacity to be sued.

Section (k). — Here it will be seen that for in rem jurisdiction, as well as for in personam jurisdiction, the Commission proposed the best notice possible to the defendant consistent with "reasonable diligence." Thus, personal service is required where reasonably possible. If it is not reasonably possible, then substituted service may be resorted to. If substituted service is not possible, then service by publication may be had.

Comment to 1969 Amendment. — These amendments are designed to simplify service of process especially substituted service upon parties outside this State.

Section (a). — Personal service outside the State is generally made by someone authorized by the law of the place where service is made. This section now also permits service outside the State to be made by anyone not a party and not less than 21 years of age. Sometimes a party (or his attorney) will find it more convenient to make service himself or through an agent rather than to employ a foreign process server. The option is given, since there is no constitutional impediment. It should be exercised with discretion, however, since the word of a disinterested official would probably be given more credence in a dispute as to whether service was validly made.

Section (j). — This section, which governs the specific manner in which service upon a party is to be made, has been substantially amended with respect to substituted service upon parties outside this State. The section is divided into eight subsections, each of which details the manner of service upon a particular type of party. A new ninth subsection governs all service outside this State.

Subsection (1)a. — A process server is no longer required to make a diligent effort to serve a natural person personally. If the party is not at home, copies of the summons and the complaint may be left at his abode with some person of suitable age and discretion then residing therein.

Subsection (1)b. — This subsection now provides that a party or his agent may alternatively be served in any manner specified by any statute.

Subsection (2). — The exception to this subsection for a minor 14 years of age or older has been excised. Thus, all minors are persons under disability for purposes of the subsection.

Subsection (6)b. — This subsection now provides that a corporation or its agent may alternatively be served in a manner specified by any statute.

Subsection (8)b. — See comment to subsection (6)b.

Subsection (9). — This subsection governs all service of process upon parties not inhabitant of or found within this State or which cannot otherwise be diligently served within this State. Such parties may, at the option of the party seeking to make service, be served personally outside this State, as provided in paragraph a, or be served by registered mail as provided in paragraph b. If the party's address, whereabouts, dwelling house or usual place of abode is unknown and cannot with due diligence be ascertained, or there has been a diligent but unsuccessful attempt to serve the party personally or by registered mail, the party may alternatively be served by publication as provided in paragraph c. When service is to be made in a foreign country, the alternative provisions of paragraph d may be employed. Except as provided in paragraph d, permission of the court to make service outside this State is never required.

Subsection (9)a. — Personal service outside this State is to be made in the same way as personal service within this State. Before judgment by default may be had on such service, the party seeking the judgment must file an affidavit with the court containing proof of such service and showing the circumstances warranting its usage.

Subsection (9)b. — This paragraph replaces, in effect, the service provisions of the now repealed nonresident motor vehicles act. It applies, however, to all parties and not just to nonresident motor vehicle tort-feasors. Copies of the summons and the complaint are to be sent registered mail, return receipt requested, directly to the party to be served, and not to any state official or other intermediary. Service by registered mail is not effected unless the letter is actually delivered to the party. Ordinarily, proof of delivery will be the signed returned receipt itself. Any other evidence of actual delivery is also acceptable. If the mailing is returned stamped "delivery refused," "letter unclaimed," "addressee unknown at the address," or "addressee moved and left no forwarding address," service has not been effected. Before judgment by default may be had on such service, the party seeking the judgment must file with the court an affidavit containing proof of such service and showing the circumstances warranting its usage.

Subsection (9)c. — The mechanics of service by publication have not been substantially changed. The notice is to be published in a newspaper that is qualified for legal advertising in accordance with N.C.G.S. §§ 1–579 [now repealed]. 1–598 and is published in the county where the action is pending. If no newspaper in the county qualifies, a qualified newspaper in an adjoining county or the same judicial district may be chosen. If the party's address is known or can with reasonable diligence be ascertained, a copy of the published notice is to be mailed to him. Upon completion of the publication, an affidavit containing proof of such service and showing the circumstances warranting its usage is to be filed with the court.

Subsection (9)d. — This paragraph establishes alternative procedures when service is to be made in a foreign country. It is based upon rule 4(i) of the Federal Rules of Civil Procedure, which is itself drawn from Section 2.01 of the Uniform Interstate and International Procedure Act. Under this paragraph one may enlist the assistance of a foreign government and its laws in making service on a defendant found within its territory, in order to insure the validity of the service and to avoid any objection by the foreign government that efforts to make service there constitute an encroachment on its sovereignty.

Subsection (9)e. — This paragraph prohibits a direct or collateral attack upon a default judgment obtained after service under this subsection (9) on the grounds that the subsection, or any other provision of section (j), required a different method of substituted or personal service. Since the various methods of substituted service provided for are all reasonably calculated to give notice of the pendency of the action, a party is not constitutionally entitled to be served under one rather than another, even though the statute itself so requires. Thus, to challenge an incorrect choice of a method of service under the statute, the party must appear in the action before judgment by default is rendered. Otherwise, the error is waived. Since this paragraph does not seek to bar constitutional objections to the service of process, it should be accorded full faith and credit by other states.

Rule 5. Service and filing of pleadings and other papers

(a) Service of orders, subsequent pleadings, discovery papers, written motions, written notices, and other similar papers – When required. – Every order required by its terms to be served, every pleading subsequent to the original complaint unless the court otherwise orders because of numerous defendants, every paper relating to discovery required to be served upon a party unless the court otherwise orders, every written motion other than one which may be heard ex parte, and every written notice, appearance, demand, offer of judgment and similar paper shall be served upon each of the parties, but no service need be made on parties in default for failure to appear except that pleadings asserting new or additional claims for relief against them shall be served upon them in the manner provided for service of summons in Rule 4.

(a1) Service of briefs or memoranda in support or opposition of certain dispositive motions. – In actions in superior court, every brief or memorandum in support of or in opposition to a motion to dismiss, a motion for judgment on the pleadings, a motion for summary judgment, or any other motion seeking a final determination of the rights of the parties as to one or more of the claims or parties in the action shall be served upon each of the parties at least two days before the hearing on the motion. If the brief or memorandum is not served on the other parties at least two days before the hearing on the motion, the court may continue the matter for a reasonable period to allow the responding party to prepare a response, proceed with the matter without considering the untimely served brief or memorandum, or take such other action as the ends of justice require. The parties may, by consent, alter the period of time for service. For the purpose of this two-day requirement only, service shall mean personal delivery, facsimile transmission, or other means such that the party actually receives the brief within the required time.

(b) Service — How made. — A pleading setting forth a counterclaim or cross claim shall be filed with the court and a copy thereof shall be served on the party against whom it is asserted or on the party's attorney of record as provided by this subsection.

With respect to all pleadings subsequent to the original complaint and other papers required or permitted to be served, service shall be made upon the party's attorney of record and, if ordered by the court, also upon the party. If the party has no attorney of record, service shall be made upon the party. With respect to such other pleadings and papers, service with due return may be made in a manner provided for service and return of process in Rule 4. Service under this subsection may also be made by one of the following methods:

(1) Upon a party's attorney of record:

a. By delivering a copy to the attorney. Delivery of a copy within this sub-subdivision means handing it to the attorney, leaving it at the attorney's office with a partner or employee, or sending it to the attorney's office by a confirmed telefacsimile transmittal for receipt by 5:00 P.M. Eastern Time on a regular business day, as evidenced by a telefacsimile receipt confirmation. If receipt of delivery by telefacsimile is after 5:00 P.M., service will be deemed to have been completed on the next business day.

b. By mailing a copy to the attorney's office.

(2) Upon a party:

a. By delivering a copy to the party. Delivery of a copy within this sub-subdivision means handing it to the party.

b. By mailing a copy to the party at the party's last known address or, if no address is known, by filing it with the clerk of court.

Service by mail shall be complete upon deposit of the pleading or paper enclosed in a post-paid, properly addressed wrapper in a post office or official depository under the exclusive care and custody of the United States Postal Service.

(b1) Service — Certificate of Service. — A certificate of service shall accompany every pleading and every paper required to be served on any party or nonparty to the litigation, except with respect to pleadings and papers whose service is governed by Rule 4. The certificate shall show the date and method of service or the date of acceptance of service and shall show the name and service address of each person upon whom the paper has been served. If one or more persons are served by facsimile transmission, the certificate shall also show the telefacsimile number of each person so served. Each certificate of service shall be signed in accordance with and subject to Rule 11 of these rules.

(c) Service – Numerous defendants. – In any action in which there are unusually large numbers of defendants, the court, upon motion or of its own initiative, may order that service of the pleadings of the defendants and replies thereto need not be made as between the defendants and that any crossclaim, counterclaim, or matter constituting an avoidance or affirmative defense contained therein shall be deemed to be denied or avoided by all other parties and that the filing of any such pleading and service thereof upon the plaintiff constitutes due notice of it to the parties. A copy of every such order shall be served upon the parties in such manner and form as the court directs.

(d) Filing. — The following papers shall be filed with the court, either before service or within five days after service:

(1) All pleadings, as defined by Rule 7(a) of these rules, subsequent to the complaint, whether such pleadings are original or amended.

(2) Written motions and all notices of hearing.

(3) Any other application to the court for an order that may affect the rights of or in any way commands any individual, business entity, governmental agency, association, or partnership to act or to forego action of any kind.

(4) Notices of appearance.

(5) Any other paper required by rule or statute to be filed.

(6) Any other paper so ordered by the court.

(7) All orders issued by the court.

All other papers, regardless of whether these rules require them to be served upon a party, should not be filed with the court unless (i) the filing is agreed to by all parties, or (ii) the papers are submitted to the court in relation to a motion or other request for relief, or (iii) the filing is permitted by another rule or statute. Briefs or memoranda provided to the court may not be filed with the clerk of court unless ordered by the court. The party taking a deposition or obtaining material through discovery is responsible for its preservation and delivery to the court if needed or so ordered.

(e)(1) Filing with the court defined. — The filing of pleadings and other papers with the court as required by these rules shall be made by filing them with the clerk of the court, except that the judge may permit the papers to be filed with him, in which event he shall note thereon the filing date and forthwith transmit them to the office of the clerk.

(2) Filing by electronic means. — If, pursuant to G.S. 7A-34 and G.S. 7A-343, the Supreme Court and the Administrative Officer of the Courts establish uniform rules, regulations, costs, procedures and specifications for the filing of pleadings or other court papers by electronic means, filing may be made by the electronic means when, in the manner, and to the extent provided therein.

Added by Laws 1967, c. 954, § 1. Amended by Laws 1971, c. 538; Laws 1971, c. 1156, § 2.5; Laws 1975, c. 762, § 1; Laws 1983, c. 201, § 1; Laws 1985, c. 546, § 1; Laws 1991, c. 168, § 1; S.L. 2000-127, § 1, eff. Oct. 1, 2000; S.L. 2001-379, § 3, eff. Oct. 1, 2001; S.L. 2001-388, § 1, eff. Aug. 26, 2001; S.L. 2004-199, § 5(a), eff. Oct. 1, 2004; S.L. 2005-138, §§ 1, 2, eff. Oct. 1, 2005; S.L. 2006-187, § 2(a), eff. Aug. 3, 2006; S.L. 2011-332, § 4.2, eff. Oct. 1, 2011.

Comment

Comment to this Rule as Originally Enacted. — *Section (a).* This section is based upon the federal rule and incorporates part of the West Virginia rule.

Former § 1-125 required that a copy of the answer be mailed to the plaintiff or his attorney of record by the clerk and prohibited the clerk from allowing the answer to be filed without a copy for that purpose. Former § 1-140 stated that if no copy of an answer containing a counterclaim was served upon the plaintiff or his attorney, the allegations in the counterclaim should be denied as a matter of law. Other statutes dealing with serving of notice included: former § 1-578, providing that no motion might be heard and no orders in the cause might be made outside the county where the action was pending unless notice of motion was served on the opposing party in accordance with the provisions of § 1-581; former § 1-568.13, service of order upon person to be examined under adverse party examination statutes; former § 1-568.14, notice to all other parties; former § 8-89, inspection of writings; former § 8-90, production of documents; former §§ 8-71 and 72, depositions; former § 1-153, motion to strike; and § 40-17, notice to parties in eminent domain proceedings.

This section is intended to include all such motions and orders. The phrase "and similar paper" indicates that the enumeration of papers is not exhaustive.

Section (b). — This section is based upon the federal rule but does not track the exact language of the federal rule. The section preserves the requirement of former § 1-140 that a counterclaim or crossclaim be served on the party against whom it is asserted or on his attorney of record.

Former §§ 1-585, 586, and 587 prescribed the form of notices and method of service, which was similar to this section. These provisions permit service upon a party or his attorney unless otherwise provided.

No statutory provision providing heretofore for notice by mail has been found, but such notice by mail was upheld by the court in a case where defendant filed a written motion to strike portions of the complaint and the court found that copies of the motion had been mailed to and received by plaintiff's attorneys. The court said in such circumstances plaintiff was not entitled to have notice of the motion to strike served on her by an officer. Heffner v. Jefferson Std. Life Ins. Co., 214 N.C. 359, 199 S.E. 293 (1938).

Section (c). — This section tracks the language of the federal rule. It should be pointed out that the rule is permissive and applies only when the court makes an order under the rule. If such an order is made, a copy of the order must be served upon all parties. If such an order is made, each defendant prepares his answer to the complaint in which he may state his defenses to the complaint, counterclaims against the plaintiff, and cross actions against any or all of the defendants. Each defendant must serve his answer upon the plaintiff within the time prescribed by Rule 12 (a) and file it with the court. The plaintiff is not required to serve and file replies to counterclaims stated in any of the answers of the defendants, and no defendant need serve and file an answer to a crossclaim asserted against him in any of the answers of the defendants. Any counterclaim, crossclaim, or matter constituting an avoidance or affirmative defense contained in any of the answers of the defendants shall be deemed denied. It should be noted that this section dispenses with service of replies to counterclaims and answers to crossclaims only. Other pleadings and all motions must be served as in other cases.

This section also provides that "the filing of any such pleading and service thereof on the plaintiff constitutes due notice of it to the parties." In all cases where an order is entered under the provisions of this section the defendant or his attorney would be required to examine the court file to determine if any crossclaim had been filed against him.

Former § 1-140 provided that if an answer containing a counterclaim was not served on the plaintiff or his attorney, the counterclaim should be deemed denied. The second paragraph of the same statute provided that if a defendant asserted a crossclaim against a codefendant, no judgment by default might be entered against such codefendant unless he had been served with a notice together with a copy of such crossclaim. Thus, the statute did not require that a counterclaim or crossclaim be "served"; it merely denied certain kinds of relief (default judgment) if such was not served.

Default provisions such as Rule 55 would obviously be inoperative if the judge made an order under this section.

Section (d). — Although this section incorporates most of the federal rule, federal Rule 5 (d) was deemed insufficient for North Carolina practice. Consequently, this section is more detailed than the federal rule. The section also incorporates part of the West Virginia rule but does not track the language of that rule. There is no provision in the federal rule with respect to acceptance of service or of a certificate indicating the method of service. It is believed that this section is more in line with North Carolina practice with respect to service or acceptance of service of summons and other process.

This section will not affect the provisions of certain other rules with respect to filing of papers, such as Rule 3, which requires the complaint to be filed before service.

In substance, this section requires the filing with the court of all papers which are required to be served. There are also papers which are not required to be served, which must also be filed, such as motions which may be heard ex parte. Good practice would indicate that all papers relating to the action should be filed with the court whether required by these rules or not.

Section (e). — This section tracks the federal rule. It reflects prior North Carolina practice.

Comment to the 1975 Amendment. — The amendment adds the words "every paper relating to discovery required to be served upon a party unless the court otherwise orders." It, therefore, makes it clear that all papers relating to discovery required to be served on any party must be served on all parties, unless the court orders otherwise. The language of the former rule expressly included notices and demands, but was not explicit as to answers or responses under Rules 33, 34, and 36. The court is given the power to vary the requirement if in a given case it proves needlessly onerous, such as where the papers are voluminous or where there are numerous parties.

Comments — 2000

The rule does not require any party to submit a brief or memorandum; it only applies in certain instances in which a party intends to submit a brief or memorandum to the court. The rule would not preclude a party from providing the judge with copies of cases or statutes at a hearing.

This addition to the Official Comment shall only be for annotation purposes and shall not be construed to be the law.

Rule 6. Time

(a) Computation. — In computing any period of time prescribed or allowed by these rules, by order of court, or by any applicable statute, including rules, orders or statutes respecting publication of notices, the day of the act, event, default or publication after which the designated period of time begins to run is not to be included. The last day of the period so computed is to be included, unless it is a Saturday, Sunday or a legal holiday when the courthouse is closed for transactions, in which event the period runs until the end of the next day which is not a Saturday, Sunday, or a legal holiday when the courthouse is closed for transactions. When the period of time prescribed or allowed is less than seven days, intermediate Saturdays, Sundays, and holidays shall be excluded in the computation. A half holiday shall be considered as other days and not as a holiday.

(b) Enlargement. — When by these rules or by a notice given thereunder or by order of court an act is required or allowed to be done at or within a specified time, the court for cause shown may at any time in its discretion with or without motion or notice order the period enlarged if request therefor is made before the expiration of the period originally prescribed or as extended by a previous order. Upon motion made after the expiration of the specified period, the judge may permit the act to be done where the failure to act was the result of excusable neglect. Notwithstanding any other provisions of this rule, the parties may enter into binding stipulations without approval of the court enlarging the time, not to exceed in the aggregate 30 days, within which an act is required or allowed to be done under these rules, provided, however, that neither the court nor the parties may extend the time for taking any action under Rules 50(b), 52, 59(b), (d), (e), 60(b), except to the extent and under the conditions stated in them.

(c) Unaffected by expiration of session. — The period of time provided for the doing of any act or the taking of any proceeding is not affected or limited by the continued existence or expiration of a session of court. The continued existence or expiration of a session of court in no way affects the power of a court to do any act or take any proceeding, but no issue of fact shall be submitted to a jury out of session.

(d) For motions, affidavits. — A written motion, other than one which may be heard ex parte, and notice of the hearing thereof shall be served not later than five days before the time specified for the hearing, unless a different period is fixed by these rules or by order of the court. Such an order may for cause shown be made on ex parte application. When a motion is supported by affidavit, the affidavit shall be served with the motion; and except as otherwise provided in Rule 59(c), opposing affidavits shall be served at least two days before the hearing. If the opposing affidavit is not served on the other parties at least two days before the hearing on the motion, the court may continue the matter for a reasonable period to allow the responding party to prepare a response, proceed with the matter without considering the untimely served affidavit, or take such other action as the ends of justice require. For the purpose of this two-day requirement only, service shall mean personal delivery, facsimile transmission, or other means such that the party actually receives the affidavit within the required time.

(e) Additional time after service by mail. — Whenever a party has the right to do some act or take some proceedings within a prescribed period after the service of a notice or other paper upon him and the notice or paper is served upon him by mail, three days shall be added to the prescribed period.

(f) Additional time for Address Confidentiality Program participants. — Whenever a person participating in the Address Confidentiality Program established by Chapter 15C of the General Statutes has a legal right to act within a prescribed period of 10 days or less after the service of a notice or other paper upon the program participant, and the notice or paper is served upon the program participant by mail, five days shall be added to the prescribed period.

Added by Laws 1967, c. 954, § 1. Amended by S.L. 2000-127, § 5, eff. Oct. 1, 2000; S.L. 2002-171, § 2, eff. Jan. 1, 2003; S.L. 2003-337, § 2, eff. Oct. 1, 2003.

Comment

Section (a). — The basic rule of excluding the first and including the last day is presently embodied in § 1-593 as to the time within which an act is to be done, and in § 1-594 as to publication of notices. Section 1-593 excludes the last day if it is a Sunday or a legal holiday. The federal rule and this section also exclude Saturdays. This section also conforms publication period time requirements to other time computations.

One other significant change is wrought by adoption of this provision. Formerly, intermediate Saturdays, Sundays, and holidays were included in computing the time, no matter how short the period was. The federal rule makes allowance for the shorter periods of time by providing that if the period is seven days or less, intermediate Saturdays, Sundays or holidays shall not be included.

Section (b). — This section, based upon the federal rule, is more detailed than former statutory provisions. However, there is no basic change in procedure. Former § 1-125 permitted the clerk to extend the time for filing answer or demurrer for a period of time not exceeding 20 days. Former § 1-152 permitted the judge in his discretion to enlarge the time for the doing of any act. Former § 1-220 permitted the clerk or the judge to relieve a party from a judgment, order, verdict or other proceeding taken against him through his mistake, inadvertence, surprise, or excusable neglect, and to supply an omission in any proceeding.

Section (c). — Self-explanatory.

Section (d). — Former § 1-581 provided for 10 days notice of motion. Thus, adoption of this section results in halving the normal period of notice.

Section (e). — There is no present statutory equivalent to this section. As to service of notice, the statutes do not contemplate service by mail. However, service of notice on plaintiff's attorneys by mail was upheld in Heffner v. Jefferson Std. Life Ins. Co., 214 N.C. 359, 199 S.E. 293 (1938). There are other instances in which service by mail is possible.

ARTICLE 3

Pleadings and Motions

Rule 7. Pleadings allowed; motions

(a) Pleadings. — There shall be a complaint and an answer; a reply to a counterclaim denominated as such; an answer to a crossclaim, if the answer contains a crossclaim; a third-party complaint if a person who was not an original party is summoned under the provisions of Rule 14; and a third-party answer, if a third-party complaint is served. If the answer alleges contributory negligence, a party may serve a reply alleging last clear chance. No other pleading shall be allowed except that the court may order a reply to an answer or a third-party answer.

(b) Motions and other papers. —

(1) An application to the court for an order shall be by motion which, unless made during a hearing or trial or at a session at which a cause is on the calendar for that session, shall be made in writing, shall state with particularity the grounds therefor, and shall set forth the relief or order sought. The requirement of writing is fulfilled if the motion is stated in a written notice of the hearing of the motion.

(2) The rules applicable to captions, signing, and other matters of form of pleadings apply to all motions and other papers provided for by these rules.

(3) A motion to transfer under G.S. 7A-258 shall comply with the directives therein specified but the relief thereby obtainable may also be sought in a responsive pleading pursuant to Rule 12(b).

(4) A motion in a civil action in a county that is part of a multicounty judicial district may be heard in another county which is part of that same judicial district with the permission of the senior resident superior court judge of that district or of that judge's designee. Except for emergencies as determined by the senior resident superior court judge or that judge's designee, a motion in a civil action to be heard outside the county in which the case is filed shall be heard at a civil session of court.

(c) Demurrers, pleas, etc., abolished. — Demurrers, pleas, and exceptions for insufficiency shall not be used.

(d) Pleadings not read to jury. — Unless otherwise ordered by the judge, pleadings shall not be read to the jury.

Added by Laws 1967, c. 954, § 1. Amended by Laws 1971, c. 1156, § 1; S.L. 2000-127, § 2, eff. Oct. 1, 2000; S.L. 2005-163, § 1, eff. Oct. 1, 2005; S.L. 2011-317, § 1, eff. Oct. 1, 2011.

Comment

Section (a). — This section defines the total permissible range of pleadings, following long established code procedure by making the reply the terminal permissible pleading in the traditional exchange between plaintiff and defendant. Furthermore, this section makes specific that which has been evolved without literal sanction under the Code, that an answer is to be filed to a crossclaim and that where additional defendants are summoned, third party complaint and answer are to be filed. The only time reply is actually required, aside from when ordered by the court, is to a counterclaim actually so denominated. This is an improvement over code procedure, which requires a reply to any counterclaim at peril of admitting its allegations, thereby putting an unjustifiable burden on the plaintiff to ascertain at his peril whether answers containing affirmative defenses may be construed to involve counterclaims. Whether or not a reply is necessary is presently extremely difficult to determine in other contexts. Compare, e.g. Little v. Stevens, 267 N.C. 328, 148 S.E.2d 201 (1966), and former § 1-159. Finally, following code practice, authority is given the courts to order replies to noncounterclaiming answers and third party answers, thus rounding out the total list of permissible pleadings under all circumstances.

Section (b)(1). — This section makes more explicit as a matter of literal statement the motion practice actually followed under present code practice. The specification that written motions shall state their grounds and the relief sought is a helpful directive. And the provision for combining the motion with the notice thereof actually gives literal sanction to a procedure of convenience frequently indulged in State court practice without such direct authorization.

Section (c). — This section rounds out the exclusive listing of pleadings and motions allowable under this approach, by making explicit what a long tradition might have resisted, that those other traditional pretrial stage procedural devices, the demurrer and the special pleas, are abolished from the practice. There are to be only the listed pleadings, and motions shaped functionally to accomplish various specific pretrial purposes formerly served by motions, demurrers and pleas. The abolition of these devices by name does not, of course, automatically do away with the possibility that the functions served by these shall continue to be served. This section must be read in the light of Rule 12, wherein the new procedure by which these functions are served is spelled out.

Section (d). — The purpose of this section is to end the practice of reading pleadings to the jury. The Commission contemplated that a brief opening statement would generally be substituted.

Comments — 2000

The 2000 amendment conforms the North Carolina rule to federal Rule 7(b). The federal courts do not apply the particularity requirement as a procedural technicality to deny otherwise meritorious motions. Rather, the federal courts apply the rule to protect parties from prejudice, to assure that opposing parties can comprehend the basis for the motion and have a fair opportunity to respond.

This addition to the Official Comment shall only be for annotation purposes and shall not be construed to be the law.

Rule 8. General rules of pleadings

(a) Claims for relief. — A pleading which sets forth a claim for relief, whether an original claim, counterclaim, crossclaim, or third-party claim shall contain

(1) A short and plain statement of the claim sufficiently particular to give the court and the parties notice of the transactions, occurrences, or series of transactions or occurrences, intended to be proved showing that the pleader is entitled to relief, and

(2) A demand for judgment for the relief to which he deems himself entitled. Relief in the alternative or of several different types may be demanded. In all actions involving a material issue related to any of the subjects listed in G.S. 7A-45.4(a)(1), (2), (3), (4), (5), or (8), the pleading shall state whether or not relief is demanded for damages incurred or to be incurred in an amount equal to or exceeding five million dollars ($5,000,000). In all negligence actions, and in all claims for punitive damages in any civil action, wherein the matter in controversy exceeds the sum or value of twenty-five thousand dollars ($25,000), the pleading shall not state the demand for monetary relief, but shall state that the relief demanded is for damages incurred or to be incurred in excess of twenty-five thousand dollars ($25,000). However, at any time after service of the claim for relief, any party may request of the claimant a written statement of the monetary relief sought, and the claimant shall, within 30 days after such service, provide such statement, which shall not be filed with the clerk until the action has been called for trial or entry of default entered. Such statement may be amended in the manner and at times as provided by Rule 15.

(b) Defenses; form of denials. — A party shall state in short and plain terms his defenses to each claim asserted and shall admit or deny the averments upon which the adverse party relies. If he is without knowledge or information sufficient to form a belief as to the truth of an averment, he shall so state and this has the effect of a denial. Denials shall fairly meet the substance of the averments denied. When a pleader intends in good faith to deny only a part of or a qualification of an averment, he shall specify so much of it as is true and material and shall deny only the remainder. Unless the pleader intends in good faith to controvert all the averments of the preceding pleading, he may make his denials as specific denials of designated averments or paragraphs, or he may generally deny all the averments except such designated averments or paragraphs as he expressly admits; but, when he does so intend to controvert all its averments, he may do so by general denial subject to the obligations set forth in Rule 11.

(c) Affirmative defenses. — In pleading to a preceding pleading, a party shall set forth affirmatively accord and satisfaction, arbitration and award, assumption of risk, contributory negligence, discharge in bankruptcy, duress, estoppel, failure of consideration, fraud, illegality, injury by fellow servant, laches, license, payment, release, res judicata, statute of frauds, statute of limitations, truth in actions for defamation, usury, waiver, and any other matter constituting an avoidance or affirmative defense. Such pleading shall contain a short and plain statement of any matter constituting an avoidance or affirmative defense sufficiently particular to give the court and the parties notice of the transactions, occurrences, or series of transactions or occurrences, intended to be proved. When a party has mistakenly designated a defense as a counterclaim or a counterclaim as a defense, the court, on terms, if justice so requires, shall treat the pleading as if there had been a proper designation.

(d) Effect of failure to deny. — Averments in a pleading to which a responsive pleading is required, other than those as to the amount of damage, are admitted when not denied in the responsive pleading. Averments in a pleading to which no responsive pleading is required or permitted shall be taken as denied or avoided.

(e) Pleading to be concise and direct; consistency. —

(1) Each averment of a pleading shall be simple, concise, and direct. No technical forms of pleading or motions are required.

(2) A party may set forth two or more statements of a claim or defense alternatively or hypothetically, either in one count or defense or in separate counts or defenses. When two or more statements are made in the alternative and one of them if made independently would be sufficient, the pleading is not made insufficient by the insufficiency of one or more of the alternative statements. A party may also state as many separate claims or defenses as he has regardless of consistency and whether based on legal or on equitable grounds or on both. All statements shall be made subject to the obligations set forth in Rule 11.

(f) Construction of pleadings. — All pleadings shall be so construed as to do substantial justice.

Added by Laws 1967, c. 954, § 1. Amended by Laws 1975 (2nd Ex. Sess.), c. 977, § 5; Laws 1979, c. 654, § 4; Laws 1985 (Reg. Sess. 1986), c. 1027, § 56; Laws 1989 (Reg. Sess. 1990), c. 995, § 1; S.L. 2014-102, § 7, eff. Aug. 6, 2014; S.L. 2014-115, § 18.5, eff. Aug. 11, 2014.

Comment

Section (a). — In prescribing what a complaint is to contain, it will be observed that while the Commission abandoned the code formulation of "a plain and concise statement of the facts constituting a cause of action," it did not adopt without change the federal rules formula, "a short and plain statement of the claim showing that the pleader is entitled to relief." The statement must be "sufficiently particular to give the court and the parties notice of the transactions or occurrences, intended to be proved..."

The Commission's objective may be summarized as follows: 1. By omitting any requirement in terms that a complaint state "facts," the Commission sought to put behind it the sterile dispute as to whether an allegation states evidentiary or ultimate facts or conclusions of law. Of course, in order to show that he is entitled to relief, a pleader will be compelled to be factual, but the new formulation saved him from floundering on the ancient distinctions.

2. By omitting any reference to "cause of action," and directing attention to the notice-giving functions served by the complaint, the Commission sought a new start on the problem of how much specificity is desirable in a complaint. It can fairly be argued, of course, that when the Commission substituted "claim" for "cause of action" that it was merely exchanging one conundrum for another. But changing the formulation does have the advantage of enabling the courts to approach the problem of specificity unembarrassed by prior decisions and with an eye to the functions that pleading can properly serve. Moreover, the new approach can take into account other procedures provided by these rules—the pretrial conference, the broadened discovery, the summary judgment.

3. By specifically requiring a degree of particularity the Commission sought to put at rest any notion that the mere assertion of a grievance will be sufficient under these rules. In this connection, the forms provided in Rule 84 should be examined. The Commission's prescription suggests that not only is it permissible under these rules for a pleader to so plead as to obviate the need for a pretrial conference or resort to the discovery procedures but that it will frequently be his duty to do so.

Section (b). — This section sets forth the basic directive for defensive pleading. It follows the basic code pattern of requiring either denials or admissions of all specific averments of the claimant for affirmative relief, or the pleading of affirmative defenses in avoidance. It is interesting to reflect that here, too, is a plain indication that Rule § 1A-1, 8(a) contemplates factual pleading, else the directive to admit or deny averments is meaningless. Sanction is given as in existing State practice to obtain the effect of a denial by stating lack of sufficient knowledge or information to form a belief. The traditional prohibition against negative pregnant pleading is stated in terms of fairly meeting the substance of averments denied.

The fairly detailed specification of the different forms that partial denials and admissions may take is a helpful one and does not appear in the code. An innovation from the standpoint of existing State practice is involved in the allowance of a true general denial, or a qualified general denial not directed specifically to each separate paragraph, which is the largest unit that may be generally denied under judicial interpretation of the Code.

Section (c) contains a helpful specific listing of numerous traditional defenses which must be specially pleaded. This enumeration is beneficial in avoiding questions as to whether this or that defense is an "affirmative defense" required to be pleaded to allow evidence in its proof. At least one change in existing law is involved in the inclusion of the defense of statute of frauds in this listing. Added to the federal listing are truth in defamation actions, and usury, to reflect existing State practice.

Section (d) states existing State practice.

Section (e)(1) contains a general homily eschewing the old technical forms of pleading and admonishing directness rather than the pomposity which frequently creeps into common law and Code pleading.

Section (e)(2) directly sanctions alternative and hypothetical pleadings, which are not literally sanctioned under the code, but generally permitted within limits. More significantly this rule directly authorizes the pleading of inconsistent claims as well as defenses. While inconsistent defenses are now permissible under the code, inconsistent affirmative claims of some types have been held to require election when their underlying legal theories (as opposed to factual theories) were substantively inconsistent.

Section (f) states a homily similarly expressed under the Code in former § 1–151.

Rule 9. Pleading special matters

(a) Capacity. — Any party not a natural person shall make an affirmative averment showing its legal existence and capacity to sue. Any party suing in any representative capacity shall make an affirmative averment showing his capacity and authority to sue. When a party desires to raise an issue as to the legal existence of any party or the capacity of any party to sue or be sued or the authority of a party to sue or be sued in a representative capacity, he shall do so by specific negative averment, which shall include such supporting particulars as are peculiarly within the pleader's knowledge.

(b) Fraud, duress, mistake, condition of the mind. — In all averments of fraud, duress or mistake, the circumstances constituting fraud or mistake shall be stated with particularity. Malice, intent, knowledge, and other condition of mind of a person may be averred generally.

(c) Conditions precedent. — In pleading the performance or occurrence of conditions precedent, it is sufficient to aver generally that all conditions precedent have been performed or have occurred. A denial of performance or occurrence shall be made specifically and with particularity.

(d) Official document or act. — In pleading an official document or official act it is sufficient to aver that the document was issued or the act done in compliance with law.

(e) Judgment. — In pleading a judgment, decision or ruling of a domestic or foreign court, judicial or quasi-judicial tribunal, or of a board or officer, it is sufficient to aver the judgment, decision or ruling without setting forth matter showing jurisdiction to render it.

(f) Time and place. — For the purpose of testing the sufficiency of a pleading, averments of time and place are material and shall be considered like all other averments of material matter.

(g) Special damage. — When items of special damage are claimed each shall be averred.

(h) Private statutes. — In pleading a private statute or right derived therefrom it is sufficient to refer to the statute by its title or the day of its ratification if ratified before January 1, 1996, or the date it becomes law if it becomes law on or after January 1, 1996, and the court shall thereupon take judicial notice of it.

(i) Libel and slander. —

(1) In an action for libel or slander it is not necessary to state in the complaint any extrinsic facts for the purpose of showing the application to the plaintiff of the defamatory matter out of which the claim for relief arose, but it is sufficient to state generally that the same was published or spoken concerning the plaintiff, and if such allegation is controverted, the plaintiff is bound to establish on trial that it was so published or spoken.

(2) The defendant may in his answer allege both the truth of the matter charged as defamatory, and any mitigating circumstances to reduce the amount of damages; and whether he proves the justification or not, he may give in evidence the mitigating circumstances.

(j) Medical malpractice.—Any complaint alleging medical malpractice by a health care provider pursuant to G.S. 90–21.11(2)a. in failing to comply with the applicable standard of care under G.S. 90–21.12 shall be dismissed unless:

(1) The pleading specifically asserts that the medical care and all medical records pertaining to the

alleged negligence that are available to the plaintiff after reasonable inquiry have been reviewed by a person who is reasonably expected to qualify as an expert witness under Rule 702 of the Rules of Evidence and who is willing to testify that the medical care did not comply with the applicable standard of care;

(2) The pleading specifically asserts that the medical care and all medical records pertaining to the alleged negligence that are available to the plaintiff after reasonable inquiry have been reviewed by a person that the complainant will seek to have qualified as an expert witness by motion under Rule 702(e) of the Rules of Evidence and who is willing to testify that the medical care did not comply with the applicable standard of care, and the motion is filed with the complaint; or

(3) The pleading alleges facts establishing negligence under the existing common-law doctrine of res ipsa loquitur.

Upon motion by the complainant prior to the expiration of the applicable statute of limitations, a resident judge of the superior court for a judicial district in which venue for the cause of action is appropriate under G.S. 1–82 or, if no resident judge for that judicial district is physically present in that judicial district, otherwise available, or able or willing to consider the motion, then any presiding judge of the superior court for that judicial district may allow a motion to extend the statute of limitations for a period not to exceed 120 days to file a complaint in a medical malpractice action in order to comply with this Rule, upon a determination that good cause exists for the granting of the motion and that the ends of justice would be served by an extension. The plaintiff shall provide, at the request of the defendant, proof of compliance with this subsection through up to ten written interrogatories, the answers to which shall be verified by the expert required under this subsection. These interrogatories do not count against the interrogatory limit under Rule 33.

(k) Punitive damages. — A demand for punitive damages shall be specifically stated, except for the amount, and the aggravating factor that supports the award of punitive damages shall be averred with particularity. The amount of damages shall be pled in accordance with Rule 8.

Added by Laws 1967, c. 954, § 1. Amended by Laws 1995, c. 20, § 10; Laws 1995, c. 309, § 2; Laws 1995, c. 514, § 3; S.L. 1998–217, § 61, eff. Oct. 31, 1998; S.L. 2001–121, § 1, eff. Oct. 1, 2001; S.L. 2011–400, § 3, eff. Oct. 1, 2011.

Comment

This rule is designed to lay down some special rules for pleading in typically recurring contexts which have traditionally caused trouble when no codified directive existed.

Section (a). — This section deals with the problem of putting in issue the legal existence, the capacity or the authority of parties. The rule as presented here requires that parties plaintiff who are not natural persons shall affirmatively aver their legal existence and capacity and that parties plaintiff suing in representative capacities shall affirmatively plead to show capacity and authority. However, the further requirement is laid down that any party actually desiring to put any of these concepts in issue shall negatively aver their nonexistence and support the averment. This section departs from federal Rule 9, which has no requirement that capacity, legal existence or representative authority be affirmatively averred. The Code nowhere deals specifically with the question whether capacity, etc., must be affirmatively pleaded. It did, of course, provide for demurrer to a complaint which affirmatively disclosed lack of capacity. Former § 1–127(2). Monfils v. Hazlewood, 218 N.C. 215, 10 S.E.2d 673 (1940) (complaint in wrongful death action affirmatively showing plaintiff a foreign administratrix). Capacity and existence are customarily pleaded affirmatively in North Carolina practice in any context where they might possibly be in issue, e.g., by parties suing in representative capacities; by corporations. There is no present Code requirement that their nonexistence or noncapacity be specifically averred and supported by pleading in order to put this in issue, and the rule does require this. This is an improvement, since it deprives parties of the easy ability, without real basis in fact, to put the opponent to needless proof of these matters.

Section (b). — This section codifies a rule applied without specific Code directive in existing State practice. See, e.g., Calloway v. Wyatt, 246 N.C. 129, 97 S.E.2d 881 (1957).

Section (c). — This section is an approximate counterpart to former § 1–155. The rule is, however, more precise on two aspects, and thereby an improvement. First it is made plain that the license to plead generally extends to "occurrence" as well as to "performance" of conditions precedent. Second, the rule requires that the party desiring to controvert performance or occurrence must specify and particularize rather than merely deny the general allegation.

Section (d). — This section had no counterpart in existing law, but is a helpful sanction to plead generally and in conclusory terms the official character of document issuance and particular acts — "facts" not logically subject to "ultimate fact" pleading.

Section (e). — This section is an approximate counterpart to former § 1–154, but makes precise some things not spelled out in that statute, i.e., that it relates to judgments of foreign as well as domestic courts and to the decisions of quasi-judicial tribunals as well as those of traditional courts of law and judicial officers.

Section (f). — This section varies the usual rule under the Code that allegations of time and place are immaterial, but in only one narrow respect, viz., that for purposes of testing the sufficiency of a pleading, i.e., on motion to dismiss or for judgment on the pleadings, such allegations are considered material. The main purpose of this is to allow the early raising of issues as to the bar of the statute of limitations. This section would actually solidify a trend in North Carolina practice toward pretrial resolutions of the issue, notwithstanding it may not technically be raised by an attack by demurrer on the pleading itself, but must be affirmatively pleaded by the party relying on the defense. Section 1–15. The practice has already evolved, however, of resolving the issue after answer filed, on pretrial motion or motion for judgment on the pleading. See, e.g., Rowland v. Beauchamp, 253 N.C. 231, 116 S.E.2d 720 (1960); Gillikin v. Bell, 254 N.C. 244, 118 S.E.2d 609 (1961). This section would carry the process one step further and allow the issue to be raised prior to filing of answer by motion to dismiss. For all other purposes, however, allegations of time and place ordinarily remain immaterial, so far as limiting proof is concerned. Of course, any question of materiality is customarily avoided by the "on or about" or "at or near" type allegation.

Section (g). — This section codifies, without attempting elaboration, the rule generally stated and followed under North Carolina Code practice. It attempts no specification of what amounts to "special damage" in particular context, so that developed case precedent on this would continue to apply. See, on this point, Brandis and Trotter, Some Observations on Pleading Damages in North Carolina, 31 N.C.L. Rev. 249 (1953).

Section (h). — This section has no counterpart in the federal rules, but is taken from former § 1–157.

Section (i). — This section has no counterpart in the federal rules, but is taken from former § 1–158.

Rule 10. Form of pleadings

(a) Caption; names of parties.—Every pleading shall contain a caption setting forth the division of the court in which the action is filed, the title of the action, and a designation as in Rule 7(a). In the complaint the title of the action shall include the names of all the parties, but in other pleadings it is sufficient to state the name of the first party on each side with an appropriate indication of other parties.

(b) Paragraphs; separate statement.—All averments of claim or defense shall be made in numbered paragraphs, the contents of each of which be limited as far as practicable to a statement of a single set of circumstances; and a paragraph may be referred to by number in all succeeding pleadings. Each claim founded upon a separate transaction or occurrence and each defense other than denials shall be stated in a separate count or defense whenever a separation facilitates the clear presentation of the matters set forth.

(c) Adoption by reference; exhibits.—Statements in a pleading may be adopted by reference in a different part of the same pleading or in another pleading or in any motion in the action. A copy of any written instrument which is an exhibit to a pleading is a part thereof for all purposes.

Added by Laws 1967, c. 954, § 1.

Comment

Section (a). — This section dealing with the formal caption and designation of parties in the pleadings generally approximates the corresponding directive found in former § 1–122(1), although the latter actually dealt literally only with the caption and party designation in the complaint. The rule literally sanctions the practice customarily followed of shortening the listing of multiple parties in all pleadings subsequent to the complaint.

Section (b). — This section deals basically with the requirement that pleadings be drafted in a format designed to promote the clear definition of fact issues—the required separate statement in numbered paragraphs of practically manageable aggregates of factual averments, each generally referable to a separate substantive concept likely to lead to one manageable issue if controverted. This is a key innovation in the Code "fact-pleading" reform in reaction to the formulary pleading of common law. Thus, comparable provisions were found in former §§ 1–122(2) (complaint) and 1–138 (answer). By carrying forward this scheme, it is made abundantly clear that these rules are designed just as are the codes to cause factual issues clearly to emerge in the unsupervised exchange of pleadings where skilled and honest pleaders are aligned in opposition. That this is the design of these rules, particularly as exemplified in Rule 10(b), see Mr. Justice Jackson's analysis and admonition in O'Donnell v. Elgin, J. & E. Ry., 338 U.S. 384, 70 S. Ct. 200, 94 L. Ed. 187, 16 A.L.R.2d 646 (1949) ("We no longer insist upon technical rules of pleading, but it will ever be difficult in a jury trial to segregate issues which counsel do not separate in their pleading, preparation or thinking"). It can be stated quite confidently that this rule contemplates a continuation of the issue-defining fact pleading approach of the Code.

Section (c). — This section's first sentence involves a change from present practice which is controlled by a rule of the Supreme Court and does not permit adoption of portions of pleadings by reference into other parts of the cause or other pleadings. Of course, this presents a critical policy question of the propriety of adopting statutes in direct conflict with existing court rules. However, the practice sanctioned in this rule is believed an improvement, all things considered. The second sentence, directly sanctioning the incorporation of attached exhibits involves no change in procedure. The phrase "for all purposes" is apt to avoid the type of decision which quibbles over whether mere attachment of an exhibit without express words purporting to incorporate particular aspects as direct allegations does have this effect.

Rule 11. Signing and verification of pleadings

(a) Signing by Attorney.—Every pleading, motion, and other paper of a party represented by an attorney shall be signed by at least one attorney of record in his individual name, whose address shall be stated. A party who is not represented by an attorney shall sign his pleading, motion, or other paper and state his address. Except when otherwise specifically provided by rule or statute, pleadings need not be verified or accompanied by affidavit. The signature of an attorney or party constitutes a certificate by him that he has read the pleading, motion, or other paper; that to the best of his knowledge, information, and belief formed after reasonable inquiry it is well grounded in fact and is warranted by existing law or a good faith argument for the extension, modification, or reversal of existing law, and that it is not interposed for any improper purpose, such as to harass or to cause unnecessary delay or needless increase in the cost of litigation. If a pleading, motion, or other paper is not signed, it shall be stricken unless it is signed promptly after the omission is called to the attention of the pleader or movant. If a pleading, motion, or other paper is signed in violation of this rule, the court, upon motion or upon its own initiative, shall impose upon the person who signed it, a represented party, or both, an appropriate sanction, which may include an order to pay to the other party or parties the amount of the reasonable expenses incurred because of the filing of the pleading, motion, or other paper, including a reasonable attorney's fee.

(b) Verification of pleadings by a party.—In any case in which verification of a pleading shall be required by these rules or by statute, it shall state in substance that the contents of the pleading verified are true to the knowledge of the person making the verification, except as to those matters stated on information and belief, and as to those matters he believes them to be true. Such verification shall be by affidavit of the party, or if there are several parties united in interest and pleading together, by at least one of such parties acquainted with the facts and capable of making the affidavit. Such affidavit may be made by the agent or attorney of a party in the cases and in the manner provided in section (c) of this rule.

(c) Verification of pleadings by an agent or attorney.—Such verification may be made by the agent or attorney of a party for whom the pleading is filed, if the action or defense is founded upon a written instrument for the payment of money only and the instrument or a true copy thereof is in the possession of the agent or attorney, or if all the material allegations of the pleadings are within the personal knowledge of the agent or attorney. When the pleading is verified by such agent or attorney, he shall set forth in the affidavit:

(1) That the action or defense is founded upon a written instrument for the payment of money only and the instrument or a true copy thereof is in his possession, or

(2) a. That all the material allegations of the pleadings are true to his personal knowledge and

b. The reasons why the affidavit is not made by the party.

(d) Verification by corporation or the State.—When a corporation is a party the verification may be made by any officer, or managing or local agent thereof upon whom summons might be served; and when the State or any officer thereof in its behalf is a party, the verification may be made by any person acquainted with the facts.

Added by Laws 1967, c. 954, § 1. Amended by Laws 1985 (Reg. Sess. 1986), c. 1027, § 55.

Comment

This rule is in form an amalgamation of federal Rule 11 and basic North Carolina statutes concerned with signing and verification of pleadings. The provision common to both, that every pleading must be signed either by a party or his attorney of record, is retained. The requirement that every pleading subsequent to a verified pleading must be verified is abandoned, and the only time any pleading must be verified is when some statute specifically requires it, as in actions for divorce (G.S. 50-8). As an alternative to the verification control on truth, the federal approach of constituting an attorney's signature to any pleading a certificate of good faith in its preparation is adopted. However, the severe explicit federal rule sanction of disciplinary action against an attorney violating this rule is dropped, retaining only the sanction of striking as sham.

Sections (b), (c), and (d) are not found in the corresponding federal rule, but are lifted as substantial counterparts from former §§ 1-145, 1-146, and 1-147.

Rule 12. Defenses and objections; when and how presented; by pleading or motion; motion for judgment on pleading

(a)(1) When Presented. — A defendant shall serve his answer within 30 days after service of the summons and complaint upon him. A party served with a pleading stating a crossclaim against him shall serve an answer thereto within 30 days after service upon him. The plaintiff shall serve his reply to a counterclaim in the answer within 30 days after service of the answer or, if a reply is ordered by the court, within 30 days after service of the order, unless the order otherwise directs. Service of a motion permitted under this rule alters these periods of time as follows, unless a different time is fixed by order of the court:

a. The responsive pleading shall be served within 20 days after notice of the court's action in ruling on the motion or postponing its disposition until the trial on the merits;

b. If the court grants a motion for a more definite statement, the responsive pleading shall be served within 20 days after service of the more definite statement.

(2) Cases Removed to United States District Court. — Upon the filing in a district court of the United States of a petition for the removal of a civil action or proceeding from a court in this State and the filing of a copy of the petition in the State court, the State court shall proceed no further therein unless and until the case is remanded. If it shall be finally determined in the United States courts that the action or proceeding was not removable or was improperly removed, or for other reason should be remanded, and a final order is entered remanding the action or proceeding to the State court, the defendant or defendants, or any other party who would have been permitted or required to file a pleading had the proceedings to remove not been instituted, shall have 30 days after the filing in such State court of a certified copy of the order of remand to file motions and to answer or otherwise plead.

(b) How Presented. — Every defense, in law or fact, to a claim for relief in any pleading, whether a claim, counterclaim, crossclaim, or third-party claim, shall be asserted in the responsive pleading thereto if one is required, except that the following defenses may at the option of the pleader be made by motion:

(1) Lack of jurisdiction over the subject matter,

(2) Lack of jurisdiction over the person,

(3) Improper venue or division,

(4) Insufficiency of process,

(5) Insufficiency of service of process,

(6) Failure to state a claim upon which relief can be granted,

(7) Failure to join a necessary party.

A motion making any of these defenses shall be made before pleading if a further pleading is permitted. The consequences of failure to make such a motion shall be as provided in sections (g) and (h). No defense or objection is waived by being joined with one or more other defenses or objections in a responsive pleading or motion. Obtaining an extension of time within which to answer or otherwise plead shall not constitute a waiver of any defense herein set forth. If a pleading sets forth a claim for relief to which the adverse party is not required to serve a responsive pleading, he may assert at the trial any defense in law or fact to that claim for relief. If, on a motion asserting the defense numbered (6), to dismiss for failure of the pleading to state a claim upon which relief can be granted, matters outside the pleading are presented to and not excluded by the court, the motion shall be treated as one for summary judgment and disposed of as provided in Rule 56, and all parties shall be given reasonable opportunity to present all material made pertinent to such a motion by Rule 56.

(c) Motion for judgment on the pleadings. — After the pleadings are closed but within such time as not to delay the trial, any party may move for judgment on the pleadings. If, on a motion for judgment on the pleadings, matters outside the pleadings are presented to and not excluded by the court, the motion shall be treated as one for summary judgment and disposed of as provided in Rule 56, and all parties shall be given reasonable opportunity to present all material made pertinent to such a motion by Rule 56.

(d) Preliminary hearings. — The defenses specifically enumerated (1) through (7) in section (b) of this rule, whether made in a pleading or by motion, and the motion for judgment on the pleadings mentioned in section (c) of this rule shall be heard and determined before trial on application of any party, unless the judge orders that the hearing and determination thereof be deferred until the trial.

(e) Motion for more definite statement. — If a pleading to which a responsive pleading is permitted is so vague or ambiguous that a party cannot reasonably be required to frame a responsive pleading, he may move for a more definite statement before interposing his responsive pleading. The motion shall point out the defects complained of and the details desired. If the motion is granted and the order of the judge is not obeyed within 20 days after notice of the order or within such other time as the judge may fix, the judge may strike the pleading to which the motion was directed or make such orders as he deems just.

(f) Motion to strike. — Upon motion made by a party before responding to a pleading or, if no responsive pleading is permitted by these rules, upon motion made by a party within 30 days after the service of the pleading upon him or upon the judge's own initiative at any time, the judge may order stricken from any pleading any insufficient defense or any redundant, irrelevant, immaterial, impertinent, or scandalous matter.

(g) Consolidation of defenses in motion. — A party who makes a motion under this rule may join with it any other motions herein provided for and then available to him. If a party makes a motion under this rule but omits therefrom any defense or objection then available to him which this rule permits to be raised by motion, he shall not thereafter make a motion based on the defense or objection so omitted, except a motion as provided in section (h)(2) hereof on any of the grounds there stated.

(h) Waiver or preservation of certain defenses. —

(1) A defense of lack of jurisdiction over the person, improper venue, insufficiency of process, or insufficiency of service of process is waived (i) if omitted from a motion in the circumstances described in section (g), or (ii) if it is neither made by motion under this rule nor included in a responsive pleading or an amendment thereof permitted by Rule 15(a) to be made as a matter of course.

(2) A defense of failure to state a claim upon which relief can be granted, a defense of failure to join a necessary party, and an objection of failure to state a legal defense to a claim may be made in any pleading permitted or ordered under Rule 7(a), or by motion for judgment on the pleadings, or at the trial on the merits.

(3) Whenever it appears by suggestion of the parties or otherwise that the court lacks jurisdiction of the subject matter, the court shall dismiss the action.

Added by Laws 1967, c. 954, § 1. Amended by Laws 1971, c. 1236; Laws 1975, c. 76, § 2.

Comment

This rule deals comprehensively with the whole mechanism, including timetables, for raising all the various defenses and objections traditionally available to defensively aligned parties at some pretrial stage, including those based merely on objections to form of pleadings, those traditionally characterized as dilatory defenses, and those based upon defenses on the merits.

Section (a) is a straightforward timetable for the filing of the traditional defensive pleadings, the answer, and the reply. The 30-day period rather than the federal rule 20-day period is adopted. All other considerations of timeliness in raising the various possible objections and defenses by other devices are related to the times for filing these responsive pleadings.

The remaining sections deal in closely inter-related fashion with the whole problem of an orderly staging of the various traditional objections and defenses, worked out to guard against dilatoriness and to encourage economy of effort and early potential raising and determination of defenses likely to be decisive, either as to the abatement of the particular action, or on the merits. The key conceptions, involving some fairly drastic changes from the Code practice, are these: (1) Only two kinds of procedural devices—the traditional defensive pleadings and functionally shaped motions—shall be utilized to raise all the objections and defenses made available. This has been presaged in the provisions of Rule 7(c), abolishing demurrers and pleas, and thus leaving only pleadings and the motion remaining as available devices out of the traditional arsenal. (2) Except for the possible objections to mere forms of pleadings, all the traditional defenses, whether characterized as merely formal, dilatory, or on the merits, may be raised together, and for the first time, in the required responsive pleadings. This departs from the traditional Code approach which required certain defenses, both dilatory and on the merits, to be raised, at peril of waiver, by demurrer, when they appear on the face of the pleading (former §§ 1-127, 1-133). Taking a different approach, this rule instead merely gives the option to any defensive pleader to raise seven enumerated objections and defenses by motion prior to filing his responsive pleading [Rule 12(b)]; and the option to either party to then have such motion-raised defenses heard preliminarily unless the court defers consideration of them to trial time [Rule 12(d)].

The third sentence in section (b) has as its purpose the clarification of the preceding sentence. Ordinarily, of course, a motion making any of the listed defenses should be made before pleading. But the failure to do so is not preclusive in all circumstances and as to all defenses, as sections (g) and (h) of this rule make clear.

The only ones of the traditional objections to mere form which are retained are the motion to make more definite and certain and the motion to strike. It must be assumed that in the context of the federal pleading approach the motion to make more definite and certain will be utilized with much more restraint, generally only when such ambiguity exists that the responsive pleader cannot reasonably be required to plead to the pleading under attack. See generally 2 Moore's Federal Practice Pars. 12.18 and 12.20.

The most direct analogue to the Code demurrer for failure to state facts sufficient to constitute a cause of action, which is abolished under this procedure, is the motion to dismiss for failure to state a claim upon which relief can be granted. [Rule 12(b)(6)]. In a general way it can be said that this motion is typically honored in federal practice under the same circumstances that a demurrer is sustained and action dismissed in State practice because the pleading attacked contains a "statement of a defective cause of action," as opposed merely to a "defective statement of good cause of action." Compare, for example, Turner v. Gastonia City Bd. of Educ., 250 N.C. 456, 109 S.E.2d 211 (1959), illustrating application of the "defective cause" rule under existing State demurrer practice, with DeLoach v. Crawley's, Inc., 128 F.2d 378 (5th Cir. 1942), illustrating dismissal rule on motion to dismiss under federal Rule 12(b)(6). Unlike the State practice demurrer, this motion to dismiss may "speak." [Rule 12(b), last sentence].

The waiver provisions of Rule 12(h) provide in effect that the defenses of failure to state a claim, or failure to join a necessary party may be raised at any time before verdict. After verdict however, the defenses of failure to state a claim and failure to join a necessary party cannot then be raised or noted for the first time. Lack of jurisdiction of the subject matter, of course, cannot be waived and is always available as a defense.

In addition to the motion to dismiss, analogous in a limited way to the demurrer as above stated, a motion for judgment on the pleadings is likewise provided in Rule 12(c). It too has "speaking" capacities.

Rule 13. Counterclaim and crossclaim

(a) Compulsory counterclaims.—A pleading shall state as a counterclaim any claim which at the time of serving the pleading the pleader has against any opposing party, if it arises out of the transaction or occurrence that is the subject matter of the opposing party's claim and does not require for its adjudication the presence of third parties of whom the court cannot acquire jurisdiction. But the pleader need not state the claim if

(1) At the time the action was commenced the claim was the subject of another pending action, or

(2) The opposing party brought suit upon his claim by attachment or other process by which the court did not acquire jurisdiction to render a personal judgment on that claim, and the pleader is not stating any counterclaim under this rule.

(b) Permissive counterclaim.—A pleading may state as a counterclaim any claim against an opposing party not arising out of the transaction or occurrence that is the subject matter of the opposing party's claim.

(c) Counterclaim exceeding opposing claim.—A counterclaim may or may not diminish or defeat the recovery sought by the opposing party. It may claim relief exceeding in amount or different in kind from that sought in the pleading of the opposing party.

(d) Counterclaim against the State of North Carolina.—These rules shall not be construed to enlarge beyond the limits fixed by law the right to assert counterclaims or to claim credit against the State of North Carolina or an officer or agency thereof.

(e) Counterclaim maturing or acquired after pleading.—A claim which either matured or was acquired by the pleader after serving his pleading may, with the permission of the court, be presented as a counterclaim by supplemental pleading.

(f) Omitted counterclaim.—When a pleader fails to set up a counterclaim through oversight, inadvertence, or excusable neglect, or when justice requires, he may by leave of court set up the counterclaim by amendment.

(g) Crossclaim against coparty.—A pleading may state as a crossclaim any claim by one party against a coparty arising out of the transaction or occurrence that is the subject matter either of the original action or of a counterclaim therein or relating to any property that is the subject matter of the original action. Such crossclaim may include a claim that the party against whom it is asserted is or may be liable to the crossclaimant for all or part of a claim asserted in the action against the crossclaimant.

(h) Additional parties may be brought in.—When the presence of parties other than those to the original action is required for the granting of complete relief in the determination of a counterclaim or crossclaim, the court shall order them to be brought in as defendants as provided in these rules, if jurisdiction of them can be obtained.

(i) Separate trial; separate judgment.—If the court orders separate trials as provided in Rule 42(b), judgment on a counterclaim or crossclaim may be rendered in accordance with the terms of Rule 54(b) when the court has jurisdiction so to do, even if the claims of the opposing party have been dismissed or otherwise disposed of.

Added by Laws 1967, c. 954, § 1.

Comment

Sections (a) through (f) deal with counterclaims that must and those that may be asserted in an action, i.e., with compulsory and permissive counterclaims.

Compulsory counterclaims. — There is no current statutory provision which in terms makes any counterclaim compulsory. However, certain counterclaims have traditionally been made compulsory in effect by application of res judicata principles. The judicially evolved rule is that a party will be barred from maintaining an action if in a prior or pending action he could have obtained the same relief by permissive counterclaim and if a judgment for plaintiff in the former or pending action would collaterally estop the plaintiff in the second in respect of determinative issues. Thus, most typically, when a party is sued for damages arising out of negligent operation of an automobile, he must assert any claim for damages he may have arising out of the same occurrence by counterclaim, at peril of being barred from thereafter asserting the claim by separate action. Allen v. Salley, 179 N.C. 147, 101 S.E. 545 (1919). Rule 13(a) states this substantially, but with more directness, and in a way which avoids some possible question about the application of the North Carolina judicial rule to a second action when plaintiff in the first action lost. Basically, this rule should cause no actual change in the practice in respect to those claims which counsel for defendants will feel under compulsion to assert by counterclaim at peril of being barred to assert them separately.

Three necessary exceptions to the basic rule of compulsion are provided in this section. A counterclaim otherwise compulsory under the rule need not be asserted: (1) If parties necessary to its adjudication cannot be subjected to jurisdiction; or (2) if the pleader has already asserted the claim in another pending action; or (3) if to counterclaim would subject the pleader to personal jurisdiction in respect of a merely quasi in rem claim by the plaintiff, as to which the pleader is not otherwise amenable to personal jurisdiction. Furthermore, possible relief against the consequences of failure to assert a normally compulsory counterclaim is provided in section (f) which gives the court discretion to allow a compulsory counterclaim to be added by amendment.

Permissive counterclaim. — Under former code practice, two types of counterclaim were permissive: (1) Any contract claim existing at the commencement of the plaintiff's action, when the plaintiff's claim is in contract, and (2) any claim arising out of the same contract or transaction which is the basis of plaintiff's action (usually compulsory under the res judicata rule).

The rule in section (b) is much broader. In fact, it is unlimited in its terms — a pleader may at his option assert any claim he may have against an opponent which he is not compelled by section (a) to assert. This approach parallels that of the unlimited joinder of claims philosophy of Rule 18. The idea is that so far as the basic structuring of the litigation at the pleading stage is concerned, there should be unlimited ability to join opposing as well as parallel claims—and that the appropriate protection against trial of an overly complex case resulting from unlimited counterclaim assertion right is by severance for separate trial subsequently under Rule 42(b).

Section (c). — This section states existing case law in North Carolina. See 1 McIntosh, North Carolina Practice and Procedure, § 1238 (2d ed. 1956).

Section (d). — This section is self-explanatory.

Section (e). — This section allows the assertion by supplemental pleading, with leave of court, of counterclaims maturing or acquired after the pleader has already filed his defensive pleading. This is a direct and simple handling of a problem as to which confusion had existed under code practice. Under former § 1–137, a counterclaim might be asserted under the contract section only if it was in existence at the time of commencement of plaintiff's action, but no such limitation was stated with respect to counterclaims under the same transaction section. But, of course, these also may arise out of contract, and some confusion existed in applying the statute. See 1 McIntosh, North Carolina Practice and Procedure, § 1242 (2d ed. 1956). This rule makes no distinction based on types of counterclaim, but simply provides that any subsequently acquired counterclaim may, if the court deems it proper on a whole view of the matter, be injected into litigation after the initial pleading has already been served.

Crossclaims between parties similarly aligned, as coplaintiffs or codefendants. — Rule 13(g), following the general philosophy of an unlimited option by pleaders to join any claims and assert any counterclaims at the pleading stage, lays down a very liberal policy for asserting crossclaims between coparties. There is, however, a limitation, not found with respect to permissive claim joinder under Rule 18, or permissive counterclaim assertion under Rule 13(b). The crossclaim must arise out of the same transaction or occurrence on which the basic claims and counterclaims are based, or must relate to property which is the subject matter of the original action. Thus, coparties cannot as a matter of right inject claims between themselves which have not even a general historical relation to the basic claims in litigation between plaintiffs and defendants. But, given the general historical relation expressed in the concept, "arising out of the same transaction or occurrence," there is no further requirement that the crossclaim relate substantively to the basic claim or counterclaim — or that it in some way affect the party asserting these basic claims. Thus, most typically, where A sues B and C for personal injury damages as alleged joint tort-feasors, B and C may crossclaim against each other in respect of independent claims for personal injury or property damage alleged to have resulted from the same occurrence out of which A's claim arose. Certainly the most common bases for crossclaims are those for contribution or indemnification in respect of the crossclaimant's alleged liability, and the last sentence Rule 13(g) specifically authorizes these bases.

This represents a substantial departure from former code practice which, without specific statutory directive, had slowly evolved a much more restrictive judicial rule for permissible crossclaims between coparties. Thus, it was held under the code that the only permissible crossclaim was one for indemnification based on a noncontractual right (e.g., primary as opposed to secondary tort liability). Specifically forbidden was any crossclaim by one codefendant against another for: (1) Personal injury or property damage to the claimant, notwithstanding it "arose out of the same occurrence" as plaintiff's primary claim. Jarrett v. Brogdon, 256 N.C. 693, 124 S.E.2d 850 (1962); (2) contribution in respect of the crossclaimant's liability to plaintiff. Bass v. Lee, 255 N.C. 73, 120 S.E.2d 570 (1961); and (3) indemnification if based on an express or implied contract to indemnify crossclaimant in respect of his liability to plaintiff. Steele v. Moore–Flesher Hauling Co., 260 N.C. 486, 133 S.E.2d 197 (1963). See generally, tracing the evolution of the permissible crossclaim rules to their present state, Note, 40 N.C.L. Rev. 633 (1962).

Section (h). — This section states existing North Carolina case law. Bullard v. Berry Coal & Oil Co., 254 N.C. 756, 119 S.E.2d 910 (1961) (when A sues B in negligence and B counterclaims, B may have C brought in to defend against counterclaim on allegations that C is vicariously liable thereon in respect of A's alleged negligence).

Here again, with respect to the liberal attitude toward allowable crossclaims, the notion is that if over-complexity results for the purposes of trial, severance and separate trials under Rule 42(b) is the appropriate action, rather than preventing the assertion of crossclaims at the pleading stage.

Section (i). — This section incorporates the provisions of Rule 54(b) to allow the entering of "final judgment" in respect to particular counterclaims or crossclaims, notwithstanding the whole action is not yet ripe for judgment.

Rule 14. Third-party practice

(a) When defendant may bring in third party.—At any time after commencement of the action a defendant, as a third-party plaintiff, may cause a summons and complaint to be served upon a person not a party to the action who is or may be liable to him for all or part of the plaintiff's claim against him. Leave to make the service need not be obtained if the third-party complaint is filed not later than 45 days after the answer to the complaint is served. Otherwise leave must be obtained on motion upon notice to all parties to the action. The person served with the summons and third-party complaint, hereinafter called the third-party defendant, shall make his defense to the third-party plaintiff's claim as provided in Rule 12 and his counterclaims against the third-party plaintiff and crossclaim against other third-party defendants as provided in Rule 13. The third-party defendant may assert against the plaintiff any defenses which the third-party plaintiff has to the plaintiff's claim. The third-party defendant may also assert any claim against the plaintiff arising out of the transaction or occurrence that is the subject matter of the plaintiff's claim against the third-party plaintiff. The plaintiff may assert any claim against the third-party defendant arising out of the transaction or occurrence that is the subject matter of the plaintiff's claim against the third-party plaintiff, and the third-party defendant thereupon shall assert his defenses as provided in Rule 12 and his counterclaims and crossclaims as provided in Rule 13. Any party may move for severance, separate trial, or dismissal of the third-party claim. A third-party defendant may proceed under this rule against any person not a party to the action who is or may be liable to him for all or part of the claim made in the action against the third-party defendant.

Where the normal statute of limitations period in an action arising on a contract is extended as provided in G.S. 1–47(2) or in any action arising on a contract or promissory note, upon motion of the defendant the court may order to be made parties additional defendants, including any party of whom the plaintiff is a subrogee, assignee, third-party beneficiary, endorsee, agent or transferee, or such other person as has received the benefit of the contract by transfer of interest.

(b) When plaintiff may bring in third party.—When a counterclaim is asserted against a plaintiff, he may cause a third party to be brought in under circumstances which under this rule would entitle a defendant to do so.

(c) Rule applicable to State of North Carolina.—Notwithstanding the provisions of the Tort Claims Act, the State of North Carolina may be made a third party under subsection (a) or a third-party defendant under subsection (b) in any tort action. In such cases, the same rules governing liability and the limits of liability of the State and its agencies shall apply as is provided for in the Tort Claims Act.

Added by Laws 1967, c. 954, § 1. Amended by Laws 1969, c. 810, § 2; Laws 1975, c. 587, § 1; Laws 1981, c. 92; Laws 1981, c. 810.

Comment

Comment to this Rule as Originally Enacted. — Certainly one of the most unsatisfactory areas of North Carolina procedural law was that concerned with what has come to be called "third-party practice." By this is meant the basis upon which and the procedure whereby an original defendant (third-party plaintiff) may implead — have brought into the action — an additional party (third-party defendant) to defend against a claim over by the original defendant/third-party plaintiff. An adequate procedural rule dealing with this important and frequently encountered problem must at least: (1) Specify the substantive grounds permitting impleader, and (2) clearly set out the procedure by which it may be accomplished. For a comprehensive coverage, it should additionally prescribe the kinds of claims which, after impleader has been accomplished, may then be asserted by the parties — originally plaintiff, third-party plaintiff, and third-party defendants — inter se. North Carolina statutory law did none of these in adequate, direct terms. Because of the desirability of allowing impleader in some situations at least, the North Carolina court constructed a set of judicial rules for impleading by drawing upon certain statutes which suggested its use peripherally or in a specific situation, but which were completely inadequate if gauged by the standards of adequate coverage above suggested. Thus, former § 1–73, providing in part that the court might cause parties to be brought in when necessary to a complete determination of the controversy; former § 1–222, providing in part that a judgment might be given for or against one or more of several defendants, might determine the rights of the parties on each side, as between themselves, and might grant a defendant any affirmative relief to which entitled; and § 1-240, cryptically providing for the impleading of alleged joint tort-feasors by an original alleged tort-feasor defendant, were drawn upon by the court. As indicated, none of these statutes dealt directly with the basic problems: (a) Of grounds for impleading (except § 1-240, dealing narrowly with contribution between joint tort-feasors); (b) Of the procedure by which a third-party plaintiff actually impleads a third-party defendant; or (c) Of the kinds of claims that may, after impleader is accomplished, be asserted by the parties inter se.

Working with this completely inadequate statutory pattern, the court has, over the years, evolved rules and sanctioned procedures for impleading which can only be found by resort to the decided cases. These rules as evolved are, aside from the difficulty of locating them, subject to criticism because of their narrowness of approach to the grounds on which impleading is allowed in the first place, and then to the question of what claims may properly be asserted after impleading by the parties inter se. Thus, the basic rule which has evolved to control impleadings permits impleading only when the claim by the third-party plaintiff is for: (1) Contribution against an alleged joint tortfeasor under § 1-240, or (2) indemnification, but only when the indemnification right arises as a matter of law, and not when it arises by express or implied contract. See, for a summary of this rule and the basis of its evolution, 1 McIntosh, North Carolina Practice and Procedure, § 722 (2d edition 1956, with 1965 Supplement). The court is not always consistent in this distinction. See Davis v. Radford, 233 N.C. 283, 63 S.E.2d 822 (1951).

Beyond this, no systematic prescription of the additional claims which may thereafter be asserted between third-party plaintiff and third-party defendant, and between plaintiff and third-party defendant has been worked out in the North Carolina cases. And, as pointed out, this is not provided in the statutes. It is clear only that an impleaded third-party defendant may, but is not compelled to, assert against the third-party plaintiff any claim which would, as to the third-party plaintiff's claim, meet the permissive counterclaim test of former § 1-123. Norris v. Johnson, 246 N.C. 179, 97 S.E.2d 773 (1957) (permissive); Morgan v. Brooks, 241 N.C. 527, 85 S.E.2d 869 (1955) (but not compulsory).

None of the statutes drawn upon prescribed the exact procedure for impleading. Thus, there was no statutory directive as to whether it shall be done by "cross complaint" in the original defendant's answer, or by separate "third-party complaint"; as to whether it requires an order of court based upon motion and notice, or an order entered ex parte; nor as to what mode of service of the third-party complaint or cross complaint shall be utilized. In the absence of any such directive, a practice, generally standardized, but with many variants has been evolved. It has received at least indirect sanction from the court by constant reference to its use without comment. See 1 McIntosh, North Carolina Practice and Procedure, § 722.5 (1965 Pocket Supplement). This practice is cumbersome, and, as indicated, not by any means completely standardized.

In contrast to this most unsatisfactory situation, federal Rule 14 provides a directive for third-party practice which is comprehensive in its coverage. The substantive test for impleading is stated directly — a party may be impleaded "who is or may be liable to [the third-party plaintiff] for all or part of the plaintiff's claim against him." This obviously gives the right to implead for contribution and indemnification, where the substantive right to those remedies exists by statute or common law. This is the limit of the impleading right judicially evolved under North Carolina practice. The federal rule is construed to go beyond this and allow impleading for indemnification where the right to be indemnified has arisen out of contract. See, e.g., Watkins v. Baltimore & O. Ry., 29 F. Supp. 700 (W.D. Pa. 1939). This would broaden the North Carolina approach. Note that it still does not allow impleading on its liberal a basis as exists for crossclaims between parties originally joined as defendants. There, under federal Rule 13, the only requirement is relation between the crossclaim and the transaction or occurrence forming the basis of plaintiff's claim.

Beyond the direct and plain statement of the substantive test for impleading, the federal rule prescribes clearly and concisely the procedure for impleading where the right exists. This, as pointed out, is not done in the North Carolina statutes.

Finally, federal Rule 14 concludes with a clear statement, likewise lacking in State statutes, of the various claims which may, after a third-party defendant is impleaded, be asserted by the various parties inter se. Here, as in the joinder statutes, the safeguard against undue complexity which might result under this rule's liberal allowance of permissible cross and counterclaims is stated to be severance of claims in advance of trial.

It should be noted that federal Rule 14 is of course entirely procedural—it does not, indeed cannot — affect any substantive rights. Thus, it does not allow impleader unless the substantive right exists under State law. Accordingly, then, adoption of this rule does not affect any of the North Carolina substantive law of contribution or indemnification.

Comment to the 1969 Amendment. — (a) G.S. 1-47(2) was amended to provide that where an action is brought on a sealed instrument, the defendant or defendants in such action may file a counterclaim arising out of the same transaction or transactions as are the subject of plaintiff's claim, although a shorter period of limitation would otherwise apply to defendant's counterclaim.

The second paragraph of Rule 14 was amended to provide that in such actions, or in any action arising on a contract or promissory note, the defendant may have additional defendants brought into the action. Such additional defendants cannot escape liability by passage of time or by transferring of contract rights.

Rule 15. Amended and supplemental pleadings

(a) Amendments.—A party may amend his pleading once as a matter of course at any time before a responsive pleading is served or, if the pleading is one to which no responsive pleading is permitted and the action has not been placed upon the trial calendar, he may so amend it at any time within 30 days after it is served. Otherwise a party may amend his pleading only by leave of court or by written consent of the adverse party; and leave shall be freely given when justice so requires. A party shall plead in response to an amended pleading within 30 days after service of the amended pleading, unless the court otherwise orders.

(b) Amendments to conform to the evidence.—When issues not raised by the pleadings are tried by the express or implied consent of the parties, they shall be treated in all respects as if they had been raised in the pleadings. Such amendment of the pleadings as may be necessary to cause them to conform to the evidence and to raise these issues may be made upon motion of any party at any time, either before or after judgment, but failure so to amend does not affect the result of the trial of these issues. If evidence is objected to at the trial on the ground that it is not within the issues raised by the pleadings, the court may allow the pleadings to be amended and shall do so freely when the presentation of the merits of the action will be served thereby and the objecting party fails to satisfy the court that the admission of such evidence would prejudice him in maintaining his action or defense upon the merits. The court may grant a continuance to enable the objecting party to meet such evidence.

(c) Relation back of amendments.—A claim asserted in an amended pleading is deemed to have been interposed at the time the claim in the original pleading was interposed, unless the original pleading does not give notice of the transactions, occurrences, or series of transactions or occurrences, to be proved pursuant to the amended pleading.

(d) Supplemental pleadings.—Upon motion of a party the court may, upon reasonable notice and upon such terms as are just, permit him to serve a supplemental pleading setting forth transactions or occurrences or events which may have happened since the date of the pleading sought to be supplemented, whether or not the original pleading is defective in its statement of a claim for relief or defense. If the court deems it advisable that the adverse party plead thereto, it shall so order, specifying the time therefor.

Added by Laws 1967, c. 954, § 1.

Comment

This rule is, except for section (c), substantially a counterpart to federal Rule 15. Section (c) is drawn from the New York Civil Practice Law and Rules, Rule 3025. As such, it deals with a most critical aspect of the whole approach of these rules to the pleading function. This is most obvious in its basic directive for the allowing of amendments to pleading. In this aspect, its approach is generally that of the codes, with the basic theme being to allow amendment as of right up to the time that the opponent has taken his initial position by responsive pleading, and thereafter to make the privilege to amend more and more difficult to obtain as the litigation progresses and positions may accordingly have become more and more hardened on the basis of the original pleadings. However, a fundamental change of approach from existing practice is taken in (1) the generality with which this basic theme is formulated and (2) this rule's abandonment in terms of the whole variance conception so integral a part of the code amendment scheme.

Section (a). — This section first states the rule for amendment as of right up to responsive pleading time, thus basically making no change in the former law, § 1-161. But then, in dealing with the whole problem of discretionary amendments after this time and up to the time that amendments are sought to conform to proof already adduced, this rule merely lays down the simple directive that leave to amend in this interval shall be freely given "when justice so requires." This is a deliberate abandonment of the typical code approach, as found in former § 1-163, which attempted in tortuous fashion to lay down detailed directives for the exercise of this discretion. The result of this code formulation has been to necessitate equally tortured judicial construction which, instructively, still continues, 100 years after the code's adoption. See, e.g., Perkins v. Langdon, 233 N.C. 240, 63 S.E.2d 565 (1951). However, the phrase "as justice requires" has acted as an effective limitation on the amendment privilege in the federal courts. For when, on a whole view of the matter, as is frequently the case, it is determined that justice does not require a particular amendment, or that, to the contrary, positive injustice to the opposing party would result, amendment has been denied. See, e.g., Friedman v. Transamerica Corp., 5 F.R.D. 115 (D. Del. 1946); Portsmouth Baseball Corp. v. Frick, 21 F.R.D. 318 (S.D.N.Y. 1958). This is a much preferable type directive to the detailed code directive which has seemed to necessitate an obviously mechanical jurisprudence in its application. Perkins v. Langdon, supra.

The last sentence of section (a) involves a departure of obvious import from the federal rule timetable.

Section (b). — This section involves the second major change in concept from code practice. Dealing with the problem of trial time amendments necessitated by the failure of proof to conform in some degree with pleadings, it deliberately abandons the laboriously constructed code scheme of immaterial variance, material variance and total failure of proof (former §§ 1–168, 1–169), and lays down a directive based directly upon the truly legitimate policy consideration which should control amendment privilege here, namely, whether, notwithstanding variance of some degree, there has nevertheless been informed consent to try the issues on the evidence presented. Here again, limitation on amendment privilege is sufficiently insured by the phrases, "when the presentation of the merits of the action will be served thereby," and its twin, "and the objecting party fails to satisfy the court that the admission of such evidence would prejudice him." Indeed, it seems quite clear that the code directive was actually designed to get the same result, but that the very detail of its formulation led to a drift into a very mechanical approach which has now largely subverted the "litigation by consent" doctrine in North Carolina. See Note, 41 N.C.L. Rev. 647 (1963). Finally, the last sentence of this section inserts a final safeguard in its reminder of the continuance possibility.

Section (c). — This section deals with the extremely difficult matter of determining when amendments should "relate back" for statute of limitation purposes by posing the broad question of the relation between the new matter and the basic aggregate of historical facts upon which the original claim or defense is based. This deliberately avoids the more abstruse inquiry under the codes as to whether the amendment involves a "wholly different cause of action or defense." It is believed that this approach is a distinct improvement in its express reliance on the truly valid consideration of identity in the historical fact sense. Wachtell's comment on the provision in the New York Civil Practice Law and Rules from which section (c) is drawn is equally pertinent here. The rule, he says, is that "a cause of action in an amended pleading will be deemed to relate back to the commencement of the action if the original pleading gave notice of the transactions, occurrences, or series of transactions or occurrences to be proved under the amended pleading. The amended pleading will therefore relate back if the new pleading merely amplifies the old cause of action, or now even if the new pleading constitutes a new cause of action, provided that the defending party had originally been placed on notice of the events involved. For example, an amended cause of action for damages for breach of a contract would relate back where the original pleading alleged an action in equity to rescind the contract for fraud. And an amended cause of action against defendants for breach of an implied warranty of agency in entering into a contract would relate back even though the original pleading had alleged a cause of action upon the contract against the defendants as principals." Wachtell, N.Y. Practice Under the C.P.L.R. (1963), p. 141.

Section (d). — This section is in effect a general counterpart to former § 1–167, without some of the specific detail. No practical change in the procedure for filing supplemental pleadings should result under this rule.

Rule 16. Pre-trial procedure; formulating issues

(a) In any action, the court may in its discretion direct the attorneys for the parties to appear before the court for a conference to consider

(1) The simplification and formulation of the issues;

(2) The necessity or desirability of amendments to the pleadings;

(3) The possibility of obtaining admissions of fact and of documents which will avoid unnecessary proof;

(4) The limitation of the number of expert witnesses;

(5) The advisability or necessity of a reference of the case, either in whole or in part;

(6) Matters of which the court is to be asked to take judicial notice;

(7) Such other matters as may aid in the disposition of the action.

If a conference is held, the judge shall make an order which recites the action taken at the conference, any amendments allowed to the pleadings, and any agreements made by the parties as to any of the matters considered, and which may limit the issues for trial to those not disposed of by admissions or agreements of counsel; and such order when entered controls the subsequent course of the action, unless modified at the trial to prevent manifest injustice. If any issue for trial as stated in the order is not raised by the pleadings in accordance with the provisions of Rule 8, upon motion of any party, the order shall require amendment of the pleadings.

(b) In a medical malpractice action as defined in G.S. 90–21.11, at the close of the discovery period scheduled pursuant to Rule 26(g), the judge shall schedule a final conference. After the conference, the judge shall refer any consent order calendaring the case for trial to the senior resident superior court judge or the chief district court judge, who shall approve the consent order unless the judge finds that:

(1) The date specified in the order is unavailable,

(2) The terms of the order unreasonably delay the trial, or

(3) The ends of justice would not be served by approving the order.

If the senior resident superior court judge or the chief district court judge does not approve the consent order, the judge shall calendar the case for trial. In calendaring the case, the court shall take into consideration the nature and complexity of the case, the proximity and convenience of witnesses, the needs of counsel for both parties concerning their respective calendars, the benefits of an early disposition and such other matters as the court may deem proper.

Added by Laws 1967, c. 954, § 1. Amended by Laws 1987, c. 859, § 4; S.L. 2011–199, § 1, eff. Oct. 1, 2011.

Comment

While the Rules of Civil Procedure do not envisage a pretrial conference in every case, they do contemplate a significant role for such conferences. The Commission knows that where former statutes have been used systematically, excellent results have been achieved. 36 N.C.L. Rev. 521 (1958).

Two significant changes are embodied in this rule. First, whether there is to be a pretrial conference is made an entirely discretionary matter with the judge. It was the Commission's view that pretrial cannot function effectively unless the judge himself is committed to the desirability of a resort to the procedure. Second, a requirement has been added that if the pretrial order contains an issue not raised by the pleadings, the court, on motion of any party, shall order an amendment.

Comment to the 2011 Amendment. — In this and other rules, an effort was made to make the rules gender neutral. Thus, the introductory material in subsection (a) changes "the judge" and "him" to "the court" and "his" to "its", and in two places in subsection (b), "he" is changed to "the judge". No substantive change is intended by those amendments.

Subsection (a). — The portion of subsection (a) that permits the judge to direct the attorneys to appear for a conference is not changed. It still is discretionary. However, if a conference is held, the judge is required to issue an order that reflects the action taken at the conference, including any amendments to the pleadings and agreements reached by the parties. The judge, in the order, may, but is not required to, limit the issues for trial to those not disposed of by admissions or agreement at the conference.

WEST'S
NORTH CAROLINA GENERAL STATUTES ANNOTATED

ARTICLE 4
Parties

Rule 17. Parties plaintiff and defendant; capacity

(a) Real party in interest. — Every claim shall be prosecuted in the name of the real party in interest; but an executor, administrator, guardian, trustee of an express trust, a party with whom or in whose name a contract has been made for the benefit of another, or a party authorized by statute may sue in his own name without joining with him the party for whose benefit the action is brought; and when a statute of the State so provides, an action for the use or benefit of another shall be brought in the name of the State of North Carolina. No action shall be dismissed on the ground that it is not prosecuted in the name of the real party in interest until a reasonable time has been allowed after objection for ratification of commencement of the action by, or joinder or substitution of, the real party in interest; and such ratification, joinder, or substitution shall have the same effect as if the action had been commenced in the name of the real party in interest.

(b) Infants, incompetents, etc. —

(1) Infants, etc., Sue by Guardian or Guardian Ad Litem. — In actions or special proceedings when any of the parties plaintiff are infants or incompetent persons, whether residents or nonresidents of this State, they must appear by general or testamentary

guardian, if they have any within the State or by guardian ad litem appointed as hereinafter provided; but if the action or proceeding is against such guardian, or if there is no such known guardian, then such persons may appear by guardian ad litem.

(2) Infants, etc., Defend by Guardian Ad Litem. — In actions or special proceedings when any of the defendants are infants or incompetent persons, whether residents or nonresidents of this State, they must defend by general or testamentary guardian, if they have any within this State or by guardian ad litem appointed as hereinafter provided; and if they have no known general or testamentary guardian in the State, and any of them have been summoned, the court in which said action or special proceeding is pending, upon motion of any of the parties, may appoint some discreet person to act as guardian ad litem, to defend in behalf of such infants, or incompetent persons, and fix and tax his fee as part of the costs. The guardian so appointed shall, if the cause is a civil action, file his answer to the complaint within the time required for other defendants, unless the time is extended by the court; and if the cause is a special proceeding, a copy of the complaint, with the summons, must be served on him. After 20 days' notice of the summons and complaint in the special proceeding, and after answer filed as above prescribed in the civil action, the court may proceed to final judgment as effectually and in the same manner as if there had been personal service upon the said infant or incompetent persons or defendants.

All orders or final judgments duly entered in any action or special proceeding prior to April 8, 1974, when any of the defendants were infants or incompetent persons, whether residents or nonresidents of this State, and were defended therein by a general or testamentary guardian or guardian ad litem, and summons and complaint or petition in said action or special proceeding were duly served upon the guardian or guardian ad litem and answer duly filed by said guardian or guardian ad litem, shall be good and valid notwithstanding that said order or final judgment was entered less than 20 days after notice of the summons and complaint served upon said guardian or guardian ad litem.

(3) Appointment of Guardian Ad Litem Notwithstanding the Existence of a General or Testamentary Guardian.—Notwithstanding the provisions of subsections (b)(1) and (b)(2), a guardian ad litem for an infant or incompetent person may be appointed in any case when it is deemed by the court in which the action is pending expedient to have the infant, or insane or incompetent person so represented, notwithstanding such person may have a general or testamentary guardian.

(4) Appointment of Guardian Ad Litem for Unborn Persons. — In all actions in rem and quasi in rem and in all actions and special proceedings which involve the construction of wills, trusts and contracts or any instrument in writing, or which involve the determination of the ownership of property or the distribution of property, if there is a possibility that some person may thereafter be born who, if then living, would be a necessary or proper party to such action or special proceeding, the court in which said action or special proceeding is pending, upon motion of any of the parties or upon its own motion, may appoint some discreet person guardian ad litem to defend on behalf of such unborn person. Service upon the guardian ad litem appointed for such unborn person shall have the same force and effect as service upon such unborn person would have had if such person had been living. All proceedings by and against the said guardian ad litem after appointment shall be governed by all provisions of the law applicable to guardians ad litem for living persons.

(5) Appointment of Guardian Ad Litem for Corporations, Trusts, or Other Entities Not in Existence. — In all actions which involve the construction of wills, trusts, contracts or written instruments, or the determination of the ownership of property or the disposition or distribution of property pursuant to the provisions of a will, trust, contract or written instrument, if such will, trust, contract or written instrument provides benefits for disposition or distribution of property to a corporation, a trust, or an entity thereafter to be formed for the purpose of carrying into effect some provision of the said will, trust, contract or written instrument, the court in which said action or special proceeding is pending, upon motion of any of the parties or upon its own motion, may appoint some discreet person guardian ad litem for such corporation, trust or other entity. Service upon the guardian ad litem appointed for such corporation, trust or other entity shall have the same force and effect as service upon such corporation, trust or entity would have had if such corporation, trust or other entity had been in existence. All proceedings by and against the said guardian ad litem after appointment shall be governed by all provisions of the law applicable to guardians ad litem for living persons.

(6) Repealed by S.L. 1981, c. 599, § 1.

(7) Miscellaneous Provisions. — The provisions of this rule are in addition to any other remedies or procedures authorized or permitted by law, and it shall not be construed to repeal or to limit the doctrine of virtual representation or any other law or rule of law by which unborn persons or nonexistent corporations, trusts or other entities may be represented in or bound by any judgment or order entered in any action or special proceeding. This rule shall apply to all pending actions and special proceedings to which it may be constitutionally applicable. All judgments and orders heretofore entered in any action in which a guardian or guardians ad litem have been appointed for any unborn person or persons or any nonexistent corporations, trusts or other entities, are hereby validated as of the several dates of entry thereof in the

same manner and to the full extent that they would have been valid if this rule had been in effect at the time of the appointment of such guardians ad litem; provided, however, that the provisions of this sentence shall be applicable only in such cases and to the extent to which the application thereof shall not be prevented by any constitutional limitation.

(c) Guardian ad litem for infants, insane or incompetent persons; appointment procedure. — When a guardian ad litem is appointed to represent an infant or insane or incompetent person, he must be appointed as follows:

(1) When an infant or insane or incompetent person is plaintiff, the appointment shall be made at any time prior to or at the time of the commencement of the action, upon the written application of any relative or friend of said infant or insane or incompetent person or by the court on its own motion.

(2) When an infant is defendant and service under Rule 4(j)(1)a is made upon him the appointment may be made upon the written application of any relative or friend of said infant, or, if no such application is made within 10 days after service of summons, upon the written application of any other party to the action or, at any time by the court on its own motion.

(3) When an infant or insane or incompetent person is defendant and service can be made upon him only by publication, the appointment may be made upon the written application of any relative or friend of said infant, or upon the written application of any other party to the action, or by the court on its own motion, before completion of publication, whereupon service of the summons with copy of the complaint shall be made forthwith upon said guardian so appointed requiring him to make defense at the same time that the defendant is required to make defense in the notice of publication.

(4) When an insane or incompetent person is defendant and service by publication is not required, the appointment may be made upon the written application of any relative or friend of said defendant, or upon the written application of any other party to the action, or by the court on its own motion, prior to or at the time of the commencement of the action, and service upon the insane or incompetent defendant may thereupon be dispensed with by order of the court making such appointment.

(d) Guardian ad litem for persons not ascertained or for persons, trusts or corporations not in being. — When under the terms of a written instrument, or for any other reason, a person or persons who are not in being, or any corporation, trust, or other legal entity which is not in being, may be or may become legally or equitably interested in any property, real or personal, the court in which an action or proceeding of any kind relative to or affecting such property is pending, may, upon the written application of any party to such action or proceeding or of other person interested, appoint a guardian ad litem to represent such person or persons not ascertained or such persons, trusts or corporations not in being.

(e) Duty of guardian ad litem; effect of judgment or decree where party represented by guardian ad litem. — Any guardian ad litem appointed for any party pursuant to any of the provisions of this rule shall file and serve such pleadings as may be required within the times specified by these rules, unless extension of time is obtained. After the appointment of a guardian ad litem under any provision of this rule and after the service and filing of such pleadings as may be required by such guardian ad litem, the court may proceed to final judgment, order or decree against any party so represented as effectually and in the same manner as if said party had been under no legal disability, had been ascertained and in being, and had been present in court after legal notice in the action in which such final judgment, order or decree is entered.

Added by Laws 1967, c. 954, § 1. Amended by Laws 1969, c. 895, §§ 5, 6; Laws 1971, c. 1156, §§ 3, 4; Laws 1973, c. 1199; Laws 1981, c. 599, § 1; Laws 1987, c. 550, § 13.

Comment

Comment to this Rule as Originally Enacted. — For historical reasons, an apparently necessary component of any procedural code or bloc of rules is a statement of the real party in interest generality, i.e., that action must be prosecuted in the name of the "real party in interest," as opposed to the name of any other person who may have a technical or nominal interest in the claim. This was deemed necessary for the purpose of allowing assignees of choses in action to sue in their own names to recover on the chose, a thing forbidden at common law — and this was probably the only thing had in mind in the original code. But the basic statement in the code was not so limited; hence, it was necessary also to add some obvious qualifications to the basic directive that actions can only be brought in the name of the presently beneficially interested — the "real" — party. Thus, certain fiduciaries should be allowed to sue in their own names on claims in which only their beneficiaries have beneficial — "real" — interests. Furthermore, the third-party contract beneficiary has well established substantive rights which he should be allowed to sue for in his own name, notwithstanding the contract parties alone are "real" parties to the contract and hence, possibly, to the rights arising under it. Finally, some exception was needed to take into account the fact that specific statutes may sometimes give rights to sue in their own names to parties not technically real parties in interest. Through what appears to be sheer whimsy in codification the original code "real party in interest" draft section, which put both the generality and its exception into one section, was modified in the North Carolina code version to separate the two components. Thus § 1-57 states the generality, while the exceptions were stated in former § 1-63. The federal Rule 17(a) dealing with the same matters, returns to the original code pattern and states both the generality and its exception as a connected whole. The rule as presented here tracks the federal rule, and rejects the State code separation of the concepts. No change of central substance is made from the present directive. Consequently, there is no reason to anticipate any change in real party in interest case law arising from this form of statement.

Closely related to the real party in interest generality and its exceptions is the problem of formal representation of persons not sui generis for the purpose of prosecuting and defending actions as to which the parties formally represented have the true beneficial interest — the problem, in short, of the appointment of, the appearance by, and the prosecution and defense of actions through guardians for infants and incompetents. Here, the present State statutory law is substantially retained, with some attempt to clean up and make more comprehensive the whole pattern.

Comment to the 1969 Amendment. — (a) The 1969 amendment to Rule 17(a) eliminates another technical ground of possible dismissal. It provides that no action is to be dismissed on the ground that it is not prosecuted in the name of the real party in interest until a reasonable time has been allowed after objection for ratification of commencement of the section by, or joinder or substitution of, the real party in interest; and such ratification, joinder, or substitution shall have the same effect as if the action had been commenced in the name of the real party in interest.

Correction and substitution of parties was known both to the common law and the code practice. This amendment is merely another step in that direction and avoids needless delay and technical disposition of a meritorious action.

(b) (6) The amendment to Rule 17 designated as (6) [now repealed] merely acknowledges that an infant who is competent to marry, and who is 18 years of age or older, is also competent to prosecute or defend the listed domestic relations action without the appointment of a guardian ad litem.

The amendment also renumbered former subsection (6) of section (b) as subsection (7).

Rule 18. Joinder of claims and remedies

(a) Joinder of claims.—A party asserting a claim for relief as an original claim, counterclaim, cross claim, or third-party claim, may join, either as independent or as alternate claims, as many claims, legal or equitable, as he has against an opposing party.

(b) Joinder of remedies; fraudulent conveyances.—Whenever a claim is one heretofore cognizable only after another claim has been prosecuted to a conclusion, the two claims may be joined in a single action; but the court shall grant relief in that action only in accordance with the relative substantive rights of the parties. In particular, a plaintiff may state a claim for money and a claim to have set aside a conveyance fraudulent as to him, without first having obtained a judgment establishing the claim for money.

Added by Laws 1967, c. 954, § 1. Amended by Laws 1969, c. 895, § 7.

Comment

General Comment on the Problems Dealt with in the Joinder Rules, Rules 18 to 21. — The fundamental problem sought to be controlled by so-called joinder rules is that of the size which a single lawsuit shall on the one hand be compelled, and, on the other hand, permitted to assume. Hence, the rules of compulsory (minimum allowable size) and permissive (maximum allowable size) joinder. Since size depends both upon the number of claims (causes of action) and parties potentially involved, the rules of joinder have traditionally been separately framed in terms of parties and claims (causes of action).

Permissive Joinder. — The underlying policy controlling maximum permissible size is clear and has always been at least tacitly agreed upon under all procedural systems—namely, that the size should be as large as is compatible with orderly handling of issues and fairness to those parties not necessarily interested in all phases of the lawsuit as finally structured. This in turn is based upon the obvious—that economy of judicial effort is achieved by the resolution in one suit of as many claims, concluding as many parties, as is possible. The rub has come in laying down workable directions which are fairly simple in statement; which nevertheless deal adequately with the potentially two-dimensional nature of the joinder problem (both parties and causes); and which, though couched in a form concrete enough for ready application, state what is essentially a quite flexibly conceived goal, i.e., maximum size commensurate with orderly handling of issues and fairness to all parties. One way to solve what is essentially a very difficult drafting problem is to lay down a fairly rigid, hence easily expressed, limitation in the kinds of cause of action which may be joined. If this is done, the problem of too many parties tends to take care of itself, since under traditional conceptions of the structure of a "cause of action," such a single judicial unit rarely has multiple parties aligned on either side of it (typically only when the substantive law contemplates the existence of parties jointly, or jointly or severally, entitled or obligated). Thus, in most cases of attempted joinder of multiple parties there will be a more basic joinder of causes of action which will come under control of the limitation applicable to joinder of causes. This was the common-law approach, which started out allowing only one claim to be made in any action, and finally relaxed only to the point of allowing joinder of causes when they all fell within one of the "forms of action." The code draftsmen, wedded to this approach, essentially codified it, merely using new terminology, e.g., "contract," in place of old "assumpsit," to define the categories within which joinder of claims is permissive. This approach is artificial, and actually loses sight of the basic policy which should control here, but it is simple to put into directive form, and it "works," albeit at the expense of legitimate considerations. When coupled, as it typically is in the codes, with procedural devices provided to attack misjoinder preliminary to trial, it produces a vast amount of skirmishing at this stage before trial is ever reached. This is the history of application of the code joinder rules. Here the emphasis is on artificial restriction of size, with leeway provided for movement in the direction of enlargement only through the power in judges to consolidate causes not technically subject to joinder.

Another approach, which is also simple of statement, is to go in exactly the opposite direction and state a basic directive for practically unlimited joinder of claims at the pleading stage, limited only by considerations of fairness to any parties not potentially interested in the totality of the lawsuit as then structured, leaving the burden on the judiciary to move in a restricted direction by exercise of the power of severance closer to trial time. This dispenses with pleading stage skirmishes over the alignment of the suit in terms of parties and claims, and defers ultimate structuring while preserving to the parties at this stage all the benefits of an ongoing uninterrupted lawsuit. This last is essentially a description of the federal rule approach to the problem of maximum permissible size or permissive joinder.

Compulsory Joinder. — Going to the problem of minimum allowable size (compulsory joinder), the Commission found that the underlying policy consideration here has traditionally been to insure that all "necessary" or "indispensable" parties should be involved in a lawsuit before it proceeds to trial, or certainly before it proceeds to judgment. Necessity and indispensability have always been viewed in this context as involving two aspects: First, necessity from the standpoint of the judicial economy of concluding in one lawsuit the total potential range of the controversy as defined in the pleadings; Second, necessity from the standpoint of avoiding undue practical prejudice to absent parties (notwithstanding they are not legally concluded) by proceeding to trial and judgment without their presence.

There has never been considered to be any corresponding necessity to compel joinder of several causes of action, hence there have not been rules of "compulsory joinder of causes." The res judicata principle of merger by judgment arises at this stage in the form of the rule against "splitting a cause of action." This, in effect, sets the minimum allowable size of a lawsuit, so far as causes of action is concerned, at one such unit. Beyond this there is no compulsion to "join." Thus, the rules of compulsory joinder have always been rules of compulsory joinder of parties. Here, too, the problem has been to draft concretely to express the essentially flexible consideration of "necessity" above summarized. There has always been general agreement that all parties jointly entitled or obligated were "necessary" in the sense compelling their joinder, and this has been the rule from common-law days, through the codes, and under federal practice. Beyond the "jointly interested" or "united in interest" area, however, the directives have had to rely simply on general formulations of necessity in the sense above discussed. There is remarkably little change in phraseology designed to express this essential notion under the federal rule formulation from that under the codes.

Multiple Causes and Parties. — A particularly difficult problem in framing permissive joinder directives is occasioned by the necessity for taking into account the possibility of both multiple causes and parties. As indicated, despite the inextricably two-dimensional nature of the joinder problem where multiple causes and parties are involved, the traditional approach has been to frame the joinder rules as if joinder of parties and causes were two separate and independent problems. Of course, where there is but a single claim (cause of action) the joinder rule directed solely at the party joinder limitations is completely adequate to control the matter. But where separately framed directives are used, they must be interrelated in some fashion in order to take into account the possibility of joinder of both claims and parties in a single suit. This poses a logical difficulty which has actually defied any but artificial solutions in any system which has sought to impose separately conceived limitations on joinder of parties and causes, and then to interrelate these limitations. Thus, one code solution has been (as in North Carolina) to resolve this logical dilemma by adding to the basic limitations on joinder of causes the all inclusive limitation that all causes must affect all parties. This is a possible solution, but it achieves relative certainty (only relative) at the expense of truly valid considerations of maximum permissible lawsuit size. Another approach, much more likely to achieve the desired goals, is to allow unlimited joinder of claims as such, and to impose limitations only in respect of parties, which limitations apply whether there is but a single or multiple causes of action (claims) involved. This is the federal rules approach and it has proven in practice not only to be more certain of application in given cases, but also to allow closer approximation to the true goals of permissive joinder, i.e., to allow as much to be concluded in any lawsuit as is commensurate with orderly handling of issues and fairness to parties not interested in the entire scope of the suit. Here again, ultimate protection against confusion of issues and unfairness can be provided by severance power reposed in the judiciary, and so it is under the federal rules approach.

Comment on Rule 18 as Originally Enacted. — This is an exact tracking of the federal rule. This reflects the view that the joinder conceptions expressed in this rule are much preferable to the code approach as previously incorporated essentially in former §§ 1-123, 1-68 and 1-69.

The first sentence of section (a) starts with the simplest possible situation by stating the basic rule for permissive joinder of claims as between just two parties. This rule is simply for potentially unlimited joinder, without regard to number and nature. If this be thought to open the door to vast confusion by encouraging an unfettered joinder of numerous completely unrelated claims, two things should be remembered. First, as a practical matter, human affairs do not often contrive to give many legal claims to any particular individual against another particular individual at times close enough together to raise even the possibility of their joinder in a single action. Furthermore, to the extent multiple claims do arise close enough in point of time to raise the joinder possibility, they are extremely likely to arise out of the same basic historical occurrences or transactions, thus presenting fair ground for inclusion in one lawsuit. Secondly, if, however, too numerous claims are allowed to be joined in the pleadings in a particular case, this does not mean that they must therefore be tried in the same case. Both Rules 20(b) and 42(b) contain express mandates to sever claims prior to trial for separate trial where orderliness and fairness require this.

The second sentence posits the more complicated situation of multiple parties and multiple claims, and reiterates the basic rule of unlimited joinder of claims in this situation but with the proviso that the limitations on permissive party joinder (as expressed in Rules 19, 20, and 22) are to be observed. As indicated in the General Comment to this bloc of rules, this is a much more preferable way in logic to handle the difficult problem of interrelating limitations on multiple claim and multiple party joinder than is the code way. The party joinder rules impose quite realistic and sufficient restrictions on unfettered joinder of claims here. For where both multiple claims and multiple parties are involved, two unifying factors in respect of the various parties vis-a-vis the various claims must exist to allow the claims to be joined, i.e., (1) all the claims must arise out of the same aggregation of historical facts (same "transaction or occurrence, etc."), and (2) there must be in respect of all parties some common question of law or fact necessarily to be determined in the action. This is a much more easily understandable and applicable restriction than is the vague "all causes must affect all parties" restriction which underlies all other tests for permissive joinder of claims under the former code approach. It also gets more truly at the valid limiting consideration which should control the maximum size, i.e., the avoidance of too numerous historically unrelated issues in a single action wherein not all the parties are interested in the resolution of all the issues.

The third sentence quite logically makes these rules for permissive joinder of claims and of parties and claims applicable to crossclaims and third-party claims when the integral requirements for prosecuting such claims are met.

By contrast with this logically conceived and well-stated directive for permissive joinder of claims in both the single and multiple party situations, the code approach in former § 1-123 was poorly conceived and has led to logically absurd and unjustifiable results. Thus, for example, in a single party context under this statute, A may sue B in one action for breach of two entirely different contracts, since both causes fall within one of the listed categories of joinable claims, Lyon v. Atlantic C.L.R.R., 165 N.C. 143, 81 S.E. 1 (1914); but A may not in one action sue B, his employer, for (1) negligent injury, and (2) wrongful discharge from employment when A refuses to sign a release as to the negligence claim, because the two causes do not fall within any of the listed categories, not even the "same transaction" category. Pressley v. Great Atl. & Pac. Tea Co., 226 N.C. 518, 39 S.E.2d 382 (1946). In the multiple party context the "joker provision" that notwithstanding claims may be otherwise joinable, they may not be joined if all of them do not affect all parties, has given rise to quite unpredictable results from case to case. For example, in Branch Banking & Trust Co. v. Pierce, 195 N.C. 717, 143 S.E. 524 (1928), against the contention that all causes did not affect all parties, plaintiff was allowed to join several claims against various officers and directors of a corporation, alleging mismanagement notwithstanding the alleged several acts extended over a period of years during all of which it did not appear all the defendants were serving; while in Gattis v. Kilgo, 125 N.C. 133, 34 S.E. 246 (1899), A was not allowed to join a cause of action against B for slander with a cause against B and three others for subsequent publication of the same slander, because all causes did not affect all parties. Legitimate considerations of trial convenience were frequently not served by this Code directive. Thus, most typically, while it will prevent A and B from joining in a negligence case against C from injuries received by the same actionable negligence of C, the courts quite frequently consolidate for trial the separate nonjoinable claims of A and B for trial convenience.

Section (b) establishes a rule of permissive joinder, whose obvious import is to avoid the circuity of action necessitated by successive actions if such joinder were not expressly authorized by rule. The effect of this rule is to codify North Carolina case law in respect of the money claim, fraudulent conveyance joinder. Dawson Bank v. Harris, 84 N.C. 206 (1881) (establishing rule consistently followed since).

Comment on 1969 Amendment to Rule 18. — (a) Although Rule 18(a) was rewritten by the 1969 amendment, it appears that together with other rules affecting joinder of claims, especially Rules 13 and 14, a very liberal joinder of claims practice will be permissible. If there are multiple parties, then the parties' rules will have to be consulted.

Rule 19. Necessary joinder of parties

(a) Necessary joinder. — Subject to the provisions of Rule 23, those who are united in interest must be joined as plaintiffs or defendants; but if the consent of anyone who should have been joined as plaintiff cannot be obtained he may be made a defendant, the reason therefor being stated in the complaint; provided, however, in all cases of joint contracts, a claim may be asserted against all or any number of the persons making such contracts.

(b) Joinder of parties not united in interest. — The court may determine any claim before it when it can do so without prejudice to the rights of any party or to the rights of others not before the court; but when a complete determination of such claim cannot be made without the presence of other parties, the court shall order such other parties summoned to appear in the action.

(c) Joinder of parties not united in interest — Names of omitted persons and reasons for nonjoinder to be pleaded. — In any pleading in which relief is asked, the pleader shall set forth the names, if known to him, of persons who ought to be parties if complete relief is to be accorded between those already parties, but who are not joined, and shall state why they are omitted.

Added by Laws 1967, c. 954, § 1.

Comment

This rule deals with the problem of the minimum allowable size of a lawsuit, from the standpoint of parties required to be joined in order to proceed to trial. There is no compulsory joinder of causes of action, separately conceived, as noted in the General Comments to this bloc of joinder rules.

As framed, this rule is essentially a recodification of existing and former North Carolina statutes. Specifically, section (a), down to the proviso, is substantially a rewrite of the first sentence of former § 1-70. The introductory phrase, "subject to the provisions of Rule 23," makes the compulsory joinder directive subject to the class-action exception, which is now separately treated in Rule 23. The proviso is substantially a recodification of § 1-72 to carry forward the option to join or not join joint contract obligors plainly stated therein. Section (b) is substantially a tracking of the first sentence of former § 1-73, to express the general notion of "necessary party" based not on substantive jointness of claim but on the more general consideration of fairness and judicial economy of effort developed in the General Comments to this bloc of joinder rules. Adoption of this language involves rejection of the more sophisticated federal rules approach which posits the more refined categories of "indispensable" and "conditionally necessary parties." The code language is retained in the belief that roughly the same functional results are reached under its directive and the case law evolution under it of "proper" and "necessary" parties, and that no sufficiently good purpose would be served by introducing the new and more refined concepts and terminology to justify the risk of confusion from their introduction.

Section (c) is a direct counterpart of federal Rule 19(c). It is adopted because it forces explanation in the first instance of that which may be otherwise extracted by separate and time consuming later motion to require joinder. As such it should save wasted motion and time, if there is an adequate reason, such as unavailability of a party, to explain his nonjoinder in the first place.

Rule 20. Permissive joinder of parties

(a) Permissive joinder.—All persons may join in one action as plaintiffs if they assert any right to relief jointly, severally, or in the alternative in respect of or arising out of the same transaction, occurrence, or series of transactions or occurrences and if any question of law or fact common to all parties will arise in the action. All persons may be joined in one action as defendants if there is asserted against them jointly, severally, or in the alternative, any right to relief in respect of or arising out of the same transaction, occurrence, or series of transactions or occurrences and if any question of law or fact common to all parties will arise in the action. A plaintiff or defendant need not be interested in obtaining or defending against all the relief demanded. Judgment may be given for one or more of the plaintiffs according to their respective rights to relief, and against one or more defendants according to their respective liabilities.

(b) Separate trial.—The court shall make such orders as will prevent a party from being embarrassed, delayed, or put to expense by the inclusion of a party against whom he asserts no claim and who asserts no claim against him, and shall order separate trials or make other orders to prevent delay or prejudice.

Added by Laws 1967, c. 954, § 1. Amended by Laws 1973, c. 75.

Comment

This is an exact counterpart of federal Rule 20, and was proposed because it was felt, as developed in the General Comment to this bloc of rules, that the federal approach to permissive joinder is a much more serviceable one than was the code approach.

As pointed out in that Comment, the only limitations in respect of joinder in the federal approach are those related literally to party joinder. These limitations contemplate both single claim actions and multiple claim actions. In the multiple party-multiple claim action they are related by reference as limitations on claim joinder, as indicated in the Comment to Rule 18.

The rule is designed generally to express the notion that the limiting factors which control maximum lawsuit size in either single claim or multiple claim (by referring party joinder limitations to the claim joinder rule) litigation are (1) that the right to relief asserted by or against each party joined in the action should arise generally out of the same general aggregation of historical facts, and (2) furthermore, that in respect of all parties joined there must be involved for necessary determination in the lawsuit as structured a common question of law or fact. Beyond these limitations designed to keep the issues within bounds of fairness to parties and orderliness of handling, there is no requirement that every party must be affected by, or interested in, all the relief sought in the total action. And it is made plain, in furtherance of this notion, that the judgment entered in lawsuits involving multiple similarly aligned parties may be conformed to the possibility that not all parties are interested in all the relief to be given.

Section (b) provides the final safeguard against dangerous oversize and complexity through joinder by laying down a specific mandate for severance or such other orders as will protect parties in multiple party cases from unfairness resulting from their lack of interest or involvement in every facet of the case as permitted to be structured by the joinder rules.

Rule 21. Procedure upon misjoinder and nonjoinder

Neither misjoinder of parties nor misjoinder of parties and claims is ground for dismissal of an action; but on such terms as are just parties may be dropped or added by order of the court on motion of any party or on its own initiative at any stage of the action. Any claim against a party may be severed and proceeded with separately.

Added by Laws 1967, c. 954, § 1.

Comment

This is an exact counterpart to federal Rule 21, with the addition of the phrase "nor misjoinder of parties and claims" appearing in the first sentence. The general purpose of the rule is clearly to solidify the basic notion under the federal approach that faulty structuring of a case in terms of joinder of improper parties should not give rise to any drastic interruption of its normal progress to trial. Rather, the safeguard of restructuring without interruption, through severance or dropping of parties, without dismissal, is provided as an adequate protection against the evils of proceeding to trial in an overly-complex structure. The phrase referring to misjoinder of parties and causes, while probably not strictly necessary from the logical standpoint, is inserted because of the developed North Carolina case law rule for dismissal rather than severance where there is "misjoinder of both parties and causes." See Brandis, Permissive Joinder of Parties and Causes in North Carolina, 25 N.C.L. Rev. 1, pp. 49–53 (1946).

Rule 22. Interpleader

(a) Persons having claims against the plaintiff may be joined as defendants and required to interplead when their claims expose or may expose the plaintiff to double or multiple liability. It is not ground for objection to the joinder that the claims of the several claimants or the titles on which their claims depend do not have a common origin or are not identical but are adverse to and independent of one another, or that the plaintiff avers that he is not liable in whole or in part to any or all of the claimants. A defendant exposed to similar liability may obtain such interpleader by way of crossclaim or counterclaim. The provisions of this rule supplement and do not in any way limit the joinder of parties permitted in Rule 20.

(b) Where funds are subject to competing claims by parties to the action, the court may order the party in possession of the funds either to deposit the funds in an interest bearing account in a bank, savings and loan, or trust company licensed to do business in this State or to deposit the funds with the clerk. If the funds are deposited in a bank, savings and loan, or trust company, the court shall specify the type of interest bearing account to be used. Funds deposited with the clerk shall be invested or deposited as provided in G.S. 7A-112 and G.S. 7A-112.1. Upon determination of the action, the judgment shall provide for disbursement of the principal and interest earned on the funds while so deposited.

Added by Laws 1967, c. 954, § 1. Amended by Laws 1989, c. 668.

Comment

This rule makes clear that a liberalized use of interpleader is to be permitted. In particular, Pomeroy's four limitations on the use of interpleader are specifically repudiated. While the North Carolina court has not yet turned its back on these limitations, it has indicated some impatience with them. See Simon v. Raleigh City Bd. of Educ., 258 N.C. 381, 128 S.E.2d 785 (1963).

Rule 23. Class actions

(a) Representation.—If persons constituting a class are so numerous as to make it impracticable to bring them all before the court, such of them, one or more, as will fairly insure the adequate representation of all may, on behalf of all, sue or be sued.

(b) Secondary action by shareholders.—In an action brought to enforce a secondary right on the part of one or more shareholders or members of a corporation or an unincorporated association because the corporation or association refuses to enforce rights which may properly be asserted by it, the complaint shall be verified by oath.

(c) Dismissal or compromise.—A class action shall not be dismissed or compromised without the approval of the judge. In an action under this rule, notice of a proposed dismissal or compromise shall be given to all members of the class in such manner as the judge directs.

(d) Tax Class Actions.—In addition to all of the requirements set out in this rule, a class action seeking the refund of a State tax paid due to an alleged unconstitutional statute may be brought and maintained only as provided in G.S. 105-241.18.

Added by Laws 1967, c. 954, § 1; S.L. 2008-107, § 28.28(a), eff. Oct. 1, 2008.

Comment

Section (a). — In respect to class actions, the Commission adheres rather closely to the statutory provisions in North Carolina. See former § 1-70. It will be seen that three requirements are present. First, there must be a "class." Second, there must be such numerosity as to make impracticable the joinder of all members of the class. Third, there must be an assurance of adequacy of representation. This last requirement, while not contained in the statute, is surely necessary if the class action is to have any binding effect on absentees. See Hansberry v. Lee, 311 U.S. 32, 61 S. Ct. 115, 85 L. Ed. 22, 132 A.L.R. 741 (1940).

Section (b). — The Commission has not followed the federal rule in this section in its requirements that a shareholder must allege that he was a shareholder at the time of the transaction of which he complains. It was the Commission's thought that such a requirement may well deprive shareholders of any remedy when the corporation has suffered grievous injury. The Commission has also chosen not to follow the federal rule in its requirement of allegations in respect to the shareholder's efforts to persuade the managing directors to take remedial action. The Commission does not, however, take the positive approach of saying such allegations are unnecessary. Rule 8 governing what a complaint must contain is a sufficient guide in this matter.

Section (c). — This section seems obviously desirable in the protection that it affords absentees.

Rule 24. Intervention

(a) Intervention of right.—Upon timely application anyone shall be permitted to intervene in an action:

(1) When a statute confers an unconditional right to intervene; or

(2) When the applicant claims an interest relating to the property or transaction which is the subject of the action and he is so situated that the disposition of the action may as a practical matter impair or impede his ability to protect that interest, unless the applicant's interest is adequately represented by existing parties.

(b) Permissive intervention.—Upon timely application anyone may be permitted to intervene in an action.

(1) When a statute confers a conditional right to intervene; or

(2) When an applicant's claim or defense and the main action have a question of law or fact in common. When a party to an action relies for ground of claim or defense upon any statute or executive order administered by a federal or State governmental officer or agency or upon any regulation, order, requirement, or agreement issued or made pursuant to the statute or executive order, such officer or agency upon timely application may be permitted to intervene in the action. In exercising its discretion the court shall consider whether the intervention will unduly delay or prejudice the adjudication of the rights of the original parties.

(c) Procedure.—A person desiring to intervene shall serve a motion to intervene upon all parties affected thereby. The motion shall state the grounds therefor and shall be accompanied by a pleading setting forth the claim or defense for which intervention is sought. The same procedure shall be followed when a statute gives a right to intervene, except when the statute prescribes a different procedure.

Added by Laws 1967, c. 954, § 1.

Comment

Section (a). — This section, providing for intervention as of right, while closely following the federal rule, spells out a practice much like that already achieved in North Carolina. Intervention now is of right in claim and delivery and in attachment by virtue of § 1-440.43 and § 1-482. In respect to subsection (2), it will be noted that the harm to the intervenor's interest is to be considered from a "practical" standpoint, rather than technically. In other words, the intervenor need not be threatened with being bound in a strict res judicata sense. Further, it should be noted that adequate representation for the proposed intervenor is not limited to purely formal representation. But a present party may, in appropriate circumstances, be relied on to protect the intervenor's interest even though there is no formal relationship. See Annot., 84 ALR 2d 1412 (1962).

It will be observed that in any case, the application to intervene must be "timely." What will be "timely" will depend on the circumstances of the case.

Section (b). — This section perhaps establishes a broader base for permissive intervention than North Carolina now has but the Commission believes that the flexibility it makes possible to be highly desirable and the Commission is confident that the stated guide to the court as to what it shall consider in deciding whether or not to permit intervention will insure adequate protection for the original parties.

Section (c). — This section with its simple statement of the required procedure should be useful.

Rule 25. Substitution of parties upon death, incompetency or transfer of interest; abatement

(a) Death. — No action abates by reason of the death of a party if the cause of action survives. In such case, the court, on motion at any time within the time specified for the presentation of claims in G.S. 28A-19-3, may order the substitution of said party's personal representative or collector and allow the action to be continued by or against the substituted party.

(b) Insanity or incompetency. — No action abates by reason of the incompetency or insanity of a party. If such incompetency or insanity is adjudicated, the court, on motion at any time within one year after such adjudication, or afterwards on a supplemental complaint, may order that said party be represented by his general guardian or trustee or a guardian ad litem, and, allow the action to be continued. If there is no adjudication, any party may suggest such incompetency or insanity to the court and it shall enter such order in respect thereto as justice may require.

(c) Abatement ordered unless action continued. — At any time after the death, insanity or incompetency of a party, the court in which an action is pending, upon notice to such person as it directs and upon motion of any party aggrieved, may order that the action be abated, unless it is continued by the proper parties, within a time to be fixed by the court, not less than six nor more than 12 months from the granting of the order.

(d) Transfer of interest. — In case of any transfer of interest other than by death, the action shall be continued in the name of the original party; but, upon motion of any party, the court may allow the person to whom the transfer is made to be joined with the original party.

(e) Death of receiver of corporation. — No action against a receiver of a corporation abates by reason of his death, but, upon suggestion of the facts on the record, it continues against his successor or against the corporation in case a new receiver is not appointed and such successor or the corporation is automatically substituted as a party.

(f) Public officers; death or separation from office. —

(1) When a public officer is a party to an action in his official capacity and during its pendency dies, resigns or otherwise ceases to hold office, the action does not abate and his successor is automatically substituted as a party. Proceedings following the substitution shall be in the name of the substituted party, but any misnomer not affecting substantial rights of the parties shall be disregarded. An order of substitution may be entered at any time, but the omission to enter such an order shall not affect the substitution.

(2) When a public officer sues or is sued in his official capacity, he may be described as a party by his official title rather than by name; but the court may require his name to be added.

(g) No abatement after verdict. — After a verdict is rendered in any action, the action does not abate by reason of the death of a party, whether or not the cause of action upon which it is based is a type which survives.

Added by Laws 1967, c. 954, § 1. Amended by Laws 1977, c. 446, § 3.

Comment

Former § 1-74 and federal Rule 25 were generally comparable in providing for no automatic abatement of actions upon death, disability or transfer of interest of parties, but, instead, for a right to continue the action by or against substituted parties. The most important difference was in their respective ways of finally cutting off the right to continue. The federal rule allows two years within which parties may be substituted so as to continue the action, then for automatic dismissal if this has not been done within the period. Former § 1-74 allowed substitution and continuance on mere motion for one year after death or disability, and afterwards on supplemental complaint. No automatic dismissal was provided, but there was further provision that a party might be forced by the opposite party to either get substitution for continuation or suffer dismissal within a time specified by the court. Furthermore, former § 1-75 in a very awkward and questionable way imposed a duty on the adverse party to suggest to the court the death or disability of his opponent, and then a duty on the clark to notify the proper representative to come in and file pleadings.

On balance, it was felt that the State procedure had served North Carolina well enough in this area and that accordingly the form of former § 1-74 should be followed. There has been an attempt, however, to dress the format up somewhat, using catchlines for separate sections and cleaning up some of the incomplete and ambiguous language.

Furthermore, there has been added section (f), tracking the language of federal Rule 25(d), relating to death and separation of public officers. There is no comparable provision in the current law.

Finally, former § 1-75 was omitted entirely, on the basis that it was ambiguous, and that in apparently requiring new pleadings by substituted parties, it was not desirable. Its requirements have in fact been overlooked by the North Carolina court which has allowed substitution and continuation of actions without compliance with its provisions. See Alexander v. Patton, 90 N.C. 557 (1884).

The only danger in this scheme is that a party may try to lie back until a successor in interest has lost all chance of proceeding successfully and then coming in with a supplemental complaint and trying to resurrect the successor to force a continuation within time specified under section (c). But the court has prevented plaintiffs from so acting. See Sawyer v. Cowell, 241 N.C. 681, 86 S.E.2d 431 (1955).

ARTICLE 5

Depositions and Discovery

Rule 26. General provisions governing discovery

(a) Discovery methods.—Parties may obtain discovery by one or more of the following methods: depositions upon oral examination or written questions; written interrogatories; production of documents or things or permission to enter upon land or other property, for inspection and other purposes; physical and mental examinations; and requests for admission.

(b) Discovery scope and limits.—Unless otherwise limited by order of the court in accordance with these rules, the scope of discovery is as follows:

(1) In General.—Parties may obtain discovery regarding any matter, not privileged, which is relevant to the subject matter involved in the pending action, whether it relates to the claim or defense of the party seeking discovery or to the claim or defense of any other party, including the existence, description, nature, custody, condition and location of any books, documents, electronically stored information, or other tangible things and the identity and location of persons having knowledge of any discoverable matter. It is not ground for objection that the information sought will be inadmissible at the trial if the information sought appears reasonably calculated to lead to the discovery of admissible evidence nor is it grounds for objection that the examining party has knowledge of the information as to which discovery is sought. For the purposes of these rules regarding discovery, the phrase "electronically stored information" includes reasonably accessible metadata that will enable the discovering party to have the ability to access such information as the date sent, date received, author, and recipients. The phrase does not include other metadata unless the parties agree otherwise or the court orders otherwise upon motion of a party and a showing of good cause for the production of certain metadata.

(1a) Limitations on Frequency and Extent.—The frequency or extent of use of the discovery methods set forth in section (a) shall be limited by the court if it determines that: (i) the discovery sought is unreasonably cumulative or duplicative, or is obtainable from some other source that is more convenient, less burdensome, or less expensive; (ii) the party seeking discovery has had ample opportunity by discovery in the action to obtain the information sought; or (iii) the discovery is unduly burdensome or expensive, taking into account the needs of the case, the amount in controversy, limitations on the parties' resources, and the importance of the issues at stake in the litigation. The court may act upon its own initiative after reasonable notice or pursuant to a motion under section (c).

(1b) Specific Limitations on Electronically Stored Information.—In addition to any limitations imposed by subdivision (b)(1a) of this rule, discovery of electronically stored information is subject to the limitations set forth in Rule 34(b). The court may specify conditions for the discovery, including allocation of discovery costs.

(2) Insurance Agreements.—A party may obtain discovery of the existence and contents of any insurance agreement under which any person carrying on an insurance business may be liable to satisfy part or all of a judgment which may be entered in the action

or to indemnify or reimburse for payments made to satisfy the judgment. Information concerning the insurance agreement is not by reason of disclosure admissible in evidence at trial. For purposes of this subsection, an application for insurance shall not be treated as part of an insurance agreement.

(3) Trial Preparation; Materials.—Subject to the provisions of subsection (b)(4) of this rule, a party may obtain discovery of documents and tangible things otherwise discoverable under subsection (b)(1) of this rule and prepared in anticipation of litigation or for trial by or for another party or by or for that other party's consultant, surety, indemnitor, insurer, or agent only upon a showing that the party seeking discovery has substantial need of the materials in the preparation of the case and that the party is unable without undue hardship to obtain the substantial equivalent of the materials by other means. In ordering discovery of such materials when the required showing has been made, the court may not permit disclosure of the mental impressions, conclusions, opinions, or legal theories of an attorney or other representative of a party concerning the litigation in which the material is sought or work product of the attorney or attorneys of record in the particular action.

A party may obtain without the required showing a statement concerning the action or its subject matter previously made by that party. Upon request, a person not a party may obtain without the required showing a statement concerning the action or its subject matter previously made by that person. If the request is refused, the person may move for a court order. The provisions of Rule 37(a)(4) apply to the award of expenses incurred in relation to the motion. For purposes of this paragraph, a statement previously made is (i) a written statement signed or otherwise adopted or approved by the person making it, or (ii) a stenographic, mechanical, electrical, or other recording, or a transcription thereof, which is a substantially verbatim recital of an oral statement by the person making it and contemporaneously recorded.

Text of (b)(4) eff. until Oct. 1, 2015

(4) Trial Preparation; Experts.—Discovery of facts known and opinions held by experts, otherwise discoverable under the provisions of subsection (b)(1) of this rule and acquired or developed in anticipation of litigation or for trial, may be obtained only as follows:

a. 1. A party may through interrogatories require any other party to identify each person whom the other party expects to call as an expert witness at trial, to state the subject matter on which the expert is expected to testify, and to state the substance of the facts and opinions to which the expert is expected to testify and a summary of the grounds for each opinion.

2. Upon motion, the court may order further discovery by other means, subject to such restrictions as to scope and such provisions, pursuant to sub-subdivision (b)(4)b. of this rule, concerning fees and expenses as the court may deem appropriate.

b. Unless manifest injustice would result, (i) the court shall require that the party seeking discovery pay the expert a reasonable fee for time spent in responding to discovery under subdivision (b)(4)a.2. of this rule; and (ii) with respect to discovery obtained under subdivision (b)(4)a.2. of this rule the court may require the party seeking discovery to pay the other party a fair portion of the fees and expenses reasonably incurred by the latter party in obtaining facts and opinions from the expert.

Text of (b)(4) eff. Oct. 1, 2015.

(4) Trial Preparation; Discovery of Experts.—Discovery of facts known and opinions held by experts, that are otherwise discoverable under the provisions of subdivision (1) of this subsection and acquired or developed in anticipation of litigation or for trial, may be obtained only as provided by this subdivision:

a. 1. In general.—In order to provide openness and avoid unfair tactical advantage in the presentation of a case at trial, a party must disclose to the other parties in accordance with this subdivision the identity of any witness it may use at trial to present evidence under Rule 702, Rule 703, or Rule 705 of the North Carolina Rules of Evidence.

2. Witnesses providing a written report.—The parties shall have the option, in connection with the disclosures required by this subdivision, of accompanying the disclosure with a written report prepared and signed by the witness if the witness is one retained or specifically employed to provide expert testimony in the case or one whose duties as the party's employee regularly involve giving expert testimony. If the parties agree to accompany their disclosure pursuant to this subdivision with a written report, the report must contain all of the following:

I. A complete statement of all opinions the witness will express and the basis and reasons for them.

II. The facts or data considered by the witness in forming them.

III. Any exhibits that will be used to summarize or support them.

IV. The witness' qualifications, including a list of all publications authored in the previous 10 years.

V. A list of all other cases in which, during the previous four years, the witness testified as an expert at trial or by deposition.

VI. A statement of the compensation to be paid for the study and testimony in the case.

3. Witnesses not providing expert reports.—Unless otherwise stipulated to by the parties, or ordered by the court, a party may through interrogatories require any other party to identify each person whom the other party expects to call as an expert witness at trial, to state the subject matter on which the expert is expected to testify pursuant to Rule 702, Rule 703, or Rule 705 of the North Carolina Rules of Evidence and to state the substance of the facts and opinions to which the expert is expected to testify and a summary of the grounds for each opinion.

b. Depositions.—

1. Depositions of an expert who may testify.—A party may depose any person who has been identified as an expert pursuant to this subdivision, with such deposition to be conducted after any written report is provided or identification by response to interrogatory has been made pursuant to sub-subdivision f. of this subdivision.

2. Expert employed only for trial preparation.—Except as otherwise provided in this sub-sub-subdivision, a party may not, by interrogatories or deposition, discover facts known or opinions held by an expert who has been retained or specially employed by another party in anticipation of litigation or to prepare for trial and who is not expected to be called as a witness at trial. A party may take such discovery only as provided in Rule 35(b) or upon showing exceptional circumstances under which it is impracticable for the party to obtain facts or opinions on the same subject by other means.

c. Payment.—Unless manifest injustice would result and absent court order, the party seeking discovery under sub-subdivision b. of this subdivision shall pay the expert a reasonable fee for the time spent at that expert's deposition.

d. Trial preparation protection for draft reports or disclosures.—Drafts of reports provided under sub-sub-subdivision 2. of sub-subdivision a. of this subdivision are protected from disclosure and are not discoverable regardless of the form in which the draft is recorded.

e. Trial preparation protection for communications between a party's attorney and expert witness.—Except as otherwise provided in this sub-subdivision, communications between a party's attorney and any witness providing a report pursuant to sub-sub-subdivision 2. of sub-subdivision a. of this subdivision or identified under sub-sub-subdivision 3. of sub-subdivision a. of this subdivision, regardless of the form of the communication, are protected from disclosure and are not discoverable. Such communications are discoverable only to the extent that the communications do any of the following:

1. Relate to compensation for the expert's study or testimony.

2. Identify facts or data that the party's attorney provided and that the expert considered in forming the opinions to be expressed.

3. Identify assumptions that the party's attorney provided and that the expert relied on in forming the opinions to be expressed.

f. Time to disclose expert witness testimony.—Parties agreeing to the submission of written reports pursuant to sub-sub-subdivision 2. of sub-subdivision a. of this subdivision or parties otherwise seeking to obtain disclosure as set forth herein by interrogatory shall, unless otherwise stipulated, set by scheduling order or otherwise ordered by the court, serve such written report or in the case of no agreement on the submission of written reports, interrogatory:

1. At least 90 days before the date set for trial or the case to be ready for trial; or

2. If the evidence is intended solely to contradict or rebut evidence on the same subject matter identified by another party under sub-subdivision a. of this subdivision, within 30 days after the other party's disclosure. If a party fails to provide timely disclosure under this rule, the court may, upon motion, take such action as it deems just, including ordering that the party may not present at trial the expert witness for whom disclosure was not timely made.

The time requirements of this sub-subdivision shall not apply if all parties had less than 120-days' notice of the trial date.

g. Supplementation.—The parties must supplement these disclosures when required under subsection (e) of this rule.

(5) Claiming Privilege or Protecting Trial-Preparation Materials.

a. Information withheld.—When a party withholds information otherwise discoverable by claiming that the information is privileged or subject to protection as trial-preparation material, the party must (i) expressly make the claim and (ii) describe the nature of the documents, communications, or tangible things not produced or disclosed, and do so in a manner that, without revealing information itself privileged or protected, will enable other parties to assess the claim.

b. Information produced.—If information subject to a claim of privilege or protection as trial-preparation material is inadvertently produced in response to a discovery request, the party that produced the material may assert the claim by notifying any party that received the information of the claim and basis for it. After being notified, a party (i) must promptly return, sequester, or destroy the specified information and any copies it has, (ii) must not use or disclose the information until the claim is resolved, (iii) must take reasonable steps to retrieve the information if the party disclosed it before being notified, and (iv) may promptly present the information to the court under seal for determination of the claim. The producing party must preserve the information until the claim is resolved.

(c) Protective orders.—Upon motion by a party or by the person from whom discovery is sought, and for good cause shown, the judge of the court in which the action is pending may make any order which justice requires to protect a party or person from unreasonable annoyance, embarrassment, oppression, or undue burden or expense, including one or more of the following: (i) that the discovery not be had; (ii) that the discovery may be had only on specified terms and conditions, including a designation of the time or place; (iii) that the discovery may be had only by a method of discovery other than that selected by the party seeking discovery; (iv) that certain matters not be inquired into, or that the scope of the discovery be limited to certain matters; (v) that discovery be conducted with no one present except persons designated by the court; (vi) that a deposition after being sealed be opened only by order of the court; (vii) that a trade secret or other confidential research, development, or commercial information not be disclosed or be disclosed only in a designated way; (viii) that the parties simultaneously file specified documents or information enclosed in sealed envelopes to be opened as directed by the court.

A party seeking a protective order on the basis that electronically stored information sought is from a source identified as not reasonably accessible because of undue burden or cost has the burden of showing that the basis exists. If the showing is made, the court may nonetheless order discovery from the source if the requesting party shows good cause, but only after considering the limitations of subsection [subdivision] (b)(1a) of this rule.

If the motion for a protective order is denied in whole or in part, the court may, on such terms and conditions as are just, order that any party or person provide or permit discovery. The provisions of Rule 37(a)(4) apply to the award of expenses incurred in relation to the motion.

(d) Sequence and timing of discovery.—Unless the court upon motion, for the convenience of parties and witnesses and in the interests of justice, orders otherwise, methods of discovery may be used in any sequence and the fact that a party is conducting discovery, whether by deposition or otherwise, shall not operate to delay any other party's discovery. Any order or rule of court setting the time within which discovery must be completed shall be construed to fix the date after which the pendency of discovery will not be allowed to delay trial or any other proceeding before the court, but shall not be construed to prevent any party from utilizing any procedures afforded under Rules 26 through 36, so long as trial or any hearing before the court is not thereby delayed.

(e) Supplementation of responses.—A party who has responded to a request for discovery with a response that was complete when made is under no duty to supplement the party's response to include information thereafter acquired, except as follows:

(1) A party is under a duty seasonably to supplement the party's response with respect to any question directly addressed to (i) the identity and location of persons having knowledge of discoverable matters, and (ii) the identity of each person expected to be called as an expert witness at trial, the subject matter on which the person is expected to testify, and the substance of the testimony.

(2) A party is under a duty seasonably to amend a prior response if the party obtains information upon the basis of which (i) the party knows that the response was incorrect when made, or (ii) the party knows that the response though correct when made is no longer true and the circumstances are such that a failure to amend the response is in substance a knowing concealment.

(3) A duty to supplement responses may be imposed by order of the court, agreement of the parties, or at any time prior to trial through new requests for supplementation of prior responses.

(f) Discovery meeting, discovery conference, discovery plan.—

(1) No earlier than 40 days after the complaint is filed in an action, any party's attorney or an unrepresented party may request a meeting on the subject of discovery, including the discovery of electronically stored information. If such a request is filed, the parties shall meet in the county in which the action is pending not less than 21 days after the initial request for a meeting is filed and served upon the parties, unless agreed otherwise by the parties or their attorneys and unless an earlier time for the meeting is ordered by the court or agreed by the parties. Even if the parties or their attorneys do not seek to have a discovery meeting, at any time after commencement of an action the court may direct the parties or their attorneys to appear before it for a discovery conference.

(2) During a discovery meeting held pursuant to subdivision (f)(1) of this rule, the attorneys and any unrepresented parties shall (i) consider the nature and basis of the parties' claims and defenses and the possibilities for promptly settling or resolving the case and (ii) discuss the preparation of a discovery plan as set forth in subdivision (f)(3) of this rule. Attorneys for the parties, and any unrepresented parties, that have appeared in the case are jointly responsible for arranging the meeting, for being prepared to discuss a discovery plan, and for attempting in good faith to agree on a discovery plan. The meeting may be held by telephone, by videoconference, or in person, or a

combination thereof, unless the court, on motion, orders the attorneys and the unrepresented parties to attend in person. If a discovery plan is agreed upon, the plan shall be submitted to the court within 14 days after the meeting, and the parties may request a conference with the court regarding the plan. If the parties do not agree upon a discovery plan, they shall submit to the court within 14 days after the meeting a joint report containing those parts of a discovery plan upon which they agree and the position of each of the parties on the parts upon which they disagree. Unless the parties agree otherwise, the attorney for the first plaintiff listed on the complaint shall be responsible for submitting the discovery plan or joint report.

(3) A discovery plan shall contain the following: (i) a statement of the issues as they then appear; (ii) a proposed plan and schedule of discovery, including the discovery of electronically stored information; (iii) with respect to electronically stored information, and if appropriate under the circumstances of the case, a reference to the preservation of such information, the media form, format, or procedures by which such information will be produced, the allocation of the costs of preservation, production, and, if necessary, restoration, of such information, the method for asserting or preserving claims of privilege or of protection of the information as trial-preparation materials if different from that provided in subdivision (b)(5) of this rule, the method for asserting or preserving confidentiality and proprietary status, and any other matters addressed by the parties; (iv) any limitations proposed to be placed on discovery, including, if appropriate under the circumstances of the case, that discovery be conducted in phases or be limited to or focused on particular issues; (v) when discovery should be completed; and (vi) if appropriate under the circumstances of the case, any limitations or conditions pursuant to subsection (c) of this rule regarding protective orders.

(4) If the parties are unable to agree to a discovery plan at a meeting held pursuant to subdivision (f)(1) of this rule, they shall, upon motion of any party, appear before the court for a discovery conference at which the court shall order the entry of a discovery plan after consideration of the report required to be submitted under subdivision (f)(2) of this rule and the position of the parties. The order may address other matters, including the allocation of discovery costs, as are necessary for the proper management of discovery in the action. An order may be altered or amended as justice may require.

The court may combine the discovery conference with a pretrial conference authorized by Rule 16. A discovery conference in a medical malpractice action shall be governed by subsection (f1) of this rule.

(f1) Medical malpractice discovery conference.—In a medical malpractice action as defined in G.S. 90-21.11, upon the case coming at issue or the filing of a responsive pleading or motion requiring a determination by the court, the judge shall, within 30 days, direct the attorneys for the parties to appear for a discovery conference. At the conference the court may consider the matters set out in Rule 16 and subdivision (f)(3) of this rule and shall:

(1) Rule on all motions;

(2) Establish an appropriate schedule for designating expert witnesses, consistent with a discovery schedule pursuant to subdivision (3), to be complied with by all parties to the action such that there is a deadline for designating all expert witnesses within an appropriate time for all parties to implement discovery mechanisms with regard to the designated expert witnesses;

(3) Establish by order an appropriate discovery schedule designated so that, unless good cause is shown at the conference for a longer time, and subject to further orders of the court, discovery shall be completed within 150 days after the order is issued; nothing herein shall be construed to prevent any party from utilizing any procedures afforded under Rules 26 through 36, so long as trial or any hearing before the court is not thereby delayed; and

(4) Approve any consent order which may be presented by counsel for the parties relating to subdivisions (2) and (3) of this subsection, unless the court finds that the terms of the consent order are unreasonable.

If a party fails to identify an expert witness as ordered, the court shall, upon motion by the moving party, impose an appropriate sanction, which may include dismissal of the action, entry of default against the defendant, or exclusion of the testimony of the expert witness at trial.

(g) Signing of discovery requests, responses, and objections.—Every request for discovery or response or objection thereto made by a party represented by an attorney shall be signed by at least one attorney of record in that attorney's name, whose address shall be stated. A party who is not represented by an attorney shall sign the request, response, or objection and state that party's address. The signature of the attorney or party constitutes a certification that the attorney or party has read the request, response, or objection and that to the best of the knowledge, information, and belief of that attorney or party formed after a reasonable inquiry it is: (1) consistent with the rules and warranted by existing law or a good faith argument for the extension, modification, or reversal of existing law; (2) not interposed for any improper purpose, such as to harass or cause unnecessary delay or needless increase in the cost of litigation; and (3) not unreasonable or unduly burdensome or expensive, given the needs of the case, the discovery already had in the case, the amount in controversy, and the importance of the issues at stake in the litigation. If a request, response, or objection is not signed, it shall be stricken unless it is signed promptly after the omission is called to the attention of the party making the request, response, or objection and a party shall not be obligated to take any action with respect to it until it is signed.

If a certification is made in violation of the rule, the court, upon motion or upon its own initiative, shall impose upon the person who made the certification, the party on whose behalf the request, response, or objection is made, or both, an appropriate sanction, which may include an order to pay the amount of the reasonable expenses incurred because of the violation, including a reasonable attorney's fee.

Added by Laws 1967, c. 954, § 1. Amended by Laws 1971, c. 750; Laws 1975, c. 762, § 2; Laws 1985, c. 603, §§ 1–4; Laws 1987, c. 859, § 3; S.L. 2011-199, § 2, eff. Oct. 1, 2011; S.L. 2015-153, § 1, eff. Oct. 1, 2015.

Comment

Comment to this Rule as Originally Enacted. — *Section (a).* — This section gives a broad right of discovery to any party to take the testimony of any person, including a party, by oral deposition, pursuant to Rule 30, or by written interrogatories, pursuant to Rule 31, for the purpose of discovery or for use as evidence or for both purposes. Under prior practice the depositions of persons might be taken and perpetuated by deposition, and under former § 1-568.1 et seq. the deposition of a party might be taken for the purpose of discovery or for use as evidence or for both purposes.

Under this rule the necessity of obtaining court authorization is avoided, except leave of court must be obtained when plaintiff seeks to take a deposition within 30 days after the commencement of the action. Under prior practice a deposition of a proposed witness might be taken without order of court (former § 8-71). Under former §§ 1-568.10 and 1-568.11, a court order was necessary for examination of an adverse party.

Attendance of witnesses may be compelled by subpoena; attendance of a party by notice. Sanctions are provided in Rule 37(d) in the event a party fails to respond to the notice.

The last sentence of section (a) is much broader than the federal rule, which refers only to "a person confined in prison."

Section (b). — This section indicates the broad scope of examination and that it may cover not only evidence for use at the trial, but also inquiry into matters in themselves inadmissible at trial but which will lead to the discovery of evidence unless the court otherwise directs under Rule 30 (b) or (d).

Aside from the limitations of Rule 30(b) and (d), section (b) contains three limitations: (1) The deponent may be examined regarding any matter which is relevant to the subject matter in the pending action. (2) The deponent may not be examined regarding a matter which is privileged. (3) The deponent shall not be required to produce or submit for inspection any writing or data prescribed in the last sentence of section (b). This limitation (3) is based upon the proposed 1946 amendment to Rule 30(b).

Section (c). — This section is the same as the federal rule.

Section (d). — The use of a deposition at the trial stage is sharply limited by section (d). To be used, a deposition must not only satisfy one of the conditions of section (d), but also the limiting phrase in the first sentence of the section, "so far as admissible under the rules of evidence."

Section (e). — This section is added out of an abundance of caution.

Comment to the 1975 Amendment. — A limited rearrangement of the discovery rules is made, whereby certain rule provisions are transferred, as follows: Existing Rule 26(a) is transferred to Rules 30(a) and 31(a). Existing Rule 26(c) is transferred to Rule 30(c). Existing Rules 26(d) and (e) are transferred to Rule 32. Revisions of the transferred provisions, if any, are discussed in the notes appended to Rules 30, 31, and 32. In addition, Rule 30(b) is transferred to Rule 26(c). The purpose of this rearrangement is to establish Rule 26 as a rule governing discovery in general.

Section (a) — Discovery Devices. — This is a new section listing all of the discovery devices provided in the discovery rules and establishing the relationship between the general provision of Rule 26 and the specific rules for particular discovery devices. The provision that the frequency of use of these methods is not limited confirms existing law. It incorporates in general form a provision now found in Rule 33.

Section (b) — Scope of Discovery. — This section is recast to cover the scope of discovery generally. It regulates the discovery obtainable through any of the discovery devices listed in Rule 26(a).

All provisions as to scope of discovery are subject to the initial qualification that the court may limit discovery in accordance with these rules. Rule 26(c) (transferred from 30(b)) confers broad powers on the courts to regulate or prevent discovery even though the materials sought are within the scope of 26(b), and these powers have always been freely exercised. The new subsections in Rule 26(b) do not change existing law with respect to such situations.

Subsection (b)(1) — In General. — The language is changed to provide for the scope of discovery in general terms, rather than being limited to the scope of depositions. The subsection, although in terms applicable only to depositions, was incorporated by reference in existing Rules 33 and 34. Since decisions as to relevance to the subject matter of the action are made for discovery purposes well in advance of trial, a flexible treatment of relevance is required and the making of discovery, whether voluntary or under court order, is not a concession or a determination of relevance for purposes of trial. The substance of the subdivision represents no substantial change from the corresponding former provision. The provision of this subsection relating to matters within the knowledge of the party conducting discovery is taken from the existing North Carolina provision. It does not appear in the federal rule.

Subsection (b)(2) — Insurance Agreements. — This represents no change from the existing North Carolina provision.

Subsection (b)(3) — Work Product. — North Carolina had adopted a version of this rule in advance of the 1970 amendments to the federal rules. The present amendment would alter the test for compelling production from "injustice or undue hardship" to "substantial need" that cannot be satisfied without "undue hardship." It would also expand the scope of the protection of mental impressions, conclusions, opinions or legal theories to those of an "other representative of a party," e.g., an insurer. The wording of this subsection varies slightly from the federal rule; the basic substance of the subsection, however, remains unchanged.

Party's Right to Own Statement. — An exception to the requirement of this subsection enables a party to secure production of his own statement without any special showing. Ordinarily, a party gives a statement without insisting on a copy because he does not yet have a lawyer and does not understand the legal consequences of his actions. Thus, the statement is given at a time when he functions at a disadvantage. Discrepancies between his trial testimony and earlier statement may result from lapse of memory or ordinary inaccuracy; a written statement produced for the first time at trial may give such discrepancies a prominence which they do not deserve. In appropriate cases the court may order a party to be deposed before his statement is produced. E.g., McCoy v. GMC, 33 F.R.D. 354 (W.D. Pa. 1963); Smith v. Central Linen Serv. Co., 39 F.R.D. 15 (D. Md. 1966); Fernandes v. United Fruit Co., 50 F.R.D. 82 (D. Md. 1970).

In order to clarify and tighten the provision on statements by a party, the term "statement" is defined. The definition is adapted from 18 U.S.C. § 3500(e) (Jencks Act). The statement of a party may of course be that of plaintiff or defendant, and it may be that of an individual or of a corporation or other organization.

Section 8-89.1, which contains a similar provision whose application is restricted to personal injury plaintiffs, is repealed in connection with the enactment of this section.

Witness' Right to Own Statement. — A second exception to the requirement of this subsection permits a nonparty witness to obtain a copy of his own statement without any special showing. Many, though not all, of the considerations supporting a party's right to obtain his statement apply also to the nonparty witness.

Subsection (b)(4) — Trial Preparation; Experts. — This is a new provision dealing with discovery of information (including facts and opinions) obtained by a party from an expert retained by that party in relation to litigation or obtained by the expert and not yet transmitted to the party. The subsection deals with those experts whom the party expects to call as trial witnesses. It should be noted that the subsection does not address itself to the expert whose information was not acquired in preparation for trial but rather because he was an actor or viewer with respect to transactions or occurrences that are part of the subject matter of the lawsuit. Such an expert should be treated as an ordinary witness.

Subdivision (b)(4)a deals with discovery of information obtained by or through experts who will be called as witnesses at trial. The provision is responsive to problems suggested by a relatively recent line of authorities. Many of these cases present intricate and difficult issues as to which expert testimony is likely to be determinative. Prominent among them are food and drug, patent, and condemnation cases.

In cases of this character, a prohibition against discovery of information held by expert witnesses produces in acute form the very evils that discovery has been created to prevent. Effective cross-examination of an expert witness requires advance preparation. The lawyer even with the help of his own experts frequently cannot anticipate the particular approach his adversary's expert will take or the data on which he will base his judgment on the stand. Similarly, effective rebuttal requires advance knowledge of the line of testimony of the other side. If the latter is foreclosed by a rule against discovery, then the narrowing of issues and elimination of surprise which discovery normally produces are frustrated.

Although the trial problems flowing from lack of discovery of expert witnesses are most acute and noteworthy when the case turns largely on experts, the same problems are encountered when a single expert testifies. Thus, subdivision (b)(4)a draws no line between complex and simple cases, or between cases with many experts and those with but one. The rule established by this subdivision is patterned substantially after the result reached by a number of courts in the former absence of such a provision in the federal rules.

Past judicial restrictions on discovery of an adversary's expert, particularly as to his opinions, reflect the fear that one side will benefit unduly from the other's better preparation. The procedure established in subdivision (b)(4)a holds the risk to a minimum. Discovery is limited to trial witnesses, and may be obtained only at a time when the parties know who their expert witnesses will be. A party must as a practical matter prepare his own case in advance of that time, for he can hardly hope to build his case out of his opponent's experts.

Subdivision (b)(4)a provides for discovery of an expert who is to testify at the trial. A party can require one who intends to use the expert to state the substance of the testimony that the expert is expected to give. The court may order further discovery, and it has ample power to regulate its timing and scope and to prevent abuse. Ordinarily, the order for further discovery shall compensate the expert for his time, and may compensate the party who intends to use the expert for past expenses reasonably incurred in obtaining facts or opinions from the expert. Those provisions are likely to discourage abusive practices.

Under subdivision (b)(4)b, the court is directed or authorized to issue protective orders, including an order that the expert be paid a reasonable fee for time spent in responding to discovery, and that the party whose expert is made subject to discovery be paid a fair portion of the fees and expenses that the party incurred in obtaining information from the expert. The court may issue the latter order as a condition of discovery, or it may delay the order until after discovery is completed. These provisions for fees and expenses meet the objection that it is unfair to permit one side to obtain without cost the benefit of an expert's work for which the other side has paid, often a substantial sum.

In ordering discovery under (b)(4)a2, the court has discretion whether to award fees and expenses to the other party; its decision should depend upon whether the discovering party is simply learning about the other party's case or is going beyond this to develop his own case.

Note: The General Assembly deleted from the drafting committee's text a proposed provision identical to Federal Rule 26(b)(4)(B) expressly providing for discovery in very limited circumstances of experts retained in anticipation of litigation or in preparation for trial, but who are not expected to be called as witnesses. Failure to adopt this provision would not appear to foreclose such discovery on a proper showing under Rule 26(b)(3) or Rule 34.

Section (c) — Protective Orders. — The provisions of existing [former] Rule 30(b) are transferred to this section (c), as part of the rearrangement of Rule 26. The language has been changed to give it application to discovery generally.

In addition, drafting changes are made to carry out and clarify the sense of the rule. Insertions are made to avoid any possible implication that a protective order does not extend to "time" as well as to "place" or may not safeguard against "undue burden or expense."

The new reference to trade secrets and other confidential commercial information reflects existing law. The courts have not given trade secrets automatic and complete immunity against disclosure, but have in each case weighed their claim to privacy against the need for disclosure. Frequently, they have been afforded a limited protection.

The section contains new matter relating to sanctions. When a motion for a protective order is made and the court is disposed to deny it, the court may go a step further and issue an order to provide or permit discovery. This will bring the sanctions of Rule 37(b) directly into play. Since the court has heard the contentions of all interested persons, an affirmative order is justified. In addition, the court may require the payment of expenses incurred in relation to the motion.

Section (d) — Sequence and Priority. — This new provision is concerned with the sequence in which parties may proceed with discovery and with related problems of timing. The principal effects of the new provision are first, to eliminate any fixed priority in the sequence of discovery, and second, to make clear and explicit the court's power to establish priority by an order issued in a particular case. North Carolina has not suffered from the problems presented by rules of priority of discovery existing in some other jurisdictions under the original federal rules. This rule will insure that we do not develop any such problems. The last sentence allows discovery to continue to the time of trial so long as it does not result in a delay of trial or of any other proceeding before the court.

Section (e) — Supplementation of Responses. — The rules do not now state whether interrogatories (and questions at deposition as well as requests for inspection and admissions) impose a "continuing burden" on the responding party to supplement his answers if he obtains new information. The issue is acute when new information renders substantially incomplete or inaccurate an answer which was complete and accurate when made. It is essential that the rules provide an answer to this question. The parties can adjust to a rule either way, once they know what it is.

Arguments can be made both ways. Imposition of a continuing burden reduces the proliferation of additional sets of interrogatories. Some courts have adopted local rules establishing such a burden. Others have imposed the burden by decision. On the other hand, there are serious objections to the burden, especially in protracted cases. Although the party signs the answers, it is his lawyer who understands their significance and bears the responsibility to bring answers up to date. In a complex case all sorts of information reaches the party, who little understands its bearing on answers previously given to interrogatories. In practice, therefore, the lawyer under a continuing burden must periodically recheck all interrogatories and canvass all new information. But a full set of new answers may no longer be needed by the interrogating party. Some issues will have been dropped from the case, some questions are now seen as unimportant, and other questions must in any event be reformulated.

Section (e) provides that a party is not under a continuing burden except as expressly provided. An exception is made as to the identity of persons having knowledge of discoverable matters because of the obvious importance to each side of knowing all witnesses and because information about witnesses routinely comes to each lawyer's attention. Many of the decisions on the issue of a continuing burden have in fact concerned the identity of witnesses. An exception is also made as to expert trial witnesses in order to carry out the provisions of Rule 26(b)(4).

Another exception is made for the situation in which a party, or more frequently his lawyer, obtains actual knowledge that a prior response is incorrect. This exception does not impose a duty to check the accuracy of prior responses, but it prevents knowing concealment by a party or attorney. Finally, a duty to supplement may be imposed by order of the court in a particular case (including an order resulting from a pretrial conference) or by agreement of the parties. A party may of course make a new discovery request which requires supplementation of prior responses.

The duty will normally be enforced, in those limited instances where it is imposed, through sanctions imposed by the trial court, including exclusion of evidence, continuance, or other action, as the court may deem appropriate.

Comment to the 2011 Amendment. — Subsection (b). — Subdivision (b)(1) previously contained two paragraphs. The second paragraph has been made "(b)(1a)" and entitled "Limitations on Frequency and Extent".

Amended subdivision (b)(1) adds "electronically stored information" to the list of illustrative "things" about which a party may seek discovery. Unlike paper documents, a large amount of electronically stored information is associated with or contains information that is not readily apparent on the screen view of the file. This additional information usually is known as "metadata". Metadata includes information about the document or file that is recorded by the computer to assist in storing and retrieving the document file. For purposes of discovery under the Rules, "electronically stored information" is defined to include not only the information contained on the screen view of the file but also reasonably accessible metadata that reflects such key information as date sent, date received, author, and recipients. Other metadata is excluded from the definition of "electronically stored information", making that metadata not subject to discovery unless the parties agree to disclosure of metadata or the court orders disclosure.

Metadata includes file designation, create and edit dates, authorship, comments, and edit history. Indeed, electronic files may contain hundreds or even thousands of pieces of such information. For instance, email has its own metadata elements that can include 1,200 or more properties. Typical word processing documents not only include changes and edits but also hidden codes that determine such features as paragraphing, font, and line spacing.

Similarly, electronically created spreadsheets may contain calculations that are not visible in a printed version or hidden columns that can only be viewed by accessing the spreadsheet in its "native" application, that is, the software application used to create or record the information.

Understanding when metadata is relevant and needs to be preserved and produced represents one of the biggest challenges in electronic discovery. Sometimes metadata is needed to authenticate a disputed document or to establish facts material to a dispute, such as, in a suit involving theft of trade secrets, when a file was accessed. In most cases, however, metadata will have no material evidentiary value – it does not matter when a document was printed, who typed the revisions, or what edits were made before the document was circulated. There is also the real danger that information recorded by the computer as application metadata may be inaccurate. For example, when a new employee uses a word processing program to create a memorandum by using a memorandum template created by a former employee, the metadata for the new memorandum may incorrectly identify the former employee as the author. (Note, most of this language comes from or is based on Commentary to Principle 12 in the Sedona Principles: Second Edition, Best Practices Recommendations and Principles for Addressing Electronic Document Production, June 2007.).

As a result, subdivision (b)(1) has been written to focus electronic discovery on the kinds of metadata that will be relevant in most cases and to encourage parties not to engage in discovery concerning other kinds of metadata unless they agree that doing so is appropriate in a given case or unless they can show the court that there is a need to do so.

The substance of subdivision (b)(1a) has not been changed. The additions were made to distinguish the general limitations contained in subdivision (b)(1a) from the specific limitations applicable to discovery of electronically stored information contained in subdivision (b)(1b).

New subdivision (b)(1b) refers to the addition in Rule 34(b) of a specific limitation on production of electronically stored information based upon an objection that information from the source from which the information may be obtained is not reasonably accessible because of undue burden or cost. This limitation is taken from Rule 26(b)(2)(B) of the Federal Rules of Civil Procedure but is placed in different parts of the North Carolina Rules of Civil Procedure because the North Carolina Rules have not adopted the federal rules approach of requiring disclosure of information without request by a party. Subdivision (b)(1b) makes it clear the limitation in Rule 34(b), as well as the limitations on discovery provided in subdivision (b)(1a), apply when a motion for a protective order or motion to compel is made in response to a request for production of electronically stored information. In addition, subdivision (b)(1b) specifically recognizes the authority of the court to specify conditions for electronic discovery, including allocation of the costs of that discovery.

Sub-subdivision (b)(5)a. specifies the procedure by which a party may withhold information otherwise discoverable on the ground that the information is privileged or is subject to protection as trial-preparation material under subdivision (b)(3). The Rule is intended to expedite the resolution of discovery disputes by requiring the party withholding information on such grounds to expressly make the claim and set out a description of the information withheld so that the requesting party can decide whether to contest the claim and the court can resolve the dispute.

Sub-subdivision (b)(5)b. provides a mechanism for addressing the inadvertent production of privileged or trial preparation material. The risks of privilege waiver, and the work necessary to avoid it, add to the costs and delay of discovery. That risk is exacerbated in cases involving electronically stored information, where the volume and format of potentially discoverable material increases substantially

Subdivision (b)(5) works in tandem with subsection (f), which now allows any party to request a meeting to discuss a discovery plan to address (among other things) the process for addressing issues of privilege or trial preparation material protection.

A party asserting a claim of privilege or protection after production must give notice to the receiving party. That notice should be in writing unless the circumstances preclude it. The notice should be as specific as possible in identifying the information and stating the basis for the claim. Because the receiving party must decide whether to challenge the claim and may sequester the information and submit it to the court for a ruling on whether the claimed privilege or protection applies and whether it has been waived, the notice should be sufficiently detailed so as to enable the receiving party and the court to understand the basis for the claim and to determine whether waiver has occurred.

After receiving notice, each party that received the information must promptly return, sequester, or destroy the information and any copies it has. The option of sequestering or destroying the information is included in part because the receiving party may have incorporated the information in protected trial-preparation materials. No receiving party may use or disclose the information pending resolution of the privilege claim. The receiving party may present to the court the questions whether the information is privileged or protected as trial-preparation material and whether the privilege or protection has been waived. If it does so, it must provide the court with the grounds for the claim of privilege or protection specified in the producing party's notice and serve all parties. In presenting the question, the party may use the content of the information only to the extent permitted by the applicable law of privilege, protection for trial-preparation material, and professional responsibility.

If a party disclosed the information to nonparties before receiving notice of a claim of privilege or protection as trial-preparation material, it must take reasonable steps to retrieve the information and to return it, sequester it until the claim is resolved, or destroy it.

Whether the information is returned or not, the producing party must preserve the information pending the court's ruling on whether the claim of privilege or protection is properly asserted and whether it has been waived.

Subsection (c). — Subsection (c) relates to amended Rule 34(b) and provides that when a protective order is sought on the basis that electronically stored information that is the subject of a discovery request is from a source not reasonably accessible because of undue burden or cost, the party seeking the protective order has the burden of showing that information from the source identified is not reasonably accessible. If that showing is made, the judge may enter a protective order that limits or denies discovery from that source or, if the requesting party shows good cause for allowing the discovery in spite of the burden or cost, allows the discovery but may allocate the cost of the discovery between or among the parties.

Subsection (e). — No substantive changes are intended.

Subsection (f). — Former subsection (f) did provide a procedure by which a discovery conference could be requested by motion of a party. However, in practice, discovery conferences were rarely held in most counties of this state, and parties and their attorneys usually would not be guided by a discovery order, the lack of which could lead to inefficiency and uncertainty. One method to provide assistance to parties is to make it easier for an attorney to seek and obtain a discovery plan, even if no other attorney wants one, if that attorney perceives a need for guidelines and express limitations regarding discovery in a particular case, especially discovery involving electronically stored information. Therefore, unlike the former rule, amended subsection (f) requires a discovery meeting and subsequent order setting forth a discovery plan if any party or party's attorney requests such a meeting.

Parties often will know very early in the course of a lawsuit whether the nature of the claims asserted is such that a discovery meeting is advisable. Considering the realities of litigation, especially during the early part of a lawsuit, a discovery meeting should not be held too soon, because defense counsel will need some time to gain at least some familiarity with the allegations of the complaint and possible defenses. On the other hand, because of the importance of holding a discovery meeting sooner than later, especially in situations where a plaintiff serves discovery upon a defendant when the complaint is filed, the rule provides that a discovery meeting can be held as early as 61 days after the complaint is filed. Parties or their counsel should balance the desire for an early discovery meeting with the preference that everyone be sufficiently familiar with the lawsuit that a discovery meeting can be meaningful. Because subdivision (f)(1) allows the parties to agree as to when the discovery meeting is to be held, parties are encouraged, when reasonably possible, to delay holding the discovery meeting until all parties can become sufficiently familiar with the issues arising in the action and the potential sources of discoverable information that a discovery meeting likely will be meaningful, beneficial, and productive. Parties are especially encouraged to delay holding the discovery meeting until all defendants have filed a pleading in response to the complaint.

Subdivision (f)(2) does not contemplate a formal hearing if the parties agree to a discovery plan. Because it ultimately is the court that controls its docket, any proposed discovery plan must be approved by the court. Courts are encouraged to view each case separately and give significant weight to a discovery plan to which all parties have agreed.

Although amended subsection (f) does provide for a discovery meeting, parties may proceed with discovery before a discovery meeting is held or before a discovery plan is submitted and approved by the court.

Subsection (f) does not govern medical malpractice actions, although the matters set forth in subdivision (f)(3), which includes electronically stored information matters, may be considered at a discovery conference in a medical malpractice action held pursuant to subsection (f1).

The 2006 Commentary for Rule 26(f) of the Federal Rules of Civil Procedure can provide guidance regarding discovery of electronically stored information where applicable, taking into account any difference between the North Carolina rules governing discovery and the federal rules.

Subsection (f1). — By cross-reference, subsection (f1) makes clear that a judge may consider in a malpractice discovery conference the matters listed in subdivision (f)(3), including discovery of electronically stored information, as well as those listed in Rule 16.

Additional amendments to Rule 26 eliminate gender-specific references or conform references to parts of sections and are not intended to affect substance.

Rule 27. Depositions before action or pending appeal

(a) Before action.—

(1) Petition.—A person who desires to perpetuate that person's own testimony or the testimony of another person regarding any matter may file a verified petition in the appropriate court in a county where any expected adverse party resides. The petition shall be entitled in the name of the petitioner and shall show: (i) that the petitioner expects that the petitioner, or the petitioner's personal representative, heirs or devisees, will be a party to an action cognizable in any court, but that the petitioner is presently unable to bring it or cause it to be brought, (ii) the subject matter of the expected action and the petitioner's reasons for desiring to perpetuate it, (iii) the facts which the petitioner desires to establish by the proposed testimony and the petitioner's reasons for desiring to perpetuate it, (iv) the names or a description of the persons the petitioner expects will be adverse parties and their addresses so far as known, and (v) the names and addresses of the persons to be examined and the substance of the testimony which the petitioner expects to elicit from each, and shall ask for an order authorizing the petitioner to take the depositions of the persons to be examined named in the petition, for the purpose of perpetuating their testimony.

(2) Notice and Service.—The petitioner shall thereafter serve a notice upon each person named in the petition as an expected adverse party, together with a copy of the petition, stating that the petitioner will apply to the court, at a time and place named therein, for the order described in the petition. At least 20 days before the date of hearing (or within such time as the court may direct) the notice shall be served in the manner provided in Rule 4(j)(1) or (2) for service of summons; but if such service cannot with due diligence be made upon any expected adverse party named in the petition, the court may make such order

as is just for service by publication or otherwise, and shall appoint, for persons not served in the manner provided in Rule 4(j)(1) or (2), an attorney who shall represent them, in case they are not otherwise represented. If any expected adverse party is a minor or incompetent the provisions of Rule 17(c) apply.

(3) Order and Examination.—If the court is satisfied that the perpetuation of the testimony may prevent a failure or delay of justice, it shall make an order designating or describing the persons whose depositions may be taken and specifying the subject matter of the examination and whether the depositions shall be taken upon oral examination or written questions. The depositions may then be taken in accordance with these rules; and the court may make orders of the character provided for by Rules 34 and 35. For the purpose of applying these rules to depositions for perpetuating testimony, each reference therein to the court in which the action is pending shall be deemed to refer to the court in which the petition for such deposition was filed.

(4) Use of Deposition.—If a deposition to perpetuate testimony is taken under these rules or if, although not so taken, it would be admissible in evidence in the courts of the United States or the state in which it is taken, it may be used in any action involving the same subject matter subsequently brought in a court of this State in accordance with the provisions of Rule 32(a), or in any other court under whose rules it is admissible.

(b) Pending appeal.—If an appeal has been taken from the determination of any court or if petition for review or certiorari has been served and filed, or before the taking of an appeal or the filing of a petition for review or certiorari if the time therefor has not expired, the court in which the determination was made may allow the taking of the depositions of witnesses to perpetuate their testimony for use in the event of further proceedings in the trial court. In such case the party who desires to perpetuate the testimony may make a motion in the trial court for leave to take the depositions, upon the same notice and service thereof as if the action was pending in the trial court. The motion shall show (i) the names and addresses of the persons to be examined and the substance of the testimony which the party expects to elicit from each; (ii) the reasons for perpetuating their testimony. If the court finds that the perpetuation of the testimony is proper to avoid a failure or delay of justice, it may make an order allowing the depositions to be taken and may make orders of the character provided for by Rules 34 and 35, and thereupon the depositions may be taken and used in the same manner and under the same conditions as are prescribed in these rules for depositions taken in actions pending in the trial court.

(c) Perpetuation by action.—This rule does not limit the power of a court to entertain an action to perpetuate testimony.

Added by Laws 1967, c. 954, § 1. Amended by Laws 1975, c. 762, § 2; S.L. 2011–284, § 5, eff. June 24, 2011.

Comment

Comment to this Rule as Originally Enacted. — The objectives here are to provide simple procedures for discovery when the purpose is preservation of testimony or the obtaining of information with which to prepare a complaint and further, in appropriate cases, to provide for discovery pending appeal.

Section (a). **— Former §§ 8–85 to 8–88 provided for a special proceeding or a civil action to perpetuate testimony. Under section (a), the most significant change in respect to perpetuating testimony is that no summons is necessary. But there is a requirement of notice.**

Section (b). **— This section deals with discovery for the purpose of obtaining information to prepare a complaint. It carries forward all of the protections to a prospective defendant incorporated in former § 1–121. But, again, no service of process is necessary. After the contemplated order is obtained, the procedure set forth in the other discovery rules will apply.**

Section (c). **— This section adds something new in providing for the situation where it may be desirable to take a deposition pending an appeal.**

Comment to the 1975 Amendment. — This amendment deletes present Rule 27(b) which provided for depositions before action to obtain information to prepare a complaint. This provision and its predecessor generated about one half of all the appeals from orders relating to discovery in the North Carolina courts, most of them determined adversely to the party who initiated the procedure. Whatever may have been the justification for this procedure under the former code pleading practice in North Carolina, the adoption of the liberalized pleading requirements of Rule 8 would appear to have eliminated the necessity for retaining it.

The former sections (c) and (d) are redesignated as sections (b) and (c) respectively.

Rule 28. Persons before whom depositions may be taken

(a) Within the United States. — Within the United States or within a territory or insular possession subject to the dominion of the United States, depositions shall be taken before a person authorized to administer oaths by the laws of this State, of the United States or of the place where the examination is held, or before a person appointed by the court in which the action is pending. A person so appointed has power to administer oaths and take testimony.

(b) In foreign countries. — Depositions may be taken in a foreign country:

(1) Pursuant to any applicable treaty or convention;

(2) Pursuant to a letter of request, whether or not captioned a letter rogatory;

(3) On notice before a person authorized to administer oaths in the place where the examination is held, either by the law thereof or by the law of the United States; or

(4) Before a person commissioned by the court, and a person so commissioned shall have the power by virtue of his commission to administer any necessary oath and take testimony. A commission or a letter of request shall be issued on application and notice and on terms that are just and appropriate. It is not requisite to the issuance of a commission or a letter of request that the taking of the deposition in any other manner is impracticable or inconvenient; and both a commission and a letter of request may be issued in proper cases. A notice or commission may designate the person before whom the deposition is to be taken either by name or descriptive title. A letter of request may be addressed "To the Appropriate Authority in (here name the country)." When a letter of request or any other device is used pursuant to any applicable treaty or convention, it shall be captioned in the form prescribed by that treaty or convention. Evidence obtained in response to a letter of request need not be excluded merely because the testimony was not taken under oath, or any similar departure from the requirements for depositions taken within the United States under these rules.

(c) Disqualification for interest. — Unless the parties agree otherwise by stipulation as provided in Rule 29, no deposition shall be taken before a person who is any of the following:

(1) A relative, employee, or attorney of any of the parties;

(2) A relative or employee of an attorney of the parties;

(3) Financially interested in the action; or

(4) An independent contractor if the contractor or the contractor's principal is under a blanket contract for the court reporting services with an attorney of the parties, party to the action, or party having a financial interest in the action. Notwithstanding the disqualification under this rule, the party desiring to take the deposition under a stipulation shall disclose the disqualification in writing in a Rule 30(b) notice of deposition and shall inform all parties to the litigation on the record of the existence of the disqualification under this rule and of the proposed stipulation waiving the disqualification. Any party opposing the proposed stipulation as provided in the notice of deposition shall give timely written notice of his or her opposition to all parties.

For the purposes of this rule, a blanket contract means a contract to perform court reporting services over a fixed period of time or an indefinite period of time, rather than on a case by case basis, or any other contractual arrangement which compels, guarantees, regulates, or controls the use of particular court reporting services in future cases.

Notwithstanding any other provision of law, a person is prohibited from taking a deposition under any contractual agreement that requires transmission of the original transcript without the transcript having been certified as provided in Rule 30(f) by the person before whom the deposition was taken.

Notwithstanding the provisions of this subsection, a person otherwise disqualified from taking a deposition under this subsection may take a deposition provided that the deposition is taken by videotape in compliance with Rule 30(b)(4) and Rule 30(f), and the notice for the taking of the deposition states the name of the person before whom the deposition will be taken and that person's relationship, if any, to a party or a party's attorney, provided that the deposition is also recorded by stenographic means by a nondisqualified person.

(d) Depositions to be used in foreign countries. —

(1) A person desiring to take depositions in this State to be used in proceedings pending in the courts of any other country may present to a judge of the superior or district court a commission, order, notice, consent, or other authority under which the deposition is to be taken, whereupon it shall be the duty of the judge to issue the necessary subpoenas pursuant to Rule 45. Orders of the character provided in Rules 30(b), 30(d), and 45(b) may be made upon proper application therefor by the person to whom such subpoena is directed. Failure by any person without adequate excuse to obey a subpoena served upon him pursuant to this rule may be deemed a contempt of the court from which the subpoena issued.

(2) The commissioner herein provided for shall not proceed to act under and by virtue of his appointment until the party seeking to obtain such deposition has deposited with him a sufficient sum of money to cover all costs and charges incident to the taking of the deposition, including such witness fees as are allowed to witnesses in this State for attendance upon the superior court. From such deposit the commissioner shall retain whatever amount may be due him for services, pay the witness fees and other costs that may have been incurred by reason of taking such deposition, and if any balance remains in his hands, he shall pay the same to the party by whom it was advanced.

Added by Laws 1967, c. 954, § 1. Amended by Laws 1975, c. 762, § 2; Laws 1995, c. 389, § 4; S.L. 1999-264, § 1, eff. Oct.

1, 1999; S.L. 2001-379, § 4, eff. Oct. 1, 2001; S.L. 2011-247, § 2, eff. Dec. 1, 2011.

Comment

Comment to this Rule as Originally Enacted. — This rule is the same as the federal rule except that "of this State" has been inserted in section (a), and section (d) has been added.

Under section (a) depositions for use in North Carolina need not be taken within the State. They may be taken wherever the party taking the deposition desires, subject to the protective provisions of Rule 30(b). However, a subpoena to require a witness to attend the deposition will not run outside the State. Many states have statutes comparable to present G.S. 8-84, making their subpoena power available to compel residents to appear for depositions to be used in foreign states.

Section (d) has no counterpart in the federal rules. It is designed to permit courts in this State to assist parties in proceedings in other states to take depositions in this State for use in such proceedings. North Carolina now has such a statute as indicated above. This rule also requires the party taking a deposition to make a deposit insuring the payment of all fees and costs incident to the taking of the deposition. This practice will be new.

Comment to the 1975 Amendment. — This section is amended slightly to conform to the federal rule, but its substance remains unchanged.

Rule 29. Stipulations regarding discovery procedure

Unless the court orders otherwise, the parties may by written stipulation (i) provide that depositions may be taken before any person, at any time or place, upon any notice, and in any manner and when so taken may be used like other depositions, and (ii) modify the procedures provided by these rules for other methods of discovery.

Added by Laws 1967, c. 954, § 1. Amended by Laws 1975, c. 762, § 1.

Comment

Comment to this Rule as Originally Enacted. — This rule is identical with federal Rule 29. In many cases, saving time and expense is just as important as strict formality. It should be noted that the stipulation relates only to the formalities of taking depositions, and not to their use at trial. Hence, parties may stipulate as to time, place, and manner of taking of a deposition without waiving objections to its admissibility under Rule 26(d).

Comment to the 1975 Amendment. — There is no provision for stipulations varying the procedures by which methods of discovery other than depositions are governed. It is common practice for parties to agree on such variations, and the amendment recognizes such agreements and provides a formal mechanism in the rules for giving them effect. Any stipulation varying the procedures may be superseded by court order.

Rule 30. Depositions upon oral examination

(a) When depositions may be taken. — After commencement of the action, any party may take the testimony of any person, including a party, by deposition upon oral examination. Leave of court, granted with or without notice, must be obtained only if the plaintiff seeks to take a deposition prior to the expiration of 30 days after service of the summons and complaint upon any defendant or service made under Rule 4(e), except that leave is not required (i) if a defendant has served a notice of taking deposition or otherwise sought discovery, or (ii) if special notice is given as provided in subsection (b)(2) of this rule. The attendance of witnesses may be compelled by subpoena as provided in Rule 45, provided that no subpoena need be served on a deponent who is a party or an officer, director or managing agent of a party, provided the party has been served with notice pursuant to subsection (b)(1) of this rule. The deposition of a person confined in prison or of a patient receiving in-patient care in or confined to an institution or hospital for the mentally ill or mentally handicapped may be taken only by leave of court on such terms as the court prescribes.

(b) Notice of examination; general requirements; place of examination; special notice; nonstenographic recording; production of documents and things; deposition of organization. —

(1) A party desiring to take the deposition of any person upon oral examination shall give notice in writing to every other party to the action. The notice shall state the time and place for taking the deposition and the name and address of each person to be examined, if known, and, if the name is not known, a general description sufficient to identify him or the particular class or group to which he belongs. If a subpoena duces tecum is to be served on the person to be examined, the designation of the materials to be produced as set forth in the subpoena shall be attached to or included in the notice. The notice shall be served on all parties at least 15 days prior to the taking of the deposition when any party required to be served resides without the State and shall be served on all parties at least 10 days prior to the taking of the deposition when all of the parties required to be served reside within the State. Depositions of parties, officers, directors or managing agents of parties or of other persons designated pursuant to subsection (b)(6) hereof to testify on behalf of a party may be taken only at the following places:

A resident of the State may be required to attend for examination by deposition only in the county wherein he resides or is employed or transacts his business in person. A nonresident of the State may be required to attend for such examination only in the county wherein he resides or within 50 miles of the place of service except that a judge, as defined by subdivision (h) of this rule, may, upon motion showing good cause, require that a party who selected the county where the action is pending as the forum for the action or an officer, director or managing agent of such a party, or a person designated pursuant to subsection (b)(6) hereof to testify on behalf of such a party present himself for the taking of his deposition in the county where the action is pending. The judge upon granting the motion may make any other orders allowed by Rule 26(c) with respect thereto, including orders with respect to the expenses of the deponent.

(2) Leave of court is not required for the taking of a deposition by plaintiff if the notice (i) states that the person to be examined is about to go out of the county where the action is pending and more than 100 miles from the place of trial, or is about to go out of the United States, or is bound on a voyage to sea, and will be unavailable for examination unless his deposition is taken before expiration of the 30–day period, and (ii) sets forth facts to support the statement. The plaintiff's attorney shall sign the notice, and his signature constitutes a certification by him that to the best of his knowledge, information, and belief the statement and supporting facts are true. The sanctions provided by Rule 11 are applicable to the certification.

If a party shows that when he was served with notice under this subsection (b)(2) he was unable through the exercise of diligence to obtain counsel to represent him at the taking of the deposition, the deposition may not be used against him.

(3) The court may for cause shown enlarge or shorten the time for taking the deposition.

(4) Unless the court orders otherwise, testimony at a deposition may be recorded by sound recording, sound-and-visual, or stenographic means. If the testimony is to be taken by other means in addition to or in lieu of stenographic means, the notice shall state the methods by which it shall be taken and shall state whether a stenographer will be present at the deposition. In the case of a deposition taken by stenographic means, the party that provides for the stenographer shall provide for the transcribing of the testimony taken. If the deposition is by sound recording only, the party noticing the deposition shall provide for the transcribing of the testimony taken. If the deposition is by sound-and-visual means, the appearance or demeanor of deponents or attorneys shall not be distorted through camera techniques. Regardless of the method stated in the notice, any party or the deponent may have the testimony recorded by stenographic means.

(5) A party deponent, deponents who are officers, directors or managing agents of parties and other persons designated pursuant to subsection (b)(6) hereof to testify on behalf of a party may not be served with a subpoena duces tecum, but the notice to a party for the deposition of such a deponent may be accompanied by a request made in compliance with Rule 34 for the production of documents and tangible things at the taking of the deposition. The procedure of Rule 34, except as to time for response, shall apply to the request. When a notice to take such a deposition is accompanied by a request made in compliance with Rule 34 the notice and the request must be served at least 15 days earlier than would otherwise be required by Rule 30(b)(1), and any objections to such a request must be served at least seven days prior to the taking of the deposition.

(6) A party may in his notice and in a subpoena name as the deponent a public or private corporation or a partnership or association or governmental agency and describe with reasonable particularity the matters on which examination is requested. In that event, the organization so named shall designate one or more officers, directors, or managing agents, or other persons who consent to testify on its behalf, and may set forth, for each person designated, the matters on which he will testify. A subpoena shall advise a nonparty organization of its duty to make such a designation. It shall not be necessary to serve a subpoena on an organization which is a party, but the notice, served on a party without an accompanying subpoena shall clearly advise such of its duty to make the required designation. The persons so designated shall testify as to matters known or reasonably available to the organization. This subsection (b)(6) does not preclude taking a deposition by any other procedure authorized in these rules.

(7) The parties may stipulate in writing or the court may upon motion order that a deposition be taken by telephone. For the purposes of this rule and Rules 28(a), 37(a)(1) and 45(d), a deposition taken by telephone is taken in the district and the place where the deponent is to answer questions propounded to him.

(c) Examination and cross-examination; record of examination; oath; objections. — Examination and cross-examination of witnesses may proceed as permitted at the trial under the provisions of Rule 43(b). The person before whom the deposition is to be taken shall put the deponent on oath and shall personally, or by someone acting under his direction and in his presence, record the testimony of the deponent. The testimony shall be taken stenographically or recorded by any other means ordered in accordance with subsection (b)(4) of this rule. If requested by one of the parties, the testimony shall be transcribed.

All objections made at the time of the examination to the qualifications of the person before whom the deposition is taken, or to the manner of taking it, or to the evidence presented, or to the conduct of any party, and any other objection to the proceedings, shall be noted upon the deposition by the person before whom the deposition is taken. Subject to any limitations imposed by orders entered pursuant to Rule 26(c) or 30(d), evidence objected to shall be taken subject to the objections. In lieu of participating in the oral examination, parties may serve written questions in a sealed envelope on the party who served the notice of taking the deposition, and he shall transmit them to the person before whom the deposition is to be taken who shall open them at the deposition, propound them to the witness and record the answers verbatim.

(d) Motion to terminate or limit examination. — At any time during the taking of the deposition, on motion of a party or of the deponent and upon a showing that the examination is being conducted in bad faith or in such manner as unreasonably to annoy, embarrass, or oppress the deponent or party, a judge of the court in which the action is pending or any judge in the county where the deposition is being taken may order before whom the examination is being taken to cease forthwith from taking the deposition, or may limit the scope and manner of the taking of the deposition as provided in Rule 26(c). If the order made terminates the examination, it shall be resumed thereafter only upon the order of a judge of the court in which the action is pending. Upon demand of the objecting party or deponent, the taking of the deposition shall be suspended for the time necessary to make a motion for an order. The provisions of Rule 37(a)(4) apply to the award of expenses incurred in relation to the motion.

(e) Submission to deponent; changes; signing. — The sound-and-visual recording, or the transcript of it, if any, the transcript of the sound recording, or the transcript of a deposition taken by stenographic means, shall be submitted to the deponent for examination and shall be reviewed by the deponent, unless such examination and review are waived by the deponent and by the parties. If there are changes in form or substance, the deponent shall sign a statement reciting such changes and the reasons given by the deponent for making them. The person administering the oath shall indicate in the certificate prescribed by subdivision (f)(1) whether any review was requested and, if so, shall append any changes made by the deponent. The certificate shall then be signed by the deponent, unless the parties by stipulation waive the signing or the deponent is ill or cannot be found or refuses to sign. If the certificate is not signed by the deponent within 30 days of its submission to him, the person before whom the deposition was taken shall sign the certificate and state on the certificate the fact of the waiver or of the illness or absence of the deponent or the fact of the refusal or failure to sign together with the reason, if any, given therefor; and the deposition may then be used as fully as though the certificate were signed unless on a motion to suppress under Rule 32(d)(4) the court holds that the reasons given for the refusal to sign require rejection of the deposition in whole or in part.

(f) Certification by person administering the oath; exhibits; copies. —

(1) The person administering the oath shall certify that the deponent was duly sworn by him and that the deposition is a true record of the testimony given by the deponent. This certificate shall be in writing and accompany the sound-and-visual or sound recording or transcript of the deposition. He shall then place the deposition in an envelope or package endorsed with the title of the action and marked "Deposition of (here insert name of witness)" and shall personally deliver it or mail it by first class mail to the party taking the deposition or his attorney who shall preserve it as the court's copy.

Documents and things produced for inspection during the examination of the deponent shall, upon the request of a party, be marked for identification and annexed to and returned with the deposition, and may be inspected and copied by any party, except that (i) the person producing the materials may substitute copies to be marked for identification, if he affords to all parties fair opportunity to verify the copies by comparison with the originals, and (ii) if the person producing the materials requests their return, the person before whom the deposition is taken shall mark them, give each party an opportunity to inspect and copy them, and return them to the person producing them, and the materials may then be used in the manner as if annexed to and returned with the deposition. Any party may move for an order that the original be annexed to and returned with the deposition to the court, pending final disposition of the case.

(2) Upon payment of reasonable charges therefor, the person administering the oath shall furnish a copy of the deposition to any party or to the deponent.

(3) Repealed by S.L. 2005-138, § 3, eff. Oct. 1, 2005.

(g) Failure to attend or to serve subpoena; expenses. —

(1) If the party giving the notice of the taking of a deposition fails to attend and proceed therewith and another party attends in person or by attorney pursuant to the notice, the judge may order the party giving the notice to pay to such other party the reasonable expenses incurred by him and his attorney in attending, including reasonable attorney's fees.

(2) If the party giving the notice of the taking of a deposition of a witness fails to serve a subpoena upon him and the witness because of such failure does not attend, and if another party attends in person or by attorney because he expects the deposition of that witness to be taken, the judge may order the party

giving the notice to pay to such other party the reasonable expenses incurred by him and his attorney in attending, including reasonable attorney's fees.

(h) Judge; definition. —

(1) In respect to actions in the superior court, a judge of the court in which the action is pending shall, for the purposes of this rule, and Rule 26, Rule 31, Rule 33, Rule 34, Rule 35, Rule 36 and Rule 37, be a superior court judge who has jurisdiction pursuant to G.S. 7A-47.1 or G.S. 7A-48 in that county.

(2) In respect to actions in the district court, a judge of the court in which the action is pending shall, for the purposes of this rule, Rule 26, Rule 31, Rule 33, Rule 34, Rule 35, Rule 36 and Rule 37, be the chief district judge or any judge designated by him pursuant to G.S. 7A-192.

(3) In respect to actions in either the superior court or the district court, a judge of the court in the county where the deposition is being taken shall, for the purposes of this rule, be a superior court judge who has jurisdiction pursuant to G.S. 7A-47.1 or G.S. 7A-48 in that county, or the chief judge of the district court or any judge designated by him pursuant to G.S. 7A-192.

Added by Laws 1967, c. 954, § 1. Amended by Laws 1973, c. 828, § 1; Laws 1973, c. 1126, §§ 1, 2; Laws 1975, c. 762, § 2; Laws 1977, c. 769; Laws 1983, c. 201, § 2; Laws 1983, c. 801, §§ 1, 2; Laws 1987 (Reg. Sess. 1988), c. 1037, § 42; Laws 1995 (Reg. Sess., 1996), c. 742, § 4; S.L. 2005-138, § 3, eff. Oct. 1, 2005.

Comment

Comment to this Rule as Originally Enacted. — This rule prescribes the procedure for taking depositions upon oral examination. Depositions upon written interrogatories are governed by Rule 31. The procedure fixed by Rule 30 governs depositions upon oral examination in all cases, whether a deposition with or without leave of court as provided in Rule 26(a), or under an order of court for the perpetuation of testimony before action under Rule 27 (a) or under order of court for the perpetuation of testimony pending appeal as provided in Rule 27(b) or under order of court as provided in Rule 27(c).

Section (a) differs from federal Rule 30 (a) in that a specific time for serving notice prior to the taking of the deposition is fixed, instead of "reasonable notice" as is found in the federal rule. Furthermore, section (a) does not authorize the court to extend or shorten the time fixed by the rule. Such a provision is contained in federal Rule 30(a).

Sections (b) and (d) provide for protection from the abuse of the discovery procedure to either the opposing party or the person to be examined. Before the taking of the deposition begins, either may apply for protection under section (b). During the taking of the deposition either may apply for protection under section (d). Under section (b) application is made to the judge of the court in which the action is pending upon motion seasonably made. "Seasonably" means as soon as the person making the motion learns that he will need the protective order. Moore's Federal Practice, § 30.05, (2nd Ed.). Such a motion must comply with Rule 7(b), be served and filed in compliance with Rule 5, and be served within the time provided in Rule 6(d).

A change has been made in federal Rule 30(c) in that a provision has been added with respect to the payment for transcribing when the transaction is requested by a party other than the party taking the deposition. In some cases the sale purpose of the deposition may be for discovery only, and not for use at the trial. Hence, the court should have this power.

The words "or by some method by which the testimony is written or typed as it is given" are inserted in section (c) for the purpose of indicating that, in the absence of agreement, testimony may be taken by any of the methods described.

As has been indicated, section (d) provides for protection during the taking of the deposition. Such a motion may be made before a judge of a court in which an action is pending or a judge of the court in which the deposition is being taken. Section (d) authorizes the judge to order either party or the deponent to pay such costs as may be deemed reasonable upon the granting or refusing of such a motion.

Section (e) changes former procedure to the extent that the deposition need not be signed by the deponent unless one of the parties or the deponent makes such a request.

Section (f) contains no provision for opening a deposition similar to former practice (repealed § 8-71). No good reason exists for continuing that practice, since in most cases all parties have copies of the deposition, and objections which have been entered at the taking of the deposition can be passed on at the time of trial.

Section (g) is identical with federal Rule 30(g). Apparently there is no provision under present statutes for the taxing of expenses under such circumstances.

Comment to the 1975 Amendment. — *Section (a).* — This section contains the provisions of existing Rule 26(a), transferred here as part of the rearrangement relating to Rule 26. Existing Rule 30(a) is transferred to 30(b). Changes in language have been made to conform to the new arrangement.

This section is further revised in regard to the requirement of leave of court for taking a deposition. The present procedure, requiring a plaintiff to obtain leave of court if he serves notice of taking a deposition within 30 days after commencement of the action, is changed in several respects. First, leave is required by reference to the time the deposition is to be taken rather than the date of serving notice of taking. Second, the 30-day period runs from the service of summons and complaint on any defendant, rather than the commencement of the action. Third, leave is not required beyond the time that defendant initiates discovery, thus showing that he has retained counsel. As under the present practice, a party not afforded a reasonable opportunity to appear at a deposition, because he has not yet been served with process, is protected against use of the deposition at trial against him. See Rule 32(a) transferred from [former] 26(d). Moreover, he can later redepose the witness if he so desires.

The purpose of requiring the plaintiff to obtain leave of court is to protect a defendant who has not had an opportunity to retain counsel and inform himself as to the nature of the suit. This protection, however, is relevant to the time of taking the deposition, not to the time that notice is served. Similarly, the protective period should run from the service of process rather than the filing of the complaint with the court. The new procedure is consistent in principle with the provisions of Rules 33, 34 and 36 as revised.

Plaintiff is excused from obtaining leave even during the initial 30-day period if he gives the special notice provided in subsection (b)(2). The required notice must state that the person to be examined is about to go out of the district where the action is pending and more than 100 miles from the place of trial, or out of the United States, or on a voyage to sea, and will be unavailable for examination unless deposed within the 30-day period. Defendant is protected by a provision that the deposition cannot be used against him if he was unable through exercise of diligence to obtain counsel to represent him.

The North Carolina modification of the former federal rule, requiring leave of court to depose mental patients as well as prisoners, is retained in substance.

The provision obviating the necessity of serving a subpoena on a deponent who is a party or an officer, director or managing agent of a party where the party has been served with notice of the deposition incorporates by rule the result reached by decision in most federal courts.

Section (b). — Existing Rule 30(b) on protective orders has been transferred to Rule 26(c), and existing former Rule 30(a) relating to the notice of taking deposition has been transferred to this section. Because new material has been added, subsection numbers have been inserted.

Subsection (b)(1). — If a subpoena duces tecum is to be served, a copy thereof or a designation of the materials to be produced must accompany the notice. Each party is thereby enabled to prepare for the deposition more effectively. The former North Carolina requirement, designating the length of notice required, is retained in preference to the standard of reasonable notice contained in the federal rules. The provision with respect to the place of deposition is removed in a modified form to this subsection from Rule 45(d)(2), where it referred only to deponents testifying under subpoena, and not to party deponents testifying pursuant to notice only.

Subsection (b)(2). — This subsection is discussed in the note to section (a), to which it relates.

Subsection (b)(3). — This provision is new, although the power of the Court to alter the time of a deposition has probably always existed.

Subsection (b)(4). — In order to facilitate less expensive procedures, provision is made for the recording of testimony by other than stenographic means—e.g., by mechanical, electronic, or photographic means. Because these methods give rise to problems of accuracy and trustworthiness, the party taking the deposition is required to apply for a court order. The order is to specify how the testimony is to be recorded, preserved, and filed, and it may contain whatever additional safeguards the court deems necessary.

Subsection (b)(5). — A provision is added to enable a party, through service of notice, to require another party to produce documents or things at the taking of his deposition. This may now be done as to a nonparty deponent through use of subpoena duces tecum as authorized by Rule 45, but some federal courts held under the former federal rule that documents could be secured from a party only under former Rule 34, which required notice, hearing and an order finding good cause for production. With the elimination of "good cause" from Rule 34, the reason for this restrictive doctrine has disappeared.

Whether production of documents or things should be obtained directly under Rule 34 or at the deposition under this rule will depend on the nature and volume of the documents or things. Both methods are made available. When the documents are few and simple, and closely related to the oral examination, ability to proceed via this rule will facilitate discovery. If the discovering party insists on examining many and complex documents at the taking of the deposition, thereby causing undue burdens on others, the latter may, under Rules 26(c) or 30(d), apply for a court order that the examining party proceed via Rule 34 alone. The provisions as to the timing of such request eliminates an ambiguity present in the new federal rule and insures that the party giving notice of the taking of a deposition will know in advance of the deposition what documents or things the deponent declines to produce. This will allow the deposing party an opportunity to seek an order to compel production under Rule 37(a) prior to the deposition if he is so advised and will serve to minimize the risk that a deposition will be adjourned because of the previously undisclosed refusal of the deponent to produce requested documents or things.

Subsection (b)(6). — A new provision is added, whereby a party may name a corporation, partnership, association or governmental agency as the deponent and designate the matters on which he requests examination, and the organization shall then name one or more of its officers, directors, or managing agents, or other persons consenting to appear and testify on its behalf with respect to matters known or reasonably available to the organization. The organization may designate persons other than officers, directors, and managing agents, but only with their consent. Thus, an employee or agent who has an independent or conflicting personal injury case—can refuse to testify on behalf of the organization.

This procedure supplements the existing practice whereby the examining party designates the corporate official to be deposed. Thus, if the examining party believes that certain officials who have not testified pursuant to this subsection have added information, he may depose them. On the other hand, a court's decision whether to issue a protective order may take account of the availability and use made of the procedures provided in this subsection.

The new procedure should be viewed as an added facility for discovery, one which may be advantageous to both sides as well as an improvement in the deposition process. It will reduce the difficulties now encountered in determining, prior to the taking of a deposition, whether a particular employee or agent is a "managing agent." It will curb the "bandying" by which officers or managing agents of a corporation are deposed in turn but each disclaims knowledge of facts that are clearly known to persons in the organization and thereby to it. The provision should also assist organizations which find that an unnecessarily large number of their officers and agents are being deposed by a party uncertain of who in the organization has knowledge. Some courts have held that under the existing rules a corporation should not be burdened with choosing which person is to appear for it. This burden is not essentially different from that of answering interrogatories under Rule 33, and is in any case lighter than that of an examining party ignorant of who in the corporation has knowledge.

This rule is so phrased that notice to parties, including a party deponent, and a subpoena to a nonparty organization are required to bring the rule into play.

The wording of this subsection is slightly altered from that of the federal rule to eliminate an ambiguity as to whether the subpoena must be issued to a party.

Section (c). — A new sentence is inserted at the beginning, representing the transfer of existing Rule 26(c) to this section. Another addition conforms to the new provision in subsection (b)(4).

The present rule provides that transcription shall be carried out unless all parties waive it. In view of the many depositions taken from which nothing useful is discovered, the revised language provides that transcription is to be performed if any party requests it.

Parties choosing to serve written questions rather than participate personally in an oral deposition are directed to serve their questions on the party taking the deposition, since the officer is often not identified in advance. Confidentiality is preserved, since the questions may be served in a sealed envelope.

Section (d). — The assessment of expenses incurred in relation to motions made under this section (d) is made subject to the provisions of Rule 37(a). The standards for assessment of expenses are more fully set out in Rule 37(a), and these standards should apply to the essentially similar motions of this section.

Section (e). — The provision relating to the refusal of a deponent to sign his deposition is tightened through insertion of a 30–day time period and a provision allowing use of the deposition upon the refusal or failure of the deponent to sign and return it within the required time.

Subsection (f)(1). — A provision is added which codifies in a flexible way the procedure for handling exhibits related to the deposition and at the same time assures each party that he may inspect and copy documents and things produced at a nonparty witness in response to a subpoena duces tecum. As a general rule and in the absence of agreement to the contrary or order of the court, exhibits produced without objection are to be annexed to and returned with the deposition, but a deponent may substitute copies for purposes of marking and he may obtain return of the exhibits. The right of the parties to inspect exhibits for identification and to make copies is assured.

The former requirement of North Carolina Rule 26(f)(1) that the original and one copy be filed with the clerk is abandoned. In practice it proved to have little utility and was generally waived or ignored.

Subsection (f)(3). — This provision clarifies the conflict between former Rule 30(f)(3) which required the party to give the notice, and [former] 32(e) which required the clerk to do so. It also eliminates the former requirement that the party taking the deposition furnish a copy to all other parties. Whatever the reason for the former requirement may have been, in practice it has penalized the party with limited means who must utilize depositions to make out his claim or defense.

Section (g). — This provision contained only minor changes in phraseology not affecting the substance of the rule.

Rule 31. Depositions upon written questions

(a) Serving questions; notice.—After commencement of the action, any party may take the testimony of any person, including a party, by deposition upon written questions. The attendance of witnesses may be compelled by the use of subpoena as provided in Rule 45 provided that no subpoena need be served on a deponent who is a party or an officer, director or managing agent of a party, provided the party has been served with notice pursuant to this rule. Such a deposition shall be taken in the county where the witness resides or is employed or transacts his business in person unless the witness agrees that it may be taken elsewhere. The deposition of a person confined in prison or of a patient receiving in-patient care in or confined to an institution or hospital for the mentally ill or mentally handicapped may be taken only by leave of court on such terms as the court prescribes.

A party desiring to take a deposition upon written questions shall serve them upon every other party with a notice stating (i) the name and address of the person who is to answer them, if known, and if the name is not known, a general description sufficient to identify him or the particular class or group to which he belongs, and (ii) the name or descriptive title and address of the officer before whom the deposition is to be taken. A deposition upon written questions may be taken of a public or private corporation or a partnership or association or governmental agency in accordance with the provisions of Rule 30(b)(6).

Within 30 days after the notice and written questions are served, a party may serve cross questions upon all other parties. Within 10 days after being served with cross questions, a party may serve redirect questions upon all other parties. Within 10 days after being served with redirect questions, a party may serve recross questions upon all other parties. The court may for cause shown enlarge or shorten the time.

(b) Person to take responses and prepare record. — A copy of the notice and copies of all questions served shall be delivered by the party taking the deposition to the person designated in the notice to take the deposition, who shall proceed promptly, in the manner provided by Rule 30(c), (e), and (f), to take the testimony of the deponent in response to the questions and to prepare, certify, and mail the deposition, attaching thereto the copy of the notice and the questions received by him.

(c) Repealed by S.L. 2005–138, § 4, eff. Oct. 1, 2005.

Added by Laws 1967, c. 954, § 1. Amended by Laws 1975, c. 762, § 2; S.L. 2005–138, § 4, eff. Oct. 1, 2005.

Comment

Comment to this Rule as Originally Enacted. — This rule provides an alternative method for taking depositions which a party may employ rather than taking the deposition on oral examination as provided for in Rule 30, and follows very closely federal Rule 31.

Under former § 8–71, when a deposition was returned to the court, the clerk was required to open and pass on it after giving parties or their attorney not less than one day's notice. Section (c) simply requires the party taking the deposition to give notice of the filing of the deposition.

"Rule 31(d) permits a party or a deponent to make a motion in the court in which the action is pending for any protective order specified in Rule 30. The motion, however, must be made prior to the taking of the testimony of the deponent. This time limitation upon the making of the motion is perfectly proper with respect to a party, but if applied also to a motion made by a deponent, it is inconsistent with the practice that the interrogatories are not to be shown to the deponent in advance of the taking of the deposition. While the time limitation imposed by Rule 30(d) upon the making of a motion for a protective order is in terms applicable to a motion by a deponent, it is believed that the proper practice should be that the interrogatories should not be shown to the deponent in advance of the taking of his deposition, except upon consent of the parties, and that the deponent should be allowed to make a motion for a protective order during the taking of the deposition as provided in Rule 30(d) for the making of a similar motion by a deponent upon an oral examination." 4 Moore's Federal Practice, § 31.06.

Comment to the 1975 Amendment. — Confusion is created by the use of the same terminology to describe both the taking of a deposition upon "written interrogatories" pursuant to this rule and the serving of "written interrogatories" upon parties pursuant to Rule 33. The distinction between these two modes of discovery will be more readily and clearly grasped through substitution of the word "questions" for "interrogatories" throughout this rule.

Section (a). — A new paragraph is inserted at the beginning of this section to conform to the rearrangement of provisions in Rules 26(a), 30(a), and 30(b).

The revised section permits designation of the deponent by general description or by class or group. This conforms to the practice for depositions on oral examination.

The new procedure provided in Rule 30(b)(6) for taking the deposition of a corporation or other organization through persons designated by the organizations is incorporated by reference.

The service of all questions, including cross, redirect, and recross, is to be made on all parties. This will inform the parties and enable them to participate fully in the procedure.

The time allowed for service of cross, redirect, and recross questions has been extended. Experience with the existing time limits under the former federal rule showed them to be unrealistically short. No special restriction is placed on the time for serving the notice of taking the deposition and the first set of questions. Since no party is required to serve cross questions less than 30 days after the notice and questions are served, the defendant has sufficient time to obtain counsel. The court may for cause shown enlarge or shorten the time.

The provision obviating the necessity of service of subpoena on a party or an officer, director or managing agent of a party conforms to revised Rule 30(a) and federal case law in the absence of a similar provision in the federal rules.

The North Carolina modification of the former federal rule, requiring leave of court to depose mental patients as well as prisoners, is retained in substance.

Section (c). — This section is amended to conform to the change in Rule 30(f)(3).

Former Section (d). — Since new Rule 26(c) provides for protective orders with respect to all discovery, and expressly provides that the court may order that one discovery device be used in place of another, section (d) is eliminated as unnecessary.

Rule 32. Use of depositions in court proceedings

(a) Use of depositions. — At the trial or upon the hearing of a motion or an interlocutory proceeding or upon a hearing before a referee, any part or all of a deposition, so far as admissible under the rules of evidence applied as though the witness were then present and testifying, may be used against any party who was present or represented at the taking of the deposition or who had reasonable notice thereof, in accordance with any of the following provisions:

(1) Any deposition may be used by any party for the purpose of contradicting or impeaching the testimony of deponent as a witness.

(2) The deposition of a person called as a witness may also be used as substantive evidence by any party adverse to the party who called the deponent as a witness and it may be used by the party calling deponent as a witness as substantive evidence of such facts stated in the deposition as are in conflict with or inconsistent with the testimony of deponent as a witness.

(3) The deposition of a party or of any one who at the time of taking the deposition was an officer, director, or managing agent, or a person designated under Rule 30(b)(6) or 31(a) to testify on behalf of a public or private corporation, partnership or association or governmental agency which is a party may be used by an adverse party for any purpose, whether or not the deponent testifies at the trial or hearing.

(4) The deposition of a witness, whether or not a party, may be used by any party for any purpose if the court finds: that the witness is dead; or that the witness is at a greater distance than 100 miles from the place of trial or hearing, or is out of the United States, unless it appears that the absence of the witness was procured by the party offering the deposition; or that the witness is unable to attend or testify because of age, illness, infirmity, or imprisonment; or that the party offering the deposition has been unable to procure the attendance of the witness by subpoena; or upon application and notice, that such exceptional circumstances exist as to make it desirable, in the interest of justice and with due regard to the importance of presenting testimony of witnesses orally in open court, to allow the deposition to be used; or the witness is an expert witness whose testimony has been procured by videotape as provided for under Rule 30(b)(4).

(5) If only part of a deposition is offered in evidence by a party, an adverse party may require him to introduce any other part which is relevant to the part introduced, and any party may introduce any other parts.

Substitution of parties pursuant to Rule 25 does not affect the right to use depositions previously taken; and, when an action in any court of the United States or of any state has been dismissed and another action involving the same subject matter is afterward brought between the same parties or their representatives or successors in interest, all depositions lawfully taken in the former action and duly prepared, certified, and delivered in accordance with Rule 30 may be used in the latter as if originally taken therefor.

(b) Objections to admissibility. — Subject to the provisions of Rules 28(b) and subsection (d)(3) of this rule, objection may be made at the trial or hearing to receiving in evidence any deposition or part thereof for any reason which would require the exclusion of the evidence if the witness were then present and testifying.

(c) Effect of taking or using depositions. — A party does not make a person his own witness for any purpose by taking his deposition. The introduction in evidence of the deposition or any part thereof for any purpose other than that of contradicting or impeaching the deponent makes the deponent the witness of the party introducing the deposition, but this shall not apply to the use by an adverse party of a deposition under subsection (a)(2) or (a)(3) of this rule. At the trial or hearing any party may rebut any relevant evidence contained in a deposition whether introduced by him or by any other party.

(d) Effect of errors and irregularities in depositions. —

(1) As to Notice. — All errors and irregularities in the notice for taking a deposition are waived unless written objection is promptly served upon the party giving the notice.

(2) As to Disqualification of Person before Whom Taken. — Objection to taking a deposition because of disqualification of the person before whom it is to be taken is waived unless made before the taking of the deposition begins or as soon thereafter as the disqualification becomes known or could be discovered with reasonable diligence.

(3) As to Taking of Deposition. —

a. Objections to the competency of a witness or to the competency, relevancy, or materiality of testimony are not waived by failure to make them before or during the taking of the deposition, unless the ground of the objection is one which might have been obviated or removed if presented at that time.

b. Errors and irregularities occurring at the oral examination in the manner of taking the deposition, in the form of the questions or answers, in the oath or affirmation, or in the conduct of parties, and errors of any kind which might be obviated, removed, or cured if promptly presented, are waived unless seasonable objection thereto is made at the taking of the deposition.

c. Objections to the form of written questions submitted under Rule 31 are waived unless served in writing upon the party propounding them within the time allowed for serving the succeeding cross or other questions and within five days after service of the last questions authorized.

(4) As to Completion and Return of Deposition. — Errors and irregularities in the manner in which the testimony is transcribed or the deposition is prepared, signed, certified, sealed, indorsed, transmitted, or otherwise dealt with by the person taking the deposition under Rules 30 and 31 are waived unless a motion to suppress the deposition or some part thereof is made with reasonable promptness after such defeat is, or with due diligence might have been, ascertained.

Added by Laws 1967, c. 954, § 1. Amended by Laws 1975, c. 762, § 2; Laws 1977, c. 984; Laws 1981, c. 599, § 2; S.L. 2005–138, §§ 5, 6, eff. Oct. 1, 2005.

Comment

Comment To This Rule as Originally Enacted. — The purpose of this rule is to require defects in the taking of depositions to be pointed out promptly in order that the erring party may have an opportunity to correct the errors and prevent waste of time and expense by a subsequent claim to suppress a deposition based upon some technical error.

Section (a) carries forward former § 1–568.23(a).

Under former law objection based upon the disqualification of the person before whom the deposition is to be taken could be made at any time up to trial. Under section (b) such an objection would be unavailable at trial.

Sections (c)(1) and (2) follow verbatim federal Rule 32 (c)(1) and (3) and former § 1–568.23(b) and (d).

Federal Rule 32(c)(2), which is the same as former § 1–568.23(c), has been omitted.

Section (d). — This section follows federal Rule 32(d) verbatim and is quite similar to former §§ 1–568.22 and 1–568.23(e) except in this rule objection must be made with "reasonable promptness," whereas, under former statutes, a motion to suppress must have been made within ten days after the deposition was filed.

Comment to the 1975 Amendment. — As part of the rearrangement of the discovery rules, existing sections (d) and (e) of Rule 26 are transferred to Rule 32 as new sections (a) and (c). The provisions of Rule 32 are retained as section (d) of Rule 32 with appropriate changes in the lettering and numbering of subheadings. The new rule is given a suitable new title. A beneficial by product of the rearrangement is that provisions which are naturally related to one another are placed in one rule.

A change is made in new Rule 32(a), whereby it is made clear that the rules of evidence are to be applied to depositions offered at trial as though the deponent were then present and testifying at trial. This eliminates the possibility of certain technical hearsay objections which are based, not on the contents of deponent's testimony, but on his absence from court. The language of present [former] Rule 26(d) does not appear to authorize these technical objections, but it is not entirely clear.

The provisions of former Rule 26(d)(2)a and b, governing use of a deposition where the deponent testifies at trial, are preserved in Rule 32(a)(1) and (2) with the added provision that any party may use a deposition to contradict or impeach a witness who testifies at trial.

Note present Rule 26(e), transferred to Rule 32(b).

An addition in Rule 32(a)(2) provides for use of a deposition of a person designated by a corporation or other organization, which is a party, to testify on its behalf. This complements the new procedure for taking the deposition of a corporation or other organization provided in Rules 30(b)(6) and 31(a). The addition is appropriate, since the deposition is in substance and effect that of the corporation or other organization which is a party.

References to other rules are changed to conform to the rearrangement, and minor verbal changes have been made for clarification. The time for objecting to written questions served under Rule 31 is slightly extended.

The somewhat unwieldy provisions of former Rule 32(e) relating to the mechanics of handling objections to all or part of a deposition are abandoned in favor of present Rule 32(b).

The absence of specific provisions relating to the time when objections of various kinds must be made has necessitated the entry of a stipulation on the subject in every carefully taken deposition. Rules 32(d)(3)a and b incorporate in the rules provisions that are almost universally stipulated by the parties in the absence of a rule.

Rule 33. Interrogatories to parties

(a) Availability; procedures for use.—Any party may serve upon any other party written interrogatories to be answered by the party served or, if the party served is a public or private corporation or a partnership or association or governmental agency, by any officer or agent, who shall furnish such information as is available to the party. Interrogatories may, without leave of court, be served upon the plaintiff after commencement of the action and upon any other party with or after service of the summons and complaint upon that party.

A party may direct no more than 50 interrogatories, in one or more sets, to any other party, except upon leave granted by the Court for good cause shown or by agreement of the other party. Interrogatory parts and subparts shall be counted as separate interrogatories for purposes of this rule.

There shall be sufficient space following each interrogatory in which the respondent may state the response. The respondent shall: (1) state the response in the space provided, using additional pages if necessary; or (2) restate the interrogatory to be followed by the response.

Each interrogatory shall be answered separately and fully in writing under oath, unless it is objected to, in which event the reasons for objection shall be stated in lieu of an answer. An objection to an interrogatory shall be made by stating the objection and the reason therefor either in the space following the interrogatory or following the restated interrogatory. The answers are to be signed by the person making them, and the objections signed by the attorney making them. The party upon whom the interrogatories have been served shall serve a copy of the answers, and objections if any, within 30 days after the service of the interrogatories, except that a defendant may serve answers or objections within 45 days after service of the summons and complaint upon the defendant. The court may allow a shorter or longer time. The party submitting the interrogatories may move for an order under Rule 37(a) with respect to any objection to or other failure to answer an interrogatory.

(b) Scope; use at trial.—Interrogatories may relate to any matters which can be inquired into under Rule 26(b), and the answers may be used to the extent permitted by the rules of evidence.

An interrogatory otherwise proper is not necessarily objectionable merely because an answer to the interrogatory involves an opinion or contention that relates to fact or the application of law to fact, but the court may order that such an interrogatory need not be answered until after designated discovery has been completed or until a pretrial conference or other later time.

(c) Option to produce business records.—Where the answer to an interrogatory may be derived or ascertained from the business records, including electronically stored information, of the party upon whom the interrogatory has been served or from an examination, audit or inspection of such business records, or from a compilation, abstract or summary based thereon, and the burden of deriving or ascertaining the answer is substantially the same for the party serving the interrogatory as for the party served, it is a sufficient answer to such interrogatory to specify the records from which the answer may be derived or ascertained and to afford to the party serving the interrogatory reasonable opportunity to examine, audit or inspect such records and to make copies, compilations, abstracts or summaries. A specification shall be in sufficient detail to permit the interrogating party to locate and to identify, as readily as can the party served, the records from which the answer may be ascertained.

Added by Laws 1967, c. 954, § 1. Amended by Laws 1971, c. 1156, § 4.5; Laws 1975, c. 99; Laws 1975, c. 762, § 2; Laws 1987, c. 73; Laws 1987, c. 613, § 1; S.L. 2011-199, § 3, eff. Oct. 1, 2011.

Comment

Comment to this Rule as Originally Enacted. — Under former § 1-568.17 a party might examine upon written interrogatories.

This rule provides that the scope of the interrogatories is the same as that for discovery generally, as set out in Rule 26(b). Hence, interrogatories may be used for purposes of discovery. Also, the use of answers to interrogatories is limited by Rule 26(d) as well as by ordinary rules of evidence.

The period in which plaintiff may not serve interrogatories without leave of court has been lengthened from 10 days, as in federal Rule 33, to 30 days. This corresponds to the time for filing answer or other pleading or motion and thus preserves the general scheme by which a defendant is given 30 days to take his first action unless the court otherwise orders.

It should be noted that this rule does not require notice to parties other than the one to be examined. Former § 1-568.17 required that a copy of the order for examination and a copy of the interrogatories be delivered to all other parties.

The problems which might be presented in cases where the interrogatories call for documents to be attached are covered in Rule 26(b), which governs the scope of the interrogatories.

Comment to the 1975 Amendment. *Section (a).* — The mechanics of the operation of Rule 33 are substantially revised by the proposed amendment, with a view to reducing court intervention. There is generally agreement that interrogatories have spawned a greater percentage of objections and motions than any other discovery device.

The procedures provided in former Rule 33 seemed calculated to encourage objections and court motions. The time period allowed for objecting to interrogatories, 10 days, was too short. The time pressures tended to encourage objections as a means of gaining time to answer. The time for objections was even shorter than for answers, and the party ran the risk that if he failed to object in time he may have waived his objections. It often seemed easier to object than to seek an extension of time. Unlike Rules 30(d) and 37(a), Rule 33 imposed no sanction of expenses on a party whose objections were clearly unjustified. Rule 33 assured that the objections led directly to court, through its requirement that they be served with a notice of hearing. Although this procedure did not preclude an out-of-court resolution of the dispute, the procedure tended to discourage informal negotiations. If answers were served and they were thought inadequate, the interrogating party could move under Rule 37(a) for an order compelling adequate answers. There was no assurance that the hearing on objections and that on inadequate answers would be heard together.

The amendment improves the procedure of Rule 33 in the following respects:

(1) The time allowed for response applies to both answers and objections, but a defendant need not respond in less than 45 days after service of the summons and complaint upon him. As is true under existing law, the responding party who believes that some parts or all of the interrogatories are objectionable may choose to seek a protective order under new Rule 26(c) or may serve objections under this rule. Unless he applies for a protective order, he is required to serve answers or objections in response to the interrogatories, subject to the sanctions provided in Rule 37(d). Answers and objections are served together, so that a response to each interrogatory is encouraged, and any failure to respond is easily noted.

(2) In view of the enlarged time permitted for response, it is no longer necessary to require leave of court for service of interrogatories. The purpose of this requirement—that defendant have time to obtain counsel before a response must be made—is adequately fulfilled by the requirement that interrogatories be served upon a party with or after service of the summons and complaint upon him.

(3) If objections are made, the burden is on the interrogating party to move under Rule 37(a) for a court order compelling answers, in the course of which the court will pass on the objections. The change in the burden of going forward does not alter the existing obligation of an objecting party to justify his objections. If the discovering party asserts that an answer is incomplete or evasive, again he may look to Rule 37(a) for relief, and he should add this assertion to his motion to overrule objections. There is no requirement that the parties consult informally concerning their differences, but the new procedure should encourage consultation.

A change is made in section (a) which is not related to the sequence of procedures. The restriction to "adverse" parties is eliminated. The courts have generally construed this restriction as precluding interrogatories unless an issue between the parties is disclosed by the pleadings—even though the parties may have conflicting interests. The resulting distinctions have often been highly technical. Eliminating the requirement of "adverse" parties from Rule 33 brings it into line with all other discovery rules.

A second change in section (a) is the addition of the term "governmental agency" to the listing of organizations whose answers are to be made by any officer or agent of the organization. This does not involve any change in existing law. Compare the similar listing in Rule 30(b)(6).

The duty of a party to supplement his answers to interrogatories is governed by a new provision in Rule 26(e).

Section (b). — There are numerous and conflicting federal decisions on the question whether and to what extent interrogatories are limited to matters "of fact," or may elicit opinions, contentions, and legal conclusions.

Rule 33 is amended to provide that an interrogatory is not objectionable merely because it calls for an opinion or contention that relates to fact or the application of law to fact. Efforts to draw sharp lines between facts and opinions have invariably been unsuccessful, and the clear trend of the cases is to permit "factual" opinions. As to requests for opinions or contentions that call for the application of law to fact, they can be most useful in narrowing and sharpening the issues, which is a major purpose of discovery. On the other hand, under the new language interrogatories may not extend to issues of "pure law," i.e., legal issues unrelated to the facts of the case.

Since interrogatories involving mixed questions of law and fact may create disputes between the parties which are best resolved after much or all of the other discovery has been completed, the court is expressly authorized to defer an answer. Likewise, the court may delay determination until pretrial conference, if it believes that the dispute is best resolved in the presence of the judge.

The use of answers to interrogatories at trial is made subject to the rules of evidence. The provisions governing use of depositions, to which this rule presently refers, are not entirely apposite to answers to interrogatories, since deposition practice contemplates that all parties will ordinarily participate through cross-examination.

Certain provisions are deleted from section (b) because they are fully covered by new Rule 26(c) providing for protective orders and Rules 26(a) and 26(d). The language of the section is thus simplified without any change of substance.

Section (c). — This is a new section relating especially to interrogatories which require a party to engage in burdensome or expensive research into his own business records in order to give an answer. The section gives the party an option to make the records available and place the burden of research on the party who seeks the information. This provision, without undermining the liberal scope of interrogatory discovery, places the burden of discovery upon its potential benefitee, and alleviates a problem which in the past has troubled federal courts. The interrogating party is protected against abusive use of this provision through the requirement that the burden of ascertaining the answer be substantially the same for both sides. A respondent may not impose on an interrogating party a mass of records as to which research is feasible only for one familiar with the records. At the same time, the respondent unable to invoke this section does not on that account lose the protection available to him under new Rule 26(c) against oppressive or unduly burdensome or expensive interrogatories. And even when the respondent successfully invokes the section, the court is not deprived of its usual power, in appropriate cases, to require that the interrogating party reimburse the respondent for the expense of assembling his records and making them intelligible.

Disclosure of trial witnesses. — Prior to the 1970 revision the federal cases were in conflict as to whether a party could be required at a proper time, in response to an interrogatory or by other discovery devices, to state the names and addresses of witnesses then known, and whom he proposed to call at trial. Probably the weight of reported authority was that a party is not required so to do. But at least the judge at pretrial under Rule 16 may require disclosure in the exercise of a sound discretion in light of all the circumstances.

And the 1970 revision provides that "A party may through interrogatories require any other party to identify each person whom the other party expects to call as an expert witness at trial, to state the subject matter on which the expert is expected to testify, and to state the substance of the facts and opinions to which the expert is expected to testify and a summary of the grounds for each opinion." Rule 26(b)(4) a 1, supra.

Obtaining copies of documents, etc., by requesting a party to attach them to his answers to interrogatories. — Formerly Rule 34 required a motion showing good cause as a prerequisite to obtaining discovery and production of documents and things for inspection, copying or photographing. Accordingly, most federal authorities held that interrogatories to a party requesting copies of documents were not proper and that copies of statements or witnesses and other documents could be obtained from a party only under Rule 34 (or Rules 26 and 45) upon a showing of good cause. The present revision eliminates the good-cause requirement in Rule 34; but section (b) of that rule sets out the procedure that should be followed in obtaining inspection, etc. Rule 34 does not, however, deal with discovery of trial preparation materials. That matter is now dealt with by Rule 26(b)(3), (4), supra. Those provisions allow a party or a witness to obtain a copy of his own written statement as of right. And a party is entitled, as of right, to obtain from any other party the names of expert witnesses whom he expects to call at trial, and a statement of the substance of the facts and opinions to which the expert is expected to testify. Rule 26(b)(4) a 1, supra. As to other trial preparation materials a party must make the showing spelled out in Rule 26(b)(3), supra. This requirement, accordingly, should not be circumvented by an improper use of Rule 33 or Rule 34.

Rule 30(b)(5) does, however, provide that "The notice to a party deponent may be accompanied by a request made in compliance with Rule 34 for the production of documents and tangible things at the taking of the deposition."

Comment to the 2011 Amendment. *Subsection (c).* — Subsection (c) is amended to parallel Rule 34(a) by recognizing the importance of electronically stored information. The term "electronically stored information" has the same broad meaning in subsection (c) as in Rule 34(a).

Special difficulties may arise in using electronically stored information, either due to its form or because it is dependent on a particular computer system. Subsection (c) allows a responding party to substitute access to documents or electronically stored information for an answer only if the burden of deriving the answer will be substantially the same for either party. Subsection (c) requires a party electing to respond to an interrogatory by providing electronically stored information to ensure that the interrogating party can locate and identify it "as readily as can the party served". In this regard, the responding party should consider using the system on which the electronically stored information is housed to generate summary reports that can be produced as the kind of "compilation, abstract or summary" contemplated by subsection (c). Such reports can be particularly helpful when they are the same kind of reports that the producing party uses in making decisions or tracking information.

Subsection (c) also provides that the responding party must give the interrogating party a "reasonable opportunity to examine, audit, or inspect" the information. Depending on the circumstances, satisfying these provisions with regard to electronically stored information may require the responding party to provide some combination of technical support, information on application software, or other assistance. The key question is whether such support enables the interrogating party to derive or ascertain the answer from the electronically stored information as readily as can the responding party. A party that wishes to invoke subsection (c) by specifying electronically stored information may be required to provide direct access to its electronic information system, but only if that is necessary to afford the requesting party an adequate opportunity to derive or ascertain the answer to the interrogatory. The necessity question will turn on whether the requesting party can show that there is some specific reason, beyond general suspicion, to doubt the information that the producing party provides from the system involved and that the burden of providing direct access is reasonable in light of the importance of the information and the circumstances of the case. In appropriate situations, the court should consider having the parties share the cost of providing such direct access. Further, in situations where direct access becomes an issue, the responding party's need to protect sensitive interests of confidentiality or privacy may mean that it must derive or ascertain and provide the answer itself rather than invoke subsection (c).

Rule 34. Production of documents, electronically stored information, and things; entry upon land for inspection and other purposes

(a) Scope.—Any party may serve on any other party a request (i) to produce and permit the party making the request, or someone acting on that party's behalf, to inspect and copy, test, or sample any designated documents, electronically stored information, or tangible things which constitute or contain matters within the scope of Rule 26(b) and which are in the possession, custody or control of the party upon whom the request is served; or (ii) to permit entry upon designated land or other property in the possession or control of the party upon whom the request is served for the purpose of inspection and measuring, surveying, photographing, testing, or sampling the property or any designated object or operation thereon, within the scope of Rule 26(b).

(b) Procedure.—The request may, without leave of court, be served upon the plaintiff after commencement of the action and upon any other party with or after service of the summons and complaint upon that party. The request shall set forth the items to be inspected either by individual item or by category, and describe each item and category with reasonable particularity. The request shall specify a reasonable time, place, and manner of making the inspection and performing the related acts. The request may specify the form or forms in which electronically stored information is to be produced.

The party upon whom the request is served shall serve a written response within 30 days after the service of the request, except that a defendant may serve a response within 45 days after service of the summons and complaint upon that defendant. The court may allow a shorter or longer time. The response shall state, with respect to each item or category, that inspection and related activities will be permitted as requested, unless the request is objected to, in which event the reasons for objection shall be stated. If objection is made to part of an item or category, the part shall be specified. In addition to other bases for objection, the response may state an objection to production of electronically stored information from sources that the party identifies as not reasonably accessible because of undue burden or cost. The response may also state an objection to a requested form for producing electronically stored information. If the responding party objects to a requested form, or if no form is specified in the request, the party must state the form or forms it intends to use. The party submitting the request may move for an order under Rule 37(a) with respect to any objection to or other failure to respond to the request or any part thereof, or any failure to permit inspection as requested.

Unless otherwise stipulated by the parties or ordered by the court, the following procedures apply to producing documents or electronically stored information:

(1) A party must produce documents as they are kept in the usual course of business or must organize and label them to correspond to the categories in the request;

(2) If a request does not specify a form for producing the electronically stored information, a party must produce it in a reasonably usable form or forms; and

(3) A party need not produce the same electronically stored information in more than one form.

(b1) Form of response.— There shall be sufficient space following each request in which the respondent may state the response. The respondent shall: (1) state the response in the space provided, using additional pages if necessary; or (2) restate the request to be followed by the response. An objection to a request shall be made by stating the objection and the reason therefor either in the space following the request or following the restated request.

(c) Persons not parties.—This rule does not preclude an independent action against a person not a party for production of documents and things and permission to enter upon land.

Added by Laws 1967, c. 954, § 1. Amended by Laws 1969, c. 895, § 8; Laws 1973, c. 923, § 1; Laws 1987, c. 613, § 2; S.L. 2011-199, § 4, eff. Oct. 1, 2011.

Comment

Comment to this Rule as Originally Enacted. — Former statutes in a pending action authorized the court to order an inspection of writings (§ 8-89) and the production of documents (§ 8-90).

The protective provisions of Rule 30(b) are incorporated in this rule by reference.

The provisions in this rule limiting the scope of the examination as permitted in Rule 26(b) and the specification in Rule 26(b) of documents which shall not be the subject of discovery would appear to provide explicit regulations on such matters and avoid complexities which have existed under the federal rules.

Comment to the 1969 Amendment. — The 1969 amendment deleted former subsection (b) which dealt with discovery of certain documents without order of court. Since this whole area is now undergoing intensive study, it was thought desirable to delay action until a later date.

Comment to the 1975 Amendment. — Rule 34 is revised to accomplish the following major changes in the existing rule: (1) To eliminate the requirement of good cause for production, which was formerly superimposed on the provisions regulating the permissible scope of discovery; (2) To have the rule operate without the necessity of the court's participation; (3) To include testing and sampling as well as inspecting or photographing tangible things; and (4) To make clear that the rule does not preclude an independent action for analogous discovery against persons not parties.

Section (a). — Good cause is eliminated because it has furnished an uncertain and erratic protection to the parties from whom production is sought and is now rendered unnecessary by virtue of the more specific provisions added to Rule 26(b) relating to materials assembled in preparation for trial and to experts retained or consulted by parties.

The good-cause requirement was originally inserted in federal Rule 34 as a general protective provision in the absence of experience with the specific problems that would arise thereunder. The overwhelming proportion of the cases in which the formula of good cause has been applied to require a specific showing are those involving trial preparation. In practice, the courts have not treated documents as having a special immunity to discovery simply because of their being documents. Protection may be afforded to claims of privacy or secrecy or of undue burden or expense under what is now Rule 26(c) (previously Rule 30(b)). To be sure, an appraisal of "undue" burden inevitably entails consideration of the needs of the party seeking discovery. With special provisions added to govern trial preparation materials and experts, there is no longer any occasion to retain the requirement of good cause.

The revision of Rule 34 to have it operate extrajudicially rather than by court order is to a large extent a reflection of existing practice.

The inclusion of testing and sampling of tangible things and objects or operations on land reflects a need frequently encountered by parties in preparation for trial. If the operation of a particular machine is the basis of a claim for negligent injury, it will often be necessary to test its operating parts or to sample and test the products it is producing.

The inclusive description of "documents" is revised to accord with changing technology. It makes clear that Rule 34 applies to electronic data compilations from which information can be obtained only with the use of detection devices, and that when the data can as a practical matter be made usable by the discovering party only through respondent's devices, respondent may be required to use his devices to translate the data into usable form. In many instances, this means that respondent will have to supply a printout of computer data. The burden thus placed on respondent will vary from case to case, and the courts have ample power under Rule 26(c) to protect respondent against undue burden or expense, either by restricting discovery or requiring that the discovering party pay costs. Similarly, if the discovering party needs to check the electronic source itself, the court may protect respondent with respect to preservation of his records, confidentiality of nondiscoverable matters, and costs.

Section (b). — The procedure provided in Rule 34 is essentially the same as that in Rule 33, as amended, and the discussion in the note appended to that rule is relevant to Rule 34 as well. Problems peculiar to Rule 34 relate to the specific arrangements that must be worked out for inspection and related acts of copying, photographing, testing, or sampling.

The rule provides that a request for inspection shall set forth the items to be inspected either by item or category, describing each with reasonable particularity, and shall specify a reasonable time, place, and manner of making the inspection.

Section (c). — Rule 34 as revised continues to apply only to parties. Comments from the bar to the drafters of the federal rule made clear that in the preparation of cases for trial it is occasionally necessary to enter land or inspect large tangible things in the possession of a person not a party, and that some federal courts had dismissed independent actions in the nature of bills in equity for such discovery on the ground that Rule 34 is preemptive. While an ideal solution to this problem is to provide for discovery against persons not parties in Rule 34, both the jurisdictional and procedural problems are very complex. For the present, this section makes clear that Rule 34 does not preclude independent actions for discovery against persons not parties.

Relation to other rules. — Rule 34 does not deal with trial preparation materials, since discovery as to those materials is specially dealt with by Rule 26(b)(3), (4). Accordingly, those provisions should not be circumvented by an improper use of Rule 33 or 34.

A request made in compliance with Rule 34 may accompany the notice to a party deponent to take his oral deposition. Rule 30(b)(5).

Comment to the 2011 Amendment. *Subsection (a).* — As originally adopted, Rule 34 focused on discovery of "documents" and "things." In 1975, Rule 34(a) was amended to include discovery of data compilations, anticipating that the use of computerized information would increase. Since then, the growth in electronically stored information and in the variety of systems for creating and storing such information has been dramatic. Lawyers and judges interpreted the term "documents" to include electronically stored information because it obviously was improper to allow a party to evade discovery obligations on the basis that the label had not kept pace with changes in information technology. But it has become increasingly difficult to say that all forms of electronically stored information, many dynamic in nature, fit within the traditional concept of a "document." Electronically stored information may exist in dynamic databases and other forms far different from fixed expression on paper. Subsection (a) is amended to confirm that discovery of electronically stored information stands on equal footing with discovery of paper documents. The change clarifies that Rule 34 applies to information that is fixed in a tangible form and to information that is stored in a medium from which it can be retrieved and examined. At the same time, a Rule 34 request for production of "documents" should be understood to encompass, and the response should include, electronically stored information unless discovery in the action has clearly distinguished between electronically stored information and "documents."

Discoverable information often exists in both paper and electronic form, and the same or similar information might exist in both. The wide variety of computer systems currently in use, and the rapidity of technological change, counsel against a limiting or precise definition of electronically stored information. "Electronically stored information" in subsection (a)(i) has the same meaning as in Rule 26(b)(1). It is expansive and includes any type of information that is stored electronically, except most metadata. A common example often sought in discovery is electronic communications, such as e-mail. The rule covers, either as documents or as electronically stored information, information "stored in any medium," to encompass future developments in computer technology. Subsection (a)(i) is intended to be broad enough to cover all current types of computer-based information and flexible enough to encompass future changes and developments. References elsewhere in the rules to "electronically stored information" should be understood to invoke this expansive approach. The term used in subsection (a)(i) appears in a number of other amendments, such as those to Rules 26(b)(1), 26(b)(1b), 26(c), 26(f)(1), 26(f)(3), 33(c), 37(a)(2), 37(b1), 45(a), 45(c), and 45(d). In each of these rules, electronically stored information has the same broad meaning it has under subsection (a)(i) of this rule.

The term "electronically stored information" is broad, but whether material that falls within this term should be produced, and in what form, are separate questions that must be addressed under Rules 26(b), 26(c), and 34(b).

Subsection (b). — Subsection (b) provides that a party must produce documents as they are kept in the usual course of business or must organize and label them to correspond with the categories in the discovery request. The production of electronically stored information should be subject to comparable requirements to protect against deliberate or inadvertent production in ways that raise unnecessary obstacles for the requesting party. Subsection (b) is amended to ensure similar protection for electronically stored information.

Subsection (b) permits the requesting party to designate the form or forms in which it wants electronically stored information produced. The form of production is more important to the exchange of electronically stored information than of hard-copy materials, although a party might specify hard copy as the requested form. Specification of the desired form or forms may facilitate the orderly, efficient, and cost-effective discovery of electronically stored information. The rule recognizes that different forms of production may be appropriate for different types of electronically stored information. Using current technology, for example, a party might be called upon to produce word processing documents, e-mail messages, electronic spreadsheets, different image or sound files, and material for databases. Requiring that such diverse types of electronically stored information all be produced in the same form could prove impossible and, even if possible, could increase the cost and burdens of producing and using the information. The rule therefore provides that the requesting party may ask for different forms of production for different types of electronically stored information.

The rule does not require that the requesting party choose a form or forms of production. The requesting party may not have a preference. In some cases, the requesting party may not know what form the producing party uses to maintain its electronically stored information, although new Rule 26(f) allows for discussion of the form of production in a discovery meeting between the parties.

The second paragraph of subsection (b) provides a specific basis for objecting to discovery of electronically stored information that is in addition to objections to more traditional discovery, i.e, an objection that the potential burden or cost to the responding party of obtaining the information from the source in which it is stored makes the requirement for production unreasonable. This amendment is taken from Federal Rules of Civil Procedure, Rule 26(b)(2)(B), but is placed in Rule 34 because the North Carolina Rules, unlike the federal rules, do not require disclosure of discoverable information without request.

The amendment to subsection (b), paragraph 2, is designed to address issues raised by difficulties in locating, retrieving, and providing discovery of some electronically stored information. Electronic storage systems often make it easy to locate and retrieve information. But some sources of electronically stored information can be assessed only with substantial burden and cost. In a particular case, these burdens and costs may make the information on such sources not reasonably accessible. It is not possible to define in a rule the different types of technological features that may affect the burdens and costs of accessing electronically stored information. The duties regarding electronically stored information not reasonably accessible outlined in Rule 45(d) also apply to Rule 34(b).

Under this rule, a responding party should produce requested electronically stored information that is relevant, not privileged, and reasonably accessible, subject to the limitations that apply to all discovery. The responding party also must identify, by category or type, sources containing potentially responsive information that it is neither searching nor producing. The identification should, to the extent possible, provide enough detail to enable the requesting party to evaluate the burdens and costs of providing the discovery and the likelihood of finding responsive information on the identified sources.

If the parties cannot agree whether, or on what terms, sources identified as not reasonably accessible should be searched and discoverable information produced, the issue may be raised either by a motion to compel discovery or by a motion for a protective order. Rules 26(c) and 37(a)(2) provide that when a motion to compel discovery or for a protective order is presented to the court, the party objecting to production bears the burden of showing that the electronically stored information is not reasonably accessible. If that showing is made, the requesting party still may obtain discovery by showing good cause, considering the limitations of Rule 26(b)(1a) that balance the costs and potential benefits of discovery and Rule 26(b)(1b) that permits the court to specify conditions for the discovery, including allocation of discovery costs.

A further provision in the second paragraph of subsection (b) provides that, if a form in which the information is to be produced is specified in the request to produce, a responding party may not simply object to providing electronically stored information in the form specified; the party must propose an alternative form or forms. If the parties are unable to resolve any disagreement about form, a judge may need to resolve the disagreement.

If the form of production is not specified by party agreement or court order, the responding party must produce electronically stored information either in a form or forms in which it ordinarily is maintained or in a form or forms that are reasonably usable. In this regard, the responding party should consider using the system on which the electronically stored information is housed to generate summary reports. Such reports can be particularly helpful when they are the same kind of reports that the producing party uses in making decisions or tracking information. Generating reports to meet the needs of the litigation also can be helpful. While a system of electronically stored information may not store information in precisely the fashion sought by a requesting party and, therefore, the responding party cannot be forced to produce information in exactly the fashion sought, it may be possible to use the same system to provide reports from existing information that will provide the information needed for the litigation even though not precisely in the fashion sought.

Under some circumstances, the responding party may need to provide some reasonable amount of technical support, information on application software, or other reasonable assistance to enable the requesting party to use the information. The Rule does not require a party to produce electronically stored information in the form in which it ordinarily is maintained, so long as it is produced in a reasonably usable form. But the option to produce in a reasonably usable form does not mean that a responding party is free to convert electronically stored information from the form in which it ordinarily is maintained to a different form that makes it more difficult or burdensome for the requesting party to use the information efficiently in the litigation. If the responding party ordinarily maintains the information it is producing in a way that makes it searchable by electronic means, the information should not be produced in a form that removes or significantly degrades this feature.

If a party that receives produced information claims that it needs to look "behind" that information or have access to the full database or system that generated the information, the question of further production or direct access will turn on whether the requesting party can show that there is some specific reason, beyond general suspicion, to doubt the information and that the burden of providing direct access is reasonable in light of the importance of the information and the circumstances of the case. If the burden is negligible in light of the circumstances, production or access probably will follow. If the burden is heavy, the requesting party will need to have a stronger rationale for additional production.

Some electronically stored information may ordinarily be maintained in a form that is not reasonably usable by any party. One example is "legacy" data that can be used only by superseded systems. Whether a producing party should be required to convert such information to a more usable form, or should be required to produce it at all, should be addressed under Rule 26(b)(1a).

Whether or not the requesting party specified the form of production, subsection (b) provides that the same electronically stored information ordinarily need be produced in only one form.

Subsection (b1). — The last paragraph of former subsection (b) has been set out separately as new subsection (b1). Its substance has not been changed.

Rule 35. Physical and mental examination of persons

(a) Order for examination. — When the mental or physical condition (including the blood group) of a party, or of an agent or a person in the custody or under the legal control of a party, is in controversy, a judge of the court in which the action is pending as defined by Rule 30(h) may order the party to submit to a physical or mental examination by a physician or to produce for examination his agent or the person in his custody or legal control. The order may be made only on motion for good cause shown and upon notice to the person to be examined and to all parties and shall specify the time, place, manner, conditions, and scope of the examination and the person or persons by whom it is to be made.

(b) Report of examining physician. —

(1) If requested by the party against whom an order is made under Rule 35(a) or the person examined, the party causing the examination to be made shall deliver to him a copy of a detailed written report of the examining physician setting out his findings, including results of all tests made, diagnoses and conclusions, together with like reports of all earlier examinations of the same condition. After such request and delivery the party causing the examination shall be entitled upon request to receive from the party against whom the order is made a like report of any examination, previously or thereafter made, of the same condition, unless, in the case of a report of examination of a person not a party, the party shows that he is unable to obtain it. The court on motion may make an order against a party requiring delivery of a report on such terms as are just, and if a physician fails or refuses to make a report the court may exclude his testimony if offered at the trial.

(2) By requesting and obtaining a report of the examination so ordered or by taking the deposition of the examiner, the party examined waives any privilege he may have in that action or any other involving the same controversy, regarding the testimony of every other person who has examined or may thereafter examine him in respect of the same mental or physical condition.

(3) This subsection applies to examinations made by agreement of the parties, unless the agreement expressly provides otherwise. This subsection does not preclude discovery of a report of an examining physician or the taking of a deposition of the physician in accordance with the provisions of any other rule.

Added by Laws 1967, c. 954, § 1. Amended by Laws 1975, c. 762, § 2.

Comment

Comment to this Rule as Originally Enacted. — *Section (a).* — This section differs from federal Rule 35(a) only in the inclusion of certain changes proposed by the Advisory Committee in its 1955 report. Such inclusions make clear the right to require a blood test in an action in which blood relationships are in controversy. The provision for the examination of a person in the custody or under the legal control of a party will permit the examination of a minor or incompetent.

This procedure is new to North Carolina practice. However, the right to require the plaintiff in a civil action to recover personal injuries to submit to a physical examination was recognized in Flythe v. Eastern Carolina Coach Co., 195 N.C. 777, 143 S.E. 865 (1928). Section 8–50.1 authorizes the court in actions in which the question of paternity arises to order a blood test.

Section (b). — This section permits the party examined to obtain the report of the physician making the examination. Since the party causing the examination could not obtain a copy of such a report made at the instance of the examined party because he might claim the report was privileged, this rule expressly provides that after the examined party requests a copy of the report of the examination made at the instance of the party causing the examination, the latter is entitled upon request to receive a report from the party examined of any examination previously or thereafter made concerning the same mental or physical examination.

The court is given the discretionary power to order that a copy of the report be furnished to any other party to the action.

Comment to the 1975 Amendment. — North Carolina adopted this provision in this form in advance of its adoption as a part of the federal rules. The provisions bringing an agent of a party within the scope of the rule is the only present change aside from the addition of subsection (b)(3).

Subsection (b)(3). — This new subsection removes any possible doubt that reports of examination may be obtained although no order for examination has been made under Rule 35(a). Examinations are very frequently made by agreement and sometimes before the party examined has an attorney. The federal courts have uniformly ordered that reports be supplied and it appears best to fill the technical gap in the present rule.

The subsection also makes clear that reports of examining physicians are discoverable not only under Rule 35(b) but under other rules as well. To be sure, if the report is privileged, then discovery is not permissible under any rule other than Rule 35(b) and it is permissible under Rule 35(b) only if the party requests a copy of the report of examination made by the other party's doctor. But if the report is unprivileged and is subject to discovery under the provisions of rules other than Rule 35(b)—such as Rules 34 or 26(b)(3) or (4)—discovery should not depend upon whether the person examined demands a copy of the report.

Rule 36. Requests for admission; effect of admission

(a) Request for admission.—A party may serve upon any other party a written request for the admission, for purposes of the pending action only, of the truth of any matters within the scope of Rule 26(b) set forth in the request that relate to statements or opinions of fact or of the application of law to fact, including the genuineness of any documents described in the request. Copies of documents shall be served with the request unless they have been or are otherwise furnished or made available for inspection and copying. The request may, without leave of court, be served upon the plaintiff after commencement of the action and upon any other party with or after service of the summons and complaint upon that party. If the request is served with service of the summons and complaint, the summons shall so state.

Each matter of which an admission is requested shall be separately set forth. The matter is admitted unless, within 30 days after service of the request, or within such shorter or longer time as the court may allow, the party to whom the request is directed serves upon the party requesting the admission a written answer or objection addressed to the matter, signed by the party or by his attorney, but, unless the court shortens the time, a defendant shall not be required to serve answers or objections before the expiration of 60 days after service of the summons and complaint upon him. If objection is made, the reasons therefor shall be stated. The answer shall specifically deny the matter or set forth in detail the reasons why the answering party cannot truthfully admit or deny the matter. A denial shall fairly meet the substance of the requested admission, and when good faith requires that a party qualify his answer or deny only a part of the matter of which an admission is requested, he shall specify so much of it as is true and qualify or deny the remainder. An answering party may not give lack of information or knowledge as a reason for failure to admit or deny unless he states that he has made reasonable inquiry and that the information known or readily obtainable by him is insufficient to enable him to admit or deny. A party who considers that a matter of which an admission has been requested presents a genuine issue for trial may not, on that ground alone, object to the request; he may, subject to the provisions of Rule 37(c), deny the matter or set forth reasons why he cannot admit or deny it.

There shall be sufficient space following each request in which the respondent may state the response. The respondent shall:

(1) State the response in the space provided, using additional pages if necessary; or

(2) Restate the request to be followed by the response. An objection to a request shall be made by stating the objection and the reason therefor either in the space following the request or following the restated request.

The party who has requested the admissions may move to determine the sufficiency of the answers or objections. Unless the court determines that an objection is justified, it shall order that an answer be served. If the court determines that an answer does not comply with the requirements of this rule, it may order either that the matter is admitted or that an amended answer be served. The court may, in lieu of these orders, determine that final disposition of the request be made at a pretrial conference or at a designated time prior to trial. The provisions of Rule 37(a)(4) apply to the award of expenses incurred in relation to the motion.

(b) Effect of admission.—Any matter admitted under this rule is conclusively established unless the court on motion permits withdrawal or amendment of the admission. Subject to the provisions of Rule 16 governing amendment of a pretrial order, the court may permit withdrawal or amendment when the presentation of the merits of the action will be subserved thereby and the party who obtained the admission fails to satisfy the court that withdrawal or amendment will prejudice him in maintaining his action or defense on the merits. Any admission made by a party under this rule is for the purpose of pending action only and is not an admission by him for any other purpose nor may it be used against him in any other proceeding.

Added by Laws 1967, c. 954, § 1. Amended by Laws 1975, c. 762, § 2; Laws 1981, c. 384, §§ 1, 2; Laws 1987, c. 613, § 3.

Comment

Comment to this Rule as Originally Enacted. — Pretrial admissions of genuineness of documents were governed by former § 8-91. The provisions of this statute regarding taxation of costs are carried forward in Rule 37(c).

The last sentence of section (a) is designed to preclude a party from offering lack of knowledge as a ground for refusing to admit when, in fact, he has the means to such knowledge reasonably within his power. To allow such a technical ground for refusal on any other basis would render the effect of the admission provision practically useless.

Section (b) does not appear in the federal rule. This section places the burden on the party serving the request to answer to interrogatories or detail reasons why he cannot.

Comment to the 1975 Amendment. — Rule 36 serves two vital purposes, both of which are designed to reduce trial time. Admissions are sought, first to facilitate proof with respect to issues that cannot be eliminated from the case, and secondly, to narrow the issues by eliminating those that can be. The changes made in the rules are designed to serve these purposes more effectively. Certain disagreements in the courts about the proper scope of the rule are resolved. In addition, the procedural operation of the rule is brought into line with other discovery procedures, and the binding effect of an admission is clarified.

Section (a). — As revised, the section provides that a request may be made to admit any matters within the scope of Rule 26(b) that relate to statements or opinions of fact or of the application of law to fact. It thereby eliminates the requirement that the matters be "of fact." This change resolves conflicts in the federal court decisions as to whether a request to admit matters of "opinion" and matters involving "mixed law and fact" is proper under the rule.

Not only is it difficult as a practical matter to separate "fact" from "opinion," but an admission on a matter of opinion may facilitate proof or narrow the issues or both. An admission of a matter involving the application of law to fact may, in a given case, even more clearly narrow the issues. For example, an admission that an employee acted in the scope of his employment may remove a major issue from the trial. The amended provision does not authorize requests for admissions of law unrelated to the facts of the case.

Requests for admission involving the application of law to fact may create disputes between the parties which are best resolved in the presence of the judge after much or all of the other discovery has been completed. Power is therefore expressly conferred upon the court to defer decision until a pretrial conference is held or until a designated time prior to trial. On the other hand, the court should not automatically defer decision; in many instances, the importance of the admission lies in enabling the requesting party to avoid the burdensome accumulation of proof prior to the pretrial conference.

Courts have also divided on whether an answering party may properly object to requests for admission as to matters which that party regards as "in dispute." The proper response in such cases is an answer. The very purpose of the request is to ascertain whether the answering party is prepared to admit or regards the matter as presenting a genuine issue for trial. In his answer, the party may deny, or he may give as his reason for inability to admit or deny the existence of a genuine issue. The party runs no risk of sanctions if the matter is genuinely in issue, since Rule 37(c) provides a sanction of costs only when there are no good reasons for a failure to admit.

On the other hand, requests to admit may be so voluminous and so framed that the answering party finds the task of identifying what is in dispute and what is not unduly burdensome. If so, the responding party may obtain a protective order under Rule 26(c). Some of the decisions sustaining objections on "disputability" grounds could have been justified by the burdensome character of the requests.

Another sharp split of authority exists on the question whether a party may base his answer on lack of information or knowledge without seeking out additional information. One line of cases has held that a party may answer on the basis of such knowledge as he has at the time he answers. A larger group of cases, supported by commentators, has taken the view that if the responding party lacks knowledge, he must inform himself in reasonable fashion.

The rule as revised adopts the majority view, as in keeping with a basic principle of the discovery rules that a reasonable burden may be imposed on the parties when its discharge will facilitate preparation for trial and ease the trial process. It has been argued against this view that one side should not have the burden of "proving" the other side's case. The revised rule requires only that the answering party make reasonable inquiry and secure such knowledge and information as are readily obtainable by him. In most instances, the investigation will be necessary either to his own case or to preparation for rebuttal. Even when it is not, the information may be close enough at hand to be "readily obtainable." Rule 36 requires only that the party state that he has taken these steps. The sanction for failure of a party to inform himself before he answers lies in the award of costs after trial, as provided in Rule 37(c).

The requirement that the answer to a request for admission be sworn is deleted in favor of a provision that the answer be signed by the party or by his attorney. The provisions of Rule 36 make it clear that admissions function very much as pleadings do. Thus, when a party admits in part and denies in part, his admission is for purposes of the pending action only and may not be used against him in any other proceeding. The broadening of the rule to encompass mixed questions of law and fact reinforces this feature. Rule 36 does not lack a sanction for false answers; Rule 37(c) furnishes an appropriate deterrent.

The existing language describing the available grounds for objection to a request for admission is eliminated as neither necessary nor helpful. The statement that objection may be made to any request which is "improper" adds nothing to the provisions that the party serve an answer or objection addressed to each matter and that he state his reasons for any objection. None of the other discovery rules sets forth grounds for objection, except so far as all are subject to the general provisions of Rule 26.

Changes are made in the sequence of procedures in Rule 36 so that they conform to the new procedures in Rules 33 and 34. The major changes are as follows:

(1) The normal time for response to a request for admissions is lengthened from 20 to 30 days, conforming more closely to prevailing practice. A defendant need not respond, however, in less than 45 days after service of the summons and complaint upon him. The court may lengthen or shorten the time when special situations require it.

(2) The present requirement that the plaintiff wait 10 days to serve requests without leave of court is eliminated. The revised provision accords with those in Rules 33 and 34.

(3) The requirement that the objecting party move automatically for a hearing on his objection is eliminated, and the burden is on the requesting party to move for an order. The change in the burden of going forward does not modify present law on burden of persuasion. The award of expenses incurred in relation to the motion is made subject to the comprehensive provisions of Rule 37(a)(4).

(4) A problem peculiar to Rule 36 arises if the responding party serves answers that are not in conformity with the requirements of the rule—for example, a denial is not "specific," or the explanation of inability to admit or deny is not "in detail." Rule 36 now makes no provision for court scrutiny of such answers before trial, and it seems to contemplate that defective answers bring about admissions just as effectively as if no answer had been served. Some cases have so held.

Giving a defective answer the automatic effect of an admission may cause unfair surprise. A responding party who purported to deny or to be unable to admit or deny will for the first time at trial confront the contention that he has made a binding admission. Since it is not always easy to know whether a denial is "specific" or an explanation is "in detail," neither party can know how the court will rule at trial and whether proof must be prepared. Some courts, therefore, have entertained motions to rule on defective answers. They have at times ordered that amended answers be served, when the defects were technical, and at other times have declared that the matter was admitted. The rule as revised conforms to the latter practice.

Section (b). — The rule does not now indicate the extent to which a party is bound by his admission. Some courts view admissions as the equivalent of sworn testimony. At least in some jurisdictions a party may rebut his own testimony, and by analogy an admission made pursuant to Rule 36 may likewise be thought rebuttable.

The new provisions give an admission a conclusively binding effect, for purposes only of the pending action, unless the admission is withdrawn or amended. In form and substance a Rule 36 admission is comparable to an admission in pleadings or a stipulation drafted by counsel for use at trial, rather than to an evidentiary admission of a party. Unless the party securing an admission can depend on its binding effect, he cannot safely avoid the expense of preparing to prove the very matters on which he has secured the admission, and the purpose of the rule is defeated.

Provision is made for withdrawal or amendment of an admission. This provision emphasizes the importance of having the action resolved on the merits, while at the same time assuring each party that justified reliance on an admission in preparation for trial will not operate to his prejudice.

Rule 37. Failure to make discovery; sanctions

(a) Motion for order compelling discovery.—A party, upon reasonable notice to other parties and all persons affected thereby, may apply for an order compelling discovery as follows:

(1) Appropriate Court.—An application for an order to a party or a deponent who is not a party may be made to a judge of the court in which the action is pending, or, on matters relating to a deposition where the deposition is being taken in this State, to a judge of the court in the county where the deposition is being taken, as defined by Rule 30(h).

(2) Motion.—If a deponent fails to answer a question propounded or submitted under Rules 30 or 31, or a corporation or other entity fails to make a designation under Rule 30(b)(6) or 31(a), or a party fails to answer an interrogatory submitted under Rule 33, or if a party, in response to a request for inspection submitted under Rule 34, fails to respond that inspection will be permitted as requested or fails to permit inspection as requested, the discovering party may move for an order compelling an answer, or a designation, or an order compelling inspection in accordance with the request. The motion must include a certification that the movant has in good faith conferred or attempted to confer with the person or party failing to make the discovery in an effort to secure the information or material without court action. When taking a deposition on oral examination, the proponent of the question shall complete the examination on all other matters before the examination is adjourned, in order to apply for an order. If the motion is based upon an objection to production of electronically stored information from sources the objecting party identified as not reasonably accessible because of undue burden or cost, the objecting party has the burden of showing that the basis for the objection exists.

If the court denies the motion in whole or in part, it may make such protective order as it would have been empowered to make on a motion made pursuant to Rule 26(c).

(3) Evasive or Incomplete Answer.—For purposes of this subdivision an evasive or incomplete answer is to be treated as a failure to answer.

(4) Award of Expenses of Motion.—If the motion is granted, the court shall, after opportunity for hearing, require the party or deponent whose conduct necessitated the motion or the party advising such conduct or both of them to pay to the moving party the reasonable expenses incurred in obtaining the order, including attorney's fees, unless the court finds that the opposition to the motion was substantially justified or that other circumstances make an award of expenses unjust.

If the motion is denied, the court shall, after opportunity for hearing, require the moving party to pay to the party or deponent who opposed the motion the reasonable expenses incurred in opposing the motion, including attorney's fees, unless the court finds that the making of the motion was substantially justified or that other circumstances make an award of expenses unjust.

If the motion is granted in part and denied in part, the court may apportion the reasonable expenses incurred in relation to the motion among the parties and persons in a just manner.

(b) Failure to comply with order.—

(1) Sanctions by Court in County Where Deposition Is Taken.—If a deponent fails to be sworn or to answer a question after being directed to do so by a judge of the court in the county in which the deposition is being taken, the failure may be considered a contempt of that court.

(2) Sanctions by Court in Which Action Is Pending.—If a party or an officer, director, or managing agent of a party or a person designated under Rule 30(b)(6) or 31(a) to testify on behalf of a party fails to obey an order to provide or permit discovery, including an order made under section (a) of this rule or Rule 35, or if a party fails to obey an order entered under Rule 26(f) a judge of the court in which the action is pending may make such orders in regard to the failure as are just, and among others the following:

a. An order that the matters regarding which the order was made or any other designated facts shall be taken to be established for the purposes of the action in accordance with the claim of the party obtaining the order;

b. An order refusing to allow the disobedient party to support or oppose designated claims or defenses, or prohibiting the party from introducing designated matters in evidence;

c. An order striking out pleadings or parts thereof, or staying further proceedings until the order is obeyed, or dismissing the action or proceeding or any part thereof, or rendering a judgment by default against the disobedient party;

d. In lieu of any of the foregoing orders or in addition thereto, an order treating as a contempt of court the failure to obey any orders except an order to submit to a physical or mental examination;

e. Where a party has failed to comply with an order under Rule 35(a) requiring the party to produce another for examination, such orders as are listed in subdivisions a, b, and c of this subsection, unless the party failing to comply shows that the party is unable to produce such person for examination.

In lieu of any of the foregoing orders or in addition thereto, the court shall require the party failing to obey the order to pay the reasonable expenses, including attorney's fees, caused by the failure, unless the court finds that the failure was substantially justified or that other circumstances make an award of expenses unjust.

(b1) Failure to provide electronically stored information.—Absent exceptional circumstances, a court may not impose sanctions under these rules on a party for failing to provide electronically stored information lost as a result of routine, good-faith operation of an electronic information system.

(c) Expenses on failure to admit.—If a party fails to admit the genuineness of any document or the truth of any matter as requested under Rule 36, and if the party requesting the admissions thereafter proves the genuineness of the document or the truth of the matter, the requesting party may apply to the court for an order requiring the other party to pay to him or her the reasonable expenses incurred in making that proof, including reasonable attorney's fees. The court shall make the order unless it finds that (i) the request was held objectionable pursuant to Rule 36(a), or (ii) the admission sought was of no substantial importance, or (iii) the party failing to admit had reasonable ground to believe that he or she might prevail on the matter, or (iv) there was other good reason for the failure to admit.

(d) Failure of party to attend at own deposition or serve answers to interrogatories or respond to request for inspection.—If a party or an officer, director, or managing agent of a party or a person designated under Rule 30(b)(6) or 31(a) to testify on behalf of a party fails (i) to appear before the person who is to take the deposition, after being served with a proper notice, or (ii) to serve answers or objections to interrogatories submitted under Rule 33, after proper service of the interrogatories, or (iii) to serve a written response to a request for inspection submitted under Rule 34, after proper service of the request, the court in which the action is pending on motion may make such orders in regard to the failure as are just, and among others it may take any action authorized under subdivisions a, b, and c of subsection (b)(2) of this rule. In lieu of any order or in addition thereto, the court shall require the party failing to act to pay the reasonable expenses, including attorney's fees, caused by the failure, unless the court finds that the failure was substantially justified or that other circumstances make an award of expenses unjust.

The failure to act described in this section may not be excused on the ground that the discovery sought is objectionable unless the party failing to act has applied for a protective order as provided by Rule 26(c).

(e), (f) Reserved for future codification purposes.

(g) Failure to participate in the framing of a discovery plan.—If a party or the party's attorney fails to participate in good faith in the framing of a discovery plan by agreement as is required by Rule 26(f), the court may, after opportunity for hearing, require such party or the party's attorney to pay to any other party the reasonable expenses, including attorney's fees, caused by the failure.

Added by Laws 1967, c. 954, § 1. Amended by Laws 1973, c. 827, § 1; Laws 1975, c. 762, § 2; Laws 1985, c. 603, §§ 5-7; S.L. 2001-379, § 5, eff. Oct. 1, 2001; S.L. 2011-199, § 5, eff. Oct. 1, 2011.

Comment

Comment to this Rule as Originally Enacted. — Under § 8-78 and former §§ 1-568.18 and 1-568.19, sanctions against either a deponent or adverse party for failure to answer or to appear are provided for. Under § 8-78 a deponent may be committed to jail upon warrant of the commissioner before whom the deposition is taken. Under former §§ 1-568.18 and 1-568.19 sanctions could be applied only upon order of court issued either by the clerk of superior court in which the action was pending or the judge having jurisdiction.

Under this rule sanctions can be applied only for failure to comply with a court order. Hence, if discovery procedure requires a court order as under Rules 34 or 35, failure to obey the order can be punished immediately under section (b)(2). But where the discovery procedure is set in motion by the parties themselves, the party seeking discovery must first obtain a court order under section (a) requiring the recalcitrant party or witness to make discovery. The only exception to this is found in section (d), which permits an immediate sanction against parties, their officers, or managing agents for a willful failure to appear.

Comment to the 1975 Amendment. — Rule 37 provides generally for sanctions against parties or persons unjustifiably resisting discovery. Experience in the federal courts brought to light a number of the defects in the language of the rule as well as instances in which it was not serving the purposes for which it was designed. In addition, changes being made in other discovery rules require conforming amendments to Rule 37.

Rule 37 sometimes refers to a "failure" to afford discovery and at other times to a "refusal" to do so. Taking note of this dual terminology, federal courts imported into "refusal" a requirement of "willfullness." In Societe Internationale v. Rogers, 357 U.S. 197, 78 S. Ct. 1087, 2 L. Ed. 2d 1255 (1958), the United States Supreme Court concluded that the rather random use of these two terms in Rule 37 showed no design to use them with consistently distinctive meanings, that "refused" in Rule 37(b)(2) meant simply a failure to comply, and that willfulness was relevant only to the selection of sanctions, if any, to be imposed. Substitution of "failure" for "refusal" throughout Rule 37 should eliminate confusion.

Section (a). — Rule 37(a) provides relief to a party seeking discovery against one who, with or without stated objections, fails to afford the discovery sought. It has always fully served this function in relation to depositions, but the amendments being made to Rules 33 and 34 give Rule 37(a) added scope and importance. Under existing Rule 33, a party objecting to interrogatories must make a motion for court hearing on his objections. The changes now made in Rules 33 and 37(a) make it clear that the interrogating party must move to compel answers, and the motion is provided for in Rule 37(a). Existing Rule 34, since it requires a court order prior to production of documents or things or permission to enter on land, has no relation to Rule 37(a). Amendments of Rules 34 and 37(a) create a procedure similar to that provided for Rule 33.

Subsection (a)(1). — This is a new provision making clear to which court a party may apply for an order compelling discovery. In relation to Rule 33 interrogatories and Rule 34 requests for inspection, the court where the action is pending is the appropriate enforcing tribunal. The new provision spells out the respective roles of the court where the action is pending and the court where the deposition is taken. In some instances, two courts are available to a party seeking to compel answers from a party deponent. The party seeking discovery may choose the court to which he will apply, but the court has power to remit the party to the other court as a more appropriate forum.

Subsection (a)(2). — This subsection contains the substance of existing provisions of Rule 37(a) authorizing motions to compel answers to questions put at depositions and to interrogatories. New provisions authorize motions for orders compelling designation under Rules 30(b)(6) and 31(a) and compelling inspection in accordance with a request made under Rule 34. If the court denies a motion, in whole or in part, it may accompany the denial with issuance of a protective order. Compare the converse provision in Rule 26(c).

Subsection (a)(3). — This new provision makes clear that an evasive or incomplete answer is to be considered, for purposes of subsection (a), a failure to answer. The federal courts have consistently held that they have the power to compel adequate answers. This power of the court is recognized and incorporated into the rule.

Subsection (a)(4). — This subsection adds provisions for award of expenses, including reasonable attorney's fees, to the prevailing party or person when a motion is made for an order compelling discovery. The prior North Carolina rule had no such provision. The provision requires that expenses be awarded unless the conduct of the losing party or person is found to have been "substantially justified." This language is intended to encourage judges to be more alert to abuses occurring in the discovery process.

On many occasions, to be sure, the dispute over discovery between the parties is genuine, though ultimately resolved one way or the other by the court. In such cases, the losing party is substantially justified in carrying the matter to court. But the rules should deter the abuse implicit in carrying or forcing a discovery dispute to court when no genuine dispute exists. And the potential or actual imposition of expenses is virtually the sole formal sanction in the rules to deter a party from pressing to a court hearing frivolous requests for or objections to discovery.

The proposed provision provides in effect that expenses should ordinarily be awarded unless a court finds that the losing party acted justifiably in carrying his point to court. At the same time, a necessary flexibility is maintained, since the court retains the power to find that other circumstances make an award of expenses unjust—as where the prevailing party also acted unjustifiably. The amendment does not significantly limit the discretion of the court, but rather presses the court to address itself to abusive practices.

Section (b). — This section deals with sanctions for failure to comply with a court order.

The scope of Rule 37(b)(2) is broadened by extending it to include any order "to provide or permit discovery," including orders issued under Rules 37(a) and 35. Various rules authorize orders for discovery—e.g., Rule 35(b)(1), Rule 26(c) as revised, Rule 37(d). Rule 37(b)(2) should provide comprehensively for enforcement of all these orders. On the other hand, the reference to Rule 34 is deleted to conform to the changed procedure in that rule.

Paragraph e provides that sanctions which have been available against a party for failure to comply with an order under Rule 35(a) to submit to examination will now be available against him for his failure to comply with a Rule 35(a) order to produce a third person for examination, unless he shows that he is unable to produce the person. In this context, "unable" means in effect "unable in good faith."

Subsection (b)(2) is amplified to provide for payment of reasonable expenses caused by the failure to obey the order. Although Rules 37(b)(2) and 37(d) have been silent as to award of expenses, federal courts have nevertheless ordered them on occasion. The provision places the burden on the disobedient party to avoid expenses by showing that his failure is justified or that special circumstances make an award of expenses unjust. Allocating the burden in this way conforms to the provisions as to expenses in Rule 37(a), and is particularly appropriate when a court order is disobeyed.

An added reference to directors of a party is similar to a change made in section (d) and is explained in the note to that section. The added reference to persons designated by a party under Rules 30(b)(6) or 31(a) to testify on behalf of the party carries out the new procedure in those rules for taking a deposition of a corporation or other organization.

Section (c). — Rule 37(c) provides a sanction for the enforcement of Rule 36 dealing with requests for admission. Rule 36 provides the mechanism whereby a party may obtain from another party in appropriate instances either (1) an admission, or (2) a sworn and specific denial, or (3) a sworn statement "setting forth in detail the reasons why he cannot truthfully admit or deny." If the party obtains the second or third of these responses, in proper form, Rule 36 does not provide for a pretrial hearing on whether the response is warranted by the evidence thus far accumulated. Instead, Rule 37(c) is intended to provide post-trial relief in the form of a requirement that the party improperly refusing the admission pay the expenses of the other side in making the necessary proof at trial.

Rule 37(c), as now written, addresses itself in terms only to the sworn denial and is silent with respect to the statement of reasons for an inability to admit or deny. There is no apparent basis for this distinction, since the sanction provided in Rule 37(c) should deter all unjustified failures to admit. This omission in the rule has caused confused and diverse treatment in the federal courts. The amendment eliminates this defect in Rule 37(c) by bringing within its scope all failures to admit.

Additional provisions in Rule 37(c) protect a party from having to pay expenses if the request for admission was held objectionable under Rule 36(a) or if the party failing to admit had reasonable ground to believe that he might prevail on the matter. The latter provision emphasizes that the true test under Rule 37(c) is not whether a party prevailed at trial but whether he acted reasonably in believing that he might prevail.

Section (d). — The scope of section (d) is broadened to include responses to requests for inspection under Rule 34, thereby conforming to the new procedures of Rule 34.

The permissible sanctions are broadened to include such orders "as are just." Although former federal Rule 37(d) in terms provided for only three sanctions, all rather severe, the federal courts had interpreted it as permitting softer sanctions than those which it set forth. The rule is changed to provide the greater flexibility as to sanctions which the cases show is needed.

The resulting flexibility as to sanctions eliminates any need to retain the requirement that the failure to appear or respond be "willful." The concept of "willful failure" is at best subtle and difficult, and the cases do not supply a bright line. Many courts have imposed sanctions without referring to willfulness. In addition, in view of the possibility of light sanctions, even a negligent failure should come within Rule 37(d). If default is caused by counsel's ignorance of federal practice, or by his preoccupation with another aspect of the case, dismissal of the action and default judgment are not justified, but the imposition of expenses and fees may well be. "Willfulness" continues to play a role, along with various other factors, in the choice of sanctions. Thus, the scheme conforms to Rule 37(b) as construed by the Supreme Court in Societe Internationale v. Rogers, 357 U.S. 197, 208, 78 S. Ct. 1087, 2 L. Ed. 2d 1255 (1958).

A provision is added to make clear that a party may not properly remain completely silent even when he regards a notice to take his deposition or a set of interrogatories or requests to inspect as improper and objectionable. If he desires not to appear or not to respond, he must apply for a protective order. Prior to the adoption of this rule, federal cases were divided on whether a protective order must be sought. The party from whom discovery is sought is afforded, through Rule 26(c), a fair and effective procedure whereby he can challenge the request made. At the same time, the total noncompliance with which Rule 37(d) is concerned may impose severe inconvenience or hardship on the discovering party and substantially delay the discovery process.

The failure of an officer or managing agent of a party to make discovery as required by present Rule 37(d) is treated as the failure of the party. The rule as revised provides similar treatment for a director of a party. There is slight warrant for the present distinction between officers and managing agents on the one hand and directors on the other. Although the legal power over a director to compel his making discovery may not be as great as over officers or managing agents, the practical differences are negligible. That a director's interests are normally aligned with those of his corporation is shown by the provisions of old Rule 26(d)(2), transferred to 32(a)(2) (deposition of director of party may be used at trial by an adverse party for any purpose) and of Rule 43(b) (director of party may be treated at trial as a hostile witness on direct examination by any adverse party). Moreover, in those rare instances when a corporation is unable through good-faith efforts to compel a director to make discovery, it is unlikely that the court will impose sanctions.

Comment to the 2011 Amendment. *Subsection (a).* — Subdivision (a)(2) relates to Rule 34(b) and provides that when a motion to compel is sought after the respondent has objected to the production of electronically stored information on the basis that the information sought is from a source not reasonably accessible because of undue burden or cost, the party objecting to production has the burden of showing that information from the source identified is not reasonably accessible.

Subsection (b). — Amendments to subsection (b) are not intended to change substance.

Subsection (b1). — Subsection (b1) is an effort to recognize a necessary balance between normal computer system operations and the needs of litigation. It focuses on a distinctive feature of computer operations - the routine alteration and deletion of information that attends ordinary use. Many steps essential to computer operation may alter or destroy information for reasons that have nothing to do with how that information might relate to litigation. As a result, the ordinary operation of computer systems creates a risk that a party may lose potentially discoverable information without culpable conduct on its part. Under subsection (b1), absent exceptional circumstances, sanctions cannot be imposed for loss of electronically stored information resulting from the routine, good-faith operation of an electronic information system.

Subsection (b1) applies only to information lost due to the "routine operation of an electronic information system", i.e., the ways in which such systems generally are designed, programmed, and implemented to meet the party's technical and business needs. The "routine operation" of computer systems includes the alteration and overwriting of information, often without the operator's specific direction or awareness - a feature with no direct counterpart in hard-copy documents. Such features are essential to the operation of electronic information systems.

Subsection (b1) applies to information lost due to the routine operation of an information system only if the operation was in good faith. Good faith in the routine operation of an information system may involve a party's intervention to modify or suspend certain features of that routine operation to prevent the loss of information, if that information is subject to a preservation obligation. A preservation obligation may arise from many sources, including common law, statutes, regulations, or a court order in the case. The good faith requirement of subsection (b1) means that a party is not permitted to exploit the routine operation of an information system to thwart discovery obligations by allowing that operation to continue so that specific stored information that it is required to preserve will be destroyed. When a party is under a duty to preserve information because of pending or reasonably anticipated litigation, intervention in the routine operation of an information system is one aspect of what is often called a "litigation hold." Among the factors that bear on a party's good faith in the routine operation of an information system are the steps the party took to comply with a court order or party agreement requiring preservation of specific electronically stored information.

Whether good faith would call for steps to prevent the loss of information on sources that the party believes are not reasonably accessible under Rule 26(b) depends on the circumstances of each case. One factor is whether the party reasonably believes that the information on such sources is likely to be discoverable and not available from reasonably accessible sources.

The protection provided by subsection (b1) applies only to sanctions "under these rules." It does not affect authority under rules of professional responsibility or other sources to impose sanctions.

This rule restricts the imposition of "sanctions." It does not prevent a court from making the kinds of adjustments frequently used in managing discovery if a party is unable to provide relevant responsive information. For example, a court could order the responding party to produce an additional witness for deposition, respond to additional interrogatories, or make similar attempts to provide substitutes or alternatives for some or all of the lost information.

Subsections (c), (d), and (g) — No substantive changes have been made.

Article 6

Trials

Rule 38. Jury trial of right

(a) Right preserved. — The right of trial by jury as declared by the Constitution or statutes of North Carolina shall be preserved to the parties inviolate.

(b) Demand. — Any party may demand a trial by jury of any issue triable of right by a jury by serving upon the other parties a demand therefor in writing at any time after commencement of the action and not later than 10 days after the service of the last pleading directed to such issue. Such demand may be made in the pleading of the party or endorsed on the pleading.

(c) Demand — Specification of issues. — In his demand a party may specify the issues which he wishes so tried; otherwise, he shall be deemed to have demanded trial by jury for all the issues so triable. If a party has demanded trial by jury for only some of the issues, any other party within 10 days after service of the last pleading directed to such issues or within 10 days after service of the demand, whichever is later, or such lesser time as the court may order, may serve a demand for trial by jury of any other or all of the issues in the action.

(d) Waiver. — Except in actions wherein jury trial cannot be waived, the failure of a party to serve a demand as required by this rule and file it as required by Rule 5(d) constitutes a waiver by him of trial by jury. A demand for trial by jury as herein provided may not be withdrawn without the consent of the parties who have pleaded or otherwise appear in the action.

(e) Right granted. — The right of trial by jury as to the issue of just compensation shall be granted to the parties involved in any condemnation proceeding brought by bodies politic, corporations or persons which possess the power of eminent domain.

Added by Laws 1967, c. 954, § 1. Amended by Laws 1973, c. 149.

Comment

This rule and Rule 39 provide for the preservation of the right to jury trial and methods for claim and waiver of that right. The principal change effected is that waiver of right to jury trial is accomplished by a failure seasonably to demand jury trial.

North Carolina Const., Art. IV, § 12, specifically provides that jury trial can be waived, and former § 1-184 set up three methods by which there could be such waiver. They were: (1) By failing to appear at the trial; (2) By written consent filed with the clerk; and (3) By oral consent entered in the minutes. All three methods are retained. See Rule 39(a). But a fourth is added which has as its object the early ascertainment of those cases in which there will be no jury. This knowledge is useful in calendaring a case and in counsel's preparation for trial.

The requirement of positive action by a party to preserve the right to jury trial is not at all new in certain areas—references and mandamus for example. In respect to references, see Simmons v. Lee, 230 N.C. 216, 53 S.E. 79 (1949). See also Rule 53 and the accompanying note. In respect to mandamus, see former § 1-513. This statute has been repealed and jury trial in respect to mandamus is now governed by this rule and Rule 39.

The procedure for demanding jury trial is simple. The demand may be within a pleading or endorsed thereon or by separate document. No particular form of words is prescribed. As to the time when the demand must be made, generally it will be "not later than 10 days after the service of the last pleading" directed to the issue in question. But it will be observed that section (c) makes it possible for a party to demand jury trial only for some of the issues. To adjust to the situation where, for example, a plaintiff in a negligence suit might have failed to demand jury trial on any issue and the defendant, at the last moment (on the 10th day after filing his answer), demands jury trial on only the damage issue, the rule allows the plaintiff 10 days after the service of the defendant's demand in which to demand jury trial on other issues.

The reference in section (d) to actions wherein jury trial cannot be waived would include actions for divorce not based on one year's separation. See § 50-10.

In keeping with present law [see J.L. Roper Lumber Co. v. Elizabeth City Lumber Co., 137 N.C. 431, 49 S.E. 946 (1905)], Rule 39(b) authorizes a judge to disregard a waiver of jury trial.

Rule 39. Trial by jury or by the court

(a) By jury.—When trial by jury has been demanded and has not been withdrawn as provided in Rule 38, the action shall be designated upon the docket as a jury action. The trial of all issues so demanded shall be by jury, unless

(1) The parties who have pleaded or otherwise appeared in the action or their attorneys of record, by written stipulation filed with the court or by an oral stipulation made in open court and entered in the minutes, consent to trial by the court sitting without a jury, or

(2) The court upon motion or of its own initiative finds that a right of trial by jury of some or all of those issues does not exist under the Constitution or statutes.

(b) By the court.—Issues not demanded for trial by jury as provided in Rule 38 shall be tried by the court; but, notwithstanding the failure of a party to demand a trial by jury in an action in which such a demand might have been made of right, the court in its discretion upon motion or of its own initiative may order a trial by jury of any or all issues.

(c) Advisory jury and trial by consent.—In all actions not triable of right by a jury the court upon motion or of its own initiative may try any issue or question of fact with an advisory jury or the court, with the consent of the parties, may order a trial with a jury whose verdict has the same effect as if trial by jury had been a matter of right. In either event the jury shall be selected in the manner provided by Rule 47(a).[1]

Added by Laws 1967, c. 954, § 1.

[1] So in original. Rule 47 does not contain any designated subdivisions.

Comment

As indicated in the note to Rule 38, this rule carries forward the essence of former § 1-184 in respect to methods of waiver and the present power of the judge to require trial by jury, even though there has been a waiver. Moreover, provision is made for trial by jury when there is no right to such trial if the judge decides such a course is desirable or if the parties consent.

Rule 40. Assignment of cases for trial; continuances

(a) The senior resident superior court judge of any superior court district or set of districts as defined in G.S. 7A–41.1 may provide by rule for the calendaring of actions for trial in the superior court division of the various counties within his district or set of districts. Calendaring of actions for trial in the district court shall be in accordance with G.S. 7A–146. Precedence shall be given to actions entitled thereto by any statute of this State.

(b) No continuance shall be granted except upon application to the court. A continuance may be granted only for good cause shown and upon such terms and conditions as justice may require. Good cause for granting a continuance shall include those instances when a party to the proceeding, a witness, or counsel of record has an obligation of service to the State of North Carolina, including service as a member of the General Assembly or the Rules Review Commission.

Added by Laws 1967, c. 954, § 1. Amended by Laws 1969, c. 895, § 9; Laws 1985, c. 603, § 8; Laws 1987 (Reg. Sess. 1988), c. 1037, § 43; S.L. 1997–34, § 10, eff. April 23, 1997.

Comment

Comment to this Rule as Originally Enacted. — This rule, as does the present Rule of Practice in the Superior Court, provides ultimately for judicial control of the calendar. The reference to the judge "senior in point of continuous service" is merely to designate the responsible judge in those districts having more than one judge.

Comment to the 1969 amendment. — The 1969 amendment added the provision concerning continuances. The previous code contained some detailed provisions on continuances. This brief provision was deemed appropriate out of an abundance of caution.

Rule 41. Dismissal of actions

(a) Voluntary dismissal; effect thereof. —

(1) By Plaintiff; by Stipulation. — Subject to the provisions of Rule 23(c) and of any statute of this State, an action or any claim therein may be dismissed by the plaintiff without order of court (i) by filing a notice of dismissal at any time before the plaintiff rests his case, or; (ii) by filing a stipulation of dismissal signed by all parties who have appeared in the action. Unless otherwise stated in the notice of dismissal or stipulation, the dismissal is without prejudice, except that a notice of dismissal operates as an adjudication upon the merits when filed by a plaintiff who has once dismissed in any court of this or any other state or of the United States, an action based on or including the same claim. If an action commenced within the time prescribed therefor, or any claim therein, is dismissed without prejudice under this subsection, a new action based on the same claim may be commenced within one year after such dismissal unless a stipulation filed under (ii) of this subsection shall specify a shorter time.

(2) By Order of Judge. — Except as provided in subsection (1) of this section, an action or any claim therein shall not be dismissed at the plaintiff's instance save upon order of the judge and upon such terms and conditions as justice requires. Unless otherwise specified in the order, a dismissal under this subsection is without prejudice. If an action commenced within the time prescribed therefor, or any claim therein, is dismissed without prejudice under this subsection, a new action based on the same claim may be commenced within one year after such dismissal unless the judge shall specify in his order a shorter time.

(b) Involuntary dismissal; effect thereof. — For failure of the plaintiff to prosecute or to comply with these rules or any order of court, a defendant may move for dismissal of an action or of any claim therein against him. After the plaintiff, in an action tried by the court without a jury, has completed the presentation of his evidence, the defendant, without waiving his right to offer evidence in the event the motion is not granted, may move for a dismissal on the ground that upon the facts and the law the plaintiff has shown no right to relief. The court as trier of the facts may then determine them and render judgment against the plaintiff or may decline to render any judgment until the close of all the evidence. If the court renders judgment on the merits against the plaintiff, the court shall make findings as provided in Rule 52(a). Unless the court in its order for dismissal otherwise specifies, a dismissal under this section and any dismissal not provided for in this rule, other than a dismissal for lack of jurisdiction, for improper venue, or for failure to join a necessary party, operates as an adjudication upon the merits. If the court specifies that the dismissal of an action commenced within the time prescribed therefor, or any claim therein, is without prejudice, it may also specify in its order that a new action based on the same claim may be commenced within one year or less after such dismissal.

(c) Dismissal of counterclaim; crossclaim, or third-party claim. — The provisions of this rule apply to the dismissal of any counterclaim, crossclaim, or third-party claim.

(d) Costs. — A plaintiff who dismisses an action or claim under section (a) of this rule shall be taxed with the costs of the action unless the action was brought in forma pauperis. If a plaintiff who has once dismissed an action in any court commences an action based upon or including the same claim against the same defendant before the payment of the costs of the action previously dismissed, unless such previous action was brought in forma pauperis, the court, upon motion of the defendant, shall make an order for the payment of such costs by the plaintiff within 30 days and shall stay the proceedings in the action until the plaintiff has complied with the order. If the plaintiff does not comply with the order, the court shall dismiss the action.

Added by Laws 1967, c. 954, § 1. Amended by Laws 1969, c. 895, § 10; Laws 1977, c. 290.

Comment

Comment to this Rule as Originally Enacted. — *Section (a).* — The absolute right of a plaintiff to take a voluntary nonsuit for any or no reason at all at any time before verdict is beyond question under present law. Southeastern Fire Ins. Co. v. Walton, 256 N.C. 345, 123 S.E.2d 780 (1962). The vice of such an arrangement appears clearly in the following excerpt from an opinion of a federal judge:

"Before the effective date of [Rule 41] it not infrequently happened ... that in a case ... which had come to issue, perhaps after disposition of preliminary motions, which had gone to trial, in the trial of which plaintiff had introduced all his testimony, for the trial of which defendant had called witnesses from great distances and incurred great expense, the plaintiff would dismiss just at the moment the court was about to direct a verdict for defendant. The next day he might bring the same suit again. And the process might be repeated time after time. It was an outrageous imposition not only on the defendant but also on the court. Rule 41 has done much to put an end to that evil.

"The evil aimed at by the rule most largely is manifested in the extreme situation described. To a lesser extent it is present in any instance in which a defendant is damaged by being dragged into court and put to expense with no chance whatever ... of having the suit determined in his favor." McCann v. Bentley Stores Corp., 34 F. Supp. 234 (W.D. Mo. 1940).

Under the rule, the plaintiff's absolute right of dismissal is confined to the period before answer or a motion for summary judgment—the period before which there has been a heavy expenditure of time and effort by the court and other parties. Thereafter, the plaintiff can dismiss only with the consent of the other parties or with the permission of the judge. This latter provision allowing dismissal with the permission of the judge should be ample to take care of the hardship case where, for quite legitimate reasons, the plaintiff is unable to press his claim. It should be noted, however, that the judge is authorized to condition the dismissal on terms. For the federal practice in respect to terms, see 5 Moore's Federal Practice, § 41.06.

It should also be observed that the first voluntary dismissal will have the same effect as is now accorded a voluntary nonsuit, i.e., it is not a judgment on the merits. But a second dismissal, no matter where the first action was brought, will be a judgment on the merits.

Section (b). — Under this section, whether the action be a nonjury action or a jury action, there may be a motion for a dismissal because of failure of a plaintiff to prosecute or for a failure "to comply with these rules or any order of court." The power of the court to dismiss for failure to prosecute is well established [see Wynne v. Conrad, 220 N.C. 355, 17 S.E.2d 514 (1941)] and the rule merely gives statutory recognition of this power.

In respect to a motion for dismissal because of noncompliance with these rules or an order of court, the propriety of a dismissal will, of course, depend on the rule or order which has not been complied with. The rule does not undertake to say in what circumstances a dismissal will be proper any more than it attempts arbitrarily to declare what is a failure to prosecute.

In an action tried by the court without a jury, the rule provides for a motion similar to the familiar motion for compulsory nonsuit under former § 1-183. It is contemplated that where there is a jury trial, Rule 50 will come into play with its motion for a directed verdict. For a discussion of the interrelation of this rule and Rule 50, see the comment to Rule 50. The practice under section (b) will be much like that under former § 1-183. But there are some changes. The court is empowered to determine that its adjudication shall be on the merits and to find the facts in appropriate cases at the close of the plaintiff's evidence.

Section (c). — This section makes clear that the rule is applicable to all situations in which a claim is capable of being pressed under these rules.

Section (d). — This section makes certain that one, other than a plaintiff suing in forma pauperis, will have paid the costs in the first action before he can maintain a second action on the same claim.

Comment to the 1969 amendment. — The most significant change produced by the 1969 amendments to Rule 41 is that a claimant's unfettered right to a voluntary, nonprejudicial dismissal endures up to the moment he rests his case. But the amended Rule specifies, as did the earlier version, that a second dismissal shall operate as an adjudication upon the merits.

There has been an attempt to make clear that the right to bring a new action within one year, after either a voluntary or an involuntary dismissal, is dependent on the original action having been commenced before the relevant statute of limitations has run. To that end, the last sentences of subsections 41(a)(1) and 41(a)(2) and section 41(b) now speak of "an action commenced within the time prescribed therefor."

Subsection 41(a)(1) has been rewritten to provide that the right to bring a new action within one year applies in the case of a dismissal by stipulation if the parties do not "specify a shorter time." Basically, the rights of the parties have not been affected because a stipulation requires unanimity among the parties. If any party objects to the extension of the statute of limitations, he may refuse to sign the stipulation and thereby compel the claimant to seek the court's permission under subsection 41(a)(2).

Section 41(b) has been rewritten, in conformity with the present federal rule, to make it clear that a motion for involuntary dismissal under Rule 41 is available at the close of the claimant's case only in an action tried by the court without a jury. When there is a jury and a defendant wishes to challenge the sufficiency of the evidence, he must resort to Rule 50.

A second objective in the rewriting of section 41(b) was to make clear that the court's power to dismiss on terms, that is, to condition the dismissal ("Unless the court in its order for dismissal otherwise specifies,...") extends to all dismissals other than voluntary dismissals under section 41(a). Thus, if there were a motion to dismiss under Rule 37(b)(2)(iii) for failure to comply with a discovery order, the court, under the amended version of Rule 41(b), could in granting the motion specify that the dismissal was without prejudice.

Rule 42. Consolidation; separate trials

(a) Consolidation.—Except as provided in subdivision (b)(2) of this section, when actions involving a common question of law or fact are pending in one division of the court, the judge may order a joint hearing or trial of any or all the matters in issue in the actions; he may order all the actions consolidated; and he may make such orders concerning proceedings therein as may tend to avoid unnecessary costs or delay. When actions involving a common question of law or fact are pending in both the superior and the district court of the same county, a judge of the superior court in which the action is pending may order all the actions consolidated, and he may make such orders concerning proceedings therein as may tend to avoid unnecessary costs or delay.

(b) Separate trials.—

(1) The court may in furtherance of convenience or to avoid prejudice and shall for considerations of venue upon timely motion order a separate trial of any claim, cross-claim, counterclaim, or third-party claim, or of any separate issue or of any number of claims, cross-claims, counterclaims, third-party claims, or issues.

(2) Upon motion of any party in an action that includes a claim commenced under Article 1G of Chapter 90 of the General Statutes involving a managed care entity as defined in G.S. 90–21.50, the court shall order separate discovery and a separate trial of any claim, cross-claim, counterclaim, or third-party claim against a physician or other medical provider.

(3) Upon motion of any party in an action in tort wherein the plaintiff seeks damages exceeding one hundred fifty thousand dollars ($150,000), the court shall order separate trials for the issue of liability and the issue of damages, unless the court for good cause shown orders a single trial. Evidence relating solely to compensatory damages shall not be admissible until the trier of fact has determined that the defendant is liable. The same trier of fact that tries the issues relating to liability shall try the issues relating to damages.

(4) Pursuant to G.S. 1–267.1, any facial challenge to the validity of an act of the General Assembly, other than a challenge to plans apportioning or redistricting State legislative or congressional districts, shall be heard by a three-judge panel in the Superior Court of Wake County if a claimant raises such a challenge in the claimant's complaint or amended complaint in any court in this State, or if such a challenge is raised by the defendant in the defendant's answer, responsive pleading, or within 30 days of filing the defendant's answer or responsive pleading. In that event, the court shall, on its own motion, transfer that portion of the action challenging the validity of the act of the General Assembly to the Superior Court of Wake County for resolution by a three-judge panel if, after all other matters in the action have been resolved, a determination as to the facial validity of an act of the General Assembly must be made in order to completely resolve any matters in the case. The court in which the action originated shall maintain jurisdiction over all matters other than the challenge to the act's facial validity and shall stay all matters that are contingent upon the outcome of the challenge to the act's facial validity pending a ruling on that challenge and until all appeal rights are exhausted. Once the three-judge panel has ruled and all appeal rights have been exhausted, the matter shall be transferred or remanded to the three-judge panel or the trial court in which the action originated for resolution of any outstanding matters, as appropriate.

Added by Laws 1967, c. 954, § 1. Amended by S.L. 2001–446, § 4.8, eff. July 1, 2002; S.L. 2011–400, § 2, eff. Oct. 1, 2011; S.L. 2014–100, § 18B.16(c), eff. Aug. 7, 2014.

Comment

Section (a), providing for consolidation of actions "involving a common question of law or fact," invokes a power that North Carolina courts have long exercised. See McIntosh, North Carolina Practice and Procedure (1st ed.) pp. 536–537, § 506. Section (b) furnishes the court with the contrasting power of severance. With the multisided lawsuit made possible by these rules, it is safe to say that there will be more frequent occasion for the exercise of this power than formerly. Indeed, the power of severance is an indispensable safety valve to guard against the occasion where a suit of unmanageable size is thrust on the court. Whether or not there should be a severance rests in the sound discretion of the judge. For occasions where severance has been thought appropriate, see 5 Moore's Federal Practice, § 42.03.

Rule 43. Evidence

(a) Form.—In all trials the testimony of witnesses shall be taken orally in open court, unless otherwise provided by these rules.

(b) Examination of hostile witnesses and adverse parties.—A party may interrogate any unwilling or hostile witness by leading questions and may contradict and impeach him in all respects as if he had been called by the adverse party. A party may call an adverse party or an agent or employee of an adverse party, or an officer, director, or employee of a public or private corporation or of a partnership or association which is an adverse party, or an officer, agent or employee of a state, county or municipal government or agency thereof which is an adverse party, and interrogate him by leading questions and contradict and impeach him in all respects as if he had been called by the adverse party.

(c) Record of excluded evidence.—In an action tried before a jury, if an objection to a question propounded to a witness is sustained by the court, the court on request of the examining attorney shall order a record made of the answer the witness would have given. The court may add such other or further statement as clearly shows the character of the evidence, the form in which it was offered, the objection made and the ruling thereon. In actions tried without a jury the same procedure may be followed, except that the court upon request shall take and report the evidence in full, unless it clearly appears that the evidence is not admissible on any grounds or that the witness is privileged.

(d) Affirmation in lieu of oath.—Whenever under these rules an oath is required to be taken, a solemn affirmation may be accepted in lieu thereof.

(e) Evidence on motions.—When a motion is based on facts not appearing of record the court may hear the matter on affidavits presented by the respective parties, but the court may direct that the matter be heard wholly or partly on oral testimony or depositions.

Added by Laws 1967, c. 954, § 1.

Comment

While these rules do not deal extensively with questions of evidence, matters dealt with by the federal rules have been considered.

Section (a). — This section continues the usual practice of testimony being taken orally in open court. The "unless" clause refers principally to the provisions for the use of depositions in Rule 26(d).

Section (b). — This section deals with the situation where a party is forced to call his adversary as a witness. Under former provisions of § 8–50, one was permitted in this situation to cross-examine the witness and to contradict him but not to impeach him. This latter restriction is removed on the theory that a party who is so desperate as to be forced to call his adversary as a witness should be allowed the greatest latitude in refuting his adversary's testimony, should that be desirable. Section (b) also enlarges and spells out in greater detail the category of witnesses to whom its special provisions apply. The former provisions of § 8–50 said only that where a corporation is a party, its "officers or agents" are within its scope.

Section (c). — This section continues present practice.

Section (d). — This section makes available to all the privilege of using an affirmation instead of an oath. Under § 11–4, only Quakers, Moravians, Dunkers and Mennonites are so privileged.

Section (e). — This section continues present practice.

Rule 44. Proof of official record

(a) Authentication of copy.—An official record or an entry therein, when admissible for any purpose, may be evidence by an official publication thereof or by a copy attested by the officer having the legal custody of the record, or by his deputy, and accompanied with a certificate that such officer has the custody. If the office in which the record is kept is without the State of North Carolina but within the United States or within a territory or insular possession subject to the dominion of the United States, the certificate may be made by a judge of a court of record of the political subdivision in which the record is kept, authenticated by the seal of the court, or may be made by any public officer having a seal of office and having official duties in the political subdivision in which the record is kept, authenticated by the seal of his office. If the office in which the record is kept is in a foreign state or country, the certificate may be made by a secretary of embassy or legation, consul general, consul, vice-consul, or consular agent or by any officer in the foreign service of the United States stationed in the foreign state or country in which the record is kept, and authenticated by the seal of his office.

(b) Proof of lack of record.—A written statement signed by an officer having the custody of an official record or by his deputy that after diligent search no record or entry of a specified tenor is found to exist in the records of his office, accompanied by a certificate as above provided, is admissible as evidence that the records of his office contain no such record or entry.

(c) Other proof.—This rule does not prevent the proof of official records specified in Title 28, U.S.C. §§ 1738 and 1739 in the manner therein provided; nor of entry or lack of entry in official records by any method authorized by any other applicable statute or by the rules of evidence at common law.

Added by Laws 1967, c. 954, § 1.

Comment

North Carolina had no general statute, applying to all official custodians of records, in respect to the proof of official records. Section (a) supplies this omission and makes unnecessary reliance on statutes applicable to particular custodians and to particular situations. For reference to and discussion of the North Carolina statutes, see Stansbury, North Carolina Evidence, § 154.

Section (b) provides a simple method for producing evidence of nonexistence of a record.

Section (c), out of an abundance of caution, leaves as alternative methods of proof any methods now existing. For various statutes, see Chapter 8 of the General Statutes, Article 2 and Article 3. 28 U.S.C., §§ 1738 and 1739 have to do with proof of records in other states and in territories and possessions of the United States. In addition, the two sections prescribe the "faith and credit" these records are to have when duly authenticated.

Rule 44.1. Determination of foreign law

A party who intends to raise an issue concerning the law of a foreign country shall give notice by pleadings or by other reasonable written notice. The court, in determining foreign law, may consider any relevant material or source, including testimony, whether or not submitted by a party or admissible under Chapter 8 of the General Statutes and State law. The court's determination shall be treated as a ruling on a question of law.

Added by Laws 1967, c. 954, § 1. Amended by Laws 1995, c. 389, § 5.

Rule 45. Subpoena

(a) Form; Issuance.—

(1) Every subpoena shall state all of the following:

a. The title of the action, the name of the court in which the action is pending, the number of the civil action, and the name of the party at whose instance the witness is summoned.

b. A command to each person to whom it is directed to attend and give testimony or to produce and permit inspection and copying of designated records, books, papers, documents, electronically stored information, or tangible things in the possession, custody, or control of that person therein specified.

c. The protections of persons subject to subpoenas under subsection (c) of this rule.

d. The requirements for responses to subpoenas under subsection (d) of this rule.

(2) A command to produce records, books, papers, electronically stored information, or tangible things may be joined with a command to appear at trial or hearing or at a deposition, or any subpoena may be issued separately. A subpoena may specify the form or forms in which electronically stored information is to be produced.

(3) A subpoena shall issue from the court in which the action is pending.

(4) The clerk of court in which the action is pending shall issue a subpoena, signed but otherwise blank, to a party requesting it, who shall complete it before service. Any judge of the superior court, judge of the district court, magistrate, or attorney, as officer of the court, may also issue and sign a subpoena.

(b) Service.—

(1) Manner.—Any subpoena may be served by the sheriff, by the sheriff's deputy, by a coroner, or by any person who is not a party and is not less than 18 years of age. Service of a subpoena upon a person named therein shall be made by delivering a copy thereof to that person or by registered or certified mail, return receipt requested. Service of a subpoena for the attendance of a witness only may also be made by telephone communication with the person named therein only by a sheriff, the sheriff's designee who is not less than 18 years of age and is not a party, or a coroner.

(2) Service of copy.—A copy of the subpoena served under subdivision (b)(1) of this subsection shall also be served upon each party in the manner prescribed by Rule 5(b).

(3) Subdivision (b)(2) of this subsection does not apply to subpoenas issued under G.S. 15A–801 or G.S. 15A–802.

(c) Protection of Persons Subject to Subpoena.—

(1) Avoid undue burden or expense.—A party or an attorney responsible for the issuance and service of a subpoena shall take reasonable steps to avoid imposing an undue burden or expense on a person subject to the subpoena. The court shall enforce this subdivision and impose upon the party or attorney in violation of this requirement an appropriate sanction that may include compensating the person unduly bur-

dened for lost earnings and for reasonable attorney's fees.

(2) For production of public records or hospital medical records.—Where the subpoena commands any custodian of public records or any custodian of hospital medical records, as defined in G.S. 8–44.1, to appear for the sole purpose of producing certain records in the custodian's custody, the custodian subpoenaed may, in lieu of personal appearance, tender to the court in which the action is pending by registered or certified mail or by personal delivery, on or before the time specified in the subpoena, certified copies of the records requested together with a copy of the subpoena and an affidavit by the custodian testifying that the copies are true and correct copies and that the records were made and kept in the regular course of business, or if no such records are in the custodian's custody, an affidavit to that effect. When the copies of records are personally delivered under this subdivision, a receipt shall be obtained from the person receiving the records. Any original or certified copy of records or an affidavit delivered according to the provisions of this subdivision, unless otherwise objectionable, shall be admissible in any action or proceeding without further certification or authentication. Copies of hospital medical records tendered under this subdivision shall not be open to inspection or copied by any person, except to the parties to the case or proceedings and their attorneys in depositions, until ordered published by the judge at the time of the hearing or trial. Nothing contained herein shall be construed to waive the physician-patient privilege or to require any privileged communication under law to be disclosed.

(3) Written objection to subpoenas.—Subject to subsection (d) of this rule, a person commanded to appear at a deposition or to produce and permit the inspection and copying of records, books, papers, documents, electronically stored information, or tangible things may, within 10 days after service of the subpoena or before the time specified for compliance if the time is less than 10 days after service, serve upon the party or the attorney designated in the subpoena written objection to the subpoena, setting forth the specific grounds for the objection. The written objection shall comply with the requirements of Rule 11. Each of the following grounds may be sufficient for objecting to a subpoena:

a. The subpoena fails to allow reasonable time for compliance.

b. The subpoena requires disclosure of privileged or other protected matter and no exception or waiver applies to the privilege or protection.

c. The subpoena subjects a person to an undue burden or expense.

d. The subpoena is otherwise unreasonable or oppressive.

e. The subpoena is procedurally defective.

(4) Order of court required to override objection.—If objection is made under subdivision (3) of this subsection, the party serving the subpoena shall not be entitled to compel the subpoenaed person's appearance at a deposition or to inspect and copy materials to which an objection has been made except pursuant to an order of the court. If objection is made, the party serving the subpoena may, upon notice to the subpoenaed person, move at any time for an order to compel the subpoenaed person's appearance at the deposition or the production of the materials designated in the subpoena. The motion shall be filed in the court in the county in which the deposition or production of materials is to occur.

(5) Motion to quash or modify subpoena.—A person commanded to appear at a trial, hearing, deposition, or to produce and permit the inspection and copying of records, books, papers, documents, electronically stored information, or other tangible things, within 10 days after service of the subpoena or before the time specified for compliance if the time is less than 10 days after service, may file a motion to quash or modify the subpoena. The court shall quash or modify the subpoena if the subpoenaed person demonstrates the existence of any of the reasons set forth in subdivision (3) of this subsection. The motion shall be filed in the court in the county in which the trial, hearing, deposition, or production of materials is to occur.

(6) Order to compel; expenses to comply with subpoena.—When a court enters an order compelling a deposition or the production of records, books, papers, documents, electronically stored information, or other tangible things, the order shall protect any person who is not a party or an agent of a party from significant expense resulting from complying with the subpoena. The court may order that the person to whom the subpoena is addressed will be reasonably compensated for the cost of producing the records, books, papers, documents, electronically stored information, or tangible things specified in the subpoena.

(7) Trade secrets; confidential information.—When a subpoena requires disclosure of a trade secret or other confidential research, development, or commercial information, a court may, to protect a person subject to or affected by the subpoena, quash or modify the subpoena, or when the party on whose behalf the subpoena is issued shows a substantial need for the testimony or material that cannot otherwise be met without undue hardship, the court may order a person to make an appearance or produce the materials only on specified conditions stated in the order.

(8) Order to quash; expenses.—When a court enters an order quashing or modifying the subpoena, the court may order the party on whose behalf the subpoena is issued to pay all or part of the subpoenaed person's reasonable expenses including attorney's fees.

(d) Duties in Responding to Subpoenas.—

(1) Form of response.—A person responding to a subpoena to produce records, books, documents, electronically stored information, or tangible things shall produce them as they are kept in the usual course of business or shall organize and label them to correspond with the categories in the request.

(2) Form of producing electronically stored information not specified.—If a subpoena does not specify a form for producing electronically stored information, the person responding must produce it in a form or forms in which it ordinarily is maintained or in a reasonably useable form or forms.

(3) Electronically stored information in only one form.—The person responding need not produce the same electronically stored information in more than one form.

(4) Inaccessible electronically stored information.—The person responding need not provide discovery of electronically stored information from sources that the person identifies as not reasonably accessible because of undue burden or cost. On motion to compel discovery or for a protective order, the person responding must show that the information is not reasonably accessible because of undue burden or cost. If that showing is made, the court may nonetheless order discovery from such sources if the requesting party shows good cause, after considering the limitations of Rule 26(b)(1a). The court may specify conditions for discovery, including requiring the party that seeks discovery from a nonparty to bear the costs of locating, preserving, collecting, and producing the electronically stored information involved.

(5) Specificity of objection.—When information subject to a subpoena is withheld on the objection that it is subject to protection as trial preparation materials, or that it is otherwise privileged, the objection shall be made with specificity and shall be supported by a description of the nature of the communications, records, books, papers, documents, electronically stored information, or other tangible things not produced, sufficient for the requesting party to contest the objection.

(d1) Opportunity for Inspection of Subpoenaed Material.—A party or attorney responsible for the issuance and service of a subpoena shall, within five business days after the receipt of material produced in compliance with the subpoena, serve all other parties with notice of receipt of the material produced in compliance with the subpoena and, upon request, shall provide all other parties a reasonable opportunity to copy and inspect such material at the expense of the inspecting party.

(e) Contempt; Expenses to Force Compliance With Subpoena.—

(1) Failure by any person without adequate excuse to obey a subpoena served upon the person may be deemed a contempt of court. Failure by any party without adequate cause to obey a subpoena served upon the party shall also subject the party to the sanctions provided in Rule 37(d).

(2) The court may award costs and attorney's fees to the party who issued a subpoena if the court determines that a person objected to the subpoena or filed a motion to quash or modify the subpoena, and the objection or motion was unreasonable or was made for improper purposes such as unnecessary delay.

(f) Discovery From Persons Residing Outside the State.—

(1) Any party may obtain discovery from a person residing in another state of the United States or a territory or an insular possession subject to its jurisdiction in any one or more of the following forms: (i) oral depositions, (ii) depositions upon written questions, or (iii) requests for production of documents and tangible things. In doing so, the party shall use and follow any applicable process and procedures required and available under the laws of the state, territory, or insular possession where the discovery is to be obtained. If required by the process or procedure of the state, territory, or insular possession where the discovery is to be obtained, a commission may issue from the court in which the action is pending in accordance with the procedures set forth in subdivision (2) of this subsection.

(2) Obtaining a commission.—

a. The party desiring a commission to obtain discovery outside the State shall prepare and file a motion indicating the party's intent to obtain a commission and requesting that the commission be issued.

b. The motion shall indicate that the moving party has conferred, or describe fully the moving party's good faith attempts to confer, with counsel for all other parties regarding the request and shall indicate whether the motion is unopposed. The motion shall also attach a copy of any proposed subpoena, notice of deposition, or other papers to be served on the person from whom the moving party is seeking to obtain discovery.

c. The motion shall indicate that counsel for the moving party has read the applicable rules and procedures of the foreign state and that the moving party will comply with those rules and procedures in obtaining the requested discovery.

d. If the motion reflects that it is unopposed or indicates that the moving party has made reasonable, good faith efforts to confer with all other parties and that no other party has indicated that it opposes the motion, the motion shall immediately be placed on the calendar for a hearing within 20 days before the court in which the action is pending where the commission shall be issued. However, if the court determines, in its discretion, that the moving party has failed to make reasonable, good faith efforts to confer with all other parties prior to filing the motion, the court shall refuse to issue the commission, and the motion shall be denied.

e. If the motion does not reflect that it is unopposed or that the moving party has made reasonable, good faith efforts to confer with all other parties and that no other party has indicated that it opposes the motion, any party wishing to oppose the motion shall file written objections to issuance of the commission within 10 days of being served with the motion, and the motion shall immediately be placed on the calendar for a hearing to be held within 20 days before the court in which the action is pending. The hearing may be held by telephone in the court's discretion. The court may refuse to issue the commission only upon a showing of substantial good cause to deny the motion.

f. If the court, in its discretion, determines that any party opposing the motion did so without good cause, the court shall require the party opposing the motion to pay the moving party the reasonable costs and expenses incurred in obtaining the order, including attorneys' fees, unless circumstances exist which make an award of expenses unjust.

(3) In addition to any terms required by the foreign jurisdiction to initiate the process of obtaining the requested discovery, the commission shall:

a. State the time and place at which the requested discovery is to occur;

b. State the name and address of the person from whom the discovery is sought, if known, and, if unknown, a general description sufficient to identify the person or the particular class or group to which he or she belongs; and

c. Attach a copy of any case management order, discovery order, local rule, or other rule or order establishing any discovery deadlines in the North Carolina action.

Added by Laws 1967, c. 954, § 1. Amended by Laws 1969, c. 886, § 1; Laws 1971, c. 159; Laws 1975, c. 762, § 3; Laws 1983, c. 665, § 1; Laws 1983, c. 722; Laws 1989, c. 262, § 1; S.L. 2003-276, § 1, eff. Oct. 1, 2003; S.L. 2007-514, § 1, eff. Oct. 1, 2007; S.L. 2011-199, § 6, eff. Oct. 1, 2011; S.L. 2011-247, § 3, eff. Dec. 1, 2011.

Comment

Comment to this Rule as Originally Enacted. — This rule would seem to be largely self-explanatory. An effort has been made to provide a convenient and highly flexible practice in respect to subpoenas. It will be noted that the subpoena is to be directed to the witness rather than to the sheriff as our present statute provides. The party obtaining the subpoena will deliver it to the appropriate sheriff or other proper person for service.

The differences between sections (a) and (c) on the one hand, and section (d) on the other should also be noted. In sections (a) and (c), it is contemplated that the subpoena will issue from the court where the action is to be tried wherever the witness is likely to be found, while in section (d) the idea is that the subpoena shall issue from the court of the county where the deposition is to be taken. The limitations of section (d) in no way affect where the subpoena may be served nor do they in any way apply to sections (a) and (c).

Comment to the 1975 Amendment. — *Section (d).* — The reference in subsection (d)(1) is amended to conform to the relocation of the section to which it refers. The second paragraph of subsection (d)(1) is borrowed from the federal rule. Former subsection (d)(2) is relocated to Rule 30(b)(1) where, as modified, it applies to all deponents, and not just those whose presence can be compelled only by subpoena.

Section (e). — This provision is amended to require service of a copy of a subpoena duces tecum by delivery or by registered or certified mail and to allow a person other than a sheriff, his deputy or a coroner to serve a subpoena for the attendance of a witness by registered or certified mail. The amendment also requires the server to be of legal age.

Comment to the 2011 Amendment. — Rule 45 is amended to conform the provisions for subpoenas to changes in other discovery rules, largely related to discovery of electronically stored information. In addition, in a number of places, words identifying parts of the rule have been changed to make this rule consistent with the language of other Rules of Civil Procedure, without an intention to change substance.

Subsection (a). — Subdivision (a)(1) is amended to recognize that electronically stored information, as defined in Rule 34(a), also can be sought by subpoena. Like Rule 34(b), subdivision (a)(2) is amended to provide that the subpoena can designate a form or forms for production of electronic data. Under subdivision (c)(3), the person served with a subpoena may object to the requested form or forms if producing in the requested form would subject the person to undue burden or expense or is otherwise unreasonable or oppressive.

Subsection (c). — As with discovery of electronically stored information from parties, complying with a subpoena for such information may impose burdens on the responding nonparty. Subsection (c) provides protection against undue impositions on nonparties. For example, subdivision (c)(1) directs that a party serving a subpoena "shall take reasonable steps to avoid imposing undue burden or expense on a person subject to the subpoena," subdivision (c)(3) permits the person served with the subpoena to object to it, and subdivision (c)(6) directs that an order requiring compliance "shall protect any person who is not a party or an agent of a party from significant expense resulting from" compliance.

Subsection (d). — As under Rule 34(b), subdivision (d)(2) is amended to provide that if the subpoena does not specify the form or forms for electronically stored information, the person served with the subpoena must produce electronically stored information in a form or forms in which it is usually maintained or in a form or forms that are reasonably usable. Subdivision (d)(3) is added to provide that the person producing electronically stored information should not have to produce the same information in more than one form.

Subdivision (d)(4) is added to provide that the responding person need not provide discovery of electronically stored information from sources the person identifies as not reasonably accessible, unless the court orders such discovery for good cause, considering the limitations of Rule 26(b)(1a), on terms that protect a nonparty against undue burden or cost. As with a party under Rule 26(c) or 37(a)(2), the person objecting to production pursuant to a subpoena bears the burden of showing the burden or cost and its unreasonableness under the circumstances. If the showing is made, the judge has the authority to quash the subpoena or, upon a showing of good cause by the requesting party and consideration of limitations on frequency and extent set out in Rule 26(b)(1a), require compliance upon condition.

Rule 46. Objections and exceptions

(a) Rulings on admissibility of evidence. –

(1) When there is objection to the admission of evidence on the ground that the witness is for a specified reason incompetent or not qualified or disqualified, it shall be deemed that a like objection has been made to any subsequent admission of evidence from the witness in question. Similarly, when there is objection to the admission of evidence involving a specified line of questioning, it shall be deemed that a like objection has been taken to any subsequent admission of evidence involving the same line of questioning.

(2) If there is proper objection to the admission of evidence and the objection is overruled, the ruling of the court shall be deemed excepted to by the party making the objection. If an objection to the admission of evidence is sustained or if the court for any reason excludes evidence offered by a party, the ruling of the court shall be deemed excepted to by the party offering the evidence.

(3) No objections are necessary with respect to questions propounded to a witness by the court or a juror but it shall be deemed that each such question has been properly objected to and that the objection has been overruled and that an exception has been taken to the ruling of the court by all parties to the action.

(b) Pretrial rulings, interlocutory orders, trial rulings, and other orders not directed to the admissibility of evidence. – With respect to pretrial rulings, interlocutory orders, trial rulings, and other orders of the court not directed to the admissibility of evidence, formal objections and exceptions are unnecessary. In order to preserve an exception to any such ruling or order or to the court's failure to make any such ruling or order, it shall be sufficient if a party, at the time the ruling or order is made or sought, makes known to the court the party's objection to the action of the court or makes known the action that the party desires the court to take and the party's grounds for its position. If a party has no opportunity to object or except to a ruling or order at the time it is made, the absence of an objection or exception does not thereafter prejudice that party.

(c) Repealed by S.L. 2001–379, § 6, eff. Oct. 1, 2001.

Added by Laws 1967, c. 954, § 1. Amended by S.L. 2001–379, § 6, eff. Oct. 1, 2001.

Comment

Section (a)(1) is aimed at situations where repeated objections in respect to the admission of evidence have been necessary in order to assure review. In Shelton v. Southern Ry., 193 N.C. 670, 139 S.E. 232 (1927), the court declared:

"It is thoroughly established in this State that, if incompetent evidence is admitted over objection, but the same evidence has theretofore or thereafter been given in other parts of the examination, the benefit of the exception is ordinarily lost."

This proposition has recently been reaffirmed in Dunes Club, Inc. v. Cherokee Ins. Co., 259 N.C. 293, 130 S.E.2d 625 (1963). Thus, apparently the only course of safety for counsel to follow under prior practice would be to object at every opportunity. It would seem that a single objection should suffice in either of the two situations specified in subsection (a)(1).

Section (a)(2) continues the present practice.

Section (a)(3) continues the present practice of making unnecessary objection or exception with respect to questions propounded by a juror or the judge. See former § 1–206(d).

Section (b), it will be noted, applies to all nonevidentiary rulings and orders. In this respect, it is new. However, the general principle of the section has been in North Carolina practice for some time in respect to rulings on motions for nonsuit. See former § 1–183.

Section (c) continues present practice. See former § 1–206, subsection (b), and the note to Rule 51.

Westlaw Electronic Research

Rule 47. Jurors

Inquiry as to the fitness and competency of any person to serve as a juror and the challenging of such person shall be as provided in Chapter 9 of the General Statutes.

Added by Laws 1967, c. 954, § 1.

Rule 48. Juries of less than twelve — majority verdict

Except in actions in which a jury is required by statute, the parties may stipulate that the jury will consist of any number less than 12 or that a verdict or a finding of a stated majority of the jurors shall be taken as the verdict or finding of the jury.

Added by Laws 1967, c. 954, § 1.

Comment

Since jury trial may be waived entirely, it is certainly appropriate with the consent of the parties that trial be by a jury of less than 12 and that the usual rule of unanimity not prevail. The rule recognizes the exception in actions for divorce provided by G.S. 50-10. Under the rule therefore, if there is a jury trial in a divorce action (there may not be: G.S. 50-10 provides for waiver when the ground alleged is one year's separation) it will be by a jury of 12 and the rule of unanimity will prevail.

Rule 49. Verdicts

(a) General and special verdicts.—The judge may require a jury to return either a general or a special verdict and in all cases may instruct the jury, if it renders a general verdict, to find upon particular questions of fact, to be stated in writing, and may direct a written finding thereon. A general verdict is that by which the jury pronounces generally upon all or any of the issues, either in favor of the plaintiff or defendant. A special verdict is that by which the jury finds the facts only.

(b) Framing of issues.—Issues shall be framed in concise and direct terms, and prolixity and confusion must be avoided by not having too many issues. The issues, material to be tried, must be made up by the attorneys appearing in the action, or by the judge presiding, and reducing to writing, before or during the trial.

(c) Waiver of jury trial on issue.—If, in submitting the issues to the jury, the judge omits any issue of fact raised by the pleadings or by the evidence, each party waives his right to a trial by jury of the issue so omitted unless before the jury retires he demands its submission to the jury. As to an issue omitted without such demand the judge may make a finding; or, if he fails to do so, he shall be deemed to have made a finding in accord with the judgment entered.

(d) Special finding inconsistent with general verdict.—Where a special finding of facts is inconsistent with the general verdict, the former controls, and the judge shall give judgment accordingly.

Added by Laws 1967, c. 954, § 1.

Comment

A distinguished scholar has said that the North Carolina verdict practice "has enabled, more than any other factor perhaps, a very small judiciary to care for the litigation of one of the larger states." Green, A New Development in Jury Trial, 13 ABAJ 715, at p. 716 (1927). The Commission shares this high opinion of the North Carolina practice and, in its more essential respects, the Commission proposed its retention. It will be observed that sections (a), (b) and (d) are practically drawn verbatim from former §§ 1-200; 1-201; § 1-202; former § 1-203.

There are some changes produced by the rule. Former § 1-203 permitted the jury "in their discretion" to return either a general or special verdict "in every action for the recovery of money only or specific real property." No instances of an exercise of this discretion were known to the Commission, and it saw no purpose in not allowing the judge to control the form of verdict. Accordingly, it omitted any reference to the jury's discretion in this respect.

Section (c) changes the law in respect to issues omitted by the judge in submitting a case to the jury. The right to jury trial on such issues would be lost in the absence of a demand for such submission and the judge would be empowered to make a finding on the issue in question. The idea is that the inadvertent omission of an issue ought not to jeopardize a whole trial when an impartial fact finder is on hand to make the requisite finding. Ample means for a party to protect his right to jury trial on all issues are clearly available. All he has to do is demand their submission "before the jury retires."

Section (c) also employs, in the case of an omitted issue and an omitted finding by the judge, a presumption of a finding in accord with the judgment. Formerly, in this situation, nothing was presumed in support of the judgment in jury cases. Tucker v. Satterthwaite, 120 N.C. 118, 27 S.E. 45 (1897).

Finally, it will be observed that the rule speaks of issues "raised in the pleadings or by the evidence." Normally, the issues will be raised by the pleadings but under Rule 15(b) provision is made for regarding the pleadings as amended whenever an issue outside the pleadings is tried with consent of the parties, express or implied. Thus, it will not be essential for the pleadings to reflect, on every occasion, all the issues.

Rule 50. Motion for a directed verdict and for judgment notwithstanding the verdict

(a) When made; effect. — A party who moves for a directed verdict at the close of the evidence offered by an opponent may offer evidence in the event that the motion is not granted, without having reserved the right so to do and to the same extent as if the motion had not been made. A motion for a directed verdict which is not granted is not a waiver of trial by jury even though all parties to the action have moved for directed verdicts. A motion for a directed verdict shall state the specific grounds therefor. The order granting a motion for a directed verdict shall be effective without any assent of the jury.

(b) Motion for judgment notwithstanding the verdict. —

(1) Whenever a motion for a directed verdict made at the close of all the evidence is denied or for any reason is not granted, the submission of the action to the jury shall be deemed to be subject to a later determination of the legal questions raised by the motion. Not later than 10 days after entry of judgment, a party who has moved for a directed verdict may move to have the verdict and any judgment entered thereon set aside and to have judgment entered in accordance with his motion for a directed verdict; or if a verdict was not returned such party, within 10 days after the jury has been discharged, may move for judgment in accordance with his motion for a directed verdict. In either case the motion shall be granted if it appears that the motion for directed verdict could properly have been granted. A motion for a new trial may be joined with this motion, or a new trial may be prayed for in the alternative. If a verdict was returned the judge may allow the judgment to stand or may set aside the judgment and either order a new trial or direct the entry of judgment as if the requested verdict had been directed. If no verdict was returned the judge may direct the entry of judgment as if the requested verdict had been directed or may order a new trial. Not later than ten (10) days after entry of judgment or the discharge of the jury if a verdict was not returned, the judge on his own motion may, with or without further notice and hearing, grant, deny, or redeny a motion for directed verdict made at the close of all the evidence that was denied or for any reason was not granted.

(2) An appellate court, on finding that a trial judge should have granted a motion for directed verdict made at the close of all the evidence, may not direct entry of judgment in accordance with the motion unless the party who made the motion for a directed verdict also moved for judgment in accordance with Rule 50(b)(1) or the trial judge on his own motion granted, denied or redenied the motion for a directed verdict in accordance with Rule 50(b)(1).

(c) Motion for judgment notwithstanding the verdict — Conditional rulings on grant of motion. —

(1) If the motion for judgment notwithstanding the verdict, provided for in section (b) of this rule, is granted, the court shall also rule on the motion for new trial, if any, by determining whether it should be granted if the judgment is thereafter vacated or reversed, and shall specify the grounds for granting or denying the motion for the new trial. If the motion for new trial is thus conditionally granted, the order thereon does not affect the finality of the judgment. In case the motion for new trial has been conditionally granted and the judgment is reversed on appeal, the new trial shall proceed unless the appellate division has otherwise ordered. In case the motion for new trial has been conditionally denied, the appellee on appeal may assert error in that denial; and if the judgment is reversed on appeal, subsequent proceedings shall be in accordance with the order of the appellate division.

(2) The party whose verdict has been set aside on motion for judgment notwithstanding the verdict may serve a motion for a new trial pursuant to Rule 59 not later than 10 days after entry of the judgment notwithstanding the verdict.

(d) Motion for judgment notwithstanding the verdict — Denial of motion. — If the motion for judgment notwithstanding the verdict is denied, the party who prevailed on that motion may, as appellee, assert grounds entitling him to a new trial in the event the appellate division concludes that the trial court erred in denying the motion for judgment notwithstanding the verdict. If the appellate division reverses the judgment, nothing in this rule precludes it from determining that the appellee is entitled to a new trial, or from directing the trial court to determine whether a new trial shall be granted.

Added by Laws 1967, c. 954, § 1. Amended by Laws 1969, c. 895, § 11.

Comment

Comment to this Rule as Originally Enacted. — It will be recalled that Rule 41(b) provides the procedure in those cases tried to the court where the party defending believes the evidence of his adversary is insufficient to permit a recovery. Section (a) of this rule provides the procedure in comparable circumstances in those cases tried by jury. It further provides a procedure whereby a claimant in a jury trial may urge that he is entitled to a recovery as a matter of law.

The rule contemplates that a party defending may move for a directed verdict at the close of his adversary's evidence or at the close of all the evidence whether or not he has made a prior motion. The rule further contemplates that any party may move for a directed verdict at the close of all the evidence.

Some important changes are effected by Rules 41(a) and 50(a) taken together. Formerly, a party defending had available the motion for nonsuit provided by former § 1-183. Judgment pursuant to a grant of the motion was not a judgment on the merits. In addition, any party had available the common-law motion for a directed verdict which does, if granted, result in a judgment on the merits. Everett v. Williams, 152 N.C. 117, 67 S.E. 265 (1910). Despite the greater potential of the directed verdict, the motion was infrequently employed because the claimant could always, under prior practice, forestall the directed verdict by taking a voluntary nonsuit.

Under the rules, at the close of the claimant's evidence, the party defending in a jury trial will be restricted to the directed verdict motion—a motion that if granted will result in a judgment on the merits disposing of the case finally in the absence of reversal on appeal. But it should be remembered that the judge will have power under Rule 41(a)(2) on the claimant's motion to allow a dismissal that is not on the merits.

The last sentence in section (a) is simply for the purpose of avoiding a useless formality. When a judge decides that a directed verdict is appropriate, actually he is deciding that the question has become one exclusively of law and that the jury has no function to serve. In these circumstances, it is an idle gesture to require the jury to go through the motions of returning the verdict directed.

Section (b), providing for a motion for judgment notwithstanding the verdict or, as it is commonly called "a judgment NOV" (an abbreviation for non obstante veredicto) introduces an entirely new procedure to North Carolina practice. It is true that North Carolina had a judgment NOV of sorts—for use in a situation where the party against whom a verdict is rendered would have been entitled to a judgment on the pleadings. See McIntosh, North Carolina Practice and Procedure (1st ed.), § 612. The judgment NOV in this rule is an altogether different affair. In essence, it involves allowing a judge to consider the question of the sufficiency of the evidence after the jury has returned a verdict.

This power has been sought — unsuccessfully it must be said — by superior court judges on more than one occasion. See, e.g., Batson v. City Laundry Co., 202 N.C. 560, 163 S.E. 600 (1932); Jones v. Dixie Fire Ins. Co., 210 N.C. 559; 187 S.E. 769 (1936). A moment's reflection will show why. A motion challenging the sufficiency of the evidence will often present a close question of great difficulty. A jury verdict for the movant eliminates this question and an appeal based on the ruling on the motion. But under prior practice, the judge was not permitted to consider the question raised by the motion after submitting the case to the jury. He was required to rule, finally, before the case was submitted.

If the motion was granted, there would likely be an appeal. If the trial judge was affirmed, it was quite possible that the appeal was unnecessary since the jury, had it been allowed to consider the evidence, might well have found for the movant. If the trial judge was reversed, there would have to be a new trial, repeating much of the expenditure in time and effort that was put into the first trial because there was no verdict on which judgment could be entered.

Under the rule, whenever a motion for a directed verdict made at the close of all the evidence is not granted, it will be deemed that the judge submitted the case to the jury having reserved for later determination the legal question raised by the motion. Thus, if there is a verdict for the nonmovant or if for some reason a verdict is not returned, the judge can reconsider the sufficiency of the evidence and, if convinced that it is insufficient, can grant the motion. If, on appeal it should prove that the judge was correct, that is, that he properly granted the motion, then the appellate court can affirm and, in appropriate cases, order judgment entered for the movant. On the other hand, if it should prove that the trial judge improperly granted the motion, the appellate court is not restricted to granting a new trial, as under the prior practice, but can order judgment entered on the verdict.

The utility of the judgment NOV must be obvious. It will certainly eliminate some appeals and it will certainly eliminate some second trials.

Turning now to the procedure for employing the motion for judgment NOV, it will be observed that making an appropriate motion for a directed verdict is an absolute prerequisite for the motion for judgment NOV. 5 Moore's Federal Practice, § 50.08 and cases cited.

Second, it will be observed that the motion can, but need not be, coupled with a motion for a new trial. If it is joined with a motion for a new trial, the proper procedure, as laid down by the Supreme Court in Montgomery Ward & Co. v. Duncan, 311 U.S. 243, 61 S. Ct. 189, 85 L. Ed. 147 (1940) and as spelled out in sections (c) and (d) is for the court to rule on both motions. If the motion for judgment is granted and this is approved on appeal, the lower court's ruling on the movant's (verdict loser's) motion for new trial becomes irrelevant. Final judgment for the movant is affirmed. If, however, the lower court is reversed on appeal as to the motion for judgment, then its ruling on the new trial motion becomes a matter of importance. If the movant (verdict loser) was granted a new trial, "the new trial shall proceed unless the appellate court has otherwise ordered." Of course, the appellate court might very well "otherwise order" since the nonmovant (verdict winner) could assert on appeal not only error in the grant of the motion for judgment but error in the grant of the new trial. If the movant was denied a new trial although granted a judgment NOV, he can, under section (c), "assert error in that denial" on appeal.

Section (d) deals with the situation where the motion for judgment is denied. The movant may have coupled with his motion a motion for new trial. If the new trial motion was also denied, then the movant could appeal in respect to both motions. If the appellate court reverses as to the motion for judgment, it can order judgment for the movant or a new trial as the case may be. If the appellate court affirms in respect to the motion for judgment, it may of course reverse or affirm in respect to the new trial motion.

Comment to the 1969 Amendment. — Rule 50, both in its old version and in the new, contemplates that when a party moves for a directed verdict and his motion is denied or for any reason is not granted, that party may, after an adverse verdict or the failure of the jury to return a verdict, move for judgment notwithstanding the verdict. When the movant for a directed verdict who is not immediately successful later moves for a judgment notwithstanding the verdict and his motion is granted or denied, and there is an appeal, the powers of the appellate court are reasonably clear, as outlined in section 50(c) and (d). But when the movant for a directed verdict later fails to move for a judgment notwithstanding the verdict, there has been in the federal courts uncertainty about the powers of an appellate court. See 5 Moore's Federal Practice, § 2365–2374. The uncertainty revolves around the question of whether an appellate court can direct entry of judgment for a party who was erroneously denied a directed verdict but who later failed to move, as the rule contemplates, for a motion for judgment notwithstanding the verdict. The Supreme Court ruled in Cone v. West Virginia Pulp & Paper Co., 330 U.S. 212, 67 S. Ct. 752, 91 L. Ed. 849 (1947), that in the circumstances outlined the appellate court was limited to directing a new trial.

It might be said that the rationale of the court's ruling in the Cone case rests on a desire that no final conclusive judgment be rendered against a party unless the trial judge has had an opportunity to consider whether the loser should be given another chance. The trial judge would not have this opportunity in the absence of some such rule as that enunciated in Cone.

The Commission has from the first embraced the Cone result. The Commission has gone further and attempted to meet some of the problems spawned by the Cone decision.

Its first effort was the rather clumsy one comprised in the last two sentences of Rule 50(b) as it was originally enacted. These two sentences have now been deleted and they should be forgotten.

In their stead, the General Assembly has added a new final sentence to what is now section 50(b)(1) and a new section 50(b)(2). These additions make clear the power of a trial judge, once there has been a motion for a directed verdict, to consider on his own motion, after entry of judgment (see Rule 58 as to when judgment is deemed to be entered), entry of judgment in accordance with the directed verdict motion. The additions also make clear that without some post-verdict consideration of a motion for judgment or the reserved motion for a directed verdict, the appellate court cannot, if it should find erroneous the failure to grant the motion for directed verdict, direct entry of judgment for the appellant but can only order a new trial.

Rule 51. Instructions to jury

(a) Judge to explain law but give no opinion on facts.—In charging the jury in any action governed by these rules, a judge shall not give an opinion as to whether or not a fact is fully or sufficiently proved and shall not be required to state, summarize or recapitulate the evidence, or to explain the application of the law to the evidence. If the judge undertakes to state the contentions of the parties, he shall give equal stress to the contentions of each party.

(b) Requests for special instructions.—Requests for special instructions must be in writing, entitled in the cause, and signed by the counsel or party submitting them. Such requests for special instructions must be submitted to the judge before the judge's charge to the jury is begun. The judge may, in his discretion, consider such requests regardless of the time they are made. Written requests for special instructions shall, after their submission to the judge, be filed with the clerk as a part of the record.

(c) Judge not to comment on verdict.—The judge shall make no comment on any verdict in open court in the presence or hearing of any member of the jury panel; and if any judge shall make any comment as herein prohibited or shall praise or criticize any jury on account of its verdict, whether such praise, criticism or comment be made inadvertently or intentionally, such praise, criticism or comment by the judge shall for any party to any other action remaining to be tried constitute valid grounds as a matter of right for a continuance of any action to a time when all members of the jury panel are no longer serving. The provisions of this section shall not be applicable upon the hearing of motions for a new trial or for judgment notwithstanding the verdict.

Added by Laws 1967, c. 954, § 1. Amended by Laws 1985, c. 537, § 2.

Comment

The effort here, except for minor changes, has been to carry forward the substance of the present law. The prohibition on comment by the judge has been retained. His duty to charge has been retained. The automatic exception to any errors in respect to the charge, formerly contained in § 1–206, subsection (c), has been retained in Rule 46.

Rule 52. Findings by the court

(a) Findings. —

(1) In all actions tried upon the facts without a jury or with an advisory jury, the court shall find the facts specially and state separately its conclusions of law thereon and direct the entry of the appropriate judgment.

(2) Findings of fact and conclusions of law are necessary on decisions of any motion or order ex mero motu only when requested by a party and as provided by Rule 41(b). Similarly, findings of fact and conclusions of law are necessary on the granting or denying of a preliminary injunction or any other provisional remedy only when required by statute expressly relating to such remedy or requested by a party.

(3) If an opinion or memorandum of decision is filed, it will be sufficient if the findings of fact and conclusions of law appear therein.

(b) Amendment. — Upon motion of a party made not later than 10 days after entry of judgment the court may amend its findings or make additional findings and may amend the judgment accordingly. The motion may be made with a motion for a new trial pursuant to Rule 59.

(c) Review on appeal. — When findings of fact are made in actions tried by the court without a jury, the question of the sufficiency of the evidence to support the findings may be raised on appeal whether or not the party raising the question has made in the trial court an objection to such findings or has made a motion to amend them or a motion for judgment, or a request for specific findings.

Added by Laws 1967, c. 954, § 1. Amended by Laws 1969, c. 895, § 12.

Comment

Comment to this Rule as Originally Enacted. — This rule largely follows prior law, incorporating little of the federal rule. Former § 1–185 called for written findings and conclusions of law "upon trial of an issue of fact by the court." In respect to motions and provisional remedies, the Commission has been guided by the North Carolina case law. See Millhiser v. Balsley, 106 N.C. 433, 11 S.E. 314 (1890); Whitehead v. Hale, 118 N.C. 601, 24 S.E. 360 (1896). The reference to Rule 41(b) has to do with the situation when the trial judge is dismissing an action at the close of the plaintiff's evidence with the determination that the dismissal shall be on the merits. In this situation, both Rules 41 and 52 contemplate that the judge shall make written findings and conclusions.

Comment to the 1969 amendment. — (a) The amendment to Rule 52(a) and the addition of subsections (1) and (2) to section (a) merely assign numbers to the paragraphs. The other change is a matter of grammar.

The amendment added subsection (3) which is new. It provides that when findings are necessary by the court, it is sufficient if the findings of fact and conclusions of law appear in the decision or memorandum. The main purpose here is to make it clear that no particular form is required, and it is sufficient if the findings of fact and conclusions of law are distinguishable.

Rule 53. Referees

(a) Kinds of reference. —

(1) By Consent. — Any or all of the issues in an action may be referred upon the written consent of the parties except in actions to annul a marriage, actions for divorce, actions for divorce from bed and board, actions for alimony without the divorce or actions in which a ground of annulment or divorce is in issue.

(2) Compulsory. — Where the parties do not consent to a reference, the court may, upon the application of any party or on its own motion, order a reference in the following cases:

a. Where the trial of an issue requires the examination of a long or complicated account; in which case the referee may be directed to hear and decide the whole issue, or to report upon any specific question of fact involved therein.

b. Where the taking of an account is necessary for the information of the court before judgment, or for carrying a judgment or order into effect.

c. Where the case involves a complicated question of boundary, or requires a personal view of the premises.

d. Where a question of fact arises outside the pleadings, upon motion or otherwise, at any stage of the action.

(b) Jury trial. —

(1) Where the reference is by consent, the parties waive the right to have any of the issues within the scope of the reference passed on by a jury.

(2) A compulsory reference does not deprive any party of his right to a trial by jury, which right he may preserve by

a. Objecting to the order of compulsory reference at the time it is made, and

b. By filing specific exceptions to particular findings of fact made by the referee within 30 days after the referee files his report with the clerk of the court in which the action is pending, and

c. By formulating appropriate issues based upon the exceptions taken and demanding a jury trial upon such issues. Such issues shall be tendered at the same time the exceptions to the referee's report are filed. If there is a trial by jury upon any issue referred, the trial shall be only upon the evidence taken before the referee.

(c) Appointment. — The parties may agree in writing upon one or more persons not exceeding three, and a reference shall be ordered to such person or persons in appropriate cases. If the parties do not agree, the court shall appoint one or more referees, not exceeding three, but no person shall be appointed referee to whom all parties in the action object.

(d) Compensation. — The compensation to be allowed a referee shall be fixed by the court and charged in the bill of costs. After appointment of a referee, the court may from time to time order advancements by one or more of the parties of sums to be applied to the referee's compensation. Such advancements may be apportioned between the parties in such manner as the court sees fit. Advancements so made shall be taken into account in the final fixing of costs and such adjustments made as the court then deems proper.

(e) Powers. — The order of reference to the referee may specify or limit his powers and may direct him to report only upon particular issues or to do or perform particular acts or to receive and report evidence only and may fix the time and place for beginning and closing the hearings and for the filing of the referee's report. Subject to the specifications and limitations stated in the order, every referee has power to administer oaths in any proceeding before him, and has generally the power vested in a referee by law. The referee shall have the same power to grant adjournments and to allow amendments to pleadings and to the summons as the judge and upon the same terms and with like effect. The referee shall have the same power as the judge to preserve order and punish all violations thereof, to compel the attendance of witnesses before him by attachment, and to punish them as for contempt for nonattendance or for refusal to be sworn or to testify. The parties may procure the attendance of witnesses before the referee by the issuance and service of subpoenas as provided in Rule 45.

(f) Proceedings. —

(1) Meetings. — When a reference is made, the clerk shall forthwith furnish the referee with a copy of the order of reference. Upon receipt thereof unless the order of reference otherwise provides, the referee shall forthwith set a time and place for the first meeting of the parties or their attorneys to be held within 20 days after the date of the order of reference and shall notify the parties or their attorneys. It is the duty of the referee to proceed with all reasonable diligence. Any party, on notice to all other parties and the referee, may apply to the court for an order requiring the referee to expedite the proceedings and to make his report. If a party fails to appear at the time and place appointed, the referee may proceed ex parte, or, in his discretion, may adjourn the proceedings to a future day, giving notice to the absent party of the adjournment.

(2) Statement of Accounts. — When matters of accounting are in issue before the referee, he may prescribe the form in which the accounts shall be submitted and in any proper case may require or receive in evidence a statement by a certified public accountant or other qualified accountant who is called as a witness. Upon objection of a party to any of the items thus submitted or upon a showing that the form of statement is insufficient, the referee may require a different form of statement to be furnished, or the accounts of specific items thereof to be proved by oral examination of the accounting parties or upon written interrogatories or in such other manner as he directs.

(3) Testimony Reduced to Writing. — The testimony of all witnesses must be reduced to writing by the referee, or by someone acting under his direction and shall be filed in the cause and constitute a part of the record.

(g) Report. —

(1) Contents and Filing. — The referee shall prepare a report upon the matters submitted to him by the order of reference and shall include therein his decision on all matters so submitted. If required to make findings of fact and conclusions of law, he shall set them forth separately in the report. He shall file the report with the clerk of the court in which the action is pending and unless otherwise directed by the order of reference, shall file with it a transcript of the

proceedings and of the evidence and the original exhibits. Before filing his report a referee may submit a draft thereof to counsel for all parties for the purpose of receiving their suggestions. The clerk shall forthwith mail to all parties notice of the filing.

(2) Exceptions and Review. — All or any part of the report may be excepted to by any party within 30 days from the filing of the report. Thereafter, and upon 10 days' notice to the other parties, any party may apply to the judge for action on the report. The judge after hearing may adopt, modify or reject the report in whole or in part, render judgment, or may remand the proceedings to the referee with instructions. No judgment may be rendered on any reference except by the judge.

Added by Laws 1967, c. 954, § 1. Amended by Laws 1969, c. 895, § 13.

Comment

Comment to this Rule as Originally Enacted. — Generally, the rules leave the reference practice as it was. But some changes are made.

Section (a). — The Commission has included all of the grounds for compulsory reference found in former § 1-189 except that providing for reference in actions "of which the courts of equity ... had exclusive jurisdiction" prior to 1868.

Section (b). — In keeping with prior practice, the rule affirms the right of jury trial in compulsory reference cases. It goes further, and spells out, as former §§ 1-188 to 1-195 did not, just how the right of jury trial is to be preserved. The method of preserving jury trial is essentially the same as that required by the case law. See Bartlett v. Hopkins, 235 N.C. 165, 69 S.E.2d 236 (1952).

Section (c). — This section essentially makes no change.

Section (d). — The Commission thought it would be useful to include, as former §§ 1-188 to 1-195 did not, some details in respect to the compensation of referees.

Section (e). — The first sentence specifying the allowable flexibility in the order of reference is new. So far as the powers of the referee are concerned, they remain essentially unchanged except as enlarged by section (f).

Section (f). — Former §§ 1-188 to 1-195 contained no equivalent to subsection (2) but the Commission believes the new authority will be useful.

Section (g). — Here, for purposes of clarity, the rules goes into more detail than did former §§ 1-188 to 1-195 but the main outlines of the prior practice are retained.

Comment to the 1969 amendment. — *Section (a).* — Rule 53(a) previously provided that all issues in an action may be referred upon the written consent of the parties except in actions to annul a marriage, and actions for divorce and separation.

There being no such action as an "action for divorce and separation," this ground has been deleted. The 1969 amendment added to the list: actions for divorce, actions for divorce from bed and board, actions for alimony without the divorce or actions in which a ground of annulment or divorce is in issue. This language now conforms to previous rules concerning reference in domestic relations cases.

ARTICLE 7

Judgment

Rule 54. Judgments

(a) Definition.—A judgment is either interlocutory or the final determination of the rights of the parties.

(b) Judgment upon multiple claims or involving multiple parties.—When more than one claim for relief is presented in an action, whether as a claim, counterclaim, crossclaim, or third-party claim, or when multiple parties are involved, the court may enter a final judgment as to one or more but fewer than all of the claims or parties only if there is no just reason for delay and it is so determined in the judgment. Such judgment shall then be subject to review by appeal or as otherwise provided by these rules or other statutes. In the absence of entry of such a final judgment, any order or other form of decision, however designated, which adjudicates fewer than all the claims or the rights and liabilities of fewer than all the parties shall not terminate the action as to any of the claims or parties and shall not then be subject to review either by appeal or otherwise except as expressly provided by these rules or other statutes. Similarly, in the absence of entry of such a final judgment, any order or other form of decision is subject to revision at any time before the entry of judgment adjudicating all the claims and the rights and liabilities of all the parties.

(c) Demand for judgment.—A judgment by default shall not be different in kind from or exceed in amount that prayed for in the demand for judgment. Except as to a party against whom a judgment is entered by default, every final judgment shall grant the relief to which the party in whose favor it is rendered is entitled, even if the party has not demanded such relief in his pleadings.

Added by Laws 1967, c. 954, § 1.

Comment

Section (a). — This section carries forward the definition of a judgment formerly contained in § 1-208.

Section (b). — These rules, with their liberalized provisions for expanding the size of a lawsuit, make it highly desirable in the multi-party and multi-claim lawsuit that there be provision for expediting appeals, in certain instances, from rulings terminating the litigation in respect to fewer than all the parties or all the claims. Otherwise, it may well be, if the aggrieved party must delay his appeal until all parties and claims have been disposed of, that the delay will be intolerable. On the other hand, there may be cases which should be presented in their entirety to the appellate court even at the price of delaying one party or another.

In considering this section, it should be remembered that § 1-277 was left intact except as it is modified by this section. In other words, appeals will continue to lie only when a "party aggrieved" has been deprived of a "substantial right," or from a final judgment. The modification here is that when there is no just reason for delay and when there is an express determination to that effect, the unit to which the finality concept shall be applied is by this rule made a smaller one. Thus, if two claims are presented to the trial court and one of them is the subject of a disputed ruling, an appeal will lie if the ruling would have been appealable in an action involving that claim alone and if the judge makes the requisite determination.

Conversely, in the absence of a determination by the trial judge, it is clear that there can be no appellate review irrespective of the nature of the ruling of the trial court, unless elsewhere expressly authorized. Section 1-277 is not such an express authorization. Thus, it will be seen that in the absence of a determination by the trial judge, a lawyer can safely delay in prosecuting his appeal. When there is such a determination, the situation will not be as clear. There must be in addition either a final judgment or a ruling affecting a "substantial right" for an appeal to lie. When these conditions obtain has not heretofore been altogether clear, and will not be under these rules. The only course of safety will be to press for review.

Section (c). — This section is a restatement of prior law.

Rule 55. Default

(a) Entry.—When a party against whom a judgment for affirmative relief is sought has failed to plead or is otherwise subject to default judgment as provided by these rules or by statute and that fact is made to appear by affidavit, motion of attorney for the plaintiff, or otherwise, the clerk shall enter his default.

(b) Judgment.—Judgment by default may be entered as follows:

(1) By the Clerk.—When the plaintiff's claim against a defendant is for a sum certain or for a sum which can by computation be made certain, the clerk upon request of the plaintiff and upon affidavit of the amount due shall enter judgment for that amount and costs against the defendant, if the defendant has been defaulted for failure to appear and if the defendant is not an infant or incompetent person. A verified pleading may be used in lieu of an affidavit when the pleading contains information sufficient to determine or compute the sum certain.

In all cases wherein, pursuant to this rule, the clerk enters judgment by default upon a claim for debt which is secured by any pledge, mortgage, deed of trust or other contractual security in respect of which foreclosure may be had, or upon a claim to enforce a lien for unpaid taxes or assessments under G.S. 105-414,[1] the clerk may likewise make all further orders required to consummate foreclosure in accordance with the procedure provided in Article 29A of Chapter 1 of the General Statutes, entitled "Judicial Sales".

(2) By the Judge. —

a. In all other cases the party entitled to a judgment by default shall apply to the judge therefor; but no judgment by default shall be entered against an infant or incompetent person unless represented in the action by a guardian ad litem or other such representative who has appeared therein. If the party against whom judgment by default is sought has appeared in the action, that party (or, if appearing by representative, the representative) shall be served with written notice of the application for judgment at least three days prior to the hearing on such application. If, in order to enable the judge to enter judgment or to carry it into effect, it is necessary to take an account or to determine the amount of damages or to establish the truth of any averment by evidence or to take an investigation of any other matter, the judge may conduct such hearings or order such references as the judge deems necessary and proper and shall accord a right of trial by jury to the parties when and as required by the Constitution or by any statute of North Carolina. If the plaintiff seeks to establish paternity under Article 3 of Chapter 49 of the General Statutes and the defendant fails to appear, the judge shall enter judgment by default.

b. A motion for judgment by default may be decided by the court without a hearing if:

1. The motion specifically provides that the court will decide the motion for judgment by default without a hearing if the party against whom judgment is sought fails to serve a written response, stating the grounds for opposing the

motion, within 30 days of service of the motion; and

2. The party against whom judgment is sought fails to serve the response in accordance with this sub-subdivision.

(c) Service by publication.—When service of the summons has been made by published notice, no judgment shall be entered on default until the plaintiff shall have filed a bond, approved by the court, conditioned to abide such order as the court may make touching the restitution of any property collected or obtained by virtue of the judgment in case a defense is thereafter permitted and sustained; provided, that in actions involving the title to real estate or to foreclose mortgages thereon or in actions in which the State of North Carolina or a county or municipality thereof is the plaintiff such bond shall not be required.

(d) Setting aside default.—For good cause shown the court may set aside an entry of default, and, if a judgment by default has been entered, the judge may set it aside in accordance with Rule 60(b).

(e) Plaintiffs, counterclaimants, cross claimants.—The provisions of this rule apply whether the party entitled to the judgment by default is a plaintiff, a third-party plaintiff, or a party who has pleaded a crossclaim or counterclaim. In all cases a judgment by default is subject to the limitations of Rule 54(c).

(f) Judgment against the State of North Carolina.—No judgment by default shall be entered against the State of North Carolina or an officer in his official capacity or agency thereof unless the claimant establishes his claim or right to relief by evidence.

Added by Laws 1967, c. 954, § 1. Amended by Laws 1971, c. 542; Laws 1971, c.1101; Laws 1977, c. 675; Laws 1991, c. 278, § 1; Laws 1993 (Reg.Sess. 1994), c. 733, § 3; S.L. 1999–187, § 1, eff. Oct. 1, 1999.

[1] Repealed by Laws 1971, c. 806, § 3.

Comment

The State statutes presented a hodgepodge. Although former § 1–211 purported by its literal terms to give an exclusive listing of all the cases in which judgment by default final might be given, there were various other authorizations for such judgments scattered throughout the procedural and substantive sections. Section 1–212 then purportedly rounded out the scheme by providing that in all other cases "except those mentioned in § 1–211," judgment by default and inquiry might be given. This was obviously in literal conflict with all sections other than former § 1–211 which specifically authorized judgment by default final.

Although failure to file appropriate responsive pleading to a claim for affirmative relief is the usual basis for default judgment, other grounds appear: e.g. failure to file required bonds (former § 1–211(4) and § 1–525), failure to comply with pretrial discovery orders (former §§ 1–568.19, 8–89), and filing of "frivolous" pleadings (former § 1–219).

By § 1–209, clerks of superior court were authorized to enter all judgments by default authorized generally by § 1–209, and former §§ 1–211 and 1–213. This jurisdiction given clerks is concurrent with that of the superior court judge. Moody v. Howell, 229 N.C. 198, 49 S.E.2d 233 (1948). But some of the other scattered statutes authorizing judgments by default apparently contemplate that in the specific situations dealt with only the judge may enter judgment (e.g. § 1–525). Where the concurrent jurisdiction existed however, the appellate jurisdiction of the superior court judge as to the clerk's entry of judgment was retained (former § 1–220).

Although not made plain in the statutes, it has been held that though there is a "right" to a judgment upon default, the court may always in the exercise of its discretion allow time to answer when motion for judgment by default is made. Kruger v. Bank of Commerce, 123 N.C. 16, 31 S.E. 270 (1898). And of course, such judgments, as others, may be set aside after entry either by the clerk who entered them (former § 1–220), or by any appropriate judge for the usual reasons, i.e., excusable neglect, mistake, surprise; etc.

The main infirmities in the prior North Carolina practice as codified were thought to be (1) a general lack of symmetry and orderliness in the style and pattern of the various statutes, and (2) as a matter of substance, too much power and too much readiness in clerks to enter judgments which may thereafter be hard to set aside.

Accordingly, it was felt that federal Rule 55, with some few modifications to accommodate certain actions found in state practice and not in federal should be adopted, partially supplanting certain of the statutes which dealt with default judgments.

The federal rule approach actually contemplates a two-stage approach to judgment by default: The entry of default by the clerk; and thereafter the entry of judgment by default. Federal Rule 55(b)(1) provides that the clerk may only enter judgments by default in a very limited context, when (a) the claim is for a sum certain or for a computable sum, and (b) the default is for want of appearance; and (c) the defaulting party is neither an infant nor incompetent. This approach of limiting the clerk's power to the purely ministerial functions of (a) making entry of default in all cases, and (b) entering judgment itself in only this very limited context is felt to be wise.

The basic federal scheme continues by providing in 55(b)(2) that in all other cases than the very limited area spelled out in 55(b)(1), judgment itself may only be entered by the judge. Thus, in all cases where (a) the claim is not for a sum certain or computable, or (b) the defaulting party has appeared, or (c) the defaulting party is an infant or incompetent, only the judge may actually enter judgment. And except where the defaulting party has made no appearance, he must be given notice, and the entry of the judgment is in all instances in the discretion of the judge. It is believed that deliberately pointing up the discretionary nature of this power to enter judgment by default at this stage is wise, and will result in an overall saving of time by prompting full inquiry into the matter at the pre-entry stage rather than, as under prior practice, having discretion in the matter exercised usually after judgment has already been entered.

Note next that the delineation between judges' and clerks' power is not the delineation between judgments by "default final" and those by "default and inquiry." This distinction indeed is not retained in literal terms in the federal rule pattern. Obviously those very limited judgments within the power of the clerk to enter are judgments by default final. But the judge may enter either type under 55(b)(2). Instead of using this terminology, however, the rule as presented approaches the matter pragmatically by providing that when in order to enter final judgment something further must be done after entry of default, e.g. when an account must be taken or a jury trial had on an issue of damages or any other, the judge orders that done which is necessary. Thus, there is no intermediate judgment by "default and inquiry," but an entry of default in all cases and a final judgment by default entered only after everything required to its entry has been done. The same conceptions were involved in former § 1-212.

Section (c). — The Commission here attempted to take abundant precaution to protect the nonappearing defendant.

Section (d). — This section provides for setting aside default entries and judgments by default and ties the basis therefor into Rule 60(b) providing generally for setting aside judgments. Former § 1-220 and existing case law expressed this conception so that this involves no real change.

Section (e). — This section makes it plain that the general provisions of the rule apply as well to defendants and third-party plaintiffs as to plaintiffs seeking affirmative relief. This conception was expressed less artfully in former § 1-213 as to defendants and North Carolina actually had no express provision for default judgments in favor of third-party plaintiffs, or crossclaims. This is necessary now particularly in view of the third-party practice liberalization provided in other rules.

Section (f). — This section seems to be self-explanatory.

Rule 56. Summary judgment

(a) For claimant.—A party seeking to recover upon a claim, counterclaim, or crossclaim or to obtain a declaratory judgment may, at any time after the expiration of 30 days from the commencement of the action or after service of a motion for summary judgment by the adverse party, move with or without supporting affidavits for a summary judgment in his favor upon all or any part thereof.

(b) For defending party.—A party against whom a claim, counterclaim, or crossclaim is asserted or a declaratory judgment is sought, may, at any time, move with or without supporting affidavits for a summary judgment in his favor as to all or any part thereof.

(c) Motion and proceedings thereon. — The motion shall be served at least 10 days before the time fixed for the hearing. The adverse party may serve opposing affidavits at least two days before the hearing. If the opposing affidavit is not served on the other parties at least two days before the hearing on the motion, the court may continue the matter for a reasonable period to allow the responding party to prepare a response, proceed with the matter without considering the untimely served affidavit, or take such other action as the ends of justice require. For the purpose of this two-day requirement only, service shall mean personal delivery, facsimile transmission, or other means such that the party actually receives the affidavit within the required time.

The judgment sought shall be rendered forthwith if the pleadings, depositions, answers to interrogatories, and admissions on file, together with the affidavits, if any, show that there is no genuine issue as to any material fact and that any party is entitled to a judgment as a matter of law. A summary judgment, interlocutory in character, may be rendered on the issue of liability alone although there is genuine issue as to the amount of damages. Summary judgment, when appropriate, may be rendered against the moving party.

(d) Case not fully adjudicated on motion.—If on motion under this rule judgment is not rendered upon the whole case or for all the relief asked and a trial is necessary, the court at the hearing of the motion, by examining the pleadings and the evidence before it and by interrogating counsel, shall if practicable ascertain what material facts exist without substantial controversy and what material facts are actually and in good faith controverted. It shall thereupon make an order specifying the facts that appear without substantial controversy, including the extent to which the amount of damages or other relief is not in controversy, and directing such further proceedings in the action as are just. Upon the trial of the action the facts so specified shall be deemed established.

(e) Form of affidavits; further testimony; defense required.—Supporting and opposing affidavits shall be made on personal knowledge, shall set forth such facts as would be admissible in evidence, and shall show affirmatively that the affiant is competent to testify to the matters stated therein. Sworn or certified copies of all papers or parts thereof referred to in an affidavit shall be attached thereto or served therewith. The court may permit affidavits to be supplemented or opposed by depositions, answers to interrogatories, or further affidavits. When a motion for summary judgment is made and supported as provided in this rule, an adverse party may not rest upon the mere allegations or denials of his pleading, but his response, by affidavits or as otherwise provided in this rule, must set forth specific facts showing that there is a genuine issue for trial. If he does not so respond, summary judgment, if appropriate, shall be entered against him.

(f) When affidavits are unavailable.—Should it appear from the affidavits of a party opposing the motion that he cannot for reasons stated present by affidavit facts essential to justify his opposition, the court may refuse the application for judgment or may order a continuance to permit affidavits to be obtained or depositions to be taken or discovery to be had or may make such other order as is just.

(g) Affidavits made in bad faith.—Should it appear to the satisfaction of the court at any time that any of the affidavits presented pursuant to this rule are presented in bad faith or solely for the purpose of delay, the court shall forthwith order the party employing them to pay to the other party the amount of the reasonable expenses which the filing of the affidavits caused him to incur, including reasonable attorney's fees.

Added by Laws 1967, c. 954, § 1. Amended by S.L. 2000–127, § 6, eff. Oct. 1, 2000.

Comment

While it has long been urged in North Carolina, see Chadbourn, A Summary Judgment Procedure for North Carolina, 14 N.C.L. Rev., 211 (1936), and while, in one form or another, it has been adopted in a majority of the states, the procedure provided by this rule is wholly new to North Carolina. It adds a powerful new weapon for the just, swift and efficient disposition of claims or defenses patently without merit. The rule provides a device whereby it can expeditiously be determined whether or not there exists between the parties a genuine issue as to any material fact. It is not the purpose of the rule to resolve disputed material issues of fact but rather to determine if such issues exist.

Under prior procedure, if the pleadings disclosed an issue of fact, a trial was generally necessary even though there might in actuality be no genuine dispute at all as to the facts. It was enough if the issue was formally raised by the pleadings. Significantly, however, the code drafters were well aware that there might indeed be no issue of material fact present even though the pleadings appeared to present one. They thus provided that sham and irrelevant defenses could be stricken, former § 1–126, that irrelevant and redundant matter might be stricken, former § 1–153, and that a frivolous demurrer, answer or reply might be disregarded, former § 1–219. But, for reasons that need not be examined here, these devices have not proved equal to the task of identifying those claims or defenses in which there was no genuine dispute as to a material fact.

The great merit of the summary judgment is that it does provide a device for identifying the factually groundless claim or defense. It does so by enabling the parties to lay before the court materials extraneous to the pleadings. If these materials reveal any dispute as to a material fact, summary judgment is precluded. But as section (e) makes clear, a party cannot necessarily rely on the pleadings to show the existence of such a dispute.

The operation of the rule can be illustrated by supposing an action to recover damages for personal injuries. The sole defense offered is that the plaintiff's exclusive remedy is afforded by the Workmen's Compensation Act. The plaintiff moves for summary judgment, supporting his motion with affidavits which on their face show that the act is inapplicable to the defendant's enterprise. At the hearing on the motion, the defendant can forestall summary judgment simply by producing an affidavit, deposition or interrogatory or oral testimony tending to show that he does come under the act. If, on the other hand, he does nothing, entry of partial summary judgment, leaving for later jury determination the amount of damages, can be entered against him. He has failed to show that there is a genuine issue as to any material fact except damages.

The defendant might also move for a summary judgment in the case supposed. If he shows, without any contrary showing by the plaintiff, that the act applies, then it would be appropriate to enter judgment for the defendant. Of course, section (f) permits the refusal of the motion when a party presents reasons for his inability to present affidavits opposing the motion.

It will be observed that section (e) requires that supporting and opposing affidavits "shall be made on personal knowledge" and "shall set forth such facts as would be admissible in evidence."

Rule 57. Declaratory judgments

The procedure for obtaining a declaratory judgment pursuant to Article 26, Chapter 1, General Statutes of North Carolina, shall be in accordance with these rules, and the right to trial by jury may be demanded under the circumstances and in the manner provided in Rules 38 and 39. The existence of another adequate remedy does not preclude a judgment for declaratory relief in cases where it is appropriate. The court may order a prompt hearing of an action for a declaratory judgment and may advance it on the calendar.

Added by Laws 1967, c. 954, § 1.

Comment

This rule tracks the language of federal Rule 57, changed only by reference to the state statutory law, which spells out in detail the scope, procedure for obtaining, and effect of declaratory judgment. The comparable federal statutory law is 28 U.S.C.A. §§ 2201, 2202, a much more general statute than the state statute. The North Carolina Declaratory Judgment Act, to which reference is made, is essentially the Uniform Declaratory Judgment Act. The Commission felt that except for one minor change in respect of jury trial, the need for which is developed below, it should retain this basic statutory law and not substitute the more general federal type formulation. Professor Borchard, father of both, felt that state declaratory judgment acts should be more specific and detailed than the basic federal statutory authority needed to be. This separate practice rule simply refers to the basic act and in effect says (what is perhaps not strictly necessary in view of the coverage rule, Rule 1) that action for this relief as other actions shall be governed by these rules.

This rule does also make specific the right to jury trial as in other actions. Although this reflects a background of separate law and equity administration with resulting problems of jury right in the federal system in "new" kinds of actions, problems not presented in the North Carolina completely fused code practice, it does no harm to leave in this reference. Indeed, the North Carolina act itself, in § 1–261, states the basic right to jury trial of fact issues in this type of action.

The provision that, "The existence of another adequate remedy does not preclude a judgment for declaratory relief..." merely states more plainly and bolsters what is implicit in the act itself when in § 1–253 it is provided that the power to grant declaratory relief exists "whether or not further relief is or could be claimed." The federal act contains similar language in § 2201, but the federal rules draftsman thought it expedient to solidify this in the rule itself. No reason appears to depart from this. The critical substantive point here is that this language preserves the discretionary right of the court when asked to declare rights to decline to do so, possibly on the basis of existence of another remedy, but not necessarily to do so.

The provision for advancing trial of declaratory actions seems wise and would not apparently violate any State procedural customs or rules, within which peremptory settings are familiar practice.

Rule 58. Entry of judgment

Subject to the provisions of Rule 54(b), a judgment is entered when it is reduced to writing, signed by the judge, and filed with the clerk of court. The party designated by the judge or, if the judge does not otherwise designate, the party who prepares the judgment, shall serve a copy of the judgment upon all other parties within three days after the judgment is entered. Service and proof of service shall be in accordance with Rule 5. If service is by mail, three days shall be added to the time periods prescribed by Rule 50(b), Rule 52(b), and Rule 59. All time periods within which a party may further act pursuant to Rule 50(b), Rule 52(b), or Rule 59 shall be tolled for the duration of any period of noncompliance with this service requirement, provided however that no time period under Rule 50(b), Rule 52(b), or Rule 59 shall be tolled longer than 90 days from the date the judgment is entered. Subject to the provisions of Rule 7(b)(4), consent for the signing and entry of a judgment out of term, session, county, and district shall be deemed to have been given unless an express objection to such action was made on the record prior to the end of the term or session at which the matter was heard.

Notwithstanding any other law to the contrary, any judgment entered by a magistrate in a small claims action pursuant to Article 19 of Chapter 7A shall be entered in accordance with this Rule except judgments announced and signed in open court at the conclusion of a trial are considered to be served on the parties, and copies of any judgment not announced and signed in open court at the conclusion of a trial shall be served by the magistrate on all parties in accordance with this Rule, within three days after the judgment is entered. If service is by mail, three days shall be added to the time periods prescribed by G.S. 7A–228. All time periods within which a party may further act pursuant to G.S. 7A–228 shall be tolled for the duration of any period of noncompliance of this service requirement, provided that no time period shall be tolled longer than 90 days from the date judgment is entered.

Added by Laws 1967, c. 954, § 1. Amended by Laws 1993 (Reg.Sess., 1994), c. 594, § 1; S.L. 2005–163, § 2, eff. Oct. 1, 2005.

Comment

[Editor's Note: This Comment was removed at the request of the Revisor of Statutes, as it was no longer considered relevant in light of the complete revision by Laws 1993 (Reg.Sess., 1994), c. 594, § 1.]

Rule 59. New trials; amendment of judgments

(a) Grounds.—A new trial may be granted to all or any of the parties and on all or part of the issues for any of the following causes or grounds:

(1) Any irregularity by which any party was prevented from having a fair trial;

(2) Misconduct of the jury or prevailing party;

(3) Accident or surprise which ordinary prudence could not have guarded against;

(4) Newly discovered evidence material for the party making the motion which he could not, with reasonable diligence, have discovered and produced at the trial;

(5) Manifest disregard by the jury of the instructions of the court;

(6) Excessive or inadequate damages appearing to have been given under the influence of passion or prejudice;

(7) Insufficiency of the evidence to justify the verdict or that the verdict is contrary to law;

(8) Error in law occurring at the trial and objected to by the party making the motion, or

(9) Any other reason heretofore recognized as grounds for new trial.

On a motion for a new trial in an action tried without a jury, the court may open the judgment if one has been entered, take additional testimony, amend findings of fact and conclusions of law or make new findings and conclusions, and direct the entry of a new judgment.

(b) Time for motion.—A motion for a new trial shall be served not later than 10 days after entry of the judgment.

(c) Time for serving affidavits.—When a motion for new trial is based upon affidavits they shall be served with the motion. The opposing party has 10 days after such service within which to serve opposing affidavits, which period may be extended for an additional period not exceeding 30 days either by the court for good cause shown or by the parties by written stipulation. The court may permit reply affidavits.

(d) On initiative of court.—Not later than 10 days after entry of judgment the court of its own initiative, on notice to the parties and hearing, may order a new trial for any reason for which it might have granted a new trial on motion of a party, and in the order shall specify the grounds therefor.

(e) Motion to alter or amend a judgment.—A motion to alter or amend the judgment under section (a) of this rule shall be served not later than 10 days after entry of the judgment.

Added by Laws 1967, c. 954, § 1. Amended by S.L. 2014-115, § 1, eff. Aug. 11, 2014.

Comment

Section (a). — Here, in listing the grounds for new trial, the rule goes beyond the prior statutory law as set forth in former § 1-207 to include all those grounds for new trial which have been approved by North Carolina case law. Former § 1-207 made express mention of only three grounds for new trial—exceptions, insufficient evidence, and excessive damages. But the court has approved new trial in a number of other situations: Where the damages are inadequate, Hinton v. Cline, 238 N.C. 136, 76 S.E.2d 162 (1953); Where the verdict is defective, Vandiford v. Vandiford, 215 N.C. 461, 2 S.E.2d 364 (1939); Where there is misconduct of or affecting the jury, Keener v. Beal, 246 N.C. 247, 98 S.E.2d 19 (1957); In re Will of Hall, 252 N.C. 70, 113 S.E.2d 1 (1960); Where there is newly discovered evidence, Crissman v. Palmer, 225 N.C. 472, 35 S.E.2d 422 (1945); Where there are irregularities in the trial, Lupton v. Spencer, 173 N.C. 126, 91 S.E. 718 (1917); Where there is surprise, Hardy v. Hardy, 128 N.C. 178, 38 S.E. 815 (1901); When equity and justice so require, Walston v. Greene, 246 N.C. 617, 99 S.E.2d 805 (1957).

Section (b). — Here there is a new requirement as to the time within which a motion for new trial must be made. It will be observed that the time is keyed to the "entry of judgment." As to what constitutes "entry of judgment," see Rule 58.

Section (c). — While the practice prescribed here did not previously enjoy statutory sanction, a similar practice had been approved by the court. See Brown v. Town of Hillsboro, 185 N.C. 368, 117 S.E. 41 (1923); Allen v. Gooding, 174 N.C. 271, 93 S.E. 740 (1917).

Section (d). — Again, no prior statute is comparable to the section, but the Commission believes the practice has been approved by the Supreme Court. See Walston v. Greene, 246 N.C. 617, 99 S.E.2d 805 (1957).

Section (e). — This section would seem to be self-explanatory.

Rule 60. Relief from judgment or order

(a) Clerical mistakes.—Clerical mistakes in judgments, orders or other parts of the record and errors therein arising from oversight or omission may be corrected by the judge at any time on his own initiative or on the motion of any party and after such notice, if any, as the judge orders. During the pendency of an appeal, such mistakes may be so corrected before the appeal is docketed in the appellate division, and thereafter while the appeal is pending may be so corrected with leave of the appellate division.

(b) Mistakes; inadvertence; excusable neglect; newly discovered evidence; fraud, etc.—On motion and upon such terms as are just, the court may relieve a party or his legal representative from a final judgment, order, or proceeding for the following reasons:

(1) Mistake, inadvertence, surprise, or excusable neglect;

(2) Newly discovered evidence which by due diligence could not have been discovered in time to move for a new trial under Rule 59(b);

(3) Fraud (whether heretofore denominated intrinsic or extrinsic), misrepresentation, or other misconduct of an adverse party;

(4) The judgment is void;

(5) The judgment has been satisfied, released, or discharged, or a prior judgment upon which it is based has been reversed or otherwise vacated, or it is no longer equitable that the judgment should have prospective application; or

(6) Any other reason justifying relief from the operation of the judgment.

The motion shall be made within a reasonable time, and for reasons (1), (2) and (3) not more than one year after the judgment, order, or proceeding was entered or taken. A motion under this section does not affect the finality of a judgment or suspend its operation. This rule does not limit the power of a court to entertain an independent action to relieve a party from a judgment, order, or proceeding, or to set aside a judgment for fraud upon the court. The procedure for obtaining any relief from a judgment, order, or proceeding shall be by motion as prescribed in these rules or by an independent action.

(c) Judgments rendered by the clerk.—The clerk may, in respect of judgments rendered by himself, exercise the same powers authorized in sections (a) and (b). The judge has like powers in respect of such judgments. Where such powers are exercised by the clerk, appeals may be had to the judge in the manner provided by law.

Added by Laws 1967, c. 954, § 1.

Comment

The prior North Carolina law was that the court could correct clerical mistakes at any time by motion in the cause, either in or out of term. The motion to correct a clerical error need not be made to the same judge who tried the cause.

There were two statutes dealing with the subject matter. Former § 1-220 provided in effect that where there had been personal service upon the defendant the court could set aside a judgment for mistake, surprise, inadvertence or excusable neglect within one year from the rendition of the judgment. Section 1-108 formerly provided in effect that where there had been constructive service only the defendant must be allowed to defend even after judgment at any time within one year after notice of the judgment but within five years after rendition of the judgment. In any such case the judge must find the facts concerning the mistake, surprise, etc., and that the defendant had a meritorious defense and he must reduce this information to writing.

In reference to section (b)(3) of the federal rule, North Carolina makes a distinction in extrinsic and intrinsic fraud and in the manner in which such judgment may be attacked.

There is not as much difference between the federal rule and the North Carolina as first blush would indicate. Actually, the federal rule uses very succinct language to incorporate most of the results obtained under the North Carolina statutes and case law. As noted above the prior North Carolina practice distinguished between the rights of a defendant who was personally served and a defendant against whom constructive notice was served.

Rule 61. Harmless error

No error in either the admission or exclusion of evidence and no error or defect in any ruling or order or in anything done or omitted by any of the parties is ground for granting a new trial or for setting aside a verdict or for vacating, modifying, or otherwise disturbing a judgment or order, unless refusal to take such action amounts to the denial of a substantial right.

Added by Laws 1967, c. 954, § 1.

Comment

The substance of this rule has been many times endorsed by the court. See e.g., Collins v. Lamb, 215 N.C. 719, 2 S.E.2d 863 (1937).

Rule 62. Stay of proceedings to enforce a judgment

(a) Automatic stay; exceptions—Injunctions and receiverships.—Except as otherwise stated herein, no execution shall issue upon a judgment nor shall proceedings be taken for its enforcement until the expiration of the time provided in the controlling statute or rule of appellate procedure for giving notice of appeal from the judgment. Unless otherwise ordered by the court, an interlocutory or final judgment in an action for an injunction or in a receivership action shall not be stayed during the period after its entry and until an appeal is taken or during the pendency of an appeal. The provisions of section (c) govern the suspending, modifying, restoring, or granting of an injunction during the pendency of an appeal.

(b) Stay on motion for new trial or for judgment.—In its discretion and on such conditions for the security of the adverse party as are proper, the court may stay the execution of or any proceedings to enforce a judgment pending the disposition of a motion for a new trial or to alter or amend a judgment made pursuant to Rule 59, or of a motion for relief from a judgment or order made pursuant to Rule 60, or of a motion for judgment made pursuant to Rule 50, or of a motion for amendment to the findings or for additional findings made pursuant to Rule 52(b). If the time provided in the controlling statute or rule of appellate procedure for giving notice of appeal from the judgment had not expired before a stay under this subsection was entered, that time shall begin to run immediately upon the expiration of any stay under this section, and no execution shall issue nor shall proceedings be taken for enforcement of the judgment until the expiration of that time.

(c) Injunction pending appeal.—When an appeal is taken from an interlocutory or final judgment granting, dissolving, or denying an injunction, the court in its discretion may suspend, modify, restore, or grant an injunction during the pendency of the appeal upon such terms as to bond or otherwise as it considers proper for the security of the rights of the adverse party.

(d) Stay upon appeal.—When an appeal is taken, the appellant may obtain a stay of execution, subject to the exceptions contained in section (a), by proceeding in accordance with and subject to the conditions of G.S. 1–289, G.S. 1–290, G.S. 1–291, G.S. 1–292, G.S. 1–293, G.S. 1–294, and G.S. 1–295.

When stay is had by giving supersedeas bond, the bond may be given at or after the time of filing the notice of appeal or of procuring the order allowing the appeal as the case may be, and stay is then effective when the supersedeas bond is approved by the court.

(e) Stay in favor of North Carolina, city, county, local board of education, or agency thereof.—When an appeal is taken by the State of North Carolina, or a city or a county thereof, a local board of education, or an officer in his official capacity or agency thereof or by direction of any department or agency of the State of North Carolina or a city or county thereof or a local board of education and the operation or enforcement of the judgment is stayed, no bond, obligation, or other security shall be required from the appellant.

(f) Power of appellate court not limited.—The provisions of this rule do not limit any power of an appellate court or of a judge or justice thereof to stay proceedings during the pendency of an appeal or to suspend, modify, restore, or grant an injunction during the pendency of an appeal or to make any order appropriate to preserve the status quo or the effectiveness of the judgment subsequently to be entered.

(g) Stay of judgment as to multiple claims or multiple parties.—When a court has ordered a final judgment under the conditions stated in Rule 54(b), the court may stay enforcement of that judgment until the entering of a subsequent judgment or judgments and may prescribe such conditions as are necessary to secure the benefit thereof to the party in whose favor the judgment is entered.

(h) Right to immediate interlocutory appeal of order granting or denying injunctive relief in as-applied constitutional challenge.—Notwithstanding any other provision of law, a party shall have the right of immediate appeal (i) from an adverse ruling by a trial court granting or denying interlocutory, temporary, or permanent injunctive or declaratory relief restraining the State or a political subdivision of the State from enforcing the operation or execution of an act of the General Assembly as applied against a party in a civil action or (ii) from an adverse ruling by a trial court denying a motion to stay an injunction restraining the State or a political subdivision of the State from enforcing the operation or execution of an act of the General Assembly as applied against a party in a civil action. This subsection only applies where the State or a political subdivision of the State is a party in the civil action. This subsection does not apply to facial challenges heard by a three-judge panel pursuant to G.S. 1–267.1.

Added by Laws 1967, c. 954, § 1. Amended by Laws 1973, c. 91; Laws 1979, c. 820, § 10; Laws 1987, c. 462, § 1; Laws 1989, c. 377, §§ 3, 4; S.L. 2014–100, § 18B.16(d), eff. Aug. 7, 2014.

Comment

While in general this rule leaves the present North Carolina law intact in this area, it does make some specific provisions in order to tie in the procedure here employed to other rules.

Rule 63. Disability of a judge

If by reason of death, sickness or other disability, resignation, retirement, expiration of term, removal from office, or other reason, a judge before whom an action has been tried or a hearing has been held is unable to perform the duties to be performed by the court under these rules after a verdict is returned or a trial or hearing is otherwise concluded, then those duties, including entry of judgment, may be performed:

(1) In actions in the superior court by the judge senior in point of continuous service on the superior court regularly holding the courts of the district. If this judge is under a disability, then the resident judge of the district senior in point of service on the superior court may perform those duties. If a resident judge, while holding court in the judge's own district suffers disability and there is no other resident judge of the district, such duties may be performed by a judge of the superior court designated by the Chief Justice of the Supreme Court.

(2) In actions in the district court, by the chief judge of the district, or if the chief judge is disabled, by any judge of the district court designated by the Director of the Administrative Office of the Courts.

If the substituted judge is satisfied that he or she cannot perform those duties because the judge did not preside at the trial or hearing or for any other reason, the judge may, in the judge's discretion, grant a new trial or hearing.

Added by Laws 1967, c. 954, § 1. Amended by S.L. 2001-379, § 7, eff. Aug. 18, 2001.

Comment

Formerly, there was no statutory prescription in respect to the problem dealt with by this rule. It can be seen, however, that in particular cases where a verdict has already been returned or findings of fact and conclusions of law filed and then the trial judge is unable to continue to function, it will be highly useful to have some judge authorized to step into the breach.

ARTICLE 8

Miscellaneous

Rule 64. Seizure of person or property

At the commencement of and during the course of an action, all remedies providing for seizure of person or property for the purpose of securing satisfaction of the judgment ultimately to be entered in the action are available under the circumstances and in the manner provided by the law of this State.

Added by Laws 1967, c. 954, § 1.

Comment

This rule seems to be self-explanatory.

Rule 65. Injunctions

(a) Preliminary injunction; notice.—No preliminary injunction shall be issued without notice to the adverse party.

(b) Temporary restraining order; notice; hearing; duration. – A temporary restraining order may be granted without written or oral notice to the adverse party or that party's attorney only if (i) it clearly appears from specific facts shown by affidavit or by verified complaint that immediate and irreparable injury, loss, or damage will result to the applicant before the adverse party or that party's attorney can be heard in opposition, and (ii) the applicant's attorney certifies to the court in writing the efforts, if any, that have been made to give the notice and the reasons supporting the claim that notice should not be required. Every temporary restraining order granted without notice shall be endorsed with the date and hour of issuance; shall be filed forthwith in the clerk's office and entered of record; shall define the injury and state why it is irreparable and why the order was granted without notice; and shall expire by its terms within such time after entry, not to exceed 10 days, as the judge fixes, unless within the time so fixed the order, for good cause shown, is extended for a like period or unless the party against whom the order is directed consents that it may be extended for a longer period. The reasons for the extension shall be entered of record. In case a temporary restraining order is granted without notice and a motion for a preliminary injunction is made, it shall be set down for hearing at the earliest possible time and takes precedence over all matters except older matters of the same character; and when the motion comes on for hearing, the party who obtained the temporary restraining order shall proceed with a motion for a preliminary injunction, and, if he does not do so, the judge shall dissolve the temporary restraining order. On two days' notice to the party who obtained the temporary restraining order without notice or on such shorter notice to that party as the judge may prescribe, the adverse party may appear and move its dissolution or modification and in that event the judge shall proceed to hear and determine such motion as expeditiously as the ends of justice require. Damages may be awarded in an order for dissolution as provided in section (e).

(c) Security.—No restraining order or preliminary injunction shall issue except upon the giving of security by the applicant, in such sum as the judge deems proper, for the payment of such costs and damages as may be incurred or suffered by any party who is found to have been wrongfully enjoined or restrained. No such security shall be required of the State of North Carolina or of any county or municipality thereof, or any officer or agency thereof acting in an official capacity, but damages may be awarded against such party in accord with this rule. In suits between spouses relating to support, alimony, custody of children, separation, divorce from bed and board, and absolute divorce no such security shall be required of the plaintiff spouse as a condition precedent to the issuing of a temporary restraining order or preliminary injunction enjoining the defendant spouse from interfering with, threatening, or in any way molesting the plaintiff spouse during pendency of the suit, until further order of the court, but damages may be awarded against such party in accord with this rule.

A surety upon a bond or undertaking under this rule submits himself to the jurisdiction of the court and irrevocably appoints the clerk of the court as his agent upon whom any papers affecting his liability on the bond or undertaking may be served. His liability may be enforced on motion without the necessity of an independent action. The motion and such notice of the motion as the court prescribes may be served on the clerk of the court, who shall forthwith mail copies to the persons giving the security and the sureties thereon if their addresses are known.

(d) Form and scope of injunction or restraining order.—Every order granting an injunction and every restraining order shall set forth the reasons for its issuance; shall be specific in terms; shall describe in reasonable detail, and not by reference to the complaint or other document, the act or acts enjoined or restrained; and is binding only upon the parties to the action, their officers, agents, servants, employees, and attorneys, and upon those persons in active concert or participation with them who receive actual notice in any manner of the order by personal service or otherwise.

(e) Damages on dissolution.—An order or judgment dissolving an injunction or restraining order may include an award of damages against the party procuring the injunction and the sureties on his undertaking without a showing of malice or want of probable cause in procuring the injunction. The damages may be determined by the judge, or he may direct that they be determined by a referee or jury.

Added by Laws 1967, c. 954, § 1. Amended by S.L. 2001–379, § 8, eff. Oct. 1, 2001.

Comment

Practice Prior to Rule. — While a plaintiff may be entitled to legal and equitable relief in a civil action, the preliminary injunction continues to be an extraordinary and provisional remedy and will not be granted except where adequate relief cannot be had without it. Town of Clinton v. Ross, 226 N.C. 682, 40 S.E.2d 593 (1946).

When temporary injunction issued. — The form of relief may be a preliminary injunction or restraining order, which may be issued:

(1) To preserve the status quo pending the action. As a rule, a mandatory order or injunction will not be made as a preliminary injunction except when the injury is immediate, pressing, irreparable, and clearly established. Seaboard Air Line Ry. v. Atlantic Coast Line Ry., 237 N.C. 88, 74 S.E.2d 430 (1953).

(2) To protect the subject matter of the action.

(3) To prevent fraudulent transfer. See § 1–485.

Time of issuing. — The preliminary injunction may be granted at the time of commencing the action or at any time afterwards, before judgment. Requisites are (a) affidavits; (b) summons.

When notice required. — When the restraining order is asked for as a preliminary motion, notice is not required, but if the judge deems it proper that the other party should be heard, he may issue a show cause order, and the defendant may, in the meantime, be restrained. A restraining order cannot be granted by a judge for a longer time than twenty days, without notice. After the defendant has answered, an injunction will not be granted except upon notice. However, the defendant may be restrained pending such action. See former §§ 1–490, 1–491, 1–492.

Undertaking. — Upon granting a restraining order or an order for an injunction, the judge shall require a written undertaking. See former § 1–496.

Appeals. — Upon appeal from a judgment vacating a restraining order or denying a perpetual injunction where the injunction is the principal relief sought, the court, in its discretion, may require plaintiff to give bond and continue the restraining order pending the appeal. See § 1–500.

Damages in injunction. — A judgment dissolving an injunction carries with it judgment for damages against the party procuring it and against his sureties without the requirement of malice or want of probable cause, which damages may be obtained by a reference or otherwise, as the judge directs. See former § 1–497.

Practice under Rule. — This rule is substantially the same as federal Rule 65.

Section (a). — This section provides that no preliminary injunction shall be issued without notice to the adverse party. While the rule does not specify the type of notice, proper service of the complaint and summons upon the party or his proper agent have been held sufficient. The court must have in personam jurisdiction. Section (b) specifies the time for hearing. On the hearing, the pleadings, if verified, and other affidavits have been held sufficient to grant a preliminary injunction.

The principal change here is the requirement of notice. Ordinarily, the purpose of the preliminary or interlocutory injunction is to preserve the status quo until the issues are determined after final hearing. Section (b) takes care of the situation where immediate action is necessary.

Section (b). — A restraining order is a temporary order, entered in an action, without notice, if necessary, and upon a summary showing of its necessity in order to prevent immediate and irreparable injury, pending a fuller hearing and determination of the rights of the parties. The ex parte restraining order is, under this section, then, subject to definite time limitations and is to preserve the status quo until the motion for a preliminary injunction can, after notice, be brought on for hearing and decision. Such ex parte order must be upon verified facts. Note, also, that such order granted without notice expires by its terms within such time after entry, not to exceed ten days, unless the time is, for good cause shown, extended.

Section (c). — The requirements with respect to security as set forth in this section are similar to the requirements of former § 1–496.

In general, there are two methods for enforcement of liability on a bond or other security given to secure the issuance of a restraining order or preliminary injunction: An independent action or motion for judgment in the injunction action. The second paragraph of section (c) deals with this second method of enforcement. Since this motion procedure is part of the "equity suit," there is no right to trial by jury on the issues raised. If, however, an independent action is brought, this would be one of law, and a right to jury would be preserved.

Section (d). — The requirement that the judge state the reasons for granting the injunction and the acts to be restrained is new. Under prior law no particular form of order was required, although the decisions hold that "the defendant shall be given authentic notification of the mandate of the court or judge." Davis v. Champion Fiber Co., 150 N.C. 84, 63 S.E. 178 (1908). There does not appear to be a statute as explicit as the final clause of section (d) with respect to the parties affected by the action.

Section (e). — This is substantially the same provision as is found in former § 1–497.

Rules 66 to 67. Omitted

Rule 68. Offer of judgment and disclaimer

(a) Offer of judgment.—At any time more than 10 days before the trial begins, a party defending against a claim may serve upon the adverse party an offer to allow judgment to be taken against him for the money or property or to the effect specified in his offer, with costs then accrued. If within 10 days after the service of the offer the adverse party serves written notice that the offer is accepted, either party may then file the offer and notice of acceptance together with proof of service thereof and thereupon the clerk shall enter judgment. An offer not accepted within 10 days after its service shall be deemed withdrawn and evidence of the offer is not admissible except in a proceeding to determine costs. If the judgment finally obtained by the offeree is not more favorable than the offer, the offeree must pay the costs incurred after the making of the offer. The fact that an offer is made but not accepted does not preclude a subsequent offer.

(b) Conditional offer of judgment for damages.—A party defending against a claim arising in contract or quasi contract may, with his responsive pleading, serve upon the claimant an offer in writing that if he fails in his defense, the damages shall be assessed at a specified sum; and if the claimant signifies his acceptance thereof in writing within 20 days of the service of such offer, and on the trial prevails, his damages shall be assessed accordingly. If the claimant does not accept the offer, he must prove his damages as if the offer had not been made. If the damages assessed in the claimant's favor do not exceed the sum stated in the offer, the party defending shall recover the costs in respect to the question of damages.

Added by Laws 1967, c. 954, § 1.

Comment

Both sections of the rule would seem to be self-explanatory. They encompass the substance of former §§ 1–541 and 1–542. Former § 1–543, permitting a disclaimer of title by the defendant in trespass actions together with an offer to make amends, was repealed on the theory that its purpose can be accomplished by use of section (a).

Rule 68.1. Confession of judgment

(a) For present or future liability.—A judgment by confession may be entered without action at any time in accordance with the procedure prescribed by this rule. Such judgment may be for money due or for money that may become due. Such judgment may also be entered for alimony or for support of minor children.

(b) Procedure.—A prospective defendant desiring to confess judgment shall file with the clerk of the superior court as provided in section (c) a statement in writing signed and verified or sworn to by such defendant authorizing the entry of judgment for the amount stated. The statement shall contain the name of the prospective plaintiff, his county of residence, the name of the defendant, his county of residence, and shall concisely show why the defendant is or may become liable to the plaintiff.

If either the plaintiff or defendant is not a natural person, for the purposes of this rule its county of residence shall be considered to be the county in which it has its principal place of business, whether in this State or not.

(c) Where entered.—Judgment by confession may be entered only in the county where the defendant resides or has real property or in the county where the plaintiff resides but the entry of judgment in any county shall be conclusive evidence that this section has been complied with.

(d) Form of entry.—When a statement in conformity with this rule is filed with the clerk of the superior court, the clerk shall enter judgment thereon for the amount confessed, and docket the judgment as in other cases, with costs, together with disbursements. The statement, with the judgment, shall become the judgment roll.

(e) Force and effect.—Judgments entered in conformity with this rule shall have the same effect as other judgments except that no judgment by confession shall be held to be res judicata as to any fact in any civil action except in an action on the judgment confessed. When such judgment is for alimony or support of minor children, the failure of the defendant to make any payments as required by such judgment shall subject him to such penalties as may be adjudged by the court as in any other case of contempt of its orders. Executions may be issued and enforced in the same manner as upon other judgments. When the full amount of the judgment is not all due, or is payable in installments, and the installments are not all due, execution may issue upon such judgment for the collection of such sums as have become due and shall be in usual form. Notwithstanding the issue and satisfaction of such execution, the judgment remains as security for the sums thereafter to become due; and whenever any further sum becomes due, execution may in like manner be issued.

Added by Laws 1967, c. 954, § 1. Amended by Laws 1987, c. 288, § 1.

Comment

While this rule largely follows former §§ 1–247, 1–248 and 1–249, there are some changes.

That part of former § 1–247 expressly allowing judgment to be confessed "to secure any person against contingent liability on behalf of the defendant" has been omitted. Otherwise, there has been no change in respect to the subject matter for which judgment may be confessed.

The provisions in respect to the particular county in which judgment may be confessed have been changed. Formerly, § 1–249 permitted a judgment to be confessed where the defendant resided or "has property." Since it would seem to be a simple matter for a defendant to have property in any county (simply by wearing his clothes there), the possibility of abuse of the procedure by nonresidents for the benefit of nonresidents is present. The rule therefore specifies that the property must be real property. More importantly, it provides that judgment may be confessed also in the county of the plaintiff's residence. It will be observed that section (c), after stating the appropriate counties for the confession of judgment, provides that entry of judgment is conclusive evidence that the section has been complied with. This, in effect, puts the responsibility on the clerks for the enforcement of this section. At any rate, it prevents any nice inquiry as to whether it has been complied with.

Rule 69. Omitted

Rule 70. Judgment for specific acts; vesting title

If a judgment directs a party to execute a conveyance of land or to deliver deeds or other documents or to perform any other specific act and the party fails to comply within the time specified, the judge may direct the act to be done at the cost of the disobedient party by some other person appointed by the judge and the act when so done has like effect as if done by the party. On application of the party entitled to performance, the clerk shall issue a writ of attachment or sequestration against the property of the disobedient party to compel obedience to the judgment. The judge may also in proper cases adjudge the party in contempt. If real or personal property is within the State, the judge in lieu of directing a conveyance thereof may enter a judgment divesting the title of any party and vesting it in others and such judgment has the effect of a conveyance executed in due form of law. When any order or judgment is for the delivery of possession, the party in whose favor it is entered is entitled to execution upon application to the clerk upon payment of the necessary fees.

Added by Laws 1967, c. 954, § 1.

Comment

While preserving the essence of the former vesting statute, § 1–227, the rule as drafted makes two changes. First, where a party has been directed in a judgment to perform an act and has failed to so perform, it imports into the statutes for the first time authorization for the court to have someone else to perform the act with "like effect as if done by the party." Perhaps this authorization is most obviously applicable to specific performance decrees, yet it should be noted that it is not limited to transfers of title but extends to all acts which the court might properly direct in a judgment. Second, the rule makes it clear that a judgment divesting title and vesting it in others "has the effect of a conveyance" without further words being added to the effect that the judgment "shall be regarded as a deed of conveyance." See Morris v. White, 96 N.C. 91, 2 S.E. 254 (1887), and Evans v. Brendle, 173 N.C. 149, 91 S.E. 723 (1917).

Rules 71 to 83. Omitted

Rule 84. Forms

The following forms are sufficient under these rules and are intended to indicate the simplicity and brevity of statement which the rules contemplate:

(1) Complaint on a Promissory Note.

1. On or about ...., ..., defendant executed and delivered to plaintiff a promissory note [in the following words and figures: (here set out the note verbatim)]; [a copy of which is hereto annexed as Exhibit A]; [whereby defendant promised to pay to plaintiff or order on ..., ..., the sum of .... dollars with interest thereon at the rate of ... percent per annum].

2. Defendant owes to plaintiff the amount of said note and interest.

Wherefore, plaintiff demands judgment against defendant for the sum of .... dollars, interest and costs.

(2) Complaint on Account.

Defendant owes plaintiff .... dollars according to the account hereto annexed as Exhibit A.

Wherefore, plaintiff demands judgment against defendant for the sum of .... dollars, interest and costs.

(3) Complaint for Negligence.

1. On ...., ..., at [name of place where accident occurred], defendant negligently drove a motor vehicle against plaintiff who was then crossing said street.

2. Defendant was negligent in that:

(a) Defendant drove at an excessive speed.

(b) Defendant drove through a red light.

(c) Defendant failed to yield the right-of-way to plaintiff in a marked crosswalk.

3. As a result plaintiff was thrown down and had his leg broken and was otherwise injured, was prevented from transacting his business, suffered great pain of body and mind, and incurred expenses for medical attention and hospitalization [in the sum of one thousand dollars] (or) [in an amount not yet determined].

Wherefore, plaintiff demands judgment against defendant in the sum of .... dollars and costs.

(4) Complaint for Negligence.

(Where Plaintiff Is Unable to Determine Definitely Whether One or the Other of Two Persons Is Responsible or Whether Both Are Responsible and Where His Evidence May Justify a Finding of Willfulness or of Recklessness or of Negligence.)

1. On ...., at ...., defendant X or defendant Y, or both defendants X and Y, willfully or recklessly or negligently drove or caused to be driven a motor vehicle against plaintiff who was then crossing said street.

2. Defendant X or defendant Y, or both defendants X and Y were negligent in that:

(a) Either defendant or both defendants drove at an excessive speed.

(b) Either defendant or both defendants drove through a red light.

(c) Either defendant or both defendants failed to yield the right-of-way to plaintiff in a marked crosswalk.

3. As a result plaintiff was thrown down and had his leg broken and was otherwise injured, was prevented from transacting his business, suffered great pain of body and mind, and incurred expenses for medical attention and hospitalization [in the sum of one thousand dollars] (or) [in an amount not yet determined].

Wherefore, plaintiff demands judgment against X or against Y or against both in the sum of .... dollars and costs.

(5) Complaint for Specific Performance.

1. On or about ...., ..., plaintiff and defendant entered into an agreement in writing, a copy of which is hereto annexed as Exhibit A.

2. In accord with the provisions of said agreement plaintiff tendered to defendant the purchase price and requested a conveyance of the land, but defendant refused to accept the tender and refused to make the conveyance.

3. Plaintiff now offers to pay the purchase price.

Wherefore, plaintiff demands (1) that defendant be required specifically to perform said agreement, (2) damages in the sum of .... dollars, and (3) that if specific performance is not granted plaintiff have judgment against defendant in the sum of .... dollars.

(6) Complaint in the Alternative.

I.

Defendant owes plaintiff .... dollars according to the account hereto annexed as Exhibit A.

II. ALTERNATIVE COUNT

Plaintiff claims in the alternative that defendant owes plaintiff .... dollars for goods sold and delivered by plaintiff to defendant between ...., ..., and ...., ...

(7) Complaint for Fraud.

1. On ...., ..., at ...., defendant with intent to defraud plaintiff represented to plaintiff that ....

2. Said representations were known by defendant to be and were false. In truth, [what the facts actually were].

3. Plaintiff believed and relied upon the false representations, and thus was induced to ....

4. As a result of the foregoing, plaintiff has been damaged [nature and amount of damage].

Wherefore, plaintiff demands judgment against defendant for .... dollars, interest and costs.

(8) Complaint for Money Paid by Mistake.

Defendant owes plaintiff .... dollars for money paid by plaintiff to defendant by mistake under the following circumstances:

1. On ...., ..., at ...., pursuant to a contract ...., plaintiff paid defendant .... dollars.

(9) Motion for Judgment on the Pleadings.

Plaintiff moves that judgment be entered for plaintiff on the pleadings, on the ground that the undisputed facts appearing therein entitle plaintiff to such judgment as a matter of law.

(10) Motion for More Definite Statement.

Defendant moves for an order directing plaintiff to file a more definite statement of the following matters: [set out]

The ground of this motion is that plaintiff's complaint is so [vague] [ambiguous] in respect to these matters that defendant cannot reasonably be required to frame an answer hereto, in that the complaint ....

(11) Answer to Complaint.

First Defense

The complaint fails to state a claim against defendant upon which relief can be granted.

Second Defense

If defendant is indebted to plaintiff as alleged in the complaint, he is indebted to plaintiff jointly with X. X is alive; is a resident of the State of North Carolina, and is subject to the jurisdiction of this court as to serve[1] of process; and has not been made a party.

Third Defense

1. Defendant admits the allegations contained in paragraphs .... and .... of the complaint.

2. Defendant alleges that he is without knowledge or information sufficient to form a belief as to the truth of the allegations contained in paragraph .... of the complaint.

3. Defendant denies each and every other allegation contained in the complaint.

Fourth Defense

The right of action set forth in the complaint did not accrue within ... year next before the commencement of this action.

Counterclaim

[Here set forth any claim as a counterclaim in the manner in which a claim is pleaded in a complaint.]

Crossclaim Against Defendant Y

[Here set forth the claim constituting a crossclaim against defendant Y in the manner in which a claim is pleaded in a complaint.] Dated: ....

....

Attorney for Defendant

(12) Motion to Bring in Third-Party Defendant.

Defendant moves for leave to make X a party to this action and that there be served upon him summons and third-party complaint as set forth in Exhibit A attached.

(13) Third-Party Complaint.

______________________,)
Plaintiff,)
v.)
______________________,) Third Party Complaint
Defendant and Third-Party Plaintiff,) Civil Action No. ______
v.)
______________________,)
Third-Party Defendant.)

1. Plaintiff .... has filed against defendant .... a complaint, a copy of which is attached as "Exhibit C."

2. [Here state the grounds upon which the defendant and third-party plaintiff is entitled to recover from the third-party defendant all or part of what plaintiff may recover from the defendant and third-party plaintiff.]

Wherefore, plaintiff demands judgment against third-party defendant .... for all sums that may be adjudged against defendant .... in favor of plaintiff.

(14) Complaint for Negligence Under Federal Employer's Liability Act.

1. During all the times herein mentioned defendant owned and operated in interstate commerce a railroad which passed through a tunnel located at .... and known as Tunnel No. ....

2. On or about June 1, ..., defendant was repairing and enlarging the tunnel in order to protect interstate trains and passengers and freight from injury and in order to make the tunnel more conveniently usable for interstate commerce.

3. In the course of thus repairing and enlarging the tunnel on said day defendant employed plaintiff as one of its workmen, and negligently put plaintiff to work in a portion of the tunnel which defendant had left unprotected and unsupported.

4. By reason of defendant's negligence in thus putting plaintiff to work in that portion of the tunnel, plaintiff was, while so working pursuant to defendant's orders, struck and crushed by a rock which fell from the unsupported portion of the tunnel, and was (here describe plaintiff's injuries).

5. Prior to these injuries, plaintiff was a strong, able-bodied man, capable of earning and actually earning .... dollars per day. By these injuries he has been made incapable of any gainful activity, has suffered great physical and mental pain, and has incurred expense in the amount of .... dollars for medicine, medical attendance, and hospitalization.

Wherefore, plaintiff demands judgment against defendant in the sum of .... dollars and costs.

(15) Complaint for Interpleader and Declaratory Relief.

1. On or about June 1, ..., plaintiff issued to G. H. a policy of life insurance whereby plaintiff promised to pay to K. L. as beneficiary the sum of . . . . dollars upon the death of G. H. The policy required the payment by G. H. of a stipulated premium on June 1, ..., and annually thereafter as a condition precedent to its continuance in force.

2. No part of the premium due June 1, ..., was ever paid and the policy ceased to have any force of effect on July 1, ...

3. Thereafter, on September 1, ..., G. H. and K. L. died as the result of a collision between a locomotive and the automobile in which G. H. and K. L. were riding.

4. Defendant C. D. is the duly appointed and acting executor of the will of G. H.; defendant E. F. is the duly appointed and acting executor of the will of K. L.; defendant X. Y. claims to have been duly designed as beneficiary of said policy in place of K. L.

5. Each of defendants, C. D., E. F., and X. Y. is claiming that the above-mentioned policy was in full force and effect at the time of the death of G. H.; each of them is claiming to be the only person entitled to receive payment of the amount of the policy and has made demand for payment thereof.

6. By reason of these conflicting claims of the defendants, plaintiff is in great doubt as to which defendant is entitled to be paid the amount of the policy, if it was in force at the death of G. H.

Wherefore plaintiff demands that the court adjudge:

(1) That none of the defendants is entitled to recover from plaintiff the amount of said policy or any part thereof.

(2) That each of the defendants be restrained from instituting any action against plaintiff for the recovery of the amount of said policy or any part thereof.

(3) That, if the court shall determine that said policy was in force at the death of G. H., the defendants be required to interplead and settle between themselves their rights to the money due under said policy, and that plaintiff be discharged from all liability in the premises except to the person whom the court shall adjudge entitled to the amount of said policy.

(4) That plaintiff recover its costs.

(16) Averment of Capacity Under Rule 9 (a).

(North Carolina Corporation)

Plaintiff is a corporation incorporated under the law of North Carolina having its principal office in [address].

(Foreign Corporation)

Plaintiff is a corporation incorporated under the law of the State of Delaware having [not having] a registered office in the State of North Carolina.

(Unincorporated Association)

Plaintiff is an unincorporated association organized under the law of the State of New York having its principal office in [address] and (if applicable) having a principal office in the State of North Carolina at [address], and as such has the capacity to sue in its own name in North Carolina.

Added by Laws 1967, c. 954, § 1. Amended by S.L. 1999-456, § 59, eff. Jan. 1, 2000.

1 Probably should read "service".

INDEX TO RULES OF CIVIL PROCEDURE

GENERAL RULES OF PRACTICE FOR THE SUPERIOR AND DISTRICT COURTS SUPPLEMENTAL TO THE RULES OF CIVIL PROCEDURE

Adopted Pursuant to G.S. § 7A–34, Effective July 1, 1970

Table of Rules

Rule 1. Philosophy of General Rules of Practice

These rules are applicable in the Superior and District Court Divisions of the General Court of Justice. They shall at all times be construed and enforced in such manner as to avoid technical delay and to permit just and prompt consideration and determination of all the business before them.

Rule 2. Calendaring of Civil Cases

Subject to the provisions of Rule 40(a), Rules of Civil Procedure and G.S. 7A–146:

(a) The Senior Resident Judge and Chief District Judge in each Judicial District shall be responsible for the calendaring of all civil cases and motions for trial or hearing in their respective jurisdictions. A case management plan for the calendaring of civil cases must be developed by the Senior Resident Judge and the Chief District Court Judge. The Administrative Office of the Courts shall be available to provide assistance to judges in developing a case management program.

The effective date of the plan and any amendments thereto shall be either January 1 or July 1. The plan must be promulgated in writing and copies of the plan must be distributed to all attorneys of record within the judicial district. In order to provide for statewide dissemination, copies of plans effective January 1 shall be filed with the Administrative Office of the Courts on or before October 31 and on or before April 30 for plans effective July 1.

In districts with Trial Court Administrators, the responsibility for carrying out the case management plan may be delegated to the Trial Court Administrator.

The case management plan must contain a provision that attorneys may request that cases may be placed on the calendar.

(b) The civil calendar shall be prepared under the supervision of the Senior Resident Judge or Chief District Court Judge. Calendars must be published and distributed by the Clerk of Court to each attorney of record (or party where there is no attorney of record) and presiding judge no later than four weeks prior to the first day of court.

(c) Except in districts served by a Trial Court Administrator, a ready calendar shall be maintained by the Clerk of Court for the District and Superior Courts. Five months after a complaint is filed, the Clerk shall place that case on a ready calendar, unless the time is extended by written order of the Senior Resident Judge or the Chief District Judge for their respective jurisdictions. In districts with Trial Court Administrators, a case tracking system shall be maintained.

(d) During the first full week in January and the first full week following the 4th of July or such other weeks as the Senior Resident Judge shall designate that are agreeable to the Chief Justice, the Senior Resident Judge of each district shall be assigned to his home district for administrative purposes. During such administrative terms, the Senior Resident Judge shall be responsible for reviewing all cases on the ready calendar, or all cases designated by the Trial Court Administrator, of each county in the judicial district. The Senior Resident Judge shall take appropriate actions to insure prompt disposition of any pending motions or other matters necessary to move the cases toward a conclusion. The Chief District Court Judge shall undertake periodically such an administrative review of the District Court Civil Docket.

(e) When an attorney is notified to appear for the setting of a calendar, pretrial conference, hearing of a motion or for trial, he must, consistent with ethical requirements, appear or have a partner, associate or another attorney familiar with the case present. Unless an attorney has been excused in advance by the judge before whom the matter is scheduled and has given prior notice to his opponent, a case will not be continued.

(f) Requests for a peremptory setting for cases involving persons who must travel long distances or numerous expert witnesses or other extraordinary reasons for such a request must be made to the Senior Resident Judge or Chief District Judge. In districts with Trial Court Administrators, requests should be made to the Trial Court Administrator. A peremptory setting shall be granted only for good and compelling reasons. A Senior Resident Judge or Chief District Judge may set a case peremptorily on his own motion.

(g) When a case on a published calendar (tentative or final) is settled, all attorneys of record must notify the Trial Court Administrator (Clerk of Court in those counties with no Trial Court Administrator) within twenty-four (24) hours of the settlement and advise who will prepare and present judgment, *and when.*

[Amended effective July 1, 1980; July 1, 1988.]

Rule 2.1. Designation of Exceptional Civil Cases and Complex Business Cases

(a) The Chief Justice may designate any case or group of cases as (a) exceptional or (b) "complex business." A senior resident superior court judge, chief district court judge, or presiding superior court judge may ex mero motu, or on motion of any party, recommend to the Chief Justice that a case or cases be designated as exceptional or complex business.

(b) Such recommendation for exceptional cases may include special areas of expertise needed by the judge to be assigned and may include a list of recommended judges. Every complex business case shall be assigned to a special superior court judge for complex business cases, designated by the Chief Justice under Rule 2.2, who shall issue a written opinion upon final disposition of the case.

(c) Such recommendation shall be communicated to the Chief Justice through the Administrative Office of the Courts.

(d) Factors which may be considered in determining whether to make such designations include: the number and diverse interests of the parties; the amount and nature of anticipated pretrial discovery and motions; whether the parties voluntarily agree to waive venue for hearing pretrial motions; the complexity of the evidentiary matters and legal issues involved; whether it will promote the efficient administration of justice; and such other matters as the Chief Justice shall deem appropriate.

(e) The Chief Justice may enter such orders as are appropriate for the pretrial, trial, and other disposition of such designated case or cases.

[Adopted effective January 5, 1988. Amended effective August 28, 1995.]

Rule 2.2. Designation of Special Superior Court Judge for Complex Business Cases

The Chief Justice shall designate one or more superior court judges as special judges to hear and decide complex business cases as provided in Rule 2.1. Any judge so designated shall be known as a Special Superior Court Judge for Complex Business Cases.

[Adopted effective August 28, 1995.]

Comment

The portion of this rule providing for the designation of a case as "exceptional" has been in effect in North Carolina since January 5, 1988, and has been utilized numerous times in various situations. The portion of this rule providing for the designation of a "complex business case" was adopted by the North Carolina Supreme Court on August 28, 1995, as a result of a recommendation in the January 1995 ANNUAL REPORT of THE NORTH CAROLINA COMMISSION ON BUSINESS LAWS AND THE ECONOMY chaired by the North Carolina Attorney General.

The North Carolina Commission on Business Laws and the Economy was established by an executive order of the Governor on April 19, 1994, to recommend "any needed changes in existing statutes and regulations which affect the operation of businesses in North Carolina, particularly Chapter 55 of the North Carolina General Statutes . . . and to recommend any needed new statutes, rules and regulations designed to assure that North Carolina offers a legal environment which provides the flexibility and support to allow businesses to operate successfully in this state and which will attract them to locate and incorporate here."

The Commission's report noted that many national corporations incorporate in the state of Delaware because of that state's Chancery Court which provides a high level of judicial expertise on corporate law issues. It also observed the desirability of a state having a substantial body of corporate law that provides predictability for business decision making. Also, it is essential that corporations litigating complex business issues receive timely and well reasoned written decisions from an expert judge.

Accordingly, the Commission recommended that the North Carolina Supreme Court amend Rule 2.1 to allow the Chief Justice to designate certain cases as complex business cases. The Commission also recommended that the Governor appoint at least one expert in corporate law matters as a Special Judge to hear cases designated by the Chief Justice pursuant to Rule 2.2.

The term "complex business case" is purposely not defined in order to give litigants the flexibility to seek a designation as such with respect to any business issue that they believe requires special judicial expertise. It is anticipated that any case involving significant issues arising under Chapters 55, 55B, 57C, 59, 78A, 78B and 78C of the General Statutes of North Carolina would be designated a complex business case.

Rule 3. Continuances

An application for a continuance shall be made to the presiding judge of the court in which the case is calendared.

[Amended February 13, 1973; August 15, 2002.]

Rule 3.1. Guidelines for Resolving Scheduling Conflicts

(a) In resolving scheduling conflicts when an attorney has conflicting engagements in different courts, the following priorities should ordinarily prevail:

1. Appellate courts should prevail over trial courts.

2. Any of the trial court matters listed in this subdivision, regardless of trial division, should prevail over any trial court matter not listed in this subdivision, regardless of trial division; there is no priority among the matters listed in this subdivision:

- any trial or hearing in a capital case;
- the trial in any case designated pursuant to Rule 2.1 of these Rules;
- the trial in a civil action that has been peremptorily set as the first case for trial at a session of superior court;
- the trial of a criminal case in superior court, when the defendant is in jail or when the defendant is charged with a Class A through E felony and the trial is reasonably expected to last for more than one week;
- the trial in an action or proceeding in district court in which any of the following is contested:
  - termination of parental rights,
  - child custody,
  - adjudication of abuse, neglect or dependency or disposition following adjudication,
  - interim or final equitable distribution,
  - alimony or post-separation support.

3. When none of the above priorities applies, priority shall be as follows: superior court, district court, magistrate's court.

(b) When an attorney learns of a scheduling conflict between matters in the same priority category, the attorney shall promptly give written notice to opposing counsel, the clerk of all courts and the appropriate judges in all cases, stating therein the circumstances relevant to resolution of the conflict under these guidelines. When the attorney learns of the conflict before the date on which the matters are scheduled to be heard, the appropriate judges are Senior Resident Superior Court Judges for matters pending in the Superior Court Division and Chief District Court Judges for matters pending in the District Court Division; otherwise the appropriate judges are the judges presiding over those matters. The appropriate judges should promptly confer, resolve the conflict, and notify counsel of the resolution.

(c) In resolving scheduling conflicts between court proceedings in the same priority category, the presiding judges should give consideration to the following:

- the comparative age of the cases;
- the order in which the trial dates were set by published calendar, order or notice;
- the complexity of the cases;
- the estimated trial time;
- the number of attorneys and parties involved;
- whether the trial involves a jury;
- the difficulty or ease of rescheduling;
- the availability of witnesses, especially a child witness, an expert witness or a witness who must travel a long distance;
- whether the trial in one of the cases had already started when the other was scheduled to begin.

(d) When settlement proceedings have been ordered in superior or district court cases, only trials, hearings upon dispositive motions, and hearings upon motions scheduled for counties with less than one court session per month shall have precedence over settlement proceedings.

(e) When a mediator, other neutral, or attorney learns of a scheduling conflict between a court proceeding and a settlement proceeding, the mediator, other neutral, unrepresented parties or attorneys shall **promptly** give written notice to the appropriate judges and request them to resolve the conflict; stating therein the circumstances relevant to a determination under (d) above.

(f) Nothing in these guidelines is intended to prevent courts from voluntarily yielding a favorable scheduling position, and judges of all courts are urged to communicate with each other in an effort to lessen the impact of conflicts and continuances on all courts.

[Adopted effective August 15, 2002. Amended effective March 4, 2004.]

Rule 4. Enlargement of Time

The judge or clerk of the court in which the action is pending may by order extend the time for filing answer.

When counsel, by consent under Rule 6(b), agree upon an enlargement of time, the agreement shall be reduced to writing and filed with the clerk.

Rule 5. Form of Pleadings

(a) If feasible, each paper presented to the court for filing shall be flat and unfolded, without manuscript cover, and firmly bound.

All papers presented to the court for filing shall be letter size (8½″ × 11″), with the exception of wills and exhibits. The Clerk of Superior Court shall require a party to refile any paper which does not conform to this size. This subsection of this rule shall become effective on July 1, 1982. Prior to that date either letter or legal size papers will be accepted.

(b) All papers filed in civil actions, special proceedings and estates shall include as the first page of the filing a cover sheet summarizing the critical elements of the filing in a format prescribed by the Administrative Office of the Courts. The Clerk of Superior Court shall not reject the filing of any paper that does not include the required cover sheet. Instead, the clerk shall file the paper, notify the filing party of the omission and grant the filing party a reasonable time not to exceed five (5) days within which to file the required cover sheet. Until such time as the party files the required cover sheet, the court shall take no further action other than dismissal in the case.

[Amended effective July 1, 1982; October 1, 1996; October 1, 1997.]

Rule 6. Motions in Civil Actions

All motions, written or oral, shall state the rule number or numbers under which the movant is proceeding. (See Rule 7 of Rules of Civil Procedure.)

Motions may be heard and determined either at the pre-trial conference or on motion calendar as directed by the presiding judge.

Every motion shall be signed by at least one attorney of record in his individual name. He shall state his office address and telephone number immediately following his signature. The signature of an attorney constitutes a certificate by him that he has read the motion; that to the best of his knowledge, information and belief, there are good grounds to support it; and that the motion is not interposed for delay. (See Rule 7(b)(2); also Rule 11).

The court in civil matters, on its motion or upon motion by a party, may in its discretion order that argument of any motion be accomplished by means of a telephone conference without requiring counsel to appear in court in person. Upon motion of any party, the court may order such argument to be recorded in such manner as the court shall direct. The court may direct which party shall pay the costs of the telephone calls. Conduct of counsel during such arguments may be subject to punishment as for direct criminal contempt of court.

[Amended effective January 1, 1985.]

Rule 7. Pre-Trial Procedure (See Rule 16)

There shall be a pre-trial conference in every civil case, unless counsel for all parties stipulate in writing to the contrary and the court approves the stipulation. Upon its own motion or upon request of any party, the court may dispense with or limit the scope of the pre-trial conference or order.

In uncontested divorce, default, and magistrate cases and magistrate appeals, a pre-trial conference or order is not required.

A party who has not requested a pre-trial conference may not move for a continuance on the ground that it has not been held.

At least twenty-one days prior to trial date, the plaintiff's attorney shall arrange a pre-trial conference with the defendant's attorney to be held not later than seven days before trial date. At such conference a pre-trial order shall be prepared and signed by the attorneys.

If, after due diligence, plaintiff's attorney cannot arrange a conference with defendant's attorney, he may apply to the presiding judge or other judge holding court in the district (or district court judge with respect to district court cases) who shall make an appropriate order. The defense attorney may initiate pre-trial under the same rules applicable to plaintiff's attorney.

The pre-trial order shall be in substance as shown on the attached sample form.

Rule 7.1. Appointment of Guardian Ad Litem 1

When any person is charged with a crime wherein the victim is a minor, or a minor is a potential witness to such crime, the court may appoint an attorney, from a list of pro bono attorneys approved by the Chief District Court Judge, as guardian ad litem for such minor victim or witness.

[Adopted effective October 1, 1990.]

1 Suggested title added by Publisher.

Rule 8. Discovery

Counsel are required to begin promptly such discovery proceedings as should be utilized in each case, and are authorized to begin even before the pleadings are completed. Counsel are not permitted to wait until the pre-trial conference is imminent to initiate discovery.

[Amended effective July 1, 1988.]

Rule 9. Opening Statements

At any time before the presentation of evidence counsel for each party may make an opening statement setting forth the grounds for his claim or defense.

The parties may elect to waive opening statements.

Opening statements shall be subject to such time and scope limitations as may be imposed by the court.

Rule 10. Opening and Concluding Arguments

In all cases, civil and criminal, if no evidence is introduced by the defendant, the right to open and close the argument to the jury shall belong to him. If a question arises as to whether the plaintiff or the defendant has the final argument to the jury, the court shall decide who is so entitled, and its decision shall be final.

In a criminal case, where there are multiple defendants, if any defendant introduces evidence the closing argument shall belong to the solicitor.

In a civil case, where there are multiple defendants, if any defendant introduces evidence, the closing argument shall belong to the plaintiff, unless the trial judge shall order otherwise.

Rule 11. Examination of Witnesses

When several counsel are employed by the same party, the examination or cross-examination of each witness for such party shall be conducted by one counsel, but the counsel may change with each successive witness or, with leave of the court, in a prolonged examination of a single witness.

Rule 12. Courtroom Decorum

Except for some unusual reason connected with the business of the court, attorneys will not be sent for when their cases are called in their regular order.

Counsel are at all times to conduct themselves with dignity and propriety. All statements and communications to the court other than objections and exceptions shall be clearly and audibly made from a standing position behind the counsel table. Counsel shall not approach the bench except upon the permission or request of the court.

The examination of witnesses and jurors shall be conducted from a sitting position behind the counsel table except as otherwise permitted by the court (see State v. Bass, 5 N.C.App. 429, 431, 168 S.E.2d 424 (1969)). Counsel shall not approach the witness except for the purpose of presenting, inquiring about, or examining the witness with respect to an exhibit, document, or diagram.

Any directions or instructions to the court reporter are to be made in open court by the presiding judge only, and not by an attorney.

Business attire shall be appropriate dress for counsel while in the courtroom.

All personalities between counsel should be avoided. The personal history or peculiarities of counsel on the opposing side should not be alluded to. Colloquies between counsel should be avoided.

Adverse witnesses and suitors should be treated with fairness and due consideration. Abusive language or offensive personal references are prohibited.

The conduct of the lawyers before the court and with other lawyers should be characterized by candor and fairness. Counsel shall not knowingly misinterpret the contents of a paper, the testimony of a witness, the language or argument of opposite counsel or the language of a decision or other authority; nor shall he offer evidence which he knows to be inadmissible. In an argument addressed to the court, remarks or statements should not be interjected to influence the jury or spectators.

Suggestions of counsel looking to the comfort or convenience of jurors should be made to the court out of the jury's hearing. Before, and during trial, a lawyer should attempt to avoid communicating with jurors, even as to matters foreign to the cause.

Counsel should yield gracefully to rulings of the court and avoid detrimental remarks both in court and out. He should at all times promote respect for the court.

Rule 13. Presence of Counsel During Jury Deliberation

The right to be present during the trial of civil cases shall be deemed to be waived by a party or his counsel by voluntary absence from the courtroom at a time when it is known that proceedings are being conducted, or are about to be conducted. In such event the proceedings, including the giving of additional instructions to the jury after they have once retired, or receiving the verdict, may go forward without waiting for the arrival or return of counsel or a party.

After the jury has retired to deliberate upon a verdict in a criminal case, at least one attorney representing the defendant shall remain in the immediate area of the courtroom so as to be available at all times during the deliberation of the jury and when the verdict is received.

Rule 14. Custody and Disposition of Evidence at Trial

Once any item of evidence has been introduced, the clerk (not the court reporter) is the official custodian thereof and is responsible for its safekeeping and availability for use as needed at all adjourned sessions of the court and for appeal.

After being marked for identification, all exhibits offered or admitted in evidence in any cause shall be placed in the custody of the clerk, unless otherwise ordered by the court.

Whenever any models, diagrams, exhibits, or materials have been offered into evidence and received by the clerk, they shall be removed by the party offering them, except as otherwise directed by the court, within 30 days after final judgment in the trial court if no appeal is taken; if the case is appealed, within 60 days after certification of a final decision from the appellate division. At the time of removal a detailed receipt shall be given to the clerk and filed in the case file.

If the party offering an exhibit which has been placed in the custody of the clerk fails to remove such article as provided herein, the clerk shall write the attorney of record (or the party offering the evidence if he has no counsel) calling attention to the provisions of this rule. If the articles are not removed within 30 days after the mailing of such notice, they may be disposed of by the clerk.

Rule 15. Electronic Media and Still Photography Coverage of Public Judicial Proceedings

(a) Definition. The terms "electronic media coverage" and "electronic coverage" are used in the generic sense to include coverage by television, motion picture and still photography cameras, broadcast microphones and recorders.

(b) Coverage Allowed. Electronic media and still photography coverage of public judicial proceedings shall be allowed in the appellate and trial courts of this state, subject to the conditions below.

(1) The presiding justice or judge shall at all times have authority to prohibit or terminate electronic media and still photography coverage of public judicial proceedings, in the courtroom or the corridors immediately adjacent thereto.

(2) Coverage of the following types of judicial proceedings is expressly prohibited: adoption proceedings, juvenile proceedings, proceedings held before clerks of court, proceedings held before magistrates, probable cause proceedings, child custody proceedings, divorce proceedings, temporary and permanent alimony proceedings, proceedings for the hearing of motions to suppress evidence, proceedings involving trade secrets, and in camera proceedings.

(3) Coverage of the following categories of witnesses is expressly prohibited: police informants, minors, undercover agents, relocated witnesses, and victims and families of victims of sex crimes.

(4) Coverage of jurors is prohibited expressly at any stage of a judicial proceeding, including that portion of a proceeding during which a jury is selected. The trial judge shall inform all potential jurors at the beginning of the jury selection process of the restrictions of this particular provision which is designated (b)(4).

(c) Location of Equipment and Personnel.

(1) The location of equipment and personnel necessary for electronic media and still photographic coverage of trial proceedings shall be at a place either inside or outside the courtroom in such a manner that equipment and personnel are completely obscured from view from within the courtroom and not heard by anyone inside the courtroom.

(i) If located within the courtroom, this area must be set apart by a booth or other partitioning device constructed therein at the expense of the media. Such construction must be in harmony with the general architectural style and decor of the courtroom and must meet the approval of the Senior Resident Superior Court Judge and the governing body of the county or municipality that owns the facility.

(ii) If located outside the courtroom, any booth or other partitioning device must be built so that passage to and from the courtroom will not be obstructed. This arrangement must meet the approval of the Senior Resident Superior Court Judge and the governing body of the county or municipality that owns the facility.

(2) Appropriate openings to allow photographic coverage of the proceedings under these rules may be made in the booth or partitioning device, provided that no one in the courtroom will see or hear any photo-

graphic or audio equipment or the personnel operating such equipment. Those in the courtroom are not to know when or if any such equipment is in operation.

(3) The presiding judge may, however, exercise his or her discretion to permit the use of electronic media and still photography coverage without booths or other restrictions set out in Rule 15(c)(1) and (c)(2) if the use can be made without disruption of the proceedings and without distraction to the jurors and other participants. Such permission may be withdrawn at any time.

(4) Video tape recording equipment which is not a component part of a television camera shall be located in an area remote from the courtroom.

(5) Media personnel shall not exit or enter the booth area or courtroom once the proceedings are in session except during a court recess or adjournment.

(6) Electronic media equipment and still photography equipment shall not be taken into the courtroom or removed from the designated media area except at the following times:

(i) prior to the convening of proceedings;

(ii) during the luncheon recess;

(iii) during any court recess with the permission of the presiding justice or judge; and

(iv) after adjournment for the day of the proceedings.

(7) The Chief Justice of the Supreme Court, and the Chief Judge of the Court of Appeals, may waive the requirements of Rule 15(c)(1) and (2) with respect to judicial proceedings in the Supreme Court and in the Court of Appeals, respectively.

(d) Official Representatives of the Media.

(1) This Court hereby designates the North Carolina Association of Broadcasters, the Radio and Television News Directors Association of the Carolinas, and the North Carolina Press Association, as the official representatives of the news media. The governing boards of these associations shall designate one person to represent the television media, one person to represent the radio broadcasters, and one person to represent still photographers in each county in which electronic media and still photographic coverage is desired. The names of the persons so designated shall be forwarded to the Senior Resident Superior Court Judge, the Director of the Administrative Office of the Courts, and the county manager or other official responsible for administrative matters in the county or municipality in which coverage is desired. Thereafter, these persons shall conduct all negotiations with the appropriate officials concerning the construction of the booths or partitioning devices referred to above. Such persons shall also be the only persons authorized to speak for the media to the presiding judge concerning the coverage of any judicial proceedings.

(2) It is the express intent and purpose of this rule to preclude judges and other officials from having to "negotiate" with various representatives of the news media. Since these rules require pooling of equipment and personnel, cooperation by the media is of the essence and the designation of three media representatives is expressly intended to prevent presiding judges from having to engage in discussion with others from the media.

(e) Equipment and Personnel.

(1) Not more than two television cameras shall be permitted in any trial or appellate court proceedings.

(2) Not more than one still photographer, utilizing not more than two still cameras with not more than two lenses for each camera and related equipment for print purposes, shall be permitted in any proceeding in a trial or appellate court.

(3) Not more than one wired audio system for radio broadcast purposes shall be permitted in any proceeding in a trial or appellate court. Audio pickup for all media purposes shall be accomplished with existing audio systems present in the court facility. If no technically suitable audio system exists in the court facility, microphones and related wiring essential for media purposes may be installed and maintained at media expense. The microphones and wiring must be unobtrusive and shall be located in places designated in advance of any proceeding by the Senior Resident Superior Court Judge of the judicial district in which the court facility is located. Such modifications or additions must be approved by the governing body of the county or municipality which owns the facility. Provided, however, hand-held audio tape recorders may be used upon prior notification to, and with the approval of, the presiding judge; such approval may be withdrawn at any time.

(4) Any "pooling" arrangements among the media required by these limitations on equipment and personnel shall be the sole responsibility of the media without calling upon the presiding judge to mediate any dispute as to the appropriate media representative or equipment authorized to cover a particular proceeding. In the absence of advance media agreement on disputed equipment or personnel issues, the presiding judge shall exclude all contesting media personnel from a proceeding.

(5) In no event shall the number of personnel in the designated area exceed the number necessary to operate the designated equipment or which can comfortably be secluded in the restricted area.

(f) Sound and Light Criteria.

(1) Only television photographic and audio equipment which does not produce distracting sound or light shall be employed to cover judicial proceedings. No artificial lighting device of any kind shall be employed in connection with the television camera.

(2) Only still camera equipment which does not produce distracting sound or light shall be employed to cover judicial proceedings. No artificial lighting device of any kind shall be employed in connection with a still camera.

(g) Courtroom Light Sources. With the concurrence of the Senior Resident Superior Court Judge of the judicial district in which a court facility is situated, modifications and additions may be made in light sources existing in the facility, provided such modifications or additions are installed and maintained without public expense and provided such modifications or additions are approved by the governing body of the county or municipality which owns the facility.

(h) Conferences of Counsel. To protect the attorney-client privilege and the right to counsel, there shall be no audio pickup or broadcast of conferences which occur in a court facility between attorneys and their clients, between co-counsel of a client, between adverse counsel, or between counsel and the presiding judge held at the bench.

(i) Impermissible Use of Media Material. None of the film, video tape, still photographs or audio reproductions developed during or by virtue of coverage of a judicial proceeding shall be admissible as evidence in the proceeding out of which it arose, any proceeding subsequent and collateral thereto, or upon any retrial or appeal of such proceedings.

[Former version of this rule suspended on an experimental basis effective October 18, 1982; amended June 13, 1990.]

Rule 16. Withdrawal of Appearance

No attorney who has entered an appearance in any civil action shall withdraw his appearance, or have it stricken from the record, except on order of the court. Once a client has employed an attorney who has entered a formal appearance, the attorney may not withdraw or abandon the case without (1) justifiable cause, (2) reasonable notice to the client, and (3) the permission of the court. (See Smith v. Bryant, 264 N.C. 208, 141 S.E.2d 303).

Rule 17. Entries On Records

No entry shall be made on the records of the Superior or District Court by any person except the clerk, his regular deputy, a person specifically directed by the presiding judge, or the judge himself.

Rule 18. Custody of Appellate Reports

The clerks of the Superior Court shall be officially responsible for the care and preservation of the volumes of the Appellate Division Reports furnished by the State pursuant to G.S. § 147–45, and for the General Statutes of North Carolina furnished by the Administrative Office of the Courts under G.S. § 7A–300(a)(9).

Each clerk of the Superior Court shall report to the presiding judge of the Superior Court at the first session of court held in January and July each year what volumes, if any, of said reports are missing or have been lost since the last report to the end that the judge may enter an appropriate order for replacement of same pursuant to G.S. § 147–51.

Rule 19. Recordari; Supersedeas; Certiorari

The Superior Court shall grant the writ of recordari only upon petition specifying the grounds of the application. The petition shall be verified and the writ may be granted with or without notice. When notice is given the petition shall be heard upon answer thereto duly verified, and upon the affidavits and other evidence offered by the parties. The decision thereupon shall be final, subject to appeal as in other cases. If the petition is granted without notice, the petitioner shall give an undertaking for costs and for the writ of supersedeas, if prayed for. In such case the writ of recordari shall be made returnable to the session of the Superior Court of the county in which the judgment or proceeding complained of was granted, and ten days' written notice shall be given to the adverse party before the session of the court to which the writ is returnable. At that session the respondent may move to dismiss, or may answer the writ, and the answer shall be verified. After hearing the application upon the petition, answer, affidavits, and evidence offered, the court shall dismiss it or order it placed on the trial docket.

In proper cases and in like manner, the court may grant the writ of certiorari. When a diminution of the record is suggested and the record is manifestly imperfect, the court may grant the writ upon motion in the cause.

Rule 20. Sureties

No member of the bar, in any case, suit, action or proceeding in which he appears as counsel, and no employee of the General Court of Justice, employee of the Sheriff's Department, or other law enforcement officer, shall act as a surety in any suit, action or proceeding pending in any division of the General Court of Justice.

Rule 21. Jury Instruction Conference

At the close of the evidence (or at such earlier time as the judge may reasonably direct) in every jury trial, civil and criminal, in the superior and district courts, the trial judge shall conduct a conference on instructions with the attorneys of record (or party, if not represented by counsel). Such conference shall be out of the presence of the jury, and shall be held for the purpose of discussing the proposed instructions to be given to the jury. An opportunity must be given to the attorneys (or party if not represented by counsel) to request any additional instructions or to object to any of those instructions proposed by the judge. Such requests, objections and the rulings of the court thereon shall be placed in the record. If special instructions are desired, they should be submitted in writing to the trial judge at or before the jury instruction conference.[1]

At the conclusion of the charge and before the jury begins its deliberations, and out of the hearing, or upon request, out of the presence of the jury, counsel shall be given the opportunity to object on the record to any portion of the charge, or omission therefrom, stating distinctly that to which he objects and the grounds of his objection.

The court may recall the jury after they have retired and give them additional instructions in order: (i) to correct or withdraw an erroneous instruction; or (ii) to inform the jury on a point of law which should have been covered in the original instructions. The provisions of the first two paragraphs of this Rule 21 also apply to the giving of all additional instructions, except that the court in its discretion shall decide whether additional argument will be permitted.

[Adopted September 15, 1981.]

[1] In criminal cases, the provisions of G.S. 15A–1231 are also applicable.

Rule 22. Local Court Rules

In order to insure general uniformity throughout each respective judicial district, all trial judges shall observe and enforce the local rules in effect in any judicial district where they are assigned to hold court. The senior resident judge shall see that each judge assigned to hold a session of court in his district is furnished with a copy of the local court rules at or before the commencement of his assignment.

[Adopted September 21, 1981.]

Rule 23. [Summary Jury Trials]

The senior resident superior court judge of any superior court district or a presiding judge unless prohibited by local rule may upon joint motion or consent of all parties order the use of a summary jury upon good cause shown and upon such terms and conditions as justice may require. The order shall describe the terms and conditions proposed for the summary jury proceeding. Such terms and conditions may include: (1) a provision as to the binding or nonbinding nature of the summary jury proceeding; (2) variations in the method for selecting jurors; (3) limitations on the amount of time provided for argument and the presentation of witnesses; (4) limitations on the method or manner of presentation of evidence; (5) appointment of a referee to preside over the summary jury trial; (6) setting the date for conducting the summary jury trial; (7) approval of a settlement agreement contingent upon the outcome of the summary jury proceeding; or (8) such other matters as would in the opinion of the court contribute to the fair and efficient resolution of the dispute. The court shall maintain jurisdiction over the case, and may, where appropriate, rule on pending motions.

[Adopted August 14, 1991.]

Comment

The summary jury trial is a dispute resolution technique pioneered in the federal courts in the early 1980s. Pursuant to reports of its success as a settlement tool, the North Carolina Supreme Court in 1987 authorized the use of summary jury trials in three judicial districts on an experimental basis. Since that time, a number of summary jury trials have been conducted.

In May, 1991, a report prepared by the Private Adjudication Center detailed the North Carolina state courts' experience with the summary jury trial. That report noted that a number of variations in the summary jury trial process had been used successfully. The report concluded with a number of recommendations subsequently endorsed by the Dispute Resolution Committee of the North Carolina Bar Association. One of the recommendations was that the North Carolina Supreme Court adopt a General Rule of Practice authorizing the use of summary jury trials throughout the state.

Pursuant to that recommendation, this General Rule provides for the use of summary jury trials based upon the voluntary agreement of the parties, manifested by way of a joint motion to the court. The rule further provides that the authority to approve the request lies with the senior resident superior court judge for the county or judicial district in which the action is pending (or a presiding judge unless prohibited by local rule). The request shall be approved if the court finds that it is in the interest of justice for good cause shown. In this context, good cause relates to a judicial determination that the use of a summary jury trial represents a fair and efficient method for pursuing settlement of the dispute.

The Rule does *not* authorize a court to mandate the use of a summary jury trial. Nothing in the rule, however, prohibits a judge or other court administrator from raising the possibility of using a summary jury trial with the parties during a pre-trial conference or other event and explaining the possible benefits of the process.

The summary jury trials conducted to date in North Carolina have employed a number of innovative techniques. These variations, many of which are detailed in the above-referenced report, have ranged from variations on the methods used to select a jury to limitations on the manner in which evidence is presented. In other cases, the parties have requested that the court appoint a referee to preside over the summary jury proceeding. In addition, the parties in several summary jury trials have agreed that the results would be binding, sometimes pursuant to a "high/low agreement" that limits both parties' risk of an aberrant result. The Rule specifically provides that the court has the power to authorize these practices in appropriate cases.

Rule 23.1. Summary Procedure for Significant Commercial Disputes

(a) The senior resident superior court judge of any superior court district, or a presiding judge unless prohibited by local rule may, upon joint motion or consent of all parties, order Summary Procedures For A Significant Commercial Dispute ("Summary Procedures") in any case within the subject matter jurisdiction of the superior court that does not include a claim for personal, physical or mental injury where 1) the amount in controversy exceeds $500,000; 2) at least one party is a North Carolina citizen, corporation or business entity (or a subsidiary of such corporation or business entity) or has its principal place of business in North Carolina; and 3) all parties agree to forego any claim of punitive damages and waive the right to a jury trial. The joint motion or consent for summary procedures must be filed with the court on or before the time the answer or other responsive pleading is due.

(b) To the extent they are not inconsistent with these Rules, the North Carolina Rules of Civil Procedure shall apply to Summary Procedures.

(c) Summary Procedures are commenced by filing with the court and serving a complaint.

(d) The complaint and any accompanying documents shall be sent, via next-day delivery, to either a person identified in the agreement between the parties to receive notice of Summary Procedures or, absent such specification, to each defendant's principal place of business or residence.

(e) The complaint must state prominently on the first page that Summary Procedures are requested. The complaint also must contain a statement of the amount in controversy exclusive of interest and costs, a statement that one of the parties is a North Carolina citizen, corporation or other business entity, or a subsidiary of such corporation or business entity, or that such citizen, corporation or business entity has its principal place of business in North Carolina, and a statement that the defendant has agreed to submit to the court's jurisdiction for Summary Procedures.

(f) Any action pending in any other jurisdiction which could have been brought initially as a Summary Procedure in this state may, subject to the procedures of the court of the other jurisdiction, be transferred to the superior courts of this state and converted to a Summary Procedure. Any pending action in this state may be converted to a Summary Procedure subject to the provisions of this Rule 23.1. Within 15 days of transfer or conversion, the court shall hold a conference at which time a schedule for the remainder of the action shall be established that will conform as closely as feasible to these Rules. Unless cause not to do so is shown, the record from any prior proceedings shall be incorporated into the record of the Summary Procedures.

(g) A defendant shall serve an answer together with any compulsory counterclaims within thirty days after service of the complaint.

(h) A plaintiff shall serve a reply to any counterclaim within twenty days after service of the counterclaim. Any answer or reply to a counterclaim shall be accompanied by a list of persons consulted, or relied upon, in connection with preparation of the answer or reply. Crossclaims, permissive counterclaims and third-party claims are not permitted absent agreement of all parties. Crossclaims, counterclaims and third-party claims, if any, are subject to the provisions of this Rule 23.1.

(i) A party may, in lieu of an answer, respond to a complaint or counterclaim by moving to dismiss. A motion to dismiss and accompanying brief must be served within thirty days after service of the complaint upon the defendant. A motion to dismiss a counterclaim and accompanying brief must be served within twenty days after service of the counterclaim. An answering brief in opposition to a motion to dismiss is due within fifteen days after service of the motion and accompanying brief. A reply brief in support of the motion to dismiss is due within ten days after service of the answering brief. The opening and answering briefs shall be limited to twenty-five pages, and the reply brief shall be limited to ten pages. Within thirty days after the filing of the final reply brief on all motions to dismiss, if no oral argument occurs, or within thirty days of oral argument if oral argument occurs, the court will either render to the parties its decision on such motions or will provide to the parties an estimate of when such decision will be rendered. Such additional time shall not normally exceed an additional thirty days. If a motion to dismiss a claim is denied, an answer to that claim shall be filed within ten days of such denial.

(j) Within seven days of filing of the answer, a plaintiff shall serve upon the answering defendant a copy of each document in the possession of plaintiff that plaintiff intends to rely upon at trial, a list of witnesses that plaintiff intends to call at trial and a list of all persons consulted or relied upon in connection with preparation of the complaint. Within thirty days of the filing of the answer, the answering defendant shall provide to all other parties a list of witnesses it intends to call at trial and all documents in its possession that it intends to rely upon at trial. A plaintiff against whom a counterclaim has been asserted shall serve upon the defendant asserting the counterclaim, within thirty days after such plaintiff receives from the defendant asserting the counterclaim the materials referred to in the preceding sentence, a list of witnesses it intends to call at trial in opposition to the counterclaim, all documents in its possession that it intends to rely upon at trial in opposition to the counterclaim and all persons consulted or relied upon in connection with preparation of the reply to the counterclaim.

(k) Any party may serve upon any other party up to ten written interrogatories (with any sub-part to be counted as a separate interrogatory) within thirty days after the filing of the last answer. Responses are due within twenty days after service of the interrogatories.

(*l*) Any party may serve on any other party a request to produce and permit the party making the request, or someone acting on his behalf, to inspect and copy any designated documents, said request to be served within thirty days after filing of the last answer. The response to a document request is due within thirty days after service of the document request and must include production of the documents at that time for inspection and copying.

(m) Any party may serve on any other party a notice of up to four depositions to begin no sooner than seven days from service of the deposition notice and subsequent to the filing of all answers. A party may also take the deposition of any person on the other party's witness list, as well as the deposition of all affiants designated under Section (s) of this Rule. The first deposition notice by a party shall be served not later than sixty days after the filing of the last answer. All depositions to be taken by a party are to be scheduled and completed within 120 days of the filing of the last answer.

(n) Any party may serve upon any other party up to ten requests for admission (with any sub-part to be counted as a separate request for admission) within thirty days of the filing of the last answer. Responses are due within twenty days after service.

(*o*) Parties are obligated to supplement promptly their witness list, the documents they intend to rely upon at trial and their discovery responses under this Rule.

(p) Discovery disputes, at the court's option, may be addressed by a referee at the expense of the parties or by the court.

(q) Unless otherwise ordered by the court, all discovery, except for discovery contemplated by Section (s) of this Rule, shall be completed within 180 days after the filing of the last answer.

(r) There shall be no motions for summary judgment in Summary Procedures.

(s) If the parties notify the court within seven days after the close of discovery that the parties have agreed to forego witnesses at the trial of the case, the parties may submit briefs and appendices in support of their cause as follows:

(1) Plaintiff's Brief—thirty days following close of discovery;

(2) Defendant's Answering Brief—within thirty days after service of plaintiff's brief; and

(3) Plaintiff's Reply Brief—within fifteen days of service after Defendant's Answering Brief.

(t) The briefs must cite to the applicable portions of the record. Affidavits may be used but all affiants must be identified prior to the close of discovery and must, at the option of any other party, be produced for deposition within two weeks from the date discovery would otherwise close. The court shall make factual findings based upon the record presented by the parties.

(u) If the parties elect to forego witnesses at trial and submit briefs pursuant to Section (s) of this Rule, trial shall consist of oral argument, or submission on briefs if oral argument is waived by the parties with the consent of the court, to be scheduled and held by the court within one week of the close of briefing pursuant to Section (s).

(v) If the parties elect to present live witnesses at trial, the trial shall be scheduled to begin between thirty and sixty days after the close of discovery. Within thirty days after the close of discovery, the parties shall provide the court with an agreed upon pre-trial order. The pre-trial order shall include a summary of the claims or defenses of each party, a list of the witnesses each party expects to introduce at trial, a description of any evidentiary disputes, a statement of facts not in dispute and a statement of disputed issues of fact. Absent contrary court order, the trial shall be limited to five days, which shall be allocated equitably between the parties. Within ten days of the close of trial, each party shall file a post-trial brief including proposed findings of fact and conclusions of law. Each brief shall not exceed fifty pages.

(w) Within thirty days after the filing of the final brief, if no oral argument occurs, or within thirty days of argument if oral argument occurs, the court will either render to the parties its decision after trial or will provide the parties an estimate of when the decision will be rendered. Such additional time shall not normally exceed an additional thirty days.

(x) The schedule for trial or decision after trial or on motion to dismiss shall not be extended unless the assigned judge certifies that:

(1) the demands of the case and its complexity make the schedule under this Rule incompatible with serving the ends of justice; or

(2) the trial cannot reasonably be held or the decision rendered within such time because of the complexity of the case or the number or complexity of pending criminal cases.

[Adopted effective August 28, 1995.]

Comment

This rule was adopted by the North Carolina Supreme Court on August 28, 1995 as a result of a recommendation in the January 1995 ANNUAL REPORT of THE NORTH CAROLINA COMMISSION ON BUSINESS LAWS AND

THE ECONOMY chaired by the North Carolina Attorney General.

In its report, the Commission observed that, historically, North Carolina has enjoyed a high quality, efficient civil justice system. In recent years, however, civil litigation (and in particular, complex commercial litigation) has become protracted and costly. This is the result of many factors, including more complex laws and regulations, legal tactics and increased caseload.

The North Carolina court system has responded by instituting a number of innovative programs designed to resolve civil disputes more efficiently. These include court-ordered arbitration and a pilot mediation program. Despite the success of these programs, resolution of complex business and commercial disputes in North Carolina can be slow and costly.

The Commission noted that a state court system that offers alternatives to the normal litigation process which can expedite the resolution of significant commercial and business disputes is an important element of a progressive, efficient business environment. States that can offer alternatives are more likely to attract new business organizations and incorporations as well as business expansions.

Accordingly, the Commission recommended that the State establish a summary procedure through which North Carolina citizens and business entities and their subsidiaries, and businesses which are headquartered in the State can more efficiently resolve significant commercial civil disputes. The Commission recommended that the availability of such a summary procedure be limited to civil actions in superior court where 1) at least $500,000 is in controversy, 2) at least one party is a North Carolina citizen or corporation, and 3) all parties consent to the summary proceeding. As part of that agreement, the parties to the summary proceeding must agree to waive punitive damages and a jury trial.

The summary procedure provided for in this Rule can be utilized only with consent of all parties. It does not restrict any parties' rights and is supplementary to, and not inconsistent with, the General Statutes. (See G.S. 7A–34.) Its purpose is to provide an alternative procedure for significant commercial disputes and thereby improve the overall efficiency of the court system.

Rule 24. Pretrial Conference in Capital Cases

There shall be a pretrial conference in every case in which the defendant stands charged with a crime punishable by death. No later than ten days after the superior court obtains jurisdiction in such a case, the district attorney shall apply to the presiding superior court judge or other superior court judge holding court in the district, who shall enter an order requiring the prosecution and defense counsel to appear before the court within forty-five days thereafter for the pretrial conference. Upon request of either party at the pretrial conference the judge may for good cause shown continue the pretrial conference for a reasonable time.

At the pretrial conference, the court and the parties shall consider:

(1) simplification and formulation of the issues, including, but not limited to, the nature of the charges against the defendant, and the existence of evidence of aggravating circumstances;

(2) timely appointment of assistant counsel for an indigent defendant when the State is seeking the death penalty; and

(3) such other matters as may aid in the disposition of the action.

The judge shall enter an order that recites that the pretrial conference took place, and any other actions taken at the pretrial conference.

This rule does not affect the rights of the defense or the prosecution to request, or the court's authority to grant, any relief authorized by law, including but not limited to appointment of assistant counsel, in advance of the pretrial conference.

[Adopted effective June 1, 1994.]

Rule 25. Motions for Appropriate Relief and Habeas Corpus Applications in Capital Cases

When considering motions for appropriate relief and/or applications for writs of habeas corpus in capital cases, the following procedures shall be followed:

(1) All appointments of defense counsel shall be in accordance with G. S. 7A–451(c), (d), and (e) and rules adopted by the Office of Indigent Defense Services;

(2) All requests for appointment of experts made prior to the filing of a motion for appropriate relief and subsequent to a denial by the Director of Indigent Defense Services shall be ruled on by the senior resident superior court judge or the senior resident superior court judge's designee in accordance with rules adopted by the Office of Indigent Defense Services;

(3) All requests for other *ex parte* and similar matters arising prior to the filing of a motion for appropriate relief shall be ruled on by the senior resident superior court judge or the senior resident superior court judge's designee in accordance with rules adopted by the Office of Indigent Defense Services;

(4) All motions for appropriate relief, when filed, shall be referred to the senior resident superior court judge or the senior resident superior court judge's designee for that judge's review and administrative action, including, as may be appropriate, dismissal, calendaring for hearing, entry of a scheduling order for subsequent events in the case, or other appropriate actions;

(5) Subsequent to direct appeal, an application for writ of habeas corpus shall not be used as a substitute for appeal and/or a motion for appropriate relief and is not available as a means of reviewing and correcting nonjurisdictional legal error. If the applicant has

been sentenced pursuant to a final judgment issued by a competent tribunal of criminal jurisdiction (i.e., by a trial court having subject matter jurisdiction to enter the sentence), the application for writ of habeas corpus shall be denied. In the event the application for writ of habeas corpus raises a meritorious challenge to the original jurisdiction of the sentencing court, and the writ is granted, the judge shall make the writ returnable before the senior resident superior court judge of the judicial district where the applicant was sentenced or the senior resident superior court judge's designee. In the event the application for writ of habeas corpus raises a meritorious nonjurisdictional challenge to the applicant's conviction and sentence, the judge shall immediately refer the matter to the senior resident superior court judge of the judicial district where the applicant was sentenced or the senior resident superior court judge's designee for disposition as a motion for appropriate relief; and

(6) All requests for and awards of attorney fees and other expenses of representation shall be made in accordance with rules adopted by the Office of Indigent Defense Services.

[Adopted effective May 1, 2003.]

Rule 26. Secure Leave Periods for Attorneys

(A) Purpose, Authorization. In order to secure for the parties to actions and proceedings pending in the Superior and District Courts, and to the public at large, the heightened level of professionalism that an attorney is able to provide when the attorney enjoys periods of time that are free from the urgent demands of professional responsibility and to enhance the overall quality of the attorney's personal and family life, any attorney may from time to time designate and enjoy one or more secure leave periods each year as provided in this Rule.

(B) Length, Number. A secure leave period shall consist of one or more complete calendar weeks. During any calendar year, an attorney's secure leave periods pursuant to this Rule and to Rule 33A of the Rules of Appellate Procedure shall not exceed, in the aggregate, three calendar weeks.

(C) Designation, Effect. To designate a secure leave period an attorney shall file a written designation containing the information required by subsection (D), with the official specified in subsection (E), and within the time provided in subsection (F). Upon such filing, the secure leave period so designated shall be deemed allowed without further action of the court, and the attorney shall not be required to appear at any trial, hearing, in-court or out-of-court deposition, or other proceeding in the Superior or District Courts during that secure leave period.

(D) Content of Designation. The designation shall contain the following information:

(1) the attorney's name, address, telephone number and state bar number,

(2) the date of the Monday on which the secure leave period is to begin and of the Friday on which it is to end,

(3) the dates of all other secure leave periods during the current calendar year that have previously been designated by the attorney pursuant to this Rule and to Rule 33A of the Rules of Appellate Procedure,

(4) a statement that the secure leave period is not being designated for the purpose of delaying, hindering or interfering with the timely disposition of any matter in any pending action or proceeding, and

(5) a statement that no action or proceeding in which the attorney has entered an appearance has been scheduled, peremptorily set or noticed for trial, hearing, deposition or other proceeding during the designated secure leave period.

(E) Where to File Designation. The designation shall be filed as follows:

(1) if the attorney has entered an appearance in any criminal action, in the office of the District Attorney for each prosecutorial district in which any such case or proceeding is pending;

(2) if the attorney has entered an appearance in any civil action, either

(a) in the office of the trial court administrator for each superior court district and district court district in which any such case is pending or,

(b) if there is no trial court administrator for a superior court district, in the office of the Senior Resident Superior Court Judge for that district,

(c) if there is no trial court administrator for a district court district, in the office of the Chief District Court Judge for that district;

(3) if the attorney has entered an appearance in any special proceeding or estate proceeding, in the office of the Clerk of Superior Court of the county in which any such matter is pending;

(4) if the attorney has entered an appearance in any juvenile proceeding, with the juvenile case calendaring clerk in the office of the Clerk of Superior Court of the county in which any such proceeding is pending.

(F) When to File Designation. To be effective, the designation shall be filed:

(1) no later than ninety (90) days before the beginning of the secure leave period, and

(2) before any trial, hearing, deposition or other matter has been regularly scheduled, peremptorily set or noticed for a time during the designated secure leave period.

(G) Procedure When Court Proceeding Scheduled Despite Designation. If, after a designation of a secure leave period has been filed pursuant to this rule, any trial, hearing, in-court deposition or other in-court proceeding is scheduled or peremptorily set for a time during the secure leave period, the attorney shall file with the official by whom the matter was calendared or set, and serve on all parties, a copy of the designation with a certificate of service attached. Any party may, within ten days after service of the copy of the designation and certificate of service, file a written objection with that official and serve a copy on all parties. The only ground for objection shall be that the designation was not in fact filed in compliance with this Rule. If no objection is filed, that official shall reschedule the matter for a time that is not within the attorney's secure leave period. If an objection is filed, the court shall determine whether the designation was filed in compliance with this Rule. If the court finds that the designation was filed as provided in this Rule, it shall reschedule the matter for a time that is not within the attorney's secure leave period. If the court finds the designation was not so filed, it shall enter any scheduling, calendaring or other order that it finds to be in the interests of justice.

(H) Procedure When Deposition Scheduled Despite Designation. If, after a designation of a secure leave period has been filed pursuant to this Rule, any deposition is noticed for a time during the secure leave period, the attorney may serve on the party that noticed the deposition a copy of the designation with a certificate of service attached, and that party shall reschedule the deposition for a time that is not within the attorney's secure leave period. Any dispute over whether the secure leave period was properly designated pursuant to this Rule shall be resolved pursuant to the portions of the Rules of Civil Procedure, G.S. 1A–1, that govern discovery.

(I) Nothing in this Rule shall limit the inherent power of the Superior and District Courts to reschedule a case to allow an attorney to enjoy a leave during a period that has not been designated pursuant to this Rule, but there shall be no entitlement to any such leave.

[Adopted May 6, 1999, effective January 1, 2000.]

FORMS

Certificate of Readiness

NORTH CAROLINA IN THE GENERAL COURT OF JUSTICE

________ COUNTY ________ COURT DIVISION

________________)
Plaintiff) File #: ________
-v-) Film #: ________
________________) Certificate of Readiness
Defendant)

As counsel of record for ______ (name the party you represent), who is a plaintiff, defendant, third party, (underline one) I hereby certify that:

A. I know of no procedural matters which would delay the trial of the case when called for jury trial;

B. All motions existing of record this date have been heard or otherwise disposed of;

C. I know of no parties or witnesses desired that will not be available on the trial date;

D. I know of no current reason that would cause me to move for a continuance;

E. I am ready for trial.

This the ______ day of ______.

____
Attorney

Order on Final Pre-Trial Conference

IN THE GENERAL COURT OF JUSTICE
________ COURT DIVISION

________________)
Plaintiff(s)) File #: ________
-v-) Film #: ________
________________)
Defendant(s))

ORDER ON FINAL PRE–TRIAL CONFERENCE

Pursuant to the provisions of Rule 16 of the State Rules of Civil Procedure, and Rule 7, General Rules of Practice, a final pretrial conference was held in the above-entitled cause on the ______ day of ______, ______, ______, Esquire, appeared as counsel for the plaintiff(s); ______, Esquire, appeared as counsel for the defendant(s).

(1) It is stipulated that all parties are properly before the court, and that the court has jurisdiction of the parties and of the subject matter.

Note: If the facts are otherwise they should be accurately stated.

(2) It is stipulated that all parties have been correctly designated, and there is no question as to misjoinder or nonjoinder of parties.

Note: If the facts are otherwise, they should be accurately stated.

(3) If any of the parties is appearing in a representative capacity, it should be set out whether there is any question concerning the validity of the appointment of the representatives. Letters or orders of appointment should be included as exhibits.

(4) Any third-party defendant(s) or cross-claimant(s) should follow the same procedure as set out in paragraphs (4) and (5) for plaintiff(s) and defendant(s).

(5) In addition to the other stipulations contained herein, the parties hereto stipulate and agree with respect to the following undisputed facts:

(a)

(b)

Note: Here set out all facts not in genuine dispute. [1]

[1] IN CONTRACT CASES, the parties may stipulate upon, or state fair contentions with respect to, where applicable (a) whether the contract relied on was oral or in writing; (b) the date thereof and the parties thereto; (c) the substance of the contract, if oral; (d) the terms of the contract which are relied upon and the portions in controversy; (e) any collateral oral agreement, if claimed, and the terms thereof; (f) any specific breach of contract claimed; (g) any misrepresentation of fact claimed; (h) if modification of the contract or waiver of covenant is claimed, what modification or waiver, and how accomplished, and (i) an itemized statement of damages claimed to have resulted from any alleged breach, the source of such information, how computed, and any books or records available to sustain such damage claimed.

IN MOTOR VEHICLE NEGLIGENCE CASES, the parties may stipulate upon, or state their contentions with respect to, where applicable (a) the owner, type and make of each vehicle involved; (b) the agency of each driver; (c) the place and time of accident, conditions of weather, and whether daylight or dark; (d) nature of terrain as to level, uphill or downhill; (e) traffic signs, signals and controls, if any, and by what authority placed; (f) any claimed obstruction of view; (g) presence of other vehicles, where significant; (h) a detailed list of acts of negligence or contributory negligence claimed; (i) specific statutes, ordinances, rules, or regulations alleged to have been violated, and upon which each of the parties will rely at the trial to establish negligence or contributory negligence; (j) a detailed list of nonpermanent personal injuries claimed, including the nature and extent thereof; (k) a detailed list of permanent personal injuries claimed, including nature and extent thereof; (*l*) the age of any party alleged to have been injured; (m) the life and work expectancy of any party seeking to recover for permanent injury; (n) an itemized statement of all special damages, such as medical, hospital, nursing, etc., with the amount and to whom paid; (*o*) if loss of earnings is claimed; (p) a detailed list of any property damages, and (q) in death cases, the decedent's date of birth, marital status, employment for five years before date of death, work expectancy, reasonable probability of promotion, rate of earnings for five years before date of death, life expectancy under mortuary table, and general physical condition immediately prior to date of death.

IN THE EVENT THIS CASE DOES NOT FALL WITHIN ANY OF THE CATEGORIES ENUMERATED ABOVE, OR ANY OF THE CATEGORIES SUGGESTED BY THIS FORM, COUNSEL SHOULD, NEVERTHELESS, SET FORTH THEIR POSITIONS WITH AS MUCH DETAIL AS POSSIBLE

(6) The following is a list of all known exhibits the plaintiff(s) may offer at the trial:

(a)

(b)

Note: Here list the pre-trial identification numbers and a brief description of each exhibit.

(7) It is stipulated and agreed that opposing counsel has been furnished a copy of each exhibit identified by the plaintiff(s), except:

Note: Here set out stipulations with respect to (a) the exhibits that have been furnished opposing counsel, (b) the arrangements made for the inspection of exhibits of the character which prohibits or makes impractical their reproduction, and (c) any waiver of the requirement to furnish opposing counsel with a copy of exhibits.

(8) It is stipulated and agreed that each of the exhibits identified by the plaintiff(s) is genuine and, if relevant and material, may be received in evidence without further identification or proof, except:

Note: Here set out with particularity the basis of objection to specific exhibits.

It is permissible to generally reserve the right to object at the trial on grounds of relevancy and materiality.

(9) The following is a list of all known exhibits the defendant(s) may offer at the trial:

(a)

(b)

Note: Here list the pre-trial identification and a brief description of each exhibit.

(10) It is stipulated and agreed that opposing counsel has been furnished a copy of each exhibit identified by the defendant(s), except:

Note: Here set out stipulations with respect to (a) the exhibits that have been furnished opposing counsel, (b) the arrangements made for the inspection of exhibits of the character which prohibits or makes impractical their reproduction, and (c) any waiver of the requirement to furnish opposing counsel with a copy of exhibits.

(11) It is stipulated and agreed that each of the exhibits identified by the defendant(s) is genuine, and, if relevant and material, may be received in evidence without further identification or proof, except:

Note: Here set out with particularity the basis of objection to specific exhibits. It is permissible to generally reserve the right to object at the trial on grounds of relevancy and materiality.

(12) Any third-party defendant(s) and cross-claimant(s) should follow the same procedure with respect to exhibits as required of plaintiff(s) and defendant(s).

Note: Attention is called to the provisions of the pre-trial rule with respect to the obligation to immediately notify opposing counsel if additional exhibits are discovered after the preparation of this order.

(13) The following is a list of the names and addresses of all known witnesses the plaintiff(s) may offer at the trial:

Note: If either plaintiff or defendant's attorney discover additional witnesses after this listing, attention is called to obligation to notify opposing counsel. There shall be no requirement that all witnesses listed by a party be used, and the court may after satisfactory explanation, in his discretion, permit the use of a witness not listed.

The trial judge may, for good cause made known to him, relieve a party of the requirement of disclosing the name of any witness.

(14) The following is a list of the names and addresses of all known witnesses the defendant(s) may offer at the trial:

(15) Any third-party defendant(s) and cross-claimant(s) should follow the same procedure with respect to witnesses as above outlined for plaintiff(s) and defendant(s). Counsel shall immediately notify opposing counsel if the names of additional witnesses are discovered after the preparation of this order.

(16) There are no pending motions, and neither party desires further amendments to the pleadings, except:

Note: Here state facts regarding pending or impending motion. If any motions are contemplated, such as motion for the physical examination of a party, motion to take the deposition of a witness for use as evidence, etc., such motions should be filed in advance of the final pretrial conference so that they may be ruled upon, and the rulings stated in the final pre-trial order. The same procedure should be followed with respect to any desired amendments to pleadings.

(17) Additional consideration has been given to a separation of the triable issues, and counsel for all parties are of the opinion that a separation of issues in this particular case would (would not) be feasible.

(18) The plaintiff(s) contends (contend) that the contested issues to be tried by the court (jury) are as follows:

(19) The defendant(s) contends (contend) that the contested issues to be tried by the court (jury) are as follows:

(20) Any third-party defendant(s) and cross-claimant(s) contends (contend) that the contested issues to be tried by the court (jury) are as follows:

Note: In all instances possible, the parties should agree upon the triable issues and include them in this order in the form of a stipulation, in lieu of the three preceding paragraphs.

(21) Counsel for the parties announced that all witnesses are available and the case is in all respects ready for trial. The probable length of the trial is estimated to be _______ days.

(22) Counsel for the parties represent to the court that, in advance of the preparation of this order, there was a full and frank discussion of settlement possibilities. Counsel for the plaintiff will immediately notify the clerk in the event of material change in settlement prospects.

Note: Counsel shall be required to conduct a frank discussion concerning settlement possibilities at the time of the conference of attorneys, and clients shall either be consulted in advance of the conference concerning settlement figures or be available for consultation at the time of the conference. The court will make inquiry at the time of trial as to whether this requirement was strictly observed.

____

Counsel for Plaintiff(s)

____

Counsel for Defendant(s)

Approved and Ordered Filed.

Date: __________

____

Judge Presiding

RULES IMPLEMENTING STATEWIDE MEDIATED SETTLEMENT CONFERENCES AND OTHER SETTLEMENT PROCEDURES IN SUPERIOR COURT CIVIL ACTIONS

Adopted October 2, 1991

Table of Rules

Rule 1. Initiating Settlement Events

A. Purpose of Mandatory Settlement Procedures. Pursuant to N.C.G.S. § 7A–38.1, these Rules are promulgated to implement a system of settlement events which are designed to focus the parties' attention on settlement rather than on trial preparation and to provide a structured opportunity for settlement negotiations to take place. Nothing herein is intended to limit or prevent the parties from engaging in settlement procedures voluntarily at any time before or after those ordered by the court pursuant to these Rules.

B. Duty of Counsel to Consult with Clients and Opposing Counsel Concerning Settlement Procedures. In furtherance of this purpose, counsel, upon being retained to represent any party to a superior court case, shall advise his or her client(s) regarding the settlement procedures approved by these Rules and shall attempt to reach agreement with opposing counsel on the appropriate settlement procedure for the action.

C. Initiating the Mediated Settlement Conference in Each Action by Court Order.

(1) *Order by Senior Resident Superior Court Judge.* The senior resident superior court judge of any judicial district shall, by written order, require all persons and entities identified in Rule 4 to attend a pre-trial mediated settlement conference in all civil actions except those actions in which a party is seeking the issuance of an extraordinary writ or is appealing the revocation of a motor vehicle operator's license. The judge may withdraw his/her order upon motion of a party pursuant to Rule 1.C(6) only for good cause shown.

(2) *Motion to Authorize the Use of Other Settlement Procedures.* The parties may move the senior resident superior court judge to authorize the use of some other settlement procedure allowed by these rules or by local rule in lieu of a mediated settlement conference, as provided in N.C.G.S. § 7A–38.1(i). Such motion shall be filed within 21 days of the order requiring a mediated settlement conference on a North Carolina Administrative Office of the Courts (NCAOC) form, and shall include:

(a) the type of other settlement procedure requested;

(b) the name, address and telephone number of the neutral selected by the parties;

(c) the rate of compensation of the neutral;

(d) that the neutral and opposing counsel have agreed upon the selection and compensation of the neutral selected; and

(e) that all parties consent to the motion.

If the parties are unable to agree to each of the above, then the senior resident superior court judge shall deny the motion and the parties shall attend the mediated settlement conference as originally ordered by the court. Otherwise, the court may order the use of any agreed upon settlement procedures authorized by Rules 10–13 herein or by local rules of the superior court in the county or district where the action is pending.

(3) *Timing of the Order.* The senior resident superior court judge shall issue the order requiring a mediated settlement conference as soon as practicable after the time for the filing of answers has expired. Rules 1.C(4) and 3.B herein shall govern the content of the order and the date of completion of the conference.

(4) *Content of Order.* The court's order shall (1) require that a mediated settlement conference be held in the case; (2) establish a deadline for the completion of the conference; (3) state clearly that the parties have the right to select their own mediator as provided by Rule 2; (4) state the rate of compensation of the court appointed mediator in the event that the parties do not exercise their right to select a mediator pursuant to Rule 2; and (5) state that the parties shall be required to pay the mediator's fee at the conclusion of the settlement conference unless otherwise ordered by the court. The order shall be on a NCAOC form.

(5) *Motion for Court Ordered Mediated Settlement Conference.* In cases not ordered to mediated settlement conference, any party may file a written motion with the senior resident superior court judge requesting that such conference be ordered. Such motion shall state the reasons why the order should be allowed and shall be served on non-moving parties. Objections to the motion may be filed in writing with the senior resident superior court judge within 10 days after the date of the service of the motion. Thereafter, the judge shall rule upon the motion without a hearing and notify the parties or their attorneys of the ruling.

(6) *Motion to Dispense with Mediated Settlement Conference.* A party may move the senior resident superior court judge to dispense with the mediated settlement conference ordered by the judge. Such motion shall state the reasons the relief is sought. For good cause shown, the senior resident superior court judge may grant the motion.

Such good cause may include, but not be limited to, the fact that the parties have participated in a settlement procedure such as non-binding arbitration or early neutral evaluation prior to the court's order to participate in a mediated settlement conference or have elected to resolve their case through arbitration.

D. Initiating the Mediated Settlement Conference by Local Rule.

(1) *Order by Local Rule.* In judicial districts in which a system of scheduling orders or scheduling conferences is utilized to aid in the administration of civil cases, the senior resident superior court judge of said districts shall, by local rule, require all persons and entities identified in Rule 4 to attend a pre-trial mediated settlement conference in all civil actions except those actions in which a party is seeking the issuance of an extraordinary writ or is appealing the revocation of a motor vehicle operator's license. The judge may withdraw his/her order upon motion of a party pursuant to Rule 1.D(6) only for good cause shown.

(2) *Scheduling Orders or Notices.* In judicial districts in which scheduling orders or notices are utilized to manage civil cases and for all cases ordered to mediated settlement conference by local rule, said order or notice shall (1) require that a mediated settlement conference be held in the case; (2) establish a deadline for the completion of the conference; (3) state clearly that the parties have the right to designate their own mediator and the deadline by which that designation should be made; (4) state the rate of compensation of the court appointed mediator in the event that the parties do not exercise their right to designate a mediator; and (5) state that the parties shall be required to pay the mediator's fee at the conclusion of the settlement conference unless otherwise ordered by the court.

(3) *Scheduling Conferences.* In judicial districts in which scheduling conferences are utilized to manage civil cases and for cases ordered to mediated settlement conferences by local rule, the notice for said scheduling conference shall (1) require that a mediated settlement conference be held in the case; (2) establish a deadline for the completion of the conference; (3) state clearly that the parties have the right to designate their own mediator and the deadline by which that designation should be made; (4) state the rate of compensation of the court appointed mediator in the event that the parties do not exercise their right to designate a mediator; and (5) state that the parties shall be required to pay the mediator's fee at the conclusion of the settlement conference unless otherwise ordered by the court.

(4) *Application of Rule 1.C.* The provisions of Rules 1.C(2), (5) and (6) shall apply to Rule 1.D except for the time limitations set out therein.

(5) *Deadline for Completion.* The provisions of Rule 3.B determining the deadline for completion of the mediated settlement conference shall not apply to mediated settlement conferences conducted pursuant to Rule 1.D. The deadline for completion shall be set by the senior resident superior court judge or designee at the scheduling conference or in the scheduling order or notice, whichever is applicable. However, the completion deadline shall be well in advance of the trial date.

(6) *Selection of Mediator.* The parties may designate or the senior resident superior court judge may appoint, mediators pursuant to the provisions of Rule 2, except that the time limits for designation and appointment shall be set by local rule. All other provisions of Rule 2 shall apply to mediated settlement conferences conducted pursuant to Rule 1.D.

(7) *Use of Other Settlement Procedures.* The parties may utilize other settlement procedures pursuant to the provisions of Rule 1.C (2) and Rule 10. However, the time limits and method of moving the court for approval to utilize another settlement procedure set out in those rules shall not apply and shall be governed by local rule.

[Amended effective December 1, 1993; October 1, 1995; December 30, 1998; September 1, 2000; November 21, 2002; March 4, 2004; March 1, 2006; March 1, 2010; January 1, 2012; April 1, 2014.]

COMMENT TO RULE 1

Comment to Rule 1.C(6).

If a party is unable to pay the costs of the conference or lives a great distance from the conference site, the court may want to consider Rules 4 or 7 prior to dispensing with mediation for good cause. Rule 4 provides a way for a party to attend electronically and Rule 7 provides a way for parties to attend and obtain relief from the obligation to pay the mediator's fee.

Rule 2. Designation of Mediator

A. Designation of Certified Mediator by Agreement of Parties. The parties may designate a mediator certified pursuant to these Rules by agreement within 21 days of the court's order. The plaintiff's attorney shall file with the court a Designation of Mediator by Agreement within 21 days of the court's order, however, any party may file the designation. The party filing the designation shall serve a copy on all parties and the mediator designated to conduct the settlement conference. Such designation shall state the name, address and telephone number of the mediator designated; state the rate of compensation of the mediator; state that the mediator and opposing counsel have agreed upon the designation and rate of compensation; and state that the mediator is certified pursuant to these Rules. The notice shall be on a NCAOC form.

B. Approval of Party Nominee Eliminated. As of January 1, 2006, the former Rule 2.B rule allowing the approval of a non-certified mediator is rescinded. Beginning on that date, the court shall appoint mediators certified by the Dispute Resolution Commission (Commission), pursuant to Rule 2.C which follows.

C. Appointment of Mediator by the Court. If the parties cannot agree upon the designation of a mediator, the plaintiff or plaintiff's attorney shall so notify the court and request, on behalf of the parties, that the senior resident superior court judge appoint a mediator. The motion must be filed within 21 days after the court's order and shall state that the attorneys for the parties have had a full and frank discussion concerning the designation of a mediator and have been unable to agree. The motion shall be on a form approved by the NCAOC.

Upon receipt of a motion to appoint a mediator, or failure of the parties to file a Designation of Mediator by Agreement with the court within 21 days of the court's order, the senior resident superior court judge shall appoint a mediator, certified pursuant to these Rules, who has expressed a willingness to mediate actions within the judge's district.

In making such appointments, the senior resident superior court judge shall rotate through the list of available certified mediators. Appointments shall be made without regard to race, gender, religious affiliation, or whether the mediator is a licensed attorney. The senior resident superior court judge shall retain discretion to depart in a specific case from a strict rotation when, in the judge's discretion, there is good cause to do so.

As part of the application or annual certification renewal process, all mediators shall designate those judicial districts for which they are willing to accept court appointments. Each designation shall be deemed to be a representation that the designating mediator has read and will abide by the local rules for, and will accept appointments from, the designated district and will not charge for travel time and expenses incurred in carrying out his/her duties associated with those appointments. A refusal to accept an appointment in a judicial district designated by the mediator may be grounds for removal from said district's court appointment list by the Commission or the senior resident superior court judge.

The Commission shall furnish to the senior resident superior court judge of each judicial district a list of those certified superior court mediators requesting appointments in that district. Said list shall contain the mediators' names, addresses and telephone numbers and shall be provided electronically through the Commission's website at www.ncdrc.org. The Commission shall promptly notify the senior resident superior court judge of any disciplinary action taken with respect to a mediator on the list of certified mediators for the judicial district.

D. Mediator Information Directory. To assist the parties in designating a mediator, the Commission shall assemble, maintain and post on its website a list of certified superior court mediators. The list shall supply contact information for mediators and identify court districts that they are available to serve. Where a mediator has supplied it to the Commission, the list shall also provide biographical information, including information about an individual mediator's education, professional experience and mediation training and experience.

E. Disqualification of Mediator. Any party may move the senior resident superior court judge of the district where the action is pending for an order disqualifying the mediator. For good cause, such order shall be entered. If the mediator is disqualified, a replacement mediator shall be designated or appointed pursuant to Rule 2. Nothing in this provision shall preclude mediators from disqualifying themselves.

[Amended effective December 1, 1993; July 1, 1994; October 1, 1995; December 30, 1998; September 1, 2000; November 21, 2002; March 1, 2006; October 1, 2008; March 1, 2010; January 1, 2012; April 1, 2014.]

Rule 3. The Mediated Settlement Conference

A. Where Conference is to be Held. The mediated settlement conference shall be held in any location agreeable to the parties and the mediator. If the parties cannot agree on a location, the mediator shall be responsible for reserving a neutral place in the county where the action is pending and making arrangements for the conference and for giving timely notice of the time and location of the conference to all attorneys, *pro se* parties, and other parties required to attend.

B. When Conference is to be Held. As a guiding principle, the conference should be held after the parties have had a reasonable time to conduct discovery but well in advance of the trial date.

The court's order issued pursuant to Rule 1.C(1) shall state a deadline for completion for the conference which shall be not less than 120 days nor more than 180 days after issuance of the court's order. The mediator shall set a date and time for the conference pursuant to Rule 6.B(5).

C. Extending Deadline for Completion. The senior resident superior court judge may extend the deadline for completion of the mediated settlement conference upon the judge's own motion, upon stipulation of the parties or upon suggestion of the mediator.

D. Recesses. The mediator may recess the conference at any time and may set times for reconvening. If the time for reconvening is set before the conference is recessed, no further notification is required for persons present at the conference.

E. The Mediated Settlement Conference is not to Delay Other Proceedings. The mediated settlement conference shall not be cause for the delay of other proceedings in the case, including the completion of discovery, the filing or hearing of motions or the trial of the case, except by order of the senior resident superior court judge.

[Amended effective December 1, 1993; October 1, 1995; December 30, 1998; September 1, 2000; November 21, 2002; March 4, 2004; January 1, 2012; April 1, 2014.]

Rule 4. Duties of Parties, Attorneys and Other Participants in Mediated Settlement Conferences

A. Attendance.

(1) The following persons shall attend a mediated settlement conference:

(a) Parties.

(i) All individual parties;

(ii) Any party that is not a natural person or a governmental entity shall be represented at the conference by an officer, employee or agent who is not such party's outside counsel and who has been authorized to decide on behalf of such party whether and on what terms to settle the action or who has been authorized to negotiate on behalf of such party and can promptly communicate during the conference with persons who have decision-making authority to settle the action; provided, however, if a specific procedure is required by law (*e.g.*, a statutory pre-audit certificate) or the party's governing documents (*e.g.*, articles of incorporation, bylaws, partnership agreement, articles of organization or operating agreement) to approve the terms of the settlement, then the representative shall have the authority to negotiate and make recommendations to the applicable approval authority in accordance with that procedure;

(iii) Any party that is a governmental entity shall be represented at the conference by an employee or agent who is not such party's outside counsel and who has authority to decide on behalf of such party whether and on what terms to settle the action; provided, if under law proposed settlement terms can be approved only by a board, the representative shall have authority to negotiate on behalf of the party and to make a recommendation to that board.

(b) Insurance Company Representatives. A representative of each liability insurance carrier, uninsured motorist insurance carrier, and underinsured motorist insurance carrier which may be obligated to pay all or part of any claim presented in the action. Each such carrier shall be represented at the conference by an officer, employee or agent, other than the carrier's outside counsel, who has the authority to make a decision on behalf of such carrier or who has been authorized to negotiate on behalf of the carrier and can promptly communicate during the conference with persons who have such decision-making authority.

(c) Attorneys. At least one counsel of record for each party or other participant, whose counsel has appeared in the action.

(2) Any party or person required to attend a mediated settlement conference shall physically attend until an agreement is reduced to writing and signed as provided in Rule 4.C. or an impasse has been declared. Any such party or person may have the attendance requirement excused or modified, including the allowance of mat party's or person's participation without physical attendance:

(a) By agreement of all parties and persons required to attend and the mediator, or

(b) By order of the senior resident superior court judge, upon motion of a party and notice to all parties and persons required to attend and the mediator.

(3) *Scheduling.* Participants required to attend shall promptly notify the mediator after designation or appointment of any significant problems they may have with dates for conference sessions before the completion deadline, and shall keep the mediator informed as to such problems as may arise before an anticipated conference session is scheduled by the mediator. After a conference session has been scheduled by the mediator, and a scheduling conflict with another court proceeding thereafter arises, participants shall promptly attempt to resolve it pursuant to Rule 3.1 of the General Rules of Practice for the Superior and District Courts, or, if applicable, the Guidelines for Resolving Scheduling Conflicts adopted by the State–Federal Judicial Council of North Carolina June 20, 1985.

B. Notifying Lien Holders. Any party or attorney who has received notice of a lien or other claim upon proceeds recovered in the action shall notify said lien holder or claimant of the date, time, and location of the mediated settlement conference and shall request said lien holder or claimant to attend the conference or make a representative available with whom to communicate during the conference.

C. Finalizing Agreement.

(1) If an agreement is reached at the conference, parties to the agreement shall reduce its terms to writing and sign it along with their counsel. By stipulation of the parties and at their expense, the agreement may be electronically recorded. If an agreement is upon all issues, a consent judgment or one or more voluntary dismissals shall be filed with the court by such persons as the parties shall designate.

(2) If the agreement is upon all issues at the conference, the parties shall give a copy of their signed agreement, consent judgment or voluntary dismissal(s) to the mediator and all parties at the conference and shall file a consent judgment or voluntary dismissal(s) with the court within 30 days or within 90 days if the state or a political subdivision thereof is a party to the action, or before expiration of the mediation deadline, whichever is longer. In all cases, consent judgments or voluntary dismissals shall be filed prior to the scheduled trial.

(3) If an agreement is reached upon all issues prior to the conference or finalized while the conference is in recess, the parties shall reduce its terms to writing and sign it along with their counsel and shall file a consent judgment or voluntary dismissal(s) disposing of all issues with the court within 30 days or within 90 days if the state or a political subdivision thereof is a party to the action or before expiration of the mediation deadline, whichever is longer.

(4) When a case is settled upon all issues, all attorneys of record must notify the senior resident judge within four business days of the settlement and advise who will file the consent judgment or voluntary dismissal(s).

D. Payment of Mediator's Fee. The parties shall pay the mediator's fee as provided by Rule 7.

E. Related Cases. Upon application by any party or person, the senior resident superior court judge may order that an attorney of record or a party in a pending superior court case or a representative of an insurance carrier that may be liable for all or any part of a claim pending in superior court shall, upon reasonable notice, attend a mediation conference that may be convened in another pending case, regardless of the forum in which the other case may be pending, provided that all parties in the other pending case consent to the attendance ordered pursuant to this rule. Any such attorney, party, or carrier representative that properly attends a mediation conference pursuant to this rule shall not be required to pay any of the mediation fees or costs related to that mediation conference. Any disputed issues concerning an order entered pursuant to this rule shall be determined by the senior resident superior court judge who entered the order.

F. No Recording. There shall be no stenographic, audio, or video recording of the mediation process by any participant. This prohibition precludes recording either surreptitiously or with the agreement of the parties.

[Amended effective October 1, 1995; July 15, 1996; December 30, 1998; September 1, 2000; November 21, 2002; March 4, 2004; March 1, 2006; January 1, 2012; April 1, 2014.]

COMMISSION COMMENTS TO RULE 4

Commission Comment to Rule 4.C.

N.C.G.S. § 7A–38.1(l) provides that no settlement shall be enforceable unless it has been reduced to writing and signed by the parties. When a settlement is reached during a mediated settlement conference, the mediator shall be sure its terms are reduced to writing and signed by the parties and their attorneys before ending the conference.

Cases in which agreement upon all issues has been reached should be disposed of as expeditiously as possible. This rule is intended to assure that the mediator and the parties move the case toward disposition while honoring the private nature of the mediation process and the mediator's duty of confidentiality. If the parties wish to keep confidential the terms of their settlement, they may timely file with the court closing documents which do not contain confidential terms, *i.e.*, voluntary dismissal(s) or a consent judgment resolving all claims. Mediators will not be required by local rules to submit agreements to the court.

Commission Comment to Rule 4.E.

Rule 4.E was adopted to clarify a senior resident superior court judge's authority in those situations where there may be a case related to a superior court case pending in a different forum. For example, it is common for there to be claims asserted against a third-party tortfeasor in a superior court case at the same time that there are related workers' compensation claims being asserted in an Industrial Commission case. Because of the related nature of such claims, the parties in the Industrial Commission case may need an attorney of record, party or insurance carrier representative in the superior court case to attend the Industrial Commission mediation conference in order to resolve the pending claims in that case. Rule 4.E specifically authorizes a senior resident superior court judge to order such attendance provided that all parties in the related Industrial Commission case consent and the persons ordered to attend receive reasonable notice. The Industrial Commission's Rules for Mediated Settlement and Neutral Evaluation Conferences contain a similar provision that provides that persons involved in an Industrial Commission case may be ordered to attend a mediation conference in a related superior court case.

Rule 5. Sanctions for Failure to Attend Mediated Settlement Conference or Pay Mediator's Fee

Any person required to attend a mediated settlement conference or to pay a portion of the mediator's fee in compliance with N.C.G.S. § 7A–38.1 and the rules promulgated by the Supreme Court of North Carolina (Supreme Court) to implement that section who fails to attend or to pay without good cause, shall be subject to the contempt powers of the court and monetary sanctions imposed by a resident or presiding superior court judge. Such monetary sanctions may include, but are not limited to, the payment of fines, attorney fees, mediator fees, expenses and loss of earnings incurred by persons attending the conference.

A party seeking sanctions against another party or person shall do so in a written motion stating the grounds for the motion and the relief sought. Said motion shall be served upon all parties and on any person against whom sanctions are being sought. The court may initiate sanction proceedings upon its own motion by the entry of a show cause order.

If the court imposes sanctions, it shall do so, after notice and a hearing, in a written order, making findings of fact and conclusions of law. An order imposing sanctions shall be reviewable upon appeal where the entire record as submitted shall be reviewed to determine whether the order is supported by substantial evidence.

[Amended effective October 1, 1995; December 30, 1998; September 1, 2000; November 21, 2002; March 1, 2010; January 1, 2012; April 1, 2014.]

Rule 6. Authority and Duties of Mediators

A. Authority of Mediator.

(1) *Control of Conference.* The mediator shall at all times be in control of the conference and the procedures to be followed. The mediator's conduct shall be governed by Standards of Professional Conduct for Mediators (Standards) promulgated by the Supreme Court.

(2) *Private Consultation.* The mediator may communicate privately with any participant prior to and during the conference. The fact that private communications have occurred with a participant shall be disclosed to all other participants at the beginning of the conference.

B. Duties of Mediator.

(1) The mediator shall define and describe the following at the beginning of the conference:

(a) The process of mediation;

(b) The differences between mediation and other forms of conflict resolution;

(c) The costs of the mediated settlement conference;

(d) That the mediated settlement conference is not a trial, the mediator is not a judge and the parties retain their right to trial if they do not reach settlement;

(e) The circumstances under which the mediator may meet and communicate privately with any of the parties or with any other person;

(f) Whether and under what conditions communications with the mediator will be held in confidence during the conference;

(g) The inadmissibility of conduct and statements as provided by N.C.G.S. § 7A–38.1;

(h) The duties and responsibilities of the mediator and the participants; and

(i) That any agreement reached will be reached by mutual consent.

(2) *Disclosure.* The mediator has a duty to be impartial and to advise all participants of any circumstances bearing on possible bias, prejudice or partiality.

(3) *Declaring Impasse.* It is the duty of the mediator to determine in a timely manner that an impasse exists and that the conference should end. To that end, the mediator shall inquire of and consider the desires of the parties to cease or continue the conference.

(4) *Reporting Results of Mediation.*

(a) The mediator shall report to the court the results of the mediated settlement conference and any settlement reached by the parties prior to or during a recess of the conference. Mediators shall also report the results of mediations held in other superior court civil cases in which a mediated settlement conference was not ordered by the court. Said report shall be filed on a NCAOC form within

10 days of the conclusion of the conference or of being notified of the settlement and shall include the names of those persons attending the mediated settlement conference if a conference was held. Local rules shall not require the mediator to send a copy of the parties' agreement to the court.

(b) If an agreement upon all issues is reached at, prior to or during a recess of the conference, the mediator's report shall state whether the action will be concluded by consent judgment or voluntary dismissal(s) and the name, address and telephone number of the person(s) designated by the parties to file such consent judgment or dismissal(s) with the court. The mediator shall advise the parties that Rule 4.C requires them to file their consent judgment or voluntary dismissal with the court within 30 days or within 90 days if the state or a political subdivision thereof is a party to the action, or before expiration of the mediation deadline, whichever is longer. The mediator shall indicate on the report that the parties have been so advised.

(c) The Commission or the NCAOC may require the mediator to provide statistical data for evaluation of the mediated settlement conference program.

(d) Mediators who fail to report as required by this rule shall be subject to sanctions by the senior resident superior court judge. Such sanctions shall include, but not be limited to, fines or other monetary penalties, decertification as a mediator and any other sanction available through the power of contempt. The senior resident superior court judge shall notify the Commission of any action taken against a mediator pursuant to this section.

(5) *Scheduling and Holding the Conference.* It is the duty of the mediator to schedule the conference and conduct it prior to the conference completion deadline set out in the court's order. The mediator shall make an effort to schedule the conference at a time that is convenient with all participants. In the absence of agreement, the mediator shall select a date and time for the conference. Deadlines for completion of the conference shall be strictly observed by the mediator unless said time limit is changed by a written order of the senior resident superior court judge.

A mediator selected by agreement of the parties shall not delay scheduling or holding a conference because one of more of the parties has not paid an advance fee deposit required by that agreement.

[Amended effective December 1, 1993; October 1, 1995; December 30, 1998; September 1, 2000; November 21, 2002; March 4, 2004; October 2, 2008; January 1, 2012; April 1, 2014.]

Rule 7. Compensation of the Mediator and Sanctions

A. By Agreement. When the mediator is stipulated by the parties, compensation shall be as agreed upon between the parties and the mediator. The terms of the parties' agreement with the mediator notwithstanding, Section D below shall apply to issues involving the compensation of the mediator. Sections E and F below shall apply unless the parties' agreement provides otherwise.

B. By Court Order. When the mediator is appointed by the court, the parties shall compensate the mediator for mediation services at the rate of $150 per hour. The parties shall also pay to the mediator a one time, per case administrative fee of $150 that is due upon appointment.

C. Change of Appointed Mediator. Pursuant to Rule 2.A, the parties may select a certified mediator to conduct their mediated settlement conference. Parties who fail to select a certified mediator and then desire a substitution after the court has appointed a mediator, shall obtain court approval for the substitution. The court may approve the substitution only upon proof of payment to the court's original appointee the $150 one time, per case administrative fee, any other amount due and owing for mediation services pursuant to Rule 7.B and any postponement fee due and owing pursuant to Rule 7.E.

D. Indigent Cases. No party found to be indigent by the court for the purposes of these rules shall be required to pay a mediator fee. Any mediator conducting a settlement conference pursuant to these rules shall waive the payment of fees from parties found by the court to be indigent. Any party may move the senior resident superior court judge for a finding of indigence and to be relieved of that party's obligation to pay a share of the mediator's fee.

Said motion shall be heard subsequent to the completion of the conference or, if the parties do not settle their case, subsequent to the trial of the action. In ruling upon such motions, the judge shall apply the criteria enumerated in N.C.G.S. § 1–110(a), but shall take into consideration the outcome of the action and whether a judgment was rendered in the movant's favor. The court shall enter an order granting or denying the party's request.

E. Postponements and Fees.

(1) As used herein, the term "postponement" shall mean reschedule or not proceed with a settlement conference once a date for a session of the settlement conference has been scheduled by the mediator. After a settlement conference has been scheduled for a specific date, a party may not unilaterally postpone the conference.

(2) A conference session may be postponed by the mediator for good cause only after notice by the movant to all parties of the reasons for the postponement and a finding of good cause by the mediator. Good cause shall mean that the reason for the postponement involves a situation over which the party seeking the postponement has no control, including but not limited to, a party or attorney's illness, a

death in a party or attorney's family, a sudden and unexpected demand by a judge that a party or attorney for a party appear in court for a purpose not inconsistent with the Guidelines established by Rule 3.1(d) of the General Rules of Practice for the Superior and District Courts or inclement weather such that travel is prohibitive. Where good cause is found, a mediator shall not assess a postponement fee.

(3) The settlement of a case prior to the scheduled date for mediation shall be good cause provided that the mediator was notified of the settlement immediately after it was reached and the mediator received notice of the settlement at least 14 calendar days prior to the date scheduled for mediation.

(4) Without a finding of good cause, a mediator may also postpone a scheduled conference session with the consent of all parties. A fee of $150 shall be paid to the mediator if the postponement is allowed, except that if the request for postponement is made within seven calendar days of the scheduled date for mediation, the fee shall be $300. The postponement fee shall be paid by the party requesting the postponement unless otherwise agreed to between the parties. Postponement fees are in addition to the one time, per case administrative fee provided for in Rule 7.B.

(5) If all parties select the certified mediator and they contract with the mediator as to compensation, the parties and the mediator may specify in their contract alternatives to the postponement fees otherwise required herein.

F. Payment of Compensation by Parties. Unless otherwise agreed to by the named parties or ordered by the court, the mediator's fee shall be paid in equal shares by the parties. For purposes of this rule, multiple parties shall be considered one party when they are represented by the same counsel. Parties obligated to pay a share of the fees shall pay them equally. Payment shall be due upon completion of the conference.

[Amended effective December 1, 1993; October 1, 1995; July 15, 1996; May 8, 1997; December 30, 1998; October 1, 1999; September 1, 2000; November 21, 2002; March 4, 2004; March 1, 2006; October 1, 2008; March 1, 2010; January 1, 2012; April 1, 2014.]

COMMENTS TO RULE 7

Comment to Rule 7.B.

Court-appointed mediators may not be compensated for travel time, mileage or any other out-of-pocket expenses associated with a court-ordered mediation.

It is not unusual for two or more related cases to be mediated collectively. A mediator shall use his or her business judgment in assessing the one time, per case administrative fee when two or more cases are mediated together and set his/her fee according to the amount of time s/he spent in an effort to schedule the matter for mediation. The mediator may charge a flat fee of $150 if scheduling was relatively easy or multiples of that amount if more effort was required.

Comment to Rule 7.E.

Non-essential requests for postponements work a hardship on parties and mediators and serve only to inject delay into a process and program designed to expedite litigation. As such, it is expected that mediators will assess a postponement fee in all instances where a request does not appear to be absolutely warranted. Moreover, mediators are encouraged not to agree to postponements in instances where, in their judgment, the mediation could be held as scheduled.

Comment to Rule 7.F.

If a party is found by a senior resident superior court judge to have failed to attend a mediated settlement conference without good cause, then the court may require that party to pay the mediator's fee and related expenses.

Rule 8. Mediator Certification and Decertification

The Commission may receive and approve applications for certification of persons to be appointed as superior court mediators. For certification, a person shall:

A. Have completed a minimum of 40 hours in a trial court mediation training program certified by the Commission, or have completed a 16–hour supplemental trial court mediation training certified by the Commission after having been certified by the Commission as a family financial mediator;

B. Have the following training, experience and qualifications:

(1) An attorney may be certified if he or she:

(a) is either:

(i) a member in good standing of the North Carolina State Bar; or

(ii) a member similarly in good standing of the bar of another state and a graduate of a law school recognized as accredited by the North Carolina Board of Law Examiners; demonstrates familiarity with North Carolina court structure, legal terminology and civil procedure; and provides to the Commission three letters of reference as to the applicant's good character, including at least one letter from a person with knowledge of the applicant's practice as an attorney; and

(b) has at least five years of experience after date of licensure as a judge, practicing attorney, law professor and/or mediator or equivalent experience.

Any current or former attorney who is disqualified by the attorney licensing authority of any state shall be ineligible to be certified under this Rule 8.B(1) or Rule 8.B(2).

(2) A non-attorney may be certified if he or she has:

(a) completed a six-hour training on North Carolina court organization, legal terminology, civil court procedure, the attorney-client privilege, the unauthorized practice of law and common legal issues arising in superior court cases, provided by a trainer certified by the Commission;

(b) provided to the Commission three letters of reference as to the applicant's good character, including at least one letter from a person with knowledge of the applicant's experience claimed in Rule 8.B(2)(c);

(c) completed either:

(i) a minimum of 20 hours of basic mediation training provided by a trainer acceptable to the Commission; and after completing the 20–hour training, mediating at least 30 disputes, over the course of at least three years, or equivalent experience, and possess a four-year college degree from an accredited institution, except that the four-year degree requirement shall not be applicable to mediators certified prior to January 1, 2005, and have four years of professional, management or administrative experience in a professional, business or governmental entity; or

(ii) ten years of professional, management or administrative experience in a professional, business or governmental entity and possess a four-year college degree from an accredited institution, except that the four-year degree requirement shall not be applicable to mediators certified prior to January 1, 2005.

C. Have completed the following observations:

(1) *All applicants.* All applicants for certification shall observe two mediated settlement conferences, at least one of which shall be of a superior court case.

(2) *Non-attorney applicants.* Non–attorney applicants for certification shall observe three mediated settlement conferences in addition to those required by (1) above and which are conducted by at least two different mediators. At least one of these additional observations shall be of a superior court case.

(3) *Conferences eligible for observation.* Conferences eligible for observation under (1) and (2) above shall be those in cases pending before the North Carolina Superior Court, the North Carolina Court of Appeals, the North Carolina Industrial Commission, the North Carolina Office of Administrative Hearings, or the United States District Courts for North Carolina that are ordered to mediation or conducted by agreement of the parties which incorporates the rules of mediation of one of those entities.

Conferences eligible for observation shall also include those conducted in disputes prior to litigation which are mediated by agreement of the parties incorporating the rules for mediation of one of the entities named above.

All such conferences shall be conducted by certified superior court mediators pursuant to rules adopted by one of the above entities and shall be observed from their beginning to settlement or impasse. Observations shall be reported on an NCAOC form.

(4) All observers shall conform their conduct to the Commission's Requirements for Observer Conduct.

D. Demonstrate familiarity with the statute, rules and practice governing mediated settlement conferences in North Carolina;

E. Be of good moral character and adhere to any standards of practice for mediators acting pursuant to these Rules adopted by the Supreme Court. An applicant for certification shall disclose on his/her application(s) any of the following: any pending criminal matters; any criminal convictions; and any disbarments or other revocations or suspensions of any professional license or certification, including suspension or revocation of any license, certification, registration or qualification to serve as a mediator in another state or country for any reason other than to pay a renewal fee. In addition, an applicant for certification shall disclose on his/her application(s) any of the following which occurred within ten years of the date the application(s) is filed with the Commission: any pending disciplinary complaint(s) filed with, or any private or public sanctions(s) imposed by, a professional licensing or regulatory body, including any body regulating mediator conduct; any judicial sanction(s); any civil judgment(s); any tax lien(s); or any bankruptcy filing(s). Once certified, a mediator shall report to the Commission within (30) days of receiving notice any subsequent criminal conviction(s); any disbarment(s) or revocation(s) of a professional license(s), other disciplinary complaint(s) filed with or actions taken by, a professional licensing or regulatory body; any judicial sanction(s); any tax lien(s); any civil judgment(s) or any filing(s) for bankruptcy.

F. Submit proof of qualifications set out in this section on a form provided by the Commission;

G. Pay all administrative fees established by the NCAOC upon the recommendation of the Commission;

H. Agree to accept as payment in full of a party's share of the mediator's fee, the fee ordered by the court pursuant to Rule 7;

I. Comply with the requirements of the Commission for continuing mediator education or training. (These requirements may include completion of training or self-study designed to improve a mediator's communication, negotiation, facilitation or mediation skills; completion of observations; service as a mentor to a less experienced mediator; being mentored by a more experienced mediator; or serving as a trainer. Mediators shall report on a Commission approved form.);

J. Once certified, agree to make reasonable efforts to assist mediator certification applicants in completing their observation requirements.

K. No mediator who held a professional license and relied upon that license to quality for certification under subsections B(l) or B(2) above shall be decertified or denied recertification because that mediator's license lapses, is relinquished or becomes inactive; provided, however, that this subsection shall not apply to any mediator whose professional license is revoked, suspended, lapsed, relinquished or becomes inactive due to disciplinary action or the threat of same from his/her licensing authority. Any mediator whose professional license is revoked, suspended, lapsed, or relinquished, or who becomes inactive, shall report such matter to the Commission.

If a mediator's professional license lapses, is relinquished or becomes inactive, s/he shall be required to complete all otherwise voluntary continuing mediator education requirements adopted by the Commission as part of its annual certification renewal process and to report completion of those hours to the Commission's office annually.

Certification may be revoked or not renewed at any time it is shown to the satisfaction of the Commission that a mediator no longer meets the above qualifications or has not faithfully observed these rules or those of any district in which he or she has served as a mediator. Any person who is or has been disqualified by a professional licensing authority of any state for misconduct shall be ineligible to be certified under this Rule.

[Amended effective December 1, 1993; July 1, 1994; October 1, 1995; July 15, 1996; May 8, 1997; December 30, 1998; September 1, 2000; November 21, 2002; March 4, 2004; March 1, 2006; October 1, 2008; January 1, 2012; April 1, 2014.]

Rule 9. Certification of Mediation Training Programs

A. Certified training programs for mediators seeking only certification as superior court mediators shall consist of a minimum of 40 hours instruction. The curriculum of such programs shall include:

(1) Conflict resolution and mediation theory;

(2) Mediation process and techniques, including the process and techniques of trial court mediation;

(3) Communication and information gathering skills;

(4) Standards of conduct for mediators including, but not limited to the Standards adopted by the Supreme Court;

(5) Statutes, rules and practice governing mediated settlement conferences in North Carolina;

(6) Demonstrations of mediated settlement conferences;

(7) Simulations of mediated settlement conferences, involving student participation as mediator, attorneys and disputants, which simulations shall be supervised, observed, and evaluated by program faculty; and

(8) Satisfactory completion of an exam by all students testing their familiarity with the statutes, rules, and practice governing mediated settlement conferences in North Carolina.

B. Certified training programs for mediators who are already certified as family financial mediators shall consist of a minimum of sixteen hours. The curriculum of such programs shall include the subjects in Rule 9.A and discussion of the mediation and culture of insured claims. There shall be at least two simulations as specified in subsection (7).

C. A training program must be certified by the Commission before attendance at such program may be used for compliance with Rule 8.A. Certification need not be given in advance of attendance.

Training programs attended prior to the promulgation of these Rules or attended in other states may be approved by the Commission if they are in substantial compliance with the standards set forth in this Rule.

D. To complete certification, a training program shall pay all administrative fees established by the NCAOC upon the recommendation of the Commission.

[Amended effective October 1, 1995; December 30, 1998; September 1, 2000; November 21, 2002; January 1, 2012; April 1, 2014.]

Rule 10. Other Settlement Procedures

A. Order Authorizing Other Settlement Procedures. Upon receipt of a motion by the parties seeking authorization to utilize a settlement procedure in lieu of a mediated settlement conference, the senior resident superior court judge may order the use of the procedure requested under these rules or under local rules unless the court finds that the parties did not agree upon all of the relevant details of the procedure, (including items a-e in Rule 1.C(2)); or that for good cause, the selected procedure is not appropriate for the case or the parties.

B. Other Settlement Procedures Authorized by These Rules. In addition to mediated settlement conferences, the following settlement procedures are authorized by these Rules:

(1) *Neutral Evaluation (Rule 11).* Neutral evaluation in which a neutral offers an advisory evaluation of the case following summary presentations by each party;

(2) *Arbitration (Rule 12).* Non-binding arbitration, in which a neutral renders an advisory decision following summary presentations of the case by the parties and binding arbitration, in which a neutral renders a binding decision following presentations by the parties; and

(3) *Summary Trials (Jury or Non–Jury) (Rule 13).* Non-binding summary trials, in which a privately procured jury or presiding officer renders an advisory verdict following summary presentations by the parties and, in the case of a summary jury trial, a

summary of the law presented by a presiding officer; and binding summary trials, in which a privately procured jury or presiding officer renders a binding verdict following summary presentations by the parties and, in the case of a summary jury trial, a summary of the law presented by a presiding officer.

C. General Rules Applicable to Other Settlement Procedures.

(1) *When Proceeding is Conducted.* Other settlement procedures ordered by the court pursuant to these rules shall be conducted no later than the date of completion set out in the court's original mediated settlement conference order unless extended by the senior resident superior court judge.

(2) *Authority and Duties of Neutrals.*

(a) Authority of neutrals.

(i) Control of proceeding. The neutral evaluator, arbitrator or presiding officer shall at all times be in control of the proceeding and the procedures to be followed.

(ii) Scheduling the proceeding. The neutral evaluator, arbitrator or presiding officer shall attempt to schedule the proceeding at a time that is convenient with the participants, attorneys and neutral(s). In the absence of agreement, such neutral shall select the date for the proceeding.

(b) Duties of neutrals.

(i) The neutral evaluator, arbitrator or presiding officer shall define and describe the following at the beginning of the proceeding.

(a) The process of the proceeding;

(b) The differences between the proceeding and other forms of conflict resolution;

(c) The costs of the proceeding;

(d) The inadmissibility of conduct and statements as provided by N.C.G.S. § 7A-38.1(l) and Rule 10.C(6) herein; and

(e) The duties and responsibilities of the neutral(s) and the participants.

(ii) Disclosure. Each neutral has a duty to be impartial and to advise all participants of any circumstance bearing on possible bias, prejudice, or partiality.

(iii) Reporting results of the proceeding. The neutral evaluator, arbitrator or presiding officer shall report the result of the proceeding to the court on a NCAOC form. The NCAOC may require the neutral to provide statistical data for evaluation of other settlement procedures on forms provided by it.

(iv) Scheduling and holding the proceeding. It is the duty of the neutral evaluator, arbitrator or presiding officer to schedule the proceeding and conduct it prior to the completion deadline set out in the court's order. Deadlines for completion of the proceeding shall be strictly observed by the neutral evaluator, arbitrator, or presiding officer unless said time limit is changed by a written order of the senior resident superior court judge.

(3) *Extensions of Time.* A party or a neutral may request the senior resident superior court judge to extend the deadline for completion of the settlement procedure. A request for an extension shall state the reasons the extension is sought and shall be served by the moving party upon the other parties and the neutral. If the court grants the motion for an extension, this order shall set a new deadline for the completion of the settlement procedure. Said order shall be delivered to all parties and the neutral by the person who sought the extension.

(4) *Where Procedure is Conducted.* The neutral evaluator, arbitrator or presiding officer shall be responsible for reserving a place agreed to by the parties, setting a time, and making other arrangements for the proceeding and for giving timely notice to all attorneys and unrepresented parties in writing of the time and location of the proceeding.

(5) *No Delay of Other Proceedings.* Settlement proceedings shall not be cause for delay of other proceedings in the case, including but not limited to the conduct or completion of discovery, the filing or hearing of motions or the trial of the case, except by order of the senior resident superior court judge.

(6) *Inadmissibility of Settlement Proceedings.* Evidence of statements made and conduct occurring in a mediated settlement conference or other settlement proceeding conducted under this section, whether attributable to a party, the mediator, other neutral, or a neutral observer present at the settlement proceeding, shall not be subject to discovery and shall be inadmissible in any proceeding in the action or other civil actions on the same claim, except:

(a) In proceedings for sanctions under this section;

(b) In proceedings to enforce or rescind a settlement of the action;

(c) In disciplinary proceedings before the State Bar or any agency established to enforce standards of conduct for mediators or other neutrals; or

(d) In proceedings to enforce laws concerning juvenile or elder abuse.

As used in this section, the term "neutral observer" includes persons seeking mediator certification, persons studying dispute resolution processes, and persons acting as interpreters.

No settlement agreement to resolve any or all issues reached at the proceeding conducted under this subsection or during its recesses shall be enforceable unless it has been reduced to writing and signed by the parties. No evidence otherwise discoverable shall be inadmissible merely because it is presented or discussed in a mediated settlement conference or other settlement proceeding. No mediator, other neutral or neutral observer present at a settlement proceeding shall be compelled to testify or produce evidence concerning statements made and conduct occurring in anticipation of, during or as a follow-up to a mediated settlement conference or other settlement proceeding pursuant to this section in any civil proceeding for any purpose, including proceedings to enforce or rescind a settlement of the action, except to attest to the signing of any agreements, and except proceedings for sanctions under this section, disciplinary hearings before the State Bar or any agency established to enforce standards of conduct for mediators or other neutrals and proceedings to enforce laws concerning juvenile or elder abuse.

(7) *No Record Made.* There shall be no record made of any proceedings under these Rules unless the parties have stipulated to binding arbitration or binding summary trial in which case any party after giving adequate notice to opposing parties may record the proceeding.

(8) *Ex Parte Communication Prohibited.* Unless all parties agree otherwise, there shall be no *ex parte* communication prior to the conclusion of the proceeding between the neutral and any counsel or party on any matter related to the proceeding except with regard to administrative matters.

(9) *Duties of the Parties.*

(a) Attendance. All persons required to attend a mediated settlement conference pursuant to Rule 4 shall attend any other settlement procedure which is non-binding in nature, authorized by these rules and ordered by the court except those persons to whom the parties agree and the senior resident superior court judge excuses. Those persons required to attend other settlement procedures which are binding in nature, authorized by these rules and ordered by the court shall be those persons to whom the parties agree. Notice of such agreement shall be given to the court and to the neutral through the filing of a motion to authorize the use of other settlement procedures within 21 days after entry of the order requiring a mediated settlement conference. The notice shall be on a NCAOC form.

(b) Finalizing agreement.

(i) If an agreement is reached on all issues at the neutral evaluation, arbitration or summary trial, the parties to the agreement shall reduce its terms to writing and sign it along with their counsel. A consent judgment or one or more voluntary dismissals shall be filed with the court by such persons as the parties shall designate within 14 days of the conclusion of the proceeding or before the expiration of the deadline for its completion, whichever is longer. The person(s) responsible for filing closing documents with the court shall also sign the report to the court. The parties shall give a copy of their signed agreement, consent judgment or voluntary dismissal(s) to the neutral evaluator, arbitrator, or presiding officer, and all parties at the proceeding.

(ii) If an agreement is reached upon all issues prior to the evaluation, arbitration or summary trial or while the proceeding is in recess, the parties shall reduce its terms to writing and sign it along with their counsel and shall file a consent judgment or voluntary dismissal(s) disposing of all issues with the court within 14 days or before the expiration of the deadline for completion of the proceeding whichever is longer.

(iii) When a case is settled upon all issues, all attorneys of record must notify the senior resident judge within four business days of the settlement and advise who will sign the consent judgment or voluntary dismissal(s).

(c) Payment of neutral's fee. The parties shall pay the neutral's fee as provided by Rule 10.C(12).

(10) *Selection of Neutrals in Other Settlement Procedures.* The parties may select any individual to serve as a neutral in any settlement procedure authorized by these rules. For arbitration, the parties may select either a single arbitrator or a panel of arbitrators. Notice of such selection shall be given to the court and to the neutral through the filing of a motion to authorize the use of other settlement procedures within 21 days after entry of the order requiring a mediated settlement conference. The notice shall be on a NCAOC form. Such notice shall state the name, address and telephone number of the neutral selected; state the rate of compensation of the neutral; and state that the neutral and opposing counsel have agreed upon the selection and compensation.

(11) *Disqualification.* Any party may move a resident or presiding superior court judge of the district in which an action is pending for an order disqualifying the neutral and, for good cause, such order shall be entered. Cause shall exist if the selected neutral has violated any standard of conduct of the State Bar or any standard of conduct for neutrals that may be adopted by the Supreme Court.

(12) *Compensation of the Neutral.* A neutral's compensation shall be paid in an amount agreed to among the parties and the neutral. Time spent reviewing materials in preparing for the neutral evaluation, conducting the proceeding, and making and reporting the award shall be compensable time.

Unless otherwise ordered by the court or agreed to by the parties, the neutral's fees shall be paid in equal shares by the parties. For purposes of this section, multiple parties shall be considered one party when they are represented by the same counsel. The presiding officer and jurors in a summary jury trial are neutrals within the meaning of these Rules and shall be compensated by the parties.

(13) *Sanctions for Failure to Attend Other Settlement Procedure or Pay Neutral's Fee.* Any person

required to attend a settlement procedure or to pay a neutral's fee in compliance with N.C.G.S. § 7A–38.1 and the rules promulgated by the Supreme Court to implement that section, who fails to attend or to pay the fee without good cause, shall be subject to the contempt powers of the court and monetary sanctions imposed by a resident or presiding superior court judge. Such monetary sanctions may include, but are not limited to, the payment of fines, attorney fees, neutral fees, expenses, and loss of earnings incurred by persons attending the procedure. A party seeking sanctions against a person or a resident or presiding judge upon his/her own motion shall do so in a written motion stating the grounds for the motion and the relief sought. Said motion shall be served upon all parties and on any person against whom sanctions are being sought. If the court imposes sanctions, it shall do so, after notice and a hearing, in a written order, making findings of fact supported by substantial evidence and conclusions of law.

[Adopted effective November 21, 2002. Amended effective March 4, 2004; March 1, 2006; March 1, 2010; January 1, 2012; April 1, 2014.]

Rule 11. Rules for Neutral Evaluation

A. Nature of Neutral Evaluation. Neutral evaluation is an informal, abbreviated presentation of facts and issues by the parties to an evaluator at an early stage of the case. The neutral evaluator is responsible for evaluating the strengths and weaknesses of the case, providing candid assessment of liability, settlement value and a dollar value or range of potential awards if the case proceeds to trial. The evaluator is also responsible for identifying areas of agreement and disagreement and suggesting necessary and appropriate discovery.

B. When Conference is to be Held. As a guiding principle, the neutral evaluation conference should be held at an early stage of the case after the time for the filing of answers has expired but in advance of the expiration of the discovery period.

C. Pre–Conference Submissions. No later than 20 days prior to the date established for the neutral evaluation conference to begin, each party shall furnish the evaluator with written information about the case and shall at the same time certify to the evaluator that they served a copy of such summary on all other parties to the case. The information provided to the evaluator and the other parties hereunder shall be a summary of the significant facts and issues in the party's case, shall not be more than five pages in length and shall have attached to it copies of any documents supporting the parties' summary. Information provided to the evaluator and to the other parties pursuant to this paragraph shall not be filed with the court.

D. Replies to Pre–Conference Submissions. No later than 10 days prior to the date established for the neutral evaluation conference to begin any party may, but is not required to, send additional written information not exceeding three pages in length to the evaluator, responding to the submission of an opposing party. The response shall be served on all other parties and the party sending such response shall certify such service to the evaluator, but such response shall not be filed with the court.

E. Conference Procedure. Prior to a neutral evaluation conference, the evaluator may request additional written information from any party. At the conference, the evaluator may address questions to the parties and give them an opportunity to complete their summaries with a brief oral statement.

F. Modification of Procedure. Subject to approval of the evaluator, the parties may agree to modify the procedures required by these rules for neutral evaluation.

G. Evaluator's Duties.

(1) *Evaluator's Opening Statement.* At the beginning of the conference the evaluator shall define and describe the following points to the parties in addition to those matters set out in Rule 10.C(2)(b):

(a) The fact that the neutral evaluation conference is not a trial, the evaluator is not a judge, the evaluator's opinions are not binding on any party, and the parties retain their right to trial if they do not reach a settlement.

(b) The fact that any settlement reached will be only by mutual consent of the parties.

(2) *Oral Report to Parties by Evaluator.* In addition to the written report to the court required under these rules at the conclusion of the neutral evaluation conference, the evaluator shall issue an oral report to the parties advising them of his or her opinions of the case. Such opinion shall include a candid assessment of liability, estimated settlement value, and the strengths and weaknesses of each party's claims if the case proceeds to trial. The oral report shall also contain a suggested settlement or disposition of the case and the reasons therefore. The evaluator shall not reduce his or her oral report to writing and shall not inform the court thereof.

(3) *Report of Evaluator to Court.* Within 10 days after the completion of the neutral evaluation conference, the evaluator shall file a written report with the court using a NCAOC form. The evaluator's report shall inform the court when and where the evaluation was held, the names of those who attended and the names of any party, attorney or insurance company representative known to the evaluator to have been absent from the neutral evaluation without permission. The report shall also inform the court whether or not an agreement upon all issues was reached by the parties and, if so, state the name of the person(s) designated to file the consent judgment or voluntary dismissal(s) with the court. Local rules shall not

require the evaluator to send a copy of any agreement reached by the parties to the court.

H. Evaluator's Authority to Assist Negotiations. If all parties to the neutral evaluation conference request and agree, the evaluator may assist the parties in settlement discussions.

[Adopted effective November 21, 2002. Amended effective March 4, 2004; January 1, 2012; April 1, 2014.]

Rule 12. Rules for Arbitration

In this form of settlement procedure the parties select an arbitrator who shall hear the case and enter an advisory decision. The arbitrator's decision is made to facilitate the parties' negotiation of a settlement and is non-binding, unless neither party timely requests a trial *de novo*, in which case the decision is entered by the senior resident superior court judge as a judgment, or the parties agree that the decision shall be binding.

A. Arbitrators.

Arbitrator's Canon of Ethics. Arbitrators shall comply with the *Canons of Ethics for Arbitrators* promulgated by the Supreme Court of North Carolina (Canons). Arbitrators shall be disqualified and must recuse themselves in accordance with the Canons.

B. Exchange of Information.

(1) *Pre-hearing Exchange of Information.* At least 10 days before the date set for the arbitration hearing the parties shall exchange in writing:

(a) Lists of witnesses they expect to testify;

(b) Copies of documents or exhibits they expect to offer into evidence; and

(c) A brief statement of the issues and contentions of the parties.

Parties may agree in writing to rely on stipulations and/or statements, sworn or unsworn, rather than a formal presentation of witnesses and documents, for all or part of the hearing. Each party shall bring to the hearing and provide to the arbitrator a copy of these materials. These materials shall not be filed with the court or included in the case file.

(2) *Exchanged Documents Considered Authenticated.* Any document exchanged may be received in the hearing as evidence without further authentication; however, the party against whom it is offered may subpoena and examine as an adverse witness anyone who is the author, custodian, or a witness through whom the document might otherwise have been introduced. Documents not so exchanged may not be received if to do so would, in the arbitrator's opinion, constitute unfair, prejudicial surprise.

(3) *Copies of Exhibits Admissible.* Copies of exchanged documents or exhibits are admissible in arbitration hearings in lieu of the originals.

C. Arbitration Hearings.

(1) *Witnesses.* Witnesses may be compelled to testify under oath or affirmation and produce evidence by the same authority and to the same extent as if the hearing were a trial. The arbitrator is empowered and authorized to administer oaths and affirmations in arbitration hearings.

(2) *Subpoenas.* Rule 45 of the North Carolina Rules of Civil Procedure (N.C.R.Civ.P.) shall apply to subpoenas for attendance of witnesses and production of documentary evidence at an arbitration hearing under these Rules.

(3) *Motions.* Designation of an action for arbitration does not affect a party's right to file any motion with the court.

(a) The court, in its discretion, may consider and determine any motion at any time. It may defer consideration of issues raised by motion to the arbitrator for determination in the award. Parties shall state their contentions regarding pending motions referred to the arbitrator in the exchange of information required by Rule 12.B(1).

(b) Pendency of a motion shall not be cause for delaying an arbitration hearing unless the court so orders.

(4) *Law of Evidence Used as Guide.* The law of evidence does not apply, except as to privilege, in an arbitration hearing but shall be considered as a guide toward full and fair development of the facts. The arbitrator shall consider all evidence presented and give it the weight and effect the arbitrator determines appropriate.

(5) *Authority of Arbitrator to Govern Hearings.* Arbitrators shall have the authority of a trial judge to govern the conduct of hearings, except for the power to punish for contempt. The arbitrator shall refer all matters involving contempt to the senior resident superior court judge.

(6) *Conduct of Hearing.* The arbitrator and the parties shall review the list of witnesses, exhibits and written statements concerning issues previously exchanged by the parties pursuant to Rule 12.B(1), above. The order of the hearing shall generally follow the order at trial with regard to opening statements and closing arguments of counsel, direct and cross-examination of witnesses and presentation of exhibits. However, in the arbitrator's discretion the order may be varied.

(7) *No Record of Hearing Made.* No official transcript of an arbitration hearing shall be made. The arbitrator may permit any party to record the arbitration hearing in any manner that does not interfere with the proceeding.

(8) *Parties must be Present at Hearings; Representation.* Subject to the provisions of Rule 10.C(9), all parties shall be present at hearings in person or through representatives authorized to make binding decisions on their behalf in all matters in controversy

before the arbitrator. All parties may be represented by counsel. Parties may appear *pro se* as permitted by law.

(9) *Hearing Concluded.* The arbitrator shall declare the hearing concluded when all the evidence is in and any arguments the arbitrator permits have been completed. In exceptional cases, the arbitrator has discretion to receive post-hearing briefs, but not evidence, if submitted within three days after the hearing has been concluded.

D. The Award.

(1) *Filing the Award.* The arbitrator shall file a written award signed by the arbitrator and filed with the clerk of superior court in the county where the action is pending, with a copy to the senior resident superior court judge within 20 days after the hearing is concluded or the receipt of post-hearing briefs whichever is later. The award shall inform the court of the absence of any party, attorney, or insurance company representative known to the arbitrator to have been absent from the arbitration without permission. An award form, which shall be a NCAOC form, shall be used by the arbitrator as the report to the court and may be used to record its award. The report shall also inform the court in the event that an agreement upon all issues was reached by the parties and, if so, state the name of the person(s) designated to file the consent judgment or voluntary dismissal(s) with the court. Local rules shall not require the arbitrator to send a copy of any agreement reached by the parties to the court.

(2) *Findings; Conclusions; Opinions.* No findings of fact and conclusions of law or opinions supporting an award are required.

(3) *Scope of Award.* The award must resolve all issues raised by the pleadings, may be in any amount supported by the evidence, shall include interest as provided by law, and may include attorney's fees as allowed by law.

(4) *Costs.* The arbitrator may include in an award court costs accruing through the arbitration proceedings in favor of the prevailing party.

(5) *Copies of Award to Parties.* The arbitrator shall deliver a copy of the award to all of the parties or their counsel at the conclusion of the healing or the arbitrator shall serve the award after filing. A record shall be made by the arbitrator of the date and manner of service.

E. Trial De Novo.

(1) *Trial De Novo as of Right.* Any party not in default for a reason subjecting that party to judgment by default who is dissatisfied with an arbitrator's award may have a trial *de novo* as of right upon filing a written demand for trial *de novo* with the court, and service of the demand on all parties, on a NCAOC form within 30 days after the arbitrator's award has been served. Demand for jury trial pursuant to N.C.R.Civ.P. 38(b) does not preserve the right to a trial *de novo*. A demand by any party for a trial *de novo* in accordance with this section is sufficient to preserve the right of all other parties to a trial *de novo*. Any trial *de novo* pursuant to this section shall include all claims in the action.

(2) *No Reference to Arbitration in Presence of Jury.* A trial *de novo* shall be conducted as if there had been no arbitration proceeding. No reference may be made to prior arbitration proceedings in the presence of a jury without consent of all parties to the arbitration and the court's approval.

F. Judgment on the Arbitration Decision.

(1) *Termination of Action Before Judgment.* Dismissals or a consent judgment may be filed at any time before entry of judgment on an award.

(2) *Judgment Entered on Award.* If the case is not terminated by dismissal or consent judgment and no party files a demand for trial *de novo* within 30 days after the award is served, the senior resident superior court judge shall enter judgment on the award, which shall have the same effect as a consent judgment in the action. A copy of the judgment shall be served on all parties or their counsel.

G. Agreement for Binding Arbitration.

(1) *Written Agreement.* The arbitrator's decision may be binding upon the parties if all parties agree in writing. Such agreement may be made at any time after the order for arbitration and prior to the filing of the arbitrator's decision. The written agreement shall be executed by the parties and their counsel and shall be filed with the clerk of superior court and the senior resident superior court judge prior to the filing of the arbitrator's decision.

(2) *Entry of Judgment on a Binding Decision.* The arbitrator shall file the decision with the clerk of superior court and it shall become a judgment in the same manner as set out in N.C.G.S. § 1–569.1ff.

H. Modification Procedure.

Subject to approval of the arbitrator, the parties may agree to modify the procedures required by these rules for court ordered arbitration.

[Adopted effective November 21, 2002. Amended effective March 4, 2004; January 1, 2012; April 1, 2014.]

Rule 13. Rules for Summary Trials

In a summary bench trial, evidence is presented in a summary fashion to a presiding officer, who shall render a verdict. In a summary jury trial, evidence is presented in summary fashion to a privately procured jury, which shall render a verdict. The goal of summary trials is to obtain an accurate prediction of the ultimate verdict of a full civil trial as an aid to the parties and their settlement efforts.

Rule 23 of the General Rules of Practice also provide for summary jury trials. While parties may request of the court permission to utilize that process, it may not be substituted in lieu of mediated settlement conferences or other procedures outlined in these rules.

A. Pre–Summary Trial Conference. Prior to the summary trial, counsel for the parties shall attend a conference with the presiding officer selected by the parties pursuant to Rule 10.C(10). That presiding officer shall issue an order which shall:

(1) Confirm the completion of discovery or set a date for the completion;

(2) Order that all statements made by counsel in the summary trial shall be founded on admissible evidence, either documented by deposition or other discovery previously filed and served, or by affidavits of the witnesses;

(3) Schedule all outstanding motions for hearing;

(4) Set dates by which the parties exchange:

(a) A list of parties' respective issues and contentions for trial;

(b) A preview of the party's presentation, including notations as to the document (*e.g.* deposition, affidavit, letter, contract) which supports that evidentiary statement;

(c) All documents or other evidence upon which each party will rely in making its presentation; and

(d) All exhibits to be presented at the summary trial.

(5) Set the date by which the parties shall enter a stipulation, subject to the presiding officer's approval, detailing the time allowable for jury selection, opening statements, the presentation of evidence and closing arguments (total time is usually limited to one day);

(6) Establish a procedure by which private, paid jurors will be located and assembled by the parties if a summary jury trial is to be held and set the date by which the parties shall submit agreed upon jury instructions, jury selection questionnaire, and the number of potential jurors to be questioned and seated;

(7) Set a date for the summary jury trial; and

(8) Address such other matters as are necessary to place the matter in a posture for summary trial.

B. Presiding Officer to Issue Order If Parties Unable to Agree. If the parties are unable to agree upon the dates and procedures set out in Section A of this Rule, the presiding officer shall issue an order which addresses all matters necessary to place the case in a posture for summary trial.

C. Stipulation to a Binding Summary Trial. At any time prior to the rendering of the verdict, the parties may stipulate that the summary trial be binding and the verdict become a final judgment. The parties may also make a binding high/low agreement, wherein a verdict below a stipulated floor or above a stipulated ceiling would be rejected in favor of the floor or ceiling.

D. Evidentiary Motions. Counsel shall exchange and file motions *in limine* and other evidentiary matters which shall be heard prior to the trial. Counsel shall agree prior to the hearing of said motions as to whether the presiding officer's rulings will be binding in all subsequent hearings or non-binding and limited to the summary trial.

E. Jury Selection. In the case of a summary jury trial, potential jurors shall be selected in accordance with the procedure set out in the pre-summary trial order. These jurors shall complete a questionnaire previously stipulated to by the parties. Eighteen jurors or such lesser number as the parties agree shall submit to questioning by the presiding officer and each party for such time as is allowed pursuant to the Summary Trial Pre-trial Order. Each party shall then have three peremptory challenges, to be taken alternately, beginning with the plaintiff. Following the exercise of all peremptory challenges, the first 12 seated jurors, or such lesser number as the parties may agree, shall constitute the panel.

After the jury is seated, the presiding officer in his/her discretion, may describe the issues and procedures to be used in presenting the summary jury trial. The jury shall not be informed of the non-binding nature of the proceeding, so as not to diminish the seriousness with which they consider the matter and in the event the parties later stipulate to a binding proceeding.

F. Presentation of Evidence and Arguments of Counsel. Each party may make a brief opening statement, following which each side shall present its case within the time limits set in the Summary Trial Pre-trial Order. Each party may reserve a portion of its time for rebuttal or surrebuttal evidence. Although closing arguments are generally omitted, subject to the presiding officer's discretion and the parties' agreement, each party may be allowed to make closing arguments within the time limits previously established.

Evidence shall be presented in summary fashion by the attorneys for each party without live testimony. Where the credibility of a witness is important, the witness may testify in person or by video deposition. All statements of counsel shall be founded on evidence that would be admissible at trial and documented by prior discovery.

Affidavits offered into evidence shall be served upon opposing parties far enough in advance of the proceeding to allow time for affiants to be deposed. Counsel may read portions of the deposition to the jury. Photographs, exhibits, documentary evidence and accurate summaries of evidence through charts, diagrams, evidence notebooks or other visual means are encouraged, but shall be stipulated by both parties or approved by the presiding officer.

G. Jury Charge. In a summary jury trial, following the presentation of evidence by both parties, the presiding officer shall give a brief charge to the jury, relying on predetermined jury instructions and such additional instructions as the presiding officer deems appropriate.

H. Deliberation and Verdict. In a summary jury trial, the presiding officer shall inform the jurors that they should attempt to return a unanimous verdict. The jury shall be given a verdict form stipulated to by the parties or approved by the presiding officer. The form may include specific interrogatories, a general liability inquiry, and/or an inquiry as to damages. If, after diligent efforts and a reasonable time, the jury is unable to reach a unanimous verdict, the presiding officer may recall the jurors and encourage them to reach a verdict quickly and/or inform them that they may return separate verdicts, for which purpose the presiding officer may distribute separate forms.

In a summary bench trial, at the close of the presentation of evidence and arguments of counsel and after allowing time for settlement discussions and consideration of the evidence by the presiding officer, the presiding officer shall render a decision. Upon a party's request, the presiding officer may allow three business days for the filing of post-hearing briefs. If the presiding officer takes the matter under advisement or allows post-hearing briefs, the decision shall be rendered no later than 10 days after the close of the hearing or filing of briefs whichever is longer.

I. Jury Questioning. In a summary jury trial the presiding officer may allow a brief conference with the jurors in open court after a verdict has been returned, in order to determine the basis of the jury's verdict. However, if such a conference is used, it should be limited to general impressions. The presiding officer should not allow counsel to ask detailed questions of jurors to prevent altering the summary trial from a settlement technique to a form of pre-trial rehearsal. Jurors shall not be required to submit to counsels' questioning and shall be informed of the option to depart.

J. Settlement Discussions. Upon the retirement of the jury in summary jury trials or the presiding officer in summary bench trials, the parties and/or their counsel shall meet for settlement discussions. Following the verdict or decision, the parties and/or their counsel shall meet to explore further settlement possibilities. The parties may request that the presiding officer remain available to provide such input or guidance as the presiding officer deems appropriate.

K. Modification of Procedure. Subject to approval of the presiding officer, the parties may agree to modify the procedures set forth in these Rules for summary trial.

L. Report of Presiding Officer. The presiding officer shall file a written report no later than 10 days after the verdict. The report shall be signed by the presiding officer and filed with the clerk of the superior court in the county where the action is pending, with a copy to the senior resident court judge. The presiding officer's report shall inform the court of the absence of any party, attorney or insurance company representative known to the presiding officer to have been absent from the summary jury or summary bench trial without permission. The report may be used to record the verdict. The report shall also inform the court in the event that an agreement upon all issues was reached by the parties and, if so, state the name of the person(s) designated to file the consent judgment or voluntary dismissal(s) with the court. Local rules shall not require the presiding officer to send a copy of any agreement reached by the parties.

[Adopted effective November 21, 2002. Amended effective March 4, 2004; March 1, 2010; January 1, 2012; April 1, 2014.]

Rule 14. Local Rule Making

The senior resident superior court judge of any district conducting mediated settlement conferences under these Rules is authorized to publish local rules, not inconsistent with these Rules and N.C.G.S. § 7A–38.1, implementing mediated settlement conferences in that district.

[Amended effective November 21, 2002; January 1, 2012; April 1, 2014.]

Rule 15. Definitions

A. The term, senior resident superior court judge, as used throughout these rules, shall refer both to said judge or said judge's designee.

B. The phrase, NCAOC forms, shall refer to forms prepared by, printed and distributed by the NCAOC to implement these Rules or forms approved by local rule which contain at least the same information as those prepared by the NCAOC. Proposals for the creation or modification of such forms may be initiated by the Commission.

[Amended effective November 21, 2002; January 1, 2012; April 1, 2014.]

Rule 16. Time Limits

Any time limit provided for by these Rules may be waived or extended for good cause shown. Service of papers and computation of time shall be governed by the N.C.R.Civ.P.

[Amended effective November 21, 2002; January 1, 2012; April 1, 2014.]

RULES IMPLEMENTING SETTLEMENT PROCEDURES IN EQUITABLE DISTRIBUTION AND OTHER FAMILY FINANCIAL CASES

Adopted December 30, 1998, effective March 1, 1999

Table of Rules

Rule 1. Initiating Settlement Procedures

A. Purpose of Mandatory Settlement Procedures. Pursuant to N.C.G.S. § 7A–38.4A, these Rules are promulgated to implement a system of settlement events which are designed to focus the parties' attention on settlement rather than on trial preparation and to provide a structured opportunity for settlement negotiations to take place. Nothing herein is intended to limit or prevent the parties from engaging in settlement procedures voluntarily at any time before or after those ordered by the court pursuant to these Rules.

B. Duty of Counsel to Consult with Clients and Opposing Counsel Concerning Settlement Procedures. In furtherance of this purpose, counsel, upon being retained to represent any party to a district court case involving family financial issues, including equitable distribution, child support, alimony, post-separation support action or claims arising out of contracts between the parties under N.C.G.S. §§ 50–20(d), 52–10, 52–10. 1 or 52B shall advise his or her client regarding the settlement procedures approved by these Rules and, at or prior to the scheduling conference mandated by N.C.G.S. § 50–21(d), shall attempt to reach agreement with opposing counsel on the appropriate settlement procedure for the action.

C. Ordering Settlement Procedures.

(1) *Equitable Distribution Scheduling Conference.* At the scheduling conference mandated by N.C.G.S. § 50–21(d) in all equitable distribution actions in all judicial districts, or at such earlier time as specified by local rule, the court shall include in its scheduling order a requirement that the parties and their counsel attend a mediated settlement conference or, if the parties agree, other settlement procedure conducted pursuant to these Rules, unless excused by the court pursuant to Rule 1.C(6) or by the court or mediator pursuant to Rule 4.A(2). The court shall dispense with the requirement to attend a mediated settlement conference or other settlement procedure only for good cause shown.

(2) *Scope of Settlement Proceedings.* All other financial issues existing between the parties when the equitable distribution settlement proceeding is ordered, or at any time thereafter, may be discussed, negotiated or decided at the proceeding. In those districts where a child custody and visitation mediation program has been established pursuant to N.C.G.S. § 7A–494, child custody and visitation issues may be the subject of settlement proceedings ordered pursuant to these Rules only in those cases in which the parties and the mediator have agreed to include them and in which the parties have been exempted from, or have fulfilled the program requirements. In those districts where a child custody and visitation mediation program has not been established pursuant to N.C.G.S. § 7A–494, child custody and visitation issues may be the subject of settlement proceedings ordered pursuant to these Rules with the agreement of all parties and the mediator.

(3) *Authorizing Settlement Procedures Other Than Mediated Settlement Conference.* The parties and their attorneys are in the best position to know which settlement procedure is appropriate for their case. Therefore, the court shall order the use of a settlement procedure authorized by Rules 10–12 herein or by local rules of the district court in the county or district where the action is pending if the parties have agreed upon the procedure to be used, the neutral to be employed and the compensation of the neutral. If the parties have not agreed on all three items, then the court shall order the parties and their counsel to attend a mediated settlement conference conducted pursuant to these Rules.

The motion for an order to use a settlement procedure other than a mediated settlement conference shall be submitted on a North Carolina Administrative Office of the Courts (NCAOC) form at the scheduling conference and shall state:

(a) the settlement procedure chosen by the parties;

(b) the name, address and telephone number of the neutral selected by the parties;

(c) the rate of compensation of the neutral; and

(d) that all parties consent to the motion.

(4) *Content of Order.* The court's order shall (1) require the mediated settlement conference or other settlement proceeding be held in the case; (2) establish a deadline for the completion of the conference or proceeding; and (3) state that the parties shall be required to pay the neutral's fee at the conclusion of the settlement conference or proceeding unless otherwise ordered by the court. Where the settlement proceeding ordered is a judicial settlement conference, the parties shall not be required to pay for the neutral.

The order shall be contained in the court's scheduling order, or if no scheduling order is entered, shall be on a NCAOC form. Any scheduling order entered at the completion of a scheduling conference held pursuant to local rule may be signed by the parties or their attorneys in lieu of submitting the forms referred to hereinafter relating to the selection of a mediator.

(5) *Court–Ordered Settlement Procedures in Other Family Financial Cases.*

(a) By Motion of a Party. Any party to an action involving family financial issues not previously ordered to a mediated settlement conference may move the court to order the parties to participate in a settlement procedure. Such motion shall be made in writing, state the reasons why the order should be allowed and be served on the non-moving party. Any objection to the motion or any request for hearing shall be filed in writing with the court within 10 days after the date of the service of the motion. Thereafter, the judge shall rule upon the motion and notify the parties or their attorneys of the ruling. If the court orders a settlement proceeding, then the proceeding shall be a mediated settlement conference conducted pursuant to these Rules. Other settlement procedures may be ordered if the circumstances outlined in subsection (3) above have been met.

(b) By Order of the Court. Upon its own motion, the court may order the parties and their attorneys to attend a mediated settlement conference pursuant to these Rules in any other action involving family financial issues and in contempt proceedings in all family financial issues.

The court may order a settlement procedure other than a mediated settlement conference only upon motion of the parties and a finding that the circumstances outlined in subsection (3) above have been met. The court shall consider the ability of the parties to pay for the services of a mediator or other neutral before ordering the parties to attend a settlement procedure pursuant to this section and shall comply with the provisions of Rule 2 with reference to the appointment of a mediator.

D. Motion to Dispense with Settlement Procedures. A party may move the court to dispense with the mediated settlement conference or other settlement procedure ordered by the judge. The motion shall state the reasons for which the relief is sought. For good cause shown, the court may grant the motion. Such good cause may include, but not be limited to, the fact that the parties have participated in a settlement procedure such as non-binding arbitration or early neutral evaluation prior to the court's order to participate in a mediated settlement conference or have elected to resolve their case through arbitration under the Family Law Arbitration Act (N.C.G.S. § 50–41 *et seq.*) or that one of the parties has alleged domestic violence.

[Adopted December 30, 1998, effective March 1, 1999. Amended effective September 1, 2000; October 16, 2001; November 21, 2002; March 1, 2006; January 1, 2012; April 1, 2014.]

Comment to Rule 1

Comment to Rule 1.C(6).

If a party is unable to pay the costs of the conference or lives a great distance from the conference site, the court may want to consider Rules 4 or 7 prior to dispensing with mediation for good cause. Rule 4 provides a way for a party to attend electronically and Rule 7 provides a way for parties to attend and obtain relief from the obligation to pay the mediator's fee.

Rule 2. Designation of Mediator

A. Designation of Certified Family Financial Mediator by Agreement of the Parties. The parties may designate a certified family financial mediator certified pursuant to these Rules by agreement by filing with the court a Designation of Mediator by Agreement at the scheduling conference. Such designation shall; state the name, address and telephone number of the mediator designated; state the rate of compensation of the mediator; state that the mediator and opposing counsel have agreed upon the designation and rate of compensation; and state that the mediator is certified pursuant to these Rules.

In the event the parties wish to designate a mediator who is not certified pursuant to these Rules, the parties may nominate said person by filing a Nomination of Non–Certified Family Financial Mediator with the court at the scheduling conference. Such nomination shall state the name, address and telephone number of the mediator; state the training, experience or other qualifications of the mediator; state the rate of compensation of the mediator; state that the mediator and opposing counsel have agreed upon the nomination and rate of compensation, if any. The court shall approve said nomination if, in the court's opinion, the nominee is qualified to serve as mediator and the parties and the nominee have agreed upon the rate of compensation.

Designations of mediators and nominations of mediators shall be made on a NCAOC form. A copy of each such form submitted to the court and a copy of the court's order requiring a mediated settlement conference shall be delivered to the mediator by the parties.

B. Appointment of Certified Family Financial Mediator by the Court. If the parties cannot agree upon the designation of a mediator, they shall so notify the court and request that the court appoint a mediator. The motion shall be filed at the scheduling conference and shall state that the attorneys for the parties have had a full and frank discussion concerning the designation of a mediator and have been unable to agree on a mediator. The motion shall be on a form approved by the NCAOC. Upon receipt of a motion to appoint a mediator, or failure of the parties to file a Designation of Mediator by Agreement with the court, the court shall appoint a family financial mediator, certified pursuant to these Rules, who has expressed a willingness to mediate actions within the court's district.

In making such appointments, the court shall rotate through the list of available certified mediators. Appointments shall be made without regard to race, gender, religious affiliation or whether the mediator is a licensed attorney. The district court judges shall retain discretion to depart in a specific case from a strict rotation when, in the judge's discretion, there is good cause to do so.

As part of the application or certification renewal process, all mediators shall designate those judicial districts for which they are willing to accept court appointments. Each designation shall be deemed to be a representation that the designating mediator has read and will abide by the local rules for, and will accept appointments from, the designated district and will not charge for travel time and expenses incurred in carrying out his/her duties associated with those appointments. A refusal to accept an appointment in a judicial district designated by the mediator may be grounds for removal from that district's court appointment list by the Commission or by the chief district court judge.

The Commission shall furnish to the district court judges of each judicial district a list of those certified family financial mediators requesting appointments in that district. That list shall contain the mediators' names, addresses and telephone numbers and shall be provided electronically through the Commission's website at www.ncdrc.org. The Commission shall promptly notify the district court judges of any disciplinary action taken with respect to a mediator on the list of certified mediators for the judicial district.

C. Mediator Information. To assist the parties in designating a mediator, the Commission shall assemble, maintain and post on its website a list of certified family financial mediators. The list shall supply contact information for mediators and identify court districts that they are available to serve. Where a mediator has supplied it to the Commission, the list shall also provide biographical information, including information about an individual mediator's education, professional experience and mediation training and experience.

D. Disqualification of Mediator. Any party may move a court of the district where the action is pending for an order disqualifying the mediator. For good cause, such order shall be entered. If the mediator is disqualified, a replacement mediator shall be selected or appointed pursuant to Rule 2. Nothing in this provision shall preclude mediators from disqualifying themselves.

[Adopted December 30, 1998, effective March 1, 1999. Amended effective September 1, 2000; October 16, 2001; November 21, 2002; March 1, 2006; October 1, 2008; March 1, 2010; January 1, 2012; April 1, 2014.]

Rule 3. The Mediated Settlement Conference

A. Where Conference is to be Held. The mediated settlement conference shall be held in any location agreeable to the parties and the mediator. If the parties cannot agree to a location, the mediator shall be responsible for reserving a neutral place in the county where the action is pending and making arrangements for the conference and for giving timely notice of the time and location of the conference to all attorneys, *pro se* parties, and other persons required to attend.

B. When Conference is to be Held. As a guiding principle, the conference should be held after the parties have had a reasonable time to conduct discovery but well in advance of the trial date. The mediator is authorized to assist the parties in establishing a discovery schedule and completing discovery.

The court's order issued pursuant to Rule 1.C(1) shall state a deadline for completion of the conference which shall be not more than 150 days after issuance of the court's order, unless extended by the court. The mediator shall set a date and time for the conference pursuant to Rule 6.B(5).

C. Extending Deadline for Completion. The district court judge may extend the deadline for completion of the mediated settlement conference upon the judge's own motion, upon stipulation of the parties or upon suggestion of the mediator.

D. Recesses. The mediator may recess the conference at any time and may set times for reconvening. If the time for reconvening is set during the conference, no further notification is required for persons present at the conference.

E. The Mediated Settlement Conference is Not to Delay Other Proceedings. The mediated settlement conference shall not be cause for the delay of other proceedings in the case, including the completion of discovery, the filing or hearing of motions or the trial of the case, except by order of the court.

[Adopted December 30, 1998, effective March 1, 1999. Amended effective September 1, 2000; November 21, 2002; January 1, 2012; April 1, 2014.]

Rule 4. Duties of Parties, Attorneys and Other Participants in Mediated Settlement Conferences

A. Attendance.

(1) The following persons shall attend a mediated settlement conference:

(a) Parties.

(b) Attorneys. At least one counsel of record for each party whose counsel has appeared in the action.

(2) Any party or person required to attend a mediated settlement conference shall physically attend until an agreement is reduced to writing and signed as provided in Rule 4.B or an impasse has been declared. Any such party or person may have the attendance requirement excused or modified, including the allowance of that party's or person's participation without physical attendance by:

(a) agreement of all parties and persons required to attend and the mediator; or

(b) order of the court, upon motion of a party and notice to all parties and persons required to attend and the mediator.

(3) *Scheduling.* Participants required to attend shall promptly notify the mediator after selection or appointment of any significant problems they may have with dates for conference sessions before the completion deadline, and shall keep the mediator informed as to such problems as may arise before an anticipated conference session is scheduled by the mediator. After a conference session has been scheduled by the mediator, and a scheduling conflict with another court proceeding thereafter arises, participants shall promptly attempt to resolve it pursuant to Rule 3.1 of the General Rules of Practice for the Superior and District Courts, or, if applicable, the Guidelines for Resolving Scheduling Conflicts adopted by the State–Federal Judicial Council of North Carolina on June 20, 1985.

B. Finalizing Agreement.

(1) If an agreement is reached at the conference, the parties shall reduce the essential terms of the agreement to writing.

(a) If the parties conclude the conference with a written document containing all of the terms of their agreement for property distribution and do **not** intend to submit their agreement to the court for approval, the agreement shall be signed by all parties and formally acknowledged as required by N.C.G.S. § 50–20(d). If the parties conclude the conference with a written document containing all of the terms of their agreement and intend to submit their agreement to the court for approval, the agreement shall be signed by all parties but need not be formally acknowledged. In all cases, the mediator shall report to the court that the matter has been settled and include in the report the name of the person responsible for filing closing documents with the court.

(b) If the parties reach an agreement at the conference for property distribution and do not later intend to submit their agreement to the court for approval, but are unable to complete a final document reflecting their settlement or have it signed and acknowledged as required by N.C.G.S. § 50–20(d), then the parties shall summarize their understanding in written form and shall use it as a memorandum and guide to writing such agreements as may be required to give legal effect to its terms. If the parties later intend to submit their agreement to the court for approval the agreement must be in writing and signed by the parties but need not be formally acknowledged. The mediator shall facilitate the writing of the summary memorandum and shall either:

(i) report to the court that the matter has been settled and include in the report the name of the person responsible for filing closing documents with the court; or, in the mediator's discretion,

(ii) declare a recess of the conference. If a recess is declared, the mediator may schedule another session of the conference if the mediator determines that it would assist the parties in finalizing a settlement.

(2) In all cases where an agreement is reached after being ordered to mediation, whether prior, during the mediation or during a recess, the parties shall file

their consent judgment or voluntary dismissal(s) with the court within 30 days of the agreement or before the expiration of the mediation deadline, whichever is later. The mediator shall report to the court that the matter has been settled and who reported the settlement.

(3) A settlement agreement resolving the distribution of property reached at a proceeding conducted under this section or during its recesses which has not been approved by a court shall not be enforceable unless it has been reduced to writing, signed by the parties and acknowledged as required by N.C.G.S. § 50–20(d).

C. Payment of Mediator's Fee. The parties shall pay the mediator's fee as provided by Rule VII.

D. No Recording. There shall be no stenographic, audio or video recording of the mediation process by any participant. This prohibition precludes recording either surreptitiously or with the agreement of the parties.

[Adopted December 30, 1998, effective March 1, 1999. Amended effective September 1, 2000; October 16, 2001; November 21, 2002; March 4, 2004; March 1, 2006; October 1, 2008; January 1, 2012; April 1, 2014.]

Comment to Rule 4

Comment to Rule 4.B.

N.C.G.S. § 7A–38.4A(j) provides that no settlement shall be enforceable unless it has been reduced to writing and signed by the parties. When a settlement is reached during a mediated settlement conference, the mediator shall be sure its terms are reduced to writing and signed by the parties and their attorneys before ending the conference.

Cases in which agreement on all issues has been reached should be disposed of as expeditiously as possible. This rule is intended to assure that the mediator and the parties move the case toward disposition while honoring the private nature of the mediation process and the mediator's duty of confidentiality. If the parties wish to keep confidential the terms of their settlement, they may timely file with the court closing documents which do not contain confidential terms, *i.e.*, voluntary dismissal(s) or a consent judgment resolving all claims. Mediators will not be required by local rules to submit agreements to the court.

Rule 5. Sanctions for Failure to Attend Mediated Settlement Conferences or Pay Mediator's Fee

Any person required to attend a mediated settlement conference or to pay a portion of the mediator's fee in compliance with N.C.G.S. § 7A–38.4A and the rules promulgated by the Supreme Court of North Carolina (Supreme Court) to implement that section who fails to attend or to pay without good cause, shall be subject to the contempt powers of the court and monetary sanctions imposed by a judge. Such monetary sanctions may include, but are not limited to, the payment of fines, attorney fees, mediator fees, expenses and loss of earnings incurred by persons attending the conference.

A party seeking sanctions against another party or person shall do so in a written motion stating the grounds for the motion and the relief sought. Said motion shall be served upon all parties and on any person against whom sanctions are being sought. The court may initiate sanction proceedings upon its own motion by the entry of a show cause order.

If the court imposes sanctions, it shall do so, after notice and a hearing, in a written order, making findings of fact and conclusions of law. An order imposing sanctions shall be reviewable upon appeal where the entire record as submitted shall be reviewed to determine whether the order is supported by substantial evidence.

[Adopted December 30, 1998, effective March 1, 1999. Amended effective September 1, 2000; October 16, 2001; November 21, 2002; March 1, 2010; January 1, 2012; April 1, 2014.]

Rule 6. Authority and Duties of Mediators

A. Authority of Mediator.

(1) *Control of Conference.* The mediator shall at all times be in control of the conference and the procedures to be followed. The mediator's conduct shall be governed by Standards of Professional Conduct for Mediators (Standards) promulgated by the Supreme Court.

(2) *Private Consultation.* The mediator may communicate privately with any participant during the conference. However, there shall be no *ex parte* communication before or outside the conference between the mediator and any counsel or party on any matter touching the proceeding, except with regard to scheduling matters. Nothing in this rule prevents the mediator from engaging in *ex parte* communications, with the consent of the parties, for the purpose of assisting settlement negotiations.

B. Duties of Mediator.

(1) The mediator shall define and describe the following at the beginning of the conference:

(a) The process of mediation;

(b) The differences between mediation and other forms of conflict resolution;

(c) The costs of the mediated settlement conference;

(d) That the mediated settlement conference is not a trial, the mediator is not a judge and the parties retain their right to trial if they do not reach settlement;

(e) The circumstances under which the mediator may meet and communicate privately with any of the parties or with any other person;

(f) Whether and under what conditions communications with the mediator will be held in confidence during the conference;

(g) The inadmissibility of conduct and statements as provided by N.C.G. S. § 7A–38.4A(j);

(h) The duties and responsibilities of the mediator and the participants; and

(i) The fact that any agreement reached will be reached by mutual consent.

(2) *Disclosure.* The mediator has a duty to be impartial and to advise all participants of any circumstance bearing on possible bias, prejudice or partiality.

(3) *Declaring Impasse.* It is the duty of the mediator to determine in a timely manner that an impasse exists and that the conference should end. To that end, the mediator shall inquire of and consider the desires of the parties to cease or continue the conference.

(4) *Reporting Results of Mediation.*

(a) The mediator shall report to the court the results of the mediated settlement conference and any settlement reached by the parties prior to or during a recess of the conference. Mediators shall also report the results of mediations held in other district court family financial cases in which a mediated settlement conference was not ordered by the court. Said report shall be filed on a NCAOC form within 10 days of the conclusion of the conference or of being notified of the settlement and shall include the names of those persons attending the mediated settlement conference if a conference was held. If partial agreements are reached at the conference, the report shall state what issues remain for trial. Local rules shall not require the mediator to send a copy of the parties' agreement to the court.

(b) If an agreement upon all issues was reached, the mediator's report shall state whether the action will be concluded by consent judgment or voluntary dismissal(s) and the name, address and telephone number of the person(s) designated by the parties to file such consent judgment or dismissal(s) with the court as required by Rule 4.B(2). The mediator shall advise the parties that consistent with Rule 4.B(2) above, their consent judgment or voluntary dismissal is to be filed with the court within 30 days or before expiration of the mediation deadline, whichever is longer, and the mediator's report shall indicate that the parties have been so advised.

(c) The Commission or the NCAOC may require the mediator to provide statistical data for evaluation of the mediated settlement conference program.

(d) Mediators who fail to report as required by this rule shall be subject to sanctions by the court. Such sanctions shall include, but not be limited to, fines or other monetary penalties, decertification as a mediator and any other sanctions available through the power of contempt. The court shall notify the Commission of any action taken against a mediator pursuant to this section.

(5) *Scheduling and Holding the Conference.* The mediator shall schedule the conference and conduct it prior to the conference completion deadline set out in the court's order. The mediator shall make an effort to schedule the conference at a time that is convenient with all participants. In the absence of agreement, the mediator shall select a date and time for the conference. Deadlines for completion of the conference shall be strictly observed by the mediator unless changed by written order of the court.

A mediator selected by agreement of the parties shall not delay scheduling or holding the conference because one or more of the parties has not paid an advance fee deposit required by that agreement.

[Adopted December 30, 1998, effective March 1, 1999. Amended effective September 1, 2000; October 16, 2001; November 21, 2002; March 4, 2004; October 1, 2008; January 1, 2012; April 1, 2014.]

Rule 7. Compensation of the Mediator and Sanctions

A. By Agreement. When the mediator is selected by agreement of the parties, compensation shall be as agreed upon between the parties and the mediator. The terms of the parties' agreement with the mediator notwithstanding, Section E. below shall apply to issues involving the compensation of the mediator. Sections D and F below shall apply unless the parties' agreement provides otherwise.

B. By Court Order. When the mediator is appointed by the court, the parties shall compensate the mediator for the mediation services at the rate of $150 per hour. The parties shall also pay the mediator a one time, per case administrative fee of $150, which accrues upon payment.

C. Change of Appointed Mediator. Pursuant to Rule 2.A, the parties may select a certified mediator or nominate a non-certified mediator to conduct their mediated settlement conference. Parties who fail to select a mediator and then desire a substitution after the court has appointed a mediator, shall obtain court approval for the substitution. The court may approve the substitution only upon proof of payment to the court's original appointee the $150 one time, per case administrative fee and any other amount due and owing for mediation services pursuant to Rule 7.B and any postponement fee due and owing pursuant to Rule 7.F.

D. Payment of Compensation by Parties. Unless otherwise agreed to by the parties or ordered by the court, the mediator's fees shall be paid in equal shares by the named parties. Payment shall be due and payable upon completion of the conference.

E. Inability to Pay. No party found by the court to be unable to pay a full share of a mediator's fee shall be required to pay a full share. Any party required to pay a share of a mediator fee pursuant to Rules 7.B and C may move the court to pay according to the court's determination of that party's ability to pay.

In ruling on such motions, the judge may consider the income and assets of the movant and the outcome of the action. The court shall enter an order granting or denying the party's motion. In so ordering, the court may require that one or more shares be paid out of the marital estate.

Any mediator conducting a settlement conference pursuant to these rules shall accept as payment in full of a party's share of the mediator's fee that portion paid by or on behalf of the party pursuant to an order of the court issued pursuant to this rule.

F. Postponement and Fees.

(1) As used herein, the term "postponement" shall mean reschedule or not proceed with a settlement conference once a date for a session of the settlement conference has been scheduled by the mediator. After a settlement conference has been scheduled for a specific date, a party may not unilaterally postpone the conference.

(2) A conference session may be postponed by the mediator for good cause only after notice by the movant to all parties of the reasons for the postponement and a finding of good cause by the mediator. Good cause shall mean that the reason for the postponement involves a situation over which the party seeking the postponement has no control, including but not limited to, a party or attorney's illness, a death in a party or attorney's family, a sudden and unexpected demand by a judge that a party or attorney for a party appear in court for a purpose not inconsistent with the Guidelines established by Rule 3.1(d) of the General Rules of Practice for the Superior and District Courts or inclement weather such that travel is prohibitive. Where good cause is found, a mediator shall not assess a postponement fee.

(3) The settlement of a case prior to the scheduled date for mediation shall be good cause provided that the mediator was notified of the settlement immediately after it was reached and the mediator received notice of the settlement at least 14 calendar days prior to the date scheduled for mediation.

(4) Without a finding of good cause, a mediator may also postpone a scheduled conference session with the consent of all parties. A fee of $150 shall be paid to the mediator if the postponement is allowed, except that if the request for postponement is made within seven calendar days of the scheduled date for mediation, the fee shall be $300. The postponement fee shall be paid by the party requesting the postponement unless otherwise agreed to between the parties. Postponement fees are in addition to the one time, per case administrative fee provided for in Rule 7.B.

(5) If all parties select the certified mediator and they contract with the mediator as to compensation, the parties and the mediator may specify in their contract alternatives to the postponement fees otherwise required herein.

[Adopted December 30, 1998, effective March 1, 1999. Amended effective September 1, 2000; October 16, 2001; November 21, 2002; March 4, 2004; October 1, 2008; March 1, 2010; January 1, 2012; April 1, 2014.]

Comments to Rule 7

Comment to Rule 7.B.

Court-appointed mediators may not be compensated for travel time, mileage or any other out-of-pocket expenses associated with a court-ordered mediation.

Comment to Rule 7.D.

If a party is found by the court to have failed to attend a family financial settlement conference without good cause, then the court may require that party to pay the mediator's fee and related expenses.

Comment to Rule 7.F.

Non-essential requests for postponements work a hardship on parties and mediators and serve only to inject delay into a process and program designed to expedite litigation. As such, it is expected that mediators will assess a postponement fee in all instances where a request does not appear to be absolutely warranted. Moreover, mediators are encouraged not to agree to postponements in instances where, in their judgment, the mediation could be held as scheduled.

Rule 8. Mediator Certification and Decertification

The Commission may receive and approve applications for certification of persons to be appointed as family financial mediators. For certification, a person must have complied with the requirements in each of the following sections.

A. Training and Experience. Each applicant for certification must demonstrate that she/he has a basic understanding of North Carolina family law. Applicants should be able to demonstrate that they have completed at least 12 hours of education in basic family law (a) by attending workshops and programs on topics such as separation and divorce, alimony and post-separation support, equitable distribution, child custody and support and domestic violence; (b) by engaging in independent study such as viewing or listening to video or audio programs on those family law topics; or (c) by demonstrating equivalent experience, including demonstrating that his or her work experience satisfies one of the categories set forth in the Commission's Policy on Interpreting and Implementing the First Unnumbered Paragraph of FFS Rule 8.A, *e.g.*, that the applicant is an experienced family law judge, board certified family lawyer and, in addition, shall:

(1) Be an Advanced Practitioner member of the Association for Conflict Resolution (ACR) and have earned an undergraduate degree from an accredited four-year college or university, or

(2) Have completed a 40–hour family and divorce mediation training approved by the Commission pursuant to Rule 9, or, if already a certified superior court mediator, have completed the 16–hour family mediation supplemental course pursuant to Rule 9, and have additional experience as follows:

(a) as a member in good standing of the NC State Bar or as a member similarly in good standing of the bar of another state and a graduate of a law school recognized as accredited by the North Carolina Board of law Examiners, with at least five years of experience after the date of licensure as a judge, practicing attorney, law professor and/or mediator or a person with equivalent experience; or

(b) as a licensed psychiatrist pursuant to N.C.G.S. § 90–9 *et seq.*, with at least five years of experience in the field after the date of licensure; or

(c) as a licensed psychologist pursuant to N.C.G.S. § 90–270.1 *et seq.*, with at least five years of experience in the field after the date of licensure; or

(d) as a licensed marriage and family therapist pursuant to N.C.G.S. § 90–270.45 *et seq.*, with at least five years of experience in the field after date of licensure; or

(e) as a licensed clinical social worker pursuant to N.C.G.S. § 90B–7 *et seq.*, with at least five years of experience in the field after date of licensure; or

(f) as a licensed professional counselor pursuant to N.C.G.S. § 90–329 *et seq.*, with at least five years of experience in the field after date of licensure; or

(g) as an accountant certified in North Carolina with at least five years of experience in the field after date of certification.

B. If not licensed to practice law in one of the United States, have completed a six-hour training on North Carolina legal terminology, court structure and civil procedure provided by a trainer certified by the Commission. Attorneys licensed to practice law in states other than North Carolina shall complete this requirement through a course of self-study as directed by the Commission's executive secretary.

C. If not licensed to practice law in North Carolina, provide three letters of reference to the Commission as to the applicant's good character, including at least one letter from a person with knowledge of the applicant's practice and experience as required by Rule 8.A.

D. Have observed as a neutral observer with the permission of the parties two mediations involving custody or family financial issues conducted by a mediator who is certified pursuant to these rules, or who is an Advanced Practitioner Member of the ACR or who is a NCAOC custody mediator. Conferences eligible for observation shall also include those conducted in disputes prior to litigation of family financial issues which are mediated by agreement of the parties and which incorporate these Rules.

If the applicant is not an attorney licensed to practice law in one of the United States, s/he must observe three additional mediations of civil or family cases or of disputes prior to litigation which are conducted by a mediator certified by the Commission and are conducted pursuant to an order of a court or agreement of the parties incorporating the mediation rules of a North Carolina state or federal court. All such conferences shall be observed from their beginning to settlement or impasse. Observations shall be reported on an NCAOC form.

All observers shall conform their conduct to the Commission's Requirements for Observer Conduct.

E. Demonstrate familiarity with the statutes, rules and standards of practice and conduct governing mediated settlement conferences conducted pursuant to these Rules.

F. Be of good moral character and adhere to any standards of practice for mediators acting pursuant to these Rules adopted by the Supreme Court. An applicant for certification shall disclose on his/her application(s) any of the following: any pending criminal matters or any criminal convictions; any disbarments or other revocations or suspensions of any professional license or certification, including suspension or revocation of any license, certification, registration or qualification to serve as a mediator in another state or country for any reason other than to pay a renewal fee. In addition, an applicant for certification shall disclose on his/her application(s) any of the following which occurred within 10 years of the date the application(s) is filed with the Commission: any pending disciplinary complaint(s) filed with, or any private or public sanction(s) imposed by, a professional licensing or regulatory body, including any body regulating mediator conduct; any judicial sanction(s); any civil judgment(s); any tax lien(s); or any bankruptcy filing(s). Once certified, a mediator shall report to the Commission within 30 days of receiving notice any subsequent criminal conviction(s); any disbarment(s) or revocation(s) of a professional license, other disciplinary complaints filed with, or actions taken by, a professional licensing or regulatory body; any judicial sanction(s); any tax lien(s); any civil judgment(s) or any filing(s) for bankruptcy.

G. Submit proof of qualifications set out in this section on a form provided by the Commission.

H. Pay all administrative fees established by the NCAOC upon the recommendation of the Commission.

I. Agree to accept as payment in full of a party's share of the mediator's fee, the fee ordered by the court pursuant to Rule 7.

J. Comply with the requirements of the Commission for continuing mediator education or training. (These requirements may include advanced divorce mediation training, attendance at conferences or seminars relating to mediation skills or process and consultation with other family and divorce mediators about cases actually mediated. Mediators seeking recertification beyond one year from the date of initial certification may also be required to demonstrate that they have completed eight hours of family law training, including tax issues relevant to divorce and property distribution and eight hours of training in family dynamics, child development and interpersonal relations at any time prior to that recertification.) Mediators shall report on a Commission approved form.

Certification may be revoked or not renewed at any time if it is shown to the satisfaction of the Commission that a mediator no longer meets the above qualifications or has not faithfully observed these rules or those of any district in which he or she has served as a mediator. Any person who is or has been disqualified by a professional licensing authority of any state for misconduct shall be ineligible to be certified under this Rule. No application for recertification shall be denied on the grounds that the mediator's training and experience does not meet the training and experience required under Rules which were promulgated after the date of his/her original certification.

K. Once certified, agree to make reasonable efforts to assist mediator certification applicants in completing their observation requirements.

L. No mediator who held a professional license and relied upon that license to qualify for certification under subsection 8.A(2) above shall be decertified or denied recertification because that mediator's license lapses, is relinquished or becomes inactive; provided, however, that this subsection shall not apply to any mediator whose professional license is revoked, suspended, lapsed, relinquished or becomes inactive due to disciplinary action or the threat of same, from his/her licensing authority. Any mediator whose professional license is revoked, suspended, lapsed, relinquished or becomes inactive shall report such matter to the Commission.

If a mediator's professional license lapses, is relinquished or becomes inactive, s/he shall be required to complete all otherwise voluntary continuing mediator education requirements as adopted by the Commission as part of its annual certification renewal process and to report completion of those hours to the Commission's office annually.

[Adopted December 30, 1998, effective March 1, 1999. Amended effective September 1, 2000; October 16, 2001; November 21, 2002; March 4, 2004; March 1, 2006; October 1, 2008; March 1, 2010; January 1, 2012; April 1, 2014.]

Rule 9. Certification of Mediation Training Programs

A. Certified training programs for mediators certified pursuant to Rule 8.A(2) shall consist of a minimum of 40 hours of instruction. The curriculum of such programs shall include the subjects in each of the following sections:

(1) Conflict resolution and mediation theory;

(2) Mediation process and techniques, including the process and techniques typical of family and divorce mediation;

(3) Communication and information gathering skills;

(4) Standards of conduct for mediators including, but not limited to the Standards adopted by the Supreme Court;

(5) Statutes, rules and practice governing mediated settlement conferences conducted pursuant to these Rules;

(6) Demonstrations of mediated settlement conferences with and without attorneys involved;

(7) Simulations of mediated settlement conferences, involving student participation as mediator, attorneys and disputants, which simulations shall be supervised, observed and evaluated by program faculty;

(8) An overview of North Carolina law as it applies to custody and visitation of children, equitable distribution, alimony, child support and post separation support;

(9) An overview of family dynamics, the effect of divorce on children and adults and child development;

(10) Protocols for the screening of cases for issues of domestic violence and substance abuse; and

(11) Satisfactory completion of an exam by all students testing their familiarity with the statutes, rules and practice governing family financial settlement procedures in North Carolina.

B. Certified training programs for mediators certified pursuant to Rule 8.A(2) shall consist of a minimum of 16 hours of instruction. The curriculum of such programs shall include the subjects listed in Rule 9.A. There shall be at least two simulations as specified in subsection (7).

C. A training program must be certified by the Commission before attendance at such program may be used for compliance with Rule 8.A. Certification need not be given in advance of attendance.

Training programs attended prior to the promulgation of these Rules or attended in other states or approved by the ACR with requirements equivalent to those in effect for the Academy of Family Mediators immediately prior to its merger with other organizations to become the ACR may be approved by the Commission if they are in substantial compliance with the Standards set forth in this rule. The Commission may require attendees of an ACR approved program to demonstrate compliance with the requirements of Rules 9.A(5) and 9.A(8) either in the ACR approved training or in some other acceptable course.

D. To complete certification, a training program shall pay all administrative fees established by the NCAOC in consultation with the Commission.

[Adopted December 30, 1998, effective March 1, 1999. Amended effective September 1, 2000; October 16, 2001; November 21, 2002; January 1, 2012; April 1, 2014.]

Rule 10. Other Settlement Procedures

A. Order Authorizing Other Settlement Procedures. Upon receipt of a motion by the parties seeking authorization to utilize a settlement procedure in lieu of a mediated settlement conference, the court may order the use of those procedures listed in Rule 10.B unless the court finds: that the parties did not agree upon the procedure to be utilized, the neutral to conduct it or the neutral's compensation; or that the procedure selected is not appropriate for the case or the parties. Judicial settlement conferences may be ordered only if permitted by local rule.

B. Other Settlement Procedures Authorized by These Rules. In addition to mediated settlement conferences, the following settlement procedures are authorized by these Rules:

(1) *Neutral Evaluation* (Rule 11), in which a neutral offers an advisory evaluation of the case following summary presentations by each party.

(2) *Judicial Settlement Conference* (Rule 12), in which a district court judge assists the parties in reaching their own settlement, if allowed by local rules.

(3) *Other Settlement Procedures* described and authorized by local rule pursuant to Rule 13.

The parties may agree to use arbitration under the Family Law Arbitration Act (N.C.G.S. § 50–41 *et seq.*) which shall constitute good cause for the court to dispense with settlement procedures authorized by these rules (Rule 1.C(6)).

C. General Rules Applicable to Other Settlement Procedures.

(1) *When Proceeding is Conducted.* The neutral shall schedule the conference and conduct it no later than 150 days from the issuance of the court's order or no later than the deadline for completion set out in the court's order, unless extended by the court. The neutral shall make an effort to schedule the conference at a time that is convenient with all participants. In the absence of agreement, the neutral shall select a date and time for the conference. Deadlines for completion of the conference shall be strictly observed by the neutral unless changed by written order of the court.

(2) *Extensions of Time.* A party or a neutral may request the court to extend the deadlines for completion of the settlement procedure. A request for an extension shall state the reasons the extension is sought and shall be served by the moving party upon the other parties and the neutral. The court may grant the extension and enter an order setting a new deadline for completion of the settlement procedure. Said order shall be delivered to all parties and the neutral by the person who sought the extension.

(3) *Where Procedure is Conducted.* Settlement proceedings shall be held in any location agreeable to the parties. If the parties cannot agree to a location, the neutral shall be responsible for reserving a neutral place and making arrangements for the conference and for giving timely notice of the time and location of the conference to all attorneys and *pro se* parties.

(4) *No Delay of Other Proceedings.* Settlement proceedings shall not be cause for delay of other proceedings in the case, including but not limited to the conduct or completion of discovery, the filing or hearing of motions or the trial of the case, except by order of the court.

(5) *Inadmissibility of Settlement Proceedings.* Evidence of statements made and conduct occurring in a mediated settlement conference or other settlement proceeding conducted under this section, whether attributable to a party, the mediator, other neutral or a neutral observer present at the settlement proceeding, shall not be subject to discovery and shall be inadmissible in any proceeding in the action or other civil actions on the same claim, except:

(a) In proceedings for sanctions under this section;

(b) In proceedings to enforce or rescind a settlement of the action;

(c) In disciplinary proceedings before the State Bar or any agency established to enforce standards of conduct for mediators or other neutrals; or

(d) In proceedings to enforce laws concerning juvenile or elder abuse.

As used in this subsection, the term "neutral observer" includes persons seeking mediator certification, persons studying dispute resolution processes, and persons acting as interpreters.

No settlement agreement to resolve any or all issues reached at the proceeding conducted under this section or during its recesses shall be enforceable unless it has been reduced to writing and signed by the parties and in all other respects complies with the requirements of Chapter 50 of the North Carolina General Statutes. No evidence otherwise discoverable shall be inadmissible merely because it is presented or discussed in a settlement proceeding.

No mediator, other neutral or neutral observer present at a settlement proceeding under this section, shall be compelled to testify or produce evidence concerning statements made and conduct occurring in anticipation of, during or as a follow-up to a mediated settlement conference or other settlement proceeding pursuant to this section in any civil proceeding for any purpose, including proceedings to enforce or rescind a settlement of the action, except to attest to the signing of any agreements, and except proceedings for sanctions under this section, disciplinary hearings before the State Bar or any agency established to enforce standards of conduct for mediators or other neutrals, and proceedings to enforce laws concerning juvenile or elder abuse.

(6) *No Record Made.* There shall be no stenographic or other record made of any proceedings under these Rules.

(7) *Ex Parte Communication Prohibited.* Unless all parties agree otherwise, there shall be no *ex parte* communication prior to the conclusion of the proceeding between the neutral and any counsel or party on any matter related to the proceeding except with regard to administrative matters.

(8) *Duties of the Parties.*

(a) Attendance. All parties and attorneys shall attend other settlement procedures authorized by Rule 10 and ordered by the court.

(b) Finalizing Agreement.

(i) If agreement is reached on all issues at the neutral evaluation, judicial settlement conference or other settlement procedure, the essential terms of the agreement shall be reduced to writing as a summary memorandum unless the parties have reduced their agreement to writing, signed it and in all other respects have complied with the requirements of Chapter 50 of the North Carolina General Statutes. The parties and their counsel shall use the summary memorandum as a guide to drafting such agreements and orders as may be required to give legal effect to its terms. Within 30 days of the proceeding, all final agreements and other dispositive documents shall be executed by the parties and notarized, and judgments or voluntary dismissals shall be filed with the court by such persons as the parties or the court shall designate.

(ii) If an agreement is reached upon all issues prior to the neutral evaluation, judicial settlement conference or other settlement procedure or finalized while the proceeding is in recess, the parties shall reduce its terms to writing and sign it along with their counsel, shall comply in all respects with the requirements of Chapter 50 of the North Carolina General Statutes and shall file a consent judgment or voluntary dismissals(s) disposing of all issues with the court within 30 days, or before the expiration of the deadline for completion of the proceeding, whichever is longer.

(iii) When a case is settled upon all issues, all attorneys of record must notify the court within four business days of the settlement and advise who will sign the consent judgment or voluntary dismissal(s).

(c) Payment of Neutral's Fee. The parties shall pay the neutral's fee as provided by Rule 10.C(12), except that no payment shall be required or paid for a judicial settlement conference.

(9) *Sanctions for Failure to Attend Other Settlement Procedure or Pay Neutral's Fee.* Any person required to attend a settlement procedure or pay a neutral's fee in compliance with N.C.G.S. § 7A–38.4A and the rules promulgated by the Supreme Court to implement that section who, fails to attend or to pay the fee without good cause, shall be subject to the contempt powers of the court and monetary sanctions imposed by the court. Such monetary sanctions may include, but are not limited to, the payment of fines, attorney fees, neutral fees, expenses and loss of earnings incurred by persons attending the procedure. A party to the action, or the court on its own motion, seeking sanctions against a party or attorney, shall do so in a written motion stating the grounds for the motion and the relief sought. Said motion shall be served upon all parties and on any person against whom sanctions are being sought. If the court imposes sanctions, it shall do so, after notice and a hearing, in a written order, making findings of fact supported by substantial evidence and conclusions of law.

(10) *Selection of Neutrals in Other Settlement Procedures.*

Selection by Agreement. The parties may select any person whom they believe can assist them with the settlement of their case to serve as a neutral in any settlement procedure authorized by these rules, except for judicial settlement conferences.

Notice of such selection shall be given to the court and to the neutral through the filing of a motion to authorize the use of other settlement procedures at the scheduling conference or the court appearance when settlement procedures are considered by the court. The notice shall be on a NCAOC form as set out in Rule 2 herein. Such notice shall state the name, address and telephone number of the neutral selected; state the rate of compensation of the neutral; and state that the neutral and opposing counsel have agreed upon the selection and compensation.

If the parties are unable to select a neutral by agreement, then the court shall deny the motion for authorization to use another settlement procedure and the court shall order the parties to attend a mediated settlement conference.

(11) *Disqualification of Neutrals.* Any party may move a court of the district in which an action is pending for an order disqualifying the neutral; and, for good cause, such order shall be entered. Cause shall exist, but is not limited to circumstances where, the selected neutral has violated any standard of conduct of the State Bar or any standard of conduct

for neutrals that may be adopted by the Supreme Court.

(12) *Compensation of Neutrals.* A neutral's compensation shall be paid in an amount agreed to among the parties and the neutral. Time spent reviewing materials in preparation for the neutral evaluation, conducting the proceeding and making and reporting the award shall be compensable time. The parties shall not compensate a settlement judge.

(13) *Authority and Duties of Neutrals.*

(a) Authority of Neutrals.

(i) Control of Proceeding. The neutral shall at all times be in control of the proceeding and the procedures to be followed.

(ii) Scheduling the Proceeding. The neutral shall make a good faith effort to schedule the proceeding at a time that is convenient with the participants, attorneys and neutral. In the absence of agreement, the neutral shall select the date and time for the proceeding. Deadlines for completion of the conference shall be strictly observed by the neutral unless changed by written order of the court.

(b) Duties of Neutrals.

(i) The neutral shall define and describe the following at the beginning of the proceeding:

(a) The process of the proceeding;

(b) The differences between the proceeding and other forms of conflict resolution;

(c) The costs of the proceeding;

(d) The admissibility of conduct and statements as provided by N.C.G.S. § 7A–38.1(l) and Rule 10.C(6) herein; and

(e) The duties and responsibilities of the neutral and the participants.

(ii) Disclosure. The neutral has a duty to be impartial and to advise all participants of any circumstance bearing on possible bias, prejudice or partiality.

(iii) Reporting Results of the Proceeding. The neutral evaluator, settlement judge or other neutral shall report the result of the proceeding to the court in writing within 10 days in accordance with the provisions of Rules 11 and 12 herein on a NCAOC form. The NCAOC, in consultation with the Commission, may require the neutral to provide statistical data for evaluation of other settlement procedures.

(iv) Scheduling and Holding the Proceeding. It is the duty of the neutral to schedule the proceeding and conduct it prior to the completion deadline set out in the court's order. Deadlines for completion of the proceeding shall be strictly observed by the neutral unless said time limit is changed by a written order of the court.

[Adopted December 30, 1998, effective March 1, 1999. Amended effective September 1, 2000; October 16, 2001; November 21, 2002; March 4, 2004; March 1, 2006; March 1, 2010; January 1, 2012; April 1, 2014.]

Rule 11. Rules for Neutral Evaluation

A. Nature of Evaluation. Neutral evaluation is an informal, abbreviated presentation of facts and issues by the parties to an evaluator at an early stage of the case. The neutral evaluator is responsible for evaluating the strengths and weaknesses of the case, providing a candid assessment of the merits of the case, settlement value and a dollar value or range of potential awards if the case proceeds to trial. The evaluator is also responsible for identifying areas of agreement and disagreement and suggesting necessary and appropriate discovery.

B. When Conference is to be Held. As a guiding principle, the neutral evaluation conference should be held at an early stage of the case, after the time for the filing of answers has expired but in advance of the expiration of the discovery period.

C. Pre–Conference Submissions. No later than 20 days prior to the date established for the neutral evaluation conference to begin, each party shall furnish the evaluator with written information about the case, and shall at the same time certify to the evaluator that they served a copy of such summary on all other parties to the case. The information provided to the evaluator and the other parties hereunder shall be a summary of the significant facts and issues in the party's case, and shall have attached to it copies of any documents supporting the parties' summary. Information provided to the evaluator and to the other parties pursuant to this paragraph shall not be filed with the court.

D. Replies to Pre–Conference Submissions. No later than 10 days prior to the date established for the neutral evaluation conference to begin, any party may, but is not required to, send additional written information to the evaluator responding to the submission of an opposing party. The response furnished to the evaluator shall be served on all other parties and the party sending such response shall certify such service to the evaluator, but such response shall not be filed with the court.

E. Conference Procedure. Prior to a neutral evaluation conference, the evaluator, if he or she deems it necessary, may request additional written information from any party. At the conference, the evaluator may address questions to the parties and give them an opportunity to complete their summaries with a brief oral statement.

F. Modification of Procedure. Subject to approval of the evaluator, the parties may agree to modify the procedures required by these rules for neutral evaluation.

G. Evaluator's Duties.

(1) *Evaluator's Opening Statement.* At the beginning of the conference the evaluator shall define and describe the following points to the parties in addition to those matters set out in Rule 10.C(2)(b):

(a) The fact that the neutral evaluation conference is not a trial, the evaluator is not a judge, the evaluator's opinions are not binding on any party and the parties retain their right to trial if they do not reach a settlement.

(b) The fact that any settlement reached will be only by mutual consent of the parties.

(2) *Oral Report to Parties by Evaluator.* In addition to the written report to the court required under these rules, at the conclusion of the neutral evaluation conference, the evaluator shall issue an oral report to the parties advising them of his or her opinions of the case. Such opinion shall include a candid assessment of the merits of the case, estimated settlement value and the strengths and weaknesses of each party's claims if the case proceeds to trial. The oral report shall also contain a suggested settlement or disposition of the case and the reasons therefor. The evaluator shall not reduce his or her oral report to writing and shall not inform the court thereof.

(3) *Report of Evaluator to Court.* Within 10 days after the completion of the neutral evaluation conference, the evaluator shall file a written report with the court using a NCAOC form, stating when and where the conference was held, the names of those persons who attended the conference and the names of any party or attorney known to the evaluator to have been absent from the neutral evaluation without permission. The report shall also inform the court whether or not any agreement was reached by the parties. If partial agreement(s) are reached at the evaluation conference, the report shall state what issues remain for trial. In the event of a full or partial agreement, the report shall state the name of the person(s) designated to file the consent judgment or voluntary dismissals with the court. Local rules shall not require the evaluator to send a copy of any agreement reached by the parties to the court.

H. Evaluator's Authority to Assist Negotiations. If all parties at the neutral evaluation conference request and agree, the evaluator may assist the parties in settlement discussions. If the parties do not reach a settlement during such discussions, however, the evaluator shall complete the neutral evaluation conference and make his or her written report to the court as if such settlement discussions had not occurred. If the parties reach agreement at the conference, they shall reduce their agreement to writing as required by Rule 10.C(8)(b).

[Adopted December 30, 1998, effective March 1, 1999. Amended effective September 1, 2000; November 21, 2002; March 4, 2004; January 1, 2012; April 1, 2014.]

Rule 12. Judicial Settlement Conference

A. Settlement Judge. A judicial settlement conference shall be conducted by a district court judge who shall be selected by the chief district court judge. Unless specifically approved by the chief district court judge, the district court judge who presides over the judicial settlement conference shall not be assigned to try the action if it proceeds to trial.

B. Conducting the Conference. The form and manner of conducting the conference shall be in the discretion of the settlement judge. The settlement judge may not impose a settlement on the parties but will assist the parties in reaching a resolution of all claims.

C. Confidential Nature of Conference. Judicial settlement conferences shall be conducted in private. No stenographic or other record may be made of the conference. Persons other than the parties and their counsel may attend only with the consent of all parties. The settlement judge will not communicate with anyone the communications made during the conference, except that the judge may report that a settlement was reached and, with the parties' consent, the terms of that settlement.

D. Report of Judge. Within 10 days after the completion of the judicial settlement conference, the settlement judge shall file a written report with the court using a NCAOC form, stating when and where the conference was held, the names of those persons who attended the conference and the names of any party or attorney known to the settlement judge to have been absent from the settlement conference without permission. The report shall also inform the court whether or not any agreement was reached by the parties. If partial agreement(s) are reached at the settlement conference, the report shall state what issues remain for trial. In the event of a full or partial agreement, the report shall state the name of the person(s) designated to file the consent judgment or voluntary dismissals with the court. Local rules shall not require the settlement judge to send a copy of any agreement reached by the parties to the court

[Adopted December 30, 1998, effective March 1, 1999. Amended effective September 1, 2000; October 16, 2001; November 21, 2002; March 4, 2004; January 1, 2012; April 1, 2014.]

Rule 13. Local Rule Making

The chief district court judge of any district conducting settlement procedures under these Rules is authorized to publish local rules, not inconsistent with these Rules and N.C.G.S. § 7A–38.4. implementing settlement procedures in that district.

[Adopted December 30, 1998, effective March 1, 1999. Amended effective September 1, 2000; November 21, 2002; January 1, 2012; April 1, 2014.]

Rule 14. Definitions

A. The word, court, shall mean a judge of the district court in the district in which an action is pending who has administrative responsibility for the action as an assigned or presiding judge, or said judge's designee, such as a clerk, trial court administrator, case management assistant, judicial assistant and trial court coordinator.

B. The phrase, NCAOC forms, shall refer to forms prepared by, printed and distributed by the NCAOC to implement these Rules or forms approved by local rule which contain at least the same information as those prepared by the NCAOC. Proposals for the creation or modification of such forms may be initiated by the Commission.

C. The term, family financial case, shall refer to any civil action in district court in which a claim for equitable distribution, child support, alimony or post separation support is made or in which there are claims arising out of contracts between the parties under N.C.G.S. §§ 50–20(d), 52–10, 52–10.1 or 52B.

[Adopted December 30, 1998, effective March 1, 1999. Amended effective September 1, 2000; October 16, 2001; November 21, 2002; January 1, 2012; April 1, 2014.]

Rule 15. Time Limits

Any time limit provided for by these rules may be waived or extended for good cause shown. Time shall be counted pursuant to the North Carolina Rules of Civil Procedure.

[Adopted December 30, 1998, effective March 1, 1999. Amended effective September 1, 2000; November 21, 2002; January 1, 2012; April 1, 2014.]

RULES REGULATING MEDIATION OF CHILD CUSTODY AND VISITATION DISPUTES

Adopted December 19, 2002

Table of Rules

CHILD CUSTODY AND VISITATION MEDIATION

Comment

Legislation establishing a statewide Custody and Visitation Program in North Carolina required that the North Carolina Administrative Office of the Courts "promulgate rules and regulations necessary and appropriate for the administration of the program" and that services provided be "uniform." G.S. 7A–494. Uniform rules will protect families receiving such services, will allow meaningful statistical comparisons to be made, and allow both mediators and the mediation program to be periodically reevaluated. The Program is to be established in phases throughout North Carolina, beginning on July 1, 1989.

[Amended effective September 1, 2012.]

Rule 1. Goals of Mediation

The goals of custody and visitation dispute mediation are centered in the reduction of the stress and anxiety experienced by children in separation and divorce by furnishing an alternative way for the parties to settle custody and visitation disputes. A trained mediator helps the parties reorganize the family, continue parenting their children despite separation, and begins an educational process which will allow parties to recognize and meet the needs of their children. Mediation provides a structured, confidential, non-adversarial setting which will help the parties make informed choices about matters involving their children, with the hope that such cooperative resolution will alleviate the acrimony between the parties, reducing attendant stress on both the parties and the child. A successful mediation will help the parties put a parenting plan in writing, will teach them to solve future problems without recourse to the courts, and thus reduce the stress of re-litigation of custody and visitation disputes.

[Adopted December 19, 2002. Amended effective September 1, 2012.]

Rule 2. Purpose of Program

The North Carolina Child Custody and Visitation Mediation Program is to provide the services of skilled mediators to further the goals set out above.

[Adopted December 19, 2002. Amended effective September 1, 2012.]

Rule 3. Definitions

3.01. Mediation. A process whereby a trained, neutral third party acts to encourage and facilitate the resolution of a dispute without prescribing what the resolution should be.

3.02. Mediator. A trained, neutral third party who acts to encourage and facilitate the resolution of a dispute without prescribing what the resolution should be.

3.03. Parenting Agreement. A written agreement reached by the parties with the assistance of the mediator, which may be presented to the court for approval and adoption as an order of the court.

[Adopted December 19, 2002. Amended effective September 1, 2012.]

Rule 4. Administration of Program

The North Carolina Administrative Office of the Courts (NCAOC) is responsible for establishing the North Carolina Child Custody and Visitation Mediation Program and is to promulgate rules and regulations for the administration of the program. The Director of the NCAOC shall appoint necessary staff to plan, organize, and administer the program on a statewide basis. The NCAOC is to cooperate with each Chief District Court Judge and other district personnel in implementation and administration of the program.

4.01. Employment of Mediators. Mediators are to be employed by the Chief District Court Judge of the judicial district, after consultation with NCAOC Court Programs and Management Services staff concerning qualifications, salary and benefits, and are to be hired as full or part-time employees.

4.02. In–House Contracts Permitted. When deemed appropriate by the NCAOC, the Chief District Court Judge may contract for delivery of mediation services. Such contracts are to be approved by the Director of the NCAOC and are exempt from competitive bidding procedures under Chapter 143 of the General Statutes.

4.03. Administration of Funds. Funds appropriated by the General Assembly for the establishment and maintenance of mediation programs are to be administered by the NCAOC.

4.04. Multi–District Programs. The NCAOC may authorize all or part of a program in one district to be operated in conjunction with that of another district or districts.

4.05. Advisory Committee Established. The Director of the NCAOC shall appoint a Custody Mediation Advisory Committee of at least five members to advise the Child Custody and Visitation Mediation Program. Members of the committee are to receive the same per diem and travel expenses as members of state boards and commissions generally.

[Adopted December 19, 2002. Amended effective September 1, 2012.]

Rule 5. Local District Programs

Each local district program is to consist of a qualified mediator, or mediators, and such clerical staff as the NCAOC, in consultation with the local program, deems necessary. Each Chief District Court Judge should develop local rules to address custody mediation practices, including issues not addressed in statute.

[Adopted December 19, 2002. Amended effective September 1, 2012.]

Rule 6. Qualifications of Mediators

A person desiring to furnish mediation services must demonstrate that he or she:

1) Has at least a master's degree in psychology, social work, family counseling, or a comparable human relations discipline; and

2) Has completed at least 40 hours of training in mediation techniques by an instructor deemed qualified by the NCAOC; and

3) Has professional training and experience relating to child development, family dynamics, or comparable areas; and

4) Meets such other criteria as specified by the NCAOC.

6.01. Initial Training Period. A person just beginning to furnish mediation services in the North Carolina Child Custody and Visitation Mediation Program shall satisfy the following requirements for training and mentoring, to be completed in 6–12 months following employment, unless some or all of the requirements are waived by the Director of the NCAOC or his designee. The new mediator shall not conduct mediations without supervision until the individual is assessed by NCAOC staff and approved by the hiring authority.

A. Minimum of 2 weeks of internship in the field to learn case management processes

B. 18 hours of court observations of domestic trials involving child custody and visitation issues

C. 18 hours of custody mediation observation with mediators approved to be mentors by the NCAOC

D. 40 hours of mediation training in a program approved by the NCAOC

E. 24 hours of co-mediation with mediators approved to be mentors by the NCAOC

F. Minimum 4 hours (2 sessions) solo mediation under observation by NCAOC staff or NCAOC approved mentor

G. Official assessment of knowledge, skills and performance of mediation conducted by NCAOC staff

H. Approval to be a NC Child Custody and Visitation Mediator signed by the hiring authority

I. Attendance at meetings/additional training (as designated by the NCAOC)

J. Regional meetings

K. Annual training meetings/workshops or clinics

L. New mediator meetings

6.02. Continuing Education. A mediator is to keep abreast of developments in the field through such professional journals and bulletins as are available; further, a mediator is to participate in at least 16 hours of continuing education, including a component on ethics, every two years in a program approved by the Director of the NCAOC or his designee. A mediator should also regularly participate as a co-mediator, preferably with mediators outside the mediator's judicial district.

6.03. Site Visits. NCAOC staff will conduct periodic site visits to the custody mediation programs in each district and report findings to the Chief District Court Judge. A report will also be kept on file at NCAOC. Staff at NCAOC shall be available to assist Chief District Court Judges in the periodic evaluation of mediators.

6.04. Professional Development. In the interest of quality assurance, program evaluation and continuous skill improvement, NCAOC staff shall provide in-service workshops, new mediator support meetings, and co-mediation and observation opportunities. Mediators are expected to participate in at least one of these events per year. Reports and assessments collected during these interactions shall be shared with the mediator.

6.05. Mediator Ethics. See *Standards of Practice for Mediators in the North Carolina Child Custody and Visitation Mediation Program.*

[Adopted December 19, 2002. Amended effective September 1, 2012.]

Rule 7. Referral to Mediation

All actions involving unresolved issues as to the custody or visitation of a minor child shall be ordered to mediation on such issues prior to the trial of the matter, unless the court waives mediation. Such actions include an action for custody or visitation in which no order has been previously entered, motions to modify orders previously entered, and actions to enforce custody and visitation orders. This mandatory referral procedure does not limit the right of the court to enter temporary and ex *parte* orders under the applicable statutory provisions, or to immediately enforce existing orders. The order of referral shall advise the parties that a show cause order may be issued, or other sanctions imposed, if they fail to appear at the orientation session, or the first mediation session. (See form AOC–CV–632, *Motion and Order to Waive Custody Mediation.*)

[Adopted December 19, 2002. Amended effective September 1, 2012.]

Comment

In the opinion of the Custody Mediation Advisory Committee, the mandatory provisions of G. S. 50–13.1(b), the statutory authority for this section, apply only to actions brought under the provisions of Chapter 50 of the General Statutes. Actions instituted under the provisions of the Juvenile Code, as found in Chapter 7B of the General Statutes, often include issues of placement and visitation at the dispositional stage; such issues may, in appropriate cases, be referred for mediation by a district court judge. Actions brought under the provisions of Chapter 50B of the General Statutes (Domestic Violence) are often inappropriate for mediation because they necessarily involve allegations of intimate partner abuse. If, however, the court finds the custody or visitation aspect of a domestic violence case to be appropriate for mediation, due consideration should be given to safety issues in the case. (See Domestic Violence Policy for the NC Custody and Visitation Mediation Program.)

Rule 8. Waiver of Mediation

On its own motion, or that of either party, the court may waive the setting of a contested custody or visitation matter for mediation. Good cause includes, but is not limited to, a showing of undue hardship to a party, an agreement between the parties for private mediation, allegations of abuse or neglect of the minor child, allegations of alcoholism, drug abuse, or domestic violence between the parents in common, or allegations of severe psychological, psychiatric, or emotional problems. Where a party resides more than 50 miles from court, such distance may be considered good cause. (See form AOC–CV–632, *Motion and Order to Waive Custody Mediation.*)

[Adopted December 19, 2002. Amended effective September 1, 2012.]

Rule 9. Orientation

Prior to mediation, an orientation session shall be held at which the goals and procedures of the mediation process shall be explained to the parties to reduce apprehension and avoidance of the process. An intake form shall be completed. The parties shall be advised that if they fail to appear for the initial mediation session, an order to show cause might be issued and the non-appearing party could be found in contempt of the court.

[Adopted December 19, 2002. Amended effective September 1, 2012.]

Rule 10. Attendance at Mediation Sessions

The mediation process shall consist of no more than three sessions, each of which shall not exceed two hours in length. A party must attend the orientation and first mediation session before deciding to withdraw from the process. The number of sessions may be extended by agreement of the parties with the permission of the Chief District Court Judge.

[Adopted December 15, 2002. Amended effective September 1, 2012.]

Rule 11. Neutral Stance of Mediator

While a mediator is to be a neutral in promoting an agreement between the parties, the mediator is to be aware of the best interests of the children involved in the case. During the mediation process, the mediator is to help the parties avoid agreements which do not promote the best interests of the child.

[Adopted December 19, 2002. Amended effective September 1, 2012.]

Rule 12. The Mediation Process

The mediator should assist the parties in focusing on the needs of their child, the need to reorganize the family and use its strengths, the need to maintain continuity of relationships and stability in the child's life, and the options available to the parties which would accomplish those goals. The mediator should help the parties select from the range of options those which are sound and workable, in an effort to reach an agreement which will reduce the conflict in the family, benefiting both the parties and child.

12.01. Authority of Mediator. The mediator shall be in control at all times of the mediation process and the procedures to be followed in the mediation. The mediator may suspend the mediation session if it becomes unsafe for any of the participants, including the mediator.

12.02. Location. The mediation proceeding shall be held in a private and safe location.

12.03. Confidentiality. The mediation proceeding shall be confidential. Neither the mediator nor any party or other person involved in mediation sessions shall be competent to testify as to communications made during or in furtherance of such mediation sessions, provided there is no privilege as to communications made in furtherance of a crime or fraud. An individual shall not, however, obtain thereby immunity from prosecution for criminal conduct or be excused from the reporting requirement of G.S. 7A–543 or G.S. 108A–102.

12.04. Parenting Plan. A detailed and clearly written parenting agreement, or parenting plan, is the desired end-product of the mediation process. The parenting plan may include a designation of the party having legal or physical custody, and what duties and responsibilities such designation includes. The plan should also include a complete schedule of the child's time with each party, including holidays, vacation time, and special events. Arrangements may be made for special day observances, such as birthdays. The need of the child to maintain relationships with persons with whom the child has a substantial relationship may be addressed.

The mediator should help the parties reduce their agreement to writing and ensure that each party understands the written document. *Before the parties sign the proposed agreement,* the mediator shall mail a copy of the proposed agreement to parties and counsel, encourage each party to have their attorneys review the agreement with them prior to their signing the plan, and afford them a reasonable opportunity to do so. The mediator shall promptly submit the initial signed agreement, or any signed modification agreement to the court. An *Order Approving Parenting Agreement* is to be attached for the judge's signature. (See form AOC–CV–631.) Signed copies will be provided to both parties and their attorneys.

12.05. Plan Incorporated in Court Order. Where an initial signed agreement or a signed modification of that agreement is submitted to the court, it shall be incorporated in a court order unless the court finds good reason not to do so. (See form AOC–CV–631, *Order Approving Parenting Agreement.)* When incorporated, the agreement is enforceable as is any other court order. Even though designated "parenting agreement," or some similar name, the incorporated agreement shall be considered a custody order or child custody determination within the meaning of Chapter 50A of the General Statutes, G.S. 14–320.1, G.S. 110–139.1, or other places where those terms appear.

12.06. Termination of Mediation. After the parties have attended at least the orientation and first mediation session, either or both of the parties may decide not to participate further in the mediation process, and the mediator shall report to the court that no agreement was reached.

Either party may move to have the mediation proceedings dismissed and the action heard in court due to the mediator's bias, undue familiarity with a party, or other prejudicial ground. Further, if the mediator determines that the case is not suitable for mediation due to a power imbalance between the parties, the presence of child abuse or neglect, or other reason, the mediator may report to the court that the case was not resolved. (See form AOC–CV–914, *Order to Calendar Custody or Visitation Dispute.)*

Where an agreement is not reached, the custody mediation office may make available information on community resources for families and children involved in a family reorganization.

12.07. Return to Mediation. The mediator shall explain to the parties that the needs of their children change over time, and encourage them to return to mediation if they are unable to resolve any problems caused by that factor, or other changes in circumstances. (See form AOC–CV–634, *Motion and Order to Return to Custody Mediation.)*

12.08. Other Participants. At the mediator's discretion and with the consent of all parties, other participants may be included in mediation sessions following the initial session.

12.09. Caucus with Parties. Although the majority of the session is conducted with all parties together, at the mediator's discretion and with consent of all parties, the mediator may utilize a caucus, speaking to each participant individually.

12.10. Evaluation of Program. The NCAOC shall evaluate the program from time to time, and **shall** prepare a summary of the program activities to be included in the North Carolina Courts Annual Report of the Administrative Office of the Courts.

Comment

In addition to evaluation of the statistics compiled and submitted by the various programs, user satisfaction might be monitored by the use of exit interviews, and follow-up questionnaires and telephone interviews in a sampling of cases at some time after the completion of the process.

12.11. Complaint Procedure. The written orientation materials provided to the parties shall advise them how a complaint about the mediator, or mediation process, can be filed with the Chief District Court Judge of the judicial district.

[Adopted December 19, 2002. Amended effective September 1, 2012.]

PERMANENCY MEDIATION PROGRAM

Comment

Legislation in G. S. 7B–202 establishing Permanency Mediation in North Carolina requires that the North Carolina Administrative Office of the Courts "establish a Permanency Mediation program" in phases statewide and to "promulgate policies and regulations necessary and appropriate for the administration of the program."

[Adopted effective September 1, 2012.]

Rule 1. Purpose of Permanency Mediation

The purpose of the Permanency Mediation Program is to provide statewide and uniform services to resolve cases in which a juvenile is alleged or has been adjudicated to be abused, neglected, or dependent, or in which a petition or motion to terminate a parent's parental rights has been filed. Participants in the mediation shall include the parties and their attorneys, including the guardian ad litem and attorney advocate for the child. Others may participate by agreement of the parties, their attorneys, and the mediator, or by order of the court.

[Adopted effective September 1, 2012.]

Rule 2. Definitions

2.01. Mediator. A party who has a contract with the North Carolina Administrative Office of the Courts (NCAOC) to perform permanency mediation services.

2.02. Permanency Mediation Agreement. Any agreement reached by the parties as a result of the mediation, whether referred to as a "placement agreement," "case plan," or some similar name, which is reduced to writing, signed by each party, and submitted to the court as soon as practicable.

[Adopted effective September 1, 2012.]

Rule 3. Administration of the Program

The NCAOC is responsible for establishing the program in phases statewide.

3.01. Contractual Services. The Director of the NCAOC is authorized to approve contractual agreements for permanency mediation services; such contracts are exempt from competitive bidding procedures.

3.02. Funding. Any funds appropriated by the General Assembly for the establishment and maintenance of permanency mediation programs shall by [1] administered by the NCAOC.

[Adopted effective September 1, 2012.]

[1] So in original.

Rule 4. Advisory Committee

The Custody Mediation Advisory Committee, established by the Director of the NCAOC, shall advise the NCAOC on matters of the Permanency Mediation Program.

[Adopted effective September 1, 2012.]

APPENDICES

APPENDIX A. STANDARDS OF PRACTICE FOR MEDIATORS IN THE NORTH CAROLINA CHILD CUSTODY AND VISITATION MEDIATION PROGRAM

I. Preamble.

Custody mediation is a family-centered conflict resolution process in which an impartial third party assists the participants in negotiating a consensual and informed parenting agreement. In mediation, decision-making authority rests with the parties. The role of the mediator includes facilitating communication between the parties, exploring solutions, and addressing the needs of the children and other persons who are involved in the dispute.

Mediation is based on principles of problem solving that focus on balance, fairness, privacy and confidentiality, self-determination, and the best interests of all relevant family members, with particular emphasis on the children.

These standards, together with the Uniform Rules Regulating Mediation of Child Custody and Visitation Disputes and Permanency Mediation under the North Carolina Child Custody and Visitation Mediation Program ("Uniform Rules"), are intended to assist and guide custody mediators in the program.

II. Initiating the Process.

II.A. Definition and Description of Mediation. The mediator shall define mediation for all participants, and distinguish the process from therapy, counseling, custody evaluation, arbitration and advocacy.

II.B. Identification of Issues. The mediator shall elicit sufficient information from the participants so they can mutually agree on the issues to be resolved in mediation.

II.C. Determination of Whether Mediation is Appropriate. After gathering information from the parties, the mediator shall evaluate whether mediation of the case is appropriate.

The mediator shall screen the parties for all statutory concerns, particularly those related to family violence, and shall terminate the proceedings if mediation cannot safely continue.

Comment

Uniform Rule 12.02 provides that the mediation proceeding be held in a safe environment, and Uniform Rule 12.01 provides that the proceeding shall be suspended if it becomes unsafe for any participant.

Uniform Rule 12.06 provides that the mediator may report to the court that the case is not suitable for mediation "due to a power imbalance between the parties, the presence of child abuse or neglect, or other reason." Under the provisions of G.S. 50–13.1(c), the court may waive mandatory mediation for "good cause," which includes "allegations of abuse or neglect of the minor child; allegations of alcoholism, drug abuse, or domestic violence between the parents in common; or allegations of severe psychological, psychiatric, or emotional problems."

II.D. Procedures. The mediator shall reach an understanding with the participants regarding the procedures to be followed in mediation. This includes, but is not limited to, the practice of separate meetings between a participant and the mediator (i.e., a caucus), confidentiality, use of legal services, the involvement of additional parties, and conditions under which mediation may be terminated by the mediator. The mediator shall also inform the parties of their right to withdraw from the mediation process.

Comment

See Uniform Rules 12.03 (Confidentiality), 12.04 (Parenting Plan), 12.08 (Other Participants), and 12.09 (Caucus with parties). See also G.S. 50–13.1(e) and (f) for the statutory provisions relating to the confidentiality of the mediation proceeding and, as a general rule, the incompetence of the mediator as a witness in court. There are specific exemptions from the privilege "as to communications made in furtherance of a crime or fraud, "and as required by the abuse reporting provisions of G.S. 7A–543 and G.S. 108A–102.

II.E. Duty of Disclosure. A mediator shall disclose any circumstance to the participants which might cause the mediator to have, or appear to have, a conflict of interest. This shall include any relationship the mediator has with any party or attorney involved in the matter being mediated, whether that relationship is past, present, or anticipated. The mediator shall also fully divulge any possible pecuniary interest the mediator has in the matter, any prior knowledge of the case being mediated, and any other matter which might reasonably appear to present a conflict. Such disclosures must be made as soon as practical after the mediator becomes aware of such interest, knowledge, or relationship. The duty to disclose continues throughout the mediation process.

II.F. Standards of Recusal. If the mediator has provided counseling or mediation services to one of the parties in the past, then the mediator must recuse himself or herself. If such services have been provided to both parties, the mediator shall not proceed unless all parties choose to do so after a full discussion of the role of the mediator in the present mediation as distinguished from the past relationship. The parties may elect to have a different mediator assigned to the case.

Any party to the mediation may request that the mediator be recused because of a conflict of interest. If the mediator believes that a conflict is such that he or she cannot carry out the mediation, then the mediator must recuse himself or herself. If, however, the mediator believes that he or she can carry out the mediation then the mediator may decline to recuse himself or herself. The party may then request that the court remove the mediator.

Comment

Uniform Rule 12.06 provides that either party may move to dismiss the mediation proceedings "due to the mediator's bias, undue familiarity with a party, or other prejudicial ground."

III. Additional Responsibilities of the Mediator.

III.A. The mediator's primary role is to assist the parties in reaching an informed and voluntary agreement. The mediator shall not allow at any time manipulative or intimidating negotiation techniques. The mediator shall not at any time coerce a participant into entering into an agreement, nor shall the mediator make any substantive decision, or act as an advisor, for any participant.

III.B. Although the mediator shall strive to maintain impartiality at all times, the mediator may promote during the mediation the participants' awareness and consideration of the rights of children and third parties who will be affected by the decision of the participants.

Comment

Uniform Rule 11 provides that the mediator is to be neutral but is to "be aware of the best interest of the children," and is to assist the parties to avoid agreements which do not promote the best interest of the child. Uniform Rule 12 provides, in part, that the mediator is to assist the parties in focusing on the needs of the child, so that an agreement benefiting both the parties and the child can be reached.

III.C. The mediator shall be sensitive to issues raised by the gender, ethnic, and cultural diversity of the parties to the mediation.

III.D. The mediator shall not share information with the participants in areas in which the mediator is not qualified by either training or experience.

III.E. The mediator shall advise the participants that each has a right to secure and consult with independent legal counsel during the course of the mediation, and prior to the execution of a formal agreement resolving the issues.

IV. Referral of Parties.

The mediator may refer participants to appropriate community resources so long as such referrals do not compromise the mediator's role as a neutral third party. The mediator shall furnish to the participants a list of at least three service providers, including both professionals in private practice and non-profit agencies.

Under no circumstances should a mediator self-refer a matter, or refer a matter to a specific agency or person with which the mediator has a continuing financial relationship. No commissions, rebates, or similar forms of remuneration shall be given or received for referral of clients.

V. Concluding Mediation.

V.A. The mediator shall inform the participants of their right to withdraw from mediation at any time and for any reason.

V.B. If the mediator believes that the participants are unable or unwilling to participate meaningfully in the mediation process, or that an impasse has been reached and an agreement is unlikely, the mediator may suspend or terminate mediation. In order to avoid unnecessary emotional-costs to the participants, the mediator should not prolong unproductive discussions.

V.C. If no agreement is reached, the mediator may give the parties information on available community resources which can assist families involved in a reorganization.

V.D. When the participants reach a full agreement, the mediator shall discuss with them the process by which the agreement may be formalized and submitted to the court for approval.

V.E. When the participants reach a partial agreement, the mediator shall discuss with them procedures available to them to resolve the remaining issues.

VI. Storage and Disposal of Records.

The mediator shall preserve the records of each case for a period of three years after the conclusion of the mediation. The mediator's records shall be stored in locked containers, and destroyed in a manner which will preserve their confidentiality.

VII. Post-Mediation Relationships.

The mediator's post-mediation professional or social relationship may compromise the mediator's continued availability as a neutral third party. If the parties return to mediation, the mediator must fully disclose any such relationship as set out above in Section II.E.

After mediation of a custody dispute as a part of a court-ordered program, a mediator shall not thereafter accept private employment to mediate other portions of the parties' dispute.

Comment

In order to preserve the integrity of the mandatory custody mediation program, it is important that the mediator avoid, insofar as possible, even the appearance of impropriety.

[Adopted effective September 1, 2012.]

APPENDIX B. DOMESTIC VIOLENCE POLICY FOR THE NC CHILD CUSTODY AND VISITATION MEDIATION PROGRAM

Preamble

While cases involving domestic violence may be exempted from mandatory mediation under the provisions of N.C. Gen. Stat. 50–13.1 (c), this policy is intended to address those cases not waived prior to referral to mediation and/or those deemed appropriate for mediation by the referral source.

Rules and Procedures

I. Orientation

A. Participants may be offered the opportunity to attend separate orientation sessions.

B. Whenever possible, bailiffs should be present at orientation sessions.

II. Screening

A. Mediation intake form questions will alert mediators to issues regarding physical and verbal violence in the relationship, the presence of a Domestic Violence Protective Order (DVPO), and/or issues of substance abuse, child abuse and/or mental illness.

1. 50B Cases

Cases that originate from Chapter 50B actions shall not be mediated.

2. Chapter 50 Cases in which Domestic Violence Is or May Be an Issue

a. When a case referred by the court involves or includes a Chapter 50B action or order, the case may be considered for mediation only if a claim for custody or visitation is pending in a Chapter 50 case.

b. Domestic cases in which violence is a central issue generally are not appropriate for mediation.

c. If there is a prior or pending Chapter 50B action between the parties or a party indicates concerns regarding alleged domestic violence, the mediator has a professional responsibility to screen immediately for safety issues and to make a determination as to the appropriateness of the case for mediation. (Refer to screening procedures outlined in II.A.3.a–e). Cases deemed inappropriate for mediation should be returned to court.

d. Mediators shall where possible obtain a copy of any Chapter 50B Order as a part of the screening process.

e. Mediators will continue to screen each case for appropriateness during mediation session(s) and/or the orientation session.

3. Chapter 50 Cases with an associated Chapter 50B

a. When domestic violence is indicated the mediator may conduct a brief separate interview (in person or by telephone) with either or both parties during the appointment setting phase, to assess the appropriateness of the case for mediation. A detailed assessment during a pre-mediation interview or caucus utilizing a standard one page violence assessment screening checklist may also be appropriate. If the case is appropriate for mediation, assessment shall continue during the mediation process.

b. If the mediator and parties jointly choose to pursue mediation following the assessment described above, the mediator shall determine the appropriate format for the mediation process.

c. Mediators in the training progression, regardless of prior experience with domestic violence, shall consult with their mentor and/or North Carolina Administrative Office of the Courts (NCAOC) staff regarding such cases, and/or arrange for a co-mediator prior to scheduling a mediation session.

d. When the assessment indicates the case is **appropriate** for mediation:

I. The mediator shall make arrangements to promote emotional and physical safety of all participants. Refer to *Triage Process*.

II. The mediator shall refer to *Differences in Parenting Contracts* regarding appropriate parenting time arrangements to maximize boundary setting, reduce reasons for contact and to minimize opportunity to create confusion and to coerce.

III. If safety issues arise during the mediation process, the mediator shall terminate the session, and return the case to the court for disposition. Refer to *Additional Screening Considerations: Indicators of Abuse That Can Be Observed During Mediation*.

e. When the assessment indicates that a case is **inappropriate** for mediation, the mediator shall return the case to the court for disposition.

III. Domestic Violence Protective Order

A Domestic Violence Protective Order (DVPO) is issued by the court. Neither the mediator nor the parties have the authority to modify a DVPO without the approval of the court. If the parties enter into a Parenting Agreement which is inconsistent with the terms of the DVPO, the Parenting Agreement is not effective until approved by the court. The mediator will attach a copy of the DVPO to the Parenting Agreement prior to submission to the judge for review and appropriate disposition.

Continuing Training and Education

I. New Mediators: (Those working to complete the training progression.)

A. Initial Training

1. The 40 hour mediation training for new mediators will include two hours of training on issues and procedures regarding domestic violence.

2. An additional training of six hours regarding screening for domestic violence issues and how these issues relate to mediation procedures and technique will be provided during the first twelve to eighteen months of employment.

B. Continuing Training

1. Recently hired mediators will work with mediators approved to be mentors by the NCAOC. The mentors will have:

a. completed the training progression.

b. demonstrated knowledge, skill and sensitivity in the issues relative to screening/mediation of domestic violence cases.

c. exhibited the ability during case management and self-evaluation to request assistance where appropriate.

2. New mediators will also be required to be involved in continuing training for heightened awareness of domestic violence issues, screening procedures and self-evaluation.

II. All Mediators: Continuing Education in Domestic Violence

Experienced mediators should continue to pursue training, to include gender sensitivity and related issues, the effect of domestic violence on various developmental stages of childhood, and self-awareness of personal issues and how they may impact the mediation process and clients.

Interagency Collaboration

All mediators are encouraged to develop collaborative working relationships with local domestic violence programs and professionals.

Safety

The mediator must, above all, promote the safety of all participants in the mediation process. The mediator shall make arrangements with the client(s) and other appropriate professionals (such as law enforcement) to promote the client's ability to participate in the mediation process safely.

[Adopted effective September 1, 2012.]

RULES IMPLEMENTING MEDIATION IN MATTERS BEFORE THE CLERK OF SUPERIOR COURT

Adopted January 26, 2006, effective March 1, 2006

Table of Rules

Rule 1. Initiating Mediation in Matters Before the Clerk

A. Purpose of Mandatory Mediation. These Rules are promulgated pursuant to N.C.G.S. § 7A-38.3B to implement mediation in certain cases within the clerk's jurisdiction. The procedures set out here are designed to focus the parties' attention on settlement and resolution rather than on preparation for contested hearings and to provide a structured opportunity for settlement negotiations to take place. Nothing herein is intended to limit or prevent the parties from engaging in other settlement efforts voluntarily either prior to or after the filing of a matter with the clerk.

B. Duty of Counsel to Consult with Clients and Opposing Counsel Concerning Settlement Procedures. In furtherance of this purpose, counsel, upon being retained to represent a party to a matter before the clerk, shall discuss the means available to the parties through mediation and other settlement procedures to resolve their disputes without resort to a contested hearing. Counsel shall also discuss with each other what settlement procedure and winch neutral third party would best suit their clients and the matter in controversy.

C. Initiating the Mediation by Order of the Clerk.

(1) *Order by The Clerk of Superior Court.* The clerk of superior court of any county may, by written order, require all persons and entities identified in Rule 4 to attend a mediation in any matter in which the clerk has original or exclusive jurisdiction, except those matters under N.C.G.S. Chapters 45 and 48 and those matters in which the jurisdiction of the clerk is ancillary.

(2) *Content of Order.* The order shall be on a North Carolina Administrative Office of the Courts (NCAOC) form and shall:

(a) require that a mediation be held in the case;

(b) establish deadlines for the selection of a mediator and completion of the mediation;

(c) state the names of the persons and entities who shall attend the mediation;

(d) state clearly that the persons ordered to attend have the right to select their own mediator as provided by Rule 2;

(e) state the rate of compensation of the court appointed mediator in the event that those persons do not exercise their right to select a mediator pursuant to Rule 2; and

(f) state that those persons shall be required to pay the mediator's fee in shares determined by the clerk.

(3) *Motion for Court Ordered Mediation.* In matters not ordered to mediation, any party, interested persons or fiduciary may file a written motion with the clerk requesting that mediation be ordered. Such motion shall state the reasons why the order should be allowed and shall be served in accordance with Rule 5 of the North Carolina Rules of Civil Procedure (N.C.R.Civ.P.) on non-moving parties, interested persons and fiduciaries designated by the clerk or identified by the petitioner in the pleadings. Objections to the motion may be filed in writing within five days after the date of the service of the motion. Thereafter, the clerk shall rule upon the motion without a

hearing and notify the parties or their attorneys of the ruling.

(4) *Informational Brochure.* The clerk shall serve a brochure prepared by the Dispute Resolution Commission (Commission) explaining the mediation process and the operations of the Commission along with the order required by Rule 1.C(1) and 1.C(3).

(5) *Motion to Dispense With Mediation.* A named party, interested person or fiduciary may move the clerk of superior court to dispense with a mediation ordered by the clerk. Such motion shall state the reasons the relief is sought and shall be served on all persons ordered to attend and the mediator. For good cause shown, the clerk may grant the motion.

(6) *Dismissal of Petition For the Adjudication of Incompetence.* The petitioner shall not voluntarily dismiss a petition for adjudication of incompetence after mediation is ordered.

[Adopted January 26, 2006, effective March 1, 2006. Amended effective January 1, 2012; April 1, 2014.]

Rule 2. Designation of Mediator

A. Designation of Certified Mediator by Agreement of Parties. The parties may designate a mediator certified by the Commission by agreement within a period of time as set out in the clerk's order. However, the parties may only designate mediators certified for estate and guardianship matters pursuant to these Rules for estate or guardianship matters.

The petitioner shall file with the clerk a Designation of Mediator within the period set out in the clerk's order; however, any party may file the designation. The party filing the designation shall serve a copy on all parties and the mediator designated to conduct the mediation. Such designation shall state the name, address and telephone number of the mediator designated; state the rate of compensation of the mediator; state that the mediator and persons ordered to attend have agreed upon the designation and rate of compensation; and state under what rules the mediator is certified. The notice shall be on a NCAOC form,

B. Appointment of Mediator by the Clerk. In the event a Designation of Mediator is not filed with the clerk within the time for filing stated in the clerk's order, the clerk shall appoint a mediator certified by the Commission. The clerk shall appoint only those mediators certified pursuant to these Rules for estate and guardianship matters to those matters. The clerk may appoint any certified mediator who has expressed a desire to be appointed to mediate all other matters within the jurisdiction of the clerk.

Except for good cause, mediators shall be appointed by the clerk by rotation from a list of those certified mediators who wish to be appointed for matters within the clerk's jurisdiction, without regard to occupation, race, gender, religion, national origin, disability or whether they are an attorney.

As part of the application or annual certification renewal process, all mediators shall designate those counties for which they are willing to accept court appointments. Each designation shall be deemed to be a representation that the designating mediator has read and will abide by the local rules for, and will accept appointments from, the designated county and will not charge for travel time and expenses incurred in carrying out his/her duties associated with those appointments. A refusal to accept an appointment in a county designated by the mediator may be grounds for removal from said county's court appointment list by the Commission or by the clerk of that county.

The Commission shall furnish to the clerk of each county a list of those superior court mediators requesting appointments in mat county who are certified in estate and guardianship proceedings, and those certified in other matters before the clerk. Said list shall contain the mediators' names, addresses and telephone numbers and shall be provided electronically through the Commission's website at www.ncdrc.org. The Commission shall promptly notify the clerk of any disciplinary action taken with respect to a mediator on the list of certified mediators for the county.

C. Mediator Information Directory. The Commission shall maintain for the consideration of the clerks of superior court and those designating mediators for matters within the clerk's jurisdiction, a directory of certified mediators who request appointments in those matters and a directory of those mediators who are certified pursuant to these Rules. Said directory shall be maintained on the Commission's website at www.ncdrc. org.

D. Disqualification of Mediator. Any person ordered to attend a mediation pursuant to these Rules may move the clerk of superior court of the county in which the matter is pending for an order disqualifying the mediator. For good cause, such order shall be entered. If the mediator is disqualified, a replacement mediator shall be designated or appointed pursuant to Rule 2. Nothing in this provision shall preclude mediators from disqualifying themselves.

[Adopted January 26, 2006, effective March 1, 2006. Amended effective March 1, 2010; January 1, 2012; April 1, 2014.]

Rule 3. The Mediation

A. Where Mediation is to be Held. The mediated settlement conference shall be held in any location agreeable to the parties and the mediator. If the parties cannot agree to a location, the mediator shall be responsible for reserving a neutral place in the county where the action is pending and making arrangements for the conference and for giving timely notice of the time and location of the conference to all attorneys, *pro se* parties, and other persons required to attend.

B. When Mediation is to be Held. The clerks order issued pursuant to Rule 1.C(3) shall state a deadline for completion of the mediation. The mediator shall set a date and time for the mediation pursuant to Rule 6.B(5) and shall conduct the mediation before that date unless the date is extended by the clerk.

C. Extending the Deadline for Completion. The clerk may extend the deadline for completion of the mediation upon the clerk's own motion, upon stipulation of the parties or upon suggestion of the mediator.

D. Recesses. The mediator may recess the mediation at any time and may set times for reconvening which are prior to the deadline for completion. If the time for reconvening is set before the mediation is recessed, no further notification is required for persons present at the mediation.

E. The Mediation is not to Delay Other Proceedings. The mediation shall not be cause for the delay of other proceedings in the matter, including the completion of discovery, the filing or hearing of motions or the hearing of the matter, except by order of the clerk of superior court.

[Adopted January 26, 2006, effective March 1, 2006. Amended effective January 1, 2012; April 1, 2014.]

Rule 4. Duties of Parties, Attorneys and Other Participants in Mediations

A. Attendance.

(1) Persons ordered by the clerk to attend a mediation conducted pursuant to these Rules shall physically attend until an agreement is reduced to writing and signed as provided in Rule 4.B or an impasse has been declared. Any such person may have the attendance requirement excused or modified, including the allowance of that person's participation by telephone or teleconference:

(a) By agreement of all persons ordered to attend and the mediator, or

(b) By order of the clerk of superior court, upon motion of a person ordered to attend and notice of the motion to all other persons ordered to attend and the mediator.

(2) Any person ordered to attend a mediation conducted pursuant to these Rules that is not a natural person or a governmental entity shall be represented at the mediation by an officer, employee or agent who is not such person's outside counsel and who has been authorized to decide on behalf of such party whether and on what terms to settle the matter.

(3) Any person ordered to attend a mediation conducted pursuant to these Rules that is a governmental entity shall be represented at the mediation by an employee or agent who is not such entity's outside counsel and who has authority to decide on behalf of such entity whether and on what terms to settle the matter; provided, however, if under law proposed settlement terms can be approved only by a governing board, the employee or agent shall have authority to negotiate on behalf of the governing board.

(4) An attorney ordered to attend a mediation pursuant to these Rules has satisfied the attendance requirement when at least one counsel of record for any person ordered to attend has attended the mediation.

(5) Other persons may participate in the mediation at the discretion of the mediator.

(6) Persons ordered to attend shall promptly notify the mediator after selection or appointment of any significant problems they may have with dates for mediation sessions before the completion deadline and shall keep the mediator informed as to such problems as may arise before an anticipated session is scheduled by the mediator.

B. Finalizing the Agreement.

(1) If an agreement is reached at the mediation, in matters that, as a matter of law, may be resolved by the parties by agreement, the parties to the agreement shall reduce its terms to writing and sign it along with their counsel. The parties shall designate a person who will file a consent judgment or one or more voluntary dismissals with the clerk and that person shall sign the mediator's report. If agreement is reached in such matters prior to the mediation or during a recess, the parties shall inform the mediator and the clerk that the matter has been settled and, within 10 calendar days of the agreement being reached, file a consent judgment or voluntary dismissal(s).

(2) In all other matters, including guardianship and estate matters, if an agreement is reached upon some or all of the issues at mediation, the persons ordered to attend shall reduce its terms to writing and sign it along with their counsel, if any. Such agreements are not binding upon the clerk but they may be offered into evidence at the hearing of the matter and may be considered by the clerk for a just and fair resolution of the matter. Evidence of statements made and conduct occurring in a mediation where an agreement is reached is admissible pursuant to N.C.G.S. § 7A–38.3B(g)(3).

All written agreements reached in such matters shall include the following language in a prominent place in the document:

"This agreement is not binding on the clerk but will be presented to the clerk as an aid to reaching a just resolution of the matter."

C. Payment of Mediator's Fee. The persons ordered to attend the mediation shall pay the mediator's fee as provided by Rule 7.

D. No Recording. There shall be no stenographic, audio or video recording of the mediation process by any participant. This prohibition precludes recording either surreptitiously or with the agreement of the parties.

[Adopted January 26, 2006, effective March 1, 2006. Amended effective January 1, 2012; April 1, 2014.]

Rule 5. Sanctions for Failure to Attend Mediation or Pay Mediator's Fee

Any person ordered to attend a mediation pursuant to these Rules who fails without good cause to attend or to pay a portion of the mediator's fee in compliance with N.C.G.S. § 7A–38.3B and the Rules promulgated by the Supreme Court of North Carolina (Supreme Court) to implement that section, shall be subject to contempt powers of the clerk and the clerk may impose monetary sanctions. Such monetary sanctions may include, but are not limited to, the payment of fines, attorney fees, mediator fees, expenses and loss of earnings incurred by persons attending the mediation.

A person seeking sanctions against another person shall do so in a written motion stating the grounds for the motion and the relief sought. Said motion shall be served upon all persons ordered to attend. The clerk may initiate sanction proceedings upon his/her own motion by the entry of a show cause order. If the clerk imposes sanctions, the clerk shall do so, after notice and a hearing, in a written order making findings of fact and conclusions of law. An order imposing sanctions is reviewable by the superior court in accordance with N.C.G.S. § 1–301.2 and N.C.G.S. § 1–301.3, as applicable, and thereafter by the appellate courts in accordance with N.C.G.S. § 7A–38.1(g).

[Adopted January 26, 2006, effective March 1, 2006. Amended effective March 1, 2010; January 1, 2012; April 1, 2014.]

Rule 6. Authority and Duties of Mediators

A. Authority of the Mediator.

(1) *Control of the Mediation.* The mediator shall at all times be in control of the mediation and the procedures to be followed. The mediator's conduct shall be governed by Standards of Professional Conduct for Mediators (Standards) promulgated by the Supreme Court.

(2) *Private Consultation.* The mediator may communicate privately with any participant or counsel prior to, during and after the mediation. The fact that private communications have occurred with a participant before the conference shall be disclosed to all other participants at the beginning of the mediation.

B. Duties of the Mediator.

(1) The mediator shall define and describe the following at the beginning of the mediation:

(a) The process of mediation;

(b) The costs of the mediation and the circumstances in which participants will not be taxed with the costs of mediation;

(c) That the mediation is not a trial, the mediator is not a judge, and the parties retain their right to a hearing if they do not reach settlement;

(d) The circumstances under which the mediator may meet and communicate privately with any of the parties or with any other person;

(e) Whether and under what conditions communications with the mediator will be held in confidence during the conference;

(f) The inadmissibility of conduct and statements as provided by N.C.G.S. § 7A–38.3B;

(g) The duties and responsibilities of the mediator and the participants; and

(h) That any agreement reached will be reached by mutual consent and reported to the clerk as provided by rule.

(2) *Disclosure.* The mediator has a duty to be impartial and to advise all participants of any circumstances bearing on possible bias, prejudice or partiality.

(3) *Declaring Impasse.* It is the duty of the mediator to determine in a timely manner that an impasse exists and that the mediation should end. To that end, the mediator shall inquire of and consider the desires of the parties to cease or continue the mediation.

(4) *Reporting Results of Mediation.*

(a) The mediator shall report to the court on a NCAOC form within five days of completion of the mediation whether or not the mediation resulted in a settlement or impasse. If settlement occurred prior to or during a recess of a mediation, the mediator shall file the report of settlement within five days of learning of the settlement and, in addition to the other information required, report who informed the mediator of the settlement.

(b) The mediator's report shall identify those persons attending the mediation, the time spent in and fees charged for mediation, and the names and contact information for those persons designated by the parties to file such consent judgment or dismissal(s) with the clerk as required by Rule 4.B. Mediators shall provide statistical data for evaluation of the mediation program as required from time to time by the Commission or the NCAOC. Mediators shall not be required to send agreements reached in mediation to the clerk, except in estate and guardianship matters and other matters which may be resolved only by order of the clerk.

(c) Mediators who fail to report as required pursuant to this Rule shall be subject to the contempt power of the court and sanctions.

(5) *Scheduling and Holding the Mediation.* It is the duty of the mediator to schedule the mediation and conduct it prior to the mediation completion deadline set out in the clerk's order. The mediator shall make an effort to schedule the mediation at a time that is convenient with all participants. In the absence of agreement, the mediator shall select a date and time for the mediation. Deadlines for completion of the mediation shall be strictly observed by the mediator unless said time limit is changed by a written order of the clerk of superior court.

[Adopted January 26, 2006, effective March 1, 2006. Amended effective January 1, 2012; April 1, 2014.]

Rule 7. Compensation of the Mediator

A. By Agreement. When the mediator is stipulated by the parties, compensation shall be as agreed upon between the parties and the mediator.

B. By Order of the Clerk. When the mediator is appointed by the clerk, the parties shall compensate the mediator for mediation services at the rate of $150 per hour. The parties shall also pay to the mediator a one-time, per case administrative fee of $150 that is due upon appointment.

C. Payment for Compensation. In matters within the clerk's jurisdiction that, as a matter of law, may be resolved by the parties by agreement the mediator's fee shall be paid in equal shares by the parties unless otherwise agreed to by the parties. Payment shall be due upon completion of the mediation.

In all other matters before the clerk, including guardianship and estate matters, the mediator's fee shall be paid in shares as determined by the clerk. A share of a mediator's fee may only be assessed against the estate of a decedent, a trust or a guardianship or against a fiduciary or interested person upon the entry of a written order making specific written findings of fact justifying the taxing of costs.

D. Change of Appointed Mediator. Parties who fail to select a certified mediator within the time set out in the clerk's order and then desire a substitution after the clerk has appointed a certified mediator, shall obtain the approval of the clerk for the substitution. The clerk may approve the substitution only upon proof of payment to the clerk's original appointee the $150 one time, per case administrative fee, any other amount due and owing for mediation services pursuant to Rule 7.B, and any postponement fee due and owing pursuant to Rule 7.F, unless the clerk determines that payment of the fees would be unnecessary or inequitable.

E. Indigent Cases. No person ordered to attend a mediation found to be indigent by the clerk for the purposes of these Rules shall be required to pay a share of the mediator's fee. Any person ordered by the clerk of superior court to attend may move the clerk for a finding of indigence and to be relieved of that person's obligation to pay a share of the mediator's fee. The motion shall be heard subsequent to the completion of the mediation or if the parties do not settle their matter, subsequent to its conclusion. In ruling upon such motions, the clerk shall apply the criteria enumerated in N.C.G.S. § 1-110(a), but shall take into consideration the outcome of the matter and whether a decision was rendered in the movant's favor. The clerk shall enter an order granting or denying the person's request. Any mediator conducting a mediation pursuant to these Rules shall waive the payment of fees from persons found by the court to be indigent.

F. Postponements.

(1) As used herein, the term "postponement" shall mean reschedule or not proceed with mediation once the mediator has scheduled a date for a session of the mediation. After mediation has been scheduled for a specific date, a person ordered to attend may not unilaterally postpone the mediation.

(2) A mediation session may be postponed by the mediator for good cause beyond the control of the movant only after notice by the movant to all persons of the reasons for the postponement and a finding of good cause by the mediator. A postponement fee shall not be charged in such circumstance.

(3) Without a finding of good cause, a mediator may also postpone a scheduled mediation session with the consent of all parties. A fee of $150 shall be paid to the mediator if the postponement is allowed or if the request is within two business days of the scheduled date the fee shall be $300. The person responsible for it shall pay the postponement fee. If it is not possible to determine who is responsible, the clerk shall assess responsibility. Postponement fees are in addition to the one time, per case administrative fee provided for in Rule 7.B. A mediator shall not charge a postponement fee when the mediator is responsible for the postponement

(4) If all persons ordered to attend select the mediator and they contract with the mediator as to compensation, the parties and the mediator may specify in their contract alternatives to the postponement fees otherwise required herein.

G. Sanctions for Failure to Pay Mediator's Fee. Willful failure of a party to make timely payment of that party's share of the mediator's fee (whether the one time, per case, administrative fee, the hourly fee for mediation services or any postponement fee) or willful failure of a party contending indigent status to promptly move the clerk of superior court for a finding of indigency, shall constitute contempt of court and may result, following notice and a hearing, in the imposition of any and all lawful sanctions by the superior court pursuant to N.C.G.S. § 5A.

[Adopted January 26, 2006, effective March 1, 2006. Amended effective October 1, 2008; March 1, 2010; January 1, 2012; April 1, 2014.]

Rule 8. Mediator Certification and Decertification

The Commission may receive and approve applications for certification of persons to be appointed as clerk of court mediators.

A. For appointment by the clerk as mediator in all cases within the clerk's jurisdiction except guardianship and estate matters, a person shall be certified by the Commission for either the superior or district court mediation programs;

B. For appointment by the clerk as mediator in guardianship and estate matters within the clerk's jurisdiction, a person shall be certified as a mediator by the Commission for either the superior or district court programs and complete a course, at least 10 hours in length, approved by the Commission pursuant to Rule 9 concerning estate and guardianship matters within the clerk's jurisdiction;

C. Submit proof of qualifications set out in this section on a form provided by the Commission;

D. Pay all administrative fees established by the NCAOC upon the recommendation of the Commission; and

E. Agree to accept, as payment in full of a party's share of the mediator's fee, the fee ordered by the clerk pursuant to Rule 7.

Certification may be revoked or not renewed at any time it is shown to the satisfaction of the Commission that a mediator no longer meets the above qualifications or has not faithfully observed these Rules or those of any county in which he or she has served as a mediator or the Standards. Any person who is or has been disqualified by a professional licensing authority of any state for misconduct shall be ineligible to be certified under this Rule.

[Adopted January 26, 2006, effective March 1, 2006. Amended effective January 1, 2012; April 1, 2014.]

Rule 9. Certification of Mediation Training Programs

A. Certified training programs for mediators seeking certification pursuant to these Rules for estate and guardianship matters within the jurisdiction of the clerk of superior court shall consist of a minimum of 10 hours instruction. The curriculum of such programs shall include:

(1) Factors distinguishing estate and guardianship mediation from other types of mediations;

(2) The aging process and societal attitudes toward the elderly, mentally ill and disabled;

(3) Ensuring full participation of respondents and identifying interested persons and nonparty participants;

(4) Medical concerns of the elderly, mentally ill and disabled;

(5) Financial and accounting concerns in the administration of estates and of the elderly, mentally ill and disabled;

(6) Family dynamics relative to the elderly, mentally ill and disabled and to the families of deceased persons;

(7) Assessing physical and mental capacity;

(8) Availability of community resources for the elderly, mentally ill and disabled;

(9) Principles of guardianship law and procedure;

(10) Principles of estate law and procedure;

(11) Statute, rules and forms applicable to mediation conducted under these Rules; and

(12) Ethical and conduct issues in mediations conducted under these Rules.

The Commission may adopt Guidelines for trainers amplifying the above topics and set out minimum time frames and materials that trainers shall allocate to each topic. Any such Guidelines shall be available at the Commission's office and posted on its website.

B. A training program must be certified by the Commission before attendance at such program may be used for compliance with Rule 8.B. Certification need not be given in advance of attendance. Training programs attended prior to the promulgation of these Rules or attended in other states may be approved by the Commission if they are in substantial compliance with the standards set forth in this Rule.

C. To complete certification, a training program shall pay all administrative fees established by the NCAOC in consultation with the Commission.

[Adopted January 26, 2006, effective March 1, 2006. Amended effective January 1, 2012; April 1, 2014.]

Rule 10. Procedural Details

The clerk of superior court shall make all those orders just and necessary to safeguard the interests of all persons and may supplement all necessary procedural details not inconsistent with these Rules.

[Adopted January 26, 2006, effective March 1, 2006. Amended effective January 1, 2012; April 1, 2014.]

Rule 11. Definitions

A. The term, clerk of superior court, as used throughout these Rules, shall refer both to said clerk or assistant clerk.

B. The phrase, NCAOC forms, shall refer to forms prepared by, printed and distributed by the

NCAOC to implement these Rules or forms approved by local rule which contain at least the same information as those prepared by the NCAOC. Proposals for the creation or modification of such forms may be initiated by the Commission.

[Adopted January 26, 2006, effective March 1, 2006. Amended effective January 1, 2012; April 1, 2014.]

Rule 12. Time Limits

Any time limit provided for by these Rules may be waived or extended for good cause shown. Service of papers and computation of time shall be governed by the N.C.R.Civ.P.

[Adopted January 26, 2006, effective March 1, 2006. Amended effective January 1, 2012; April 1, 2014.]

RULES IMPLEMENTING THE PRELITIGATION FARM NUISANCE MEDIATION PROGRAM

Adopted April 10, 1996

Table of Rules

Rule 1. Submission of Dispute to Prelitigation Farm Nuisance Mediation

A. Mediation shall be initiated by the filing of a Request for Prelitigation Mediation of Farm Nuisance Dispute (Request) (Form AOC–CV–820) with the clerk of superior court in a county in which the action may be brought. The Request shall be on a form prescribed by the North Carolina Administrative Office of the Courts (NCAOC) and posted on the NCAOC's website at www.nccourts.org. The party filing the Request shall mail a copy of the Request by certified U.S. mail, return receipt requested, to each party to the dispute.

B. The clerk of superior court shall accept the Request and shall file it in a miscellaneous file under the name of the requesting party.

[Adopted April 10, 1996. Amended effective September 1, 2000; January 1, 2012; April 1, 2014.]

Rule 2. Exemption from N.C.G.S. § 7A–38.1

A dispute mediated pursuant to N.C.G.S. § 7A–38.3, shall be exempt from an order referring the dispute to a mediated settlement conference entered pursuant to N.C.G.S. § 7A–38.1.

[Adopted April 10, 1996. Amended effective September 1, 2000; January 1, 2012; April 1, 2014.]

Rule 3. Selection of Mediator

A. Time Period for Selection. The parties to the dispute shall have 21 days from the date of the filing of the Request to select a mediator to conduct their mediation and to file Notice of Selection of Certified Mediator by Agreement.

B. Selection of Certified Mediator by Agreement. The clerk shall provide each party to the dispute with a list of certified superior court mediators serving the judicial district encompassing the county in which the Request was filed. If the parties are able to agree on a mediator from that list to conduct their mediation, the party who filed the Request shall notify the clerk by filing with the clerk a Notice of Selection of Certified Mediator by Agreement (Notice) (Form AOC–CV–821). Such Notice shall state the name, address and telephone number of the certified mediator selected; state the rate of compensation to be paid the mediator; and state that the mediator and the parties to the dispute have agreed on the selection and the rate of compensation. The Notice shall be on a form prepared and distributed by the NCAOC and available on the court's website.

C. Court Appointment of Mediator. If the parties to the dispute cannot agree on selection of a certified superior court mediator, the party who filed the Request shall file with the clerk a Motion for Court Appointment of Mediator (Motion) and the senior resident superior court judge shall appoint a certified superior court mediator. The Motion shall be filed with the clerk within 21 days of the date of the filing of the Request. The Motion shall be on a form prepared and distributed by the NCAOC (Form AOC–CV–821). The Motion shall state whether any party prefers a certified attorney mediator, and if so, the senior resident superior court judge shall appoint a certified attorney mediator. The Motion may state that all parties prefer a certified non-attorney mediator, and if so, the senior resident judge shall appoint a certified non-attorney mediator. If no preference is expressed, the senior resident superior court judge may appoint any certified superior court mediator.

As part of the application or annual renewal certification process, all mediators shall designate those judicial districts for which they are willing to accept court appointments. Each designation shall be deemed to be a representation that the designating mediator has read and will abide by the local rules for, and will accept appointments from, the designated district and will not charge for travel time and expenses incurred in carrying out his/her duties associated with those appointments. A refusal to accept an appointment in a judicial district designated by the mediator may be grounds for removal from that district's court appointment list by the Commission or by the senior resident superior court judge.

The Commission shall furnish to the senior resident superior court judge of each judicial district a list of those certified superior court mediators requesting appointments in that district. Said list shall contain the mediators' names, addresses and telephone numbers and shall be provided electronically through the Commission's website at www.ncdrc.org. The Commission shall promptly notify the senior resident superior court judge of any disciplinary action taken with respect to a mediator on the list of certified mediators for the judicial district.

D. Mediator Information Directory. To assist parties in learning more about the qualifications and experience of certified mediators, the Dispute Resolution Commission (Commission) shall post a list of certified superior court mediators on its website at www.ncdrc.org accompanied by contact, availability and biographical information, including information identifying mediators who wish to mediate farm nuisance matters.

[Adopted April 10, 1996. Amended effective September 1, 2000; January 1, 2012; April 1, 2014.]

Rule 4. The Prelitigation Farm Mediation

A. When Mediation is to be Completed. The mediation shall be completed within 60 days of the Notice or the date of the order appointing a mediator to conduct the mediation.

B. Extending Deadline for Completion. The senior resident superior court judge may extend the deadline for completion of the mediation upon the judge's own motion, upon stipulation of the parties or upon suggestion of the mediator.

C. Where Mediation is to be Held. The mediated settlement conference shall be held in any location agreeable to the parties and the mediator. If the parties cannot agree to a location, the mediator shall be responsible for reserving a neutral place in the county where the action is pending and making arrangements for the conference and for giving timely notice of the time and location of the conference to all attorneys, *pro se* parties and other persons required to attend.

D. Recesses. The mediator may recess the mediation at any time and may set a time for reconvening, except that such time shall fall within a 30 day period from the date of the order appointing the mediator. No further notification is required for persons present at the recessed mediation session.

E. Duties of the Parties, Attorneys, and Other Participants. Rule 4 of the Rules Implementing Mediated Settlement Conferences in Superior Court Civil Actions is hereby incorporated by reference.

F. Sanctions for Failure to Attend. Rule 5 of the Rules Implementing Mediated Settlement Conferences in Superior Court Civil Actions is hereby incorporated by reference.

[Adopted April 10, 1996. Amended effective September 1, 2000; January 1, 2012; April 1, 2014.]

Rule 5. Authority and Duties of the Mediator

A. Authority of Mediator.

(1) *Control of Mediation.* The mediator shall at all times be in control of the mediation and the procedures to be followed. The mediator's conduct shall be governed by Standards of Professional Conduct for Mediators (Standards) promulgated by the Supreme Court.

(2) *Private Consultation.* The mediator may communicate privately with any participant prior to and during the mediation. The fact that private communications have occurred with a participant shall be disclosed to all other participants at the beginning of the mediation.

(3) *Scheduling the Mediation.* The mediator shall make a good faith effort to schedule the mediation at a time that is convenient for the participants, attorneys and mediator. In the absence of agreement, the mediator shall select the date for the mediation.

B. Duties of Mediator.

(1) The mediator shall define and describe the following at the beginning of the mediation:

(a) The process of mediation;

(b) The differences between mediation and other forms of conflict resolution;

(c) The costs of mediation;

(d) The fact that the mediation is not a trial, the mediator is not a judge and that the parties may pursue their dispute in court if mediation is not successful and they so choose;

(e) The circumstances under which the mediator may meet and communicate privately with any of the parties or with any other person;

(f) Whether and under what conditions communications with the mediator will be held in confidence during the mediation;

(g) The inadmissibility of conduct and statements as provided by N.C.G.S. § 7A–38.t(1);

(h) The duties and responsibilities of the mediator and the participants; and

(i) The fact that any agreement reached will be reached by mutual consent.

(2) *Disclosure.* The mediator has a duty to be impartial and to advise all participants of any circumstance bearing on possible bias, prejudice or partiality.

(3) *Declaring Impasse.* It is the duty of the mediator to determine timely that an impasse exists and that the mediation should end.

(4) *Scheduling and Holding the Mediation.* It is the duty of the mediator to schedule the mediation and to conduct it within the time frame established by Rule 4 above. Rule 4 shall be strictly observed by the mediator unless an extension has been granted in writing by the senior resident superior court judge.

(5) *No Recording.* There shall be no stenographic, audio or video recording of the mediation process by any participant. This prohibition precludes recording either surreptitiously or with the agreement of the parties.

[Adopted April 10, 1996. Amended effective September 1, 2000; January 1, 2012; April 1, 2014.]

Rule 6. Compensation of the Mediator

A. By Agreement. When the mediator is stipulated to by the parties, compensation shall be as agreed upon between the parties and the mediator, except that no administrative fees or fees for services shall be assessed any party if all parties waive mediation prior to the occurrence of an initial mediation meeting.

B. By Court Order. When the mediator is appointed by the court, the parties shall compensate the mediator for mediation services at the rate of $150 per hour. The parties shall also pay to the mediator a one time, per case administrative fee of $150, except that no administrative fees or fees for services shall be assessed any party if all parties waive mediation prior to the occurrence of an initial mediation meeting.

C. Indigent Cases. No party found to be indigent by the court for the purposes of these rules shall be required to pay a mediator fee. Any mediator conducting a mediation pursuant to these rules shall waive the payment of fees from parties found by the court to be indigent. Any party may move the senior resident superior court judge for a finding of indigency and to be relieved of that party's obligation to pay a share of the mediator's fee.

Said motion shall be heard subsequent to the completion of the mediation or, if the parties do not settle their cases, subsequent to the trial of the action. In ruling upon such motions, the judge shall apply the criteria enumerated in N.C.G.S. § 1–110(a), but shall take into consideration the outcome of the action and whether a judgment was rendered in the movant's favor. The court shall enter an order granting or denying the party's request.

D. Postponement Fee. As used herein, the term "postponement" shall mean reschedule or not proceed with a mediation once a date for the mediation has been agreed upon and scheduled by the parties and the mediator. After a mediation has been scheduled for a specific date, a party may not unilaterally postpone the mediation. A mediation may be postponed only after notice to all parties of the reason for the postponement, payment of a postponement fee to the mediator and consent of the mediator and the opposing attorney. If a mediation is postponed within seven business days of the scheduled date, the fee shall be $150. If the mediation is postponed within three business days of the scheduled date, the fee shall be $300. Postponement fees shall be paid by the party requesting the postponement unless otherwise agreed to between the parties. Postponement fees are in addition to the one time, per case administrative fee provided for in Rule 6. B.

E. Payment of Compensation of Parties. Unless otherwise agreed to by the parties or ordered by the court, the mediator's fee shall be paid in equal shares by the parties. For purposes of this rule, multiple parties shall be considered one party when they are represented by the same counsel. Parties obligated to pay a share of the fees shall pay them equally. Payment shall be due upon completion of the mediation.

F. Sanctions for Failure to Pay Mediator's Fee. Willful failure of a party to make timely payment of that party's share of the mediator's fee (whether the one time, per case, administrative fee, the hourly fee for mediation services, or any postponement fee) or willful failure of a party contending indigent status to promptly move the senior resident superior court judge for a finding of indigency, shall constitute contempt of court and may result, following notice, in a hearing and the imposition of monetary sanctions by a resident or presiding superior court judge.

[Adopted April 10, 1996. Amended June 12, 1996; amended effective September 1, 2000; January 1, 2012; April 1, 2014.]

COMMENTS TO RULE 6

Comment to Rule 6.B.

Court-appointed mediators may not be compensated for travel time, mileage or any other out-of-pocket expenses.

Comment to Rule 6.D.

Though Rule 6.D provides that mediators "shall" assess the postponement fee, it is understood there may be rare situations where the circumstances occasioning a request for a postponement are beyond the control of the parties, for example, an illness, serious accident, unexpected and unavoidable trial conflict. When the party or parties take steps to notify the mediator as soon as possible in such circumstances, the mediator, may, in his or her discretion, waive the postponement fee.

Non-essential requests for postponements work a hardship on parties and mediators and serve only to inject delay into a process and program designed to expedite settlement. As such, it is expected that mediators will assess a postponement fee in all instances where a request does not appear to be absolutely warranted. Moreover, mediators are encouraged not to agree to postponements in instances where, in their judgment, the mediation could be held as scheduled.

Comment to Rule 6.E.

If a party is found by a senior resident superior court judge to have failed to attend a mediation without good cause, then the court may require that party to pay the mediator's fee and related expenses.

Comment to Rule 6.F.

If the Prelitigation Farm Nuisance Mediation Program is to be successful, it is essential that mediators, both party-selected and court-appointed, be compensated for their services. Rule 6.F is intended to give the court express authority to enforce payment of fees owed both court-appointed and party-selected mediators. In instances where the mediator is party-selected, the court may enforce fees which exceed the caps set forth in 6.B (hourly fee and administrative fee) and 6.D (postponement/cancellation fee) or which provide for payment of services or expenses not provided for in Rule 6 but agreed to among the parties, for example, payment for travel time or mileage.

Rule 7. Waiver of Mediation

All parties to a farm nuisance dispute may waive mediation by informing the mediator of their waiver in writing. The Waiver of Prelitigation Mediation in Farm Nuisance Dispute (Waiver) shall be on a form prescribed by the NCAOC (Form AOC–CV–822). The party who requested mediation shall file the Waiver with the clerk and mail a copy to the mediator and all parties named in the Request.

[Adopted April 10, 1996. Amended effective September 1, 2000; January 1, 2012; April 1, 2014.]

Rule 8. Mediator's Certification that Mediation Concluded

A. Contents of Certification. Following the conclusion of mediation or the receipt of a Waiver signed by all parties to the farm nuisance dispute, the mediator shall prepare a Mediator's Certification in Prelitigation Farm Nuisance Dispute (Certification) on a form prescribed by the NCAOC (Form AOC–CV–823). If a mediation was held, the Certification shall state the date on which the mediation was concluded and report the general results. If a mediation was not held, the Certification shall state why the mediation was not held and identify any parties named in the Request who failed, without good cause, to attend or participate in mediation or shall state that all parties waived mediation in writing pursuant to Rule 7 above.

B. Deadline for Filing Mediator's Certification. The mediator shall file the completed Certification with the clerk within seven days of the completion of the mediation, the failure of the mediation to be held or the receipt of a signed waiver of mediation. The mediator shall serve a copy of the Certification on each of the parties named in the Request.

[Adopted April 10, 1996. Amended effective September 1, 2000; January 1, 2012; April 1, 2014.]

Rule 9. Certification of Mediation Training Programs

The Commission may specify a curriculum for a farm mediation training program and may set qualifications for trainers.

[Adopted April 10, 1996. Amended effective September 1, 2000; January 1, 2012; April 1, 2014.]

RULES OF THE NORTH CAROLINA SUPREME COURT FOR THE DISPUTE RESOLUTION COMMISSION

Effective November 1, 1996

Table of Rules

Rule I. Officers of the Commission

A. Officers. The North Carolina Dispute Resolution Commission (Commission) shall establish the offices of chair and vice chair.

B. Appointment; Elections.

(1) The chair shall be appointed for a two-year term and shall serve at the pleasure of the Chief Justice of the Supreme Court of North Carolina. (Supreme Court).

(2) The vice chair shall be elected by vote of the full Commission for a two-year term and shall serve in the absence of the chair.

C. Committees.

(1) The chair may appoint such standing and *ad hoc* committees as are needed and designate Commission members to serve as committee chairs.

(2) The chair may appoint ex-officio members to serve on either standing or *ad hoc* committees. Ex–officio members shall have particular expertise in dispute resolution or be representatives of dispute resolution programs or organizations. Ex–officio members may not vote upon issues before committees or before the Commission, but may attend committee and Commission meetings and participate in discussions.

[Effective November 1, 1996. Amended effective December 19, 2002; March 1, 2010; January 1, 2012; April 1, 2014.]

Rule II. Commission Office; Staff

A. Office. The chair, in consultation with the director of the North Carolina Administrative Office of the Courts (NCAOC), is authorized to establish and maintain an office for the conduct of Commission business.

B. Staff. The chair, in consultation with the director of the NCAOC, is authorized to appoint an executive secretary and to: (1) fix his or her terms of employment, salary, and benefits; (2) determine the scope of his or her authority and duties; and (3) delegate to the executive secretary the authority to employ necessary secretarial and staff assistants, with the approval of the director of the NCAOC.

[Effective November 1, 1996. Amended effective January 1, 2012; April 1, 2014.]

Rule III. Commission Membership

A. Vacancies. Upon the death, resignation, or permanent incapacitation of a member of the Commission, the chair shall notify the appointing authority and request that the vacancy created by the death, resignation, or permanent incapacitation be filled. The appointment of a successor shall be for the former member's unexpired term.

B. Disqualifications. If, for any reason, a Commission member becomes disqualified to serve, that member's appointing authority shall be notified and requested to take appropriate action. If a member resigns or is removed, the appointment of a successor shall be for the former member's unexpired term.

C. Conflicts of Interest and Recusals. All Commission members must:

(1) Disclose any present or prior interest or involvement in any matter pending before the Commission or its committees for decision upon which the member is entitled to vote;

(2) Recuse himself or herself from voting on any such matter if his or her impartiality might reasonably be questioned; and

(3) Continue to inform themselves and to make disclosures of subsequent facts and circumstances requiring recusal.

An ex-officio member who has a conflict of interest with regard to a matter before a committee or the Commission shall disclose his/her conflict before engaging in any discussion related to the matter.

D. Compensation. Pursuant to N.C.G.S. § 138–5, ex-officio members of the Commission shall receive no compensation for their services but may be reimbursed for their out-of-pocket expenses necessarily incurred on behalf of the Commission and for their mileage, subsistence, and other travel expenses at the per diem rate established by statutes and regulations applicable to state boards and commissions.

[Effective November 1, 1996. Amended effective January 1, 2012; April 1, 2014.]

Rule IV. Meetings of the Commission

A. Meeting Schedule. The Commission shall meet at least twice each year pursuant to a schedule set by the Commission and in special sessions at the call of the chair or other officer acting for the chair.

B. Quorum. A majority of Commission members shall constitute a quorum. Decisions shall be made by a majority of the members present and voting except that decisions to dismiss complaints or impose sanctions pursuant to Rule IX of these Rules or to deny certification or certification renewal or to revoke certification pursuant to Rule X of these Rules shall require an affirmative vote consistent with those Rules.

C. Public Meetings. All meetings of the Commission for the general conduct of business and minutes of such meetings shall be open and available to the public except that meetings, portions of meetings, or hearings conducted pursuant to Rules IX and X of these Rules may be closed to the public in accordance with those Rules.

D. Matters Requiring Immediate Action. If, in the opinion of the chair, any matter requires a decision or other action before the next regular meeting of the Commission and does not warrant the call of a special meeting, it may be considered and a vote or other action taken by correspondence, telephone, facsimile, or other practicable method; provided, all formal Commission decisions taken are reported to the executive secretary and included in the minutes of Commission proceedings.

E. Committee Meetings. Committees shall meet as needed. A majority of committee members eligible to vote shall constitute a quorum for purposes of standing and *ad hoc* committee meetings. Decisions shall be made by a majority of the members eligible to vote who are present and voting except that decisions to dismiss complaints or impose sanctions pursuant to Rule DC of these Rules or to deny certification or certification renewal or to revoke certification pursuant to Rule X of these Rules shall require an affirmative vote consistent with those Rules.

[Effective November 1, 1996. Amended effective December 19, 2002; March 1, 2006; January 1, 2012; April 1, 2014.]

Rule V. Commission's Budget

The Commission, in consultation with the director of the NCAOC, shall prepare an annual budget. The budget and supporting financial information shall be public records.

[Effective November 1, 1996. Amended effective January 1, 2012.]

Rule VI. Powers and Duties of the Commission

The Commission shall have the authority to undertake activities to expand public awareness of dispute resolution procedures, to foster growth of dispute resolution services in this state, and to ensure the availability of high quality mediation training programs and the competence of mediators. Specifically, the Commission is authorized and directed to do the following:

A. Review and approve or disapprove applications of (1) persons seeking to have training programs certified; (2) persons seeking certification as qualified to provide mediation training; (3) attorneys and nonattorneys seeking certification as qualified to conduct mediated settlement conferences and mediations; and (4) persons or organizations seeking reinstatement following a prior suspension or decertification.

B. Review applications as against criteria for certification set forth in rules adopted by the Supreme Court for mediated settlement conference/mediation programs operating under the Commission's jurisdiction and as against such other requirements of the Commission which amplify and clarify those rules. The Commission may adopt application forms and require their completion for approval.

C. Compile and maintain lists of certified trainers and training programs along with the names of contact persons, addresses, and telephone numbers and make those lists available on-line or upon request.

D. Institute periodic review of training programs and trainer qualifications and re-certify trainers and training programs that continue to meet criteria for certification. Trainers and training programs that are not re-certified shall be removed from the lists of certified trainers and certified training programs.

E. Compile, keep current, and make available on-line lists of certified mediators which specify the judicial districts in which each mediator wishes to practice.

F. Prepare, keep current, and make available on-line biographical information submitted to the Commission by certified mediators in order to make such information accessible to court staff, lawyers, and the wider public.

G. Make reasonable efforts on a continuing basis to ensure that the judiciary, clerks of court, court administration personnel, attorneys, and to the extent feasible, parties to mediation, are aware of the Commission and its office and the Commission's duty to receive and hear complaints against mediators and mediation trainers and training programs.

[Effective November 1, 1996. Amended effective December 19, 2002; March 1, 2010; January 1, 2012; April 1, 2014.]

Rule VII. Mediator Conduct

The conduct of all mediators, mediation trainers, and managers of mediation training programs must conform to the Standards of Professional Conduct for Mediators (Standards) adopted by the Supreme Court and enforceable by the Commission and the standards of any professional organization of which such person is a member that are not in conflict nor inconsistent with the Standards, A certified mediator shall inform the Commission of any criminal convictions, disbarments or other revocations or suspensions of a professional license, complaints filed against the mediator or disciplinary actions imposed upon the mediator by any professional organization, judicial sanctions, civil judgments, tax liens or filings for bankruptcy. Failure to do so is a violation of these Rules. Violations of the Standards or other professional standards or any conduct otherwise discovered reflecting a lack of moral character or fitness to conduct mediations or which discredits the Commission, the courts or the mediation process may subject a mediator to disciplinary proceedings by the Commission.

[Effective November 1, 1996. Amended effective March 1, 2006; March 1, 2010; January 1, 2012; April 1, 2014.]

Rule VIII. Standards and Advisory Opinions Committee

A. The Standards and Advisory Opinions Committee. The Commission's chair shall appoint a standing committee on Standards and Advisory Opinions to address the matters listed below in Rule VIII.B. Members of the Standards and Advisory Opinions Committee shall recuse themselves from discussing or deliberating on any matter in which they cannot act impartially or about which they have a conflict of interest. Pursuant to Rule I.C(2) only Commission members may vote on matters before the Standards and Advisory Opinions Committee.

B. Matters to Be Considered by the Standards and Advisory Opinions Committee. The Standards and Advisory Opinions Committee shall review and consider the following:

(1) Matters relating to the Standards, including making recommendations for revisions to the Standards.

(2) Commission staff requests for assistance in responding to inquiries from mediators and the public regarding matters of ethics and Standards interpretation and the drafting of advisory opinions pursuant to the Commission's Advisory Opinion Policy.

(3) Matters relating to mediator advertising, including advertising or related materials, asserting that the individual or training program featured in the advertisement is certified or eligible to be certified.

(4) Matters that interface with the N.C. State Bar or other professional regulatory agencies regarding inconsistencies and/or conflicts between DRC Rules and the rules of those entities.

C. Initial Staff Review.

(1) Commission staff may respond in writing to requests for advice under VIII.B and may respond orally when time is of the essence. Written requests for formal advisory opinions shall be referred to the Chair of the Standards and Advisory Opinions Committee in compliance with procedures established by the committee. The referral procedure shall ensure that the case file number, names of parties, and other identifying information are deleted so that any decision cannot be influenced by this information.

(2) All requests for informal advice shall be logged by Commission staff and the requesting party's confidentiality shall be maintained unless otherwise requested by the requesting party.

D. Review by Standards and Advisory Opinions Committee.

(1) If the Standards and Advisory Opinions Committee Chair determines that a formal Commission advisory opinion is not warranted under Rule VIII.B, the requesting party shall be so advised in writing and provided with informal advice if requested.

(2) If the Standards and Advisory Opinions Committee Chair determines that a Commission advisory opinion is warranted under Rule VIII.B, the matter shall be considered by the Standards and Advisory Opinions Committee, and if the Standards and Advisory Opinions Committee concurs, a proposed advisory

opinion shall be prepared and submitted to the Commission for its consideration. If the Standards and Advisory Opinions Committee determines that a formal Commission advisory opinion is not warranted under Rule VIII.B, the requesting person shall be so advised in writing and provided with informal advice if requested.

[Effective November 1, 1996. Amended effective December 19, 2002; March 1, 2006; March 1, 2010; January 1, 2012; April 1, 2014.]

Rule IX. Grievance and Disciplinary Committee

A. Grievance and Disciplinary Committee. The Commission's chair shall appoint a standing committee entitled the Grievance and Disciplinary Committee to address the matters listed below in Paragraph B. Members of the Committee shall shall recuse themselves from discussing or deliberating on any matter in which they cannot act impartially or about which they have a conflict of interest. Pursuant to Rule I.C(2) only Commission members may vote on matters before the Grievance and Disciplinary Committee.

B. Matters to Be Considered by the Grievance and Disciplinary Committee. The Grievance and Disciplinary Committee shall review and consider the following:

(1) Matters relating to the moral character, conduct, or fitness to practice of an applicant for mediator certification or certification renewal or of a certified mediator and appeals of staff decisions to deny an application for mediator certification or certification renewal on the basis of the applicant's moral character, conduct, or fitness to practice.

(2) Matters relating to the moral character, conduct, or fitness to practice of any trainer or manager affiliated with a certified mediator training program or a training program that is an applicant for certification or certification renewal and appeals of staff decisions to deny an application for mediator training program certification or certification renewal on the basis of the moral character, conduct, or fitness to practice of any trainer or manager affiliated with the program.

(3) Complaints by a member of the Commission, its staff, a judge, court staff, or any member of the public regarding the moral character, conduct, or fitness to practice of a mediator under the Commission's jurisdiction or a trainer or manager affiliated with a certified mediator training program.

C. Initial Staff Review and Determination.

(1) *Review and Referral of Matters Relating to Moral Character, Conduct, or Fitness to Practice.* Commission staff shall review information relating to the moral character, conduct, or fitness to practice of applicants seeking mediator certification or certification renewal, including matters which applicants are required to report under program rules, and information relating to the moral character, conduct, or fitness to practice of trainers and managers affiliated with mediator training programs seeking certification or certification renewal (applicants).

Commission staff may contact applicants to discuss matters reported and may conduct background checks on applicants. Any third party with knowledge of any information relating to the moral character, conduct, or fitness to practice of an applicant may notify the Commission. Commission staff shall seek to verify any such third party reports and may disregard those that cannot be verified. Commission staff may contact any agency where complaints about an applicant have been filed or any agency or judge that has imposed discipline on an applicant.

All such reported matters or any other information gathered by Commission staff and bearing on moral character, conduct, or fitness to practice shall be forwarded directly to the Grievance and Disciplinary Committee for its review, except those matters expressly exempted from review by the Guidelines for Reviewing Pending Grievances/Complaints, Disciplinary Actions Taken, Convictions, Civil Judgments, Tax Liens, Bankruptcies, and Other Matters Relevant to Good Moral Character (Guidelines). Matters that are exempted by the Guidelines may be processed by Commission staff and will not act as a bar to certification or certification renewal.

Commission staff or the Grievance and Disciplinary Committee may elect to take any matter relating to an applicant's moral character, conduct, or fitness to practice, including matters reported by third parties or revealed by background check, and process it as a complaint pursuant to Rule IX.C(3) below. Commission staff may consult with the Grievance and Disciplinary Committee's chair prior to making such election.

(2) *Commission Staff Review of Oral or Written Complaints.* Commission staff shall review oral and written complaints made to the Commission regarding the moral character, conduct, or fitness to practice of a mediator under the jurisdiction of the Commission or a trainer or manager affiliated with a certified mediator training program (respondents), except that Commission staff shall not act on anonymous complaints unless staff can independently verify the allegations made.

(a) Oral complaints. If after reviewing an oral complaint, Commission staff determines it is necessary to contact any third parties about the matter including any witnesses identified by the complaining party or other third parties identified by staff during its review of the complaint, or to refer the matter to the Grievance and Disciplinary Committee, the Commission staff shall first make a summary of the complaint and forward it to the complaining party who shall be asked to sign the summary along with a release and to return it to the Commission's office, except that when complaints are initiated by a member of the Commission, the Grievance and Disciplinary Committee, the Standards and Advisory Opinions Committee or by Commission staff, judges, other court officials, or court staff, they need not be in writing and may be filed anonymously.

(b) Written complaints. Commission staff shall acknowledge all written complaints within 30 days of receipt. Written complaints may be made by letter, email or filed on the Commission's approved complaint form. If a complaint is not made on the approved form, Commission staff shall require the complaining party to sign a release before contacting any third parties in the course of an investigation.

(c) If a complaining party refuses to sign a complaint summary prepared by Commission staff or to sign a release or otherwise seeks to withdraw a complaint after filing it with the Commission, Commission staff or a Grievance and Disciplinary Committee member may pursue the complaint. In determining whether to pursue a complaint independently, Commission staff or a Grievance and Disciplinary Committee member shall consider why the complaining party is unwilling to pursue the matter further, whether the complaining party is willing to testify if a hearing is necessary, whether the complaining party has specifically asked to withdraw the complaint, the seriousness of the allegations made in the complaint, whether the circumstances complained of may be independently verified without the complaining party's participation, and whether there have been previous complaints filed regarding the respondent's conduct.

(d) If Commission staff asks a respondent to respond in writing to an oral or written complaint, the respondent shall be provided with a summary of or a copy of the complaint and any supporting evidence provided by the complaining party. The respondent shall have 30 days from the date of the letter transmitting the complaint to respond. Upon request, the respondent may be afforded 10 additional days to respond to the complaint

(e) Any complaint made pursuant to Rule IX.C above regarding the conduct of a certified mediator during a mediation, from appointment or selection through conclusion by settlement or impasse, not filed within one (1) year of the conclusion of such mediation shall be deemed untimely and shall be subject to summary dismissal.

(3) *Initial Determination on Oral and Written Complaints.* After reviewing a Rule IX,B(3) complaint and any additional information gathered, including information supplied by the respondent and any witnesses or other third parties contacted, Commission staff shall determine whether to;

(a) Recommend dismissal. Commission staff shall make a recommendation to dismiss a complaint upon concluding that the complaint does not allege facts sufficient to constitute a violation of a rule, standard, or guideline enforceable under the jurisdiction of the Commission. Such recommendation shall be made to the chair of the Grievance and Disciplinary Committee. If after giving the complaint due consideration, the Grievance and Disciplinary Committee chair disagrees with the recommendation to dismiss, s/he may direct staff to refer the matter for conciliation or to the full Grievance and Disciplinary Committee for review. If the chair agrees with the recommendation, the complaint shall be dismissed with notification to the complaining party, the respondent, and any witnesses or others contacted. The complaining party and respondent shall be notified of the dismissal by certified U.S. mail, return receipt requested and such service shall be deemed sufficient for purposes of these Rules. Commission staff shall note for the file why a determination was made to dismiss the complaint and shall report on such dismissals to the Grievance and Disciplinary Committee. Dismissed complaints shall remain on file with the Commission for at least five years and the Grievance and Disciplinary Committee may take such complaints into consideration if additional complaints are later made against the same respondent.

The complaining party shall have 30 days from the date of the letter notifying him or her of the dismissal to appeal the determination in writing to the full Grievance and Disciplinary Committee.

(b) Refer to conciliation. If Commission staff determines that the complaint appears to be largely the result of a misunderstanding between the respondent and complainant or raises a best practices concern(s) or involves technical or relatively minor rule violation(s) resulting in minimal harm to the complainant, the matter may be referred for conciliation if the parties are willing to discuss the basis of the complaint. Once a matter is referred for conciliation, Commission staff may serve as a resource to the parties, but shall not act as their mediator. Prior to or at the time a matter is referred for conciliation, Commission staff shall provide written information to the complainant explaining the conciliation process and advising him/her that the complaint will be deemed to be resolved and the file closed if the complainant does not notify the Commission within 90 days of the referral that conciliation either failed to occur or did not resolve the matter. If either the complaining party or the respondent refuses conciliation or the complaining party notifies Commission staff that conciliation failed, Commission staff may refer the matter to the Grievance and Disciplinary Committee for review or to the Grievance and Disciplinary Committee chair with a recommendation for dismissal.

(c) Refer to the Grievance and Disciplinary Committee. Following initial investigation, including contacting the respondent, any witnesses, or other third parties as necessary, Commission staff shall refer all Rule IX.B(3) matters to the fall Grievance and Disciplinary Committee when such matters raise concerns about possible significant program rule or Standards violations or raise a significant question about a respondent's moral character, conduct, or fitness to practice. No matter shall be referred to the Grievance and Disciplinary Committee until the respondent has been forwarded a copy of the complaint or a summary and a copy of these Rules and allowed a 30 day period in which to respond.

The respondent's response to the complaint and the responses of any witnesses or others contacted during the investigation shall not be forwarded to the complainant, except as provided for in N.C.G.S. § 7A–38.2(h) and there shall be no opportunity for rebuttal. The response shall be included in the materials forwarded to the Grievance and Disciplinary Committee. If any witnesses or others were contacted, any written responses or summaries of responses shall also be included in the materials forwarded to the Grievance and Disciplinary Committee.

(4) *Confidentiality.* Commission staff will create and maintain files for all matters considered pursuant to Rule IX.B. All information in those files pertaining to applicants for certification or certification renewal shall remain confidential in accordance with N.C.G.S. § 7A–38.2(h). Information pertaining to complaints regarding the character, conduct, or fitness to practice of mediators or trainers or managers affiliated with certified training programs shall remain confidential until such time as the Grievance and Disciplinary Committee completes its preliminary investigation and finds probable cause pursuant to Rule IX.D(2) and N.C.G.S. § 7A–38. 2(h).

Commission staff shall reveal the names of applicants and respondents to the Grievance and Disciplinary Committee and the Grievance and Disciplinary Committee shall keep the names of applicants and respondents and other identifying information confidential except as provided for in N.C.G.S. § 7A–38.2(h).

D. Grievance and Disciplinary Committee Review and Determination on Matters Referred by Staff.

(1) *Grievance and Disciplinary Committee Review of Applicant Moral Character Issues and Complaints.* The Grievance and Disciplinary Committee shall review matters brought before it by Commission staff pursuant to the provisions of Rule IX.B above and may contact any other persons or entities with knowledge of the matter for additional information. The chair may in his/her discretion appoint members of the Grievance and Disciplinary Committee to serve on a subcommittee to investigate a particular matter brought to the Grievance and Disciplinary Committee by Commission staff. The chair of the Grievance and Disciplinary Committee or his/her designee may issue subpoenas for the attendance of witnesses and for the production of books, papers, or other documentary evidence deemed necessary or material to the Grievance and Disciplinary Committee's investigation and review of the matter.

(2) *Grievance and Disciplinary Committee Deliberation.* The Grievance and Disciplinary Committee shall deliberate to determine whether probable cause exists to believe that an applicant or respondent's conduct:

(a) is a violation of the Standards of Professional Conduct for Mediators or any other standards of professional conduct that are not in conflict with nor inconsistent with the Standards and to which the mediator, trainer, or manager is subject;

(b) is a violation of Supreme Court program rules or any other program rules for mediated settlement conference/mediation programs;

(c) is inconsistent with good moral character (Mediated Settlement Conference Program Rule 8.E, Family Financial Settlement Conference Rule 8.F, and District Criminal Court Rule 7.E);

(d) reflects a lack of fitness to conduct mediated settlement conferences/mediations or to serve as a trainer or training program manager (Rule VII above); and/or

(e) serves to discredit the Commission, the courts, or the mediation process (Rule VII above).

(3) *Grievance and Disciplinary Committee Determination.* Following deliberation, the Grievance and Disciplinary Committee shall determine whether to dismiss a matter, make a referral, or impose sanctions.

(a) To dismiss. If a majority of Grievance and Disciplinary Committee members reviewing an issue of moral character, conduct, or fitness to practice or a complaint and eligible to vote finds no probable cause, the Grievance and Disciplinary Committee shall dismiss the matter and instruct Commission staff to:

(i) certify or recertify the applicant, if an application is pending, or to notify the mediator or training program by certified U.S. mail, return receipt requested, that no further action will be taken in the matter, or

(ii) notify the complaining party and the respondent that no further action will be taken and that the matter is dismissed.

(b) To refer. If after reviewing an application for certification or certification renewal or a complaint, a majority of Grievance and Disciplinary Committee members eligible to vote determines that:

(i) any violation of the program rules or Standards that occurred was technical or relatively minor in nature, caused minimal harm to a complainant, and did not discredit the program, courts, or Commission, the Grievance and Disciplinary Committee may:

(1) dismiss the complaint with a letter to the complaining party and respondent notifying them of the dismissal, citing the violation and advising the mediator to avoid such conduct in the future, or

(2) refer the respondent to one or more members of the Grievance and Disciplinary Committee to discuss the matter and explore ways that the respondent may avoid similar complaints in the future.

(ii) respondent's conduct involves no violations, but raises best practices or professionalism concerns, the Grievance and Disciplinary Committee may:

(1) direct staff to dismiss the complaint with a letter to the respondent advising him/her of the Grievance and Disciplinary Committee's concerns and providing guidance;

(2) direct the respondent to meet with one or more members of the Grievance and Disciplinary Committee who will informally discuss the Grievance and Disciplinary Committee's concerns and provide counsel; or

(3) refer the respondent to the Chief Justice's Commission on Professionalism for counseling and guidance.

(iii) the applicant or respondent's conduct raises significant concerns about his/her fitness to practice, including concerns about mental instability, mental health, lack of mental acuity or possible dementia, or concerns about possible alcohol or substance abuse, the Grievance and Disciplinary Committee may, in lieu of or in addition to imposing sanctions, refer the applicant or respondent to the North Carolina State Bar's Lawyer Assistance Program (LAP) for evaluation, or if the applicant or respondent is not a lawyer, to a physician, other licensed mental health professional, or to a substance abuse counselor or organization.

A complaining party shall have no right of appeal from a Grievance and Disciplinary Committee determination to dismiss a complaint or to refer a mediator pursuant to subsections (a) or (b) above.

Neither letters regarding conduct nor referrals are to be considered sanctions under Rule IX. E(10) below. Rather, such are intended as opportunities to address concerns and to help applicants and respondents perform more effectively as mediators. There may, however, be instances that are more serious in nature where the Grievance and Disciplinary Committee may both make a referral and impose sanctions under Rule IX. E(10).

In the event that an applicant or respondent is referred to one or more members of the Grievance and Disciplinary Committee for counsel, to LAP, or to some other professional entity and fails to cooperate regarding the referral, refuses to sign releases or to provide any resulting evaluations to the Grievance and Disciplinary Committee, or should any resulting discussions or evaluation(s) suggest that the applicant or respondent is not currently capable of serving as a mediator, trainer, or manager, the Grievance and Disciplinary Committee reserves the right to make further determinations in the matter, including decertification. During a referral under (iii) above, the Grievance and Disciplinary Committee may require respondent to cease practicing as a mediator, trainer, or manager during the referral period and until such time as the Grievance and Disciplinary Committee has authorized his/her return to active practice. The Grievance and Disciplinary Committee may condition a certification or certification renewal on the applicant's successful completion of the referral process.

Any costs associated with a referral, *e.g.*, costs of evaluation or treatment, shall be borne entirely by the applicant or respondent.

(c) To propose sanctions. If a majority of Grievance and Disciplinary Committee members eligible to vote find(s) probable cause pursuant to Rule IX.D(2) above, the Grievance and Disciplinary Committee shall propose sanctions on the applicant or respondent pursuant to Rule IX.E(10), except as provided for in Rule IX.D(3)(b)(i).

Within the 30–day period set forth in Rule IX. D(4) below, an applicant or respondent may contact the Grievance and Disciplinary Committee and object to any referral made or sanction imposed on the applicant or respondent, including objecting to any public posting of a sanction, and seek to negotiate some other outcome with the Grievance and Disciplinary Committee. The Grievance and Disciplinary Committee shall have the authority to engage in such negotiations with the applicant or respondent. During the negotiation period, the applicant or respondent may request an extension of the time in which to request an appeal under Rule IX.D(4) below. Commission staff, in consultation with the Grievance and Disciplinary Committee chair, may extend the appeal period up to an additional 30 days in order to allow more time to complete negotiations.

Notification of any dismissal, referral, or sanction imposed pursuant to subsections (a), (b), or (c) above shall be by certified U.S. mail, return receipt requested, and such service shall be deemed sufficient for purposes of these Rules. All witnesses and any others contacted by staff or committee member shall be notified, if feasible, of any dismissal.

(4) *Right of Appeal.* If a referral is made or sanctions are imposed, the applicant or respondent shall have 30 days from the date of the letter sent by U.S. certified mail, return receipt requested, transmitting the Grievance and Disciplinary Committee's findings and actions to appeal. Notification of appeal must be made to the Commission's office in writing. If no appeal is received within 30 days, the applicant or respondent shall be deemed to have accepted the Grievance and Disciplinary Committee's findings and proposed sanctions. The complainant does not have a right of appeal.

E. Appeal to the Commission.

(1) *The Commission Shall Meet to Consider Appeals.* An appeal of the Grievance and Disciplinary Committee's determination pursuant to Rule IX.D(4) above shall be heard by the members of the Commission, except that all members of the Grievance and Disciplinary Committee who participated in issuing the determination on appeal shall be recused and shall not participate in the Commission's deliberations. No matter shall be heard and decided by less than three Commission members. Members of the Commission shall recuse themselves when they cannot act impartially. Any challenges questioning the neutrality of a member shall be decided by the Commission's chair.

(2) *Conduct of the Hearing.*

(a) At least 30 days prior to the hearing before the Commission, Commission staff shall forward to all parties, special counsel to the Commission, and members of the Commission who will hear the matter, copies of all documents considered by the Grievance and Disciplinary Committee and summaries of witness or other third party interviews and/or character recommendations.

(b) Hearings conducted by the Commission pursuant to this rule shall be *de novo*.

(c) Applicants, complainants, respondents, and any witnesses or others identified as having relevant information about the matter may appear at the hearing with or without counsel.

(d) All hearings will be open to the public except that for good cause shown the presiding officer may exclude from the hearing room all persons except the parties, counsel, and those engaged in the hearing. No hearing will be closed to the public over the objection of an applicant or respondent.

(e) In the event that the applicant, complainant, or respondent fails to appear without good cause, the Commission shall proceed to hear from those parties and witnesses who are present and to make a determination based on the evidence presented at the proceeding.

(f) Proceedings before the Commission shall be conducted informally, but with decorum.

(g) The Commission, through its counsel, and applicant or respondent may present evidence in the form of sworn testimony and/or written documents. The Commission, through its counsel, and the applicant or respondent may cross-examine any witness called to testify by the other. Commission members may question any witness called to testify at the hearing. The Rules of Evidence shall not apply, except as to privilege, but shall be considered as a guide toward full and fair development of the facts. The Commission shall consider all evidence presented and give it appropriate weight and effect.

(h) The Commission's chair or designee shall serve as the presiding officer. The presiding officer shall have such jurisdiction and powers as are necessary to conduct a proper and speedy investigation and disposition of the matter on appeal. The presiding officer may administer oaths and may issue subpoenas for the attendance of witnesses and the production of books, papers, or other documentary evidence.

(3) *Date of Hearing.* An appeal of any sanction proposed by the Grievance and Disciplinary Committee shall be heard by the Commission within 180 days of the date the notice of appeal is filed with the Commission.

(4) *Notice of Hearing.* The Commission's office shall serve on all parties by certified U.S. mail, return receipt requested, notice of the date, time, and place of the hearing no later than 60 days prior to the hearing and such service shall be deemed sufficient for purposes of these Rules.

(5) *Ex Parte Communications.* No person shall have any *ex parte* communication with members of the Commission concerning the subject matter of the appeal. Communications regarding scheduling matters shall be directed to Commission staff.

(6) *Attendance.* All parties, including applicants, complainants, and respondents, shall attend in person. The presiding officer may, in his or her discretion, permit an attorney to represent a party by telephone or through video conference or to allow witnesses to testify by telephone or through video conference with such limitations and conditions as are just and reasonable. If an attorney or witness appears by telephone or video conference, the Commission's staff must be notified at least 20 days prior to the proceeding. At least five days prior to the proceeding, the Commission's staff must be provided with contact information for those who will participate by telephone or video conference.

(7) *Witnesses.* The presiding officer shall exercise discretion with respect to the attendance and number of witnesses who appear, voluntarily or involuntarily, for the purpose of ensuring the orderly conduct of the proceeding. Each party shall forward to the Commis-

sion's office and to all other parties at least 10 days prior to the hearing, the names of all witnesses who will be called to testify.

(8) *Transcript.* The Commission shall retain a court reporter to keep a record of the proceeding. Any party who wishes to obtain a transcript of the record may do so at his/her own expense by contacting the court reporter directly. The only official record of the proceeding shall be the one made by the court reporter retained by the Commission. Copies of tapes, non-certified transcripts therefrom, or a record made by a court reporter retained by a party are not part of the official record,

(9) *Commission Decision.* After the hearing, a majority of the Commission members hearing the appeal may;

(a) find that there is not clear and convincing evidence to support the referral or imposition of sanctions and, therefore, dismiss the complaint or direct Commission staff to certify or recertify the mediator or mediator training program, or

(b) find that there is clear and convincing evidence that grounds exist to refer or to impose sanctions. The Commission may impose the same or different sanctions than imposed by the Grievance and Disciplinary Committee or make the same or a different referral. The Commission shall set forth its findings, conclusions, referral and/or sanctions, or other action, in writing and serve its decision on the parties within 60 days of the date of the hearing. Notification of the decision shall be sent by certified U.S. mail, return receipt requested, and such service shall be deemed sufficient for purposes of these Rules.

(10) *Sanctions.* The sanctions that may be proposed by the Grievance and Disciplinary Committee or imposed by the Commission include, but are not limited to, the following;

(a) Private, written admonishment;

(b) Public, written admonishment;

(c) Completion of additional training;

(d) Restriction on types of cases to be mediated in the future;

(e) Reimbursement of fees paid to the mediator or training program;

(f) Suspension for a specified term;

(g) Probation for a specified term;

(h) Certification or renewal of certification upon conditions;

(i) Denial of certification or certification renewal;

(j) Decertification;

(k) Prohibition on participation as a trainer or manager of a certified mediator training program either indefinitely or for a period of time; and

(*l*) Any other sanction deemed appropriate by the Grievance and Disciplinary Committee/Commission.

(11) *Publication of Grievance and Disciplinary Committee/Commission Decisions.*

(a) Names of respondents who have been reprimanded privately or applicants who have never been certified and have been denied certification shall not be published in the Commission's newsletter nor on its web site.

(b) Names of respondents or applicants who are sanctioned under any other provision of Rule IX. E(10) above and who have been denied reinstatement under Rule IX.E(13) below shall be published in the Commission's newsletter and on its website along with a short summary of the facts involved and the discipline imposed. For good cause shown, the Commission may waive this requirement.

(c) Chief district court judges and/or senior resident superior court judges in judicial districts in which a mediator serves, the NC State Bar and any other professional licensing/certification bodies to which a mediator Is subject, and other trial forums or agencies having mandatory programs and using mediators certified by the Commission shall be notified of any sanction imposed upon a mediator except those named in Rule IX.E(11)(a) above.

(d) If the Commission imposes sanctions as a result of a complaint filed by a third party, the Commission's office shall, on request, release copies of the complaint, response, and Commission/Grievance and Disciplinary Committee decision.

(12) *Appeal.* The General Court of Justice, Superior Court Division, in Wake County shall have jurisdiction over appeals of Commission decisions imposing sanctions or denying applications for mediator or mediator training program certification or certification renewal. An order imposing sanctions or denying applications for mediator or mediator training program certification or certification renewal shall be reviewable upon appeal and the entire record as submitted shall be reviewed to determine whether the order is supported by substantial evidence. Notice of appeal shall be filed in the Superior Court in Wake County within 30 days of the date of the Commission's decision.

(13) *Reinstatement.* An applicant, mediator, trainer, or manager who has been sanctioned under this rule may be certified or reinstated as a certified mediator or training program or as an active trainer or manager pursuant to Rule IX.E(13)(h) below. Except as otherwise provided by the Grievance and Disciplinary Committee or Commission, no application for reinstatement may be tendered within two years of the date of the sanction or denial.

(a) A petition for reinstatement shall be made in writing, verified by the petitioner, and filed with the Commission's office.

(b) The petition for reinstatement shall contain;

(i) the name and address of the petitioner;

(ii) the reasons why certification was denied or the moral character, conduct, or fitness concerns upon which the suspension or decertification or the bar to serving as a trainer or training program manager was based; and

(iii) a concise statement of facts claimed to justify certification or reinstatement as a certified mediator, certified training program or a trainer or program manager affiliated with a certified training program.

(c) The petition for reinstatement may also contain a request for a hearing on the matter to consider any additional evidence which the petitioner wishes to put forth, including any third party testimony regarding his or her character, competency, or fitness to practice as a mediator, trainer, or manager.

(d) The Commission's staff shall refer the petition to the Commission for review,

(e) If the petitioner does not request a hearing, the Commission shall review the petition and shall make a decision within 60 days of the filing of the petition. That decision shall be final. If the petitioner requests a hearing, it shall be held within 180 days of the filing of the petition. The Commission shall conduct the hearing consistent with Rule IX. E(2) above. At the hearing, the petitioner may:

(i) appear personally and be heard;

(ii) be represented by counsel;

(iii) call and examine witnesses;

(iv) offer exhibits; and

(v) cross-examine witnesses.

(f) At the hearing, the Commission may call witnesses, offer exhibits, and examine the petitioner and witnesses.

(g) The burden of proof shall be upon the petitioner to establish by clear and convincing evidence:

(i) that the petitioner has rehabilitated his/her character; addressed and resolved any conditions which led to his/her denial of certification or suspension or decertification; completed additional training in mediation theory and practice to ensure his/her competency as a mediator, trainer or manager; and/or taken steps to address and resolve any other matter(s) which led to the petitioner's denial, suspension, decertification, or prohibition from serving as a trainer or manager;

(ii) the petitioner's certification will not be detrimental to the Mediated Settlement Conference, Family Financial Settlement, Clerk Mediation, District Criminal Court Mediation Program, or other program rules, or to the Commission, courts, or public; and

(iii) that the petitioner has completed any paperwork required for certification or reinstatement and paid any required reinstatement and/or certification fees.

(h) If the petitioner is found to have rehabilitated him or herself and is fit to serve as a mediator, trainer, or manager, the Commission shall certify or reinstate the petitioner as a certified mediator or training program or as an active trainer or manager. Certification or reinstatement may be conditioned upon the completion of additional training and observations as needed to refresh skills and awareness of program rules and requirements.

(i) The Commission shall set forth its decision to certify or reinstate a petitioner or to deny certification or reinstatement in writing, making findings of fact and conclusions of law. Notification of the decision shall be sent by certified U.S. mail, return receipt requested, within 30 days of the date of the hearing, and such service shall be deemed sufficient for purposes of these Rules.

(j) If a petition seeking certification or reinstatement is denied, the petitioner may not apply again pursuant to this section until two years have lapsed from the date the denial was issued.

(k) The General Court of Justice, Superior Court Division, in Wake County shall have jurisdiction over appeals of Commission decisions to deny certification or reinstatement. An order denying reinstatement shall be reviewable upon appeal, and the entire record as submitted shall be reviewed to determine whether the order is supported by substantial evidence. Notice of appeal shall be filed in the Superior Court in Wake County within 30 days of the date of the Commission's decision.

[Effective November 1, 1996. Amended effective March 1, 2006; March 1, 2010; January 1, 2012; April 1, 2014.]

Rule X. Mediator Certification and Training Committee

A. Mediator Certification and Training Committee. The chair of the Commission shall appoint a standing committee entitled the Mediator Certification and Training Committee to review the matters set forth in Rule X.B below. Members of the Certification Committee shall recuse themselves from discussing and deliberating on any matter in which they cannot act impartially or about which they have a conflict of interest. Pursuant to Rule I.C(2) only Commission members may vote on matters before the Committee.

B. Matters to Be Considered by the Mediator Certification and Training Committee. The Mediator Certification and Training Committee shall review and consider the following matters:

(1) Appeals of staff decisions to deny an application filed by a person or mediator training program seek-

ing certification or certification renewal based on deficiencies in the applicant's qualifications unrelated to moral character, conduct, or fitness to practice. Deficiencies relating to moral character, conduct, or fitness to practice shall be considered pursuant to Rule IX above.

(2) Complaints filed by a member of the Commission, its staff, court personnel, or any member of the public regarding the qualifications of an applicant for certification or certification renewal, or the qualifications of a mediator or mediator training program, its managers, or trainers, except that, complaints relating to the moral character, conduct, or fitness to practice of an applicant, mediator, trainer, or manager shall be considered pursuant to Rule DC above.

C. Staff Investigation of Qualifications.

(1) *Information obtained during the certification or renewal process..* Commission staff shall review all pending applications for certification and certification renewal to determine whether the applicant meets qualifications unrelated to moral character, conduct, or fitness to practice set out in program rules adopted by the Supreme Court for mediated settlement conference/mediation programs under the jurisdiction of the Commission and any guidelines or other policies adopted by the Commission for the purpose of implementing those rules. Commission staff may contact those reporting to request additional information and may consider any other information acquired during the review process that bears on the applicant's eligibility for certification or certification renewal.

(2) *Complaints about mediator or mediator training program qualifications filed with the Commission.* Commission staff shall forward written complaints about the qualifications of an applicant, certified mediator, certified mediator training program, or any trainer or manager affiliated with such program, that do not pertain to moral character, conduct, or fitness to practice filed by any member of the general public, the Commission, or its staff, to the Mediator Certification and Training Committee for investigation. Copies of such complaints shall be served on the subject of the complaint by certified U.S. mail, return receipt requested, and such service shall be deemed sufficient for purposes of these Rules.

However, in instances where Commission staff cannot verify the allegations in the complaint or has otherwise verified that the applicant, mediator, or mediator training program meet qualifications for certification or certification renewal set forth in program rules and Commission policies intended to implement those rules, the Commission staff may refer the matter to the Mediator Certification and Training Committee's chair rather than to the Mediator Certification and Training Committee as set forth above. If after giving the complaint due consideration, the chair agrees with the staffs assessment of the matter, the chair may dismiss the complaint with notification to the complaining party. Such notification shall be by certified U.S. mail, return receipt requested, and such service shall be deemed sufficient for purposes of these Rules. The complaining party shall have 30 days from the date of the notification to appeal the chair's determination to the full Mediator Certification and Training Committee. The appeal shall be in writing and directed to the Commission's office. If the chair disagrees with the staff's assessment, staff shall refer the matter to the Mediator Certification and Training Committee.

D. Investigation by the Mediator Certification and Training Committee.

(1) The Mediator Certification and Training Committee shall investigate all matters brought before it by staff pursuant to the provisions of Rule X.C. above. The chair may in his/her discretion appoint members of the Mediator Certification and Training Committee to serve on a subcommittee to investigate a particular matter brought to the committee by Commission staff. The chair or his or her designee may issue subpoenas for the attendance of witnesses and for the production of books, papers, or other documentary evidence deemed necessary or material to any such investigation. The chair or designee may contact the following persons and entities for information concerning such application or complaint:

(a) all references, employers, colleges, and other individuals and entities cited in applications for mediator certification, including any and all other professional licensing or certification bodies to which the applicant is subject and any additional persons or entities identified by Commission staff during the course of its review as having relevant information about the applicant's qualifications;

(b) personnel affiliated with an applicant for mediator training program certification or certification renewal or personnel affiliated with a certified mediator training program and participants who attended or completed the training program; and

(c) all parties bringing complaints about the qualifications of an applicant for certification or certification renewal, a mediator, or a mediator training program (respondent) unrelated to moral character, conduct, or fitness to practice and any other person or entity with information about the respondent and identified by Commission staff or the Mediator Certification and Training Committee during the course of its review of the complaint.

All information in Commission files pertaining to the initial certification of a mediator or mediator training program or to renewals of such certifications shall be confidential, except as provided in N.C.G.S. § 7A-38.2(h) or these Rules.

(2) *Probable Cause Determination.* Those members of the Mediator Certification and Training Committee reviewing the matter and eligible to vote shall

deliberate to determine whether probable cause exists to believe that the applicant or respondent:

(a) does not meet qualifications for mediator certification or certification renewal unrelated to moral character, conduct, or fitness to practice as set forth in program rules adopted by the Supreme Court for mediated settlement conference/mediation programs under the jurisdiction of the Commission or guidelines and other policies adopted by the Commission for the purpose of implementing those rules, or

(b) does not meet the qualifications for mediator training program certification or certification renewal as set forth in program rules adopted by the Supreme Court for mediated settlement conference/mediation programs under the jurisdiction of the Commission or guidelines and other policies adopted by the Commission for the purpose of implementing those rules.

If probable cause is found, the application for certification or certification renewal shall be denied or the respondent's certification shall be revoked.

(3) *Authority of Mediator Certification and Training Committee to Deny Certification or Certification Renewal or to Revoke Certification.*

(a) If a majority of Mediator Certification and Training Committee members reviewing a matter and eligible to vote finds no probable cause pursuant to Rule X.D(2) above, Commission staff shall certify or re-certify the applicant. If the investigation was initiated by the filing of a written complaint, the Mediator Certification and Training Committee shall dismiss the complaint and notify the complaining party and the respondent in writing that the complaint has been dismissed. Notification of dismissal shall be sent by certified U.S. mail, return receipt requested, and such service shall be deemed sufficient for purposes of these Rules. A complaining party shall have no right of appeal from the Mediator Certification and Training Committee's decision to dismiss a complaint or to certify or re-certify an applicant.

(b) If a majority of Mediator Certification and Training Committee members reviewing a matter and eligible to vote finds probable cause pursuant to Rule X.D(2) above, the Mediator Certification and Training Committee shall deny certification or certification renewal or revoke certification. The Mediator Certification and Training Committee's findings, conclusions, and denial or revocation shall be in writing and forwarded to applicant or respondent. Notification of the determination shall be sent by certified U.S. mail, return receipt requested, and such service shall be deemed sufficient for purposes of these Rules.

(c) If the Mediator Certification and Training Committee denies Certification or certification renewal or revokes certification, the applicant or respondent may appeal the denial or revocation to the Commission within 30 days from the date of the letter transmitting the Mediator Certification and Training Committee's findings and determination. Notification of appeal must be in writing and directed to the Commission's office. If no appeal is filed within 30 days, the applicant or respondent shall be deemed to have accepted the Mediator Certification and Training Committee's findings and determination.

E. Appeal of the Denial to the Commission.

(1) *The Commission Shall Meet.* An appeal of a denial or revocation by the Mediator Certification and Training Committee pursuant to Rule X.D(2) above shall be heard by the members of the Commission, except that all members of the Mediator Certification and Training Committee who participated in issuing the determination that is on appeal shall recuse themselves from participating. No matter shall be heard and decided by less than three Commission members. Members of the Commission shall recuse themselves when they cannot act impartially. Any challenges raised by the appealing party or any other party questioning the neutrality of a member shall be decided by the Commission's chair.

(2) *Conduct of the Hearing.*

(a) At least 30 days prior to the hearing before the Commission, Commission staff shall forward to all parties, special counsel to the Commission, if appointed and members of the Commission who will hear the matter, copies of all documents considered by the Mediator Certification and Training Committee and summaries of witness interviews and/or character recommendations.

(b) Hearings conducted by the Commission will be a *de novo* review of the Mediator Certification and Training Committee's decision.

(c) The Commission's chair or his/her designee shall serve as the presiding officer. The presiding officer shall have such jurisdiction and powers as are necessary to conduct a proper and speedy investigation and disposition of the matter on appeal. The presiding officer may administer oaths and may issue subpoenas for the attendance of witnesses and the production of books, papers, or other documentary evidence.

(d) Special counsel supplied either by the North Carolina Attorney General at the request of the Commission or employed by the Commission may present the evidence in support of the denial or revocation of certification. Commission members may question any witnesses called to testify at the hearing.

(e) The Commission, through its counsel, and the applicant or respondent or his/her/its representative may present evidence in the form of sworn testimony and/or written documents. The Commission, through its counsel, and the applicant or respondent, may cross-examine any witness called to testify at the hearing. The Rules of Evidence shall not apply, except as to privilege, but shall be considered as a guide toward full and fair development of the facts. The Commission shall consider all evidence presented and give it appropriate weight and effect.

(f) All hearings shall be conducted in private, unless the applicant or respondent requests a public hearing.

(g) In the event that the complainant, respondent, or applicant fails to appear without good cause, the Commission shall proceed to hear from those parties and witnesses who are present and make a determination based on the evidence presented at the proceeding.

(h) Proceedings before the Commission shall be conducted informally but with decorum.

(3) *Date of Hearing.* An appeal of any denial or revocation by the Mediator Certification and Training Committee shall be heard by the Commission within 180 days of the date of the letter transmitting the Mediator Certification and Training Committee's findings and determination.

(4) *Notice of Hearing.* The Commission's office shall serve on all parties by certified U.S. mail, return receipt requested, notice of the date, time, and place of the hearing no later than 60 days prior to the hearing and such service shall be deemed sufficient for purposes of these Rules.

(5) *Ex Parte Communications.* No person shall have any *ex parte* communication with members of the Commission concerning the subject matter of the appeal. Communications regarding scheduling matters shall be directed to Commission staff.

(6) *Attendance.* All parties, including complaining parties, respondents, and applicants, or their representatives in the case of a training program, shall attend in person. The presiding officer may, in his or her discretion, permit an attorney to represent a party by telephone or through video conference or to allow witnesses to testify by telephone or through video conference with such limitations and conditions as are just and reasonable. If an attorney or witness appears by telephone or video conference, the Commission's staff must be notified at least 20 days prior to the proceeding. At least five days prior to the proceeding, the Commission's staff must be provided with contact information for those who will participate by telephone or video conference.

(7) *Witnesses.* The presiding officer shall exercise his/her discretion with respect to the attendance and number of witnesses who appear, voluntarily or involuntarily, for the purpose of ensuring the orderly conduct of the proceeding. Each party shall forward to the Commission's office at least 10 days prior to the hearing the names of all witnesses who will testify for them.

(8) *Transcript.* The Commission shall retain a court reporter to keep a record of the proceeding. Any party who wishes to obtain a transcript of the record may do so at his or her own expense by contacting the court reporter directly. The only official record of the proceeding shall be the one made by the court reporter retained by the Commission. Copies of tapes, non-certified transcripts therefrom, or a record made by a court reporter retained by a party are not part of the official record.

(9) *Commission Decision.* After the hearing, a majority of the Commission members hearing the appeal may;

(a) find that there is not clear and convincing evidence to support the denial or revocation and, therefore dismiss the complaint or direct commission staff to certify or recertify the applicant, or

(b) find that there is clear and convincing evidence to affirm the committee's findings and denial or revocation. The Commission shall set forth its findings, conclusions, and denial determination in writing and serve it on the parties within 60 days of the date of the hearing by certified U.S. mail, return receipt requested. Such service shall be deemed adequate for purposes of these Rules.

(10) *Publication of Mediator Certification and Training Committee/Commission Decisions.*

(a) Names of applicants for mediator certification or names of mediator training programs that are denied certification or certification renewal or who have had their certification revoked pursuant to this rule shall not be published in the Commission's newsletter or on its web site and the determination shall not be generally publicized.

(b) Chief district court judges, senior resident superior court judges, or Clerks in districts which the mediator serves, and other trial forums or agencies having mandatory programs and using mediators certified by the Commission shall be notified of any revocation of certification or denial of a renewal.

(11) *Appeals.* The General Court of Justice, Superior Court Division, in Wake County shall have jurisdiction over appeals of Commission decisions denying an application or revoking a certification. An order denying or revoking certification pursuant to this rule shall be reviewable upon appeal where the entire record as submitted shall be reviewed to determine whether the order is supported by substantial evidence. Notice of appeal shall be filed in the Superior Court in Wake County within 30 days of the date of the Commission's decision.

(12) *Reinstatement of Certification.* A mediator or training program whose certification renewal has been denied or whose certification has been revoked under this rule may be reinstated as a certified mediator or mediation training program pursuant to Rule X.E(12)(g) below. An application for reinstatement

may be tendered at any time the applicant believes that he/she/it has become qualified to be reinstated.

(a) A petition for reinstatement shall be made in writing, verified by the petitioner, and filed with the Commission's office.

(b) The petition for reinstatement shall contain:

(i) the name and address of the petitioner;

(ii) a concise statement of the reasons upon which the denial of certification renewal or revocation was based; and

(iii) a concise statement of facts claimed to justify certification renewal or reinstatement as a certified mediator or mediator training program.

(c) The petition seeking reinstatement may also contain a request for a hearing on the matter to consider any additional evidence that the petitioner wishes to put forth.

(d) The Commission's staff shall refer the petition to the Commission for review.

(e) If the petitioner does not request a hearing, the Commission shall review the petition and shall make a decision within 90 days of the filing of the petition. That decision shall be final. If the petitioner requests a hearing, it shall be held within 180 days of the filing of the petition. The Commission shall conduct the hearing consistent with Rule X.E(2) above. At the hearing, the petitioner may:

(i) appear personally and be heard;

(ii) be represented by counsel;

(iii) call and examine witnesses;

(iv) offer exhibits; and

(v) cross-examine witnesses.

(f) At the hearing, the Commission may call witnesses, offer exhibits and examine the petitioner and witnesses.

(g) The burden of proof shall be upon the petitioner to establish by clear and convincing evidence that:

(i) the petitioner has satisfied the qualifications that led to the denial or revocation, and

(ii) the petitioner has completed any paperwork required for reinstatement and paid any required reinstatement and/or certification fees.

(h) If the petitioner is found to have met the qualifications and is entitled to have his/her/its certification reinstated, the Commission shall so certify.

(i) If a petition for reinstatement is denied, the petitioner may apply again pursuant to this section at any time after the qualifications are met.

(j) The Commission shall set forth its decision to certify a mediator or mediator training program or to deny certification in writing, making findings of fact and conclusions of law, and serve the decision on the petitioner by certified U.S. mail, return receipt requested, within 60 days of the date of the hearing. Such service shall be deemed sufficient for purposes of these Rules.

(k) The General Court of Justice, Superior Court Division, in Wake County shall have jurisdiction over appeals of Commission decisions to deny reinstatement. An order denying reinstatement shall be reviewable upon appeal, and the entire record as submitted shall be reviewed to determine whether the order is supported by substantial evidence. Notice of review shall be filed in the Superior Court in Wake County within 30 days of the date of the Commission's decision.

[Effective November 1, 1996. Amended effective January 1, 2012; April 1, 2014.]

Rule XI. Other Standing Committees

A. Superior Court Oversight Committee. The Commission's chair shall appoint a standing committee on Superior Court Oversight, including the Mediated Settlement Conference (MSC), Clerk Mediation, and Farm Nuisance Mediation programs. The Superior Court Oversight Committee shall support and monitor these programs to insure that each operates effectively pursuant to the rules for each program. The Superior Court Oversight Committee shall consider and make recommendations to the Commission regarding statutory or program rule changes. Members of the Superior Court Oversight Committee shall recuse themselves from discussing or deliberating on any matter in which they cannot act impartially or about which they have a conflict of interest. Pursuant to Rule 1.C(2) only Commission members may vote on matters before the Superior Court Oversight Committee.

B. District Court Oversight Committee. The Commission's chair shall appoint a standing committee on District Court Oversight, including the Equitable Distribution and Other Family Financial Cases (FFS), and District Criminal Court (DCC) programs. The District Court Oversight Committee shall support and monitor these programs to insure that each operates effectively pursuant to the rules for each program. The District Court Oversight Committee shall consider and make recommendations to the Commission regarding statutory or program rule changes. Members of the District Court Oversight Committee shall recuse themselves from discussing or deliberating on any matter in which they cannot act impartially or about which they have a conflict of interest. Pursuant to Rule 1.C(2) only Commission members may vote on matters before the District Court Oversight Committee.

C. Executive Committee. The Commission's chair shall appoint an Executive Committee of the Commission. The Executive Committee shall consider matters related to legislation, finances and budget, personnel, and emergent matters when necessary. Members of the Executive Committee shall recuse themselves from discussing or deliberating on any matter in which they cannot act impartially or about which they have a conflict of interest. Pursuant to Rule 1.C(2) only Commission members may vote on matters before the Executive Committee.

[Adopted effective April 1, 2014.]

Rule XII. Internal Operating Procedures

A. The Commission may adopt and publish internal operating procedures and policies for the conduct of Commission business.

B. The Commission's procedures and policies may be changed as needed on the basis of experience.

[Adopted effective April 1, 2014.]

STANDARDS OF PROFESSIONAL CONDUCT FOR MEDIATORS

Adopted by the North Carolina Supreme Court December 30, 1998

Preamble

These Standards of Professional Conduct for Mediators (Standards) shall apply to all mediators who are certified by the North Carolina Dispute Resolution Commission (Commission) or who are not certified, but are conducting court-ordered mediations in the context of a program or process that is governed by statutes, as amended from time to time, which provide for the Commission to regulate the conduct of mediators participating in the program or process. Provided, however, that if there is a specific statutory provision that conflicts with these Standards, then the statute shall control.

These Standards are intended to instill and promote public confidence in the mediation process and to provide minimum standards for mediator conduct. As with other forms of dispute resolution, mediation must be built upon public understanding and confidence. Persons serving as mediators are responsible to the parties, the public and the courts to conduct themselves in a manner that will merit that confidence. (See Rule VII of the Rules of the North Carolina Supreme Court for the Dispute Resolution Commission.)

It is the mediator's role to facilitate communication and understanding among the parties and to assist them in reaching an agreement. The mediator should aid the parties in identifying and discussing issues and in exploring options for settlement. The mediator should not, however, render a decision on the issues in dispute. In mediation, the ultimate decision whether and on what terms to resolve the dispute belongs to the parties and the parties alone.

[Adopted effective December 30, 1998. Amended June 29, 1999, effective October 1, 1999; amended effective August 16, 2001; October 20, 2004; March 1, 2006; March 1, 2010; January 1, 2012.]

Standard I. Competency

A mediator shall maintain professional competency in mediation skills and, where the mediator lacks the skills necessary for a particular case, shall decline to serve or withdraw from serving.

A. A mediator's most important qualification is the mediator's competence in procedural aspects of facilitating the resolution of disputes rather than the mediator's familiarity with technical knowledge relating to the subject of the dispute. Therefore a mediator shall obtain necessary skills and substantive training appropriate to the mediator's areas of practice and upgrade those skills on an ongoing basis.

B. If a mediator determines that a lack of technical knowledge impairs or is likely to impair the mediator's effectiveness, the mediator shall notify the parties and withdraw if requested by any party.

C. Beyond disclosure under the preceding paragraph, a mediator is obligated to exercise his/her judgment as to whether his/her skills or expertise are sufficient to the demands of the case and, if they are not, to decline from serving or to withdraw.

[Adopted effective December 30, 1998. Amended June 29, 1999, effective October 1, 1999; August 16, 2001; October 20, 2004; March 1, 2010; January 1, 2012.]

Standard II. Impartiality

A mediator shall, in word and action, maintain impartiality toward the parties and on the issues in dispute.

A. Impartiality means absence of prejudice or bias in word and action. In addition, it means a commitment to aid all parties, as opposed to a single party, in exploring the possibilities for resolution.

B. As early as practical and no later than the beginning of the first session, the mediator shall make full disclosure of any known relationships with the parties or their counsel that may affect or give the appearance of affecting the mediator's impartiality.

C. The mediator shall decline to serve or shall withdraw from serving if:

(1) a party objects to his/her serving on grounds of lack of impartiality, and after discussion, the party continues to object; or

(2) the mediator determines he/she cannot serve impartially.

[Adopted effective December 30, 1998. Amended June 29, 1999, effective October 1, 1999; August 16, 2001; October 20, 2004; March 1, 2010; January 1, 2012.]

Standard III. Confidentiality

A mediator shall, subject to exceptions set forth below, maintain the confidentiality of all information obtained within the mediation process.

A. A mediator shall not disclose, directly or indirectly, to any non-participant, any information communicated to the mediator by a participant within the mediation process, whether the information is obtained before, during or after the mediated settlement conference. A mediator's filing with the appropriate court a copy of an agreement reached in mediation pursuant to a statute that mandates such filing shall not be considered to be a violation of this paragraph.

B. A mediator shall not disclose, directly or indirectly, to any participant, information communicated to the mediator in confidence by any other participant in the mediation process, whether the information is obtained before, during or after the mediated settlement conference, unless that other participant gives the mediator permission to do so. A mediator may encourage a participant to permit disclosure, but absent such permission, the mediator shall not disclose.

C. A mediator shall not disclose to court officials or staff any information communicated to the mediator by any participant within the mediation process, whether before, during or after the mediated settlement conference, including correspondence or communications regarding scheduling or attendance, except as required to complete a report of mediator for the court; provided, however, when seeking to collect a fee for services, the mediator may share correspondence or communications from a participant relating to the fees of the mediator. The confidentiality provisions above notwithstanding, if a mediator believes that communicating certain procedural matters to court personnel will aid the mediation, then with the consent of the parties to the mediation, the mediator may do so. In making any permitted disclosure, a mediator shall refrain from expressing personal opinions about a participant or any aspect of the case with court officials or staff.

D. The confidentiality provisions set forth in A, B, and C above notwithstanding, a mediator may report otherwise confidential conduct or statements made in preparation for, during or as a follow-up to mediation in the circumstances set forth in sections (1) and (2) below:

(1) A statute requires or permits a mediator to testify or to give an affidavit or to tender a copy of any agreement reached in mediation to the official designated by the statute.

If, pursuant to Family Financial Settlement (FFS) and Mediated Settlement Conference (MSC) Rule 5, a mediator has been subpoenaed by a party to testify about who attended or failed to attend a mediated settlement conference/mediation, the mediator shall limit his/her testimony to providing the names of those who were physically present or who attended by electronic means.

If, pursuant to FFS and MSC Rule 5, a mediator has been subpoenaed by a party to testify about a party's failure to pay the mediator's fee, the mediator's testimony shall be limited to information about the amount of the fee and who had or had not paid it and shall not include statements made by any participant about the merits of the case.

(2) To a participant, non-participant, law enforcement personnel or other persons affected by the harm intended where public safety is an issue, in the following circumstances:

(i) a party or other participant in the mediation has communicated to the mediator a threat of serious bodily harm or death to be inflicted on any person, and the mediator has reason to believe the party has the intent and ability to act on the threat; or

(ii) a party or other participant in the mediation has communicated to the mediator a threat of significant damage to real or personal property and the mediator has reason to believe the party has the intent and ability to act on the threat; or

(iii) a party's or other participant's conduct during the mediation results in direct bodily injury or death to a person.

If the mediator is a North Carolina lawyer and a lawyer made the statements or committed the conduct reportable under subsection D(2) above, then the mediator shall report the statements or conduct to the North Carolina State Bar (State Bar) or the court having jurisdiction over the matter in accordance with North Carolina State Bar Rule of Professional Conduct 8.3(e).

E. Nothing in this Standard prohibits the use of information obtained in a mediation for instructional purposes or for the purpose of evaluating or monitoring the performance of a mediator, mediation organization or dispute resolution program, so long as the parties or the specific circumstances of the parties' controversy are not identified or identifiable.

F. Nothing in this Standard shall prohibit a mediator from revealing communications or conduct occurring prior to, during or after a mediation in the event that a party to or a participant in a mediation has filed a complaint regarding the mediator's professional conduct, moral character or fitness to practice as a mediator and the mediator reveals the communication or conduct for the purpose of defending him/herself against the complaint. In making any such disclosures, the mediator should make every effort to protect the confidentiality of non-complaining parties to or participants in the mediation and avoid disclosing the specific circumstances of the parties' controversy. The mediator may consult with non-complaining parties or witnesses to consider their input regarding disclosures.

[Adopted effective December 30, 1998. Amended June 29, 1999, effective October 1, 1999; August 16, 2001; October 20, 2004; March 1, 2006; March 1, 2010; January 1, 2012; April 1, 2014.]

Standard IV. Consent

A mediator shall make reasonable efforts to ensure that each party understands the mediation process, the role of the mediator and the party's options within the process.

A. A mediator shall discuss with the participants the rules and procedures pertaining to the mediation process and shall inform the parties of such matters as applicable rules require.

B. A mediator shall not exert undue pressure on a participant, whether to participate in mediation or to accept a settlement; nevertheless, a mediator shall encourage parties to consider both the benefits of participation and settlement and the costs of withdrawal and impasse.

C. If a party appears to have difficulty comprehending the process, issues or settlement options or difficulty participating in a mediation, the mediator shall explore the circumstances and potential accommodations, modifications or adjustments that would facilitate the party's capacity to comprehend, participate and exercise self-determination. If the mediator then determines that the party cannot meaningfully participate in the mediation, the mediator shall recess or discontinue the mediation. Before discontinuing the mediation, the mediator shall consider the context and circumstance of the mediation, including subject matter of the dispute, availability of support persons for the party and whether the party is represented by counsel.

D. In appropriate circumstances, a mediator shall inform the parties of the importance of seeking legal, financial, tax or other professional advice before, during or after the mediation process.

[Adopted effective December 30, 1998. Amended June 29, 1999, effective October 1, 1999; August 16, 2001; October 20, 2004; March 1, 2010; January 1, 2012.]

Standard V. Self Determination

A mediator shall respect and encourage self-determination by the parties in their decision whether, and on what terms, to resolve their dispute and shall refrain from being directive and judgmental regarding the issues in dispute and options for settlement.

A. A mediator is obligated to leave to the parties full responsibility for deciding whether and on what terms to resolve their dispute. He/She may assist them in making informed and thoughtful decisions, but shall not impose his/her judgment or opinions for those of the parties concerning any aspect of the mediation.

B. A mediator may raise questions for the participants to consider regarding their perceptions of the dispute as well as the acceptability of proposed options for settlement and their impact on third parties. Furthermore, a mediator may suggest for consideration options for settlement in addition to those conceived of by the parties themselves.

C. A mediator shall not impose his/her opinion about the merits of the dispute or about the acceptability of any proposed option for settlement. A mediator should resist giving his/her opinions about the dispute and options for settlement even when he/she is requested to do so by a party or attorney. Instead, a mediator should help that party utilize his/her own resources to evaluate the dispute and the options for settlement.

This section prohibits imposing one's opinions, advice and/or counsel upon a party or attorney. It does not prohibit the mediator's expression of an opinion as a last resort to a party or attorney who requests it and the mediator has already helped that party utilize his/her own resources to evaluate the dispute and options.

D. Subject to Standard IV.D above, if a party to a mediation declines to consult an independent counsel or expert after the mediator has raised this option, the mediator shall permit the mediation to go forward according to the parties' wishes.

E. If, in the mediator's judgment, the integrity of the process has been compromised by, for example, inability or unwillingness of a party to participate meaningfully, inequality of bargaining power or ability, unfairness resulting from non-disclosure or fraud by a participant or other circumstance likely to lead to a grossly unjust result, the mediator shall inform the parties of the mediator's concern. Consistent with the confidentiality required in Standard III, the mediator may discuss with the parties the source of the concern. The mediator may choose to discontinue the mediation in such circumstances but shall not violate the obligation of confidentiality.

[Adopted effective December 30, 1998. Amended June 29, 1999, effective October 1, 1999; amended effective August 16, 2001; October 20, 2004; March 1, 2010; January 1, 2012.]

Standard VI. Separation of Mediation from Legal and Other Professional Advice

A mediator shall limit himself or herself solely to the role of mediator, and shall not give legal or other professional advice during the mediation.

A mediator may provide information that the mediator is qualified by training or experience to provide only if the mediator can do so consistent with these Standards. Mediators may respond to a party's request for an opinion on the merits of the case or suitability of settlement proposals only in accordance with Section V.C above.

[Adopted effective December 30, 1998. Amended June 29, 1999, effective October 1, 1999; amended effective August 16, 2001; October 20, 2004; March 1, 2010; January 1, 2012; April 1, 2014.]

Commission Official Comment

Although mediators shall not provide legal or other professional advice, mediators may respond to a party's request for an opinion on the merits of the case or the suitability of settlement proposals only in accordance with Section V.C above, and mediators may provide information that they are qualified by training or experience to provide only if it can be done consistent with these Standards.

Standard VII. Conflicts of Interest

A mediator shall not allow any personal interest to interfere with the primary obligation to impartially serve the parties to the dispute.

A. The mediator shall place the interests of the parties above the interests of any court or agency which has referred the case, if such interests are in conflict.

B. Where a party is represented or advised by a professional advocate or counselor, the mediator shall place the interests of the party over his/her own interest in maintaining cordial relations with the professional, if such interests are in conflict.

C. A mediator who is a lawyer, therapist or other professional and the mediator's professional partners or co-shareholders shall not advise, counsel or represent any of the parties in future matters concerning the subject of the dispute, an action closely related to the dispute or an out growth of the dispute when the mediator or his/her staff has engaged in substantive conversations with any party to the dispute. Substantive conversations are those that go beyond discussion of the general issues in dispute, the identity of parties or participants and scheduling or administrative issues. Any disclosure that a party might expect the mediator to hold confidential pursuant to Standard III is a substantive conversation.

A mediator who is a lawyer, therapist or other professional may not mediate the dispute when the mediator or the mediator's professional partners or co-shareholders has advised, counseled or represented any of the parties in any matter concerning the subject of the dispute, an action closely related to the dispute, a preceding issue in the dispute or an out growth of the dispute.

D. A mediator shall not charge a contingent fee or a fee based on the outcome of the mediation.

E. A mediator shall not use information obtained or relationships formed during a mediation for personal gain or advantage.

F. A mediator shall not knowingly contract for mediation services which cannot be delivered or completed as directed by a court or in a timely manner.

G. A mediator shall not prolong a mediation for the purpose of charging a higher fee.

H. A mediator shall not give or receive any commission, rebate or other monetary or non-monetary form of consideration from a party or representative of a party in return for referral or expectation of referral of clients for mediation services, except that a mediator may give or receive de minimis offerings such as sodas, cookies, snacks or lunches served to those attending mediations conducted by the mediator and intended to further those mediations or intended to show respect for cultural norms.

A mediator should neither give nor accept any gift, favor, loan or other item of value that raises a question as to the mediator's actual or perceived impartiality.

[Adopted effective December 30, 1998. Amended June 29, 1999, effective October 1, 1999; amended effective August 16, 2001; October 20, 2004; March 1, 2010; January 1, 2012; April 1, 2014.]

Standard VIII. Protecting the Integrity of the Mediation Process

A mediator shall encourage mutual respect between the parties and shall take reasonable steps, subject to the principle of self-determination, to limit abuses of the mediation process.

A. A mediator shall make reasonable efforts to ensure a balanced discussion and to prevent manipulation or intimidation by either party and to ensure that each party understands and respects the concerns and position of the other even if they cannot agree.

B. If a mediator believes that the statements or actions of any participant, including those of a lawyer who the mediator believes is engaging in or has engaged in professional misconduct, jeopardize or will jeopardize the integrity of the mediation process, the mediator shall attempt to persuade the participant to cease his/her behavior and take remedial action. If the mediator is unsuccessful in this effort, s/he shall take appropriate steps including, but not limited to, postponing, withdrawing from or terminating the mediation. If a lawyer's statements or conduct are reportable under Standard III.C(2), the mediator shall report the lawyer to the State Bar or the court having jurisdiction over the matter in accordance with North Carolina State Bar Rule of Professional Conduct 8.3.

[Adopted effective December 30, 1998. Amended June 29, 1999, effective October 1, 1999; amended effective August 16, 2001; March 1, 2010; January 1, 2012.]

RESTRUCTURE OF THE ALTERNATIVE DISPUTE RESOLUTION COMMITTEE OF THE STATE JUDICIAL COUNCIL

On July 13, 2000, the Supreme Court created the Alternative Dispute Resolution Committee of the State Judicial Council composed of twenty-four members to advise the Council and the Court on policy directions for the court-sponsored dispute resolution programs and to provide coordination and evaluation of those programs from time to time as needed. The ADR Committee has met regularly to fulfill its charge until the budget crisis of 2006 cut off any funding for meetings.

During his tenure as Chair, Judge Ralph Walker appointed a subcommittee to review the structure, charge, and operation of the Committee. After the Subcommittee's report was submitted and discussed, the full Committee voted to recommend that its charge remain unchanged, its operations streamlined, and its membership reduced.

Upon this recommendation, the Supreme Court hereby adopts the following rule, restructuring the Alternative Dispute Resolution Committee of the North Carolina State Judicial Council.

1. The duties of the Committee shall remain the same, which are as follows:

- To provide ongoing coordination and policy direction for court-sponsored dispute resolution programs in the state;
- To provide a forum for the consideration of issues affecting the future direction of the court-sponsored dispute resolution movement within the North Carolina court system;
- To recommend to the State Judicial Council guidelines for the appropriate form of dispute resolution to be used as a case management tool in cases heard in the general Court of Justice;
- To monitor the effectiveness of dispute resolution programs and report its findings to the State Judicial Council;
- To provide a forum for the resolution of inter-program issues that arise among the various programs sponsored by the court system; and
- To serve as a clearing-house for rules that affect dispute resolution programs before they are submitted to the Supreme Court for review and adoption.

2. The membership of the Committee shall be reduced from twenty-four to fifteen members. The fifteen members shall be appointed by the Chief Justice as follows:

- Two Superior Court Judges, one from a single county district and one from a multi county district;
- Two District Court judges, one from a single county district and one from a multi county district;
- The Chair of the Dispute Resolution Commission or his/her designee from among the members of the Commission;
- Five attorneys licensed to practice law in NC recommended by the President of the NC Bar Association, two of whom shall be familiar with the operations and procedures of the District Court;
- The Chair of the Child Custody Mediation Advisory Committee or his/her designee from among the members of that committee;
- A Trial Court Administrator or Judicial Assistant;
- A citizen interested in dispute resolution programs;
- The Director of the Administrative Office of the Courts or his/her designee; and
- A person appointed by the Chief Justice as Chair.

3. All terms shall be for four years and that the fact that a person serves in any other official capacity in an activity related to a dispute resolution program does not disqualify that person from serving on the Committee if the person is otherwise qualified to serve.

4. The Chair is authorized to appoint as ex-officio members of the Committee persons who represent the following programs or entities: the Supreme Court, Court of Appeals, the Industrial Commission, the NCBA's Dispute Resolution Section, Dispute Settlement Centers, the Fourth Circuit mediation program, and any other group interested in court-sponsored dispute resolution programs and that those ex-officio members are permitted to serve and vote on subcommittees as established by the Committee.

5. A member whose term has expired, but whose replacement has not been appointed shall continue to serve until such replacement is appointed.

6. Any person interested in court sponsored dispute resolution programs, who makes that interest known to the Chair of the Committee, shall be given notice of the meetings and business of the Committee whether those meetings are conducted in person or by phone.

7. It is recommended that there be at least two public meetings of the Committee each year, and that other meetings may be conducted by phone or in person as called by the Chair.

8. Routine rule changes and program modifications may be circulated among the membership and others who request notification by electronic means

and that those changes be deemed approved unless a member objects to their adoption. In that event, an attempt should be made to circulate an amended draft in an effort to reach a decision without a meeting. In the event a meeting is necessary, the Chair may conduct a meeting by phone on issues that s/he determines are routine in nature.

9. The State Judicial Council may delegate other duties to the Committee and the State Judicial Council may also establish supplemental procedures and policies to regulate the work of the Committee.

[Adopted effective October 5, 2010.]

RULES IMPLEMENTING MEDIATION IN MATTERS PENDING IN DISTRICT CRIMINAL COURT

Adopted and effective November 8, 2007

Table of Rules

Rule 1. Initiating Voluntary Mediation in District Criminal Court

A. Purpose of Mediation. Pursuant to N.C.G.S. § 7A–38.3D, these Rules are promulgated to implement programs for voluntary mediation of certain cases within the jurisdiction of the district criminal courts. These procedures are intended to assist private parties, with the help of a neutral mediator, in discussing and resolving their disputes and in conserving judicial resources. The chief district court judge, the district attorney and the community mediation center shall determine whether to establish a program in a district court judicial district. Because participation in this program and in the mediation process is voluntary, no defendant, complaining witness or any other person who declines to participate in mediation or whose case cannot be settled in mediation, shall face any adverse consequences as a result of his/her failure to participate or reach an agreement and the case shall simply be returned to court. Consistent with N.C.G.S. § 7A–38.3D(j) a party's participation or failure to participate in mediation is to be held confidential and not revealed to the court or the district attorney.

B. Definitions.

(1) *Court.* The term "court" as used throughout these rules, shall refer both to a criminal district court judge or his/her designee, including a district attorney or designee, or personnel affiliated with a community mediation center.

(2) *Mediation Process.* The term "mediation process" as used throughout these rules, shall encompass intake, screening and mediation through impasse or until the case is dismissed.

(3) *District Attorney.* The term "district attorney" as used throughout these rules, shall refer to the district attorney, assistant district attorneys and any staff or designee of the district attorney.

C. Initiating the Mediation.

(1) *Suggestion by the Court.* In districts that establish a program, the court may encourage private parties to attend mediation in certain cases or categories of cases. In determining whether to encourage mediation in a case or category of cases, the judge or designee may consider among other factors:

(a) whether the parties are willing to participate;

(b) whether continuing prosecution is in the best interest of the parties or of any non-parties impacted by the dispute;

(c) whether the private parties involved in the dispute have an expectation of a continuing relationship and there are issues underlying their dispute that have not been addressed and which may create later conflict or require court involvement;

(d) whether cross-warrants have been filed in the case; and

(e) whether the case might otherwise be subject to voluntary dismissal.

(2) *Multiple Charges.* Multiple charges pending in the same court against a single defendant or pending against multiple defendants and involving the same complainant or complainants may be consolidated for purposes of holding a single mediation in the matter. Charges pending in multiple courts may be consolidated for purposes of mediation with the consent of those courts.

(3) *Timing of Suggestion.* The court shall encourage parties to attend and participate in mediation as

soon as practicable. Since there is no possibility of incarceration resulting from any agreement reached in mediation, the judge is not required to provide a court-appointed attorney to a defendant prior to his/her mediation.

(4) *Notice to Parties.* The court shall provide to parties who have agreed to attend mediation notice of the following either orally or in writing on a North Carolina Administrative Office of the Courts (NCAOC) approved form: (1) the deadline for completion of the mediation process; (2) the name of the mediator who will mediate the dispute or the name of the community mediation center who will provide the mediator; and (3) and that the defendant may be required to pay the dismissal fee set forth in Rule 5.B(2). In lieu of providing this information orally or in writing, the court may refer the complaining witness and defendant to a community mediation center whose staff shall advise the parties of the above information.

(5) *Motion for Mediation.* Any complainant or defendant may file an oral or written request with the court to have a mediation conducted in his or her dispute and the court shall determine whether the dispute is appropriate for referral. If in writing, the motion may be on a NCAOC form.

(6) *Screening.* A mediator as defined by Rule 7 below or a community mediation center to which the parties are referred for mediation shall advise the court, if it is determined upon screening of the case or parties, that the matter is not appropriate for mediation.

[Adopted November 8, 2007, effective November 8, 2007. Amended effective January 1, 2012; April 1, 2014.]

Rule 2. Program Administration

Pursuant to N.C.G.S. § 7A–38.3D(c), a community mediation center may assist a judicial district in administering and operating its mediation program for district court criminal matters. The court may delegate to a center responsibility for the scheduling of cases and the center may provide volunteer and/or staff mediators to conduct the mediations. The center shall also maintain files in such mediations; record caseload statistics and other information as required by the court, the Dispute Resolution Commission (Commission) or the (NCAOC), including tracking the number of cases referred to mediation and the outcome of those mediations; and, in accordance with N.C.G.S. § 7A–38.7 and N.C.G.S. § 7A–38.3D(m), oversee the dismissal process for cases resolved in mediation.

[Adopted November 8, 2007, effective November 8, 2007. Amended effective January 1, 2012; April 1, 2014.]

Rule 3. Appointment of Mediator

A. Authority to Appoint. When the parties have agreed to attend mediation, the court shall appoint a community mediation center mediator by name or shall designate a center to appoint a mediator to conduct the mediation. The mediator appointed shall be certified pursuant to Rule 7 of these rules or shall be working toward certification under the supervision of the center to whom the dispute is referred for mediation.

B. Disqualification of Mediator. For good cause shown, a complainant or defendant may move the court to disqualify the mediator appointed to conduct their mediation. If the mediator is disqualified, the court or designee shall appoint a new one to conduct the mediation. Nothing in this provision shall preclude a mediator from disqualifying him or herself.

[Adopted November 8, 2007, effective November 8, 2007. Amended effective January 1, 2012; April 1, 2014.]

Rule 4. The Mediation

A. Scheduling Mediation. The mediator appointed to conduct the mediation or the community mediation center to which the matter has been referred by the court for appointment of a mediator, shall be responsible for any scheduling that must be done prior to the mediation, any reporting required by these rules or local rules and the maintenance of any files pertaining to the mediation.

B. Where Mediation is to be Held. Mediation shall be held in the courthouse or if suitable space is available, in the offices of a community mediation center or at any other place as agreed upon between the mediator and parties.

C. Extending Deadline for Completion. The court may extend the deadline for completion of the mediation process upon its own motion or upon suggestion of community mediation center staff.

D. Recessed. The mediator may recess the mediation at any time and may set times for reconvening. If the time for reconvening is set before the mediation is recessed, no further notification is required for persons present at the mediation. In recessing a matter, the mediator shall take into account whether the parties wish to continue mediating and whether they are making progress toward resolving their dispute.

E. No Recording. There shall be no stenographic, audio or video recording of the mediation process by any participant. This prohibition precludes recording either surreptitiously or with the agreement of the parties.

[Adopted November 8, 2007, effective November 8, 2007. Amended effective January 1, 2012; April 1, 2014.]

Rule 5. Duties of the Parties

A. Attendance.

(1) Complainant(s) and defendant(s) who agree to attend mediation will physically attend the proceeding until an agreement is reached or the mediator has declared an impasse.

(2) The following may attend and participate in mediation:

(a) Parents or guardians of a minor party. Parent(s) or guardian(s) of a minor complainant or defendant who have been encouraged by the court to attend. However, a court shall encourage attendance by a parent or guardian only in consultation with the mediator and a mediator may later excuse the participation of a parent or guardian if the mediator determines his/her presence is not helpful to the process.

(b) Attorneys. Attorneys representing parties may physically attend and participate in mediation. Alternatively, lawyers may participate indirectly by advising clients before, during and after mediation sessions, including monitoring compliance with any agreements reached.

(c) Others. In the mediator's discretion, others whose presence and participation is deemed helpful to resolving the dispute or to addressing any issues underlying it, may be permitted to attend and participate unless and until the mediator determines their presence is no longer helpful. Mediators may exclude anyone wishing to attend and participate, but whose presence and participation the mediator deems would likely be disruptive or counter-productive.

(3) *Exceptions to Physical Attendance.* A party or other person may be excused from physically attending the mediation and allowed to participate by telephone or through any attorney:

(a) by agreement of the complainant(s) and defendant(s) and the mediator, or

(b) by order of the court.

(4) *Scheduling.* The complainant(s) and defendant(s) and any parent, guardian or attorney who will be attending the mediation will:

(a) Make a good faith effort to cooperate with the mediator or community mediation center to schedule the mediation at a time that is convenient for all participants;

(b) Promptly notify the mediator or community mediation center to which the case has been referred of any significant scheduling concerns which may impact that person's ability to be present for mediation; and

(c) Notify the mediator or the center about any other concerns that may impact a party or person's ability to attend and participate meaningfully, *e.g.,* the need for wheelchair access or for a deaf or foreign language interpreter.

B. Finalizing Agreement.

(1) *Written Agreement.* If an agreement is reached at the mediation, the complainant and defendant are to insure that the terms are reduced to writing and signed. Agreements that are not reduced to writing and signed will not be deemed enforceable. If no agreement is reached in mediation, an impasse will be declared and the matter will be referred back to the court or its designee.

(2) *Dismissal Fee.* To be dismissed by the district attorney, the defendant, unless the parties agree to some other apportionment, shall pay a dismissal fee as set by N.C.G.S. § 7A–38.7 and N.C.G.S. § 7A–38.3D(m) to the clerk of superior court in the county where the case was filed and supply proof of payment to the community mediation center administering the program for the judicial district. Payment is to be made in accordance with the terms of the parties' agreement. The center shall, thereafter, provide the district attorney with a dismissal form, which may be an approved NCAOC form. In his or her discretion, a judge or his/her designee may waive the dismissal fee pursuant to N.C.G.S. § 7A–38.3D(m) when the defendant is indigent, unemployed, a full-time college or high school student, is a recipient of public assistance or for any other appropriate reason. The mediator shall advise the parties where and how to pay the fee.

[Adopted November 8, 2007, effective November 8, 2007. Amended effective January 1, 2012; April 1, 2014.]

Rule 6. Authority and Duties of the Mediator

A. Authority of the Mediator.

(1) *Control of Mediation.* The mediator shall at all times be in control of the mediation process and the procedures to be followed. The mediator's conduct shall be governed by Standards of Professional Conduct for Mediators (Standards) promulgated by the Supreme Court.

(2) *Private Consultation.* The mediator may communicate privately with any participant or counsel prior to and during the mediation. The fact that previous communications have occurred with a participant shall be disclosed to all other participants at the beginning of the mediation.

(3) *Inclusion and Exclusion of Participants at Mediation.* In the mediator's discretion, he or she may encourage or allow persons other than the parties or their attorneys, to attend and participate in mediation, provided that the mediator has determined the presence of such persons to be helpful to resolving the dispute or to addressing issues underlying it. Mediators may also exclude persons other that the parties and their attorneys whose presence the mediator

deems would likely be or which has, in fact, been counter-productive.

(4) *Scheduling the Mediation.* The mediator or community mediation center staff involved in scheduling shall make a good faith effort to schedule the mediation at a time that is convenient for the parties and any parent(s), guardian(s) or attorney(s) who will be attending. In the absence of agreement, the mediator or community mediation center staff shall select the date for the mediation and notify those who will be participating. Parties are to cooperate with the mediator in scheduling the mediation, including providing the information required by Rule 5.A(4).

B. Duties of the Mediator.

(1) The mediator shall define and describe the following at the beginning of the mediation:

(a) The process of mediation;

(b) That the mediation is not a trial and the mediator is not a judge, attorney or therapist;

(c) That the mediator is present only to assist the parties in reaching their own agreement;

(d) The circumstances under which the mediator may meet and communicate privately with any of the parties or with any other person;

(e) Whether and under what conditions communications with the mediator will be held in confidence during the mediation;

(f) The inadmissibility of conduct and statements as provided in N.C.G.S. § 7A-38.3D(i);

(g) The duties and responsibilities of the mediator and the participants;

(h) That any agreement reached will be by mutual consent;

(i) That if the parties are unable to agree and the mediator declares an impasse, that the parties and the case will return to court; and

(j) That if an agreement is reached in mediation and the parties agree to request a dismissal of the charges pending in the case, the defendant, unless the parties agree to some other apportionment, shall pay a dismissal fee in accordance with N.C.G.S. § 7A-38.7 and N.C.G.S. § 7A-38.3D(m), unless a judge in his or her discretion has waived the fee for good cause. Payment of the dismissal fee shall be made to the clerk of superior court in the county where the case was filed and the community mediation center must provide the district attorney with a dismissal form and proof that the defendant has paid the dispute resolution fee before the charges can be dismissed.

(2) *Disclosure.* Consistent with the Standards of Professional Conduct for Mediators (Standards), the mediator has a duty to be impartial and to advise all participants of any circumstances bearing on possible bias, prejudice or partiality.

(3) *Declaring Impasse.* Consistent with the Standards, it is the duty of the mediator to determine in a timely manner that an impasse exists and that the mediation should conclude. To that end, the mediator shall inquire of and consider the desires of the parties to cease or continue the mediation.

(4) *Reporting Results of Mediation.* The mediator or community mediation center shall report the outcome of mediation to the court or its designee in writing on a NCAOC approved form by the date the case is next calendared. If the criminal court charges are on the court docket the same day as the mediation, the mediator shall inform the attending district attorney of the outcome of the mediation before close of court on that date unless alternative arrangements are approved by the district attorney.

(5) *Scheduling and Holding the Mediation.* It is the duty of the mediator and community mediation center staff to schedule the mediation and conduct it prior to any deadline set by the court or its designee. Deadlines shall be strictly observed by the mediator and center staff unless the deadline is extended orally or in writing by a judge or his/her designee.

[Adopted November 8, 2007, effective November 8, 2007. Amended effective January 1, 2012; April 1, 2014.]

Rule 7. Mediator Certification and Decertification

The Commission may receive and approve applications for certification of persons to be appointed as district criminal court mediators. For certification, an applicant shall:

A. At the time of application, be affiliated with a community mediation center established pursuant to N.C.G.S. § 7A-38.5 as either a volunteer or staff mediator and have received the center's endorsement that he or she possesses the training, experience, and skills necessary to conduct district court criminal mediations.

B. Have the following training and experience:

(1) Have both:

(a) Attended at least 24 hours of training in a district criminal court mediation training program certified by the Commission; and

(b) Have a four-year degree from an accredited college or university or have four years of post high school education through an accredited college, university or junior college or four years of full-time work experience, or any combination thereof; or have two years experience as a staff or volunteer mediator at a community mediation center; or

(2) Be a mediated settlement conference or family financial settlement mediator certified by the Commission or be an Advanced Practitioner Member of the Association for Conflict Resolution.

C. Observations and Mediation Experience:

(1) Observe at least two court-referred criminal district court mediations conducted by a mediator certified pursuant to these rules or for a one-year period following the initial adoption of these rules, observe any mediator who is affiliated with a community mediation center established pursuant to N.C.G.S. § 7A–38.5 and who has mediated at least 10 criminal district court cases.

(2) Co-mediate or mediate at least three court-referred district criminal court mediations under the observation of staff affiliated with a community mediation center whose criminal district court mediation training program has been certified by the Commission pursuant to Rule 9 of these Rules.

D. Demonstrate familiarity with the statutes, rules and practice governing district criminal court mediations in North Carolina.

E. Be of good moral character, submit to a criminal background check within one year prior to applying for certification under these Rules and adhere to any standards of practice for mediators acting pursuant to these Rules adopted by the Supreme Court of North Carolina. Applicants for certification and recertification and all certified district criminal court mediators shall report to the Commission any pending criminal matters or any criminal convictions, disbarments or other disciplinary complaints and actions or any judicial sanctions as soon as the applicant or mediator has notice of them.

F. Commit to serving the district court as a mediator under the direct supervision of a community mediation center authorized under N.C.G.S. § 7A–38.5 for a period of at least two years.

G. Comply with the requirements of the Commission for continuing mediator education or training.

H. Submit proof of qualifications set out in this Section on a form provided by the Commission.

Community mediation centers participating in the program shall assist the Commission in implementing the certification process established by this Rule by:

(1) Documenting Sections A–F for the mediator and Commission;

(2) Reviewing its documentation with the mediator in a face-to-face meeting scheduled no less than 30 days from the mediator's request to apply for certification;

(3) Making a written recommendation on the applicant's certification to the Commission; and

(4) Forwarding the documentation for Sections A–F and its recommendation to the Commission along with the mediator's completed certification application form.

Certification may be revoked or not renewed at any time it is shown to the satisfaction of the Commission that a mediator no longer meets the above qualifications or has not faithfully observed these Rules or those of any district in which he or she has served as a mediator. Any person who is or has been disqualified by a professional licensing authority of any state for misconduct shall be ineligible to be certified under this Rule. Certification renewal shall be required every two years.

A community mediation center may withdraw its affiliation with a mediator certified pursuant to these Rules. Such disaffiliation does not revoke said mediator's certification. A mediator's certification is portable and a mediator may agree to be affiliated with a different center. However to mediate under this program in the district criminal court, a mediator must be affiliated with the community mediation center providing services in that court. A mediator may be affiliated with more than one center and provide services in the county served by those centers.

[Adopted November 8, 2007, effective November 8, 2007. Amended effective January 1, 2012; April 1, 2014.]

Rule 8. Certification of Mediation Training Programs

A. Certified training programs for mediators seeking certification as district criminal court mediators shall consist of a minimum of 24 hours instruction. The curriculum of such programs shall include:

(1) Conflict resolution and mediation theory;

(2) Mediation process and techniques, including the process and techniques of district court criminal mediation;

(3) Agreement writing;

(4) Communication and information gathering;

(5) Standards of conduct for mediators including, but not limited to the Standards adopted by the Supreme Court;

(6) Statutes, rules, forms and practice governing mediations in North Carolina's district criminal courts;

(7) Demonstrations of district criminal court mediations;

(8) Simulations of district criminal court mediations, involving student participation as mediator, victim, offender and attorneys which shall be supervised, observed and evaluated by program faculty;

(9) Courtroom protocol;

(10) Domestic violence awareness; and

(11) Satisfactory completion of an exam by all students testing their familiarity with the statutes, rules and practice governing district court mediations in North Carolina.

B. A training program must be certified by the Commission before attendance at such program may be deemed as satisfying Rule 8.

Training programs attended prior to the promulgation of these rules or attended in other states may be approved by the Commission if they are in substantial compliance with the standards set forth in this Rule.

C. Renewal of certification shall be required every two years.

[Adopted November 8, 2007, effective November 8, 2007. Amended effective January 1, 2012; April 1, 2014.]

Rule 9. Local Rule Making

The chief district court judge of any district conducting mediations under these Rules is authorized to publish local rules, not inconsistent with these Rules and N.C.G.S. § 7A–38.3D, implementing mediation in that district.

[Adopted November 8, 2007, effective November 8, 2007. Amended effective January 1, 2012; April 1, 2014.]

SUPPLEMENTAL RULES OF PRACTICE AND PROCEDURE FOR THE NORTH CAROLINA eFILING PILOT PROJECT

Effective May 15, 2009

Table of Rules

Rule 1. Introduction

1.1—Citation to Rules. These rules shall be known as the "Supplemental Rules of Practice and Procedure for the North Carolina eFiling Pilot Project," and may be cited as the "eFiling Rules." A particular rule may be cited as "eFiling Rule ___."

1.2—Authority and Effective Date. The eFiling Rules are promulgated by the Supreme Court of North Carolina pursuant to G.S. 7A–49.5. They are effective as of May 15, 2009, and as amended from time to time.

1.3—Scope and Purpose. The eFiling Rules apply to civil superior court cases and to foreclosures under power of sale filed on or after the effective date in Chowan and Davidson Counties. Upon addition of Wake County to the pilot project by the North Carolina Administrative Office of the Courts (the "AOC"), these rules shall apply to civil superior court cases and to foreclosures under power of sale filed in Wake County on or after the effective date of the implementation of the pilot project in Wake County, and the public announcement thereof by AOC. In addition, these rules apply to any designated case types and in any counties upon the implementation of the eFiling project in any other counties and the public announcement thereof by the AOC. In general, these rules initially allow, but do not mandate, electronic filing by North Carolina licensed attorneys and court officials of pleadings and other documents required to be filed with the court by the North Carolina Rules of Civil Procedure ("Rules of Civil Procedure"), or otherwise under North Carolina law, and permit electronic notification of the electronic filing of documents between attorneys. Initially, they do not permit electronic filing by *pro se* parties or attorneys not licensed by the State of North Carolina, and they do not permit electronic filing of documents in cases not initially filed electronically. Upon the addition of Alamance County or other counties to the pilot project by the AOC, the electronic filing of civil domestic violence cases by pro se parties, acting through domestic violence center personnel approved by the Chief District Court Judge, shall be permitted upon the implementation of the eFiling project in any such counties and the public announcement thereof by AOC.

1.4—Integration with Other Rules. These rules supplement the Rules of Civil Procedure and the General Rules of Practice for Superior and District Courts (the "General Rules"). The filing and service of documents in accordance with the eFiling Rules is deemed to comply with the Rules of Civil Procedure and the General Rules. If a conflict exists between the eFiling Rules and the Rules of Civil Procedure or the General Rules, the eFiling Rules shall control.

[Effective May 15, 2009. Amended effective June, 24, 2013.]

Rule 2. Definitions

2.1—"Cloak" means the process by which portions of an original document within the court's document management system are obscured when viewed electronically by all non-court personnel other than parties to the case.

2.2—"Document" means data filed electronically under the eFiling Rules.

2.3—"eFiler" means a holder who makes, or who attempts, under eFiling Rule 5, to make an electronic filing or who authorizes another person to make an electronic filing using the holder's electronic identity.

2.4—"Electronic Identity" means the combination of username and password issued to a person by the AOC under eFiling Rule 3.1.

2.5—"Holder" means a person with an AOC approved electronic identity.

[Effective May 15, 2009. Amended effective June, 24, 2013.]

Rule 3. Electronic Identities

3.1—Issuance. Upon application and upon completion of the training, if any, required by the AOC, the AOC shall issue an electronic identity to clerk personnel, judicial support staff, domestic violence center personnel, county sheriff personnel, magistrates, and judges in the affected counties, who are approved by the Chief District Court Judge and Senior Resident Superior Court Judge (and, for inquiry purposes only, law enforcement officers or other authorized users), as well as to any attorney who

(a) is licensed to practice law in this state;

(b) has pending or intends to file or appear in a civil superior court case or a foreclosure under power of sale in a pilot county;

(c) designates a valid and operational email address; and

(d) provides all other information required by the AOC,

3.2—Scope of Electronic Identity. Electronic identities are not case specific.

3.3—Responsibility of Holder. Each holder is responsible for the confidentiality, security, and use of the holder's electronic identity. If an electronic identity becomes compromised, or any organization or affiliation change occurs, the holder shall immediately notify the AOC and request a change to the holder's user name, password or profile information as appropriate,

3.4—Effect of Use. Use of an electronic identity constitutes:

(a) an agreement by the holder to comply with the eFiling Rules;

(b) an appearance in the matter by the holder; and

(c) acknowledgement that the holder's designated email address is current.

3.5—Use by Others. If a holder authorizes another person to file using the holder's electronic identity, the holder retains full responsibility for any filing by the authorized person, and the filing has the same effect as use by the holder. An electronic filing by use of an electronic identity is deemed to have been made with the authorization of the holder unless the contrary is shown by the holder to the satisfaction of the trier of fact by clear and convincing evidence. A filing made by use of an electronic identity without authorization of the holder is void.

[Effective May 15, 2009. Amended effective June, 24, 2013.]

Rule 4. Signatures and Authenticity

4.1—Signatures. An electronically filed document requiring a signature is deemed to be signed by the eFiler pursuant to Rule 11 of the Rules of Civil Procedure, regardless of the existence of a handwritten signature on the paper, and must contain the name, postal address, e-mail address, and State Bar number of the eFiler, and the name of the eFiler preceded by the symbol "/s/" in the location at which a handwritten signature normally would appear. However, affidavits and exhibits to pleadings with the original handwritten signatures must be scanned and filed in Portable Document Format (PDF) or TIFF format. Verification or notarization of documents to be filed by domestic violence victims may be done in person or before a magistrate or authorized clerk personnel via telephone audio/visual transmission through an AOC approved system.

4.2—Signature of Person(s) Other than eFiler. An eFiler who files a document signed by two or more persons representing different parties shall confirm that all persons signing the document have agreed to its content, represent to the court in the body of the document or in an accompanying affidavit that the agreement has been obtained, and insert in the location where each handwritten signature otherwise would appear the typed signature of each person, other than the person filing, preceded by the symbol "/s/" and followed by the words "by permission." Thus, the correct format for the typed signature of a person other than the person filing is: "/s/ Jane Doe by permission." Unless required by these Rules, a document filed electronically should not be filed in an optically scanned format displaying an actual signature.

4.3—Authenticity. Documents filed electronically in accordance with the eFiling Rules and accurate printouts of such documents shall be deemed authentic.

4.4—Preservation of Originals. The eFiler shall retain originals of each filed document until a final determination of the case is made by a court of competent jurisdiction. The court may order the eFiler to produce the original document.

[Effective May 15, 2009. Amended effective June, 24, 2013.]

Rule 5. Electronic Filing and Service

5.1—Permissive Electronic Filing. Pending implementation of revised rules by the North Carolina Supreme Court, electronic filing is permitted only to commence a proceeding or in a proceeding that was commenced electronically. Electronic filing is not required to commence a proceeding. Subsequent filings made in a proceeding commenced electronically may be electronic or non-electronic at the option of the filer.

5.2—Exceptions to Electronic Delivery. Pleadings required to be served under Rule 4 and subpoenas issued pursuant to Rule 45 of the Rules of Civil Procedure must be served as provided in those rules and not by use of the electronic filing and service system. Unless otherwise provided in a case management order or by stipulation, filing by or service upon a *pro se* party is governed by eFiling Rule 5.3.

5.3—*Pro se* Parties. Except as otherwise permitted in these Rules, a party not represented by counsel shall file, serve and receive documents pursuant to the Rules of Civil Procedure and the General Rules.

5.4—Format. Documents must be filed in PDF or TIFF format, or in some other format approved by the court, in black and white only, unless color is required to protect the evidentiary value of the document, and scanned at 300 dots per inch resolution.

5.5—Cover Sheet Not Required. Completion of the case initiation requirements of the electronic filing and service system, if it contains all the required fields and critical elements of the filing, shall constitute compliance with the General Rules as well as G.S. 7A–34.1, and no separate AOC cover sheet is required.

5.6—Payment of Filing Fees. Payment of any applicable filing and convenience fees must be done at the time of filing through the electronic payment component of the electronic filing and service system. Payments shall not include service of process fees or any other fees payable to any entity other than the clerk of superior court.

5.7—Effectiveness of Filing. Transmission of a document to the electronic filing system in accordance with the eFiling Rules, together with the receipt by the eFiler of the automatically generated notice showing electronic receipt of the submission by the court, constitutes filing under the North Carolina General Statutes, the Rules of Civil Procedure, and the General Rules. An electronic filing is not deemed to be received by the court without receipt by the eFiler of such notice. If, upon review by the staff of the clerk of superior court, it appears that the filing is inaccessible or unreadable, or that prior approval is required for the filing under G.S. 1–110, or for any other authorized reason, the clerk's office shall send an electronic notice thereof to the eFiler. Upon review and acceptance of a completed filing, personnel in the clerk's office shall send an electronic notice thereof to the eFiler. If the filing is of a case initiating pleading, personnel in the clerk's office shall assign a case number to the filing and include that case number in said notice. As soon as reasonably possible thereafter, the clerk's office shall index or enter the relevant information into the court's civil case processing system (VCAP).

5.8—Certificate of Service. Pending implementation of the court's document management system, and the integration of the electronic filing and service system with the court's civil case processing system, a notice to the eFiler showing electronic receipt by the court of a filing does not constitute proof of service of a document upon any party. A certificate of service must be included with all documents, including those filed electronically, indicating thereon that service was or will be accomplished for applicable parties and indicating how service was or will be accomplished as to those parties.

5.9—Procedure When No Receipt Is Received. If a receipt with the status of "Received" is not received by the eFiler, the eFiler should assume the filing has not occurred. In that case, the eFiler shall make a paper filing with the clerk and serve the document on all other parties by the most reasonably expedient method of transmission available to the eFiler, except that pleadings required to be served under Rule 4 and subpoenas issued pursuant to Rule 45 of the Rules of Civil Procedure must be served as provided in those rules.

5.10—Retransmission of Filed Document. After implementation of the court's document management system, if, after filing a document electronically, a party discovers that the version of the document available for viewing through the electronic filing and service system is incomplete, illegible, or otherwise does not conform to the document as transmitted when filed, the party shall notify the clerk immediately and, if necessary, transmit an amended document, together with an affidavit explaining the necessity for the transmission.

5.11—Determination of Filing Date and Time. Documents may be electronically filed 24 hours a day, except when the system is down for maintenance, file saves or other causes. For the purpose of determining the timeliness of a filing received pursuant to Rule 5.7, the filing is deemed to have occurred at the date and time recorded on the receipt showing a status of "Received."

5.12—Issuance of Summons. At case initiation, the eFiler shall include in the filing one or more summons to be issued by the clerk. Upon the electronic filing of a counterclaim, crossclaim, or third-party complaint, the eFiler may include in the filing one or more summons to be issued by the clerk. Pursuant to Rule 4 of the Rules of Civil Procedure, the clerk shall sign and issue those summons and scan them into the electronic filing and service system. In civil domestic violence cases, magistrates are authorized to sign and issue summons electronically or in paper form. The eFiler shall print copies of the filed pleading and summons to be used for service of process. Copies of documents to be served, any summons, and all fees associated with service shall be delivered by the eFiler to the process server. Copies of civil domestic violence summons, complaints, orders, and other ease documents may be transmitted by the magistrate or clerk to the sheriff electronically or in paper form for service of printed copies thereof. Documents filed subsequent to the initial pleading shall contain a certificate of service as provided in Rule 5.8, Returns of service by sheriff's personnel of civil domestic violence summons, complaints, orders, and other case documents may be transmitted to and filed with the clerk of superior court via the electronic filing system or in paper form.

[Effective May 15, 2009. Amended effective June, 24, 2013.]

Rule 6. Sealed Documents and Private Information

6.1—Filing of Sealed Documents. A motion to file a document under seal may be filed electronically or in paper form and designated "Motion to Seal." A document which is the subject of a motion to seal must be submitted to the court in paper form for *in camera* review. Documents submitted under seal in paper form shall be retained by the clerk under seal until a final ruling is made on the motion to seal. The court may partially grant the motion and order the submission of a redacted version to be made a part of the record. If the court authorizes the filing of a redacted version, the filer shall perform the redaction authorized by the court, and re-file the redacted version in paper form. A paper copy of any order authorizing the filing of a document under seal or the filing of a redacted document must be attached to the document and delivered to the clerk's office. Upon implementation of the court's document management system, documents for which a motion to seal was denied, documents unsealed by order of the court, and redacted versions ordered filed by the court shall be scanned into the electronic filing and service system by personnel in the clerk's office as soon as reasonably possible. Sealed documents and original versions of documents later ordered filed in redacted form shall be retained in paper form under seal pending further orders of the court.

6.2—Requests by a Party for Sealing of Previously Filed Documents. Any attorney licensed in North Carolina and representing a party may file, electronically or in paper form, a motion to seal all or part of any previously filed document, regardless of who previously filed that document. A party not represented by counsel may file such a motion in paper form only. The court may partially grant the motion and order the movant to submit a redacted version to be made a part of the record. A paper copy of any order authorizing the filing of a redacted replacement document must be attached to the redacted version and delivered to the clerk's office. As soon as practicable after receiving the order sealing a previously filed document or replacing it with a newly filed redacted version, the clerk shall print, seal and retain the original document in paper form pending further orders of the court, and, when so ordered, remove and replace the original document in the electronic filing and service system with the redacted version.

6.3—Private Information. Except where otherwise expressly required by law, filers must comply with G.S. 132–1.10(d) to exclude or partially describe sensitive, personal or identifying information such as any social security, employer taxpayer identification, drivers license, state identification, passport, checking account, savings account, credit card, or debit card number, or personal identification (PIN) code or passwords from documents filed with the court. In addition, minors may be identified by initials, and, unless otherwise required by law, social security numbers may be identified by the last four numbers. It is the sole responsibility of the filer to omit or redact non-public and unneeded sensitive information within a document. The clerk of superior court will not review any document to determine whether it includes personal information.

6.4—Requests for Redaction or Removal of a Document by a Non–party. Any person not a party to a proceeding has the right to request the removal or redaction of all or part of a document previously filed and available on-line for public viewing in the electronic filing and service system, if the document contains sensitive, personal or identifying information about the requester, by filing a request in compliance with G.S. 132–1.10(f). As soon as practicable after the receipt of such a request, the clerk shall (1) prepare a redacted version of the electronic document removing the identifying information identified by the requester, or (2) otherwise cloak the affected portions of the document in the electronic filing and service system, so that the designated portions of the document are not viewable by the public on-line. The request for redaction or removal is not a public record and access thereto is restricted to the clerk of superior court or the clerk's staff, or upon order of the court. The original unredacted or uncloaked electronic version of the document shall remain available to parties to the proceeding.

[Effective May 15, 2009. Amended effective June, 24, 2013.]

Rule 7. Communication of Material Not Filed

7.1—Communication with Court. A communication with the court that is not filed electronically must be simultaneously sent by the author to all attorneys for parties in the case. If a party is not represented by counsel, or if an attorney cannot receive e-mail, the communication shall be sent to such party or attorney by the most reasonably expedient method available to the sending party. The communication to other parties shall contain an indication, such as "cc via e-mail," indicating the method of transmission.

7.2—Discovery. Discovery and other materials required to be served on other counsel or a party, and not required to be filed with the court, shall not be electronically filed with the court.

[Effective May 15, 2009. Amended effective June, 24, 2013.]

Rule 8. Good Faith Efforts

Parties shall endeavor reasonably, and in good faith, to resolve technical incompatibilities or other obstacles to electronic communications among them, provided that no extensive manual reformatting of documents is required. If a party asserts that it did not receive an e-mail communication or could not fully access its contents, the sending party shall promptly forward the communication to the party by other means. Any attempt or effort to avoid, compromise or alter any security element of the electronic filing and service system is strictly prohibited and may subject the offending party to civil and criminal liability. Any person becoming aware of evidence of such an occurrence shall immediately notify the court.

[Effective May 15, 2009. Amended effective June, 24, 2013.]

Rule 9. Orders, Decrees and Judgments

9.1—Proposed Order or Judgment. Any proposed order or judgment shall be tendered to the court in paper form or as an electronic filing in Microsoft Office Word 2000 format or other file format approved by the court.

9.2—Entry of Order, Judgment and Other Matters. Upon implementation of the document management component of the electronic filing and service system, a judge, or the clerk of superior court when acting as the trier of fact, or a magistrate in civil domestic violence matters, may file electronically all orders, decrees, judgments and other docket matters. Such filing shall constitute entry of the order, decree, judgment or other matter pursuant to Rule 58 of the Rules of Civil Procedure. Each order, judgment, or decree, or other document must bear the date and the name of the judge, or clerk, or magistrate issuing the order. Signed orders, decrees, judgments, and other matters in paper form shall be forwarded as soon as reasonably possible by the judge or magistrate to the clerk of superior court, and shall be deemed entered under Rule 58 of the Rules of Civil Procedure when filed with the clerk. As soon as reasonably possible, personnel in the clerk's office shall scan the document into the electronic filing and service system.

9.3—Notice of Entry. After implementation of the court's document management system and the integration of the electronic filing and service system with the court's civil case processing system, immediately upon the electronic entry of an order, decree, judgment or other matter, the electronic filing and service system shall broadcast a notification of electronic filing to all persons registered electronically to participate in the case. Transmission of the notice of entry constitutes service pursuant to Rule 58 of the Rules of Civil Procedure.

[Effective May 15, 2009. Amended effective June, 24, 2013.]

RULES OF THE NORTH CAROLINA COMMISSION ON INDIGENT DEFENSE SERVICES

Effective July 1, 2001

Table of Rules

PERFORMANCE GUIDELINES FOR ATTORNEYS REPRESENTING INDIGENT PARENT RESPONDENTS IN ABUSE, NEGLECT, DEPENDENCY AND TERMINATION OF PARENTAL RIGHTS PROCEEDINGS AT THE TRIAL LEVEL

PERFORMANCE GUIDELINES FOR INDIGENT DEFENSE REPRESENTATION IN NON–CAPITAL CRIMINAL CASES AT THE TRIAL LEVEL

PERFORMANCE GUIDELINES FOR APPOINTED COUNSEL IN JUVENILE DELINQUENCY PROCEEDINGS AT THE TRIAL LEVEL

PART 1. RULES FOR THE CONTINUED DELIVERY OF SERVICES IN NON-CAPITAL CRIMINAL AND NON-CRIMINAL CASES AT THE TRIAL LEVEL

This first part addresses the procedure for appointing and compensating counsel in all cases subject to the oversight of the Office of Indigent Defense Services (IDS Office), except for capital cases, which are covered by Part 2 of these rules, appellate cases, which are covered by Part 3 of these rules, and cases in which the State is obligated to provide legal assistance and access to the courts to inmates in the custody of the Department of Correction, which are covered by Part 4 of these rules. Parts 1 through 3 of these rules are authorized by the Indigent Defense Services Act of 2000 (IDS Act), S.L. 2000–144, Senate Bill 1323, and apply to cases pending on or after July

1, 2001. Part 4 of these rules is authorized by § 14.9(a) of S.L. 2005–276, Senate Bill 622.

The principal aim of this first part is to ensure that the system for appointing and compensating counsel at the trial level in non-capital criminal and non-criminal cases is not disrupted. Because of the sheer number of such cases handled by appointed counsel, these rules continue most of the current practices and procedures, allowing the IDS Office to consider and implement changes over time after considering the suggestions and advice of the bar, bench, and other interested persons.

The rules are drawn in large part from the North Carolina General Statutes (G.S.), as revised by the IDS Act, and Section D.0400 and D.0500 of the Rules and Regulations of the North Carolina State Bar (State Bar Rules). That section of the State Bar Rules is no longer effective beginning July 1, 2001, because the authorization for those rules, in former G.S. 7A–459, was repealed effective that date.

Whenever the term "IDS Director" is used in these rules, it means the Director of the Office of Indigent Defense Services or his or her designee. Whenever the term "IDS Office" is used in these rules, it means the Office of Indigent Defense Services or its designee. Whenever the term "IDS Commission" is used in these rules, it means the Commission on Indigent Defense Services or its designee.

These rules may be changed by the IDS Commission pursuant to its authority.

Rule 1.1. Coverage and Definitions

(1) This part applies to all non-capital criminal and non-criminal cases at the trial level, including cases in which a court has appointed counsel pursuant to G.S. 7A–451(a)(3) and G.S. 15A–1421 and the applicable case law to investigate, and, if appropriate, prepare, file, and litigate a non-capital motion for appropriate relief or other non-capital post-conviction motion in state court. The terms "non-capital criminal case" and "non-criminal case" refer only to such cases in which the IDS Office is responsible for the provision and oversight of legal representation. The term "trial level" includes all cases in district or superior court.

(2) Except as otherwise provided in these rules, this part does not apply to capital cases, as defined in Part 2 of these rules, at the trial, appellate, or post-conviction level. The term "capital offense" means any case involving a first-degree murder charge or charge in which the degree of murder is undesignated, except cases in which the defendant was under 18 years of age at the time of the offense and not potentially punishable by death, and any non-capital criminal charge brought contemporaneously with or subsequently joined with such murder charge. The term "capital appeal" means any appeal of right taken from a sentence of death, any appeal from offenses joined with a capital appeal, and any petition for extraordinary writ that is filed in the Appellate Division prior to the entry of final judgment in the Trial Division on behalf of a defendant charged with a capital offense. The term "capital post-conviction" mean any case in which a death sentence has been affirmed on direct appeal by the Supreme Court of North Carolina.

(3) Except as otherwise provided in these rules, this part does not apply to appellate cases, as defined in Part 3 of these rules. The term "appellate case" means any case in which a person is entitled to representation in the appellate courts pursuant to G.S. 7A–451 and Part 3 of these rules, including a petition for writ of certiorari or other extraordinary writ that is filed in the Appellate Division prior to the entry of final judgment in the Trial Division.

(3a) Except as otherwise provided in these rules, this part does not apply to cases in which the State is obligated to provide legal assistance and access to the courts to inmates in the custody of the Division of Adult Correction pursuant to G.S. 7A–498.3(a)(2a), as defined in Part 4 of these rules.

(4) When these rules describe the functions that a court performs, the term "court" includes clerks of superior court.

[Subsection (1) amended effective March 15, 2010]
[Subsection (2) amended effective May 6, 2005]
[Subsection (3) amended effective February 27, 2009]
[New subsection (3a) adopted effective March 15, 2010 and amended effective May 29, 2015]
[*Commentary* to Rule 1.1, subsection (1) amended effective November 4, 2005, July 1, 2009, and May 29, 2015]

Authority: G.S. 7A–452(c)(1); 7A–498.3(a)

Commentary

Subsection (1): G.S. 7A–498.3(a) places virtually all cases in which a person is entitled to counsel at state expense under the oversight of the IDS Office. The cases covered are:

1. cases in which an indigent person is entitled to legal representation under G.S. 7A–451 and G.S. 7A–451.1;

2. cases in which the IDS Office is designated by other statutes as responsible for providing legal representation; and

3. cases in which an indigent person is subject to a deprivation of liberty or other constitutionally protected interest, and is entitled by law to legal representation.

Most of the cases in which a person has a right to counsel fall within the first category—that is, cases designated in G.S. 7A–451 and 7A–451.1. Readers should consult those statutes for a complete listing of proceedings.

The General Assembly has recognized a right to counsel in miscellaneous proceedings not covered by G.S. 7A–451 and 7A–451.1, and with respect to most of those proceedings the provision of counsel is subject to the oversight of the IDS Office. The covered cases include:

- cases in which a law enforcement officer has seized property from an unknown or unapprehended defendant, or from a defendant willfully absent from the jurisdiction, and the lawful owner petitions a court for return of the property pursuant to G.S. 15A–11.1(b);

• cases in which a person is subject to a non-testimonial identification procedure under G.S. 15A–279(d);

• cases in which a material witness appears for a hearing on a motion for an order assuring his or her attendance at a criminal proceeding under G.S. 15A–803(d);

• cases in which a criminal defendant elects to represent himself or herself and the court determines that standby counsel should be appointed pursuant to G.S. 15A–1243;

• cases in which a person is taken or charged on any order of arrest for default of bail, or on surrender of bail, or in execution of arrest for any debt or damages rendered in any action, and such person petitions the court for provisional release pursuant to G.S. 23–30.1; and

• cases in which a minor has been voluntarily admitted to a mental health or substance abuse facility pursuant to G.S. 122C–224.1.

The third category of cases under IDS oversight are cases in which the courts have recognized a right to appointed counsel. For example, the defendant has a constitutional right to counsel in child support contempt proceedings in which the defendant faces a sentence of actual imprisonment. *See McBride v. McBride*, 334 N.C. 124, 431 S.E.2d 14 (1993) (finding right to counsel whether contempt proceeding is designated as civil or criminal).

Subsections (2) and (3): Capital cases are addressed in a separate part because of the differing treatment of those cases in the IDS Act. In non-capital criminal cases, the court appoints counsel pursuant to rules adopted by the IDS Office. In capital cases, the IDS Director appoints counsel directly. *See* G.S. 7A–452(a) (generally); *see also* G.S. 7A–451(c) (capital post-conviction cases). Appellate cases are also dealt with separately because of the relatively small number of such cases. The IDS Office is in a position to establish and administer procedures for the appointment and compensation of appellate counsel, relieving trial judges of that burden.

Effective May 6, 2005, subsection (2) was amended to clarify that the term "capital case" refers only to cases in which the defendant is eligible to receive the death penalty, and does not refer to those cases in which life imprisonment without parole is the maximum possible punishment because the defendant was under the age of 18 at the time of the offense. *See* G.S. 14–17; *Roper v. Simmons*, 2005 U.S. LEXIS 2200, 125 S. Ct. 1183 (2005). Effective February 27, 2009, subsection (3) was amended to clarify the definition of an "appellate case" and to provide that litigation of an extraordinary writ in the Appellate Division prior to the entry of a final judgment in the Trial Division is not within the scope of appointed trial counsel's representation.

Rule 1.2. Entitlement to Counsel

[No rules adopted; reserved for future use]

Commentary

Under revised G.S. 7A–452(a), the court continues to determine whether a person is entitled to counsel at state expense. In making this determination, the court must decide, first, whether the person is indigent, although in some matters, such as juvenile delinquency proceedings, the person is presumed to be indigent. Second, the court must determine whether the person is entitled to counsel in the particular proceeding. Rule 1.4, below, governs the first inquiry concerning indigency. The IDS Office has not adopted rules concerning the second inquiry, the right to counsel in particular proceedings, because the IDS Act did not change the extent of a person's rights under the United States and North Carolina constitutions, statutes, and case law; it only transferred to the IDS Office the authority to oversee the provision of legal representation in such cases. For a list of cases subject to IDS Office oversight, *see* commentary to Rule 1.1, above. In cases subject to this part, once the court determines that a person is indigent and has a right to counsel, appointment of counsel is governed by Rule 1.5, below.

In some instances, North Carolina law authorizes someone other than a judge to make at least a preliminary determination of indigency and entitlement to counsel. The IDS Act did not materially change those provisions, although it did provide that appointment of counsel is subject to rules adopted by the IDS Office. For example, G.S. 7A–452(c) continues to authorize the clerk of court to determine whether a person is indigent and entitled to counsel, subject to review by a judge. *See also* G.S. 122C–269(b) (describing clerk's responsibilities in involuntary commitment proceedings). In counties with a public defender office, G.S. 7A–452(a) continues to provide that the Public Defender may make this determination preliminarily and may assign himself or herself or an assistant public defender to represent the person, subject to review by the court.

Rule 1.3. Notice of Rights

(a) Generally

[No rules adopted; reserved for future use]

(b) Responsibilities of Public Defenders and Clerks for In–Custody Defendants

In counties with a public defender office, the authority having custody of a person who is without counsel for more than 48 hours after being taken into custody shall so inform the Public Defender. The Public Defender shall make a preliminary determination of the person's entitlement to his or her services and shall proceed accordingly, including notifying the court of the person's status or appointing himself or herself to represent the person pending a determination of the court. The court shall make the final determination. In counties without a public defender office, the authority having custody of a person who is without counsel for more than 48 hours after being taken into custody shall so inform the clerk of superior court, who shall proceed accordingly, including bringing the person's situation to the attention of a district court judge for determination of the right to counsel and review of pretrial release conditions.

Authority: G.S. 7A–452; 7A–453

Commentary

Subsection (a): A number of statutes obligate judicial officials to notify individuals of their right to counsel, describing the timing and basic content of the notice. In criminal cases, for example, *see* G.S. 15A–511 (notice by magistrate at initial appearance); G.S. 15A–603 (notice by district court judge at first appearance in felony case); G.S. 15A–942 (notice by superior court judge at arraignment); G.S. 15A–1101 (procedure for trial of misdemeanors in district court is in accordance with trial procedure in superior court, including requirement that district court judge notify defendant of right to counsel when arraigning defendant). The IDS Act did not alter these requirements. The IDS Office is considering adopting additional procedures to assist judicial officials in notifying individuals of their right to counsel, after considering the suggestions and advice of the bar, bench, and other interested persons.

Subsection (b): This subsection implements the requirements of revised G.S. 7A–453, which deals with the situation in which a person has been in custody for more than 48 hours and has no counsel. Revised G.S. 7A–453 is not materially different than the former version of that statute; it has always required that notice be given, either to the Public Defender or clerk, concerning in-custody defendants without counsel. The revised statute merely provides that in counties designated by the IDS Office, the custodian of the person must notify the IDS Office's designee. In counties not designated by the IDS Office, the custodian must notify the clerk of superior court. Through the above rule, the IDS Office makes the Public Defender its designee in counties that have a public defender office. In counties that do not have a public defender office, the IDS Office makes no designation; therefore, the custodian should continue to notify the clerk of court.

If a person is in custody without counsel, the Public Defender should bring the person's situation to the attention of the court, which may appoint counsel in accordance with Rule 1.5, below. The Public Defender also may tentatively assign himself or herself to represent the person pursuant to G.S. 7A–452(a).

Likewise, the clerk of court should bring the person's situation to the attention of a judge as soon as feasible; pursuant to G.S. 7A–452(c) and Rule 1.5, below, the clerk also may appoint counsel. If the clerk does not appoint counsel for an in-custody defendant, it is particularly important for the clerk to alert a district court judge, especially in cases involving probation violations, orders for arrest for failing to appear, surrenders by sureties, and misdemeanors in those judicial districts that do not routinely hold first appearances. In those cases, a defendant's first-scheduled court date may be several days or even weeks after he or she is taken into custody. If counsel is not appointed until that first court date, the case will likely have to be continued to a later date, resulting in inefficient use of court time, longer pretrial custody for defendants, and greater demands on limited jail resources.

Rule 1.4. Indigency

(a) Standard

An indigent person is a person who is financially unable to secure legal representation or provide other necessary expenses of representation at the time the expenses are required.

(b) Procedure for Determining Indigency

(1) Before appointing counsel in cases in which indigency is a condition of appointment, the court shall require the defendant or respondent to complete and sign under oath an affidavit of indigency on a form approved by the IDS Director.

(2) The court shall make reasonable inquiry of the defendant or respondent under oath to determine the truth of the statements made in the affidavit of indigency.

(3) The affidavit of indigency shall be filed in the records of the case.

(4) Based on the affidavit of indigency, the affiant's statements to the court on this subject, and such other information as may be brought to the attention of the court during the proceedings, the court shall determine whether the defendant or respondent is indigent.

(5) The question of indigency may be determined or redetermined by the court at any stage of the action or proceeding.

(6) If at any stage in the action or proceeding a person previously determined to be indigent becomes financially able to secure legal representation and provide other necessary expenses of representation, he or she must inform counsel appointed to represent him or her of that fact, who must promptly inform the court.

Authority: G.S. 7A–450; 7A–452; 7A–498.3(b); 7A–498.5(c)(8)

Commentary

Revised G.S. 7A–452 continues to require the court in most cases to determine whether a person is indigent for purposes of receiving counsel at state expense; however, under G.S. 7A–498.3(b) and 7A–489.5(c)(8), the determination is to be made in accordance with policies and procedures adopted by the IDS Office.

Subsection (a): The IDS Act did not alter the basic statutory definition of indigency in G.S. 7A–450(a), which is set forth in this rule. The court should continue to follow that definition and the North Carolina cases interpreting it. *See, e.g., State v. Hoffman*, 281 N.C. 727, 190 S. E.2d 842 (1972) ("An indigent is one who does not have available, at the time they are required, adequate funds to pay a necessary cost of his defense.").

The North Carolina cases direct that various factors, such as the person's employment, income, and assets, be weighed in determining whether a person is indigent. The cases do not establish a precise measure of indigency, however. The specific dollar amounts discussed in older cases are not particularly useful guides in assessing a person's ability to hire a lawyer now. To assist judicial officials and others in determining indigency, the IDS Office is working on developing more detailed standards and expanding on the basic statutory definition of indigency.

Subsection (b): Subsections (1) through (4) substantially repeat the procedure for determining indigency in former Rule D.0402 of the State Bar Rules. The form affidavit of indigency referred to in subsection (1) is the same form that has been used by the AOC (AOC–CR–226). Subsections (5) and (6) substantially repeat the requirements in G.S. 7A–450(c) and (d). Courts should continue to follow any other statutory requirements to assure that counsel is provided as appropriate. For example, although a district court judge reviews indigency at the defendant's first appearance in a felony case, a superior court judge must re-examine the question if the defendant appears without counsel in superior court. *See* G.S. 15A–942 (requiring superior court to do so at arraignment).

Subsection (b) also recognizes that in some cases, indigency is not a condition of appointment of counsel, for example, in cases in which a juvenile is alleged to be delinquent. *See* G.S. 7B–2000.

Rule 1.5. Appointment Procedure

(a) Districts Without a Public Defender Office

(1) In judicial districts that do not have a public defender office, each judicial district bar or county bar association shall adopt a plan or plans for the appointment by the court of qualified members of the private bar to represent indigent persons in all cases subject to this part. Any plan adopted by a judicial district bar or county bar association shall provide for appointment of counsel on a systematic and impartial basis. To the extent a judicial district bar or county bar association plan does not address any categories of cases, the court shall appoint counsel in those cases on a systematic and impartial basis. A plan may be applicable to the entire district, or, at the election of the judicial district bar or county bar association, separate plans may be adopted for use in each separate county within the district.

(2) Except as otherwise provided by the IDS Office, the plan or plans for a district or county in effect on June 30, 2001, shall govern the method by which counsel are thereafter selected in that district or county for appointment in non-capital criminal and non-criminal cases at the trial level. A plan is considered to be "in effect" on June 30, 2001, if by that date it has been adopted by the judicial district bar or county bar association, approved by the North Carolina State Bar, and certified to the clerk of superior court of the county to which the plan is applicable by the Secretary of the North Carolina State Bar.

(3) Beginning July 1, 2001, any revisions in a district or county plan must be adopted by the judicial district bar or county bar association and approved by the IDS Commission, following which the IDS Director shall certify the revised plan or plans to the clerk of superior court to which the plan or plans are applicable.

(4) Any provisions in district or county plans concerning appointment of counsel in capital or appellate cases, as defined in Parts 2 and 3 of these rules, shall be of no effect as of July 1, 2001.

(5) Any provisions in district or county plans that are inconsistent with rules now or hereafter adopted by the IDS Office shall be of no effect as of July 1, 2001.

(b) Districts with a Public Defender Office

(1) No later than November 1, 2001, in judicial districts with a public defender office, the Public Defender shall submit to the IDS Director a proposed plan for the appointment of counsel in all cases subject to this part. The proposed plan shall provide for the making of appointments under the oversight of and pursuant to procedures adopted by the Public Defender.

(2) In developing the proposed plan, the Public Defender shall consult with the IDS Director and with the judicial district bench and bar in which the public defender's office is located. The IDS Director shall thereafter submit the proposed plan to the IDS Commission, which may approve the plan as submitted, modify it, or reject it. The plan adopted by the IDS Commission shall become the plan for appointment of counsel in that judicial district.

(3) After the Commission has adopted the initial plan for a judicial district with a public defender office, the IDS Director may, after consulting with the Public Defender, modify the plan and the requirements and procedures for appointing counsel in that judicial district as necessary to effectuate the purposes of the IDS Act. If any modifications being considered by the IDS Director substantially change the plan, the IDS Director shall submit the proposed changes to the IDS Commission for approval.

(4) Until a Public Defender's plan is approved by the IDS Commission, the court shall continue to appoint counsel in accordance with current procedure.

(5) The Public Defender shall not be appointed to represent, and shall not assign counsel to represent, a juvenile alleged to be abused, neglected, or dependent.

(c) Districts with a Special Counsel Office.

In judicial districts with a special counsel program, the court shall continue to appoint special counsel, pursuant to G.S. 122C–270, to represent all indigent respondents at all hearings, rehearings, and supplemental hearings held at the state facility. For cases assigned to a special counsel office that the office is unable to handle, the special counsel office shall adopt a plan for assigning such cases to qualified members of the private bar. The special counsel office shall submit any plan for approval and certification by the IDS Director.

(d) Appointments Pursuant to Plans

(1) Except as otherwise provided by the IDS Director, all appointments of counsel in cases subject to this part shall be made in conformity with the plans described in this rule, unless the judge in cases subject to subsection (a), above, or the authority authorized to make appointments in cases subject to subsections (b) and (c), above, deems it proper in the furtherance of justice to appoint as counsel for a person a lawyer who is not on the certified plan or list or who is not next in sequence on the list.

(2) No attorney shall be appointed as counsel for a person in a non-capital criminal or non-criminal case in a court of any district unless the attorney has

consented to placement of his or her name on the list of attorneys subject to appointment or, if the attorney has not agreed to do so, has otherwise consented to be appointed. The attorney named in the appointment order shall not delegate to another attorney any material responsibilities to the client, including representation at critical stages of the case, unless the court finds in open court that the substitute attorney practices in the same law firm as the appointed attorney and is on the list of attorneys who are eligible for appointment to the particular case or has a contract with IDS to handle that type of case, that the client and the substitute attorney both consent to the delegation, and that the delegation is in the best interests of the client.

(3) No person for whom counsel is appointed shall be entitled to select or specify the attorney assigned to defend him or her.

(d1) Right of Review from Denial of Attorney Application for Placement on Appointment List or Removal of Attorney from Appointment List.

If an attorney is denied placement on or removed from one or more lists of attorneys subject to appointment in a judicial district or county pursuant to a plan authorized by subsection (a), (b), or (c), above, the attorney may seek review of that decision by the IDS Director or his or her designee in accordance with policies and procedures adopted by the IDS Office.

(e) Record Keeping

(1) In districts without a public defender office, the clerk of superior court of each county, under the direction of the Administrative Office of the Courts pursuant to G.S. 7A–343(3) and (10), shall continue to file in his or her office, maintain, and keep current the plan for assignment of counsel in non-capital criminal and non-criminal cases, and a record of all counsel eligible for appointment under the plan, applicable to said county as certified by the Secretary of the North Carolina State Bar or IDS Director, as the case may be.

(2) No later than November 1, 2001, in districts with a public defender office, the Public Defender shall file in his or her office, maintain, and keep current the plan for assignment of counsel in non-capital criminal and non-criminal cases pursuant to subsection (b), above, and a record of all counsel eligible for appointment under the plan, applicable to said district as certified by the IDS Director.

(3) In districts with a special counsel program, the special counsel shall file in his or her office, maintain, and keep current the plan for assignment of counsel pursuant to subsection (c), above, and a record of all counsel eligible for appointment under the plan, applicable to said district as certified by the IDS Director.

(4) Orders for the appointment of counsel shall be entered by the court on a form approved by the IDS Director.

(f) Authority to Implement Other Programs, Plans, and Contracts.

Nothing in these rules shall prohibit assignment of otherwise qualified counsel to represent indigent defendants or respondents pursuant to programs, plans, or contracts that may be implemented from time to time to improve quality, efficiency, and economy where such programs, plans, or contracts are approved by the IDS Director. Nothing in these rules shall preclude the IDS Commission from adopting and enforcing rules that supercede a plan for appointment of counsel in any district.

[Subsection (a) amended effective February 10, 2005 and December 10, 2010]

[Subsections (b) amended effective November 16, 2001 and July 1, 2009]

[Subsection (c) amended effective December 10, 2010 and May 29, 2015]

[Subsection (d) amended effective July 8, 2005, February 16, 2007, and May 29, 2015]

[New subsection (d1) adopted effective February 1, 2010]

[Subsection (f) amended effective November 16, 2001 and May 29, 2015]

Authority: G.S. 7A–452(a); 7A–498.3(a), (c) 7A–495.5(c), (d), and (e); 122C-270

Commentary

G.S. 7A–498.3 and 7A–498.5 grant the IDS Office broad authority to adopt rules, procedures, and standards for the appointment of counsel. *See also* G.S. 7A–452(a) (counsel shall be appointed by the court in non-capital criminal cases in accordance with rules adopted by the IDS Office). Because of the sheer number of non-capital criminal and non-criminal cases handled by appointed counsel each year, the IDS Office is not presently able to consider or adopt improvements in the method for appointing counsel in such cases across the state. Accordingly, this rule continues much of the current practice and procedure. The text of this rule is based in large part on former Rule D.0404 of the State Bar Rules.

Subsection (a): The IDS Commission recognizes the continuing importance of district and county bar plans to the operation of the system, and in most respects this rule keeps the current plans in effect until the IDS Commission and IDS Office consider and implement changes. If a district bar or county bar association wishes to make changes to a plan after July 1, 2001, the changes must be approved by the IDS Commission rather than the North Carolina State Bar, which reflects the changes in authority implemented by the IDS Act. Many district and county bar plans that were in effect on June 30, 2001 do not specifically address non-criminal cases. If a plan does not address such cases, the court should appoint counsel on a systematic and impartial basis.

Subsection (b): Currently, in some districts with a public defender office, the judge assigns most indigent cases to the Public Defender, who then assigns to private counsel those cases that the office is unable to handle (either because of workload or conflict-of-interest reasons). All public defender offices are currently drafting plans that will expand this procedure to all districts with such an office. However, because all public defender offices are not in a position to begin performing this duty as of July 1, 2001, subsection (1) leaves current practices undisturbed until the Public Defender in the district submits a plan, which the IDS Director approves and certifies. The rule requires all Public Defenders to ensure that such a plan has been submitted, approved, and certified no later than November 1, 2001. Any plan adopted pursuant to this provision should address, among other things, the procedure to be followed when the public defender office has a conflict of interest. Subsection (b)(5) was amended effective July 1, 2009 to remove a reference to the appointment of guardians ad litem for juveniles in cases in which the Administrative Office of the Courts' guardian ad litem program is unable to represent the juvenile due to a conflict. The Administrative Office of the Courts is responsible for the appointment and compensation of guardians ad litem in those cases.

Subsection (c): This subsection establishes a procedure similar to subsection (b), requiring special counsel offices (in districts where located) to develop plans for assigning to private counsel cases that the office is unable to handle. This subsection was amended effective December 10, 2010 to delete a prior reference to special counsel continuing to represent indigent respondents on direct appeal. For all civil commitment appeals filed on or after October 1, 2006, S.L. 2006–264 directs that appellate counsel for the indigent respondent shall be appointed in accordance with rules adopted by the IDS Office. As with all other indigent appeals, Rule 3.2(b) was subsequently revised to provide that, for civil commitment appeals filed on or after October 1, 2006, the court shall appoint the Office of the Appellate Defender to represent the respondent.

Subsection (d): As in the past, appointments should be made in accordance with the plans for each district. The subsection makes some changes, however. First, subsection (1) clarifies that in the interest of justice an attorney may be appointed who is not on the list regardless of whether the attorney regularly practices in the district. Second, subsection (2) prohibits appointment of an attorney unless the attorney consents to appointment, either by agreeing to be on the list or, if not on the list, by consenting to being appointed. Subsection (d)(2) was amended effective July 8, 2005 and again February 16, 2007 to clarify that an attorney appointed to a case may not delegate material responsibility for that case to another attorney who is not named in the appointment order. *See State v. Carter*, 66 N.C. App. 21, 23, 311 S.E.2d 5, 7 (1984); RPC 58 (1989). If an appointed attorney is unable to appear at a scheduled court appearance due to a conflict in another court, secured leave, illness, or a family emergency, subsection (d) does not prohibit the attorney from asking another lawyer to appear on his or her behalf and seek a continuance or argue a bond reduction motion for an incarcerated client. Subsection (d) also does not prohibit an appointed attorney who is unavailable from sending another lawyer to interview an incarcerated client. In exceptional cases where the appointed attorney is unavailable, the court may allow the appointed attorney to delegate client responsibilities at critical stages of a case if the court makes the specified findings. Subsection (d)(2) was amended effective May 29, 2015 to clarify that the same policies apply to delegated responsibilities in cases handled by attorneys who have a contract with IDS.

Subsection (d1): This subsection was adopted effective February 1, 2010 to provide that an attorney who has been denied placement on a local indigent list or removed from a local indigent list by a local indigent committee has the right to seek review of that decision by the IDS Director. This subsection does not create a right to seek review by the IDS Director of an order imposed by a court pursuant to its concurrent jurisdiction over the conduct of the lawyers who appear before it.

Subsection (e): The clerk of superior court continues to keep a record of current district or county bar plans and eligibility lists in districts without a public defender office. Public defender and special counsel offices will keep their plans on file in their offices. The court (judge or clerk) continues to make a record of appointments by entering the order of appointment on a revised version of the form that has been used by the AOC (AOC–CR–224).

Subsection (f): This subsection recognizes the authority of the IDS Office to modify appointment procedures and to adopt different methods for delivering services (such as contracting with attorneys rather than appointing them on a case-by-case basis). *See* G.S. 7A–498.3; G.S. 7A–498.5.

Rule 1.6. Waiver of Counsel

(a) Standard.

An indigent person who has been informed of his or her right to be represented by counsel at any in-court proceeding may, in writing, waive the right to in-court representation by counsel. Any such waiver of counsel shall be effective only if the court finds of record that at the time of waiver the indigent person acted with full awareness of his or her rights and of the consequences of the waiver. In making such a finding, the court shall follow the requirements of G.S. 15A–1242 and shall consider, among other things, such matters as the person's age, education, familiarity with the English language, mental condition, and the complexity of the matter.

(b) Standby Counsel in Criminal Cases.

In a criminal case, if the defendant has elected to proceed without the assistance of counsel, the trial judge in his or her discretion may determine that standby counsel should be appointed to assist the defendant when called upon, and to bring to the judge's attention matters favorable to the defendant upon which the judge should rule on his or her own motion.

[Subsection (a) amended effective May 29, 2015]

Authority: G.S. 7A-457; 15A-1243

Commentary

Subsection (a): Revised G.S. 7A–457(a) provides that waivers of in- court representation shall be in accordance with rules adopted by the IDS Office. The above rule restates the requirements for a valid waiver in G.S. 7A–457(a) and is intended to continue current practice and procedure on taking waivers until the IDS Office develops any additional rules or procedures. Until the IDS Office develops any such additional rules or procedures, courts can continue to use the same waiver of counsel form that has been used by the AOC (AOC–CR–227). This rule does not affect the standard in G.S. 7A–457(c) with respect to waiver of counsel at out-of-court proceedings, such as during interrogation, which the IDS Act did not revise. This rule also does not deal with waiver of retained counsel by a non-indigent person. If a person has no counsel, the court should determine whether the person wishes to waive the right to both appointed and retained counsel. In criminal cases, if the person wishes to represent himself or herself, the court must conduct the inquiry required by G.S. 15A–1242 on self-representation.

The IDS Act also did not affect the statutes that recognize that in some circumstances a person may lack the capacity to waive counsel. For example, G.S. 122C–268(d) provides that in cases in which a person is alleged to be mentally ill and subject to in-patient commitment, counsel shall be appointed if the person is indigent or refuses to retain counsel although financially able to do so. *See also* G.S. 35A–1107 (appointment of guardian ad litem for person alleged to be incompetent); G.S. 108A–105(b) (appointment of guardian ad litem for disabled adult). Similar provisions apply to minors who have a right to counsel. *See* G.S. 7B–600 and –601 (juvenile abuse and neglect proceedings); G.S. 7B–1101 (termination of parental rights where parent is a minor); G.S. 7B–2000 (juvenile delinquency proceedings).

Subsection (b): G.S. 15A–1243 provides that, in cases in which a defendant has elected to represent himself or herself, appointment of standby counsel shall be in accordance with rules adopted by the IDS Office. For non-capital criminal cases, the above rule restates the provisions on appointment of standby counsel in G.S. 15A–1243 and is intended to continue the current practice and procedure.

Rule 1.7. Withdrawal of Appointed Counsel

(a) Scope of Obligation

Unless otherwise provided by law, counsel appointed in a case subject to this part is required to continue with the representation through judgment at the trial level, discussion with the client about his or her right to appeal, and entry of notice of appeal or expiration of the time for giving notice of appeal. Nothing in these rules shall be construed as permitting or requiring an attorney of record to deviate from applicable laws of this State, the Rules of Professional Conduct administered by the North Carolina State Bar, or other legal or ethical obligations of an attorney as an officer of the court.

(a1) Identification of Conflicts

Upon appointment to a case subject to this part, counsel shall make prompt and reasonable efforts to determine if the representation would cause any conflict of interest. If counsel identifies a nonwaivable conflict of interest, counsel shall file a timely motion to withdraw pursuant to subsection (b) of this rule. If counsel identifies a waivable conflict of interest, counsel shall either obtain the informed written consent of the client in accordance with the Rules of Professional Conduct or file a timely motion to withdraw pursuant to subsection (b) of this rule.

(b) Withdrawal

At any time during or pending the trial or retrial of a case subject to this part, a judge of a court of competent jurisdiction may, upon application of the attorney appointed to the case and for good cause shown, permit the attorney to withdraw from the case. If the judge allows the attorney to withdraw, appointment of new counsel shall be in accordance with Rule 1.5 of these rules.

(c) Contract Counsel

Withdrawal from a case by an attorney performing work under contract with the IDS Office shall be in accordance with the terms of the contract. If the contract does not specify a method of withdrawal, an attorney may withdraw in accordance with subsections (a) and (b) of this rule.

[New subsection (a1) adopted effective September 24, 2010]

Authority: G.S. 7A–498.2(b); 7A–498.3(a), (c); 7A–498.5(c), (d); 15A–143; 15A–144

Commentary

Subsection (a): G.S. 15A–143 states that an attorney making a general appearance in a criminal case is obligated to represent the defendant "until entry of final judgment." Subsection (a) is intended to emphasize the attorney's further responsibility to advise the client concerning appeal and to enter notice of appeal if requested. This rule applies that requirement to all cases subject to this part unless otherwise provided by law.

Subsection (a1): This subsection was added effective September 24, 2010. If appointed counsel moves to withdraw due to a conflict, in determining the appropriate amount of time to approve for compensation purposes pursuant to Rule 1.9(a)(1b), below, the trial judge shall consider the timeliness of counsel's efforts to identify the conflict and to file the motion to withdraw.

Subsection (b): This subsection restates the provisions in former Rule D.0405 of the State Bar Rules on withdrawal from a case at the trial level. If a person other than appointed counsel (such as the client, prosecutor, or IDS Director) requests that a judge of a court of competent jurisdiction remove counsel for good cause, the judge shall follow established law. *See, e.g., State v. Poole*, 305 N.C. 308, 289 S.E.2d 335 (1982); *State v. Hutchins*, 303 N.C. 321, 279 S.E.2d 788 (1981); *see also State v. Robinson*, 330 N.C. 1, 409 S.E.2d 288 (1991).

Subsection (c): This subsection is new. Although contracts entered into by the IDS Office may require that attorneys obtain a judge's approval to withdraw from a case, they potentially may provide for a different method of reassigning cases.

Rule 1.8. Contracts

The IDS Office is authorized to enter into contracts for legal representation and related services in cases in which the IDS Office is responsible for the provision and oversight of legal representation of a person. Contracts may provide for, among other things, appointment of particular counsel to handle certain cases and compensation at a specified rate. Any contracts for legal representation or related services in cases under the oversight of the IDS Office must be approved by the IDS Director.

Authority: G.S. 7A–498.2(b); 7A–498.3(a), (c), (d); 7A–498.5(c), (d), (f)

Commentary

This rule reflects the authority granted the IDS Office to contract for services in cases in which the IDS Office is responsible for the provision of legal services, and to control the expenditure of funds for quality legal representation and related services in such cases.

Rule 1.9. Payment of Appointed Counsel

(a) Compensation at Trial.

(1a) If an attorney seeks compensation for time spent waiting in court for multiple cases to be called or working on multiple cases simultaneously, the attorney's time shall be prorated among each of the cases involved. For all cases finally disposed at the trial level on or after July 1, 2005, final attorney fee applications must be signed by the appointed attorney and submitted to the trial judge within no more than one year after the date on which the case was finally disposed at the trial level. For all cases finally disposed at the trial level before July 1, 2005, final attorney fee applications must be signed by the appointed attorney and submitted to the trial judge by January 1, 2006. In accordance with policies and procedures approved by the IDS Commission, an attorney may apply to the IDS Director for one advance extension of the applicable deadline or for a waiver of the applicable deadline.

(1b) Upon completion of the representation of a person by appointed counsel in the trial court in a non-capital criminal or non-criminal case, the trial judge shall, upon application, enter an order fixing the fee to which the attorney is entitled. In doing so, the judge shall review the amount of time claimed by the attorney, and shall approve an appropriate amount of time based on the factors normally considered in fixing attorneys' fees, such as the nature of the case, and the effort and responsibility involved.

(2) Absent extraordinary circumstances and advance written approval of the IDS Director, once the judge approves an appropriate amount of time pursuant to subsection (1b), above, the hourly rate for attorney compensation in such cases in both district and superior court, for both in-court and out-of-court time, shall be an amount approved by the IDS Commission and specified in the applicable IDS policy. In the event of changes in the availability of funding, the IDS Commission shall determine the effective date of any adjustment to the hourly rates for attorney compensation in cases in district and superior court.

(3) Even if the trial, hearing, or other proceeding is never held, preparation therefore is nevertheless compensable and, in extraordinary cases pending in superior court, the presiding judge may allow a fee for services rendered and payment for expenses incurred pending final determination of the case. In such cases, the time approved and hourly rate paid shall be set pursuant to subsections (1b) and (2), above.

(4) Fees shall be fixed by the district court judge who hears the case for actions or proceedings finally determined in the district court, and by the superior court judge who hears the case for actions or proceedings originating in superior court. In cases that are heard on appeal from district to superior court, fees may be fixed by the presiding district or superior court judge, provided that the defendant is given notice and an opportunity to be heard.

(5) This section does not preclude districts from compensating attorneys in the above cases based on methods other than hours per case, such as per case fee schedules or per session rates, provided that the alternative compensation method or rate is approved by the IDS Director. Any district using or proposing an alternative compensation method shall notify the IDS Director, and the IDS Director may approve the method used or proposed provided it is consistent with the purposes of the IDS Act.

(b) Orders for Payment. Orders for the payment of compensation to appointed counsel for representation shall be entered by the judge on a form approved by the IDS Director. A copy of the order for the payment of fees shall be forwarded by the clerk of superior court to IDS Financial Services Division, Courier Box 56–10–50, Raleigh, N.C. If no courier is available, a copy of the order shall be mailed to P.O. Box 2448, Raleigh, N.C. 27602.

(c) Fee Schedules. The IDS Director may authorize or require the use of fee schedules for the compensation of attorneys and the payment for services related to legal representation in non-capital criminal and non-criminal cases.

(d) Compensation of Contract Counsel. Compensation of attorneys performing work under contract with the IDS Office shall be paid in accordance with the terms of the contract.

(e) Outside Compensation Prohibited. Once counsel has been appointed to represent a person in a case subject to this part, counsel shall not accept any fees for the representation other than that awarded by the court or the IDS Director. If a third party contributes funds to non-counsel services, counsel shall place the funds in trust and account to the third party and the IDS Director about the use of the funds.

[Subsection (a) amended effective February 15, 2002, May 6, 2005, August 13, 2007,
February 1, 2008, February 27, 2009, June 5, 2009, June 1, 2011, and May 29, 2015]
[Subsection (b) amended effective May 6, 2005]
[Subsection (e) amended effective September 15, 2006]
[Commentary to subsection (e) amended effective March 7, 2014]

Authority: G.S. 7A–458; 7A–498.5(f)

Commentary

This rule effectively continues the current practice on compensating appointed counsel in non-capital criminal and non-criminal cases. It incorporates substantial portions of former Rule D.0406 of the State Bar Rules and of G.S. 7A–458 before it was revised by the IDS Act. Representation is complete within the meaning of this rule when counsel has fulfilled the obligations set forth in Rule 1.7(a), above. Courts using fee schedules in effect before the effective date of the IDS Act should notify the IDS Office of any such schedules. Because of the sheer number of non-capital criminal and non-criminal cases handled by appointed attorneys, the IDS Office is not presently in a position to assume responsibility for determining compensation throughout the state.

Subsection (a): Effective April 1, 2002, subsection (a) established a standard hourly rate of $65 in all non-capital and non-criminal cases at the trial level. The subsection was amended effective February 1, 2008 to increase that rate to $75 per hour for all fee applications signed by judges on or after February 1, 2008. Due to significant funding reductions by the 2011 General Assembly and the Commission's decision to implement a reduced and variable rate structure for different types of cases, the subsection was amended effective June 1, 2011 to provide that the hourly rates for non-capital and non-criminal cases shall be as approved by the Commission and specified in the applicable IDS policy. The subsection was also amended effective May 6, 2005 to clarify that attorneys can not double-bill the state for time spent waiting in court or working on multiple cases simultaneously. For all cases finally disposed at the trial level on or after July 1, 2005, the subsection was amended to require attorneys to submit fee applications to the presiding judge within one year of the date of final disposition. Effective August 13, 2007, the subsection was amended to allow attorneys to apply for an advance extension or waiver of the deadline in accordance with policies and procedures approved by the IDS Commission. Attorney fee applications submitted more than one year after the date of final disposition without an approved extension or waiver will not be paid from state funds. Subsection (a)(4) was amended effective February 27, 2009 to clarify that, in cases that are appealed de novo to superior court, fees may be set by the presiding district or superior court judge, depending on local practice. Subsection (a)(2) was amended effective June 5, 2009 to remove a provision that set a minimum fee equivalent to one hour of work for cases in which an attorney claims and the court approves less than one hour.

Subsection (b): In entering orders for payment, courts should continue to use a revised version of the fee application form that has been used by the AOC (AOC–CR–225). Effective May 6, 2005, the clerk is no longer required to certify every individual fee application. However, fee applications must be sent to IDS Financial Services in a secure packet directly from the clerk's office.

Subsection (e): Subsection (e) was amended effective September 15, 2006 to clarify that, to avoid any potential for overreaching or the appearance of impropriety, an appointed attorney cannot subsequently accept fees as retained counsel from the client or the client's family. If family or friends of an indigent client want to contribute to non-counsel services, such as expert or support services, nothing in this subsection precludes them from doing so. However, the appointed attorney must place any such funds in his or her trust account and provide an accounting to the contributing family member and the IDS Director.

This commentary was amended effective March 7, 2014 to clarify a new exception to the general prohibition against accepting a retainer in a case after an attorney has been appointed. Effective for offenses committed on or after December 1, 2013, the General Assembly amended G.S. 15A–1340.23 to provide that, unless otherwise noted, the maximum punishment for a person who is convicted of a Class 3 misdemeanor and who has no more than three prior convictions shall be a $200 fine. Thus, unless otherwise noted, an indigent defendant who is charged with committing a Class 3 misdemeanor on or after that date and who has no more than three prior convictions is not entitled to appointed counsel pursuant to G.S. 7A–451(a)(1). However, if a defendant who is not entitled to counsel for a Class 3 misdemeanor pursuant to G.S. 7A–451(a)(1) is in custody at the time the court determines entitlement to counsel and the court does not modify the pretrial detainee's conditions of release to allow him or her to be released pending trial without posting a secured bond, the court may appoint counsel to represent the pretrial detainee during the period of pretrial confinement on the Class 3 misdemeanor charge to ensure that he or she has meaningful access to the courts. This type of appointment constitutes a limited appearance pursuant to G.S. 15A–141(3) and G.S. 15A–143 and the appointment ends at the time of the defendant's release from custody. In such a case, there is less risk of overreaching or the appearance of impropriety than with other indigent appointments, and the attorney may be retained by the client after the client's release from custody to continue the representation in the case.

If, during the course of representation as appointed counsel, an attorney learns that a client who was previously determined to be indigent has become financially able to pay for the representation, G.S. 7A–450(d) directs the attorney to inform the court. *But cf.* RPC 52 (Jan. 13, 1989) (directing counsel to "call upon his client to reveal that circumstance to the tribunal" and, if the client refuses to permit disclosure, to move to withdraw). If the court finds that the client is no longer indigent, the appointed attorney may move to withdraw or continue the representation *pro bono*.

Rule 1.10. Supporting Services

In non-capital criminal and non-criminal cases, the court may approve fees for the service of expert witnesses, investigators, and others providing services related to legal representation in accordance with all applicable IDS rules and policies.

[Amended eff. Dec. 9, 2011.]

Authority: G.S. 7A–454; 7A–498.3(c); 7A–498.5(c)(6)

Commentary

The above statutes, as revised, provide that appointment and compensation of experts, investigators, and others providing services related to legal representation shall be in accordance with IDS rules. For non-capital criminal and non-criminal cases, this rule is intended to restate in general terms the current statutory and case law on such services. This section was amended December 9, 2011 to clarify that court orders approving fees for experts and investigators shall comply with all applicable IDS rules and policies, including the standardized expert rates set by the IDS Commission pursuant to G.S. 7A–498.5(f). For capital cases, see Part 2, Rules 2D.1 through 2D.5.

Commentary

The above statutes, as revised, provide that appointment and compensation of experts, investigators, and others providing services related to legal representation shall be in accordance with IDS rules. For noncapital criminal and noncriminal cases, this rule is intended to restate in general terms the current statutory and case law on such services. For capital cases, *see* Part 2, Rules 2D.1 through 2D.5.

Rule 1.11. Recoupment of Fees

(a) Generally

To the extent required by law, individuals who have been appointed counsel under this part shall continue to be responsible for repaying the fees paid to such counsel or, in the case of representation by a public defender office or contract counsel, the value of services rendered by counsel. The judge setting the fee to be paid or the value of services rendered shall determine the amount to be recouped if recoupment is required by law. The court shall ensure that the person potentially responsible for paying the fees is notified of the potential liability, and that the person has a reasonable opportunity to be heard on the issue.

(b) Value of Public Defender or Contract Services

For legal representation rendered by attorneys working in a public defender office or under contract with the IDS Office, the value of services pursuant to G.S. 7A–455(b) shall be determined in the same manner in which appointed counsel's compensation is determined pursuant to Rules 1.9(a)(1b) and 1.9(a)(2), above, if recoupment is required by law.

[Subsections (a) and (b) and commentary amended effective September 19, 2014.]

Authority: G.S. 7A–450.1 through –450.4; 7A–455; 7A–498.5(c)(8)

Commentary

Subsection (a): For the most part, this rule is intended to continue current practice in non-capital criminal and non-criminal cases with respect to recoupment of the cost of appointed counsel. In criminal cases, recoupment is governed by G.S. 7A–455. The IDS Act made only one change to that statute. It required that the value of services reflected in a judgment against a defendant be set in accordance with rules adopted by the IDS Office. The Public Defender remains obligated to inform the judge of the value of legal services rendered to the defendant. The form judgment is a revised version of the same fee application form that has been used by the AOC (AOC–CR–225).

In some non-criminal cases, recoupment of fees is also required, although the procedure for recoupment differs somewhat from the procedure in criminal cases. *See* G.S. 7A–450.1 through –450.4. The IDS Act did not alter those procedures.

This rule also provides that a person potentially liable for fees should be given reasonable notice and an opportunity to be heard. In most cases covered by this part, the person will be present at the time judgment is entered, and the court can give the person an opportunity to be heard on the amount proposed to be entered.

Subsection (b): G.S. 7A–455(b) provides that "[t]he value of services [rendered by assigned counsel, the public defender, or the appellate defender] shall be determined in accordance with rules adopted by the Office of Indigent Defense Services," and G.S. 7A–498.5(c)(8) directs the IDS Commission to develop standards for "assessing and collecting the costs of legal representation." Pursuant to that authority, subsection (b) was revised effective September 19, 2014 to clarify that, when a court determines the value of services provided by a public defender or contract attorney, the court should apply the same hourly rates that the IDS Commission sets for private assigned counsel services.

PART 2. RULES FOR PROVIDING LEGAL REPRESENTATION IN CAPITAL CASES

This second part addresses the procedure to be followed in capital cases. The rules are authorized by the Indigent Defense Services Act of 2000 (IDS Act), S.L. 2000–144, Senate Bill 1323, and apply to cases pending on or after July 1, 2001. Fee applications for capital representation filed on or after that date will be governed by these rules.

These rules are intended to set forth a comprehensive system for providing legal representation in cases that potentially may be tried capitally or that have resulted in a sentence of death. Unlike the Rules for Continued Delivery of Services in Non–Capital Criminal and Non–Criminal Cases, described in Part 1, this part departs significantly from previous practice and procedure. The approach taken below reflects the intent of the IDS Act, which places with the Office of Indigent Defense Services (IDS Office) the responsibility for appointing and compensating counsel in capital cases.

This part is divided into four subparts, corresponding to the major areas requiring attention in capital litigation:

- Appointment and Compensation of Trial Counsel
- Appointment and Compensation of Appellate Counsel
- Appointment and Compensation of Post–Conviction Counsel
- Appointment and Compensation of Experts and Others Providing Services Related to Legal Representation

This part also includes an appendix containing standards that attorneys must meet to be considered for appointment as trial, appellate, or post-conviction counsel in capital cases.

The rules are authorized by Chapters 7A and 15A of the North Carolina General Statutes (G.S.), and by the IDS Act. The rules supercede the provisions on capital representation in Section D. of the Rules and Regulations of the North Carolina State Bar (State Bar Rules) and any provisions on capital representation in local bar plans issued pursuant to the State Bar Rules. As of July 1, 2001, those rules, which were authorized by former G.S. 7A-459, are no longer effective.

Whenever the term "IDS Director" is used in these rules and appendix, it means the Director of the Office of Indigent Defense Services or his or her designee. Whenever the term "IDS Office" is used in these rules and appendix, it means the Office of Indigent Defense Services or its designee. Whenever the term "IDS Commission" is used in these rules and appendix, it means the Commission on Indigent Defense Services or its designee.

These rules may be changed by the IDS Commission pursuant to its authority.

PART 2A. APPOINTMENT AND COMPENSATION OF TRIAL COUNSEL IN CAPITAL CASES

2A.1. Coverage of this Subpart

(a) Applies to Capital Trials. This subpart applies to all capital offenses and all non-capital criminal charges brought contemporaneously with or subsequently joined with a capital offense. A "capital offense" means any first-degree murder charge or charge of murder where the degree is undesignated, except cases in which the defendant was under 18 years of age at the time of the offense and not potentially punishable by death. The term "capital defendant" means a defendant charged with a capital offense.

(b) Authority to Implement Other Programs, Plans, and Contracts. Nothing in these rules shall prohibit assignment of otherwise qualified counsel to represent indigent defendants in capital trials pursuant to programs, plans, or contracts that may be implemented from time to time to improve quality, efficiency, and economy where such programs, plans, or contracts are approved by the IDS Director.

[Subsection (a) amended effective May 6, 2005]

Authority: G.S. 7A-498.2(b); 7A-498.3(a); 7A-498.5(c)(7), (c)(8), (d)

Commentary

Effective May 6, 2005, subsection (a) was amended to clarify that the term "capital case" refers only to cases in which the defendant is eligible to receive the death penalty, and does not refer to those cases in which life imprisonment without parole is the maximum possible punishment because the defendant was under the age of 18 at the time of the offense. *See* G.S. 14-17; *Roper v. Simmons*, 2005 U.S. LEXIS 2200, 125 S. Ct. 1183 (2005).

2A.2. Appointment of Trial Counsel

(a) Provisional Appointment of Counsel. Upon learning that a defendant has been charged with a capital offense, the IDS Director may immediately appoint a lawyer on a provisional basis to conduct a preliminary investigation and determine whether the defendant is indigent and needs appointed counsel. Provisional counsel shall report the results of his or her investigation to the IDS Director. If the defendant has not had a first appearance in court, the IDS Director may authorize provisional counsel to attend the defendant's first appearance and advise the court whether the case is a capital case as defined by these rules and therefore subject to the appointment procedures in this subpart. Provisional counsel is authorized to take steps to protect the capital defendant's rights pending appointment of trial counsel by the IDS Director, but the IDS Director may impose limitations on the scope of services to be provided by provisional counsel.

(b) Assignment of IDS Office. At the defendant's first appearance in district court, the court shall determine whether the defendant is indigent pursuant to paragraph 1.4 of the Rules for the Continued Delivery of Services in Non-Capital Criminal and Non-Criminal Cases, and charged with a capital offense as defined in paragraph 2A.1(a) above. If the court so finds, it shall notify the IDS Director of the need to appoint counsel for the capital defendant in accordance with these rules. If the defendant is charged with a capital offense in an indictment and his or her first appearance is in superior court, the court shall determine whether the defendant is indigent and is charged with a capital offense as defined in paragraph 2A.1(a) above. If the court so finds, the court shall ensure that the IDS Director is notified of the need to appoint counsel for the capital defendant, in accordance with these rules, by email, facsimile, or telephone.

(c) Appointment of First Trial Counsel. The IDS Director shall appoint at least one lawyer for a capital defendant as early in the process as possible. The IDS Director shall maintain a list of lawyers eligible for appointment as lead or associate counsel. The list shall consist of lawyers who are eligible to be lead or associate counsel pursuant to the procedures in Appendix 2A of these rules, and may include attorneys in private practice, public defenders and assistant public defenders, and attorneys with whom the IDS Office contracts or employs to provide representation in capital cases. If the first lawyer appointed will serve as lead trial counsel, the IDS Director shall appoint that lawyer from the list of lawyers eligible for appointment as lead counsel. If the first lawyer appointed will serve as associate trial counsel, the IDS Director shall appoint that lawyer from the list of lawyers eligible for appointment as lead or associate counsel. Appointment orders, signed by the IDS Director, shall be distributed to the clerk of superior court, the district attorney, the appointed attorney, and the defendant.

(d) Appointment of Second Trial Counsel. Upon request by and consultation with the current appointed lawyer, the IDS Director may appoint a second lawyer for a capital defendant prior to a declaration at a hearing pursuant to Rule 24 of the General Rules of Practice that the case will be prosecuted capitally, if the IDS Director finds good cause justifying an earlier appointment. If a second lawyer has not been appointed prior to a hearing pursuant to Rule 24 of the General Rules of Practice at which a judge determines that the state may prosecute the case capitally, the current appointed lawyer shall immediately notify the IDS Director of the judicial determination and the IDS Director shall immediately appoint a second lawyer. The IDS Director shall maintain a list of lawyers eligible for appointment as lead or associate counsel. The list shall consist of lawyers eligible to be lead or associate counsel pursuant to the procedures in Appendix 2A of these rules, and may include attorneys in private practice, public defenders and assistant public defenders, and attorneys with whom the IDS Office contracts or employs to provide representation in capital cases. If the second lawyer appointed will serve as lead trial counsel, the IDS Director shall appoint that lawyer from the list of lawyers eligible for appointment as lead counsel. If the second lawyer appointed will serve as associate trial counsel, the IDS Director shall appoint that lawyer from the list of lawyers eligible for appointment as lead or associate counsel. The IDS Director shall consult with the first lawyer appointed about the appointment of the second lawyer. Appointment orders, signed by the IDS Director, shall be distributed to the clerk of superior court, the district attorney, the appointed attorney, and the defendant.

(d1) Identification of Conflicts. Upon appointment to a case subject to this part, counsel shall make prompt and reasonable efforts to determine if the representation would cause any conflict of interest. If counsel identifies a nonwaivable conflict of interest, counsel shall file a timely motion to withdraw. If counsel identifies a waivable conflict of interest, counsel shall either obtain the informed written consent of the client in accordance with the Rules of Professional Conduct or file a timely motion to withdraw.

(e) No Subsequent Appointment of Retained Counsel. If a retained attorney becomes unable to continue representing a capital defendant because the defendant or any third party can not fulfill the terms of the financial agreement between the attorney and the defendant or any third party, the retained attorney may file with the court a motion to withdraw. If the court permits the retained attorney to withdraw, that attorney is not eligible to be appointed to represent the defendant.

(f) Litigation of Extraordinary Writ in Appellate Division Outside Scope of Appointed Trial Counsel's Representation. Counsel appointed to represent a capital defendant in the Trial Division is not authorized to prepare, file, or litigate a petition for writ of certiorari or other extraordinary writ in the Appellate Division prior to the entry of final judgment in the Trial Division. If counsel appointed pursuant to paragraph 2A.2(c) or 2A.2(d), above, determines that a petition for an extraordinary writ in the Appellate Division is warranted, counsel shall notify the Office of Appellate Defender. The Office of Appellate Defender or counsel appointed by the Appellate Defender pursuant to paragraph 2B.2(c), below, shall file the petition only if it will present a potentially meritorious issue for review.

[Subsection (a) amended effective January 10, 2011 and May 20, 2011]
[Subsection (d) amended effective June 6, 2008]
[New subsection (d1) adopted effective September 24, 2010]
[New subsection (e) adopted effective May 6, 2005]
[New subsection (f) adopted effective February 27, 2009]

Authority: G.S. 7A–450(b), (b1); 7A–451(b); 7A–452(a); 7A–498.3(b), (c); 7A–498.5(d), (h)

Commentary

Subsection (a): This provision, allowing for designation of provisional counsel, is in recognition of the importance of affording counsel to capital defendants as soon as possible. The IDS Office expects that it will receive daily information from the Administrative Office of the Court's Automated Criminal Information System (ACIS) about the murder warrants issued in each county. This information is entered into ACIS automatically and immediately in those counties in which the computerized Magistrate System is installed, and manually by clerks of court in the remaining counties. Once a day, the IDS Office will receive email generated by ACIS listing all murder warrants entered into the system in the previous twenty-four hours.

Subsection (b): When a district or superior court judge finds a capital defendant indigent, he or she will notify the IDS Director by the most convenient immediate means—either email, facsimile, or telephone—of the defendant's name, the docket numbers of each of the warrants or indictments for which the defendant needs appointed counsel (including contemporaneously charged non-capital offenses), and the offenses charged. The IDS Director will approve and make available a form (AOC–CR–427) on which the judge will record the means by which the IDS Director was notified. The judge will file the form with the clerk of superior court.

Subsections (c) and (d): In capital cases, G.S. 7A–452(a) provides that, where practicable, either lead or associate defense counsel shall be a member of the bar in that judicial division.

These subsections authorize the IDS Director to appoint lead or associate trial counsel, or both. Subsection (d) was amended effective June 6, 2008 to limit the circumstances in which the IDS Director may appoint a second attorney to represent a capital defendant prior to a declaration at a Rule 24 hearing that the case will be prosecuted capitally. If a case is declared non-capital after the IDS Director has appointed two counsel, the IDS Director will consult with appointed counsel and may remove one counsel.

Subsection (d1): This subsection was added effective September 24, 2010. If appointed counsel moves to withdraw due to a conflict, in determining the appropriate amount of compensation pursuant to Rule 2A.4(a), below, the IDS Director shall consider the timeliness of counsel's efforts to identify the conflict and to file the motion to withdraw.

Subsection (f): This subsection was added effective February 27, 2009 to clarify that litigation of an extraordinary writ in the Appellate Division prior to the entry of a final judgment in the Trial Division is not within the scope of appointed trial counsel's representation in a capital case and to provide a procedure for pursuing such litigation if trial counsel deems it necessary.

2A.3. Waiver of Counsel

(a) Standard. An indigent capital defendant who has been informed of his or her right to be represented by counsel at any in-court-proceeding may, in writing, waive the right to in-court representation by counsel. Any such waiver of counsel shall be effective only if the court finds of record that at the time of waiver the defendant acted with full awareness of his or her rights and of the consequences of the waiver. In making such a finding, the court shall follow the requirements of G.S. 15A–1242 and shall consider, among other things, such matters as the defendant's age, education, familiarity with the English language, mental condition, and the complexity of the matter.

(b) Standby counsel in capital cases. If a capital defendant has elected to proceed without the assistance of counsel, the trial judge shall immediately notify the IDS Director, who may appoint, in his or her discretion, standby counsel to assist the defendant when called upon, and to bring to the judge's attention matters favorable to the defendant upon which the judge should rule on his or her own motion.

[Subsection (a) amended effective May 29, 2015.]

Authority: G.S. 7A–457; 15A–1243

Commentary

Subsection (a): Revised G.S. 7A–457(a) provides that waivers of in-court representation shall be in accordance with rules adopted by the IDS Office. The above rule restates the requirements for a valid waiver in G.S. 7A–457(a) and is intended to continue current practice and procedure on taking waivers until the IDS Office develops any additional rules or procedures. Until the IDS Office develops any such additional rules or procedures, courts can continue to use the same waiver of counsel form that has been used by the AOC (AOC–CR–227). This rule does not affect the standard in G.S. 7A–457(c) with respect to waiver of counsel at out-of-court proceedings, such as during interrogation, which the IDS Act did not revise. This rule also does not deal with waiver of retained counsel by a non- indigent capital defendant. If a capital defendant has no counsel, the court should determine whether the defendant wishes to waive the right to both appointed and retained counsel. If a capital defendant wishes to represent himself or herself, the court must conduct the inquiry required by G.S. 15A–1242 on self-representation.

Subsection (b): G.S. 15A–1243 provides that, in cases in which a defendant has elected to represent himself or herself, appointment of standby counsel shall be in accordance with rules adopted by the IDS Office. For capital cases, the above rule directs the trial judge to immediately notify the IDS Director, who may appoint standby trial counsel.

2A.4. Compensation and Recoupment

(a) Compensation. Appointed counsel who represented an indigent capital defendant at trial shall submit to the IDS Director an itemized fee application on a form prescribed by the IDS Director, showing the time counsel spent in trial representation of the defendant. If an attorney seeks compensation for time spent working on multiple cases simultaneously, the attorney's time shall be prorated among each of the cases involved. Following review of the fee application, the IDS Director shall determine the amount of compensation and forward the award to IDS Financial Services for payment. If counsel is required pursuant to paragraph 2A.5(a)(iv) below to meet with the IDS Director to review the representation, the fee shall include compensation for time spent in that review. Private counsel appointed to represent an indigent capital defendant may apply for and receive interim payments in the discretion of the IDS Director. For all cases finally disposed at the trial level on or after July 1, 2005, final attorney fee applications must be signed by the appointed attorney and submitted to the IDS Director within no more than one year after the date on which the case was finally disposed at the trial level. For all cases finally disposed at the trial level before July 1, 2005, final attorney fee applications must be signed by the appointed attorney and submitted to the IDS Director by January 1, 2006. In accordance with policies and procedures approved by the IDS Commission, an attorney may apply to the IDS Director for one advance extension of the applicable deadline or for a waiver of the applicable deadline. Counsel may make a written request for a review of the amount of compensation approved by the IDS Director from a committee of the IDS Commission designated by the IDS Commission to conduct such review. A retained attorney is not eligible to receive state funds to supplement the amount of compensation he or she has received from a capital defendant or any third party.

(b) Recoupment of Fees Generally. To the extent required by law, capital defendants for whom counsel has been appointed under this part shall continue to be responsible for repaying the fees paid to such counsel or, in the case of representation by a public defender office, the value of services rendered by counsel. After the IDS Director sets the fee to be paid or the value of services rendered, the IDS Director shall notify the defendant of the potential liability, and afford the defendant a reasonable opportunity to be heard on the issue. The trial judge or other appropriate judicial official shall then determine the amount to be recouped if recoupment is required by law.

(c) Recoupment for Contract Services. For legal representation rendered by attorneys working under contract with the IDS Office, the value of services, and the procedures for entry of any appropriate orders or judgments, shall be determined in accordance with the terms of the contract if recoupment is required by law.

(d) Outside Compensation Prohibited. Once counsel has been appointed to represent a person in a case subject to this part, counsel shall not accept any fees for the representation other than that awarded by the IDS Director. If a third party contributes funds to non-counsel services, counsel shall place the funds in trust and account to the third party and the IDS Director about the use of the funds.

[Subsection (a) amended effective May 6, 2005, August 13, 2007, and May 29, 2015.]
[Subsection (b) amended effective March 7, 2008]
[New subsection (d) adopted effective November 12, 2004. Subsection (d) amended effective September 15, 2006]

Authority: G.S. 7A–450.1 through –450.4; G.S. 7A–452(b); 7A–455; 7A–458; 7A–498.1(4), (5); 7A–498.3(c), (d); 7A–498.5(c)(8), (f)

Commentary

Subsection (a): Counsel should continue to use a revised version of the capital case fee application that has been used by the AOC (AOC–CR–425) to document fee and expense applications. Subsection (a) was amended May 6, 2005 to clarify that attorneys can not double-bill the state for time spent working on multiple cases simultaneously. For all cases finally disposed at the trial level on or after July 1, 2005, the subsection was also amended to require attorneys to submit fee applications to the IDS Director within one year of the date of final disposition. Effective August 13, 2007, the subsection was amended to allow attorneys to apply for an advance extension or waiver of the deadline in accordance with policies and procedures approved by the IDS Commission. Attorney fee applications submitted more than one year after the date of final disposition without an approved extension or waiver will not be paid from state funds. Finally, the subsection was amended to provide that an attorney who was retained to represent a capital defendant can not seek additional compensation from the state.

Subsection (b): In capital cases, recoupment of the cost of court- appointed counsel is governed by G.S. 7A–455. The IDS Act made only one change to that statute. It required that the value of services reflected in a judgment against a defendant be set in accordance with rules adopted by the IDS Office. Since Rule 2A.4(a) authorizes the IDS Director to set fees for counsel and supporting services, this rule requires the IDS Director to notify the defendant of the potential liability and afford the defendant a reasonable opportunity to be heard on the issue, before the trial judge can set the amount of any judgment. The subsection was amended effective March 7, 2008 to clarify that judgments for attorney fees can be ordered by the trial judge or another appropriate judicial official. The Public Defender is obligated to inform the IDS Director of the value of legal services rendered to the defendant. The form judgment is a revised version of the form that has been used by the AOC (AOC–CR-425).

Subsection (d): Subsection (d) was amended effective September 15, 2006 to clarify that, to avoid any potential for overreaching or the appearance of impropriety, an appointed attorney cannot subsequently accept fees as retained counsel from the client or the client's family. If family or friends of an indigent client want to contribute to non-counsel services, such as expert or support services, nothing in this subsection precludes them from doing so. However, the appointed attorney must place any such funds in his or her trust account and provide an accounting to the contributing family member and the IDS Director. This commentary was amended effective September 19, 2008 to clarify that, if family or friends of an indigent client hire an attorney to represent the client, the appointed attorney shall file a motion to withdraw from the representation. If, during the course of representation as appointed counsel, an attorney learns that a client who was previously determined to be indigent has become financially able to pay for the representation, G.S. 7A–450(d) directs the attorney to inform the court. *But cf.* RPC 52 (Jan. 13, 1989) (directing counsel to "call upon his client to reveal that circumstance to the tribunal" and, if the client refuses to permit disclosure, to move to withdraw). If the court finds that the client is no longer indigent, the appointed attorney may move to withdraw or continue the representation *pro bono*.

2A.5. Conditions of Appointment

(a) Requirements. The IDS Director may set additional conditions of appointment, including requiring attorneys appointed under this subpart to:

(i) consult with the IDS Director or his or her designee at regular intervals during the pendency of the representation, as required by the IDS Director;

(ii) attend training and/or continuing legal education in the area of capital trial representation as directed by the IDS Director;

(iii) follow the procedures required in Part 2D of these rules concerning appointment and compensation of experts, and other expenses of representation; and

(iv) meet with the IDS Director following a verdict in the case and prior to final payment of counsel fees to review the course of the representation.

(b) Substitution of Counsel. For good cause, the IDS Director may request *ex parte* that a judge of a court of competent jurisdiction replace lead or associate counsel previously appointed with new counsel selected by the IDS Director.

(c) Withdrawal of One Counsel After Non–Capital Declaration. Absent exceptional circumstances and the prior approval of the IDS Director, if second counsel has been appointed to a case pursuant to paragraph 2A.2(d) above, and there is a subsequent declaration that the case will be prosecuted non-capitally, one of the appointed lawyers shall move to withdraw. Counsel shall consult with the IDS Director or his or her designee prior to deciding which assigned counsel will so move, and shall notify the IDS Director or his or her designee of the court's ruling on the motion to withdraw.

[New subsection (c) adopted effective March 26, 2010]

Authority: G.S. 7A–498.1(1), (2); 7A–498.5(a), (c)(4), (c)(7), (h); 7A–498.6(b)(8)

Commentary

Subsection (b): This subsection permits the IDS Director to request *ex parte* that a judge remove an attorney previously appointed. It would be impossible to note all the circumstances that reasonably might cause the IDS Director to make such a request. Such circumstances might not in themselves constitute ineffective assistance of counsel. *See State v. Sweezy,* 291 N.C. 366, 371–72, 230 S.E.2d 524 (1976); *see also State v. Kuplin,* 316 N.C. 387, 396, 343 S.E.2d 793 (1986) ("Each case must be examined on an individual basis. In the absence of a constitutional violation, the decision about whether appointed counsel shall be replaced is a matter solely for the discretion of the trial court."). Reasonable tactical disagreements between the IDS Director and appointed counsel will not constitute grounds for the IDS Director to request substitution of counsel. If the judge determines that the attorney is rendering ineffective assistance of counsel or that the attorney has an impermissible conflict of interest, substitution is required as a matter of law. *See State v. Moorman,* 320 N.C. 387, 358 S.E.2d 502 (1987); *State v. James,* 111 N.C. App. 785, 433 S.E.2d 755 (1993).

Subsection (c): This subsection was adopted effective March 26, 2010 to clarify that, if two attorneys have been appointed to represent a capital defendant and the case is subsequently declared non-capital, one of the attorneys must move to withdraw, unless there are exceptional circumstances and the IDS Director has given prior approval for both attorneys to continue the representation. If a case is declared non-capital within 30 days of a scheduled trial date and the two appointed attorneys have divided the associated work and responsibility, the IDS Director generally will approve both attorneys continuing the representation at the trial.

PART 2B. APPOINTMENT AND COMPENSATION OF APPELLATE COUNSEL IN CAPITAL CASES

2B.1. Coverage of this Subpart

(a) Applies to Capital Appeals. This subpart applies to capital appeals and all appeals from offenses joined with a capital appeal. The term "capital appeal" includes appeals of right taken from a sentence of death and petitions for writ of certiorari or other extraordinary writs that are filed in the Appellate Division prior to the entry of final judgment in the Trial Division on behalf of a defendant charged with a capital offense.

(b) Authority to Implement Other Programs, Plans, and Contracts. Nothing in these rules shall prohibit assignment of otherwise qualified counsel to represent indigent defendants in capital appeals pursuant to programs, plans, or contracts that may be implemented from time to time to improve quality, efficiency, and economy where such programs, plans, or contracts are approved by the IDS Director.

[Subsection (a) amended effective February 27, 2009]

Authority: G.S. 7A–498.2(b); 7A–498.3(a); 7A–498.5(c)(7), (c)(8), (d)

2B.2. Appointment of Appellate Counsel

(a) Provisional Appointment of the Office of Appellate Defender. In extraordinary circumstances and in the absence of a court appointment pursuant to paragraph 2B.2(b) below, the Appellate Defender may appoint the Office of the Appellate Defender on a provisional basis to make a preliminary determination of the defendant's entitlement to appointed counsel in the Appellate Division, and to file a petition for an appropriate extraordinary writ in the Appellate Division.

(a1) Appointment of the Office of Appellate Defender by the Court for Litigation of Extraordinary Writ in Appellate Division Prior to Entry of Final Judgment in Trial Division. The trial court may appoint the Office of Appellate Defender to represent a defendant charged with a capital offense for the purpose of preparing, filing, and litigating a petition for writ of certiorari or other extraordinary writ in the Appellate Division prior to final entry of judgment in the Trial Division. If appointed for this purpose, the Office of Appellate Defender or counsel appointed by the Appellate Defender pursuant to paragraph 2B.2(c), below, shall file the petition only if it will present a potentially meritorious issue for review.

(b) Appointment of the Office of Appellate Defender by the Court for Appeals of Right. Following entry of a judgment imposing a death sentence, the IDS Director shall appoint the Office of Appellate Defender as appellate counsel in the capital case, and in any joined non-capital case upon which the court enters judgment, if the court determines that the capital defendant is indigent. It shall not be necessary for the IDS Director to file an order appointing the Office of Appellate Defender. The appellate entries made by the court following entry of a death judgment against an indigent defendant shall reflect that appeal is taken by operation of law pursuant to G.S. 15A–2000(d)(1), and that the IDS Director has appointed the Office of Appellate Defender. The appellate entries shall be mailed or transmitted by facsimile to the Office of Appellate Defender as soon as practicable following entry of judgment.

(c) Representation by Appellate Defender; Assignment of Other Appellate Counsel. The Appellate Defender shall represent on appeal as many of the defendants with capital appeals as possible to maximize the effectiveness of the Office of Appellate Defender, consistent with the other goals and responsibilities of that office. For the defendants that the Office of Appellate Defender does not represent on appeal, the Appellate Defender shall appoint one or two lawyers to represent the defendant on appeal. The Appellate Defender shall maintain a list of lawyers eligible to represent capital defendants on appeal pursuant to the procedures in Appendix 2B to these rules. The Appellate Defender shall appoint from that list pursuant to rules approved by the IDS Director. Appointment orders, signed by the Appellate Defender, shall be distributed to the appellant, trial judge, prosecuting attorney, defense attorneys at trial, clerk of superior court for the county where the trial took place, and court reporter(s).

(d) Conflicts. If the Office of Appellate Defender is appointed to represent a capital defendant whose case would create a conflict of interest with a current or previous client of the Office of Appellate Defender, the Appellate Defender shall immediately notify the IDS Director, and the IDS Director shall appoint counsel in the new case pursuant to the rules under which the Appellate Defender would appoint counsel. If the Appellate Defender is appointed to represent co-appellants, the Appellate Defender may appoint the Office of the Appellate Defender to represent a co-appellant and may appoint counsel for the remaining co-appellants so long as the Appellate Defender previously has not undertaken representation of a co-appellant.

(e) Evidentiary Hearings on Remand from the Appellate Courts Pending Direct Appeal and Assignment of Counsel by the Appellate Defender. After consulting with appointed appellate counsel, the Appellate Defender or IDS Director may appoint one or two additional lawyers to represent the appellant at an evidentiary hearing in the Trial Division on remand from the Appellate Division when the direct appeal is still pending. If additional counsel is appointed for that purpose, that counsel must be on the roster of attorneys who are approved to represent indigent capital defendants in the Trial Division pursuant to Rule 2A.2(d)(App.). Compensation of counsel appointed under this subsection shall be governed by Rule 2B.3. Appointment and compensation of experts and payment of other expenses related to litigation at the evidentiary hearing as authorized under this subsection shall be governed by Part 2D of these rules.

[[New subsection (a) adopted effective July 9, 2004]
[New subsection (a1) adopted effective February 27, 2009]
[Subsection (b) amended effective February 27, 2009]
[Subsection (c) amended effective November 4, 2005]
[Subsection (d) amended effective January 18, 2002]
[New subsection (e) adopted effective November 4, 2005]

Authority: G.S. 7A–450(b); 7A–452(a); 7A–498.3(b), (c); 7A–498.5(d), (h); 7A–498.8(b)(1), (b)(6)

Commentary

The superior court shall continue to use a revised version of the appellate entries form that has been used by the AOC (AOC–CR–350) to appoint the Office of Appellate Defender to represent the defendant in a capital appeal. The form will memorialize the automatic appeal of the conviction and sentence pursuant to G.S. 15A–2000(d)(1), the defendant's indigency status, the appointment of the Office of Appellate Defender by operation of these rules, and other relevant information common to all appeals of right from criminal convictions in superior court.

Subsection (a): This provision was added in July 2004 to authorize the Appellate Defender to provisionally appoint the Office of the Appellate Defender in certain circumstances. The need for this authority has typically arisen in three types of cases: 1) cases in which the Appellate Defender believes that a trial court has erroneously denied indigency status after a person who the court previously determined was indigent entered notice of appeal, and that a petition for an extraordinary writ should be filed on the person's behalf; 2) cases in which a trial court has determined that a person is indigent but denied appointed appellate counsel, and the Appellate Defender believes that the person has a right to appointed appellate counsel and that a petition for an extraordinary writ should be filed on the person's behalf; and 3) cases in which the Appellate Defender is contacted by appointed trial counsel concerning the need for immediate review of a pre-trial ruling, and the Appellate Defender agrees that the ruling should be challenged in the appellate courts by means of a petition for an extraordinary writ.

Subsection (a1): Subsection (a1) was adopted effective February 27, 2009 to clarify that the trial court may appoint the Office of Appellate Defender for litigating an extraordinary writ in the Appellate Division prior to the entry of a final judgment in the Trial Division on behalf of a defendant charged with a capital offense.

Subsection (b): This subsection was amended effective February 27, 2009 to clarify that it governs direct appeals of right in capital cases.

Subsection (e): This provision was added in November 2005 to authorize the Appellate Defender or IDS Director to appoint counsel to litigate an evidentiary hearing in the Trial Division on remand from the Appellate Division when the direct appeal is still pending.

2B.3. Compensation and Recoupment

(a) Compensation. Appointed counsel who represented an indigent capital defendant on appeal shall submit to the IDS Director an itemized fee application on a form prescribed by the IDS Director, showing the time counsel spent in appellate representation of the defendant. If an attorney seeks compensation for time spent working on multiple cases simultaneously, the attorney's time shall be prorated among each of the cases involved. Following review of the fee application, the IDS Director shall determine the amount of compensation and forward the award to IDS Financial Services for payment. If counsel is required pursuant to paragraph 2B.4(b)(iii) below to meet with the Appellate Defender or others to review the representation, the fee shall include compensation for time spent in that review. Private counsel appointed to represent an indigent capital defendant may apply for and receive interim payments in the discretion of the IDS Director. For all cases finally disposed at the appellate level on or after July 1, 2005, final attorney fee applications must be signed by the appointed attorney and submitted to the Appellate Defender or IDS Director within no more than one year after the date on which the appeal was finally disposed. For all cases finally disposed at the appellate level before July 1, 2005, final attorney fee applications must be signed by the appointed attorney and submitted to the Appellate Defender or IDS Director by January 1, 2006. In accordance with policies and procedures approved by the IDS Commission, an attorney may apply to the IDS Director for one advance extension of the applicable deadline or for a waiver of the applicable deadline. Counsel may make a written request for a review of the amount of compensation determined by the IDS Director from a committee of the IDS Commission designated by the IDS Commission to conduct such review.

(b) Recoupment of Fees Generally. To the extent required by law, capital defendants for whom counsel has been appointed under this part shall continue to be responsible for repaying the fees paid to such counsel or, in the case of representation by a public defender or appellate defender office, the value of services rendered by counsel. After the IDS Director sets the fee to be paid or the value of services rendered, the IDS Director shall notify the defendant of the potential liability, and afford the defendant a reasonable opportunity to be heard on the issue. The trial judge or other appropriate judicial official shall then determine the amount to be recouped if recoupment is required by law.

(c) Recoupment for Contract Services. For legal representation rendered by attorneys working under contract with the IDS Office, the value of services, and the procedures for entry of any appropriate orders or judgments, shall be determined in accordance with the terms of the contract if recoupment is required by law.

(d) Outside Compensation Prohibited. Once counsel has been appointed to represent a person in a case subject to this part, counsel shall not accept any fees for the representation other than that awarded by the IDS Director. If a third party contributes funds to non-counsel services, counsel shall place the funds in trust and account to the third party and the IDS Director about the use of the funds.

[Subsection (a) amended effective May 6, 2005, August 13, 2007, and May 29, 2015]
[Subsection (b) amended effective March 7, 2008]
[New subsection (d) adopted effective November 12, 2004. Subsection (d) amended effective September 15, 2006]

Authority: G.S. 7A–450.1 through –450.4; 7A–452(b); 7A–455; 7A–458; 7A–498.1(4), (5); 7A–498.3(c), (d); 7A–498.5(c)(8), (f)

Commentary

See the commentary to Rule 2A.4, above.

2B.4. Conditions of Appointment

(a) Petitions for Certiorari, Oppositions to Petitions for Certiorari, and Representation in the Supreme Court of the United States. If the defendant does not receive sentencing relief in the Supreme Court of North Carolina, the appointed appellate lawyer shall prepare and file in the Supreme Court of the United States a timely petition for writ of certiorari to the Supreme Court of North Carolina, unless relieved of this responsibility by the IDS Director or Appellate Defender. If the defendant receives sentencing relief in the Supreme Court of North Carolina, but the Supreme Court of the United States arguably has certiorari jurisdiction on an issue that could result in guilt-phase relief, the appointed appellate lawyer will be compensated for preparing and filing in the Supreme Court of the United States a timely petition for writ of certiorari to the Supreme Court of North Carolina only if the lawyer obtains prior written authorization from the IDS Director or Appellate Defender. If the defendant receives relief in the Supreme Court of North Carolina and the state files a petition for writ of certiorari, the appointed appellate lawyer shall prepare and file a timely response in opposition to the petition, unless relieved of this responsibility by the IDS Director or Appellate Defender. If the Supreme Court of the United States grants certiorari, the appointed appellate lawyer shall represent the defendant in proceedings before the Supreme Court, unless relieved of this responsibility by the IDS Director or Appellate Defender.

If the IDS Director or Appellate Defender relieves the appointed appellate lawyer of any of these responsibilities or declines to authorize appointed appellate counsel to file a writ of certiorari on an issue that could result in guilt-phase relief, the Appellate Defender may undertake the representation directly or appoint one or two other qualified appellate attorneys from the list of lawyers eligible to represent capital defendants on appeal. The Appellate Defender also may appoint the Office of Appellate Defender or another qualified appellate attorney from the list of lawyers eligible to represent capital defendants on appeal as co-counsel with appointed appellate counsel. Compensation of counsel for work performed pursuant to this subsection shall be governed by Rule 2B.3.

(b) Other Requirements. The IDS Director or Appellate Defender may set additional conditions of appointment, including requiring attorneys appointed under this subpart to:

(i) consult with the Appellate Defender or his or her designee during the pendency of the representation in the Appellate Division or in the Supreme Court of the United States as provided by paragraph 2B.4(a), above, participate in practice oral arguments, and submit briefs for pre-filing review, as required by the Appellate Defender;

(ii) attend training and/or continuing legal education in the area of capital appellate representation as approved by the IDS Director; and

(iii) meet with the Appellate Defender and any others designated by the IDS Director following an appellate decision and prior to final payment of counsel fees to review the course of the representation.

(c) Substitution of Counsel. For good cause, the IDS Director may request *ex parte* that a court of competent jurisdiction replace an appellate attorney previously appointed with new counsel selected by the IDS Director.

[Subsection (a) amended effective September 14, 2007]
[Subsection (b) amended effective September 14, 2007]

Authority: G.S. 7A–451(b)(7), 7A–498.1(1), (2); 7A–498.5(a), (c)(4), (c)(7), (h); 7A–498.6(b)(8); 7A–498.8(b)(3), (b)(4), (b)(6a)

Commentary

Subsection (a): Subsection (a) was amended effective September 14, 2007 to address defense petitions for certiorari in the Supreme Court of the United States on issues that could lead to guilt-phase relief, oppositions to state petitions for certiorari, and the responsibility for representation in the Supreme Court of the United States if that Court grants certiorari review. The amendments reflect statutory revisions that were enacted during the 2007 legislative session, which extended the entitlement to counsel to "review of any judgment or decree rendered on direct appeal by the Supreme Court of North Carolina pursuant to the certiorari jurisdiction of the United States Supreme Court." S.L. 2007–323, § 14.19(a).

Subsection (b): Based on the same statutory revisions described in the commentary to subsection 2B.4(a), above, this subsection was amended effective September 14, 2007 to clarify that the Appellate Defender may set additional conditions of appointment for representation in the Supreme Court of the United States, including requiring consultations, reviews of draft petitions and briefs, and practice oral arguments.

Subsection (c): See the commentary to Rule 2A.5(b), above.

PART 2C. APPOINTMENT OF POST–CONVICTION COUNSEL IN CAPITAL CASES

2C.1. Coverage of this Part

(a) Applies to Capital Post–Conviction. This subpart applies to capital defendants whose death sentences are on direct appeal to the Supreme Court of North Carolina or have been affirmed on direct appeal by the Supreme Court of North Carolina.

(b) Authority to Implement Other Programs, Plans, and Contracts. Nothing in these rules shall prohibit assignment of otherwise qualified counsel to represent indigent defendants in capital post-conviction proceedings pursuant to programs, plans, or contracts that may be implemented from time to time to improve quality, efficiency, and economy where such programs, plans, or contracts are approved by the IDS Director.

Authority: G.S. 7A–451(c), (d); 7A–498.2(b); 7A–498.3(a); 7A–498. 5(c)(7), (c)(8), (d)

2C.2. Appointment of Post–Conviction Counsel and Scope of Representation

(a) Appointment of Counsel. The IDS Director shall appoint two lawyers as post-conviction counsel in each indigent capital post-conviction case in accordance with G.S. 7A–451(c). The IDS Director shall maintain a list of lawyers eligible to represent capital defendants in post-conviction proceedings pursuant to the procedures in Appendix 2C of these rules. Appointment orders, signed by the IDS Director, shall be distributed to the defendant, clerk of superior court for the county where the trial took place, district attorney, attorney general, and lawyers appointed as post-conviction counsel.

(b) Scope of Representation. If a Motion for Appropriate Relief is denied by the superior court, appointed capital post-conviction counsel are authorized to prepare, file, and litigate a petition for writ of certiorari in the Supreme Court of North Carolina. Counsel are also authorized to prepare, file, and litigate a petition for writ of certiorari or other extraordinary writ seeking review of an interlocutory ruling of the superior court. If a petition for writ of certiorari is denied by the Supreme Court of North Carolina or if that court grants certiorari review but denies relief, counsel who seek to be compensated for preparing, filing, or litigating a petition for writ of certiorari in the Supreme Court of the United States must obtain prior authorization from the Appellate Defender.

Absent exceptional circumstances and the prior approval of the IDS Director, if the superior court vacates a death sentence and resentences a defendant to life imprisonment without the possibility of parole, but there is one or more guilt-phase claims in a pending Motion for Appropriate Relief, one of the appointed lawyers shall move to withdraw. Counsel shall consult with the IDS Director or his or her designee about the pending guilt-phase claims prior to deciding which assigned counsel will so move, and shall notify the IDS Director or his or her designee of the court's ruling on the motion to withdraw. Subject to policies and procedures adopted by the IDS Office, the remaining appointed lawyer shall continue the litigation of the pending guilt-phase claims until they are finally resolved in the Trial Division. If the guilt-phase claims are ultimately denied, subject to policies and procedures adopted by the IDS Office, the remaining appointed lawyer may also prepare, file, and litigate a petition for writ of certiorari in the Appellate Division. If a petition for writ of certiorari is denied by the Appellate Division or if that Division grants certiorari review but denies relief, counsel who seek to be compensated for preparing, filing, or litigating a petition for writ of certiorari in the Supreme Court of the United States must obtain prior authorization from the Appellate Defender.

[Section amended effective February 27, 2009 and September 24, 2010]

Authority: G.S. 7A–450(b); 7A–451(c), (d); 7A–498.3(b), (c); 7A–498.5(d), (h)

Commentary

Subsection (a): Pursuant to G.S. 7A–451(c), an indigent capital defendant may apply to the IDS Office for appointment of post-conviction counsel. If the defendant was previously adjudicated indigent for purposes of trial or direct appeal, the defendant shall be presumed indigent and the IDS Office shall appoint two counsel to represent the defendant in post-conviction proceedings. If the defendant was not previously adjudicated indigent, the IDS Office shall request that the superior court of the district in which the defendant was indicted determine whether the defendant is indigent. In such cases, if the court finds that the defendant is indigent and desires counsel, it shall appoint the IDS Office, which shall in turn appoint two counsel to represent the defendant. The IDS Director will approve and make available a form to facilitate the court's appointment of the IDS Office (AOC–CR–427). The court can notify the IDS Director that it has appointed the IDS Office by mail, facsimile, or email.

Subsection (b): This subsection was amended effective February 27, 2009 to clarify the scope of appointed capital post-conviction counsel's representation and to provide a mechanism for seeking advance approval to litigate a certiorari petition in the Supreme Court of the United States. The subsection was amended again effective September 24, 2010 to address the procedure if a judge vacates a defendant's death sentence but does not issue a final ruling on one or more guilt-phase claims in a pending Motion for Appropriate Relief. Under those circumstances, this provision would allow one of the previously appointed post-conviction counsel to continue the representation.

2C.3. Compensation and Recoupment

(a) Compensation. Appointed counsel who represented an indigent capital defendant in post-conviction proceedings shall submit to the IDS Director an itemized fee application on a form prescribed by the IDS Director, showing the time counsel spent in post-conviction representation of the defendant. If an attorney seeks compensation for time spent working on multiple cases simultaneously, the attorney's time shall be prorated among each of the cases involved. Following review of the fee application, the IDS Director shall determine the amount of compensation and forward the award to IDS Financial Services for payment. If counsel is required pursuant to paragraph 2C.4(a)(iv) below to meet with the IDS Director to review the representation, the fee shall include compensation for time spent in that review. Private counsel appointed to represent a capital defendant on post-conviction may apply for and receive interim payments in the discretion of the IDS Director. For all cases finally disposed at the post-conviction level on or after July 1, 2005, final attorney fee applications must be signed by the appointed attorney and submitted to the IDS Director within no more than one year after the date on which the post-conviction proceedings were finally disposed. For all cases finally disposed at the post-conviction level before July 1, 2005, final attorney fee applications must be signed by the appointed attorney and submitted to the IDS Director by January 1, 2006. In accordance with policies and procedures approved by the IDS Commission, an attorney may apply to the IDS Director for one advance extension of the applicable deadline or for a waiver of the applicable deadline. Counsel may make a written request for a review of the amount of compensation determined by the IDS Director from a committee of the IDS Commission designated by the IDS Commission to conduct such review.

(b) Recoupment of Fees Generally. To the extent required by law, capital defendants for whom counsel has been appointed under this part shall continue to be responsible for repaying the fees paid to such counsel or, in the case of representation by a public defender or appellate defender office, the value of services rendered by counsel. After the IDS Director sets the fee to be paid or the value of services rendered, the IDS Director shall notify the defendant of the potential liability, and afford the defendant a reasonable opportunity to be heard on the issue. The trial judge or other appropriate judicial official shall then determine the amount to be recouped if recoupment is required by law.

(c) Recoupment for Contract Services. For legal representation rendered by attorneys working under contract with the IDS Office, the value of services, and the procedures for entry of any appropriate orders or judgments, shall be determined in accordance with the terms of the contract if recoupment is required by law.

(d) Outside Compensation Prohibited. Once counsel has been appointed to represent a person in a case subject to this part, counsel shall not accept any fees for the representation other than that awarded by the IDS Director. If a third party contributes funds to non-counsel services, counsel shall place the funds in trust and account to the third party and the IDS Director about the use of the funds.

[Subsection (a) amended effective May 6, 2005, August 13, 2007, and May 29, 2015]

[Subsection (b) amended effective March 7, 2008]

[New subsection (d) adopted effective November 12, 2004. Subsection (d) amended effective September 15, 2006]

Authority: G.S. 7A–450.1 through –450.4; 7A–452(b); 7A–455; 7A–458; 7A–498.1(4), (5); 7A–498.3(c), (d); 7A–498.5(c)(8), (f)

Commentary

See the commentary to Rule 2A.4, above.

2C.4. Conditions of Appointment

(a) Requirements. The IDS Director may set additional conditions of appointment, including requiring attorneys appointed under this subpart to:

(i) consult with the IDS Director during the pendency of the representation and submit the Motion for Appropriate Relief or other filings for pre-filing review, as required by the IDS Director;

(ii) attend training and/or continuing legal education in the area of capital post-conviction representation as approved by the IDS Director;

(iii) follow the procedures required in Part 2D of these rules concerning appointment and compensation of experts, and other expenses of representation; and

(iv) meet with the IDS Director following the end of the representation and prior to final payment of counsel fees to review the course of the representation.

(b) Substitution of Counsel. For good cause, the IDS Director may request *ex parte* that a judge of a court of competent jurisdiction replace post-conviction counsel previously appointed with new counsel selected by the IDS Director.

Authority: G.S. 7A–498.1(1), (2); 7A–498.5(a), (c)(4), (c)(7), (h); 7A–498.6(b)(8)

Commentary

See the commentary to Rule 2A.5(b), above.

PART 2D. APPOINTMENT AND COMPENSATION OF EXPERTS AND PAYMENT OF OTHER EXPENSES RELATED TO LEGAL REPRESENTATION IN CAPITAL CASES

2D.1. Initial Application

Defense counsel shall make application to the IDS Director for authorization to retain experts or for other substantial expenses necessary to the defense of the capital defendant before applying to a court for such authorization, and before incurring a financial obligation for which defense counsel will apply to the IDS Director for payment by the IDS Office. The application shall be in writing, unless exceptional or extraordinary circumstances necessitate an oral motion. Defense counsel will be required to make at least as specific an application to retain experts as would be required by a fair but exacting trial judge applying G.S. 7A–450(a) and *Ake v. Oklahoma* and its progeny. The IDS Director may require counsel to make a more particularized application before approving or disapproving the application.

[Amended eff. May 20, 2011.]

Authority: G.S. 7A–450(b); 7A–454; 7A–498.1(1); 7A–498.3(a), (c),(d); 7A–498.5(c)(6), (f)

Commentary

Routine expenses, such as typical long-distance telephone calls, are not substantial expenses within the meaning of this rule. Counsel can resolve any question about whether an expense requires prior approval of the IDS Director by communication with the IDS Director by telephone or email.

Ordinarily, counsel should submit to the IDS Director a written application for expert funding. However, in exceptional or extraordinary circumstances, counsel may apply for expert funding by telephone or email.

2D.2. Confidentiality of Application

The IDS Director will maintain the application in a confidential file open only to the IDS Office and the defense team.

Authority: G.S. 7A–498.3(a), (c); 7A–498.5(c)(6), (f)

2D.3. Disapproval of Application

If the IDS Director disapproves the application, timely written notice of disapproval of the application will be delivered to counsel. The IDS Director will maintain the notice of disapproval in a confidential file open only to the IDS Office and the defense team.

Authority: G.S. 7A–498.3(a), (c), (d); 7A–498.5(c)(6), (f)

2D.4. Application to Court

Defense counsel may apply to a court for appointment of experts or for other expenses following disapproval by the IDS Director. However, in no event may counsel apply to a court for a deviation from the standardized expert hourly rates following disapproval of a requested deviation by the IDS Director. If counsel applies to a court for appointment of experts or for other expenses, counsel may not submit an application to a court that includes information not contained in the application made to the IDS Director unless exceptional or extraordinary circumstances necessitate submitting such new or additional information directly to a court. If counsel makes application to a court following the IDS Director's disapproval, counsel shall submit with its application to the court a complete copy of the IDS Director's written notice of disapproval and a complete copy of the written application made to the IDS Director. Counsel must immediately forward to the IDS Director a complete copy of any court order approving funds previously disapproved by the IDS Director and a complete copy of the application made to the court. Such court order and application will be maintained in a confidential file open only to the IDS Office and the defense team.

[Amended eff. December 9, 2011.]

Authority: G.S. 7A–454; 7A–498.3(a), (c), (d); 7A–498.5(c)(6), (f)

Commentary

If, after denial of an initial application to the IDS Director for appointment or compensation of experts or other supporting services, defense counsel discovers new or additional information that is relevant to such application, counsel ordinarily should submit a new application to the IDS Director before submitting an application to a court. Counsel may submit to a court an application that contains new or additional information only in exceptional or extraordinary circumstances. This section was amended December 9, 2011 to clarify that counsel may not seek judicial review of the IDS Director's decision to deny a deviation from the standardized expert hourly rates set by the IDS Commission pursuant to G.S. 7A–498.5(f).

Commentary

If, after denial of an initial application to the IDS Director for appointment or compensation of experts or other supporting services, defense counsel discovers new or additional information that is relevant to such application, counsel ordinarily should submit a new application to the IDS Director before submitting an application to a court. Counsel may submit to a court an application that contains new or additional information only in exceptional or extraordinary circumstances.

2D.5. Authority to Implement other Programs, Plans, and Contracts

Nothing in these rules shall prohibit appointment or compensation of otherwise qualified experts pursuant to programs, plans, or contracts that may be implemented from time to time to improve quality, efficiency, and economy where such programs, plans, or contracts are approved by the IDS Director.

Authority: G.S. 7A–454; 7A–498.1(1), (3); 7A–498.3(a), (c); 7A–498.5(c)(6), (d), (f)

APPENDIX TO PART 2

The following three appendices set eligibility standards for trial, appellate, and post-conviction counsel in capital cases.

APPENDIX 2A. STANDARDS FOR LEAD AND ASSOCIATE TRIAL COUNSEL IN CAPITAL CASES

2A.1 (App.) Trial Qualifications and Experience

(a) Lead Counsel

To be eligible to be appointed as lead counsel in a capital case, an attorney must demonstrate that he or she has the required legal knowledge and skill necessary for representation as lead counsel in a capital case and will apply that knowledge and skill with appropriate thoroughness and preparation, and that he or she meets the requirements listed below. However, if an attorney cannot meet one or more of the requirements set forth below, the IDS Director may waive any requirement(s) pursuant to paragraph 2A.1(c) (App.) below.

A candidate for appointment must demonstrate that he or she:

(i) has at least six years of criminal or civil litigation experience; or has at least four years of concentrated criminal litigation experience as a public defender, prosecutor, or attorney in a capital defense organization;

(ii) is familiar with ethics requirements, current criminal practice and procedure in North Carolina, and capital jurisprudence established by the Supreme Court of the United States and Supreme Court of North Carolina;

(iii) has participated as trial counsel in at least ten jury trials to verdict or to hung jury;

(iv) has tried a capital case to verdict or to hung jury as lead defense counsel; or has tried two capital cases to verdict or to hung jury as associate defense counsel; or has represented to disposition at the trial level defendants in four homicides cases; and

(v) has substantial familiarity with and experience in the use of expert witnesses and scientific and medical evidence, including mental health, social history, and pathology evidence.

(b) Associate Counsel

To be eligible to be appointed as associate counsel in a capital case, an attorney must demonstrate that he or she has the required legal knowledge and skill necessary for representation as associate counsel in a capital case and will apply that knowledge and skill with appropriate thoroughness and preparation, and that he or she meets the requirements listed below. However, if an attorney cannot meet one or more of the requirements set forth below, the IDS Director may waive any requirement(s) pursuant to paragraph 2A.1(c) (App.) below.

A candidate for appointment must demonstrate that he or she:

(i) has at least three years of criminal or civil litigation experience;

(ii) is familiar with ethics requirements, current criminal practice and procedure in North Carolina, and capital jurisprudence established by the Supreme Court of the United States and Supreme Court of North Carolina;

(iii) has participated as trial counsel in at least four jury trials to verdict or to hung jury; or has spent two years in practice in a capital defense organization; and

(iv) has substantial familiarity with scientific and medical evidence, including mental health, social history, and pathology evidence.

(c) Waiver

If an attorney cannot meet one or more of the requirements set forth above, the IDS Director, upon determination that the attorney has the required legal knowledge and skill necessary for representation as lead or associate counsel in a capital case, and will apply that knowledge and skill with appropriate thoroughness and preparation, may either waive such requirement(s) or defer any requirement(s) for a reasonable time and in the interim place the attorney on the roster of qualified lead or associate counsel.

2A.2 (App.) Applications

(a) Application.

An attorney who seeks to be appointed as lead or associate counsel in a capital case shall submit to the IDS Director an application on a form prescribed by the IDS Director. The application shall require the attorney to demonstrate that he or she has fully satisfied the requirements set forth above. The attorney shall specify for which Judicial Division roster(s) of qualified lead counsel and associate counsel he or she seeks to be considered. The attorney shall also identify any requirement(s) that he or she requests be waived, and shall set forth in detail his or her trial experience or other exceptional qualifications that justify waiver.

(b) Required Submissions.

In support of an application, an attorney shall submit to the IDS Director:

(i) a list of all first-degree murder cases in which the attorney has appeared within the past five years, including the name of the case, the county, the trial judge, the prosecuting attorney, any co-counsel, the result or verdict, and any reported appellate decision in the case;

(ii) at least two examples of substantial written legal work product prepared by the attorney at the trial or appellate level in connection with separate felony cases;

(iii) a description of specialized criminal defense training programs attended within the past five years, such as those sponsored by the North Carolina Advocates for Justice, the North Carolina Bar Association, or the Center for Death Penalty Litigation;

(iv) the names, addresses, and phone numbers of two superior court judges, two prosecutors, and two defense attorneys familiar with the attorney's work as an advocate; and

(v) any additional material that may assist the IDS Director in evaluating the applicant's trial qualifications and experience.

(c) Waiver or Deferral of Required Submissions.

If an attorney has not provided each of the above items, the IDS Director, upon determination that the attorney has the required legal knowledge and skill necessary for representation as lead or associate counsel in a capital case, and will apply that knowledge and skill with appropriate thoroughness and preparation as either lead or associate counsel, may either waive such submission(s) or defer submission of any item(s) for a reasonable time and in the interim place the attorney on the roster of qualified lead or associate counsel.

(d) Creation of Capital Trial Roster.

Following review of each application to determine that it is complete, the IDS Director will investigate the contents of the submission, contact references, and determine whether the attorney is qualified for appointment as lead or associate counsel in a capital case. The IDS Director shall thereafter create and maintain a roster of attorneys qualified for and willing to accept appointments as lead and associate counsel in each Judicial Division.

(e) Appeal to the IDS Commission.

If the IDS Director determines that an attorney is not qualified for appointment as lead or associate counsel in a capital case or otherwise declines to place the attorney's name on the capital trial roster, the attorney may make a written request for a review of the IDS Director's decision from a committee of the IDS Commission designated by the IDS Commission to conduct such review.

[Subsection (b) amended effective May 29, 2015]
[Subsection (e) amended effective February 10, 2006]

2A.3 (App.) Retention and Eligibility

(a) On–Going Training.

To remain eligible for appointment as lead or associate counsel in a capital case, an attorney must attend capital training sessions as prescribed by the IDS Director, and consult regularly and frequently with the IDS Director with respect to each capital case to which the attorney is appointed.

(b) Removal from Roster.

The IDS Director may remove from the roster of attorneys qualified for appointment as lead or associate counsel in a capital case any attorney who has ignored requirements for appointment as lead or associate counsel; has failed to continue to demonstrate that he or she has the required legal knowledge and skill necessary for representation as lead or associate counsel; or has failed to continue to demonstrate that he or she is willing to apply that knowledge and skill with appropriate thoroughness and preparation as lead or associate counsel. The IDS Director may also remove an attorney from a roster if, as part of a periodic review of the roster, the IDS Director determines that a smaller roster of attorneys will better serve the goals of ensuring the best possible representation of indigent capital defendants and of delivering quality services in the most efficient and cost-effective manner. If the IDS Director removes an attorney from the capital trial roster, the attorney may make a written request for a review of the IDS Director's decision from a committee of the IDS Commission designated by the IDS Commission to conduct such review.

[Subsection (b) amended effective February 10, 2006 and May 29, 2015]

APPENDIX 2B. STANDARDS FOR APPELLATE COUNSEL IN CAPITAL CASES

2B.1 (App.) Appellate Qualifications and Experience

(a) Appellate Counsel

To be eligible to be appointed as appellate counsel on direct appeal in a capital case, an attorney must demonstrate that he or she has the required legal knowledge and skill necessary for representation as appellate counsel in a capital case and will apply that knowledge and skill with appropriate thoroughness and preparation, and that he or she meets the requirements listed below. However, if an attorney cannot meet one or more of the requirements set forth below, the IDS Director may waive any requirement(s) pursuant to paragraph 2B.1(b) (App.) below.

A candidate for appointment must demonstrate that he or she:

(i) has at least five years of criminal, appellate, or post-conviction experience; or has at least three years of concentrated criminal litigation experience as a public defender, prosecutor, or attorney in a capital defense organization; or is currently serving as the Appellate Defender or an Assistant Appellate Defender;

(ii) is familiar with ethics requirements, current criminal practice and procedure in North Carolina, and capital jurisprudence established by the Supreme Court of the United States and the Supreme Court of North Carolina;

(iii) is familiar with practice and procedure in the trial and appellate courts of North Carolina; and

(iv) has had primary responsibility for the appeal of at least five felony convictions in any state or federal court, at least three of which were on behalf of the defendant, and at least three of which were orally argued by the attorney.

(b) Waiver

If an attorney cannot meet one or more of the requirements set forth above, the IDS Director, upon determination that the attorney has the required legal knowledge and skill necessary for representation as appellate counsel in a capital case, and will apply that knowledge and skill with appropriate thoroughness and preparation, may either waive such requirement(s) or defer any requirement(s) for a reasonable time and in the interim place the attorney on the roster of qualified appellate counsel.

2B.2 (App.) Applications

(a) Application

An attorney who seeks to be appointed as appellate counsel in a capital case shall submit to the Appellate Defender an application on a form prescribed by the IDS Director. The application shall require the attorney to demonstrate that he or she has fully satisfied the requirements set forth above. The attorney shall also identify any requirement(s) that he or she requests be waived, and shall set forth in detail his or her appellate experience or other exceptional qualifications that justify waiver.

(b) Required Submissions

In support of an application, an attorney shall submit to the Appellate Defender:

(i) at least two appellate briefs, written exclusively or primarily by the applicant, the opposing briefs, and the appellate court's decision;

(ii) a description of specialized capital or other criminal appellate advocacy, or other criminal practice program, attended in the past five years;

(iii) the names, addresses, and phone numbers of two prosecutors and two defense attorneys, current or former, including at least one appellate adversary, who are familiar with the applicant's work as an advocate; and

(iv) any additional material that may assist the IDS Director in evaluating the applicant's appellate qualifications and experience.

The applicant may submit the name, address, and phone number of one appellate judge, if the judge is familiar with the applicant's work as an advocate.

(c) Waiver or Deferral of Required Submissions

If an attorney has not provided each of the above items, the IDS Director, upon determination that the attorney has the required legal knowledge and skill necessary for representation as appellate counsel in a capital case, and will apply that knowledge and skill with appropriate thoroughness and preparation as appellate counsel, may either waive such submission(s) or defer submission of any item(s) for a reasonable time and in the interim place the attorney on the roster of qualified appellate counsel.

(d) Creation of Capital Appeals Roster

Following review of each application to determine that it is complete, the Appellate Defender will investigate the contents of the submission, contact references, and make any further investigation deemed necessary. The Appellate Defender shall then make a recommendation to the IDS Director as to whether the attorney is qualified for appointment as appellate counsel in a capital case. The IDS Director shall make the final determination as to whether an attorney should be included on the capital appeals roster. The Appellate Defender shall thereafter create and maintain a roster of attorneys qualified for and willing to accept appointments as appellate counsel.

(e) Appeal to the IDS Commission

If the IDS Director determines that an attorney is not qualified for appointment as appellate counsel in a capital case or otherwise declines to place the attorney's name on the capital appeals roster, the attorney may make a written request for a review of the IDS Director's decision from a committee of the IDS Commission designated by the IDS Commission to conduct such review.

[Subsection (e) amended effective February 10, 2006]

2B.3 (App.) Retention and Eligibility

(a) On–Going Training.

To remain eligible for appointment as counsel on a capital appeal, an attorney must attend and successfully complete training sessions as prescribed by the Appellate Defender, and consult regularly and frequently with the Appellate Defender with respect to each capital case to which the attorney is appointed.

(b) Removal from Roster.

The IDS Director may remove from the roster of attorneys qualified for appointment as appellate counsel in a capital case any attorney who has ignored requirements for appointment as appellate counsel; has failed to continue to demonstrate that he or she has the required legal knowledge and skill necessary for representation as appellate counsel; or has failed to continue to demonstrate that he or she is willing to apply that knowledge and skill with appropriate thoroughness and preparation as appellate counsel. The IDS Director may also remove an attorney from the roster if, as part of a periodic review of the roster, the IDS Director determines that a smaller roster of attorneys will better serve the goals of ensuring the best possible representation of indigent capital defendants and of delivering quality services in the most efficient and cost-effective manner. If the IDS Director removes an attorney from the capital appeals roster, the attorney may make a written request for a review of the IDS Director's decision from a committee of the IDS Commission designated by the IDS Commission to conduct such review.

[Subsection (b) amended effective February 10, 2006 and May 29, 2015]

APPENDIX 2C. STANDARDS FOR STATE POST–CONVICTION COUNSEL IN CAPITAL CASES

2C.1 (App.) State Post–Conviction Qualifications and Experience

(a) State Post–Conviction Counsel

To be eligible to be appointed as counsel on a Motion for Appropriate Relief and any appeal therefrom in a capital case, an attorney must demonstrate that he or she has the required legal knowledge and skill necessary for representation as post-conviction counsel in a capital case and will apply that knowledge and skill with appropriate thoroughness and preparation, and that he or she meets the requirements listed below. However, if an attorney cannot meet one or more of the requirements set forth below, the IDS Director may waive any requirement(s) pursuant to paragraph 2C.1(b) (App.) below.

A candidate for appointment must demonstrate that he or she:

(i) has at least five years criminal or civil trial experience; or has at least five years criminal or civil appellate experience; or has at least five years state or federal post-conviction experience; or has at least three years of concentrated criminal litigation experience as a public defender, prosecutor, or attorney in a public or private capital defense organization; or is currently in practice in a capital defense organization;

(ii) is familiar with ethics requirements, current criminal practice and procedure in North Carolina, and capital jurisprudence established by the Supreme Court of the United States and the Supreme Court of North Carolina;

(iii) is familiar with the practice and procedure of the trial and appellate courts of North Carolina, including the practice and procedure for filing a Motion for Appropriate Relief, and with the practice and procedure of the federal courts with regard to federal habeas corpus petitions;

(iv) has had primary responsibility for representing a party in at least three criminal or civil appeals, or criminal post-conviction proceedings; and

(v) has substantial familiarity with and experience in the use of expert witnesses and scientific and medical evidence, including mental health, social history, and pathology evidence.

(b) Waiver

If an attorney cannot meet one or more of the requirements set forth above, the IDS Director, upon determination that the attorney has the required legal knowledge and skill necessary for representation as post-conviction counsel in a capital case, and will apply that knowledge and skill with appropriate thoroughness and preparation, may either waive such requirement(s) or defer any requirement(s) for a reasonable time and in the interim place the attorney on the roster of qualified post-conviction counsel.

2C.2 (App.) Applications

(a) Application

An attorney who seeks to be appointed as post-conviction counsel in a capital case shall submit to the IDS Director an application on a form prescribed by the IDS Director. The application shall require the attorney to demonstrate that he or she has fully satisfied the requirements set forth above. The attorney shall also identify any requirement(s) that he or she requests be waived, and shall set forth in detail his or her criminal or civil litigation, appellate and/or post-conviction experience, or other exceptional qualifications that justify waiver.

(b) Required Submissions

In support of an application, an attorney shall submit to the IDS Director:

(i) at least two examples of substantial written legal work product prepared by the attorney in connection with separate cases, or at least two appellate briefs, written exclusively or primarily by the applicant, the opposing briefs, and the appellate court's decision in the case;

(ii) a description of specialized trial, appellate, or post-conviction capital defense training programs attended in the past five years;

(iii) the names, addresses, and phone numbers of two prosecutors and two defense attorneys, current or former, including at least one adversary, who are familiar with the applicant's work as an advocate; and

(iv) any additional material that may assist the IDS Director in evaluating the applicant's post-conviction qualifications and experience.

The applicant may submit the name, address, and phone number of one judge, if the judge is familiar with the applicant's work as an advocate.

(c) Waiver or Deferral of Required Submissions

If an attorney has not provided each of the above items, the IDS Director, upon determination that the attorney has the required legal knowledge and skill necessary for representation as post-conviction counsel in a capital case, and will apply that knowledge and skill with appropriate thoroughness and preparation as post-conviction counsel, may either waive such submission(s) or defer submission of any item(s) for a reasonable time and in the interim place the attorney on the roster of qualified post-conviction counsel.

(d) Creation of Post–Conviction Roster

Following review of each application to determine that it is complete, the IDS Director will investigate the contents of the submission, contact references, and determine whether the attorney is qualified for appointment as post-conviction counsel in a capital case. The IDS Director shall thereafter create and maintain a roster of attorneys qualified for and willing to accept appointments as post-conviction counsel.

(e) Appeal to the IDS Commission

If the IDS Director determines that an attorney is not qualified for appointment as post-conviction counsel in a capital case or otherwise declines to place the attorney's name on the capital post-conviction roster, the attorney may make a written request for a review of the IDS Director's decision from a committee of the

IDS Commission designated by the IDS Commission to conduct such review.

[Subsection (e) amended effective February 10, 2006]

2C.3 (App.) Retention and Eligibility

(a) On–Going Training.

To remain eligible for appointment as counsel on an initial Motion for Appropriate Relief and any appeal therefrom, an attorney must attend and successfully complete capital training sessions as prescribed by the IDS Director, and consult regularly and frequently with the IDS Director with respect to each capital case to which the attorney is appointed.

(b) Removal from Post–Conviction Roster.

The IDS Director may remove from the roster of attorneys qualified for appointment as post-conviction counsel in a capital case any attorney who has ignored requirements for appointment as post-conviction counsel; has failed to continue to demonstrate that he or she has the required legal knowledge and skill necessary for representation as post-conviction counsel; or has failed to continue to demonstrate that he or she is willing to apply that knowledge and skill with appropriate thoroughness and preparation as post-conviction counsel. The IDS Director may also remove an attorney from the roster if, as part of a periodic review of the roster, the IDS Director determines that a smaller roster of attorneys will better serve the goals of ensuring the best possible representation of indigent capital defendants and of delivering quality services in the most efficient and cost-effective manner. If the IDS Director removes an attorney from the capital post-conviction roster, the attorney may make a written request for a review of the IDS Director's decision from a committee of the IDS Commission designated by the IDS Commission to conduct such review.

[Subsection (b) amended effective February 10, 2006 and May 29, 2015]

PART 3. RULES FOR PROVIDING LEGAL REPRESENTATION IN NON–CAPITAL CRIMINAL APPEALS AND NON–CRIMINAL APPEALS

This third part addresses the procedure to be followed when a person is entitled to appointed counsel on appeal to the Appellate Division from adverse decisions in the Trial Division in both non-capital criminal proceedings and non-criminal proceedings. The rules are authorized by the Indigent Defense Services Act of 2000 (IDS Act), S.L. 2000–144, Senate Bill 1323, and apply to cases pending on or after July 1, 2001. Fee applications for appellate representation filed on or after that date will be governed by these rules.

The rules supercede the provisions on appellate representation in Section D. of the Rules and Regulations of the North Carolina State Bar (State Bar Rules) and any provisions on appellate representation in local bar plans issued pursuant to the State Bar Rules. As of July 1, 2001, those rules, which were authorized by former G.S. 7A–459, are no longer effective.

Whenever the term "IDS Director" is used in these rules, it means the Director of the Office of Indigent Defense Services or his or her designee. Whenever the term "IDS Office" is used in these rules, it means the Office of Indigent Defense Services or its designee. Whenever the term "IDS Commission" is used in these rules, it means the Commission on Indigent Defense Services or its designee.

These rules may be changed by the IDS Commission pursuant to its authority.

Rule 3.1. Coverage of this Part

This part applies to cases in which an indigent person is entitled to appointed appellate counsel pursuant to G.S. 7A–498.3 on appeal of right or other review to the Appellate Division from an adverse ruling in the Trial Division, including a petition for writ of certiorari or other extraordinary writ that is filed before or after entry of final judgment in the Trial Division, other than a judgment imposing a sentence of death or a non-capital judgment joined with a judgment imposing a sentence of death.

[Section amended effective November 15, 2002 and February 27, 2009]

Authority: G.S. 7A–451(b); 7A–452; 7A–498.3(a)

Commentary

The bulk of the cases governed by this subsection will be indigent non-capital criminal appeals. However, G.S. 7A–451(a) identifies eighteen types of "actions and proceedings" in which persons are entitled to appointed counsel.

Where a right to appellate review of an adverse ruling is authorized by statute in any of these actions and proceedings, a person is entitled to appointed appellate counsel. Subsection (b) of G.S. 7A–451 reads in relevant part as follows:

(b) In each of the actions and proceedings enumerated in subsection (a) of this section, entitlement to the services of counsel begins as soon as feasible after the indigent is taken into custody or service is made upon him of the charge, petition, notice or other initiating process. Entitlement continues through any critical stage of the action or proceeding, including, if applicable: . . . (6) Review of any judgment or decree pursuant to G.S. 7A–27, 7A–30(1), 7A–30(2), and Subchapter XIV of Chapter 15A of the General Statutes.

Three of the four statutory references in subsection (6) are specific. G.S. 7A–30(1) and –30(2) extend a person's right to counsel to appeals of right from decisions of the North Carolina Court of Appeals to the Supreme Court of North

Carolina based either on a substantial constitutional question or on a dissent in the Court of Appeals. Subchapter XIV of Chapter 15A governs motions for appropriate relief and appeals of right from criminal convictions returned in the Trial Division, including appeals from superior court to the Appellate Division.

G.S. 7A–27, the fourth statutory reference in G.S. 7A–451(b), broadly concerns "appeals of right" from the Trial Division. Subsection (a) mandates that appeals in death cases go directly to the Supreme Court of North Carolina. Subsection (b) directs that appeals from "any final judgment of a superior court," other than those in death cases or those based on a guilty or no contest plea, go directly to the Court of Appeals, as do civil district court appeals and appeals from certain interlocutory orders in civil cases. Subsection (b) also states that appeals of right "[f]rom any other order or judgment of the superior court from which an appeal is authorized by statute" go to the Court of Appeals."

Rule 3.2. Appointment of Appellate Counsel

(a1) Provisional Appointment of the Office of the Appellate Defender to File a Petition for an Extraordinary Writ

In extraordinary circumstances and in the absence of a court appointment pursuant to paragraph 3.2(b) below, the Appellate Defender may appoint the Office of the Appellate Defender, or an attorney on the roster of counsel who are qualified and willing to accept appointment to represent persons in the Appellate Division, on a provisional basis to make a preliminary determination of the person's entitlement to appointed counsel in the Appellate Division, and to file a petition for an appropriate extraordinary writ in the Appellate Division.

(a2) Provisional Appointment of the Office of the Appellate Defender in Proceedings Under Subchapter I of Chapter 7B of the General Statutes

In the absence of a court appointment pursuant to paragraph 3.2(b) below, when the Appellate Defender is notified by trial counsel of an appealable ruling adverse to the respondent in an action brought under Subchapter I of Chapter 7B of the General Statutes, the Appellate Defender may appoint the Office of the Appellate Defender, or an attorney on the roster of counsel who are qualified and willing to accept appointment to represent persons in the Appellate Division, on a provisional basis to make a preliminary determination of the respondent's entitlement to appointed counsel in the Appellate Division, and to represent the respondent in contemplation of an appeal, or to consult with trial counsel and the respondent on the decision of whether to enter notice of appeal.

(b) Appointment of the Office of Appellate Defender by the Court

When a person enters notice of appeal or seeks to file a petition for writ of certiorari or other extraordinary writ in the Appellate Division in a case subject to this part and requests appointment of appellate counsel, the trial court shall make a determination of the person's indigency in accordance with Part 1, paragraph 1.4(b) of these rules. In its discretion, the court may rely on a previous determination of indigency. If the court determines that the person is indigent, the court shall appoint the Office of Appellate Defender to represent the person in the Appellate Division, except that, in cases subject to G.S. 122C–270(e) and 122C–289 where the appeal was filed before October 1, 2006, the district court shall appoint as appellate counsel of record the attorney who represented the person in district court. These rules, including provisions relating to standards and compensation, govern all other aspects of appointment of counsel appointed under the foregoing exception. If the Office of Appellate Defender is appointed to file a petition for an extraordinary writ, the Office of Appellate Defender or counsel appointed by the Appellate Defender pursuant to paragraph 3.2(d), below, shall file the petition only if it will present a potentially meritorious issue for review.

(c) Transmittal of Judgment and Forms

Following the appointment of the Office of Appellate Defender to represent a person in a case subject to this part, the clerk of superior court shall immediately send to the Office of Appellate Defender, by United States mail or by facsimile, a copy of the judgment or decree from which the appeal was taken, as well as any written appellate entries or rulings the court makes with respect to the appeal.

(d) Assignment of Counsel by the Appellate Defender

If the Appellate Defender determines that, to insure quality appellate representation, a person's appeal should not be assigned to the Office of Appellate Defender, the Appellate Defender shall assign the person's case to private counsel or a public defender or assistant public defender listed on the roster of qualified appellate counsel maintained by the Appellate Defender pursuant to paragraph 3.4 below and rules approved by the IDS Director. Such counsel is thereafter appellate counsel of record, subject to the limitations and conditions of appointment in paragraph 3.2(i), below.

(e) Conflicts

If the Office of Appellate Defender is appointed to represent a person whose case would create a conflict of interest with a current or previous client of the Office of Appellate Defender, the Appellate Defender shall immediately notify the IDS Director, and the IDS Director shall appoint counsel in the new case pursuant to the rules under which the Appellate Defender would appoint counsel. If the Appellate Defender is appointed to represent co-appellants, the Appellate Defender may appoint the Office of the Appellate Defender to represent a co-appellant and may appoint counsel for the remaining co-appellants so long as the Appellate Defender previously has not undertaken representation of a co-appellant.

(f) Notice of Assignment and Request for Record Following the Appellate Defender's decision to assign an appeal to other counsel, or following the IDS Director's assignment of counsel in case of a conflict, the assigning authority shall immediately notify assigned counsel of the appointment, and shall also notify the clerk of superior court, the court reporter(s) or other custodian(s) of the recorded proceedings, and the adverse parties of the name, address, and telephone number of assigned counsel. The Office of Appellate Defender shall transmit to assigned appellate counsel a copy of the documents forwarded to the Office of Appellate Defender by the clerk of superior court pursuant to paragraph 3.2(b) above, and shall request that the clerk transmit to assigned counsel the complete file maintained by the clerk in the case.

(g1) Litigation of Non–Capital Motions for Appropriate Relief Pending Direct Appeal and Assignment of Counsel by the Appellate Defender

Appellate counsel appointed pursuant to Part 3 of these rules who seeks to be compensated for preparing, filing, or litigating a non-capital Motion for Appropriate Relief ("MAR") pending direct appeal pursuant to G.S. 15A–1418 must obtain prior authorization from the Appellate Defender. If the Appellate Defender declines to authorize MAR litigation, appointed appellate counsel may seek authorization from the IDS Director. After consulting with appointed appellate counsel, the Appellate Defender or IDS Director may appoint one additional counsel to represent the appellant for purposes of preparing, filing, or litigating an MAR. If additional counsel is appointed to prepare, file, or litigate the MAR, that counsel must be on a roster of counsel in some North Carolina jurisdiction who are qualified to represent defendants at trial charged with the highest offense the appellant has appealed, or a higher offense. Compensation of counsel appointed under this subsection shall be governed by Rule 3.3. Appointment and compensation of experts and payment of other expenses related to MAR litigation authorized under this subsection shall be governed by Part 2D of these rules.

(g2) Evidentiary Hearings on Remand from the Appellate Courts Pending Direct Appeal and Assignment of Counsel by the Appellate Defender

After consulting with appointed appellate counsel, the Appellate Defender or IDS Director may appoint one additional lawyer to represent the appellant at an evidentiary hearing in the Trial Division on remand from the Appellate Division when the direct appeal is still pending. If additional counsel is appointed for that purpose in a criminal case, that counsel must be on a roster of counsel in some North Carolina jurisdiction who are qualified to represent indigent defendants in the Trial Division charged with the highest offense that is being remanded, or a higher offense. If additional counsel is appointed for that purpose in a case brought under Chapter 7B of the General Statutes, that counsel must be on a roster of counsel in some North Carolina jurisdiction who are qualified to represent indigent persons in the Trial Division in the applicable type of case. Compensation of counsel appointed under this subsection shall be governed by Rule 3.3. Appointment and compensation of experts and payment of other expenses related to litigation at the evidentiary hearing as authorized under this subsection shall be governed by Part 2D of these rules.

(h) Litigation of Motions to Modify Dispositional Orders Pending Direct Appeal in Juvenile Delinquency Cases and Assignment of Counsel by the Appellate Defender

Appellate counsel appointed to a juvenile delinquency case pursuant to Part 3 of these rules who seeks to be compensated for preparing, filing, or litigating a motion to modify a dispositional order pending direct appeal pursuant to G.S. 7B–2600 must obtain prior authorization from the Appellate Defender. If the Appellate Defender declines to authorize the litigation, appointed appellate counsel may seek authorization from the IDS Director. After consulting with appointed appellate counsel and the Juvenile Defender, the Appellate Defender or IDS Director may appoint one additional counsel to represent the appellant for purposes of preparing, filing, or litigating a motion to modify a dispositional order. If additional counsel is appointed to prepare, file, or litigate the motion, that counsel must be on a roster of counsel in some North Carolina jurisdiction who are qualified to represent juveniles in district court delinquency proceedings charged with the highest offense the appellant has appealed, or a higher offense. Compensation of counsel appointed under this subsection shall be governed by Rule 3.3. Appointment and compensation of experts and payment of other expenses related to the motion to modify the dispositional order authorized under this subsection shall be governed by Part 2D of these rules.

(i) Petitions for Certiorari, Oppositions to Petitions for Certiorari, and Representation in the Supreme Court of the United States

If appellate counsel appointed pursuant to Part 3 of these rules seeks to be compensated for any of the following, counsel must obtain prior written authorization from the Appellate Defender:

(i) preparing and filing a petition for certiorari seeking review of federal constitutional issues in the Supreme Court of the United States following an unfavorable final ruling in the North Carolina Appellate Division;

(ii) preparing and filing an opposition in response to a petition for certiorari review filed by the state in the Supreme Court of the United States following a favorable final ruling in the North Carolina Appellate Division; and

(iii) representation in the Supreme Court of the United States if certiorari is granted.

After consulting with appointed appellate counsel, as an alternative to authorizing appointed appellate counsel to undertake any of the above representation, the Appellate Defender may relieve appointed appellate counsel of this responsibility and undertake the representation directly or appoint another qualified appellate attorney from the list of lawyers eligible to represent non-capital defendants or respondents on appeal. The Appellate Defender also may appoint the Office of Appellate Defender or another qualified appellate attorney from the list of lawyers eligible to represent non-capital defendants or respondents on appeal as co-counsel with appointed appellate counsel. The appointed appellate counsel may seek review of the Appellate Defender's decision from the IDS Director. Compensation of counsel for work performed pursuant to this subsection shall be governed by Rule 3.3.

(j) Litigation of Motions Challenging Adjudicatory, Dispositional, or Other Final Orders Pending Direct Appeal in Abuse, Neglect, Dependency, or Termination of Parental Rights Cases and Assignment of Counsel by the Appellate Defender

Appellate counsel appointed to represent a respondent in an abuse, neglect, dependency, or termination of parental rights case pursuant to Part 3 of these rules who seeks to be compensated for preparing, filing, or litigating a motion in district court challenging an adjudicatory, dispositional, or other final order pending direct appeal must obtain prior authorization from the Appellate Defender. If the Appellate Defender declines to authorize the litigation, appointed appellate counsel may seek authorization from the IDS Director. After consulting with appointed appellate counsel, the Appellate Defender or IDS Director may appoint one additional counsel to represent the appellant for purposes of preparing, filing, or litigating such a motion. If additional counsel is appointed to prepare, file, or litigate the motion, that counsel must be on a roster of counsel in some North Carolina jurisdiction who are qualified to represent respondents in district court abuse, neglect, dependency, or termination of parental rights proceedings. Compensation of counsel appointed under this subsection shall be governed by Rule 3.3. Appointment and compensation of experts and payment of other expenses related to the motion authorized under this subsection shall be governed by Part 2D of these rules.

(k) Litigation of Motions Challenging Civil Contempt or Other Final Orders Pending Direct Appeal in Child Support Contempt Cases and Assignment of Counsel by the Appellate Defender.

Appellate counsel appointed to represent a defendant in a child support contempt case pursuant to Part 3 of these rules who seeks to be compensated for preparing, filing, or litigating a motion in district court challenging a finding of civil contempt or other final order pending direct appeal must obtain prior authorization from the Appellate Defender. If the Appellate Defender declines to authorize the litigation, appointed appellate counsel may seek authorization from the IDS Director. After consulting with appointed appellate counsel, the Appellate Defender or IDS Director may appoint one additional counsel to represent the appellant for purposes of preparing, filing, or litigating such a motion. If additional counsel is appointed to prepare, file, or litigate the motion, that counsel must be on a roster of counsel in some North Carolina jurisdiction who are qualified to represent defendants in child support contempt proceedings. Compensation of counsel appointed under this subsection shall be governed by Rule 3.3. Appointment and compensation of experts and payment of other expenses related to the motion authorized under this subsection shall be governed by Part 2D of these rules.

[New subsection (a1) adopted effective July 9, 2004]
[New subsection (a2) adopted effective February 10, 2006]
[Subsection (b) amended effective September 15, 2006, December 8, 2006, and February 27, 2009]
[Subsection (d) amended effective September 14, 2007]
[Subsection (e) amended effective January 18, 2002]
[New subsection (g1) adopted effective November 15, 2002]
[New subsection (g)(2) adopted effective November 4, 2005]
[New subsection (h) adopted effective July 8, 2005]
[New subsection (i) adopted effective September 14, 2007]
[New subsection (j) adopted effective September 19, 2008]
[New subsection (k) adopted effective December 7, 2012]

Authority: G.S. 7A–450(b); 7A–451(b)(6), (b)(8); 7A–452(a); 7A–498.3; 7A–498.5(d), (h); 7A–498.8(b)(1), (b)(6), (b)(6a)

Commentary

In all actions and proceedings in which courts previously appointed appellate counsel, the court shall appoint the Office of Appellate Defender.

Subsection (a1): This provision was added in July 2004 to authorize the Appellate Defender to provisionally appoint the Office of the Appellate Defender or a private appellate attorney in certain circumstances. The need for this authority has typically arisen in three types of cases: 1) cases in which the Appellate Defender believes that a trial court has erroneously denied indigency status after a person who the court previously determined was indigent entered notice of appeal, and that a petition for an extraordinary writ should be filed on the person's behalf; 2) cases in which a trial court has determined that a person is indigent but denied appointed appellate counsel, and the Appellate Defender believes that the person has a right to appointed appellate counsel and that a petition for an extraordinary writ should be filed on the person's behalf; and 3) cases in which the Appellate Defender is contacted by appointed trial counsel concerning the need for immediate review of a pre-trial ruling, and the Appellate Defender agrees that the ruling should be challenged in the appellate courts by means of a petition for an extraordinary writ.

Subsection (a2): This provision was added in February 2006 to authorize the Appellate Defender to provisionally appoint the Office of the Appellate Defender or a private appellate attorney on a provisional basis in proceedings brought under Subchapter I of Chapter 7B of the General Statutes. The need for this authority arose when the Supreme Court of North Carolina adopted Rule 3A of the North Carolina Rules of Appellate Procedure, which is designed to expedite appeals in abuse, neglect, or dependency and termination of parental rights cases. Effective October 1, 2009, Rule 3A was renamed Rule 3.1.

Subsection (b): This subsection was revised in September 2006 to conform with amendments to G.S. 122C–270 and 122C–289 in the 2005 Technical Corrections Act. *See* S.L. 2006–264. Previously, G.S. 122C–270 and 122C–289 provided that the attorney appointed to represent the respondent in district court was also responsible for perfecting and concluding any appeal. For all civil commitment appeals filed on or after October 1, 2006, S.L. 2006–264 directs that appellate counsel for the indigent respondent shall be appointed in accordance with rules adopted by the IDS Office. As with all other indigent appeals, this subsection was subsequently revised to provide that, for civil commitment appeals filed on or after October 1, 2006, the court shall appoint the Office of the Appellate Defender to represent the respondent. Civil commitment appeals filed before October 1, 2006 continue to be the responsibility of the attorney assigned at the initial district court hearing. This subsection was further revised in December 2006 to clarify that the trial court is the proper body to determine an appellant's indigency and appoint the Office of the Appellate Defender. The subsection was further revised in February 2009 to clarify that it addresses appointments to file petitions for extraordinary writs, as well as direct appeals of right.

Subsection (g1): This provision was added in November 2002 to authorize the Appellate Defender or IDS Director to appoint counsel to litigate a non-capital motion for appropriate relief pending direct appeal.

Subsection (g2): This provision was added in November 2005 to authorize the Appellate Defender or IDS Director to appoint counsel to litigate an evidentiary hearing in the Trial Division on remand from the Appellate Division when the direct appeal is still pending.

Subsection (h): This provision was added in July 2005 to authorize the Appellate Defender or IDS Director to appoint counsel to litigate a motion to modify a juvenile dispositional order in district court pending appeal. G.S. 7B–2600(b) gives the district court authority to reduce the nature or duration of an illegally imposed disposition order in a juvenile delinquency case.

Subsection (i): This new subsection was adopted effective September 14, 2007 to address petitions for certiorari and oppositions in response to petitions for certiorari in the Supreme Court of the United States in cases involving important issues of federal law, as well as the responsibility for representation in the Supreme Court of the United States if that Court grants certiorari review. The amendments reflect statutory revisions that were enacted during the 2007 legislative session, which, subject to the IDS Rules, extended the entitlement to counsel to review of certain judgments or decrees rendered on direct appeal by a court of the North Carolina Appellate Division. S.L. 2007–323, § 14.19(a). Before requesting authorization to seek certiorari review by the Supreme Court of the United States from a ruling of the North Carolina Court of Appeals, appointed appellate counsel must seek review of the federal constitutional issues in question by the Supreme Court of North Carolina in a petition for discretionary review or an appeal based on a dissent in the North Carolina Court of Appeals. The decision to authorize compensation will be in the Appellate Defender's discretion, subject to review by the IDS Director, based on the criteria set forth in G.S. 7A–451(b)(8).

Subsection (j): This provision was added in September 2008 to authorize the Appellate Defender or IDS Director to appoint counsel to litigate a motion in district court challenging an adjudicatory, dispositional, or other final order in an abuse, neglect, dependency, or termination of parental rights case pending appeal.

Subsection (k): This provision was added in December 2012 to authorize the Appellate Defender or IDS Director to appoint counsel to litigate a motion in district court challenging a finding of civil contempt or other final order in a child support contempt case pending appeal.

Rule 3.3. Compensation of Appellate Counsel

(a) Setting of Fee.

Assigned private appellate counsel of record shall be compensated in an amount determined by the IDS Director following consultation with the Appellate Defender, except that the IDS Director shall not consult with the Appellate Defender concerning the fee to be paid to counsel assigned by the IDS Director pursuant to paragraph 3.2(e) above. If counsel is required pursuant to paragraph 3.4(f)(iii) below to meet with the Appellate Defender to review the representation, the fee shall include compensation for time spent in that review.

(b) Fee Application.

After a person's appeal becomes final, assigned private counsel shall submit to the Appellate Defender, or to the IDS Director in a conflict case, an itemized fee application on a form prescribed by the Appellate Defender, showing the time counsel spent in appellate representation of the person. If an attorney seeks compensation for time spent working on multiple cases simultaneously, the attorney's time shall be prorated among each of the cases involved. Following review of the fee application, the Appellate Defender shall forward the application to the IDS Director with a recommendation concerning the amount to be paid. The IDS Director shall fix the fee to be paid and forward the award to IDS Financial Services for payment. Private counsel appointed to represent an indigent defendant or respondent on direct appeal may apply for and receive interim payments in the discretion of the IDS Director. For all cases finally disposed at the appellate level on or after July 1, 2005, final attorney fee applications must be signed by the appointed attorney and submitted to the Appellate Defender or IDS Director within no more than one year after the date on which the appeal was finally disposed. For all cases finally disposed at the appellate level before July 1, 2005, final attorney fee applications must be signed by the appointed attorney and submitted to the Appellate Defender or IDS Director by January 1, 2006. In accordance with policies and procedures approved by the IDS Commission, an attorney may apply to the IDS Director for one advance extension of the applicable deadline or for a waiver of the applicable deadline. Counsel may make a written request for a review of the amount of compensation approved by the IDS Director from a committee of the IDS Commission designated by the IDS Commission to conduct such review.

(c) Recoupment of Fees Generally.

To the extent required by law, persons who have been appointed counsel under this part shall continue to be responsible for repaying the fees paid to such counsel or, in the case of representation by a public defender or appellate defender office, the value of services rendered by counsel. After the IDS Director sets the fee to be paid or the value of services rendered, the IDS Director shall notify the person potentially responsible for paying the fees of the potential liability, and afford the person a reasonable opportunity to be heard on the issue. The trial judge or other appropriate judicial official shall then determine the amount to be recouped if recoupment is required by law.

(d) Recoupment for Contract Services.

For legal representation rendered by attorneys working under contract with the IDS Office, the value of services, and the procedures for entry of any appropriate orders or judgments, shall be determined in accordance with the terms of the contract if recoupment is required by law.

(e) Outside Compensation Prohibited.

Once counsel has been appointed to represent a person in a case subject to this part, counsel shall not accept any fees for the representation other than that awarded by the IDS Director. If a third party contributes funds to non-counsel services, counsel shall place the funds in trust and account to the third party and the IDS Director about the use of the funds.

[Subsection (a) amended effective May 6, 2005, August 13, 2007, and May 26, 2010]
[Subsection (b) amended effective May 29, 2015]
[Subsection (c) amended effective March 7, 2008]
[New subsection (e) adopted effective November 12, 2004. Subsection (e) amended effective September 15, 2006]

Authority: G.S. 7A–450.1 through –450.4;7A–452(b); 7A–455; 7A–458; 7A–498.1(4), (5); 7A–498.3(c), (d); 7A–498.5(c)(8), (f); 7A–498.8(b)

Commentary

Subsection (b): The Appellate Defender will make available to counsel a form approved by the Appellate Defender (AOC–CR–426) to document fee and expense applications. Subsection (b) was amended effective May 6, 2005 to clarify that attorneys can not double-bill the state for time spent working on multiple cases simultaneously. For all cases finally disposed at the appellate level on or after July 1, 2005, the subsection was also amended to require attorneys to submit fee applications to the Appellate Defender or IDS Director within one year of the date of final disposition. Effective August 13, 2007, the subsection was amended to allow attorneys to apply for an advance extension or waiver of the deadline in accordance with policies and procedures approved by the IDS Commission. Attorney fee applications submitted more than one year after the date of final disposition without an approved extension or waiver will not be paid from state funds.

Subsection (c): In appellate cases, recoupment of the cost of court-appointed counsel is governed by G.S. 7A–455. The IDS Act made only one change to that statute. It required that the value of services reflected in a judgment against a defendant be set in accordance with rules adopted by the IDS Office. Since Rules 3.3(a) and (b) authorize the IDS Director to set fees for appellate counsel, this rule requires the IDS Director to notify the person potentially responsible for paying the fees of the potential liability and afford the person a reasonable opportunity to be heard on the issue, before the trial judge sets the amount of any judgment. The subsection was amended effective March 7, 2008 to clarify that judgments for attorney fees can be ordered by the trial judge or another appropriate judicial official. The Public Defender and Appellate Defender are obligated to inform the IDS Director of the value of legal services rendered to a defendant. The form judgment is a new form (AOC–CR–426) that is similar to the form previously used by the AOC.

Subsection (e): Subsection (e) was amended effective September 15, 2006 to clarify that, to avoid any potential for overreaching or the appearance of impropriety, an appointed attorney cannot subsequently accept fees as retained counsel from the client or the client's family. If family or friends of an indigent client want to contribute to non-counsel services, such as expert or support services, nothing in this subsection precludes them from doing so. However, the appointed attorney must place any such funds in his or her trust account and provide an accounting to the contributing family member and the IDS Director. If, during the course of representation as appointed counsel, an attorney learns that a client who was previously determined to be indigent has become financially able to pay for the representation, G.S. 7A–450(d) directs the attorney to inform the court. *But cf.* RPC 52 (Jan. 13, 1989) (directing counsel to "call upon his client to reveal that circumstance to the tribunal" and, if the client refuses to permit disclosure, to move to withdraw). If the court finds that the client is no longer indigent, the appointed attorney may move to withdraw or continue the representation *pro bono*.

Rule 3.4. Standards for Appellate Counsel

(a) Maintenance of Roster

The Appellate Defender shall maintain a roster of attorneys who are qualified and willing to accept appointment by the Appellate Defender or IDS Director to represent persons in the Appellate Division pursuant to these rules.

(b) Qualifications

To be eligible for appointment to represent persons in the Appellate Division, an attorney must demonstrate that he or she is proficient in legal writing and oral advocacy, has the required legal knowledge and skill necessary for appellate representation, and will apply that knowledge and skill with appropriate thoroughness and preparation.

(c) Submission of Application

An attorney who desires to be on the roster of qualified appellate counsel shall submit to the Appellate Defender an application on a form prescribed by the Appellate Defender, accompanied by the following materials:

(i) a complete resume of the applicant's educational and legal experience;

(ii) four samples of the applicant's legal writing, which may include pleadings, memoranda of law, or appellate briefs;

(iii) three letters of recommendation from attorneys licensed in North Carolina for five or more years, or from professors of law familiar with the applicant's legal writing and oral advocacy skills;

(iv) unless the applicant is currently serving as the Appellate Defender or an Assistant Appellate Defender, a listing of three cases in which the applicant represented an appellant to judgment in the Appellate Division; and

(v) any additional materials that may assist the Appellate Defender in evaluating the applicant's appellate qualifications and experience.

(d) Waiver

If an attorney cannot supply one or more of the submissions set forth in paragraph (c), the Appellate Defender, upon demonstration that the attorney has the required legal knowledge and skill necessary for representation as appellate counsel, and will apply that knowledge and skill with appropriate thoroughness and preparation, may either waive such submission(s) or defer such submission(s) for a reasonable time and in the interim place the attorney on the roster of qualified appellate counsel.

(e) Review of Application and Creation of Appellate Roster

Following receipt of the application to be on the roster of qualified appellate counsel, the Appellate Defender shall consider the submitted materials, conduct such investigation as is appropriate, and determine whether the attorney is qualified for appointment as appellate counsel in a non-capital criminal or non-criminal case. The Appellate Defender shall notify the applicant in writing whether he or she will be placed on the roster of qualified appellate counsel. If the Appellate Defender determines that an attorney is not qualified for appointment as appellate counsel in a non-capital criminal or non-criminal case or otherwise declines to place the attorney's name on the appellate roster, the attorney may make a written request for a review of the Appellate Defender's decision from a committee of the IDS Commission designated by the IDS Commission to conduct such review.

(f) Conditions of Appointment

The Appellate Defender or IDS Director may set additional conditions of appointment, including requiring attorneys appointed under this subpart to:

(i) consult with the Appellate Defender or his or her designee during the pendency of the representation in the Appellate Division or in the Supreme Court of the United States as provided by paragraph 3.2(i), above, participate in practice oral arguments, and submit briefs for pre-filing review, as required by the Appellate Defender;

(ii) promptly notify the Appellate Defender by mail, facsimile, or email upon the filing of each brief or substantive motion or memorandum in the case, include in the notification a copy of the Questions Presented in each brief, and upon request by the Appellate Defender, transmit to the Appellate Defender a copy of the entire brief, motion, or memorandum, or portions thereof; and

(iii) meet with the Appellate Defender or his or her designee following an appellate decision and prior to final payment of counsel fees to review the course of the representation.

(g) Retention of Eligibility

To remain eligible for appointment as counsel in a non-capital criminal or noncriminal appeal, an attorney must attend and successfully complete any training sessions prescribed by the Appellate Defender.

[Subsection (e) amended effective February 10, 2006]

[Subsection (f) amended effective September 14, 2007]

Authority: G.S. 7A–450(b); 7A–451(b)(8); 7A–498.1(1), (2); 7A–498.5(c)(2), (c)(4), (h); 7A–498.6(b)(8); 7A–498.8(b)(3), (b)(4), (b)(6a)

Commentary

Subsection (f): Based on statutory revisions that were enacted during the 2007 legislative session, which extended the entitlement to counsel to review of certain judgments or decrees rendered on direct appeal by a court of the North Carolina Appellate Division, see S.L. 2007–323, § 14. 19(a), this subsection was amended effective September 14, 2007 to clarify that the Appellate Defender may set additional conditions of appointment for representation in the Supreme Court of the United States, including requiring consultations, reviews of draft petitions and briefs, and practice oral arguments.

Rule 3.5. Substitution of Counsel

For good cause, the Appellate Defender or IDS Director may request *ex parte* that a judge of a court of competent jurisdiction replace appellate counsel previously appointed with new counsel selected by the Appellate Defender or IDS Director.

Authority: G.S. 7A–498.1(1), (2); 7A–498.5(c)(4), (h); 7A–498.6(b)(8); 7A–498.8(b)

Commentary

This rule permits the Appellate Defender or IDS Director to request *ex parte* that a judge remove an attorney previously appointed. It would be impossible to note all the circumstances that reasonably might cause the Appellate Defender or IDS Director to make such a request. Such circumstances might not in themselves constitute ineffective assistance of counsel. *See State v. Sweezy,* 291 N.C. 366, 371–72, 230 S.E.2d 524 (1976); *see also State v. Kuplin*, 316 N.C. 387, 396, 343 S.E.2d 793 (1986) ("Each case must be examined on an individual basis. In the absence of a constitutional violation, the decision about whether appointed counsel shall be replaced is a matter solely for the discretion of the trial court."). Reasonable tactical disagreements between the Appellate Defender and appointed counsel, or between the IDS Director and appointed counsel, will not constitute grounds for the Appellate Defender or IDS Director to request substitution of counsel. If the judge determines that the attorney is rendering ineffective assistance of counsel or that the attorney has an impermissible conflict of interest, substitution is required as a matter of law. *See State v. Moorman*, 320 N.C. 387, 358 S.E.2d 502 (1987); *State v. James*, 111 N.C. App. 785, 433 S.E.2d 755 (1993).

Rule 3.6. Removal from Roster

Following consultation with the IDS Director, the Appellate Defender may remove from the roster of attorneys qualified for appointment as appellate counsel any attorney who has ignored requirements for appointment as appellate counsel; has failed to continue to demonstrate that he or she has the required legal knowledge and skill necessary for representation as appellate counsel; or has failed to continue to demonstrate that he or she is willing to apply that knowledge and skill with appropriate thoroughness and preparation as appellate counsel. Following consultation with the IDS Director, the Appellate Defender may also remove an attorney from the roster if, as part of a periodic review of the roster, the Appellate Defender determines that a smaller roster of attorneys will better serve the goals of ensuring the best possible appellate representation of indigent persons and of delivering quality services in the most efficient and cost-effective manner. If the Appellate Defender removes an attorney from the appellate roster, the attorney may make a written request for a review of the Appellate Defender's decision from a committee of the IDS Commission designated by the IDS Commission to conduct such review.

[Section amended effective February 10, 2006 and May 29, 2015]

Authority: G.S. 7A–498.1(1), (2); 7A–498.5(c)(4), (h); 7A–498.8(b)

Rule 3.7. Authority to Implement other Programs, Plans, and Contracts

Nothing in these rules shall prohibit assignment of otherwise qualified counsel to represent indigent defendants and respondents on appeal pursuant to programs, plans, or contracts that may be implemented from time to time to improve quality, efficiency, and economy where such programs, plans, or contracts are approved by the IDS Director.

[Section amended effective May 29, 2015.]

Authority: G.S. 7A–498.1; 7A–498.3(a), (c); 7A–498.5(c), (d), (f)

PART 4. RULES FOR PROVIDING LEGAL ASSISTANCE AND ACCESS TO THE COURTS TO INMATES IN THE CUSTODY OF THE DIVISION OF ADULT CORRECTION

The IDS Office is responsible for establishing, supervising, and maintaining a system for providing inmates in the custody of the Division of Adult Correction with legal assistance and access to the courts. This fourth part addresses the procedure to be followed in such cases. The rules are authorized by § 14.9(a) of S.L. 2005–276, Senate Bill 622, and by Chapters 7A and 15A of the North Carolina General Statutes (G.S.), and apply to cases pending on or after March 15, 2010.

Whenever the term "IDS Director" is used in these rules, it means the Director of the Office of Indigent Defense Services or his or her designee. Whenever the term "IDS Office" is used in these rules, it means the Office of Indigent Defense Services or its designee. Whenever the term "IDS Commission" is used in these rules, it means the Commission on Indigent Defense Services or its designee.

These rules may be changed by the IDS Commission pursuant to its authority. All references to the "Department of Correction" in prior versions of these rules were changed to the "Division of Adult Correction" effective June 13, 2014.

[Amended effective June 13, 2014.]

Rule 4.1. Coverage and Definitions

(1) This part applies to cases in which the State is obligated to provide legal assistance and access to the courts to inmates in the custody of the Division of Adult Correction pursuant to G.S. 7A–498.3(a)(2a). This part does not apply to cases in which a court has appointed counsel pursuant to G.S. 7A–451(a)(3) and G.S. 15A–1421 and the applicable case law to investigate, and, if appropriate, prepare, file, and litigate a non-capital motion for appropriate relief or other non-capital post-conviction motion in state court on behalf

of a defendant, regardless of whether the defendant is in the custody of the Division of Adult Correction. Cases in which the court has appointed counsel to represent a defendant in non-capital post-conviction are governed by Part 1 of these rules.

(2) This part does not apply to capital post-conviction cases, as defined in Part 2 of these rules.

[Adopted effective March 15, 2010. Amended effective June 13, 2014.]

Authority: G.S. 7A–498.3; *Bounds v. Smith,* 430 U.S. 817 (1977); *Lewis v. Casey,* 518 U.S. 343 (1996)

Rule 4.2. Entitlement to Counsel

There is no requirement that the court determine indigency or entitlement to counsel or that counsel be appointed as provided in G.S. 7A–452 in cases subject to this part. If an inmate is released during the pendency of litigation subject to this part, which arose during confinement and is not mooted by release, representation shall continue in accordance with Rules 4.3 and 4.4 of these rules.

[Adopted effective March 15, 2010.]

Authority: G.S. 7A–498.3(a)(2a), (b)

Rule 4.3. Case Screening, Investigation, and Appointment Procedures

(a) Principal Contract

The IDS Office is authorized to enter into contracts with North Carolina Prisoner Legal Services, Inc. (NCPLS) or other similar entity to provide legal assistance and access to the courts to inmates in the custody of the Division of Adult Correction. Any contracts for legal assistance and access to the courts for inmates must be approved by the IDS Director. All requests for representation by inmates in the custody of the Division of Adult Correction shall initially be made to NCPLS or other similar entity. If NCPLS or other similar entity accepts representation pursuant to the contract, NCPLS or other similar entity shall continue to represent the inmate in accordance with the terms of the contract, except as otherwise provided herein. With respect to non-capital post-conviction claims filed in state district or superior court, if the court grants an evidentiary hearing, NCPLS or other similar entity may continue the representation at the evidentiary hearing or ask the IDS Director to appoint qualified local counsel to continue the representation at the evidentiary hearing. Compensation for services rendered at the evidentiary hearing or pursuant to an appointment by the IDS Director shall be governed by Rule 4.5(b) of these rules.

(b) Conflicts of Interest

In cases in which NCPLS or other similar entity with which the IDS Office has entered into a contract pursuant to subsection (a) of this rule has a conflict of interest and cannot represent an inmate in state court post-conviction, the IDS Office is authorized to enter into additional contracts with organizations or individual attorneys or to appoint counsel to perform case screening and investigation, and, if appropriate, to prepare and file a motion for appropriate relief or other post-conviction motion in state court on behalf of the inmate. Any contracts or appointments in conflict cases must be approved by the IDS Director. If the court grants an evidentiary hearing, contract or appointed counsel may continue the representation at the evidentiary hearing or ask the IDS Director to appoint qualified local counsel to continue the representation at the evidentiary hearing. Compensation for services rendered at the evidentiary hearing or pursuant to an appointment by the IDS Director shall be governed by Rule 4.5(b) of these rules.

[Adopted effective March 15, 2010. Subsection (a) amended effective June 13, 2014; December 5, 2014.]

Authority: G.S. 7A–498.2(b); 7A–498.3(a)(2a), (c), (d); 7A–498.5(c), (d)

Commentary

Subsection (a): Subsection (a) was amended effective December 5, 2014 to clarify that it applies to non-capital post-conviction claims filed in state district court where the court grants an evidentiary hearing.

Rule 4.4. Scope of Services

(a) Scope of Obligation

(1) Unless otherwise provided by law or herein, the scope of services to be provided by NCPLS or an organization or attorney under contract with the IDS Office or appointed by the IDS Director shall be governed by the terms of the contract or appointment. Counsel appointed by the IDS Director to represent an inmate at an evidentiary hearing shall continue with the representation until the action is resolved in state district or superior court, unless the inmate is released during the pendency of the post-conviction litigation and the issue is mooted by release or unless otherwise provided by law. If NCPLS or other similar entity that is representing an inmate pursuant to Rule 4.3(a) of these rules believes that a petition for writ of certiorari to the Appellate Division or a federal habeas petition is warranted, the filing of those petitions shall be governed by the terms of the contract. If an attorney who has contracted with the IDS Office or been appointed by the IDS Director to represent an inmate pursuant to Rule 4.3(b) of these rules believes that a petition for writ of certiorari to the Appellate Division is warranted, the attorney shall petition the court to appoint the Office of the Appellate Defender for that purpose and shall send a copy of the request for appointment to the Office of the Appellate Defender. An attorney who has contracted with the IDS Office or been appointed by the IDS

Director to represent an inmate pursuant to Rule 4.3(b) of these rules shall not be compensated under Rule 4.5 of these rules for filing a federal habeas petition without the advance written approval of the IDS Director.

(2) Nothing in these rules shall be construed as permitting or requiring an attorney of record to deviate from applicable laws of this State, the Rules of Professional Conduct administered by the North Carolina State Bar, or other legal or ethical obligations of an attorney as an officer of the court.

(b) Withdrawal

If an attorney is under contract with the IDS Office or has been appointed by the IDS Director to represent an inmate at an evidentiary hearing, a judge of a court of competent jurisdiction may, upon application of the attorney and for good cause shown, permit the attorney to withdraw from the case. If the judge allows the attorney to withdraw, appointment of new counsel shall be in accordance with Rule 4.3 of these rules.

[Adopted effective March 15, 2010. Subsection (a)(1) amended effective June 13, 2014. Subsection (a) amended effective December 5, 2014.]

Authority: G.S. 7A–498.3(a)(2a); 7A–498.5(c), (d); 15A–143; 15A–144

Commentary

Subsection (a): Subsection (a) was amended effective December 5, 2014 to provide that counsel appointed by the IDS Director to represent an inmate at an evidentiary hearing generally shall continue with the representation until the action is resolved in state district or superior court.

Rule 4.5. Compensation of Counsel

(a) Compensation of Contract Counsel

Compensation of counsel who represents an inmate pursuant to a contract authorized by Rule 4.3 of these rules shall be governed by the terms of the contract. If NCPLS or other similar entity under contract with IDS continues the representation of an inmate at an evidentiary hearing, in addition to the compensation provided pursuant to the contract, NCPLS or other similar entity may request attorney fees for work performed after the date of the court order granting the evidentiary hearing and during the pendency of the proceeding in state district or superior court, in the manner provided in subsection (b), below.

(b) Compensation of Appointed Counsel

(1) Upon completion of the representation, counsel who represented an inmate pursuant to an appointment authorized by Rule 4.3 of these rules shall submit to the IDS Director an itemized fee application on a form prescribed by the IDS Director, showing the time counsel spent in representation of the inmate. Counsel also may apply for and receive interim payments in the discretion of the IDS Director. Following review of the fee application, the IDS Director shall determine the amount of compensation based on the hourly rate established by Rule 1.9(a) of these rules. In doing so, the IDS Director shall review the amount of time claimed by the attorney, and shall approve an appropriate amount of time based on the factors normally considered in fixing attorneys' fees, such as the nature of the case, and the effort and responsibility involved.

(2) For all cases subject to this part that are finally disposed in district or superior court on or after March 15, 2010, final attorney fee applications must be signed by the appointed attorney and submitted to the IDS Director within no more than one year after the date on which the proceedings were finally disposed in district or superior court. In accordance with policies and procedures approved by the IDS Commission, an attorney may apply to the IDS Director for one advance extension of the applicable deadline or for a waiver of the applicable deadline.

(3) Counsel may make a written request for a review of the amount of compensation determined by the IDS Director from a subcommittee of the IDS Commission designated by the IDS Commission to conduct such review.

[Adopted effective March 15, 2010. Subsection (a) amended effective December 5, 2014. Subsection (b)(2) amended effective December 5, 2014.]

Authority: G.S. 7A–498.3; 7A–498.5(c), (d), (f)

Commentary

Subsection (a): Subsection (a) was amended effective December 5, 2014 to clarify that NCPLS or other similar entity may request attorney fees for work performed after the date of a court order granting an evidentiary hearing and during the pendency of the proceeding in state district or superior court.

Subsection (b): Subsection (b)(2) was amended effective December 5, 2014 to clarify that the one-year deadline for submission of fee applications applies to cases finally disposed in district court, as well as cases finally disposed in superior court.

Rule 4.6. Experts and Supporting Services

(a) Initial Application to IDS Office

(1) Counsel providing representation in a case subject to this part, including a case in which NCPLS or other similar entity continues the representation at an evidentiary hearing pursuant to Rule 4.3(a) of these rules, must make application to the IDS Director for authorization to retain experts or for other substantial expenses necessary to the representation of an inmate before applying to a court for such authorization and before incurring a financial obligation for which defense counsel will apply to the IDS Director for payment by the IDS Office. The application shall be in writing, unless exceptional or extraordinary circumstances necessitate an oral motion. Defense counsel

will be required to make at least as specific an application to retain experts as would be required by a fair but exacting trial judge applying G.S. 7A-450(a) and *Ake v. Oklahoma* and its progeny. The IDS Director may require counsel to make a more particularized application before approving or disapproving the application.

(2) The IDS Director shall maintain the application in a confidential file open only to the IDS Office and the defense team.

(3) If the IDS Director disapproves the application, timely written notice of disapproval of the application will be delivered to counsel. The IDS Director shall maintain the notice of disapproval in a confidential file open only to the IDS Office and the defense team.

(b) Application to Court

Counsel providing representation in a case subject to this part may apply to a court for appointment of experts or for other expenses following disapproval by the IDS Director, but counsel may not submit an application to a court that includes information not contained in the application made to the IDS Director unless exceptional or extraordinary circumstances necessitate submitting such new or additional information directly to a court. If counsel makes application to a court following the IDS Director's disapproval, counsel shall submit with its application to the court a complete copy of the IDS Director's written notice of disapproval and a complete copy of the written application made to the IDS Director. Counsel must immediately forward to the IDS Director a complete copy of any court order approving funds previously disapproved by the IDS Director and a complete copy of the application made to the court. Such court order and application shall be maintained in a confidential file open only to the IDS Office and the defense team.

[Adopted eff. March 15, 2010. Subsection (a)(1) amended effective June 13, 2014.]

Authority: G.S. 7A-450(b); 7A-454; 7A-498.1(1); 7A-498.3(a), (c), (d); 7A-498.5(c)(6), (f)

Commentary

Subsection (a): Routine expenses, such as typical long-distance telephone calls, are not substantial expenses within the meaning of this rule. Counsel can resolve any question about whether an expense requires prior approval of the IDS Director through advance written communication with the IDS Director.

Subsection (a)(1) was amended effective June 13, 2014 to clarify that requests for experts and other substantial expenses should be directed to the IDS Director if NCPLS or other similar entity accepts representation in a case pursuant to the principal contract with IDS and continues the representation at an evidentiary hearing pursuant to Rule 4.3(a) of these rules. Requests for experts and other substantial expenses should be directed to the court if NCPLS or other similar entity is appointed by the court outside of that principal contract.

Subsection (b): If, after denial of an initial application to the IDS Director for appointment or compensation of experts or other supporting services, counsel discovers new or additional information that is relevant to such application, counsel ordinarily should submit a new application to the IDS Director before submitting an application to a court. Counsel may submit to a court an application that contains new or additional information only in exceptional or extraordinary circumstances.

Rule 4.7. Authority to Implement Other Programs, Plans, and Contracts

Nothing in these rules shall prohibit assignment of otherwise qualified counsel to provide legal assistance and access to the courts to inmates in the custody of the Division of Adult Correction pursuant to programs, plans, or contracts that may be implemented from time to time to improve quality, efficiency, and economy where such programs, plans, or contracts are approved by the IDS Director.

[Adopted effective March 15, 2010. Amended effective June 13, 2014.]

Authority: G.S. 7A-454; 7A-498.1; 7A-498.3; 7A-498.5(c), (d), (f)

PERFORMANCE GUIDELINES FOR ATTORNEYS REPRESENTING INDIGENT PARENT RESPONDENTS IN ABUSE, NEGLECT, DEPENDENCY AND TERMINATION OF PARENTAL RIGHTS PROCEEDINGS AT THE TRIAL LEVEL

Adopted December 14, 2007

Preface

The primary goal of the IDS Commission is to ensure that indigent persons in North Carolina who are entitled to counsel at state expense are afforded high quality legal representation. *See* G.S. 7A-498.1(2). To further that goal, the Indigent Defense Services Act of 2000 directs the Commission to establish "[s]tandards for the performance of public defenders and appointed counsel." G.S. 7A-498.5(c)(4).

The initial draft of these performance guidelines was based on a review of standards and guidelines that have been adopted in several other jurisdictions—including California, Maryland, Oregon, South Carolina, and the District of Columbia—as well as resources published by the American Bar Association, the National Council of Juvenile and Family Court Judges, and Texas Lawyers for Children. For several months, a Parent Attorney Performance Guidelines Committee reviewed drafts of these guidelines and revised them to fit the nuances of North Carolina law and practice. Once a final proposed draft was complete, it was distributed to all private appointed counsel and assistant public defenders who handle abuse, neglect, dependency, and termination of parental rights cases, as well as all district court judges and representatives of the Department of Social Services and the state Guardian ad Litem program, for their comments and feedback. Based on the comments that were received, the Committee made a number of improvements to the guidelines. The full IDS Commission then adopted the attached performance guidelines on December 14, 2007.

These performance guidelines cover all indigent abuse, neglect, dependency, and termination of parental rights cases in North Carolina district court. The guidelines are intended to identify issues that may arise at each stage of the proceedings and to recommend effective approaches to resolving those issues. These guidelines do not replace or supersede statutes, case law, ethical rules or responsibilities, local rules, or the parent attorney's best tool of all, his or her judgment about what course of action is best in any given situation. These guidelines are intended to be a fluid document, subject to changes in the law and the practical experiences of the attorneys who use them. Because all provisions will not be applicable in all cases, the guidelines direct counsel to use his or her best professional judgment in determining what steps to undertake in specific cases. The Commission hopes these guidelines will be useful as a training tool and resource for new and experienced parent attorneys, as well as a tool for potential systemic reform in some areas. The guidelines are not intended to serve as a benchmark for ineffective assistance of counsel claims or attorney disciplinary proceedings.

The IDS Commission believes that providing high quality representation of parents who are facing the possible loss of their children is a difficult and challenging endeavor, which requires great skill and dedication. That skill and dedication is demonstrated by parent attorneys across North Carolina on a daily basis, and the Commission commends those counsel. The Commission recognizes that the goals embodied in these guidelines will not be attainable without sufficient funding and resources, and hopes the North Carolina General Assembly will continue its support of both quality indigent defense services and appropriate community services for parents to help keep children with their families whenever possible.

The IDS Commission thanks all of the attorneys who zealously represent indigent parents across the state. In addition, the Commission thanks everyone who worked on the drafting of these performance guidelines and who offered comments. The Commission plans to review and revise the guidelines on a regular basis to ensure that they continue to comply with North Carolina law and reflect quality performance, and invites ongoing feedback from the parents bar and juvenile court community.

Overview of North Carolina Juvenile Court for New Parent Attorneys

Before representing a respondent parent in an abuse, neglect, dependency, or termination of parental rights proceeding, counsel should become familiar with the relevant juvenile court laws, procedures, timelines, and actors in North Carolina. The following brief overview of some of the laws, procedures, timelines, and actors is intended to aid new parent attorneys in acquiring some basic familiarity. It is not intended to be a substitute for reading and researching the applicable statutes, case law, and local rules.

1. General Provisions

(a) Juvenile Court hosts two primary categories of juvenile cases:

(1) Abuse, neglect, dependency, and termination of parental rights matters, in which counsel is appointed to represent the indigent parent(s); and

(2) Juvenile delinquency and undisciplined matters, in which counsel is appointed to represent a juvenile who is alleged to be delinquent or in contempt of a court order finding the juvenile to be undisciplined.

These performance guidelines address abuse, neglect, dependency, and termination of parental rights proceedings, not delinquency or undisciplined contempt proceedings.

(b) The identity and roles of the major participants in abuse, neglect, dependency, and termination of parental rights actions include:

(1) The judge hears the case and renders decisions. The judge may hear only juvenile actions in larger counties or districts, or may appear in juvenile court only when assigned in smaller counties. More populous judicial districts and all Family Court districts follow the "one case, one judge" model, whereby a judge is assigned to hear all aspects of a case after it is filed. In other counties, judges rotate their assignments and many judges may hear different phases of a case.

(2) The parent attorney represents a respondent parent. When more than one parent is a party to the case, each parent should have separate counsel,

even when their interests appear to be consistent with one another.

(3) The Department of Social Services ("DSS") attorney represents and advocates for the position of the county DSS Director and his or her agents. The burden of proof is on DSS in abuse, neglect, and dependency cases, and in termination of parental rights actions initiated by DSS, and the DSS attorney presents evidence to meet this burden. The DSS attorney may be a county attorney, work for DSS as a full-time staff attorney, or be in private practice and work for DSS on a contract basis.

(4) The social worker is the agent of the DSS Director. The social worker works with the parent unless DSS has been relieved of reunification efforts by the court, directs the child's care if the child is in custody, helps prepare court reports, and testifies when needed.

(5) The guardian ad litem ("GAL") and GAL attorney advocate represent the best interests of the child. The GAL is typically an unpaid trained volunteer, and the GAL attorney advocate is an attorney paid by the state GAL program to represent and advocate for the position of the GAL. Each judicial district has a GAL supervisor who assists the volunteers in completing written court reports and may appear in court.

(6) The juvenile clerk of court is the person from the Office of the Clerk of Superior Court who is assigned to the courtroom. The juvenile clerk maintains the confidential court file, issues summonses and assigns provisional counsel when a petition is filed, issues notices of hearing dates to the parties as required by law, maintains custody of the exhibits introduced in any hearing, and ensures that a digital or audiotape record of the proceedings is made for appellate review purposes. The juvenile clerk may also complete and obtain necessary signatures on the request for transcript and appellate entries forms when a trial order is appealed, and may assist with having a writ issued to bring an incarcerated client in for court.

(c) A case plan is a written document between DSS and the respondent parent setting forth the services to be delivered to the parent, the tasks each party must undertake, and the objectives or goals to be met by each party. Case plans set deadlines for these activities and are typically revised, renewed, or updated every 90 days.

(d) Throughout an abuse, neglect, or dependency proceeding, DSS is required by statute to make reasonable efforts to prevent the removal of the child from the home or to return the child to the home, and has a duty to continue reunification efforts unless and until relieved of that duty by the court. DSS can be relieved of reasonable efforts under the circumstances set forth in G.S. 7B–507(b), including when such efforts clearly are futile or inconsistent with the juvenile's health or safety, when any of the aggravated circumstances defined by G.S. 7B–101(2) exist, when the parent's rights to another child have been involuntarily terminated, or when the parent has committed certain violent crimes against another child of the parent. Because concurrent planning is permitted by the Juvenile Code, DSS may simultaneously pursue efforts toward reunification and another permanent plan, such as guardianship or adoption.

(e) Abuse, neglect, dependency, and termination of parental rights actions are civil proceedings, and the Rules of Civil Procedure apply unless a different procedure is provided by the Juvenile Code or case law. The Rules of Evidence apply at some, but not all, of the hearings in these proceedings.

(f) In some counties, the judge calls the calendar, while in other counties, the DSS attorney calls the cases. New parent attorneys should understand the procedure followed locally to ensure that counsel, the client, and any defense witnesses appear in court at the correct date and time.

2. Pre–Adjudication Proceedings

(a) An abuse, neglect, or dependency matter is initiated in court by the filing of a petition and issuance of a summons. If DSS determines that immediate removal of the child from the home is necessary, a social worker or law enforcement officer may take the child into temporary custody without a court order and prior to the filing of the petition, but must release the child within 12 hours (or 24 hours on a weekend or holiday) unless DSS files a petition and obtains a nonsecure custody order from the court within that time in accordance with G.S. 7B–502 through G.S. 7B–504.

(b) When DSS files an abuse, neglect, or dependency petition, the clerk is required to appoint provisional counsel for each respondent parent. While local practice may vary, provisional counsel typically is the attorney for the parent pending the parent appearing, applying for court-appointed counsel, and being found to be indigent. If the court finds the parent indigent when he or she first appears, the same attorney usually will be appointed as counsel of record. While the Juvenile Code states that the court shall dismiss provisional counsel if the parent does not appear at the initial hearing, local practice may vary as to counsel's obligations if the parent client fails to appear. New parent attorneys should become familiar with local practices so they understand the scope and extent of provisional appointments.

(c) If the child is placed in nonsecure custody after DSS files an abuse, neglect, or dependency petition, "day-one" or pre-hearing conferences are scheduled in some districts before the initial nonsecure custody hearing. These are informal meetings, usually without the judge, to explain the proceedings and resolve as much as possible about the child's placement pending the adjudicatory hearing. These conferences may be combined with the initial nonsecure hearing or that hearing may occur on a different date.

(d) The purpose of nonsecure custody hearings is to determine whether the child should remain in DSS custody pending the adjudicatory hearing and, if so, to ensure that the child is in the most appropriate placement. If the child is in nonsecure custody, an initial hearing on the need for him or her to remain in custody must be held within seven calendar days after the child was taken into custody, unless the respondent parent and other parties consent to a continuance for up to 10 business days. If the court orders that a juvenile remain in nonsecure custody, unless waived by the respondent parent, the second nonsecure custody hearing must be held within seven business days after the initial hearing, and subsequent nonsecure custody hearings must be held at least every 30 calendar days thereafter until the adjudicatory hearing.

(e) The standard of proof at a nonsecure custody hearing is clear and convincing evidence that the juvenile's placement in custody is necessary. Per statute, the Rules of Evidence do not apply at nonsecure custody hearings.

3. Adjudication and Disposition Hearings

(a) The purpose of the adjudicatory phase in an abuse, neglect, or dependency case is to determine the existence or nonexistence of the conditions alleged in the petition. The adjudicatory hearing must occur no later than 60 days after the filing of the petition, unless the court orders a continuance.

(b) The standard of proof at an adjudicatory hearing is clear and convincing evidence. The Rules of Evidence apply at adjudicatory hearings.

(c) The purpose of the dispositional phase in an abuse, neglect, or dependency case is to determine the needs of the parent and child and ways to fulfill those needs, and to set a further review date for the court to receive reports from all parties about progress in meeting those needs. The dispositional hearing occurs after the adjudication, often on the same date but perhaps later if additional time is needed to investigate resources or obtain information requested by the court.

(d) There is no standard of proof at a dispositional hearing. Per statute, the Rules of Evidence do not apply at dispositional hearings and the court may consider any information that is relevant, reliable, and necessary to determine the best interest of the juvenile.

4. Review and Permanency Planning Hearings

(a) The purpose of review hearings is to enable the court to review and assess the progress of the case, including the services that have been provided to the parent and the parent's compliance with his or her obligations under the dispositional order. Review hearings must occur within 90 days after the dispositional hearing and at least every six months thereafter. The court may order that review hearings be held less frequently if the criteria set forth in G.S. 7B–906(b) are met, but the court may not refuse to conduct a review hearing if any party files a motion seeking one.

(b) There is no standard of proof at a review hearing. Per statute, the Rules of Evidence do not apply at review hearings and the court may consider any information that is relevant, reliable, and necessary to determine the needs of the juvenile.

(c) The purpose of a permanency planning hearing is to develop a plan to achieve a safe, permanent home for the juvenile within a reasonable period of time. The permanency planning hearing must occur within 30 calendar days after any court order directing the cessation of reasonable efforts toward reunification, and within 12 months of the initial order removing the child from the parental home. The permanency planning hearing may be combined with a review hearing.

(d) There is no standard of proof at a permanency planning hearing. Per statute, the Rules of Evidence do not apply at permanency planning hearings, and the court may consider any information that is relevant, reliable, and necessary to determine the needs of the juvenile.

(e) Pursuant to G.S. 7B–907(d), DSS must file a petition or motion to terminate parental rights any time the juvenile has been in placement outside the home for 12 of the most recent 22 months, a court has determined that the parent abandoned the child, or the parent has committed one of the criminal offenses specified in G.S. 7B–907(d). That requirement does not apply, however, if the court finds that the permanent plan for the child is custody or guardianship with a relative or other suitable person; that filing a petition to terminate parental rights would not be in the child's best interest; or that DSS has not been relieved of the duty to pursue reunification and efforts are still required to enable the juvenile's return home.

5. Termination of Parental Rights

(a) Termination of parental rights may be initiated by a new petition or by a motion in the cause in an underlying abuse, neglect, or dependency case. A petition or motion to terminate parental rights may be filed by a DSS that has custody of the child, by the child's GAL, or by a private party. If termination of parental rights is necessary to accomplish the permanent plan for the child, DSS must file a petition or motion to terminate parental rights within 60 calendar days of the date of the permanency planning hearing at which the plan was approved, unless the court makes written findings about why it cannot be filed within that time. Regardless of the identity of the petitioner, the respondent parent is entitled to appointed counsel if found to be indigent.

(b) Local practice varies as to the appointment of counsel in a termination of parental rights case. In some counties, counsel appointed in the underlying abuse, neglect, or dependency case continues automatically as counsel for the termination case. In other counties, the respondent parent must complete a new affidavit of indigency and, if approved by the court, counsel for the underlying abuse, neglect, or dependency case will be newly appointed to the termination case or different counsel will be appointed to the termination case. New parent attorneys should become familiar with the local practice so they understand the scope and extent of case appointments.

(c) Local practice also varies as to the assignment of case file numbers when there are multiple cases involving the same child. Pursuant to the Administrative Office of the Court's Rules of Record-Keeping, a juvenile should have only one file in a county, but that file may be broken down into various subparts, and a termination of parental rights petition or motion should be assigned the underlying abuse, neglect, or dependency file number with an extension. However, in some counties, there may be multiple files involving the same juvenile, and a termination of parental rights petition or motion may be given a new file number. New parent attorneys should become familiar with the local practice so they are aware of all files that may be introduced in cases.

(d) The purposes and goals of the major stages of proceedings in termination of parental rights actions, and the required timelines for those stages, are as follows:

(1) The purpose of a pre-hearing (or "special hearing") under G.S. 7B-1108 is to determine the issues raised by the termination petition or motion and the respondent's answer or response. The pre-hearing is required only if an answer or response is filed. A respondent should receive between 10 and 30 days notice of the hearing. Local practice varies as to the timing of the pre-hearing relative to the adjudicatory hearing.

(2) The purpose of the adjudicatory phase in a termination of parental rights proceeding is to determine the existence or non-existence of any of the grounds for termination alleged in the petition or motion. The adjudicatory hearing must occur within 90 calendar days after the filing of the petition or motion, unless the judge for good cause orders that it be held at a later time. The adjudication order must be filed within 30 calendar days of the conclusion of the adjudicatory hearing.

(3) The standard of proof during the adjudicatory phase of a termination of parental rights case is clear, cogent, and convincing evidence. The Rules of Evidence apply during the adjudicatory phase.

(4) If grounds to terminate are found to exist at the adjudicatory hearing, the purpose of the dispositional phase in a termination of parental rights proceeding is to determine whether termination is in the best interest of the juvenile. While the dispositional hearing usually occurs immediately following the finding of grounds to terminate, there is no statutory deadline for the hearing. The dispositional order must be filed within 30 calendar days of the conclusion of the dispositional hearing.

(5) There is no standard of proof during the dispositional phase of a termination of parental rights case. Per statute, the Rules of Evidence do not apply during the dispositional phase, and the court may consider any information to determine whether termination of parental rights is in the best interest of the juvenile.

(6) Pursuant to G.S. 7B-908, following the termination of parental rights, the court must review the placement of the child at least every six months until the juvenile is the subject of a decree of adoption. Once a parent's rights have been terminated, the parent will not be a party to these post-termination placement reviews, unless an appeal of the termination order is pending and a court has stayed the order pending the appeal.

Adopted December 14, 2007.

SECTION 1: General Provisions

Guideline 1.1. Function of the Performance Guidelines

(a) The Commission on Indigent Defense Services hereby adopts these performance guidelines to promote one of the purposes of the Indigent Defense Services Act of 2000—improving the quality of indigent representation in North Carolina—and pursuant to G.S. 7A-498.5(c)(4).

(b) These guidelines are intended to serve as a guide for attorneys representing indigent parent respondents in abuse, neglect, or dependency and termination of parental rights proceedings at the trial level, and to contain a set of considerations and recommendations to assist counsel in providing quality representation for indigent parent respondents. The guidelines also may be used as a training tool.

(c) These are performance guidelines, not standards. The steps covered in these guidelines are not to be undertaken automatically in every case. Instead, the steps actually taken should be tailored to the requirements of a particular case. In deciding what steps are appropriate, counsel should use his or her best professional judgment.

Adopted December 14, 2007.

Guideline 1.2. General Role of the Parent Attorney

(a) The paramount obligations of parent counsel are to provide zealous and quality representation to their clients at all stages of the proceedings, and to preserve, protect, and promote their clients' rights and expressed interests throughout the proceedings. Parent attorneys also have an obligation to conduct themselves professionally, abide by the Revised Rules of Professional Conduct of the North Carolina State Bar and other ethical norms, and act in accordance with all rules of court. Unless inconsistent with the client's interests, parent counsel should cooperate with and promote a productive relationship between all parties and attorneys in the case.

(b) Parent counsel are the professional representatives of their clients. Counsel should candidly advise clients regarding the probable success and consequences of adopting any posture in the proceedings, and provide clients with all information necessary to make informed decisions. Counsel does not have an obligation to execute any directive of a client that does not comport with law or standards of ethics or professional conduct.

Adopted December 14, 2007.

Guideline 1.3. Education, Knowledge, Training, and Experience of the Parent Attorney

(a) Before accepting appointment to an indigent abuse, neglect, dependency or termination of parental rights case, counsel has an ethical obligation to ensure that he or she has available sufficient time, resources, knowledge, and experience to afford quality representation to the parent in the particular matter. If it later appears that counsel is unable to afford quality representation in the case, counsel should move to withdraw. If counsel is allowed to withdraw, he or she should cooperate with new counsel to the extent that such cooperation is in the best interests of the client and in accord with the Revised Rules of Professional Conduct.

(b) To provide quality representation of respondent parents, counsel must be familiar with the North Carolina Juvenile Code and case law interpreting it. The following articles in Subchapter I of Chapter 7B of the General Statutes are of particular interest to the parent attorney:

(1) Article 1, Purposes and Definitions: G.S. 7B–100–101;

(2) Article 2, Jurisdiction: G.S. 7B–200–201;

(3) Article 3, Screening of Abuse and Neglect Complaints: G.S. 7B–300–311;

(4) Article 4, Venue and Petitions: G.S. 7B–400–408;

(5) Article 5, Temporary and Nonsecure Custody: G.S. 7B–500–508;

(6) Article 6, Basic Rights: G.S. 7B–600–603;

(7) Article 7, Discovery: G.S. 7B–700;

(8) Article 8, Hearing Procedures: G.S. 7B–800–808;

(9) Article 9, Dispositions: G.S. 7B–900–911;

(10) Article 10, Modification and Enforcement of Dispositional Orders, and Appeals: G.S. 7B–1000–1004; and

(11) Article 11, Termination of Parental Rights: G.S. 7B–1100–1112.

(c) Parent attorneys should also be familiar with the following laws, rules, and resources:

(1) The provisions in G.S. Chapter 50 related to child custody and support;

(2) The Uniform Child Custody Jurisdiction and Enforcement Act (UCCJEA), G.S. Chapter 50A;

(3) The North Carolina Rules of Civil Procedure, G.S. Chapter 1A;

(4) The North Carolina Rules of Evidence, G.S. Chapter 8C;

(5) The North Carolina Rules of Appellate Procedure, with a particular focus on Rule 3A;

(6) Any applicable local rules;

(7) The North Carolina DSS Family Support and Child Welfare Manual, *available at* http://info.dhhs.state.—nnc.us/ olm/manuals/manuals.aspx?dc=dss;

(8) The North Carolina GAL Attorney Manual, *available at* http://www.nccourts.org/Citizens/GAL/Manual.asp;

(9) Local agencies that provide services pursuant to a contract with DSS, as well as any agencies in the community that might offer help to respondent parents in meeting their case plans; and

(10) Any relevant local interagency protocols or agreements.

(d) Counsel should be generally familiar with the Adoption and Safe Families Act (ASFA), 42 U.S.C. §§ 620–679 and the ASFA Regulations, 45 C.F.R. Parts 1355–1357. Counsel should understand that ASFA is relevant to abuse, neglect, or dependency and termination of parental rights proceedings in North Carolina only to the extent that its requirements are reflected in North Carolina law, but that noncompliance with ASFA can affect DSS's funding.

(e) When warranted by the facts of the case, parent counsel should also review and consult the following:

(1) The Indian Child Welfare Act (ICWA), 25 U.S.C. §§ 1901–1963, the ICWA Regulations, 25 C.F.R. Part 23, and the Guidelines for State Courts: Indian Child Custody Proceedings, 44 Fed. Reg. 67, 584 (Nov. 26, 1979);

(2) The Multi–Ethnic Placement Act (MEPA), as amended by the Inter–Ethnic Adoption Provisions of 1996 (MEPA–IEP), 42 U.S.C. §§ 622(b)(9), 671(a)(18), 1996(b) (1998);

(3) The Child Abuse Prevention and Treatment Act (CAPTA), P.L. 108–36;

(4) The Interstate Compact on the Placement of Children (ICPC), G.S. 7B–3800–3806, and the ICPC Regulations, *available at* http://info.dhhs.state.nc.us/olm/manuals/dss/csm–70/man/CS1605–01.htm;

(5) The Health Insurance Portability and Accountability Act (HIPAA), P.L. 104–191, including the privacy requirements in 45 C.F.R. Parts 160, 162, and 164; and

(6) Immigration laws relating to child welfare and child custody.

(f) Counsel should understand the standard of proof that applies at every stage of the proceedings in abuse, neglect, or dependency and termination of parental rights cases.

(g) Counsel should develop a basic knowledge of:

(1) Criminal law and procedure;

(2) Child development;

(3) Alcohol and drug abuse;

(4) Domestic violence;

(5) Sexual, physical, and emotional abuse;

(6) How children may be affected by abuse, neglect, and dependency;

(7) How parents and children may be affected by DSS involvement in the family unit; and

(8) The unique issues that may arise when a minor child in DSS custody becomes pregnant.

(h) Counsel should be aware that cultural and ethnic differences exist as to child rearing.

(i) Counsel should be familiar with available programs and services that can aid older children, such as LINKS life skills services offered through the North Carolina Foster Care Independence Program for youth who are between 13 and 21 years of age, and Contractual Agreements for Continued Residential Services ("CARS Agreements") for youth who are between 18 and 21 years of age. Information about those programs can be found in Chapter IV, Section VIII of the North Carolina DSS Family Support and Child Welfare Manual. When appropriate, counsel should inform the parent client of the availability and benefits of such programs.

(j) New parent attorneys should seek opportunities to observe various phases of juvenile court proceedings, and consider reviewing the following:

(1) The American Bar Association Standards of Practice for Attorneys Representing Parents in Abuse and Neglect Cases (2006), *available at* http://www.abanet.org;

(2) Representing Parents in Child Welfare Cases: A Basic Introduction for Attorneys (American Bar Association 2000), *available at* http://www.abanet.org/child/rclji/RepresentParents.pdf;

(3) North Carolina Juvenile Court: Child Protection Hearings, A Handbook for Parents, Guardians, Custodians and Children (North Carolina Court Improvement Services); and

(4) Improving Outcomes for Older Youth: What Judges and Attorneys Need to Know (National Child Welfare Resource Center for Youth Development 2004), *available at* http://www.nrcys.ou.edu/ yd/resources/publications/pdfs/improveoutcomes.pdf.

(k) Where appropriate to provide competent representation, counsel should consult with more experienced attorneys to acquire necessary knowledge and information, including information about the practices of the local DSS, judges, and other court personnel.

(*l*) Counsel should keep abreast of changes in this area of the law, and should seek continuing legal education in juvenile court representation and general civil trial practice.

Adopted December 14, 2007.

Guideline 1.4. General Duties of the Parent Attorney

(a) Counsel should take all reasonable steps to maintain adequate and appropriate contact with the parent client throughout the proceedings. When the client is subject to a court order or case plan, counsel should attempt to communicate regularly with the client to assess whether the client is performing as he or she should pursuant to the order or plan. If counsel loses contact with a client, counsel should make a reasonable effort to reestablish contact, which may entail seeking information from family members, DSS, law enforcement, local adult probation offices, and other sources.

(b) Counsel should avoid conflicts of interest involving the parent client, any additional respondent parent(s), and prior clients. Counsel should understand that each parent should have his or her own attorney, and that one attorney should not represent both parents absent some unusual circumstances and express written consent. Where appropriate, counsel should consider seeking an advisory opinion on any potential conflicts from the North Carolina State Bar. Although counsel may interview the non-client parent, it must be done with the permission of that parent's attorney.

(c) Counsel should be familiar with the applicable Revised Rules of Professional Conduct and the obligation of counsel to withdraw in certain circumstances. If, at anytime during the course of representation, the client makes it known to counsel that he or she no longer wants counsel to represent him or her, counsel should inform the client of the potential consequences of withdrawal, including delay in the progress of the case. Counsel should be aware that mere tactical disagreements between counsel and the client ordinarily do not justify withdrawal from a case. If it is necessary for counsel to move to withdraw, counsel should do so in a way that protects the client's rights and interests, and does not violate counsel's ethical duties to the client.

(d) Counsel must understand at which hearings the Rules of Evidence apply in these proceedings and at which hearings they do not. Even at hearings that are not governed by the Rules of Evidence, counsel should make appropriate objections to information and testimony that is blatantly unreliable, inflammatory, immaterial, inaccurate, or incapable of being verified.

(e) Counsel must be aware of the time requirements imposed by the North Carolina Juvenile Code. Counsel should consider developing a tickler system to keep track of all required stages and hearings, to determine whether they took place within the mandated time periods, and to enable counsel to make appropriate objections to untimely hearings to preserve issues for possible appellate review.

(f) Counsel should take all reasonable steps to ensure that the parent client is notified in advance of all court dates. Counsel should also provide the client with copies of all petitions, court orders, case plans, and other important documents in the case.

(g) Because children are often displaced during these proceedings and because deadlines are imposed by the Juvenile Code, counsel should attempt to avoid continuances by any party for frivolous reasons. If counsel determines that it is necessary to request a continuance on behalf of the parent or that a continuance would materially benefit the parent's case, counsel should file a written motion for a continuance that clearly states good cause or compelling reasons. Counsel should object to continuance motions by other parties where necessary and appropriate.

(h) Counsel should review the court file before each court date, and attempt to seek enforcement of any local rules requiring that court reports and attachments be distributed to parties in advance of the court date. Counsel should move to continue hearings where significant and detrimental recommendations are made in court reports that were not timely delivered to counsel so counsel can prepare to meet or challenge the recommendations.

(i) At all hearings in abuse, neglect, or dependency and termination of parental rights proceedings, counsel should consider whether a motion to close the courtroom to the public pursuant to G.S. 7B–801 is justified and appropriate.

(j) Where appropriate, counsel should advise the respondent parent and all potential defense witnesses as to suitable courtroom dress and demeanor.

(k) Counsel should appear on time for all scheduled court hearings in a client's case. If scheduling conflicts arise, counsel should resolve them in accordance with Rule 3.1 of the General Rules of Practice and any applicable local rules.

(*l*) If a parent client can not be located during the pendency of the proceedings and counsel is unaware of the client's objectives, counsel should act in accordance with any applicable ethics opinions, including filing a motion to withdraw if appropriate.

(m) If counsel is allowed to withdraw or is discharged by the court at any point in the proceedings, counsel should take reasonable steps to notify the parent of the withdrawal or discharge, the next scheduled court date, and the parent's right to reapply for appointed counsel at the next court date.

(n) Counsel should never give preference to retained clients over appointed clients, or suggest that retained clients should or would receive preference.

Adopted December 14, 2007.

Guideline 1.5. Clients with Diminished Capacity and Guardians ad Litem

(a) Counsel must take into account the client's objectives when the client is mentally competent. When a client's capacity to make adequately considered decisions in connection with the representation is diminished, counsel should act in accordance with Rule 1.14 of the Revised Rules of Professional Conduct and any applicable statutory and case law.

(b) Counsel should be fully familiar with Rule 17 of the Rules of Civil Procedure, G.S. 7B–602, G.S. 7B–1101.1, and any applicable case law governing appointment of a GAL for a respondent parent. If counsel believes his or her client is entitled to a GAL due to age, incompetency, diminished capacity, or other reasons, counsel should file a motion seeking appointment of a GAL.

(c) If another party seeks appointment of a GAL for the respondent parent, counsel should consider all relevant factors in determining whether to oppose or consent to the appointment, including the services a GAL would provide and any inferences about the client's capacity or parenting ability that may be drawn from counsel's position or the appointment of a GAL.

(d) If a court appoints a GAL for the parent client, counsel for the parent should familiarize himself or herself with the GAL's role and duties under any applicable statutory and case law and ethics opinions.

Adopted December 14, 2007.

Guideline 1.6. Incarcerated Clients

(a) Counsel should understand that an incarcerated client can actively participate in his or her case, and should determine if the client is being held in a Department of Correction facility that offers parenting, anger management, and other classes that may be required under the case plan or court order. If the incarcerated client is being held in a local county jail, counsel should determine if any of the services that are required under the case plan or court order can be provided at the local jail. If appropriate, counsel should attempt to make arrangements with the prison or jail for a contact visit between a service provider and the incarcerated client.

(b) Unless otherwise directed by the parent client, counsel should take steps to ensure that a writ is issued to have an incarcerated client brought to court for all hearings. Because local practice surrounding issuance of a writ may vary, counsel should become familiar with the local practice. If the client is incarcerated in another state or is in federal custody, counsel should be aware that a writ likely will not be available and should consider all alternative means of communication between the court and the client, including a telephone link during the hearing or a deposition of the client before the court date.

(c) Counsel should encourage an incarcerated client to write letters, send small gifts or cards to the child through DSS, pay small amounts of child support if possible, and otherwise attempt to maintain contact with the child despite the incarceration.

(d) Counsel should attempt to involve the state prison social worker or the client's case manager in the process, in order to identify relevant services that might be available inside the prison and to help coordinate communication with the client.

Adopted December 14, 2007.

SECTION 2: Case Review, Investigation, and Preparation

Guideline 2.1. General Obligations of Counsel Upon Appointment

(a) Counsel shall obtain and review copies of the petition and other documents in the court file, and determine DSS's grounds for alleging abuse, neglect, or dependency, or DSS's or a private party's grounds for seeking termination of parental rights.

(b) If counsel is provisionally appointed, counsel should attempt to make contact with the parent client before the initial court date if contact information is available and time permits. If the client appears at the initial hearing, counsel should ensure that the client is informed of his or her rights to have counsel appointed, to hire an attorney, or to represent himself or herself, and that the client will need to make a choice concerning representation on the first court date. If the parent client chooses to have counsel appointed at the first court date, provisional counsel may also assist the client in applying for appointed counsel.

Adopted December 14, 2007.

Guideline 2.2. Theory of the Case

During case review, investigation, and preparation for all hearings, counsel should develop and continually reassess a theory of the case. A theory of the case is one central theory that organizes the facts, emotions, and legal basis in support of the client's position. The theory of the case furnishes the basic position from which counsel determines all preparation and actions in a case.

Adopted December 14, 2007.

Guideline 2.3. The Initial Interview

(a) Counsel shall attempt to arrange for an initial interview with the respondent parent as soon as practicable after being assigned to the client's case. If necessary, counsel may arrange for a designee to conduct the initial interview.

(b) The purpose of the initial interview is to acquire information from the respondent parent concerning the client, the child, potential witnesses, and the allegations in the petition; to provide the client with information concerning the case; to explain the client's options; and to determine the client's expressed interests. Counsel should try to ensure at this and all successive interviews and proceedings that barriers to communication, such as disabilities or differences in language or literacy, are overcome. If appropriate, counsel should file a motion to have a foreign language or sign language interpreter appointed by the court and present at the initial interview. Counsel should also consider utilizing the services of any professionals who are already providing services to the parent client.

(c) Information that should be acquired during the initial interview includes, but is not limited to:

(1) General information about the client, including his or her family and social support, and housing, transportation, financial, employment, and immigration status (if applicable);

(2) General information about any physical or mental health problems, or alcohol or substance abuse, which may have contributed to the allegations and/or impair the client's ability to work toward reunification;

(3) Information about the client's criminal history, if any, and any prior involvement with DSS;

(4) The existence of any companion criminal charges against the client arising out of the same facts or circumstances alleged in the juvenile petition, including the names of any appointed or retained criminal defense counsel;

(5) The client's version of the facts and circumstances surrounding the allegations and the client's view of any possible defenses;

(6) Information about any potential relative placements, including contact information and relevant background information, such as any substance abuse or criminal history;

(7) Information about the current visitation schedule between the parent and child if the child is not in the parental home, and the client's wishes regarding visitation;

(8) Information about services provided prior to removal of the child from the parental home, if any, as well as services that might have avoided the need for removal if DSS had provided them;

(9) Information about any documents that have been signed by the parent client at the request of DSS, if any, and the client's state of mind at the time of signing;

(10) Any evidence that should be preserved;

(11) Any photographs relevant to the defense of the allegations that may exist or should be taken as soon as possible; and

(12) The names of potential witnesses to the facts and circumstances underlying the petition, and permission from the client to contact those persons.

(d) Information that should be provided to the client at the initial interview includes, but is not limited to:

(1) An overview of the juvenile court process and actors, the possible timeline of the case, and an explanation that the client's level of effort and cooperation will be taken into account by DSS and the court;

(2) An explanation of the attorney-client privilege;

(3) The nature and elements of the allegations in the petition;

(4) How counsel may be reached by the client and when counsel plans to have contact with the client next;

(5) An explanation that the client should make and keep appointments with the attorney, appear in court when required, maintain a phone number, address, or both where the attorney can reach the client or leave a message for the client, and the possible consequences of failing to maintain contact with counsel;

(6) The requirements of any case plan and the possible consequences of failing to abide by the plan;

(7) Any recommended evaluations or treatment and the possible consequences of failing to obtain them;

(8) The client's rights to visitation;

(9) The role of any foster parent(s) and the importance of developing a positive relationship with the foster parent(s), if possible; and

(10) Realistic answers, where possible, to the client's most urgent questions.

(e) Counsel should explain to the client his or her position concerning the client discussing the case with DSS personnel, the GAL for the child, service providers, forensic evaluators, any foster parent(s), and other persons outside of counsel's presence, and should ask to be informed of all such contacts. Counsel's position regarding contact with other parties should take into account the seriousness of the allegations, whether the client appears capable of determining if contact will be beneficial or detrimental to his or her interests, the need for social workers to have access to the client to pursue reunification, counsel's ability to be present for all contacts without unnecessarily delaying reunification efforts, and counsel's ethical obligations to the client. Regardless of counsel's position on third party contact with the client, the parent attorney should instruct the respondent parent not to sign any documents presented by any party, including a proposed case plan, without first consulting with counsel.

(f) After the initial interview of the client, counsel should follow up with the client in writing if appropriate and practicable, and should consider communicating in writing with all other parties about counsel's position on contact with the parent client.

Adopted December 14, 2007.

Guideline 2.4. Counsel's Responsibilities After the Initial Interview

(a) Counsel has a duty to conduct an independent case review and investigation of the allegations in the petition, including but not limited to:

(1) Review of all pleadings and applicable statutes and case law;

(2) Review of all court files;

(3) Review of DSS files to the extent permitted by local rules or court order; and

(4) An additional in-depth interview or interviews of the client.

(b) If applicable, counsel should obtain and review all previous court files concerning the juvenile. If counsel is denied access to any such files in violation of G.S. 7B–2901(a)(4), counsel should seek a court order allowing that review.

(c) Counsel should make all reasonable efforts to obtain information in the possession of third parties, such as DSS, law enforcement, and the GAL. Counsel should make prompt requests for such information, including but not limited to physical evidence, social service records, medical or mental health records or reports, substance abuse treatment results, information about the client's attendance at anger management and parenting classes, and information about the client's education, employment, and housing status. Where appropriate, counsel should ask the client to sign a release authorizing counsel to access confidential information.

(d) Counsel should identify all potential witnesses and determine priorities regarding which persons to interview. Potential witnesses include, but are not limited to:

(1) Mental health workers who have worked with the parent or child;

(2) School personnel;

(3) Law enforcement;

(4) Physicians;

(5) Relatives;

(6) Neighbors and landlords;

(7) Employers;

(8) Caseworkers;

(9) Foster parents and other caretakers;

(10) Alcohol and drug counselors;

(11) Ministers, clergy, and other faith leaders; and

(12) Parenting instructors.

If potential witnesses are represented by counsel, the parent attorney should obtain permission from that counsel and the interview should take place in the presence of that counsel, unless the witness waives that right.

(e) If the parent client also faces criminal charges arising out of the allegations in the juvenile petition and the parent attorney does not represent the client in criminal court, the parent attorney should consult with the parent's criminal defense attorney.

(f) If counsel determines that it is necessary to interview the child, counsel should obtain permission from the GAL attorney advocate, even if the child is not in nonsecure custody. If an interview is conducted, counsel should be careful to utilize interviewing techniques that are age appropriate and take into account the alleged abuse or neglect the child may have suffered.

(g) Counsel should determine whether any of the following items should be brought to the immediate attention of DSS, the GAL, and/or the court:

(1) Possible placements for the child, including potential relative or kinship placements;

(2) Services that might enable reunification or physical placement of the child in the parental home while DSS retains legal custody, if applicable;

(3) The client's wishes regarding visitation; and

(4) The client's and child's immediate physical and mental needs, if any.

(h) Counsel should evaluate DSS's efforts to reunify the respondent parent and the child, and ask DSS to provide appropriate services for the parent client, such as:

(1) Mental or physical exam of a party;

(2) A modification or increase in visitation;

(3) Relative placement of a child who is in nonsecure custody; and

(4) Funds, transportation, or other services aimed at assisting the parent in overcoming the conditions that led to the filing of the petition and in pursing reunification.

Counsel should maintain documentation of all requests for services that are made to DSS, when they are made, and the agency's response. Whenever possible and appropriate, counsel should encourage communication between service providers for the parent and the child.

(i) If appropriate, counsel should consider contacting a foreign consulate to obtain necessary evaluations or services.

Adopted December 14, 2007.

Guideline 2.5. Evaluation of the Pleadings and Written Answers

(a) In an abuse, neglect, or dependency case, counsel should review the petition, summons, and return of service and, unless there are sound tactical reasons for not doing so, move to dismiss the pleadings if there are defects, such as:

(1) The petition does not contain the name, date of birth, and address of the juvenile, and the name and last known address of the parent, guardian, or custodian;

(2) The petition was not properly verified by the DSS Director or his or her designee;

(3) The petition does not contain sufficient factual allegations to convey subject matter jurisdiction and personal jurisdiction over the parent; or

(4) The petition and summons were not properly and timely served on the parent client.

(b) In a termination of parental rights case, counsel should review the petition or motion and, unless there are sound tactical reasons for not doing so, move to dismiss the pleadings if there are defects, such as:

(1) The petition or motion does not contain the name of the juvenile, date and place of the juvenile's birth, the county where the juvenile is currently residing, and the name and last known address of the parent, guardian, or custodian;

(2) The petition or motion does not contain the name and address of the petitioner or movant, and sufficient facts to identify the petitioner or movant as someone who is authorized by statute to file the petition or motion;

(3) The petition or motion was not properly verified by the petitioner or movant;

(4) The petition or motion does not contain sufficient factual allegations to warrant a determination that grounds for termination exist; or

(5) The petition or motion was not properly and timely served on the parent client.

(c) If termination of parental rights is initiated by a motion in the cause in the underlying abuse, neglect, or dependency case, counsel should determine if the motion was accompanied by a notice to the respondent parent that meets the requirements of G.S. 7B–1106.1. If no such notice accompanied the motion, or if the notice does not meet the statutory requirements, counsel should consider moving to dismiss the motion in the cause.

(d) In an abuse, neglect, or dependency case, after reasonable inquiry, counsel should consider filing a timely written answer to the petition and raising any applicable affirmative defenses. In a termination of parental rights case, unless there are sound tactical reasons for not doing so, counsel should file a written answer to the petition to terminate, or a response to the motion to terminate, within 30 calendar days after service of the petition or motion.

(e) Even if the pleadings are adequate, counsel should be sufficiently familiar with the language of the pleadings to recognize if DSS subsequently moves to amend them in a way that would change the nature of the conditions upon which the pleadings were based in violation of G.S. 7B–800.

Adopted December 14, 2007.

Guideline 2.6. Case Plans

(a) Counsel should be aware that a case plan may have been entered into between the parent and DSS prior to the filing of an abuse, neglect, or dependency petition in an attempt to avoid filing. Counsel should also be aware that, where nonsecure custody of the child is taken at the time the petition is filed, a case plan may have been entered into between the parent and DSS prior to the adjudicatory hearing.

(b) Counsel should review any proposed or signed case plan with the client to, among other things, verify that it requires services and service providers that are appropriate and tailored to the needs of the parent client and that it conceivably could be completed within the time allowed by the plan. Counsel should consider negotiating with DSS about the specific requirements of the proposed case plan if, after consultation with the client, counsel believes that modifications to the required services, the service providers, or the time frame for completion would be favorable to the client. If possible, counsel should ask DSS to provide a list of approved service providers and allow the parent client to choose an appropriate provider from the list. Counsel should also consider negotiating with DSS about the extent of and limitations on information that will be given to DSS in reports by service providers in order to facilitate a therapeutic relationship between the parent client and the service providers.

(c) After consultation with the client and taking into account the client's objectives and needs, counsel should advise the client whether to agree to and sign a proposed case plan, whether to sign a proposed case plan after crossing through those items with which the client disagrees, or whether to sign a proposed case plan after adding language in the "comments" section of the plan. If counsel and the parent client agree that the client will not sign a proposed case plan, counsel should instruct the client to write on the case plan "refused to sign on advice of counsel." Counsel should also advise the client that a refusal to sign a proposed plan may cause DSS to view the client as uncooperative and may be admitted into evidence and relied upon by the court.

(d) Whenever a case plan is signed, counsel should advise the client of his or her responsibilities under the plan, and of any potential consequences of not following the plan.

(e) If it later becomes relevant that the client could not have completed an objective of a signed case plan within the time allowed, counsel should consider gathering evidence for presentation at the next hearing about the impossibility of performance.

Adopted December 14, 2007.

Guideline 2.7. Nonsecure Custody Hearings

(a) In preparation for a nonsecure custody hearing, counsel should ascertain the client's goals and the best strategy for achieving those goals, including contesting whether there is a reasonable factual basis for the allegations in the petition or presenting evidence in support of other reasonable placements or means of protecting the juvenile. In doing so, counsel should consider the tactical advantages and disadvantages of contesting the factual basis for any allegations at such an early stage in the proceedings, including the possibility that the client may be prejudiced by evidence that is elicited.

(b) If a nonsecure custody order has been granted, counsel should review the order with the client and explain the meaning of nonsecure custody. Counsel should also determine whether the client consents to DSS having nonsecure custody for seven additional business days, consents until the adjudication and waives his or her right to additional nonsecure custody hearings, or does not consent and desires a hearing. If the parent does not waive nonsecure custody hearings, counsel should take steps to ensure that the client gets all nonsecure hearings to which he or she is entitled by statute.

(c) Counsel should be familiar with the placement options generally available in that county and any potential placement options in the case, including relative placements, and should advocate for the client's wishes regarding placement at all nonsecure hearings. Counsel should request that any potential placement individual(s) attend the next nonsecure custody hearing to facilitate the court ordering placement if appropriate.

(d) Counsel should be aware of all inquiries that the court must make at nonsecure custody hearings under G.S. 7B–506, including whether the criteria for continued custody under G.S. 7B–503 continue to exist, the identity and location of any missing parent, whether paternity is at issue, potential relative placements, and the status of other children in the home, and should present appropriate evidence pertaining to those inquiries.

(e) Counsel should advise the court and DSS if the child has any specific medical or psychiatric needs of which counsel is aware.

(f) If necessary and appropriate, counsel should ask the court to provide local juvenile or mental health experts who can perform a psychological evaluation of the parent or child.

(g) If the court sets out placement or visitation conditions for the parent in the nonsecure custody order, counsel should explain to the client those conditions and any potential consequences of failing to comply.

(h) Counsel should be aware that nonsecure custody orders must contain appropriate findings of fact pursuant to G.S. 7B–507 as to whether DSS has made reasonable efforts to eliminate the need for the child's out-of-home placement and to reunify the parent and child, or relieving DSS of the obligation to make reasonable efforts. If necessary, counsel should ask the court to make appropriate findings on the record.

Adopted December 14, 2007.

Guideline 2.8. Pre–Adjudication Motions

(a) The decision to file pre-adjudication motions should be made after thorough investigation and after considering the applicable law in light of the circumstances of each case, as well as the need to preserve issues for appellate review. Pre-adjudication motions that counsel should consider filing include, but are not limited to:

(1) Discovery motions;

(2) Motions for an in camera inspection;

(3) Motions to dismiss the petition or other motions related to the insufficiency of the pleadings under Rule 12(b) of the North Carolina Rules of Civil Procedure;

(4) Motions to divulge the identity and contact information for witnesses and others;

(5) Motions for medical, psychological, or psychiatric evaluations;

(6) Evidentiary motions and motions in *limine*;

(7) Motions for appointment of a GAL for the respondent parent, if appropriate;

(8) Motions for the appropriation of funds to enable the respondent parent to receive appropriate evaluations and services; and

(9) Motions for any non-licensed placement provider to receive the county share of the applicable monthly foster care rate.

(b) Motions should be filed in a timely manner, comport with the formal requirements of statute and court rules, and succinctly inform the court of the authority relied upon.

(c) When a hearing is scheduled on a pre-adjudication motion, counsel's preparation for the hearing should include, but is not limited to:

(1) Investigation, discovery, and research relevant to the claim(s) advanced;

(2) Preparing and filing written briefs and memoranda on applicable points of law, if necessary and appropriate; and

(3) Developing a full understanding of the standard of proof, evidentiary principles, and procedures that will apply at the hearing.

Adopted December 14, 2007.

Guideline 2.9. Pre–Adjudication Conferences

(a) Counsel should be aware that, by local rule, some judicial districts conduct a pre-adjudication conference to clarify all issues for trial. Counsel should be familiar with all applicable local rules and should know what issues must be raised at a pre-adjudication conference to be preserved for the adjudicatory hearing. In districts that do not require a pre-adjudication conference by local rule, counsel should consider requesting a conference.

(b) Counsel should also be aware of any local rules requiring the parties to exchange at the pre-adjudication conference witness lists and documents they intend to introduce at the adjudicatory hearing, and should comply with those local rules.

Adopted December 14, 2007.

Guideline 2.10. Discovery

(a) Counsel for respondent parents should be aware that they may use the discovery tools and procedures that are available to the parties in any civil matter, unless limited or prohibited by the court or local rules. Counsel should consider utilizing all available informal and formal discovery methods, including informal written requests, depositions, interrogatories, requests for admissions, subpoenas for persons, subpoenas *duces tecum* for the production of documents, and other methods.

(b) Unless there are sound tactical reasons for not requesting discovery, counsel should seek discovery of relevant information to the broadest extent permitted under state and federal law, including but not limited to:

(1) The complete files of DSS, including the social worker's notes and reports about every contact with the respondent parent, child, and any other person material to the case;

(2) The complete files of the GAL for the child;

(3) Police records and reports;

(4) Records in the possession of medical or mental health professionals, with a release from the client;

(5) Records in the possession of alcohol or substance abuse treatment facilities, with a release from the client;

(6) School records for the child and/or the respondent parent, with a release from the client; and

(7) Impeachment evidence, such as prior convictions or similar evidence of other misconduct by or bias of a DSS witness.

(c) If discovery is not timely provided to counsel, the parent attorney should consider filing a motion to compel production and/or seeking a continuance of the applicable hearing.

(d) Counsel should be aware that the court may deny, restrict, or defer discovery in a juvenile case. If counsel's discovery requests are denied, counsel should ask for an in camera inspection by the court and submit affidavits or statements in support of that request in accordance with G.S. 7B–700. Counsel should preserve any discovery issues for appeal by objecting to the court's ruling on the record and making any appropriate offers of proof.

(e) If counsel receives discovery requests from DSS or any other party, counsel should comply with the requests to the extent required by the Rules of Civil Procedure and should object to any requests that do not tend to elicit admissible or relevant information. If necessary and appropriate, counsel should consider seeking a protective order from the court in response to discovery requests by DSS or the GAL attorney advocate.

(f) Counsel should be generally familiar with federal law providing that medical records regarding an evaluation, diagnosis, or treatment for alcohol or substance abuse are confidential and may not be released or disclosed without the patient's consent or a court order that meets federal requirements. If counsel is aware of any such relevant records regarding the client, counsel should ask the client to execute a release form.

(g) Counsel should be generally familiar with federal law prohibiting the release of educational records without the student's consent if he or she is now 18 years of age or older, a parent's consent if the student is still under 18 years of age, or a court order that meets federal requirements. If counsel is aware of any such relevant records regarding the child or the respondent parent, counsel should ask the client to execute a release form.

Adopted December 14, 2007.

Guideline 2.11. Experts and Support Services

(a) Throughout case review and investigation, and in preparation for each hearing in an abuse, neglect, dependency, or termination of parental rights case, the parent attorney should consider whether the assistance of an investigator, licensed clinical social worker, family preservation specialist, mental health expert, or other expert is necessary and appropriate. If necessary and appropriate, counsel should file a motion with the court setting forth a particularized showing of necessity and requesting funds to secure the assistance of an expert whose evaluation, consultation, or testimony may assist the client at each phase of the proceedings. Counsel should be aware that local practice varies as to whether a motion for experts or support services can be heard *ex parte*.

(b) If counsel believes an expert evaluation of the child is necessary and appropriate, counsel should serve any motion for expert funding on the legal custodian of the child and the GAL attorney advocate.

(c) If appropriate, counsel should obtain reports from experts and prepare them to testify. Counsel should also prepare the respondent parent for any evaluation by explaining the nature of the procedure and encouraging the client's cooperation.

(d) If appropriate, counsel should file a motion to have a foreign language or sign language interpreter appointed by the court.

(e) Counsel should take all necessary steps to preserve for appeal any denial of investigative, expert, or interpreter funding.

(f) If, at any hearing in an abuse, neglect, dependency, or termination of parental rights case, the parent attorney learns that DSS or another party intends to call an expert witness to testify, counsel should take steps to determine whether the witness is qualified as an expert in the relevant field. If counsel believes the witness is qualified to testify in a given field, counsel should consider stipulating to the tender. If counsel believes the witness is not qualified or the testimony will address a subject matter outside of the witness's expertise, unless there are sound tactical reasons for not doing so, counsel should challenge the witness's qualifications and conduct a *voir dire* of the witness on the record to preserve the issue for possible appellate review.

Adopted December 14, 2007.

SECTION 3: Negotiating

Guideline 3.1. Negotiating a Consent Judgment

(a) After appropriate investigation and case review, counsel should explore with the client and DSS the possibility and desirability of reaching a negotiated consent judgment, and should be aware that DSS will often dismiss one of the grounds alleged in the petition in exchange for a stipulation to another ground. In doing so, counsel should understand that an adjudication of dependency is generally considered a better outcome for the client than an adjudication of abuse or neglect. Counsel should also understand that, while an adjudication of abuse or neglect is *res judicata* in a subsequent termination of parental rights proceeding, an adjudication of dependency may or may not be *res judicata* depending on the basis for the dependency.

(b) Counsel should be familiar with the conditions under which consent judgments are permissible under G.S. 7B–902, including that all parties must be present and consent, all parties must be represented by counsel or have waived counsel, and the court must make appropriate findings of fact.

(c) Throughout negotiations, counsel should consider any concessions the client might offer to DSS, including but not limited to:

(1) Foregoing a hearing on uncontroverted allegations;

(2) Refraining from asserting or litigating a well-grounded pre-trial motion;

(3) Consenting to continued nonsecure custody; and

(4) Stipulating to the admissibility of evidence that requires the use of live witnesses, where the information is known to be admissible and relevant.

(d) Counsel should also consider any concessions DSS might offer to the client, including but not limited to:

(1) Foregoing obtaining a nonsecure custody order;

(2) Allowing suitable relatives to supervise visits;

(3) Allowing visits between the parent and child at locations other than the DSS office;

(4) Placing children in foster care closer to the parent's home; and

(5) Providing gasoline and public transportation vouchers.

(e) Counsel should explain to the client all possible consequences of stipulating to one or more facts or circumstances or entering into a consent judgment, including the possible waiver of appellate rights. If counsel is not familiar with appellate practice, counsel should consider consulting with the Office of the Appellate Defender.

(f) Counsel must keep the client fully informed of all offers made by DSS with respect to a consent judgment, and should discuss with the client the advantages, disadvantages, and consequences of accepting any offers, including the possibility that the ultimate resolution could be termination of the parent's rights to the child.

(g) Notwithstanding the existence of ongoing tentative negotiations with DSS, counsel should continue to prepare and investigate the case to the extent necessary to protect the client's rights and interests in the event that negotiations fail.

Adopted December 14, 2007.

Guideline 3.2. The Decision to Consent to a Judgment

Counsel should discuss with the client the goals the client seeks to achieve, and should thoroughly inform the client of his or her alternatives, the chances of prevailing at a hearing, and the advantages, disadvantages, and potential consequences of any consent judgment. If the parent client also faces criminal charges arising out of the allegations in the juvenile petition and the parent attorney does not represent the client in criminal court, the parent attorney should consult with the parent's criminal defense attorney. However, the decision to consent to a judgment ultimately rests with the client.

Adopted December 14, 2007.

SECTION 4: Adjudication and Disposition

Guideline 4.1. Preserving the Record on Appeal During Adjudication and Disposition

(a) Counsel should establish a proper record for appellate review throughout adjudication and disposition, including but not limited to:

(1) Making appropriate objections to testimony or information in any reports or prior orders that DSS or the GAL seeks to have admitted into evidence;

(2) Making appropriate offers of proof regarding excluded evidence; and

(3) Requesting recordation of the proceedings pursuant to G.S. 7B–806. If something non-verbal transpires during adjudication or disposition that is rele-

vant and important, counsel should ask to have the record reflect what happened.

(b) Counsel should also take steps to ensure that the court's ruling on any objection is on the record and that any stricken information or evidence does not appear in the record.

Adopted December 14, 2007.

Guideline 4.2. The Adjudicatory Phase Generally

(a) Throughout preparation and the adjudicatory hearing, counsel should consider the theory of the case and ensure that counsel's decisions and actions are consistent with that theory.

(b) Counsel should be familiar with the Rules of Evidence and the law relating to all stages of the adjudicatory process, as well as all legal and evidentiary issues that reasonably can be anticipated to arise at the adjudicatory hearing based on the pleadings, investigation, and discovery, and should be prepared to make appropriate objections. If, at the adjudicatory hearing, DSS or the GAL makes material allegations about facts or circumstances that are not contained in the petition, counsel should consider seeking a continuance or objecting to preserve the issue for appellate review.

(c) In advance of the adjudicatory hearing, counsel should take all steps necessary to complete appropriate and thorough investigation, discovery, and research, including but not limited to:

(1) Interviewing and subpoenaing all potentially helpful defense witnesses that have been identified by the client and by counsel's review of the pleadings and evidence, including medical personnel or other professionals that are referenced in the DSS files, as well as the DSS or GAL reports and attachments, if available to counsel pursuant to local rules;

(2) Interviewing and subpoenaing any needed adverse witnesses, including the child if necessary and appropriate;

(3) Examining and subpoenaing all potentially helpful physical or documentary evidence;

(4) Obtaining copies of all DSS and GAL reports and attachments, if available to counsel pursuant to local rules, so that counsel can be prepared with rebuttal witnesses and evidence;

(5) Making a timely motion in advance of the hearing for funds for investigators or other experts if warranted, and arranging for defense experts to consult and/or testify on issues that are potentially helpful;

(6) Obtaining and reading transcripts of any prior proceedings in the case or related cases, if applicable;

(7) Obtaining any photographs or preparing charts, maps, diagrams, or other visual aids of all scenes, persons, objects, or information that may help the court better understand the case; and

(8) Meeting with the client to review the DSS and GAL reports and attachments, if available to counsel pursuant to local rules, and to discuss the defense and prepare the client's testimony.

(d) Where appropriate, counsel should have the following information and materials available at the time of the adjudicatory hearing:

(1) Copies of all relevant documents filed in the case, including the petition;

(2) A copy of the Juvenile Code and other critical statutes and cases related to anticipated issues;

(3) The DSS and GAL reports and attachments, if available to counsel pursuant to local rules;

(4) Any expert reports;

(5) Copies of subpoenas;

(6) A list of all exhibits to be offered and the witnesses through whom they will be introduced;

(7) Any reports from assessments or counseling that the client has completed;

(8) Documentation concerning the client's employment and housing status;

(9) Documentation regarding any special achievements of the child while in the custody of the parent;

(10) Negative drug screen results, if any;

(11) A plan, outline, or draft of opening statement;

(12) Cross-examination plans for all possible adverse witnesses;

(13) Direct-examination plans for all prospective defense witnesses;

(14) A plan, outline, or draft of closing argument;

(15) Proposed amendments to the petition, if applicable; and

(16) Proposed findings of fact and conclusions of law to be offered to the judge at the end of the hearing.

(e) Counsel should consider seeking an advance ruling on issues likely to arise at the adjudicatory hearing, by requesting a pre-trial conference, filing a motion in *limine*, or other means.

(f) Counsel should avoid unnecessarily having young children testify and should be sensitive to the nature of young children as witnesses. Where appropriate, counsel should ask for an in camera interview of child witnesses in the presence of all attorneys, or for the court to allow remote testimony or other accommodations.

(g) Counsel should consider whether there are tactical reasons to stipulate to damaging facts that are readily provable and uncontroverted, such as the possibility that the facts will have less impact on the court if they are summarized rather than the subject of lengthy testimony, and the possibility that the court will view the client as accepting responsibility for the stipulated facts or circumstances.

(h) If counsel is entitled by local rules to the DSS or GAL reports and attachments prior to the hearing, but has been unable to obtain them, counsel should consider asking for a continuance to discuss the reports with the client and prepare rebuttal evidence.

(i) Counsel should be familiar with and advise the client of the direct and collateral consequences of an adjudication of abuse, neglect, or dependency, including the effect on any future allegations regarding this child or other children.

(j) If the adjudicatory hearing was not held within the time required by G.S. 7B–801(c), unless there are sound tactical reasons for not doing so, counsel should object and move to dismiss the petition to preserve the issue for possible appellate review.

(k) If the adjudicatory order does not contain appropriate findings of fact and conclusions of law or was not reduced to writing within 30 calendar days after the hearing, unless there are sound tactical reasons for not doing so, counsel should object and move to dismiss the petition to preserve the issue for possible appellate review.

(*l*) If the client is facing criminal charges or might face future criminal charges due to the allegations in the juvenile petition, the parent attorney should consider asking the court to place any adjudication order under seal and to direct all parties to maintain the confidentiality of the order.

Adopted December 14, 2007.

Guideline 4.3. Confronting the Evidence at the Adjudicatory Hearing

(a) Counsel should anticipate weaknesses in DSS's proof, and research and prepare to argue corresponding motions, including motions to dismiss.

(b) Unless sound tactical reasons exist for not doing so, counsel should make timely and appropriate objections and motions to strike improper DSS or GAL evidence, and should assert all possible grounds for exclusion of the evidence.

(c) In preparing for cross-examination, counsel should:

(1) Consider the need to integrate cross-examination, the theory of the case, and closing argument;

(2) Be thoroughly familiar with the DSS file, as well as the DSS and GAL reports and attachments, if available to counsel pursuant to local rules;

(3) Consider whether cross-examination of each individual witness is likely to generate helpful information, and avoid asking questions that are unnecessary or might elicit responses harmful to the parent's case;

(4) Anticipate the witnesses DSS or the GAL might call, including the parent client, and consider a cross-examination plan for each anticipated witness;

(5) Be alert to inconsistencies, variations, and contradictions within each witness's testimony;

(6) Be alert to inconsistencies, variations, and contradictions between different witnesses' testimony; and

(7) Be alert to issues relating to bias and credibility of witnesses.

(d) If DSS or the GAL attempts to present a disposition report to the court prior to the conclusion of the adjudication phase in violation of G.S. 7B–808(a), counsel should make appropriate objections.

(e) At the close of DSS's case, counsel should move to dismiss the petition for insufficient evidence. Where appropriate, counsel should be prepared to present argument in support of the motion, including supporting case law.

Adopted December 14, 2007.

Guideline 4.4. Presenting the Parent's Case at the Adjudicatory Hearing

(a) Counsel should develop, in consultation with the client, an overall defense strategy. In deciding on defense strategy, counsel should consider whether the client's interests are best served by not presenting evidence on behalf of the parent, and instead relying on the evidence and inferences, or lack thereof, from DSS's case.

(b) Counsel should discuss with the parent client all of the considerations relevant to the client's decision to testify, as well as the possibility that another party may call the parent client to testify, including but not limited to the likelihood of cross-examination and impeachment, and the possibility that the client might incriminate himself or herself by testifying in the juvenile proceeding if the client is also facing criminal prosecution. Counsel should also discuss with the client the possibility that, by invoking his or her Fifth Amendment privilege against self-incrimination when responding to questions about potentially criminal activity, the juvenile court may infer an answer unfavorable to the client.

(c) In preparing to present the parent's case, counsel should, where appropriate:

(1) Develop a plan for direct examination of each potential defense witness;

(2) Determine the implications that the order of witnesses may have on the parent's case;

(3) Consider the possible use of character witnesses and any negative consequences that may flow from such testimony;

(4) Consider the use of demonstrative evidence and the order of exhibits;

(5) Be fully familiar with North Carolina statutory and case law on objections, motions to strike, offers of proof, and preserving the record on appeal; and

(6) Be fully familiar with North Carolina statutory and case law on the admissibility of documentary evidence, the foundation necessary to secure introduction of evidence, and any hearsay exceptions that might permit introduction of documentary evidence without authentication.

(d) In developing and presenting the parent's case, counsel should consider the implications it may have for rebuttal by DSS.

(e) Counsel should prepare all defense witnesses for direct examination and possible cross-examination.

(f) If a DSS objection is sustained or defense evidence is improperly excluded, counsel should make appropriate efforts to rephrase the question(s) and/or make an offer of proof. Counsel should take appropriate steps to preserve for appellate review any issues regarding the exclusion of evidence by placing on the record a forecast of the evidence, by describing the documentary or physical evidence sought to be introduced, or by conducting a *voir dire* examination of the witness.

(g) Counsel should conduct redirect examination as appropriate.

(h) At the close of all of the evidence, counsel should renew the motion to dismiss the petition for insufficient evidence.

Adopted December 14, 2007.

Guideline 4.5. The Dispositional Phase Generally

(a) Throughout preparation and the dispositional hearing, counsel should consider the theory of the case and ensure that counsel's decisions and actions are consistent with that theory. Counsel should also consider whether asking for a continuance of the dispositional hearing would be in the client's best interest.

(b) Counsel should be aware that the Rules of Evidence do not apply at the dispositional hearing, and that the court may generally accept into evidence information from any source reasonably related to determining the best interests of the child. However, counsel should still be prepared to object on the record to information and testimony that is blatantly unreliable, inflammatory, immaterial, inaccurate, or incapable of being verified.

(c) If DSS or the GAL provides to counsel in advance of the dispositional hearing any reports or documentary evidence that they intend to offer at the hearing, counsel should review them carefully with the parent client to determine whether any information in the reports or evidence may be inaccurate or susceptible to impeachment. Counsel should also consider subpoenaing the authors of the reports to be cross-examined if counsel knows DSS or the GAL does not intend to utilize them as live witnesses.

Adopted December 14, 2007.

Guideline 4.6. Confronting the Evidence at the Dispositional Hearing

(a) Counsel should anticipate and be prepared to respond to any inaccurate or unfavorable information that is presented at the dispositional hearing by DSS or the GAL.

(b) Where appropriate, counsel should cross-examine any witnesses whose testimony is damaging to the respondent parent's interests, and challenge the accuracy, credibility, and weight of any reports or other evidence before the court.

(c) If any reports or documentary evidence that DSS or the GAL offers at the dispositional hearing have not been timely provided to counsel prior to court in compliance with the Juvenile Code and any applicable local rules, counsel should consider moving to continue the dispositional hearing to allow time for review of the reports or evidence, or filing a motion in *limine* to prohibit the introduction of the reports or evidence.

(d) Counsel should be aware that dispositional orders must contain appropriate findings of fact pursuant to G.S. 7B–507 as to whether DSS has made reasonable efforts to eliminate the need for the child's out-of-home placement and to reunify the parent and child, or relieving DSS of the obligation to make reasonable efforts. If necessary, counsel should ask the court to make appropriate findings on the record.

Adopted December 14, 2007.

Guideline 4.7. Presenting the Parent's Case at the Dispositional Hearing

(a) Counsel should be prepared to present all mitigating and favorable information regarding the parent client to the court at the dispositional hearing—including evidence of the parent's achievements and progress after the filing of the petition—through documentary evidence, photographs, and the testimony of the respondent parent and other witnesses. Potential mitigating and favorable information includes, but is not limited to, medical, psychiatric, psychological, social, employment, and educational information.

(b) If appropriate, counsel should present to the court an alternative dispositional plan or report on behalf of the parent client, including placement of the child in the parental home or viable alternative placements for the child that are favorable to the client. Counsel should present evidence in support of the alternative plan or report, including but not limited to:

(1) Supporting testimony of the client, relatives, and others;

(2) Supporting testimony of experts, if necessary and appropriate; and

(3) Supporting affidavits, reports, and hearsay evidence, as long as such documents and evidence have been provided to opposing counsel in advance of the hearing to avoid a motion in *limine* to prohibit the introduction of the evidence.

(c) Counsel should be aware of the dispositional alternatives set forth in G.S. 7B–903, and should advocate for those that are consistent with the client's wishes and well grounded in fact and law.

(d) At the dispositional hearing, counsel should request that the court direct appropriate placements for the child and specific visitation schedules with the respondent parent. If appropriate, counsel should ask the court to direct DSS to conduct a home study of the client's home, a potential relative placement, or another suitable placement for the child.

(e) Counsel should also request orders for DSS to provide or make referrals for services that may benefit the parent client and aid in reunification, including but not limited to:

(1) Family preservation services;

(2) Medical and mental health services;

(3) Alcohol or drug treatment;

(4) Parenting education;

(5) Housing assistance;

(6) Domestic violence counseling;

(7) Anger management counseling; and

(8) Other social services.

Adopted December 14, 2007.

Guideline 4.8. Post–Disposition

(a) Counsel should discuss with the parent client the result of the dispositional hearing, all responsibilities of the parent pursuant to the court's ruling, any available post-disposition motions to set aside an adverse decision, and the parent's right to appeal.

(b) Counsel should review any proposed order or orders and suggest amendments, if necessary to be consistent with the court's findings, conclusions, and decree. If counsel is not permitted to review the proposed order in advance of signing in violation of the Rules of Civil Procedure and there are errors in the order, counsel should consider filing a motion to set aside the court order, to have it stricken from the record, and to have an amended order entered.

(c) If the order was not timely filed within 30 calendar days of the hearing, counsel should consider objecting and moving to dismiss the petition to preserve the issue for possible appellate review.

(d) If the order does not contain all findings of fact that are required by G.S. 7B–807 and G.S. 7B–905, as well as all findings of fact regarding reasonable efforts that are required by G.S. 7B–507 if DSS has custody, counsel should consider filing a motion for rehearing or for an amended order.

(e) If necessary and appropriate, counsel should file any applicable motions for rehearing, for an amended order, or for relief from the order in accordance with the Rules of Civil Procedure, as well as any notices of appeal in compliance with Rule 3A of the Rules of Appellate Procedure.

(f) Counsel should take all reasonable steps to monitor the client's compliance with the court's order, as well as any barriers to the client's compliance such as a lack of transportation, and to monitor the provision of services.

Adopted December 14, 2007.

SECTION 5: Review and Permanency Planning

Guideline 5.1. Preserving the Record on Appeal During Review and Permanency Planning

(a) Counsel should be aware that there are statutory limits on the appealability of review and permanency planning orders and that an order ceasing reunification efforts can only be appealed in compliance with G.S. 7B–507(c) and G.S. 7B–1001(a)(5).

(b) Counsel should establish a proper record for appellate review throughout all review and permanency planning hearings, including but not limited to:

(1) Making appropriate objections to testimony or information in any reports or prior orders that DSS or the GAL seeks to have admitted into evidence;

(2) Making appropriate offers of proof regarding excluded evidence; and

(3) Requesting recordation of the proceedings pursuant to G.S. 7B–806. If something non-verbal transpires during the hearing that is relevant and important, counsel should ask to have the record reflect what happened.

(c) Counsel should also take steps to ensure that the court's ruling on any objection is on the record and that any stricken information or evidence does not appear in the record.

Adopted December 14, 2007.

Guideline 5.2. Review and Permanency Planning Generally

(a) Counsel should be aware that the Rules of Evidence do not apply at review and permanency planning hearings, and that the court may generally accept into evidence information from any source reasonably related to determining the best interests of the child. However, counsel should still be prepared to object on the record to information and testimony that is blatantly unreliable, inflammatory, immaterial, inaccurate, or incapable of being verified. Counsel should also take steps to ensure that the court's ruling on any objection is on the record and that any stricken information or evidence does not appear in the record.

(b) In preparation for review and permanency planning hearings, counsel should conduct appropriate investigation and consider interviewing potential witnesses. In accordance with all applicable local rules and ethical standards governing interviews of represented parties, counsel should consider interviewing the foster parent(s), caseworker, and any professionals who are providing services to the parent. Counsel should also meet with the parent client, review the applicable DSS or GAL reports and attachments, and anticipate and prepare to counter any negative information or inferences about the client.

(c) Counsel should verify that any reports or documentary evidence that DSS, the GAL, or the GAL attorney advocate seeks to have admitted at a review or permanency planning hearing have been provided to counsel prior to court in compliance with any applicable local rules. If any reports or documentary evidence have not been timely provided to counsel, counsel should consider moving to continue the hearing to allow time for review of the reports or evidence, or filing a motion in *limine* to prohibit the introduction of the reports or evidence. When reports are provided to counsel in advance, counsel should consider subpoenaing the authors of the reports to be cross-examined if counsel knows DSS or the GAL does not intend to utilize them as live witnesses.

(d) Counsel should assess DSS's reunification efforts and consider whether any special limitations of the respondent parent warrant specific increased reunification efforts. If applicable, counsel should argue in favor of increased reunification efforts and against ceasing reunification efforts.

(e) Counsel should verify that DSS has provided all services and visitation promised or directed in prior orders and case plans, and should consider calling the parent to testify about any previously ordered services that were not provided.

(f) At review and permanency planning hearings, counsel should present favorable documentary and photographic evidence and testimony about the parent client's progress in meeting his or her case plan. Evidence counsel should consider presenting includes, but is not limited to:

(1) Improvements in the parent's educational, employment, or housing status;

(2) The parent's payment of child support obligations;

(3) The parent's payment of mortgages, rent, and utilities;

(4) Proper licensure and insurance of a motor vehicle;

(5) The parent's attendance at group or individual therapy;

(6) The parent's attendance at alcohol or substance abuse treatment programs or meetings;

(7) The parent's regular communication and visitation with the child; and

(8) The parent's compliance with other court orders, including probationary judgments.

(g) Counsel should ask the court to make specific findings on the record as to the reunification efforts expended by DSS and whether those efforts were sufficient and reasonable. If counsel believes reunification efforts have not been reasonable, counsel should object on the record to preserve the issue for possible appellate review.

(h) If a review order also serves as a cease reunification order pursuant to G.S. 7B–507, or as a permanency planning order pursuant to G.S. 7B–907, and does not contain the required findings of fact, counsel should consider filing a motion for rehearing or for an amended order.

(i) If necessary and appropriate, counsel should file any applicable motions for rehearing, for an amended order, or for relief from the order in accordance with the Rules of Civil Procedure, as well as any notices of appeal in compliance with G.S. 7B–1001 and Rule 3A of the Rules of Appellate Procedure.

Adopted December 14, 2007.

Guideline 5.3. Review Hearings

(a) Counsel should request a review hearing if the need for additional services arises, if any event occurs that may significantly affect the need for continued placement, or if it otherwise becomes necessary to protect the client's interests. If necessary and appropriate, counsel should consider filing a motion for an order to show cause why another party should not be held in contempt for non-compliance with a court order.

(b) Counsel should be aware that review orders must contain appropriate findings of fact pursuant to G.S. 7B–507 as to whether DSS has made reasonable efforts to eliminate the need for the child's out-of-home placement and to reunify the parent and child, or relieving DSS of the obligation to make reasonable efforts. If necessary, counsel should ask the court to make appropriate findings on the record.

Adopted December 14, 2007.

Guideline 5.4. Permanency Planning Hearings

(a) Counsel should explain to the parent client that a permanency planning hearing could result in a plan of adoption for the child, which would require DSS to initiate termination proceedings within 60 days of the hearing unless waived by the court.

(b) Counsel should be prepared at the permanency planning hearing to present an alternative long-term plan for the child and to present evidence in support of the alternative plan.

(c) If reunification with the parent is adopted as the permanent plan or a concurrent plan for the juvenile, counsel should take all reasonable steps to ensure that the judge's findings of fact and order clearly state the parent's and DSS's obligations, the time the parent has to comply, and the possibility of return to the parental home if the parent complies.

(d) If the court enters a permanency planning order that changes the permanent plan to adoption, counsel should advocate that reunification, or custody or guardianship with a relative or other suitable adult, be adopted as a concurrent plan where appropriate. Counsel should also explain to the client that, even when adoption is the primary permanent plan for the juvenile, the parent may still pursue reunification efforts on his or her own and the court may subsequently revise the permanent plan to direct reunification. Counsel should consider advising the respondent parent that, because the proceedings are now adversarial, the client should no longer cooperate with DSS except for purposes of scheduling visitation. Counsel should also consider asking to have the record reflect that advice.

(e) Counsel should advise the client when service of a petition or motion to terminate is expected to be made soon, such as at the conclusion of the permanency planning hearing where the court approves a permanent plan that requires termination of parental rights. Counsel should be aware that, depending on local practice, counsel may not be served as attorney of record for the client and may not receive a copy of the petition or motion from the petitioner's attorney. If warranted by local practice, counsel should ask DSS and the GAL attorney advocate to provide him or her with a copy of the petition or motion to terminate, or instruct the client to inform counsel immediately upon receipt of a petition or motion. With the permission of the client, counsel should consider arranging with the attorney for the petitioner to accept service of the petition or motion on behalf of the client.

Adopted December 14, 2007.

SECTION 6: Termination of Parental Rights

Guideline 6.1. Preserving the Record on Appeal During Termination Proceedings

(a) Counsel should establish a proper record for appellate review throughout the termination proceedings, including but not limited to:

(1) Making appropriate objections to testimony or information in any reports or prior orders that the petitioner or the GAL seeks to have admitted into evidence;

(2) Making appropriate offers of proof regarding excluded evidence; and

(3) Requesting recordation of the proceedings under G.S. 7B-806. If something nonverbal transpires that is relevant and important, counsel should ask to have the record reflect what happened.

(b) Counsel should also take steps to ensure that the court's ruling on any objection is on the record and that any stricken information or evidence does not appear in the record.

Adopted December 14, 2007.

Guideline 6.2. Termination of Parental Rights Generally

(a) Counsel should develop, in consultation with the client, an overall theory of the case. Throughout preparation and the termination hearing, counsel should consider the theory of the case and ensure that counsel's decisions and actions are consistent with that theory.

(b) If the petition or motion to terminate is not timely filed, and the court has not entered an order finding good cause for the late filing, counsel should move to dismiss the petition or motion, unless there are sound tactical reasons for not doing so.

(c) Counsel should confer with the client as soon as possible after a petition or motion to terminate is filed about all issues related to the defense of the petition or motion, including but not limited to:

(1) Witnesses that should be interviewed and possibly subpoenaed;

(2) Documentary and photographic evidence that should be gathered and/or subpoenaed; and

(3) Any prior court files, both for the subject juvenile and any other child of the parent client, which may be relied upon or introduced into evidence by the petitioner or the GAL.

If appropriate, counsel should also discuss with the client whether there are tactical reasons to stipulate to any allegations in the petition or motion, other than ultimate facts that could themselves constitute a ground for termination, such as facts that are uncontroverted and/or readily capable of determination or proof. The decision to stipulate ultimately rests with the client.

(d) If the parent client also faces criminal charges arising out of the allegations in the juvenile petition and the parent attorney does not represent the client in criminal court, the parent attorney should consult with the parent's criminal defense attorney prior to filing any answer or response to the petition or motion.

(e) The decision to file pre-trial motions should be made after thorough investigation and after considering the applicable law in light of the circumstances of each case, as well as the need to preserve issues for appellate review. Pre-trial motions that counsel should consider filing include, but are not limited to:

(1) Discovery motions;

(2) Motions for an in camera inspection;

(3) Motions to dismiss the petition or motion on the grounds of insufficiency of the pleadings under Rule 12(b) of the North Carolina Rules of Civil Procedure;

(4) Motions to divulge the identity and contact information for witnesses and others;

(5) Motions for medical, psychological, or psychiatric evaluations;

(6) Evidentiary motions and motions in *limine*; and

(7) Motions for appointment of a GAL for the respondent parent, if appropriate.

Motions should be filed in a timely manner, comport with the formal requirements of statute and court rules, and succinctly inform the court of the authority relied upon.

(f) Unless there are sound tactical reasons for not doing so, counsel should consider utilizing all available informal and formal discovery methods and should seek discovery to the broadest extent permitted by law, including but not limited to:

(1) The identity of all lay witnesses who will be called to testify at the termination hearing and a summary of the testimony to be elicited;

(2) The identity of all expert witnesses who will be called to testify at the termination hearing and copies of the witnesses' curriculum vitae and any reports prepared by the witnesses; and

(3) A list of all reunification services that were provided to the parent prior to the filing of the petition or motion to terminate.

If discovery is not timely provided to counsel, the parent attorney should consider filing a motion to compel production and/or seeking a continuance of the termination hearing.

(g) After an answer or response is filed, counsel should take any necessary steps to enforce the parent's right to a special hearing within the time set forth in G.S. 7B–1108. At the special hearing, counsel should raise any pre-trial motions that may require an evidentiary hearing prior to the adjudication of the termination petition or motion, such as discovery motions or motions in *limine*.

(h) In advance of the termination hearing, counsel should take all steps necessary to complete appropriate and thorough investigation, discovery, and research, including but not limited to:

(1) Interviewing and subpoenaing all potentially helpful defense witnesses that have been identified by the client and by counsel's review of the pleadings and evidence, including medical personnel or other professionals that are referenced in the DSS files, or DSS or GAL reports and attachments;

(2) Interviewing and subpoenaing any needed adverse witnesses, including the child if necessary and appropriate;

(3) Examining and subpoenaing all potentially helpful physical or documentary evidence;

(4) Obtaining copies of all DSS and GAL reports and attachments so that counsel can be prepared with rebuttal witnesses and evidence;

(5) Making a timely motion in advance of the hearing for funds for investigators or other experts if warranted, and arranging for defense experts to consult and/or testify on issues that are potentially helpful;

(6) Obtaining and reading transcripts of any prior proceedings in the case or related cases, if applicable;

(7) Obtaining any photographs or preparing charts, maps, diagrams, or other visual aids of all scenes, persons, objects, or information that may help the judge better understand the case; and

(8) Meeting with the client to review the DSS and GAL reports and attachments, discuss the defense, and prepare the client's testimony.

(i) Counsel should be familiar with the Rules of Evidence and the statutory and case law relating to all stages of a termination proceeding, as well as all legal and evidentiary issues that reasonably can be anticipated to arise at the termination hearing based on the pleadings, investigation, and discovery, and should be prepared to make appropriate objections. If, at the termination hearing, the petitioner makes material allegations about facts or circumstances that are not contained in the petition or motion, counsel should consider seeking a continuance or objecting to preserve the issue for appellate review.

(j) Where appropriate, counsel should have the following information and materials available at the time of the termination hearing;

(1) Copies of all relevant documents filed in the case, including the petition or motion;

(2) A copy of the Juvenile Code and other critical statutes and cases related to anticipated issues;

(3) The DSS and GAL reports and attachments;

(4) Any expert reports;

(5) Copies of subpoenas;

(6) A list of all exhibits to be offered and the witnesses through whom they will be introduced;

(7) Any reports from assessments or counseling that the client has completed;

(8) Documentation concerning the client's employment and housing status;

(9) Documentation regarding any special achievements of the child while in the custody of the parent;

(10) Negative drug screen results, if any;

(11) A plan, outline, or draft of opening statement;

(12) Cross-examination plans for all possible adverse witnesses;

(13) Direct-examination plans for all prospective defense witnesses;

(14) A plan, outline, or draft of closing argument; and

(15) Proposed findings of fact and conclusions of law to be offered to the judge at the end of the hearing.

(k) Counsel should avoid unnecessarily having young children testify, and should be sensitive to the nature of young children as witnesses. Where appropriate, counsel should ask the court for any appropriate accommodations and take steps to ensure that the substance of any testimony by child witnesses is placed on the record.

(*l*) If the adjudicatory and dispositional phases of the termination proceedings are not concluded within the time periods mandated by statute, counsel should move to dismiss the petition or motion, unless there are sound tactical reasons for not doing so.

Adopted December 14, 2007.

Guideline 6.3. Confronting the Evidence During the Adjudication Phase of the Termination Hearing

(a) Counsel should anticipate the petitioner's theory of the case, all evidence the petitioner can reasonably be expected to introduce during the adjudication phase of the termination hearing, and any weaknesses in that evidence. Counsel should research and prepare to argue corresponding motions, including motions to dismiss.

(b) Unless sound tactical reasons exist for not doing so, counsel should make timely and appropriate objections and motions to strike improper evidence offered by the petitioner or GAL, and should assert all possible grounds for exclusion of the evidence.

(c) In preparing for cross-examination, counsel should:

(1) Consider the need to integrate cross-examination, the theory of the case, and closing argument;

(2) Be thoroughly familiar with the DSS file, as well as the previously submitted DSS and GAL reports and attachments;

(3) Consider whether cross-examination of each individual witness is likely to generate helpful information, and avoid asking questions that are unnecessary or might elicit responses harmful to the parent's case;

(4) Anticipate the adverse witnesses that might be called, including the parent client, and consider a cross-examination plan for each anticipated witness;

(5) Be alert to inconsistencies, variations, and contradictions within each witness's testimony;

(6) Be alert to inconsistencies, variations, and contradictions between different witnesses' testimony; and

(7) Be alert to issues relating to bias and credibility of witnesses.

(d) If DSS or the GAL attempts to present dispositional evidence or a dispositional report to the court prior to the conclusion of the adjudication phase, counsel should make appropriate objections.

(e) At the close of the petitioner's case, counsel should move to dismiss the petition or motion for insufficient evidence. Where appropriate, counsel should be prepared to present argument in support of the motion, including supporting case law.

Adopted December 14, 2007.

Guideline 6.4. Presenting the Parent's Case During the Adjudication Phase of the Termination Hearing

(a) Counsel should consider whether the client's interests are best served by not presenting evidence on behalf of the parent, and instead relying on the evidence and inferences, or lack thereof, from the petitioner's case.

(b) Counsel should discuss with the parent client all of the considerations relevant to the client's decision to testify, including but not limited to the likelihood of cross-examination and impeachment, and the possibility that the client might incriminate himself or herself by testifying in the juvenile proceeding if the client is also facing criminal prosecution. Counsel should also discuss with the client the possibility that, by invoking his or her Fifth Amendment privilege against self-incrimination when responding to questions about potentially criminal activity, the juvenile court may infer an answer unfavorable to the client.

(c) Counsel should comply with any local rules of court that may require counsel to divulge to the petitioner and other parties a witness list or other information prior to the termination hearing.

(d) Counsel should address and defend all allegations in the petition or motion that are capable of a defense. In preparing to present the parent's case, counsel should, where appropriate:

(1) Develop a plan for direct examination of each potential defense witness;

(2) Determine the implications that the order of witnesses may have on the parent's case;

(3) Consider the possible use of character witnesses and any negative consequences that may flow from such testimony;

(4) Consider the use of demonstrative evidence and photographs, and the order of exhibits;

(5) Be fully familiar with North Carolina statutory and case law on objections, motions to strike, offers of proof, and preserving the record on appeal; and

(6) Be fully familiar with North Carolina statutory and case law on the admissibility of documentary evidence, the foundation necessary to secure introduction of evidence, and any hearsay exceptions that might permit introduction of documentary evidence without authentication.

(e) In developing and presenting the parent's case, counsel should consider the implications it may have for rebuttal by DSS.

(f) Counsel should prepare all defense witnesses, including the parent client, for direct examination and possible cross-examination.

(g) If a DSS objection is sustained or defense evidence is improperly excluded, counsel should make appropriate efforts to rephrase the question(s) and/or make an offer of proof. Counsel should take appropriate steps to preserve for appellate review any issues regarding the exclusion of evidence by placing on the record a forecast of the evidence, by describing the documentary or physical evidence sought to be introduced, or by conducting a *voir dire* examination of the witness.

(h) Counsel should conduct redirect examination as appropriate.

(i) At the close of all of the evidence, counsel should renew the motion to dismiss the termination petition or motion, or any part thereof, for insufficient evidence.

Adopted December 14, 2007.

Guideline 6.5. Confronting the Evidence During the Dispositional Phase of the Termination Hearing

(a) Counsel should be aware that, during the dispositional phase of a termination hearing, the court may receive any information that would assist it in determining the factors set forth in G.S. 7B–1110. However, counsel should still be prepared to object on the record to any information or testimony that is blatantly unreliable, inflammatory, immaterial, inaccurate, or incapable of being verified.

(b) If any reports or documentary evidence that the petitioner, GAL, or GAL attorney advocate offers at the dispositional hearing have not been timely provided to counsel prior to court in compliance with the Juvenile Code and any applicable local rules, counsel should consider moving to continue the dispositional hearing to allow time for review of the reports or evidence, or filing a motion in *limine* to prohibit the introduction of the reports or evidence.

Adopted December 14, 2007.

Guideline 6.6. Presenting the Parent's Case During the Dispositional Phase of the Termination Hearing

(a) If the court determines that grounds to terminate parental rights exist and the case enters the dispositional phase, counsel should be prepared to present to the court at the dispositional hearing all mitigating and favorable information on behalf of the parent client—including evidence of the parent's achievements and progress after the filing of the petition and evidence of the child's expressed interests regarding adoption—through documentary evidence, photographs, and the testimony of the respondent parent and other witnesses. Potential mitigating and favorable information includes, but is not limited to, medical, psychiatric, psychological, social, employment, and educational information. During the dispositional phase, counsel's goal is to demonstrate that, while grounds to terminate may exist, termination would not be in the best interest of the juvenile.

(b) If appropriate, counsel should present to the court an alternative dispositional plan to termination and adoption, including viable alternative placements for the child that are favorable to the client. Counsel should present evidence in support of the alternative plan, including but not limited to:

(1) Supporting testimony of the parent client, relatives, and others;

(2) Supporting testimony of experts, if necessary and appropriate; and

(3) Supporting affidavits, reports, and other hearsay evidence, as long as such documents and evidence have been provided to opposing counsel in advance of the hearing to avoid a motion in *limine* to prohibit the introduction of the evidence.

(c) Counsel should be aware that a dispositional order must contain appropriate findings of fact pursuant to G.S. 7B–1110. If necessary, counsel should ask the court to make appropriate findings on the record.

Adopted December 14, 2007.

Guideline 6.7. Relinquishment and Other Alternatives to Termination

(a) Counsel should be familiar with the statutory and case law governing voluntary relinquishment of parental rights, as well as the local DSS policy concerning relinquishments. If appropriate, counsel should discuss with the parent client his or her option of relinquishing parental rights to a specific person or persons rather than to DSS.

(b) Counsel should fully explain to the parent client the advantages, disadvantages, and consequences of voluntary relinquishment, including but not limited to:

(1) The fact that the parent's child support obligations will continue after relinquishment, until a final decree of adoption for the child is entered;

(2) The fact that, unlike a termination order by the court, voluntary relinquishment is not a ground for the future termination of rights to other children; and

(3) The possibility that visitation could continue until a final decree of adoption is entered.

(c) Counsel should fully explain to the parent client the applicable deadline for revocation of a relinquishment and the procedure to be followed if the parent decides to revoke within that time.

(d) If a parent client decides to voluntarily relinquish his or her parental rights, when possible, counsel should take steps to ensure that the relinquishment is executed during a court session and in the presence of multiple witnesses. Counsel should also consider tendering the client to the court for the court to make inquiry as to the knowing and voluntary nature of the relinquishment.

(e) Counsel should be familiar with and fully explain to the client all other termination alternatives, including placement of the child in the custody or guardianship of a relative or other suitable person who is agreeable to the petitioner and the respondent parent. Counsel should explain to the client that a custodial arrangement would allow the parent later to seek a change in visitation or custodial status by filing a motion to modify the dispositional order or a custody action pursuant to Chapter 50 of the North Carolina General Statutes.

Adopted December 14, 2007.

SECTION 7: Appeal and Post-Representation

Guideline 7.1. Appeal to the Appellate Division

(a) Counsel should inform the parent client of his or her right to appeal to the appellate division any appealable judgments of the court that are listed in G.S. 7B–1001, and the action that must be taken to perfect that appeal.

(b) Whenever the taking of an appeal is reasonably anticipated, counsel should immediately notify the Office of the Appellate Defender so that provisional appellate counsel can be appointed promptly.

(c) If the respondent parent has a right to appeal and wants to file an appeal, counsel shall preserve the parent's right to do so by filing and serving a notice of appeal in accordance with the procedures and timelines set forth in G.S. 7B–1001 and Rule 3A of the Rules of Appellate Procedure, including obtaining the client's signature on the notice of appeal and signing the notice of appeal as trial counsel of record. Counsel shall file any signed notice of appeal and certificate of service with the Clerk of Superior Court within the appropriate deadline and shall serve all parties to the action. Counsel should also take steps to ensure that the appellate entries form is prepared and filed.

(d) If the respondent parent does not have a right to appeal and counsel believes there is a meritorious issue in the case that might be raised in the appellate division by means of a petition for writ of *certiorari*, counsel should inform the parent of his or her opinion and consult with the Office of the Appellate Defender about the appropriate procedure.

(e) Pursuant to Rule 33(a) of the North Carolina Rules of Appellate Procedure and Rules 1.7(a) and 3.2(a) of the Rules of the Commission on Indigent Defense Services, the entry of notice of appeal does not constitute a general appearance as counsel of record in the appellate division.

(f) If notice of appeal has been entered, counsel should consider filing a motion for a stay pending appeal in accordance with the Rules of Civil Procedure. When an appeal is pending for orders other than termination of parental rights, or when a termination of parental rights order has been stayed pending appeal, counsel should continue zealously representing the respondent parent and promoting the parent's rights and expressed interests at all subsequent proceedings. If the appeal is from a termination of parental rights order and a stay is denied, counsel should encourage the client to comply with prior court orders while the appeal is pending. Counsel should also inform the respondent parent of the need to maintain regular contact with the appellate attorney throughout the appeal.

(g) If counsel believes that the client has a right to appeal and continues to be indigent, but the trial court denies indigency status for purposes of appeal, trial counsel should consult with the Office of the Appellate Defender about the client's options and inform the client of those options.

Adopted December 14, 2007.

Guideline 7.2. Trial Counsel's Duty to Assist Appellate Counsel

(a) Trial counsel should be generally familiar with the requirements of Rule 3A of the North Carolina Rules of Appellate Procedure and all applicable policies of the Office of Indigent Defense Services and Office of the Appellate Defender, including but not limited to, trial counsel's obligation to notify the Office of the Appellate Defender immediately following the conclusion of a hearing at which a decision was made adverse to the client when the client is considering entering notice of appeal, and the division of responsibilities between trial and appellate counsel in the preparation of the proposed record on appeal.

(b) Trial counsel should take all reasonable steps to assist the appellate attorney with securing needed documents from the court file, including the appellate entries. Upon request, trial counsel should also assist the appellate counsel in identifying issues for appeal. However, the ultimate responsibility for decisions in all phases of the appellate representation, and for compliance with all required appellate rules and procedures, rests with appellate counsel.

Adopted December 14, 2007.

Guideline 7.3. Other Post–Representation Obligations

(a) Even after representation is complete, counsel should comply with the respondent parent's reasonable requests for information and material that is part of counsel's file.

(b) Pursuant to Rule 3A of the Rules of Appellate Procedure, trial counsel should promptly respond to any requests for information or documents from the appellate attorney, when applicable.

Adopted December 14, 2007.

PERFORMANCE GUIDELINES FOR INDIGENT DEFENSE REPRESENTATION IN NON–CAPITAL CRIMINAL CASES AT THE TRIAL LEVEL

Adopted November 12, 2004

Preface

The primary goal of the Commission on Indigent Defense Services ("IDS Commission") is to ensure that indigent defendants in North Carolina are afforded high quality legal representation. *See* G.S. 7A–498.1(2). To further that goal, the Indigent Defense Services Act of 2000 directs the Commission to establish "[s]tandards for the performance of public defenders and appointed counsel." G.S. 7A–498.5(c)(4).

These performance guidelines are based largely on the "Performance Guidelines for Criminal Defense Representation" that have been promulgated by the National Legal Aid and Defender Association, as well as a review of standards and guidelines in several other jurisdictions, including Connecticut, Kansas, Massachusetts, New Mexico, New York City, Oregon, and Washington. Over a period of several months, a Committee of the IDS Commission reviewed a draft of these guidelines and revised them to fit the nuances of North Carolina law and practice. Initial proposed guidelines were then sent to 70 public and private defense attorneys around the state, with a request that they provide feedback. Based on the comments that were received, the Committee made a number of changes to that earlier draft. In August 2004, the revised guidelines were mailed to all public defenders and assistant public defenders, more than 2,000 private defense attorneys, all active district and superior court judges, and all elected district attorneys for comments. Again, based on the comments that were received, the Committee made a number of improvements to the guidelines. The full IDS Commission then adopted the attached performance guidelines on November 12, 2004.

These performance guidelines cover all indigent adult non-capital criminal cases in district and superior court. The guidelines are intended to identify issues that may arise at each stage of a criminal proceeding, and to recommend effective approaches to resolving those issues. Because all provisions will not be applicable in all cases, the guidelines direct counsel to use his or her best professional judgment in determining what steps to undertake in specific cases. The Commission hopes these guidelines will be useful as a training tool and resource for new and experienced defense attorneys, as well as a tool for potential systemic reform in some areas. The guidelines are not intended to serve as a benchmark for ineffective assistance of counsel claims or attorney disciplinary proceedings.

The IDS Commission believes that providing high quality criminal defense representation is a difficult and challenging endeavor, which requires great skill and dedication. That skill and dedication is demonstrated by defense counsel across North Carolina on a daily basis, and the Commission commends those counsel. The Commission recognizes that the goals embodied in these guidelines will not be attainable without sufficient funding and resources, and hopes the North Carolina General Assembly will continue its support of quality indigent defense services.

The IDS Commission thanks all of the defense attorneys who zealously represent indigent defendants across the state. In addition, the Commission thanks everyone who worked on the drafting of these performance guidelines and who offered comments. The Commission plans to review and revise the guidelines on a regular basis to ensure that they continue to comply with North Carolina law and reflect quality performance, and invites ongoing feedback from the defense bar and criminal justice community.

SECTION 1

Guideline 1.1. Function of Performance Guidelines

(a) The Commission on Indigent Defense Services hereby adopts these performance guidelines to promote one of the purposes of the Indigent Defense Services Act of 2000—improving the quality of indigent defense representation in North Carolina—and pursuant to G.S. 7A–498.5(c)(4).

(b) These guidelines are intended to serve as a guide for attorney performance in non-capital criminal cases at the trial level, and contain a set of considerations and recommendations to assist counsel in providing quality representation for indigent criminal defendants. The guidelines also may be used as a training tool.

(c) These are performance guidelines, not standards. The steps covered in these guidelines are not to be undertaken automatically in every case. Instead, the steps actually taken should be tailored to the requirements of a particular case. In deciding what steps are appropriate, counsel should use his or her best professional judgment.

Guideline 1.2. Role of Defense Counsel

(a) The paramount obligations of criminal defense counsel are to provide zealous and quality representation to their clients at all stages of the criminal process, and to preserve, protect, and promote their clients' rights and interests throughout the criminal proceedings. Attorneys also have an obligation to conduct themselves professionally, abide by the Revised Rules of Professional Conduct of the North Carolina State Bar and other ethical norms, and act in accordance with all rules of court.

(b) Defense counsel are the professional representatives of their clients. Counsel should candidly advise clients regarding the probable success and consequences of adopting any posture in the proceedings, and provide clients with all information necessary to make informed decisions. Counsel does not have an obligation to execute any directive of a client that does not comport with law or standards of ethics or professional conduct.

Guideline 1.3. Education, Training and Experience of Defense Counsel

(a) To provide quality representation, counsel must be familiar with the substantive criminal law and the law of criminal procedure and its application in North Carolina. Counsel should also be informed of any applicable local rules, including those set forth in the district's case docketing plan, as well as the practices of the specific judge before whom a case is pending.

(b) Counsel has an ongoing obligation to stay abreast of changes and developments in criminal law and procedure, and to continue his or her legal education, skills training, and professional development.

(c) Prior to accepting appointment to an indigent criminal matter, counsel should have sufficient experience, skills, training, and supervision to provide quality representation. Where appropriate to provide competent representation, counsel should consult with more experienced attorneys to acquire necessary knowledge and information, including information about the practices of judges, prosecutors, and other court personnel.

Guideline 1.4. General Duties of Defense Counsel

(a) Before accepting appointment to an indigent criminal case, an attorney has an obligation to ensure that he or she has available sufficient time, resources, knowledge, and experience to afford quality representation to a defendant in a particular matter. If it later appears that counsel is unable to afford quality representation in the case, counsel should move to withdraw. If counsel is allowed to withdraw, he or she should cooperate with new counsel to the extent that such cooperation is in the best interests of the client and in accord with the Revised Rules of Professional Conduct.

(b) Counsel must be alert to all actual and potential conflicts of interest that would impair their ability to represent a client. If counsel identifies an actual conflict of interest, counsel should immediately move to withdraw. If counsel identifies a potential conflict of interest, counsel should fully disclose the conflict to all affected clients and, if appropriate, obtain informed consent to proceed on behalf of those clients. Where appropriate, counsel may seek an advisory opinion on any potential conflicts from the North Carolina State Bar. Mere tactical disagreements between counsel and a client ordinarily do not justify withdrawal from a case. If it is necessary for counsel to withdraw, counsel should do so in a way that protects the client's rights and interests, and does not violate counsel's ethical duties to the client.

(c) Counsel has an obligation to maintain regular contact with the client and keep the client informed of the progress of the case. Counsel should promptly comply with a client's reasonable requests for information, and reply to client correspondence and telephone calls.

(d) Counsel should appear on time for all scheduled court hearings in a client's case. If scheduling conflicts arise, counsel should resolve them in accordance with Rule 3.1 of the General Rules of Practice.

(e) Counsel should never give preference to retained clients over appointed clients, or suggest that retained clients should or would receive preference.

SECTION 2

Guideline 2.1. General Obligations of Counsel Regarding Pretrial Release

Where appropriate, counsel has an obligation to attempt to secure the prompt pretrial release of the client under the conditions most favorable to the client.

Guideline 2.2. Initial Interview

(a) Counsel shall arrange for an initial interview with the client as soon as practicable after being assigned to the client's case. Absent exceptional circumstances, if the client is in custody, the initial interview should take place within three business days after counsel receives notice of assignment to the client's case. If necessary, counsel may arrange for a designee to conduct the initial interview.

(b) *Preparation*:

Prior to conducting the initial interview, the attorney should, where possible:

(1) be familiar with the charges against the client, as well as the elements and potential punishment of each charged offense;

(2) obtain copies of any relevant documents that are available, including copies of any charging documents, recommendations and reports made by pretrial service or detention agencies concerning pretrial release, and law enforcement reports;

(3) be familiar with the legal criteria for determining pretrial release conditions and the procedures that will be followed in setting those conditions;

(4) be familiar with the different types of pretrial release conditions the court may set, as well as any written policies of the judicial district, and whether any pretrial service or other agencies are available to act as a custodian for the client's release; and

(5) be familiar with any procedures available for reviewing the trial judge's setting of bail.

(c) *The Interview*:

(1) The purpose of the initial interview is to acquire information from the client concerning pretrial release and, where appropriate, the facts of the case, and to provide the client with information concerning the case. Counsel should try to ensure at this and all successive interviews and proceedings that barriers to communication, such as differences in language or literacy, be overcome. If appropriate, counsel should file a motion to have a foreign language or sign language interpreter appointed by the court and present at the initial interview.

(2) Information that should be acquired during the initial interview includes, but is not limited to:

(A) the client's ties to the community, including the length of time he or she has lived at the current and former addresses, family relationships, employment record and history, and immigration status (if applicable);

(B) the client's physical and mental health, including any impairing conditions such as substance abuse or learning disabilities, and educational and armed services history;

(C) the client's immediate medical and/or mental health needs;

(D) the client's past criminal history, if any, including arrests and convictions for adult and juvenile offenses and prior history of court appearances or failure to appear in court;

(E) the existence of any other pending charges against the client and the identity of any other appointed or retained counsel;

(F) whether the client is on probation or parole, and the client's past or present performance under supervision;

(G) the ability of the client to meet any financial conditions of release; and

(H) the names of individuals or other sources that counsel can contact to verify the information provided by the client, and the permission of the client to contact those individuals.

(3) Information to be provided to the client during the initial interview includes, but is not limited to:

(A) an explanation of the procedures that will be followed in setting the conditions of pretrial release;

(B) an explanation of the type of information that will be requested in any interview that may be conducted by a pretrial release agency, and an explanation that the client is not required to and should not make statements concerning the offense;

(C) an explanation of the attorney-client privilege and instructions not to talk to anyone about the facts of the case without first consulting the attorney;

(D) the nature of the charges and potential penalties;

(E) a general procedural overview of the progression of the case, where possible;

(F) how counsel can be reached and when counsel plans to have contact with the client next;

(G) realistic answers, where possible, to the client's most urgent questions; and

(H) what arrangements will be made or attempted for the satisfaction of the client's most pressing needs, such as medical or mental health attention, and contact with family members.

(4) Where appropriate, counsel should be prepared at the initial interview to ask the client to sign a release authorizing counsel to access confidential information.

(d) *Additional Information*

Whenever possible, counsel should use the initial interview to gather additional information relevant to preparation of the defense. Such information may include, but is not limited to:

(1) the facts surrounding the charges against the client and the client's view of any potential defenses;

(2) any evidence of improper police investigative practices or prosecutorial conduct that may affect the client's rights;

(3) any possible witnesses who should be located;

(4) any evidence that should be preserved; and

(5) where appropriate, evidence of the client's competence to stand trial and/or mental state at the time of the offense.

Guideline 2.3. Pretrial Release Proceedings in Misdemeanor and Felony Cases

(a) As soon as possible after appointment, where the client has not been able to obtain pretrial release, counsel should consider filing a motion to reduce bond or otherwise modify any pretrial release conditions that were set by the magistrate or other judicial official at the client's initial appearance.

(b) Counsel should be prepared to present to the appropriate judicial official a statement of the factual circumstances and the legal criteria supporting release and, where appropriate, to make a proposal concerning conditions of release. Counsel should consider the potential consequences of allowing the client to make statements at any bond reduction hearing.

(c) In counties with a pretrial service program, counsel should consider utilizing the services of that program where it would be likely to benefit the client.

(d) Counsel should fully inform the client of his or her conditions of release after such conditions have been set by the court.

(e) If the court sets conditions of release that require the posting of a monetary bond or the posting of real property as collateral for release, counsel should be familiar with and explain to the client the available options and the procedures that must be followed in posting such assets. Where appropriate, counsel should advise the client and others acting in his or her behalf how properly to post such assets.

(f) Where the client is incarcerated and unable to obtain pretrial release, counsel should alert the jail, and if appropriate the court, to any special medical or psychiatric and security needs of the client that are known to counsel.

Guideline 2.4. Probable Cause Hearing in Felony Cases

(a) Counsel should discuss with the client the meaning of probable cause and the procedural aspects surrounding a probable cause determination, and should consider the tactical advantages and disadvantages of having a probable cause hearing. Counsel should consider any concessions the prosecution might make if the defendant waives, or does not oppose a continuance of, a probable cause hearing. Before waiving a probable cause hearing, counsel should consider the possible benefits of a hearing, including the potential for discovery and the development of impeachment evidence. Counsel also should be aware of all consequences if the client waives a probable cause hearing, including the effect of waiver on the statutory deadline for requesting voluntary discovery under G.S. 15A–902(d).

(b) In preparing for a probable cause hearing, counsel should consider:

(1) the elements of each of the offenses alleged;

(2) the law for establishing probable cause;

(3) factual information that is available concerning the existence or lack of probable cause;

(4) the tactics of full or partial cross-examination;

(5) additional factual information and impeachment evidence that could be discovered by counsel during the hearing; and

(6) any continuing need to pursue modification of the conditions of release if the client is in custody.

Counsel ordinarily should not call the client or defense witnesses to testify at the probable cause hearing unless there are sound tactical reasons for doing so.

Guideline 2.5. Charging Language in Criminal Pleadings

(a) Counsel should review the criminal pleadings in all cases and, unless there are sound tactical reasons for not doing so, move to dismiss the pleading if there are defects in the charging language, including but not limited to:

(1) the pleading does not list all of the essential elements of the charged offense; and

(2) the pleading contains more than one charge in a single count.

(b) Even if the pleading adequately charges a crime, counsel should be sufficiently familiar with the language of the pleading to recognize a fatal variance at trial and move to dismiss the charge if the evidence is insufficient to support the charge as pled.

(c) Counsel should be aware of all time limits applicable to challenges to defects in the charging language of a criminal pleading. Counsel also should be aware of the potential consequences of alerting the prosecution to defects in the charging language.

Guideline 2.6. Indictments and Bills of Information in Felony Cases

(a) Upon return of a bill of indictment, unless there are sound tactical reasons for not doing so, counsel should consider any potential grounds for quashing the indictment or challenges to the grand jury proceedings, including, but not limited to:

(1) improper composition of the grand jury as a whole, including any systematic exclusion of qualified persons either in the drawing of the list of potential grand jurors or the selecting of grand jurors from the list;

(2) the inclusion of a grand juror who does not meet the requirements of G.S. 9–3;

(3) the bill of indictment lacks the signatures and markings required by G.S. 15A–644;

(4) the bill of indictment was not found to be true by at least twelve grand jurors and/or was not returned in open court; and

(5) the bill of indictment was based entirely on the testimony of witnesses who were disqualified or evidence that is incompetent.

(b) Counsel should be aware of all time limits applicable to motions to quash the indictment or challenges to the grand jury proceedings.

(c) Where applicable, counsel should consider, and inform the client of, the advantages and disadvantages of waiving a bill of indictment and consenting to a bill of information pursuant to G.S. 15A–642 and G.S. 15A–923.

Guideline 2.7. Arraignment in Felony Cases

Counsel should consider whether to request arraignment under G.S. 15A–941(d). Counsel should be aware that some pretrial motions may be waived if they are not filed at or before arraignment (or within the time limit prescribed by G.S. 15A–952 if arraignment is waived), including a motion to continue, motion challenging venue or for change of venue, motion to join or sever offenses, motion challenging grand jury composition, motion for a bill of particulars, and motion challenging non-jurisdictional pleading defects. Counsel should also consult local calendaring rules to determine whether they establish different deadlines for pretrial motions.

SECTION 3

Guideline 3.1. Search Warrants and Prosecution Requests for Non-Testimonial Evidence

(a) Counsel should be familiar with the law governing search warrants under G.S. 15A–241 *et seq.* and applicable case law, including, but not limited to, the requirements for a search warrant application, the basis for issuing a search warrant, the required form and content of a search warrant, the execution and service of a search warrant, and the permissible scope of the search.

(b) Counsel should be familiar with the law governing the prosecution's power to require a defendant to provide non-testimonial evidence (such as participation in an in-person lineup, handwriting exemplars, and physical specimens), the potential consequences if a defendant refuses to comply with a non-testimonial identification order issued pursuant to G.S. 15A–271 *et seq.*, and the extent to which counsel may participate in or observe the proceedings.

Guideline 3.2. Client's Competence and Capacity to Proceed

(a) When defense counsel has a good faith doubt as to the client's capacity to proceed in a criminal case, counsel may:

(1) file an *ex parte* motion to obtain the services of a mental health expert and thereby determine whether to raise the client's competency before the court; or

(2) file a motion questioning the client's competence to stand trial or enter a plea under G.S. 15A–1001(a) and applicable case law, in which case the court may order a mental health examination at a state mental

health facility or by the appropriate local forensic examiner.

(b) While the client's wishes ordinarily control, counsel may question competency without the client's assent or over the client's objection if necessary.

(c) After counsel receives and reviews the report from any court-ordered competency examination, counsel should consider whether to file a motion requesting a formal hearing on the client's capacity to proceed.

(d) Whenever competency is at issue, counsel still has a continuing duty to prepare the case for all anticipated court proceedings.

(e) If the court enters an order finding the client incompetent and orders involuntary commitment proceedings to be initiated, defense counsel ordinarily will not represent the client at those proceedings, but should cooperate with the commitment attorney upon request.

SECTION 4

Guideline 4.1. Case Review, Investigation, and Preparation

(a) Counsel has a duty to conduct an independent case review and investigation. The client's admissions or statements to counsel of facts constituting guilt do not necessarily obviate the need for such independent review and investigation. The review and investigation should be conducted as promptly as possible.

(b) Sources of review and investigative information may include the following:

(1) *Charging Documents, Statutes, and Case Law*

Copies of all charging documents in the case should be obtained and examined to determine the specific charges that have been brought against the client. The relevant statutes and precedents should be examined to identify:

(A) the elements of the offense(s) with which the client is charged;

(B) the defenses, ordinary and affirmative, that may be available, as well as the proper manner and timeline for asserting any available defenses; and

(C) any defects in the charging documents, constitutional or otherwise, such as statute of limitations, double jeopardy, or irregularities in the grand jury proceedings.

(2) *The Client*

An in-depth interview or interviews of the client should be used to:

(A) seek information concerning the incident or events giving rise to the charge(s);

(B) elicit information concerning possible improper police investigative practices or prosecutorial conduct that may affect the client's rights;

(C) explore the existence of other potential sources of information relating to the offense or client, including school, work, jail, probation, and prison records;

(D) collect information relevant to sentencing; and

(E) continue to assess the client's medical and/or mental health needs.

(3) *Potential Witnesses*

Counsel should consider whether to interview the potential witnesses, including any complaining witnesses and others adverse to the client. If the attorney conducts such interviews of potential witnesses, he or she should attempt to do so in the presence of a third person who will be available, if necessary, to testify as a defense witness at trial. Alternatively, counsel should have an investigator conduct such interviews.

(4) *The Police and Prosecution*

Counsel should utilize available discovery procedures to secure information in the possession of the prosecution or law enforcement authorities, including police reports, unless a sound tactical reason exists for not doing so (*e.g.*, defense obligations under G.S. 15A–905).

(5) *The Courts*

If possible, counsel should request and review any tapes or transcripts from previous hearings in the case. Counsel should also review the client's prior court file(s) where appropriate.

(6) *Information in the Possession of Third Parties*

Where appropriate, counsel should seek a release or court order to obtain necessary confidential information about the client, co-defendant(s), witness(es), or victim(s) that is in the possession of third parties. Counsel should be aware of privacy laws and other requirements governing disclosure of the type of confidential information being sought.

(7) *Physical Evidence*

Where appropriate, counsel should make a prompt request to the police or investigative agency for any physical evidence or expert reports relevant to the offense or sentencing. Counsel should view the physical evidence consistent with case needs.

(8) *The Scene*

Where appropriate, counsel or an investigator should view the scene of the alleged offense. This should be done under circumstances as similar as possible to those existing at the time of the alleged incident (*e.g.*, weather, time of day, lighting conditions, and seasonal changes). Counsel should consider the taking of photographs and the creation of diagrams or charts of the actual scene of the alleged offense.

(9) *Assistance from Experts, Investigators, and Interpreters*

Counsel should consider whether expert or investigative assistance, including consultation and testimony, is necessary or appropriate to:

(A) prepare a defense;

(B) adequately understand the prosecution's case;

(C) rebut the prosecution's case; and/or

(D) investigate the client's competence to proceed, mental state at the time of the offense, and/or capacity to make a knowing and intelligent waiver of constitutional rights.

If counsel determines that expert or investigative assistance is necessary and appropriate, counsel should file an *ex parte* motion setting forth the particularized showing of necessity required by *Ake v. Oklahoma, State v. Ballard*, and their progeny. If appropriate, counsel should file a motion to have a foreign language or sign language interpreter appointed by the court. Counsel should take all necessary steps to preserve for appeal any denial of expert, investigative, or interpreter funding.

(c) During case preparation and throughout trial, counsel should identify potential legal issues and the corresponding objections. Counsel should consider the tactics of when and how to raise those objections. Counsel should also consider how best to respond to objections that could be raised by the prosecution.

Guideline 4.2. Discovery in Cases Within the Original Jurisdiction of the Superior Court

(a) Counsel has a duty to pursue discovery procedures provided by the applicable rules of criminal procedure within the time periods prescribed by G.S. 15A–902, and to pursue such informal discovery methods as may be available to supplement the factual investigation of the case.

(b) Prior to filing a formal motion with the court, counsel must first serve the prosecutor with a written request for voluntary discovery unless counsel and the prosecutor agree in writing to comply voluntarily with G.S. 15A–901 *et seq.* Counsel must file a motion to compel discovery if the prosecution's response is unsatisfactory or delayed. Regardless of the prosecution's response, counsel should file a motion to compel discovery if the case is proceeding to trial.

(c) In exceptional cases, counsel should consider not making a discovery request or signing a written agreement under G.S. 15A–902(a), on the ground that it will trigger a defense obligation to disclose evidence under G.S. 15A–905.

(d) Unless there is a sound tactical reason for not requesting discovery or signing a written agreement under G.S. 15A–902(a) (*e.g.*, defense obligations under G.S. 15A–905), counsel should seek discovery to the broadest extent permitted under federal and state law, including but not limited to, the following items:

(1) all information to which the defendant is entitled under G.S. 15A–903;

(2) all potential exculpatory information and evidence to which the defense is entitled under *Brady v. Maryland* and its progeny, including but not limited to:

(A) impeachment evidence, such as a witness' prior convictions or other misconduct; bias of a witness; a witness' capacity to observe, perceive, or recollect; and psychiatric evaluations of a witness;

(B) evidence discrediting police investigation and credibility;

(C) evidence undermining the identification of the client;

(D) evidence tending to show the guilt of another;

(E) the identity of favorable witnesses; and

(F) exculpatory physical evidence; and

(3) to the extent not provided under statutory discovery, any other information necessary to the defense of the case, including but not limited to:

(A) the names, addresses, and availability of state witnesses;

(B) the details of the circumstances under which any oral or written statements by the accused or a co-defendant were made;

(C) any evidence of prior bad acts that the prosecution may intend to use against the client;

(D) the data underlying any expert reports; and

(E) any evidence necessary to enable counsel to determine whether to file a motion to suppress evidence under G.S. 15A–971 *et seq.*

(e) Counsel should seek the timely production and preservation of discoverable evidence. If the prosecution fails to disclose or belatedly discloses discoverable evidence, counsel should consider requesting one or more of the sanctions provided by G.S. 15A–910.

(f) If counsel believes the state may destroy or consume in testing evidence that is significant to the case (*e.g.*, rough notes of law enforcement interviews, 911 tapes, drugs, or blood samples), counsel should also file a motion to preserve the evidence in the event that it is discoverable.

(g) Counsel should timely comply with all of the requirements in G.S. 15A–905 governing disclosure of evidence by the defendant and notice of defenses and expert witnesses. Counsel also should be aware of the possible sanctions for failure to comply with those requirements under G.S. 15A–910.

Guideline 4.3. Theory of the Case

During case review, investigation, and trial preparation, counsel should develop and continually reassess a theory of the case. A theory of the case is one central theory that organizes the facts, emotions, and legal basis for the client's acquittal or conviction of a lesser offense, while also telling the defense story of innocence, reduced culpability, or unfairness. The theory of the case furnishes the basic position from which counsel determines all actions in a case.

SECTION 5

Guideline 5.1. The Decision to File Pretrial Motions

(a) Counsel should consider filing appropriate pretrial motions whenever there exists a good-faith reason to believe that the applicable law may entitle the client to relief which the court has authority to grant.

(b) The decision to file pretrial motions should be made after thorough investigation and after considering the applicable law in light of the circumstances of each case, as well as the need to preserve issues for appellate review. Among the issues that counsel should consider addressing in pretrial motions are:

(1) the pretrial custody of the client and a motion to review conditions of release;

(2) the constitutionality of the implicated statute or statutes;

(3) any potential defects in the grand jury composition or charging process;

(4) the sufficiency of the charging document under all applicable statutory and constitutional provisions;

(5) the dismissal of a charge on double jeopardy grounds;

(6) the need for a bill of particulars;

(7) the propriety and prejudice of any joinder or severance of charges or defendants;

(8) the statutory and constitutional discovery obligations of the prosecution;

(9) the suppression of evidence gathered as the result of violations of the North Carolina Constitution and the United States Constitution, including:

(A) the fruits of illegal searches or seizures;

(B) involuntary statements or confessions;

(C) statements or confessions obtained in violation of the client's right to counsel, or privilege against self-incrimination; and

(D) unreliable identification evidence that would give rise to a substantial likelihood of irreparable misidentification;

(10) the suppression of evidence gathered in violation of any right, duty, or privilege arising out of North Carolina law;

(11) access to necessary support or investigative resources or experts;

(12) the need for a change of venue;

(13) the defendant's speedy trial rights and/or calendaring rights under G.S. 7A–49.4;

(14) the defendant's right to a continuance in order adequately to prepare his or her case;

(15) matters of trial evidence that may be appropriately litigated by means of a pretrial motion in *limine*;

(16) the suppression of a prior conviction obtained in violation of the defendant's right to counsel;

(17) the recusal of the trial judge;

(18) the full recordation of all proceedings pursuant to G.S. 15A–1241;

(19) matters of trial or courtroom procedure; and

(20) notice of affirmative defenses if required by G.S. 15A–905(c) and G.S. 15A–959.

(c) Counsel should be aware of all time limits on the filing of pretrial motions, and should know whether a motion must or may be accompanied by a factual affidavit.

(d) Unless there are sound tactical reasons for not doing so, counsel should request that the court rule on all previously filed defense motions.

Guideline 5.2. Filing and Arguing Pretrial Motions

(a) Motions should be filed in a timely manner, should comport with the formal requirements of statute and court rules, and should succinctly inform the court of the authority relied upon.

(b) When a hearing on a motion requires the taking of evidence, counsel's preparation for the evidentiary hearing should include:

(1) investigation, discovery, and research relevant to the claim(s) advanced;

(2) the subpoenaing of all helpful evidence, and the subpoenaing and preparation of all helpful witnesses;

(3) full understanding of the burdens of proof, evidentiary principles and procedures applying to the hearing, including the benefits and costs of having the client and other defense witnesses testify;

(4) obtaining the assistance of an expert witness where appropriate and necessary; and

(5) preparation and submission of a memorandum of law where appropriate.

(c) If a hearing on a pretrial motion is held in advance of trial, counsel should attempt to obtain the transcript of the hearing for use at trial where appropriate.

Guideline 5.3. Subsequent Filing and Renewal of Pretrial Motions

Counsel should be prepared to raise during the subsequent proceedings any issue that is appropriately raised pretrial, but could not have been so raised because the facts supporting the motion were unknown or not reasonably available. Further, counsel should be prepared to renew pretrial motions or file additional motions at any subsequent stage of the proceedings if new supporting information is later disclosed or made available. Counsel should also renew pretrial motions and object to the admission of challenged evidence at trial as necessary to preserve the motions and objections for appellate review.

SECTION 6

Guideline 6.1. The Plea Negotiation Process and the Duties of Counsel

(a) After appropriate investigation and case review, counsel should explore with the client the possibility and desirability of reaching a negotiated disposition of the charges rather than proceeding to trial. In doing so, counsel should fully explain to the client the rights that would be waived by a decision to enter a plea and not proceed to trial.

(b) Counsel should keep the client fully informed of any plea discussions and negotiations, and convey to the client any offers made by the prosecution for a negotiated settlement. Counsel may not accept any plea agreement without the client's express authorization.

(c) Counsel should explain to the client those decisions that ultimately must be made by the client, as well as the advantages and disadvantages inherent in those choices. The decisions that must be made by the client after full consultation with counsel include whether to plead guilty or not guilty, whether to accept a plea agreement, and whether to testify at the plea hearing. Counsel should also explain to the client the impact of the decision to enter a guilty plea on the client's right to appeal. Although the decision to enter a plea of guilty ultimately rests with the client, if counsel believes the client's decisions are not in his or her best interest, counsel should attempt to persuade the client to change his or her position.

(d) Notwithstanding the existence of ongoing tentative plea negotiations with the prosecution, counsel should continue to prepare and investigate the case to the extent necessary to protect the client's rights and interests in the event that plea negotiations fail.

(e) Counsel should not allow a client to plead guilty based on oral conditions that are not disclosed to the court. Counsel should ensure that all conditions and promises comprising a plea arrangement between the prosecution and defense are included in writing in the transcript of plea.

Guideline 6.2. The Contents of the Negotiations

(a) In conducting plea negotiations, counsel should attempt to become familiar with any practices and policies of the particular district, judge, and prosecuting attorney that may affect the content and likely results of a negotiated plea bargain.

(b) To develop an overall negotiation plan, counsel should be fully aware of, and fully advise the client of:

(1) the maximum term of imprisonment that may be ordered under the applicable sentencing laws, including any habitual offender statutes, sentencing enhancements, mandatory minimum sentence requirements, and mandatory consecutive sentence requirements;

(2) the possibility of forfeiture of assets seized in connection with the case;

(3) any registration requirements, including sex offender registration;

(4) the likelihood that a conviction could be used for sentence enhancement in the event of future criminal cases, such as sentencing in the aggravated range, habitual offender status, or felon in possession of a firearm;

(5) the possibility of earned-time credits;

(6) the availability of appropriate diversion or rehabilitation programs;

(7) the likelihood of the court imposing financial obligations on the client, including the payment of attorney fees, court costs, fines, and restitution; and

(8) the effect on the client's appellate rights.

Counsel should also discuss with the client that there may be other potential collateral consequences of entering a plea, such as deportation or other effects on immigration status; motor vehicle or other licensing; parental rights; possession of firearms; voting rights; employment, military, and government service considerations; and the potential exposure to or impact on any federal charges.

(c) In developing a negotiation strategy, counsel should be completely familiar with:

(1) concessions that the client might offer the prosecution as part of a negotiated settlement, including but not limited to:

(A) declining to assert the right to proceed to trial on the merits of the charges;

(B) refraining from asserting or litigating any particular pretrial motion(s);

(C) agreeing to fulfill specified restitution conditions and/or participation in community work or service programs, or in rehabilitation or other programs;

(D) providing the prosecution with assistance in prosecuting or investigating the present case or other alleged criminal activity;

(E) waiving challenges to validity or proof of prior convictions; and

(F) waiving the right to indictment and consenting to a bill of information on a related but unindicted offense;

(2) benefits the client might obtain from a negotiated settlement, including but not limited to, an agreement:

(A) that the prosecution will not oppose the client's release on bail pending sentencing or appeal;

(B) that the client may enter a conditional plea to preserve the right to litigate and contest the denial of a suppression motion;

(C) to dismiss or reduce one or more of the charged offenses either immediately, or upon completion of a deferred prosecution agreement;

(D) that the client will not be subject to further investigation or prosecution for uncharged alleged criminal conduct;

(E) that the client will receive, with the agreement of the court, a specified sentence or sanction or a sentence or sanction within a specified range;

(F) that at the time of sentencing and/or in communications with the preparer of a sentencing services plan or presentence report, the prosecution will take, or refrain from taking, a specified position with respect to the sanction to be imposed on the client by the court; and

(G) that at the time of sentencing and/or in communications with the preparer of a sentencing services plan or presentence report, the prosecution will not present certain information;

(3) information favorable to the client concerning such matters as the offense, mitigating factors and relative culpability, prior offenses, personal background, employment record and opportunities, educational background, and family and financial status;

(4) information that would support a sentencing disposition other than incarceration, such as the potential for rehabilitation or the nonviolent nature of the crime; and

(5) information concerning the availability of treatment programs, community treatment facilities, and community service work opportunities.

(d) In conducting plea negotiations, counsel should be familiar with:

(1) the various types of pleas that may be agreed to, including a plea of guilty, a plea of *nolo contendere*, a conditional plea of guilty in which the defendant retains the right to appeal the denial of a suppression motion, and a plea in which the defendant is not required to personally acknowledge his or her guilt (*Alford* plea);

(2) the advantages and disadvantages of each available plea according to the circumstances of the case; and

(3) whether the plea agreement is binding on the court and prison authorities.

Guideline 6.3. The Decision to Enter a Plea of Guilty

(a) Counsel shall inform the client of any tentative negotiated agreement reached with the prosecution, and explain to the client the full content of the agreement, including its advantages, disadvantages, and potential consequences.

(b) When counsel reasonably believes that acceptance of a plea offer is in the client's best interests, counsel should attempt to persuade the client to accept the plea offer. However, the decision to enter a plea of guilty ultimately rests with the client.

Guideline 6.4. Entry of the Plea before the Court

(a) Prior to the entry of a plea, counsel should:

(1) fully explain to the client the rights he or she will waive by entering the plea;

(2) fully explain to the client the conditions and limits of the plea agreement and the maximum punishment, sanctions, and other consequences the client will be exposed to by entering a plea; and

(3) fully explain to the client the nature of the plea hearing and prepare the client for the role he or she may play in the hearing, including answering questions of the judge and providing a statement concerning the offense.

(b) When entering the plea, counsel should ensure that the full content and conditions of the plea agreement between the prosecution and defense are made part of the transcript of plea.

(c) Subsequent to the acceptance of a plea, counsel should review and explain the plea proceedings to the client, and respond to any client questions and concerns.

SECTION 7

Guideline 7.1. General Trial Preparation

(a) Throughout preparation and trial, counsel should consider the theory of the defense and ensure that counsel's decisions and actions are consistent with that theory.

(b) The decision to proceed to trial rests solely with the client. Counsel should discuss with the client the relevant strategic considerations of this decision. When appropriate, counsel should also explain to the client that decisions concerning trial strategy are ordinarily to be made by counsel, after consultation with the client and investigation of the applicable facts and law. However, counsel should be aware that, under North Carolina law, if counsel and a fully informed competent client reach an absolute impasse as to tactical decisions, the client's wishes may control.

(c) In advance of trial, counsel should take all steps necessary to complete thorough investigation, discovery, and research. Among the steps counsel should consider in preparation are:

(1) interviewing and subpoenaing all potentially helpful witnesses;

(2) examining and subpoenaing all potentially helpful physical or documentary evidence;

(3) obtaining funds for defense investigators and experts, and arranging for defense experts to consult and/or testify on issues that are potentially helpful;

(4) obtaining and reading transcripts of any prior proceedings in the case or related proceedings; and

(5) obtaining photographs or preparing charts, maps, diagrams, or other visual aids of all scenes, persons, objects, or information that may aid the fact finder in understanding the defense case.

(d) Where appropriate, counsel should have the following information and materials available at the time of trial:

(1) copies of all relevant documents filed in the case;

(2) relevant documents prepared by investigators;

(3) reports, test results, and other materials disclosed by the prosecution pursuant to G.S. 15A–901 *et seq.*;

(4) *voir dire* topics, plans, or questions;

(5) a plan, outline, or draft of opening statement;

(6) cross–examination plans for all possible prosecution witnesses;

(7) direct–examination plans for all prospective defense witnesses;

(8) copies of defense subpoenas;

(9) prior statements of all prosecution witnesses (*e.g.*, transcripts, police reports);

(10) prior statements of all defense witnesses;

(11) reports from defense experts;

(12) a list of all defense exhibits, and the witnesses through whom they will be introduced;

(13) originals and copies of all documentary exhibits;

(14) proposed jury instructions with supporting case citations;

(15) copies of critical statutes and cases; and

(16) a plan, outline, or draft of closing argument.

(e) Counsel should be fully informed as to the rules of evidence and the law relating to all stages of the trial process, and should be familiar with legal and evidentiary issues that reasonably can be anticipated to arise in the trial.

(f) Counsel should be familiar with case law concerning making admissions of guilt to the jury without the client's consent.

(g) Counsel should decide if it is beneficial to secure an advance ruling on issues likely to arise at trial (*e.g.*, use of prior convictions to impeach the defendant) and, where appropriate, should prepare motions and memoranda for such advance rulings.

(h) Where appropriate, counsel should advise the client as to suitable courtroom dress and demeanor. If the client is incarcerated, counsel should try to ensure that the client does not appear before the jury in jail or other inappropriate clothing, or in shackles or handcuffs. If an incarcerated client is brought before the jury in jail clothing, shackles, or handcuffs, counsel should object and seek appropriate relief from the court.

(i) Counsel should plan with the client, court personnel, and/or sheriff's office for the most convenient system for conferring throughout the trial.

(j) Throughout preparation and trial, counsel should consider the potential effects that particular actions may have upon sentencing if there is a finding of guilt.

Guideline 7.2. Preserving the Record on Appeal

Counsel should establish a proper record for appellate review throughout the trial process, including requesting recordation of all significant portions of the trial under G.S. 15A–1241(b). If something non-verbal transpires during trial that is relevant and important, counsel should ask to have the record reflect what happened.

Guideline 7.3. *Voir Dire* and Jury Selection

(a) *Preparation*

(1) Counsel should be familiar with the procedures by which a jury panel is selected, and should be alert to any potential legal challenges to the composition or selection of the panel.

(2) Counsel should be familiar with the local practices and the individual trial judge's procedures for selecting a jury from the panel, and should be alert to any potential legal challenges to those procedures.

(3) Prior to jury selection, counsel should seek to obtain a prospective juror list where feasible, and should develop a method for tracking juror selection and seating.

(4) Counsel should be familiar with any juror questionnaire that may be used by the court or prosecution and, where appropriate, should develop a defense questionnaire and file a pretrial motion to authorize its use.

(5) In advance of trial, counsel should develop *voir dire* topics, plans, or questions that are tailored to the specific case. Among the purposes *voir dire* questions should be designed to serve are:

(A) to elicit information about the attitudes of individual jurors, which will inform the use of peremptory strikes and challenges for cause;

(B) to determine the jurors' attitudes toward legal principles that are critical to the defense case, including, where appropriate, the client's decision not to testify; and

(C) to present the client, preview the defense case, and assess the impact of damaging information on the jurors' ability to fairly consider the case.

In conducting *voir dire*, counsel should be aware that jurors may develop impressions of counsel and the defendant, and should recognize the importance of establishing a relationship of credibility.

(6) Counsel should be familiar with the law concerning mandatory and discretionary *voir dire* inquiries so as to be able to defend any request to ask particular questions of prospective jurors.

(7) Counsel should be familiar with the law concerning challenges for cause and peremptory strikes. Counsel also should be aware of the statutory and case law directing that peremptory challenges need to be exhausted in order to preserve for appeal the denial of any challenges for cause.

(b) *Examining the Prospective Jurors*

(1) Counsel should personally conduct the *voir dire* examination of the panel.

(2) If the court denies counsel's request to ask questions during *voir dire* that are significant or necessary to the defense of the case, counsel should take all steps necessary to protect the *voir dire* record for appeal, including filing a written motion listing the proposed *voir dire* questions or otherwise making proposed questions part of the record.

(3) If the *voir dire* questions may elicit sensitive answers or where otherwise appropriate, counsel should request individual *voir dire*.

(c) *Challenges and Objections*

(1) Counsel should consider challenging for cause all persons who are subject to challenge under G.S. 15A–1212, including all persons about whom a legitimate argument can be made for actual prejudice or bias relevant to the case, when it is likely to benefit the client.

(2) When a challenge for cause is denied, counsel should consider exercising a peremptory challenge to remove the juror. Counsel should be aware of the requirements in G.S. 15A–1214(h) for preserving the denial of a challenge for cause for appellate review.

(3) In exercising challenges for cause and peremptory strikes, counsel should consider both the panelists who may replace a person who is removed and the total number of peremptory challenges available.

(4) Counsel should object to and preserve for appellate review all issues relating to the unconstitutional exclusion of jurors by the prosecution or court.

Guideline 7.4. Opening Statement

(a) Prior to delivering an opening statement, counsel should consider whether to ask for sequestration of witnesses.

(b) Counsel should be familiar with North Carolina law and the individual trial judge's practices regarding the permissible content of an opening statement. Counsel should consider the need to, and if appropriate, ask the court to instruct the prosecution not to mention in opening statement contested evidence for which the court has not determined admissibility.

(c) Counsel should consider the strategic advantages and disadvantages of disclosure of particular information during opening statement.

(d) Counsel's objectives in making an opening statement may include the following:

(1) to introduce the theory of the defense case;

(2) to provide an overview of the defense case;

(3) to identify the weaknesses of the prosecution's case;

(4) to emphasize the prosecution's burden of proof;

(5) to summarize the anticipated testimony of witnesses, and the role of each in relationship to the entire case;

(6) to describe the exhibits that will be introduced and the role of each in relationship to the entire case;

(7) to clarify the jurors' responsibilities;

(8) to state the ultimate inferences counsel wants the jury to draw;

(9) to personalize the client and counsel for the jury; and

(10) to prepare the jury for the client's testimony or decision not to testify.

(e) Counsel should consider incorporating the promises of proof the prosecutor makes to the jury during opening statement into the defense opening statement and summation.

(f) Whenever the prosecutor oversteps the bounds of a proper opening statement, counsel should consider objecting, requesting a mistrial, or seeking cautionary instructions, unless sound tactical considerations weigh against any such objections or requests. Such tactical considerations may include, but are not limited to:

(1) the significance of the prosecutor's error; and

(2) the possibility that an objection might enhance the significance of the information in the jurors' minds, or otherwise negatively affect the jury.

Guideline 7.5. Confronting the Prosecution's Case

(a) Counsel should anticipate weaknesses in the prosecution's proof, and research and prepare to argue corresponding motions for judgment of dismissal or nonsuit.

(b) Counsel should consider the advantages and disadvantages of entering into stipulations concerning the prosecution's case.

(c) Unless sound tactical reasons exist for not doing so, counsel should make timely objections and motions to strike improper state evidence, and assert all possible statutory and constitutional grounds for exclusion of the evidence. If evidence is admissible only for a limited purpose, counsel should consider requesting an appropriate limiting instruction.

(d) In preparing for cross-examination, counsel should be familiar with North Carolina law and procedures concerning cross-examination and impeachment of witnesses. Counsel should be prepared to question witnesses as to the existence and content of prior statements.

(e) In preparing for cross-examination, counsel should:

(1) consider the need to integrate cross-examination, the theory of the defense, and closing argument;

(2) consider whether cross-examination of each individual witness is likely to generate helpful information, and avoid asking questions that are unnecessary or might elicit responses harmful to the defense case;

(3) anticipate those witnesses the prosecution might call in its case-in-chief or in rebuttal, and consider a cross-examination plan for each of the anticipated witnesses;

(4) be alert to inconsistencies, variations, and contradictions within each witness' testimony;

(5) be alert to inconsistencies, variations, and contradictions between different witnesses' testimony;

(6) if applicable, review all prior statements of the witnesses and any prior relevant testimony of the prospective witnesses;

(7) where appropriate, review relevant statutes and local police regulations for possible use in cross-examining police witnesses;

(8) be alert to issues relating to witness credibility, including bias and motive for testifying; and

(9) be fully familiar with North Carolina statutory and case law on objections, motions to strike, offers of proof, and preserving the record on appeal.

(f) Counsel should consider conducting a *voir dire* examination of potential prosecution witnesses who may not be competent to give particular testimony, including expert witnesses whom the prosecutor may call. Counsel should be aware of the law concerning competency of witnesses in general, and admission of expert testimony in particular, to be able to raise appropriate objections.

(g) Before beginning cross-examination, counsel should ascertain whether the prosecutor provided copies of all prior statements of prosecution witnesses as required by G.S. 15A–903(a). If disclosure was not properly made, counsel should request relief as appropriate under G.S. 15A–910, including:

(1) a cautionary instruction;

(2) adequate time to review the documents or investigate and prepare further before commencing cross-examination, including a continuance or recess if necessary;

(3) exclusion of the witness' testimony and all evidence affected by that testimony;

(4) a mistrial;

(5) dismissal of the case; and/or

(6) any other sanctions counsel believes would remedy the violation.

(h) At the close of the prosecution's case and out of the presence of the jury, counsel should move for a judgment of dismissal or nonsuit on each count charged. Where appropriate, counsel should be prepared with supporting case law.

Guideline 7.6. Presenting the Defense Case

(a) Counsel should develop, in consultation with the client, an overall defense strategy. In deciding on defense strategy, counsel should consider whether the client's interests are best served by not presenting defense evidence, and instead relying on the evidence and inferences, or lack thereof, from the prosecution's case.

(b) Counsel should discuss with the client all of the considerations relevant to the client's decision to testify, including but not limited to, the likelihood of cross-examination and impeachment concerning prior convictions and prior bad acts that affect credibility.

(c) Counsel should be aware of the elements of any affirmative defense(s) and know whether the defense bears a burden of persuasion or production. Counsel should be familiar with the notice requirements for affirmative defenses and introduction of expert testimony that are imposed by G.S. 15A–905(c), G.S. 15A–959, and North Carolina case law.

(d) In preparing for presentation of a defense case, counsel should, where appropriate:

(1) develop a plan for direct examination of each potential defense witness;

(2) determine the implications that the order of witnesses may have on the defense case;

(3) consider the possible use of character witnesses and any negative consequences that may flow from such testimony;

(4) consider the need for expert witnesses;

(5) consider the use of demonstrative evidence and the order of exhibits; and

(6) be fully familiar with North Carolina statutory and case law on objections, motions to strike, offers of proof, and preserving the record on appeal.

(e) In developing and presenting the defense case, counsel should consider the implications it may have for rebuttal by the prosecution.

(f) Counsel should prepare all defense witnesses for direct examination and possible cross-examination. Where appropriate, counsel should also advise witnesses and the defendant of suitable courtroom dress and demeanor.

(g) If a prosecution objection is sustained or defense evidence is improperly excluded, counsel should make appropriate efforts to rephrase the question(s) and/or make an offer of proof.

(h) Counsel should conduct redirect examination as appropriate.

(i) At the close of all of the evidence, counsel should renew the motion for judgment of dismissal or nonsuit on each charged count.

Guideline 7.7. Closing Argument

(a) Counsel should be familiar with the substantive limits on both prosecution and defense summation, including the law governing closing arguments under G.S. 7A–97 and G.S. 15A–1230, Rule 10 of the General Rules of Practice for the Superior and District Courts, and North Carolina case law.

(b) In developing closing argument, counsel should review the proceedings to determine what aspects can be used in support of defense summation and, where appropriate, should consider:

(1) highlighting weaknesses in the prosecution's case;

(2) describing favorable inferences to be drawn from the evidence;

(3) incorporating into the argument:

(A) the theory of the defense case;

(B) helpful testimony from direct and cross-examinations;

(C) verbatim instructions drawn from the expected jury charge;

(D) responses to anticipated prosecution arguments; and

(E) visual aids and exhibits; and

(4) the effects of the defense argument on the prosecution's rebuttal argument.

(c) Whenever the prosecutor exceeds the scope of permissible argument, counsel should consider objecting, seeking cautionary instructions, or requesting a mistrial unless sound tactical considerations suggest otherwise. Such tactical considerations may include, but are not limited to:

(1) the possibility that an objection or cautionary instruction might enhance the significance of the information in the jurors' minds;

(2) whether, with respect to a motion for mistrial, counsel believes that the case will result in a favorable verdict for the client; and

(3) the need to preserve the objection for appellate review.

Guideline 7.8. Jury Instructions

(a) Counsel should be familiar with the law and the individual judge's practices concerning ruling on proposed instructions, charging the jury, use of pattern charges, and preserving objections to the instructions.

(b) Pursuant to G.S. 15A–1231, counsel should submit in writing proposed special instructions or modifications of the pattern jury instructions in light of the particular circumstances of the case, including the desirability of seeking a verdict on a lesser included offense. Where possible, counsel should provide case law in support of the proposed instructions. Counsel should try to ensure that all jury instruction discussions are on the record.

(c) Where appropriate, counsel should object to and argue against improper instructions proposed by the prosecution.

(d) If the court does not adopt instructions requested by counsel, or gives instructions over counsel's objection, counsel should take all steps necessary to preserve the record for appeal, including filing a copy of proposed instructions pursuant to G.S. 15A–1231.

(e) During delivery of the charge, counsel should be alert to any deviations from the judge's planned instructions, object to deviations unfavorable to the client, and, if necessary, request additional or curative instructions.

(f) If there are grounds for objecting to any jury instructions, counsel should object before the verdict form is submitted to the jury and the jury is allowed to begin deliberations.

(g) If the court proposes giving supplemental instructions to the jury, either upon request of the jurors or upon their failure to reach a verdict, counsel should ask the judge to state the proposed charge to counsel before it is delivered to the jury. Counsel should also try to ensure that any supplemental instructions are given to the entire jury in open court pursuant to G.S. 15A–1234(d).

SECTION 8

Guideline 8.1. Obligations of Counsel in Sentencing

Counsel's obligations in the sentencing process include:

(a) where a defendant chooses not to proceed to trial, to attempt to negotiate a plea agreement with consideration of the sentencing, correctional, and financial implications;

(b) to try to ensure the client is not harmed by inaccurate information or information that is not properly before the court in determining the sentence to be imposed;

(c) to ensure that all reasonably available mitigating and favorable evidence, which is likely to benefit the client, is presented to the court;

(d) to develop a plan that seeks to achieve the sentencing alternative most favorable to the client, and that reasonably can be obtained based on the facts and circumstances of the offense, the defendant's background, the applicable sentencing provisions, and other information pertinent to the sentencing decision;

(e) to try to ensure that all information presented to the court which may harm the client, if inaccurate, untruthful, or otherwise improper, is stricken from the text of any sentencing services plan or presentence report;

(f) to consider the need for and availability of sentencing specialists, or mental health or mental retardation professionals; and

(g) to identify and preserve potential issues for appeal.

Guideline 8.2. Sentencing Options, Consequences, and Procedures

(a) Counsel should be familiar with and advise the client of the sentencing provisions and options applicable to the case, including:

(1) the applicable sentencing laws, including any habitual offender statutes, sentencing enhancements, mandatory minimum sentence requirements, mandatory consecutive sentence requirements, and constitutional limits on sentences;

(2) deferred prosecution, prayer for judgment continued, probation without a conviction, and diversionary programs;

(3) probation or suspension of sentence, and mandatory and permissible conditions of probation;

(4) confinement in a mental institution;

(5) forfeiture of assets seized in connection with the case;

(6) any mandatory registration requirements, including sex offender registration, or mandatory DNA testing; and

(7) the possibility of expungement and sealing of records.

(b) Counsel should be familiar with and advise the client of the direct and collateral consequences of the judgment and sentence, including:

(1) credit for pretrial detention;

(2) the likelihood that the conviction could be used for sentence enhancement in the event of future criminal cases, such as sentencing in the aggravated range, habitual offender status, or felon in possession of a firearm;

(3) the possibility of earned-time credits;

(4) the availability of correctional programs and work release;

(5) the availability of drug rehabilitation programs, psychiatric treatment, and health care; and

(6) the likelihood of the court imposing financial obligations on the client, including the payment of attorney fees, court costs, fines, and restitution.

Counsel should also discuss with the client that there may be other potential collateral consequences of the judgment and sentence, such as deportation or other effects on immigration status; motor vehicle or other licensing; parental rights; possession of firearms; voting rights; employment, military, and government service considerations; and the potential exposure to or impact on any federal charges.

(c) Counsel should be familiar with the sentencing procedures, including:

(1) the effect that plea negotiations may have upon the sentencing discretion of the court;

(2) the procedural operation of the applicable sentencing system, including concurrent and consecutive sentencing;

(3) the practices of those who prepare the sentencing services plan or presentence report, and the defendant's rights in that process;

(4) access to the sentencing services plan or presentence report by counsel and the defendant;

(5) the defense sentencing presentation and/or sentencing memorandum;

(6) the opportunity to challenge information presented to the court for sentencing purposes;

(7) the availability of an evidentiary hearing to challenge information, and the applicable rules of evidence and burdens of proof at such a hearing; and

(8) the participation that victims and prosecution or defense witnesses may have in the sentencing proceedings.

Guideline 8.3. Preparation for Sentencing

In preparing for sentencing, counsel should consider the need to:

(a) inform the client of the applicable sentencing requirements, options, and alternatives, and the sentencing judge's practices and procedures if known;

(b) maintain regular contact with the client prior to the sentencing hearing, and inform the client of the steps being taken in preparation for sentencing;

(c) obtain from the client relevant information concerning such subjects as his or her background and personal history, prior criminal record, employment history and skills, education, medical and mental health history and condition, and financial status, and obtain from the client sources through which the information provided can be corroborated;

(d) inform the client of his or her right to speak at the sentencing proceeding and assist the client in preparing the statement, if any, to be made to the court, after considering the possible consequences that any admission of guilt may have on an appeal, subsequent retrial, or trial on other offenses;

(e) inform the client of the effects that admissions and other statements may have on an appeal, retrial, or other judicial proceedings, such as collateral or restitution proceedings;

(f) inform the client if counsel will ask the court to consider a particular sentence or range of sentences; and

(g) collect and present documents and affidavits to support the defense position and, where relevant, prepare and present witnesses to testify at the sentencing hearing.

Guideline 8.4. The Sentencing Services Plan or Presentence Report

(a) Counsel should be familiar with the procedures concerning the preparation and submission of a sentencing services plan or presentence report, and should consider the tactical implications of requesting that a plan be prepared.

(b) If a plan is prepared, counsel should:

(1) provide to the official preparing the plan relevant information favorable to the client, including, where appropriate, the client's version of the offense;

(2) prepare the client to be interviewed by the person preparing the plan;

(3) review the completed plan and discuss it with the client;

(4) try to ensure the client has adequate time to examine the completed plan; and

(5) take appropriate steps to ensure that erroneous or misleading information that may harm the client is challenged or deleted from the plan.

Guideline 8.5. The Prosecution's Sentencing Position

Unless there is a sound tactical reason for not doing so, counsel should attempt to determine whether the prosecution will advocate that a particular type or length of sentence be imposed, including the factual basis for any sentence in the aggravated range.

Guideline 8.6. The Defense Sentencing Theory

Counsel should prepare a defense sentencing presentation and, where appropriate, a defense sentencing memorandum. Among the topics counsel may wish to include in the sentencing presentation or memorandum are:

(a) information favorable to the defendant concerning such matters as the offense, mitigating factors and relative culpability, prior offenses, personal background, employment record and opportunities, educational background, and family and financial status;

(b) information that would support a sentencing disposition other than incarceration, such as the potential for rehabilitation or the nonviolent nature of the crime;

(c) information concerning the availability of treatment programs, community treatment facilities, and community service work opportunities;

(d) challenges to incorrect or incomplete information, and inappropriate inferences and characterizations that are before the court; and

(e) a defense sentencing proposal.

Guideline 8.7. The Sentencing Process

(a) Counsel should be prepared at the sentencing proceeding to take the steps necessary to advocate fully for the requested sentence and to protect the client's legal rights and interests.

(b) Where appropriate, counsel should be prepared to present supporting evidence, including testimony of witnesses, affidavits, letters, and public records, to establish the facts favorable to the defendant.

(c) Where the court has the authority to do so, counsel should request specific orders or recommendations from the court concerning the place of confinement and psychiatric treatment or drug rehabilitation, and against deportation or exclusion of the defendant.

(d) Where appropriate, counsel should prepare the client to personally address the court. In addition, counsel should prepare any expert and other witnesses to address the court.

(e) After the sentencing hearing is complete, counsel should fully explain to the client the terms of the sentence, including any conditions of probation.

SECTION 9

Guideline 9.1. Appeal of Misdemeanor Conviction for Trial *De Novo* in Superior Court

(a) When a defendant has been convicted of a misdemeanor in district court, except where the defendant explicitly waives his or her right to appeal as part of a plea agreement, counsel should advise the client of the right to appeal for trial *de novo* with a jury in superior court. Counsel should also advise the client of the potential advantages and disadvantages of exercising that right.

(b) Counsel should be aware of, and advise the client of, the time limit for *de novo* appeal set forth in G.S. 15A–1431(c).

Guideline 9.2. Motion for Appropriate Relief in the Trial Division

(a) Counsel should be familiar with the procedures available under G.S. 15A–1411 *et seq.* to seek a new trial, dismissal of charges, or other relief. Counsel should be aware of the grounds for relief that must be asserted within 10 days after entry of judgment, and the grounds that may be asserted more than 10 days after entry of judgment.

(b) When a judgment has been entered against the defendant after trial, counsel should consider whether it is appropriate to file a motion for appropriate relief with the trial court pursuant to G.S. 15A–1414. In deciding whether to file such a motion, the factors counsel should consider include:

(1) the likelihood of success of the motion, given the nature of the error or errors that can be raised; and

(2) the effect that such a motion might have on the client's appellate rights, including whether the filing of such a motion will assist in preserving the defendant's right to raise on appeal the issues that might be raised in the motion for appropriate relief.

Guideline 9.3. Right to Appeal to the Appellate Division

(a) Counsel should inform the defendant of his or her right to appeal the judgment of the court to the appellate division and the action that must be taken to perfect an appeal.

(b) If the defendant has a right to appeal and wants to file an appeal, the attorney shall preserve the defendant's right to do so by entering notice of appeal in accordance with the procedures and timelines set forth in G.S. 15A–1448 and the Rules of Appellate Procedure. Pursuant to Rule 33(a) of the North Carolina Rules of Appellate Procedure and Rules 1.7(a) and 3.2(a) of the Rules of the Commission on Indigent Defense Services, the entry of notice of appeal does not constitute a general appearance as counsel of record in the appellate division.

(c) If the defendant does not have a right to appeal and counsel believes there is a meritorious issue in the case that might be raised in the appellate division by means of a petition for writ of *certiorari*, counsel should inform the defendant of his or her opinion and consult with the Office of the Appellate Defender about the appropriate procedure.

(d) If counsel believes the defendant has a right to appeal and continues to be indigent, but the trial court denies appointed appellate counsel or denies indigency status for purposes of appeal, trial counsel should consult with the Office of the Appellate Defender about the defendant's options and inform the defendant of those options.

(e) Where the client takes an appeal, trial counsel should cooperate in providing information to appellate counsel concerning the proceedings in the trial court, and should timely respond to reasonable requests from appellate counsel for additional information about the case.

Guideline 9.4. Bail Pending Appeal

(a) Where a client indicates a desire to appeal the judgment and/or sentence of the court, counsel should inform the client of any right that may exist under G.S. 15A–536 to be released on bail pending the disposition of the appeal and, prior to the appointment of appellate counsel, make such a motion where appropriate.

(b) Where an appeal is taken and after appellate counsel is appointed, trial counsel should cooperate with appellate counsel in providing information if appellate counsel pursues a request for bail.

Guideline 9.5. Post-Disposition Obligations

Even after counsel's representation in a case is complete, counsel should comply with a client's reasonable requests for information and materials that are part of counsel's file. Counsel should also take reasonable steps to correct clerical or other errors in court documents, including jail credit calculations.

PERFORMANCE GUIDELINES FOR APPOINTED COUNSEL IN JUVENILE DELINQUENCY PROCEEDINGS AT THE TRIAL LEVEL

Adopted December 14, 2007

Preface

The primary goal of the Commission on Indigent Defense Services ("IDS Commission") is to ensure that indigent persons in North Carolina who are entitled to counsel at state expense are afforded high quality legal representation. *See* G.S. 7A–498.1(2). To further that goal, the Indigent Defense Services Act of 2000 directs the Commission to establish "[s]tandards for the performance of public defenders and appointed counsel." G.S. 7A–498.5(c)(4).

These performance guidelines are based largely on the "Performance Guidelines for Indigent Defense Representation in Non–Capital Criminal Cases at the Trial Level" that have been promulgated by the IDS Commission, as well as a review of standards and guidelines in Georgia and Kentucky and the Juvenile Defender Delinquency Notebook published by the National Juvenile Defender Center. For several months, a Juvenile Delinquency Performance Guidelines Committee reviewed drafts of these guidelines and revised them to fit the nuances of North Carolina law and practice. Once a final proposed draft was complete, it was distributed to all private appointed counsel and assistant public defenders who handle delinquency proceedings, as well as all district court judges and other interested persons, for their comments and feedback. Based on the comments that were received, the Committee made a number of improvements to the guidelines. The full IDS Commission then adopted the attached performance guidelines on December 14, 2007.

These performance guidelines cover all juvenile delinquency cases in North Carolina. The guidelines are intended to identify issues that may arise at each stage of a delinquency proceeding and to recommend effective approaches to resolving those issues. Because all provisions will not be applicable in all cases, the guidelines direct counsel to use his or her best professional judgment in determining what steps to undertake in specific cases. The Commission hopes these guidelines will be useful as a training tool and resource for new and experienced juvenile defense attorneys, as well as a tool for potential systemic reform in some areas. The guidelines are not intended to serve as a benchmark for ineffective assistance of counsel claims or attorney disciplinary proceedings.

The IDS Commission believes that providing high quality juvenile defense representation is a difficult and challenging endeavor, which requires great skill and dedication. That skill and dedication is demonstrated by juvenile defense counsel across North Carolina on a daily basis, and the Commission commends those counsel. The Commission recognizes that the goals embodied in these guidelines will not be attainable without sufficient funding and resources and hopes the North Carolina General Assembly will continue its support of both quality indigent defense services and appropriate dispositional options for juveniles.

The IDS Commission thanks all of the juvenile defense attorneys who zealously represent juveniles across the state. In addition, the Commission thanks everyone who assisted in drafting these performance guidelines and who offered comments. The Commission plans to review and revise the guidelines on a regular basis to ensure that they continue to comply with North Carolina law and reflect quality performance, and it invites ongoing feedback from the defense bar and juvenile defense community.

SECTION 1: General Provisions

Guideline 1.1. Function of the Performance Guidelines

(a) The Commission on Indigent Defense Services hereby adopts these performance guidelines to promote one of the purposes of the Indigent Defense Services Act of 2000—improving the quality of indigent defense representation in North Carolina—and pursuant to G.S. 7A–498.5(c)(4).

(b) These guidelines are intended to serve as a guide for counsel's performance in juvenile delinquency proceedings at the district court level and to contain a set of considerations and recommendations to assist appointed counsel in providing quality representation for juveniles. The guidelines also may be used as a training tool.

(c) These are performance guidelines, not standards. The steps covered in these guidelines are not to be undertaken automatically in every case. Instead, the steps actually taken should be tailored to the requirements of a particular case. In deciding what steps are appropriate, counsel should use his or her best professional judgment.

Adopted December 14, 2007.

Guideline 1.2. Definitions

(a) Juvenile. Any person under the age of eighteen who is not married, emancipated, or a member of the armed forces of the United States, or any person who is 18 to 20 years of age and has been adjudicated delinquent and committed to a youth development center.

(b) Juvenile delinquent or delinquent juvenile. A juvenile who has been adjudicated delinquent of an offense that would be a crime if committed by an adult.

(c) Appointed counsel. An attorney appointed to represent a juvenile in a juvenile delinquency proceeding.

(d) Expressed interests. The stated desires of the juvenile client about the direction and objectives of the case.

Adopted December 14, 2007.

SECTION 2: Role, Qualifications, and Duties of Defense Counsel

Guideline 2.1. Role of Defense Counsel

(a) An attorney in a juvenile delinquency proceeding is the juvenile's voice to the court, representing the expressed interests of the juvenile at every stage of the proceedings. The attorney owes the same duties to the juvenile under the North Carolina Rules of Professional Conduct, including the duties of loyalty and confidentiality, as an attorney owes to a client who is an adult criminal defendant.

(b) The attorney for a juvenile is bound to advocate the expressed interests of the juvenile. In addition, the attorney has a responsibility to counsel the juvenile, recommend to the juvenile actions consistent with the juvenile's interests, and advise the juvenile as to potential outcomes of various courses of action.

(c) An attorney in a juvenile delinquency proceeding should be familiar with the "Role of Defense Counsel in Delinquency Proceedings" approved by the Commission on Indigent Defense Services, available at www.ncids.org under the "Juvenile Defender" link.

Adopted December 14, 2007.

Guideline 2.2. Education, Training, and Experience of Defense Counsel

(a) To provide quality representation, counsel must be familiar with the Juvenile Code and the substantive criminal law and procedure in North Carolina. Counsel should also be familiar with any applicable local rules of the judicial district, which can be obtained in the local clerk's office and may be available at www.nccourts.org, as well as the practices of the specific judge before whom a case is pending.

(b) Counsel has an ongoing obligation to stay abreast of changes and developments in juvenile law and procedure and criminal law and procedure and to continue his or her legal education, skills training, and professional development.

(c) Before accepting appointment to a juvenile delinquency case, counsel should have sufficient experience, knowledge, skill, and training in areas such as communication techniques with children and adolescents, adolescent brain development, motions practice, detention advocacy, pre-adjudication preparation, and adjudication, disposition and post-disposition advocacy to provide quality representation. Counsel should have knowledge and understanding of the practice and procedures of the local court counselor's office and the role and functions of other court actors. If appropriate, counsel is encouraged to consult with other attorneys to acquire pertinent additional knowledge and information, including information about the practices of judges, prosecutors, and other court personnel.

Adopted December 14, 2007.

Guideline 2.3. General Duties of Defense Counsel

(a) Before accepting appointment to a juvenile delinquency case, counsel has an obligation to ensure that he or she has sufficient time, resources, knowledge, and experience to provide quality representation to the juvenile. If it later appears that counsel is unable to provide quality representation, counsel should move to withdraw. If counsel is allowed to withdraw, he or she should cooperate with new counsel to the extent that such cooperation is in accord with the North Carolina Rules of Professional Conduct.

(b) Counsel must be alert to all actual and potential conflicts of interest that would impair his or her ability to represent a juvenile client. If counsel identifies a potential conflict of interest, counsel should fully disclose the conflict to all affected persons and, if appropriate, obtain informed consent to proceed on behalf of the juvenile or move to withdraw. Counsel may seek an advisory opinion on any potential conflicts from the North Carolina State Bar. Mere tactical disagreements between counsel and a juvenile ordinarily do not justify withdrawal from a case. If it is necessary for counsel to withdraw, counsel should do so in a way that protects the juvenile's rights and interests and does not violate counsel's ethical duties to the juvenile.

(c) Counsel has an obligation to maintain regular contact with his or her juvenile client and to keep the juvenile informed of the progress of the case. Counsel should promptly comply with any reasonable request by the juvenile for information and reply to correspondence and telephone calls from the juvenile.

(d) Counsel should maintain a relationship with the juvenile client's parent or guardian, but should not allow that relationship to interfere with counsel's duties to the juvenile or the expressed interests of the juvenile.

(e) Counsel should appear on time for all scheduled court hearings in a juvenile's case. If scheduling conflicts arise, counsel should resolve them in accordance with Rule 3.1 of the General Rules of Practice and any applicable local rules.

(f) Counsel should never give preference to retained clients over juveniles for whom counsel has been appointed.

Adopted December 14, 2007.

SECTION 3: Interviewing the Juvenile

Guideline 3.1. Preparation for the Initial Interview

(a) Counsel should arrange for an initial interview with the juvenile as soon as practicable after being assigned to the juvenile's case. Absent exceptional circumstances, if the juvenile is in detention, the initial interview should take place within three business days after counsel receives notice of assignment to the juvenile's case. If necessary, counsel may arrange for a designee to conduct the initial interview.

(b) Before conducting the initial interview, the attorney should, if possible:

(1) be familiar with the charges against the juvenile and the elements of and potential dispositions for each charged offense;

(2) obtain copies of all relevant documents that are available, including copies of any petitions and related documents, recommendations and reports made by the court counselor's office, and law enforcement reports; and

(3) if the juvenile is detained:

(A) be familiar with the legal criteria governing the circumstances under which the court may order release and the procedures that will be followed in setting those conditions;

(B) be familiar with the different types of pre-adjudication release conditions the court may set, any written policies of the judicial district, and whether any person or agency is available to act as a custodian for the juvenile's release; and

(C) be familiar with any procedures available for reviewing the trial judge's determination to continue custody.

Adopted December 14, 2007.

Guideline 3.2. The Initial Interview

(a) The purposes of the initial interview are to acquire information from the juvenile concerning the facts of the case and to provide the juvenile with information concerning the case. If the juvenile remains in secure custody, counsel should also acquire information from the juvenile concerning pre-adjudication release.

(b) Counsel should communicate with the juvenile in a manner that will be effective, considering the juvenile's maturity, intellectual ability, language, educational level, special education needs, cultural background, gender, and physical, mental, and emotional health. If appropriate, counsel should file a motion to have a foreign language or sign language interpreter appointed by the court and present at the initial interview.

(c) Information about the juvenile that counsel should attempt to acquire during the initial interview includes, but is not limited to:

(1) the juvenile's current living arrangements, family relationships, and ties to the community, including the length of time his or her family has lived at the current and former addresses, as well as the juvenile's supervision when at home;

(2) the immigration status of the juvenile and his or her family members, if applicable;

(3) the juvenile's educational history, including current grade level and attendance and any disciplinary history;

(4) the juvenile's physical and mental health, including any impairing conditions such as substance abuse or learning disabilities, and any prescribed medications and other immediate needs;

(5) the juvenile's delinquency history, if any, including arrests, detentions, diversions, adjudications, and failures to appear in court;

(6) whether there are any other pending charges against the juvenile and the identity of any other appointed or retained counsel;

(7) whether the juvenile is on probation or post-release supervision and, if so, the name of his or her court counselor and the juvenile's past or present performance under supervision;

(8) the options available to the juvenile for release if the juvenile is in secure custody; and

(9) the names of individuals or other sources that counsel can contact to verify the information provided by the juvenile, and the permission of the juvenile to contact those sources.

(d) Information about the specific juvenile delinquency matter that counsel should attempt to acquire from the juvenile includes, but is not limited to:

(1) the facts surrounding the juvenile delinquency matter;

(2) any evidence of improper police or other governmental conduct, including interrogation procedures, that may affect the juvenile's rights;

(3) any possible witnesses and where they may be located;

(4) any evidence that should be preserved; and

(5) evidence of the juvenile's capacity to stand trial and mental state at the time of the offense.

(e) When appropriate, counsel should be prepared at the initial interview to ask the juvenile to sign a release authorizing counsel to access confidential information, such as school records and medical or mental health records.

(f) Information counsel should provide to the juvenile during the initial interview includes, but is not limited to:

(1) an explanation of the procedures that will be followed in setting the conditions of pre-adjudication release if the juvenile remains in secure custody;

(2) an explanation of the type of information that will be requested in any future interview that may be conducted by a court counselor, and an explanation that the juvenile is not required to and should not make statements concerning the offense;

(3) an explanation of the attorney-client privilege and instructions not to talk to anyone about the facts of the case without first consulting counsel;

(4) the nature of the charges and potential penalties;

(5) a general procedural overview of the progression of the case, where possible;

(6) how counsel can be reached and when counsel plans to have contact with the juvenile next;

(7) the date and time of the next scheduled court proceeding in the case;

(8) realistic answers, where possible, to the juvenile's questions; and

(9) what arrangements will be made or attempted for the satisfaction of the juvenile's most pressing needs, such as medical or mental health attention, and contact with family members.

Adopted December 14, 2007.

SECTION 4: Proceedings Before the Adjudicatory Hearing

Guideline 4.1. General Obligations of Counsel Regarding Pre–Adjudication Release

(a) Unless contrary to the expressed interests of the juvenile, counsel has an obligation to attempt to secure the prompt pre-adjudication release of the juvenile under the conditions most favorable to the juvenile.

(b) While hearings in delinquency proceedings are open pursuant to G.S. 7B–2402, counsel should consider moving the court to close any initial proceedings, including secure custody, first appearance, probable cause, and transfer hearings. Factors counsel should consider when making this request include the age of the juvenile, the nature of the charges, and any information that may be discussed during the hearing that could harm the juvenile. If requested by the juvenile, counsel should move to close the proceedings.

(c) If the juvenile is detained, counsel should try to ensure, prior to any initial court hearing, that the juvenile does not appear before the judge in inappropriate clothing or in shackles or handcuffs. If a detained juvenile is brought before the judge in detention clothing, shackles, or handcuffs, counsel should object and seek relief from the court pursuant to G.S. 7B–2402.1.

Adopted December 14, 2007.

Guideline 4.2. Secure Custody Hearings

(a) Counsel should make all reasonable efforts to interview the juvenile prior to the initial secure custody hearing.

(b) At a secure custody hearing, counsel should be prepared to present to the court a statement of the factual circumstances and factors supporting release and to propose conditions of release, including those in G.S. 7B–1906(f). Counsel should consider preparing for the court a proposed release order that includes conditions of release. Counsel should consider the potential consequences of statements made by the juvenile at any secure custody hearing and advise the juvenile accordingly.

(c) If the juvenile is released, counsel should fully explain the conditions of release to the juvenile and advise him or her of the potential consequences of a violation of those conditions.

(d) If the juvenile remains in detention, counsel should alert the detention facility in writing and, if appropriate, the court, to any special medical, psychiatric, or educational needs of the juvenile that are known to counsel.

Adopted December 14, 2007.

Guideline 4.3. First Appearance in Felony Cases

(a) Counsel should be aware of all statutory time limits for first appearance hearings in felony cases and should make any appropriate objections and motions.

(b) If counsel has not met with the juvenile before the first appearance hearing, counsel should meet with the juvenile as soon as possible after the first appearance and before the next hearing.

Adopted December 14, 2007.

Guideline 4.4. Probable Cause Hearing in Felony Cases

(a) Counsel should be aware of all statutory time limits for probable cause hearings in felony cases involving a juvenile who is at least 13 years of age and should make any appropriate objections and motions.

(b) Counsel should discuss with the juvenile the meaning of probable cause and the procedural aspects surrounding a probable cause determination. Counsel should consider any concessions the prosecution might make if the juvenile waives, or does not oppose a continuance of, a probable cause hearing. Before waiving a probable cause hearing, counsel should consider the possible benefits of a hearing, including the potential for discovery and the development of impeachment evidence. Counsel also should be aware of all consequences if the juvenile waives a probable cause hearing, including the effect of waiver on the outcome of a transfer hearing. Counsel should be aware of local customs with respect to probable case hearings, including whether or not waiver of probable cause ensures that the juvenile's case will remain in delinquency court.

(c) In preparing for a probable cause hearing, counsel should be familiar with Article 22 of the Juvenile Code and should specifically consider:

(1) the elements of each of the offenses alleged;

(2) the law for establishing probable cause;

(3) the procedure for conducting a probable cause hearing under G.S. 7B–2202;

(4) factual information that is available concerning the existence or lack of probable cause;

(5) tactical considerations for whether to conduct cross-examination, full or partial, of prosecution witnesses;

(6) whether additional factual information and impeachment evidence could be discovered by counsel during the hearing;

(7) any continuing need to pursue release of the juvenile if the juvenile is in custody; and

(8) that counsel should not call the juvenile or defense witnesses to testify at the probable cause hearing unless there are sound tactical reasons for doing so.

(d) Counsel should make reasonable efforts to ensure that the probable cause hearing is recorded and, with permission of the court, should consider utilizing a personal recording device in case the court recording device fails.

Adopted December 14, 2007.

Guideline 4.5. Transfer Hearings in Felony Cases

(a) Counsel should be aware of all statutory time limits for transfer hearings in felony cases involving a juvenile who is at least 13 years of age and should make any appropriate objections and motions.

(b) Counsel should prepare for a transfer hearing to the same degree as for an adjudicatory hearing and should be aware that the decision to transfer a juvenile to adult court may only be reversed upon a finding of abuse of discretion by the superior court.

(c) In preparation for the transfer hearing, counsel should be familiar with the procedures of a transfer hearing, with a particular focus on the eight factors the court must consider pursuant to G.S. 7B–2203.

(d) At the transfer hearing, counsel should review all information provided to the court by the prosecution and should be prepared to cross-examine any witnesses the prosecution presents.

(e) Unless the juvenile directs otherwise, counsel should present any evidence to the court that counsel believes will support a decision not to transfer. Evidence may include, but is not limited to, the juvenile's record, performance on court supervision, educational history, mental and emotional state, intellectual functioning, developmental issues, and family history. Counsel should be prepared to present testimony to prevent transfer, including testimony by people who can provide helpful insight into the juvenile's character, such as teachers, counselors, psychologists, community members, probation officers, religious affiliates, family members, friends, employers, or other persons with a positive personal or professional view of the juvenile.

(f) Counsel should make reasonable efforts to ensure that the transfer hearing is recorded and, with permission of the court, should consider utilizing a personal recording device in case the court recording device fails.

(g) If the court orders transfer of jurisdiction to adult court, counsel should consider appealing the matter to superior court to request remand to district court and to preserve the issue for possible review in the appellate division.

Adopted December 14, 2007.

SECTION 5: Incriminating Evidence and Capacity to Proceed

Guideline 5.1. Search Warrants, Interrogations, and Prosecution Requests for Non–Testimonial Evidence

(a) Counsel should be familiar with the law governing search warrants under G.S. 15A–24 *et seq.* and applicable case law, including the requirements for a search warrant application, the basis for issuing a warrant, the required form and content of a warrant, the execution and service of a warrant, and the permissible scope of the search.

(b) Counsel should be familiar with the law governing a juvenile's protection against self-incrimination, including G.S. 7B–2101 and applicable case law.

(c) Counsel should be familiar with the law governing the prosecution's power to require a juvenile to provide non-testimonial evidence (such as participation in an in-person lineup, handwriting exemplars, and physical specimens), the potential consequences if a juvenile refuses to comply with a non-testimonial identification order issued pursuant to G.S. 7B–2103 *et seq.*, and the extent to which counsel may participate in or observe the proceedings.

Adopted December 14, 2007.

Guideline 5.2. Juvenile's Capacity to Proceed

(a) When defense counsel has a good faith doubt as to the juvenile's capacity to proceed in a delinquency case, counsel should consider consulting the capacity to proceed sections in the North Carolina Civil Commitment Manual and the North Carolina Defender Manual, available at www.ncids.org, and should:

(1) file an *ex parte* motion to obtain the services of a mental health expert and thereby determine whether to raise the juvenile's capacity to proceed; or

(2) file a motion questioning the juvenile's capacity to proceed or enter an admission under G.S. 7B–2401, G.S. 15A–1001(a), and applicable case law, in which case the court may order a mental health examination at a state facility or by the appropriate local forensic examiner.

(b) Although the juvenile's expressed interests ordinarily control, counsel may question capacity to proceed without the juvenile's assent or over the juvenile's objection, if necessary.

(c) After counsel receives and reviews the report from any court-ordered examination, counsel should consider whether to file a motion requesting a formal hearing on the juvenile's capacity to proceed.

(d) If capacity to proceed is at issue, counsel still has a duty to continue to prepare the case for all anticipated court proceedings.

(e) If the court enters an order finding the juvenile incapable of proceeding and orders involuntary commitment proceedings to be initiated, defense counsel ordinarily will not represent the juvenile at those proceedings but should cooperate with the commitment attorney upon request.

Adopted December 14, 2007.

SECTION 6: Case Review, Preparation, and Discovery

Guideline 6.1. Charging Language in Delinquency Petition

(a) Counsel should review the delinquency petition in all cases and determine whether there are any defects, such as:

(1) the petition does not list all of the essential elements of the charged offense;

(2) the petition contains more than one charge in a single count; and/or

(3) the petition does not allege a crime for which the juvenile may be charged.

If there are defects, counsel should determine whether to move to dismiss the petition after considering all relevant factors, including but not limited to the type of defect, the likelihood of obtaining a favorable ruling, and the likelihood that the charge will be refiled. Counsel also should be aware of all potential consequences of a motion to dismiss, including alerting the prosecution to defects in the charging language.

(b) Even if the petition adequately charges an offense that would be a crime if committed by an adult, counsel should be sufficiently familiar with the language of the petition to recognize a fatal variance at trial and move to dismiss the charge if the evidence is insufficient to support the charge as pled.

(c) Counsel should be aware of all time limits under G.S. 7B–1703 that are applicable to the filing of a delinquency petition and should consider moving to dismiss the petition if the statutory time limits are not followed.

Adopted December 14, 2007.

Guideline 6.2. Case Review, Investigation, and Preparation

(a) Counsel has a duty to conduct an independent case review and investigation. The juvenile's admissions of responsibility or other statements to counsel do not necessarily obviate the need for independent review and investigation. The review and investigation should be conducted as promptly as possible.

(b) Counsel should be aware that under G.S. 7B–2408, no statement made to the intake court counselor is admissible prior to the dispositional hearing.

(c) Sources of review and investigative information may include the following:

(1) *Petitions, Statutes, and Case Law.* Counsel should obtain and examine copies of all petitions in the case to determine the specific charges that have been brought against the juvenile. The relevant statutes and precedents should be examined to identify:

(A) the elements of the offense(s) with which the juvenile is charged;

(B) the defenses, ordinary and affirmative, that may be available, as well as the proper manner for asserting any available defenses; and

(C) any defects in the petitions, constitutional or otherwise, such as statute of limitations, double jeopardy, or others.

(2) *The Juvenile.* Counsel should conduct an in-depth interview or interviews of the juvenile as outlined in Section 3, *supra.*

(3) *Potential Witnesses.* Counsel should consider whether to interview potential witnesses, including any complaining witnesses and others adverse to the juvenile. If counsel conducts interviews of potential witnesses, he or she should attempt to do so in the presence of a third person who will be available, if necessary, to testify as a defense witness at the adjudicatory hearing. Alternatively, counsel should have an investigator conduct the interviews.

(4) *The Police and Prosecution.* Counsel should utilize available discovery procedures to secure information in the possession of the prosecution or law enforcement authorities, including police reports, unless sound tactical reasons exist for not doing so (*e.g.*, defense obligations under G.S. 7B–2301). *See* Guideline 6.3, *infra.*

(5) *The Courts.* If possible, counsel should request and review tapes or transcripts from any previous hearings in the case. Counsel should also review the juvenile's prior court file(s) and request that the court counselor provide the juvenile's prior court history from North Carolina Juvenile Online Information Network (NCJOIN).

(6) *Information in the Possession of Third Parties.* When appropriate, counsel should seek a release or court order to obtain necessary confidential information about the juvenile, co-juvenile(s), witness(es), or victim(s) that is in the possession of third parties. Counsel should be aware of privacy laws and other requirements governing disclosure of the type of confidential information being sought.

(7) *Physical Evidence.* When appropriate, counsel should make a prompt request to the police or investigative agency for any physical evidence or expert reports relevant to the offense or sentencing. Counsel should view the physical evidence consistent with case needs.

(8) *The Scene.* When appropriate, counsel or an investigator should view the scene of the alleged offense. This should be done under circumstances as similar as possible to those existing at the time of the alleged incident (*e.g.*, weather, time of day, lighting conditions, and seasonal changes). Counsel should consider taking photographs and creating diagrams or charts of the actual scene of the alleged offense.

(9) *Assistance from Experts, Investigators, and Interpreters.* Counsel should consider whether expert or investigative assistance, including consultation and testimony, is necessary or appropriate to:

(A) prepare a defense;

(B) adequately understand the prosecution's case;

(C) rebut the prosecution's case; or

(D) investigate the juvenile's capacity to proceed, mental state at the time of the offense, and capacity to make a knowing and intelligent waiver of constitutional rights.

If counsel determines that expert or investigative assistance is necessary and appropriate, counsel should file an *ex parte* motion setting forth the particularized showing of necessity required by *Ake v. Oklahoma*, 470 U.S. 68, 105 S. Ct. 1087 (1985), *State v. Ballard*, 333 N. C. 515, 428 S.E.2d 178 (1993), and their progeny. If appropriate, counsel should also file a motion to have a foreign language or sign language interpreter appointed by the court. Counsel should preserve for appeal any denial of expert, investigative, or interpreter funding by making all proper objections and motions on the record.

(d) During case preparation and throughout the adjudicatory hearing, counsel should identify potential legal issues and the corresponding objections. Counsel should consider the strategy of making objections, including the proper timing and method. Counsel should also consider how best to respond to objections that could be raised by the prosecution.

Adopted December 14, 2007.

Guideline 6.3. Discovery

(a) Counsel has a duty to pursue discovery procedures provided by the applicable rules of criminal procedure and the Juvenile Code (G.S. 7B–2300 *et seq.*) and to pursue such informal discovery methods as may be available to supplement the factual investigation of the case.

(b) Before filing a formal motion with the court, counsel must serve the prosecutor with a written request for voluntary disclosure, unless counsel and the prosecutor agree in writing to comply voluntarily with G.S. 7B–2300 *et seq.* Counsel must file a motion to compel discovery if the prosecution's response is unsatisfactory or delayed. Regardless of the prosecution's response, counsel should file a motion to compel discovery if the case is proceeding to an adjudicatory hearing.

(c) In exceptional cases, counsel should consider not making a discovery request or signing a written agreement under G.S. 7B–2300 on the ground that it will trigger a defense obligation to disclose evidence under G.S. 7B–2301.

(d) Unless there are sound tactical reasons for not requesting discovery or signing a written agreement under G.S. 7B–2300 (*e.g.*, defense obligations under G.S. 7B–2301), counsel should seek discovery to the broadest extent permitted under federal and state law, including but not limited to the following items:

(1) all information to which the juvenile is entitled under G.S. 7B–2300;

(2) all potential exculpatory information and evidence to which the defense is entitled under *Brady v. Maryland*, 373 U.S. 83, 83 S. Ct. 1194 (1963) and its progeny, including but not limited to:

(A) impeachment evidence, such as a witness's prior adjudications or convictions, misconduct, or juvenile court record; bias of a witness; a witness's capacity to observe, perceive, or recollect; and psychiatric evaluations of a witness;

(B) evidence discrediting police investigation and credibility;

(C) evidence undermining the identification of the juvenile;

(D) evidence tending to show the guilt or responsibility of another;

(E) the identity of favorable witnesses; and

(F) exculpatory physical evidence; and

(3) to the extent not provided under statutory discovery, any other information necessary to the defense of the case, including but not limited to:

(A) the names, addresses, and availability of prosecution witnesses;

(B) the details of the circumstances under which any oral or written statements by the accused or a co-juvenile were made;

(C) any evidence of prior bad acts that the prosecution may intend to use against the juvenile;

(D) the data underlying any expert reports; and

(E) any evidence necessary to enable counsel to determine whether to file a motion to suppress evidence.

(e) Counsel should seek the timely production and preservation of discoverable evidence. If the prosecution fails to disclose or belatedly discloses discoverable evidence, counsel should consider requesting one or more sanctions, akin to those provided by G.S. 15A–910.

(f) If counsel believes the prosecution may destroy or consume in testing evidence that is significant to the case (*e.g.*, rough notes of law enforcement interviews, 911 tapes, drugs, or blood samples), counsel should file a motion to preserve the evidence in the event that it is discoverable.

(g) Counsel should timely comply with all of the requirements in G.S. 7B–2301 governing disclosure of evidence by the juvenile and notice of defenses and expert witnesses.

Adopted December 14, 2007.

Guideline 6.4. Theory of the Case

During case review, investigation, and preparation for the adjudicatory hearing, counsel should develop and continually reassess a theory of the case. A theory of the case is one central theory that organizes the facts, emotions, and legal basis for a finding of not responsible or adjudication of a lesser offense, while also telling the juvenile's story of innocence, reduced culpability, or unfairness. The theory of the case furnishes the basic position from which counsel determines all actions in a case.

Adopted December 14, 2007.

SECTION 7: Pre-Adjudication Motions

Guideline 7.1. The Decision to File Pre–Adjudication Motions

(a) Counsel should consider filing appropriate pre-adjudication motions whenever there exists a good faith reason to believe that the applicable law may entitle the juvenile to relief which the court has authority to grant.

(b) Counsel should consult the local rules of the judicial district to determine whether they establish deadlines for pre-adjudication motions and should comply with any such rules.

(c) The decision to file pre-adjudication motions should be made after thorough investigation and after considering the applicable law in light of the circumstances of each case, as well as the need to preserve issues for appellate review. Among the issues that counsel should consider addressing in pre-adjudication motions are:

(1) the constitutionality of the implicated statute(s);

(2) the sufficiency of the petition under all applicable statutory and constitutional provisions;

(3) the dismissal of a charge on double jeopardy grounds;

(4) the propriety and prejudice of any joinder or severance of charges or juveniles;

(5) the statutory and constitutional discovery obligations of the prosecution;

(6) the suppression of evidence gathered as the result of violations of the North Carolina Constitution, the United States Constitution, and applicable federal and state statutes, including:

(A) the fruits of any illegal searches or seizures;

(B) any statements or confessions obtained in violation of the juvenile's right to counsel, privilege against self-incrimination, or rights protected under G.S. 7B–2101; and

(C) the fruits of any unconstitutional identification procedures;

(7) whether there are grounds to prevent discovery or testimony or other evidence based on privilege;

(8) access to necessary support or investigative resources or experts;

(9) the need for a change of venue;

(10) the juvenile's calendaring rights under the Juvenile Code;

(11) the juvenile's right to a continuance in order adequately to prepare his or her case;

(12) matters of trial evidence that may be appropriately litigated by means of a pre-adjudication motion *in limine*, including exclusion of any pre-adjudication statements the juvenile may have made at intake;

(13) recusal of the trial judge;

(14) the full recordation of all proceedings;

(15) matters of courtroom procedure; and

(16) notice of affirmative defenses.

Adopted December 14, 2007.

Guideline 7.2. Filing and Arguing Pre–Adjudication Motions

(a) Motions should be filed in a timely manner, comport with the formal requirements of statute and court rules, and succinctly inform the court of the authority relied upon.

(b) When a hearing on a motion requires the taking of evidence, counsel's preparation for the evidentiary hearing should include:

(1) investigation, discovery, and research relevant to the claim(s) advanced;

(2) subpoenaing of all helpful evidence, and subpoenaing and preparation of all helpful witnesses;

(3) full understanding of the burdens of proof, evidentiary principles, and procedures applicable to the hearing, including the potential advantages and disadvantages of having the juvenile and other defense witnesses testify;

(4) obtaining the assistance of an expert witness when appropriate; and

(5) preparation and submission of a memorandum of law when appropriate.

(c) Unless there are sound tactical reasons for not doing so, counsel should request that the court rule on all previously filed defense motions prior to the adjudicatory hearing.

(d) If a hearing on a pre-adjudication motion is held in advance of an adjudicatory hearing, counsel should attempt to obtain the transcript of the hearing for use at the adjudicatory hearing, if appropriate.

Adopted December 14, 2007.

Guideline 7.3. Subsequent Filing and Renewal of Pre–Adjudication Motions

(a) Counsel should be prepared to raise during the adjudication proceedings any issue that is appropriately raised pre-adjudication, but could not have been so raised because the facts supporting the motion were unknown or not reasonably available.

(b) Counsel should be prepared to renew pre-adjudication motions or file additional motions at any subsequent stage of the proceedings if new supporting information is later disclosed or made available.

Counsel should also renew pre-adjudication motions and object to the admission of challenged evidence at the adjudicatory hearing to preserve the motions and objections for appellate review pursuant to Rule 10(b) of the North Carolina Rules of Appellate Procedure and *State v. Tutt*, 171 N.C. App. 518, 615 S. E.2d 688 (2005).

Adopted December 14, 2007.

SECTION 8: Pleas

Guideline 8.1. Advising the Juvenile About Pleas

(a) Counsel should explain to the juvenile that certain decisions concerning a possible plea ultimately must be made by the juvenile, as well as the advantages and disadvantages inherent in those choices. The decisions that must be made by the juvenile include whether to admit or deny the allegations of the petition, whether to accept a plea agreement, and whether to testify at a plea hearing.

(b) After appropriate investigation and case review, counsel should explore with the juvenile the possibility and desirability of negotiating a plea to the charges rather than proceeding to an adjudicatory hearing. In doing so, counsel should fully explain to the juvenile the rights that would be waived by a decision to enter a plea and not proceed to the adjudicatory hearing, including the fact that an admission of the allegations of the petition is the same as an adjudication, and the impact of the decision on the juvenile's right to appeal.

Adopted December 14, 2007.

Guideline 8.2. Preparation for Plea Negotiations

(a) In preparing for plea negotiations, counsel should attempt to become familiar with any practices and policies of the particular district, judge, prosecuting attorney and, when applicable, court counselor's office, which may affect the content and likely results of a negotiated plea bargain.

(b) Counsel should be familiar with:

(1) the various types of pleas that may be agreed to, including an admission of responsibility, a plea of no contest, a conditional admission in which the juvenile retains the right to appeal the denial of a suppression motion, a plea in which the juvenile is not required personally to acknowledge his or her involvement (*Alford* plea), and a plea to dismiss the case after adjudication under G.S. 7B-2501(d);

(2) the advantages and disadvantages of each available plea according to the circumstances of the case; and

(3) whether a proposed plea agreement is binding on the court.

(c) To develop an overall negotiation plan, counsel should be fully aware and advise the juvenile of the possible results of an adjudication, including:

(1) the maximum term of confinement for the offense;

(2) any requirements for registration such as sex offender registration, and for being fingerprinted and photographed;

(3) the possibility that an adjudication or admission of the offense could be used for cross-examination or sentence enhancement in the event of future criminal cases;

(4) the availability of appropriate dispositional options; and

(5) the potential collateral consequences of entering a plea, such as deportation or other effects on immigration status; effects on motor vehicle or other licensing; educational notifications; distribution of fingerprint and photographic information; and the potential exposure to or impact on any federal charges.

(d) In developing a negotiation strategy, counsel should be completely familiar with:

(1) concessions that the juvenile might offer the prosecution as part of a negotiated agreement, such as:

(A) waiving the probable cause hearing;

(B) declining to assert the right to proceed to the adjudicatory hearing on the merits of the charge;

(C) refraining from asserting or litigating a particular pre-adjudication motion;

(D) agreeing to fulfill specified restitution conditions or to participate in community work or service programs or other dispositional options;

(E) assisting the prosecution in investigating the present case or other alleged delinquent activity; and

(F) waiving a challenge to the validity or proof of a prior adjudication;

(2) benefits the juvenile might obtain from a negotiated agreement, such as:

(A) that the prosecution will not seek transfer;

(B) that the juvenile may enter an admission and preserve the right to litigate and contest the denial of a suppression motion;

(C) dismissal or reduction of one or more of the charged offenses, either immediately or upon completion of conditions of a deferred adjudication;

(D) that the juvenile will not be subject to further investigation or prosecution for uncharged alleged delinquent conduct;

(E) that the prosecution will not oppose the juvenile's release pending disposition or appeal;

(F) that the juvenile will receive, with the agreement of the court, a specified disposition;

(G) that at the disposition hearing, the prosecution will take, or refrain from taking, a specified position with respect to the sanction to be imposed on the juvenile by the court; and

(H) that at the disposition hearing, the prosecution will not present certain information;

(3) information favorable to the juvenile concerning matters such as the offense, mitigating factors and relative culpability, prior offenses, personal background, familial status, and educational and other relevant social information;

(4) information that would support a disposition other than confinement, such as the potential for rehabilitation or the nonviolent nature of the crime; and

(5) information concerning the availability of dispositional options, such as treatment programs, community treatment facilities, and community service work opportunities.

Adopted December 14, 2007.

Guideline 8.3. Ongoing Preparation During Plea Negotiations

(a) Notwithstanding plea negotiations with the prosecution, counsel should continue to prepare and investigate the case to the extent necessary to protect the juvenile's rights and interests in the event that plea negotiations fail.

(b) Counsel should keep the juvenile fully informed of any plea discussions and negotiations and convey to the juvenile any offers made by the prosecution for a negotiated agreement.

Adopted December 14, 2007.

Guideline 8.4. The Decision to Enter a Plea

(a) If counsel and the prosecution reach a tentative negotiated agreement, counsel should explain to the juvenile the full content of the agreement, including its advantages, disadvantages, and potential consequences. Counsel should also inform the juvenile that any plea agreement may be rejected by the court and the consequences of a rejection.

(b) Counsel should again advise the juvenile of the possible results of an adjudication as set forth in Guideline 8.2(c), *supra*.

(c) Counsel may not accept or reject a plea agreement without the juvenile's express authorization. Although the decision to accept or reject a plea agreement ultimately rests with the juvenile, if counsel believes the juvenile's decisions are not in his or her best legal interests, counsel should make every effort to ensure that the juvenile understands all of the potential consequences before the juvenile makes a final decision.

Adopted December 14, 2007.

Guideline 8.5. Preparing the Juvenile for Entry of Plea

If the juvenile agrees to a negotiated plea, prior to the entry of a plea, counsel should:

(1) fully explain to the juvenile the nature of the plea hearing and the meaning of the questions on the transcript of admission;

(2) fully explain to the juvenile the conditions and limits of the plea agreement and the maximum punishment, sanctions, and other consequences the juvenile will be exposed to by entering a plea; and

(3) fully explain to the juvenile the plea hearing process, the role he or she may play in the hearing, including answering questions of the judge, the need to speak clearly and audibly before the court, and the need to behave appropriately and respond in a respectful manner to the court.

Adopted December 14, 2007.

Guideline 8.6. Entry of Plea

(a) Counsel should not allow a juvenile to plead responsible based on oral conditions that are not disclosed to the court.

(b) When the juvenile enters a plea, counsel should ensure that the full content and conditions of the plea agreement between the prosecution and defense are legibly recorded on the transcript of admission.

(c) Subsequent to the acceptance of a plea by the court, counsel should review and explain the plea proceedings to the juvenile and respond to any questions and concerns of the juvenile.

Adopted December 14, 2007.

SECTION 9: The Adjudicatory Hearing

Guideline 9.1. General Adjudicatory Hearing Preparation

(a) Counsel should explain to the juvenile that, although it is the juvenile's decision whether to deny the allegations of the petition and proceed to an adjudicatory hearing, decisions concerning adjudication strategy are ordinarily to be made by counsel, after consultation with the juvenile and investigation of the applicable facts and law. However, counsel should be aware that, under the North Carolina Rules of Professional Conduct, if counsel and a fully informed competent juvenile reach an absolute impasse as to tactical decisions, the juvenile's wishes may control.

(b) Throughout preparation and adjudication, counsel should develop a theory of the defense and ensure that counsel's decisions and actions are consistent with that theory.

(c) In advance of the adjudicatory hearing, counsel should take all steps necessary to complete thorough investigation, discovery, and research. Among the steps counsel should take in preparation are:

(1) interviewing and subpoenaing all potentially helpful witnesses;

(2) subpoenaing any potentially helpful physical or documentary evidence;

(3) filing applicable pre-trial motions, with supporting briefs, memorandum, case law, and other supporting documentation, if appropriate;

(4) when appropriate, obtaining funds for defense investigators and experts and arranging for defense experts to consult and/or testify on issues that are potentially helpful;

(5) obtaining and reading transcripts of any prior proceedings in the case or related proceedings; and

(6) obtaining photographs or preparing charts, maps, diagrams, or other visual aids of any scenes, persons, objects, or information that may aid the court in understanding the juvenile's defense.

(d) When appropriate, counsel should have the following relevant information and materials available at the time of the adjudicatory hearing:

(1) copies of all documents filed in the case;

(2) documents prepared by investigators;

(3) reports, test results, and other materials disclosed by the prosecution pursuant to G.S. 7B–2300 *et seq.*;

(4) a plan, outline, or draft of an opening statement, if appropriate;

(5) cross-examination plans for all possible prosecution witnesses;

(6) direct-examination plans for all prospective defense witnesses;

(7) copies of defense subpoenas;

(8) any prior statements of all prosecution witnesses (*e.g.*, transcripts and police reports);

(9) any prior statements of all defense witnesses;

(10) reports from defense experts;

(11) a list of all defense exhibits and the witnesses through whom they will be introduced;

(12) originals and copies of all defense documentary exhibits;

(13) copies of statutes and cases; and

(14) a plan, outline, or draft of the closing argument.

(e) Counsel should be familiar with the rules of evidence that apply in adjudicatory proceedings, the law relating to all stages of the adjudicatory process, including the standards of proof in each proceeding, and the legal and evidentiary issues that reasonably can be anticipated to arise during the adjudicatory hearing.

(f) Counsel should decide if it is beneficial to obtain an advance ruling on issues likely to arise at the adjudicatory hearing (*e.g.*, use of prior adjudications to impeach the juvenile) and, if appropriate, prepare motions and memoranda for such advance rulings.

(g) Counsel should arrange with court personnel and/or the sheriff's office for counsel to be able to confer with the juvenile in a confidential setting during the adjudicatory hearing.

(h) Counsel should consider moving the court under G.S. 7B–2402 to close any initial proceedings. Factors counsel should consider when making this request include the age of the juvenile, the nature of the charges, and any information that may be discussed during the hearing that could harm the juvenile. If requested by the juvenile, counsel should move to close the proceedings.

(i) Throughout preparation and adjudication, counsel should consider the potential effects that particular actions may have upon disposition if there is a finding of delinquency.

(j) Counsel should consider moving the court to sequester any witnesses who may be called to testify at the adjudicatory hearing.

Adopted December 14, 2007.

Guideline 9.2. Juvenile Dress and Demeanor at the Adjudicatory Hearing

(a) When appropriate, counsel should advise the juvenile as to suitable courtroom dress and demeanor.

(b) If the juvenile is detained, counsel should try to ensure, prior to the court hearing, that the juvenile does not appear before the judge in inappropriate clothing or in shackles or handcuffs. If a detained juvenile is brought before the judge in detention clothing, shackles, or handcuffs, counsel should object and seek appropriate relief from the court pursuant to G.S. 7B–2402.1.

Adopted December 14, 2007.

Guideline 9.3. Preserving the Record on Appeal

Throughout the adjudicatory process, counsel should establish a proper record for appellate review, including making reasonable efforts to ensure that the adjudicatory hearing is recorded. If a relevant and important non-verbal event occurs during the adjudicatory hearing, counsel should ask to have the record reflect what happened. With permission of the court, counsel should also consider utilizing a personal recording device in case the court recording device fails.

Adopted December 14, 2007.

Guideline 9.4. Opening Statement

(a) Though an opening statement is not always presented at a bench hearing, counsel should consider the potential benefits of making an opening statement. If counsel decides to make an opening statement, counsel should consider whether to ask for sequestration of witnesses before the statement.

(b) Counsel should be familiar with North Carolina law and the individual trial judge's practices regarding the permissible content of an opening statement. If appropriate, counsel should ask the court to instruct the prosecution not to mention in opening statement contested evidence for which the court has not determined admissibility.

(c) Counsel should consider the strategic advantages and disadvantages of disclosure of particular information during opening statement.

(d) Counsel should have a clear understanding of his or her objectives in making an opening statement. Appropriate objectives include:

(1) introducing the theory of the defense case;

(2) providing an overview of the defense case;

(3) identifying the weaknesses of the prosecution's case;

(4) emphasizing the prosecution's burden of proof; and

(5) preparing the court for the juvenile's testimony or decision not to testify.

(e) Whenever the prosecutor oversteps the bounds of a proper opening statement, counsel should consider objecting, requesting a mistrial, or seeking cautionary instructions, unless sound tactical considerations weigh against any such objections or requests. Such tactical considerations may include, but are not limited to:

(1) the significance of the prosecutor's error; and

(2) the possibility that an objection might enhance the significance of the information in the court's mind, or otherwise negatively affect the court.

Adopted December 14, 2007.

Guideline 9.5. Preparing for and Confronting the Prosecution's Case

(a) Counsel should anticipate weaknesses in the prosecution's proof, and research and prepare to argue corresponding motions for judgment of dismissal or not delinquent.

(b) Counsel should consider the advantages and disadvantages of entering into stipulations concerning the prosecution's case.

(c) Unless sound tactical reasons exist for not doing so, counsel should make timely objections and motions to strike improper prosecution evidence and assert all possible statutory and constitutional grounds for exclusion of the evidence. If evidence offered by the prosecution is admissible only for a limited purpose, counsel generally should request that the court limit consideration to the proper purpose.

(d) Counsel should seek to ensure that any statements made by the juvenile to the court counselor during the preliminary hearing and evaluation process be excluded from the adjudicatory hearing pursuant to G.S. 7B–2408.

(e) In preparing for cross-examination, counsel should:

(1) be familiar with North Carolina law and procedures concerning cross-examination and impeachment of witnesses;

(2) be prepared to question witnesses as to the existence and content of prior statements;

(3) consider the need to integrate cross-examination, the theory of the defense, and closing argument;

(4) determine what counsel expects to accomplish by cross-examination of each witness and avoid asking questions that are unnecessary or might elicit responses harmful to the defense case;

(5) anticipate witnesses the prosecution might call in its case-in-chief or in rebuttal, and consider a cross-examination plan for each of the anticipated witnesses;

(6) be alert to inconsistencies, variations, and contradictions within each witness's testimony;

(7) be alert to inconsistencies, variations, and contradictions between different witnesses' testimony;

(8) review any prior statements and prior relevant testimony of the prospective witnesses;

(9) when appropriate, review relevant statutes and local police regulations for possible use in cross-examining police witnesses; and

(10) be alert to issues relating to witness credibility, including bias and motive for testifying.

(f) Counsel should consider conducting a *voir dire* examination of potential prosecution witnesses who may not be competent to give particular testimony, including expert witnesses and younger witnesses. Counsel should be aware of the law concerning competency of witnesses in general, and admission of expert testimony in particular, to be able to raise appropriate objections.

(g) Before beginning cross-examination, counsel should ascertain whether the prosecutor provided copies of all prior statements of prosecution witnesses as required by G.S. 7B–2300. If disclosure was not properly made, counsel should request appropriate relief similar to that found in G.S. 15A–910, including:

(1) adequate time to review the documents or investigate and prepare further before commencing cross-examination, including a continuance or recess if necessary;

(2) exclusion of the witness's testimony and all evidence affected by that testimony;

(3) a mistrial;

(4) dismissal of the case; and/or

(5) any other sanctions counsel believes would remedy the violation.

(h) At the close of the prosecution's case, counsel should move for a judgment of dismissal on each count charged. Where appropriate, counsel should be prepared with supporting case law.

Adopted December 14, 2007.

Guideline 9.6. Presenting the Defense Case

(a) In consultation with the juvenile, counsel should develop an overall defense strategy. In deciding on defense strategy, counsel should consider whether the juvenile's interests are best served by not presenting defense evidence and relying instead on the evidence and inferences, or lack thereof, from the prosecution's case.

(b) Counsel should discuss with the juvenile all of the considerations relevant to the juvenile's decision to testify, including the likelihood of cross-examination and impeachment concerning prior adjudications and prior bad acts that affect credibility.

(c) Counsel should be aware of the elements of any affirmative defense(s) and know whether the defense bears a burden of persuasion or production.

(d) In preparing for presentation of the defense case, counsel should, where appropriate:

(1) develop a plan for direct examination of each potential defense witness;

(2) determine the effect that the order of witnesses may have on the defense case;

(3) consider the possible use of character witnesses and any negative consequences that may flow from such testimony;

(4) consider the need for expert witnesses;

(5) consider the use of demonstrative evidence and the most effective order of exhibits; and

(6) be fully familiar with North Carolina statutory and case law on objections, motions to strike, offers of proof, and preserving the record on appeal.

(e) In developing and presenting the defense case, counsel should consider the implications it may have for rebuttal by the prosecution.

(f) Counsel should prepare all defense witnesses for direct examination and possible cross-examination. When appropriate, counsel should also advise witnesses of suitable courtroom dress and demeanor.

(g) If a prosecution objection to a proper question is sustained or defense evidence is improperly excluded, counsel should rephrase the question or make an offer of proof.

(h) Counsel should conduct redirect examination as appropriate.

(i) At the close of all of the evidence, counsel should renew the motion for judgment of dismissal on each charged count.

Adopted December 14, 2007.

Guideline 9.7. Closing Argument

(a) In developing a closing argument, counsel should review the proceedings to determine what aspects can be used in support of defense summation and should:

(1) highlight any weaknesses in the prosecution's case;

(2) point out favorable inferences to be drawn from the evidence;

(3) incorporate into the argument:

(A) the theory of the defense case;

(B) helpful testimony from direct and cross-examinations;

(C) responses to anticipated prosecution arguments; and

(D) any relevant visual aids and exhibits; and

(4) consider the effects of the defense argument on the prosecution's rebuttal argument.

(b) Whenever the prosecutor exceeds the scope of permissible argument, counsel should object or request a mistrial unless sound tactical considerations suggest otherwise. Such tactical considerations may include, but are not limited to:

(1) the significance of the prosecution's error;

(2) the possibility that an objection might enhance the significance of the information in the court's mind;

(3) whether, with respect to a motion for mistrial, counsel believes that the case will result in a favorable decision for the juvenile; and

(4) the need to preserve the objection for appellate review.

Adopted December 14, 2007.

SECTION 10: The Dispositional Hearing

Guideline 10.1. Dispositional Procedures

Counsel should be familiar with applicable dispositional procedures, including:

(1) the effect that plea negotiations may have on the dispositional discretion of the court;

(2) the procedural operation of disposition;

(3) the practices of the court counselor's office in preparation of the pre-dispositional report, and the juvenile's rights in that process;

(4) the right of access by counsel and the juvenile to the pre-dispositional report;

(5) the defense dispositional presentation and/or memorandum;

(6) the opportunity to challenge information presented to the court for disposition;

(7) the availability of an evidentiary hearing to challenge information, and the applicable rules of evidence and burden of proof at such a hearing; and

(8) the participation that victims and prosecution or defense witnesses may have in the dispositional proceedings.

Adopted December 14, 2007.

Guideline 10.2. Advising the Juvenile About Disposition

(a) If the juvenile enters a plea or is found delinquent, counsel should be familiar with and advise the juvenile of the dispositional requirements, options, and alternatives applicable to the offense, including:

(1) the applicable disposition laws, including the dispositional chart, calculation of the juvenile's delinquency history, and exposure to commitment to a youth development center;

(2) disposition continued;

(3) probation or suspension of confinement and mandatory and permissible conditions of probation;

(4) any mandatory requirements for registration, such as sex offender registration, or for fingerprinting and photographing; and

(5) the possibility of expunction and sealing of records.

(b) Counsel should be familiar with and advise the juvenile of the direct and collateral consequences of the adjudication and disposition including, as appropriate:

(1) credit for pre-adjudication detention;

(2) the likelihood that the adjudication could be used for sentence enhancement in the event of future criminal cases; and

(3) if applicable, other potential collateral consequences of the adjudication and disposition, such as deportation or other effects on immigration status; effects on motor vehicle or other licensing; and the potential exposure to or impact on any federal charges, educational notification, and distribution of fingerprint and photographic information.

Adopted December 14, 2007.

Guideline 10.3. Preparation for Disposition

In preparing for disposition, counsel should:

(1) be aware and inform the juvenile of the judge's practices and procedures, if possible;

(2) maintain regular contact with the juvenile prior to the dispositional hearing, and inform the juvenile and his or her parent or guardian of the steps being taken in preparation for disposition and what to expect at the dispositional hearing;

(3) obtain from the juvenile relevant information concerning such subjects as his or her background and personal history, prior record, educational history, mental health history and condition, and employment history, if any, and obtain from the juvenile sources through which the information provided can be corroborated;

(4) utilize dispositional experts, including mental health, developmental, or educational professionals, if applicable;

(5) inform the juvenile of his or her right to speak at the dispositional proceeding, and assist the juvenile in preparing the statement, if any, to be made to the court, after considering the possible consequences that any admission or other statement may have on an appeal, subsequent adjudicatory hearing, adjudication on other offenses, or other judicial proceedings, such as collateral or restitution proceedings;

(6) inform the juvenile if counsel will ask the court to consider a particular disposition;

(7) collect and present documents and affidavits to support the defense position and, when relevant, prepare and present witnesses to testify at the dispositional hearing;

(8) prepare any expert or other witnesses to address the court;

(9) consult with any child and family treatment team, if appropriate and possible; and

(10) unless there are sound tactical reasons for not doing so, attempt to determine whether the prosecution will advocate that a particular type or length of confinement be imposed.

Adopted December 14, 2007.

Guideline 10.4. The Pre–Dispositional Report

(a) Counsel should be familiar with the procedures concerning the preparation and submission of a predispositional report by the court counselor's office.

(b) If a pre-dispositional report is prepared, counsel should:

(1) provide to the court counselor preparing the report relevant information favorable to the juvenile, including, where appropriate, the juvenile's version of the offense;

(2) prepare the juvenile to be interviewed by the court counselor preparing the report, if the juvenile has not already been interviewed;

(3) make reasonable efforts to review the completed report and discuss it with the juvenile before going to court;

(4) try to ensure the juvenile has adequate time to examine the report, unless directed by the court not to disclose information in the report pursuant to G.S. 7B–2413; and

(5) take appropriate steps to ensure that erroneous or misleading information that may harm the juvenile is challenged or deleted from the report.

Adopted December 14, 2007.

Guideline 10.5. The Defense Dispositional Plan

Counsel should prepare a defense dispositional plan and, where appropriate, a dispositional memorandum. Among the topics counsel may wish to include in the dispositional presentation or memorandum are:

(1) information favorable to the juvenile concerning such matters as the offense, mitigating factors and relative culpability, prior adjudications, personal background, educational history, employment record and opportunities, and familial and financial status;

(2) information that would support a disposition other than confinement, such as the potential for rehabilitation or the nonviolent nature of the crime;

(3) information concerning the availability of treatment programs, community treatment facilities, and community service work opportunities;

(4) challenges to incorrect or incomplete information and inappropriate inferences and characterizations that are before the court; and

(5) a defense confinement proposal, if necessary.

Adopted December 14, 2007.

Guideline 10.6. The Dispositional Hearing

(a) At the dispositional hearing, counsel should take the steps necessary to advocate fully for the requested disposition and to protect the juvenile's legal rights and interests.

(b) If appropriate, counsel should present supporting evidence, including testimony of the juvenile and witnesses, affidavits, letters, and public records to establish the facts favorable to the juvenile. Counsel should also try to ensure that the juvenile is not harmed by inaccurate information or information that is not properly before the court in determining the disposition to be imposed.

(c) If the court has the authority to do so, counsel should request specific orders or recommendations from the court concerning the place of confinement and any psychiatric treatment or drug rehabilitation, and against deportation or exclusion of the juvenile, if applicable.

(d) Counsel should identify and preserve potential issues for appeal, including making reasonable efforts to ensure that the dispositional hearing is recorded. With permission of the court, counsel should also consider utilizing a personal recording device in case the court recording device fails.

Adopted December 14, 2007.

SECTION 11: Post-Disposition Obligations and Appeals

Guideline 11.1. Explaining the Disposition to the Juvenile

After the dispositional hearing is complete, counsel should fully explain to the juvenile the terms of the disposition, including any conditions of probation and implications of violating probation.

Adopted December 14, 2007.

Guideline 11.2. Motion to Modify or Vacate

Counsel should be familiar with the procedures available under G.S. 7B–2600 to seek relief from the dispositional order and should utilize those procedures when appropriate.

Adopted December 14, 2007.

Guideline 11.3. Right to Appeal to the Appellate Division

(a) Counsel should inform the juvenile of his or her right to appeal the judgment of the court to the appellate division, the action that must be taken to perfect an appeal, and the possible outcomes of a decision to appeal.

(b) If the juvenile has a right to appeal and wants to appeal, the attorney should enter notice of appeal in accordance with the procedures and timelines set forth in G.S. 7B–2602 *et seq.* and the Rules of Appellate Procedure, and should consider offering to the court a completed form appellate entries (AOC–J–470) appointing the Office of the Appellate Defender. Pursuant to Rule 33(a) of the North Carolina Rules of Appellate Procedure and Rules 1.7(a) and 3.2(a) of the Rules of the Commission on Indigent Defense Services, the entry of notice of appeal does not constitute a general appearance as counsel of record in the appellate division.

(c) If the juvenile does not have a right to appeal and counsel believes there is a meritorious issue in the case that might be raised in the appellate division by means of a petition for writ of *certiorari*, counsel should inform the juvenile of his or her opinion and consult with the Office of the Appellate Defender about the appropriate procedure.

(d) Where the juvenile takes an appeal, trial counsel should cooperate in providing information to appellate counsel concerning the proceedings in the trial court and should timely respond to reasonable requests from appellate counsel for additional information about the case.

Adopted December 14, 2007.

Guideline 11.4. Disposition Pending Appeal

(a) If a juvenile decides to appeal the adjudication or disposition of the court, counsel should inform the juvenile of any right that may exist under G.S. 7B–2605 to be released pending disposition of the appeal and, prior to the appointment of appellate counsel, make such a motion when appropriate. Counsel should also consult with the juvenile as to the possible outcomes of such a motion.

(b) If an appeal is taken and appellate counsel is appointed, trial counsel should cooperate with appellate counsel in providing information if appellate counsel pursues a request for release.

Adopted December 14, 2007.

Guideline 11.5. Post–Disposition Obligations

Even after counsel's representation in a case is complete, counsel should comply with a juvenile's reasonable requests for information and materials that are part of counsel's file. Counsel should also take reasonable steps to correct clerical or other errors in court documents.

Adopted December 14, 2007.

GENERAL RULES OF PRACTICE AND PROCEDURE FOR THE NORTH CAROLINA BUSINESS COURT

Adopted March 9, 2000

Table of Rules

Rule 1. Philosophy and Goals

1.1—Citation to Rules. These rules shall be known and cited as the General Rules of Practice and Procedure for the North Carolina Business Court. They may also be referred to in abbreviated form as "BCR" or "Business Court Rules" (e.g., this section may be cited as "BCR 1.1").

1.2—Purpose. The Business Court Rules are designed to facilitate the pretrial and trial of cases by the North Carolina Business Court and any other court(s) with comparable and compatible technical capabilities and otherwise subject to the North Carolina Rules of Civil Procedure and the General Rules of Practice for Superior and District Courts. They are intended to take advantage of computer-assisted methods of information processing and the transmission of such information by advanced communications equipment: (1) where feasible, (2) where elected by one or more parties and (3) where approved by the Court. They are not, however, intended to operate to the exclusion of paper-driven methods of handling litigation, absent prior agreement.

1.3—Environment. These rules are designed to accommodate litigation and trial of cases utilizing electronic methods which include but are not limited to electronic filing, scanning, storage and reproduction of written material in machine-readable form suitable for transmission through a variety of communications media, as well as litigation and trial of cases in non-electronic form dependent upon the physical manipulation of paper writings.

1.4—Goals. These rules and the equipment and methods they enable are intended to provide better access to Court information for litigants, counsel, and the public; increase the efficiency and understanding of Court personnel, counsel, and witnesses; decrease costs for litigants and others involved in the court system; and facilitate the efficient and effective presentation of evidence in the courtroom. Whether applied in an electronic or non-electronic environment, these rules shall be construed and enforced to avoid technical delay, encourage civility, permit just and prompt determination of all proceedings and promote the efficient administration of justice.

1.5—Integration with Other Rules. These rules are intended to supplement, not supplant, the North Carolina Rules of Civil Procedure and the General Rules of Practice for Superior and District Courts. Should any conflict be deemed to exist between the

Business Court Rules and the North Carolina Rules of Civil Procedure or the General Rules of Practice for Superior and District Courts, the latter Rules shall control.

[Adopted March 9, 2000. Amended effective July 31, 2006.]

Rule 2. Definitions

2.1—"Electronic Identity" means the combination of Username and Password issued to a person by the Court and utilized by that person for the purpose of filing an electronic record.

2.2—"Electronic" means relating to technology having electrical, digital, magnetic, wireless, optical, electromagnetic, or similar capabilities.

2.3—"Electronic Agent" means a computer program or an electronic or other automated means used independently to initiate an action or respond to electronic records or performances in whole or in part, without review or action by an individual.

2.4—"Electronic Record" means a record created, generated, sent, communicated, received, or stored by electronic means. All electronic records shall be capable of being printed as paper, or transferred to archival media, without loss of content or material alteration of appearance.

2.5—"Electronic Security Procedure" means a procedure employed for the purpose of verifying that an electronic signature, record, or performance is that of a specific person or for detecting changes or errors in the information in an electronic record.

2.6—"Record" means information that is inscribed on a tangible medium or that is stored in an electronic or other medium and is retrievable in perceivable form.

2.7—"Document" means a related and paginated grouping of information items contained on a record.

2.8—"Information" means data, text, images, sounds, or codes, manipulated manually or by computer hardware and software.

2.9—"Information Processing System" means a system for creating, generating, sending, receiving, storing, displaying, or processing information on paper or in an electronic medium.

2.10—"Paper" means any item subject to filing, service, or another use contemplated by these Rules.

[Adopted March 9, 2000. Amended effective July 31, 2006.]

Rule 3. Mandatory Business Court Jurisdiction

3.1—Compliance with N.C. Gen. Stat. § 7A–45.1.

(a) A party shall file a Notice of Designation of an action as a mandatory complex business case under N.C. Gen. Stat. § 7A–45.4 by using Form 1 appearing at the end of these Rules. The time period for filing the Notice of Designation is explicitly set forth in N.C. Gen. Stat. § 7A–45.4. If the time period for filing a Notice of Designation expires with respect to a party, such party may not proceed under N.C. Gen. Stat. § 7A–45.4, but may seek assignment of the action to the Business Court under General Rule of Practice 2.1.

(b) In the event that a party amends a pleading under N.C. R. Civ. P. 15 (either by right or with leave of Court), if the amendment raises a new material issue listed in subsections (a)(1) through (a)(6) of N.C. Gen. Stat. § 7A–45.4, then a Notice of Designation (with respect to the entire action) may be filed with respect to such new material issue within the time periods set forth in subsection (d) of N.C. Gen. Stat. § 7A–45.4. Such time periods will be calculated and determined by reference to the amended pleading and all permitted responses thereto. A party shall refrain from filing a Notice of Designation based on an amended pleading unless the new material issue presented by the amended pleading substantially alters the nature of the action and other considerations support assignment of the case to the Business Court. The Notice of Designation procedure shall not be utilized in connection with an amended pleading for the purpose of interfering with or delaying ongoing or upcoming proceedings, or where assignment of the action to Business Court would be inconsistent with the interests of justice given the status of the proceedings in the Superior Court where the action is pending.

(c) Service of a party's Notice of Designation upon the Special Superior Court Judge for Complex Business Cases who is then the Chief Business Court Judge as required by N.C. Gen. Stat. 7A–45.4(b) shall be effected in the same manner (i.e., by e-mail or facsimile transmission) in which the party sends the Notice of Designation to the Chief Justice of the Supreme Court.

3.2—Contents of Notice of Designation. N.C. Gen. Stat. 7A–45.4 provides an expedited method for certain types of actions to be assigned to the Business Court. In setting forth the categories of cases within the "mandatory" jurisdiction of the Business Court, the General Assembly afforded the Court flexibility to determine (on its own motion or the motion of a party) that the action should not be retained as a Business Court case. In order to allow the Court to make such a determination on its own motion, Form 1 requires that the party filing the Notice of Designation explain why and how the action falls within one of the specific categories set forth in N.C. Gen. Stat. § 7A–45.4(a) and invites that party to supply any additional information that may be helpful in determining whether the Court should retain the action. When completing Form 1, the party should briefly and succinctly explain the nature of the dispute and the material issues likely to be presented in the action (including any material issues not listed in N.C. Gen. Stat.

§ 7A–45.4(a)). In addition, the party should identify for the Court any other factors that may assist the Court in deciding whether to retain the case, including but not limited to (i) the amount in issue, (ii) the novelty of the issues, (iii) the degree to which the interests of justice will be advanced by adjudication of the action under the Business Court's rules and procedures, and (iv) any other potential impacts on the parties or the Court that would be associated with retention of the action.

3.3—Opposition to Notice of Designation. N.C. Gen. Stat. 7A–45.4(e) provides that a party may file an opposition to the Notice of Designation. In the event that a party files such an opposition, all other parties to the action shall be entitled to file responses supporting or opposing retention of the action in the Business Court. Such responses shall be filed within fifteen days of service of the opposition or in such shorter time as the Court may direct.

3.4—Payment of Fee for Cases Assigned to the Business Court. The fee for cases assigned to the Business Court shall be paid to the Clerk of Superior Court in the judicial district in which the matter is pending and is due immediately upon receipt of an Order assigning the case to the Business Court. This fee is non-refundable in the event an Order is subsequently entered remanding the case to the Superior Court in the County in which the case was originally filed.

[Adopted effective July 31, 2006.]

Rule 4. Case Identification and Electronic Identities

4.1—Case Identification Numbers. On designation or assignment of any case to the Business Court, the matter shall retain the civil action number assigned to it by the clerk in the county in which the action originated.

4.2—Electronic Identities. Upon application of any person having a matter before the Business Court, the Court shall issue an Electronic Identity to such person which shall be used in connection with, and shall authorize, the electronic filing of information by such person in the Business Court. Electronic Identities are not case specific. The issuance of an Electronic Identity without utilization shall not constitute an appearance in any matter. The utilization of an Electronic Identity in connection with any electronic filing in the Business Court shall constitute (a) the agreement of the person to whom the Electronic Identity has been issued that such person shall use the Electronic Identity in compliance with the rules and procedures of the Business Court for electronic filing and all other rules applicable to the Business Court and (b) an appearance in the matter in which the filing is made of the person to whom the Electronic Identity is issued.

4.3—Recipients of Electronic Identification. Each person to whom an Electronic Identity is issued (the "Recipient") shall be responsible for the security and use of such Electronic Identity. Any electronic filing made utilizing an Electronic Identity shall be deemed to be made with the authorization of the Recipient, unless and until the contrary is demonstrated by the Recipient to the satisfaction of the Court by clear and convincing evidence.

[Adopted March 9, 2000. Redesignated from Rule 3 and amended effective July 31, 2006.]

Rule 5. Signatures and Authenticity

5.1—Signatures. Information filed with the Court electronically shall be deemed to be signed by a person (the "Signatory"), regardless of the existence of a handwritten signature on the paper, provided that such paper is filed by the Signatory using an Electronic Identity, and that the paper contains the name, postal address, e-mail address and State Bar number (if applicable) of the Signatory and the typed signature of the person preceded by the symbol "/s/" in the location at which a handwritten signature would normally appear if filed in paper form. Unless required by the circumstances, information filed electronically need not and should not be filed in an optically scanned format displaying an actual signature.

5.2—Stipulations or Other Information Involving Multiple Signatures. In the case of a stipulation or other information to be signed by two or more persons representing different parties, the person who files such information shall confirm that all persons due to sign the information are agreeable to the content of the document, shall represent to the Court in the body of the information or in an accompanying filing that such agreement has been obtained, and shall insert the typed signature of persons other than the person filing preceded by the symbol "/s/" and followed by the words "by permission" in the location where such handwritten signature would otherwise appear. Thus, the correct format for the typed signature of a person other than the person filing is: "/s/ Jane Doe by permission."

5.3—Original Document. Information filed electronically in accordance with these Rules as it resides in the Court's computer system, and true and accurate printouts of such information, shall be considered authentic. To the extent that the original of a document is not required by these Rules to be filed in the office of the Clerk of Superior Court in the judicial district in which the matter is pending, the Court may require the party to produce that original document, document attachment, or exhibit, even though a copy of it has already been filed electronically. A screen display or paper printout of an electronic filing is equivalent to the electronic original for purposes of the Best Evidence Rule, if the display or printout is at a degree of optical resolution equal to the resolution at which the document is stored in the records of the Court.

[Adopted March 9, 2000. Redesignated from Rule 4 and amended effective July 31, 2006.]

Rule 6. Electronic Filing and Service

6.1—Business Court Preference for Electronic Filing. For all papers filed with the Business Court, the parties are strongly encouraged to use the Business Court's Electronic filing and service system to effect transmittal and filing of those papers and to serve them on all parties. However, except as provided in a Case Management Order, nothing in these Rules shall require the filing of any information in the Business Court by electronic means.

6.2—Attributes of Acceptable Electronic Filing. Electronic filing may be conducted only through authorized use of a valid Electronic Identity in accordance with these Rules. All electronic filings shall be made using only those file formats approved by the Court, and the format for each electronic filing shall be designated by using a generally recognized file extension that identifies a particular format. The manipulation of any file or the use of any technique or format for the purpose of impairing access or display of any file is strictly prohibited.

6.3—Certification of Electronically Filed Document. For the purposes of Rule 11 of the North Carolina Rules of Civil Procedure and these Business Court Rules, any electronically filed information shall be deemed signed by one or more counsel of record or unrepresented parties (each, a "Signatory") pursuant to Rule 5 of these Rules.

6.4—Notice of Electronic Filing. Electronic transmission of a paper to the Business Court file server in accordance with these Rules, together with the receipt of a Notice of Electronic Filing automatically generated by the Electronic filing and service system as authorized by the Court, shall constitute filing of the paper with the Business Court for purposes of timing under the North Carolina General Statutes, the North Carolina Rules of Civil Procedure, and the Business Court Rules, and shall constitute entry of that paper on the Business Court Docket. An electronic filing with the Business Court is deemed complete only upon receipt of such Notice of Electronic Filing by the person filing the paper.

6.5—Substituted Electronic Service. Service of pleadings and other communications with the Court shall be governed by Rules 6, 7, and the Case Management Order. Until an order regarding service of written papers is entered by the Court, and in the absence of a written stipulation, the parties shall serve documents upon each other in compliance with N.C. R. Civ. P. 5. Where a Business Court order calls for use of Electronic Filing in a matter, receipt by e-mail of a Notice of Electronic Filing at the e-mail address specified in the Case Management Order shall constitute an adequate and timely substitute for service pursuant to the North Carolina Rules of Civil Procedure. Each person who may be served by e-mail shall be responsible for the timely monitoring of receipt of e-mail messages, the proper operation of the person's e-mail service and the prompt notification of the Court and all other persons involved in a matter of any change in e-mail address.

6.6—Date and Time of Filing. When information has been filed electronically, the official information of record is the electronic recording of the information as stored on the Court's file server, and the filing date and time is deemed to be the date and time recorded on the Court's file server for transmission of the Notice of Electronic Filing, which date and time is stated in the body of such Notice. In the event that information is timely filed, the date and time of the electronic filing shall govern the creation or performance of any further right, duty, act, or event required or permitted under North Carolina law or applicable rule, unless the Court rules that the enforcement of such priority on a particular occasion would result in manifest injustice.

6.7—Submission of Filing. An electronic filing may be submitted to the Court at any time of the day or night. For purposes of determining the timeliness of a filing, if the submission of the filing began during normal business hours of the Business Court (8:00 a.m.—5:00 p.m., Monday through Friday, excluding holidays), the filing is deemed to have occurred on that date. If the submission of the filing began after normal business hours of the Business Court, the filing is deemed to have occurred on the next day the Business Court is open for business.

6.8—Information Not Filed With the Court. The parties may choose to electronically serve information that is not filed with the court (e.g., discovery).

(a) *Service.* All information that is served electronically, but not filed electronically in the Business Court, shall be served on all persons or entities required to be served in the manner designated in the Case Management Order. Service by e-mail shall be deemed satisfied by transmitting the information by e-mail in a format approved by the Court or agreed upon by the parties.

(b) *Time service occurs.* Service of an electronically transmitted document shall be deemed to occur one hour after it is sent, provided that (i) documents sent after 5 p.m. shall be deemed sent at 8 a.m. the following day; and (ii) documents sent by electronic means that are not in a format in which the content is readily accessible to the recipient shall not be deemed served until actually received in a form in which the content is readily accessible to the receiving party.

6.9—Informal Communications. All communications with the Court that are not filed in the Business Court Electronic filing and service system (e.g., letters to the Court) shall be simultaneously sent to all other parties in the case via e-mail (and if a party cannot receive e-mail, by the most reasonably expedient method available to the sending party (facsimile transmission, hand delivery, or mail)). The transmitting party shall promptly notify the Court if the party is unable to comply with this rule.

6.10—Additional Time Upon Electronic Service. Electronic service shall be treated the same as service by mail for the purpose of adding three (3) days to the prescribed period to respond under N.C. R. Civ. P. 6(e).

6.11—Notice and Entry of Orders, Judgments, and Other Matters. The Court shall file electronically all orders, decrees, judgments, and proceedings of the Court, and all other docket matters, which shall constitute entry of the order, decree, judgment, or proceeding on the Court's Docket, pursuant to applicable law and procedure. Each order shall bear a date and a typed signature of the Business Court Judge issuing the order. Immediately upon the entry of such matter on the Docket, the Court shall transmit to each e-mail address of record a notice of the entry. Transmission of such Notice of Entry shall constitute service pursuant to N.C. R. Civ. P. 58. The Business Court shall be responsible for filing copies of its orders with the Clerk of Superior Court in the judicial district in which the matter is pending.

6.12—Good Faith Efforts With Respect to Electronic Communications. The parties shall make all reasonable endeavors in good faith to resolve technical incompatibilities or other obstacles to electronic communications, provided that no purchase of hardware or software shall be required and no extensive "manual" reformatting of documents shall be expected. Parties shall, for example, attempt to identify and correct problems which render content of communications inaccessible and shall save or transmit documents in electronic formats that are mutually available to all parties receiving them. It shall not be consistent with the rules for a party to object to use of electronic communications and fail to cooperate in resolving a problem upon which the objection is based. In the event that a party asserts that it did not receive an e-mail communication or could not fully access its contents, the sending party shall promptly forward the communication to the party by other means, notify the Court that the information has been sent by other means and make reasonable efforts to assure that the receiving party obtains and is able to access the communication at issue and subsequent communications. No party shall encrypt the contents of a message or change the electronic format in a manner which prevents a party from having access to all information made available to the Court.

6.13—Determination of Failure and Effect on Due Date. The Court shall deem the Electronic filing and service system to be subject to a technical failure on a given day if the Court server is unable to receive and accept filings in accordance with these Rules, either continuously or intermittently over the course of any period of time that, after 12:00 noon on such day, amounts in the aggregate to more than one hour. In the event of a technical failure, filings due that day which were not filed due solely to such technical failures shall become due the next business day. Such delayed filings shall be rejected unless accompanied by a declaration or affidavit attesting to the filing person's failed attempts to file electronically at least two times after 12:00 noon separated by at least one hour on each day of delay due to such technical failure.

6.14—Procedure Where Notice of Electronic Filing Not Received. If a Notice of Electronic Filing is not received from the Court in response to a transmission of information for filing, the information will not be deemed filed. The person making the filing shall attempt to re-file the information electronically until such a Notice is received, consistent with the provisions of subparagraph 6.13 permitting delayed filings. Each person using the Electronic filing and service system is solely responsible for the proper operation of all equipment and facilities used to transmit an electronic filing.

6.15—Retransmission of Electronic Filing. If, after filing information electronically, any party discovers that the version of the information available for viewing through the Electronic filing and service system is incomplete, garbled, or otherwise does not conform to the information as transmitted when filed, such party shall notify the Court immediately and retransmit the filing if necessary.

[Adopted March 9, 2000. Redesignated from Rule 5 and amended effective July 31, 2006.]

Rule 7. Filing Other Than by Electronic Means

When a party is unable to use the Business Court's electronic filing and service system, any information required or permitted to be filed with the Business Court may be filed by facsimile transmission, by hand delivery, or by delivery through the United States Mail.

7.1—Facsimile Transmission. The Business Court may maintain one or more facsimile machines for the purpose of receiving filings and communications from parties. Numbers for such facsimile machines shall be posted on the Business Court web site. Except as provided in a Case Management Order, any information required or permitted to be filed by facsimile shall be transmitted to the facsimile machine for the Business Court Judge to whom a case has been assigned located at the Business Court of the assigned Judge. In the absence of an assigned Business Court Judge, facsimile transmissions shall be directed to the facsimile machine of the Chief Business Court Judge. The date and time recorded for completion of such facsimile transmission by the Business Court facsimile system shall establish the time of delivery to the Business Court. Any person or entity submitting a filing by such facsimile method shall assume all risk of error, malfunction, misdirection, or other error that causes a failure in transmission or otherwise prevents receipt by the Court of a complete and accurate filing. In the event of a filing by facsimile, the filing party shall use its best efforts to serve the document on all parties by the means most reasonably calculated to insure receipt of the document by all parties the same day. If unable to serve by facsimile after diligent efforts, the filing party may serve by hand delivery or overnight courier for receipt the next business day if within the state, and by the day following the next business day if outside the state. The Court may receive a facsimile transmission into a computer file, rather than receiving such a transfer onto paper, and shall image such facsimile transmission for further system use.

7.2—Hand Delivery. Except as provided in a Case Management Order, documents may be filed with the Business Court by hand delivery to the Business Court at the chambers of the Business Court Judge assigned to a case or, in the absence of an assignment, to the chambers of the Chief Business Court Judge. Filing by hand delivery shall be deemed complete only upon actual receipt by authorized Business Court personnel of a document.

7.3—Mail. Except as provided in a Case Management Order, documents may be filed with the Business Court by U.S. Mail but such a filing shall be deemed complete only when actually received by the Business Court. The Court will maintain mailing addresses on its web site. In cases assigned to a particular Business Court Judge, mail shall be directed to the Judge's chambers. In the absence of an assignment, mail shall be directed to the chambers of the Chief Business Court Judge.

[Adopted effective July 31, 2006.]

Rule 8. Filings With the Clerk of Superior Court

8.1—Required Filings with the Clerk of Superior Court. In accordance with the provisions of N.C. R. Civ. P. 5(d), all documents and materials submitted to the Business Court shall also be filed within five (5) business days with the Clerk of Superior Court in the judicial district in which the matter is pending. Where such documents and materials have been electronically filed with the Business Court, the certificate of service for filings with the Clerk of Superior Court shall additionally be signed in handwriting above or in lieu of the electronic signature line.

[Adopted effective July 31, 2006.]

Rule 9. Time

9.1—Clarification Concerning Time Calculations. In the event that the time prescribed for taking any action by any statute, rule of procedure, or any order of the Court is less than seven days, then even if the additional day allowed as a result of service by telefacsimile after 5:00 pm (or the equivalent service by electronic filing or email under these Rules) or the additional three days for electronic service or service by mail extends the time prescribed to seven days or more, intermediate Saturdays, Sundays, and holidays shall nevertheless be excluded in calculation of time (in the manner specified in N.C. R. Civ. P. 6(a)). In such event, if time is enlarged further pursuant to Rules 9.2 or 9.3, then intermediate Saturdays, Sundays, and holidays shall be included in calculating time only with respect to the period of the enlargement.

9.2—Enlargements of Time—Motions. Once a case has been assigned or designated to the Business Court, all motions to extend any of the times prescribed or allowed by these Rules, the North Carolina Rules of Civil Procedure, or by court order, shall be directed to the Business Court Judge assigned to the case. If the case has not yet been assigned to a particular judge, the motion to extend time shall be directed to the Chief Business Court Judge. The motion for extension of time shall not be considered to have been made until it is received by the Business Court. After assignment or designation to the Business Court, a party shall not seek an order to extend time from the Clerk of Superior Court in the judicial district in which the matter is pending, notwithstanding the party's obligation to file a hard copy of such material with said Clerk of Superior Court.

The movant shall have a good faith basis for requesting any such extension of time and, except in extraordinary cases, the movant shall first consult with any opposing party and reflect that party's position in the motion and indicate whether the opposing party wishes to be heard on the motion. Provided that there is such a good faith basis, the filing of the motion for extension of time shall automatically extend the time for filing or the performance of the act for which the extension is sought until the earlier of the expiration of the extension requested, ten calendar days, or a ruling by the court. In the event that the motion for extension of time is denied, the filing shall be made or the act done no later than the second business day following filing of the court's order unless a different time is provided by the court's order.

9.3—Enlargements of Time—No Motion Required. With the exception of papers for which time cannot be enlarged (as explicitly provided in N.C. R. Civ. P. 6(b) or in other court rules or statutes), if a statute, any rule of procedure, or any order of the Court requires that a paper be filed or served less than twenty days after the Chief Justice designates an action as a complex business case under General Rule of Practice 2.1 and/or N.C. Gen. Stat. § 7A–45.4, then the time for filing or service of such paper (and for filing of service of papers responsive thereto or dependent thereon) is hereby automatically enlarged so that filing or service will be due on the twentieth (20th) day following such assignment. No motion or order shall be submitted to the Court in such event.

[Adopted effective July 31, 2006.]

Rule 10. Protective Orders for Information Deemed Confidential or Proprietary

10.1—Protective Order Respecting Proprietary Rights. In connection with the electronic filing of any information in the Business Court, any person may apply by motion for an order prohibiting the electronic filing in the matter of certain specifically identified information on the grounds that such information is subject to a proprietary right or a right of confidentiality and that electronic filing is likely to result in substantial prejudice to those rights. A motion for such an order shall be filed not less than three business days before the information to which the motion pertains is due to be filed with the Court. Nothing in this paragraph shall be construed to change any requirement or standard that otherwise would be applicable for issuance of a protective order per se or in connection with information contained in a paper record.

[Adopted March 9, 2000. Redesignated from Rule 7 and amended effective July 31, 2006.]

Rule 11. Security

11.1—Confidentiality of Electronic Identity. Each person shall maintain as confidential, except as expressly provided in these rules, the Electronic Identity issued to that person by the Court. Upon learning about information constituting reasonable evidence of the likely compromise of the confidentiality of the Electronic Identity, an individual shall immediately notify the Court.

11.2—Use of Electronic Identity by Additional Person. A person to whom an Electronic Identity has been issued may authorize another person to file a paper using his number and signature; however, the authorizing person shall retain full responsibility for any paper so filed or for other use of such number and signature.

11.3—Compromise of Security. Any attempt or effort to avoid, compromise or alter any security element of the Electronic filing and service system is strictly prohibited. Any person receiving information constituting reasonable evidence of a likely occurrence of such an attempt or effort shall immediately notify and cooperate with the Court concerning such information.

[Adopted March 9, 2000. Redesignated from Rule 8 and amended effective July 31, 2006.]

Rule 12. Videoconferencing

Rule 12.1—By Agreement. By mutual agreement, counsel may arrange for any proceeding or conference to be held by videoconference by coordinating a schedule for such meeting that is convenient with the Business Court. All Counsel and other participants shall be subject to the same rules of procedure and decorum as if the meeting were held in the courtroom of the Business Court.

Rule 12.2—Responsibility for Videoconferencing Facilities. The parties are responsible for obtaining all communications facilities and arranging all details as may be required to connect and interface with the videoconferencing equipment available to the Business Court. The Business Court will endeavor to make reasonable technical assistance available to the parties concerning the specifications and requirements of the Court's equipment, but all responsibility for planning and executing all technical considerations required to hold a videoconference successfully shall remain solely with the parties.

Rule 12.3—Allocation of Videoconferencing Costs. In the absence of a contrary agreement among the parties, each party participating by videoconference shall bear its own costs of participating in the conference.

Rule 12.4—Court Reporter. Where any proceeding or conference is held by videoconference, the court reporter transcribing such proceeding or conference will be present in the Business Court.

[Adopted March 9, 2000. Redesignated from Rule 10 and amended effective July 31, 2006.]

Rule 13. Undertakings of Parties and Limitation of Court Liability

13.1—Undertakings. Parties wishing to utilize the computer-assisted facilities of the Business Court agree by accessing such facilities to abide by all aspects of these rules, including conditions of access and use and security procedures set out herein and as they may subsequently be published by the Business Court.

13.2—No Business Court Liability. Attorneys, litigants, and all other persons granted access to the computer-assisted facilities of the Business Court agree that the Business Court shall not be liable to them for damages of any kind resulting from the negligent misuse of Court facilities. Such misuse may result in Court sanctions or, in the instance of an aggrieved party, in a right to pursue compensatory damages from a party who intentionally or negligently misuses Court facilities. Such misuse shall be deemed to include the introduction of computer viruses into information handling systems of the Court or other parties, where virus control software recommended by the Court is not being used.

13.3—Viruses. Any party filing electronically shall check each file to be transmitted for viruses before transmitting. Any electronic filing submitted to the Court containing viruses will be rejected by the Court's computer system.

[Adopted March 9, 2000. Redesignated from Rule 11 and amended effective July 31, 2006.]

Rule 14. Calendaring and Commencement of Actions

14.1—Preparation of Calendar. The calendar for each of the Business Court Judges shall be prepared by that Business Court Judge and published on the Business Court Web Site. Where e-mail addresses have been provided to the Business Court, Notices of Hearing shall be distributed by e-mail to each attorney of record (or party where there is no attorney of record) no later than five (5) business days prior to the day of the hearing unless otherwise specified by the Case Management Order. An attorney or party who has not provided an e-mail address to the Court will receive Notices of Hearing via facsimile, or where no facsimile number is available, by first class mail.

14.2—Appearances. An attorney and/or unrepresented party who is notified to appear for the setting of a calendar, pretrial conference, hearing of a motion, or for trial, shall, consistent with ethical requirements, appear or have a partner, associate, or another attorney familiar with the case present. Unless an attorney has been excused in advance by the Business Court Judge and has given prior notice to opponent(s), a case will not be continued for failure of appearance.

14.3—Notification of Settlement. When a case is settled, counsel for the plaintiff and each unrepresented plaintiff of record shall notify the Business Court Judge or the Judge's designee within twenty-four (24) hours of the settlement and shall advise the Court of the identity of the party or parties who will prepare and present the judgment, dismissal, or stipulation of dismissal, which shall be presented within thirty (30) days of the notification of settlement.

[Adopted March 9, 2000. Redesignated from Rule 12 and amended effective July 31, 2006.]

Rule 15. Motion Practice

15.1—All Motions to Be Filed in Business Court. After a case has been assigned or designated to the Business Court, and for as long as the case is pending in this Court, parties shall seek rulings on all motions in the case from this Court, and not from Superior Court Judges or Clerks in the counties where cases originate.

15.2—Form. All motions, unless made orally during a hearing or a trial, shall be in paper writing or electronic form and shall be accompanied by a brief, except as provided in Rules 15.10 and 15.12. Each motion shall be set out in a separate paper. Where the terms "Motion," "Brief," "Affidavit," "Document," "Deposition" and like designations are used herein, they shall refer to such items in paper writing or electronic form as determined appropriate under these rules.

15.3—Content. All motions shall state with particularity the grounds therefor, shall cite any statute or rule of procedure relied upon and shall set forth the relief or order sought.

15.4—Motions Decided on Papers and Briefs.

(a) Motions shall be considered and decided by the Court on the pleadings, admissible evidence, the official court file, and briefs, without hearing or oral argument, unless otherwise ordered by the Court. Special considerations thought by counsel sufficient to warrant a hearing or oral argument may be brought to the Court's attention in the motion or response.

(b) If the Court grants oral argument on any motion, it shall give the parties at least five (5) business days' notice of the date and place of oral argument. The Court, however, for good cause shown, may shorten the five (5)–day notice period. The Court may in its discretion conduct any oral argument by telephone or videoconference.

15.5—Movant's Supporting Documents and Brief. If allegations of facts not appearing of record are relied upon to support a motion, affidavits, parts of depositions, and other pertinent documents then available shall accompany the motion. If supporting documents are not then available, the moving party may move for an extension of time in accordance with Rule 9.2.

15.6—Response to Motion and Brief. The respondent, if opposing a motion, shall file a response, including brief, within twenty (20) days after service of the brief supporting the motion (or thirty (30) days if the motion is for summary judgment). If supporting documents are not then available, the respondent may move for an extension of time in accordance with Rule 9.2. For good cause appearing therefor, a respondent may be required by the Court to file any response and supporting documents, including brief, within such shorter period of time as the Court may specify.

15.7—Reply Brief. A reply brief may be filed within ten (10) days after service of the response. A reply brief is limited to discussion of matters newly raised in the response.

15.8—Limitations on Length of Briefs. The Court favors concise briefs. Unless the following limits are modified by the Court for good cause shown, briefs in support of motions and responsive briefs shall be double-spaced and limited in length to a maximum of seven thousand, five hundred (7,500) words. Reply briefs shall also be double-spaced and may not exceed three thousand, seven hundred and fifty (3,750) words. Headings, footnotes, quotations, and citations count toward these word-count limitations. The case caption on the first page of a brief, any table of contents, any table of authorities, and any required certificates of counsel or of a party do not count toward these word-count limitations.

Requests for expansion of word limitations shall be made five (5) business days prior to filing the brief for which expansion of word limitations is sought. Requests for expansion of word limitations that are filed simultaneously with the brief shall be denied.

Each brief shall include a certificate by the attorney or party that the brief complies with this Rule 15.8. The attorney or party may rely upon the word count of the word-processing system used to prepare the brief.

Unless a Case Management Order or another order of the Court expressly provides otherwise, all parties who are jointly represented by any law firm shall join together in a single brief. Unless otherwise ordered by the Court, that single brief may not exceed the length limit stated above.

15.9—Suggestion of Subsequently Decided Authority. As an addendum to a brief, response brief, or reply brief, a suggestion of subsequently decided controlling authority, without argument, may be filed at any time prior to the Court's ruling and shall contain only the citation to the case relied upon, if published, or a copy of the opinion if the case is unpublished.

15.10—Motions Not Requiring Briefs. No brief is required by either movant or respondent, unless otherwise directed by the Court, with respect to the following motions:

(a) discovery motions in which the parties have agreed to the expedited procedures described in Rule 15.12;

(b) for extension of time for the performance of an act required or allowed to be done, provided request therefor is made before the expiration of the period originally prescribed or extended by previous orders;

(c) to continue a pre-trial conference, hearing, or the trial of an action;

(d) to add parties;

(e) to amend the pleadings;

(f) to file supplemental pleadings;

(g) to appoint a next friend or guardian ad litem;

(h) for substitution of parties;

(i) to stay proceedings to enforce judgment; and

(j) for pro hac vice admission of counsel who are not members of the North Carolina State Bar.

The above motions, which are not required to be accompanied by a brief, shall state good cause therefor and cite any applicable rule, statute, or other authority justifying the relief sought. These motions shall be accompanied by a proposed order.

15.11—Failure to File and Serve Motion Materials. The failure to file a brief or response within the time specified in this rule shall constitute a waiver of the right thereafter to file such brief or response, except upon a showing of excusable neglect. A motion unaccompanied by a required brief may, in the discretion of the Court, be summarily denied. If a respondent fails to file a response within the time required by this rule, the motion will be considered and decided as an uncontested motion, and ordinarily will be granted without further notice.

15.12—Determination of Discovery Motions Through Oral Argument Without Briefs. With the consent of both parties and as allowed by the Court, the parties may present motions and the Court may resolve disputes regarding discovery matters through the use of an expedited oral argument procedure. Such motions will routinely be limited to matters which can be argued and determined in one hour or less.

[Adopted March 9, 2000. Redesignated from Rule 13 and amended effective July 31, 2006.]

Rule 16. Presentation Technology

16.1—Generally. Electronic presentations and technologically generated demonstrative evidence should be used to enhance the trier-of-fact's understanding of facts in the action or to further the convenience or efficiency of the litigation process. Presentations which contain technological aspects that primarily add dramatization or "special effects" may be excluded pursuant to North Carolina Rule of Evidence 403. In making such determination, the Court will consider, in addition to any other matters it deems pertinent, the extent to which the presentation serves proper purposes, the extent to which the manner of the presentation may enhance a party's factual contentions without adequate foundation, and the opposing party's technological resources, means, and ability to prepare to rebut the presentation.

16.2—Foundation. No graphic reconstructions, dramatizations, or other technologically manufactured representations shall be permitted unless:

(a) all representations made or conveyed in the presentation that may be probative to issues in the case or prejudicial to another party are supported by other competent evidence presented in the trial; and

(b) the opposing party has been given an adequate notice and opportunity, determined under the circumstances of the case, to review the presentation and obtain any relevant information concerning its preparation prior to it being presented to the trier-of-fact.

16.3—Virus Prevention. Any media brought into the Business Court for presentation purposes shall be checked for viruses using appropriate virus scanning software before such media are used in the courtroom.

16.4—Presentation Formats. All presentation software not in conformance with the file formats accepted by the Court may not be utilized in the courtroom without the prior express approval of the Court.

[Adopted March 9, 2000. Redesignated from Rule 14 and amended effective July 31, 2006.]

Rule 17. Case Management Meetings, Reports, Conferences, and Orders

17.1—Case Management Meeting. Within thirty (30) days of filing of assignment or designation of a case to the Business Court, or such shorter or longer time as the Court shall order, the parties shall meet to discuss case management issues, as well as the potential content of a Case Management Order. Unless the parties agree otherwise, counsel for the first plaintiff listed in the complaint is responsible for initiating the scheduling of the Case Management Meeting. In initiating the scheduling of the Case Management Meeting, plaintiff's counsel should contact each law firm that he or she knows will appear in the case, even if that law firm has not yet entered a formal appearance.

The parties' Case Management Meeting should cover at least the following subjects:

(a) The length of the discovery period, the number of fact and expert depositions to be permitted, and, as appropriate, the length and sequence of such depositions.

(b) A preliminary schedule for depositions of such persons and entities as the parties are able to identify.

(c) The date by which parties shall complete disclosure of expert information pursuant to N.C. R. Civ. P. 26(b)(4)(a).

(d) The identity and number of any Motions to Dismiss or other preliminary or pre-discovery motions which shall be filed and the time period in which they shall be filed, briefed, and argued.

(e) Which parties should be required to file joint briefs for purposes of the length limitations on briefs under Rule 15.8.

(f) The time period after the close of discovery within which post-discovery dispositive motions shall be filed, briefed, and argued and a tentative schedule for such activities.

(g) A tentative date by which the parties will be prepared for trial.

(h) The timing of any mediated settlement conference (see Rule 19) and the selection of a mediator or group of mediators.

(i) An estimate of the volume of documents and/or electronic information likely to be the subject of discovery in the case from parties and nonparties and whether there are technological means, including but not limited to production of electronic images rather than paper documents and any associated protocol, that may render document discovery more manageable at an acceptable cost.

(j) The number of interrogatories which shall be allowed each party.

(k) The advisability of using special master(s) for fact finding, mediation of discovery disputes or such other matters as the parties may agree upon.

(*l*) The situs of pretrial and trial proceedings.

(m) An identification of any disputes concerning personal jurisdiction, subject matter jurisdiction, or venue, or a stipulation that no such controversies exist at the time of the Case Management Meeting.

(n) Whether or not a party or parties desire to use the electronic filing, case tracking, scanning, videographic, and real-time court reporting capabilities of the Court, and, to the extent this is the case, a determination of:

(1) Fairness issues, including but not necessarily limited to use of such capabilities by some but not all parties and/or by parties whose resources permit or require variations in the use of such capabilities;

(2) Issues related to compatibility of Court and party facilities and equipment;

(3) Issues related to the use of demonstrative exhibits and any balancing of relevance and potential prejudice which may need to occur in connection with such exhibits;

(4) Such other issues related to the use of the Court's and Parties' special technological facilities as may be raised by any party or the Court or its technological advisor, given the nature of the case and the resources of the parties.

(*o*) A good faith estimate by counsel for each party based upon consultation with each such party of the costs each party is likely to incur in pursuing the litigation through trial court adjudication, provided, however, that any party may, instead of disclosing this information in a Case Management Meeting or Case Management Report, file this information with the Court under seal and without service of the information on any other party, or discuss this information privately with the Court at the Case Management Conference.

(p) A preliminary listing of the principal legal and factual issues which counsel believe will need to be decided in the case.

(q) A preliminary listing of any issues in the case that any party believes are governed by law other than North Carolina law or federal law.

(r) The need for retention of potentially relevant documents, including but not limited to documents stored electronically and the need to suspend all automatic deletions of electronic documents or overwriting of backup tapes which may contain potentially relevant information. The parties shall also discuss the need for a document preservation order.

(s) The need for cost-shifting of expenses related to discovery of information stored electronically, including the restoration of back-up tapes and forensic examination of computers, and the possibility of obtaining the desired information from alternate sources at reduced expense.

(t) The format in which the electronic records are to be produced, and procedures to avoid unnecessary burden and expense associated with such production. If metadata is to be produced, the parties shall discuss a protocol for producing such information, including the format for production (e.g., native, copy, original), and the ability to search such information.

(u) The need for security measures to be adopted to protect any information that is produced in electronic format or that will be converted into electronic format and stored on counsel's computer systems. Such discussion should encompass whether and under what circumstances clients will be afforded access to the information produced by another party and what security measures should be used for such access.

(v) Such other matters as the Court may assign to the parties for their consideration.

17.2—Case Management Report. The views of each party on the matters set forth in Section 17.1 above, as expressed through counsel or any pro se litigant(s), shall be reduced to writing, circulated for amendment or modification by each party, and filed with the Court in the form of a Case Management Report. Unless the parties agree otherwise, counsel for the first plaintiff listed in the complaint is responsible to prepare and circulate the initial draft of the Case Management Report to all counsel, who shall have five days within which to propose revisions to the report or raise issues about which the parties disagree. If the parties disagree on any issues in the Case Management Report, they shall nonetheless file a single Case Management Report that, in any areas of disagreement, states the views of each party. The final Case Management Report shall be signed by counsel for each party and shall be filed with the Court within fifteen (15) days of the Case Management Meeting.

17.3—Case Management Conference. Within twenty (20) days of the case management meeting of the parties or such longer period as the Court may prescribe, the Court will convene a Case Management Conference with attendance by counsel for all parties and their clients (or in the case of a business entity, such representative as has authority to make all binding litigation-related decisions) unless the Court shall, in its discretion, excuse the attendance of clients. Such conference will be conducted with as much informality as possible and with the active participation of clients encouraged. The Court will hear the views of counsel and/or clients on such issues listed in Rule 17.1 above as are pertinent to the case and/or on which there are material differences of opinion.

17.4—Case Management Order. Following the Case Management Conference, the Court shall issue a Case Management Order in the form appended to these Rules as Form 2. The Case Management Order will deal with such issues developed in the Case Management Meeting and/or the Case Management Conference as may be determined at the time, given the nature and status of the case. The provisions of the Case Management Order may not be deviated from without notice, grant of a hearing which is discretionary with the Court, good cause shown and entry of an order by the Court. The Case Management Order shall also specify a schedule of status conferences to assess the functioning of the Case Management Order, assess the progress of the case, and enter such further orders or revisions in the Case Management Order, including a trial date, as the Court may deem necessary or appropriate.

17.5—Effect on Other Rules. This Rule 17 is intended to supplement, not substitute for, the provisions of Rule 7 of the General Rules of Practice for Superior and District Courts and its related sample form dealing with pre-trial conferences and orders.

[Adopted March 9, 2000. Redesignated from Rule 15 and amended effective July 31, 2006.]

Rule 18. Discovery

18.1—North Carolina Rules of Civil Procedure Applicable. Except as expressly supplemented by these rules, the North Carolina Rules of Civil Procedure governing the conduct of depositions and discovery in State Courts shall control in the Business Court.

18.2—Presumptive Limits on Discovery Procedures. Subject to an order modifying discovery procedures for good cause shown, the Court expects discovery in cases assigned to the Business Court to be completed within nine (9) months from issuance of the Case Management Order. Parties are free, however, to begin discovery prior to issuance of the Case Management Order. Presumptively, subject to stipulation of the parties and order of the Court for good cause shown, interrogatories (including sub–parts) and requests for admission are limited to fifty (50) in number by each party. Depositions are presumptively limited to twelve (12) depositions each (not including depositions of testifying experts) by the plaintiffs, by the defendants, and by any third-party defendants, subject to alteration by the Court.

18.3—Depositions. The Court expects counsel to conduct discovery in good faith and to cooperate and be courteous with each other in all phases of the discovery process. Depositions shall be conducted in accordance with the following guidelines:

(a) Counsel shall not direct or request that a witness not answer a question, unless that counsel has objected to the question on the ground that the answer is protected by a privilege or a limitation on evidence directed by the Court.

(b) Counsel shall not make objections or statements which might suggest an answer to a witness. Counsel's statements when making objections should be succinct, stating briefly the basis of the objection and nothing more.

(c) Counsel and any witness/client shall not engage in private, off the record conferences while the deposition is proceeding in session, except for the purpose of deciding whether to assert a privilege.

(d) Deposing counsel shall provide to counsel for the witness and counsel for all parties present a copy of all documents shown to the witness during the deposition. The copy may be provided either before the deposition begins or contemporaneously with the showing of each document to the witness. The witness and counsel for the witness may not discuss documents privately before the witness answers questions about them.

18.4—No Filing of Discovery Materials. Depositions and deposition notices, interrogatories, requests for documents, requests for admission, and answers and responses thereto shall not be filed electronically on the Court's Electronic filing and service system unless the Court so orders or unless the Court will need such documents in a pretrial proceeding. All discovery materials shall be served on other counsel or parties, and may be served electronically pursuant to Rule 6.8 above. The party taking a deposition or obtaining any material through discovery (including through third party discovery) is responsible for the preservation and delivery of such material to the Court when needed or ordered in the form specified by the Court. Any party seeking to compel discovery or other pre-trial relief based upon discovery material which has not been filed shall identify the specific portion of the material which is directly relevant and ensure that it is filed as an attachment to the application for relief.

18.5—Discovery with Respect to Expert Witnesses. Discovery with respect to experts, including expert depositions and disclosure of expert information, shall be conducted within the discovery period set forth in the Case Management Order.

18.6—Conference of Attorneys with Respect to Motions and Objections Relating to Discovery.

(a) The Court will not consider motions and objections relating to discovery unless moving counsel files a certificate that, after personal consultation and diligent attempts to resolve differences, the parties are unable to reach an accord. The certificate shall set forth the date of the conference, the names of the participating attorneys, and the specific results achieved. It shall be the responsibility of counsel for the movant to arrange for the conference and, in the absence of an agreement to the contrary, the conference shall be held in the office of the attorney nearest to the Court where the case was originally filed. Alternatively, at any party's request, the conference may be held by telephone.

(b) Prior to filing motions and objections relating to discovery of information stored electronically, the parties shall discuss the possibility of shifting costs for electronic discovery, the use of Rule 30(b)(6) depositions of information technology personnel, and informal means of resolving disputes regarding technology and electronically stored information. The certificate required by Rule 18.6(a) shall address efforts to resolve the dispute through these and any other means related to discovery of information stored electronically.

18.7—Expedited Resolution of Some Discovery Disputes. If, after a conference as required by Rule 18.6, the parties agree that a discovery dispute can be ruled upon in a telephone or videoconference of no more than thirty (30) minutes, the Court will schedule such a conference and rule on the dispute without briefing by the parties. Alternatively, if the parties agree that the dispute can be ruled upon in an in-court hearing of no more than one hour, without briefing, subject to Rule 15.12 the Court will schedule a hearing of such matter at the earliest date reasonably available to the Court and the parties. The fact that these proceedings are expedited and are conducted without briefing does not alter the application of N.C. R. Civ. P. 37(a)(4) relating to the imposition of sanctions and the award of expenses.

18.8—Completion of Discovery. The requirement that discovery be completed within a specified time means that adequate provisions must be made for interrogatories and requests for admission to be answered, for documents to be produced, and for depositions to be held within the discovery period. Normally the Court will not entertain motions relating to discovery conducted after the close of the discovery period as set forth in the Court's Case Management Order.

18.9—Extension of the Discovery Period or Request for More Discovery. Motions seeking an extension of the discovery period or permission to take more discovery than is permitted under the Case Management Order shall be made or presented prior to the expiration of the time within which discovery is required to be completed. Such motions must set forth good cause justifying the additional time or additional discovery and will be granted or approved only upon such a showing of good cause and a showing that the parties have diligently pursued discovery. The Court will permit additional depositions usually only upon a showing of exceptionally good cause.

18.10—Trial Preparation After the Close of Discovery. For good cause appearing therefor, the physical or mental examination of a party may be ordered at any time prior to or during trial. Ordinarily, the deposition of a material witness not subject to subpoena should be taken during discovery. However, the deposition of a material witness who agrees to appear for trial, but later becomes unavailable or refuses to attend, may be ordered at any time prior to or during trial.

[Adopted March 9, 2000. Redesignated from Rule 16 and amended effective July 31, 2006.]

Rule 19. Mediation

19.1—Mediation Mandatory in All Cases. Mediation is a valued tool in the resolution of litigated matters. As such, all cases pending in the Business Court shall be subject to the Rules Implementing Statewide Mediated Settlement Conferences in Superior Court Civil Actions and such other Rules or orders consistent therewith as may be established or entered by the Business Court.

19.2—Approved List of Business Court Mediators. The Business Court maintains on its website a list of mediators who have had experience with cases within the jurisdiction of the Business Court. Parties are not, however, required to select a mediator from this list. In the event the parties to a Business Court case are unable to agree on a mediator, upon notice from a party, the Business Court will appoint a mediator from the Business Court's approved list to act as mediator in that case.

[Adopted March 9, 2000. Redesignated from Rule 17 and amended effective July 31, 2006.]

Rule 20. Openings and Closings

20.1—Opening Statements. At any time before the presentation of evidence, counsel for each party may make an opening statement setting forth the grounds of claim or defense. The parties may elect to waive opening statements. Opening statements may be limited in time and scope in the discretion of the Court.

20.2—Closing Argument. If no evidence is produced by the defendant, the right to open and close the argument to the jury shall belong to the defendant. If a question arises as to whether the plaintiff or the defendant has the final argument to the jury, the Court shall decide who is so entitled.

In a case where there are multiple defendants, if any defendant introduces evidence, the closing argument shall belong to the plaintiff, unless the Business Court Judge in his discretion orders otherwise.

[Adopted March 9, 2000. Redesignated from Rule 18 and amended effective July 31, 2006.]

Rule 21. Examination of Witnesses

21.1—When several counsel are employed by the same party, the examination or cross-examination of each witness for such party shall be conducted by one counsel, but examining counsel may change with each successive witness or, with leave of the Court, during a prolonged examination of a single witness.

[Adopted March 9, 2000. Redesignated from Rule 19 and amended effective July 31, 2006.]

Rule 22. Courtroom Decorum

22.1—Communications and Position. Counsel are at all times to conduct themselves with dignity and propriety. All statements and communications to the Court shall be clearly and audibly made from a standing position behind the counsel table or the computer-assisted podium. Counsel shall not approach the bench except upon the permission or request of the Court.

Colloquies between and disrespectful references to opposing counsel shall be strictly avoided. Adverse witnesses and parties shall be treated with fairness and due consideration. Abusive language or offensive personal references are strictly prohibited.

The examination of witnesses and jurors shall be conducted from a sitting position behind the counsel table or from the computer-assisted podium, except as otherwise permitted by the Court. Counsel may only approach a witness for the purpose of presenting, inquiring about, or examining that witness with respect to an exhibit, document, or diagram.

22.2—Professional Demeanor. The conduct of the lawyers before the Court and with other lawyers should be characterized by candor and fairness. Counsel shall not knowingly misrepresent the contents of documents or other exhibits, the testimony of a witness, the language or argument of opposing counsel or the language of a decision or other authority; nor shall counsel offer evidence known to be inadmissible or cross-examine without a good faith basis for doing so. In an argument addressed to the Court, remarks or statements may not be interjected to improperly influence or mislead the jury.

Counsel shall yield gracefully to rulings of the Court and avoid disrespectful remarks both in Court and out. Counsel shall at all times conduct themselves in a manner which promotes respect for the Court and the judicial process.

[Adopted March 9, 2000. Redesignated from Rule 20 and amended effective July 31, 2006.]

Rule 23. Juries

23.1—Jury Instruction Conference. At the close of the evidence (or at such earlier time as the judge may reasonably direct) in every jury trial, the judge shall conduct a conference on instructions with the attorneys of record (or party, if not represented by counsel). Such conference shall be out of the presence of the jury, and shall be held for the purpose of discussing the proposed instructions to be given to the jury. If special instructions are desired, they must be submitted in writing to the trial judge at or before the jury instruction conference.

23.2—Objections to Instructions. An opportunity shall be given to the attorneys (or party, if not represented by counsel) to request any additional instructions or to object to any of those instructions proposed by the judge. Any such requests, objections, and the rulings of the Court thereon shall be placed on the record.

At the conclusion of the charge and before the jury begins its deliberations (and out of the hearing, or upon request, out of the presence of the jury), counsel (or party, if not represented by counsel) shall be given an opportunity to object on the record to any portion of the charge as given, or omission therefrom, stating with particularity the objection and grounds therefor.

23.3—Treatment of Instructions during Jury Deliberations. The Court may recall the jury after they have retired and give them additional instructions in order: (i) to correct or withdraw an erroneous instruction; (ii) to inform the jury on a point of law which should have been covered in the original instructions; or (iii) to respond to questions posed by the jury. The provisions of Rule 23.2 above are also applicable to any such additional instructions or other information provided at this stage of the proceeding. The Court, in its discretion, may give a copy of the instructions to the foreperson or to all members of the jury.

23.4—Contacts with Jurors Prohibited. All parties, witnesses, and attorneys shall avoid any extra-judicial contact or communications with a member of a jury venire or panel who has been or may be selected in a case in which that person is involved. No person may have any extra-judicial contact or communication, either directly or indirectly, with a member of a jury venire or panel which may reasonably have the effect of influencing, or which is intended to influence, the potential juror or sitting juror. Attorneys for parties shall inform their clients and witnesses of this rule.

No person shall approach a juror, either directly or through any member of his immediate family, in an effort to secure information concerning the juror's background. No provision of this rule is intended to prohibit communication with a juror after the juror has been dismissed from further service, so long as the communication does not tend to harass, humiliate, or intimidate the juror in any fashion.

23.5—Presence of Counsel during Jury Deliberation. The right to be present during the trial of civil cases shall be deemed to be waived by a party or counsel by voluntary absence from the courtroom at a time when it is known that proceedings are being conducted or are about to be conducted. In such event the proceedings, including the giving of additional instructions to the jury after they have once retired, or receipt of the verdict, may go forward without waiting for the arrival or return of counsel or a party.

[Adopted March 9, 2000. Redesignated from Rule 21 and amended effective July 31, 2006.]

Rule 24. Trial Dates and Final Pretrial Preparation

24.1—Trial Date. Trial shall commence on the date established by the Court, normally through revisions to the Case Management Order, or in such other manner as the Court shall deem appropriate. The Court will consider a request to continue a trial date only if the request is signed by both the party and counsel for the party.

24.2—Final Pretrial Preparation. Except in cases deemed by the Court to require different arrangements, no later than twenty (20) days before trial, the parties shall file trial briefs, along with proposed instructions on the issues in jury cases or findings of fact and conclusions of law in non-jury cases. The parties will also file at this time any motions in limine or other motions they wish to have considered prior to trial. The Court may in its discretion schedule a final pretrial conference to deal with such motions or other pretrial matters as deemed appropriate. Any party, or the Court on its own motion, may request a pretrial hearing or a telephone or videoconference to address matters relating to final pretrial preparation or settlement of a case. This rule is not intended to prevent submission of proposed jury instructions as provided for in Rule 23.1.

[Adopted March 9, 2000. Redesignated from Rule 22 and amended effective July 31, 2006.]

Rule 25. Court Reporting Considerations

25.1—Scheduling of Court Reporters. Barring extenuating circumstances, official court reporters will be used to report all hearings in the Business Court; however, if both parties agree to hire a freelance reporter, that reporter would then become the official reporter for the particular hearing or trial that he or she was hired to report. Where feasible, the same court reporter will be used to report all hearings in a case. The scheduling of court reporters will be handled through a joint effort of the local scheduling coordinator and the Judicial Scheduling Coordinator for the Administrative Office of the Courts.

25.2—Request for Real–Time Transcription. A request for real-time transcription of the proceedings before the Court shall be made, to the extent possible, during the Case Management Conference. The parties will use the appropriate AOC Form to make such a request and shall submit the same to the Judicial

Scheduling Coordinator for the Administrative Office of the Courts. Prior to the proceeding for which transcription is needed, the parties shall confer with the reporter assigned to the case regarding specific needs (e.g., real-time feed, rough ASCII, daily copy) and shall arrange for compensation directly with the reporter. The parties, prior to trial, will provide the reporter with information particular to the case to aid in clarity of transcription, e.g., pleadings, deposition transcripts, glossary of unique terms, etc.

25.3—Realtime Feeds or Rough-Draft Transcripts. A "realtime feed" or "rough-draft transcript"—that which is displayed simultaneously with proceedings occurring before the Court or that which is provided by e-mail or ASCII disk prior to certification—may be referred to or quoted from during a proceeding, provided, however, that any dispute concerning the accuracy of the transcription of a realtime feed or rough draft transcript will be resolved by the Court in its discretion after consultation with the reporter.

25.4—Publication of Transcripts. Transcripts of proceedings before the Business Court shall be published on the Court's Web Site in the sole discretion of the Business Court Judge. See Rule 27. Access to such transcripts via the Web Site, however, shall only be made available to those counsel, pro se litigants or members of the public with authorization codes issued by the Court after payment of the reporter's transcription fee or under such other conditions as are set by the Court.

25.5—Storage and Retention of Court Reporters' Notes. Per N.C. Gen. Stat. § 7A-95, if stenograph, shorthand, or voice writing equipment is used to record proceedings in Superior Court, the original tapes, notes, discs, or other records are the property of the state of North Carolina, and the Clerk of Superior Court is the ultimate custodian of the notes; therefore, when a hearing or trial is completed, the court reporter shall leave his or her notes with the clerk. The court reporter shall not take those notes with him or her for any reason other than to prepare the transcript in the case. If a transcript has been ordered and the reporter signs out the tapes, notes, etc. from the clerk, that court reporter shall return those tapes, notes, etc. to the clerk's office upon completion of the transcript. This rule applies to both official and freelance court reporters.

[Adopted March 9, 2000. Redesignated from Rule 23 and amended effective July 31, 2006.]

Rule 26. Appellate Record Considerations

26.1—Filing of Transcripts. Certified original transcripts and other record items shall be filed in accordance with Rule 7 of the North Carolina Rules of Appellate Procedure and shall be subject to any further requirement that the appellate court deems appropriate. Parties are encouraged to assist the Court in transmitting original transcripts and other records electronically in addition to the format required by Rule 7 of the North Carolina Rules of Appellate Procedure to the end that the entire appellate record may be transmitted to the appeals court as efficiently and expeditiously as possible.

26.2—Signatures on Appellate Materials. Electronically filed transcripts shall contain such means of signature as may be specified by the appellate courts.

[Redesignated from Rule 25 and amended effective July 31, 2006.]

Rule 27. Web Site and Publication

27.1—Web Site. The Business Court shall maintain a site on the World Wide Web for ready access to members of the bar and to the public generally. The Web Site shall be located at the uniform resource locator www.ncbusinesscourt.net. The Web Site will store for ready retrieval basic information about the Business Court, including but not limited to these Rules and the procedure for Complex Business Case designation. In addition, the Web Site will store, in the sole discretion of the Business Court Judges:

(a) the Court's address, facsimile machine numbers, and the mailing and physical addresses of the chambers of Business Court Judges;

(b) the Court's docket;

(c) pleadings filed with the Court;

(d) motions filed with the Court;

(e) briefs filed with the Court;

(f) the opinions of the Court; and

(g) rough-draft and/or official transcripts of proceedings before the Court.

27.2—Citation to Business Court Opinions. Citation to the opinions of the Business Court shall be to the year of the opinion, followed by "NCBC," followed by the opinion number, e.g., "1999 NCBC 1." Pinpoint notations to Business Court opinions shall be made to the numbered paragraph in which the cited material appears, e.g., "1999 NCBC 1 ¶1."

[Redesignated from Rule 24 and amended effective July 31, 2006.]

Form 1. Notice of Designation of Action As Mandatory Complex Business Case

STATE OF NORTH CAROLINA

COUNTY OF

IN THE GENERAL COURT OF JUSTICE
COURT DIVISION
CIVIL ACTION NO:

John Doe,
Plaintiff,
v.

ABC Corporation,
Defendant.

NOTICE OF DESIGNATION OF ACTION AS MANDATORY COMPLEX BUSINESS CASE UNDER N.C. GEN. STAT. § 7A–45.4

Pursuant to N.C. Gen. Stat. § 7A–45.4, ______ (insert name of party) ______ hereby designates the above-captioned action as a mandatory complex business case. In good faith and based on information reasonably available, ______ (insert name of party) ______, through counsel, hereby certifies that this action meets the following criteria for designation as a mandatory complex business case pursuant N.C. Gen. Stat. § 7A–45.4(a), and should be adjudicated in the Business Court:

______ (1) The law governing corporations, partnerships, limited liability companies, and limited liability partnerships.

______ (2) Securities law.

______ (3) Antitrust law, except claims based solely on unfair competition under N.C. Gen. Stat. § 75–1.1.

______ (4) State trademark or unfair competition law, except claims based solely on unfair competition under N.C. Gen. Stat. § 75–1.1.

______ (5) Intellectual property law.

______ (6) The Internet, electronic commerce, and biotechnology.

Briefly explain (attach additional sheets if necessary) why the action falls within the specific categories of N.C. Gen. Stat. 7A–45.4(a) checked above, as well as any additional information you believe may be helpful to the Court in determining whether the Business Court should retain jurisdiction of this matter:

A copy of all pleadings listed in N.C. R. Civ. P. 7(a) that have been filed to date in this action are attached hereto as Appendix A for the convenience of the Court.

This ___ day of ______, 20 ___.

____
Attorney for ______________

[Added effective July 31, 2006.]

Form 2. Case Management Order

STATE OF NORTH CAROLINA — IN THE GENERAL COURT OF JUSTICE
COURT DIVISION
COUNTY OF — CIVIL ACTION NO:

John Doe,
Plaintiff,
v.
ABC Corporation,
Defendant.

CASE MANAGEMENT ORDER

THIS MATTER is before the Court pursuant to Rule 17 of the Business Court Rules. This case has been designated as an exceptional case pursuant to Rule 2.1 of the General Rules of Practice. The parties have conferred in advance and have agreed that the Court should enter an order covering scheduling and case management issues in order to facilitate the fair and efficient disposition of this action.

THEREFORE, IT IS ORDERED, ADJUDGED, AND DECREED that:

I. SCOPE OF ORDER

A. *General Scope of Order*

This order establishes certain procedures to be used and sets deadlines for various matters likely to arise through trial. It shall remain in effect until rescinded by the Court or superseded by subsequent orders. The North Carolina Rules of Civil Procedure, the General Rules of Practice for the Superior and District Courts, and the Local Rules for the North Carolina Business Court shall govern all matters not expressly covered by this Order.

B. *Application of Order*

This Order, as well as any subsequent case management orders entered by the Court, shall bind all parties to this action and all parties added hereafter unless the Court orders to the contrary.

C. *Modification of this Order*

The Court may amend or supplement this Order as deemed appropriate by the Court upon the motion of any party or by the Court.

II. COMMUNICATION WITH THE COURT AND AMONG THE PARTIES

A. The parties are represented locally by the following: (hereinafter "Liaison Counsel"):

1. ________, of ________, representing Plaintiff(s);
2. ________, of ________, representing Defendant(s).

B. The Court will communicate with counsel and counsel shall have the responsibility for notifying all parties that it represents of all communications from the Court.

C. All communications with the Court, including a copy of any paper, pleading, order or proposed order, and all exhibits, attachments or enclosures thereto filed in this action shall be sent to the Business Court Judge assigned to the case.

The following parties have agreed to use the Business Court's electronic filing and service in accordance with Rule 6:

____

____

____

Any communication filed electronically automatically will be served on all parties equipped to receive electronic mail.

D. A copy of any paper, pleading, order or proposed order (including all attachments or enclosures, or any other written or electronic communication with the Court, whether filed or not filed) generated by counsel for any party shall be delivered, e-mailed or telecopied to counsel for the other party or parties at least five (5) business days before any scheduled hearing on a matter to which such documents relate.

III. JURISDICTION AND VENUE

A. This Court has subject matter jurisdiction over the disputes raised in this action.

B. The parties ☐ do ☐ do not *(check one)* stipulate that all of the defendants have been properly served with the summons and complaint, and the Court has personal jurisdiction over each of the parties.

C. The parties ☐ do ☐ do not *(check one)* stipulate that venue is proper in this action.

D. All pretrial and trial proceedings in this matter shall occur in the following location: __________.

IV. ISSUES, DISCOVERY, MOTIONS, AND TRIAL

A. *ISSUES*

The principal legal and factual issues which counsel presently believe will need to be decided in this case are as follows:

____

____

____

____

The issues in this case which counsel presently believe are governed by the law of any state other than North Carolina law or federal law are as follows:

____

____

____

____

B. *DISCOVERY*

At a hearing on ___, the Court heard discussion and arguments of counsel regarding discovery in this case. Having considered the record and arguments of counsel, the Court hereby incorporates into this Case Management Order the following provisions regarding discovery on the merits:

The parties are instructed to conduct fact discovery first, then move on to expert witness discovery. The parties shall have until __________ to conduct fact discovery on the merits issues. The parties shall be permitted no more than ______ fact depositions each. The parties shall be allowed __________ interrogatories each. The parties shall submit to the Court any proposed protective orders by ________. There will be a subsequent sixty (60) day period for discovery of expert witnesses, if necessary, though and including __________. This additional sixty (60) day period is reserved solely for discovery of expert witnesses, and shall not apply if expert discovery is unnecessary. The parties shall be permitted no more than ______ expert depositions each.

A preliminary schedule for depositions of such persons and entities as the parties presently are able to identify is as follows: ____________________

____

____

____

The parties shall produce electronic records shall in the following format: ______.

The parties shall adopt the following procedures to avoid unnecessary burden and expense associated with production of electronic records: ______

______

______

______

The parties shall adopt the following procedures for retention of potentially relevant documents, including but not limited to documents stored electronically and the need to suspend all automatic deletions of electronic documents or overwriting of backup tapes which may contain potentially relevant information:

______

______

______

______

The parties shall adopt the following security measures to protect any information that is produced in electronic format or that will be converted into electronic format and stored on counsel's computer systems:

______

______

______

______

The following further limitations and guidelines are hereby placed on discovery:

1. Depositions shall be conducted in accordance with the following guidelines:

(a) All parties or employees will be made available for deposition on ten days' notice to counsel.

(b) Counsel shall not direct or request that a witness not answer a question, unless counsel has objected to the question on the ground that the answer is protected by privilege or a limitation on evidence directed by the Court.

(c) Counsel shall not make objections or statements which might suggest an answer to a witness. Counsel's statements when making objections should be succinct, stating the basis of the objection and nothing more.

(d) Counsel and their witness-clients shall not engage in private, off-the-record conferences while the deposition is proceeding in session, except for the purpose of deciding whether to assert a privilege.

(e) Deposing counsel shall provide to the witness's counsel a copy of all documents shown to the witness during the deposition. The copies shall be provided either before the deposition begins or contemporaneously with the showing of each document to the witness. The witness and the witness's counsel do not have the right to discuss documents privately before the witness answers questions about them.

2. The parties may conduct only that discovery specifically provided for in this Order.

3. No extensions of time shall be granted without written consent of the opposing party or by Order of the Court.

C. *MOTIONS*

The parties intend to file the following Motions to Dismiss or other preliminary or pre-discovery motions, and have designated the following time periods in which such motions shall be filed, briefed, and argued: ______

______

It is further ordered that the setting of the ________________ deadline for completion of discovery shall not limit any party from filing summary judgment motions as to merits issues during such period, but any such motions should be very narrowly drawn so as to address only issues on which fact discovery has been completed. If there are still motions pending after the discovery period, the Court will set a briefing schedule at that time.

After the close of discovery, the parties shall have until ______ to file post-discovery dispositive motions.

For the purposes of the length limitations on briefs under Rule 15.8, the following parties shall be required to file joint briefs: ____________________.

The parties have selected ________________ as a mediator and mediation shall be completed by __________.

D. *TRIAL*

The tentative date by which the parties will be prepared for trial is: ______.

The following parties have indicated a desire to use case tracking, scanning, videographic, and real-time court reporting services: ____________________

____

____

SO ORDERED, this the ____ day of __________.

The Honorable ______________

Business Court Judge Presiding

[Redesignated from Exhibit A and amended effective July 31, 2006.]

NORTH CAROLINA RULES OF EVIDENCE

(G.S. § 8C–1)
and
OFFICIAL COMMENTARY
Effective July 1, 1984

---

§ 8C–1. Rules of Evidence

The North Carolina Rules of Evidence are as follows:

ARTICLE 1
General Provisions

Rule 101. Scope

These rules govern proceedings in the courts of this State to the extent and with the exceptions stated in Rule 1101.

Added by Laws 1983, c. 701, § 1.

North Carolina Commentary

This rule differs from Fed.R.Evid. 101 only in that "courts of this State" has been substituted for "courts of the United States and before United States magistrates." Rule 1101 provides greater details regarding the applicability of these rules in various proceedings.

Rule 102. Purpose and construction

(a) In general.—These rules shall be construed to secure fairness in administration, elimination of unjustifiable expense and delay, and promotion of growth and development of the law of evidence to the end that the truth may be ascertained and proceedings justly determined.

(b) Subordinate divisions.—For the purpose of these rules only, the subordinate division of any rule which is labeled with a lower case letter shall be a subdivision.

Added by Laws 1983, c. 701, § 1.

North Carolina Commentary

This rule differs from Fed.R.Evid. 102 by the addition of subdivision (b) which is explained below. The commentary to each rule indicates whether the rule is identical to or different from its counterpart in the federal rules. The intent is to make applicable, as an aid in construction, the federal decisional law construing identical or similar provisions of the Federal Rules of Evidence.

Of course, federal precedents are not binding on the courts of this State in construing these rules. Nonetheless, these rules are not adopted in a vacuum. A substantial body of law construing these rules exists and should be looked to by the courts for enlightenment and guidance in ascertaining the intent of the General Assembly in adopting these rules. Uniformity of evidence rulings in the courts of this State and federal courts is one motivating factor in adopting these rules and should be a goal of our courts in construing those rules that are identical.

Problems of construction may arise that have not been settled by federal precedents. In these instances, our courts should examine North Carolina cases as well as federal cases for enlightenment.

Although these rules answer the vast majority of evidence questions that arise in our courts, there are some evidentiary questions that are not within the coverage of these rules. In these instances, North Carolina precedents will continue to control unless changed by our courts.

The commentary to each rule indicates whether the rule is consistent with current North Carolina practice. The discussion of North Carolina law is included to highlight the changes made by these rules.

Wherever the commentary refers to "the Advisory Committee's Note", the reference is to the Advisory Committee on Rules of Evidence appointed by United States Chief Justice Warren on March 8, 1965. See Saltzburg and Redden, Federal Rules of Evidence Manual, p. 2–4 (3d ed.1982).

Rule 102 provides that these rules shall be construed to promote growth and development of the law of evidence. Of course, this provision is not intended to give discretion to construe the rules unfettered by the language of the rules. Rather, the language of Rule 102 permits a flexible approach to problems not explicitly covered by the rules.

Subdivision (b) was added to this rule to make it clear that the scheme of subordinate divisions being followed is that of the federal rules. The North Carolina statutory scheme would term the subordinate divisions referred to as "subsections." It was felt by the drafters of the North Carolina rules and commentary that following the federal scheme would avoid confusion in comparing the federal rules to the North Carolina rules and in applying authorities which refer to the federal rules.

Rule 103. Rulings on evidence

(a) Effect of erroneous ruling.—Error may not be predicated upon a ruling which admits or excludes evidence unless a substantial right of the party is affected, and

(1) Objection.—In case the ruling is one admitting evidence, a timely objection or motion to strike appears of record. No particular form is required in order to preserve the right to assert the alleged error upon appeal if the motion or objection clearly presented the alleged error to the trial court;

(2) Offer of proof. — In case the ruling is one excluding evidence, the substance of the evidence was made known to the court by offer or was apparent from the context within which questions were asked.

Once the court makes a definitive ruling on the record admitting or excluding evidence, either at or before trial, a party need not renew an objection or offer of proof to preserve a claim of error for appeal.

(b) Record of offer and ruling.—The court may add any other or further statement which shows the character of the evidence, the form in which it was offered, the objection made, and the ruling thereon. It may direct the making of an offer in question and answer form.

(c) Hearing of jury.—In jury cases, proceedings shall be conducted, to the extent practicable, so as to prevent inadmissible evidence from being suggested to the jury by any means, such as making statements or offers of proof or asking questions in the hearing of the jury.

(d) Review of errors where justice requires.—Notwithstanding the requirements of subdivision (a) of this rule, an appellate court may review errors affecting substantial rights if it determines, in the interest of justice, it is appropriate to do so.

Added by Laws 1983, c. 701, § 1; S.L. 2003-101, § 1, eff. Oct. 1, 2003; S.L. 2006-264, § 30.5, eff. Aug. 27, 2006.

North Carolina Commentary

This rule is identical to Fed.R.Evid. 103, except for subsection (1) of subdivision (a), and subdivision (d).

Subdivision (a) adopts the "substantial rights" language used in the majority of states in testing for harmless error. North Carolina Civ.Pro.Rule 61 provides that no error is grounds for reversal unless the error amounts to the denial of a substantial right. Subdivision (a) is not intended to affect the additional requirement in criminal cases that a reasonable possibility exist that a different result would have been reached if the error had not been committed. See G.S. 15A-1443.

Subdivision (a) also provides that rulings on evidence cannot be assigned as error unless the nature of the error was called to the attention of the judge, so as to alert him to the proper course of action and enable opposing counsel to take proper corrective measures. This is in accord with North Carolina practice. See Brandis on North Carolina Evidence § 27, at 107 (1982); G.S. 15A-1446. The wording of subsection (1) differs from the federal rule by borrowing the language of G.S. 15A-1446(a) to describe the minimum requirements of an objection or motion to strike.

The provisions of **subdivision (b)** are substantially the same as current North Carolina practice. North Carolina Civ.Pro.Rule 43(c) and G.S. 15A-1446(a) should be amended where necessary to conform to Rule 103.

Subdivision (c) is in accord with North Carolina practice.

Subdivision (d) differs from Fed.R.Evid. 103(d). The federal rule provides that, although an error was not brought to the court's attention (as required by subdivision (a)), the court may nevertheless review "plain error affecting substantial rights." Subdivision (d) of this rule borrows its language from G.S. 15A-1446(b), which applies in criminal proceedings, and makes that the standard for both criminal and civil proceedings, but with the addition that "substantial rights" must be affected. This represents an expansion of the areas in civil cases in which North Carolina appellate courts may review error where no proper objection or motion was previously made. See Brandis on North Carolina Evidence § 27 (1982).

It is anticipated that in civil cases appellate courts will rarely exercise the authority to take notice of errors that were not brought to the attention of the trial court. G.S. 15A-1446(b) should be amended to reflect the adoption of Rule 103(d).

Rule 104. Preliminary questions

(a) Questions of admissibility generally.—Preliminary questions concerning the qualification of a person to be a witness, the existence of a privilege, or the admissibility of evidence shall be determined by the court, subject to the provisions of subdivision (b). In making its determination it is not bound by the rules of evidence except those with respect to privileges.

(b) Relevancy conditioned on fact.—When the relevancy of evidence depends upon the fulfillment of a condition of fact, the court shall admit it upon, or subject to, the introduction of evidence sufficient to support a finding of the fulfillment of the condition.

(c) Hearing of jury.—Hearings on the admissibility of confessions or other motions to suppress evidence in criminal trials in Superior Court shall in all cases be conducted out of the hearing of the jury. Hearings on other preliminary matters shall be so conducted when the interests of justice require or, when an accused is a witness, if he so requests.

(d) Testimony by accused.—The accused does not, by testifying upon a preliminary matter, subject himself to cross-examination as to other issues in the case.

(e) Weight and credibility.—This rule does not limit the right of a party to introduce before the jury evidence relevant to weight or credibility.

Added by Laws 1983, c. 701, § 1.

North Carolina Commentary

This rule is identical to Fed.R.Evid. 104 with the exception of subdivision (c) which is discussed below.

Subdivision (a) states as a general rule that preliminary questions shall be determined by the judge. This is in accord with North Carolina practice. See H. Brandis, Brandis on North Carolina Evidence, § 8 (1982). The Advisory Committee's Note to the federal rule states:

"The applicability of a particular rule of evidence often depends upon the existence of a condition. Is the alleged expert a qualified physician? Is a witness whose former testimony is offered unavailable? Was a stranger present during a conversation between attorney and client? In each instance the admissibility of evidence will turn upon the answer to the question of the existence of the condition. Accepted practice, incorporated in the rule, places on the judge the responsibility for these determinations. McCormick § 53; Morgan, Basic Problems of Evidence 45–50 (1962).

"To the extent that these inquiries are factual, the judge acts as a trier of fact. Often, however, rulings on evidence call for an evaluation in terms of a legally set standard. Thus when a hearsay statement is offered as a declaration against interest, a decision must be made whether it possesses the required against-interest characteristics. These decisions, too, are made by the judge.

"In view of these considerations, this subdivision refers to preliminary requirements generally by the broad term 'question,' without attempt at specification.

"This subdivision is of general application. It must, however, be read as subject to the special provisions for 'conditional relevancy' in subdivision (b) and those for confessions in subdivision (d)."

The second sentence of subdivision (a) provides that in making its determination on preliminary questions, the court is not bound by the rules of evidence except those with respect to privileges. The Advisory Committee's Note states:

"If the question is factual in nature, the judge will of necessity receive evidence pro and con on the issue. The rule provides that the rules of evidence in general do not apply to this process. McCormick § 53, p. 123, n. 8, points out that the authorities are 'scattered and inconclusive,' and observes:

" 'Should the exclusionary law of evidence, "the child of the jury system" in Thayer's phrase, be applied to this hearing before the judge? Sound sense backs the view that it should not, and that the judge should be empowered to hear any relevant evidence, such as affidavits or other reliable hearsay.'

"This view is reinforced by practical necessity in certain situations. An item, offered and objected to, may itself be considered in ruling on admissibility, though not yet admitted in evidence. Thus the content of an asserted declaration against interest must be considered in ruling whether it is against interest. . . . Another example is the requirement of Rule 602 dealing with personal knowledge. In the case of hearsay, it is enough, if the declarant 'so far as appears [has] had an opportunity to observe the fact declared'. McCormick § 10, p. 19.

"If concern is felt over the use of affidavits by the judge in preliminary hearings on admissibility, attention is directed to the many important judicial determinations made on the basis of affidavits. . . .

"The Rules of Civil Procedure are more detailed. Rule 43(e), dealing with motions generally, provides:

" 'When a motion is based on facts not appearing of record the court may hear the matter on affidavits presented by the respective parties, but the court may direct that the matter be heard wholly or partly on oral or testimony or depositions.'

". . . Rule 56 provides in detail for the entry of summary judgment based on affidavits. Affidavits may supply the foundation for temporary restraining orders under Rule 65(b)."

Subdivision (b) concerns relevancy conditioned on fact. The Advisory Committee's Note states:

"In some situations, the relevancy of an item of evidence, in the large sense, depends on the existence of a particular preliminary fact. Thus, when a spoken statement is relied upon to prove notice to X, it is without probative value unless X heard it. Or if a letter purporting to be from Y is relied upon to establish an admission by him, it has no probative value unless Y wrote or authorized it. Relevance in this sense has been labelled 'conditional relevancy'. Morgan, Basic Problems of Evidence 45–46 (1962). Problems arising in connection with it are to be distinguished from problems of logical relevancy, e.g., evidence in a murder case that accused on the day before purchased a weapon of the kind used in the killing, treated in Rule 401.

"If preliminary questions of conditional relevancy were determined solely by the judge, as provided in subdivision (1), the functioning of the jury as a trier of fact would be greatly restricted and in some cases virtually destroyed. These are appropriate questions for juries. Accepted treatment, as provided in the rule, is consistent with that given fact questions generally. The judge makes a preliminary determination whether the foundation evidence is sufficient to support a finding of fulfillment of the condition. If so, the item is admitted. If after all the evidence on the issue is in, pro and con, the jury could reasonably conclude that fulfillment of the condition is not established, the issue is for them. If the evidence is not such as to allow a finding, the judge withdraws the matter from their consideration. . . .

"The order of proof here, as generally, is subject to the control of the judge."

Subdivision (b) is in accord with North Carolina practice in making an exception to the general rule that preliminary questions are for the court. When the relevancy of evidence depends upon the existence of some other fact which also requires proof, the determination of the preliminary fact question is for the jury. Brandis on North Carolina Evidence § 8, p. 27–28 (1982).

Subdivision (c) concerns when hearings on preliminary questions will be out of the hearing of the jury. The Advisory Committee's Note states:

"Preliminary hearings on the admissibility of confessions must be conducted outside the hearing of the jury. See Jackson v. Denno, 378 U.S. 368, 84 S.Ct. 1774, 12 L.Ed.2d 908 (1964). Otherwise, detailed treatment of when preliminary matters should be heard outside the hearing of the jury is not feasible. The procedure is time consuming. Not infrequently the same evidence which is relevant to the issue of establishment of fulfillment of a condition precedent to admissibility is also relevant to weight or credibility, and time is saved by taking foundation proof in the presence of the jury. Much evidence on preliminary questions, though not relevant to jury issues, may be heard by the jury with no adverse effect. A great deal must be left to the discretion of the judge who will act as the interests of justice require."

Subdivision (c) has been changed from the federal rule by the addition of language requiring other motions to suppress evidence in criminal cases in superior court to be conducted out of the hearing of the jury. This is in accord with G.S. 15A–977(e) which should be amended to reflect the adoption of this rule.

Subdivision (d) provides that the accused does not, by testifying upon a preliminary matter, subject himself to cross-examination as to other issues in the case. As the Advisory Committee's Note states:

"The limitation upon cross-examination is designed to encourage participation by the accused in the determination of preliminary matters. He may testify concerning them without exposing himself to cross-examination generally. The provision is necessary because of the breadth of cross-examination under Rule 611(b).

"The rule does not address itself to questions of the subsequent use of testimony given by an accused at a hearing on a preliminary matter. See Walder v. United States, 347 U.S. 62 [74 S.Ct. 354, 98 L.Ed. 503] (1954); Simmons v. United States, 390 U.S. 377 [88 S.Ct. 967, 19 L.Ed.2d 1247] (1968); Harris v. New York, 401 U.S. 222 [91 S.Ct. 643, 28 L.Ed.2d 1] (1971)."

There are no North Carolina cases on this point.

Subdivision (e) makes it clear that after the court makes its determination on a preliminary question of fact, the party opposing the ruling is entitled to introduce before the jury evidence that relates to the weight or credibility of certain evidence. For example, even if the court determines that a confession was not coerced, the defendant may introduce evidence of coercion, since this is relevant to the weight of the evidence.

Subdivision (e) is in accord with North Carolina practice.

Rule 105. Limited admissibility

When evidence which is admissible as to one party or for one purpose but not admissible as to another party or for another purpose is admitted, the court, upon request, shall restrict the evidence to its proper scope and instruct the jury accordingly.

Added by Laws 1983, c. 701, § 1.

North Carolina Commentary

This rule is identical to Fed.R.Evid. 105. The Advisory Committee's Note states:

"A close relationship exists between this rule and Rule 403 which requires exclusion when 'probative value is substantially outweighed by the danger of unfair prejudice, confusion of the issues, or misleading the jury.' The present rule recognizes the practice of admitting evidence for a limited purpose and instructing the jury accordingly. The availability and effectiveness of this practice must be taken into consideration in reaching a decision whether to exclude for unfair prejudice under Rule 403. In Bruton v. United States, 389 U.S. 818, 88 S.Ct. 126, 19 L.Ed.2d 70 (1968), the Court ruled that a limiting instruction did not effectively protect the accused against the prejudicial effect of admitting in evidence the confession of a codefendant which implicated him. The decision does not, however, bar the use of limited admissibility with an instruction where the risk of prejudice is less serious."

Rule 105 is in accord with the general rule in North Carolina that evidence that is inadmissible for one purpose may be admitted for other and proper purposes. See Brandis on North Carolina Evidence § 79 (1982).

Rule 106. Remainder of or related writings or recorded statements

When a writing or recorded statement or part thereof is introduced by a party, an adverse party may require him at that time to introduce any other part or any other writing or recorded statement which ought in fairness to be considered contemporaneously with it.

Added by Laws 1983, c. 701, § 1.

North Carolina Commentary

This rule is identical to Fed.R.Evid. 106. The Advisory Committee's Note states:

"The rule is an expression of the rule of completeness. McCormick § 56. It is manifested as to depositions in Rule 32(a)(4) of the Federal Rules of Civil Procedure, of which the proposed rule is substantially a restatement.

"The rule is based on two considerations. The first is the misleading impression created by taking matters out of context. The second is the inadequacy of repair work when delayed to a point later in the trial. . . . The rule does not in any way circumscribe the right of the adversary to develop the matter on cross-examination or as part of his own case.

"For practical reasons, the rule is limited to writings and recorded statements and does not apply to conversations."

N.C.Civ.Pro.Rule 32(a)(5), which applies to depositions, is similar to Rule 106.

ARTICLE 2

Judicial Notice

Rule 201. Judicial notice of adjudicative facts

(a) Scope of rule.—This rule governs only judicial notice of adjudicative facts.

(b) Kinds of facts.—A judicially noticed fact must be one not subject to reasonable dispute in that it is either (1) generally known within the territorial jurisdiction of the trial court or (2) capable of accurate and ready determination by resort to sources whose accuracy cannot reasonably be questioned.

(c) When discretionary.—A court may take judicial notice, whether requested or not.

(d) When mandatory.—A court shall take judicial notice if requested by a party and supplied with the necessary information.

(e) Opportunity to be heard.—In a trial court, a party is entitled upon timely request to an opportunity to be heard as to the propriety of taking judicial notice and the tenor of the matter noticed. In the absence of prior notification, the request may be made after judicial notice has been taken.

(f) Time of taking notice.—Judicial notice may be taken at any stage of the proceeding.

(g) Instructing jury.—In a civil action or proceeding, the court shall instruct the jury to accept as conclusive any fact judicially noticed. In a criminal case, the court shall instruct the jury that it may, but is not required to, accept as conclusive any fact judicially noticed.

Added by Laws 1983, c. 701, § 1.

North Carolina Commentary

This rule is identical to Fed.R.Evid. 201, except subdivision (e) which is discussed below. The Advisory Committee's Note states:

"This is the only evidence rule on the subject of judicial notice. It deals only with judicial notice of 'adjudicative' facts. No rule deals with judicial notice of 'legislative' facts. . . .

"The omission of any treatment of legislative facts results from fundamental differences between adjudicative facts and legislative facts. Adjudicative facts are simply the facts of the particular case. Legislative facts, on the other hand, are those which have relevance to legal reasoning and the lawmaking process, whether in the formulation of a legal principle or ruling by a judge or court or in the enactment of a legislative body. . . .

"What, then, are 'adjudicative' facts? Davis refers to them as those 'which relate to the parties,' or more fully:

" 'When a court or an agency finds facts concerning the immediate parties—who did what, where, when, how, and with what motive or intent—the court or agency is performing an adjudicative function, and the facts are conveniently called adjudicative facts. . . .

" 'Stated in other terms, the adjudicative facts are those to which the law is applied in the process of adjudication. They are the facts that normally go to the jury in a jury case. They relate to the parties, their activities, their properties, their businesses.' 2 Administrative Law Treatise 353."

Current North Carolina law does not deal with procedure for taking judicial notice of facts. Judicial notice of domestic and foreign law is dealt with in G.S. Chapter 8, Article 1, which remains in force.

Subdivision (b) concerns the kinds of facts that may be judicially noticed. The Advisory Committee's Note states:

"With respect to judicial notice of adjudicative facts, the tradition has been one of caution in requiring that the matter be beyond reasonable controversy. This tradition of circumspection appears to be soundly based, and no reason to depart from it is apparent."

Subdivision (b) is consistent with current North Carolina practice. See Brandis on North Carolina Evidence § 11 (1982).

Subdivisions (c) and (d) govern when judicial notice is discretionary and when it is mandatory. The Advisory Committee's Note states:

"Under subdivision (c) the judge has a discretionary authority to take judicial notice, regardless of whether he is so requested by a party.

"The taking of judicial notice is mandatory under subdivision (d), only when a party requests it and the necessary information is supplied. This scheme is believed to reflect existing practice. It is simple and workable. It avoids troublesome distinctions in the many situations in which the process of taking judicial notice is not recognized as such."

Subdivisions (c) and (d) are in accord with North Carolina practice. See Brandis on North Carolina Evidence § 11 (1982).

Subdivision (e) entitles a party, upon timely request, to an opportunity to be heard as to the propriety of taking judicial notice. It differs from the federal rule by its limitation to a trial court. The Advisory Committee's Note states:

"Basic considerations of procedural fairness demand an opportunity to be heard on the propriety of taking judicial notice and the tenor of the matter noticed. The rule requires the granting of that opportunity upon request. No formal scheme of giving notice is provided. An adversely affected party may learn in advance that judicial notice is in contemplation, either by virtue of being served with a copy of a request by another party under subdivision (d) that judicial notice be taken, or through an advance indication by the judge. Or he may have no advance notice at all. The likelihood of the latter is enhanced by the frequent failure to recognize judicial notice as such. And in the absence of advance notice, a request made after the fact could not in fairness be considered untimely. . . ."

Subdivision (e) departs from current North Carolina practice which generally does not require an opportunity to be heard prior to the court taking judicial notice on its own initiative. See Brandis on North Carolina Evidence § 11 (1982).

With respect to notice at administrative hearings, see G.S. 150A-30.

Subdivision (f) is in accord with North Carolina practice in allowing judicial notice to be taken at any stage of the proceedings, whether in the trial court or on appeal.

Subdivision (g) concerns instructing the jury with respect to judicially noticed facts. The Advisory Committee's Note states:

"Within its relatively narrow area of adjudicative facts, the rule contemplates there is to be no evidence before the jury in disproof. The judge instructs the jury to take judicially noticed facts as established. This position is justified by the undesirable effects of the opposite rule in limiting the rebutting party, though not his opponent, to admissible evidence, in defeating the reasons for judicial notice, and in affecting the substantive law to an extent and in ways largely unforeseeable. Ample protection and flexibility are afforded by the broad provision for opportunity to be heard on request, set forth in subdivision (e)."

Subdivision (g) is in accord with North Carolina practice in civil cases by not allowing evidence to be introduced to dispute a fact that has been judicially noticed. See Brandis on North Carolina Evidence § 11, at 34 (1982).

However, subdivision (g) differs from North Carolina practice by permitting evidence to be introduced in a criminal trial to rebut a fact that has been judicially noticed. In adopting subdivision (g), Congress was of the view that a mandatory instruction to a jury in a criminal case to accept as conclusive any fact judicially noticed is contrary to the spirit of the right to a jury trial.

ARTICLE 3

Presumptions in Civil Actions and Proceedings

Rule 301. Presumptions in general in civil actions and proceedings

In all civil actions and proceedings when not otherwise provided for by statute, by judicial decision, or by these rules, a presumption imposes on the party against whom it is directed the burden of going forward with evidence to rebut or meet the presumption, but does not shift to such party the burden of proof in the sense of the risk of nonpersuasion, which remains throughout the trial upon the party on whom it was originally cast. The burden of going forward is satisfied by the introduction of evidence sufficient to permit reasonable minds to conclude that the presumed fact does not exist. If the party against whom a presumption operates fails to meet the burden of producing evidence, the presumed fact shall be deemed proved, and the court shall instruct the jury accordingly. When the burden of producing evidence to meet a presumption is satisfied, the court must instruct the jury that it may, but is not required to, infer the existence of the presumed fact from the proved fact.

Added by Laws 1983, c. 701, § 1.

North Carolina Commentary

The first sentence of this rule is identical to Fed.R.Evid. 301, except that the phrase "by statute, by judicial decision" is used in lieu of the phrase "by Act of Congress." The last three sentences of the rule, which were modeled upon Alaska Rule of Evidence 301 (1979), clarify the effect of the rule.

A presumption is an assumption of fact resulting from a rule of law which requires such fact to be assumed or inferred from another fact established in the action. The term "basic fact" is used to designate the fact from which the assumption or inference is made and the term "presumed fact" is used to indicate the fact assumed or inferred.

The rule does not apply to "conclusive presumptions", which are merely statements of substantive law and have nothing to do with the law of evidence. See Brandis on North Carolina Evidence § 215, at 170 (1982).

In some situations, when the basic fact has been established, the presumed fact may (but need not) be found to exist. The existence of the presumed fact is for the trier of fact to determine from all the evidence pro and con. The term "permissive presumption" is used to describe this situation. Id. at 171. Or it is said that the basic fact is prima facie evidence of the fact to be inferred. Rule 301 does not apply in situations where a statute or judicial decision creates a "permissive presumption" or merely provides that one fact shall be "prima facie" evidence of another.

The term "mandatory presumption" is used when the presumed fact *must* be found when the basic fact has been established, unless sufficient evidence of the nonexistence of the presumed fact is forthcoming. Id. at 171. Rule 301 is intended to govern mandatory presumptions.

Care should be taken to determine whether the presumption in question is within the scope of this rule since the term presumption is often misused. The first sentence of the rule makes it clear that the General Assembly and the courts retain power to create presumptions having an effect different from that provided for in this rule. Nonetheless, a presumption created by a prior statute or judicial decision should be construed to come within the scope of this rule unless it is clear that the presumption was not intended to be a "mandatory presumption."

Under Rule 301, the presumption satisfies the burden of producing evidence of the presumed fact. Evidence sufficient to prove the basic fact is sufficient proof of the presumed fact to survive a directed verdict at the end of the proponent's case-in-chief. This is in accord with North Carolina practice.

The general rule in North Carolina is in accord with Rule 301 in that a presumption does not shift the burden of proof. Id. § 218, at 179. However, with respect to some presumptions in North Carolina, the opponent has the burden of persuading the jury, by a preponderance of the evidence or otherwise, that the presumed fact does not exist. Id. If by statute or judicial decision a particular presumption shifts the burden of proof, Rule 301 does not apply.

Proof of the basic fact not only discharges the proponent's burden of producing evidence of the presumed fact but also places upon the opponent the burden of producing evidence that the presumed fact does not exist. If the opponent does not introduce any evidence, or the evidence is not sufficient to permit reasonable minds to conclude that the presumed fact does not exist, the proponent is entitled to a peremptory instruction that the presumed fact shall be deemed proved. This is in accord with North Carolina practice. Id. § 222, at 189.

If the opponent introduces evidence sufficient to permit reasonable minds to conclude that the presumed fact does not exist, no peremptory instruction should be given. Rather, the court must instruct the jury that it may, but is not required to, infer the existence of the presumed fact from proof of the basic fact.

Of course, the opponent may avoid the effect of a presumption by proving that the basic fact does not exist.

Rule 302. Applicability of federal law in civil actions and proceedings

In civil actions and proceedings, the effect of a presumption respecting a fact which is an element of a claim or defense as to which federal law supplies the rule of decision is determined in accordance with federal law.

Added by Laws 1983, c. 701, § 1.

North Carolina Commentary

This rule differs from Fed.R.Evid. 302 in that "federal law" has been substituted for "state law." The Comment to Rule 302 of the Uniform Rules of Evidence (1974) explains the purpose of the change:

> "Parallel jurisdiction in state and federal courts exists in many instances. The rule prescribes that when a federally created right is litigated in a state court, any prescribed federal presumption shall be applied."

ARTICLE 4

Relevancy and Its Limits

Rule 401. Definition of "relevant evidence"

"Relevant evidence" means evidence having any tendency to make the existence of any fact that is of consequence to the determination of the action more probable or less probable than it would be without the evidence.

Added by Laws 1983, c. 701, § 1.

North Carolina Commentary

This rule is identical to Fed.R.Evid. 401. The Advisory Committee's Note states:

> "Problems of relevancy call for an answer to the question whether an item of evidence, when tested by the processes of legal reasoning, possesses sufficient probative value to justify receiving it in evidence. Thus, assessment of the pro-

bative value of evidence that a person purchased a revolver shortly prior to a fatal shooting with which he is charged is a matter of analysis and reasoning.

"The variety of relevancy problems is coextensive with the ingenuity of counsel in using circumstantial evidence as a means of proof. An enormous number of cases fall in no set pattern, and this rule is designed as a guide for handling them. On the other hand, some situations recur with sufficient frequency to create patterns susceptible of treatment by specific rules. Rule 404 and those following it are of that variety; they also serve as illustrations of the application of the present rule as limited by the exclusionary principles of Rule 403.

"Passing mention should be made of so-called 'conditional' relevancy. Morgan, Basic Problems of Evidence 45–46 (1962). In this situation, probative value depends not only upon satisfying the basic requirement of relevancy as described above but also upon the existence of some matter of fact. For example, if evidence of a spoken statement is relied upon to prove notice, probative value is lacking unless the person sought to be charged heard the statement. The problem is one of fact, and the only rules needed are for the purpose of determining the respective functions of judge and jury. See Rules 104(b) and 901. The discussion which follows in the present note is concerned with relevancy generally, not with any particular problem of conditional relevancy.

"Relevancy is not an inherent characteristic of any item of evidence but exists only as a relation between an item of evidence and a matter properly provable in the case. Does the item of evidence tend to prove the matter sought to be proved? Whether the relationship exists depends upon principles evolved by experience or science, applied logically to the situation at hand. James, Relevancy, Probability and the Law, 29 Calif.L.Rev. 689, 696, n. 15 (1941), in Selected Writings on Evidence and Trial 610, 615, n. 15 (Fryer ed.1957). The rule summarizes this relationship as a 'tendency to make the existence' of the fact to be proved 'more probable or less probable.' Compare Uniform Rule 1(2) which states the crux of relevancy as 'a tendency in reason,' thus perhaps emphasizing unduly the logical process and ignoring the need to draw upon experience or science to validate the general principle upon which relevancy in a particular situation depends.

"The standard of probability under the rule is 'more . . . probable than it would be without the evidence.' Any more stringent requirement is unworkable and unrealistic. As McCormick § 152, p. 317, says, 'A brick is not a wall,' or, as Falknor, Extrinsic Policies Affecting Admissibility, 10 Rutgers L.Rev. 574, 576 (1956), quotes Professor McBaine, '[I]t is not to be supposed that every witness can make a home run.' . . . Dealing with probability in the language of the rule has the added virtue of avoiding confusion between questions of admissibility and questions of the sufficiency of the evidence.

"The rule uses the phrase 'fact that is of consequence to the determination of the action' to describe the kind of fact to which proof may properly be directed. The language is that of California Evidence Code § 210; it has the advantage of avoiding the loosely used and ambiguous word 'material.' . . . The fact to be proved may be ultimate, intermediate, or evidentiary; it matters not, so long as it is of consequence in the determination of the action. Cf. Uniform Rule 1(2) which requires that the evidence relate to a 'material' fact.

"The fact to which the evidence is directed need not be in dispute. While situations will arise which call for the exclusion of evidence offered to prove a point conceded by the opponent, the ruling should be made on the basis of such considerations as waste of time and undue prejudice (see Rule 403), rather than under any general requirement that evidence is admissible only if directed to matters in dispute. Evidence which is essentially background in nature can scarcely be said to involve disputed matter, yet it is universally offered and admitted as an aid to understanding. Charts, photographs, views of real estate, murder weapons, and many other items of evidence fall in this category. A rule limiting admissibility to evidence directed to a controversial point would invite the exclusion of this helpful evidence, or at least the raising of endless questions over its admission."

While North Carolina courts have used slightly different definitions of relevant evidence, the rule is unlikely to alter significantly North Carolina practice. See Brandis on North Carolina Evidence § 78 (1982). Although the rule speaks in terms of relevancy, the definition includes what is often referred to in our courts as materiality. Id. § 77.

Rule 402. Relevant evidence generally admissible; irrelevant evidence inadmissible

All relevant evidence is admissible, except as otherwise provided by the Constitution of the United States, by the Constitution of North Carolina, by Act of Congress, by Act of the General Assembly or by these rules. Evidence which is not relevant is not admissible.

Added by Laws 1983, c. 701, § 1.

North Carolina Commentary

This rule is identical to Fed.R.Evid. 402 except that the phrases "by the Constitution of North Carolina" and "by Act of the General Assembly" were added and the phrase "by other rules prescribed by the Supreme Court pursuant to statutory authority" was deleted. The Advisory Committee's Note states:

"The provisions that all relevant evidence is admissible, with certain exceptions, and that evidence which is not relevant is not admissible are 'a presupposition involved in the very conception of a rational system of evidence.' Thayer, Preliminary Treatise on Evidence 264 (1898). They constitute the foundation upon which the structure of admission and exclusion rests. . . .

"Not all relevant evidence is admissible. The exclusion of relevant evidence occurs in a variety of situations and may be called for by these rules, by the Rules of Civil . . . Procedure . . ., by Act of Congress, or by constitutional considerations.

"Succeeding rules in the present article, in response to the demands of particular policies, require the exclusion of evidence despite its relevancy. In addition, . . . Article VI imposes limitations upon witnesses and the manner of dealing with them; Article VII specifies requirements with respect to opinions and expert testimony; Article VIII excludes hearsay not falling within an exception; Article IX spells out the handling of authentication and identification; and Article X restricts the manner of proving the contents of writings and recordings.

"The Rules of Civil . . . Procedure in some instances require the exclusion of relevant evidence. For example, . . . the Rules of Civil Procedure, by imposing requirements of notice and unavailability of the deponent, place limits on the use of relevant depositions.

. . .

"The rule recognizes but makes no attempt to spell out the constitutional considerations which impose basic limitations upon the admissibility of relevant evidence. Examples are evidence obtained by unlawful search and seizure. Weeks v. United States, 232 U.S. 383, 34 S.Ct. 341, 58 L.Ed. 652 (1914); Katz v. United States, 389 U.S. 347, 88 S.Ct. 507, 19 L.Ed.2d 576 (1967); incriminating statement elicited from an accused in violation of right to counsel, Massiah v. United States, 377 U.S. 201, 84 S.Ct. 1199, 12 L.Ed.2d 246 (1964)."

Rule 402 is consistent with North Carolina practice.

Rule 403. Exclusion of relevant evidence on grounds of prejudice, confusion, or waste of time

Although relevant, evidence may be excluded if its probative value is substantially outweighed by the danger of unfair prejudice, confusion of the issues, or misleading the jury, or by considerations of undue delay, waste of time, or needless presentation of cumulative evidence.

Added by Laws 1983, c. 701, § 1.

North Carolina Commentary

This rule is identical to Fed.R.Evid. 403. The Advisory Committee's Note states:

"The case law recognizes that certain circumstances call for the exclusion of evidence which is of unquestioned relevance. These circumstances entail risks which range all the way from inducing decision on a purely emotional basis, at one extreme, to nothing more harmful than merely wasting time, at the other extreme. Situations in this area call for balancing the probative value of and need for the evidence against the harm likely to result from its admission. . . . The rules which follow in this Article are concrete applications evolved for particular situations. However, they reflect the policies underlying the present rule, which is designed as a guide for the handling of situations for which no specific rules have been formulated.

"Exclusion for risk of unfair prejudice, confusion of issues, misleading the jury, or waste of time, all find ample support in the authorities. 'Unfair prejudice' within its context means an undue tendency to suggest decision on an improper basis, commonly, though not necessarily, an emotional one.

"The rule does not enumerate surprise as a ground for exclusion, in this respect following Wigmore's view of the common law. 6 Wigmore § 1849. Cf. McCormick § 152, p. 320, n. 29, listing unfair surprise as a ground for exclusion but stating that it is usually 'coupled with the danger of prejudice and confusion of issues'. . . . While it can scarcely be doubted that claims of unfair surprise may still be justified despite procedural requirements of notice and instrumentalities of discovery, the granting of a continuance is a more appropriate remedy than exclusion of the evidence. . . . Moreover, the impact of a rule excluding evidence on the ground of surprise would be difficult to estimate."

The rule is substantially in accord with North Carolina practice. See Brandis on North Carolina Evidence § 77 et seq. (1982). In North Carolina, unfair surprise appears to be a ground for exclusion of evidence. Id. § 77, p. 287. However, as the Advisory Committee states, the rule does not enumerate surprise as a ground for exclusion. Nonetheless, surprise may be covered by unfair prejudice, confusion of issues, or undue delay. See Wright and Graham, Federal Practice and Procedure: Evidence § 5218, at 298.

The Advisory Committee's Note states that:

"In reaching a decision whether to exclude on grounds of unfair prejudice, consideration should be given to the probable effectiveness or lack of effectiveness of a limiting instruction. See Rule 106 and Advisory Committee's Note thereunder. The availability of other means of proof may also be an appropriate factor."

Rule 404. Character evidence not admissible to prove conduct; exceptions; other crimes

(a) Character evidence generally.—Evidence of a person's character or a trait of his character is not admissible for the purpose of proving that he acted in conformity therewith on a particular occasion, except:

(1) Character of accused.—Evidence of a pertinent trait of his character offered by an accused, or by the prosecution to rebut the same;

(2) Character of victim.—Evidence of a pertinent trait of character of the victim of the crime offered by an accused, or by the prosecution to rebut the same, or evidence of a character trait of peacefulness of the victim offered by the prosecution in a homicide case to rebut evidence that the victim was the first aggressor;

(3) Character of witness.—Evidence of the character of a witness, as provided in Rules 607, 608, and 609.

(b) Other crimes, wrongs, or acts.—Evidence of other crimes, wrongs, or acts is not admissible to prove the character of a person in order to show that he acted in conformity therewith. It may, however, be admissible for other purposes, such as proof of motive, opportunity, intent, preparation, plan, knowledge, identity, or absence of mistake, entrapment or accident. Admissible evidence may include evidence of an offense committed by a juvenile if it would have been a Class A, B1, B2, C, D, or E felony if committed by an adult.

Added by Laws 1983, c. 701, § 1. Amended by Laws 1994, Ex. Sess., c. 7, § 3; Laws 1995, c. 509, § 7.

North Carolina Commentary

This rule is identical to Fed.Evid.Rule 404, except for the addition of the word "entrapment" in the last sentence of subdivision (b).

Subdivision (a) deals with the basic question whether character evidence should be admitted. The Advisory Committee's Note states:

"Once the admissibility of character evidence in some form is established under this rule, reference must then be made to Rule 405, which follows, in order to determine the appropriate method of proof. If the character is that of a witness, see Rules 608 and 610 for methods of proof.

"Character questions arise in two fundamentally different ways. (1) Character may itself be an element of a crime, claim, or defense. A situation of this kind is commonly referred to as 'character in issue.' Illustrations are: the chastity of the victim under a statute specifying her chastity as an element of the crime of seduction, or the competency of the driver in an action for negligently entrusting a motor vehicle to an incompetent driver. No problem of the general relevancy of character evidence is involved, and the present rule therefore has no provision on the subject. The only question relates to allowable methods of proof, as to which see Rule 405, immediately following. (2) Character evidence is susceptible of being used for the purpose of suggesting an inference that the person acted on the occasion in question consistently with his character. This use of character is often described as 'circumstantial.' Illustrations are: evidence of a violent disposition to prove that the person was the aggressor in an affray, or evidence of honesty in disproof of a charge of theft. This circumstantial use of character evidence raises questions of relevancy as well as questions of allowable methods of proof."

The rule is consistent with North Carolina practice in that character evidence is generally not admissible as circumstantial evidence of conduct.

Subdivision (a)(1) creates an exception which permits an accused to introduce pertinent evidence of good character, in which event the prosecution may rebut with evidence of bad character. The exception is consistent with North Carolina practice except that subdivision (a)(1) speaks in terms of a "pertinent trait of his character". This limits the exception to relevant character traits, whereas North Carolina Practice permits use of evidence of general character. Professor Brandis states that:

"The North Carolina rule on this subject is unique, and appears to have had its origin in a misinterpretation of the earlier opinions.

"In a majority of jurisdictions, character evidence must be confined to the particular trait of character involved in the conduct which is being investigated: In the case of a witness, his character for truth and veracity; of a defendant charged with a crime of violence, his peaceable or violent character; of an alleged embezzler, his honesty and integrity, etc.; a few courts will *also* admit evidence of general moral character, and this view was adopted by the North Carolina Court at an early date. For at least eighty years it was permissible to prove either the general character or the specific relevant trait of character of the person in question. When, during this period, the Court stated that only 'general character' could be shown, it meant that the only method of proving character was by general reputation, as distinguished from 'particular facts and the opinion of witnesses.' In State v. Hairston the principle of the earlier cases seems to have been misunderstood, and the rule was stated: 'A party introducing a witness as to character can only prove the general character of the person asked about. The witness, of his own motion, may say in what respect it is good or bad.' . . .

"When the witness is asked whether he knows the general 'reputation' or 'reputation and character' of the subject, if he answers 'No' he should be stood aside; but if he answers 'Yes' it seems that he need not confine his testimony to that reputation, but may testify to reputation for some specific trait of character. This may be highly relevant, as when witness character is at stake and the answer deals with reputation for veracity. However, it may deal with reputation for liquor-selling, or horse trading, or domestic cruelty, even though the trait is wholly irrelevant to any issue in the case.

"The Court recently reviewed the history of the rule, but did not change it. It explicitly held that it is proper for counsel to prepare his witness by explaining the rule that this does not render the specific trait evidence inadmissible unless, at counsel's suggestion, it is false. To this writer this is convincing proof that the rule should be scrapped. When counsel ascertains in advance a trait which the witness will specify, his question to elicit it should surely not merely be allowed, but be required to deal with that trait. In such case, objection may be made to the question and relevance rationally appraised. As it is, the question is foolproof and there is no opportunity to object until the specific trait evidence is actually given and the damage is done." Brandis on North Carolina Evidence § 114 (1982) (footnotes omitted).

Brandis also notes that:

"At best the present rule requires use of an ambiguous and misleading formula in examining character witnesses. At worst it has positively undesirable consequences. It opens the door to evidence of character traits which are irrelevant and prejudicial, and permits the prosecution, under the guise of impeaching the defendant as a witness, to prove traits having no relation to veracity but which are relevant on the issue of guilt, thus evading the rule (see § 104) prohibiting the State from attacking the defendant's character unless he first puts it in issue. These consequences would be avoided, and logic and symmetry restored, by confining the inquiry to traits relevant for the particular purpose and holding the witness to responsive answers." Id. at 114, n. 91.

Subdivision (a)(2) creates an exception to permit an accused to introduce pertinent evidence of the character of the victim and to permit the prosecution to introduce similar evidence in rebuttal of the character evidence. The subdivision extends the exception recognized in North Carolina homicide and assault and battery cases to include all criminal cases. See Brandis on North Carolina Evidence § 106 (1982).

North Carolina practice permits evidence of the character of the victim tending to show that the defendant had a reasonable apprehension of death or bodily harm. Id. Such evidence when introduced to show the reasonable apprehension of death or bodily harm to the accused, rather than to prove that the victim acted in conformity with his character trait on a particular occasion, would not be within the ban created by subdivision (a).

North Carolina practice also permits evidence of the character of the victim tending to show that the victim was the first aggressor. Unlike Rule 404, current North Carolina practice permits such evidence to be introduced only if the State's evidence is wholly circumstantial or the nature of the transaction is in doubt.

Subdivision (a)(2) permits proof of any pertinent trait of the victim. North Carolina practice has confined the evidence to character for violence. Id.

Subdivision (a)(2) is consistent with North Carolina practice in that evidence of the character of the victim for peace and quiet would be admissible to rebut evidence of the deceased's character for violence and evidence of the victim's good general character would not. Id. at 397.

The second part of subdivision (a)(2) permits introduction of "evidence of a character trait of peacefulness of the victim offered by the prosecution in a homicide case to rebut evidence that the victim was the first aggressor." In North Carolina the prosecution may offer evidence of the deceased's character for peace and quiet only if the defendant has introduced evidence of the deceased's character for violence. See Nance v. Fike, 244 N.C. 368, 372 [93 S.E.2d 443] (1956). Thus in North Carolina the accused can apparently claim self-defense without opening the door to character evidence relating to the victim. Subdivision (a)(2) would alter this practice and permit the prosecution to offer evidence of the peacefulness of the victim to rebut any evidence that the victim was the first aggressor.

The North Carolina exception, unlike the rule, applies to cases of civil assault and battery. See Brandis on North Carolina Evidence § 106, at 393 (1982). The Advisory Committee's Note states:

"The argument is made that circumstantial use of character ought to be allowed in civil cases to the same extent as in criminal cases, i.e., evidence of good (nonprejudicial) character would be admissible in the first instance, subject to rebuttal by evidence of bad character. . . . The difficulty with expanding the use of character evidence in civil cases is set forth by the California Law Revision Commission . . . :

" 'Character evidence is of slight probative value and may be very prejudicial. It tends to distract the trier of fact from the main question of what actually happened on the particular occasion. It subtly permits the trier of fact to reward the good man and to punish the bad man because of their respective characters despite what the evidence in the case shows actually happened.' "

Subdivision (a)(3) creates an exception to the general rule and permits the introduction of evidence of the character of a witness, as provided in Rules 607, 608, and 609, to prove that he acted in conformity therewith on a particular occasion.

Subdivision (b) permits the introduction of specific "crimes, wrongs, or acts" for a purpose other than to prove the conduct of a person. The Advisory Committee's Note states:

"Subdivision (b) deals with a specialized but important application of the general rule excluding circumstantial use of character evidence. Consistently with that rule, evidence of other crimes, wrongs, or acts is not admissible to prove character as a basis for suggesting the inference that conduct on a particular occasion was in conformity with it. However, the evidence may be offered for another purpose, such as proof of motive, opportunity, and so on, which does not fall within the prohibition. In this situation the rule does not require that the evidence be excluded. No mechanical solution is offered. The determination must be made whether the danger of undue prejudice outweighs the probative value of the evidence, in view of the availability of other means of proof and other factors appropriate for making decisions of this kind under Rule 403."

The list in the last sentence of subdivision (b) is nonexclusive and the fact that evidence cannot be brought within a category does not mean that the evidence is inadmissible.

Subdivision (b) is consistent with North Carolina practice.

Relevance of the complainant's past behavior in a rape or sex offense case is governed by Rule 412.

Rule 405. Methods of proving character

(a) Reputation or opinion.—In all cases in which evidence of character or a trait of character of a person is admissible, proof may be made by testimony as to reputation or by testimony in the form of an opinion. On cross-examination, inquiry is allowable into relevant specific instances of conduct. Expert testimony on character or a trait of character is not admissible as circumstantial evidence of behavior.

(b) Specific instances of conduct.—In cases in which character or a trait of character of a person is an essential element of a charge, claim, or defense, proof may also be made of specific instances of his conduct.

Added by Laws 1983, c. 701, § 1.

North Carolina Commentary

This rule is identical to Fed.R.Evid. 405 except for the addition of the last sentence to subdivision (a).

The Advisory Committee's Note states:

"The rule deals only with allowable methods of proving character, not with admissibility of character evidence, which is covered by Rule 404.

"Of the three methods of proving character provided by the rule, evidence of specific instances of conduct is the most convincing. At the same time it possesses the greatest capacity to arouse prejudice, to confuse, to surprise, and to consume time. Consequently the rule confines the use of evidence of this kind to cases in which character is, in the strict sense, in issue and hence deserving of a searching inquiry. When character is used circumstantially and hence occupies a lesser status in the case, proof may be only by reputation and opinion. These latter methods are also available when character is in issue."

With respect to specific instances of conduct and reputation, this treatment is consistent with North Carolina practice. See Brandis on North Carolina Evidence § 110 (1982).

With respect to opinion evidence, the Advisory Committee's Note states:

"In recognizing opinion as a means of proving character, the rule departs from usual contemporary practice in favor of that of an earlier day. See 7 Wigmore § 1986, pointing out that the earlier practice permitted opinion and arguing strongly for evidence based on personal knowledge and belief as contrasted with 'the second-hand, irresponsible product of multiplied guesses and gossip which we term "reputation".' It seems likely that the persistence of reputation evidence is due to its largely being opinion in disguise. Traditionally character has been regarded primarily in moral overtones of good and bad: chaste, peaceable, truthful, honest. Nevertheless, on occasion nonmoral considerations crop up, as in the case of the incompetent driver, and this seems bound to happen increasingly. If character is defined as the kind of person one is, then account must be taken of varying ways of arriving at the estimate. . . . No effective dividing line exists between character and mental capacity, and the latter traditionally has been provable by opinion."

In permitting opinion evidence as a means of proving character, the rule departs from current North Carolina practice. The general practice in this State is to frame questions in terms of reputation. However, if the witness is questioned concerning the "general character" or the "reputation and character" of another person, it is understood that the real subject of inquiry is reputation. State v. King, 224 N.C. 329 [30 S.E.2d 230] (1944); State v. Hicks, 200 N.C. 539 [157 S.E. 851] (1933); State v. Cathey, 170 N.C. 794 [87 S.E. 532] (1916). Professor Brandis points out that:

"If as, e.g., in the initial question in State v. Cathey . . . 'reputation' is entirely omitted from the question, or if the question refers, as in State v. Hicks . . . to 'reputation and character,' the judge and counsel may know that the witness should confine himself to reputation, but, in the absence of further enlightenment, it seems most doubtful that the witness is so legally learned. Therefore, the practical result may well be to admit opinion evidence while giving lip service to the prohibition against it. Since, additionally, as a practical matter, many witnesses will in fact give opinion in answering a question ostensibly calling only for reputation, it seems to the author of this edition that it would be much more realistic for the Court to scrap the present stated rule and frankly admit either opinion or reputation testimony." Stansbury's North Carolina Evidence (Brandis ed.) § 110, at 338, n. 99.

Since Fed.R.Evid. 405 opens up the possibility of proving character by means of expert witnesses, the last sentence was added to subdivision (a) to prohibit expert testimony on character as it relates to the likelihood of whether or not the defendant committed the act he is accused of. This sentence is not intended to exclude expert testimony of a personality or character change as it relates to the issue of damages.

The second sentence of subdivision (a) permits inquiry on cross-examination into relevant specific instances of conduct. The Advisory Committee's Note states:

"According to the great majority of cases, on cross-examination inquiry is allowable as to whether the reputation witness has heard of particular instances of conduct pertinent to the trait in question. . . . The theory is that, since the reputation witness relates what he has heard, the inquiry tends to shed light on the accuracy of his hearing and reporting. Accordingly, the opinion witness would be asked whether he knew, as well as whether he had heard. The fact is, of course, that these distinctions are of slight if any practical significance, and the second sentence of subdivision (a) eliminates them as a factor in formulating questions. This recognition of the propriety of inquiring into specific instances of conduct does not circumscribe inquiry otherwise into the bases of opinion and reputation testimony."

Under current North Carolina practice, inquiry into specific instances of conduct on cross-examination is available only on the cross-examination of the person whose character is in question. Brandis on North Carolina Evidence §§ 111, 115 (1982). It is not permissible in North Carolina to ask a character witness whether he has heard of the person in question having committed a particular act. Id. § 115. However, to some extent the North Carolina rule may be circumvented by cross-examination as to specific traits. Id.

Also, the Advisory Committee's Note states:

"The express allowance of inquiry into specific instances of conduct on cross-examination in subdivision (a) and the express allowance of it as part of a case in chief when character is actually in issue in subdivision (b) contemplate that testimony of specific instances is not generally permissible on the direct examination of an ordinary opinion witness to character. Similarly as to witnesses to the character of witnesses under Rule 608(b). Opinion testimony on direct in these situations ought in general to correspond to reputation testimony as now given, i.e., be confined to the nature and extent of observation and acquaintance upon which the opinion is based. See Rule 701."

Rule 406. Habit; routine practice

Evidence of the habit of a person or of the routine practice of an organization, whether corroborated or not and regardless of the presence of eyewitnesses, is relevant to prove that the conduct of the person or organization on a particular occasion was in conformity with the habit or routine practice.

Added by Laws 1983, c. 701, § 1.

North Carolina Commentary

This rule is identical to Fed.R.Evid. 406.

The Advisory Committee's Note states:

"An oft-quoted paragraph, McCormick § 162, p. 340, describes habit in terms effectively contrasting it with character.

" 'Character and habit are close akin. "Character" is a generalized description of one's disposition, or of one's disposition in respect to a general trait, such as honesty, temperance, or peacefulness. "Habit," in modern usage, both lay and psychological, is more specific. It describes one's regular response to a repeated specific situation. If we speak of character for care, we think of the person's tendency to act prudently in all the varying situations of life, in business, family life, in handling automobiles and in walking across the street. A habit, on the other hand, is the person's regular practice of meeting a particular kind of situation with a specific type of conduct, such as the habit of going down a particular stairway two stairs at a time, or of giving the hand-signal for a left turn, or of alighting from railway cars while they are moving. The doing of the habitual acts may become semi-automatic.'

"Equivalent behavior on the part of a group is designated 'routine practice of an organization' in the rule. Agreement is general that habit evidence is highly persuasive as proof of conduct on a particular occasion. Again quoting McCormick § 162, p. 341:

" 'Character may be thought of as the sum of one's habits though doubtless it is more than this. But unquestionably the uniformity of one's response to habit is far greater than the consistency with which one's conduct conforms to character or disposition. Even though character comes in only exceptionally as evidence of an act, surely any sensible man in investigating whether X did a particular act would be greatly helped in his inquiry by evidence as to whether he was in the habit of doing it.'

"When disagreement has appeared, its focus has been upon the question of what constitutes habit, and the reason for this is readily apparent. The extent to which instances must be multiplied and consistency of behavior maintained in order to rise to the status of habit inevitably gives rise to difference of opinion. Lewan, Rationale of Habit Evidence, 16 Syracuse L.Rev. 39, 49 (1964). While adequacy of sampling and uniformity of response are key factors, precise standards for measuring their sufficiency for evidence purposes cannot be formulated.

"The rule is consistent with prevailing views. Much evidence is excluded simply because of failure to achieve the status of habit. Thus, evidence of intemperate 'habits' is generally excluded when offered as proof of drunkenness in accident cases, Annot., 46 A.L.R.2d 103, and evidence of other assaults is inadmissible to prove the instant one in a civil assault action, Annot., 66 A.L.R.2d 806. In Levin v. United States, 119 U.S.App.D.C. 156, 338 F.2d 265 (1964), testimony as to the religious 'habits' of the accused, offered as tending to prove that he was at home observing the Sabbath rather than out obtaining money through larceny by trick, was held properly excluded:

" 'It seems apparent to us that an individual's religious practices would not be the type of activities which would lend themselves to the characterization of "invariable regularity." (1 Wigmore 520.) Certainly the very volitional basis of the activity raises serious questions as to its invariable nature, and hence its probative value.' Id. at 272.

"These rulings are not inconsistent with the trend towards admitting evidence of business transactions between one of the parties and a third person as tending to prove that he made the same bargain or proposal in the litigated situation. Slough, Relevancy Unraveled, 6 Kan.L.Rev. 38–41 (1957). Nor are they inconsistent with such cases as Whittemore v. Lockheed Aircraft Corp., 65 Cal.App.2d 737, 151 P.2d 670 (1944), upholding the admission of evidence that plaintiff's intestate had on four other occasions flown planes from defendant's factory for delivery to his employer airline, offered to prove that he was piloting rather than a guest on a plane which crashed and killed all on board while en route for delivery.

"A considerable body of authority has required that evidence of the routine practice of an organization be corroborated as a condition precedent to its admission in evidence. Slough, Relevancy Unraveled, 5 Kan.L.Rev. 404, 449 (1957). This requirement is specifically rejected by the rule on the ground that it relates to the sufficiency of the evidence rather than admissibility. . . . The rule also rejects the requirement of the absence of eyewitnesses, sometimes encountered with respect to admitting habit evidence to prove freedom from contributory negligence in wrongful death cases."

Rule 406 is consistent with North Carolina practice. See Brandis on North Carolina Evidence § 95 (1982).

Rule 407. Subsequent remedial measures

When, after an event, measures are taken which, if taken previously, would have made the event less likely to occur, evidence of the subsequent measures is not admissible to prove negligence or culpable conduct in connection with the event. This rule does not require the exclusion of evidence of subsequent measures when offered for another purpose, such as proving ownership, control, or feasibility of precautionary measures, if those issues are controverted, or impeachment.

Added by Laws 1983, c. 701, § 1.

North Carolina Commentary

This rule is identical to Fed.R.Evid. 407 except that the phrase "those issues are" has been inserted to clarify what must be controverted.

The Advisory Committee's Note states:

"The rule incorporates conventional doctrine which excludes evidence of subsequent remedial measures as proof of an admission of fault. The rule rests on two grounds. (1) The conduct is not in fact an admission, since the conduct is equally consistent with injury by mere accident or through contributory negligence. Or, as Baron Bramwell put it, the rule rejects the notion that 'because the world gets wiser at it gets older, therefore it was foolish before'. Hart v. Lancashire & Yorkshire Ry. Co., 21 L.T.R.N.S. 261, 263 (1869). Under a liberal theory of relevancy this ground alone would not support exclusion as the inference is still a possible one. (2) The other, and more impressive, ground for exclusion rests on a social policy of encouraging people to take, or at least not discouraging them from taking, steps in furtherance of added safety. The courts have applied this principle to exclude evidence of subsequent repairs, installation of safety devices, changes in company rules, and discharge of employees, and the language of the present rule is broad enough to encompass all of them. See Falknor, Extrinsic Policies Affecting Admissibility, 10 Rutgers L.Rev. 574, 590 (1956).

"The second sentence of the rule directs attention to the limitations of the rule. Exclusion is called for only when the evidence of subsequent remedial measures is offered as proof of negligence or culpable conduct. In effect it rejects the suggested inference that fault is admitted. Other purposes are, however, allowable, including ownership or control, existence of duty, and feasibility of precautionary measures, if controverted, and impeachment. 2 Wigmore § 283; Annot., 64 A.L.R.2d 1296. Two recent federal cases are illustrative. Boeing Airplane Co. v. Brown, 291 F.2d 310 (9th Cir.1961), an action against an airplane manufacturer for using an allegedly defectively designed alternator shaft which caused a plane crash, upheld the admission of evidence of subsequent design modification for the purpose of showing that design changes and safeguards were feasible. And Powers v. J.B. Michael & Co., 329 F.2d 674 (6th Cir.1964), an action against a road contractor for negligent failure to put out warning signs, sustained the admission of evidence that defendant subsequently put out signs to show that the portion of the road in question was under defendant's control. The requirement that the other purpose be controverted calls for automatic exclusion unless a genuine issue be present and allows the opposing party to lay the groundwork for exclusion by making an admission. Otherwise the factors of undue prejudice, confusion of issues, misleading the jury, and waste of time remain for consideration under Rule 403."

The increasing tendency of federal courts is to hold that Rule 407 is not applicable to product liability cases. North Carolina courts have applied the rule excluding evidence of subsequent remedial measures in product liability cases. See Jenkins v. Helgren, 26 N.C.App. 653 [217 S.E.2d 120] (1975). It is the intent of the Committee that the rule should apply to all types of actions.

Rule 407 is consistent with North Carolina practice. See Brandis on North Carolina Evidence § 180 (1982).

Rule 408. Compromise and offers to compromise

Evidence of (1) furnishing or offering or promising to furnish, or (2) accepting or offering or promising to accept, a valuable consideration in compromising or attempting to compromise a claim which was disputed as to either validity or amount, is not admissible to prove liability for or invalidity of the claim or its amount. Evidence of conduct or evidence of statements made in compromise negotiations is likewise not admissible. This rule does not require the exclusion of any evidence otherwise discoverable merely because it is presented in the course of compromise negotiations. This rule also does not require exclusion when the evidence is offered for another purpose, such as proving bias or prejudice of a witness, negativing a contention of undue delay, or proving an effort to obstruct a criminal investigation or prosecution.

Added by Laws 1983, c. 701, § 1.

North Carolina Commentary

This rule is identical to Fed.R.Evid. 408 except that the words "evidence of" were added to the second sentence. The addition is for the purpose of clarification and is not intended as a material change. The Advisory Committee's Note states:

"As a matter of general agreement, evidence of an offer to compromise a claim is not receivable in evidence as an admission of, as the case may be, the validity or invalidity of the claim. As with evidence of subsequent remedial measures, dealt with in Rule 407, exclusion may be based on two grounds. (1) The evidence is irrelevant, since the offer may be motivated by a desire for peace rather than from any concession of weakness of position. The validity of this position will vary as the amount of the offer varies in relation to the size of the claim and may also be influenced by other circumstances. (2) A more consistently impressive ground is promotion of the public policy favoring the compromise and settlement of disputes. McCormick §§ 76, 251. While the rule is ordinarily phrased in terms of offers of compromise, it is apparent that a similar attitude must be taken with respect to completed compromise when offered against a party thereto. This latter situation will not, of course, ordinarily occur except when a party to the present litigation has compromised with a third person."

North Carolina practice is consistent with Rule 408 in that an offer of compromise, as such, is not admissible to prove liability for or invalidity of a claim or its amount. See Brandis on North Carolina Evidence § 180 (1982). The same rule applies to an offer to settle, or the actual settlement of, a third person's claim arising out of the transaction in litigation. Id. at 56. The words "the claim" in the first sentence should be interpreted to include the claim that is the subject of the lawsuit and any other claim arising out of the same occurrence.

The Advisory Committee's Note states:

"The policy considerations which underlie the rule do not come into play when the effort is to induce a creditor to settle an admittedly due amount for a lesser sum. McCormick § 251, p. 540. Hence the rule requires that the claim be disputed as to either validity or amount."

The phrase "which was disputed" should be interpreted consistently with North Carolina decisional law concerning what constitutes a dispute. See Wilson County Board of Education v. Lamm, 276 N.C. 487 [173 S.E.2d 281] (1970).

With respect to the second sentence of the rule, the Advisory Committee's Note states:

"The practical value of the common law rule has been greatly diminished by its inapplicability to admissions of fact, even though made in the course of compromise negotiations, unless hypothetical, stated to be 'without prejudice,' or so connected with the offer as to be inseparable from it. McCormick § 251, pp. 540–541. An inevitable effect is to inhibit freedom of communication with respect to compromise, even among lawyers. Another effect is the generation of controversy over whether a given statement falls within or without the protected area. These considerations account for the expansion of the rule herewith to include evidence of conduct or statements made in compromise negotiations, as well as the offer or completed compromise itself."

Thus Rule 408 changes the current North Carolina practice that allows a "distinct admission of an independent fact" made during compromise negotiations to be received in evidence. See Brandis on North Carolina Evidence § 180, at 56–57 (1982).

Policy reasons for the compromise rule do not apply to evidence discoverable outside of settlement negotiations. Thus the third sentence of Rule 408 states that evidence otherwise discoverable need not be excluded merely because it is presented in compromise discussions. There is not any North Carolina case law on this point.

The Advisory Committee's Note states that:

"The final sentence of the rule serves to point out some limitations upon its applicability. Since the rule excludes only when the purpose is proving the validity or invalidity of the claim or its amount, an offer for another purpose is not within the rule. The illustrative situations mentioned in the rule are supported by the authorities. As to proving bias or prejudice of a witness, see Annot., 161 A.L.R. 395, contra, Fenberg v. Rosenthal, 348 Ill.App. 510, 109 N.E.2d 402 (1952), and negativing a contention of lack of due diligence in presenting a claim, 4 Wigmore § 1061. An effort to 'buy off' the prosecution or a prosecuting witness in a criminal case is not within the policy of the rule of exclusion. McCormick, § 251, p. 542."

The final sentence of the rule is consistent with North Carolina practice in that an offer for a purpose other than to prove the validity or invalidity of the claim or its amount is not within the rule. See Brandis on North Carolina Evidence § 180, at 55, 56 (1982).

Rule 409. Payment of medical and other expenses

Evidence of furnishing or offering or promising to pay medical, hospital, or other expenses occasioned by an injury is not admissible to prove liability for the injury.

Added by Laws 1983, c. 701, § 1.

North Carolina Commentary

This rule is identical to Fed.R.Evid. 409, except that the phrase "other expenses" has been substituted for the phrase "similar expenses."

The Advisory Committee's Note states:

"The considerations underlying this rule parallel those underlying Rules 407 and 408, which deal respectively with subsequent remedial measures and offers of compromise. As stated in Annot., 20 A.L.R.2d 291, 293:

"'[G]enerally, evidence of payment of medical, hospital, or similar expenses of an injured party by the opposing party, is not admissible, the reason often given being that such payment or offer is usually made from humane impulses and not from an admission of liability, and that to hold otherwise would tend to discourage assistance to the injured person.'"

Under current North Carolina law, rendering aid to an injured person or promising to render aid is not an admission of fault.

Rule 409 does not cover rendering aid but does not change existing North Carolina law that rendering aid to an injured person or promising to render aid is not an admission of fault. Brandis on North Carolina Evidence § 180, at 58 (1982).

Unlike the federal rule, which applies to "medical, hospital, or similar expenses," this rule applies to "medical, hospital, or other expenses." The phrase "other expenses" is intended to include, but is not limited to, lost wages and damage to property. The phrase "occasioned by an injury" is intended to include a property injury as well as a personal injury. The rule's coverage of nonmedical expenses occasioned by either a personal or property injury is an expansion of the current North Carolina rule. See Id. However, this rule is intended to apply only to tort claims and not to claims in other actions such as child support.

Rule 409 is consistent with North Carolina practice in that evidence inadmissible under the rule to prove liability may be admissible for another purpose. See Id. § 180, at 58–59 (1982). The rule is also consistent with North Carolina practice in that it does not bar evidence of conduct and statements outside of the simple act of furnishing or offering to pay medical expenses. As the Advisory Committee's Note states:

"Contrary to Rule 408, dealing with offers of compromise, the present rule does not extend to conduct or statements not a part of the act of furnishing or offering or promising to pay. This difference in treatment arises from fundamental differences in nature. Communication is essential if compromises are to be effected, and consequently broad protection of statements is needed. This is not so in cases of payments or offers or promises to pay medical expenses, where factual statements may be expected to be incidental in nature."

Rule 410. Inadmissibility of pleas, plea discussions, and related statements

Except as otherwise provided in this rule, evidence of the following is not, in any civil or criminal proceeding, admissible for or against the defendant who made the plea or was a participant in the plea discussions:

(1) A plea of guilty which was later withdrawn;

(2) A plea of no contest;

(3) Any statement made in the course of any proceedings under Article 58 of Chapter 15A of the General Statutes or comparable procedure in district court, or proceedings under Rule 11 of the Federal Rules of Criminal Procedure or comparable procedure in another state, regarding a plea of guilty which was later withdrawn or a plea of no contest;

(4) Any statement made in the course of plea discussions with an attorney for the prosecuting authority which do not result in a plea of guilty or which result in a plea of guilty later withdrawn.

However, such a statement is admissible in any proceeding wherein another statement made in the course of the same plea or plea discussions has been introduced and the statement ought in fairness be considered contemporaneously with it.

Added by Laws 1983, c. 701, § 1.

North Carolina Commentary

This rule is identical to Fed.R.Evid. 410, except as noted below.

The Advisory Committee's Note states:

"Withdrawn pleas of guilty were held inadmissible in federal prosecutions in Kercheval v. United States, 274 U.S. 220, 47 S.Ct. 582, 71 L.Ed. 1009 (1927). The Court pointed out that to admit the withdrawn plea would effectively set at naught the allowance of withdrawal and place the accused in a dilemma utterly inconsistent with the decision to award him a trial. The New York Court of Appeals, in People v. Spitaleri, 9 N.Y.2d 168, 212 N.Y.S.2d 53, 173 N.E.2d 35 (1961), reexamined and overturned its earlier decisions which had allowed admission. In addition to the reasons set forth in *Kercheval*, which was quoted at length, the court pointed out that the effect of admitting the plea was to compel defendant to take the stand by way of explanation and to open the way for the prosecution to call the lawyer who had represented him at the time of entering the plea. State court decisions for and against admissibility are collected in Annot., 86 A.L.R.2d 326."

Subsection (2), regarding pleas of no contest is the same as the federal rule and is consistent with North Carolina law. Brandis on North Carolina Evidence § 177, at 41, 42 (1982).

The third paragraph differs from Fed.R.Evid. 410 by making a reference to Article 58 of General Statutes Chapter 15A, which specifies the procedure relating to guilty pleas in superior court. The third paragraph also refers to comparable procedures in district court, although no statutory scheme regulates plea negotiations in district court. See Official Commentary to G.S. Ch. 15A, Art. 58.

Prior to the 1979 amendments to Fed.R.Evid. 410 and Fed.R.Crim.P. 11(e)(6), it was questionable whether an otherwise voluntary admission to law enforcement officials was rendered inadmissible merely because it was made in hope of obtaining leniency by a plea. The Notes of the Advisory Committee on the amendment to Fed.R.Crim.P. 11(e)(6) state that the rule:

"makes inadmissible statements made 'in the course of any proceedings under this rule regarding' either a plea of guilty later withdrawn or a plea of no contest later withdrawn and also statements 'made in the course of plea discussions with an attorney for the government which do not result in a plea of guilty or which result in a plea of guilty later withdrawn.' It is not limited to statements by the defendant himself, and thus would cover statements by defense counsel regarding defendant's incriminating admissions to him. It thus fully protects the plea discussion process . . . without attempting to deal with confrontations between suspects and law enforcement agents, which involve problems of quite different dimensions . . .. This change, it must be emphasized, does not compel the conclusion that statements made to law enforcement agents, especially when the agents purport to have authority to bargain, are inevitably admissible. Rather, the point is that such cases . . . must be resolved by that body of law dealing with police interrogations."

If there has been a plea of guilty later withdrawn or a plea of no contest, the third paragraph of Rule 410 makes inadmissible statements made in the course of any proceedings relating to guilty pleas in the superior or district courts. This includes, for example, admissions by the defendant when he makes his plea in court and also admissions made to provide the factual basis for the plea. However, the rule is not limited to statements made in court. If the court were to defer its decision on a plea agreement pending examination of the presentence report, statements made to the probation officer in connection with the preparation of that report would come within the third paragraph. See Notes of Advisory Committee on the Amendment to Fed. R.Crim.P. 11(e)(6).

The last sentence of Rule 410 provides an exception to the general rule of nonadmissibility of the described statements. Such a statement is admissible "in any proceedings wherein another statement made in the course of the same plea or plea discussions has been introduced and the statement ought in fairness be considered contemporaneously with it."

". . . when evidence of statements made in the course of or as a consequence of a certain plea or plea discussions are introduced under circumstances not prohibited by this rule (e.g., not 'against' the person who made the plea), other statements relating to the same plea or plea discussions may also be admitted when relevant to the matter at issue. For example, if a defendant upon a motion to dismiss a prosecution on some ground were able to admit certain statements made in aborted plea discussions in his favor, then other relevant statements made in the same plea discussions should be admissible against the defendant in the interest of determining the truth of the matter at issue. The language . . follows closely that in Fed.R.Evid. 106, as the considerations involved are very similar." Id.

Unlike the federal rule, Rule 410 does not contain an exception permitting a statement made by the defendant under oath, on the record, and in the presence of counsel to be introduced in a criminal proceeding for perjury or false statement.

Rule 410 differs from the federal rule by making the described evidence inadmissible in favor of the defendant as well as against him. North Carolina practice in this area is governed in part by G.S. 15A-1025 which is consistent with this rule. G.S. 15A-1025 should be amended after Rule 410 is adopted.

Rule 411. Liability insurance

Evidence that a person was or was not insured against liability is not admissible upon the issue whether he acted negligently or otherwise wrongfully. This rule does not require the exclusion of evidence of insurance against liability when offered for another purpose, such as proof of agency, ownership, or control, or bias or prejudice of a witness.

Added by Laws 1983, c. 701, § 1.

North Carolina Commentary

This rule is identical to Fed.R.Evid. 411. The Advisory Committee's Note states:

"The courts have with substantial unanimity rejected evidence of liability insurance for the purpose of proving fault, and absence of liability insurance as proof of lack of fault. At best the inference of fault from the fact of insurance coverage is a tenuous one, as is its converse. More important, no doubt, has been the feeling that knowledge of the presence or absence of liability insurance would induce juries to decide cases on improper grounds. McCormick § 168; Annot., 4 A.L.R.2d 761. The rule is drafted in broad terms so as to include contributory negligence or other fault of a plaintiff as well as fault of a defendant.

"The second sentence points out the limits of the rule, using well established illustrations. Id."

Rule 411 is consistent with North Carolina practice in barring evidence of insurance unless offered for a purpose other than to prove negligence. See Brandis on North Carolina Evidence § 88 (1982).

Rule 412. Rape or sex offense cases; relevance of victim's past behavior

(a) As used in this rule, the term "sexual behavior" means sexual activity of the complainant other than the sexual act which is at issue in the indictment on trial.

(b) Notwithstanding any other provision of law, the sexual behavior of the complainant is irrelevant to any issue in the prosecution unless such behavior:

(1) Was between the complainant and the defendant; or

(2) Is evidence of specific instances of sexual behavior offered for the purpose of showing that the act or acts charged were not committed by the defendant; or

(3) Is evidence of a pattern of sexual behavior so distinctive and so closely resembling the defendant's version of the alleged encounter with the complainant as to tend to prove that such complainant consented to the act or acts charged or behaved in such a manner as to lead the defendant reasonably to believe that the complainant consented; or

(4) Is evidence of sexual behavior offered as the basis of expert psychological or psychiatric opinion that the complainant fantasized or invented the act or acts charged.

(c) Sexual behavior otherwise admissible under this rule may not be proved by reputation or opinion.

(d) Notwithstanding any other provision of law, unless and until the court determines that evidence of sexual behavior is relevant under subdivision (b), no reference to this behavior may be made in the presence of the jury and no evidence of this behavior may be introduced at any time during the trial of:

(1) A charge of rape or a lesser included offense of rape;

(2) A charge of a sex offense or a lesser included offense of a sex offense; or

(3) An offense being tried jointly with a charge of rape or a sex offense, or with a lesser included offense of rape or a sex offense.

Before any questions pertaining to such evidence are asked of any witness, the proponent of such evidence shall first apply to the court for a determination of the relevance of the sexual behavior to which it relates. The proponent of such evidence may make application either prior to trial pursuant to G.S. 15A-952, or during the trial at the time when the proponent desires to introduce such evidence. When application is made, the court shall conduct an in camera hearing, which shall be transcribed, to consider the proponent's offer of proof and the argument of counsel, including any counsel for the complainant, to determine the extent to which such behavior is relevant. In the hearing, the proponent of the evidence shall establish the basis of admissibility of such evidence. Notwithstanding subdivision (b) of Rule 104, if the relevancy of the evidence which the proponent seeks to offer in the trial depends upon the fulfillment of a condition of fact, the court, at the in camera hearing or at a subsequent in camera hearing scheduled for that purpose, shall accept evidence on the issue of whether that condition of fact is fulfilled and shall determine that issue. If the court finds that the evidence is relevant, it shall enter an order stating that the evidence may be admitted and the nature of the questions which will be permitted.

(e) The record of the in camera hearing and all evidence relating thereto shall be open to inspection only by the parties, the complainant, their attorneys and the court and its agents, and shall be used only as necessary for appellate review. At any probable cause hearing, the judge shall take cognizance of the evidence, if admissible, at the end of the in camera hearing without the questions being repeated or the evidence being resubmitted in open court.

Added by Laws 1983, c. 701, § 1.

North Carolina Commentary

This rule differs substantially from Fed.R.Evid. 412. Except as noted below, the rule is the same as the current shield law, G.S. 8–58.6.

Subdivision (c), which is derived from the federal rule, was added to the current shield law to make it clear that sexual behavior otherwise admissible under this rule may not be proved by reputation or opinion.

The next to the last sentence of **subdivision (d),** which is derived from the federal rule, was added to the shield law to address the issue of conditional relevancy. The sentence provides that, notwithstanding Rule 104(b), if the relevancy of the evidence depends upon the fulfillment of a condition of fact, the court will hear evidence in the in camera proceeding and decide whether the condition of fact is fulfilled. The court should decide whether the defendant has presented sufficient evidence for a reasonable jury to find the proposition asserted to be true. If so, the defendant's evidence should be admitted. If not, the evidence should be excluded. See S. Saltzburg and K. Redden, Federal Rules of Evidence Manual, at 221–27 (3d ed.1982). Evidence should not be admitted on behalf of the defendant subject to connecting-up. The court should make sure, before any evidence of prior sexual activity is admitted, that the conditional relevance analysis has been satisfied. Id. at 90.

Rule 413. Medical actions; statements to ameliorate or mitigate adverse outcome

Statements by a health care provider apologizing for an adverse outcome in medical treatment, offers to undertake corrective or remedial treatment or actions, and gratuitous acts to assist affected persons shall not be admissible to prove negligence or culpable conduct by the health care provider in an action brought under Article 1B of Chapter 90 of the General Statutes.

Added by S.L. 2004-149, § 3.1, eff. Aug. 2, 2004.

Rule 414. Evidence of medical expenses

Evidence offered to prove past medical expenses shall be limited to evidence of the amounts actually paid to satisfy the bills that have been satisfied, regardless of the source of payment, and evidence of the amounts actually necessary to satisfy the bills that have been incurred but not yet satisfied. This rule does not impose upon any party an affirmative duty to seek a reduction in billed charges to which the party is not contractually entitled.

Added by S.L. 2011-283, § 1.1, eff. Oct. 1, 2011.

Editor's Note

S.L. 2011-283, §§ 4.1 and 4.2 provide:

"Section 4.1. Severability.—If any provision of this act or its application to any person or circumstance is held invalid, the remainder of this act or the application of the provision to other persons or circumstances is not affected."

"Section 4.2. Section 4.1(a) of this act is effective when it becomes law. The remainder of this act becomes effective October 1, 2011, and applies to actions arising on or after that date." [Amended by S.L. 2011-317, § 1.1, eff. Oct. 1, 2011.]

ARTICLE 5

Privileges

Rule 501. General rule

Except as otherwise required by the Constitution of the United States, the privileges of a witness, person, government, state, or political subdivision thereof shall be determined in accordance with the law of this State.

Added by Laws 1983, c. 701, § 1.

North Carolina Commentary

This rule differs from Fed.R.Evid. 501. After reviewing the rules on privilege proposed by the Supreme Court, Congress rejected the proposal and substituted a rule that applies the common law of privileges in federal civil and criminal cases. In civil actions in which state law supplies the rule of decision, the state law on privileges applies.

The Uniform Rules of Evidence (1974) adopted the federal draft and several states have modeled their privilege laws on the federal draft. However, there is not a great deal of uniformity among the federal courts and various states with respect to privileges. Adoption of the federal draft would modify and delete privileges currently recognized in North Carolina and add other privileges currently not recognized in North Carolina.

Because of the extensive effort needed to clarify this confused area, the Committee decided not to draft new rules of privilege at this time but to continue the present statutory and common law system. See generally Brandis on North Carolina Evidence § 54 et seq. (1982).

ARTICLE 6

Witnesses

Rule 601. General rule of competency; disqualification of witness

(a) General rule.—Every person is competent to be a witness except as otherwise provided in these rules.

(b) Disqualification of witness in general.—A person is disqualified to testify as a witness when the court determines that the person is (1) incapable of expressing himself or herself concerning the matter as to be understood, either directly or through interpretation by one who can understand him or her, or (2) incapable of understanding the duty of a witness to tell the truth.

(c) Disqualification of interested persons.—Upon the trial of an action, or the hearing upon the merits of a special proceeding, a party or a person interested in the event, or a person from, through or under whom such a party or interested person derives his or her interest or title by assignment or otherwise, shall not be examined as a witness in his or her own behalf or interest, or in behalf of the party succeeding to his or her title or interest, against the executor, administrator or survivor of a deceased person, or the guardian of an incompetent person, or a person deriving his or her title or interest from, through or under a deceased or incompetent person by assignment or otherwise, concerning any oral communication between the witness and the deceased or incompetent person. However, this subdivision shall not apply when:

(1) The executor, administrator, survivor, guardian, or person so deriving title or interest is examined in his or her own behalf regarding the subject matter of the oral communication.

(2) The testimony of the deceased or incompetent person is given in evidence concerning the same transaction or communication.

(3) Evidence of the subject matter of the oral communication is offered by the executor, administrator, survivor, guardian or person so deriving title or interest.

Nothing in this subdivision shall preclude testimony as to the identity of the operator of a motor vehicle in any case.

Added by Laws 1983, c. 701, § 1. Amended by S.L. 2011–29, § 2, eff. April 7, 2011.

North Carolina Commentary

Subdivision (a) is identical to the first sentence of Fed.R.Evid. 601. The second sentence of Fed. R.Evid. 601 concerns the application of state law in diversity cases and was omitted. Fed.R.Evid. 601 does not contain subdivision (b) on disqualification of a witness.

This rule eliminates all grounds of incompetency not specifically recognized in subdivision (b) or (c) of the succeeding rules in this Article.

At common law husband and wife were incompetent to testify in an action to which either was a party. However, by statute, each spouse has been competent to testify for or against the other in all civil actions and proceedings, with two rigidly defined exceptions. One exception makes one spouse incompetent to testify "for or against the other . . . in any action or proceeding for or on account of criminal conversation . . .." G.S. 8–56. With respect to this exception Professor Brandis states:

> "It is hard to find a purpose except one based on notions of delicacy, and even this is frustrated by permitting the plaintiff husband to testify to his wife's improper relations with the defendant. Danger of collusion would seem to be no greater than in any other case, and the interest of the state in the marriage relation, which only doubtfully justifies extreme measures to prevent collusion in divorce litigation, is no excuse for a rule of incompetency in criminal conversation actions." Brandis on North Carolina Evidence § 58, at 232, n. 28 (1982).

The other exception bars a spouse from testifying "for or against the other in any action or proceeding in consequence of adultery." G.S. 8–56. This exception is supplemented by G.S. 50–10 which provides that in divorce actions "neither the husband nor the wife shall be a competent witness to prove the adultery of the other, nor shall the admissions of either party be received as evidence to prove such fact." With respect to this exception, Professor Brandis notes that if the original purpose was to prevent collusion in divorce actions, "[I]t would seem that the prohibition should have been repealed when a relatively short period of separation was made a ground for divorce." Brandis on North Carolina Evidence § 58, at 230, n. 20 (1982).

At common law the spouse of a criminal defendant was incompetent to testify. This incompetence was removed by G.S. 8–57 so far as testifying for the defendant was concerned. With respect to testimony against the other spouse, G.S. 8–57 left in force the common law rule of incompetence. In State v. Freeman, 302 N.C. 591 [276 S.E.2d 450] (1981), the court removed the incompetence to testify against the other spouse (except to the extent that it preserved the privilege against disclosure of confidential communications). During the 1983 Legislative Session G.S. 8–57 was rewritten and now provides that the spouse of the defendant is competent but not compellable to testify for the State against the defendant except that the spouse is both competent and compellable to testify in the following cases:

(1) In a prosecution for bigamy or criminal cohabitation, to prove the fact of marriage and facts tending to show the absence of divorce or annulment;

(2) In a prosecution for assaulting or communicating a threat to the other spouse;

(3) In a prosecution for trespass in or upon the separate lands or residence of the other spouse when living separate and apart from each other by mutual consent or court order;

(4) In a prosecution for abandonment of or failure to provide support for the other spouse or their child;

(5) In a prosecution of one spouse for any other criminal offense against the minor child of either spouse, including any illegitimate or adopted or foster child of either spouse.

The provisions of the previous G.S. 8–57 which provided that the spouse is a competent witness for the defendant in a criminal action and which also provided that a spouse was not compellable to disclose any confidential communication made by one to the other during their marriage are retained in the rewrite of the statute.

Upon adoption of Rule 601, G.S. 8–56 and 50–10 should be rewritten to make it clear that a husband or wife are competent to testify. The privilege against disclosure of confidential communications should be retained.

Subdivision (b) establishes a minimum standard for competency of a witness and is consistent with North Carolina practice. See Brandis on North Carolina Evidence § 55 (1982).

Subdivision (c) represents a narrowing of the scope of G.S. 8–51, the Dead Man's Statute. The Dead Man's Statute will now be applicable only to oral communications between the party interested in the event and the deceased person or lunatic, rather than to "a personal transaction or communication between the witness and the deceased person or lunatic." Subdivision (c) preserves the exceptions already existing in G.S. 8–51 and adds subsection (3) which is a statement of the North Carolina case law having to do with one way in which "the door can be opened." See Carswell v. Greene, 253 N.C. 266, 270 [116 S.E.2d 801] (1960); Brandis on North Carolina Evidence § 75, at 282, 283 (1982).

It was not the intent of the drafters of subdivision (c) to change any existing cases where the Dead Man's Statute has been held to be inapplicable, or where, because of the actions of one party or the other the protection of the rule has been held to be waived. For example, subdivision (c) would not change the results in Smith v. Perdue, 258 N.C. 686 [129 S.E.2d 293] (1963) or In re Chisman, 175 N.C. 420 [95 S.E. 769] (1918). The report of the Legislative Research Commission's Study Committee on the Laws of Evidence to the 1983 General Assembly did not contain subdivision (c), nor did the original versions of House Bill 96 and Senate Bill 43. This would have completely eliminated the Dead Man's Statute, which has been much criticized. In Professor Brandis' view, for example:

> "[T]he statute has fostered more injustice than it has prevented and has led to an unholy waste of the time and ingenuity of judges and counsel. The situation calls for more than legislative tinkering. What is needed is repeal of the statute." Brandis on North Carolina Evidence § 66 at 258, n. 62 (1982).

However, subdivision (c) was added to Rule 601 because of a concern that fraud and hardship could result if an interested party could testify concerning an oral communication with the deceased or lunatic.

G.S. 8–51 should be repealed after this rule is adopted.

Rule 602. Lack of personal knowledge

A witness may not testify to a matter unless evidence is introduced sufficient to support a finding that he has personal knowledge of the matter. Evidence to prove personal knowledge may, but need not, consist of the testimony of the witness himself. This rule is subject to the provisions of Rule 703, relating to opinion testimony by expert witnesses.

Added by Laws 1983, c. 701, § 1.

North Carolina Commentary

This rule, which is identical to Fed.R.Evid. 602, restates the traditional common-law rule in North Carolina barring a witness from testifying to a fact of which he has no direct personal knowledge. See Robbins v. C.W. Myers Trading Post, Inc., 251 N.C. 663 [111 S.E.2d 884] (1960). A witness who testifies to a fact which can be perceived by the senses must have had an opportunity to observe and must have actually observed the facts. The Advisory Committee's Note states that:

> "These foundation requirements may, of course, be furnished by the testimony of the witness himself; hence personal knowledge is not an absolute but may consist of what the witness thinks he knows from personal perception. . . . It will be observed that the rule is in fact a specialized application of the provisions of Rule 104(b) on conditional relevancy."

Preliminary determination of personal knowledge need not be explicit but may be implied from the witness' testimony.

Rule 602 applies to hearsay statements admitted under the hearsay exception rules in that admissibility of a hearsay statement is predicated on the foundation requirement of the witness' personal knowledge of the making of the statement itself. However, it is not intended that firsthand knowledge be required where a hearsay exception necessarily embraces secondhand knowledge (e.g. Rules 803(8)(C) and 803(23)).

Rule 602 is subject to Rule 703 relating to expert witnesses.

Rule 603. Oath or affirmation

Before testifying, every witness shall be required to declare that he will testify truthfully, by oath or affirmation administered in a form calculated to awaken his conscience and impress his mind with his duty to do so.

Added by Laws 1983, c. 701, § 1.

North Carolina Commentary

This rule is identical to Fed.R.Evid. 603 and is in accord with North Carolina practice. The Advisory Committee's Note states that:

> "The rule is designed to afford the flexibility required in dealing with religious adults, atheists, conscientious objectors, mental defectives, and children. Affirmation is simply a solemn undertaking to tell the truth; no special verbal formula is required."

Rule 604. Interpreters

An interpreter is subject to the provisions of these rules relating to qualification as an expert and the administration of an oath or affirmation that he will make a true translation.

Added by Laws 1983, c. 701, § 1.

North Carolina Commentary

This rule is identical to Fed.R.Evid. 604. There are no North Carolina cases on this point.

Rule 605. Competency of judge as witness

The judge presiding at the trial may not testify in that trial as a witness. No objection need be made in order to preserve the point.

Added by Laws 1983, c. 701, § 1.

North Carolina Commentary

This rule, which is identical to Fed.R.Evid. 605, prevents a judge from testifying in a trial over which he is presiding. The Advisory Committee's Note states that:

"The rule provides for an 'automatic objection'. To require an actual objection would confront the opponent with a choice between not objecting, with the result of allowing the testimony, and objecting, with the probable result of excluding the testimony but at the price of continuing the trial before a judge likely to feel that his integrity had been attacked by the objector."

G.S. 15A–1223 requires a judge in a criminal case to disqualify himself if he is a witness in the case upon motion of the State or the defendant. Upon adoption of Rule 605, a conforming amendment should be made to G.S. 15A–1223 to remove the requirement for a motion to disqualify.

The question of whether a judge may testify in civil proceedings over which he is presiding does not appear to have arisen in North Carolina. See Brandis on North Carolina Evidence § 53, at 198 (1982).

Rule 606. Competency of juror as witness

(a) At the trial.—A member of the jury may not testify as a witness before that jury in the trial of the case in which he is sitting as a juror. If he is called so to testify, the opposing party shall be afforded an opportunity to object out of the presence of the jury.

(b) Inquiry into validity of verdict or indictment.—Upon an inquiry into the validity of a verdict or indictment, a juror may not testify as to any matter or statement occurring during the course of the jury's deliberations or to the effect of anything upon his or any other juror's mind or emotions as influencing him to assent to or dissent from the verdict or indictment or concerning his mental processes in connection therewith, except that a juror may testify on the question whether extraneous prejudicial information was improperly brought to the jury's attention or whether any outside influence was improperly brought to bear upon any juror. Nor may his affidavit or evidence of any statement by him concerning a matter about which he would be precluded from testifying be received for these purposes.

Added by Laws 1983, c. 701, § 1.

North Carolina Commentary

This rule is identical to Fed.R.Evid. 606.

Subdivision (a) provides that a juror may not testify as a witness in the trial in which he is sitting as a juror. There are no North Carolina cases on this point.

The Advisory Committee's Note to subdivision (a) states:

"The considerations which bear upon the permissibility of testimony by a juror in the trial in which he is sitting as juror bear an obvious similarity to those evoked when the judge is called as a witness. See Advisory Committee's Note to Rule 605. The judge is not, however, in this instance so involved as to call for departure from usual principles requiring objection to be made; hence the only provision on objection is that opportunity be afforded for its making out of the presence of the jury. Compare Rule 605."

Subdivision (b) concerns an inquiry into the validity of a verdict or indictment. The Advisory Committee's Note states:

"Whether testimony, affidavits, or statements of jurors should be received for the purpose of invalidating or supporting a verdict or indictment, and if so, under what circumstances, has given rise to substantial differences of opinion. The familiar rubric that a juror may not impeach his own verdict, dating from Lord Mansfield's time, is a gross oversimplification. The values sought to be promoted by excluding the evidence include freedom of deliberation, stability and finality of verdicts, and protection of jurors against annoyance and embarrassment. McDonald v. Pless, 238 U.S. 264 [35 S.Ct. 783, 59 L.Ed. 1300] (1915). On the other hand, simply putting verdicts beyond effective reach can only promote irregularity and injustice. The rule offers an accommodation between these competing considerations.

"The mental operations and emotional reactions of jurors in arriving at a given result would, if allowed as a subject of inquiry, place every verdict at the mercy of jurors and invite tampering and harassment. . . . The authorities are in virtually complete accord in excluding the evidence. . . . As to matters other than mental operations and emotional reactions of jurors, substantial authority refuses to allow a juror to disclose irregularities which occur in the jury room, but allows his testimony as to irregularities occurring outside and allows outsiders to testify as to occurrences both inside and out. . . . However, the door of the jury room is not necessarily a satisfactory dividing point, and the Supreme Court has refused to accept it for every situation. Mattox v. United States, 146 U.S. 140 [13 S.Ct. 50, 36 L.Ed. 917], . . . (1892). Under the federal decisions the central focus has been upon insulation in the manner in which the jury reached its verdict, and this protection extends to each of the components of deliberation, including arguments, statements, discussions, mental and emotional reactions, votes, and any other feature of the process. Thus testimony or affidavits of jurors have been held incompetent to show a compromise verdict, Hyde v. United States, 225 U.S. 347, 382 [32 S.Ct. 793, 56 L.Ed. 1114] (1912); a quotient verdict, McDonald v. Pless, 238 U.S. 264 [35 S.Ct. 783, 59 L.Ed. 1300] (1915); speculation as to insurance coverage, Holden v. Porter, 405 F.2d 878 (10th Cir.1969); Farmers Coop. Elev. Ass'n v. Strand, 382 F.2d 224, 230 (8th Cir.1967), cert. denied, 389 U.S. 1014 [88 S.Ct. 589, 19 L.Ed.2d 659]; misinterpretation of instructions, Farmers Coop. Elev. Ass'n v. Strand, supra; mistake in returning verdict, United States v. Chereton, 309 F.2d 197 (6th Cir.1962); interpretation of guilty plea by one defendant as implicating others, United States v. Crosby, 294 F.2d 928, 949 (2d Cir. 1961). The policy does not, however, foreclose testimony by jurors as to prejudicial extraneous information or influences injected into or brought to bear upon the deliberative process. Thus a juror is recognized as competent to testify to statements by the bailiff or the introduction of a prejudicial newspaper account into the jury room, Mattox v. United States, 146 U.S. 140 [13 S.Ct. 50, 36 L.Ed. 917] (1892). See also Parker v. Gladden, 385 U.S. 363 [87 S.Ct. 468, 17 L.Ed.2d 420] (1966)."

The exclusion is intended to encompass testimony about mental processes and testimony about any matter or statement occurring during the deliberations, except that testimony of either of these two types can be admitted if it relates to extraneous prejudicial information or improper outside influence.

The general rule in North Carolina has been that a juror's testimony or affidavit will not be received to impeach the verdict of the jury. Brandis on North Carolina Evidence § 65 (1982). The North Carolina rule, unlike Rule 606, does not apply to attempts to support a verdict. Id. An express, though limited exception to the anti-impeachment rule is provided in G.S. 15A-1240, which should be amended to conform to Rule 606.

Also, the Advisory Committee's Note states:

"This rule does not purport to specify the substantive grounds for setting aside verdicts for irregularity; it deals only with the competency of jurors to testify concerning those grounds. Allowing them to testify as to matters other than their own inner reactions involves no particular hazard to the values sought to be protected. The rule is based upon this conclusion. It makes no attempt to specify the substantive grounds for setting aside verdicts for irregularity."

Rule 607. Who may impeach

The credibility of a witness may be attacked by any party, including the party calling him.

Added by Laws 1983, c. 701, § 1.

North Carolina Commentary

This rule is identical to Fed.R.Evid. 607. The rule abandons the traditional common law rule that a party "vouches" for a witness by calling him and, therefore, may not impeach his own witness. The traditional rule has been the subject of numerous exceptions. See N.C.Civ.Pro.Rule 43(b); Brandis on North Carolina Evidence § 40 (1982). The substantial inroads into the old rule made by statutes and decisions are evidence of doubts as to its basic soundness and workability. As the Advisory Committee's Note states:

"The traditional rule against impeaching one's own witness is abandoned as based on false premises. A party does not hold out his witnesses as worthy of belief, since he rarely has a free choice in selecting them. Denial of the right leaves the party at the mercy of the witness and the adversary."

The impeaching proof must be relevant within the meaning of Rule 401 and Rule 403 and must in fact be impeaching. See Ordover, Surprise! That Damaging Turncoat Witness Is Still With Us, 5 Hofstra L.Rev. 65, 70 (1976).

Rule 608. Evidence of character and conduct of witness

(a) Opinion and reputation evidence of character.—The credibility of a witness may be attacked or supported by evidence in the form of reputation or opinion as provided in Rule 405(a), but subject to these limitations: (1) the evidence may refer only to character for truthfulness or untruthfulness, and (2) evidence of truthful character is admissible only after the character of the witness for truthfulness has been attacked by opinion or reputation evidence or otherwise.

(b) Specific instances of conduct.—Specific instances of the conduct of a witness, for the purpose of attacking or supporting his credibility, other than conviction of crime as provided in Rule 609, may not be proved by extrinsic evidence. They may, however, in the discretion of the court, if probative of truthfulness or untruthfulness, be inquired into on cross-examination of the witness (1) concerning his character for truthfulness or untruthfulness, or (2) concerning the character for truthfulness or untruthfulness of another witness as to which character the witness being cross-examined has testified.

The giving of testimony, whether by an accused or by any other witness, does not operate as a waiver of his privilege against self-incrimination when examined with respect to matters which relate only to credibility.

Added by Laws 1983, c. 701, § 1.

North Carolina Commentary

This rule is identical to Fed.R.Evid. 608, except for the addition of the phrase "as provided in Rule 405(a)" to subdivision (a).

Subdivision (a) allows the credibility of a witness to be attacked or supported by evidence in the form of reputation or opinion. Admitting opinion evidence to prove character is a change in North Carolina practice. See Commentary to Rule 405. The reference to Rule 405(a) is to make it clear that expert testimony on the credibility of a witness is not admissible.

The rule in North Carolina has been that evidence of a specific trait of character is admissible only if asked on cross-examination or if "volunteered" by the witness on direct examination in answer to a question which asks if the witness knows the general reputation or reputation and character of the subject. In both cases, the witness may testify to character traits that are wholly irrelevant to any issue in the case. Brandis on North Carolina Evidence §§ 114, 115 (1982). The North Carolina rule is unique, and appears to have its origin in a misinterpretation of earlier opinions. Id. § 114.

The first limitation of subdivision (a) changes this result by confining evidence of specific traits of a witness to character for truthfulness or untruthfulness and permitting counsel to ask questions regarding these traits on direct examination or cross-examination. However, evidence of *truthfulness* is permitted only after the character of the witness for truthfulness has been attacked.

In North Carolina the necessity for impeachment as a prerequisite to corroboration has been more theoretical than real. Id. § 50. Adoption of this rule strengthens the limitation. The Advisory Committee's Note states that:

"Opinion or reputation that the witness is untruthful specifically qualifies as an attack under the rule, and evidence of misconduct, including conviction of crime, and of corruption also fall within this category. Evidence of bias or interest does not. McCormick § 49; 4 Wigmore §§ 1106, 1107. Whether evidence in the form of contradiction is an attack upon the character of the witness must depend upon the circumstances. McCormick § 49. (Cf. 4 Wigmore §§ 1108, 1109)."

As to the use of specific instances on direct by an opinion witness, see the Commentary to Rule 405, supra.

Subdivision (b) generally bars evidence of specific instances of conduct of a witness for the purpose of attacking or supporting his credibility. Evidence of wrongful acts admissible under Rule 404(b) is not within this rule and is admissible by extrinsic evidence or by cross-examination of any witness.

There are two exceptions under subdivision (b). Conviction of a crime as a technique of impeachment is treated in detail in Rule 609 and is merely recognized in this rule as an exception to the general rule excluding evidence of specific incidents for impeachment purposes.

The second exception allows particular instances of conduct, though not the subject of criminal conviction, to be inquired into on cross-examination of the principal witness himself or of a witness who testifies concerning his character for truthfulness. Current North Carolina practice allows only inquiry concerning the specific acts of the principal witness himself. Brandis on North Carolina Evidence §§ 111, 115 (1982). The Advisory Committee's Note states that:

"Effective cross-examination demands that some allowance be made for going into matters of this kind, but the possibilities of abuse are substantial. Consequently safeguards are erected in the form of specific requirements that the instances inquired into be probative of truthfulness or its opposite and not remote in time. Also, the overriding protection of Rule 403 requires that the probative value not be outweighed by danger of unfair prejudice, confusion of issues, or misleading the jury, and that of Rule 611 bars harassment and undue embarrassment."

The last sentence of Rule 608 constitutes a rejection of the doctrine of such cases as State v. Foster, 284 N.C. 259 [200 S.E.2d 782] (1973), that any past criminal act relevant to credibility may be inquired into on cross-examination, in apparent disregard of the privilege against self-incrimination. As the Advisory Committee's Note states:

"While it is clear that an ordinary witness cannot make a partial disclosure of incriminating matter and then invoke the privilege on cross-examination, no tenable contention can be made that merely by testifying he waives his right to foreclose inquiry on cross-examination into criminal activities for the purpose of attacking his credibility. So to hold would reduce the privilege to a nullity. While it is true that an accused, unlike an ordinary witness, has an option whether to testify, if the option can be exercised only at the price of opening up inquiry as to any and all criminal acts committed during his lifetime, the right to testify could scarcely be said to possess much vitality. In Griffin v. California, 380 U.S. 609, 85 S.Ct. 1229, 14 L.Ed.2d 106 (1965), the Court held that allowing comment on the election of an accused not to testify exacted a constitutionally impermissible price, and so here. While no specific provision in terms confers constitutional status on the right of an accused to take the stand in his own defense, the existence of the right is so completely recognized that a denial of it or substantial infringement upon it would surely be of due process dimensions. See Ferguson v. Georgia, 365 U.S. 570, 81 S.Ct. 756, 5 L.Ed.2d 783 (1961); McCormick § 131; 8 Wigmore § 2276 (McNaughton Rev.1961). In any event, wholly aside from constitutional considerations, the provision represents a sound policy."

See Brandis on North Carolina Evidence § 111, at 409, n. 28 (1982).

Rule 609. Impeachment by evidence of conviction of crime

(a) General rule.—For the purpose of attacking the credibility of a witness, evidence that the witness has been convicted of a felony, or of a Class A1, Class 1, or Class 2 misdemeanor, shall be admitted if elicited from the witness or established by public record during cross-examination or thereafter.

(b) Time limit.—Evidence of a conviction under this rule is not admissible if a period of more than 10 years has elapsed since the date of the conviction or of the release of the witness from the confinement imposed for that conviction, whichever is the later date, unless the court determines, in the interests of justice, that the probative value of the conviction supported by specific facts and circumstances substantially outweighs its prejudicial effect. However, evidence of a conviction more than 10 years old as calculated herein is not admissible unless the proponent gives to the adverse party sufficient advance written notice of intent to use such evidence to provide the adverse party with a fair opportunity to contest the use of such evidence.

(c) Effect of pardon.—Evidence of a conviction is not admissible under this rule if the conviction has been pardoned.

(d) Juvenile adjudications.—Evidence of juvenile adjudications is generally not admissible under this rule. The court may, however, in a criminal case allow evidence of a juvenile adjudication of a witness other than the accused if conviction of the offense would be admissible to attack the credibility of an adult and the court is satisfied that admission in evidence is necessary for a fair determination of the issue of guilt or innocence.

(e) Pendency of appeal.—The pendency of an appeal therefrom does not render evidence of a conviction inadmissible. Evidence of the pendency of an appeal is admissible.

Added by Laws 1983, c. 701, § 1. Amended by S.L. 1999-79, § 1.

North Carolina Commentary

Subdivision (a) differs from Fed.R.Evid. 609(a), which permits, for purposes of attacking the credibility of a witness, evidence of conviction of a felony or a crime that involves dishonesty or false statement. The current practice in North Carolina is that any sort of criminal offense may be the subject of inquiry for the purpose of attacking credibility.

Subdivision (a) provides that evidence of a crime punishable by more than 60 days confinement shall be admissible. This is the standard used in the Fair Sentencing Act in defining an aggravating factor. See G.S. 15A-1340.4(a)(1)(*o*). This includes convictions occurring in other states, the District of Columbia, and the United States even though the crime for which the defendant was convicted would not have been a crime if committed in this state.

Under current North Carolina practice a witness' denial of a prior conviction "may not be contradicted by introducing the record of his conviction or otherwise proving by other witnesses that he was, in fact, convicted." However, this prohibition has often been circumvented. Brandis on North Carolina Evidence § 112, at 414 (1982). Subdivision (a) allows the record of the conviction to be introduced.

Subdivision (a) also deletes the requirement in Fed.R.Evid. 609(a) that the court determine that the probative value of admitting evidence of the prior conviction outweighs its prejudicial effect to the defendant.

Subdivision (b) is identical to Fed.R.Evid. 609(b) and departs from the common law in North Carolina in providing a time limit on the use of prior convictions. Generally, evidence of a prior conviction is not admissible under subdivision (b) if more than 10 years has elapsed since the date of the conviction or of the release of the witness from confinement imposed for the conviction, whichever is the later date. Evidence of such a conviction is admissible, however, if the court determines, in the interests of justice, that the probative value of the conviction supported by specific facts and circumstances substantially outweighs its prejudicial effect. A party must give written notice if he intends to use a conviction falling outside the 10-year period.

Subdivision (c) differs from Fed.R.Evid. 609(c) and provides an absolute prohibition of evidence of a conviction that has been pardoned. Current North Carolina practice does not prohibit evidence of such convictions.

Subdivision (d) is identical to Fed.R.Evid. 609(d) and provides that evidence of a juvenile adjudication is generally inadmissible. However, the court in a criminal case may "allow evidence of a juvenile adjudication of a witness other than the accused if conviction of the offense would be admissible to attack the credibility of an adult and the court is satisfied that admission in evidence is necessary for a fair determination of the issue of guilt or innocence." This is intended to satisfy the requirement of Davis v. Alaska, 415 U.S. 308 [94 S.Ct. 1105, 39 L.Ed.2d 347] (1974). G.S. 7A-677, which provides that the defendant or another witness in a criminal case may be ordered to testify with respect to whether he was adjudicated delinquent, should be amended to conform to this subdivision. Conforming amendments also should be made to G.S. 15-223(b), G.S. 90-96, and G.S. 90-113.14.

Subdivision (e) is the same as Fed.R.Evid. 609(e) and conforms to current North Carolina practice. See Brandis on North Carolina Evidence § 112, at 411 (1982).

Rule 610. Religious beliefs or opinions

Evidence of the beliefs or opinions of a witness on matters of religion is not admissible for the purpose of showing that by reason of their nature his credibility is impaired or enhanced; provided, however, such evidence may be admitted for the purpose of showing interest or bias.

Added by Laws 1983, c. 701, § 1.

North Carolina Commentary

This rule is identical to Fed.R.Evid. 610 except for the proviso that explicitly states that evidence of religious beliefs or opinions may be admitted to show interest or bias. The rule clarifies unsettled law in North Carolina concerning whether, for impeachment purposes, a witness may be cross-examined as to his religious beliefs. See Brandis on North Carolina Evidence § 55, at 205 (1982). Evidence probative of something other than veracity is not prohibited by the rule.

Rule 611. Mode and order of interrogation and presentation

(a) Control by court.—The court shall exercise reasonable control over the mode and order of interrogating witnesses and presenting evidence so as to (1) make the interrogation and presentation effective for the ascertainment of the truth, (2) avoid needless consumption of time, and (3) protect witnesses from harassment or undue embarrassment.

(b) Scope of cross-examination.—A witness may be cross-examined on any matter relevant to any issue in the case, including credibility.

(c) Leading questions.—Leading questions should not be used on the direct examination of a witness except as may be necessary to develop his testimony. Ordinarily leading questions should be permitted on cross-examination. When a party calls a hostile witness, an adverse party, or a witness identified with an adverse party, interrogation may be by leading questions.

Added by Laws 1983, c. 701, § 1.

North Carolina Commentary

This rule, except for subdivision (b), is identical to Fed.R.Evid. 611.

The rule sets forth the objectives the court should seek to obtain rather than spelling out detailed rules. Specific statutes relating to the mode and order of interrogating witnesses and presenting evidence, e.g., G.S. 15A–1226 dealing with when rebuttal evidence may be presented, will not be overridden by the general guidelines set by this rule.

The Advisory Committee's Note says that:

"Item (1) restates in broad terms the power and obligation of the judge as developed under common law principles. It covers such concerns as whether testimony shall be in the form of a free narrative or responses to specific questions, McCormick § 5, the order of calling witnesses and presenting evidence, 6 Wigmore § 1867, the use of demonstrative evidence, McCormick § 179, and the many other questions arising during the course of a trial which can be solved only by the judge's common sense and fairness in view of the particular circumstances.

"Item (2) is addressed to avoidance of needless consumption of time, a matter of daily concern in the disposition of cases. A companion piece is found in the discretion vested in the judge to exclude evidence as a waste of time in Rule 403(b).

"Item (3) calls for a judgment under the particular circumstances whether interrogation tactics entail harassment or undue embarrassment. Pertinent circumstances include the importance of the testimony, the nature of the inquiry, its relevance to credibility, waste of time, and confusion. McCormick § 42. In Alford v. United States, 282 U.S. 687, 694, 51 S.Ct. 218, 75 L.Ed. 624 (1931), the Court pointed out that, while the trial judge should protect the witness from questions which 'go beyond the bounds of proper cross-examination merely to harass, annoy or humiliate,' this protection by no means forecloses efforts to discredit the witness. Reference to the transcript of the prosecutor's cross-examination in Berger v. United States, 295 U.S. 78, 55 S.Ct. 629, 79 L.Ed. 1314 (1935), serves to lay at rest any doubts as to the need for judicial control in this area.

"The inquiry into specific instances of conduct of a witness allowed under Rule 608(b) is, of course, subject to this rule."

Subdivision (b) deals with the scope of cross-examination. "In North Carolina the substantive cross-examination is not confined to the subject matter of direct testimony plus impeachment, but may extend to any matter relevant to the issues." Brandis on North Carolina Evidence § 35, at 143 (1982). Subdivision (b) rejects the more restricted approach to cross-examination found in Fed.R.Evid. 611(b) and adopts the current North Carolina wide-open cross-examination rule.

Subdivision (c) continues the traditional view that the suggestive powers of the leading question are as general propositions undesirable. Within this tradition numerous exceptions have achieved recognition: The witness who is hostile, unwilling or biased; the child witness or the adult with communication problems; the witness whose recollection is exhausted; and undisputed preliminary matters. 3 Wigmore §§ 774–778; State v. Greene, 285 N.C. 482 [206 S.E.2d 229] (1974). As the Advisory Committee's Note points out: "The matter clearly falls within the area of control by the judge over the mode and order of interrogation and presentation and accordingly is phrased in words of suggestion rather than command."

The Note states that:

"The rule also conforms to tradition in making the use of leading questions on cross-examination a matter of right. The purpose of the qualification 'ordinarily' is to furnish a basis for denying the use of leading questions when the cross-examination is cross-examination in form only and not in fact, as for example the 'cross-examination' of a party by his own counsel after being called by the opponent (savoring more of redirect) or of an insured defendant who proves to be friendly to the plaintiff."

The last sentence of subdivision (c) deals with categories of witnesses automatically regarded and treated as hostile. N.C.Civ.Pro.Rule 43(b) permits leading questions to "an adverse party or an agent or employee of an adverse party, or an officer, director, or employee of a private corporation or of a partnership or association which is an adverse party, or an officer, agent or employee of a state, county or municipal government or agency thereof which is an adverse party." The phrase of the rule "witness identified with" an adverse party is designed to enlarge the category of witnesses who may safely be regarded as hostile without further demonstration. Upon adoption of this rule, N.C.Civ.Pro.Rule 43(b) should be repealed. N.C.Civ.Pro.Rule 30 should be amended to state that depositions are subject to the North Carolina Rules of Evidence.

Rule 612. Writing or object used to refresh memory

(a) While testifying.—If, while testifying, a witness uses a writing or object to refresh his memory, an adverse party is entitled to have the writing or object produced at the trial, hearing, or deposition in which the witness is testifying.

(b) Before testifying.—If, before testifying, a witness uses a writing or object to refresh his memory for the purpose of testifying and the court in its discretion determines that the interests of justice so require, an adverse party is entitled to have those portions of any writing or of the object which relate to the testimony produced, if practicable, at the trial, hearing, or deposition in which the witness is testifying.

(c) Terms and conditions of production and use.—A party entitled to have a writing or object produced under this rule is entitled to inspect it, to cross-examine the witness thereon, and to introduce in evidence those portions which relate to the testimony of the witness. If production of the writing or object at the trial, hearing, or deposition is impracticable, the court may order it made available for inspection. If it is claimed that the writing or object contains privileged information or information not directly related to the subject matter of the testimony, the court shall examine the writing or object in camera, excise any such portions, and order delivery of the remainder to the party entitled thereto. Any portion withheld over objections shall be preserved and made available to the appellate court in the event of an appeal. If a writing or object is not produced, made available for inspection, or delivered pursuant to order under this rule, the court shall make any order justice requires, but in criminal cases if the prosecution elects not to comply, the order shall be one striking the testimony or, if justice so requires, declaring a mistrial.

Added by Laws 1983, c. 701, § 1.

North Carolina Commentary

This rule is a reorganization of Fed.R.Evid. 612 and differs substantively from the federal rule in five ways. The rule omits a reference to the Jencks Act. Also, it states explicitly that it applies to trials, hearings and depositions and that it applies to objects as well as writings. The rule explicitly provides for inspection of the writing or object if production of the object or writing at the trial is impracticable. Finally, subsection (c) adds privileged information to the grounds which may be the basis of an in camera examination and excision by the court.

If the writing is used by the witness while testifying to refresh his memory, the adverse party is entitled to production. If the writing is used before testifying for the purpose of testifying, disclosure is in the discretion of the court. Requiring disclosure of writings used before testifying is a change in North Carolina practice. See, e.g., State v. Cross, 293 N.C. 296 [237 S.E.2d 734] (1977).

As the Advisory Committee's Note points out:

"The purpose of the phrase 'for the purpose of testifying' is to safeguard against using the rule as a pretext for wholesale exploration of an opposing party's files and to insure that access is limited only to those writings which may fairly be said in fact to have an impact upon the testimony of the witness."

The phrase "for the purpose of testifying" read together with the phrase "and the court in its discretion determines that the interests of justice so require" are intended to maintain the work product "privilege" for lawyers and others who assist in preparation for trial and in most instances it is likely that the judge will exercise his discretion in such a manner to prevent discovery of statements used before testifying to refresh a witness' recollection. Saltzburg and Redden, Federal Rules of Evidence Manual, p. 417 (3d ed. 1982).

In subsection (c), by adding privileged information to those items which the court may consider in camera with possible excision of the material, the intention was to make it clear that the rule does not invade the existing authority of the court in areas such as protecting the confidentiality of the informants.

On the other hand, exculpatory writings are available to criminal defendants irrespective of Rule 612. See United States v. Aqurs, 427 U.S. 97 [96 S.Ct. 2392, 49 L.Ed.2d 342] (1976); United States v. Nobles, 422 U.S. 225 [95 S.Ct. 2160, 45 L.Ed.2d 141] (1975); Brady v. Maryland, 373 U.S. 83 [83 S.Ct. 1194, 10 L.Ed.2d 215] (1963); State v. Hardy, 293 N.C. 105 [235 S.E.2d 828] (1977).

Rule 613. Prior statements of witnesses

In examining a witness concerning a prior statement made by him, whether written or not, the statement need not be shown nor its contents disclosed to him at that time, but on request the same shall be shown or disclosed to opposing counsel.

Added by Laws 1983, c. 701, § 1.

North Carolina Commentary

This rule is identical to subdivision (a) of Fed. R.Evid. 613. There are no North Carolina cases on the subject matter of subdivision (a).

The Advisory Committee's Note states:

"The Queen's Case, 2 Br. & B. 284, 129 Eng. Rep. 976 (1820), laid down the requirement that a cross-examiner, prior to questioning the witness about his own prior statement in writing, must first show it to the witness. Abolished by statute in the country of its origin, the requirement nevertheless gained currency in the United States. The rule abolishes this useless impediment to cross-examination. . . . Both oral and written statements are included.

"The provision for disclosure to counsel is designed to protect against unwarranted insinuations that a statement has been made when the fact is to the contrary.

"The rule does not defeat the application of Rule 1002 relating to production of the original when the contents of a writing are sought to be proved. Nor does it defeat the application of Rule 26(b)(3) of the Rules of Civil Procedure, as revised, entitling a person on request to a copy of his own statement, though the operation of the latter may be suspended temporarily."

The federal rule includes a subdivision (b) barring evidence of a prior inconsistent statement unless the witness has been given an opportunity to explain or deny it. Since subdivision (b) is omitted, foundation requirements for admitting inconsistent statements will be governed by case law. See Brandis on North Carolina Evidence § 48 (1982).

Rule 614. Calling and interrogation of witnesses by court

(a) Calling by court.—The court may, on its own motion or at the suggestion of a party, call witnesses, and all parties are entitled to cross-examine witnesses thus called.

(b) Interrogation by court.—The court may interrogate witnesses, whether called by itself or by a party.

(c) Objections.—No objections are necessary with respect to the calling of a witness by the court or to questions propounded to a witness by the court but it shall be deemed that proper objection has been made and overruled.

Added by Laws 1983, c. 701, § 1.

North Carolina Commentary

Subdivisions (a) and (b) of this rule are identical to Fed.R.Evid. 614(a) and (b).

Subdivision (a) authorizes the court to call witnesses and is consistent with North Carolina practice. See Brandis on North Carolina Evidence § 37 (1982).

Subdivision (b) authorizes the court to examine witnesses, whether called by itself or by a party, and is consistent with North Carolina practice. Id.

It is anticipated that the court will exercise its authority to call or interrogate a witness only in extraordinary circumstances.

The court may not in calling or interrogating a witness do so in a manner as to suggest an opinion as to the weight of the evidence or the credibility of the witness in violation of G.S. 15A-1222 or G.S. 1A-1, Rule 51(a). Id.

Subdivision (c) differs from Fed.R.Evid. 614(c) by providing for an automatic objection to the calling or interrogation of witnesses by the court. Subdivision (c) is consistent with N.C.Civ.Pro.Rule 46(a)(3) which provides that no objections are necessary with respect to questions propounded to a witness by the court.

Rule 615. Exclusion of witnesses

At the request of a party the court may order witnesses excluded so that they cannot hear the testimony of other witnesses, and it may make the order of its own motion. This rule does not authorize exclusion of (1) a party who is a natural person, or (2) an officer or employee of a party that is not a natural person designated as its representative by its attorney, or (3) a person whose presence is shown by a party to be essential to the presentation of his cause, or (4) a person whose presence is determined by the court to be in the interest of justice.

Added by Laws 1983, c. 701, § 1.

North Carolina Commentary

This rule is similar to Fed.R.Evid. 615 except that the word "shall" in the first sentence has been changed to "*may* order witnesses excluded," and the phrase "a person whose presence is determined by the court to be in the interest of justice" has been added as a fourth exception.

The use of "*may* order witnesses excluded" rather than "shall," as in the federal rule, is intended to preserve discretion in the trial judge, allowing him to take into account such things as the physical setting of the trial. However, the practice should be to sequester witnesses on request of either party unless some reason exists not to.

In North Carolina the usual practice has been to separate witnesses and send them out of the hearing of the court when requested, but this has been discretionary with the trial judge and not a matter of right. See Brandis on North Carolina Evidence § 20 (1982). G.S. 15A-1225, which codifies this practice, should be amended to conform to Rule 615.

The Advisory Committee's Note states:

"The efficacy of excluding or sequestering witnesses has long been recognized as a means of discouraging and exposing fabrication, inaccuracy and collusion. 6 Wigmore §§ 1837-1838. The authority of the judge is admitted, the only question being whether the matter is committed to his discretion or one of right. The rule takes the latter position. No time is specified for making the request.

"Several categories of persons are excepted. (1) Exclusion of persons who are parties would raise serious problems of confrontation and due process. Under accepted practice they are not subject to exclusion. 6 Wigmore § 1841. (2) As the equivalent of the right of a natural-person party to be present, a party which is not a natural person is entitled to have a representative present. Most of the cases have involved allowing a police officer who has been in charge of an investigation to remain in court despite the fact that he will be a witness. . . . Designation of the representative by the attorney rather than by the client may at first glance appear to be an inversion of the attorney-client relationship, but it may be assumed that the attorney will follow the wishes of the client, and the solution is simple and workable. . . . (3) The category contemplates such persons as an agent who handled the transaction being litigated or an expert needed to advise counsel in the management of the litigation. See 6 Wigmore § 1841, n. 4."

A government investigative agent would be within the second exception. See S. Rept. No. 93-1277, 93d Cong., 2d Sess. (1974). The third category would include an expert listening to testimony for the purpose of testifying in his capacity as an expert.

A fourth exception to Rule 615 was added to provide that the rule does not authorize the exclusion of a person whose presence is determined by the court to be in the interest of justice. For example, when a minor child is testifying the court may determine that it is in the interest of justice for the parent or guardian to be present even though the parent or guardian is to be called subsequently. When this exception is relied upon the court should state the reasons supporting its determination that the presence of the person is in the interest of justice.

Rule 616. Alternative testimony of witnesses with developmental disabilities or mental retardation in civil cases and special proceedings

(a) Definitions.—The following definitions apply to this section:

(1) The definitions set out in G.S. 122C–3.

(2) "Remote testimony" means a method by which a witness testifies outside of an open forum and outside of the physical presence of a party or parties.

(b) Remote Testimony Authorized.—A person with a developmental disability or a person with mental retardation who is competent to testify may testify by remote testimony in a civil proceeding or special proceeding if the court determines by clear and convincing evidence that the witness would suffer serious emotional distress from testifying in the presence of a named party or parties or from testifying in an open forum and that the ability of the witness to communicate with the trier of fact would be impaired by testifying in the presence of a named party or parties or from testifying in an open forum.

(c) Hearing Procedure.—Upon motion of a party or the court's own motion, and for good cause shown, the court shall hold an evidentiary hearing to determine whether to allow remote testimony. The hearing shall be recorded unless recordation is waived by all parties. The presence of the witness is not required at the hearing unless so ordered by the presiding judge.

(d) Order.—An order allowing or disallowing the use of remote testimony shall state the findings and conclusions of law that support the court's determination. An order allowing the use of remote testimony also shall do all of the following:

(1) State the method by which the witness is to testify.

(2) List any individual or category of individuals allowed to be in or required to be excluded from the presence of the witness during testimony.

(3) State any special conditions necessary to facilitate the cross-examination of the witness.

(4) State any condition or limitation upon the participation of individuals in the presence of the witness during the testimony.

(5) State any other conditions necessary for taking or presenting testimony.

(e) Testimony.—The method of remote testimony shall allow the trier of fact and all parties to observe the demeanor of the witness as the witness testifies in a similar manner as if the witness were testifying in the open forum. Except as provided in this section, the court shall ensure that the counsel for all parties is physically present where the witness testifies and has a full and fair opportunity for examination and cross-examination of the witness. In a proceeding where a party is representing itself, the court may limit or deny the party from being physically present during testimony if the court finds that the witness would suffer serious emotional distress from testifying in the presence of the party. A party may waive the right to have counsel physically present where the witness testifies.

(f) Nonexclusive Procedure and Standard.—Nothing in this section shall prohibit the use or application of any other method or procedure authorized or required by law for the introduction into evidence of statements or testimony of a person with a developmental disability or a person with mental retardation.

Added by S.L. 2009–514, § 1, eff. Dec. 1, 2009.

ARTICLE 7

Opinions and Expert Testimony

Rule 701. Opinion testimony by lay witness

If the witness is not testifying as an expert, his testimony in the form of opinions or inferences is limited to those opinions or inferences which are (a) rationally based on the perception of the witness and (b) helpful to a clear understanding of his testimony or the determination of a fact in issue.

Added by Laws 1983, c. 701, § 1.

North Carolina Commentary

This rule is identical to Fed.R.Evid. 701.

Limitation (a) retains the traditional requirement that lay opinion be based on firsthand knowledge or observation. See Brandis on North Carolina Evidence § 122, at 468 (1982).

Limitation (b) is phrased in terms of requiring testimony to be helpful in resolving issues. This is a different test from the more traditional "collective facts exception" which allows lay opinions or inferences only where a shorthand expression is "necessary" because articulation of more primary components is impossible or highly impracticable. P. Rothstein, Rules of Evidence for United States Courts and Magistrates, at 257 (1980). See Brandis on North Carolina Evidence § 125, at 474–76 (1982). Nothing in the rule would bar evidence that is commonly referred to as a "shorthand statement of fact." Id. at 476.

As the Advisory Committee's Note points out:

"[N]ecessity as a standard for permitting opinions and conclusions has proved too elusive and too unadaptable to particular situations for purposes of satisfactory judicial administration. The rule assumes that the natural characteristics of the adversary system will generally lead to an acceptable result, since the detailed account carries more conviction than the broad assertion, and a lawyer can be expected to display his witness to the best advantage. If he fails to do so, cross-examination and argument will point up the weakness. . . . If, despite these considerations, attempts are made to introduce meaningless assertions which amount to little more than choosing up sides, exclusion for lack of helpfulness is called for by the rule."

Rule 702. Testimony by experts

(a) If scientific, technical or other specialized knowledge will assist the trier of fact to understand the evidence or to determine a fact in issue, a witness qualified as an expert by knowledge, skill, experience, training, or education, may testify thereto in the form of an opinion, or otherwise, if all of the following apply:

(1) The testimony is based upon sufficient facts or data.

(2) The testimony is the product of reliable principles and methods.

(3) The witness has applied the principles and methods reliably to the facts of the case.

(a1) A witness, qualified under subsection (a) of this section and with proper foundation, may give expert testimony solely on the issue of impairment and not on the issue of specific alcohol concentration level relating to the following:

(1) The results of a Horizontal Gaze Nystagmus (HGN) Test when the test is administered by a person who has successfully completed training in HGN.

(2) Whether a person was under the influence of one or more impairing substances, and the category of such impairing substance or substances. A witness who has received training and holds a current certification as a Drug Recognition Expert, issued by the State Department of Health and Human Services, shall be qualified to give the testimony under this subdivision.

(b) In a medical malpractice action as defined in G.S. 90–21.11, a person shall not give expert testimony on the appropriate standard of health care as defined in G.S. 90–21.12 unless the person is a licensed health care provider in this State or another state and meets the following criteria:

(1) If the party against whom or on whose behalf the testimony is offered is a specialist, the expert witness must:

a. Specialize in the same specialty as the party against whom or on whose behalf the testimony is offered; or

b. Specialize in a similar specialty which includes within its specialty the performance of the procedure that is the subject of the complaint and have prior experience treating similar patients.

(2) During the year immediately preceding the date of the occurrence that is the basis for the action, the expert witness must have devoted a majority of his or her professional time to either or both of the following:

a. The active clinical practice of the same health profession in which the party against whom or on whose behalf the testimony is offered, and if that party is a specialist, the active clinical practice of the same specialty or a similar specialty which includes within its specialty the performance of the procedure that is the subject of the complaint and have prior experience treating similar patients; or

b. The instruction of students in an accredited health professional school or accredited residency or clinical research program in the same health profession in which the party against whom or on whose behalf the testimony is offered, and if that party is a specialist, an accredited health professional school or accredited residency or clinical research program in the same specialty.

(c) Notwithstanding subsection (b) of this section, if the party against whom or on whose behalf the testimony is offered is a general practitioner, the expert witness, during the year immediately preceding the date of the occurrence that is the basis for the action, must have devoted a majority of his or her professional time to either or both of the following:

(1) Active clinical practice as a general practitioner; or

(2) Instruction of students in an accredited health professional school or accredited residency or clinical research program in the general practice of medicine.

(d) Notwithstanding subsection (b) of this section, a physician who qualifies as an expert under subsection (a) of this Rule and who by reason of active clinical practice or instruction of students has knowledge of the applicable standard of care for nurses, nurse practitioners, certified registered nurse anesthetists, certified registered nurse midwives, physician assistants, or other medical support staff may give expert testimony in a medical malpractice action with respect to the standard of care of which he is knowledgeable of nurses, nurse practitioners, certified registered nurse anesthetists, certified registered nurse midwives, physician assistants licensed under Chapter 90 of the General Statutes, or other medical support staff.

(e) Upon motion by either party, a resident judge of the superior court in the county or judicial district in which the action is pending may allow expert testimony on the appropriate standard of health care by a witness who does not meet the requirements of subsection (b) or (c) of this Rule, but who is otherwise qualified as an expert witness, upon a showing by the movant of extraordinary circumstances and a determination by the court that the motion should be allowed to serve the ends of justice.

(f) In an action alleging medical malpractice, an expert witness shall not testify on a contingency fee basis.

(g) This section does not limit the power of the trial court to disqualify an expert witness on grounds other than the qualifications set forth in this section.

(h) Notwithstanding subsection (b) of this section, in a medical malpractice action as defined in G.S. 90–21.11(2)b. against a hospital, or other health care or medical facility, a person shall not give expert testimony on the appropriate standard of care as to administrative or other nonclinical issues unless the person has substantial knowledge, by virtue of his or her training and experience, about the standard of care among hospitals, or health care or medical facilities, of the same type as the hospital, or health care or medical facility, whose actions or inactions are the subject of the testimony situated in the same or similar communities at the time of the alleged act giving rise to the cause of action.

(i) A witness qualified as an expert in accident reconstruction who has performed a reconstruction of a crash, or has reviewed the report of investigation, with proper foundation may give an opinion as to the speed of a vehicle even if the witness did not observe the vehicle moving.

Added by Laws 1983, c. 701, § 1. Amended by Laws 1995, c. 309, § 1; S.L. 2006–253, § 6, eff. Aug. 21, 2006; S.L. 2011–283, § 1.3, eff. Oct. 1, 2011; S.L. 2011–400, § 4, eff. Oct. 1, 2011.

North Carolina Commentary

The rule is identical to Fed.R.Evid. 702, except that the words "or otherwise" which appear at the end of the federal rule after the word "opinion" have been deleted.

The rule is identical to G.S. 8–58.13, which should be repealed when Rule 702 becomes effective. The rule is consistent with North Carolina practice. Brandis on North Carolina Evidence § 134, at 520, n. 25 (1982).

Rule 703. Bases of opinion testimony by experts

The facts or data in the particular case upon which an expert bases an opinion or inference may be those perceived by or made known to him at or before the hearing. If of a type reasonably relied upon by experts in the particular field in forming opinions or inferences upon the subject, the facts or data need not be admissible in evidence.

Added by Laws 1983, c. 701, § 1.

North Carolina Commentary

This rule is identical to Fed.R.Evid. 703.

Under the rule, facts or data upon which an expert bases an opinion may be derived from three possible sources. The first is the personal observation of the witness. The second source is presentation at trial by a hypothetical question or by having the expert attend the trial and hear the testimony establishing the facts. The third source consists of presentation of data to the expert outside of court. See Comment, Expert Medical Testimony: Differences Between the North Carolina Rules and the Federal Rules of Evidence, 12 W.F.L.R. 833, 837 (1976).

In State v. Wade, 296 N.C. 454 [251 S.E.2d 407] (1978), the Court stated that a "physician, as an expert witness, may give his opinion, including a diagnosis, based either on personal knowledge or observation or on information supplied him by others, including the patient, if such information is inherently reliable even though it is not independently admissible into evidence." Although the rule requires that the facts or data "be of a type reasonably relied upon by experts in the particular field" rather than that they be "inherently reliable," the thrust of State v. Wade is consistent with the rule. See W. Blakey, Examination of Expert Witnesses in North Carolina, 61 N.C.L.Rev. 1, 20–32 (1982).

The rule provides that the facts or data need not be admissible in evidence if of a type reasonably relied upon by experts in the particular field. In State v. Wade the Court stated that: "If his opinion is admissible the expert may testify to the information he relied on in forming it for the purpose of showing the basis of the opinion." Thus an expert may testify as to the facts upon which his opinion is based, even though the facts would not be admissible as substantive evidence.

Rule 704. Opinion on ultimate issue

Testimony in the form of an opinion or inference is not objectionable because it embraces an ultimate issue to be decided by the trier of fact.

Added by Laws 1983, c. 701, § 1.

North Carolina Commentary

This rule is identical to Fed.R.Evid. 704.

The rule would abrogate the doctrine that excludes evidence in the form of an opinion if it purports to resolve the "ultimate issue" to be decided by the trier of fact.

In State v. Wilkerson, 295 N.C. 559 [247 S.E.2d 905] (1978), the Court held that admissibility of expert opinion depends not on whether it would invade the jury's province, but rather on "whether the witness . . . is in a better position to have an opinion . . . than is the trier of fact." Professor Brandis states that: "It is hoped that a comparable reexamination of the rule as applied to lay testimony will be forthcoming. The rule has been condemned by thoughtful commentators, and judicial expressions of doubt are not wanting." Brandis on North Carolina Evidence § 126, at 480–81 (1982) (footnotes omitted).

The Advisory Committee's Note states:

"The abolition of the ultimate issue rule does not lower the bars so as to admit all opinions. Under Rules 701 and 702, opinions must be helpful to the trier of fact, and Rule 403 provides for exclusion of evidence which wastes time. These provisions afford ample assurance against the admission of opinions which would merely tell the jury what result to reach, somewhat in the manner of the oath-helpers of an earlier day. They also stand ready to exclude opinions phrased in terms of inadequately explored legal criteria. Thus the question, 'Did T have capacity to make a will?' would be excluded, while the question, 'Did T have sufficient mental capacity to know the nature and extent of his property and the natural objects of his bounty and to formulate a rational scheme of distribution?' would be allowed. McCormick § 12."

Rule 705. Disclosure of facts or data underlying expert opinion

The expert may testify in terms of opinion or inference and give his reasons therefor without prior disclosure of the underlying facts or data, unless an adverse party requests otherwise, in which event the expert will be required to disclose such underlying facts or data on direct examination or voir dire before stating the opinion. The expert may in any event be required to disclose the underlying facts or data on cross-examination. There shall be no requirement that expert testimony be in response to a hypothetical question.

Added by Laws 1983, c. 701, § 1.

North Carolina Commentary

This rule differs from Fed.R.Evid. 705 in two respects.

Fed.R.Evid. 705 leaves it to the court, rather than opposing counsel, to determine whether to require prior disclosure of the underlying facts. Rule 705 is consistent with G.S. 8–58.14, which should be repealed after the rule is adopted.

The second difference is that the last sentence of this rule does not appear in the Fed.R.Evid. 705. This sentence is identical to G.S. 8–58.12 which should be repealed after this rule is adopted. Although hypothetical questions are no longer required, neither the rule nor G.S. 8–58.12 prohibits their voluntary use.

Prior to 1982, when the facts upon which an opinion was based were within the expert's own knowledge, the court had discretion to permit the expert to give his opinion first and leave the facts to be brought out by cross-examination. Brandis on North Carolina Evidence § 136 (1982). Facts not within the personal knowledge of the expert had to be incorporated into a hypothetical question and thus disclosed prior to the opinion. Id. The 1981 legislation eliminated the requirement of the hypothetical question and allowed the expert to give his opinion without prior disclosure of the underlying facts unless an adverse party requests otherwise. G.S. 8–58.14. Upon the request of an adverse party, the judge must require the expert to disclose the underlying facts on direct examination or voir dire before stating the opinion. This rule continues that requirement.

The second sentence of Rule 705 gives the opposing side the right to require disclosure of the underlying facts or data on cross-examination. The cross-examiner is under no compulsion to bring out any facts or data except those unfavorable to the opinion. N.C.Civ.Pro.Rule 26(b)(4) provides for substantial discovery of the facts underlying the opinion prior to trial.

Under Rule 611, the court exercises control over the mode and order of interrogating witnesses and presenting evidence. The court may allow the opposing party to cross-examine concerning the factual basis of the opinion immediately after the opinion is given rather than at a later point in the trial.

Except where an adverse party requests it, this rule eliminates the requirement that the basis of an expert opinion must be stated. However, the requirement that there must be a basis for the expert opinion would not be abolished. See W. Blakey, Examination of Expert Witnesses in North Carolina, 61 N.C.L.Rev. 1, 9 (1982).

Rule 706. Court appointed experts

(a) Appointment.—The court may on its own motion or on the motion of any party enter an order to show cause why expert witnesses should not be appointed, and may request the parties to submit nominations. The court may appoint any expert witnesses agreed upon by the parties, and may appoint witnesses of its own selection. An expert witness shall not be appointed by the court unless he consents to act. A witness so appointed shall be informed of his duties by the court in writing, a copy of which shall be filed with the clerk, or at a conference in which the parties shall have opportunity to participate. A witness so appointed shall advise the parties of his findings, if any; his deposition may be taken by any party; and he may be called to testify by the court or any party. He shall be subject to cross-examination by each party, including a party calling him as a witness.

(b) Compensation.—Expert witnesses so appointed are entitled to reasonable compensation in whatever sum the court may allow. The compensation thus fixed is payable from funds which may be provided by law in criminal cases and civil actions and proceedings involving just compensation for the taking of property. In other civil actions and proceedings the compensation shall be paid by the parties in such proportion and at such time as the court directs, and thereafter charged in like manner as other costs.

(c) Disclosure of appointment.—In the exercise of its discretion, the court may authorize disclosure to the jury of the fact that the court appointed the expert witness.

(d) Parties' experts of own selection.—Nothing in this rule limits the parties in calling expert witnesses of their own selection.

Added by Laws 1983, c. 701, § 1.

North Carolina Commentary

This rule is identical to Fed.R.Evid. 706 except that "for the taking of property" has been inserted in subdivision (b) in lieu of "under the Fifth Amendment".

A trial judge has the discretion to call an expert witness. State v. Horne, 171 N.C. 787 [88 S.E. 433] (1916). This rule provides the procedure for calling such a witness.

Subdivision (b) provides the method of compensating experts called by the court but does not require an additional appropriation.

ARTICLE 8

Hearsay

Rule 801. Definitions and exception for admissions of a party-opponent

The following definitions apply under this Article:

(a) Statement.—A "statement" is (1) an oral or written assertion or (2) nonverbal conduct of a person, if it is intended by him as an assertion.

(b) Declarant.—A "declarant" is a person who makes a statement.

(c) Hearsay.—"Hearsay" is a statement, other than one made by the declarant while testifying at the trial or hearing, offered in evidence to prove the truth of the matter asserted.

(d) Exception for Admissions by a Party-Opponent.—A statement is admissible as an exception to the hearsay rule if it is offered against a party and it is (A) his own statement, in either his individual or a representative capacity, or (B) a statement of which he has manifested his adoption or belief in its truth, or (C) a statement by a person authorized by him to make a statement concerning the subject, or (D) a statement by his agent or servant concerning a matter within the scope of his agency or employment, made during the existence of the relationship or (E) a statement by a coconspirator of such party during the course and in furtherance of the conspiracy.

Added by Laws 1983, c. 701, § 1.

North Carolina Commentary

This rule is identical to Fed.R.Evid. 801, except for subdivision (d) which is discussed below.

Subdivision (a) defines "statement" for purposes of the hearsay rule. The Advisory Committee's Note states:

"The definition of 'statement' assumes importance because the term is used in the definition of hearsay in subdivision (c). The effect of the definition of 'statement' is to exclude from the operation of the hearsay rule all evidence of conduct, verbal or nonverbal, not intended as an assertion. The key to the definition is that nothing is an assertion unless intended to be one.

"It can scarcely be doubted that an assertion made in words is intended by the declarant to be an assertion. Hence verbal assertions readily fall into the category of 'statement'. Whether nonverbal conduct should be regarded as a statement for purposes of defining hearsay requires further consideration. Some nonverbal conduct, such as the act of pointing to identify a suspect in a lineup, is clearly the equivalent of words, assertive in nature, and to be regarded as a statement. Other nonverbal conduct, however, may be offered as evidence that the person acted as he did because of his belief in the existence of the condition sought to be proved, from which belief the existence of the condition may be inferred. This sequence is, arguably, in effect an assertion of the existence of the condition and hence properly includable within the hearsay concept. . . . Admittedly evidence of this character is untested with respect to the perception, memory, and narration (or their equivalents) of the actor, but the Advisory Committee is of the view that these dangers are minimal in the absence of an intent to assert and do not justify the loss of the evidence on hearsay grounds. No class of evidence is free of the possibility of fabrication, but the likelihood is less with nonverbal than with assertive verbal conduct. The situations giving rise to the nonverbal conduct are such as virtually to eliminate questions of sincerity. Motivation, the nature of the conduct, and the presence or absence of reliance will bear heavily upon the weight to be given the evidence. . . . Similar considerations govern nonassertive verbal conduct and verbal conduct which is assertive but offered as a basis for inferring something other than the matter asserted, also excluded from the definition of hearsay by the language of subdivision (c)."

Subdivision (a) differs from current North Carolina law by excluding from the hearsay rule all evidence of conduct, verbal or nonverbal, not intended as an assertion. Some North Carolina cases have barred evidence of conduct even though the conduct was nonassertive. In other cases, comparable evidence has been admitted, either as nonhearsay or without noticing its possible hearsay nature. Brandis on North Carolina Evidence § 142 (1982).

With respect to subdivision (a), the Advisory Committee's Note also states:

"When evidence of conduct is offered on the theory that it is not a statement, and hence not hearsay, a preliminary determination will be required to determine whether an assertion is intended. The rule is so worded as to place the burden upon the party claiming that the intention existed; ambiguous and doubtful cases will be resolved against him and in favor of admissibility. The determination involves no greater difficulty than many other preliminary questions of fact."

Subdivision (b) which defines declarant as a person who makes a statement, is consistent with North Carolina practice.

Subdivision (c) defines hearsay as a statement, other than one made by the declarant while testifying at the trial or hearing, offered to prove the truth of the matter asserted. The Advisory Committee's Note states:

"The definition follows along familiar lines in including only statements offered to prove the truth of the matter asserted. McCormick § 225; 5 Wigmore § 1361, 6 id. § 1766. If the significance of an offered statement lies solely in the fact that it was made, no issue is raised as to the truth of anything asserted, and the statement is not hearsay. . . . The effect is to exclude from hearsay the entire category of 'verbal acts' and 'verbal parts of an act,' in which the statement itself affects the legal rights of the parties or is a circumstance bearing on conduct affecting their rights.

"The definition of hearsay must, of course, be read with reference to the definition of statement set forth in subdivision (a).

"Testimony given by a witness in the course of court proceedings is excluded since there is compliance with all the ideal conditions for testifying."

This definition of hearsay is consistent with the definitions used by North Carolina courts. See Brandis on North Carolina Evidence § 138 (1982). With respect to the definition of hearsay excluding "verbal acts" from the hearsay ban, see Brandis, § 141.

Subdivision (d)(1) of Fed.R.Evid. 801 departs markedly from the common law in North Carolina by excluding from the hearsay ban several statements that come within the common law definition of hearsay. Accordingly, the language of Fed. R.Evid. 801(d), which provides that in certain circumstances prior inconsistent statements, prior consistent statements, and out-of-court identifications are not hearsay, was deleted. See Brandis on North Carolina Evidence § 46 (prior inconsistent statements), §§ 51 and 52 (prior consistent statements); State v. Neville, 175 N.C. 751 [95 S.E. 55] (1918) (identification).

Subdivision (d)(2) of Fed.R.Evid. 801 excludes certain admissions of a party-opponent from the hearsay ban by stating that such statements are not hearsay. Subdivision (d) of Rule 801 achieves the same result in a manner consistent with current North Carolina practice by providing that such a statement may be admitted as an exception to the hearsay rule.

Subdivision (d) specifies five categories of statements for which the responsibility of a party is considered sufficient to justify reception in evidence against the party.

With respect to category (A), a party's own statement is the classic example of an admission.

Category (A) is in accord with North Carolina practice. See Brandis on North Carolina Evidence §§ 167, 176 (1982).

With respect to category (B), the Advisory Committee's Note states:

"Under established principles an admission may be made by adopting or acquiescing in the statement of another. While knowledge of contents would ordinarily be essential, this is not inevitably so: 'X is a reliable person and knows what he is talking about.' See McCormick § 246, p. 527, n. 15. Adoption or acquiescence may be manifested in any appropriate manner. When silence is relied upon, the theory is that the person would, under the circumstances, protest the statement made in his presence, if untrue. The decision in each case calls for an evaluation in terms of probable human behavior. In civil cases, the results have generally been satisfactory. In criminal cases, however, troublesome questions have been raised by decisions holding that failure to deny is an admission: the inference is a fairly weak one, to begin with; silence may be motivated by advice of counsel or realization that 'anything you say may be used against you'; unusual opportunity is afforded to manufacture evidence; and encroachment upon the privilege against self-incrimination seems inescapably to be involved. However, recent decisions of the Supreme Court relating to custodial interrogation and the right to counsel appear to resolve these difficulties. Hence the rule contains no special provisions concerning failure to deny in criminal cases."

Admission of a statement of which a party has adopted is in accord with North Carolina practice. See Brandis on North Carolina Evidence § 179 (1982).

With respect to category (C), the Advisory Committee's Note states:

"No authority is required for the general proposition that a statement authorized by a party to be made should have the status of an admission by the party. However, the question arises whether only statements to third persons should be so regarded, to the exclusion of statements by the agent to the principal. The rule is phrased broadly so as to encompass both. While it may be argued that the agent authorized to make statement to his principal does not speak for him, Morgan, Basic Problems of Evidence 273 (1962), communication to an outsider has not generally been thought to be an essential characteristic of an admission. Thus a party's books or records are usable against him, without regard to any intent to disclose to third persons. 5 Wigmore § 1557. See also McCormick § 78, pp. 159–161."

North Carolina courts currently admit statements when an agent is, in fact, authorized to speak for the principal. Brandis on North Carolina Evidence § 169, at 15 (1982). However, it is unclear whether such statements are admissible when the statement was made only to the principal. Id. at 17. The rule would clarify North Carolina law by encompassing statements by an agent to the principal or to a third party.

With respect to category (D), the Advisory Committee's Note states:

"The tradition has been to test the admissibility of statement by agents, as admissions, by applying the usual test of agency. Was the admission made by the agent acting in the scope of his employment? Since few principals employ agents for the purpose of making damaging statements, the usual result was exclusive of the statement. Dissatisfaction with this loss of valuable and helpful evidence has been increasing. A substantial trend favors admitting statements related to a matter within the scope of the agency or employment."

In Hubbard v. [Southern] R.R., 203 N.C. 675 [166 S.E. 802] (1932), the Court states:

"What an agent or employee says relative to an act presently being done by him within the scope of his agency or employment is admissible . . . against the principal or employer, but what he says afterwards, and merely narrative of a past occurrence, though his agency or employment may continue as to other matters, or generally, is only hearsay and is not competent as against the principal or employer."

The North Carolina rule has been the subject of several dissenting opinions and has been criticized by Professor Brandis. See Branch v. Dempsey, 265 N.C. 733 [145 S.E.2d 395] (1965) (Sharp, J., dissenting); Pearce v. Telephone Co., 299 N.C. 64 [261 S.E.2d 176] (1980) (Copeland, Carlton and Exum, J.J., dissenting); Brandis on North Carolina Evidence § 169 (1982). Rule 801(d)(D) would change North Carolina practice and make admissible any statements related to a matter within the scope of the agency or employment. The only additional requirement is that the statement be made during the existence of the relationship.

With respect to category (E), the Advisory Committee's Note states:

"The limitation upon the admissibility of statement of co-conspirators to those made 'during the course and in furtherance of the conspiracy' is in the accepted pattern. While the broadened view of agency taken in item (iv) might suggest wider admissibility of statements of co-conspirators, the agency theory of conspiracy is at best a fiction and ought not to serve as a basis for admissibility beyond that already established. . . . The rule is consistent with the position of the Supreme Court in denying admissibility to statements made after the objectives of the conspiracy have either failed or been achieved. Krulewitch v. United States, 336 U.S. 440, 69 S.Ct. 716, 93 L.Ed. 790 (1949); Wong Sun v. United States, 371 U.S. 471, 490, 83 S.Ct. 407, 9 L.Ed.2d 441 (1963)."

Rule 801(d)(E) is in accord with North Carolina practice. See Brandis on North Carolina Evidence § 173 (1982).

Rule 802. Hearsay rule

Hearsay is not admissible except as provided by statute or by these rules.

Added by Laws 1983, c. 701, § 1.

North Carolina Commentary

This rule is identical to Fed.R.Evid. 802 except that the phrase "by statute or by these rules" is used in lieu of the phrase "by these rules or by other rules prescribed by the Supreme Court pursuant to statutory authority or by Act of Congress."

Rule 802 provides for the standard exclusion of hearsay evidence; hearsay is simply inadmissible unless an exception is applicable. This is in accord with North Carolina practice. Unless an exception to the hearsay rule is provided in these rules, the courts are not free to create new hearsay exceptions by adjudication. Rules 803(24) and 804(b)(5) allow for the admission of evidence in particular cases, but not for more general policy formulation.

Rule 803. Hearsay exceptions; availability of declarant immaterial

The following are not excluded by the hearsay rule, even though the declarant is available as a witness:

(1) Present Sense Impression.—A statement describing or explaining an event or condition made while the declarant was perceiving the event or condition, or immediately thereafter.

(2) Excited Utterance.—A statement relating to a startling event or condition made while the declarant was under the stress of excitement caused by the event or condition.

(3) Then Existing Mental, Emotional, or Physical Condition.—A statement of the declarant's then existing state of mind, emotion, sensation, or physical condition (such as intent, plan, motive, design, mental feeling, pain, and bodily health), but not including a statement of memory or belief to prove the fact remembered or believed unless it relates to the execution, revocation, identification, or terms of declarant's will.

(4) Statements for Purposes of Medical Diagnosis or Treatment—Statements made for purposes of medical diagnosis or treatment and describing medical history, or past or present symptoms, pain, or sensations, or the inception or general character of the cause or external source thereof insofar as reasonably pertinent to diagnosis or treatment.

(5) Recorded Recollection.—A memorandum or record concerning a matter about which a witness once had knowledge but now has insufficient recollection to enable him to testify fully and accurately, shown to have been made or adopted by the witness when the matter was fresh in his memory and to reflect that knowledge correctly. If admitted, the memorandum or record may be read into evidence but may not itself be received as an exhibit unless offered by an adverse party.

(6) Records of Regularly Conducted Activity.—A memorandum, report, record, or data compilation, in any form, of acts, events, conditions, opinions, or diagnoses, made at or near the time by, or from information transmitted by, a person with knowledge, if kept in the course of a regularly conducted business activity, and if it was the regular practice of that business activity to make the memorandum, report, record, or data compilation, all as shown by the testimony of the custodian or other qualified witness, unless the source of information or the method or circumstances of preparation indicate lack of trustworthiness. The term "business" as used in this paragraph includes business, institution, association, profession, occupation, and calling of every kind, whether or not conducted for profit.

(7) Absence of Entry in Records Kept in Accordance with the Provisions of Paragraph (6).—Evidence that a matter is not included in the memoranda, reports, records, or data compilations, in any form, kept in accordance with the provisions of paragraph (6), to prove the nonoccurrence or nonexistence of the matter, if the matter was of a kind of which a memorandum, report, record, or data compilation was regularly made and preserved, unless the sources of information or other circumstances indicate lack of trustworthiness.

(8) Public Records and Reports.—Records, reports, statements, or data compilations, in any form, of public offices or agencies, setting forth (A) the activities of the office or agency, or (B) matters observed pursuant to duty imposed by law as to which matters there was a duty to report, excluding, however, in criminal cases matters observed by police officers and other law-enforcement personnel, or (C) in civil actions and proceedings and against the State in criminal cases, factual findings resulting from an investigation made pursuant to authority granted by law, unless the sources of information or other circumstances indicate lack of trustworthiness.

(9) Records of Vital Statistics.—Records or data compilations, in any form, of births, fetal deaths, deaths, or marriages, if the report thereof was made to a public office pursuant to requirements of law.

(10) Absence of Public Record or Entry.—To prove the absence of a record, report, statement, or data compilation, in any form, or the nonoccurrence or nonexistence of a matter of which a record, report, statement, or data compilation, in any form, was regularly made and preserved by a public office or agency, evidence in the form of a certification in accordance with Rule 902, or testimony, that diligent search failed to disclose the record, report, statement, or data compilation, or entry.

(11) Records of Religious Organizations.—Statements of births, marriages, divorces, deaths, legitimacy, ancestry, relationship by blood or marriage, or other similar facts of personal or family history, contained in a regularly kept record of a religious organization.

(12) Marriage, Baptismal, and Similar Certificates.—Statements of fact contained in a certificate that the maker performed a marriage or other cere-

mony or administered a sacrament, made by a clergyman, public official, or other person authorized by the rules or practices of a religious organization or by law to perform the act certified, and purporting to have been issued at the time of the act or within a reasonable time thereafter.

(13) Family Records.—Statements of fact concerning personal or family history contained in family Bibles, genealogies, charts, engravings on rings, inscriptions on family portraits, engravings on urns, crypts, or tombstones, or the like.

(14) Records of Documents Affecting an Interest in Property.—The record of a document purporting to establish or affect an interest in property, as proof of the content of the original recorded document and its execution and delivery by each person by whom it purports to have been executed, if the record is a record of a public office and an applicable statute authorizes the recording of documents of that kind in that office.

(15) Statements in Documents Affecting an Interest in Property.—A statement contained in a document purporting to establish or affect an interest in property if the matter stated was relevant to the purpose of the document, unless dealings with the property since the document was made have been inconsistent with the truth of the statement or the purport of the document.

(16) Statements in Ancient Documents.—Statements in a document in existence 20 years or more the authenticity of which is established.

(17) Market Reports, Commercial Publications.—Market quotations, tabulations, lists, directories, or other published compilations, generally used and relied upon by the public or by persons in particular occupations.

(18) Learned Treatises.—To the extent called to the attention of an expert witness upon cross-examination or relied upon by him in direct examination, statements contained in published treatises, periodicals, or pamphlets on a subject of history, medicine, or other science or art, established as a reliable authority by the testimony or admission of the witness or by other expert testimony or by judicial notice. If admitted, the statements may be read into evidence but may not be received as exhibits.

(19) Reputation Concerning Personal or Family History.—Reputation among members of his family by blood, adoption, or marriage, or among his associates, or in the community, concerning a person's birth, adoption, marriage, divorce, death, legitimacy, relationship by blood, adoption, or marriage, ancestry, or other similar fact of his personal or family history.

(20) Reputation Concerning Boundaries or General History.—Reputation in a community, arising before the controversy, as to boundaries of or customs affecting lands in the community, and reputation as to events of general history important to the community or state or nation in which located.

(21) Reputation as to Character.—Reputation of a person's character among his associates or in the community.

(22) Reserved.

(23) Judgment as to Personal, Family or General History, or Boundaries.—Judgments as proof of matters of personal, family or general history, or boundaries, essential to the judgment, if the same would be provable by evidence of reputation.

(24) Other Exceptions.—A statement not specifically covered by any of the foregoing exceptions but having equivalent circumstantial guarantees of trustworthiness, if the court determines that (A) the statement is offered as evidence of a material fact; (B) the statement is more probative on the point for which it is offered than any other evidence which the proponent can procure through reasonable efforts; and (C) the general purposes of these rules and the interests of justice will best be served by admission of the statement into evidence. However, a statement may not be admitted under this exception unless the proponent of it gives written notice stating his intention to offer the statement and the particulars of it, including the name and address of the declarant, to the adverse party sufficiently in advance of offering the statement to provide the adverse party with a fair opportunity to prepare to meet the statement.

Added by Laws 1983, c. 701, § 1.

North Carolina Commentary

This rule is identical to Fed.R.Evid. 803, except as noted below. The Advisory Committee's Note states:

> "The exceptions are phrased in terms of nonapplication of the hearsay rule, rather than in positive terms of admissibility, in order to repel any implication that other possible grounds for exclusion are eliminated from consideration.
>
> "The present rule proceeds upon the theory that under appropriate circumstances a hearsay statement may possess circumstantial guarantees of trustworthiness sufficient to justify nonproduction of the declarant in person at the trial even though he may be available. The theory finds vast support in the many exceptions to the hearsay rule developed by the common law in which unavailability of the declarant is not a relevant factor. The present rule is a synthesis of them, with revision where modern developments and conditions are believed to make that course appropriate.
>
> "In a hearsay situation, the declarant is, of course, a witness, and neither this Rule nor Rule 804 dispenses with the requirement of firsthand knowledge. It may appear from his statement or be inferable from circumstances. See Rule 602."

As the Advisory Committee's Note indicates, the exceptions are phrased in terms of nonapplication of the hearsay rule. Evidence that is otherwise inadmissible may be stricken from a writing.

Exception (1) concerns present sense impressions and **Exception (2)** concerns excited utterances. The Advisory Committee's Note states:

"In considerable measure these two examples overlap, though based on somewhat different theories. The most significant practical difference will lie in the time lapse allowable between event and statement.

"The underlying theory of Exception (1) is that substantial contemporaneity of event and statement negative the likelihood of deliberate or conscious misrepresentation. Moreover, if the witness is the declarant, he may be examined on the statement. If the witness is not the declarant, he may be examined as to the circumstances as an aid in evaluating the statement. (Citation omitted.)

"The theory of Exception (2) is simply that circumstances may produce a condition of excitement which temporarily stills the capacity of reflection and produces utterances free of conscious fabrication. 6 Wigmore § 1747, p. 135. Spontaneity is the key factor in each instance, though arrived at by somewhat different routes. Both are needed in order to avoid needless niggling. . . .

"With respect to the *time element*, Exception (1) recognizes that in many, if not most, instances precise contemporaneity is not possible, and hence a slight lapse is allowable. Under Exception (2) the standard of measurement is the duration of the state of excitement. 'How long can excitement prevail? Obviously there are no pat answers and the character of the transaction or event will largely determine the significance of the time factor.' "

North Carolina courts have recognized a hearsay exception for spontaneous utterances that is substantially the same as Exception (2). See Brandis on North Carolina Evidence § 164 (1982). Exception (2) would clarify discordant rulings in this area, particularly as to the element of time. Id. at 650. Exception (1) would be a new exception to the hearsay rule in North Carolina. Id. at 653.

Exception (3) concerns statements of the declarant's then existing mental, emotional or physical condition. The Advisory Committee's Note states:

"The exclusion of 'statements of memory or belief to prove the fact remembered or believed' is necessary to avoid the virtual destruction of the hearsay rule which would otherwise result from allowing state of mind, provable by a hearsay statement, to serve as the basis for an inference of the happening of the event which produced the state of mind."

Exception (3) is similar to the corresponding North Carolina exception to the hearsay rule. See Brandis on North Carolina Evidence § 161 (1982). However, the North Carolina exception differs from Exception (3) in that in North Carolina declarations that are made in a criminal case after the commission of the crime are generally not included within the exception for fear that admissibility would permit the defendant to create evidence for himself. Id. at 636.

In North Carolina, when the issue is one of undue influence or fraud with respect to the execution of a will, the declarations of a testator are admitted only as corroborative evidence and are not alone sufficient to establish the previous conduct of another person by means of which the alleged fraud was perpetrated or the undue influence exerted. Brandis on North Carolina Evidence § 163, at 647–48. Exception (3) would change this result and permit such declarations to be admitted as substantive proof.

Exception (4) concerns statements made for purposes of medical diagnosis and treatment. The Advisory Committee's Note states:

"Even those few jurisdictions which have shied away from generally admitting statements of present condition have allowed them if made to a physician for purposes of diagnosis and treatment in view of the patient's strong motivation to be truthful. . . . The same guarantee of trustworthiness extends to statements of past conditions and medical history, made for purposes of diagnosis or treatment. It also extends to statements as to causation, reasonably pertinent to the same purposes, in accord with the current trend. . . . Statements as to fault would not ordinarily qualify under this latter language. Thus a patient's statement that he was struck by an automobile would qualify but not his statement that the car was driven through a red light. Under the exception the statement need not have been made to a physician. Statements to hospital attendants, ambulance drivers, or even members of the family might be included."

Under current North Carolina practice, statements of past condition made by a patient to a treating physician or psychiatrist, when relevant to diagnosis or treatment and therefore inherently reliable, are admissible to show the basis for the expert's opinion. Brandis on North Carolina Evidence § 161, at 635 (1982). In some instances, a statement to a nontreating physician is currently admissible. State v. Franks, 300 N.C. 1 [265 S.E.2d 177] (1980). Professor Brandis states that when qualifying as basis for the expert's opinion statements of past condition "should be (though, as yet, they are not) admissible as substantive evidence as an exception to the hearsay rule." Brandis, supra, at 636.

Exception (5) concerns past recollection recorded, which is currently admissible in North Carolina. See Brandis on North Carolina Evidence § 33 (1982).

The phrase "or adopted by a witness" was added by Congress to make it clear that statements adopted by a witness would come within the rule. The language chosen by Congress may be read to suggest that the statement does not qualify for admission unless the witness made the recordation himself or actually adopted the recordation of another. The exception should be construed so as not to require that the recordation of another be actually adopted by the witness. Thus the statement may be one that was made by the witness, one that was adopted by the witness, or one that was made by the witness and recorded by another. This construction would be in accord with North Carolina practice which permits use of the recorded statement if the witness is able to testify that he saw it at a time when the facts were fresh in his memory, and that it actually represented his recollection at the time. See Brandis, supra, at 127.

To prevent a jury from giving too much weight to a written statement that cannot be effectively cross-examined, the last sentence of Exception (5) provides that the memorandum or record may be read into evidence but may not be received as an exhibit unless offered by an adverse party. Current North Carolina practice apparently permits the writing itself, or a reading thereof by the authenticating witness, to be admitted. Brandis, supra, at 126, n. 75.

Exception (6) concerns records of regularly conducted activity. The exception is derived from the traditional business records exception. The exception is limited to business records, but business is defined to include the records of institutions and associations like schools, churches and hospitals. This appears to be a slight expansion of the current North Carolina business records exception. See Brandis, supra, § 155.

The exception is consistent with North Carolina practice in that the person making the record is not required to have personal knowledge of the transactions entered. See Brandis, supra, § 155, at 617. However, it must be shown that the record was actually based (or it was the regular practice of the activity to base the record) upon a person with knowledge acting pursuant to a regularly conducted activity.

The exception specifically includes both diagnoses and opinions, in addition to acts, events and conditions, as proper subjects of admissible entries. See State v. DeGregory, 285 N.C. 122 [203 S.E.2d 794] (1977).

In addition, the Advisory Committee's Note states that:

"Problems of the motivation of the informant have been a source of difficulty and disagreement. . . .

"The formulation of specific terms which would assure satisfactory results in all cases is not possible. Consequently the rule proceeds from the base that records made in the course of a regularly conducted activity will be taken as admissible but subject to authority to exclude if 'the sources of information or other circumstances indicate lack of trustworthiness.'"

Apparently, there are no North Carolina cases on this point.

The rule is in accord with North Carolina practice in that it includes computer storage. Brandis, supra, § 155, at 619.

Exception (7) concerns the absence of an entry in the records of regularly conducted activity. As the Advisory Committee's Note states: "Failure of a record to mention a matter which would ordinarily be mentioned is satisfactory evidence of its nonexistence." This is existing North Carolina law. See Brandis on North Carolina Evidence § 155 (1982).

Exception (8) differs from Fed.R.Evid. 803(8) in that the word "State" is used in lieu of the word "government".

Part (A) of the exception is for records, reports, statements or data compilations setting forth the activities of the public office or agency. Part (A) is in accord with North Carolina practice. See Brandis on North Carolina Evidence § 153 (1982).

Part (B) covers matters observed pursuant to duty imposed by law when there is also a duty to report. Part (B) is in general accord with North Carolina practice. Id. In criminal cases, Part (B) does not cover matters observed by police officers and other law enforcement personnel. Note that the right to confrontation may exclude evidence in criminal cases even if the matter is not one observed by law enforcement personnel.

Part (C) covers factual findings resulting from an investigation made pursuant to legal authority. The term "factual findings" is not intended to preclude the introduction of evaluative reports containing conclusions or opinions. Apparently North Carolina courts currently exclude statements in reports that only amount to an expression of opinion. Id. at 609.

The Advisory Committee's Note states:

"Factors which may be of assistance in passing upon the admissibility of evaluative reports include: (1) the timeliness of the investigation . . .; (2) the special skill or experience of the official . . .; (3) whether a hearing was held and the level at which conducted; (4) possible motivation problems suggested by Palmer v. Hoffman, 318 U.S. 109 [63 S.Ct. 477, 87 L.Ed. 645] . . . (1943). Others no doubt could be added.

"The formulation of an approach which would give appropriate weight to all possible factors in every situation is an obvious impossibility. Hence the rule, as in Exception (6), assumes admissibility in the first instance but with ample provision for escape if sufficient negative factors are present. In one respect, however, the rule with respect to evaluative reports under item (c) is very specific: they are admissible only in civil cases and against the government in criminal cases in view of the almost certain collision with confrontation rights which would result from their use against the accused in a criminal case."

The phrase "unless the sources of information or other circumstances indicate lack of trustworthiness" applies to all three parts of the exception.

Public records and reports that are not admissible under Exception (8) are not admissible as business records under Exception (6).

Exception (9) excludes from the hearsay ban records of vital statistics and is similar to G.S. 130-49 and G.S. 130-66.

One purpose of the exception is to admit a death certificate to prove that a death occurred. G.S. 130-66 also provides that a death certificate is prima facie evidence of the cause of death. However, in State v. Watson, 281 N.C. 221 [188 S.E.2d 289] (1972), the Court held that the admission of the "hearsay and conclusory statement" of the cause of death in the victim's death certificate violated the right to confrontation. Exception (9) is not intended to permit the use of statements of the cause of death in a death certificate against a defendant in a criminal case.

Exception (10) concerns the absence of a public record or entry. The Advisory Committee's Note states:

"The principle of proving nonoccurrence of an event by evidence of the absence of a record which would regularly be made of its occurrence, developed in Exception (7) with respect to regularly conducted activities, is here extended to public records of the kind mentioned in Exceptions (8) and (9). 5 Wigmore § 1633(6), p. 519. Some harmless duplication no doubt exists with Exception (7). . . .

"The rule includes situations in which absence of a record may itself be the ultimate focal point of inquiry, e.g., People v. Love, 310 Ill. 558, 142 N.E. 204 (1923), certificate of secretary of state admitted to show failure to file documents required by Securities Law, as well as cases where the absence of a record is offered as proof of the nonoccurrence of an event ordinarily recorded."

Exception (10) is similar to G.S. 1A-1, Civ. Pro.Rules 44(b) and 44(c). See also Brandis on North Carolina Evidence § 153, at 610 (1982).

Exception (11) concerns records of religious organizations. The Advisory Committee's Note states:

"Records of activities of religious organizations are currently recognized as admissible at least to the extent of the business records exception to the hearsay rule, 5 Wigmore § 1523, p. 371, and Exception (6) would be applicable. However, both the business record doctrine and Exception (6) require that the person furnishing the information be one in the business or activity. The result is such decisions as Daily v. Grand Lodge, 311 Ill. 184, 142 N.E. 478 (1924), holding a church record admissible to prove fact, date, and place of baptism, but not age of child except that he had at least been born at the time. In view of the unlikelihood that false information would be furnished on occasions of this kind, the rule contains no requirement that the information be in the course of the activity."

Currently in North Carolina records of activities of religious organizations are admissible to the extent of the business records exception to the hearsay rule. See Brandis on North Carolina Evidence § 155 (1982).

Exception (12) concerns marriage, baptismal, and similar certificates. The Advisory Committee's Note states:

"The principle of proof by certification is recognized as to public officials in Exceptions (8) and (10), and with respect to authentication in Rule 902. The present exception is a duplication to the extent that it deals with a certificate by a public official, as in the case of a judge who performs a marriage ceremony. The area covered by the rule is, however, substantially larger and extends the certification procedure to clergymen and the like who perform marriages and other ceremonies or administer sacraments. Thus certificates of such matters as baptism or confirmation, as well as marriage, are included. In principle they are as acceptable evidence as certificates of public officers. See 5 Wigmore § 1645, as to marriage certificates. When the person executing the certificate is not a public official, the self-authenticating character of documents purporting to emanate from public officials, see Rule 902, is lacking and proof is required that the person was authorized and did make the certificate. The time element, however, may safely be taken as supplied by the certificate, once authority and authenticity are established, particularly in view of the presumption that a document was executed on the date it bears."

Under current North Carolina practice, these items are admissible only to the extent they are part of a public record.

Exception (13) concerns family records.

The North Carolina exception for family records is more restrictive in that statements of family history and pedigree are admissible only if the declarant (1) is unavailable; (2) made the statement before the beginning of the controversy; and (3) bore a relationship to the family such that he was likely to have known the truth. Brandis on North Carolina Evidence § 149 (1982).

Exception (14) concerns records of documents affecting an interest in property. The Advisory Committee's Note states:

"The recording of title documents is a purely statutory development. Under any theory of the admissibility of public records, the records would be receivable as evidence of the contents of the recorded document, else the recording process would be reduced to a nullity. When, however, the record is offered for the further purpose of proving execution and delivery, a problem of lack of firsthand knowledge by the recorder, not present as to contents, is presented. This problem is solved, seemingly in all jurisdictions, by qualifying for recording only those documents shown by a specified procedure, either acknowledgement or a form of probate, to have been executed and delivered. 5 Wigmore §§ 1647-1651."

Exception (14) is consistent with North Carolina practice. See G.S. 47-20 through 47-20.4; G.S. 47-14; and G.S. 47-17.

Exception (15) concerns statements in documents affecting an interest in property. The Advisory Committee's Note states:

"Dispositive documents often contain recitals of fact. Thus a deed purporting to have been executed by an attorney in fact may recite the existence of the power of attorney, or a deed may recite that the grantors are all the heirs of the last record owner. Under the rule, these recitals are exempted from the hearsay rule. The circumstances under which dispositive documents are executed and the requirement that the recital be germane to the purpose of the document are believed to be adequate guarantees of trustworthiness, particularly in view of the nonapplicability of the rule if dealings with the property have been inconsistent with the document. The age of the document is of no significance, though in practical application the document will most often be an ancient one."

The extent to which recitals of fact in a deed or other dispositive documents are admissible in North Carolina is not entirely certain. Brandis on North Carolina Evidence § 152 (1982). Adoption of Exception (15) would somewhat expand admissibility and clarify North Carolina law in this area.

Exception (16) concerns statements in ancient documents. The Advisory Committee's Note states:

"Authenticating a document as ancient, essentially in the pattern of the common law, as provided in Rule 901(b)(8), leaves open as a separate question the admissibility of assertive statements contained therein as against a hearsay objection. 7 Wigmore § 2145a. Wigmore further states that the ancient document technique of authentication is universally conceded to apply to all sorts of documents, including letters, records, contracts, maps, and certificates, in addition to title documents, citing numerous decisions. Id. § 2145. Since most of these items are significant evidentially only insofar as they are assertive, their admission in evidence must be as a hearsay exception. But see 5 id. § 1573, p. 429, referring to recitals in ancient deeds as a 'limited' hearsay exception. The former position is believed to be the correct one in reason and authority. As pointed out in McCormick § 298, danger of mistake is minimized by authentication requirements, and age affords assurance that the writing antedates the present controversy."

North Carolina courts currently recognize as exceptions to the hearsay rule recitals in deeds more than 30 years old. "The North Carolina cases have involved deeds, but it may be assumed that the rule extends here, as it does elsewhere, to other dispositive instruments such as wills and powers of attorney." Brandis on North Carolina Evidence § 152, at 604 (1982). Exception (16) would expand the North Carolina exception to include statements in many types of documents more than 20 years old.

Exception (17) concerns market reports and commercial publications. The Advisory Committee's Note states:

"Ample authority at common law supported the admission in evidence of items falling in this category. While Wigmore's text is narrowly oriented to lists, etc., prepared for the use of a trade or profession, 6 Wigmore § 1702, authorities are cited which include other kinds of publications, for example, newspaper market reports, telephone directories, and city directories. Id. §§ 1702–1706. The basis of trustworthiness is general reliance by the public or by a particular segment of it, and the motivation of the compiler to foster reliance by being accurate."

North Carolina courts have admitted into evidence a variety of published compilations used or relied on by the public or particular professions. See Brandis on North Carolina Evidence § 165 (1982).

Exception (18) concerns learned treatises. The Advisory Committee's Note states:

"The writers have generally favored the admissibility of learned treatises . . ., but the great weight of authority has been that learned treatises are not admissible as substantive evidence though usable in the cross-examination of experts. The foundation of the minority view is that the hearsay objection must be regarded as unimpressive when directed against treatises since a high standard of accuracy is engendered by various factors: the treatise is written primarily and impartially for professionals, subject to scrutiny and exposure for inaccuracy, with the reputation of the writer at stake. . . . Sound as this position may be with respect to trustworthiness, there is, nevertheless, an additional difficulty in the likelihood that the treatise will be misunderstood and misapplied without expert assistance and supervision. This difficulty is recognized in the cases demonstrating unwillingness to sustain findings relative to disability on the basis of judicially noticed medical texts. . . . The rule avoids the danger of misunderstanding and misapplication by limiting the use of treatises as substantive evidence to situations in which an expert is on the stand and available to explain and assist in the application of the treatise if desired. The limitation upon receiving the publication itself physically in evidence, contained in the last sentence, is designed to further this policy.

. . .

"The rule does not require that the witness rely upon or recognize the treatise as authoritative, thus avoiding the possibility that the expert may at the outset block cross-examination by refusing to concede reliance or authoritativeness. . . . Moreover, the rule avoids the unreality of admitting evidence for the purpose of impeachment only, with an instruction to the jury not to consider it otherwise."

Exception (18) is substantially the same as G.S. 8–40.1. Although G.S. 8–40.1 was modeled after Exception (18), there has been some doubt whether the statements, once received, are substantive evidence or are merely for impeachment or corroboration. Brandis on North Carolina Evidence § 136, at

543 (1982). It is intended that Exception (18) authorize admission of such statements as substantive evidence.

The last sentence of G.S. 8–40.1 differs from Exception (18) by providing that the statements may not be received as exhibits "unless agreed to by counsel for the parties." The quoted language was viewed as superfluous since evidence excluded by this rule and other rules may be admitted upon stipulation by counsel for the parties.

Exception (19) concerns matters of personal and family history. The Advisory Committee's Note states:

> "Marriage is universally conceded to be a proper subject of proof by evidence of reputation in the community. . . . As to such items as legitimacy, relationship, adoption, birth, and death, the decisions are divided. . . . All seem to be susceptible to being the subject of well founded repute. The 'world' in which the reputation may exist may be family, associates, or community. This world has proved capable of expanding with changing times from the single uncomplicated neighborhood, in which all activities take place, to the multiple and unrelated worlds of work, religious affiliation, and social activity, in each of which a reputation may be generated."

Under current North Carolina law only reputation among family members is admissible concerning matters of family history and pedigree, except for marriage which may be proved by both family and community reputation. Brandis on North Carolina Evidence § 149, at 599 (1982). Exception (19) would permit proof by reputation among family and associates, or in the community.

Exception (20) concerns reputation as to land boundaries or general history. The Advisory Committee's Note states:

> "The first portion of Exception (20) is based upon the general admissibility of evidence of reputation as to land boundaries and land customs, expanded in this country to include private as well as public boundaries. McCormick § 299, p. 625. The reputation is required to antedate the controversy, though not to be ancient. The second portion is likewise supported by authority, id., and is designed to facilitate proof of events when judicial notice is not available. The historical character of the subject matter dispenses with any need that the reputation antedate the controversy with respect to which it is offered."

Exception (20) is in accord with North Carolina practice. See Brandis on North Carolina Evidence § 150 (1982).

Exception (21) concerns reputation as to character. The Advisory Committee's Note states:

> "Exception (21) recognizes the traditional acceptance of reputation evidence as a means of proving human character. McCormick §§ 44, 158. The exception deals only with the hearsay aspect of this kind of evidence. Limitations upon admissibility based on other grounds will be found in Rules 404, relevancy of character evidence generally, and 608, character of witness. The exception is in effect a reiteration, in the context of hearsay, of Rule 405(a)."

Exception (21) is consistent with North Carolina practice.

Exception (22) is reserved for future codification. Fed.R.Evid. 803(22) concerns use of a judgment of previous conviction to prove a fact essential to sustain the judgment. Under current North Carolina practice, the judgment or finding of a court generally cannot be used in another case as evidence of the fact found, except where the principle of res judicata is involved. Brandis on North Carolina Evidence § 143 (1982). By not adopting a hearsay exception for judgments of previous conviction, it is intended that North Carolina practice with respect to previous convictions remain the same.

Exception (23) concerns a judgment as proof of matters of personal, family or general history, or boundaries. The Advisory Committee's Note states:

> "A hearsay exception in this area was originally justified on the ground that verdicts were evidence of reputation. As trial by jury graduated from the category of neighborhood inquests, this theory lost its validity. It was never valid as to chancery decrees. Nevertheless the rule persisted, though the judges and writers shifted ground and began saying that the judgment or decree was as good evidence as reputation. . . . The shift appears to be correct, since the process of inquiry, sifting, and scrutiny which is relied upon to render reputation reliable is present in perhaps greater measure in the process of litigation. While this might suggest a broader area of application, the affinity to reputation is strong, and paragraph (23) goes no further, not even including character."

A judgment admitted under this exception is some evidence of the matter essential to the judgment, but is not a binding determination of the matter for purposes of the current proceeding.

Generally, a judgment cannot be used under current North Carolina practice to prove a fact essential to the judgment, except where the principle of res judicata is involved. Brandis on North Carolina Evidence § 143 (1982).

Exception (24) differs from Fed.R.Evid. 803(24) in that the last sentence of the federal rule does not require written notice. Also, Exception (24) requires the notice to be given sufficiently in advance of offering the statement while Fed.R.Evid. 803(24) requires the notice to be given sufficiently in advance of the trial or hearing.

This exception makes admissible a hearsay statement not specifically covered by any of the previous twenty-three exceptions if the statement has equivalent circumstantial guarantees of trustworthiness and the court makes the determinations required by the rule. This exception does not contemplate an unfettered exercise of judicial discretion, but it does provide for treating new and presently unanticipated situations which demonstrate a trustworthiness within the spirit of the specifically stated exceptions.

Writing for the majority in State v. Vestal, 278 N.C. 561, 589 [180 S.E.2d 755] (1971), Justice Lake stated that:

"No branch of the law should be less firmly bound to a past century than the rules of evidence. The purpose of the rules of evidence is to assist the jury to arrive at the truth. Exceptions to the hearsay rule, evolved by the experience and wisdom of our predecessors for that purpose, should not be transformed by us into rigid molds precluding all testimony not capable of being squeezed neatly into one of them."

North Carolina courts have admitted hearsay evidence in many instances on the ground that the evidence was part of the "res gestae." The res gestae formula has been frequently resorted to in cases that would seem to be more appropriately governed by independent hearsay rules. See Brandis on North Carolina Evidence § 158 (1982). The phrase res gestae "has been accountable for so much confusion that it had best be denied any place whatever in legal terminology." U.S. v. Matot, 146 F.2d 197 (2d Cir. 1944) (Learned Hand). Although evidence previously governed by the res gestae formula may now fall within the specific hearsay exceptions or the catch-all in Exception 24, the res gestae formula should not be relied on by the courts.

Rule 804. Hearsay exceptions; declarant unavailable

(a) Definition of unavailability.—"Unavailability as a witness" includes situations in which the declarant:

(1) Is exempted by ruling of the court on the ground of privilege from testifying concerning the subject matter of his statement; or

(2) Persists in refusing to testify concerning the subject matter of his statement despite an order of the court to do so; or

(3) Testifies to a lack of memory of the subject matter of his statement; or

(4) Is unable to be present or to testify at the hearing because of death or then existing physical or mental illness or infirmity; or

(5) Is absent from the hearing and the proponent of his statement has been unable to procure his attendance (or in the case of a hearsay exception under subdivision (b)(2), (3), or (4), his attendance or testimony) by process or other reasonable means.

A declarant is not unavailable as a witness if his exemption, refusal, claim of lack of memory, inability, or absence is due to the procurement or wrongdoing of the proponent of his statement for the purpose of preventing the witness from attending or testifying.

(b) Hearsay exceptions.—The following are not excluded by the hearsay rule if the declarant is unavailable as a witness:

(1) Former Testimony.—Testimony given as a witness at another hearing of the same or a different proceeding, or in a deposition taken in compliance with law in the course of the same or another proceeding, if the party against whom the testimony is now offered, or, in a civil action or proceeding, a predecessor in interest, had an opportunity and similar motive to develop the testimony by direct, cross, or redirect examination.

(2) Statement Under Belief of Impending Death.—A statement made by a declarant while believing that his death was imminent, concerning the cause or circumstances of what he believed to be his impending death.

(3) Statement Against Interest.—A statement which was at the time of its making so far contrary to the declarant's pecuniary or proprietary interest, or so far tended to subject him to civil or criminal liability, or to render invalid a claim by him against another, that a reasonable man in his position would not have made the statement unless he believed it to be true. A statement tending to expose the declarant to criminal liability is not admissible in a criminal case unless corroborating circumstances clearly indicate the trustworthiness of the statement.

(4) Statement of Personal or Family History.—(A) A statement concerning the declarant's own birth, adoption, marriage, divorce, legitimacy, relationship by blood, adoption, or marriage, ancestry, or other similar fact of personal or family history, even though declarant had no means of acquiring personal knowledge of the matter stated; or (B) a statement concerning the foregoing matters, and death also, of another person, if the declarant was related to the other by blood, adoption, or marriage or was so intimately associated with the other's family as to be likely to have accurate information concerning the matter declared.

(5) Other Exceptions.—A statement not specifically covered by any of the foregoing exceptions but having equivalent circumstantial guarantees of trustworthiness, if the court determines that (A) the statement is offered as evidence of a material fact; (B) the statement is more probative on the point for which it is offered than any other evidence which the proponent can procure through reasonable efforts; and (C) the general purposes of these rules and the interests of justice will best be served by admission of the statement into evidence. However, a statement may not be admitted under this exception unless the proponent of it gives written notice stating his intention to offer the statement and the particulars of it, including the name and address of the declarant, to the adverse party sufficiently in advance of offering the statement

to provide the adverse party with a fair opportunity to prepare to meet the statement.

Added by Laws 1983, c. 701, § 1.

North Carolina Commentary

This rule is identical to Fed.R.Evid. 804 except for the last sentence of Exception (3), which is discussed below.

Subdivision (a) defines unavailability. The Advisory Committee's Note states:

"The definition of unavailability implements the division of hearsay exceptions into two categories by Rules 803 and 804(b).

"At common law the unavailability requirement was evolved in connection with particular hearsay exceptions rather than along general lines. . . . However, no reason is apparent for making distinctions as to what satisfies unavailability for the different exceptions. The treatment in the rule is therefore uniform. . . .

"Five instances of unavailability are specified:

"(1) Substantial authority supports the position that exercise of a claim of privilege by the declarant satisfies the requirement of unavailability (usually in connection with former testimony). . . . A ruling by the judge is required, which clearly implies that an actual claim of privilege must be made.

"(2) A witness is rendered unavailable if he simply refuses to testify concerning the subject matter of his statement despite judicial pressures to do so, a position supported by similar considerations of practicality. . . .

"(3) The position that a claimed lack of memory by the witness of the subject matter of his statement constitutes unavailability likewise finds support in the cases, though not without dissent. If the claim is successful, the practical effect is to put the testimony beyond reach, as in the other instances. In this instance, however, it will be noted that the lack of memory must be established by the testimony of the witness himself, which clearly contemplates his production and subjection to cross-examination.

"(4) Death and infirmity find general recognition as grounds. . . .

"(5) Absence from the hearing coupled with inability to compel attendance by process or other reasonable means also satisfies the requirement. . . .

"If the conditions otherwise constituting unavailability result from the procurement or wrongdoing of the proponent of the statement, the requirement is not satisfied. The rule contains no requirement that an attempt be made to take the deposition of a declarant."

Under North Carolina law the unavailability requirement varies with respect to particular hearsay requirements.

Under the hearsay exception for former testimony, North Carolina courts recognize grounds (1), (4), and (5). Brandis on North Carolina Evidence § 145 (1982). Although grounds (2) and (3) are not explicitly accepted or rejected by existing North Carolina precedents, Professor Brandis asserts that they should be accepted when occasion arises. Id. at 575.

Under the hearsay exception for dying declarations, G.S. 8-51.1 requires that the declarant be dead.

Under the exception for statements against interest, apparently any legitimate reason for unavailability is sufficient. Brandis on North Carolina Evidence § 147, at 589, n. 80 (1982).

With respect to statements of family history, it was said in the older cases that the declarant must be dead. However, Professor Brandis asserts that any legitimate reason for unavailability should be acceptable. Id. at 597.

The Advisory Committee's Note states:

"If the conditions otherwise constituting unavailability result from the procurement or wrongdoing of the proponent of the statement, the requirement is not satisfied. The rule contains no requirement that an attempt be made to take the deposition of a declarant."

Exception (1) concerns former testimony.

In North Carolina, the "testimony must have been given at a former trial of the same cause, or a preliminary stage of the same cause, or the trial of another cause involving the issue and subject matter to which the testimony is directed at the current trial." Brandis on North Carolina Evidence § 145, at 575–76 (1982) (footnotes omitted). The Advisory Committee's Note states:

"The common law did not limit the admissibility of former testimony to that given in an earlier trial of the same case, although it did require identity of issues as a means of insuring that the former handling of the witness was the equivalent of what would now be done if the opportunity were presented. Modern decisions reduce the requirement to 'substantial' identity. McCormick § 233. Since identity of issues is significant only in that it bears on motive and interest in developing fully the testimony of the witness, expressing the matter in the latter terms is preferable. Id."

Also, the Advisory Committee's Note states:

"Under the exception, the testimony may be offered (1) against the party *against* whom it was previously offered or (2) against the party *by* whom it was previously offered. In each instance the question resolves itself into whether fairness allows imposing, upon the party against whom now offered, the handling of the witness on the earlier occasion. (1) If the party against whom now offered is the one *against* whom the testimony was offered previously, no unfairness is apparent in requiring him to accept his own prior conduct of cross-examination or decision not to cross-examine. Only demeanor has been lost, and that is inherent in the situation. (2) If the party against whom now offered is the one *by* whom the testimony was offered previously, a satisfactory answer becomes somewhat more difficult. One possibility is to proceed somewhat along the line of an adoptive admission, i.e., by offering the testimony proponent in effect adopts it. However, this theory savors of discarded concepts of witnesses' belonging to a party, of litigants' ability to pick and choose witnesses, and of vouching for one's own witnesses. . . . A more direct and acceptable approach is simply to recognize direct and redirect examination of one's own witness as the equivalent of cross-examining an opponent's witness. . . . Allowable techniques for dealing with hostile, double-crossing, forgetful, and mentally deficient witnesses leave no substance to a claim that one could not adequately develop his own witness at the former hearing. An even less appealing argument is presented when failure to develop fully was the result of a deliberate choice."

North Carolina practice currently permits testimony against the party *against* whom it was offered. Brandis on North Carolina Evidence § 145, at 577 (1982). There are no North Carolina cases concerning testimony offered against the party *by* whom it was previously offered.

With respect to identity of the parties, the Advisory Committee's Note states:

"As a further assurance of fairness in thrusting upon a party the prior handling of the witness, the common law also insisted upon identity of parties, deviating only to the extent of allowing substitution of successors in a narrowly construed privity. Mutuality as an aspect of identity is now generally discredited, and the requirement of identity of the offering party disappears except as it might affect motive to develop the testimony. . . The question remains whether strict identity, or privity, should continue as a requirement with respect to the party against whom offered."

North Carolina practice apparently departs from the privity requirement to the extent of allowing former testimony "if the party against whom it was admitted had not merely an opportunity for cross-examination but the same motive for cross-examination as the party against whom it is offered." Brandis on North Carolina Evidence § 145, at 577 (1982). Exception (1) permits former testimony in civil cases if a predecessor in interest had an opportunity and similar motive to develop the testimony.

Under certain circumstances, Exception (1) permits a broader use of depositions than does N.C.Civ.Pro.Rule 32. See also G.S. 8–83.

Exception (2) differs from Fed.R.Evid. 804(b)(2) in that it omits the phrase "In a prosecution for homicide or in a civil action or proceeding".

The exception is similar to G.S. 8–51.1. Unlike Fed.R.Evid. 804(b)(2) which limits admissibility of dying declarations in criminal cases to homicide prosecution, Exception (2) and G.S. 8–51.1 permit dying declarations to be admitted in all types of criminal and civil actions and proceedings. Under G.S. 8–51.1 the declarant must have died from the causes or circumstances on which he commented. Upon adoption of Exception (2), G.S. 8–51.1 should be repealed.

Exception (3) concerns statements against interest and differs from Fed.R.Evid. 804(b)(3) as noted below. The Advisory Committee's Note states:

"The circumstantial guaranty of reliability for declarations against interest is the assumption that persons do not make statements which are damaging to themselves unless satisfied for good reason that they are true. . . . If the statement is that of a party, offered by his opponent, it comes in as an admission, . . . and there is no occasion to inquire whether it is against interest, this not being a condition precedent to admissibility of admissions by opponents."

North Carolina cases have recognized declarations against pecuniary or proprietary interest as an exception to the hearsay rule. See Brandis on North Carolina Evidence § 147 (1982). In State v. Haywood, 295 N.C. 709, the North Carolina Supreme Court abandoned the Court's previous approach that excluded from the exception declarations against penal interest.

The last sentence of Fed.R.Evid. 804(b)(3) provides that: "A statement tending to expose the declarant to criminal liability and offered to exculpate the accused is not admissible unless corroborating circumstances clearly indicate the trustworthiness of the statement." Requiring corroborating circumstances to indicate clearly the trustworthiness of statements exculpating the accused while imposing no such requirement with respect to statements implicating the accused raises serious constitutional questions. Accordingly, Exception (3) differs from Fed.R.Evid. 804(b)(3) in that it imposes the requirement of corroborating circumstances with respect to both exculpating and implicating statements.

In *Haywood,* the Court listed several very restrictive requirements that a declaration against penal interest must meet. The exception should not be construed to add requirements in addition to the requirement that "corroborating circumstances clearly indicate the trustworthiness of the statement." As the Advisory Committee's Note states: "The requirement of corroboration should be construed in such a manner as to effectuate its purpose of circumventing fabrication."

Declarations against penal interests are admissible in both criminal and civil cases. However, the requirement of corroborating circumstances applies only in criminal cases.

The exception does not purport to deal with questions of the right to confrontation.

Exception (4) concerns statements of personal or family history.

The common law requirement in North Carolina that a declaration in this area must have been made before the beginning of the controversy was dropped in Fed.R.Evid. 804(b)(3), which is identical to this exception, as bearing more appropriately on weight than admissibility. See Brandis on North Carolina Evidence § 149 (1982); Advisory Committee's Note. Unlike North Carolina law that requires that the declarant be dead, Rule 804 merely requires that the declarant be unavailable. See Brandis supra.

The first part of the rule specifically disclaims any need of first-hand knowledge respecting declarant's own personal history. Advisory Committee's Note.

The second part of the rule deals with declarations concerning the history of another person. North Carolina common law provides that the declarant is qualified if related by blood or marriage. Brandis, supra. In addition, and contrary to the common law in North Carolina, the declarant qualifies under the exception by virtue of intimate association with the family.

The Advisory Committee's Note states that: "The requirement sometimes encountered that when the subject of the statement is the relationship between two other persons the declarant must qualify as to both is omitted. Relationship is reciprocal." There are no North Carolina cases on this point.

Exception (5) is identical to Rule 803(24) and differs from the federal rule. See commentary to Rule 803(24).

Rule 805. Hearsay within hearsay

Hearsay included within hearsay is not excluded under the hearsay rule if each part of the combined statements conforms with an exception to the hearsay rule provided in these rules.

Added by Laws 1983, c. 701, § 1.

North Carolina Commentary

This rule is identical to Fed.R.Evid. 805. The Advisory Committee's Note states:

"On principle it scarcely seems open to doubt that the hearsay rule should not call for exclusion of a hearsay statement which includes a further hearsay statement when both conform to the requirements of a hearsay exception. Thus a hospital record might contain an entry of the patient's age based on information furnished by his wife. The hospital record would qualify as a regular entry except that the person who furnished the information was not acting in the routine of the business. However, her statement independently qualifies as a statement of pedigree (if she is unavailable) or as a statement made for purposes of diagnosis or treatment, and hence each link in the chain falls under sufficient assurance. Or, further to illustrate, a dying declaration may incorporate a declaration against interest by another declarant. See McCormick § 290, p. 611."

Rule 805 is consistent with North Carolina practice. See, e.g., State v. Connley, 295 N.C. 327 [245 S.E.2d 663] (1978).

Rule 806. Attacking and supporting credibility of declarant

When a hearsay statement has been admitted in evidence, the credibility of the declarant may be attacked, and if attacked may be supported, by any evidence which would be admissible for those purposes if declarant had testified as a witness. Evidence of a statement or conduct by the declarant at any time, inconsistent with his hearsay statement, is not subject to any requirement that he may have been afforded an opportunity to deny or explain. If the party against whom a hearsay statement has been admitted calls the declarant as a witness, the party is entitled to examine him on the statement as if under cross-examination.

Added by Laws 1983, c. 701, § 1.

North Carolina Commentary

This rule is identical to Fed.R.Evid. 806 except that the phrase "or a statement defined in 801(d)(2)(C), (D), or (E)" has been omitted from the first sentence. Fed.R.Evid. 801 treats admissions by a party-opponent as statements that are not hearsay. Since Rule 801 treats such statements as exceptions to the hearsay rule, the above phrase is superfluous.

The Advisory Committee's Note states:

"The declarant of a hearsay statement which is admitted in evidence is in effect a witness. His credibility should in fairness be subject to impeachment and support as though he had in fact testified. See Rules 608 and 609. There are however, some special aspects of the impeaching of a hearsay declarant which require consideration. These special aspects center upon impeachment by inconsistent statement, arise from factual differences which exist between the use of hearsay and an actual witness and also between various kinds of hearsay, and involve the question of applying to declarants the general rule disallowing evidence of an inconsistent statement to impeach a witness unless he is afforded an opportunity to deny or explain. . . .

"The principal difference between using hearsay and an actual witness is that the inconsistent statement will in the case of the witness almost inevitably of necessity in the nature of things be a prior statement, which it is entirely possible and feasible to call to his attention, while in the case of hearsay the inconsistent statement may well be a subsequent one, which practically precludes calling it to the attention of the declarant. The result of insisting upon observation of this impossible requirement in the hearsay situation is to deny the opponent, already barred from cross-examination, any benefit of this important technique of impeachment. The writers favor allowing the subsequent statement. McCormick § 37, p. 69; 3 Wigmore § 1033. . . .

"When the impeaching statement was made prior to the hearsay statement, differences in the kinds of hearsay appear which arguably may justify differences in treatment. If the hearsay consisted of a simple statement by the witness, e.g., a dying declaration or a declaration against interest, the feasibility of affording him an opportunity to deny or explain encounters the same practical impossibility as where the statement is a subsequent one, just discussed, although here the impossibility arises from the total absence of anything resembling a hearing at which the matter could be put to him. The courts by a large majority have ruled in favor of allowing the statement to be used, under these circumstances. McCormick § 37, p. 69; 3 Wigmore § 1033. If however, the hearsay consists of former testimony or a deposition, the possibility of calling the prior statement to the attention of the witness or deponent is not ruled out, since the opportunity to cross-examine was available. It might thus be concluded that with former testimony or depositions the conventional foundation should be insisted upon. Most of the cases involve depositions, and Wigmore describes them as divided. 3 Wigmore § 1031. Deposition procedures at best are cumbersome and expensive, and to require the laying of the foundation may impose an undue burden. Under the federal practice, there is no way of knowing with certainty at the time of taking a deposition whether it is merely for discovery or will ultimately end up in evidence. With respect to both former testimony and depositions the possibility exists that knowledge of the statement might not be acquired until after the time of the cross-examination. Moreover, the expanded admissibility of former testimony and depositions under Rule 804(b)(1) calls for a correspondingly expanded approach to impeachment. The rule dispenses with the requirement in all hearsay situations, which is readily administered and best calculated to lead to fair results."

In Hooper v. Moore, 48 N.C. [3 Jones] 428 (1856), the court stated that in order to impeach the credibility of a declarant by showing an inconsistent statement made before the time when a deposition was taken, the declarant must be given an opportunity to explain. Professor Brandis is uncertain whether the requirement of an opportunity to explain bars proof of statements or conduct showing bias on the part of a hearsay declarant not present to testify; but in his view it should not. Brandis on North Carolina Evidence § 48, p. 183 (1982).

The provision for cross-examination of a declarant upon his hearsay statement is a corollary of general principles of cross-examination and is consistent with North Carolina practice. See N.C.Civ.Pro. Rule 32(c).

ARTICLE 9

Authentication and Identification

Rule 901. Requirement of authentication or identification

(a) General provision.—The requirement of authentication or identification as a condition precedent to admissibility is satisfied by evidence sufficient to support a finding that the matter in question is what its proponent claims.

(b) Illustrations.—By way of illustration only, and not by way of limitation, the following are examples of authentication or identification conforming with the requirements of this rule:

(1) Testimony of Witness with Knowledge.—Testimony that a matter is what it is claimed to be.

(2) Nonexpert Opinion on Handwriting.—Nonexpert opinion as to the genuineness of handwriting, based upon familiarity not acquired for purposes of the litigation.

(3) Comparison by Trier or Expert Witness.—Comparison by the trier of fact or by expert witnesses with specimens which have been authenticated.

(4) Distinctive Characteristics and the Like.—Appearance, contents, substance, internal patterns, or other distinctive characteristics, taken in conjunction with circumstances.

(5) Voice Identification.—Identification of a voice, whether heard firsthand or through mechanical or electronic transmission or recording, by opinion based upon hearing the voice at any time under circumstances connecting it with the alleged speaker.

(6) Telephone Conversations.—Telephone conversations, by evidence that a call was made to the number assigned at the time by the telephone company to a particular person or business, if (A) in the case of a person, circumstances, including self-identification, show the person answering to be the one called, or (B) in the case of a business, the call was made to a place of business and the conversation related to business reasonably transacted over the telephone.

(7) Public Records or Reports.—Evidence that a writing authorized by law to be recorded or filed and in fact recorded or filed in a public office, or a purported public record, report, statement, or data compilation, in any form, is from the public office where items of this nature are kept.

(8) Ancient Documents or Data Compilations.—Evidence that a document or data compilation, in any form, (A) is in such condition as to create no suspicion concerning its authenticity, (B) was in a place where it, if authentic, would likely be, and (C) has been in existence 20 years or more at the time it is offered.

(9) Process or System.—Evidence describing a process or system used to produce a result and showing that the process or system produces an accurate result.

(10) Methods Provided by Statute.—Any method of authentication or identification provided by statute.

Added by Laws 1983, c. 701, § 1.

North Carolina Commentary

This rule is identical to Fed.R.Evid. 901 except that in example (10) the word "statute" is inserted in lieu of the phrase "Act of Congress or by other rules prescribed by the Supreme Court pursuant to statutory authority."

The Advisory Committee's Note states:

"**Subdivision (a).** Authentication and identification represent a special aspect of relevancy. . . . Thus a telephone conversation may be irrelevant because on an unrelated topic or because the speaker is not identified. The latter aspect is the one here involved. Wigmore describes the need for authentication as 'an inherent logical necessity.' 7 Wigmore § 2129, p. 564.

"This requirement of showing authenticity or identity falls in the category of relevancy dependent upon fulfillment of a condition of fact and is governed by the procedure set forth in Rule 104(b).

"The common law approach to authentication of documents has been criticized as an 'attitude of agnosticism,' McCormick, Cases on Evidence 388, n. 4 (3rd ed. 1956), as one which 'departs sharply from men's customs in ordinary affairs,' and as presenting only a slight obstacle to the introduction of forgeries in comparison to the time and expense devoted to proving genuine writings which correctly show their origin on their face, McCormick § 185, pp. 395, 396. Today, such available procedures as requests to admit and pretrial conference afford the means of eliminating much of the need for authentication or identification. Also, significant inroads upon the traditional insistence on authentication and identification have been made by accepting as at least prima facie genuine items of the kind treated in Rule 902, infra. However, the need for suitable methods of proof still remains, since criminal cases pose their own obstacles to the use of preliminary procedures, unforeseen contingencies may arise, and cases of genuine controversy will still occur."

Subdivision (a) is in accord with North Carolina practice.

With respect to **subdivision (b)**, the Advisory Committee's Note states:

"The treatment of authentication and identification draws largely upon the experience embodied in the common law and in statutes to furnish illustrative applications of the general principle set forth in subdivision (a). The examples are not intended as an exclusive enumeration of allowable methods but are meant to guide and suggest, leaving room for growth and development in this area of the law.

"The examples relate for the most part to documents, with some attention given to voice communications and computer printouts. As Wigmore noted, no special rules have been developed for authenticating chattels. Wigmore, Code of Evidence § 2086 (3rd ed. 1942).

"It should be observed that compliance with requirements of authentication or identification by no means assures admission of an item into evidence, as other bars, hearsay for example, may remain.

"**Example (1)** contemplates a broad spectrum ranging from testimony of a witness who was present at the signing of a document to testimony establishing narcotics as taken from an accused and accounting for custody through the period until trial, including laboratory analysis."

Example (1) is in accord with North Carolina practice.

The Advisory Committee's Note states:

"**Example (2)** states conventional doctrine as to lay identification of handwriting, which recognizes that a sufficient familiarity with the handwriting of another person may be acquired by seeing him write, by exchanging correspondence, or by other means, to afford a basis for identifying it on subsequent occasions. McCormick § 189. . . . Testimony based upon familiarity acquired for purposes of the litigation is reserved to the expert under the example which follows."

Example (2) is in accord with North Carolina practice. See Brandis on North Carolina Evidence § 197 (1982).

Example (3) is comparison by the trier of fact or by expert witnesses with specimens that have been authenticated. In State v. LeDuc, 306 N.C. 62 (1982), the Court permitted handwriting comparisons by the jury unaided by lay or expert testimony. G.S. 8–40, which should be repealed upon enactment of this rule, requires that the exemplar used for comparison be "proved to the satisfaction of the judge to be genuine". However, the Advisory Committee's Note states:

"The history of common law restrictions upon the technique of proving or disproving the genuineness of a disputed specimen of handwriting through comparison with a genuine specimen, by either the testimony of expert witnesses or direct viewing by the triers themselves, is detailed in 7 Wigmore §§ 1991–1994. In breaking away, the English Common Law Procedure Act of 1854, 17 and 18 Vict., c. 125, § 27, cautiously allowed expert or trier to use exemplars 'proved to the satisfaction of the judge to be genuine' for purposes of comparison. The language found its way into numerous statutes in this country, e.g., California Evidence Code §§ 1417, 1418. While explainable as a measure of prudence in the process of breaking with precedent in the handwriting situation, the reservation to the judge of the question of the genuineness of exemplars and the imposition of an unusually high standard of persuasion are at variance with the general treatment of relevancy which depends upon fulfillment of a condition of fact. Rule 104(b). No similar attitude is found in other comparison situations, e.g., ballistics comparison by jury . . . or by experts . . . and no reason appears for its continued existence in handwriting cases. Consequently Example (3) sets no higher standard for handwriting specimens and treats all comparison situations alike, to be governed by Rule 104(b).

"Precedent supports the acceptance of visual comparison as sufficiently satisfying preliminary authentication requirements for admission in evidence. . . .

"**Example (4).** The characteristics of the offered item itself, considered in the light of circumstances, afford authentication techniques in great variety. Thus a document or telephone conversation may be shown to have emanated from a particular person by virtue of its disclosing knowledge of facts known peculiarly to him . . .; similarly, a letter may be authenticated by content and circumstances indicating it was in reply to a duly authenticated one. . . . Language patterns may indicate authenticity or its opposite."

Example (4) is in accord with North Carolina practice. See generally Brandis, supra, §§ 195, 236.

The Advisory Committee's Note states:

"**Example (5).** Since aural voice identification is not a subject of expert testimony, the requisite familiarity may be acquired either before or after the particular speaking which is the subject of the identification, in this respect resembling visual identification of a person rather than identification of handwriting. Cf. Example (2), supra."

Example (5) is in accord with North Carolina practice. See generally Brandis, supra, § 96.

The Advisory Committee's Note states:

"**Example (6).** The cases are in agreement that a mere assertion of his identity by a person talking on the telephone is not sufficient evidence of the authenticity of the conversation and that additional evidence of his identity is required. The additional evidence need not fall in any set pattern. Thus the content of his statements or the reply technique, under Example (4), supra, or voice identification, under Example (5), may furnish the necessary foundation. Outgoing calls made by the witness involve additional factors bearing upon authenticity. The calling of a number assigned by the telephone company reasonably supports the assumption that the listing is correct and that the number is the one reached. If the number is that of a place of business, the mass of authority allows an ensuing conversation if it relates to business reasonably transacted over the telephone, on the theory that the maintenance of the telephone connection is an invitation to do business without further identification. Otherwise, some additional circumstance of identification of the speaker is required. The authorities divide on the question whether the self-identifying statement of the person answering suffices. Example (6) answers in the affirmative on the assumption that usual conduct respecting telephone calls furnish adequate assurances of regularity, bearing in mind that the entire matter is open to exploration before the trier of fact."

Part (A) of Example (6) is in accord with North Carolina practice. See Brandis, supra, § 96. Part (B) permits identity to be established by evidence that the call was made to a place of business and the conversation related to business reasonably transacted over the telephone. There are no North Carolina cases directly on this point.

The Advisory Committee's Note states:

"**Example (7).** Public records are regularly authenticated by proof of custody, without more. McCormick § 191; 7 Wigmore §§ 2158, 2159. The example extends the principle to include data stored in computers and similar methods, of which increasing use in the public records area may be expected."

Example (7) is in accord with North Carolina practice. See Brandis, supra, § 195.

The Advisory Committee's Note states:

"**Example (8).** The familiar ancient document rule of the common law is extended to include data stored electronically or by other similar means. Since the importance of appearance diminishes in this situation, the importance of custody or place where found increases correspondingly. This expansion is necessary in view of the widespread use of methods of storing data in forms other than conventional written records.

"Any time period selected is bound to be arbitrary. The common law period of 30 years is here reduced to 20 years, with some shift of emphasis from the probable unavailability of witnesses to the unlikeliness of a still viable fraud after the lapse of time. . . .

"The application of Example (8) is not subject to any limitation to title documents or to any requirement that possession, in the case of a title document, has been consistent with the document. See McCormick § 190."

Example (8) is in accord with North Carolina practice, except that the period of 30 years is reduced to 20 years. See Brandis, supra, § 196.

The Advisory Committee's Note states:

"**Example (9)** is designed for situations in which the accuracy of a result is dependent upon a process or system which produces it. X-rays afford a familiar instance. Among more recent developments is the computer. . . . Example (9) does not, of course, foreclose taking judicial notice of the accuracy of the process or system."

Example (9) is in accord with North Carolina practice.

Example (10) makes clear that methods of authentication provided by the Rules of Civil Procedure or other statutes are not intended to be superseded. Illustrative are the provisions for authentication of official records in Civil Procedure Rule 44 and for the authentication of depositions in Civil Procedure Rule 30(f).

Rule 902. Self-authentication

Extrinsic evidence of authenticity as a condition precedent to admissibility is not required with respect to the following:

(1) Domestic Public Documents Under Seal.—A document bearing a seal purporting to be that of the United States, or of any state, district, commonwealth, territory or insular possession thereof, or the Trust Territory of the Pacific Islands, or of a political subdivision, department, officer, or agency thereof, and a signature purporting to be an attestation or execution.

(2) Domestic Public Documents Not Under Seal.—A document purporting to bear the signature in his official capacity of an officer or employee of any entity included in paragraph (1) hereof, having no seal, if a public officer having a seal and having official duties in the district or political subdivision of the officer or employee certifies under seal that the signer has the official capacity and that the signature is genuine.

(3) Foreign Public Documents.—A document purporting to be executed or attested in his official capacity by a person authorized by the laws of a foreign country to make the execution or attestation, and accompanied by a final certification as to the genuineness of the signature and official position (A) of the executing or attesting person, or (B) of any foreign official whose certificate of genuineness of signature and official position relates to the execution or attestation or is in a chain of certificates of genuineness of signature and official position relating to the execution or attestation. A final certification may be made by a secretary of embassy or legation, consul general, consul, vice consul, or consular agent of the United States, or a diplomatic or consular official of the foreign country assigned or accredited to the United States. If reasonable opportunity has been given to all parties to investigate the authenticity and accuracy of official documents, the court may, for good cause shown, order that they be treated as presumptively authentic without final certification or permit them to be evidenced by an attested summary with or without final certification.

(4) Certified Copies of Public Records.—A copy of an official record or report or entry therein, or of a document authorized by law to be recorded or filed and actually recorded or filed in a public office, including data compilations in any form, certified as correct by the custodian or other person authorized to make the certification, by certificate complying with paragraph (1), (2), or (3) or complying with any law of the United States or of this State.

(5) Official Publications.—Books, pamphlets, or other publications purporting to be issued by public authority.

(6) Newspapers and Periodicals.—Printed materials purporting to be newspapers or periodicals.

(7) Trade Inscriptions and the Like.—Inscriptions, signs, tags, or labels purporting to have been affixed in the course of business and indicating ownership, control, or origin.

(8) Acknowledged Documents.—Documents accompanied by a certificate of acknowledgment executed in the manner provided by law by a notary public or other officer authorized by law to take acknowledgments.

(9) Commercial Paper and Related Documents.—Commercial paper, signatures thereon, and documents relating thereto to the extent provided by general commercial law.

(10) Presumptions Created by Law.—Any signature, document, or other matter declared by any law of the United States or of this State to be presumptively or prima facie genuine or authentic.

Added by Laws 1983, c. 701, § 1.

North Carolina Commentary

This rule differs from Fed.R.Evid. 902 in that the phrase "or the Panama Canal Zone" has been deleted from paragraph (1). Paragraph (4) differs from the federal rule in that the phrase "any law of the United States or of this State" has been substituted in lieu of the phrase "of this Rule or complying with any Act of Congress or rule prescribed by the Supreme Court pursuant to statutory authority." Paragraph (10) differs from the federal rule in that the phrase "any law of the United States or of this State" is used in lieu of the phrase "Act of Congress".

The Advisory Committee's Note states:

"Case law and statutes have, over the years, developed a substantial body of instances in which authenticity is taken as sufficiently established for purposes of admissibility without extrinsic evidence to that effect, sometimes for reasons of policy but perhaps more often because practical considerations reduce the possibility of unauthenticity to a very small dimension. The present rule collects and incorporates these situations, in some instances expanding them to occupy a larger area which their underlying considerations justify. In no instance is the opposite party foreclosed from disputing authenticity."

Paragraph (1) provides that a document bearing the seal of an officer of the government and a signature purporting to be an attestation or execution does not require extrinsic evidence of authenticity as a condition precedent to admissibility. See Brandis on North Carolina Evidence § 153, at 610 (1982). The Advisory Committee's Note states:

"The acceptance of documents bearing a public seal and signature, most often encountered in practice in the form of acknowledgments or certificates authenticating copies of public records, is actually of broad application. Whether theoretically based in whole or in part upon judicial notice, the practical underlying considerations are that forgery is a crime and detection is fairly easy and certain. 7 Wigmore § 2161, p. 638. . . ."

Paragraph (2) is derived from Federal Civil Procedure Rule 44. North Carolina Civil Procedure Rule 44, which is similar, should be amended to conform to Rule 902. Paragraph (2) applies to documents as well as public records. The Advisory Committee's Note states:

"While statutes are found which raise a presumption of genuineness of purported official signatures in the absence of an official seal, 7 Wigmore § 2167 . . . the greater ease of effecting a forgery under these circumstances is apparent. Hence this paragraph of the rule calls for authentication by an officer who has a seal. Notarial acts by members of the Armed Forces and other special situations are covered in paragraph (10)."

Paragraph (3) is derived from Federal Civil Procedure Rule 44(a)(2), which was amended in 1966 to provide for greater clarity, efficiency, and flexibility in the procedure for authenticating copies of foreign official records. North Carolina Civil Procedure Rule 44 should be amended to conform to Rule 902. Paragraph (3) applies to public documents rather than being limited to public records.

Paragraph (4) is confined to official records and reports, and documents authorized to be recorded or filed and actually recorded or filed. The Advisory Committee's Note states:

"The common law and innumerable statutes have recognized the procedure of authenticating copies of public records by certificate. The certificate qualifies as a public document, receivable as authentic when in conformity with paragraphs (1), (2), or (3). . . . It will be observed that the certification procedure here provided extends only to public records, reports, and recorded documents, all including data compilations, and does not apply to public documents generally. Hence documents provable when presented in original form under paragraphs (1), (2), or (3) may not be provable by certified copy under paragraph (4)."

G.S. 1A–1, Rule 44, G.S. 8–34, G.S. 8–35, G.S. 8–18, G.S. 8–20, G.S. 47–31, and G.S. 47–34 should be amended to conform to Rule 902.

Paragraph (5) has the same effect as North Carolina Civil Procedure Rule 44(a), which should be amended to conform to Rule 902. The Advisory Committee's Note states:

"Dispensing with preliminary proof of the genuineness of purportedly official publications, most commonly encountered in connection with statutes, court reports, rules, and regulations, has been greatly enlarged by statutes and decisions. 5 Wigmore § 1684. Paragraph (5), it will be noted, does not confer admissibility upon all official publications; it merely provides a means whereby their authenticity may be taken as established for purposes of admissibility. Rule 44(a) of the Rules of Civil Procedure has been to the same effect."

Paragraph (6) changes North Carolina practice by providing that printed materials purporting to be newspapers or periodicals are self-authenticating. The Advisory Committee's Note states:

"The likelihood of forgery of newspapers or periodicals is slight indeed. Hence no danger is apparent in receiving them. Establishing the authenticity of the publication may, of course, leave still open questions of authority and responsibility for items therein contained. See 7 Wigmore § 2150."

Paragraph (7) changes North Carolina practice by providing that inscriptions, signs, tags, or labels purporting to have been affixed in the course of business and indicating ownership, control, or origin are self-authenticating. The Advisory Committee's Note states:

"Several factors justify dispensing with preliminary proof of genuineness of commercial and mercantile labels and the like. The risk of forgery is minimal. Trademark infringement involves serious penalties. Great efforts are devoted to inducing the public to buy in reliance on brand names, and substantial protection is given them."

Paragraph (8) extends the exception for acknowledged title documents to include other acknowledged documents. The Advisory Committee's Note states:

"In virtually every state, acknowledged title documents are receivable in evidence without further proof. Statutes are collected in 5 Wigmore § 1676. If this authentication suffices for documents of the importance of those affecting titles, logic scarcely permits denying this method when other kinds of documents are involved."

Paragraph (9) provides that commercial paper, signatures thereon, and documents relating thereto are authenticated to the extent provided by general commercial law. The term "general commercial law" refers to the Uniform Commercial Code, except that federal commercial law will apply when federal commercial paper is involved. Pertinent provisions of the Uniform Commercial Code are G.S. 25–1–202, 25–3–307, and 25–3–510, dealing with third-party documents, signatures on negotiable instruments, protests, and statements of dishonor.

Paragraph (10) provides for the authentication of any signature, document, or other matter declared by any federal or North Carolina statute to be presumptively or prima facie genuine or authentic.

Rule 903. Subscribing witness' testimony unnecessary

The testimony of a subscribing witness is not necessary to authenticate a writing unless required by the laws of the jurisdiction whose laws govern the validity of the writing.

Added by Laws 1983, c. 701, § 1.

North Carolina Commentary

This rule is identical to Fed.R.Evid. 903.

The Advisory Committee's Note states:

"The common law required that attesting witnesses be produced or accounted for. Today the requirement has generally been abolished except with respect to documents which must be attested to be valid, e.g., wills in some states."

The requirement of proof by the attesting witness was abolished by G.S. 8-38, which should be repealed upon enactment of Rule 903. Rule 903 is not intended to affect the method and manner of proving instruments for registration.

ARTICLE 10

Contents of Writings, Recordings and Photographs

Rule 1001. Definitions

For the purposes of this Article the following definitions are applicable:

(1) Writings and Recordings.—"Writings" and "recordings" consist of letters, words, sounds, or numbers, or their equivalent, set down by handwriting, typewriting, printing, photostating, photographing, magnetic impulse, mechanical or electronic recording, or other form of data compilation.

(2) Photographs.—"Photographs" include still photographs, x-ray films, video tapes, and motion pictures.

(3) Original.—An "original" of a writing or recording is the writing or recording itself or any counterpart intended to have the same effect by a person executing or issuing it. An "original" of a photograph includes the negative or any print therefrom. If data are stored in a computer or similar device, any printout or other output readable by sight, shown to reflect the data accurately, is an "original."

(4) Duplicate.—A "duplicate" is a counterpart produced by the same impression as the original, or from the same matrix, or by means of photography, including enlargements and miniatures, or by mechanical or electronic re-recording, or by chemical reproduction, or by other equivalent techniques which accurately reproduce the original.

Added by Laws 1983, c. 701, § 1.

North Carolina Commentary

This rule is identical to Fed.R.Evid. 1001 except that the word "sounds" has been added to paragraph (1) between "words" and "or numbers."

The Advisory Committee's Note states:

"**Paragraph (1).** Traditionally the rule requiring the original centered upon accumulations of data and expressions affecting legal relations set forth in words and figures. This meant that the rule was one essentially related to writings. Present day techniques have expanded methods of storing data, yet the essential form which the information ultimately assumes for usable purposes is words and figures. Hence the considerations underlying the rule dictate its expansion to include computers, photographic systems, and other modern developments."

Paragraph (1) clarifies North Carolina law by providing that the best evidence rule applies to recordings and photographs. See Brandis on North Carolina Evidence § 190 (1982).

With respect to **Paragraph** (3), the Advisory Committee's Note states:

"In most instances, what is an original will be self-evident and further refinement will be unnecessary. However, in some instances particularized definition is required. A carbon copy of a contract executed in duplicate becomes an original, as does a sales ticket carbon copy given to a customer. While strictly speaking the original of a photograph might be thought to be only the negative, practicality and common usage require that any print from the negative be regarded as an original. Similarly, practicality and usage confer the status of original upon any computer printout."

Paragraph (3) is substantially in accord with North Carolina practice. See Brandis, supra, § 190; G.S. 55-37.1 and G.S. 55A-27.1.

With respect to **Paragraph** (4), the Advisory Committee's Note states:

"The definition describes 'copies' produced by methods possessing an accuracy which virtually eliminates the possibility of error. Copies thus produced are given the status of originals in large measure by Rule 1003, infra. Copies subsequently produced manually, whether handwritten or typed, are not within the definition. It should be noted that what is an original for some purposes may be a duplicate for others. Thus a bank's microfilm record of checks cleared is the original as a record. However, a print offered as a copy of a check whose contents are in controversy is a duplicate."

Rule 1002. Requirement of original

To prove the content of a writing, recording, or photograph, the original writing, recording, or photograph is required, except as otherwise provided in these rules or by statute.

Added by Laws 1983, c. 701, § 1.

North Carolina Commentary

This rule is identical to Fed.R.Evid. 1002.

The rule is the familiar "best evidence rule" expanded to include explicitly writings, recordings, and photographs, as defined in Rule 1001(1) and (2), supra. See Brandis on North Carolina Evidence § 190, at 100 (1982). However, the requirement for the original is overridden in many instances by other rules such as Rule 1003, which allows duplicates to be admitted.

The rule in North Carolina is consistent with Rule 1002 in that it requires the original of a writing only when its content is sought to be proved. Id.

The Advisory Committee's Note states:

"Application of the rule requires a resolution of the question whether contents are sought to be proved. Thus an event may be proved by nondocumentary evidence, even though a written record of it was made. If, however, the event is sought to be proved by the written record, the rule applies. For example, payment may be proved without producing the written receipt which was given. Earnings may be proved without producing books of account in which they are entered. . . . Nor does the rule apply to testimony that books or records have been examined and found not to contain any reference to a designated matter.

"The assumption should not be made that the rule will come into operation on every occasion when use is made of a photograph in evidence. On the contrary, the rule will seldom apply to ordinary photographs. In most instances a party *wishes* to introduce the item and the question raised is the propriety of receiving it in evidence. Cases in which an offer is made of the testimony of a witness as to what he saw in a photograph or motion picture, without producing the same, are most unusual. The usual course is for a witness on the stand to identify the photograph or motion picture as a correct representation of events which he saw or of a scene with which he is familiar. In fact he adopts the picture as his testimony, or, in common parlance, uses the picture to illustrate his testimony. Under these circumstances, no effort is made to prove the contents of the picture, and the rule is inapplicable. . . .

"On occasion, however, situations arise in which contents are sought to be proved. Copyright, defamation, and invasion of privacy by photograph or motion picture fall in this category. Similarly as to situations in which the picture is offered as having independent probative value, e.g., automatic photograph of bank robber. . . . The most commonly encountered of this latter group is of course, the X-ray, with substantial authority calling for production of the original.

"It should be noted, however, that Rule 703, supra, allows an expert to give an opinion based on matters not in evidence, and the present rule must be read as being limited accordingly in its application. Hospital records which may be admitted as business records under Rule 803(6) commonly contain reports interpreting X-rays by the staff radiologist, who qualifies as an expert, and these reports need not be excluded from the records by the instant rule."

Rule 1003. Admissibility of duplicates

A duplicate is admissible to the same extent as an original unless (1) a genuine question is raised as to the authenticity of the original or (2) in the circumstances it would be unfair to admit the duplicate in lieu of the original.

Added by Laws 1983, c. 701, § 1.

North Carolina Commentary

This rule is identical to Fed.R.Evid. 1003.

Rule 1003 departs from the common law in North Carolina and other jurisdictions by providing that a duplicate is admissible to the same extent as an original unless a genuine question as to the authenticity of the original is raised or it would be unfair to admit the duplicate in the particular case. Traditionally, in North Carolina no special showing has been necessary in order to require production of the original.

The Advisory Committee's Note states:

"When the only concern is with getting the words or other contents before the court with accuracy and precision, then a counterpart serves equally as well as the original, if the counterpart is the product of a method which insures accuracy and genuineness. By definition in Rule 1001(4), supra, a 'duplicate' possesses this character. Therefore, if no genuine issue exists as to authenticity and no other reason exists for requiring the original, a duplicate is admissible under the rule. Other reasons for requiring the original may be present when only a part of the original is reproduced and the remainder is needed for cross-examination or may disclose matters qualifying the part offered or otherwise useful to the opposing party."

Courts should be liberal in permitting questions of genuineness to be raised. The court should examine the quality of the duplicate, the specificity and sincerity of the challenge, the importance of the evidence to the case, and the burdens of producing the original before determining whether a genuine question of authenticity is raised.

Rule 1004. Admissibility of other evidence of contents

The original is not required, and other evidence of the contents of a writing, recording, or photograph is admissible if:

(1) Originals Lost or Destroyed.—All originals are lost or have been destroyed, unless the proponent lost or destroyed them in bad faith; or

(2) Original Not Obtainable.—No original can be obtained by any available judicial process or procedure; or

(3) Original in Possession of Opponent.—At a time when an original was under the control of a party against whom offered, he was put on notice, by the pleadings or otherwise, that the contents would be a subject of proof at the hearing, and he does not produce the original at the hearing; or

(4) Collateral Matters.—The writing, recording, or photograph is not closely related to a controlling issue.

Added by Laws 1983, c. 701, § 1.

North Carolina Commentary

This rule is identical to Fed.R.Evid. 1004.

The Advisory Committee's Note states:

"Basically the rule requiring the production of the original as proof of contents has developed as a rule of preference: if failure to produce the original is satisfactorily explained, secondary evidence is admissible. The instant rule specifies the circumstances under which production of the original is excused.

"The rule recognizes no 'degrees' of secondary evidence."

Paragraph (1) provides that loss or destruction of the original, unless due to bad faith of the proponent, is a satisfactory explanation of nonproduction. See McCormick § 201. This paragraph is consistent with current North Carolina practice. See Brandis on North Carolina Evidence § 192 (1982).

Paragraph (2) provides that when the original is in the possession of a third person, inability to procure it from him by resort to process or other judicial procedure is a sufficient explanation of nonproduction. The Advisory Committee's Note states that: "Judicial procedure includes subpoena duces tecum as an incident to the taking of a deposition in another jurisdiction. No further showing is required. See McCormick § 202." Extreme expense and inconvenience in obtaining the document will not constitute unavailability.

Paragraph (3) is consistent with North Carolina practice in that secondary evidence of the contents of a writing is admissible if the opponent who is in possession of the original fails, after notice, to produce it at the trial. See Brandis on North Carolina Evidence § 193 (1982). The Advisory Committee's Note states:

"A party who has an original in his control has no need for the protection of the rule if put on notice that proof of contents will be made. He can ward off secondary evidence by offering the original. The notice procedure here provided is not to be confused with orders to produce or other discovery procedures, as the purpose of the procedure under this rule is to afford the opposite party an opportunity to produce the original, not to compel him to do so. McCormick § 203."

Under the rule, notice may be given by the pleadings. There are no North Carolina cases on this point.

Paragraph (4) is consistent with North Carolina cases in that production of the original is not required if the writing is only collaterally involved in the case. See Brandis on North Carolina Evidence § 191 (1982). The Advisory Committee's Note states:

"While difficult to define with precision, situations arise in which no good purpose is served by production of the original. Examples are the newspaper in an action for the price of publishing defendant's advertisement, Foster-Holcomb Investment Co. v. Little Rock Publishing Co., 151 Ark. 449, 236 S.W. 597 (1922), and the streetcar transfer of plaintiff claiming status as a passenger, Chicago City Ry. Co. v. Carroll, 206 Ill. 318, 68 N.E. 1087 (1903). Numerous cases are collected in McCormick § 200, p. 412, n. 1."

Rule 1005. Public records

The contents of an official record, or of a document authorized to be recorded or filed and actually recorded or filed, including data compilations in any form, if otherwise admissible, may be proved by copy, certified as correct in accordance with Rule 902 or testified to be correct by a witness who has compared it with the original. If a copy which complies with the foregoing cannot be obtained by the exercise of reasonable diligence, then other evidence of the contents may be given.

Added by Laws 1983, c. 701, § 1.

North Carolina Commentary

This rule is identical to Fed.R.Evid. 1005.

Admission of certified copies of registered instruments and official records are currently governed by G.S. 8–18, G.S. 8–34, and G.S. 1A–1, Rule 44.

The Advisory Committee's Note states:

"Public records call for somewhat different treatment. Removing them from their usual place of keeping would be attended by serious inconvenience to the public and to the custodian. As a consequence judicial decisions and statutes commonly hold that no explanation need be given for failure to produce the original of a public record. McCormick § 204; 4 Wigmore §§ 1215–1228. This blanket dispensation from producing or accounting for the original would open the door to the introduction of every kind of secondary evidence of contents of public records were it not for the preference given certified or compared copies. Recognition of degrees of secondary evidence in this situation is an appropriate quid pro quo for not applying the requirement of producing the original."

Rule 1006. Summaries

The contents of voluminous writings, recordings, or photographs which cannot conveniently be examined in court may be presented in the form of a chart, summary, or calculation. The originals, or duplicates, shall be made available for examination or copying, or both, by other parties at a reasonable time and place. The court may order that they be produced in court.

Added by Laws 1983, c. 701, § 1.

North Carolina Commentary

This rule is identical to Fed.R.Evid. 1006.

Where documents are so voluminous that it would be impracticable to produce and examine them in court, North Carolina Courts have allowed a qualified witness to testify to the results of his examination of the documents. Brandis on North Carolina Evidence § 192 (1982).

Rule 1007. Testimony or written admission of party

Contents of writings, recordings, or photographs may be proved by the testimony or deposition of the party against whom offered or by his written admission, without accounting for the nonproduction of the original.

Added by Laws 1983, c. 701, § 1.

North Carolina Commentary

This rule is identical to Fed.R.Evid. 1007.

This rule is consistent with North Carolina practice in that the original writing need not be produced where the opponent admits that the copy offered in evidence is correct. See Brandis on North Carolina Evidence § 192, at 113 (1982). The rule clarifies North Carolina law by not allowing proof of contents by oral evidence of an oral admission. See Norcum v. Savage, 140 N.C. 472 [53 S.E. 289] (1906). The Advisory Committee's Note states:

"While the parent case, Slatterie v. Pooley, 6 M. & W. 664, 151 Eng.Rep. 579 (Exch.1840), allows proof of contents by evidence of an oral admission by the party against whom offered, without accounting for nonproduction of the original, the risk of inaccuracy is substantial and the decision is at odds with the purpose of the rule giving preference to the original. See 4 Wigmore § 1255. The instant rule follows Professor McCormick's suggestion of limiting this use of admissions to those made in the course of giving testimony or in writing. McCormick § 208, p. 424. The limitation, of course, does not call for excluding evidence of an oral admission when nonproduction of the original has been accounted for and secondary evidence generally has become admissible. Rule 1004, supra."

Rule 1008. Functions of court and jury

When the admissibility of other evidence of contents of writings, recordings, or photographs under these rules depends upon the fulfillment of a condition of fact, the question whether the condition has been fulfilled is ordinarily for the court to determine in accordance with the provisions of Rule 104. However, when an issue is raised (a) whether the asserted writing ever existed, or (b) whether another writing, recording, or photograph produced at the trial is the original, or (c) whether other evidence of contents correctly reflects the contents, the issue is for the trier of fact to determine as in the case of other issues of fact.

Added by Laws 1983, c. 701, § 1.

North Carolina Commentary

This rule is identical to Fed.R.Evid. 1008.

The Advisory Committee's Note states:

"Most preliminary questions of fact in connection with applying the rule preferring the original as evidence of contents are for the judge, under the general principles announced in Rule 104, supra. Thus, the question whether the loss of the originals has been established, or of the fulfillment of other conditions specified in Rule 1004, supra, is for the judge. However, questions may arise which go beyond the mere administration of the rule preferring the original and into the merits of the controversy. For example, plaintiff offers secondary evidence of the contents of an alleged contract, after first introducing evidence of loss of the original, and defendant counters with evidence that no such contract was ever executed. If the judge decides that the contract was never executed and excludes the secondary evidence, the case is at an end without ever going to the jury on a central issue. Levin, Authentication and Content of Writings, 10 Rutgers L.Rev. 632, 644 (1956). The latter portion of the instant rule is designed to insure treatment of these situations as raising jury questions. The decision is not one for uncontrolled discretion of the jury but is subject to the control exercised generally by the judge over jury determinations. See Rule 104(b), supra."

Although there are no North Carolina cases directly on point, Rule 1008 follows the division of function between the court and the jury with respect to competency and conditional relevancy. See Brandis on North Carolina Evidence § 8 (1982).

ARTICLE 11

Miscellaneous Rules

Rule 1101. Applicability of rules

(a) Proceedings generally.—Except as otherwise provided in subdivision (b) or by statute, these rules apply to all actions and proceedings in the courts of this State.

(b) Rules inapplicable.—The rules other than those with respect to privileges do not apply in the following situations:

(1) Preliminary Questions of Fact.—The determination of questions of fact preliminary to admissibility of evidence when the issue is to be determined by the court under Rule 104(a).

(2) Grand Jury.—Proceedings before grand juries.

(3) Miscellaneous Proceedings.—Proceedings for extradition or rendition; first appearance before district court judge or probable cause hearing in criminal cases; sentencing, or granting or revoking probation; issuance of warrants for arrest, criminal summonses, and search warrants; proceedings with respect to release on bail or otherwise.

(4) Contempt Proceedings.—Contempt proceedings in which the court is authorized by law to act summarily.

Added by Laws 1983, c. 701, § 1. Amended by Laws 1983(Reg. Sess. 1984), c. 1037, § 14; Laws 1985, c. 509, § 2.

North Carolina Commentary

This rule resembles Fed.R.Evid. 1101 with appropriate modifications.

Subdivision (b)(1) restates, for convenience, the provisions of the second sentence of Rule 104(a), supra. See Advisory Committee's Note to that rule.

Current North Carolina practice with respect to voir dire, sentencing hearings, probation revocation hearings, and juvenile proceedings is not meant to be changed by adoption of these rules.

Rule 1102. Short title

These rules shall be known and may be cited as the "North Carolina Rules of Evidence."

Added by Laws 1983, c. 701, § 1.

INDEX TO RULES OF EVIDENCE

NORTH CAROLINA RULES OF APPELLATE PROCEDURE

Revised 2009

Table of Rules

ARTICLE I. APPLICABILITY OF RULES

Rule 1. Scope of Rules: Trial Tribunal Defined

(a) Title. The title of these rules is "North Carolina Rules of Appellate Procedure." They may be so cited either in general references or in reference to particular rules. In reference to particular rules the abbreviated form of citation, "N.C. R. App. P. ___," is also appropriate.

(b) Scope of Rules. These rules govern procedure in all appeals from the courts of the trial division to the courts of the appellate division; in appeals in civil and criminal cases from the Court of Appeals to the Supreme Court; in direct appeals from administrative agencies, boards, and commissions to the appellate division; and in applications to the courts of the appellate division for writs and other relief which the courts or judges thereof are empowered to give.

(c) Rules Do Not Affect Jurisdiction. These rules shall not be construed to extend or limit the jurisdiction of the courts of the appellate division as that is established by law.

(d) Definition of Trial Tribunal. As used in these rules, the term "trial tribunal" includes the superior courts, the district courts, and any administrative agencies, boards, or commissions from which appeals lie directly to the appellate division.

[Adopted: 13 June 1975. Amended: 27 November 1984—1(a), (c)—effective 1 February 1985. Reenacted and Amended: 2 July 2009—added 1(a) and renumbered remaining subsections—effective 1 October 2009 and applies to all cases appealed on or after that date.]

Rule 2. Suspension of Rules

To prevent manifest injustice to a party, or to expedite decision in the public interest, either court of the appellate division may, except as otherwise expressly provided by these rules, suspend or vary the requirements or provisions of any of these rules in a case pending before it upon application of a party or upon its own initiative, and may order proceedings in accordance with its directions.

[Adopted: 13 June 1975. Reenacted: 2 July 2009—effective 1 October 2009 and applies to all cases appealed on or after that date.]

ARTICLE II. APPEALS FROM JUDGMENTS AND ORDERS OF SUPERIOR COURTS AND DISTRICT COURTS

Rule 3. Appeal in Civil Cases—How and When Taken

(a) Filing the Notice of Appeal. Any party entitled by law to appeal from a judgment or order of a superior or district court rendered in a civil action or special proceeding may take appeal by filing notice of appeal with the clerk of superior court and serving copies thereof upon all other parties within the time prescribed by subsection (c) of this rule.

(b) Special Provisions. Appeals in the following types of cases shall be taken in the time and manner set out in the General Statutes and appellate rules sections noted:

(1) Juvenile matters pursuant to N.C.G.S. § 7B–2602; the identity of persons under the age of eighteen at the time of the proceedings in the trial division shall be protected pursuant to Rule 3.1(b).

(2) Appeals pursuant to N.C.G.S. § 7B–1001 shall be subject to the provisions of Rule 3.1.

(c) Time for Taking Appeal. In civil actions and special proceedings, a party must file and serve a notice of appeal:

(1) within thirty days after entry of judgment if the party has been served with a copy of the judgment within the three day period prescribed by Rule 58 of the Rules of Civil Procedure; or

(2) within thirty days after service upon the party of a copy of the judgment if service was not made within that three day period; provided that

(3) if a timely motion is made by any party for relief under Rules 50(b), 52(b) or 59 of the Rules of Civil Procedure, the thirty day period for taking appeal is tolled as to all parties until entry of an order disposing of the motion and then runs as to each party from the date of entry of the order or its untimely service upon the party, as provided in subdivisions (1) and (2) of this subsection (c).

In computing the time for filing a notice of appeal, the provision for additional time after service by mail in Rule 27(b) of these rules and Rule 6(e) of the N.C. Rules of Civil Procedure shall not apply.

If timely notice of appeal is filed and served by a party, any other party may file and serve a notice of appeal within ten days after the first notice of appeal was served on such party.

(d) Content of Notice of Appeal. The notice of appeal required to be filed and served by subsection (a) of this rule shall specify the party or parties taking the appeal; shall designate the judgment or order from which appeal is taken and the court to which appeal is taken; and shall be signed by counsel of record for the party or parties taking the appeal, or by any such party not represented by counsel of record.

(e) Service of Notice of Appeal. Service of copies of the notice of appeal may be made as provided in Rule 26.

[Adopted: 13 June 1975. Amended: 14 April 1976; 8 December 1988—3(a), (b), (c), (d)—effective for all judgments of the trial tribunal entered on or after 1 July 1989; 8 June 1989—3(b)—effective for all judgments of the trial tribunal entered on or after 1 July 1989; 28 July 1994—3(c)—1 October 1994; 6 March 1997—3(c)—effective upon adoption 6 March 1997; 18 October 2001—3(c)—effective 31 October 2001; 1 May 2003—3(b)(1), (2); 6 May 2004—3(b)—effective 12 May 2004; 27 April 2006—3(b)—effective 1 May 2006 and applies to all cases appealed on or after that date. Reenacted and Amended: 2 July 2009—amended 3(b)—effective 1 October 2009 and applies to all cases appealed on or after that date.]

Rule 3.1. Appeal in Qualifying Juvenile Cases—How and When Taken; Special Rules

(a) Filing the Notice of Appeal. Any party entitled by law to appeal from a trial court judgment or order rendered in a case involving termination of parental rights and issues of juvenile dependency or juvenile abuse and/or neglect, appealable pursuant to N.C.G.S. § 7B–1001, may take appeal by filing notice of appeal with the clerk of superior court and serving copies thereof upon all other parties in the time and manner set out in Chapter 7B of the General Statutes of North Carolina. Trial counsel or an appellant not represented by counsel shall be responsible for filing and serving the notice of appeal in the time and manner required. If the appellant is represented by counsel, both the trial counsel and appellant must sign the notice of appeal, and the appellant shall cooperate with counsel throughout the appeal. All such appeals shall comply with the provisions set out in subsection (b) of this rule and, except as hereinafter provided by this rule, all other existing Rules of Appellate Procedure shall remain applicable.

(b) Protecting the Identity of Juveniles. For appeals filed pursuant to this rule and for extraordinary writs filed in cases to which this rule applies, the identity of involved persons under the age of eighteen at the time of the proceedings in the trial division (covered juveniles) shall be referenced only by the use of initials or pseudonyms in briefs, petitions, and all other filings, and shall be similarly redacted from all documents, exhibits, appendixes, or arguments submitted with such filings. If the parties desire to use pseudonyms, they shall stipulate in the record on appeal to the pseudonym to be used for each covered juvenile. Courts of the appellate division are not bound by the stipulation, and case captions will utilize initials. Further, the addresses and social security numbers of all covered juveniles shall be excluded from all filings and documents, exhibits, appendixes, and arguments. In cases subject to this rule, the first document filed in the appellate courts and the record on appeal shall contain the notice required by Rule 9(a).

The substitution and redaction requirements of this rule shall not apply to settled records on appeal; supplements filed pursuant to Rule 11(c); objections, amendments, or proposed alternative records on appeal submitted pursuant to Rule 3.1(c)(2); and any verbatim transcripts submitted pursuant to Rule 9(c). Pleadings and filings not subject to substitution and redaction requirements shall include the following notice on the first page of the document immediately underneath the title and in uppercase typeface: FILED PURSUANT TO RULE [3(b)(1)] [3.1(b)] [4(e)]; SUBJECT TO PUBLIC INSPECTION ONLY BY ORDER OF A COURT OF THE APPELLATE DIVISION.

Filings in cases governed by this rule that are not subject to substitution and redaction requirements will not be published on the Court's electronic filing site and will be available to the public only with the permission of a court of the appellate division. In addition, the juvenile's address and social security number shall be excluded from all filings, documents, exhibits, or arguments with the exception of sealed verbatim transcripts submitted pursuant to Rule 9(c).

(c) Expediting Filings. Appeals filed pursuant to these provisions shall adhere strictly to the expedited procedures set forth below:

(1) *Transcripts.* Within one business day after the notice of appeal has been filed, the clerk of superior court shall notify the court reporting coordinator of the Administrative Office of the Courts of the date the notice of appeal was filed and the names of the parties to the appeal and their respective addresses or addresses of their counsel. Within two business days of receipt of such notification, the court reporting coordinator shall assign a transcriptionist to the case.

When there is an order establishing the indigency of the appellant, the transcriptionist shall prepare and deliver a transcript of the designated proceedings to the appellant and provide copies to the office of the clerk of the Court of Appeals and to the respective parties to the appeal at the addresses provided within thirty-five days from the date of assignment.

When there is no order establishing the indigency of the appellant, the appellant shall have ten days from the date that the transcriptionist is assigned to make written arrangements with the assigned transcriptionist for the production and delivery of the transcript of the designated proceedings. If such written arrangement is made, the transcriptionist shall prepare and deliver a transcript of the designated proceedings to the appellant and provide copies to the office of the clerk of the Court of Appeals and to the respective parties to the appeal at the addresses provided within forty-five days from the date of assignment. The non-indigent appellant shall bear the cost of the appellant's copy of the transcript.

When there is no order establishing the indigency of the appellee, the appellee shall bear the cost of receiving a copy of the requested transcript.

Motions for extensions of time to prepare and deliver transcripts are disfavored and will not be allowed by the Court of Appeals absent extraordinary circumstances.

(2) *Record on Appeal.* Within ten days after receipt of the transcript, the appellant shall prepare and serve upon all other parties a proposed record on appeal constituted in accordance with Rule 9. Trial counsel for the appealing party shall have a duty to assist appellate counsel, if separate counsel is appointed or retained for the appeal, in preparing and serving a proposed record on appeal. Within ten days after service of the proposed record on appeal upon an appellee, the appellee may serve upon all other parties:

1. a notice of approval of the proposed record;
2. specific objections or amendments to the proposed record on appeal, or
3. a proposed alternative record on appeal.

If the parties agree to a settled record on appeal within twenty days after receipt of the transcript, the appellant shall file three legible copies of the settled record on appeal in the office of the clerk of the Court of Appeals within five business days from the date the record was settled. If all appellees fail within the times allowed them either to serve notices of approval or to serve objections, amendments, or proposed alternative records on appeal, the appellant's proposed record on appeal shall constitute the settled record on appeal, and the appellant shall file three legible copies thereof in the office of the clerk of the Court of Appeals within five business days from the last date upon which any appellee could have served such objections, amendments, or proposed alternative record on appeal. If an appellee timely serves amendments, objections, or a proposed alternative record on appeal and the parties cannot agree to the settled record within thirty days after receipt of the transcript, each party shall file three legible copies of the following documents in the office of the clerk of the Court of Appeals within five business days after the last day upon which the record can be settled by agreement:

1. the appellant shall file his or her proposed record on appeal, and
2. an appellee shall file his or her objections, amendments, or proposed alternative record on appeal.

No counsel who has appeared as trial counsel for any party in the proceeding shall be permitted to withdraw, nor shall such counsel be otherwise relieved of any responsibilities imposed pursuant to this rule, until the record on appeal has been filed in the office of the clerk of the Court of Appeals as provided herein.

(3) *Briefs.* Within thirty days after the record on appeal has been filed with the Court of Appeals, the appellant shall file his or her brief in the office of the clerk of the Court of Appeals and serve copies upon all other parties of record. Within thirty days after the appellant's brief has been served on an appellee, the appellee shall file his or her brief in the office of the clerk of the Court of Appeals and serve copies upon all other parties of record. Motions for extensions of time to file briefs will not be allowed absent extraordinary circumstances.

(d) No–Merit Briefs. In an appeal taken pursuant to N.C.G.S. § 7B–1001, if, after a conscientious and thorough review of the record on appeal, appellate counsel concludes that the record contains no issue of merit on which to base an argument for relief and that the appeal would be frivolous, counsel may file a no-merit brief. In the brief, counsel shall identify any issues in the record on appeal that might arguably support the appeal and shall state why those issues lack merit or would not alter the ultimate result. Counsel shall provide the appellant with a copy of the no-merit brief, the transcript, the record on appeal, and any Rule 11(c) supplement or exhibits that have been filed with the appellate court. Counsel shall also advise the appellant in writing that the appellant has the option of filing a *pro se* brief within thirty days of the date of the filing of the no-merit brief and shall attach to the brief evidence of compliance with this subsection.

(e) Calendaring Priority. Appeals filed pursuant to this rule will be given priority over other cases being considered by the Court of Appeals and will be calendared in accordance with a schedule promulgated by the Chief Judge. Unless otherwise ordered by the Court of Appeals, cases subject to the expedited procedures set forth in this rule shall be disposed of on the record and briefs and without oral argument.

[Adopted: 28 April 2006—effective 1 May 2006 and applies to all cases appealed on or after that date. Amended: 11 June 2008—3A(b)(1)—effective 1 December 2008; Recodified former Rule 3A as Rule 3.1 and Reenacted Rule 3.1 as amended: 2 July 2009—rewrote 3.1(b); renumbered subsections (c) & (e); amended 3.1(c)(1) & (2); added 3.1(d) — effective 1 October 2009 and applies to all cases appealed on or after that date.]

Rule 4. Appeal in Criminal Cases— How and When Taken

(a) Manner and Time. Any party entitled by law to appeal from a judgment or order of a superior or district court rendered in a criminal action may take appeal by

(1) giving oral notice of appeal at trial, or

(2) filing notice of appeal with the clerk of superior court and serving copies thereof upon all adverse

parties within fourteen days after entry of the judgment or order or within fourteen days after a ruling on a motion for appropriate relief made during the fourteen day period following entry of the judgment or order. Appeals from district court to superior court are governed by N.C.G.S. §§ 15A–1431 and –1432.

(b) Content of Notice of Appeal. The notice of appeal required to be filed and served by subdivision (a)(2) of this rule shall specify the party or parties taking the appeal; shall designate the judgment or order from which appeal is taken and the court to which appeal is taken; and shall be signed by counsel of record for the party or parties taking the appeal, or by any such party not represented by counsel of record.

(c) Service of Notice of Appeal. Service of copies of the notice of appeal may be made as provided in Rule 26.

(d) To Which Appellate Court Addressed. An appeal of right from a judgment of a superior court by any person who has been convicted of murder in the first degree and sentenced to death shall be filed in the Supreme Court. In all other criminal cases, appeal shall be filed in the Court of Appeals.

(e) Protecting the Identity of Juvenile Victims of Sexual Offenses. For appeals filed pursuant to this rule and for extraordinary writs filed in cases to which this rule applies, the identities of all victims of sexual offenses the trial court record shows were under the age of eighteen when the trial division proceedings occurred, including documents or other materials concerning delinquency proceedings in district court, shall be protected pursuant to Rule 3.1(b).

[Adopted: 13 June 1975. Amended: 4 October 1978—4(a)(2)—effective 1 January 1979; 13 July 1982—4(d); 3 September 1987—4(d)—effective for all judgments of the superior court entered on or after 24 July 1987; 8 December 1988—4(a)—effective for all judgments of the trial tribunal entered on or after 1 July 1989; 8 June 1989—4(a)—8 December 1988 amendment rescinded prior to effective date; 18 October 2001—4(a)(2), (d) (subsection (d) amended to conform with N.C.G.S. § 7A–27)—effective 31 October 2001; 1 May 2003—4(a)(2). Reenacted and Amended: 2 July 2009—added 4(e)—effective 1 October 2009 and applies to all cases appealed on or after that date.]

Rule 5. Joinder of Parties On Appeal

(a) Appellants. If two or more parties are entitled to appeal from a judgment, order, or other determination and their interests are such as to make their joinder in appeal practicable, they may file and serve a joint notice of appeal in accordance with Rules 3 and 4; or they may join in appeal after timely taking of separate appeals by filing notice of joinder in the office of the clerk of superior court and serving copies thereof upon all other parties, or in a criminal case they may give a joint oral notice of appeal.

(b) Appellees. Two or more appellees whose interests are such as to make their joinder on appeal practicable may, by filing notice of joinder in the office of the clerk of superior court and serving copies thereof upon all other parties, so join.

(c) Procedure after Joinder. After joinder, the parties proceed as a single appellant or appellee. Filing and service of papers by and upon joint appellants or appellees is as provided by Rule 26(e).

[Adopted: 13 June 1975. Reenacted and Amended: 2 July 2009—amended 5(a)—effective 1 October 2009 and applies to all cases appealed on or after that date.]

Rule 6. Security for Costs On Appeal

(a) In Regular Course. Except in pauper appeals, an appellant in a civil action must provide adequate security for the costs of appeal in accordance with the provisions of N.C.G.S. §§ 1–285 and –286.

(b) In Forma Pauperis Appeals. A party in a civil action may be allowed to prosecute an appeal in forma pauperis without providing security for costs in accordance with the provisions of N.C.G.S. § 1–288.

(c) Filed with Record on Appeal. When security for costs is required, the appellant shall file with the record on appeal a certified copy of the appeal bond or a cash deposit made in lieu of bond.

(d) Dismissal for Failure to File or Defect in Security. For failure of the appellant to provide security as required by subsection (a) or to file evidence thereof as required by subsection (c), or for a substantial defect or irregularity in any security provided, the appeal may on motion of an appellee be dismissed by the appellate court where docketed, unless for good cause shown the court permits the security to be provided or the filing to be made out of time, or the defect or irregularity to be corrected. A motion to dismiss on these grounds shall be made and determined in accordance with Rule 37. When the motion to dismiss is made on the grounds of a defect or irregularity, the appellant may as a matter of right correct the defect or irregularity by filing a proper bond or making proper deposit with the clerk of the appellate court within ten days after service of the motion upon appellant or before the case is called for argument, whichever first occurs.

(e) No Security for Costs in Criminal Appeals. Pursuant to N.C.G.S. § 15A–1449, no security for costs is required upon appeal of criminal cases to the appellate division.

[Adopted: 13 June 1975. Amended: 27 November 1984—6(e)—effective 1 February 1985; 26 July 1990—6(c)—effective 1 October 1990. Reenacted and Amended: 2 July 2009—amended 6(b)—effective 1 October 2009 and applies to all cases appealed on or after that date.]

Rule 7. Preparation of the Transcript; Court Reporter's Duties

(a) Ordering the Transcript.

(1) *Civil Cases.* Within fourteen days after filing the notice of appeal the appellant shall contract for the transcription of the proceedings or of such parts of the proceedings not already on file, as the appellant deems necessary, in accordance with these rules, and shall provide the following information in writing: a designation of the parts of the proceedings to be transcribed; the name and address of the court reporter or other neutral person designated to prepare the transcript; and, where portions of the proceedings have been designated to be transcribed, a statement of the issues the appellant intends to raise on appeal. The appellant shall file the written documentation of this transcript contract with the clerk of the trial tribunal, and serve a copy of it upon all other parties of record and upon the person designated to prepare the transcript. If the appellant intends to urge on appeal that a finding or conclusion of the trial court is unsupported by the evidence or is contrary to the evidence, the appellant shall cite in the record on appeal the volume number, page number, and line number of all evidence relevant to such finding or conclusion. If an appellee deems a transcript of other parts of the proceedings to be necessary, the appellee, within fourteen days after the service of the written documentation of the appellant, shall contract for the transcription of any additional parts of the proceedings or such parts of the proceedings not already on file, in accordance with these rules. The appellee shall file with the clerk of the trial tribunal, and serve on all other parties of record, written documentation of the additional parts of the proceedings to be transcribed and the name and address of the court reporter or other neutral person designated to prepare the transcript.

In civil cases and special proceedings where there is an order establishing the indigency of a party entitled to appointed appellate counsel, the ordering of the transcript shall be as in criminal cases where there is an order establishing the indigency of the defendant as set forth in Rule 7(a)(2).

(2) *Criminal Cases.* In criminal cases where there is no order establishing the indigency of the defendant for the appeal, the defendant shall contract for the transcription of the proceedings as in civil cases.

When there is an order establishing the indigency of the defendant, unless the trial judge's appeal entries specify or the parties stipulate that parts of the proceedings need not be transcribed, the clerk of the trial tribunal shall order a transcript of the proceedings by serving the following documents upon either the court reporter(s) or neutral person designated to prepare the transcript: a copy of the appeal entries signed by the judge; a copy of the trial court's order establishing indigency for the appeal; and a statement setting out the name, address, telephone number and e-mail address of appellant's counsel. The clerk shall make an entry of record reflecting the date these documents were served upon the court reporter(s) or transcriptionist.

(b) Production and Delivery of Transcript.

(1) *Production.* In civil cases: from the date the requesting party serves the written documentation of the transcript contract on the person designated to prepare the transcript, that person shall have sixty days to prepare and electronically deliver the transcript.

In criminal cases where there is no order establishing the indigency of the defendant for the appeal: from the date the requesting party serves the written documentation of the transcript contract upon the person designated to prepare the transcript, that person shall have sixty days to produce and electronically deliver the transcript in non-capital cases and one hundred twenty days to produce and electronically deliver the transcript in capitally tried cases.

In criminal cases where there is an order establishing the indigency of the defendant for the appeal: from the date listed on the appeal entries as the "Date order delivered to transcriptionist," that person shall have sixty-five days to produce and electronically deliver the transcript in non-capital cases and one hundred twenty-five days to produce and electronically deliver the transcript in capitally tried cases.

The transcript format shall comply with Appendix B of these rules.

Except in capitally tried criminal cases which result in the imposition of a sentence of death, the trial tribunal, in its discretion and for good cause shown by the appellant, may extend the time to produce the transcript for an additional thirty days. Any subsequent motions for additional time required to produce the transcript may only be made to the appellate court to which appeal has been taken. All motions for extension of time to produce the transcript in capitally tried cases resulting in the imposition of a sentence of death shall be made directly to the Supreme Court by the appellant.

(2) *Delivery.* The court reporter, or person designated to prepare the transcript, shall electronically deliver the completed transcript, with accompanying PDF disk to the parties including the district attorney and Attorney General of North Carolina in criminal cases, as ordered, within the time provided by this rule, unless an extension of time has been granted under Rule 7(b)(1) or Rule 27(c). The court reporter or transcriptionist shall certify to the clerk of the trial tribunal that the transcript has been so delivered and shall send a copy of such certification to the appellate court to which the appeal is taken. The appellant shall promptly notify the court reporter when the record on appeal has been filed. Once the court reporter, or person designated to prepare the tran-

script, has been notified by the appellant that the record on appeal has been filed with the appellate court to which the appeal has been taken, the court reporter must electronically file the transcript with that court using the docket number assigned by that court.

(3) *Neutral Transcriptionist.* The neutral person designated to prepare the transcript shall not be a relative or employee or attorney or counsel of any of the parties, or a relative or employee of such attorney or counsel, or be financially interested in the action unless the parties agree otherwise by stipulation.

[Adopted: 13 June 1975. REPEALED: 1 July 1978. (See note following Rule 17.) Re-adopted: 8 December 1988—effective for all judgments of the trial tribunal entered on or after 1 July 1989. Amended: 8 June 1989—effective for all judgments of the trial tribunal entered on or after 1 July 1989; 26 July 1990—7(a)(1), (a)(2), and (b)(1)—effective 1 October 1990; 21 November 1997—effective 1 February 1998; 8 April 1999—7(b)(1), para. 5; 18 October 2001—7(b)(1), para. 4—effective 31 October 2001; 15 August 2002—7(a)(1), para. 2; 25 January 2007—7(b)(1), paras. 3, 5; 7(b)(2)—effective 1 March 2007 and applies to all cases appealed on or after that date. Reenacted and Amended: 2 July 2009—amended 7(a)(1) & (2), 7(b)(1) & (2) —effective 1 October 2009 and applies to all cases appealed on or after that date.]

Rule 8. Stay Pending Appeal

(a) Stay in Civil Cases. When appeal is taken in a civil action from a judgment, order, or other determination of a trial court, stay of execution or enforcement thereof pending disposition of the appeal must ordinarily first be sought by the deposit of security with the clerk of the superior court in those cases for which provision is made by law for the entry of stays upon deposit of adequate security, or by application to the trial court for a stay order in all other cases. After a stay order or entry has been denied or vacated by a trial court, an appellant may apply to the appropriate appellate court for a temporary stay and a writ of supersedeas in accordance with Rule 23. In any appeal which is allowed by law to be taken from an agency to the appellate division, application for the temporary stay and writ of supersedeas may be made to the appellate court in the first instance. Application for the temporary stay and writ of supersedeas may similarly be made to the appellate court in the first instance when extraordinary circumstances make it impracticable to obtain a stay by deposit of security or by application to the trial court for a stay order.

(b) Stay in Criminal Cases. When a defendant has given notice of appeal, those portions of criminal sentences which impose fines or costs are automatically stayed pursuant to the provisions of N.C.G.S. § 15A–1451. Stays of imprisonment or of the execution of death sentences must be pursued under N.C.G.S. § 15A–536 or Rule 23.

[Adopted: 13 June 1975. Amended: 27 November 1984—8(b)—effective 1 February 1985; 6 March 1997—8(a)—effective 1 July 1997. Reenacted and Amended: 2 July 2009—amended 8(a)—effective 1 October 2009 and applies to all cases appealed on or after that date.]

Rule 9. The Record on Appeal

(a) Function; Notice in Cases Involving Juveniles; Composition of Record. In appeals from the trial division of the General Court of Justice, review is solely upon the record on appeal, the verbatim transcript of proceedings, if one is designated, and any other items filed pursuant to this Rule 9. Parties may cite any of these items in their briefs and arguments before the appellate courts.

All filings involving juveniles covered by Rules 3(b)(1), 3.1(b), or 4(e) shall include the following notice in uppercase typeface:

FILED PURSUANT TO RULE [3(b)(1)] [3.1(b)] [4(e)]; SUBJECT TO PUBLIC INSPECTION ONLY BY ORDER OF A COURT OF THE APPELLATE DIVISION.

(1) *Composition of the Record in Civil Actions and Special Proceedings.* The record on appeal in civil actions and special proceedings shall contain:

a. an index of the contents of the record, which shall appear as the first page thereof;

b. a statement identifying the judge from whose judgment or order appeal is taken, the session at which the judgment or order was rendered, or if rendered out of session, the time and place of rendition, and the party appealing;

c. a copy of the summons with return, or of other papers showing jurisdiction of the trial court over person or property, or a statement showing same;

d. copies of the pleadings, and of any pretrial order on which the case or any part thereof was tried;

e. so much of the litigation, set out in the form provided in Rule 9(c)(1), as is necessary for an understanding of all issues presented on appeal, or a statement specifying that the verbatim transcript of proceedings is being filed with the record pursuant to Rule 9(c)(2), or designating portions of the transcript to be so filed;

f. where an issue presented on appeal relates to the giving or omission of instructions to the jury, a transcript of the entire charge given; and identification of the omitted instruction by setting out the requested instruction or its substance in the record on appeal immediately following the instruction given;

g. copies of the issues submitted and the verdict, or of the trial court's findings of fact and conclusions of law;

h. a copy of the judgment, order, or other determination from which appeal is taken;

i. a copy of the notice of appeal, of all orders establishing time limits relative to the perfecting of the appeal, of any order finding a party to the appeal to be a civil pauper, and of any agreement, notice of approval, or order settling the record on appeal and settling the verbatim transcript of proceedings if one is filed pursuant to Rule 9(c)(2) and (c)(3);

j. copies of all other papers filed and statements of all other proceedings had in the trial court which are necessary to an understanding of all issues presented on appeal unless they appear in the verbatim transcript of proceedings which is being filed with the record pursuant to Rule 9(c)(2);

k. proposed issues on appeal set out in the manner provided in Rule 10;

l. a statement, where appropriate, that the record of proceedings was made with an electronic recording device;

m. a statement, where appropriate, that a supplement compiled pursuant to Rule 11(c) is filed with the record on appeal; and

n. any order (issued prior to the filing of the record on appeal) ruling upon a motion by an attorney who is not licensed to practice law in North Carolina to be admitted pursuant to N.C.G.S. § 84–4.1 to appear in the appeal. In the event such a motion is filed prior to the filing of the record but has not yet been ruled upon when the record is filed, the record shall include a statement that such a motion is pending and the date that motion was filed.

(2) *Composition of the Record in Appeals from Superior Court Review of Administrative Boards and Agencies.* The record on appeal in cases of appeal from judgments of the superior court rendered upon review of the proceedings of administrative boards or agencies, other than those specified in Rule 18(a), shall contain:

a. an index of the contents of the record, which shall appear as the first page thereof;

b. a statement identifying the judge from whose judgment or order appeal is taken, the session at which the judgment or order was rendered, or if rendered out of session, the time and place of rendition, and the party appealing;

c. a copy of the summons, notice of hearing, or other papers showing jurisdiction of the board or agency over the persons or property sought to be bound in the proceeding, or a statement showing same;

d. copies of all petitions and other pleadings filed in the superior court;

e. copies of all items properly before the superior court as are necessary for an understanding of all issues presented on appeal;

f. so much of the litigation in the superior court, set out in the form provided in Rule 9(c)(1), as is necessary for an understanding of all issues presented, or a statement specifying that the verbatim transcript of proceedings is being filed with the record pursuant to Rule 9(c)(2), or designating portions of the transcript to be so filed;

g. a copy of any findings of fact and conclusions of law and of the judgment, order, or other determination of the superior court from which appeal is taken;

h. a copy of the notice of appeal from the superior court, of all orders establishing time limits relative to the perfecting of the appeal, of any order finding a party to the appeal to be a civil pauper, and of any agreement, notice of approval, or order settling the record on appeal and settling the verbatim transcript of proceedings, if one is filed pursuant to Rule 9(c)(2) and (c)(3);

i. proposed issues on appeal relating to the actions of the superior court, set out in the manner provided in Rule 10; and

j. any order (issued prior to the filing of the record on appeal) ruling upon any motion by an attorney who is not licensed to practice law in North Carolina to be admitted pursuant to N.C.G.S. § 84–4.1 to appear in the appeal. In the event such a motion is filed prior to the filing of the record but has not yet been ruled upon when the record is filed, the record shall include a statement that such a motion is pending and the date that motion was filed.

(3) *Composition of the Record in Criminal Actions.* The record on appeal in criminal actions shall contain:

a. an index of the contents of the record, which shall appear as the first page thereof;

b. a statement identifying the judge from whose judgment or order appeal is taken, the session at which the judgment or order was rendered, or if rendered out of session, the time and place of rendition, and the party appealing;

c. copies of all warrants, informations, presentments, and indictments upon which the case has been tried in any court;

d. copies of docket entries or a statement showing all arraignments and pleas;

e. so much of the litigation, set out in the form provided in Rule 9(c)(1), as is necessary for an understanding of all issues presented on appeal, or a statement specifying that the entire verbatim transcript of the proceedings is being filed with the record pursuant to Rule 9(c)(2), or designating portions of the transcript to be so filed;

f. where an issue presented on appeal relates to the giving or omission of instructions to the jury, a transcript of the entire charge given; and identification of the omitted instruction by setting out the requested instruction or its substance in the record on appeal immediately following the instruction given;

g. copies of the verdict and of the judgment, order, or other determination from which appeal is taken; and in capitally tried cases, a copy of the jury verdict sheet for sentencing, showing the aggravating and mitigating circumstances submitted and found or not found;

h. a copy of the notice of appeal or an appropriate entry or statement showing appeal taken orally; of all orders establishing time limits relative to the perfecting of the appeal; of any order finding defendant indigent for the purposes of the appeal and assigning counsel; and of any agreement, notice of approval, or order settling the record on appeal and settling the verbatim transcript of proceedings, if one is to be filed pursuant to Rule 9(c)(2);

i. copies of all other papers filed and statements of all other proceedings had in the trial courts which are necessary for an understanding of all issues presented on appeal, unless they appear in the verbatim transcript of proceedings which is being filed with the record pursuant to Rule 9(c)(2);

j. proposed issues on appeal set out in the manner provided in Rule 10;

k. a statement, where appropriate, that the record of proceedings was made with an electronic recording device;

l. a statement, where appropriate, that a supplement compiled pursuant to Rule 11(c) is filed with the record on appeal; and

m. any order (issued prior to the filing of the record on appeal) ruling upon any motion by an attorney who is not licensed to practice law in North Carolina to be admitted pursuant to N.C.G.S. § 84–4.1 to appear in the appeal. In the event such a motion is filed prior to the filing of the record but has not yet been ruled upon when the record is filed, the record shall include a statement that such a motion is pending and the date that motion was filed.

(4) *Exclusion of Social Security Numbers from Record on Appeal.* Social security numbers shall be deleted or redacted from any document before including the document in the record on appeal.

(b) Form of Record; Amendments. The record on appeal shall be in the format prescribed by Rule 26(g) and the appendixes to these rules.

(1) *Order of Arrangement.* The items constituting the record on appeal should be arranged, so far as practicable, in the order in which they occurred or were filed in the trial tribunal.

(2) *Inclusion of Unnecessary Matter; Penalty.* It shall be the duty of counsel for all parties to an appeal to avoid including in the record on appeal matter not necessary for an understanding of the issues presented on appeal, such as social security numbers referred to in Rule 9(a)(4). The cost of including such matter may be charged as costs to the party or counsel who caused or permitted its inclusion.

(3) *Filing Dates and Signatures on Papers.* Every pleading, motion, affidavit, or other paper included in the record on appeal shall show the date on which it was filed and, if verified, the date of verification and the person who verified. Every judgment, order, or other determination shall show the date on which it was entered. The typed or printed name of the person signing a paper shall be entered immediately below the signature.

(4) *Pagination; Counsel Identified.* The pages of the printed record on appeal shall be numbered consecutively, be referred to as "record pages," and be cited as "(R p ___)." Pages of the Rule 11(c) or Rule 18(d)(3) supplement to the record on appeal shall be numbered consecutively with the pages of the record on appeal, the first page of the record supplement to bear the next consecutive number following the number of the last page of the printed record on appeal. These pages shall be referred to as "record supplement pages" and be cited as "(R S p ___)." Pages of the verbatim transcript of proceedings filed under Rule 9(c)(2) shall be referred to as "transcript pages" and be cited as "(T p ___)." At the end of the record on appeal shall appear the names, office addresses, telephone numbers, State Bar numbers, and e-mail addresses of counsel of record for all parties to the appeal.

(5) *Additions and Amendments to Record on Appeal.*

(a) *Additional Materials in the Record on Appeal.* If the record on appeal as settled is insufficient to respond to the issues presented in an appellant's brief or the issues presented in an appellee's brief pursuant to Rule 10(c), the responding party may supplement the record on appeal with any items that could otherwise have been included pursuant to this Rule 9. The responding party shall serve a copy of those items on opposing counsel and shall file three copies of the items in a volume captioned "Rule 9(b)(5) Supplement to the Printed Record on Appeal." The supplement shall be filed no later than the responsive brief or within the time allowed for filing such a brief if none is filed.

(b) *Motions Pertaining to Additions to the Record.* On motion of any party or on its own initiative, the appellate court may order additional portions of a trial court record or transcript sent up and added to the record on appeal. On motion of any party, the appellate court may order any portion of the record on appeal or transcript amended to correct error shown as to form or content. Prior to the filing of the record on appeal in the appellate court, such motions may be filed by any party in the trial court.

(c) Presentation of Testimonial Evidence and Other Proceedings. Testimonial evidence, voir dire, statements and events at evidentiary and non-evidentiary hearings, and other trial proceedings necessary to be presented for review by the appellate court may be included either in the record on appeal in the form specified in Rule 9(c)(1) or by designating the verbatim transcript of proceedings of the trial tribunal as provided in Rule 9(c)(2) and (c)(3). When an issue presented on appeal relates to the giving or omission of instructions to the jury, a transcript of the entire charge given shall be included in the record on appeal. Verbatim transcripts or narration utilized in a case subject to Rules 3(b)(1), 3.1(b), or 4(e) initiated in the trial division under the provisions of Subchapter I of Chapter 7B of the General Statutes shall be prepared and delivered to the office of the clerk of the appellate court to which the appeal has been taken in the manner specified by said rules.

(1) *When Testimonial Evidence, Voir Dire, Statements and Events at Evidentiary and Non-Evidentiary Hearings, and Other Trial Proceedings Narrated—How Set Out in Record.* When an issue is presented on appeal with respect to the admission or exclusion of evidence, the question and answer form shall be utilized in setting out the pertinent questions and answers. Other testimonial evidence, voir dire, statements and events at evidentiary and non-evidentiary hearings, and other trial proceedings required by Rule 9(a) to be included in the record on appeal shall be set out in narrative form except where such form might not fairly reflect the true sense of the evidence received, in which case it may be set out in question and answer form. Parties shall use that form or combination of forms best calculated under the circumstances to present the true sense of the required testimonial evidence concisely and at a minimum of expense to the litigants. Parties may object to particular narration on the basis that it does not accurately reflect the true sense of testimony received, statements made, or events that occurred; or to particular questions and answers on the basis that the testimony might with no substantial loss in accuracy be summarized in narrative form at substantially less expense. When a judge or referee is required to settle the record on appeal under Rule 11(c) and there is dispute as to the form, the judge or referee shall settle the form in the course of settling the record on appeal.

(2) *Designation that Verbatim Transcript of Proceedings in Trial Tribunal Will Be Used.* Appellant may designate in the record on appeal that the testimonial evidence will be presented in the verbatim transcript of the evidence of the trial tribunal in lieu of narrating the evidence and other trial proceedings as permitted by Rule 9(c)(1). When a verbatim transcript of those proceedings has been made, appellant may also designate that the verbatim transcript will be used to present voir dire, statements and events at evidentiary and non-evidentiary hearings, or other trial proceedings when those proceedings are the basis for one or more issues presented on appeal. Any such designation shall refer to the page numbers of the transcript being designated. Appellant need not designate all of the verbatim transcript that has been made, provided that when the verbatim transcript is designated to show the testimonial evidence, so much of the testimonial evidence must be designated as is necessary for an understanding of all issues presented on appeal. When appellant has narrated the evidence and other trial proceedings under Rule 9(c)(1), the appellee may designate the verbatim transcript as a proposed alternative record on appeal.

(3) *Verbatim Transcript of Proceedings—Settlement, Filing, Copies, Briefs.* Whenever a verbatim transcript is designated to be used pursuant to Rule 9(c)(2):

a. it shall be settled, together with the record on appeal, according to the procedures established by Rule 11;

b. appellant shall cause the settled record on appeal and transcript to be filed pursuant to Rule 7 with the clerk of the appellate court in which the appeal has been docketed;

c. in criminal appeals, upon settlement of the record on appeal, the district attorney shall notify the Attorney General of North Carolina that the record on appeal and transcript have been settled; and

d. the briefs of the parties must comport with the requirements of Rule 28 regarding complete statement of the facts of the case and regarding appendixes to the briefs.

(4) *Presentation of Discovery Materials.* Discovery materials offered into evidence at trial shall be brought forward, if relevant, as other evidence. In all instances in which discovery materials are considered by the trial tribunal, other than as evidence offered at trial, the following procedures for presenting those materials to the appellate court shall be used: Depositions shall be treated as testimonial evidence and shall be presented by narration or by transcript of the deposition in the manner prescribed by this Rule 9(c). Other discovery materials, including interrogatories and answers, requests for admission, responses to requests, motions to produce, and the like, pertinent to issues presented on appeal, may be set out in the record on appeal or may be sent up as documentary exhibits in accordance with Rule 9(d)(2).

(5) *Electronic Recordings.* When a narrative or transcript has been prepared from an electronic re-

cording, the parties shall not file a copy of the electronic recording with the appellate division except at the direction or with the approval of the appellate court.

(d) Exhibits.

Any exhibit filed, served, submitted for consideration, admitted, or made the subject of an offer of proof may be made a part of the record on appeal if a party believes that its inclusion is necessary to understand an issue on appeal.

(1) *Documentary Exhibits Included in the Printed Record on Appeal.* A party may include a documentary exhibit in the printed record on appeal if it is of a size and nature to make inclusion possible without impairing the legibility or original significance of the exhibit.

(2) *Exhibits Not Included in the Printed Record on Appeal.* A documentary exhibit that is not included in the printed record on appeal can be made a part of the record on appeal by filing three copies with the clerk of the appellate court. The three copies shall be paginated. If multiple exhibits are filed, an index must be included in the filing. Copies that impair the legibility or original significance of the exhibit may not be filed. An exhibit that is a tangible object or is an exhibit that cannot be copied without impairing its legibility or original significance can be made a part of the record on appeal by having it delivered by the clerk of superior court to the clerk of the appellate court. When a party files a written request with the clerk of superior court that the exhibit be delivered to the appellate court, the clerk must promptly have the exhibit delivered to the appellate court in a manner that ensures its security and availability for use in further trial proceedings. The party requesting delivery of the exhibit to the appellate court shall not be required to move in the appellate court for delivery of the exhibit.

(3) *Exclusion of Social Security Numbers from Exhibits.* Social security numbers must be deleted or redacted from copies of exhibits.

(4) *Removal of Exhibits from Appellate Court.* All models, diagrams, and exhibits of material placed in the custody of the clerk of the appellate court must be taken away by the parties within ninety days after the mandate of the Court has issued or the case has otherwise been closed by withdrawal, dismissal, or other order of the Court, unless notified otherwise by the clerk. When this is not done, the clerk shall notify counsel to remove the articles forthwith; and if they are not removed within a reasonable time after such notice, the clerk shall destroy them, or make such other disposition of them as to the clerk may seem best.

[Adopted: 13 June 1975. Amended: 10 June 1981—9(c)(1)—applicable to all appeals docketed on or after 1 October 1981; 12 January 1982—9(c)(1)—applicable to all appeals docketed after 15 March 1982; 27 November 1984—applicable to all appeals in which the notice of appeal is filed on or after 1 February 1985; 8 December 1988—9(a), (c)—effective for all judgments of the trial tribunal entered on or after 1 July 1989; 8 June 1989—9(a)—effective for all judgments of the trial tribunal entered on or after 1 July 1989; 26 July 1990—9(a)(3)h and 9(d)(2)—effective 1 October 1990; 6 March 1997—9(b)(5)—effective upon adoption 6 March 1997; 21 November 1997—9(a)(1)(j)–(*l*), 9(a)(3)(i)–(k), 9(c)(5)—effective 1 February 1998; 18 October 2001—9(d)(2)—effective 31 October 2001; 6 May 2004—9(a), 9(a)(4), 9(b)(2), 9(b)(6), 9(c), 9(c)(2), 9(c)(3)(c), 9(d)(1), 9(d)(3)—effective 12 May 2004; 25 January 2007—added 9(a)(1)(m) & 9(a)(3)(*l*); amended 9(b)(4)—effective 1 March 2007 and applies to all cases appealed on or after that date. Reenacted and Amended: 2 July 2009—amended and rewrote portions of 9(a), (b), (c), & (d)—effective 1 October 2009 and applies to all cases appealed on or after that date. Amended: 28 February2013—9(d)—effective 15 April 2013.]

Rule 10. Preservation of Issues at Trial; Proposed Issues on Appeal

(a) Preserving Issues During Trial Proceedings.

(1) *General.* In order to preserve an issue for appellate review, a party must have presented to the trial court a timely request, objection, or motion, stating the specific grounds for the ruling the party desired the court to make if the specific grounds were not apparent from the context. It is also necessary for the complaining party to obtain a ruling upon the party's request, objection, or motion. Any such issue that was properly preserved for review by action of counsel taken during the course of proceedings in the trial tribunal by objection noted or which by rule or law was deemed preserved or taken without any such action, including, but not limited to, whether the judgment is supported by the verdict or by the findings of fact and conclusions of law, whether the court had jurisdiction over the subject matter, and whether a criminal charge is sufficient in law, may be made the basis of an issue presented on appeal.

(2) *Jury Instructions.* A party may not make any portion of the jury charge or omission therefrom the basis of an issue presented on appeal unless the party objects thereto before the jury retires to consider its verdict, stating distinctly that to which objection is made and the grounds of the objection; provided that opportunity was given to the party to make the objection out of the hearing of the jury, and, on request of any party, out of the presence of the jury.

(3) *Sufficiency of the Evidence.* In a criminal case, a defendant may not make insufficiency of the evidence to prove the crime charged the basis of an issue presented on appeal unless a motion to dismiss the action, or for judgment as in case of nonsuit, is made at trial. If a defendant makes such a motion after the State has presented all its evidence and has rested its case and that motion is denied and the defendant then introduces evidence, defendant's motion for dismissal or judgment in case of nonsuit made at the close of State's evidence is waived. Such a waiver precludes

the defendant from urging the denial of such motion as a ground for appeal.

A defendant may make a motion to dismiss the action, or for judgment as in case of nonsuit, at the conclusion of all the evidence, irrespective of whether defendant made an earlier such motion. If the motion at the close of all the evidence is denied, the defendant may urge as ground for appeal the denial of the motion made at the conclusion of all the evidence. However, if a defendant fails to move to dismiss the action, or for judgment as in case of nonsuit, at the close of all the evidence, defendant may not challenge on appeal the sufficiency of the evidence to prove the crime charged.

If a defendant's motion to dismiss the action, or for judgment as in case of nonsuit, is allowed, or shall be sustained on appeal, it shall have the force and effect of a verdict of "not guilty" as to such defendant.

(4) *Plain Error.* In criminal cases, an issue that was not preserved by objection noted at trial and that is not deemed preserved by rule or law without any such action nevertheless may be made the basis of an issue presented on appeal when the judicial action questioned is specifically and distinctly contended to amount to plain error.

(b) Appellant's Proposed Issues on Appeal. Proposed issues that the appellant intends to present on appeal shall be stated without argument at the conclusion of the record on appeal in a numbered list. Proposed issues on appeal are to facilitate the preparation of the record on appeal and shall not limit the scope of the issues presented on appeal in an appellant's brief.

(c) Appellee's Proposed Issues on Appeal as to an Alternative Basis in Law. Without taking an appeal, an appellee may list proposed issues on appeal in the record on appeal based on any action or omission of the trial court that was properly preserved for appellate review and that deprived the appellee of an alternative basis in law for supporting the judgment, order, or other determination from which appeal has been taken. An appellee's list of proposed issues on appeal shall not preclude an appellee from presenting arguments on other issues in its brief.

Portions of the record or transcript of proceedings necessary to an understanding of such proposed issues on appeal as to an alternative basis in law may be included in the record on appeal by agreement of the parties under Rule 11(a), may be included by the appellee in a proposed alternative record on appeal under Rule 11(b), or may be designated for inclusion in the verbatim transcript of proceedings, if one is filed under Rule 9(c)(2).

[Adopted: 13 June 1975. Amended: 10 June 1981—10(b)(2), applicable to every case the trial of which begins on or after 1 October 1981; 7 July 1983—10(b)(3); 27 November 1984—applicable to appeals in which the notice of appeal is filed on or after 1 February 1985; 8 December 1988—effective for all judgments of the trial tribunal entered on or after 1 July 1989. Reenacted and Amended: 2 July 2009—changed title of rule; deleted former 10(a); renumbered and amended remaining subsections as (a)—(c)—effective 1 October 2009 and applies to all cases appealed on or after that date.]

Rule 11. Settling the Record on Appeal

(a) By Agreement. This rule applies to all cases except those subject to expedited schedules in Rule 3.1.

Within thirty-five days after the reporter or transcriptionist certifies delivery of the transcript, if such was ordered (seventy days in capitally tried cases), or thirty-five days after appellant files notice of appeal, whichever is later, the parties may by agreement entered in the record on appeal settle a proposed record on appeal prepared by any party in accordance with Rule 9 as the record on appeal.

(b) By Appellee's Approval of Appellant's Proposed Record on Appeal. If the record on appeal is not settled by agreement under Rule 11(a), the appellant shall, within the same times provided, serve upon all other parties a proposed record on appeal constituted in accordance with the provisions of Rule 9. Within thirty days (thirty-five days in capitally tried cases) after service of the proposed record on appeal upon an appellee, that appellee may serve upon all other parties a notice of approval of the proposed record on appeal, or objections, amendments, or a proposed alternative record on appeal in accordance with Rule 11(c). If all appellees within the times allowed them either serve notices of approval or fail to serve either notices of approval or objections, amendments, or proposed alternative records on appeal, appellant's proposed record on appeal thereupon constitutes the record on appeal.

(c) By Agreement, by Operation of Rule, or by Court Order After Appellee's Objection or Amendment. Within thirty days (thirty-five days in capitally tried cases) after service upon appellee of appellant's proposed record on appeal, that appellee may serve upon all other parties specific amendments or objections to the proposed record on appeal, or a proposed alternative record on appeal. Amendments or objections to the proposed record on appeal shall be set out in a separate paper and shall specify any item(s) for which an objection is based on the contention that the item was not filed, served, submitted for consideration, admitted, or made the subject of an offer of proof, or that the content of a statement or narration is factually inaccurate. An appellant who objects to an appellee's response to the proposed record on appeal shall make the same specification in its request for judicial settlement. The formatting of the proposed record on appeal and the order in which items appear in it are the responsibility of the appellant.

If any appellee timely serves amendments, objections, or a proposed alternative record on appeal, the record on appeal shall consist of each item that is either among those items required by Rule 9(a) to be in the record on appeal or that is requested by any party to the appeal and agreed upon for inclusion by all other parties to the appeal. If a party requests that an item be included in the record on appeal but not all other parties to the appeal agree to its inclusion, then that item shall not be included in the printed record on appeal, but shall be filed by the appellant with the printed record on appeal in three copies of a volume captioned "Rule 11(c) Supplement to the Printed Record on Appeal," along with any verbatim transcripts, narrations of proceedings, documentary exhibits, and other items that are filed pursuant to Rule 9(c) or 9(d); provided that any item not filed, served, submitted for consideration, or admitted, or for which no offer of proof was tendered, shall not be included. Subject to the additional requirements of Rule 28(d), items in the Rule 11(c) supplement may be cited and used by the parties as would items in the printed record on appeal.

If a party does not agree to the wording of a statement or narration required or permitted by these rules, there shall be no judicial settlement to resolve the dispute unless the objection is based on a contention that the statement or narration concerns an item that was not filed, served, submitted for consideration, admitted, or tendered in an offer of proof, or that a statement or narration is factually inaccurate. Instead, the objecting party is permitted to have inserted in the settled record on appeal a concise counter-statement. Parties are strongly encouraged to reach agreement on the wording of statements in records on appeal. Judicial settlement is not appropriate for disputes that concern only the formatting of a record on appeal or the order in which items appear in a record on appeal.

The Rule 11(c) supplement to the printed record on appeal shall contain an index of the contents of the supplement, which shall appear as the first page thereof. The Rule 11(c) supplement shall be paginated as required by Rule 9(b)(4) and the contents should be arranged, so far as practicable, in the order in which they occurred or were filed in the trial tribunal. If a party does not agree to the inclusion or specification of an exhibit or transcript in the printed record, the printed record shall include a statement that such items are separately filed along with the supplement.

If any party to the appeal contends that materials proposed for inclusion in the record or for filing therewith pursuant to Rule 9(c) or 9(d) were not filed, served, submitted for consideration, admitted, or made the subject of an offer of proof, or that a statement or narration permitted by these rules is not factually accurate, then that party, within ten days after expiration of the time within which the appellee last served with the appellant's proposed record on appeal might have served amendments, objections, or a proposed alternative record on appeal, may in writing request that the judge from whose judgment, order, or other determination appeal was taken settle the record on appeal. A copy of the request, endorsed with a certificate showing service on the judge, shall be filed forthwith in the office of the clerk of the superior court and served upon all other parties. Each party shall promptly provide to the judge a reference copy of the record items, amendments, or objections served by that party in the case.

The functions of the judge in the settlement of the record on appeal are to determine whether a statement permitted by these rules is not factually accurate, to settle narrations of proceedings under Rule 9(c)(1), and to determine whether the record accurately reflects material filed, served, submitted for consideration, admitted, or made the subject of an offer of proof, but not to decide whether material desired in the record by either party is relevant to the issues on appeal, non-duplicative, or otherwise suited for inclusion in the record on appeal.

The judge shall send written notice to counsel for all parties setting a place and a time for a hearing to settle the record on appeal. The hearing shall be held not later than fifteen days after service of the request for hearing upon the judge. The judge shall settle the record on appeal by order entered not more than twenty days after service of the request for hearing upon the judge. If requested, the judge shall return the record items submitted for reference during the judicial settlement process with the order settling the record on appeal.

If any appellee timely serves amendments, objections, or a proposed alternative record on appeal, and no judicial settlement of the record is timely sought, the record is deemed settled as of the expiration of the ten day period within which any party could have requested judicial settlement of the record on appeal under this Rule 11(c).

Provided that, nothing herein shall prevent settlement of the record on appeal by agreement of the parties at any time within the times herein limited for settling the record by judicial order.

(d) Multiple Appellants; Single Record on Appeal. When there are multiple appellants (two or more), whether proceeding separately or jointly, as parties aligned in interest, or as cross-appellants, there shall nevertheless be but one record on appeal. The proposed issues on appeal of the several appellants shall be set out separately in the single record on appeal and attributed to the several appellants by any clear means of reference. In the event multiple appellants cannot agree to the procedure for constituting a proposed record on appeal, the judge from whose judgment, order, or other determination the appeals are taken shall, on motion of any appellant with notice to all other appellants, enter an order settling the procedure, including the allocation of costs.

(e) Extensions of Time. The times provided in this rule for taking any action may be extended in accordance with the provisions of Rule 27(c).

[Adopted: 13 June 1975. Amended: 27 November 1984—11(a), (c), (e), (f)—applicable to appeals in which the notice of appeal is filed on or after 1 February 1985; 8 December 1988—11(a), (b), (c), (e), (f)—effective for all judgments of the trial tribunal entered on or after 1 July 1989; 26 July 1990—11(b), (c), (d)—effective 1 October 1990; 6 March 1997—11(c)—effective upon adoption 6 March 1997; 21 November 1997—effective 1 February 1998; 6 May 2004—11(b), (c), (d)—effective 12 May 2004; 25 January 2007—11(c), paras. 1, 2, 5, 6; added paras. 3, 4, 8—effective 1 March 2007 and applies to all cases appealed on or after that date. Reenacted and Amended: 2 July 2009—amended 11(a) & (d); added 11(e) —effective 1 October 2009 and applies to all cases appealed on or after that date.]

Rule 12. Filing the Record; Docketing the Appeal; Copies of the Record

(a) Time for Filing Record on Appeal. Within fifteen days after the record on appeal has been settled by any of the procedures provided in Rule 11 or Rule 18, the appellant shall file the record on appeal with the clerk of the court to which appeal is taken.

(b) Docketing the Appeal. At the time of filing the record on appeal, the appellant shall pay to the clerk the docket fee fixed pursuant to N.C.G.S. § 7A–20(b), and the clerk shall thereupon enter the appeal upon the docket of the appellate court. If an appellant is authorized to appeal in forma pauperis as provided in N.C.G.S. §§ 1–288 or 7A–450 et seq., the clerk shall docket the appeal upon timely filing of the record on appeal. An appeal is docketed under the title given to the action in the trial division, with the appellant identified as such. The clerk shall forthwith give notice to all parties of the date on which the appeal was docketed in the appellate court.

(c) Copies of Record on Appeal. The appellant shall file one copy of the record on appeal, three copies of each exhibit designated pursuant to Rule 9(d), three copies of any supplement to the record on appeal submitted pursuant to Rule 11(c) or Rule 18(d)(3) and shall cause the transcript to be filed electronically pursuant to Rule 7. The clerk will reproduce and distribute copies as directed by the court, billing the parties pursuant to these rules.

[Adopted: 13 June 1975. Amended: 27 November 1984—applicable to appeals in which the notice of appeal is filed on or after 1 February 1985; 8 December 1988—12(a), (c)—effective for all judgments of the trial tribunal entered on or after 1 July 1989; 6 March 1997—12(c)—effective upon adoption 6 March 1997; 1 May 2003—12(c); 25 January 2007—12(a), (c)—effective 1 March 2007 and applies to all cases appealed on or after that date. Reenacted and Amended: 2 July 2009—amended 12(c)—effective 1 October 2009 and applies to all cases appealed on or after that date.]

Rule 13. Filing and Service of Briefs

(a) Time for Filing and Service of Briefs.

(1) *Cases Other Than Death Penalty Cases.* Within thirty days after the clerk of the appellate court has mailed the printed record to the parties, the appellant shall file a brief in the office of the clerk of the appellate court and serve copies thereof upon all other parties separately represented. The mailing of the printed record is not service for purposes of Rule 27(b); therefore, the provision of that rule allowing an additional three days after service by mail does not extend the period for the filing of an appellant's brief. Within thirty days after appellant's brief has been served on an appellee, the appellee shall similarly file and serve copies of a brief. An appellant may file and serve a reply brief as provided in Rule 28(h).

(2) *Death Penalty Cases.* Within sixty days after the clerk of the Supreme Court has mailed the printed record to the parties, the appellant in a criminal appeal which includes a sentence of death shall file a brief in the office of the clerk and serve copies thereof upon all other parties separately represented. The mailing of the printed record is not service for purposes of Rule 27(b); therefore, the provision of that rule allowing an additional three days after service by mail does not extend the period for the filing of an appellant's brief. Within sixty days after appellant's brief has been served, the appellee shall similarly file and serve copies of a brief. An appellant may file and serve a reply brief as provided in Rule 28(h).

(b) Copies Reproduced by Clerk. A party need file but a single copy of a brief. At the time of filing the party may be required to pay to the clerk of the appellate court a deposit fixed by the clerk to cover the cost of reproducing copies of the brief. The clerk will reproduce and distribute copies of briefs as directed by the court.

(c) Consequence of Failure to File and Serve Briefs. If an appellant fails to file and serve a brief within the time allowed, the appeal may be dismissed on motion of an appellee or on the court's own initiative. If an appellee fails to file and serve its brief within the time allowed, the appellee may not be heard in oral argument except by permission of the court.

[Adopted: 13 June 1975. Amended: 7 October 1980—13(a)—effective 1 January 1981; 27 November 1984—13(a), (b)—effective 1 February 1985; 30 June 1988—13(a)—effective 1 September 1988; 8 June 1989—13(a)—effective 1 September 1989; 1 May 2003—13(a)(1), (b); 23 August 2005—13(a)(1), (2)—effective 1 September 2005. Reenacted and Amended: 2 July 2009—amended 13(a)(1) & (2)—effective 1 October 2009 and applies to all cases appealed on or after that date. Amended: 28 February 2013—13(a)(1) and 13(a)(2)—effective 15 April 2013.]

ARTICLE III. REVIEW BY SUPREME COURT OF APPEALS ORIGINALLY DOCKETED IN COURT OF APPEALS: APPEALS OF RIGHT; DISCRETIONARY REVIEW

Rule 14. Appeals of Right From Court of Appeals to Supreme Court Under N.C.G.S. § 7A–30

(a) Notice of Appeal; Filing and Service. Appeals of right from the Court of Appeals to the Supreme Court are taken by filing notices of appeal with the clerk of the Court of Appeals and with the clerk of the Supreme Court and serving notice of appeal upon all other parties within fifteen days after the mandate of the Court of Appeals has been issued to the trial tribunal. For cases which arise from the Industrial Commission, a copy of the notice of appeal shall be served on the Chair of the Industrial Commission. The running of the time for filing and serving a notice of appeal is tolled as to all parties by the filing by any party within such time of a petition for rehearing under Rule 31 of these rules, and the full time for appeal thereafter commences to run and is computed as to all parties from the date of entry by the Court of Appeals of an order denying the petition for rehearing. If a timely notice of appeal is filed by a party, any other party may file a notice of appeal within ten days after the first notice of appeal was filed. A petition prepared in accordance with Rule 15(c) for discretionary review in the event the appeal is determined not to be of right or for issues in addition to those set out as the basis for a dissenting opinion may be filed with or contained in the notice of appeal.

(b) Content of Notice of Appeal.

(1) *Appeal Based Upon Dissent in Court of Appeals.* In an appeal which is based upon the existence of a dissenting opinion in the Court of Appeals, the notice of appeal shall specify the party or parties taking the appeal; shall designate the judgment of the Court of Appeals from which the appeal is taken; shall state the basis upon which it is asserted that appeal lies of right under N.C.G.S. § 7A–30; and shall state the issue or issues which are the basis of the dissenting opinion and which are to be presented to the Supreme Court for review.

(2) *Appeal Presenting Constitutional Question.* In an appeal which is asserted by the appellant to involve a substantial constitutional question, the notice of appeal shall specify the party or parties taking the appeal; shall designate the judgment of the Court of Appeals from which the appeal is taken; shall state the issue or issues which are the basis of the constitutional claim and which are to be presented to the Supreme Court for review; shall specify the articles and sections of the Constitution asserted to be involved; shall state with particularity how appellant's rights thereunder have been violated; and shall affirmatively state that the constitutional issue was timely raised (in the trial tribunal if it could have been, in the Court of Appeals if not) and either not determined or determined erroneously.

(c) Record on Appeal.

(1) *Composition.* The record on appeal filed in the Court of Appeals constitutes the record on appeal for review by the Supreme Court. However, the Supreme Court may note de novo any deficiencies in the record on appeal and may take such action in respect thereto as it deems appropriate, including dismissal of the appeal.

(2) *Transmission; Docketing; Copies.* Upon the filing of a notice of appeal, the clerk of the Court of Appeals will forthwith transmit the original record on appeal to the clerk of the Supreme Court, who shall thereupon file the record and docket the appeal. The clerk of the Supreme Court will procure or reproduce copies of the record on appeal for distribution as directed by the Court, and may require a deposit from appellant to cover the cost of reproduction.

(d) Briefs.

(1) *Filing and Service; Copies.* Within thirty days after filing notice of appeal in the Supreme Court, the appellant shall file with the clerk of the Supreme Court and serve upon all other parties copies of a new brief prepared in conformity with Rule 28, presenting only those issues upon which review by the Supreme Court is sought; provided, however, that when the appeal is based upon the existence of a substantial constitutional question or when the appellant has filed a petition for discretionary review for issues in addition to those set out as the basis of a dissent in the Court of Appeals, the appellant shall file and serve a new brief within thirty days after entry of the order of the Supreme Court which determines for the purpose of retaining the appeal on the docket that a substantial constitutional question does exist or allows or denies the petition for discretionary review in an appeal based upon a dissent. Within thirty days after service of the appellant's brief upon appellee, the appellee shall similarly file and serve copies of a new brief. An appellant may file and serve a reply brief as provided in Rule 28(h)

The parties need file but single copies of their respective briefs. The clerk will reproduce and distribute copies as directed by the Court, billing the parties pursuant to these rules.

(2) *Failure to File or Serve.* If an appellant fails to file and serve its brief within the time allowed, the

appeal may be dismissed on motion of an appellee or on the Court's own initiative. If an appellee fails to file and serve its brief within the time allowed, it may not be heard in oral argument except by permission of the Court.

[Adopted: 13 June 1975. Amended: 31 January 1977—14(d)(1); 7 October 1980—14(d)(1)—effective 1 January 1981; 27 November 1984—14(a), (b), (d)—applicable to appeals in which the notice of appeal is filed on or after 1 February 1985; 30 June 1988—14(b)(2), (d)(1)—effective 1 September 1988; 8 June 1989—14(d)(1)—effective 1 September 1989; 6 March 1997—14(a)—effective 1 July 1997; 1 May 2003—14(c)(2), (d)(1); 23 August 2005—14(d)(1)—effective 1 September 2005. Reenacted and Amended: 2 July 2009—amended 14(d)(1) & (2)—effective 1 October 2009 and applies to all cases appealed on or after that date. Amended: 28 February2013—14(d)(1)—effective 15 April 2013.]

Rule 15. Discretionary Review on Certification by Supreme Court under G.S. § 7A–31

(a) Petition of Party. Either prior to or following determination by the Court of Appeals of an appeal docketed in that court, any party to the appeal may in writing petition the Supreme Court upon any grounds specified in N.C.G.S. § 7A–31 to certify the cause for discretionary review by the Supreme Court; except that a petition for discretionary review of an appeal from the Industrial Commission, the North Carolina State Bar, the Property Tax Commission, the Board of State Contract Appeals, or the Commissioner of Insurance may only be made following determination by the Court of Appeals; and except that no petition for discretionary review may be filed in any postconviction proceeding under N.C.G.S. Ch. 15A, Art. 89, or in valuation of exempt property under N.C.G.S. Ch. 1C.

(b) Same; Filing and Service. A petition for review prior to determination by the Court of Appeals shall be filed with the clerk of the Supreme Court and served on all other parties within fifteen days after the appeal is docketed in the Court of Appeals. For cases that arise from the Industrial Commission, a copy of the petition shall be served on the Chair of the Industrial Commission. A petition for review following determination by the Court of Appeals shall be similarly filed and served within fifteen days after the mandate of the Court of Appeals has been issued to the trial tribunal. Such a petition may be contained in or filed with a notice of appeal of right, to be considered by the Supreme Court in the event the appeal is determined not to be of right, as provided in Rule 14(a). The running of the time for filing and serving a petition for review following determination by the Court of Appeals is terminated as to all parties by the filing by any party within such time of a petition for rehearing under Rule 31 of these rules, and the full time for filing and serving such a petition for review thereafter commences to run and is computed as to all parties from the date of entry by the Court of Appeals of an order denying the petition for rehearing. If a timely petition for review is filed by a party, any other party may file a petition for review within ten days after the first petition for review was filed.

(c) Same; Content. The petition shall designate the petitioner or petitioners and shall set forth plainly and concisely the factual and legal basis upon which it is asserted that grounds exist under N.C.G.S. § 7A–31 for discretionary review. The petition shall state each issue for which review is sought and shall be accompanied by a copy of the opinion of the Court of Appeals when filed after determination by that court. No supporting brief is required, but supporting authorities may be set forth briefly in the petition.

(d) Response. A response to the petition may be filed by any other party within ten days after service of the petition upon that party. No supporting brief is required, but supporting authorities may be set forth briefly in the response. If, in the event that the Supreme Court certifies the case for review, the respondent would seek to present issues in addition to those presented by the petitioner, those additional issues shall be stated in the response. A motion for extension of time is not permitted.

(e) Certification by Supreme Court; How Determined and Ordered.

(1) *On Petition of a Party.* The determination by the Supreme Court whether to certify for review upon petition of a party is made solely upon the petition and any response thereto and without oral argument.

(2) *On Initiative of the Court.* The determination by the Supreme Court whether to certify for review upon its own initiative pursuant to N.C.G.S. § 7A–31 is made without prior notice to the parties and without oral argument.

(3) *Orders; Filing and Service.* Any determination to certify for review and any determination not to certify made in response to a petition will be recorded by the Supreme Court in a written order. The clerk of the Supreme Court will forthwith enter such order, deliver a copy thereof to the clerk of the Court of Appeals, and mail copies to all parties. The cause is docketed in the Supreme Court upon entry of an order of certification by the clerk of the Supreme Court.

(f) Record on Appeal.

(1) *Composition.* The record on appeal filed in the Court of Appeals constitutes the record on appeal for review by the Supreme Court. However, the Supreme Court may note de novo any deficiencies in the record on appeal and may take such action in respect thereto as it deems appropriate, including dismissal of the appeal.

(2) *Filing; Copies.* When an order of certification is filed with the clerk of the Court of Appeals, he or she will forthwith transmit the original record on

appeal to the clerk of the Supreme Court. The clerk of the Supreme Court will procure or reproduce copies thereof for distribution as directed by the Court. If it is necessary to reproduce copies, the clerk may require a deposit by the petitioner to cover the costs thereof.

(g) Filing and Service of Briefs.

(1) *Cases Certified Before Determination by Court of Appeals.* When a case is certified for review by the Supreme Court before being determined by the Court of Appeals, the times allowed the parties by Rule 13 to file their respective briefs are not thereby extended. If a party has filed its brief in the Court of Appeals and served copies before the case is certified, the clerk of the Court of Appeals shall forthwith transmit to the clerk of the Supreme Court the original brief and any copies already reproduced for distribution, and if filing was timely in the Court of Appeals this constitutes timely filing in the Supreme Court. If a party has not filed its brief in the Court of Appeals and served copies before the case is certified, the party shall file its brief in the Supreme Court and serve copies within the time allowed and in the manner provided by Rule 13 for filing and serving in the Court of Appeals.

(2) *Cases Certified for Review of Court of Appeals Determinations.* When a case is certified for review by the Supreme Court of a determination made by the Court of Appeals, the appellant shall file a new brief prepared in conformity with Rule 28 in the Supreme Court and serve copies upon all other parties within thirty days after the case is docketed in the Supreme Court by entry of its order of certification. The appellee shall file a new brief in the Supreme Court and serve copies upon all other parties within thirty days after a copy of appellant's brief is served upon the appellee. An appellant may file and serve a reply brief as provided in Rule 28(h)

(3) *Copies.* A party need file, or the clerk of the Court of Appeals transmit, but a single copy of any brief required by this Rule 15 to be filed in the Supreme Court upon certification for discretionary review. The clerk of the Supreme Court will thereupon procure from the Court of Appeals or will reproduce copies for distribution as directed by the Supreme Court. The clerk may require a deposit by any party to cover the costs of reproducing copies of its brief.

In civil appeals in forma pauperis a party need not pay the deposit for reproducing copies, but at the time of filing its original new brief shall also deliver to the clerk two legible copies thereof.

(4) *Failure to File or Serve.* If an appellant fails to file and serve its brief within the time allowed by this Rule 15, the appeal may be dismissed on motion of an appellee or upon the Court's own initiative. If an appellee fails to file and serve its brief within the time allowed by this Rule 15, it may not be heard in oral argument except by permission of the Court.

(h) Discretionary Review of Interlocutory Orders. An interlocutory order by the Court of Appeals, including an order for a new trial or for further proceedings in the trial tribunal, will be certified for review by the Supreme Court only upon a determination by the Court that failure to certify would cause a delay in final adjudication which would probably result in substantial harm to a party.

(i) Appellant, Appellee Defined. As used in this Rule 15, the terms "appellant" and "appellee" have the following meanings:

(1) With respect to Supreme Court review prior to determination by the Court of Appeals, whether on petition of a party or on the Court's own initiative, "appellant" means a party who appealed from the trial tribunal; "appellee" means a party who did not appeal from the trial tribunal.

(2) With respect to Supreme Court review of a determination of the Court of Appeals, whether on petition of a party or on the Court's own initiative, "appellant" means the party aggrieved by the determination of the Court of Appeals; "appellee" means the opposing party; provided that, in its order of certification, the Supreme Court may designate either party an appellant or appellee for purposes of proceeding under this Rule 15.

[Adopted: 13 June 1975. Amended: 7 October 1980—15(g)(2)—effective 1 January 1981; 18 November 1981—15(a); 30 June 1988—15(a), (c), (d), (g)(2)—effective 1 September 1988; 8 December 1988—15(i)(2)—effective 1 January 1989; 8 June 1989—15(g)(2)—effective 1 September 1989; 6 March 1997—15(b)—effective 1 July 1997; 18 October 2001—15(d)—effective 31 October 2001; 23 August 2005—15(g)(2)—effective 1 September 2005. Reenacted and Amended: 2 July 2009—amended 15(c) & (d)—effective 1 October 2009 and applies to all cases appealed on or after that date. Amended: 28 February 2013—15(g)(2)—effective 15 April 2013.]

Rule 16. Scope of Review of Decisions of Court of Appeals

(a) How Determined. Review by the Supreme Court after a determination by the Court of Appeals, whether by appeal of right or by discretionary review, is to determine whether there is error of law in the decision of the Court of Appeals. Except when the appeal is based solely upon the existence of a dissent in the Court of Appeals, review in the Supreme Court is limited to consideration of the issues stated in the notice of appeal filed pursuant to Rule 14(b)(2) or the petition for discretionary review and the response thereto filed pursuant to Rule 15(c) and (d), unless further limited by the Supreme Court, and properly presented in the new briefs required by Rules 14(d)(1) and 15(g)(2) to be filed in the Supreme Court.

(b) Scope of Review in Appeal Based Solely Upon Dissent. When the sole ground of the appeal of right is the existence of a dissent in the Court of Appeals, review by the Supreme Court is limited to a consideration of those issues that are (1) specifically set out in the dissenting opinion as the basis for that dissent, (2) stated in the notice of appeal, and (3) properly presented in the new briefs required by Rule 14(d)(1) to be filed in the Supreme Court. Other issues in the case may properly be presented to the Supreme Court through a petition for discretionary review pursuant to Rule 15, or by petition for writ of certiorari pursuant to Rule 21.

(c) Appellant, Appellee Defined. As used in this Rule 16, the terms "appellant" and "appellee" have the following meanings when applied to discretionary review:

(1) With respect to Supreme Court review of a determination of the Court of Appeals upon petition of a party, "appellant" means the petitioner and "appellee" means the respondent.

(2) With respect to Supreme Court review upon the Court's own initiative, "appellant" means the party aggrieved by the decision of the Court of Appeals and "appellee" means the opposing party; provided that, in its order of certification, the Supreme Court may designate either party an "appellant" or "appellee" for purposes of proceeding under this Rule 16.

[Adopted: 13 June 1975. Amended: 3 November 1983—16(a), (b)—applicable to all notices of appeal filed in the Supreme Court on and after 1 January 1984; 30 June 1988—16(a), (b)—effective 1 September 1988; 26 July 1990—16(a)—effective 1 October 1990. Reenacted and Amended: 2 July 2009—amended 16(a) & (b)—effective 1 October 2009 and applies to all cases appealed on or after that date.]

Rule 17. Appeal Bond in Appeals Under N.C.G.S. §§ 7A–30, 7A–31

(a) Appeal of Right. In all appeals of right from the Court of Appeals to the Supreme Court in civil cases, the party who takes appeal shall, upon filing the notice of appeal in the Supreme Court, file with the clerk of that Court a written undertaking, with good and sufficient surety in the sum of $250, or deposit cash in lieu thereof, to the effect that all costs awarded against the appealing party on the appeal will be paid.

(b) Discretionary Review of Court of Appeals Determination. When the Supreme Court on petition of a party certifies a civil case for review of a determination of the Court of Appeals, the petitioner shall file an undertaking for costs in the form provided in subsection (a). When the Supreme Court on its own initiative certifies a case for review of a determination of the Court of Appeals, no undertaking for costs shall be required of any party.

(c) Discretionary Review by Supreme Court Before Court of Appeals Determination. When a civil case is certified for review by the Supreme Court before being determined by the Court of Appeals, the undertaking on appeal initially filed in the Court of Appeals shall stand for the payment of all costs incurred in either the Court of Appeals or the Supreme Court and awarded against the party appealing.

(d) Appeals in Forma Pauperis. No undertakings for costs are required of a party appealing in forma pauperis.

[Adopted: 13 June 1975. Amended: 19 June 1978—effective 1 July 1978; 26 July 1990—17(a)—effective 1 October 1990. Reenacted: 2 July 2009—effective 1 October 2009 and applies to all cases appealed on or after that date.]

ARTICLE IV. DIRECT APPEALS FROM ADMINISTRATIVE AGENCIES TO APPELLATE DIVISION

Rule 18. Taking Appeal; Record on Appeal—Composition and Settlement

(a) General. Appeals of right from administrative agencies, boards, or commissions (hereinafter "agency") directly to the appellate division under N.C.G.S. § 7A–29 shall be in accordance with the procedures provided in these rules for appeals of right from the courts of the trial divisions, except as provided in this Article.

(b) Time and Method for Taking Appeals.

(1) The times and methods for taking appeals from an agency shall be as provided in this Rule 18 unless the statutes governing the agency provide otherwise, in which case those statutes shall control.

(2) Any party to the proceeding may appeal from a final agency determination to the appropriate court of the appellate division for alleged errors of law by filing and serving a notice of appeal within thirty days after receipt of a copy of the final order of the agency. The final order of the agency is to be sent to the parties by Registered or Certified Mail. The notice of appeal shall specify the party or parties taking the appeal; shall designate the final agency determination from which appeal is taken and the court to which appeal is taken; and shall be signed by counsel of record for the party or parties taking the appeal, or by any such party not represented by counsel of record.

(3) If a transcript of fact-finding proceedings is not made by the agency as part of the process leading up to the final agency determination, the appealing party may contract with the reporter for production of such

parts of the proceedings not already on file as it deems necessary, pursuant to the procedures prescribed in Rule 7.

(c) Composition of Record on Appeal. The record on appeal in appeals from any agency shall contain:

(1) an index of the contents of the record on appeal, which shall appear as the first page thereof;

(2) a statement identifying the commission or agency from whose judgment, order, or opinion appeal is taken; the session at which the judgment, order, or opinion was rendered, or if rendered out of session, the time and place of rendition; and the party appealing;

(3) a copy of the summons with return, notice of hearing, or other papers showing jurisdiction of the agency over persons or property sought to be bound in the proceeding, or a statement showing same;

(4) copies of all other notices, pleadings, petitions, or other papers required by law or rule of the agency to be filed with the agency to present and define the matter for determination, including a Form 44 for all workers' compensation cases which originate from the Industrial Commission;

(5) a copy of any findings of fact and conclusions of law and a copy of the order, award, decision, or other determination of the agency from which appeal was taken;

(6) so much of the litigation before the agency or before any division, commissioner, deputy commissioner, or hearing officer of the agency, set out in the form provided in Rule 9(c)(1), as is necessary for an understanding of all issues presented on appeal, or a statement specifying that the verbatim transcript of proceedings is being filed with the record pursuant to Rule 9(c)(2) and (c)(3);

(7) when the agency has reviewed a record of proceedings before a division or an individual commissioner, deputy commissioner, or hearing officer of the agency, copies of all items included in the record filed with the agency which are necessary for an understanding of all issues presented on appeal;

(8) copies of all other papers filed and statements of all other proceedings had before the agency or any of its individual commissioners, deputies, or divisions which are necessary to an understanding of all issues presented on appeal, unless they appear in the verbatim transcript of proceedings being filed pursuant to Rule 9(c)(2) and (c)(3);

(9) a copy of the notice of appeal from the agency, of all orders establishing time limits relative to the perfecting of the appeal, of any order finding a party to the appeal to be a civil pauper, and of any agreement, notice of approval, or order settling the record on appeal and settling the verbatim transcript of proceedings if one is filed pursuant to Rule 9(c)(2) and (c)(3);

(10) proposed issues on appeal relating to the actions of the agency, set out as provided in Rule 10;

(11) a statement, when appropriate, that the record of proceedings was made with an electronic recording device;

(12) a statement, when appropriate, that a supplement compiled pursuant to Rule 18(d)(3) is filed with the record on appeal; and

(13) any order (issued prior to the filing of the record on appeal) ruling upon any motion by an attorney who is not licensed to practice law in North Carolina to be admitted pursuant to N.C.G.S. § 84–4.1 to appear in the appeal. In the event such a motion is filed prior to the filing of the record but has not yet been ruled upon when the record is filed, the record shall include a statement that such a motion is pending and the date that motion was filed.

(d) Settling the Record on Appeal. The record on appeal may be settled by any of the following methods:

(1) *By Agreement.* Within thirty-five days after filing of the notice of appeal, or after production of the transcript if one is ordered pursuant to Rule 18(b)(3), the parties may by agreement entered in the record on appeal settle a proposed record on appeal prepared by any party in accordance with this Rule 18 as the record on appeal.

(2) *By Appellee's Approval of Appellant's Proposed Record on Appeal.* If the record on appeal is not settled by agreement under Rule 18(d)(1), the appellant shall, within thirty-five days after filing of the notice of appeal, or after production of the transcript if one is ordered pursuant to Rule 18(b)(3), serve upon all other parties a proposed record on appeal constituted in accordance with the provisions of Rule 18(c). Within thirty days after service of the proposed record on appeal upon an appellee, that appellee may serve upon all other parties a notice of approval of the proposed record on appeal or objections, amendments, or a proposed alternative record on appeal. Amendments or objections to the proposed record on appeal shall be set out in a separate paper and shall specify any item(s) for which an objection is based on the contention that the item was not filed, served, submitted for consideration, admitted, or made the subject of an offer of proof, or that the content of a statement or narration is factually inaccurate. An appellant who objects to an appellee's response to the proposed record on appeal shall make the same specification in its request for judicial settlement. The formatting of the proposed record on appeal and the order in which items appear in it is the responsibility of the appellant. Judicial settlement is not appropriate for disputes concerning only the formatting or the order in which items appear in the settled record on appeal. If all appellees within the times allowed them either file notices of approval or fail to file either notices of approval or objections, amendments, or proposed al-

ternative records on appeal, appellant's proposed record on appeal thereupon constitutes the record on appeal.

(3) *By Agreement, by Operation of Rule, or by Court Order After Appellee's Objection or Amendment.* If any appellee timely files amendments, objections, or a proposed alternative record on appeal, the record on appeal shall consist of each item that is either among those items required by Rule 9(a) to be in the record on appeal or that is requested by any party to the appeal and agreed upon for inclusion by all other parties to the appeal, in the absence of contentions that the item was not filed, served, or offered into evidence. If a party requests that an item be included in the record on appeal but not all parties to the appeal agree to its inclusion, then that item shall not be included in the printed record on appeal, but shall be filed by the appellant with the record on appeal in a volume captioned "Rule 18(d)(3) Supplement to the Printed Record on Appeal," along with any verbatim transcripts, narrations of proceedings, documentary exhibits, and other items that are filed pursuant to Rule 18(b) or 18(c); provided that any item not filed, served, submitted for consideration, admitted, or for which no offer of proof was tendered shall not be included. Subject to the additional requirements of Rule 28(d), items in the Rule 18(d)(3) supplement may be cited and used by the parties as would items in the printed record on appeal.

If a party does not agree to the wording of a statement or narration required or permitted by these rules, there shall be no judicial settlement to resolve the dispute unless the objection is based on a contention that the statement or narration concerns an item that was not filed, served, submitted for consideration, admitted, or tendered in an offer of proof, or that a statement or narration is factually inaccurate. Instead, the objecting party is permitted to have inserted in the settled record on appeal a concise counter-statement. Parties are strongly encouraged to reach agreement on the wording of statements in records on appeal.

The Rule 18(d)(3) supplement to the printed record on appeal shall contain an index of the contents of the supplement, which shall appear as the first page thereof. The Rule 18(d)(3) supplement shall be paginated consecutively with the pages of the record on appeal, the first page of the supplement to bear the next consecutive number following the number of the last page of the record on appeal. These pages shall be referred to as "record supplement pages," and shall be cited as "(R S p ___)." The contents of the supplement should be arranged, so far as practicable, in the order in which they occurred or were filed in the trial tribunal. If a party does not agree to the inclusion or specification of an exhibit or transcript in the printed record, the printed record shall include a statement that such items are separately filed along with the supplement.

If any party to the appeal contends that materials proposed for inclusion in the record or for filing therewith pursuant to Rule 18(b) or 18(c) were not filed, served, submitted for consideration, admitted, or offered into evidence, or that a statement or narration permitted by these rules is not factually accurate, then that party, within ten days after expiration of the time within which the appellee last served with the appellant's proposed record on appeal might have filed amendments, objections, or a proposed alternative record on appeal, may in writing request that the agency head convene a conference to settle the record on appeal. A copy of that request, endorsed with a certificate showing service on the agency head, shall be served upon all other parties. Each party shall promptly provide to the agency head a reference copy of the record items, amendments, or objections served by that party in the case.

The functions of the agency head in the settlement of the record on appeal are to determine whether a statement permitted by these rules is not factually accurate, to settle narrations of proceedings under Rule 18(c)(6), and to determine whether the record accurately reflects material filed, served, submitted for consideration, admitted, or made the subject of an offer of proof, but not to decide whether material desired in the record by either party is relevant to the issues on appeal, non-duplicative, or otherwise suited for inclusion in the record on appeal.

Upon receipt of a request for settlement of the record on appeal, the agency head shall send written notice to counsel for all parties setting a place and time for a conference to settle the record on appeal. The conference shall be held not later than fifteen days after service of the request upon the agency head. The agency head or a delegate appointed in writing by the agency head shall settle the record on appeal by order entered not more than twenty days after service of the request for settlement upon the agency. If requested, the settling official shall return the record items submitted for reference during the settlement process with the order settling the record on appeal.

When the agency head is a party to the appeal, the agency head shall forthwith request the Chief Judge of the Court of Appeals or the Chief Justice of the Supreme Court, as appropriate, to appoint a referee to settle the record on appeal. The referee so appointed shall proceed after conference with all parties to settle the record on appeal in accordance with the terms of these rules and the appointing order.

If any appellee timely serves amendments, objections, or a proposed alternative record on appeal, and no judicial settlement of the record is sought, the record is deemed settled as of the expiration of the ten day period within which any party could have requested judicial settlement of the record on appeal under this Rule 18(d)(3).

Nothing herein shall prevent settlement of the record on appeal by agreement of the parties at any time within the times herein limited for settling the record by agency order.

(e) Further Procedures and Additional Materials in the Record on Appeal. Further procedures for perfecting and prosecuting the appeal shall be as provided by these rules for appeals from the courts of the trial divisions.

(f) Extensions of Time. The times provided in this rule for taking any action may be extended in accordance with the provisions of Rule 27(c).

[Adopted: 13 June 1975. Amended: 21 June 1977; 7 October 1980—18(d)(3)—effective 1 January 1981; 27 February 1985—applicable to all appeals in which the notice of appeal is filed on or after 15 March 1985; 26 July 1990—18(b)(3), (d)(1), (d)(2)—effective 1 October 1990; 6 March 1997—18(c)(2), (c)(4)—effective 1 July 1997; 21 November 1997—18(c)(11)—effective 1 February 1998; 6 May 2004—18(c)(1), (d)(2)–(3)—effective 12 May 2004; 25 January 2007—18(d)(2); 18(d)(3), paras. 1, 4, 5; added 18(d)(3), paras. 2, 3, 8—effective 1 March 2007 and applies to all cases appealed on or after that date. Reenacted and Amended: 2 July 2009—amended 18(c)(6), (7), (8) & (10); added 18(c)(13); amended title of 18(e)—effective 1 October 2009 and applies to all cases appealed on or after that date.]

Rule 19. [Reserved]

[Adopted: 13 June 1975. Amended: 21 June 1977—19(d). REPEALED: 27 February 1985—effective 15 March 1985.]

Rule 20. Miscellaneous Provisions of Law Governing Agency Appeals

Specific provisions of law pertaining to stays pending appeals from any agency to the appellate division, to pauper appeals therein, and to the scope of review and permissible mandates of the Court of Appeals therein shall govern the procedure in such appeals notwithstanding any provisions of these rules that may prescribe a different procedure.

[Adopted: 13 June 1975. Amended: 27 February 1985—effective 15 March 1985. Reenacted: 2 July 2009—effective 1 October 2009 and applies to all cases appealed on or after that date.]

ARTICLE V. EXTRAORDINARY WRITS

Rule 21. Certiorari

(a) Scope of the Writ.

(1) *Review of the Judgments and Orders of Trial Tribunals.* The writ of certiorari may be issued in appropriate circumstances by either appellate court to permit review of the judgments and orders of trial tribunals when the right to prosecute an appeal has been lost by failure to take timely action, or when no right of appeal from an interlocutory order exists, or for review pursuant to N.C.G.S. § 15A–1422(c)(3) of an order of the trial court ruling on a motion for appropriate relief.

(2) *Review of the Judgments and Orders of the Court of Appeals.* The writ of certiorari may be issued by the Supreme Court in appropriate circumstances to permit review of the decisions and orders of the Court of Appeals when the right to prosecute an appeal of right or to petition for discretionary review has been lost by failure to take timely action, or for review of orders of the Court of Appeals when no right of appeal exists.

(b) Petition for Writ; to Which Appellate Court Addressed. Application for the writ of certiorari shall be made by filing a petition therefor with the clerk of the court of the appellate division to which appeal of right might lie from a final judgment in the cause by the tribunal to which issuance of the writ is sought.

(c) Same; Filing and Service; Content. The petition shall be filed without unreasonable delay and shall be accompanied by proof of service upon all other parties. For cases which arise from the Industrial Commission, a copy of the petition shall be served on the Chair of the Industrial Commission. The petition shall contain a statement of the facts necessary to an understanding of the issues presented by the application; a statement of the reasons why the writ should issue; and certified copies of the judgment, order, or opinion or parts of the record which may be essential to an understanding of the matters set forth in the petition. The petition shall be verified by counsel or the petitioner. Upon receipt of the prescribed docket fee, the clerk will docket the petition.

(d) Response; Determination by Court. Within ten days after service of the petition any party may file a response thereto with supporting affidavits or certified portions of the record not filed with the petition. Filing shall be accompanied by proof of service upon all other parties. The court for good cause shown may shorten the time for filing a response. Determination will be made on the basis of the petition, the response, and any supporting papers. No briefs or oral argument will be received or allowed unless ordered by the court upon its own initiative.

(e) Petition for Writ in Postconviction Matters; to Which Appellate Court Addressed. Petitions for writ of certiorari to review orders of the trial court denying motions for appropriate relief upon grounds listed in N.C.G.S. § 15A–1415(b) by persons who have been convicted of murder in the first degree and sentenced to death shall be filed in the Supreme Court. In all other cases such petitions shall be filed in and determined by the Court of Appeals, and the

Supreme Court will not entertain petitions for certiorari or petitions for further discretionary review in these cases. In the event the petitioner unreasonably delays in filing the petition or otherwise fails to comply with a rule of procedure, the petition shall be dismissed by the court. If the petition is without merit, it shall be denied by the court.

(f) Petition for Writ in Postconviction Matters—Death Penalty Cases. A petition for writ of certiorari to review orders of the trial court on motions for appropriate relief in death penalty cases shall be filed in the Supreme Court within sixty days after delivery of the transcript of the hearing on the motion for appropriate relief to the petitioning party. The responding party shall file its response within thirty days of service of the petition.

[Adopted: 13 June 1975. Amended: 18 November 1981—21(a), (e); 27 November 1984—21(a)—effective 1 February 1985; 3 September 1987—21(e)—effective for all judgments of the superior court entered on and after 24 July 1987; 8 December 1988—21(f)—applicable to all cases in which the superior court order is entered on or after 1 July 1989; 6 March 1997—21(c), (f)—effective 1 July 1997; 15 August 2002—21(e). Reenacted: 2 July 2009—effective 1 October 2009 and applies to all cases appealed on or after that date. Amended: 10 April 2015—21(a).]

Rule 22. Mandamus and Prohibition

(a) Petition for Writ; to Which Appellate Court Addressed. Applications for the writs of mandamus or prohibition directed to a judge, judges, commissioner, or commissioners shall be made by filing a petition therefor with the clerk of the court to which appeal of right might lie from a final judgment entered in the cause by the judge, judges, commissioner, or commissioners to whom issuance of the writ is sought.

(b) Same; Filing and Service; Content. The petition shall be filed without unreasonable delay after the judicial action sought to be prohibited or compelled has been undertaken, or has occurred, or has been refused, and shall be accompanied by proof of service on the respondent judge, judges, commissioner, or commissioners and on all other parties to the action. The petition shall contain a statement of the facts necessary to an understanding of the issues presented by the application; a statement of the issues presented and of the relief sought; a statement of the reasons why the writ should issue; and certified copies of any order or opinion or parts of the record that may be essential to an understanding of the matters set forth in the petition. The petition shall be verified by counsel or the petitioner. Upon receipt of the prescribed docket fee, the clerk shall docket the petition.

(c) Response; Determination by Court. Within ten days after service of the petition the respondent or any party may file a response thereto with supporting affidavits or certified portions of the record not filed with the petition. Filing shall be accompanied by proof of service upon all other parties. The court for good cause shown may shorten the time for filing a response. Determination will be made on the basis of the petition, the response, and any supporting papers. No briefs or oral argument will be received or allowed unless ordered by the court upon its own initiative.

[Adopted: 13 June 1975. Reenacted: 2 July 2009—effective 1 October 2009 and applies to all cases appealed on or after that date.]

Rule 23. Supersedeas

(a) Pending Review of Trial Tribunal Judgments and Orders.

(1) *Application—When Appropriate.* Application may be made to the appropriate appellate court for a writ of supersedeas to stay the execution or enforcement of any judgment, order, or other determination of a trial tribunal which is not automatically stayed by the taking of appeal when an appeal has been taken, or a petition for mandamus, prohibition, or certiorari has been filed to obtain review of the judgment, order, or other determination; and (i) a stay order or entry has been sought by the applicant by deposit of security or by motion in the trial tribunal and such order or entry has been denied or vacated by the trial tribunal, or (ii) extraordinary circumstances make it impracticable to obtain a stay by deposit of security or by application to the trial tribunal for a stay order.

(2) *Same—How and to Which Appellate Court Made.* Application for the writ is by petition which shall in all cases, except those initially docketed in the Supreme Court, be first made to the Court of Appeals. Except when an appeal from a superior court is initially docketed in the Supreme Court, no petition will be entertained by the Supreme Court unless application has been made first to the Court of Appeals and denied by that Court.

(b) Pending Review by Supreme Court of Court of Appeals Decisions. Application may be made in the first instance to the Supreme Court for a writ of supersedeas to stay the execution or enforcement of a judgment, order, or other determination mandated by the Court of Appeals when a notice of appeal of right or a petition for discretionary review has been or will be timely filed, or a petition for review by certiorari, mandamus, or prohibition has been filed to obtain review of the decision of the Court of Appeals. No prior motion for a stay order need be made to the Court of Appeals.

(c) Petition; Filing and Service; Content. The petition shall be filed with the clerk of the court to which application is being made and shall be accompanied by proof of service upon all other parties. The petition shall be verified by counsel or the petitioner. Upon receipt of the required docket fee, the clerk will docket the petition.

For stays of the judgments of trial tribunals, the petition shall contain a statement that stay has been sought in the court to which issuance of the writ is sought and denied or vacated by that court, or shall contain facts showing that it was impracticable there to seek a stay. For stays of any judgment, the petition shall contain: (1) a statement of any facts necessary to an understanding of the basis upon which the writ is sought; and (2) a statement of reasons why the writ should issue in justice to the applicant. The petition may be accompanied by affidavits and by any certified portions of the record pertinent to its consideration. It may be included in a petition for discretionary review by the Supreme Court under N.C.G.S. § 7A–31, or in a petition to either appellate court for certiorari, mandamus, or prohibition.

(d) Response; Determination by Court. Within ten days after service of the petition any party may file a response thereto with supporting affidavits or certified portions of the record not filed with the petition. Filing shall be accompanied by proof of service upon all other parties. The court for good cause shown may shorten the time for filing a response. Determination will be made on the basis of the petition, the response, and any supporting papers. No briefs or oral argument will be received or allowed unless ordered by the court upon its own initiative.

(e) Temporary Stay. Upon the filing of a petition for supersedeas, the applicant may apply, either within the petition or by separate paper, for an order temporarily staying enforcement or execution of the judgment, order, or other determination pending decision by the court upon the petition for supersedeas. If application is made by separate paper, it shall be filed and served in the manner provided for the petition for supersedeas in Rule 23(c). The court for good cause shown in such a petition for temporary stay may issue such an order *ex parte*. In capital cases, such stay, if granted, shall remain in effect until the period for filing a petition for certiorari in the United States Supreme Court has passed without a petition being filed, or until certiorari on a timely filed petition has been denied by that Court. At that time, the stay shall automatically dissolve.

[Adopted: 13 June 1975. Amended: 2 December 1980—23(b)—effective 1 January 1981; 6 March 1997—23(e)—effective 1 July 1997. Reenacted: 2 July 2009—effective 1 October 2009 and applies to all cases appealed on or after that date.]

Rule 24. Form of Papers; Copies

A party need file with the appellate court but a single copy of any paper required to be filed in connection with applications for extraordinary writs. The court may direct that additional copies be filed. The clerk will not reproduce copies.

[Adopted: 13 June 1975. Reenacted: 2 July 2009—effective 1 October 2009 and applies to all cases appealed on or after that date.]

ARTICLE VI. GENERAL PROVISIONS

Rule 25. Penalties for Failure to Comply with Rules

(a) Failure of Appellant to Take Timely Action. If after giving notice of appeal from any court, commission, or commissioner the appellant shall fail within the times allowed by these rules or by order of court to take any action required to present the appeal for decision, the appeal may on motion of any other party be dismissed. Prior to the filing of an appeal in an appellate court, motions to dismiss are made to the court, commission, or commissioner from which appeal has been taken; after an appeal has been filed in an appellate court, motions to dismiss are made to that court. Motions to dismiss shall be supported by affidavits or certified copies of docket entries which show the failure to take timely action or otherwise perfect the appeal and shall be allowed unless compliance or a waiver thereof is shown on the record, or unless the appellee shall consent to action out of time, or unless the court for good cause shall permit the action to be taken out of time.

Motions heard under this rule to courts of the trial divisions may be heard and determined by any judge of the particular court specified in Rule 36 of these rules; motions made under this rule to a commission may be heard and determined by the chair of the commission; or if to a commissioner, then by that commissioner. The procedure in all motions made under this rule to trial tribunals shall be that provided for motion practice by the N.C. Rules of Civil Procedure; in all motions made under this rule to courts of the appellate division, the procedure shall be that provided by Rule 37 of these rules.

(b) Sanctions for Failure to Comply with Rules. A court of the appellate division may, on its own initiative or motion of a party, impose a sanction against a party or attorney or both when the court determines that such a party or attorney or both substantially failed to comply with these appellate rules, including failure to pay any filing or printing fees or costs when due. The court may impose sanctions of the type and in the manner prescribed by Rule 34 for frivolous appeals.

[Adopted: 13 June 1975. Amended: 8 December 1988—effective 1 July 1989; 6 March 1997—25(a)—effective upon adoption 6 March 1997. Reenacted: 2 July 2009—effective 1 October 2009 and applies to all cases appealed on or after that date. Amended effective March 15, 2012.]

Rule 26. Filing and Service

(a) Filing. Papers required or permitted by these rules to be filed in the trial or appellate divisions shall be filed with the clerk of the appropriate court. Filing may be accomplished by mail or by electronic means as set forth in this rule.

(1) *Filing by Mail.* Filing may be accomplished by mail addressed to the clerk but is not timely unless the papers are received by the clerk within the time fixed for filing, except that motions, responses to petitions, the record on appeal, and briefs shall be deemed filed on the date of mailing, as evidenced by the proof of service.

(2) *Filing by Electronic Means.* Filing in the appellate courts may be accomplished by electronic means by use of the electronic filing site at www.ncappellatecourts.org. All documents may be filed electronically through the use of this site. A document filed by use of the official electronic web site is deemed filed as of the time that the document is received electronically.

Responses and motions may be filed by facsimile machines, if an oral request for permission to do so has first been tendered to and approved by the clerk of the appropriate appellate court.

In all cases in which a document has been filed by facsimile machine pursuant to this rule, counsel must forward the following items by first class mail, contemporaneously with the transmission: the original signed document, the electronic transmission fee, and the applicable filing fee for the document, if any. The party filing a document by electronic means shall be responsible for all costs of the transmission, and neither they nor the electronic transmission fee may be recovered as costs of the appeal. When a document is filed to the electronic filing site at www.ncappellatecourts.org, counsel may either have his or her account drafted electronically by following the procedures described at the electronic filing site, or counsel must forward the applicable filing fee for the document by first class mail, contemporaneously with the transmission.

(b) Service of All Papers Required. Copies of all papers filed by any party and not required by these rules to be served by the clerk shall, at or before the time of filing, be served on all other parties to the appeal.

(c) Manner of Service. Service may be made in the manner provided for service and return of process in Rule 4 of the N.C. Rules of Civil Procedure and may be so made upon a party or upon its attorney of record. Service may also be made upon a party or its attorney of record by delivering a copy to either or by mailing a copy to the recipient's last known address, or if no address is known, by filing it in the office of the clerk with whom the original paper is filed. Delivery of a copy within this rule means handing it to the attorney or to the party, or leaving it at the attorney's office with a partner or employee. Service by mail is complete upon deposit of the paper enclosed in a postpaid, properly addressed wrapper in a post office or official depository under the exclusive care and custody of the United States Postal Service, or, for those having access to such services, upon deposit with the State Courier Service or Inter–Office Mail. When a document is filed electronically to the official web site, service also may be accomplished electronically by use of the other counsel's correct and current electronic mail address(es), or service may be accomplished in the manner described previously in this subsection.

(d) Proof of Service. Papers presented for filing shall contain an acknowledgment of service by the person served or proof of service in the form of a statement of the date and manner of service and of the names of the persons served, certified by the person who made service. Proof of service shall appear on or be affixed to the papers filed.

(e) Joint Appellants and Appellees. Any paper required by these rules to be served on a party is properly served upon all parties joined in the appeal by service upon any one of them.

(f) Numerous Parties to Appeal Proceeding Separately. When there are unusually large numbers of appellees or appellants proceeding separately, the trial tribunal, upon motion of any party or on its own initiative, may order that any papers required by these rules to be served by a party on all other parties need be served only upon parties designated in the order, and that the filing of such a paper and service thereof upon the parties designated constitutes due notice of it to all other parties. A copy of every such order shall be served upon all parties to the action in such manner and form as the court directs.

(g) Documents Filed with Appellate Courts.

(1) *Form of Papers.* Papers presented to either appellate court for filing shall be letter size (8½ × 11″) with the exception of wills and exhibits. All printed matter must appear in at least 12–point type on unglazed white paper of 16–20 pound substance so as to produce a clear, black image, leaving a margin of approximately one inch on each side. The body of text shall be presented with double spacing between each line of text. No more than twenty-seven lines of double-spaced text may appear on a page, even if proportional type is used. Lines of text shall be no wider than 6½ inches. The format of all papers presented for filing shall follow the additional instructions found in the appendixes to these rules. The format of briefs shall follow the additional instructions found in Rule 28(j).

(2) *Index required.* All documents presented to either appellate court other than records on appeal, which in this respect are governed by Rule 9, shall, unless they are less than ten pages in length, be preceded by a subject index of the matter contained therein, with page references, and a table of authorities, i.e., cases (alphabetically arranged), constitutional

provisions, statutes, and textbooks cited, with references to the pages where they are cited.

(3) *Closing.* The body of the document shall at its close bear the printed name, post office address, telephone number, State Bar number and e-mail address of counsel of record, and in addition, at the appropriate place, the manuscript signature of counsel of record. If the document has been filed electronically by use of the official web site at www.ncappellatecourts.org, the manuscript signature of counsel of record is not required.

(4) *Protecting the Identity of Certain Juveniles.* Parties shall protect the identity of juveniles covered by Rules 3(b)(1), 3.1(b), or 4(e) pursuant to said rules.

[Adopted: 13 June 1975. Amended: 5 May 1981—26(g)—effective for all appeals arising from cases filed in the court of original jurisdiction after 1 July 1982; 11 February 1982—26(c); 7 December 1982—26(g)—effective for documents filed on and after 1 March 1983; 27 November 1984—26(a)—effective for documents filed on and after 1 February 1985; 30 June 1988—26(a), (g)—effective 1 September 1988; 26 July 1990—26(a)—effective 1 October 1990; 6 March 1997—26(b), (g)—effective 1 July 1997; 4 November 1999—effective 15 November 1999; 18 October 2001—26(g), para. 1—effective 31 October 2001; 15 August 2002—26(a)(1); 3 October 2002—26(g)—effective 7 October 2002; 1 May 2003—26(a)(1); 6 May 2004—26(g)(4)—effective 12 May 2004. Reenacted and Amended: 2 July 2009—amended 26(g)(3) & (4)—effective 1 October 2009 and applies to all cases appealed on or after that date.]

Rule 27. Computation and Extension of Time

(a) Computation of Time. In computing any period of time prescribed or allowed by these rules, by order of court, or by any applicable statute, the day of the act, event, or default after which the designated period of time begins to run is not included. The last day of the period so computed is to be included, unless it is a Saturday, Sunday, or a legal holiday, in which event the period runs until the end of the next day which is not a Saturday, Sunday, or a legal holiday.

(b) Additional Time After Service. Except as to filing of notice of appeal pursuant to Rule 3(c), whenever a party has the right to do some act or take some proceedings within a prescribed period after the service of a notice or other paper and the notice or paper is served by mail, or by electronic mail if allowed by these rules, three days shall be added to the prescribed period.

(c) Extensions of Time; By Which Court Granted. Except as herein provided, courts for good cause shown may upon motion extend any of the times prescribed by these rules or by order of court for doing any act required or allowed under these rules, or may permit an act to be done after the expiration of such time. Courts may not extend the time for taking an appeal or for filing a petition for discretionary review or a petition for rehearing or the responses thereto prescribed by these rules or by law.

(1) *Motions for Extension of Time in the Trial Division.* The trial tribunal for good cause shown by the appellant may extend once for no more than thirty days the time permitted by Rule 11 or Rule 18 for service of the proposed record on appeal.

Motions for extensions of time made to a trial tribunal may be made orally or in writing and without notice to other parties and may be determined at any time or place within the state.

Motions made under this Rule 27 to a court of the trial division may be heard and determined by any of those judges of the particular court specified in Rule 36 of these rules. Such motions made to a commission may be heard and determined by the chair of the commission; or if to a commissioner, then by that commissioner.

(2) *Motions for Extension of Time in the Appellate Division.* All motions for extensions of time other than those specifically enumerated in Rule 27(c)(1) may be made only to the appellate court to which appeal has been taken.

(d) Motions for Extension of Time; How Determined. Motions for extension of time made in any court may be determined *ex parte*, but the moving party shall promptly serve on all other parties to the appeal a copy of any order extending time; provided that motions made after the expiration of the time allowed in these rules for the action sought to be extended must be in writing and with notice to all other parties and may be allowed only after all other parties have had an opportunity to be heard.

[Adopted: 13 June 1975. Amended: 7 March 1978—27(c); 4 October 1978—27(c)—effective 1 January 1979; 27 November 1984—27(a), (c)—effective 1 February 1985; 8 December 1988—27(c)—effective for all judgments of the trial tribunal entered on or after 1 July 1989; 26 July 1990—27(c), (d)—effective 1 October 1990; 18 October 2001—27(c)—effective 31 October 2001. Reenacted and Amended: 2 July 2009—amended 27(b)—effective 1 October 2009 and applies to all cases appealed on or after that date. Amended: 28 February 2013—27(b)—effective 15 April 2013.]

Rule 28. Briefs: Function and Content

(a) Function. The function of all briefs required or permitted by these rules is to define clearly the issues presented to the reviewing court and to present the arguments and authorities upon which the parties rely in support of their respective positions thereon. The scope of review on appeal is limited to issues so presented in the several briefs. Issues not presented and discussed in a party's brief are deemed abandoned. Similarly, issues properly presented for review in the Court of Appeals, but not then stated in the notice of appeal or the petition accepted by the Supreme Court for review and discussed in the new briefs required by Rules 14(d)(1) and 15(g)(2) to be filed in the Supreme Court for review by that Court, are deemed abandoned.

Parties shall protect the identity of juveniles covered by Rules 3(b)(1), 3.1(b), or 4(e) pursuant to said rules.

(b) Content of Appellant's Brief. An appellant's brief shall contain, under appropriate headings and in the form prescribed by Rule 26(g) and the appendixes to these rules, in the following order:

(1) A cover page, followed by a subject index and table of authorities as required by Rule 26(g).

(2) A statement of the issues presented for review. The proposed issues on appeal listed in the record on appeal shall not limit the scope of the issues that an appellant may argue in its brief.

(3) A concise statement of the procedural history of the case. This shall indicate the nature of the case and summarize the course of proceedings up to the taking of the appeal before the court.

(4) A statement of the grounds for appellate review. Such statement shall include citation of the statute or statutes permitting appellate review. When an appeal is based on Rule 54(b) of the Rules of Civil Procedure, the statement shall show that there has been a final judgment as to one or more but fewer than all of the claims or parties and that there has been a certification by the trial court that there is no just reason for delay. When an appeal is interlocutory, the statement must contain sufficient facts and argument to support appellate review on the ground that the challenged order affects a substantial right.

(5) A full and complete statement of the facts. This should be a non-argumentative summary of all material facts underlying the matter in controversy which are necessary to understand all issues presented for review, supported by references to pages in the transcript of proceedings, the record on appeal, or exhibits, as the case may be.

(6) An argument, to contain the contentions of the appellant with respect to each issue presented. Issues not presented in a party's brief, or in support of which no reason or argument is stated, will be taken as abandoned.

The argument shall contain a concise statement of the applicable standard(s) of review for each issue, which shall appear either at the beginning of the discussion of each issue or under a separate heading placed before the beginning of the discussion of all the issues.

The body of the argument and the statement of applicable standard(s) of review shall contain citations of the authorities upon which the appellant relies. Evidence or other proceedings material to the issue may be narrated or quoted in the body of the argument, with appropriate reference to the record on appeal, the transcript of proceedings, or exhibits.

(7) A short conclusion stating the precise relief sought.

(8) Identification of counsel by signature, typed name, post office address, telephone number, State Bar number, and e-mail address.

(9) The proof of service required by Rule 26(d).

(10) Any appendix required or allowed by this Rule 28.

(c) Content of Appellee's Brief; Presentation of Additional Issues. An appellee's brief shall contain a subject index and table of authorities as required by Rule 26(g), an argument, a conclusion, identification of counsel, and proof of service in the form provided in Rule 28(b) for an appellant's brief, and any appendix required or allowed by this Rule 28. It need contain no statement of the issues presented, of the procedural history of the case, of the grounds for appellate review, of the facts, or of the standard(s) of review, unless the appellee disagrees with the appellant's statements and desires to make a restatement or unless the appellee desires to present issues in addition to those stated by the appellant.

Without taking an appeal, an appellee may present issues on appeal based on any action or omission of the trial court that deprived the appellee of an alternative basis in law for supporting the judgment, order, or other determination from which appeal has been taken. Without having taken appeal or listing proposed issues as permitted by Rule 10(c), an appellee may also argue on appeal whether a new trial should be granted to the appellee rather than a judgment notwithstanding the verdict awarded to the appellant when the latter relief is sought on appeal by the appellant. If the appellee presents issues in addition to those stated by the appellant, the appellee's brief must contain a full, non-argumentative summary of all material facts necessary to understand the new issues supported by references to pages in the record on appeal, the transcript of proceedings, or the appendixes, as appropriate, as well as a statement of the applicable standard(s) of review for those additional issues.

An appellee may supplement the record with any materials pertinent to the issues presented on appeal, as provided in Rule 9(b)(5).

(d) Appendixes to Briefs. Whenever the transcript of proceedings is filed pursuant to Rule 9(c)(2), the parties must file verbatim portions of the transcript as appendixes to their briefs, if required by this Rule 28(d). Parties must modify verbatim portions of the transcript filed pursuant to this rule in a manner consistent with Rules 3(b)(1), 3.1(b), or 4(e).

(1) *When Appendixes to Appellant's Brief Are Required.* Except as provided in Rule 28(d)(2), the appellant must reproduce as appendixes to its brief:

a. those portions of the transcript of proceedings which must be reproduced verbatim in order to understand any issue presented in the brief;

b. those portions of the transcript showing the pertinent questions and answers when an issue presented in the brief involves the admission or exclusion of evidence;

c. relevant portions of statutes, rules, or regulations, the study of which is required to determine issues presented in the brief;

d. relevant items from the Rule 11(c) or Rule 18(d)(3) supplement to the printed record on appeal, the study of which are required to determine issues presented in the brief.

(2) *When Appendixes to Appellant's Brief Are Not Required.* Notwithstanding the requirements of Rule 28(d)(1), the appellant is not required to reproduce an appendix to its brief with respect to an issue presented:

a. whenever the portion of the transcript necessary to understand an issue presented in the brief is reproduced verbatim in the body of the brief;

b. to show the absence or insufficiency of evidence unless there are discrete portions of the transcript where the subject matter of the alleged insufficiency of the evidence is located; or

c. to show the general nature of the evidence necessary to understand an issue presented in the brief if such evidence has been fully summarized as required by Rule 28(b)(4) and (5).

(3) *When Appendixes to Appellee's Brief Are Required.* An appellee must reproduce appendixes to its brief in the following circumstances:

a. Whenever the appellee believes that appellant's appendixes do not include portions of the transcript or items from the Rule 11(c) or Rule 18(d)(3) supplement to the printed record on appeal that are required by Rule 28(d)(1), the appellee shall reproduce those portions of the transcript or supplement it believes to be necessary to understand the issue.

b. Whenever the appellee presents a new or additional issue in its brief as permitted by Rule 28(c), the appellee shall reproduce portions of the transcript or relevant items from the Rule 11(c) or Rule 18(d)(3) supplement to the printed record on appeal as if it were the appellant with respect to each such new or additional issue.

(4) *Format of Appendixes.* The appendixes to the briefs of any party shall be in the format prescribed by Rule 26(g) and shall consist of clear photocopies of transcript pages that have been deemed necessary for inclusion in the appendix under this Rule 28(d). The pages of the appendix shall be consecutively numbered, and an index to the appendix shall be placed at its beginning.

(e) References in Briefs to the Record. References in the briefs to parts of the printed record on appeal and to parts of the verbatim transcript or parts of documentary exhibits shall be to the pages where those portions appear.

(f) Joinder of Multiple Parties in Briefs. Any number of appellants or appellees in a single cause or in causes consolidated for appeal may join in a single brief even though they are not formally joined on the appeal. Any party to any appeal may adopt by reference portions of the briefs of others.

(g) Additional Authorities. Additional authorities discovered by a party after filing its brief may be brought to the attention of the court by filing a memorandum thereof with the clerk of the court and serving copies upon all other parties. The memorandum may not be used as a reply brief or for additional argument, but shall simply state the issue to which the additional authority applies and provide a full citation of the authority. Authorities not cited in the briefs or in such a memorandum may not be cited and discussed in oral argument.

Before the Court of Appeals, the party shall file an original and three copies of the memorandum; in the Supreme Court, the party shall file an original and fourteen copies of the memorandum.

(h) Reply Briefs. Within fourteen days after an appellee's brief has been served on an appellant, the appellant may file and serve a reply brief, subject to the length limitations set forth in Rule 28(j). Any reply brief which an appellant elects to file shall be limited to a concise rebuttal of arguments set out in the appellee's brief and shall not reiterate arguments set forth in the appellant's principal brief. Upon motion of the appellant, the Court may extend the length limitations on such a reply brief to permit the appellant to address new or additional issues presented for the first time in the appellee's brief. Otherwise, motions to extend reply brief length limitations or to extend the time to file a reply brief are disfavored.

(i) Amicus Curiae Briefs. A brief of an amicus curiae may be filed only by leave of the appellate court wherein the appeal is docketed or in response to a request made by that court on its own initiative.

A person desiring to file an amicus curiae brief shall present to the court a motion for leave to file, served upon all parties. The motion shall state concisely the nature of the applicant's interest, the reasons why an amicus curiae brief is believed desirable, the issues of law to be addressed in the amicus curiae brief, and the applicant's position on those issues. The proposed amicus curiae brief may be conditionally filed with the motion for leave. Unless otherwise ordered by the court, the application for leave will be determined solely upon the motion and without responses thereto or oral argument.

The clerk of the appellate court will forthwith notify the applicant and all parties of the court's action upon the application. Unless other time limits are set out in the order of the court permitting the brief, the amicus curiae shall file the brief within the time allowed for the filing of the brief of the party supported or, if in support of neither party, within the time allowed for filing appellant's brief. Motions for leave to file an amicus curiae brief submitted to the court after the time within which the amicus curiae brief normally would be due are disfavored in the absence of good cause. Reply briefs of the parties to an amicus curiae brief will be limited to points or authorities presented in the amicus curiae brief which are not presented in the main briefs of the parties. No reply brief of an amicus curiae will be received.

A motion of an amicus curiae to participate in oral argument will be allowed only for extraordinary reasons.

(j) Length Limitations Applicable to Briefs Filed in the Court of Appeals. Each brief filed in the Court of Appeals, whether filed by an appellant, appellee, or amicus curiae, formatted according to Rule 26 and the appendixes to these rules, shall have either a page limit or a word-count limit, depending on the type style used in the brief:

(1) *Type.*

(A) *Type style.* Documents must be set in a plain roman style, although italics or boldface may be used for emphasis. Case names must be italicized or underlined. Documents may be set in either proportionally spaced or nonproportionally spaced (monospaced) type.

(B) *Type size.*

1. Nonproportionally spaced type (e.g., Courier or Courier New) may not contain more than ten characters per inch (12–point).

2. Proportionally spaced type (e.g., Times New Roman) must be 14–point or larger.

3. Documents set in Courier New 12–point type or Times New Roman 14–point type will be deemed in compliance with these type size requirements.

(2) *Document.*

(A) *Page limits for briefs using nonproportional type.* The page limit for a principal brief that uses nonproportional type is thirty-five pages. The page limit for a reply brief is fifteen pages. Unless otherwise ordered by the court, the page limit for an amicus curiae brief is fifteen pages. A page shall contain no more than twenty-seven lines of double-spaced text of no more than sixty-five characters per line. Covers, indexes, tables of authorities, certificates of service, and appendixes do not count toward these page limits. The court may strike or require resubmission of briefs with excessive single-spaced passages or footnotes that are used to circumvent these page limits.

(B) *Word-count limits for briefs using proportional type.* A principal brief that uses proportional type may contain no more than 8,750 words. A reply brief may contain no more than 3,750 words. Unless otherwise ordered by the court, an amicus curiae brief may contain no more than 3,750 words. Covers, indexes, tables of authorities, certificates of service, certificates of compliance with this rule, and appendixes do not count against these word-count limits. Footnotes and citations in the text, however, do count against these word-count limits. Parties who file briefs in proportional type shall submit with the brief, immediately before the certificate of service, a certification, signed by counsel of record, or in the case of parties filing briefs *pro se*, by the party, that the brief contains no more than the number of words allowed by this rule. For purposes of this certification, counsel and parties may rely on word counts reported by word-processing software, as long as footnotes and citations are included in those word counts.

[Adopted: 13 June 1975. Amended: 27 January 1981—repeal 28(d)—effective 1 July 1981; 10 June 1981—28(b), (c)—effective 1 October 1981; 12 January 1982—28(b)(4)—effective 15 March 1982; 7 December 1982—28(i)—effective 1 January 1983; 27 November 1984—28(b), (c), (d), (e), (g), (h)—effective 1 February 1985; 30 June 1988—28(a), (b), (c), (d), (e), (h), (i)—effective 1 September 1988; 8 June 1989—28(h), (j)—effective 1 September 1989; 26 July 1990—28(h)(2)—effective 1 October 1990; 18 October 2001—28(b)(4)–(10), (c), (j)—effective 31 October 2001; 3 October 2002—28(j)—effective 7 October 2002; 6 May 2004—28(d), (h), (j)(2), (k)—effective 12 May 2004; 23 August 2005—28(b)(6), (c), (h)(4)—effective 1 September 2005; 25 January 2007—28(b)(6), para. 1; 28(d(3)(a), (b); 28(i), paras. 2, 3,; 28(j)(2)(A)(1) & (2); added 28(d)(1)(d)—effective 1 March 2007 and applies to all cases appealed on or after that date. Reenacted and Amended: 2 July 2009—amended 28(a), (b), (c), (d), (e), (h), (i), (j); deleted former 28(k) and replaced with new language in 28(a) — effective 1 October 2009 and applies to all cases appealed on or after that date. Amended: 28 February 2013—28(h), 28(j)(2)(A), and 28(j)(2)(B)—effective 15 April 15 2013.]

Rule 29. Sessions of Courts; Calendar of Hearings

(a) Sessions of Court.

(1) *Supreme Court.* The Supreme Court shall be in continuous session for the transaction of business. Unless otherwise scheduled by the Court, hearings in appeals will be held during the months of February through May and September through December. Additional settings may be authorized by the Chief Justice.

(2) *Court of Appeals.* Appeals will be heard in accordance with a schedule promulgated by the Chief Judge. Panels of the Court will sit as scheduled by the Chief Judge. For the transaction of other busi-

ness, the Court of Appeals shall be in continuous session.

(b) Calendaring of Cases for Hearing. Each appellate court will calendar the hearing of all appeals docketed in the court. In general, appeals will be calendared for hearing in the order in which they are docketed, but the court may vary the order for any cause deemed appropriate. On motion of any party, with notice to all other parties, the court may determine without hearing to give an appeal peremptory setting or otherwise to vary the normal calendar order. Except as advanced for peremptory setting on motion of a party or the court's own initiative, no appeal will be calendared for hearing at a time less than thirty days after the filing of the appellant's brief. The clerk of the appellate court will give reasonable notice to all counsel of record of the setting of an appeal for hearing by mailing a copy of the calendar.

[Adopted: 13 June 1975. Amended: 3 March 1982—29(a)(1); 3 September 1987—29(a)(1); 26 July 1990—29(b)—effective 1 October 1990. Reenacted and Amended: 2 July 2009—amended 29(a)(1)—effective 1 October 2009 and applies to all cases appealed on or after that date.]

Rule 30. Oral Argument and Unpublished Opinions

(a) Order and Content of Argument.

(1) The appellant is entitled to open and conclude the argument. The opening argument shall include a fair statement of the case. Oral arguments should complement the written briefs, and counsel will therefore not be permitted to read at length from briefs, records, and authorities.

(2) In cases involving juveniles covered by Rules 3(b)(1), 3.1(b), or 4(e), counsel shall refrain from using a juvenile's name in oral argument and shall refer to the juvenile pursuant to said rules.

(b) Time Allowed for Argument.

(1) *In General.* Ordinarily a total of thirty minutes will be allowed all appellants and a total of thirty minutes will be allowed all appellees for oral argument. Upon written or oral application of any party, the court for good cause shown may extend the times limited for argument. Among other causes, the existence of adverse interests between multiple appellants or between multiple appellees may be suggested as good cause for such an extension. The court of its own initiative may direct argument on specific points outside the times limited.

Counsel is not obliged to use all the time allowed, and should avoid unnecessary repetition; the court may terminate argument whenever it considers further argument unnecessary.

(2) *Numerous Counsel.* Any number of counsel representing individual appellants or appellees proceeding separately or jointly may be heard in argument within the times herein limited or allowed by order of court. When more than one counsel is heard, duplication or supplementation of argument on the same points shall be avoided unless specifically directed by the court.

(c) Non–Appearance of Parties. If counsel for any party fails to appear to present oral argument, the court will hear argument from opposing counsel. If counsel for no party appears, the court will decide the case on the written briefs unless it orders otherwise.

(d) Submission on Written Briefs. By agreement of the parties, a case may be submitted for decision on the written briefs, but the court may nevertheless order oral argument before deciding the case.

(e) Unpublished Opinions.

(1) In order to minimize the cost of publication and of providing storage space for the published reports, the Court of Appeals is not required to publish an opinion in every decided case. If the panel that hears the case determines that the appeal involves no new legal principles and that an opinion, if published, would have no value as a precedent, it may direct that no opinion be published.

(2) The text of a decision without published opinion shall be posted on the Administrative Office of the Courts' North Carolina Court System Internet web site and reported only by listing the case and the decision in the advance sheets and the bound volumes of the North Carolina Court of Appeals Reports.

(3) An unpublished decision of the North Carolina Court of Appeals does not constitute controlling legal authority. Accordingly, citation of unpublished opinions in briefs, memoranda, and oral arguments in the trial and appellate divisions is disfavored, except for the purpose of establishing claim preclusion, issue preclusion, or the law of the case. If a party believes, nevertheless, that an unpublished opinion has precedential value to a material issue in the case and that there is no published opinion that would serve as well, the party may cite the unpublished opinion if that party serves a copy thereof on all other parties in the case and on the court to which the citation is offered. This service may be accomplished by including the copy of the unpublished opinion in an addendum to a brief or memorandum. A party who cites an unpublished opinion for the first time at a hearing or oral argument must attach a copy of the unpublished opinion relied upon pursuant to the requirements of Rule 28(g). When citing an unpublished opinion, a party must indicate the opinion's unpublished status.

(4) Counsel of record and *pro se* parties of record may move for publication of an unpublished opinion, citing reasons based on Rule 30(e)(1) and serving a copy of the motion upon all other counsel and *pro se* parties of record. The motion shall be filed and served within ten days of the filing of the opinion. Any objection to the requested publication by counsel

or *pro se* parties of record must be filed within five days after service of the motion requesting publication. The panel that heard the case shall determine whether to allow or deny such motion.

(f) Pre-Argument Review; Decision of Appeal Without Oral Argument.

(1) At any time that the Supreme Court concludes that oral argument in any case pending before it will not be of assistance to the Court, it may dispose of the case on the record and briefs. In those cases, counsel will be notified not to appear for oral argument.

(2) The Chief Judge of the Court of Appeals may from time to time designate a panel to review any pending case, after all briefs are filed but before argument, for decision under this rule. If all of the judges of the panel to which a pending appeal has been referred conclude that oral argument will not be of assistance to the Court, the case may be disposed of on the record and briefs. Counsel will be notified not to appear for oral argument.

[Adopted: 13 June 1975. Amended: 18 December 1975—30(e); 3 May 1976—30(f); 5 February 1979—30(e); 10 June 1981—30(f)—effective 1 July 1981; 18 October 2001—30(e)(2), (4)—effective 1 January 2002; 3 October 2002—30(e)(3)—effective 7 October 2002; 6 May 2004—30(a)(2)—effective 12 May 2004; 23 August 2005—30, 30(e) (titles)—effective 1 September 2005. Reenacted and Amended: 2 July 2009—amended 30(a)(2), 30(b)(1)—effective 1 October 2009 and applies to all cases appealed on or after that date.]

Rule 31. Petition for Rehearing

(a) Time for Filing; Content. A petition for rehearing may be filed in a civil action within fifteen days after the mandate of the court has been issued. The petition shall state with particularity the points of fact or law that, in the opinion of the petitioner, the court has overlooked or misapprehended and shall contain such argument in support of the petition as petitioner desires to present. It shall be accompanied by a certificate of at least two attorneys who for periods of at least five years, respectively, shall have been members of the bar of this State and who have no interest in the subject of the action and have not been counsel for any party to the action, that they have carefully examined the appeal and the authorities cited in the decision, and that they consider the decision in error on points specifically and concisely identified. Oral argument in support of the petition will not be permitted.

(b) How Addressed; Filed. A petition for rehearing shall be addressed to the court that issued the opinion sought to be reconsidered.

(c) How Determined. Within thirty days after the petition is filed, the court will either grant or deny the petition. A determination to grant or deny will be made solely upon the written petition; no written response will be received from the opposing party and no oral argument by any party will be heard. Determination by the court is final. The rehearing may be granted as to all or fewer than all points suggested in the petition. When the petition is denied, the clerk shall forthwith notify all parties.

(d) Procedure When Granted. Upon grant of the petition the clerk shall forthwith notify the parties that the petition has been granted. The case will be reconsidered solely upon the record on appeal, the petition to rehear, new briefs of both parties, and the oral argument if one has been ordered by the court. The briefs shall be addressed solely to the points specified in the order granting the petition to rehear. The petitioner's brief shall be filed within thirty days after the case is certified for rehearing, and the opposing party's brief, within thirty days after petitioner's brief is served. Filing and service of the new briefs shall be in accordance with the requirements of Rule 13. No reply brief shall be received on rehearing, If the court has ordered oral argument, the clerk shall give notice of the time set therefor, which time shall be not less than thirty days after the filing of the petitioner's brief on rehearing.

(e) Stay of Execution. When a petition for rehearing is filed, the petitioner may obtain a stay of execution in the trial court to which the mandate of the appellate court has been issued. The procedure is as provided by Rule 8 of these rules for stays pending appeal.

(f) Waiver by Appeal from Court of Appeals. The timely filing of a notice of appeal from, or of a petition for discretionary review of, a determination of the Court of Appeals constitutes a waiver of any right thereafter to petition the Court of Appeals for rehearing as to such determination or, if a petition for rehearing has earlier been filed, an abandonment of such petition.

(g) No Petition in Criminal Cases. The courts will not entertain petitions for rehearing in criminal actions.

[Adopted: 13 June 1975. Amended: 27 November 1984—31(a)—effective 1 February 1985; 3 September 1987—31(d); 8 December 1988—31(b), (d)—effective 1 January 1989; 18 October 2001—31(b)—effective 31 October 2001. Reenacted: 2 July 2009—effective 1 October 2009 and applies to all cases appealed on or after that date.]

Rule 32. Mandates of the Courts

(a) In General. Unless a court of the appellate division directs that a formal mandate shall issue, the mandate of the court consists of certified copies of its judgment and of its opinion and any direction of its clerk as to costs. The mandate is issued by its transmittal from the clerk of the issuing court to the clerk or comparable officer of the tribunal from which appeal was taken to the issuing court.

(b) Time of Issuance. Unless a court orders otherwise, its clerk shall enter judgment and issue the mandate of the court twenty days after the written opinion of the court has been filed with the clerk.

[Adopted: 13 June 1975. Amended: 27 November 1984—32(b)—effective 1 February 1985. Reenacted: 2 July 2009—effective 1 October 2009 and applies to all cases appealed on or after that date.]

Rule 33. Attorneys

(a) Appearances. An attorney will not be recognized as appearing in any case unless he or she is entered as counsel of record therein. The signature of an attorney on a record on appeal, motion, brief, or other document permitted by these rules to be filed in a court of the appellate division constitutes entry of the attorney as counsel of record for the parties designated and a certification that the attorney represents such parties. The signature of a member or associate in a firm's name constitutes entry of the firm as counsel of record for the parties designated. Counsel of record may not withdraw from a case except by leave of court. Only those counsel of record who have personally signed the brief prior to oral argument may be heard in argument.

(b) Signatures on Electronically Filed Documents. If more than one attorney is listed as being an attorney for the party(ies) on an electronically filed document, it is the responsibility of the attorney actually filing the document by computer to (1) list his or her name first on the document, and (2) place on the document under the signature line the following statement: "I certify that all of the attorneys listed below have authorized me to list their names on this document as if they had personally signed it."

(c) Agreements. Only those agreements of counsel which appear in the record on appeal or which are filed in the court where an appeal is docketed will be recognized by that court.

(d) Limited Practice of Out-of-State Attorneys. Attorneys who are not licensed to practice law in North Carolina, but desire to appear before the appellate courts of North Carolina in a matter shall submit a motion to the appellate court fully complying with the requirements set forth in N.C.G. S. § 84–4.1. This motion shall be filed prior to or contemporaneously with the out-of-state attorney signing and filing any motion, petition, brief, or other document in any appellate court. Failure to comply with this provision may subject the attorney to sanctions and shall result in the document being stricken, unless signed by another attorney licensed to practice in North Carolina. If an attorney is admitted to practice before the Court of Appeals in a matter, the attorney shall be required to file another motion should the case proceed to the Supreme Court. However, if the required fee has been paid to the Court of Appeals, another fee shall not be due at the Supreme Court.

[Adopted: 13 June 1975. Amended: 18 October 2001—33(a)–(c)—effective 31 October 2001. Reenacted and Amended: 2 July 2009—added 33(d)—effective 1 October 2009 and applies to all cases appealed on or after that date.]

Rule 33.1. Secure Leave Periods for Attorneys

(a) Purpose, Authorization. In order to secure for the parties to actions and proceedings pending in the appellate division, and to the public at large, the heightened level of professionalism that an attorney is able to provide when the attorney enjoys periods of time that are free from the urgent demands of professional responsibility and to enhance the overall quality of the attorney's personal and family life, any attorney may from time to time designate and enjoy one or more secure leave periods each year as provided in this rule.

(b) Length, Number. A secure leave period shall consist of one or more complete calendar weeks. During any calendar year, an attorney's secure leave periods pursuant to this rule and to Rule 26 of the General Rules of Practice for the Superior and District Courts shall not exceed, in the aggregate, three calendar weeks.

(c) Designation, Effect. To designate a secure leave period, an attorney shall file a written designation containing the information required by subsection (d), with the official specified in subsection (e), and within the time provided in subsection (f). Upon such filing, the secure leave period so designated shall be deemed allowed without further action of the court, and the attorney shall not be required to appear at any argument or other in-court proceeding in the appellate division during that secure leave period.

(d) Content of Designation. The designation shall contain the following information: (1) the attorney's name, address, telephone number, State Bar number, and e-mail address; (2) the date of the Monday on which the secure leave period is to begin and of the Friday on which it is to end; (3) the dates of all other secure leave periods during the current calendar year that have previously been designated by the attorney pursuant to this rule and to Rule 26 of the General Rules of Practice for the Superior and District Courts; (4) a statement that the secure leave period is not being designated for the purpose of delaying, hindering, or interfering with the timely disposition of any matter in any pending action or proceeding; (5) a statement that no argument or other in-court proceeding has been scheduled during the designated secure leave period in any matter pending in the appellate division in which the attorney has entered an appearance; and (6) a listing of all cases, by caption and docket number, pending before the appellate court in which the designation is being filed. The designation shall apply only to those cases pending in that appellate court on the date of its filing. A separate designation shall be filed as to any cases on appeal subsequently filed and docketed.

(e) Where to File Designation. The designation shall be filed as follows: (1) if the attorney has entered an appearance in the Supreme Court, in the office of the clerk of the Supreme Court, even if the designation was filed initially in the Court of Appeals; (2) if the attorney has entered an appearance in the Court of Appeals, in the office of the clerk of the Court of Appeals.

(f) When to File Designation. The designation shall be filed: (1) no later than ninety days before the beginning of the secure leave period, and (2) before any argument or other in-court proceeding has been scheduled for a time during the designated secure leave period.

[Adopted: 6 May 1999—effective 1 January 2000 for all actions and proceedings pending in the appellate division on and after that date. Recodified former Rule 33A as Rule 33.1 and Reenacted Rule 33.1 as amended: 2 July 2009—amended 33.1(d) & (e) —effective 1 October 2009 and applies to all cases appealed on or after that date.]

Rule 34. Frivolous Appeals; Sanctions

(a) A court of the appellate division may, on its own initiative or motion of a party, impose a sanction against a party or attorney or both when the court determines that an appeal or any proceeding in an appeal was frivolous because of one or more of the following:

(1) the appeal was not well grounded in fact and was not warranted by existing law or a good faith argument for the extension, modification, or reversal of existing law;

(2) the appeal was taken or continued for an improper purpose, such as to harass or to cause unnecessary delay or needless increase in the cost of litigation;

(3) a petition, motion, brief, record, or other paper filed in the appeal was grossly lacking in the requirements of propriety, grossly violated appellate court rules, or grossly disregarded the requirements of a fair presentation of the issues to the appellate court.

(b) A court of the appellate division may impose one or more of the following sanctions:

(1) dismissal of the appeal;

(2) monetary damages including, but not limited to,

a. single or double costs,

b. damages occasioned by delay,

c. reasonable expenses, including reasonable attorney fees, incurred because of the frivolous appeal or proceeding;

(3) any other sanction deemed just and proper.

(c) A court of the appellate division may remand the case to the trial division for a hearing to determine one or more of the sanctions under subdivisions (b)(2) or (b)(3) of this rule.

(d) If a court of the appellate division remands the case to the trial division for a hearing to determine a sanction under subsection (c) of this rule, the person subject to sanction shall be entitled to be heard on that determination in the trial division.

[Adopted: 13 June 1975. Amended: 8 December 1988—effective 1 July 1989; 8 April 1999—34(d). Reenacted: 2 July 2009—effective 1 October 2009 and applies to all cases appealed on or after that date.]

Rule 35. Costs

(a) To Whom Allowed. Except as otherwise provided by law, if an appeal is dismissed, costs shall be taxed against the appellant unless otherwise agreed by the parties or ordered by the court; if a judgment is affirmed, costs shall be taxed against the appellant unless otherwise ordered by the court; if a judgment is reversed, costs shall be taxed against the appellee unless otherwise ordered; if a judgment is affirmed in part, reversed in part, or modified in any way, costs shall be allowed as directed by the court.

(b) Direction as to Costs in Mandate. The clerk shall include in the mandate of the court an itemized statement of costs taxed in the appellate court and a designation of the party against whom such costs are taxed.

(c) Costs of Appeal Taxable in Trial Tribunals. Any costs of an appeal that are assessable in the trial tribunal shall, upon receipt of the mandate, be taxed as directed therein and may be collected by execution of the trial tribunal.

(d) Execution to Collect Costs in Appellate Courts. Costs taxed in the courts of the appellate division may be made the subject of execution issuing from the court where taxed. Such execution may be directed by the clerk of the court to the proper officers of any county of the state; may be issued at any time after the mandate of the court has been issued; and may be made returnable on any day named. Any officer to whom such execution is directed is subject to the penalties prescribed by law for failure to make due and proper return.

[Adopted: 13 June 1975. Reenacted: 2 July 2009—effective 1 October 2009 and applies to all cases appealed on or after that date.]

Rule 36. Trial Judges Authorized to Enter Orders Under These Rules

(a) When Particular Judge Not Specified by Rule. When by these rules a trial court or a judge thereof is permitted or required to enter an order or to take some other judicial action with respect to a pending appeal and the rule does not specify the particular judge with authority to do so, the following judges of the respective courts have such authority with respect to causes docketed in their respective divisions:

(1) *Superior Court.* The judge who entered the judgment, order, or other determination from which appeal was taken, and any regular or special superior judge resident in the district or assigned to hold court in the district wherein the cause is docketed;

(2) *District Court.* The judge who entered the judgment, order, or other determination from which appeal was taken; the chief district court judge of the district wherein the cause is docketed; and any judge designated by such chief district court judge to enter interlocutory orders under N.C.G.S. § 7A–192.

(b) Upon Death, Incapacity, or Absence of Particular Judge Authorized. When by these rules the authority to enter an order or to take other judicial action is limited to a particular judge and that judge is unavailable by reason of death, mental or physical incapacity, or absence from the state, the Chief Justice will, upon motion of any party, designate another judge to act in the matter. Such designation will be by order entered *ex parte,* copies of which will be mailed forthwith by the clerk of the Supreme Court to the judge designated and to all parties.

[Adopted: 13 June 1975. Reenacted: 2 July 2009—effective 1 October 2009 and applies to all cases appealed on or after that date.]

Rule 37. Motions in Appellate Courts

(a) Time; Content of Motions; Response. An application to a court of the appellate division for an order or for other relief available under these rules may be made by filing a motion for such order or other relief with the clerk of the court, with service on all other parties. Unless another time is expressly provided by these rules, the motion may be filed and served at any time before the case is called for oral argument. The motion shall contain or be accompanied by any matter required by a specific provision of these rules governing such a motion and shall state with particularity the grounds on which it is based and the order or relief sought. If a motion is supported by affidavits, briefs, or other papers, these shall be served and filed with the motion. Within ten days after a motion is served or until the appeal is called for oral argument, whichever period is shorter, a party may file and serve copies of a response in opposition to the motion, which may be supported by affidavits, briefs, or other papers in the same manner as motions. The court may shorten or extend the time for responding to any motion.

(b) Determination. Notwithstanding the provisions of Rule 37(a), a motion may be acted upon at any time, despite the absence of notice to all parties and without awaiting a response thereto. A party who has not received actual notice of such a motion, or who has not filed a response at the time such action is taken, and who is adversely affected by the action may request reconsideration, vacation, or modification thereof. Motions will be determined without argument, unless the court orders otherwise.

(c) Protecting the Identity of Certain Juveniles. Parties shall protect the identity of juveniles covered by Rules 3(b)(1), 3.1(b), or 4(e) pursuant to said rules.

(d) Withdrawal of Appeal in Criminal Cases. Withdrawal of appeal in criminal cases shall be in accordance with N.C.G.S. § 15A–1450. In addition to the requirements of N.C.G.S. § 15A–1450, after the record on appeal in a criminal case has been filed in an appellate court but before the filing of an opinion, the defendant shall also file a written notice of the withdrawal with the clerk of the appropriate appellate court.

(e) Withdrawal of Appeal in Civil Cases.

(1) Prior to the filing of a record on appeal in the appellate court, an appellant or cross-appellant may, without the consent of the other party, file a notice of withdrawal of its appeal with the tribunal from which appeal has been taken. Alternatively, prior to the filing of a record on appeal, the parties may file a signed stipulation agreeing to dismiss the appeal with the tribunal from which the appeal has been taken.

(2) After the record on appeal has been filed, an appellant or cross-appellant or all parties jointly may move the appellate court in which the appeal is pending, prior to the filing of an opinion, for dismissal of the appeal. The motion must specify the reasons therefor, the positions of all parties on the motion to dismiss, and the positions of all parties on the allocation of taxed costs. The appeal may be dismissed by order upon such terms as agreed to by the parties or as fixed by the appellate court.

(f) Effect of Withdrawal of Appeal. The withdrawal of an appeal shall not affect the right of any other party to file or continue such party's appeal or cross-appeal.

[Adopted: 13 June 1975. Amended: 6 May 2004—37(c)—effective 12 May 2004; 25 January 2007—added 37(d)–(f)—effective 1 March 2007 and applies to all cases appealed on or after that date. Reenacted and Amended: 2 July 2009—rewrote 37(c)—effective 1 October 2009 and applies to all cases appealed on or after that date.]

Rule 38. Substitution of Parties

(a) Death of a Party. No action abates by reason of the death of a party while an appeal may be taken or is pending, if the cause of action survives. If a party acting in an individual capacity dies after appeal is taken from any tribunal, the personal representative of the deceased party in a personal action, or the successor in interest of the deceased party in a real action may be substituted as a party on motion filed by the representative or the successor in interest or by any other party with the clerk of the court in which the action is then docketed. A motion to substitute made by a party shall be served upon the personal representative or successor in interest in addition to all other parties. If such a deceased party in a personal action has no personal representative, any party may in writing notify the court of the death, and the court in which the action is then docketed shall direct the proceedings to be had in order to substitute a personal representative.

If a party against whom an appeal may be taken dies after entry of a judgment or order but before appeal is taken, any party entitled to appeal therefrom may proceed as appellant as if death had not occurred; and after appeal is taken, substitution may then be effected in accordance with this subdivision. If a party entitled to appeal dies before filing a notice of appeal, appeal may be taken by the personal representative, or, if there is no personal representative, by the attorney of record within the time and in the manner prescribed in these rules; and after appeal is taken, substitution may then be effected in accordance with this rule.

(b) Substitution for Other Causes. If substitution of a party to an appeal is necessary for any reason other than death, substitution shall be effected in accordance with the procedure prescribed in subsection (a).

(c) Public Officers; Death or Separation From Office. When a person is a party to an appeal in an official or representative capacity and during its pendency dies, resigns, or otherwise ceases to hold office, the action does not abate and the person's successor is automatically substituted as a party. Prior to the qualification of a successor, the attorney of record for the former party may take any action required by these rules. An order of substitution may be made, but neither failure to enter such an order nor any misnomer in the name of a substituted party shall affect the substitution unless it be shown that the same affected the substantial rights of a party.

[Adopted: 13 June 1975. Reenacted: 2 July 2009—effective 1 October 2009 and applies to all cases appealed on or after that date.]

Rule 39. Duties of Clerks; When Offices Open

(a) General Provisions. The clerks of the courts of the appellate division shall take the oaths and give the bonds required by law. The courts shall be deemed always open for the purpose of filing any proper paper and of making motions and issuing orders. The offices of the clerks with the clerks or deputies in attendance shall be open during business hours on all days except Saturdays, Sundays, and legal holidays, but the respective courts may provide by order that the offices of their clerks shall be open for specified hours on Saturdays or on particular legal holidays or shall be closed on particular business days.

(b) Records to Be Kept. The clerk of each of the courts of the appellate division shall keep and maintain the records of that court, on paper, microfilm, or electronic media, or any combination thereof. The records kept by the clerk shall include indexed listings of all cases docketed in that court, whether by appeal, petition, or motion, and a notation of the dispositions attendant thereto; a listing of final judgments on appeals before the court, indexed by title, docket number, and parties, containing a brief memorandum of the judgment of the court and the party against whom costs were adjudicated; and records of the proceedings and ceremonies of the court.

[Adopted: 13 June 1975. Amended: 8 December 1988—39(b)—effective 1 January 1989. Reenacted: 2 July 2009—effective 1 October 2009 and applies to all cases appealed on or after that date.]

Rule 40. Consolidation of Actions on Appeal

Two or more actions that involve common issues of law may be consolidated for hearing upon motion of a party to any of the actions made to the appellate court wherein all are docketed, or upon the initiative of that court. Actions so consolidated will be calendared and heard as a single case. Upon consolidation, the parties may set the course of argument, within the times permitted by Rule 30(b), by written agreement filed with the court prior to oral argument. This agreement shall control unless modified by the court.

[Adopted: 13 June 1975. Amended: 18 October 2001—effective 31 October 2001. Reenacted and Amended: 2 July 2009—effective 1 October 2009 and applies to all cases appealed on or after that date.]

Rule 41. Appeal Information Statement

(a) The Court of Appeals has adopted an Appeal Information Statement (Statement) which will be revised from time to time. The purpose of the Statement is to provide the Court the substance of an appeal and the information needed by the Court for effective case management.

(b) Each appellant shall complete, file, and serve the Statement as set out in this rule.

(1) The clerk of the Court of Appeals shall furnish a Statement form to all parties to the appeal when the record on appeal is docketed in the Court of Appeals.

(2) Each appellant shall complete and file the Statement with the clerk of the Court of Appeals at or before the time his or her appellant's brief is due and shall serve a copy of the statement upon all other parties to the appeal pursuant to Rule 26. The Statement may be filed by mail addressed to the clerk and, if first class mail is utilized, is deemed filed on the date of mailing as evidenced by the proof of service. Parties shall protect the identity of juveniles covered by Rules 3(b)(1), 3.1(b), or 4(e) pursuant to said rules.

(3) If any party to the appeal concludes that the Statement is in any way inaccurate or incomplete, that

party may file with the Court of Appeals a written statement setting out additions or corrections within seven days of the service of the Statement and shall serve a copy of the written statement upon all other parties to the appeal pursuant to Rule 26. The written statement may be filed by mail addressed to the clerk and, if first class mail is utilized, is deemed filed on the date of mailing as evidenced by the proof of service.

[Adopted: 3 March 1994—effective: 15 March 1994. Amended: 6 May 2004—41(b)(2)—effective 12 May 2004. Reenacted and Amended: 2 July 2009—amended 41(b)(2)—effective 1 October 2009 and applies to all cases appealed on or after that date.]

Rule 42. [Reserved]

[Adopted: 13 June 1975. Renumbered: Effective 15 March 1994. Amended: 18 October 2001—effective 31 October 2001. Recodified as Rule 1(a): 2 July 2009—effective 1 October 2009.]

APPENDICES TO NORTH CAROLINA RULES OF APPELLATE PROCEDURE

Adopted July 1, 1989

Appendix A. Timetables for Appeals

TIMETABLE OF APPEALS FROM TRIAL DIVISION AND ADMINISTRATIVE AGENCIES UNDER ARTICLES II AND IV OF THE RULES OF APPELLATE PROCEDURE

Action	*Time (Days)*	*From date of*	*Rule Ref.*
Taking appeal (civil)	30	entry of judgment (unless tolled)	3(c)
Cross appeal	10	service and filing of a timely notice of appeal	3(c)
Taking appeal (agency)	30	receipt of final agency order unless statutes provide otherwise)	18(b)(2)
Taking appeal (criminal)	14	entry of judgment (unless tolled)	4(a)
Ordering transcript (civil, agency)	14	filing notice of appeal	7(a)(1) 18(b)(3)
Ordering transcript (criminal indigent)	14	order filed by clerk of superior court	7(a)(2)
Preparing & delivering transcript (civil, non-capital criminal) (capital criminal)	 60 120	service of order for transcript	7(b)(1)
Serving proposed record on appeal (civil, non-capital criminal) (agency)	 35 35	notice of appeal (no transcript) or reporter's certificate of delivery of transcript	11(b) 18(d)
Serving proposed record on appeal (capital)	70	reporter's certificate of delivery	11(b)

Action	Time (Days)	From date of	Rule Ref.
Serving objections or proposed alternative record on appeal		service of proposed record	11(c)
(civil, non-capital criminal)	30		
(capital criminal)	35		
(agency)	30	service of proposed record	18(d)(2)
Requesting judicial settlement of record	10	expiration of the last day within which an appellee served could serve objections, etc.	11(c) 18(d)(3)
Judicial settlement of record	20	service on judge of request for settlement	11(c) 18(d)(3)
Filing record on appeal in appellate court	15	settlement of record on appeal	12(a)
Filing appellant's brief (or mailing brief under Rule 26(a))	30	Clerk's mailing of printed record (60 days in Death Cases)	13(a)
Filing appellee's brief (or mailing brief under Rule 26(a))	30	service of appellant's brief (60 days in Death Cases)	13(a)
Oral Argument	30	filing appellant's brief (usual minimum time)	29
Certification or Mandate	20	issuance of opinion	32
Petition for Rehearing (civil action only)	15	mandate	31(a)

TIMETABLE OF APPEALS FROM TRIAL DIVISION UNDER ARTICLE II, RULE 3.1, OF THE RULES OF APPELLATE PROCEDURE

Action	Time (Days)	From date of	Rule Ref.
Taking appeal	10	entry of judgment	3.1(a); N.C.G.S. § 7B–1001
Notifying court reporting coordinator (clerk of superior court)	1 (business)	filing notice of appeal	3.1(c)(1)
Assigning transcriptionist (court reporting coordinator)	2 (business)	receipt of notification from court reporting coordinator	3.1(c)(1)
Preparing and delivering a transcript of designated proceedings (indigent appellant)	35	assignment by court reporting coordinator	3.1(c)(1)
Preparing and delivering a transcript of designated proceedings (non- indigent appellant)	45	assignment of transcriptionist	3.1(c)(1)

Action	*Time (Days)*	*From date of*	*Rule Ref.*
Serving proposed record on appeal	10	receipt of transcript	3.1(c)(2)
Serving notice of approval, or objections, or proposed alternative record on appeal	10	service of proposed record	3.1(c)(2)
Filing record on appeal when parties agree to a settled record within 20 days of receipt of transcript	5 (business)	settlement of record	3.1(c)(2)
Filing record on appeal if *all* appellees fail either to serve notices of approval, or objections, or proposed alternative records on appeal	5 (business)	last date on which *any* appellee could so serve	3.1(c)(2)
Appellant files proposed record on appeal and appellee(s) files objections and amendments or an alternative proposed record on appeal when parties cannot agree to a settled record on appeal within 30 days after receipt of the transcript	5 (business)	last date on which the record could be settled by agreement	3.1(c)(2)
Filing appellant's brief	30	filing of record on appeal	3.1(c)(3)
Filing appellee's brief	30	service of appellant's brief	3.1(c)(3)

TIMETABLE OF APPEALS TO THE SUPREME COURT FROM THE COURT OF APPEALS UNDER ARTICLE III OF THE RULES OF APPELLATE PROCEDURE

Action	*Time (Days)*	*From date of*	*Rule Ref.*
Petition for Discretionary Review prior to determination	15	docketing appeal in Court of Appeals	15(b)
Notice of Appeal and/or Petition for Discretionary Review	15	mandate of Court of Appeals (or from order of Court of Appeals denying petition for rehearing)	14(a) 15(b)
Cross–Notice of Appeal	10	filing of first notice of appeal	14(a)
Response to Petition for Discretionary Review	10	service of petition	15(d)
Filing appellant's brief (or mailing brief under Rule 26(a))	30	filing notice of appeal certification of review	14(d) 15(g)(2)
Filing appellee's brief (or mailing brief under Rule 26(a))	30	service of appellant's brief	14(d) 15(g)

Action	Time (Days)	From date of	Rule Ref.
Oral Argument	30	filing appellee's brief (usual minimum time)	29
Certification or Mandate	20	issuance of opinion	32
Petition for Rehearing (civil action only)	15	mandate	31(a)

[Appendix A amended effective 1 October 1990; 6 March 1997; 31 October 2001; 1 May 2003; 1 September 2005; 1 October 2009.]

Appendix B. Format and Style

All documents for filing in either appellate court are prepared on 8½ × 11″, plain, white unglazed paper of 16 to 20 pound weight. Typing is done on one side only, although the document will be reproduced in two-sided format. No vertical rules, law firm marginal return addresses, or punched holes will be accepted. The papers need not be stapled; a binder clip or rubber bands are adequate to secure them in order.

Papers shall be prepared using at least 12–point type so as to produce a clear, black image. Documents shall be set either in nonproportional type or in proportional type, defined as follows: Nonproportional type is defined as 10–character-per-inch Courier (or an equivalent style of Pica) type that devotes equal horizontal space to each character. Proportional type is defined as any non-italic, non-script font, other than nonproportional type, that is 14–point or larger. Under Appellate Rule 28(j), briefs in nonproportional type are governed by a page limit, and briefs in proportional type are governed by a word-count limit. To allow for binding of documents, a margin of approximately one inch shall be left on all sides of the page. The formatted page should be approximately 6½ inches wide and 9 inches long. Tabs are located at the following distances from the left margin: ½″, 1″, 1½″, 2″, 4¼″ (center), and 5″.

CAPTIONS OF DOCUMENTS

All documents to be filed in either appellate court shall be headed by a caption. The caption contains: the number to be assigned the case by the clerk; the Judicial District from which the case arises; the appellate court to whose attention the document is addressed; the style of the case showing the names of all parties to the action, except as provided by Rules 3(b)(1), 3.1(b), and 4(e); the county from which the case comes; the indictment or docket numbers of the case below (in records on appeal and in motions and petitions in the cause filed prior to the filing of the record); and the title of the document. The caption shall be placed beginning at the top margin of a cover page and again on the first textual page of the document.

No. _____ (Number) DISTRICT

(SUPREME COURT OF NORTH CAROLINA)

(or)

(NORTH CAROLINA COURT OF APPEALS)

STATE OF NORTH CAROLINA)
or)
(Name of Plaintiff)) From (Name) County
) No._____
v)
(Name of Defendant))

(TITLE OF DOCUMENT)

The caption should reflect the title of the action (all parties named except as provided by Rules 3(b)(1), 3.1(b), and 4(e)) as it appeared in the trial division. The appellant or petitioner is not automatically given topside billing; the relative positions of the plaintiff and defendant should be retained.

The caption of a record on appeal and of a notice of appeal from the trial division should include directly below the name of the county, the indictment or docket numbers of the case in the trial division. Those numbers, however, should not be included in other documents, except a petition for writ of certiorari or other petitions and motions in which no record on appeal has yet been created in the case. In notices of appeal or petitions to the Supreme Court from decisions of the Court of Appeals, the caption should show the Court of Appeals docket number in similar fashion.

Immediately below the caption of each document, centered and underlined, in all capital letters, should be the title of the document, e.g., PETITION FOR DISCRETIONARY REVIEW UNDER N.C.G.S. § 7A–31, or DEFENDANT–APPELLANT'S BRIEF. A brief filed in the Supreme Court in a case previously heard and decided by the Court of Appeals is entitled NEW BRIEF.

INDEXES

A brief or petition that is ten pages or more in length and all appendixes to briefs (Rule 28) must contain an index to the contents.

The index should be indented approximately 3/4″ from each margin, providing a 5″ line. The form of the index for a record on appeal should be as follows (indexes for briefs are addressed in Appendix E):

(Record)

INDEX

USE OF THE TRANSCRIPT OF EVIDENCE WITH RECORD ON APPEAL

Those portions asterisked (*) in the sample index above would be omitted if the transcript option were selected under Appellate Rule 9(c). In their place in the record, counsel should place a statement in substantially the following form:

"Per Appellate Rule 9(c) the transcript of proceedings in this case, taken by (name), court reporter, from (date) to (date) and consisting of (# of pages) pages, numbered (1) through (last page#), and bound in (# of volumes) volumes is filed contemporaneously with this record."

The transcript should be prepared with a clear, black image on 8½ × 11″ paper of 16–20 pound substance. Enough copies should be reproduced to assure the parties of a reference copy and one file copy in the appellate court. In criminal appeals, the district attorney is responsible for conveying a copy to the Attorney General (Rule 9(c)).

The transcript should not be inserted into the record on appeal, but rather should be separately bound and submitted for filing in the proper appellate court with the record. Transcript pages inserted into the record on appeal will be treated as a narration and will be printed at the standard page charge. Counsel should note that the separate transcript will not be reproduced with the record on appeal, but will be treated and used as an exhibit.

TABLE OF CASES AND AUTHORITIES

Immediately following the index and before the inside caption, all briefs, petitions, and motions that are ten pages or greater in length shall contain a table of cases and authorities. Cases should be arranged alphabetically, followed by constitutional provisions, statutes, regulations, and other textbooks and authorities. The format should be similar to that of the index. Citations should be made according to the most recent edition of A Uniform System of Citation. Citations to regional reporters shall include parallel citations to official state reporters.

FORMAT OF BODY OF DOCUMENT

The body of the record on appeal should be single-spaced with double spaces between paragraphs. The body of petitions, notices of appeal, responses, motions, and briefs should be double-spaced, with captions, headings, issues, and long quotes single-spaced.

Adherence to the margins is important since the document will be reproduced front and back and will be bound on the side. No part of the text should be obscured by that binding.

Quotations of more than three lines in length should be indented ¾″ from each margin and should be single-spaced. The citation should immediately follow the quote.

References to the record on appeal should be made through a parenthetic entry in the text. (R pp 38–40) References to the transcript, if used, should be made in similar manner. (T p 558, line 21)

TOPICAL HEADINGS

The various sections of the brief or petition should be separated (and indexed) by topical headings, centered and underlined, in all capital letters.

Within the argument section, the issues presented should be set out as a heading in all capital letters and in paragraph format from margin to margin. Sub-issues should be presented in similar format, but block indented ½″ from the left margin.

NUMBERING PAGES

The cover page containing the caption of the document (and the index in records on appeal) is unnumbered. The index and table of cases and authorities are on pages numbered with lowercase roman numerals, e.g., i, ii, iv.

While the page containing the inside caption and the beginning of the substance of the petition or brief bears no number, it is page 1. Subsequent pages are sequentially numbered by arabic numbers, flanked by dashes, at the center of the top margin of the page, e.g. –4–.

An appendix to the brief should be separately numbered in the manner of a brief.

SIGNATURE AND ADDRESS

Unless filed *pro se*, all original papers filed in a case will bear the original signature of at least one counsel participating in the case, as in the example below.

The name, address, telephone number, State Bar number, and e-mail address of the person signing, together with the capacity in which that person signs the paper, will be included. When counsel or the firm is retained, the firm name should be included above the signature; however, if counsel is appointed in an indigent criminal appeal, only the name of the appointed counsel should appear, without identification of any firm affiliation. Counsel participating in argument must have signed the brief in the case prior to that argument.

(Retained) [LAW FIRM NAME]

By: ____________________
[Name]

By: ____________________
[Name]
Attorneys for Plaintiff–Appellants
P. O. Box 0000
Raleigh, NC 27600
(919) 999–9999
State Bar No. ______
[e-mail address]

(Appointed) ____________________
[Name]
Attorney for Defendant–Appellant
P. O. Box 0000
Raleigh, NC 27600
(919) 999–9999
State Bar No. ______
[e-mail address]

[Appendix B amended effective 31 October 2001; 15 August 2002; 7 October 2002; 12 May 2004; 1 September 2005; 1 October 2009.]

Appendix C. Arrangement of Record on Appeal

Only those items listed in the following tables and that are required by Rule 9(a) in the particular case should be included in the record. See Rule 9(b)(2) for sanctions for including unnecessary items in the record. The items marked by an asterisk (*) could be omitted from the printed record if the transcript option of Rule 9(c) is used and a transcript of the items exists.

Table 1

SUGGESTED ORDER IN APPEAL FROM CIVIL JURY CASE

1. Title of action (all parties named) and case number in caption, per Appendix B
2. Index, per Rule 9(a)(1)a
3. Statement of organization of trial tribunal, per Rule 9(a)(1)b
4. Statement of record items showing jurisdiction, per Rule 9(a)(1) c
5. Complaint
6. Pre-answer motions of defendant, with rulings thereon
7. Answer
8. Motion for summary judgment, with rulings thereon (* if oral)
9. Pretrial order

*10. Plaintiff's evidence, with any evidentiary rulings that a party to the appeal contends are erroneous

*11. Motion for directed verdict, with ruling thereon

*12. Defendant's evidence, with any evidentiary rulings that a party to the appeal contends are erroneous

*13. Plaintiff's rebuttal evidence, with any evidentiary rulings that a party to the appeal contends are erroneous

14. Issues tendered by parties
15. Issues submitted by court
16. Court's instructions to jury, per Rule 9(a)(1)f
17. Verdict
18. Motions after verdict, with rulings thereon (* if oral)
19. Judgment
20. Items, including Notice of Appeal, required by Rule 9(a)(1)i
21. Statement of transcript option as required by Rule 9(a)(1)i and 9(a)(1)*l*
22. Statement required by Rule 9(a)(1)m when a record supplement will be filed
23. Entries showing settlement of record on appeal, extensions of time, etc.
24. Proposed Issues on Appeal per Rule 9(a)(1)k
25. Names, office addresses, telephone numbers, State Bar numbers, and e-mail addresses of counsel for all parties to the appeal

Table 2

SUGGESTED ORDER IN APPEAL FROM SUPERIOR COURT REVIEW OF ADMINISTRATIVE AGENCY DECISION

1. Title of action (all parties named) and case number in caption, per Appendix B
2. Index, per Rule 9(a)(2)a
3. Statement of organization of superior court, per Rule 9(a)(2)b
4. Statement of record items showing jurisdiction of the board or agency, per Rule 9(a)(2)c
5. Copy of petition or other initiating pleading
6. Copy of answer or other responsive pleading
7. Copies of all pertinent items from administrative proceeding filed for review in superior court, including evidence

*8. Evidence taken in superior court, in order received
9. Copies of findings of fact, conclusions of law, and judgment of superior court
10. Items required by Rule 9(a)(2)h
11. Entries showing settlement of record on appeal, extensions of time, etc.
12. Proposed issues on appeal, per Rule 9(a)(2)i
13. Names, office addresses, telephone numbers, State Bar numbers, and e-mail addresses of counsel for all parties to the appeal

Table 3

SUGGESTED ORDER IN APPEAL OF CRIMINAL CASE

1. Title of action (all parties named) and case number in caption, per Appendix B
2. Index, per Rule 9(a)(3)a
3. Statement of organization of trial tribunal, per Rule 9(a)(3)b
4. Warrant
5. Judgment in district court (where applicable)
6. Entries showing appeal to superior court (where applicable)
7. Bill of indictment (if not tried on original warrant)
8. Arraignment and plea in superior court
9. *Voir dire* of jurors
*10. State's evidence, with any evidentiary rulings that a party to the appeal contends are erroneous
11. Motions at close of State's evidence, with rulings thereon (* if oral)
*12. Defendant's evidence, with any evidentiary rulings that a party to the appeal contends are erroneous
13. Motions at close of defendant's evidence, with rulings thereon (* if oral)
*14. State's rebuttal evidence, with any evidentiary rulings that a party to the appeal contends are erroneous
15. Motions at close of all evidence, with rulings thereon (* if oral)
16. Court's instructions to jury, per Rules 9(a)(3)f and 10(a)(2)
17. Verdict
18. Motions after verdict, with rulings thereon (* if oral)
19. Judgment and order of commitment
20. Appeal entries
21. Entries showing settlement of record on appeal, extensions of time, etc.
22. Proposed issues on appeal, per Rule 9(a)(3)j
23. Names, office addresses, telephone numbers, State Bar numbers, and e-mail addresses of counsel for all parties to the appeal

Table 4

PROPOSED ISSUES ON APPEAL

A. Examples related to pretrial rulings in civil actions

1. Did the trial court err in denying defendant's motion to dismiss for lack of personal jurisdiction under N.C. R. Civ. P. 12(b)(2)?
2. Did the trial court err in denying defendant's motion to dismiss for failure to state a claim upon which relief may be granted under N.C. R. Civ. P. 12(b)(6)?
3. Did the trial court err in denying defendant's motion to require plaintiff to submit to an independent physical examination under N.C. R. Civ. P. 35?
4. Did the trial court err in denying defendant's motion for summary judgment under N.C. R. Civ. P. 56?

B. Examples related to civil jury trial rulings

1. Did the trial court err in admitting the hearsay testimony of E.F.?
2. Did the trial court err in denying defendant's motion for a directed verdict?
3. Did the trial court err in instructing the jury on the doctrine of last clear chance?
4. Did the trial court err in instructing the jury on the doctrine of sudden emergency?
5. Did the trial court err in denying defendant's motion for a new trial?

C. Examples related to civil non-jury trials

1. Did the trial court err in denying defendant's motion to dismiss at the close of plaintiff's evidence?
2. Did the trial court err in its finding of fact No. 10?
3. Did the trial court err in its conclusion of law No. 3?

[Appendix C amended effective 1 October 1990; 31 October 2001; 1 October 2009.]

Appendix D. Forms

Captions for all documents filed in the appellate division should be in the format prescribed by Appendix B, addressed to the Court whose review is sought.

1. NOTICES OF APPEAL

a. To Court of Appeals from trial division

Appropriate in all appeals of right from district or superior court except appeals from criminal judgments imposing sentences of death.

(Caption)

TO THE HONORABLE COURT OF APPEALS OF NORTH CAROLINA:

(Plaintiff)(Defendant), (Name of Party), hereby gives notice of appeal to the Court of Appeals of North Carolina (from the final judgment)(from the order) entered on (date) in the (District)(Superior) Court of (name) County, (describing it).

Respectfully submitted this the ___ day of ________, 2___.

s/ ____________________
Attorney for (Plaintiff)(Defendant)–Appellant
(Address, Telephone Number, State Bar Number, and E-mail Address)

b. To Supreme Court from a Judgment of the Superior Court Including a Sentence of Death

(Caption)

TO THE HONORABLE SUPREME COURT OF NORTH CAROLINA:

(Name of Defendant), Defendant, hereby gives notice of appeal to the Supreme Court of North Carolina from the final judgment entered by (name of Judge) in the Superior Court of (name) County on (date), which judgment included a conviction of murder in the first degree and a sentence of death.

Respectfully submitted this the ___ day of ________, 2___.

s/ ____________________
Attorney for Defendant–Appellant
(Address, Telephone Number, State Bar Number, and E-mail Address)

c. To Supreme Court from a Judgment of the Court of Appeals

Appropriate in all appeals taken as of right from opinions and judgments of the Court of Appeals to the Supreme Court under N.C.G.S. § 7A–30. The appealing party shall enclose a clear copy of the opinion of the Court of Appeals with the notice. To take account of the possibility that the Supreme Court may determine that the appeal does not lie of right, an alternative petition for discretionary review may be filed with the notice of appeal.

(Caption)

TO THE HONORABLE SUPREME COURT OF NORTH CAROLINA:

(Plaintiff)(Defendant), (Name of Party), hereby appeals to the Supreme Court of North Carolina from the judgment of the Court of Appeals (describe it), which judgment . . .

(Constitutional question—N.C.G.S. § 7A–30(1)) . . . directly involves a substantial question arising under the Constitution(s) (of the United States)(and)(or)(of the State of North Carolina) as follows:

(Here describe the specific issues, citing constitutional provisions under which they arise and showing how such issues were timely raised below and are set out in the record of appeal, e.g.:)

Issue 1: Said judgment directly involves a substantial question arising under the Fourth and Fourteenth Amendments to the Constitution of the United States and under Article 1, Section 20 of the Constitution of the State of North Carolina, in that it deprives rights secured thereunder to the defendant by overruling defendant's challenge to the denial of (his) (her) Motion to Suppress Evidence Obtained by a Search Warrant, thereby depriving defendant of the constitutional right to be secure in his or her person, house, papers, and effects against unreasonable searches and seizures and violating constitutional prohibitions against warrants issued without probable cause and warrants not supported by evidence. This constitutional issue was timely raised in the trial tribunal by defendant's Motion to Suppress Evidence Obtained by a Search Warrant made prior to trial of defendant (R pp 7–10). This constitutional issue was determined erroneously by the Court of Appeals.

In the event the Court finds this constitutional question to be substantial, petitioner intends to present the following issues in its brief for review:

(Here list all issues to be presented in appellant's brief to the Supreme Court, not limited to those which are the basis of the constitutional question claim. An issue may not be briefed if it is not listed in the notice of appeal.)

(Dissent—N.C.G.S. § 7A–30(2)) . . . was entered with a dissent by Judge (name), based on the following issue(s):

(Here state the issue or issues that are the basis of the dissenting opinion in the Court of Appeals. Do not state additional issues. Any additional issues desired to be raised in the Supreme Court when the appeal of right is based solely on a dissenting opinion must be presented by a petition for discretionary review as to the additional issues.)

Respectfully submitted this the ___ day of ________, 2___.

s/ ____________________
Attorney for (Plaintiff)(Defendant)–Appellant
(Address, Telephone Number, State Bar Number, and E-mail Address)

2. [Reserved.]

3. PETITION FOR DISCRETIONARY REVIEW UNDER N.C.G.S. § 7A–31

To seek review of the opinion and judgment of the Court of Appeals when petitioner contends the case involves issues of public interest or jurisprudential significance. May also be filed as a separate paper in conjunction with a notice of appeal to the Supreme Court when the appellant contends that such appeal lies of right due to substantial constitutional questions under N.C.G.S. § 7A–30, but desires to have the Court consider discretionary review should it determine that appeal does not lie of right in the particular case.

(Caption)

TO THE HONORABLE SUPREME COURT OF NORTH CAROLINA:

(Plaintiff)(Defendant),(Name of Party), respectfully petitions the Supreme Court of North Carolina to certify for discretionary review the judgment of the Court of Appeals (describing it) on the basis that (here set out the grounds from N.C.G.S. § 7A–31 that provide the basis for the petition). In support of this petition, (Plaintiff)(Defendant) shows the following:

Facts

(Here state first the procedural history of the case through the trial division and the Court of Appeals. Then set out factual background necessary for understanding the basis of the petition.)

Reasons Why Certification Should Issue

(Here set out factual and legal arguments to justify certification of the case for full review. While some substantive argument will certainly be helpful, the focus of the argument in the petition should show how the opinion of the Court of Appeals conflicts with prior decisions of the Supreme Court or how the case is significant to the jurisprudence of the State or of significant public interest. If the Court is persuaded to take the case, the appellant may deal thoroughly with the substantive issues in the new brief.)

Issues to be Briefed

In the event the Court allows this petition for discretionary review, petitioner intends to present the following issues in its brief for review:

(Here list all issues to be presented in appellant's brief to the Supreme Court, not limited to those that are the basis of the petition. An issue may not be briefed if it is not listed in the petition.)

Respectfully submitted this the ___ day of ______, 2__.

s/ ______________________

Attorney for (Plaintiff)(Defendant)–Appellant

(Address, Telephone Number, State Bar Number, and E-mail Address)

Attached to the petition shall be a certificate of service upon the opposing parties and a clear copy of the opinion of the Court of Appeals in the case.

4. PETITION FOR WRIT OF CERTIORARI

To seek review: (1) by the appropriate appellate court of judgments or orders of trial tribunals when the right to prosecute an appeal has been lost or when no right to appeal exists; and (2) by the Supreme Court of decisions and orders of the Court of Appeals when no right to appeal or to petition for discretionary review exists or when such right has been lost by failure to take timely action.

(Caption)

TO THE HONORABLE (SUPREME COURT)(COURT OF APPEALS) OF NORTH CAROLINA:

(Plaintiff)(Defendant), (Name of Party), respectfully petitions this Court to issue its writ of certiorari pursuant to Rule 21 of the N.C. Rules of Appellate Procedure to review the (judgment)(order)(decree) of the [Honorable (name), Judge Presiding, (Superior)(District) Court, (name) County][North Carolina Court of Appeals], dated (date), (here describe the judgment, order, or decree appealed from), and in support of this petition shows the following:

Facts

(Here set out factual background necessary for understanding the basis of the petition: e.g., failure to perfect appeal by reason of circumstances constituting excusable neglect; nonappealability of right of an interlocutory order, etc.) (If circumstances are that transcript could not be procured from court reporter, statement should include estimate of date of availability and supporting affidavit from the reporter.)

Reasons Why Writ Should Issue

(Here set out factual and legal arguments to justify issuance of writ: e. g., reasons why interlocutory order makes it impracticable for petitioner to proceed further in trial court; meritorious basis of petitioner's proposed issues, etc.)

Attachments

Attached to this petition for consideration by the Court are certified copies of the (judgment)(order)(decree) sought to be reviewed, and (here list any other certified items from the trial court record and any affidavits attached as pertinent to consideration of the petition).

Wherefore, petitioner respectfully prays that this Court issue its writ of certiorari to the [(Superior)(District) Court (name) County] [North Carolina Court of Appeals] to permit review of the (judgment)(order)(decree) above specified, upon issues stated as follows: (here list the issues, in the manner provided for in the petition for discretionary review);

and that the petitioner have such other relief as to the Court may seem proper.

Respectfully submitted this the ___ day of ________, 2___.

s/ ____________________
Attorney for Petitioner
(Address, Telephone Number, State Bar Number, and E-mail Address)

(Verification by petitioner or counsel)

(Certificate of service upon opposing parties)

(Attach a clear copy of the opinion, order, etc. which is the subject of the petition and other attachments as described in the petition.)

5. PETITION FOR WRIT OF SUPERSEDEAS UNDER RULE 23 AND MOTION FOR TEMPORARY STAY

A writ of supersedeas operates to stay the execution or enforcement of any judgment, order, or other determination of a trial court or of the Court of Appeals in civil cases under Appellate Rule 8 or to stay imprisonment or execution of a sentence of death in criminal cases (other portions of criminal sentences, e.g. fines, are stayed automatically pending an appeal of right).

A motion for temporary stay under Rule 23(e) is appropriate to seek an immediate stay of execution on an *ex parte* basis pending the Court's decision on the petition for supersedeas or the substantive petition in the case.

(Caption)

TO THE HONORABLE (COURT OF APPEALS)(SUPREME COURT) OF NORTH CAROLINA:

(Plaintiff)(Defendant), (Name of Party), respectfully petitions this Court to issue its writ of supersedeas to stay (execution)(enforcement) of the (judgment)(order)(decree) of the [Honorable ________, Judge Presiding, (Superior)(District) Court, ________ County][North Carolina Court of Appeals] dated ________, pending review by this Court of said (judgment)(order)(decree) which (here describe the judgment, order, or decree and its operation if not stayed); and in support of this petition shows the following:

Facts

(Here set out factual background necessary for understanding the basis of the petition and justifying its filing under Rule 23: e.g., trial judge has vacated the entry upon finding security deposited under N.C.G.S. § ___ inadequate; trial judge has refused to stay execution upon motion therefor by petitioner; circumstances make it impracticable to apply first to trial judge for stay, etc.; and showing that review of the trial court judgment is being sought by appeal or extraordinary writ.)

Reasons Why Writ Should Issue

(Here set out factual and legal arguments for justice of issuing the writ; e.g., that security deemed inadequate by trial judge is adequate under the circumstances; that irreparable harm will result to petitioner if it is required to obey decree pending its review; that petitioner has meritorious basis for seeking review, etc.)

Attachments

Attached to this petition for consideration by the court are certified copies of the (judgment)(order)(decree) sought to be stayed and (here list any other certified items from the trial court record and any affidavits deemed necessary to consideration of the petition).

Wherefore, petitioner respectfully prays that this Court issue its writ of supersedeas to the [(Superior)(District) Court, ________ County)][North Carolina Court of Appeals] staying (execution)(enforcement) of its (judgment) (order)(decree) above specified, pending issuance of the mandate to this Court following its review and determination of the(appeal)(discretionary review)(review by extraordinary writ)(now pending)(the petition for which will be timely filed); and that the petitioner have such other relief as to the Court may seem proper.

Respectfully submitted this the ___ day of ________, 2___.

s/ ____________________
Attorney for Petitioner
(Address, Telephone Number, State Bar Number, and E-mail Address)

(Verification by petitioner or counsel.)

(Certificate of Service upon opposing party.)

Rule 23(e) provides that in conjunction with a petition for supersedeas, either as part of it or separately, the petitioner may move for a temporary stay of execution or enforcement pending the Court's ruling on the petition for supersedeas. The following form is illustrative of such a motion for temporary stay, either included as part of the main petition or filed separately.

Motion for Temporary Stay

(Plaintiff)(Defendant) respectfully applies to the Court for an order temporarily staying (execution)(enforcement) of the (judgment)(order)(decree) that is the subject of (this)(the accompanying) petition for writ of supersedeas, such order to be in effect until determination by this Court whether it shall issue its writ. In support of this Application, movant shows that (here set out the legal and factual arguments for the issuance of such a temporary stay order; e.g., irreparable harm practically threatened if petitioner must obey decree of trial court during interval before decision by Court whether to issue writ of supersedeas).

Motion for Stay of Execution

In death cases, the Supreme Court uses an order for stay of execution of death sentence in lieu of the writ of supersedeas. Counsel should promptly apply for such a stay after the judgment of the Superior Court imposing the death sentence. The stay of execution order will provide that it remains in effect until dissolved. The following form illustrates the contents needed in such a motion.

(Caption)

TO THE HONORABLE SUPREME COURT OF NORTH CAROLINA:

Now comes the defendant, (name), who respectfully shows the Court:

1. That on (date of judgment), The Honorable ________, Judge Presiding, Superior Court, ________ County, sentenced the defendant to death, execution being set for (date of execution).

2. That pursuant to N.C.G.S. § 15A–2000(d)(1), there is an automatic appeal of this matter to the Supreme Court of North Carolina, and defendant's notice of appeal was given (describe the circumstances and date of notice).

3. That the record on appeal in this case cannot be served and settled, the matter docketed, the briefs prepared, the arguments heard, and a decision rendered before the date scheduled for execution.

WHEREFORE, the defendant prays the Court to enter an Order staying the execution pending judgment and further orders of this Court.

Respectfully submitted this the ___ day of ________, 2___.

s/________________________
Attorney for Defendant–Appellant
(Address, Telephone Number, State Bar Number, and E-mail Address)

(Certificate of Service on Attorney General, District Attorney, and Warden of Central Prison)

6. PROTECTING THE IDENTITY OF CERTAIN JUVENILES; NOTICE

In cases governed by Rules 3(b), 3.1(b), and 4(e), the notice requirement of Rules 3.1(b) and 9(a) is as follows:

(Caption)

TO THE HONORABLE (COURT OF APPEALS)(SUPREME COURT) OF NORTH CAROLINA:

FILED PURSUANT TO RULE [3(b)(1)][3.1(b)][4(e)]; SUBJECT TO PUBLIC INSPECTION ONLY BY ORDER OF A COURT OF THE APPELLATE DIVISION.

[Appendix D amended effective 6 March 1997; 31 October 2001; 1 March 2007; 1 October 2009.

Appendix E. Content of Briefs

CAPTION

Briefs should use the caption as shown in Appendix B. The Title of the Document should reflect the position of the filing party both at the trial level and on the appeal, e.g., DEFENDANT–APPELLANT'S BRIEF, PLAINTIFF–APPELLEE'S BRIEF, or BRIEF FOR THE STATE. A brief filed in the Supreme Court in a case decided by the Court of Appeals is captioned a "New Brief" and the position of the filing party before the Supreme Court should be reflected, e.g., DEFENDANT–APPELLEE'S NEW BRIEF (when the State has appealed from the Court of Appeals in a criminal matter).

The cover page should contain only the caption of the case. Succeeding pages should present the following items, in order.

INDEX OF THE BRIEF

Each brief should contain a topical index beginning at the top margin of the first page following the cover, in substantially the following form:

INDEX

TABLE OF CASES AND AUTHORITIES ii
ISSUES PRESENTED 1
STATEMENT OF THE CASE 2
STATEMENT OF THE FACTS 2
ARGUMENT:

I. THE TRIAL COURT COMMITTED REVERSIBLE ERROR IN DENYING THE DEFENDANT'S MOTION TO SUPPRESS HIS INCULPATORY STATEMENT BECAUSE THAT STATEMENT WAS THE PRODUCT OF AN ILLEGAL DETENTION 6

* * *

IV. THE TRIAL COURT COMMITTED REVERSIBLE ERROR IN DENYING THE DEFENDANT'S MOTION TO SUPPRESS THE FRUITS OF A WARRANTLESS SEARCH OF HIS APARTMENT BECAUSE THE CONSENT GIVEN WAS THE PRODUCT OF POLICE COERCION 18

* * * * *

TABLE OF CASES AND AUTHORITIES

This table should begin at the top margin of the page following the index. Page references should be made to each citation of authority, as shown in the example below.

TABLE OF CASES AND AUTHORITIES

Dunaway v. New York, 442 U.S. 200, 99 S. Ct. 2248, 60 L. Ed. 2d 824 (1979) 11
State v. Perry, 298 N.C. 502, 259 S.E.2d 496 (1979) 14
State v. Reynolds, 298 N.C. 380, 259 S.E.2d 843 (1979) 12
United States v. Mendenhall, 446 U.S. 544, 100 S. Ct. 1870, 64 L. Ed. 2d 497 (1980) 14

4th Amendment, U. S. Constitution 28
14th Amendment, U. S. Constitution 28

N.C.G.S. § 15A–221 29
N.C.G.S. § 15A–222 28
N.C.G.S. § 15A–223 29

* * * * *

ISSUES PRESENTED

The inside caption is on page 1 of the brief, followed by the Issues Presented. The phrasing of the issues presented need not be identical to that set forth in the proposed issues on appeal in the record. The appellee's brief need not restate the issues unless the appellee desires to present additional issues to the Court.

ISSUES PRESENTED

I. DID THE TRIAL COURT COMMIT REVERSIBLE ERROR IN DENYING THE DEFENDANT'S MOTION TO SUPPRESS HIS INCULPATORY STATEMENT BECAUSE THAT STATEMENT WAS THE PRODUCT OF AN ILLEGAL DETENTION?

* * *

STATEMENT OF THE CASE

If the Issues Presented carry beyond page 1, the Statement of the Case should follow them, separated by the heading. If the Issues Presented do not carry over, the Statement of the Case should begin at the top of page 2 of the brief.

Set forth a concise chronology of the course of the proceedings in the trial court and the route of appeal, including pertinent dates. For example:

STATEMENT OF THE CASE

The defendant, [name], was convicted of first-degree rape at the [date], Criminal Session of the Superior Court, [name] County, the Honorable [name] presiding, and received ________ sentence for the ________ felony. The defendant gave written notice of appeal in open court to the Supreme Court of North Carolina at the time of the entry of judgment on [date]. The transcript was ordered on [date] and was delivered to the parties on [date].

A motion to extend the time for serving and filing the record on appeal was allowed by the Supreme Court on [date]. The record was filed and docketed in the Supreme Court on [date].

STATEMENT OF THE GROUNDS FOR APPELLATE REVIEW

Set forth the statutory basis for permitting appellate review. For example, in an appeal from a final judgment to the Court of Appeals, the appellant might state that the ground for appellate review is a final judgment of the superior court under N.C.G.S. § 7A–27(b). If the appeal is based on N.C. R. Civ. P. 54(b), the appellant must also state that there has been a final judgment as to one or more but fewer than all of the claims or parties and that there has been a certification by the trial court that there is no just reason for delay. If the appeal is from an interlocutory order or determination based on a substantial right, the appellant must present, in addition to the statutory authorization, facts and argument showing the substantial right that will be lost, prejudiced, or less than adequately protected absent immediate appellate review.

STATEMENT OF THE FACTS

The facts constitute the basis of the dispute or criminal charges and the procedural mechanics of the case if they are significant to the issues presented. The facts should be stated objectively and concisely and should be limited to those that are relevant to the issue or issues presented.

Do not include verbatim portions of the record or other matters of an evidentiary nature in the statement of the facts. Summaries and record or transcript citations should be used instead. No appendix should be compiled simply to support the statement of the facts.

The appellee's brief need contain no statement of the case or facts if there is no dispute. The appellee may state additional facts where deemed necessary, or, if there is a dispute over the facts, may restate the facts as they appear from the appellee's viewpoint.

ARGUMENT

Each issue will be set forth in uppercase typeface as the party's contention, e.g.,

I. THE TRIAL COURT COMMITTED REVERSIBLE ERROR IN DENYING THE DEFENDANT'S MOTION TO SUPPRESS HIS INCULPATORY STATEMENT BECAUSE THAT STATEMENT WAS THE PRODUCT OF AN ILLEGAL DETENTION.

The standard of review for each issue presented shall be set out in accordance with Rule 28(b)(6).

Parties should feel free to summarize, quote from, or cite to the record or transcript during the presentation of argument. If the transcript option is selected under Rule 9(c), the appendix to the brief may be needed, as described in Rule 28 and below.

When statutory or regulatory materials are cited, the relevant portions should be quoted in the body of the argument or placed in the appendix to the brief, as required by Rule 28(d)(1)c.

CONCLUSION

State briefly and clearly the specific objective or relief sought in the appeal. It is not necessary to restate the party's contentions, since they are presented both in the index and as headings to the individual arguments.

SIGNATURE AND CERTIFICATE OF SERVICE

Following the conclusion, the brief must be dated and signed, with the attorney's typed or printed name, mailing address, telephone number, State Bar number, and e-mail address, all indented to the center of the page.

The Certificate of Service is then shown with a centered, uppercase heading. The certificate itself, describing the manner of service upon the opposing party with the complete mailing address of the party or attorney served, is followed by the date and the signature of the person certifying the service.

APPENDIX TO THE BRIEF UNDER THE TRANSCRIPT OPTION

Rules 9(c) and 28 require additional steps to be taken in the brief to point the Court to appropriate excerpts from the transcript considered essential to the understanding of the arguments presented.

Counsel are encouraged to cite, narrate, and quote freely within the body of the brief. However, if because of length a verbatim quotation is not included in the body of the brief, that portion of the transcript and others like it shall be compiled into an appendix to the brief to be placed at the end of the brief, following all signatures and certificates. Counsel should not attach the entire transcript as an appendix to support issues involving a directed verdict, sufficiency of the evidence, or the like.

The appendix should be prepared to be clear and readable, distinctly showing the transcript page or pages from which each passage is drawn. Counsel may reproduce transcript pages themselves, clearly indicating those portions to which attention is directed.

The appendix should include a table of contents, showing the items contained in the appendix and the pages in the appendix where those items appear. The appendix shall be paginated separately from the text of the brief. For example:

CONTENTS OF APPENDIX

* * * * *

The appendix will be printed as submitted with the brief to which it is appended. Therefore, clarity of image is extremely important.

[Appendix E amended effective 31 October 2001; 15 August 2002; 1 September 2005; 1 October 2009.]

Appendix F. Fees and Costs

Fees and costs are provided by order of the Supreme Court and apply to proceedings in either appellate court. There is no fee for filing a motion in a cause; other fees are as follows and should be submitted with the document to which they pertain, made payable to the clerk of the appropriate appellate court:

Notice of Appeal, Petition for Discretionary Review, Petition for Writ of Certiorari or other extraordinary writ, Petition for Writ of Supersedeas—docketing fee of $10.00 for each document, i.e., docketing fees for a notice of appeal and petition for discretionary review filed jointly would be $20.00.

Petitions to rehear require a docketing fee of $20.00. (Petitions to rehear are only entertained in civil cases.)

An appeal bond or cash deposit of $250.00 is required in civil cases per Rules 6 and 17. The bond should be filed contemporaneously with the record in the Court of Appeals and with the notice of appeal in the Supreme Court. The bond will not be required in cases brought by petition for discretionary review or certiorari unless and until the court allows the petition.

Costs for printing documents are $1.75 per printed page. The appendix to a brief under the transcript option of Rules 9(c) and 28(b) and (c) will be reproduced as is, but billed at the rate of the printing of the brief. Both appellate courts will bill the parties for the costs of printing their documents.

Court costs on appeal total $9.00, plus the cost of copies of the opinion to each party filing a brief, and are imposed when a notice of appeal is withdrawn or dismissed, or when the mandate is issued following the opinion in a case.

Photocopying charges are $.20 per page. The facsimile transmission fee for documents sent from the clerk's office, which is in addition to standard photocopying charges, is $5.00 for the first twenty-five pages and $.20 for each page thereafter.

The fee for a certified copy of an appellate court decision, in addition to photocopying charges, is $10.00.

[Appendix F amended effective 31 October 2001; 1 October 2009.]

INDEX TO RULES OF APPELLATE PROCEDURE

RULES FOR COURT–ORDERED ARBITRATION IN NORTH CAROLINA

Adopted Effective September 14, 1989

Table of Rules

Rule 1. Definitions

(a) *"Court"* as used in these rules means:

(1) The chief district court judge or the delegate of such judge; or

(2) Any assigned judge exercising the court's jurisdiction and authority in an action.

(b) *"Living Human Being"* for purposes of these Rules is defined as a natural person, not to include any legally created person(s), as identified in N.C.G.S. § 12–3(6).

Administrative History: Authority—Order of the North Carolina Supreme Court, August 28, 1986, pilot rules adopted; pilot rule amended effective March 4, 1987; permanent rule adopted, by order of the North Carolina Supreme Court, September 14, 1989; Arb. Rule 1(a), formerly Arb. Rule 8(f), amended March 8, 1990, and amended December 19, 2002 and renumbered as Arb. Rule 1(a), effective ______, 2011; New Arb. Rule 1(b) adopted ______, 2011, effective immediately as to all cases filed on or after ______, 2012.

[Pilot Rule Adopted: 28 August 1986. Pilot rule amended: 4 March 1987; permanent rule adopted: 14 September 1989; amended: 8 March 1990—(a) and (d); amended: 19 December 2002 —(a) through (d); amended effective 1 January 2012.]

Comment

The purpose of these rules is to create an efficient, economical alternative to traditional litigation for prompt resolution of disputes in District Court. Subject to the opt-in of Superior Court cases under Arb.Rule 1(b), the rules provide for court-ordered arbitration of District Court actions because District Court actions are typically suitable for consideration in the manner provided in these rules and Superior Court actions are covered by another dispute resolution program. The $15,000 jurisdictional limit by statute and Arb.Rule 1 applies only to the claim(s) actually asserted, even though the claim(s) is or are based on a statute providing for multiple damages, e.g. N.C.Gen.Stat. §§ 1–538, 75–16. An arbitrator may award damages in any amount which a party is entitled to recover. These rules do not affect the jurisdiction or functions of the magistrates where they have been assigned such jurisdiction. Counsel are expected to value their cases reasonably without Court involvement.

"Family law matters" in Arb.Rule 1(a)(1)(iv) includes all family law cases such as divorce, guardianship, adoptions, juvenile matters, child support, custody, and visitation. "Summary ejectments" and "special proceedings", referred to in Arb.Rule 1(a)(vi), are actions so designated by the General Statutes.

Rule 2. Actions Subject To Arbitration

(a) By Order of the Court.

(1) All civil actions filed in the district court division are subject to court-ordered arbitration under these rules in accordance with the authority set forth in N.C.G.S. § 7A–37.1(c), except actions:

(i) Which are assigned to a magistrate, provided that appeals from judgments of magistrates are subject to court-ordered arbitration under these rules except appeals from summary ejectment actions and actions in which the sole claim is an action on an account;

(ii) In which class certification is sought;

(iii) In which a request has been made for a preliminary injunction or a temporary restraining order including claims filed under N.C.G.S. Chapter 50C;

(iv) Involving family law matters including claims filed under N.C.G.S. chapters 50, 50A, SOB, 51, 52, 52B and 52C;

(v) Involving title to real estate;

(vi) Which are special proceedings; or

(vii) In which the sole claim is an action on an account.

(2) *Requests for jury trial.* Cases otherwise eligible for arbitration shall be arbitrated regardless of whether a party made a request for a jury trial.

(3) *Identification of Actions for Arbitration.* The clerk shall identify actions eligible for arbitration upon the filing of the complaint or docketing of an appeal from a magistrate's judgment, in accordance with Arb. Rule 2(a)(1) and notify the court that the case has been identified for arbitration.

(4) *Notice to Parties.* The court shall serve notice upon the parties or their counsel as soon as practicable after the filing of the last required responsive pleading or the expiration of time for the last required responsive pleading or the docketing of an appeal from a magistrate's judgment.

(5) *Arbitration by Agreement.* The parties in any other civil action pending in the district court division may, upon joint written motion, request to submit the action to arbitration under these rules. The court may approve the motion if it finds that arbitration under these rules is appropriate. The consent of the parties shall not be presumed, but shall be stated by the parties expressly in writing.

(b) Exemption and Withdrawal From Arbitration. The court may exempt or withdraw any action from arbitration on its own motion, or on the motion of a party, made not less than 10 days before the arbitration hearing and a showing that:

(1) the action is excepted from arbitration under Arb. Rule 2(a)(1) or

(2) there is a compelling reason to do so.

Administrative History: Authority—Order of the North Carolina Supreme Court, August 28, 1986, pilot rules adopted; pilot rule amended effective March 4, 1987; permanent rule adopted, by order of the North Carolina Supreme Court, September 14, 1989; Arb. Rule 2(a)(1) and Arb. Rule 2(a)(2), formerly Arb. Rule 1(a) were amended March 8, 1990 and December 19, 2002 and renumbered __________, 2011; (d) was amended March 8, 1990 and December 19, 2002; Arb. Rule 2(a)(3), formerly Arb. Rule 8(a), was amended March 8, 1990 and December 19, 2002, and renumbered as Arb. Rule 2(a)(3), __________, 2011.

[Pilot Rule Adopted: 28 August 1986. Pilot rule amended: 4 March 1987; permanent rule adopted: 14 September 1989; amended: 8 March 1990—(a) and (b); amended: 1 August 1995—(b); amended effective 19 December 2002; 1 January 2005; 1 January 2012.]

COMMENT

The purpose of these rules is to create an efficient, economical alternative to traditional litigation for prompt resolution of disputes in district court. The rules provide for court-ordered arbitration of district court actions because district court actions are typically suitable for consideration in the manner provided in these rules.

An arbitrator may award damages in any amount which a party is entitled to recover. These rules do not affect the jurisdiction or functions of the magistrates where they have been assigned such jurisdiction.

In a case involving multiple defendants when there is an appeal from a magistrate's judgment, and one or more defendants have been dismissed, an appeal by a remaining defendant does not operate to rejoin the dismissed defendant(s) in the action absent properly filed pleadings in accordance with N.C.R.Civ.P. 13.

"Family law matters" in Arb.Rule 2(a)(1)(iv) includes all family law cases such as divorce, guardianship, adoptions, juvenile matters, child support, custody, and visitation. "Summary ejectments", referred to in Arb.Rule 2(a)(1)(i) and "special proceedings", referred to in Arb.Rule 2(a)(1)(vi), are actions so designated by the North Carolina General Statutes.

Arb. Rule 2(a)(3) contemplates that the clerk or designee shall determine whether an action is eligible for arbitration after reviewing the pleadings. The rule further contemplates that the clerk or designee will look beyond the cover sheet and filing codes to make this determination. The purpose of these rules is to be inclusive of the cases eligible for arbitration.

"An action on an account" as referenced and excluded in Arb. Rule 2(a)(1)(f) and 2(a)(1)(vii) includes all cases involving an account wherein the account holder is authorized to complete multiple transactions. These actions should only include accounts in which the account holder has the ability to make more than one purchase during different periods. This exemption should not include cases wherein there was one transaction, even if multiple payments are included in the agreement. The accrual of interest does not constitute multiple transactions. Action on an account, as excluded by Arb. Rule 2(a)(1)(i) and Arb. Rule 2(a)(1)(vii), does not include the exclusion of monies owed claims. Cases in which attorneys' fees are requested are not "actions in which the sole claim is an action on an account" and are therefore not excluded under Arb. Rule 2(a)(1)(vii).

No case should be excluded from the mandatory arbitration process pursuant to Arb.Rule 2(a)(1)(vii) for the action on account exception unless the original petition is accompanied by a verified itemized statement which evidences multiple transactions. All other cases shall be treated as a claim for monies owed and should be arbitrated. The court or their designee shall review any petition alleging it is an action on an account and verify that the verified itemized statement is attached. If there is no such attachment, the matter shall be deemed a petition for monies owed and the matter shall be noticed for arbitration. N.C.G.S. § 8-45.

Comment

Under Arb.Rule 2(a) the parties have a right to choose one arbitrator from the list if they wish to do so, but they have *the burden of taking the initiative if they want to make the selection,* and they must do it promptly.

When assigning arbitrators to serve in cases, the Court is encouraged to regularly use all arbitrators on the Court's list as established in Arb.Rule 2(a).

The parties in a particular case may choose a person to be an arbitrator who is not on the list required by Arb.Rule 2(a)(1), provided that person consents, the choice is approved by the Chief District Court Judge, and the person otherwise meets the requirements of Arb.Rule 2. The stipulation of agreement on an arbitrator, the arbitrator's consent, and the order approving such stipulation and consent must be filed within the 20–day period mentioned in Arb.Rule 2(a)(1).

Under Arb.Rule 2(c) filing of the award is the final act at which payment should be made, closing the matter for the arbitrator. The arbitrator should make the award when the hearing is concluded. Hearings must be brief and expedited so that an arbitrator can hear at least three per day. See Arb.Rule 3(n).

Payments and expense reimbursements authorized by Arb. Rule 2(c) are made subject to Court approval to insure conservation and judicial monitoring of the use of funds available for the program.

Rule 3. Eligibility of Arbitrators

(a) Qualification Requirements for Arbitrators. The chief district court judge shall receive and approve applications for persons to be appointed as arbitrators. Arbitrators so approved shall serve at the pleasure of the appointing court. A person seeking to be added to the list of eligible arbitrators shall:

(1) Be a member in good standing of the North Carolina State Bar;

(2) Have been licensed to practice law for five years;

(3) Shall have been admitted in North Carolina for at least the last two years of the five-year period. Admission outside North Carolina may be considered for the balance of the five-year period, so long as the arbitrator was admitted as a duly licensed member of the bar of a state(s) or a territory(ies) of the United States or the District of Columbia;

(4) Shall complete the arbitrator training course prescribed by the Administrative Office of the Courts or their training designee;

(5) Shall observe at least one arbitration conducted by an arbitrator already on the list of approved arbitrators as provided for herein; and

(6) Have a valid email address.

(b) Application Process. The person seeking eligibility as an arbitrator shall submit:

(1) a completed application on an approved form provided by the Administrative Office of the Courts; and

(2) documented proof of the qualifications as set forth in Arb. Rule 3(a) shall be attached to the application form and submitted to the chief district court judge or designee in each judicial district in which the applicant intends to serve as an arbitrator.

(c) Oath of Office. Arbitrators shall take an oath or affirmation similar to that prescribed in N.C.G.S. § 11–11, on a form promulgated by the Administrative Office of the Courts, before conducting any hearings. Said oath shall be administered by the chief district court judge or designee. A copy of the oath shall be filed by the applicant with the clerk in each county in which they serve.

(d) Arbitrator Ethics; Disqualification. Arbitrators shall comply with the Canons of Ethics for Arbitrators promulgated by the Supreme Court of North Carolina. Arbitrators shall be disqualified and must recuse themselves in accordance with the Canons.

(e) Conflict. An arbitrator shall be prohibited from participating, serving or being involved in any capacity, in any case wherein they previously served as an arbitrator. An arbitrator shall also be prohibited from participating in other cases, in any capacity, wherein the parties and/or issues arise from a case over which the arbitrator presided.

(f) Complaints. All complaints against an arbitrator shall be filed with the chief district court judge or designee for the county in which the arbitration giving rise to the complaint was conducted using a form promulgated by the Administrative Office of the Courts.

Administrative History: Authority—Order of the North Carolina Supreme Court, August 28, 1986; New Arb. Rule 3 adopted __________, 2011 (a) is former Arb. Rule 2(b) and was adopted September 14, 1989, amended March 8, 1990, amended August 1, 1995, amended December 19, 2005 and amended and renumbered __________, 2011, (c) is former Arb. Rule 2(d) and was adopted September 14, 1989 and was amended and renumbered __________, 2011; (d) is former Arb. Rule 2(e) and was adopted September 14, 1989, amended December 19, 2002 and renumbered __________, 2011.

[Pilot Rule Adopted: 28 August 1986. Pilot rule amended: 4 March 1987; permanent rule adopted: 14 September 1989; amended: 8 March 1990—(b), (j), (o), and (q); amended: 19 December 2002—(a), (b), (g), (j), (*l*), (n), (o), (p), and (q); amended effective 1 January 2012.]

Comment

Good faith compliance with Arb.Rule 3(b) is required by professional courtesy and fairness as well as the spirit of these rules. Failure to comply with Arb.Rule 3(b) may justify a sanction of limiting of evidence otherwise admissible under Arb.Rules 3(c)–3(f) and 3(g).

Arb.Rule 3(d) contemplates that the arbitrator shall return all evidence submitted when the hearing is concluded and the award has been made. Original documents and exhibits should not be marked in any way to identify them with the arbitration, to avoid possible prejudice in any future trial.

The purpose of Arb.Rule 3(n) is to ensure that hearings are limited and expedited. Failure to limit and expedite the hearings defeats the purpose of these rules. In this connection, note the option in Arb.Rule 3(b) for use of prehearing stipulations and/or sworn or unsworn statements to meet time limits.

Under Arb.Rule 3(*o*) the declaration that the hearing is concluded by the arbitrator formally marks the end of the hearing. Note Arb.Rule 4(a), which requires the arbitrator to file the award within three days after the hearing is concluded or post-hearing briefs are received. The usual practice should be a statement of the award at the close of the hearing, without submission of briefs. In the unusual case where an arbitrator is willing to receive post-hearing briefs, the arbitrator should specify the points to be addressed promptly and succinctly. Time limits in these rules are governed by N.C.R. Civ. P. 6 and N.C.Gen.Stat. §§ 103–4, 103–5.

Arb.Rule 3(p) requires that all parties be present in person or through counsel. The presence of the parties or their counsel is necessary for presentation of the case to the arbitrator. Rule 3(p) does not require that a party or any representative of a party have authority to make binding decisions on the party's behalf in the matters in controversy.

The rules do not establish a separate standard for pro se representation in court-ordered arbitrations. Instead, pro se representation in court-ordered arbitrations is governed by applicable principles of North Carolina law in that area. See Arb.Rule 3(p). Conformance of practice in court-ordered arbitrations with the applicable law, whatever it may provide, is ensured by providing that pro se representation be "as permitted by law."

Under Arb.Rule 3(q)(1), the Court will rule on prehearing motions which dispose of all or part of the case on the pleadings, or which relate to procedural management of the case. The Court will normally defer to the arbitrator's consideration motions addressed to the merits of a claim requiring a hearing, the taking of evidence, or examination of records and documents other than the pleadings and motion papers, except in cases in which an N.C.R.Civ.P. 12(b) motion is filed in lieu of a responsive pleading.

Rule 4. Assignment of Arbitrator

(a) Appointment. The court shall appoint an arbitrator in the following manner:

(1) The court shall rotate through the list for their district, set forth in subsection Arb. Rule 3(a), of available qualified arbitrators and appoint the next eligible arbitrator from the list and notify the parties of the arbitrator selected.

(2) Appointments shall be made without regard to race, gender, religious affiliation or political affiliation. The chief district court judge shall retain the discretion to depart in a specific case from a strict rotation when, in the judge's discretion, there is good cause shown.

(b) Fees and Expenses. Arbitrators shall be paid the maximum allowable fee as set forth in N.C.G.S. § 7A–37.1(c1) after an award is filed with the court. The arbitrator shall make application with the court on the proper NCAOC form within thirty (30) days of the filing of the award. An arbitrator may be paid a reasonable fee not exceeding the maximum allowable fee for work on a case not resulting in a hearing upon the arbitrator's written application to and approval by the chief district court judge. This fee shall be shared by the parties as set forth by these rules.

(c) Replacement of Arbitrator. Any party may move the chief district court judge of the district where the action is pending for an order removing the arbitrator from that case so long as the motion is file more than 7 days before the scheduled arbitration hearing. For good cause, such an order shall be entered. If an arbitrator is removed, recused, unable or unwilling to serve, a replacement shall be appointed by the court from the list of arbitrators in accordance with Arb. Rule 4(a).

Administrative History Pilot Rule Adopted: August 28, 1986; Pilot Rule Amended: March 4, 1987; Permanent Rule Adopted: September 14, 1989; (a) was amended March 8, 1990, December 19, 2002 and ________, 2011; former (b) was amended on March 8, 1990, August 1, 1995, December 19, 2002 and was renumbered and reorganized as Arb. Rule 3(a), ________, 2011; former (c) was amended March 8, 1991, December 19, 2002, January 1, 2005 and amended and renumbered as Arb. Rule 4(d), ________, 2011; former (d) was renumbered as Arb. Rule 3(c), ________, 2011; former (e) was adopted September 14, 1989, amended December 19, 2002 and amended and renumbered as Arb,. Rule 3(d), ________, 2011; former (f) was adopted September 14, 2989, amended December 19, 2002 and amended and renumbered as Arb. Rule 4(d), ________, 2011.

[Amended effective 1 January 2012.]

COMMENT

The court shall regularly use all arbitrators on the court's list as established in Arb. Rule 4(a). In counties or districts where arbitrators are assigned for multiple cases in a day, the court shall rotate through the list and appoint the next available arbitrator on the list for each day, rather than appointing a different arbitrator for each case. Under Arb. Rule 4(a)(2), consideration should be given to distance of travel and availability of arbitrators.

In accordance with Arb. Rule 4(b), filing of the award is the final act at which payment should be requested, closing the matter for the arbitrator. The arbitrator should make the award when the hearing is concluded. Hearings must be brief and expedited so that an arbitrator can hear at feast three per day. See Arb.Rule 6(q).

Payments authorized by Arb. Rule 4(b) are made subject to court approval to ensure conservation and judicial monitoring of the use of funds available for the program. Arbitrators shall not be paid a fee for continued hearings.

An agreement by all parties to remove an arbitrator may constitute good cause under Arb Rule 4(c).

Comment

Ordinarily, the arbitrator should issue the award at the conclusion of the hearing. See Arb.Rule 4(a). If the arbitrator wants post-hearing briefs, the arbitrator must receive them within three days, consider them, and file the award within three days thereafter. See Arb.Rule 3(*o*) and its Comment. If the arbitrator deems it appropriate, the arbitrator may explain orally the basis of the award.

Rule 5. Fees and Costs

(a) Arbitration Costs. The arbitrator may include, in an award, court costs accruing through the arbitration proceedings in favor of the prevailing party. Costs may not include the arbitrator fee or any portion of said fee, which shall be equally divided between the parties in accordance with these rules.

(b) Arbitrator Fee. The arbitrator's fee shall be equally divided among all parties to that action pursuant to Arb. Rule 5(c). No party shall be required to be responsible for any more than their pro rata share of the arbitrator's fee.

(c) Payment of Arbitrator's Fee.

(1) *By Non Indigent Parties.* Each party not found by the clerk to be indigent shall pay, into the clerk of court, an equal share of the arbitrator fee prior to the arbitration hearing. Failure to pay the fee shall not be a ground for continuance of the arbitration. The clerk, to whom the fee is paid, shall document each party that pays or is found to be indigent in the file on the proper form promulgated by the Administrative Office of the Court. This form shall be placed in the file.

(2) *By Indigent or Partially Indigent Parties.*

(i) Partially Indigent Persons. If, in the opinion of the clerk or court, an indigent person is financially able to pay a portion, but not all, of their pro rata share of the arbitrator's fee, the court shall require the partially indigent person to pay such portion prior to the arbitration. Failure to pay the fee shall not be a ground for continuance of the arbitration. The clerk, to whom the fee is paid, shall document each party that pays the proper amount or is found to be indigent in the file on the proper form promulgated by the Administrative Office of the Courts. This form shall be placed in the file. The clerk shall apply the criteria enumerated in N.C.G.S. § 1–110(a).

(ii) Fully Indigent Persons. Upon a finding that the party is indigent, that party shall not be required to pay their portion of the arbitration fee prior to the arbitration.

(3) *Liens.* In all cases, wherein any portion of a party's pro rata share of the arbitrator's fee is not paid in full, the court shall direct that a judgment be entered in the office of the clerk of superior court for the unpaid portion of that party's pro rata share of the arbitrator's fee, which shall constitute a lien as prescribed by the general law of the State applicable to judgments. Any reimbursement to the State as provided in this rule or any funds collected by reason of such judgment shall be deposited in the State treasury and credited against the judgment. A district court judge shall direct entry of judgment for actions or proceedings filed in district court or for those matters appealed from a magistrate's award.

(4) *Judgment for Fee.* The order or judgment shall become effective and the judgment shall be docketed and indexed pursuant to N.C.G.S. § 1–233 et seq., in the amount of the partially indigent or indigent party's share of the arbitrator's fee. Each judgment docketed against a person shall include the social security number, if any, of the judgment debtor.

Administrative History Pilot Rules Adopted August 28, 1996; Pilot Rules Amended March 4, 1987; (a) is former Arb. Rule 7(a) and was adopted September 14, 1989, was amended and renumbered ________, 2011; (b) and (c) were adopted ________, 2011; (d) is former Arb. Rule 7(b) and was adopted September 14, 1989, amended December 19, 2002 and renumbered ________, 2011.

[Pilot Rule Adopted: 28 August 1986. Pilot rule amended: 4 March 1987; permanent Rule Adopted: 14 September 1989; amended: 8 March 1990—(a), (b), (e), and (f); amended: 19 December 2002—(a), (b), (c), and (d); amended effective 1 January 2012.]

COMMENT

When determining each party's equal share of the fee in accordance with Arb. Rule 5(b), take the total arbitrator fee and divide it by the total number of parties in the action. If one party has been granted relief to sue as an indigent, include that party in the number by which the fee is divided to calculate other parties' equal share. Multiple plaintiffs and defendants shall be counted individually and not as one party. These fees are non-refundable.

For purposes of Arb Rule 5, a person shall apply for indigency before the clerk if requesting indigent status as it relates to the arbitration fee by completing and submitting AOC–G–106 or similar form if this form is modified and/or replaced by the Administrative Office of the Courts.

For purposes of Arb. Rule 5, if a party that is not a living human being, as defined by Arb. Rule 1, is listed as a party and a living human being, who is an owner, share holder or has any other ownership interest in that non-human being party is also listed as a party, then each shall be counted as an individual party.

Comment

Arb. Rule 5(c) does not preclude cross examination of a witness in a later proceeding concerning prior inconsistent statements during arbitration proceedings, if done in such a manner as not to violate the intent of Arb. Rules 5(c) and 5(d).

See also the *Comment* to Arb. Rule 6 regarding demand for trial de novo.

Rule 6. Arbitration Hearings

(a) Hearing Scheduled by the Court. Arbitration hearings shall be scheduled by the court and held in a courtroom, if available, or in any other public room suitable for conducting judicial proceedings and shall be open to the public.

(1) *Scheduling.* The court shall schedule hearings with notice to the parties to begin within 60 days after:

(i) the docketing of an appeal from a magistrate's judgment,

(ii) the filing of the last responsive pleading, or

(iii) the expiration of the time allowed for the filing of such pleading.

(b) Date of Hearing Advanced by Agreement. A hearing may be held earlier than the date set by the court, by agreement of the parties with court approval.

(c) Hearings Rescheduled; Continuance; Cancellation. A hearing may be scheduled, rescheduled, or continued to a date after the time allowed by this rule only by the court before whom the case is pending, and may be upon a written motion filed at least 24 hours prior to the scheduled arbitration hearing, and a showing of a strong and compelling reason to do so. In the event a consent judgment or dismissal is not filed with the clerk and notice provided to the court more than 24 hours prior to the scheduled arbitration hearing, all parties shall be liable for the arbitrator fee in accordance with Arb. Rule 5. Any settlement reached prior to the scheduled arbitration hearing must be reported by the parties to the court official administering the arbitration. The parties must file dismissals or consent judgments prior to the scheduled hearing to close the case without a hearing. If the dismissals or consent judgments are not filed before the scheduled hearing, the parties should appear at the hearing to have their agreement entered as the award of the arbitrator.

(d) Prehearing Exchange of Information. At least 10 days before the date set for the hearing, the parties shall exchange:

(1) Lists of witnesses they expect to testify;

(2) Copies of documents or exhibits they expect to offer in evidence; and

(3) A brief statement of the issues and their contentions.

Parties may agree in writing to rely on stipulations and/or statements, sworn or unsworn, rather than a formal presentation of witnesses and documents, for all or part of the hearing. Failure to comply with Arb. Rule 6(n) may be cause for sanctions under Arb. Rule 6(*o*). Each party shall bring to the hearing and provide to the arbitrator a copy of these materials. These materials shall not be filed with the court or included in the case file.

(e) Exchanged Documents Considered Authenticated. Any document exchanged may be received in the hearing as evidence without further authentication; however, the party against whom it is offered may subpoena and examine as an adverse witness anyone who is the author, custodian, or a witness through whom the document might otherwise have been introduced. Documents not so exchanged may not be received if to do so would, in the arbitrator's opinion, constitute unfair, prejudicial surprise.

(f) Copies of Exhibits Admissible. Copies of exchanged documents or exhibits are admissible in arbitration hearings.

(g) Witnesses. Witnesses may be compelled to testify under oath or affirmation and produce evidence by the same authority and to the same extent as if the hearing were a trial. The arbitrator is empowered and authorized to administer oaths and affirmations in arbitration hearings.

(h) Subpoenas. N.C.R.Civ.P. 45 shall apply to subpoenas for attendance of witnesses and production of documentary evidence at an arbitration hearing under these rules.

(i) Authority of Arbitrator to Govern Hearings. Arbitrators shall have the authority of a trial judge to govern the conduct of hearings, except the arbitrator may not issue contempt orders, issue sanctions or dismiss the action. The arbitrator shall refer all contempt matters and dispositive matters to the court.

(j) Law of Evidence Used as Guide. The law of evidence does not apply, except as to privilege, in an arbitration hearing but shall be considered as a guide toward full and fair development of the facts. The arbitrator shall consider all evidence presented and give it the weight and effect the arbitrator determines appropriate.

(k) No Ex Parte Communications With Arbitrator. No ex parte communications between parties or their counsel and arbitrators are permitted.

(*l*) Failure to Appear, Defaults; Rehearing. If a party who has been notified of the date, time and place of the hearing fails to appear, or fails to appear with counsel for cases in which counsel is mandated by law, without good cause therefor, the hearing shall proceed and an award may be made by the arbitrator against the absent party upon the evidence offered by the parties present, but not by default or dismissal for failure to appear. If a party is in default for any other reason but no judgment has been entered upon the default pursuant to N.C.R.Civ.P. 55(b) before the hearing, the arbitrator may hear evidence and may issue an award against the party in default. The court may order a rehearing of any case in which an award was made against a party who failed to obtain a continuance of a hearing and failed to appear for reasons beyond the party's control. Such motion for rehearing shall be filed with the court within the time allowed for demanding trial de novo stated in Arb. Rule 9(a).

(m) No Record of Hearing Made. No official transcript of an arbitration hearing shall be made. The arbitrator may permit any party to record the arbitration hearing in any manner that does not interfere with the proceeding.

(n) Parties Must Be Present at Hearings; Representation. All parties shall be present at hearings in person or through counsel. Parties may appear pro se as permitted by law.

(*o*) Sanctions. Any party failing to attend an arbitration proceeding in person or through counsel shall be subject to those sanctions available to the court in N.C.R.Civ.P. 11, 37(b)(2)(A)- 37(b)(2)(D) and N.C.G.S. § 6–21.5 on the motion of a party, report of the arbitrator, or by the court on its own motion.

(p) Proceedings in Forma Pauperis. The right to proceed in forma pauperis is not affected by these rules.

(q) Limits of Hearings. Arbitration hearings shall be limited to one hour unless the arbitrator determines at the hearing that more time is necessary to ensure fairness and justice to the parties.

(1) A written application for a substantial enlargement of time for a hearing must be filed with the court and the arbitrator if the arbitrator has been assigned, and must be served on opposing parties at the earliest practicable time, and no later than the date for prehearing exchange of information under Arb. Rule 6(d). The court will rule on these applications after consulting the arbitrator if an arbitrator has been assigned.

(2) An arbitrator is not required to receive repetitive or cumulative evidence.

(r) Hearing Concluded. The arbitrator shall declare the hearing concluded when all the evidence is in and any arguments the arbitrator permits have been completed. In exceptional cases, the arbitrator has discretion to receive post-hearing briefs, but not evidence, if submitted within three days after the hearing has been concluded.

(s) Motions. Designation of an action for arbitration does not affect a party's right to file any motion with the court.

(1) The court, in its discretion, may consider and determine any motion at any time. It may defer consideration of issues raised by motion to the arbitrator for determination in the award. Parties shall state their contentions regarding pending motions referred to the arbitrator in the exchange of information required by Arb. Rule 6(d).

(2) Pendency of a motion shall not be cause for delaying an arbitration hearing unless the court so orders.

(t) Binding Hearing. All parties to an action may agree that any award by the arbitrator be binding. Such agreement shall be in writing on a form promulgated by the Administrative Office of the Courts and shall be executed by all parties. The consent shall be filed with the clerk's office in the county in which the action is pending. Parties consenting to a binding hearing may not request a trial de novo after the arbitration award is issued. Once all parties agree to binding arbitration, no party may dismiss an appeal from a magistrate's award or dismiss the action in full except by consent. The clerk or court shall enter judgment on the award at the time the award is filed if the action has not been dismissed by consent.

Administrative History Pilot Rule Adopted August 28, 1986. Pilot Rule Amended March 4, 1987. Permanent Rule Adopted September 14, 1989. This is former Arb. Rule 3 renumbered ________, 2011, (b), (j), (*o*), and (q) were amended March 8, 1990; (a), (b), (g), (j), (*l*), (n), (*o*), (p) and (q) were amended December 19, 2002; (r) was adopted ________, 201 land applies to all cases filed on or after ________, 2011.

[Pilot Rule Adopted: 28 August 1986. Pilot rule amended: 4 March 1987; permanent rule adopted: 14 September 1989; amended: 8 March 1990—(b); amended: 19 December 2002—(a) and (b); amended effective 1 January 2012.]

COMMENT

The 60 days in Arb. Rule 6(a)(1) will allow for discovery, trial preparation, pretrial motions, disposition and calendaring. A motion to continue a hearing will be heard by a judge mindful of this goal. Continuances may be granted when a party or counsel is entitled to such under law, e.g. N.C.R.Civ.P. 40(b); rule of court, e.g. N.C.Prac.R. 3; or customary practice.

Under Arb. Rule 6(c), both parties are responsible for notifying the court personnel responsible for scheduling arbitration hearings that a consent judgment or dismissal has been filed. The notice required under Arb. Rule 6(c) should be filed with the court personnel responsible for scheduling the arbitration hearings. Failure to do so will result in assessment of the arbitrator fee. The "court official administering the arbitration" is the arbitration coordinator, judicial assistant or other staff member managing the arbitration program, as may vary from county to county.

Arb. Rule 6(d)(3) contemplates that the arbitrator shall return all evidence submitted when the hearing is concluded and the award has been made. Original documents and exhibits should not be marked in any way to identify them with the arbitration to avoid possible prejudice in any future trial.

For purposes of Arb. Rule 6(g), the arbitrator shall have such authority to administer oaths if such authorization is consistent with the laws of North Carolina.

As articulated in Arb Rule 6(i), the arbitrator is to rule upon the evidence presented at the hearing, or lack thereof. Thus an arbitrator may enter a $0 award or an award for the defendant if the evidence presented at the hearing does not support an award for the plaintiff.

Arb. Rule 6(n) requires that all parties be present in person or through counsel. The presence of the parties or their counsel is necessary for presentation of the case to the arbitrator. Rule 6(n) does not require that a party or any representative of a party have authority to make binding decisions on the party's behalf in the matters in controversy, beyond those reasonably necessary to present evidence, make arguments and adequately represent the party during the arbitration. Specifically, a representative is not required to have the authority to make binding settlement decisions.

Arb. Rule 6(n) sets forth that parties may appear pro se, as permitted by law. In accordance with applicable state law, only parties that are natural persons may appear pro se at arbitrations. Any business, corporation, limited liability corporation, unincorporated association or other professional parties, including but not limited to, businesses considered to be a separate legal entity shall be represented by counsel in accordance with the North Carolina General Statutes. See Case Notes Below.

The rules do not establish a separate standard for pro se representation in court-ordered arbitrations. Instead, pro se representation in court-ordered arbitrations is governed by applicable principles of North Carolina law in that area. See Arb. Rule 6(n). Conformance of practice in court-ordered arbitrations with the applicable law is ensured by providing that pro se representation be "as permitted by law."

The purpose of Arb. Rule 6(q) is to ensure that hearings are limited and expedited. Failure to limit and expedite the hearings defeats the purpose of these rules. In this connection, note the option in Arb. Rule 6(d) for use of prehearing stipulations and/or sworn or unsworn statements to meet time limits.

Under Arb. Rule 6(r), the declaration that the hearing is concluded by the arbitrator formally marks the end of the hearing. Note Arb. Rule 7(a), which requires the arbitrator to file the award within three days after the hearing is concluded or post-hearing briefs are received. The usual practice should be a statement of the award at the close of the hearing, without submission of briefs. In the unusual case where an arbitrator is willing to receive post-hearing briefs, the arbitrator should specify the points to be addressed promptly and succinctly. Time limits in these rules are governed by N.C.R. Civ. P. 6 and N.C.G.S. §§ 103–4, 103–5.

Under Arb. Rule 6(s)(1), the court will rule on prehearing motions which dispose of all or part of the case on the pleadings, or which relate to procedural management of the case.

No party shall be deemed to have consented to binding arbitration unless it is documented on the proper form, which is executed after the filing date of the action. No executed contract, lien, lease or other legal document, other than the proper form designating the arbitration as binding, shall be used to make an arbitration binding upon either party.

Case Notes—For note discussing representation of parties who are not living human beings, see Lexis-Nexis v Travishan Corp., 155 N.C. App. 205, 573 S.E.2d 547 (2002).

Comment

A judgment entered on the arbitrator's award is not appealable because there is no record for review by an appellate court. A trial de novo is not an "appeal," in the sense of an appeal to the North Carolina Court of Appeals from Superior Court or District Court, from the arbitrator's award. By failing to demand a trial de novo the right to appeal is waived.

Rule 7. The Award

(a) Filing the Award. The award shall be in writing, signed by the arbitrator and filed with the clerk within three days after the hearing is concluded or the receipt of post-hearing briefs, whichever is later. The arbitrator shall file a complete award indicating any award, the rate of any applicable interest and any accrued interest.

(b) Findings; Conclusions; Opinions. No findings of fact and conclusions of law or opinions supporting an award are required.

(c) Scope of Award. The award must resolve all issues raised by the pleadings, may be in any amount supported by the evidence, shall include interest as provided by law, and may include attorney's fees as allowed by law.

(d) Copies of Award to Parties. The arbitrator shall deliver a copy of the award to all of the parties or their counsel at the conclusion of the hearing or the clerk shall serve, in accordance with the N.C.R.Civ.P. 5, the award within three (3) days after filing. A record shall be made by the arbitrator or the court of the date and manner of service.

Administrative History Pilot Rules Adopted August 28, 1986; Pilot Rules Amended: March 4, 1987; Permanent Rule Adopted September 14, 1989; This is former Arb. Rule 4, renumbered ________, 2011. (a), (c) and (d) were adopted ________, 2011; (a) and (d) were amended ________, 2011.

[Pilot Rule Adopted: 28 August 1986. Pilot rule amended: 4 March 1987; permanent rule adopted: 14 September 1989; amended: 8 March 1990—(c); amended: 19 December 2002—(b) and (c); amended effective 1 January 2012.]

COMMENT

Ordinarily, the arbitrator should issue the award at the conclusion of the hearing. See Arb. Rule 7(a). If the arbitrator wants post-hearing briefs, the arbitrator must receive them within three days, consider them, and file the award within three days thereafter. See Arb. Rule 6(r) and its Comment. If the arbitrator deems it appropriate, the arbitrator may explain orally the basis of the award.

If an award is incomplete or unclear, the clerk should request clarification from the arbitrator and the arbitrator should amend the award to make the award, including any interest, evident. In the event this occurs after the award was announced to the parties, the court should serve the amended order on all parties in accordance with Arb. Rule 7(d). The service of an amended order shall cause the period for demanding a trial de novo to restart in accordance with Arb. Rule 8.

Rule 8. The Court's Judgment

(a) Termination of Action Before Judgment. Dismissals or a consent judgment may be filed at any time before entry of judgment on an award.

(b) Judgment Entered on Award. If the case is not terminated by dismissal or consent judgment and no party files a demand for trial de novo within 30 days after the award is served, the clerk or the court shall enter judgment on the award, which shall have the same effect as a consent judgment in the action. A copy of the judgment shall be served on all parties or their counsel by mail in accordance with N.C.R.Civ.P. 5(b).

(c) Judgment upon dismissal or withdrawal of a demand for trial de novo. If the case is noticed for trial de novo and all parties consent to withdraw the demand for the trial de novo in accordance with Rule 9(a)(3), the clerk or court shall immediately enter judgment on the award. A copy of the judgment shall be served on all parties or their counsel by the clerk in accordance with N.C.R.Civ.P. 5. A certificate of service shall be executed by the clerk and shall be filed.

Administrative History Pilot Rule Adopted August 28, 1986. Pilot Rule Amended March 4, 1987. Permanent Rule Adopted September 14, 1989. This is former Arb. Rule 6, renumbered ________, 2011. (a) was amended December 19, 2002; (b) was amended March 8, 1990 and December 19, 2002; (c) was adopted ________, 2011 and applies to all cases filed on or after ________, 2011.

[Pilot Rule Adopted: 28 August 1986. Pilot rule amended: 4 March 1987; permanent rule adopted: 14 September 1989; amended: 8 March 1990—(a), (b), (d), and (f); amended: 19 December 2002—(a), (b), (c), (e), and (f); amended effective 1 January 2012.]

COMMENT

No appeal lies from an arbitration award to the appellate courts of this State. The remedy available to a party aggrieved by the award is to demand a trial de novo in the district court. In the absence of such a demand within the 30 day period set forth in Arb. Rule 8(b), the clerk or the court will enter judgment on the award.

Comment

One goal of these rules is to expedite disposition of claims filed in District Court. See Arb.Rule 8(a). The 60 days in Arb.Rule 8(b)(1) will allow for discovery, trial preparation, pretrial motions disposition and calendaring. A motion to continue a hearing will be heard by a judge mindful of this goal. Continuances may be granted when a party or counsel is entitled to such under law, e.g. N.C.R.Civ.P. 40(b); rule of court, e.g. N.C.Prac.R. 3; or customary practice.

Any settlement reached prior to the scheduled arbitration hearing must be reported by the parties to the Court official administering the arbitration. The parties must file dismissals or a consent judgment prior to the scheduled hearing to close the case without a hearing. If the dismissals or consent judgment are not filed before the scheduled hearing, the parties should appear at the hearing to have their agreement entered as the award of the arbitrator.

Rule 9. Trial De Novo

(a) Trial De Novo as of Right.

(1) Any party not in default for a reason subjecting that party to judgment by default who is dissatisfied with an arbitrator's award may have a trial de novo as of right upon filing a written demand for trial de novo with the court, and service of the demand on all parties, on form promulgated by the Administrative Office of the Courts within 30 days after the arbitrator's award has been served on all parties, or within 10 days after an adverse determination of an Arb. Rule 6(*l*) motion to rehear. Demand for jury trial pursuant to N.C.R.Civ.P. 38(b) does not preserve the right to a trial de novo. A demand by any party for a trial de novo in accordance with this section is sufficient to preserve the right of all other parties to a trial de novo. Any trial de novo pursuant to this section shall include all claims in the action. No rulings by the arbitrator shall be binding on the court at a trial de novo.

(2) Upon the demand of a trial de novo by any party pursuant to these Rules, that demand shall be deemed to have preserved the rights of all parties and all issues in the case for trial de novo. No party shall lose a right to a trial de novo of any eligible issue as a result of the failure of the party initially demanding the trial de novo to proceed for any reason. In the event the party initiating the trial de novo fails to proceed for any reason, any other party may request that the trial de novo be calendared for all issues.

(3) The court shall, upon any party demanding a trial de novo of any issue, calendar all parties and issues before the court for a de novo trial. All issues and parties shall remain as pending matters and shall be calendared by the court in a timely manner for the trial de novo hearing unless and until such time as all parties agree to dismiss the demand for a trial de novo. Any such agreement shall be recorded on a form promulgated by the Administrative Office of the Courts, executed by all parties and filed with the clerk in the county in which the action is pending prior to the trial de novo.

(b) Trial De Novo Fee.

(1) The first party filing a demand for trial de novo in cases wherein the initiating party has not properly moved the court for indigent relief and relief from payment of the trial de novo fee, in accordance with Arb. Rule 9(b)(2)(H), shall pay a filing fee at the time the written demand for trial de novo is filed with the clerk, equivalent to the arbitrator's compensation, as set forth in Arb. Rule 4(b), which shall be held by the clerk until the case is terminated. The fee shall be returned to the demanding party only upon written order of the trial judge finding that the position of the demanding party has been improved over the arbitrator's award. Otherwise, the filing fee shall be deposited into the Judicial Department's General Fund at the expiration of thirty days from the final judgment from a court of competent jurisdiction or the expiration of the time for filing any available appeals, whichever is later. No party may make application for the return of this fee after the expiration of thirty days from the final judgment.

(2) If a party properly moves the court by proper motion which includes that party's social security number for indigent status and requests relief from the payment of the trial de novo fee prior to the trial de novo hearing, that party shall not be required to pay the trial de novo fee at the time of demanding the trial de novo. Said motion shall be heard subsequent to the completion of the trial de novo. In a ruling

upon such motions, the judge shall apply the criteria enumerated in N.C.G.S. § 1-110(a), but shall take into consideration the outcome of the trial de novo and the previous arbitration and whether a judgment was rendered in the indigent's favor. A judge may find that the party was indigent at the time of arbitration, but not indigent at the time of the trial de novo and make a ruling on the fees due accordingly. The court shall enter an order granting, in part or in full, or denying the party's request and:

(i) if the party is denied indigent relief, that party shall pay the trial de novo fee within ten (10) days of a final judgment from a court of competent jurisdiction or the expiration of time for all available appeals, whichever is later. In the event the party fails to pay the trial de novo fee as directed by the court, the clerk shall follow the procedure set forth in this rule for entry of judgment in the amount of the trial de novo fee as if the person had been found indigent.

(ii) If the party is granted indigent relief for any portion of the trial de novo fee, the court shall direct that a judgment be entered in the clerk's office in the county in which the action is pending for the unpaid portion of that party's pro rata share of the trial de novo fee, which shall constitute a lien as prescribed by the general law of the State applicable to judgments. The order or judgment shall become effective and the judgment shall be docketed and indexed pursuant to N.C. Gen. Stat. § 1-233 et seq., in the amount of the partially indigent or indigent party's share of the trial de novo fee. Each judgment docketed against a person shall include the social security number, if any, of the judgment debtor.

(c) No Reference to Arbitration in Presence of Jury. A trial de novo shall be conducted as if there had been no arbitration proceeding. No reference may be made to prior arbitration proceedings in the presence of a jury without consent of all parties to the arbitration and the court's approval.

(d) No Evidence of Arbitration Admissible. No evidence that there have been arbitration proceedings or of statements made and conduct occurring in arbitration proceedings may be admitted in a trial de novo, or in any subsequent proceeding involving any of the issues in or parties to the arbitration, without the consent of all parties to the arbitration and the court's approval.

(e) Arbitrator Not to Be Called as Witness. An arbitrator may not be deposed or called as a witness to testify concerning anything said or done in an arbitration proceeding in a trial de novo or any subsequent civil or administrative proceeding involving any of the issues in or parties to the arbitration. The arbitrator's notes are privileged and not subject to discovery.

(f) Judicial Immunity. The arbitrator shall have judicial immunity to the same extent as a trial judge with respect to the arbitrator's actions in the arbitration proceeding.

(g) Exclusion of Issues. All parties to an action may consent to limit the issues to be considered by the court in a trial de novo. Any such consent shall be in writing and executed by all parties or their respective counsel, filed with the clerk and submitted to the court at the trial de novo. The consent document shall set forth the issues upon which agreement has been reached and all issues remaining for consideration by the court.

Administrative History Pilot Rule Adopted August 28, 1986; Pilot Rule Amended March 4, 1987; Permanent Rule Adopted September 14, 1989; This is former Arb. Rule 5 and was renumbered ________, 2011; (a)(1) was formerly Arb. Rule 5(a), was amended March 8, 1990, December 19, 2002 and was amended and renumbered ________, 2011; Arb. Rule (a)(2) and Arb. Rule(a)(3) were adopted ________, 2011 and apply to all cases filed on or after ________, 2011; (b)(1) was amended March 8, 1990, December 19, 2002 and was amended and renumbered ________, 2011; Arb. Rule (b)(2) was adopted ________, 2011 and applies to all cases filed on or after ________, 2011; (e) and (f) were amended March 8, 1990; (c)(d) were amended December 19, 2002; (g) was adopted ________, 2011 and applies to all cases filed on or after ________, 2011

[Pilot Rule Adopted: 28 August 1986. Pilot rule amended: 4 March 1987; permanent rule adopted: 14 September 1989; amended: 8 March 1990; amended: 19 December 2002; amended effective 1 January 2012.]

COMMENT

Arb. Rule 9(a)(2) and 9(a)(3) clarify that each party is not required to notice their respective issues for a trial de novo. Once a trial de novo has been demanded, it shall be heard unless all parties consent otherwise in writing.

Under Arb. Rule 9(b)(1), if a party prevails but does not improve their position at the trial novo hearing, that party shall not be eligible for reimbursement of the trial de novo filing fee.

Arb. Rule 9(c) does not preclude cross-examination of a witness in a later proceeding concerning prior inconsistent statements during arbitration proceedings, if done in such a manner as not to violate the intent of Arb. Rules 9(c) and 9(d).

In a case involving multiple defendants and where one or more defendants have been dismissed, a demand for trial de novo by a remaining defendant does not operate to rejoin the dismissed defendant in the action absent properly filed pleadings in accordance with N.C.R.Civ.P. 13.

In the event a party has previously requested a trial by jury, the trial de novo shall be a jury trial. See also the Comment to Arb. Rule 8 regarding demand for trial de novo.

Final judgment of a court of competent jurisdiction as referenced in Arb. Rule 9(b)(1) shall mean the final judgment once all parties have availed themselves of all possible appellate processes and no avenues of appeal remain, either because the appeal has been heard and judgment has been rendered, the court has declined to consider the appeal or the time for properly filing all appeals has expired.

For purposes of Arb. Rule 9(b)(2), a person shall apply for indigency relief before the district court judge by completing and submitting AOC–G–106 or similar form if this form is modified and/or replaced by the Administrative Office of the Courts.

For purposes of Arb. Rule 9, if a party that is not a living human being, as defined by Arb. Rule 1, is listed as a party and a living human being, who is an owner, share holder or has any other ownership interest in that non-human being party is also listed as a party, then each shall be counted as an individual party.

Comment

A common set of rules has been adopted. These rules may be amended only by the Supreme Court of North Carolina. The enabling legislation, G.S. §§ 7A–37 and 7A–37.1, vests rule-making authority in the Supreme Court, and this includes amendments.

Rule 10. Administration

(a) Forms. Forms for use in these arbitration proceedings must be approved by the Administrative Office of the Courts.

(b) Delegation of Nonjudicial Functions. To conserve judicial resources and facilitate the effectiveness of these rules, the court may delegate nonjudicial, administrative duties and functions to supporting court personnel and authorize them to require compliance with these rules.

(c) Local Rules. The chief district court judge may publish local rules, not inconsistent with the Rules and N.C.G.S. 7A–37.1, implementing arbitration.

Administrative History: Authority—Order of the North Carolina Supreme Court, August 28, 1986, pilot rule adopted; pilot rule amended effective March 4, 1987; permanent rule adopted, by order of the North Carolina Supreme Court, September 14, 1989; Arb. Rule 8(a), renumbered as Arb. Rule 2(3), effective _________, 2011, was amended March 8, 1990 and December 19, 2002; Arb. Rule 8(b), renumbered as Arb. Rule 8(b)(1) and former Arb. Rule 8(b)(2), effective _________, 2011, was amended March 8, 1990 and December 19, 2002; Arb. Rule (d) was amended March 8, 1990 and (f), renumbered as Arb. Rule 1(b), effective _________, 2011, was amended March 8, 1990 and December 19, 2002; Amended December 19, 2002—(c) and (e); Effective _________, 2011, former (a), (b), (c) were renumbered, reorganized and amended; Effective _________, 2011, Arb. Rule 10(d) was reorganized as Arb. Rule 10(a) and Arb. Rule 10(e) was reorganized as Arb. Rule 10(b).

[Amended effective 1 January 2012.]

Rule 11. Application Of Rules

These Rules shall apply to cases filed on or after the effective date of these rules and to pending cases submitted by agreement of the parties under Arb. Rule 2(b) or referred to arbitration by order of the court in those districts designated for court-ordered arbitration in accordance with N.C.G.S. § 7A–37.1.

Administrative History: Authority—Order of the North Carolina Supreme Court, August 28, 1986, pilot rules adopted; pilot rule amended effective March 4, 1987; permanent rule adopted, by order of the North Carolina Supreme Court, September 14, 1989; Amended March 8, 1990; Amended December 19, 2002; Amended _________, 2011, effective immediately to all cases filed on or before _________, 2011.

[Amended effective 1 January 2012.]

COMMENT

A common set of rules has been adopted. These rules may be amended only by the Supreme Court of North Carolina. The enabling legislation, N.C.G.S. § 7A–37.1, vests rule-making authority in the Supreme Court, and this includes amendments.

Editor's note.—As to the applicability of the Rules for Court–Ordered Arbitration, see the order of the Supreme Court preceding these rules.

CANONS OF ETHICS FOR ARBITRATORS

Adopted August 19, 1999, Effective October 1, 1999

Table of Canons

Order Adopting the North Carolina Canons of Ethics for Arbitrators

WHEREAS, section 7A–37.1 of the North Carolina General Statutes authorizes court-ordered nonbinding arbitration as an alternative to civil procedure, and

WHEREAS, N.C.G.S. § 7A–37.1(b) provides for this Court to adopt rules governing this procedure,

NOW, THEREFORE, pursuant to N.C.G.S. § 7A–37.1(b), the North Carolina Canons of Ethics for Arbitrators are hereby adopted, to read as in the following pages, for court-ordered nonbinding arbitration in the State of North Carolina. The supervising Chief District Court Judge or Senior Resident Superior Court Judge shall be the enforcing authority for these Canons. These Canons shall be effective on the 1st day of October, 1999.

Adopted by the Court in conference the 19th day of August, 1999. The Appellate Division Reporter shall publish the North Carolina Canons of Ethics for Arbitrators in their entirety, as amended through this action, at the earliest practicable date.

I. An Arbitrator Shall Uphold the Integrity and Fairness of the Arbitration Process

A. Fair and just processes for resolving disputes are indispensable in our society. Arbitration is an important method for deciding many types of disputes. For arbitration to be effective, there must be broad public confidence in and understanding of the integrity and fairness of the process. Therefore, an arbitrator has a responsibility not only to the parties but also to the courts, the public and the process of arbitration itself and must observe high standards of conduct so that the integrity and fairness of the process will be preserved. Accordingly, an arbitrator has a responsibility to the public, parties whose rights will be decided, the courts, and other participants in the proceeding. These Canons shall be construed and applied to further these objectives.

B. It may be inconsistent with the integrity of the arbitration process for persons to solicit appointment for themselves. However, persons may indicate a general willingness to serve as arbitrators, e.g., by listing themselves with institutions that sponsor arbitration, or with courts that have court-annexed arbitration programs. Arbitrators may advertise, consistent with the law.

C. Persons may accept appointment as arbitrators only if they believe that they can be available to conduct the arbitration promptly. They shall exercise judgment whether their skills or expertise are sufficient to support demands of the arbitration and, if these skills or expertise are not sufficient, they shall decline to serve or withdraw from the arbitration, with the court's approval in court-administered arbitration, and notice to the parties.

D. After accepting appointment and while serving as an arbitrator, a person shall avoid entering into any financial, business, professional, family or social relationship, or acquiring any financial or personal interest likely to affect impartiality or which might reasonably create the appearance of partiality or bias. For one year after decision of a case, persons who have served as arbitrators shall avoid entering into any such relationship, or acquiring any such interest, in the circumstances which might reasonably create the appearance that they had been influenced in the arbitration by the anticipation or expectation of the relationship or interest, unless all parties to the arbitration consent to any such relationship or acquiring any such interest.

E. Arbitrators shall conduct themselves in a way that is fair, in word and action, to all parties and must not be swayed by outside pressure, public clamor, fear of criticism or self-interest. If an arbitrator determines that he or she cannot serve impartially, that arbitrator shall decline appointment or withdraw from serving and shall notify the parties, and the court in court-administered arbitrations.

F. When an arbitrator's authority is derived from the parties' agreement, the arbitrator shall not exceed that authority nor do less than required to exercise that authority completely. Where the parties' agreement sets forth procedures to be followed in conducting the arbitration or refers to rules to be followed, the arbitrator must comply with such procedures or rules.

G. An arbitrator shall make all reasonable efforts to prevent delaying tactics, harassment of parties or other participants, or other abuse or disruption of the arbitration process.

H. An arbitrator's ethical obligations begin upon acceptance of appointment and continue throughout all stages of the proceeding. In addition, wherever specifically set forth in these Canons, certain ethical obligations begin as soon as a person is asked to serve as an arbitrator and continue for one year after the decision in the case has been given to the parties.

I. An experienced arbitrator should participate in development of new practitioners in the field and should engage in efforts to educate the public about the value and use of arbitration procedures. An arbitrator should provide pro bono services, as appropriate.

[Adopted August 19, 1999, effective October 1, 1999.]

Comment

References to "commercial" in American Bar Association & American Arbitration Association, Code of Ethics for Arbitrators in Commercial Disputes, Canon I (1977) (Code), 33 Bus. Law. 311 (1977), from which these Canons have been adapted, have been deleted. Excess verbiage has been deleted. The catchline has been changed from "should" to "shall" to underscore the mandatory nature of the principle; "should" has been omitted in Canon I.A in the penultimate sentence, and the language amended, to underscore this. "Should" in the last sentence has been changed to "shall". "Should" has been changed to "shall" or "must" in other parts of the Canon.

Other additions in Canon I.A follow the Preamble to North Carolina Dispute Resolution Commission, Standards of Conduct for Mediators, 344 N.C. 753 (Standards). The addition in Canon I.B gives examples of circumstances in which persons may offer services as arbitrators. It is consistent with N.C. Ct-Ord. Arb. R.2(a). Unlike the Canon I.B says it "may be" inconsistent with the integrity of the arbitration process to solicit appointment as an arbitrator. This is because of the difficulty, e.g., in drawing a line between advertisement permitted by law and solicitation that is condemned in some professional standards, e.g., those for lawyers. Arbitrators must be mindful of fairness, neutrality, disclosure and conflict of interest principles stated in these Canons. The last sentence in Canon I.B makes it clear that the Canons should not be read to forbid arbitrator advertising where, e.g., commercial free speech principles under the Constitution allow it. The addition in Canon I.C is taken from Standards I.B–I.C and covers situations of court-appointed arbitrators under, e.g., the Uniform Arbitration Act, N.C. Gen. Stat. § 1–567.4, or in court-annexed arbitrations; these arbitrators are subject to court order appointing them, and the court is the final arbiter of these issues. The thrust of Canon I.C is consistent with Revised North Carolina Rules of Professional Conduct 1.1(Rule), although the latter deals with competence of a lawyer, and the Canon governs competence to serve as an arbitrator. Canon I.D states a one-year rule instead of the "reasonable time" principle of the Code. The one-year rule has been substituted to coincide with the time in the Federal Arbitration Act, 9 U.S.C. § 9–11, during which a party can move to set aside an award. The Uniform Act, N.C. Gen. Stat. §§ 1–567.13—1–567.14, requires set-aside applications to be made within 90 days of an award. Fed. R. Civ. P. 60(b) and N.C.R. Civ. P. (60B) limit certain judgment set-aside motions to one year. One year has been chosen as the time when nearly all conflict issues would arise and be resolved. The addition to Canon I.D, penultimate sentence, follows consent rule in Rule 1. 12(a). Additions in Canon II.E follow Standard II.C, with additions to cover court-annexed arbitration or arbitrations where a court has appointed an arbitrator under, e.g., the Uniform Act. "Asked" replaces "requested" in Canon I.H. The phrase "continues for one year" has been added to coincide with the one-year rule for Canon I.D.

Canon I.I has been adapted from Society of Professionals in Dispute Resolution, Ethical Standards of Professional Conduct, Support of the Profession (1987) (SPIDR Standards), reprinted in Rena A. Gorlin, Codes of Professional Responsibility 327 (2d ed. 1990); unlike standards applicable to arbitrators in proceedings, Canon I.I is hortatory, not mandatory. The Rules do not include the equivalent of ABA, Model Rules of Professional Conduct, Rule 6. 1, which says a lawyer should aspire to provide 50 hours of public service a year. See Alice Neece Moseley et al., An Overview of the Revised North Carolina Rules of Professional Conduct: An examination of the Interests Promoted and Subordinated. 32 Wake Forest L. Rev. 939, 990–91 (1997). Since these Canons would apply to all arbitrators, including non-lawyers, and Canon I.I states aspirations to provide continuing education, there is no inconsistency with the Rules. Canon I.I is consistent with North Carolina attorneys' obligations to take 12 hours of continuing legal education a year. Other lawyers teach this CLE, and these lawyers have the same role as Canon I.I would contemplate for experienced arbitrators.

The Canon's language has been tightened.

Canon I generally parallels North Carolina Code of Judicial Conduct, Canons 1–3 (Code of Judicial Conduct). See also National Academy of Arbitrators et al., Code of Professional Responsibility for Arbitrators of Labor–Management Disputes, ¶¶ 1.A–1.C.2, III.A (May 30, 1996) (Academy Code); International Bar Association, Ethics for International Arbitrators, Arts. 1–2 (1986)(IBA Ethics), 26 Int'l Legal Mat'ls

584 (1987), 6A Benedict on Admiralty, Doc. No. 7–12D (Frank L. Wiswall, Jr. ed., 7th rev. ed. 1999); SPIDR Standards, General Responsibilities & Responsibilities to the Parties § 1, Background and Qualifications.

II. An Arbitrator Shall Disclose Any interest or Relationship Likely to Affect Impartiality or Which Might Create an Appearance of Partiality or Bias

A. Persons asked to serve as arbitrators shall, before accepting, disclose:

(1) any direct or indirect financial or personal interest in the outcome of the arbitration;

(2) any existing or past financial, business, professional, family or social relationships which are likely to affect impartiality or which might reasonably create an appearance of partiality or bias. Persons asked to serve as arbitrators shall disclose any such relationships which they personally have with any parry or its lawyer, or with any individual whom they have been told will be a witness. They shall also disclose any such relationships involving their spouses or minor children residing in the household or their current employers, partners or business associates; and

(3) any information required by a court in the case of court-administered arbitrations.

B. Persons asked to accept appointment as arbitrators shall make a reasonable effort to inform themselves of any interests or relationships described in Canon II.A.

C. The obligation to disclose interests or relationships described in Canon II.A is a continuing duty which requires a person accepting appointment as an arbitrator to disclose, at any stage of the arbitration, any such interests or relationships which may arise, or which are recalled or discovered.

D. Disclosure shall be made to all parties unless other disclosure procedures are provided in the rules or practices of an institution or court administering the arbitration. Where more than one arbitrator has been appointed, the other arbitrators shall be informed of interests and relationships which have been disclosed.

E. If an arbitrator is asked by all parties to withdraw, the arbitrator shall do so, provided however, if a court is administering the arbitration, the arbitrator shall inform the court of the request and shall comply with court orders. If an arbitrator is asked to withdraw by less than all of the parties because of alleged partiality or bias, the arbitrator shall withdraw unless any of these circumstances exists:

(1) If the parties' agreement, or arbitration rules to which the parties have agreed, establish procedures for determining challenges to arbitrators, those procedures shall be followed;

(2) If the arbitrator, after carefully considering the matter, determines that the reason for the challenge is not substantial, and that he or she can nevertheless act and decide the case impartially and fairly, and that withdrawal would cause unfair delay or expense to another party or would be contrary to the interest of justice; or

(3) The court administering the arbitration decides otherwise.

F. The parties may waive disqualification of an arbitrator upon full disclosure of any basis for disqualification, and upon approval of the court in court-administered arbitrations.

[Adopted August 19, 1999, effective October 1, 1999.]

Comment

Excess verbiage has been deleted. "Asked" has been substituted for "requested." "Shall" has been substituted for "should" throughout the Canon; see Comment for Canon I.

Canon II.A's provisions have been stated clearly in the conjunctive ("and"). Canon II.A(2) has been amended to follow Code of Judicial Conduct, Canon 3(C)(2) as to spouses and minor children. Canon II.A(3) has been added for court-annexed arbitration or arbitration administered by a court under, e.g., the Uniform Act. Although Canon VIII.B generally provides that these Canons state principles paramount to institutional (e.g., the Code) ethics standards, Canon VII.B states an exception for Canon II.D's disclosure principles. Canon II.E has been modified to account for situations where a court administers arbitration, e.g., court-annexed arbitration, but also where a court appoints an arbitrator, e.g., pursuant to the Uniform Act, N.C. Gen. Stat. § 1–567.4. Canon II.F has been added; it is taken from N.C. Ct–Ord. Arb. R. 2(e); however, court approval is required only if a court has appointed an arbitrator in a court-annexed arbitration or pursuant to, e.g., the Uniform Act.

Canon II generally follows Code of Judicial Conduct, Canon 3(C), although Canon II does not specify degrees of kinship as the Code of Judicial Conduct does. See also Academy Code, ¶¶ 2.B, 3.A; IBA Ethics, Arts. 1, 3–4; SPIDR Standards, Responsibilities to the Parties § 4.

III. An Arbitrator, in Communicating With Parties, Shall Avoid Impropriety or the Appearance of Impropriety

A. If the parties' agreement or arbitration rules referred to in that agreement establish the manner or content of communications between the arbitrator and the parties, the arbitrator shall follow those procedures notwithstanding any contrary provision in Canons III.B and III.C.

B. Unless otherwise provided in applicable arbitration rules or in the parties' agreement, arbitrators shall not discuss a case with any party in the absence of other parties, except in these circumstances:

(1) Discussions may be had with a party concerning such matters as setting the time and place of hearings or making other arrangements for conducting proceedings. The arbitrator shall promptly inform other

parties of the discussion and shall not make any final determination concerning the matter discussed before giving each absent party an opportunity to express its views.

(2) If all parties request or consent to it, such discussion may take place.

C. Unless otherwise provided in applicable arbitration rules or in the parties' agreement, whenever an arbitrator communicates in writing with one party, the arbitrator shall send a copy of the communication to other parties at the same time. Whenever the arbitrator receives a written communication concerning the case from a party which has not already been sent to other parties, the arbitrator shall send that communication to other parties.

[Adopted August 19, 1999, effective October 1, 1999.]

Comment

"Shall" has been substituted for "should" throughout Canon III; see Comment to Canon I. Code III.B(2), stating "If a party fails to be present at a hearing after having been given due notice, the arbitrator may discuss the case with any party present," has been deleted as redundant with Canon IV.F. Revisions have also tightened the text; the last phrase clarifies "to do so." See also Code of Judicial Conduct, Canon 2, for which Canon III is a rough parallel in some respects; Academy Code, ¶ 2.D; IBA Ethics, Art. 5.

IV. An Arbitrator Shall Conduct Proceedings Fairly and Diligently

A. An arbitrator shall conduct proceedings in an evenhanded manner and treat all parties with equality and fairness at all stages of the proceedings.

B. An arbitrator shall perform duties diligently and conclude the case as promptly as circumstances reasonably permit.

C. An arbitrator shall be patient, dignified and courteous to parties, their lawyers, witnesses, and all others with whom the arbitrator deals in that capacity and shall encourage similar conduct by all participants in the proceedings. This does not preclude an arbitrator's imposing sanctions if permitted by law or by the parties' agreement.

D. Unless otherwise agreed by the parties or provided in arbitration rules to which the parties have agreed, an arbitrator shall accord to all parties the right to appear in person and to be heard after due notice of the time and place of hearing.

E. An arbitrator shall not deny a party the opportunity to be represented by counsel.

F. If a party fails to appear after due notice, an arbitrator may proceed with the arbitration when authorized to do so by the parties or by law. An arbitrator may do so only after receiving assurance that notice has been given to the absent party.

G. When an arbitrator determines that more information than has been presented by the parties is required to decide a case, it is not improper for the arbitrator to ask questions, call witnesses, and request documents or other evidence.

H. It is not improper for an arbitrator to suggest to the parties that they discuss settling the case. An arbitrator may not be present or otherwise participate in settlement discussions unless asked to do so by all parties. An arbitrator may not pressure a party to settle.

I. Nothing in these Canons is intended to prevent a person from acting as a mediator, conciliator or other neutral in a dispute in which he or she has been appointed as an arbitrator, if asked to do so by all parties or where authorized or required to do so by applicable law or rules.

J. Where there is more than one arbitrator, the arbitrators shall afford each other full opportunity to participate in all aspects of the proceedings.

K. In court-annexed arbitrations where one or more of the parties is proceeding without counsel, at the hearing the arbitrator shall discuss the nature of the arbitration process with all parties and counsel present, including the arbitrator's role, time allotted for each party's case, order of proceedings, and the right to trial de novo (if applicable) if a party not in default is dissatisfied with the arbitrator's award, unless parties waive these explanations.

[Adopted August 19, 1999, effective October 1, 1999.]

Comment

Language has been tightened, and excess verbiage has been deleted. "Shall" or "may" has been substituted for "should" throughout Canon IV; to Canon I.

Canon IV.C has been amended to follow Code o f Judicial Conduct Canon 3(A)(3). The final sentence recognizes that arbitrators may be empowered to impose sanctions in, e.g., court-annexed arbitration or by the parties' agreement, in addition to the arbitrator's ethical obligation to encourage proper conduct. Canon IV.H is consistent with Standard IV.B. Canon IV.I has been modified to take into account procedures other than mediation or conciliation, e.g., early neutral evaluation, etc. Canon IV.K has been added; it only applies to court-annexed arbitration. Where there has been an agreement to arbitrate governed by, e.g., the Uniform Act, but parties have not appointed an arbitrator pursuant to the Act and the court does so under, e.g., N.C. Gen. Stat. § 1-567.4, there is no reason to require that arbitrator to explain the nature of arbitration. Many court-annexed arbitrations involve small claims where parties may appear without counsel; fairness and efficiency suggest that an explanation at the beginning of the hearing, unless waived, will expedite the proceeding; Parties in court-annexed arbitration may agree to binding arbitration with no trial de novo; if this is the case, there is no need to explain a right to trial de novo. Canon IV.K was suggested by Standard IV.A.

See also Academy Code, ¶¶ 1.A, 2.J, 4–5; IBA Ethics, Arts. 7–8; SPIDR Standards, Responsibilities to the Parties §§ 2, 5–6. The Uniform Act and the International Commercial Arbitration and Conciliation Act provide for representation by counsel. N.C. Gen. Stat. § 1.567.7, 1–567.48(b).

V. An Arbitrator Shall Make Decisions in a Just, Independent and Deliberate Manner

A. An arbitrator shall, after careful deliberation, decide all issues submitted for determination. An arbitrator may decide no other issues.

B. An arbitrator shall decide all issues justly, exercising independent judgment, and shall not permit outside pressure to affect the decision.

C. An arbitrator shall not delegate the duty to decide to any other person, unless the parties agree to such delegation.

D. If all parties agree to settle issues in dispute and ask an arbitrator to embody that agreement in an award, an arbitrator may do so but is not required to do so unless satisfied with the propriety of the settlement terms. Whenever an arbitrator embodies the parties' settlement in an award, the arbitrator shall state in the award that it is based on the parties' agreement.

[Adopted August 19, 1999, effective October 1, 1999.]

Comment

Revisions tighten the text and omit excess verbiage. "Shall" has been substituted for "should" throughout Canon V; See Comment to Canon I. The new material in Canon V.C makes it clear that parties can agree that an arbitrator may delegate decision making in whole or in part, e.g., to conciliators as provided in the North Carolina International Commercial Arbitration and Conciliation Act. See also Academy Code, ¶¶ 2.G–2.I, 6.

VI. An Arbitrator Shall Be Faithful to the Relationship of Trust and Confidentiality Inherent in That Office

A. An arbitrator is in a relationship of trust to the parties and shall not at any time use confidential information acquired during the arbitration proceeding to gain personal advantage or advantage for others or to affect adversely the interest of another.

B. Unless the parties agree otherwise, or the law or applicable rules require, an arbitrator shall keep confidential all matters relating to the arbitration proceedings and decision.

C. It is not proper at any time for an arbitrator to inform anyone of the decision before it is given to all parties. Where there is more than one arbitrator, it is not proper at any time for an arbitrator to inform anyone concerning the arbitrators' deliberations. After an arbitration award has been made, it is not proper for an arbitrator to assist in post-arbitral proceedings, except as required by law, or as agreed by the parties.

D. In many types of arbitrations is customary for arbitrators to serve without pay. In some types of cases it is customary for arbitrators to receive compensation for services and reimbursement for expenses. Where such payments are to be made, all persons asked to serve, or who serve as arbitrators, shall be governed by the same high standards of integrity and fairness as apply to their other activities in the case. Accordingly, such persons shall scrupulously avoid bargaining with parties over the amount of payments, or engaging in communications concerning payments, which would create an appearance of coercion or other impropriety. Absent provisions in the parties' agreement, in rules to which the parties have agreed, or in applicable law, certain practices relating to payments are generally recognized as preferable to preserve the integrity and fairness of the arbitration process. These practices include:

(1) It is preferable that before the arbitrator finally accepts appointment, the basis of payment be established and that all parties be informed in writing.

(2) In cases conducted under the rules or administration of an institution that is available to assist in making arrangements for payments, payments shall be arranged by the institution to avoid the necessity for arbitrators' communicating directly with parties concerning the subject.

(3) Where no institution is available to assist in making arrangements for payments, it is preferable that any discussions with arbitrators concerning payments take place in the presence of all parties.

(4) In cases where arbitration is court-administered, court rules, orders and practices shall be followed.

[Adopted August 19, 1999, effective October 1, 1999.]

Comment

Excess verbiage has been deleted, and language has been tightened. "Shall" replaces "should" throughout Canon VI, except in Canon VI.D(3), where "should" has been omitted. Canon VI.C has been modified to allow parties to agree to use the arbitrator in other neutral roles, e.g., as a post-award mediator. Although Canon VIII.B generally provides that these Canons state principles paramount to institutional (e.g., the Code) ethics standards, Canon VIII.B states an exception for Canon VI.D(2)'s payment principles. Canon VI.D(4) has been added to take into account, e.g., court-annexed arbitration. See also Academy Code, ¶¶ 2.C, 2.K, 3.A; IBA Ethics, Arts. 6, 9; SPIDR Standards; Responsibilities to the Parties § 3, Disclosure of Fees.

VII. Ethical Considerations Relating to Arbitrators Appointed by One Party

A. Obligations under Canon I. Non-neutral party-appointed arbitrators shall observe Canon I obligations to uphold the integrity and fairness of the arbitration process, subject to these provisions:

(1) Non-neutral arbitrators may be predisposed to the party appointing them but in all other respects are obligated to act in good faith and with integrity and fairness. For example, non-neutral arbitrators shall not engage in delaying tactics or harassment of a party or witness and shall not knowingly make untrue or misleading statements to other arbitrators.

(2) Provisions of Canon I.D relating to relationships and interests do not apply to non-neutral arbitrators.

B. Obligations under Canon II. Non-neutral party-appointed arbitrators shall disclose to all parties, and to other arbitrators, interests and relationships which Canon II requires to be disclosed. Disclosure required by Canon II is for the benefit party appointing the non-neutral arbitrator and for the benefit of other parties and arbitrators so that they may know of bias which may exist or appear to exist. This obligation is subject to these provisions:

(1) Disclosure by non-neutral arbitrators must be sufficient to describe the general nature and scope of any interest or relationship, but need not include as detailed information as is expected from persons appointed as neutral arbitrators.

(2) Non-neutral arbitrators are not obliged to withdraw if asked to do so by a party who did not appoint them, notwithstanding Canon II.E.

C. Obligations under Canon III. Non-neutral party-appointed arbitrators shall observe Canon III's obligations concerning communications with parties, subject to these provisions:

(1) In an arbitration in which two party-appointed arbitrators are expected to appoint the third arbitrator, non-neutral arbitrators may consult with the party who appointed them concerning acceptability of persons under consideration for appointment as the third arbitrator.

(2) Non-neutral arbitrators may communicate with the party who appointed them concerning any other aspect of the case, provided they first inform the other arbitrators and the parties that they intend to do so. If such communication occurred before the person was appointed as arbitrator, or before the first hearing or other meeting of parties with the arbitrators, the non-neutral arbitrator shall, at the first hearing or meeting, disclose that such communication has taken place. In complying with Canon VII. C(2), it is sufficient that there be disclosure that such communication has occurred without disclosing the content of the communication. It is also sufficient to disclose at any time the intention to follow the procedure of having such communications in the future, and there is no requirement thereafter that there be disclosure before each separate occasion when such a communication occurs.

(3) When non-neutral arbitrators communicate in writing with a party that appointed them concerning any matter as to which communication is permitted under these Canons, they are not required to send copies of such writing to other parties or arbitrators.

D. Obligations under Canon IV. Non-neutral party-appointed arbitrators shall observe Canon IV's obligations to conduct proceedings fairly and diligently.

E. Obligations under Canon V. Non-neutral party-appointed arbitrators shall observe Canon V's obligations concerning making decisions, but such arbitrators may be predisposed toward deciding in favor of the party who appointed them.

F. Obligations under Canon VI. Non-neutral party-appointed arbitrators shall observe Canon VI's obligations to be faithful to the relationship of trust inherent in the office of arbitrator, but such arbitrators are not subject to Canon VI.D's provisions with respect to payments by the party appointing them.

[Adopted August 19, 1999, effective October 1, 1999.]

Comment

"Shall" or "must" has been substituted for "should" in Canon VII; See Comment to Canon I. Excess verbiage has been deleted; sentences have been tightened; Canons VII.E and VII.F have been rewritten to convey the same sense as the Code. Nothing in Rule 1,.2(d) conflicts with Canon VII.

VIII. Canons Are Subject to Laws and Professional Responsibility Principles; Choice of Law

A. These Canons are subject to applicable constitutional, statutory, decisional or administrative rules, State or federal, and when these conflict with these Canons, the Canon provision shall be deemed superseded if it is not possible to give effect to the rule and these Canons.

B. These Canons and other ethics or similar rules which may apply to an arbitrator in any other capacity e.g., as a professional, shall be read in pari materia, giving effect to these Canons and the ethics rules if possible. If an arbitrator is subject to other arbitrator ethics rules, e.g., the ABA–AAA Code of Ethics for Arbitrators in Commercial Disputes, and these Canons, these Canons shall govern if there is a conflict of standards; provided however, that the principle of primacy in Canon VIIIB shall not apply to disclosure principles in Canon II.D and payment principles in Canon VI.D(2).

C. These Canons apply to arbitrations in North Carolina, or arbitrations administered by a court in North Carolina, to arbitrations where the parties choose North Carolina law exclusive of conflict of laws principles in the contract or other agreement, or where it is determined that North Carolina law exclusive of conflict of laws principles applies, regardless of where the arbitration is conducted.

[Adopted August 19, 1999, effective October 1, 1999.]

Comment

Canon VIII is not part of the Code. However, given the possibility of conflicting rules of court, professional responsibility rules, legislation or constitutional principles, statement of the obvious in Canon VIII.A–B seems appropriate. Canon VIII.B provides that if an arbitrator is subject to professional or other ethics rules because of that arbitrator's status as, e.g., a lawyer, these Canons and the professional ethics rules shall be read in pari materia, giving effect to both if possible.

Rule 8.5 suggested Canon VIII.C, which is intended to cover court-annexed arbitrations, arbitrations where a court has appointed an arbitrator pursuant to, e.g., the Uniform Act, N.C. Gen. Stat. § 1–567.4, and arbitrations where parties have chosen North Carolina law or where North Carolina law, exclusive of conflict of laws principles, applies. This means that parties and the arbitrator cannot step across a state line and escape these principles.

CODE OF JUDICIAL CONDUCT

Adopted September 26, 1973

Table of Canons

Preamble

An independent and honorable judiciary is indispensable to justice in our society, and to this end and in furtherance thereof, this Code of Judicial Conduct is hereby established. A violation of this Code of Judicial Conduct may be deemed conduct prejudicial to the administration of justice that brings the judicial office into disrepute, or willful misconduct in office, or otherwise as grounds for disciplinary proceedings pursuant to Article 30 of Chapter 7A of the General Statutes of North Carolina. No other code or proposed code of judicial conduct shall be relied upon in the interpretation and application of this Code of Judicial Conduct.

[Adopted effective September 1, 1997. Amended April 2, 2003; amended effective January 31, 2006.]

Canon 1. A Judge Should Uphold the Integrity and Independence of the Judiciary

A judge should participate in establishing, maintaining, and enforcing, and should personally observe, appropriate standards of conduct to ensure that the integrity and independence of the judiciary shall be preserved.

[Amended April 2, 2003. Amended effective January 31, 2006.]

Canon 2. A Judge Should Avoid Impropriety in all the Judge's Activities

A. A judge should respect and comply with the law and should conduct himself/herself at all times in a manner that promotes public confidence in the integrity and impartiality of the judiciary.

B. A judge should not allow the judge's family, social or other relationships to influence the judge's judicial conduct or judgment. The judge should not lend the prestige of the judge's office to advance the private interest of others; nor should the judge convey or permit others to convey the impression that they are in a special position to influence the judge. A judge may, based on personal knowledge, serve as a personal reference or provide a letter of recommendation. A judge should not testify voluntarily as a character witness.

C. A judge should not hold membership in any organization that practices unlawful discrimination on the basis of race, gender, religion or national origin.

[Canon 2B amended effective September 1, 1997; Canon 2C adopted effective September 1, 1997. Amended April 2, 2003; amended effective January 31, 2006.]

Canon 3. A Judge Should Perform the Duties of the Judge's Office Impartially and Diligently

The judicial duties of a judge take precedence over all the judge's other activities. The judge's judicial duties include all the duties of the judge's office prescribed by law. In the performance of these duties, the following standards apply.

A. **Adjudicative responsibilities.**

(1) A judge should be faithful to the law and maintain professional competence in it. A judge should be unswayed by partisan interests, public clamor, or fear of criticism.

(2) A judge should maintain order and decorum in proceedings before the judge.

(3) A judge should be patient, dignified and courteous to litigants, jurors, witnesses, lawyers and others with whom the judge deals in the judge's official capacity, and should require similar conduct of lawyers, and of the judge's staff, court officials and others subject to the judge's direction and control.

(4) A judge should accord to every person who is legally interested in a proceeding, or the person's lawyer, full right to be heard according to law, and, except as authorized by law, neither knowingly initiate nor knowingly consider *ex parte* or other communications concerning a pending proceeding. A judge, however, may obtain the advice of a disinterested expert on the law applicable to a proceeding before the judge.

(5) A judge should dispose promptly of the business of the court.

(6) A judge should abstain from public comment about the merits of a pending proceeding in any state or federal court dealing with a case or controversy arising in North Carolina or addressing North Carolina law and should encourage similar abstention on the part of court personnel subject to the judge's direction and control. This subsection does not prohibit a judge from making public statements in the course of official duties; from explaining for public information the proceedings of the Court; from addressing or discussing previously issued judicial decisions when serving as faculty or otherwise participating in educational courses or programs; or from addressing educational, religious, charitable, fraternal, political, or civic organizations.

(7) A judge should exercise discretion with regard to permitting broadcasting, televising, recording, or taking photographs in the courtroom and areas immediately adjacent thereto during civil or criminal sessions of court or recesses between sessions, pursuant to the provisions of Rule 15 of the General Rules of Practice for the Superior and District Courts.

B. **Administrative responsibilities.**

(1) A judge should diligently discharge the judge's administrative responsibilities, maintain professional competence in judicial administration, and facilitate the performance of the administrative responsibilities of other judges and court officials.

(2) A judge should require the judge's staff and court officials subject to the judge's direction and control to observe the standards of fidelity and diligence that apply to the judge.

(3) A judge should take or initiate appropriate disciplinary measures against a judge or lawyer for unprofessional conduct of which the judge may become aware.

(4) A judge should not make unnecessary appointments. A judge should exercise the judge's power of appointment only on the basis of merit, avoiding nepotism and favoritism. A judge should not approve compensation of appointees beyond the fair value of services rendered.

C. **Disqualification.**

(1) On motion of any party, a judge should disqualify himself/herself in a proceeding in which the judge's impartiality may reasonably be questioned, including but not limited to instances where:

(a) The judge has a personal bias or prejudice concerning a party, or personal knowledge of disputed evidentiary facts concerning the proceedings;

(b) The judge served as lawyer in the matter in controversy, or a lawyer with whom the judge previously practiced law served during such association as a lawyer concerning the matter, or the judge or such lawyer has been a material witness concerning it;

(c) The judge knows that he/she, individually or as a fiduciary, or the judge's spouse or minor child residing in the judge's household, has a financial interest in the subject matter in controversy or in a party to the proceeding, or any other interest that could be substantially affected by the outcome of the proceeding;

(d) The judge or the judge's spouse, or a person within the third degree of relationship to either of them, or the spouse of such a person:

(i) Is a party to the proceeding, or an officer, director, or trustee of a party;

(ii) Is acting as a lawyer in the proceeding;

(iii) Is known by the judge to have an interest that could be substantially affected by the outcome of the proceeding;

(iv) Is to the judge's knowledge likely to be a material witness in the proceeding.

(2) A judge should inform himself/herself about the judge's personal and fiduciary financial interests, and make a reasonable effort to inform himself/herself about the personal financial interests of the judge's spouse and minor children residing in the judge's household.

(3) For the purposes of this section:

(a) The degree of relationship is calculated according to the civil law system;

(b) "Fiduciary" includes such relationships as executor, administrator, trustee and guardian;

(c) "Financial interest" means ownership of a substantial legal or equitable interest (*i.e.*, an interest that would be significantly affected in value by the outcome of the subject legal proceeding), or a relationship as director or other active participant in the affairs of a party, except that:

(i) ownership in a mutual or common investment fund that holds securities is not a "financial interest" in such securities unless the judge participates in the management of the fund;

(ii) an office in an educational, cultural, historical, religious, charitable, fraternal or civic organization is not a "financial interest" in securities held by the organization.

D. Remittal of disqualification.

Nothing in this Canon shall preclude a judge from disqualifying himself/herself from participating in any proceeding upon the judge's own initiative. Also, a judge potentially disqualified by the terms of Canon 3C may, instead of withdrawing from the proceeding, disclose on the record the basis of the judge's potential disqualification. If, based on such disclosure, the parties and lawyers, on behalf of their clients and independently of the judge's participation, all agree in writing that the judge's basis for potential disqualification is immaterial or insubstantial, the judge is no longer disqualified, and may participate in the proceeding. The agreement, signed by all lawyers, shall be incorporated in the record of the proceeding. For purposes of this section, *pro se* parties shall be considered lawyers.

[Canon 3A(7) suspended on an experimental basis effective October 18, 1982; amended effective June 13, 1990; Canon 3A(6) amended effective September 1, 1997. Amended April 3, 2003; amended effective January 31, 2006.]

Canon 4. A Judge may Participate in Cultural or Historical Activities or Engage in Activities Concerning the Legal, Economic, Educational, or Governmental System, or the Administration of Justice

A judge, subject to the proper performance of the judge's judicial duties, may engage in the following quasi-judicial activities, if in doing so the judge does not cast substantial doubt on the judge's capacity to decide impartially any issue that may come before the judge:

A. A judge may speak, write, lecture, teach, participate in cultural or historical activities, or otherwise engage in activities concerning the economic, educational, legal, or governmental system, or the administration of justice.

B. A judge may appear at a public hearing before an executive or legislative body or official with respect to activities permitted under Canon 4A or other provision of this Code, and the judge may otherwise consult with an executive or legislative body or official.

C. A judge may serve as a member, officer or director of an organization or governmental agency concerning the activities described in Canon 4A, and may participate in its management and investment decisions. A judge may not actively assist such an organization in raising funds but may be listed as a contributor on a fund-raising invitation. A judge may make recommendations to public and private fund-granting agencies regarding activities or projects undertaken by such an organization.

[Amended April 2, 2003. Amended effective January 31, 2006.]

Canon 5. A Judge Should Regulate the Judge's Extra-Judicial Activities to Ensure that they Do Not Prevent the Judge from Carrying Out the Judge's Judicial Duties

A. Avocational activities. A judge may write, lecture, teach, and speak on legal or non-legal subjects, and engage in the arts, sports, and other social and recreational activities, if such avocational activities do not substantially interfere with the performance of the judge's judicial duties.

B. Civic and charitable activities. A judge may participate in civic and charitable activities that do not reflect adversely upon the judge's impartiality or interfere with the performance of the judge's judicial duties. A judge may serve as an officer, director, trustee, or non-legal advisor of an educational, religious, charitable, fraternal or civic organization subject to the following limitations.

(1) A judge should not serve if it is likely that the organization will be engaged in proceedings that would ordinarily come before the judge.

(2) A judge may be listed as an officer, director or trustee of any cultural, educational, historical, religious, charitable, fraternal or civic organization. A judge may not actively assist such an organization in raising funds but may be listed as a contributor on a fund-raising invitation.

(3) A judge may serve on the board of directors or board of trustees of such an organization even though the board has the responsibility for approving investment decisions.

C. Financial activities.

(1) A judge should refrain from financial and business dealings that reflect adversely on the judge's impartiality, interfere with the proper performance of the judge's judicial duties, exploit the judge's judicial position or involve the judge in frequent transactions with lawyers or persons likely to come before the court on which the judge serves.

(2) Subject to the requirements of subsection (1), a judge may hold and manage the judge's own personal investments or those of the judge's spouse, children,

or parents, including real estate investments, and may engage in other remunerative activity not otherwise inconsistent with the provisions of this Code but should not serve as an officer, director or manager of any business.

(3) A judge should manage his/her investments and other financial interests to minimize the number of cases in which the judge is disqualified.

(4) Neither a judge nor a member of the judge's family residing in the judge's household should accept a gift from anyone except as follows:

(a) A judge may accept a gift incident to a public testimonial to the judge; books supplied by publishers on a complimentary basis for official or academic use; or an invitation to the judge and the judge's spouse to attend a bar-related function, a cultural or historical activity, or an event related to the economic, educational, legal, or governmental system, or the administration of justice;

(b) A judge or a member of the judge's family residing in the judge's household may accept ordinary social hospitality; a gift, favor or loan from a friend or relative; a wedding, engagement or other special occasion gift; a loan from a lending institution in its regular course of business on the same terms generally available to persons who are not judges; or a scholarship or fellowship awarded on the same terms applied to other applicants;

(c) Other than as permitted under subsection C.(4) (b) of this Canon, a judge or a member of the judge's family residing in the judge's household may accept any other gift only if the donor is not a party presently before the judge and, if its value exceeds $500, the judge reports it in the same manner as the judge reports compensation in Canon 6C.

(5) For the purposes of this section "member of the judge's family residing in the judge's household" means any relative of a judge by blood or marriage, or a person treated by a judge as a member of the judge's family, who resides in the judge's household.

(6) A judge is not required by this Code to disclose his/her income, debts or investments, except as provided in this Canon and Canons 3 and 6.

(7) Information acquired by a judge in the judge's judicial capacity should not be used or disclosed by the judge in financial dealings or for any other purpose not related to the judge's judicial duties.

D. Fiduciary activities. A judge should not serve as the executor, administrator, trustee, guardian or other fiduciary, except for the estate, trust or person of a member of the judge's family, and then only if such service will not interfere with the proper performance of the judge's judicial duties. "Member of the judge's family" includes a spouse, child, grandchild, parent, grandparent or any other relative of the judge by blood or marriage. As a family fiduciary a judge is subject to the following restrictions:

(1) A judge should not serve if it is likely that as a fiduciary the judge will be engaged in proceedings that would ordinarily come before the judge, or if the estate, trust or ward becomes involved in adversarial proceedings in the court on which the judge serves or one under its appellate jurisdiction.

(2) While acting as a fiduciary a judge is subject to the same restrictions on financial activities that apply to the judge in his/her personal capacity.

E. Arbitration. A judge should not act as an arbitrator or mediator. However, an emergency justice or judge of the Appellate Division designated as such pursuant to Article 6 of Chapter 7A of the General Statutes of North Carolina, and an Emergency Judge of the District Court or Superior Court commissioned as such pursuant to Article 8 of Chapter 7A of the General Statutes of North Carolina may serve as an arbitrator or mediator when such service does not conflict with or interfere with the justice's or judge's judicial service in emergency status. A judge of the Appellate Division may participate in any dispute resolution program conducted at the Court of Appeals and authorized by the Supreme Court.

F. Practice of law. A judge should not practice law.

G. Extra–judicial appointments. A judge should not accept appointment to a committee, commission, or other body concerned with issues of fact or policy on matters other than those relating to cultural or historical matters, the economic, educational, legal or governmental system, or the administration of justice. A judge may represent his/her country, state or locality on ceremonial occasions or in connection with historical, educational or cultural activities.

[Canon 5E amended effective March 4, 1992. Amended April 2, 2003; amended effective January 31, 2006.]

Canon 6. A Judge Should Regularly File Reports of Compensation Received for Quasi-Judicial and Extra-Judicial Activities

A judge may receive compensation, honoraria and reimbursement of expenses for the quasi-judicial and extra-judicial activities permitted by this Code, subject to the following restrictions:

A. Compensation and honoraria. Compensation and honoraria should not exceed a reasonable amount.

B. Expense reimbursement. Expense reimbursement should be limited to the actual cost of travel, food and lodging reasonably incurred by the judge and, where appropriate to the occasion, by the judge's spouse. Any payment in excess of such an amount is compensation.

C. Public reports. A judge shall report the name and nature of any source or activity from which the judge received more than $2,000 in income during the calendar year for which the report is filed. Any required report shall be made annually and filed as a public document as follows: The members of the Supreme Court shall file such reports with the Clerk of the Supreme Court; the members of the Court of Appeals shall file such reports with the Clerk of the Court of Appeals; and each Superior Court Judge, regular, special, and emergency, and each District Court Judge, shall file such report with the Clerk of the Superior Court of the county in which the judge resides. For each calendar year, such report shall be filed, absent good cause shown, not later than May 15th of the following year.

[Amended December 30, 1974; Canon 6C amended effective with reports covering calendar year 1983 which are to be filed not later than May 15, 1984. Amended April 2, 2003; amended effective January 31, 2006.]

Canon 7. A Judge may Engage in Political Activity Consistent with the Judge's Status as a Public Official

The provisions of Canon 7 are designed to strike a balance between two important but competing considerations: (1) the need for an impartial and independent judiciary and (2) in light of the continued requirement that judicial candidates run in public elections as mandated by the Constitution and laws of North Carolina, the right of judicial candidates to engage in constitutionally protected political activity. To promote clarity and to avoid potentially unfair application of the provisions of this Code, subsection B of Canon 7 establishes a safe harbor of permissible political conduct.

A. Terminology. For the purposes of this Canon only, the following definitions apply.

(1) A "candidate" is a person actively and publicly seeking election to judicial office. A person becomes a candidate for judicial office as soon as the person makes a public declaration of candidacy, declares or files as a candidate with the appropriate election authority, authorizes solicitation or acceptance of contributions or public support, or sends a letter of intent to the chair of the Judicial Standards Commission. The term "candidate" has the same meaning when applied to a judge seeking election to a non-judicial office.

(2) To "solicit" means to directly, knowingly and intentionally make a request, appeal or announcement, public or private, oral or written, whether in person or through the press, radio, television, telephone, Internet, billboard, or distribution and circulation of printed materials, that expressly requests other persons to contribute, give, loan or pledge any money, goods, labor, services or real property interest to a specific individual's efforts to be elected to public office.

(3) To "endorse" means to knowingly and expressly request, appeal or announce publicly, orally or in writing, whether in person or through the press, radio, television, telephone, Internet, billboard or distribution and circulation of printed materials, that other persons should support a specific individual in that person's efforts to be elected to public office.

B. Permissible political conduct. A judge or a candidate may:

(1) attend, preside over, and speak at any political party gathering, meeting or other convocation, including a fund-raising function for himself/herself, another individual or group of individuals seeking election to office and the judge or candidate may be listed or noted within any publicity relating to such an event, so long as he/she does not expressly endorse a candidate (other than himself/herself) for a specific office or expressly solicit funds from the audience during the event;

(2) if a judge is a candidate, endorse any individual seeking election to any office or conduct a joint campaign with and endorse other individuals seeking election to judicial office, including the solicitation of funds for a joint judicial campaign;

(3) identify himself/herself as a member of a political party and make financial contributions to a political party or organization; provided, however, that he/she may not personally make financial contributions or loans to any individual seeking election to office (other than himself/herself) except as part of a joint judicial campaign as permitted in subsection B(2);

(4) personally solicit campaign funds and request public support from anyone for his/her own campaign or, alternatively, and in addition thereto, authorize or establish committees of responsible persons to secure and manage the solicitation and expenditure of campaign funds;

(5) become a candidate either in a primary or in a general election for a judicial office provided that the judge should resign the judge's judicial office prior to becoming a candidate either in a party primary or in a general election for a non-judicial office;

(6) engage in any other constitutionally protected political activity.

C. Prohibited political conduct. A judge or a candidate should not:

(1) solicit funds on behalf of a political party, organization, or an individual (other than himself/herself) seeking election to office, by specifically asking for such contributions in person, by telephone, by electronic media, or by signing a letter, except as permitted under subsection B of this Canon or otherwise within this Code;

(2) endorse a candidate for public office except as permitted under subsection B of this Canon or otherwise within this Code;

(3) intentionally and knowingly misrepresent his/her identity or qualifications.

D. Political conduct of family members. The spouse or other family member of a judge or a candidate is permitted to engage in political activity.

[Amended March 16, 1976; amended effective September 1, 1997; amended effective February 17, 1998. Amended April 2, 2003; amended effective January 31, 2006.]

Limitation of Proceedings

Disciplinary proceedings to redress alleged violations of Canon 7 of this Code must be commenced within three months of the act or omission allegedly giving rise to the violation. Disciplinary proceedings to redress alleged violations of all other provisions of this Code must be commenced within three years of the act or omission allegedly giving rise to the violation; provided, however, that disciplinary proceedings may be instituted at any time against a judge convicted of a felony during the judge's tenure in judicial office.

[Adopted April 2, 2003. Amended effective January 31, 2006.]

Scope and Effective Date of Compliance

The provisions of Canon 7 of this Code shall apply to judges and candidates for judicial office. The other provisions of this Code shall become effective as to a judge upon the administration of the judge's oath to the office of judge; provided, however, that it shall be permissible for a newly installed judge to facilitate or assist in the transfer of the judge's prior duties as legal counsel but the judge may not be compensated therefor.

[Amended April 2, 2003. Amended effective January 31, 2006.]

RULES OF THE JUDICIAL STANDARDS COMMISSION

Adopted Effective January 1, 2007

Table of Rules

Rule 1. Authority

These rules are promulgated pursuant to the authority contained in N.C. Gen. Stat. § 7A–375(g), and § 97–78.1, and are effective September 1, 2014. The term "judge" shall at all times refer to any member of the General Court of Justice of North Carolina or any commissioner or deputy commissioner of the North Carolina Industrial Commission.

[Amended effective September 1, 2014.]

Rule 2. Organization

(a) The Commission shall have a Chairperson, who is the Court of Appeals member and two Vice–Chairpersons, each of whom shall be a superior court judge. A Vice–Chairperson shall preside in the absence of the Chairperson during Commission recommendation hearings. The Executive Director shall serve as the secretary to the full Commission and to each panel, and shall perform such duties as the full Commission or a panel may assign.

(b) The Chairperson shall divide the Commission into two six (6) member panels, one to be designated Panel A and the other Panel B. Each panel shall include one (1) superior court judge, one (1) district court judge, two (2) members appointed by the North Carolina State Bar, one (1) citizen appointed by the Governor, and one (1) citizen appointed by the General Assembly. Membership on the panels may rotate in a manner determined by the Chairperson of the Commission, provided that no member, other than the Chairperson, shall sit on both the hearing and investigative panel for the same proceeding. The Chairperson of the Commission shall preside over all panel meetings. The two Vice–Chairpersons shall be assigned to different panels and each shall preside over their respective panel meetings in the absence of the Chairperson. No member, other than the Commission Chairperson who shall preside over all disciplinary recommendation hearings, who has served on an investigative panel for a particular inquiry shall serve upon the hearing panel for the same matter. Should both panels of the Commission meet jointly, and the Chairperson not be present, then the Vice–Chairperson with the longest tenure of service on the Commission shall preside.

(c) The full Commission shall meet on the call of the Chairperson or upon the written request of any five (5) members. Each panel of the Commission shall meet every other month, unless prevented by exigent circumstances, such as inclement weather, emergency, or unresolvable conflict with court calendars, alternating such meetings with the other panel, or upon the call of the Chairperson. Hearing panels shall also meet as needed to conduct disciplinary recommendation hearings upon the call of the Chairperson. Each member of the Commission, including the Chairperson, Vice–Chairpersons, or other presiding member shall be a voting member.

(d) A quorum for the conduct of business of the full Commission shall consist of any nine (9) members. A quorum for the conduct of the business of a panel shall consist of five (5) members. A quorum for the conduct of any disciplinary recommendation proceeding instituted pursuant to Rule 12 shall consist of five (5) members of the panel assigned to hear the proceeding. The affirmative vote of five (5) members of a hearing panel is required to make a recommendation to the Supreme Court that a judge be issued a public reprimand, censured, suspended, or removed from office.

(e) The Commission shall ordinarily meet in Raleigh, but may meet anywhere in the State. The Commission's address is P.O. Box 1122, Raleigh, N.C. 27602.

[Amended effective September 1, 2014.]

Rule 3. Executive Director

The Executive Director shall have duties and responsibilities prescribed by the Commission including but not limited to:

(1) Receive and screen complaints and allegations as to misconduct or disability, and make preliminary evaluations with respect thereto;

(2) Maintain the Commission's records;

(3) Maintain statistics concerning the operation of the Commission and make them available to the Commission and to the Supreme Court;

(4) Administer the funds for the Commission's budget, as prepared by the Administrative Office of the Courts;

(5) Employ and supervise other members of the Commission's staff;

(6) Prepare an annual report of the Commission's activities for presentation to the Commission, to the Supreme Court and to the public;

(7) Employ, with the approval of the Chairperson, a special counsel, and an investigator as necessary to investigate and process matters before the Commission and before the Supreme Court.

[Amended effective September 1, 2014.]

Rule 4. Counsel

Commission counsel shall have duties and responsibilities prescribed by the Commission including but not limited to:

(1) Advise the Commission during its investigations and draft decisions, orders, reports and other documents;

(2) Direct investigations involving alleged misconduct or disability;

(3) Direct letters of notice to respondents when directed to do so by the Commission;

(4) Prosecute disciplinary recommendation proceedings before the Commission;

(5) Appear on behalf of the Commission in the Supreme Court in connection with any recommendation made by the Commission;

(6) Perform other duties at the direction of the Executive Director or Commission Chairperson.

[Amended effective September 1, 2014.]

Rule 5. Investigator

The Investigator shall have duties and responsibilities prescribed by the Commission including, but not limited to:

(1) Conduct preliminary investigations;

(2) Conduct formal investigations, upon authorization of the Commission;

(3) Assist Counsel in the preparation and coordination of disciplinary recommendation proceedings initiated pursuant to Rule 12;

(4) Maintain records of the investigations and subsequent proceedings as set forth above;

(5) Perform other duties at the direction of the Executive Director or Commission Chairperson.

[Amended effective September 1, 2014.]

Rule 6. Confidentiality

(a) During Investigative and Initial Disciplinary Recommendation Proceedings.

(1) Except as otherwise provided herein, or unless a written waiver is provided by the subject judge, at all times unless and until the Supreme Court orders any disciplinary action taken, all Commission proceedings including Commission deliberations, investigative files, records, papers and matters submitted to the Commission, shall be held confidential by the Commission, its Executive Director, Counsel, Investigator and staff except as follows:

(A) With the approval of the Commission, the investigative officer may notify respondent that a complaint has been received and may disclose to respondent the name of the person making the complaint.

(B) The Commission may inform a complainant or potential witness of the date when respondent is first notified that a complaint alleging misconduct or incapacity has been filed with the Commission.

(C) When the Commission has determined that there is a need to notify another person or agency in order to protect the public or the administration of justice.

(D) In any case in which a complaint filed with the Commission is made public by the complainant, the judge involved, independent sources, or by rule of law, the Commission may issue such statements of clarification and correction as it deems appropriate in the interest of maintaining confidence in the justice system. Such statements may address the status and procedural aspects of the proceeding, the judge's right to a fair hearing in accordance with due process requirements, and any official action of disposition by the Commission, including release of its written notice to the complainant or the judge of such action or disposition.

(E) In any case in which the Commission initiates a formal investigation that would create a reasonable conflict of interest for the respondent judge if he or she were to proceed in adjudicating a matter involving the complainant, the identity of the complainant may be made known to the respondent judge to facilitate recusal.

(2) The fact that a complaint has been made, or that a statement has been given to the Commission, shall be confidential during the investigation and initial proceeding except as provided in this Rule.

(3) No person providing information to the Commission shall disclose information they have obtained from the Commission concerning the investigation, including the fact that an investigation is being conducted, unless and until the Supreme Court orders any disciplinary action taken against the respondent.

(4) The work product of the Commission members, its Executive Director, Commission Counsel and investigator shall be confidential and shall not be disclosed.

(5) Where a complaint has been made to the State Ethics Commission and the Ethics Commission has forwarded the complaint to the Judicial Standards Commission and, as required by statute, notified the respondent judge of the complaint, the Judicial Standards Commission may, at its discretion, confirm the receipt and disposition of the complaint upon inquiry of the judge so notified.

(b) Commission Deliberations. All deliberations of the Commission in reaching a decision on the statement of charges or a recommendation to the Supreme Court shall be confidential and shall not be disclosed.

(c) General Applicability.

(1) No person shall disclose information obtained from Commission proceedings or papers filed only with the Commission, except information obtained from documents disclosed to the public by the Commission pursuant to this Rule.

(2) Any person violating the confidentiality requirements of this Rule 6 may be subject to punishment for contempt.

(3) A judge shall not intimidate, coerce, or otherwise attempt to induce any person to disclose, conceal or alter records, papers, or information made confidential by the Rule. A violation of this subsection may be charged as a separate violation of the Code of Judicial Conduct.

(4) All written communications from the Commission or its employees to a judge or his or her counsel which are deemed confidential pursuant to these rules shall be enclosed in a securely sealed inner envelope which is clearly marked "Confidential".

(d) After Investigation by the Commission and Findings of Misconduct by the Supreme Court.

(1) If, after an investigation is completed, the Commission concludes that disciplinary proceedings should be instituted, the notice and statement of charges filed by the Commission, along with the answer and all other pleadings, remain confidential. Disciplinary hearings ordered by the Commission are confidential, and recommendations of the Commission to the Supreme Court, along with the record filed in support of such recommendations are confidential. Testimony and other evidence presented to the Commission is privileged in any action for defamation.

(2) Upon issuance of a public reprimand, censure, suspension, or removal by the Supreme Court, the notice and statement of charges filed by the Commission along with the answer and all other pleadings, and recommendations of the Commission to the Supreme Court along with the record filed in support of such recommendations, are no longer confidential.

[Amended effective September 1, 2014.]

Rule 7. Disqualification

A judge who is a member of the Commission is disqualified from acting in any case in which he or she is a respondent, except in his or her own defense.

[Amended effective September 1, 2014.]

Rule 8. Advisory Opinions

(a) A judge may seek an informal advisory opinion as to whether conduct, actual or contemplated, conforms to the requirements of the Code of Judicial Conduct. Such informal advisory opinion may be requested verbally or in writing. The Chairperson, Executive Director, or Counsel may grant or deny a request for an informal advisory opinion. Information contained in a request for an informal advisory opinion shall be confidential, however, when a request for an informal advisory opinion discloses actual conduct which may be actionable as a violation of the Code of Judicial Conduct, the Chairperson, Executive Director, or Counsel shall refer the matter to an investigative panel of the Commission for consideration. The Chairperson, Executive Director, or Counsel may issue an informal advisory opinion to guide the inquiring judge's own prospective conduct if the inquiry is routine, the responsive advice if readily available from the Code of Judicial Conduct and formal Commission opinions, or the inquiry requires immediate response to protect the inquiring judge's right or interest. An informal advisory opinion may be issued verbally, but shall be confirmed in writing and shall approve or disapprove only the matter in issue and shall not otherwise serve as precedent and shall not be published. An inquiry requesting an opinion concerning past conduct or that presents a matter of first impression shall be referred to the Commission for formal opinion. Such informal advisory opinions shall be reviewed periodically by the Commission and, if upon such review, a majority of the Commission present and voting decided that such informal advisory opinion should be withdrawn or modified, the inquiring judge shall be notified in writing by the Executive Director. Until such notification, the judge shall be deemed to have acted in good faith if he or she acts in conformity with the informal advisory opinion which is later withdrawn or modified. If an inquiring judge disagrees with the informal advisory opinion issued by the Chairperson, Executive Director, or Counsel, such judge may submit a written request, in accordance with subsection (b), for consideration of the inquiry by the Commission at its next regularly scheduled meeting.

(b) Any person may request that the Commission issue a formal opinion as to whether actual or contemplated conduct on the part of a judge conforms to the requirements of the Code of Judicial Conduct. Such requests for formal opinions shall be submitted to the Executive Director. Information contained in a request for a formal opinion shall not be confidential. The Commission shall determine whether to issue a formal opinion in response to such request; if the Commission determines to issue a formal opinion, it shall prepare a formal written opinion which shall state its conclusion with respect to the question asked and the reason therefor. Such formal opinions shall be provided to interested parties in the manner deemed appropriate by the Chairperson and a copy shall be provided the Appellate Reporter for publication and such Reporter shall, from time to time as directed by the Commission, publish an index of advisory opinions. Formal advisory opinions shall have precedential value in determining whether similar conduct conforms to the Code of Judicial Conduct, but shall not constitute controlling legal authority for the purposes of review of a disciplinary recommendation by a reviewing court. A formal opinion may be reconsidered or withdrawn by the Commission in the same manner in which it was issued. Until a formal advisory opinion is modified or withdrawn by the Commission or overturned by a reviewing court, a judge shall be deemed to have acted in good faith if he or she acts in conformity therewith.

(c) All inquiries, whether requesting a formal opinion or an informal advisory opinion, shall present in detail all operative facts upon which the inquiry is based, but should not disclose privileged or sensitive information which is not necessary to the resolution of the question presented.

[Amended effective September 1, 2014.]

Rule 9. Procedure Upon Receipt of Complaint or Information

(a) The Executive Director and Commission Counsel shall review each complaint or information received by the Commission to determine whether the complaint or information, if true, discloses facts indicating that a judge has engaged in conduct which is in violation of the Code of Judicial Conduct, has engaged in willful misconduct in office, has willfully and persistently failed to perform the duties of his or her judicial office, has engaged in conduct prejudicial to the administration of justice that brings the judicial office into disrepute, or is habitually intemperate, or alleging that a judge is suffering from a mental or physical incapacity interfering with the performance of his duties, which incapacity is, or is likely to become, permanent.

(1) If such initial review discloses no such facts so that the complaint is obviously unfounded or frivolous, the Executive Director shall notify the Chairperson who, if he or she agrees, may dismiss the complaint. The Chairperson shall inform the investigative panel of any such dismissal at the panel's next meeting and, upon the request of any member, such determination may be reconsidered; otherwise the dismissal of the complaint shall be final and the complainant shall be notified.

(2) If such initial review discloses no such facts so that the complaint is obviously unfounded and frivolous, and the complaint substantially conforms to an abuse of the complaint process, the Executive Director shall notify the Chairperson, who, if he or she agrees, may dismiss the complaint and recommend that the complainant be barred from further complaints to the Commission. The Chairperson shall inform the investigative panel of any such dismissal and recommended bar at the panel's next meeting and, upon the request of any member, such dismissal may be reconsidered. Provided, a recommended bar of further complaints by the complainant shall be ordered only upon the affirmative finding of the panel, by clear and convincing evidence, that the complainant has abused the complaint process by one or more of the following:

(A) Abusive or threatening language directed toward the staff, Commission, or judiciary;

(B) Knowingly filing false information with the Commission;

(C) Repeated demands to rehear a complaint already reviewed and dismissed with no new or significantly different allegations or evidence, or repeated demands to rehear a complaint already determined to be outside of the time period allowed for review of alleged misconduct by the Commission;

(D) Complaints which maintain that the complainant is not subject to the authority of the State of North Carolina, its laws, rules, or procedures and refuse to recognize the authority of the General Statutes of North Carolina over the Commission's operations and procedures;

(b) If a complaint or information is not dismissed as frivolous or unfounded, the Executive Director and Investigator shall conduct such preliminary review as may be necessary to apprise the investigative panel of the nature thereof, and such panel shall review the complaint or information at the next meeting occurring after the complaint or information is received.

(c) If the investigative panel, by the affirmative vote of not less than five (5) members, determines that the complaint alleges, or information discloses, facts indicating that a judge has engaged in conduct which is in violation of the Code of Judicial Conduct, has engaged in willful misconduct in office, has willfully and persistently failed to perform the duties of his or her judicial office, has engaged in conduct prejudicial to the administration of justice that brings the judicial office into disrepute, or is habitually intemperate, or alleging that a judge is suffering from a mental or physical incapacity interfering with the performance of his duties, which incapacity is, or is likely to become, permanent, such panel shall order a formal investigation to determine whether disciplinary proceedings or health-related retirement should be recommended.

(d) The judge shall be notified of the formal investigation, the nature of the allegations which the Commission is investigating, and whether the formal investigation is on the Commission's own motion or upon written complaint. The notice shall afford the judge a reasonable opportunity to present such relevant information as he or she may deem advisable. Such notice shall be in writing and may be personally delivered by the Chairperson, Executive Director, Commission Counsel, or Investigator, or it may be delivered by certified mail, return receipt requested.

(e) If, upon ordering a formal investigation in accordance with subparagraph (d) above, the investigative panel determines that immediate suspension of the judge is required for the proper administration of justice, it may recommend to the Chief Justice that such judge be temporarily suspended from the performance of his or her judicial duties pending final disposition of the inquiry. A copy of such recommendation shall be provided the judge by certified mail, return receipt requested.

[Amended effective September 1, 2014.]

Rule 10. Record of Proceedings

The Commission shall keep a record of all formal investigations and disciplinary recommendation proceedings concerning a judge. In disciplinary recommendation hearings, testimony shall be recorded verbatim by a court reporter and by video recording and, if the Commission recommends to the Supreme Court that the judge be disciplined, a transcript of the evidence and all proceedings therein shall be prepared, including a video recording of the testimony of all witnesses who testify at the disciplinary recommendation hearing, and made a part of the record.

[Amended effective September 1, 2014.]

Rule 11. Letter of Caution

If the inquiry discloses conduct by a judge which requires attention but is not of such a nature as to warrant a recommendation by Commission that the judge be disciplined by the Supreme Court, the investigative panel may issue a letter of caution to the judge. No letter of caution may be issued after a disciplinary recommendation proceeding has been initiated pursuant to Rule 12.

[Amended effective September 1, 2014.]

Rule 12. Initiation of Disciplinary Recommendation Proceedings

If, after completion of the formal investigation, the investigative panel determines, by the affirmative vote of not less than five (5) members, that probable cause exists that a judge has:

(a) violated the Code of Judicial Conduct and engaged in conduct prejudicial to the administration of justice and that such conduct, if proven, would warrant a recommendation by the Commission that the judge receive a public reprimand by the Supreme Court, that may require that the judge follow a corrective course of action or, be disciplined by the Supreme Court; or

(b) that a judge is temporarily incapacitated or is suffering from an incapacity which is, or is likely to become, permanent; then,

the Commission shall initiate disciplinary recommendation proceedings by the filing, at the Commission offices, a Statement of Charges alleging the charge or charges. The Statement of Charges shall identify the complainant and state the charge or charges in plain and concise language and in sufficient detail to give fair and adequate notice of the nature of the alleged conduct or incapacity. The Statement of Charges shall be entitled "BEFORE THE JUDICIAL STANDARDS COMMISSION, Inquiry Concerning a Judge No. ___." A copy of the Statement of Charges shall be personally served upon the respondent judge by the Chairperson, the Executive Director, the Commission's Investigator, or by some person of suitable age and discretion designated by the Commission. If, after reasonable efforts to do so, personal service upon the respondent judge cannot be effected, service may be made by registered or certified mail with a delivery receipt, and proof of service in accordance with N.C. Gen. Stat. § 1–75.10(4) shall be filed with the Commission. Service of a copy of the Statement of Charges shall constitute notice to the respondent judge of the initiation of disciplinary recommendation proceedings.

[Amended effective September 1, 2014.]

Rule 13. Answer

Unless the time is extended by order of the Commission, the respondent judge shall file at the Commission offices, within twenty (20) days after service of the Statement of Charges, a written original and 10 copies of an Answer, which shall be verified. The Statement of Charges and Answer shall constitute the pleadings. No further pleadings may be filed, and no motions may be filed against any of the pleadings. The assertion of a mental or physical condition as a defense by the respondent judge shall constitute a waiver of medical privilege for the purpose of the Commission proceeding.

Failure to answer the Statement of Charges shall constitute an admission of the factual allegations contained in the Statement of Charges.

[Amended effective September 1, 2014.]

Rule 14. Ex Parte Contacts

After the filing of a Statement of Charges and disciplinary recommendation proceedings by the Commission, members of the Commission shall not engage in *ex parte* communications regarding the matter with the respondent judge, counsel for the respondent judge, Commission counsel, or any witness, except that Commission members may communicate with Commission staff and others with respect to procedural and administrative matters as may be required to perform their duties in accordance with these rules.

[Amended effective September 1, 2014.]

Rule 15. Discovery

(a) Upon written demand after the time for filing an Answer has expired, Commission Counsel and respondent judge will each disclose to the other, within 20 days after such demand, the following:

(1) the name and address of each witness the party expects to offer at the disciplinary recommendation hearing;

(2) a brief summary of the expected testimony of each witness;

(3) copies of any written statement and a transcript of any electronically recorded statement made by any person the party anticipates calling as a witness;

(4) copies of documentary evidence which may be offered;

(b) Failure to disclose the name of any witness, or to provide any material required to be disclosed by section (a) may result in the exclusion of the testimony of such witness or the documentary evidence which was not provided.

(c) Commission Counsel shall provide the respondent judge with any exculpatory evidence of which he or she is aware and which is relevant to the allegations of the complaint.

(d) Both Commission Counsel and respondent judge shall have a continuing duty to supplement information required to be exchanged under this rule.

(e) The taking of depositions, serving of requests for admission, and other discovery procedures authorized by the Rules of Civil Procedure, shall be permitted only by stipulation of the parties or by order of the Commission Chairperson for good cause shown, and in such manner and upon such conditions as the Chairperson may prescribe.

(f) Disputes concerning discovery shall be determined by the Chairperson, whose decision may not be appealed prior to the conclusion of the disciplinary recommendation hearing and the entry of a recommendation for discipline or other final order by the Commission.

(g) Unless the time is extended by order of the Commission, all discovery shall be completed within 60 days of the filing of the answer.

[Amended effective September 1, 2014.]

Rule 16. Amendments to Notice or Answer

At any time prior to the conclusion of the disciplinary recommendation hearing, the hearing panel may allow or require amendments to the Statement of Charges or to the Answer. The Statement of Charges may be amended to conform to the proof or to set forth additional facts, whether occurring before or after the commencement of the disciplinary recommendation hearing. In the event of an amendment setting forth additional facts, the respondent judge shall be given a reasonable time to answer the amendment and to prepare and present his or her defense to the matters charged thereby.

[Amended effective September 1, 2014.]

Rule 17. Disciplinary Recommendation Hearing

Upon the filing of an Answer, or upon the expiration of the time allowed for its filing, the hearing panel shall order a disciplinary recommendation hearing before it upon the charges contained in the Statement of Charges. The disciplinary recommendation hearing shall be held no sooner than 60 days after filing of the Answer or, if no Answer is filed, 60 days after the expiration of time allowed for its filing, unless the judge consents to an earlier disciplinary recommendation hearing. The Commission shall serve a notice of the disciplinary recommendation hearing upon the respondent judge in the same manner as service of the Statement of Charges under Rule 12.

Upon the date set for the disciplinary recommendation hearing, such disciplinary recommendation hearing shall proceed whether or not the respondent judge has filed an Answer, and whether or not he or she appears in person or through counsel. At least six members, or alternates, shall be present continually during the presentation of evidence at the disciplinary recommendation hearing.

Commission Counsel, or other counsel appointed by the Commission for that purpose, shall present evidence in support of the charges alleged in the Statement of Charges. Commission counsel may call the respondent judge as a witness.

The disciplinary recommendation hearing shall be recorded verbatim in accordance with the provisions of Rule 10.

[Amended effective September 1, 2014.]

Rule 18. Rights of Respondent; Burden of Proof

The respondent judge shall have the right to representation by counsel and the opportunity to defend against the charges by the introduction of evidence, examination and cross-examination of witnesses and to address the hearing panel in argument at the conclusion of the disciplinary recommendation hearing. The respondent judge shall also have the right to the issuance of subpoenas to compel the attendance of witnesses or the production of documents and other evidentiary material.

Upon the entry of an appearance by counsel for the respondent judge, a copy of any notices, pleadings, or other written communications sent to the respondent judge shall be furnished to such counsel by the Executive Director.

Commission Counsel shall have the burden of proving the existence of grounds for a recommendation of discipline by clear, cogent and convincing evidence, as that term is defined by the Supreme Court.

[Amended effective September 1, 2014.]

Rule 19. Witnesses; Oaths; Subpoenas

The respondent judge and the Commission shall have the right to call witnesses to testify to the character of the respondent and any genuine dispute of material facts between the parties in the disciplinary recommendation hearing. Neither the respondent judge nor the Commission shall call more than four character witnesses in such a proceeding. Additional character witnesses may submit affidavits or be identified and tendered for the record. Neither the respondent judge nor the Commission shall be limited in the number of witnesses called to testify to material facts in a disciplinary recommendation hearing.

Every witness who testifies before the hearing panel at a disciplinary recommendation hearing shall be required to declare, by oath or affirmation, to testify truthfully. The oath or affirmation may be administered by any member of the Commission. A subpoena to compel the attendance of a witness at a disciplinary recommendation hearing before the Commission, or a subpoena for the production of documentary evidence, shall be issued in the name of the State upon request of any party, and shall be signed by a member of the Commission, by the Executive Director, or by Commission Counsel. A subpoena shall be served, without fee, by any officer authorized to serve a subpoena pursuant to the provisions of N.C. Gen. Stat. § 1A–1, Rule 45(b).

Witnesses shall be reimbursed in the manner provided in civil cases in the General Court of Justice, and their expenses shall be borne by the party calling them unless, when mental or physical disability of the judge is in issue, in which case the Commission shall bear the reasonable expenses of the witnesses whose testimony is related to the disability. Vouchers authorizing disbursements by the Commission for witnesses shall be signed by the Chairperson or Executive Director.

[Amended effective September 1, 2014.]

Rule 20. Rules of Evidence

Except as otherwise provided in these rules, the Rules of Evidence as set forth in Chapter 8C of the North Carolina General Statutes shall apply in all disciplinary recommendation hearings under these rules. Rulings on evidentiary matters shall be made by the Chairperson, or by member presiding in the absence of the Chairperson.

[Amended effective September 1, 2014.]

Rule 21. Medical Examination

When the mental or physical condition or health of the respondent judge is in issue, a denial of the alleged condition shall constitute a waiver of medical privilege for the purpose of the Commission proceeding, and the respondent judge shall be required to produce, upon request of Commission Counsel, his or her medical records relating to such condition. The respondent judge shall also be deemed to have consented to a physical or mental examination by a qualified licensed physician or physicians designated by the Commission. A copy of the report of such examination shall be provided to the respondent judge and to the Commission. The examining physician or physicians shall receive the fee of an expert witness, to be set by the Commission.

[Amended effective September 1, 2014.]

Rule 22. Stipulations

At any time prior to the conclusion of a disciplinary recommendation hearing, the respondent judge may stipulate to any or all of the allegations of the Statement of Charges in exchange for a stated disposition, which may include a stated recommendation to the Supreme Court for discipline. The stipulation shall be in writing and shall set forth all material facts relating to the proceeding and the conduct of respondent. The stipulation shall be signed by the respondent judge, his or her counsel, and by Commission Counsel. The stipulation shall be submitted to the hearing panel, which shall either approve the stipulation or reject it. If the stipulation provides for a stated recommendation for discipline, it must be approved by the affirmative vote of not less than five members of the hearing panel. If the stipulation is rejected by the hearing panel, it shall be deemed withdrawn and will not be considered in any proceedings before, or deliberations of, the hearing panel. If the hearing panel approves the stipulation, it shall prepare a written recommendation to the Supreme Court consistent therewith and transmit such recommendation in accordance with the provisions of Rules 24 and 25.

[Amended effective September 1, 2014.]

Rule 23. Contempt Powers

The Commission has the same power as a trial court of the General Court of Justice to punish for contempt, or for refusal to obey lawful orders or process of the Commission. See N.C. Gen. Stat. § 7A-377(d).

[Amended effective September 1, 2014.]

Rule 24. Procedure Following Disciplinary Recommendation Hearing

At the conclusion of the disciplinary recommendation hearing, the hearing panel shall deliberate and determine whether to dismiss the proceeding or to file a recommendation with the Supreme Court. In all cases, the Executive Director shall notify the respondent judge in writing of the decision of the hearing panel within 60 days after the conclusion of the disciplinary recommendation hearing, unless the time is extended by order of the Chairperson.

At least five members of the Commission must concur in any recommendation to issue a public reprimand, censure, suspend, or remove any judge. If the hearing panel reaches a decision to recommend the public reprimand, censure, suspension or removal of a judge, the Executive Director shall prepare a proposed record of the proceedings and a written decision setting forth the hearing panel's findings of fact, conclusions of law, and recommendation. The proposed record of the proceeding shall include a verbatim transcript of the disciplinary recommendation hearing as well as a copy of the video recording of such disciplinary recommendation hearing. Such proposed record and decision shall be served upon the respondent judge and his or her counsel, if any, in the same manner as service of the complaint under Rule 12.

[Amended effective September 1, 2014.]

Rule 25. Transmittal of Record to the Supreme Court

A respondent who is recommended for public reprimand, censure, suspension, or removal is entitled to a copy of the proposed record to be filed with the Supreme Court, and if the respondent has objections to it, to have the record settled by the Commission's chair. Unless the respondent judge files objections to the proposed record, or a proposed alternative record, within 10 days after the proposed record and the recommendation of the hearing panel have been served upon him or her, the proposed record shall constitute the official record. If the respondent judge files objections or a proposed alternative record, the Commission Chairperson shall send written notice to Commission Counsel and to the respondent judge and his or her counsel, setting a time and place for a hearing to settle the record, and the record as settled by the Commission Chairperson shall be the official record.

Within 10 days after the official record has been settled, the Executive Director shall certify the record and decision of the Commission and file it with the Clerk of the Supreme Court. The Executive Director shall concurrently serve upon the respondent judge, in the same manner as service of the complaint under Rule 12, a notice of the filing of such record and decision, specifying the date upon which it was filed in the Supreme Court. The Executive Director shall also transmit to the respondent judge copies of any changes to the official record occurring as a result of the settlement of the record.

[Amended effective September 1, 2014.]

Rule 26. Proceedings in the Supreme Court

The respondent is entitled to present a brief and to argue the respondent's case, in person and through counsel, to the Supreme Court. Proceedings in the Supreme Court shall be as prescribed by Supreme Court Rule. See N.C. Gen. Stat. § 7A-33 and The Rules for Review of Recommendations of the Judicial Standards Commission.

[Amended effective September 1, 2014.]

RULES FOR SUPREME COURT REVIEW OF RECOMMENDATIONS OF THE JUDICIAL STANDARDS COMMISSION

Adopted September 25, 1975

Table of Rules

Rule 1. Definitions

In these rules, unless the context or subject matter otherwise requires:

(a) Commission means the Judicial Standards Commission.

(b) Judge or respondent means a justice or judge of the General Court of Justice who has been recommended for censure or removal under N.C.Gen.Stat. ch. 7A, art. 30 (1974 Supp.).

(c) Court means the Supreme Court of North Carolina. Clerk means the Clerk of the Supreme Court.

(d) Commission's attorney means the attorney who represented the Commission at the hearing which resulted in the recommendation under consideration by the Court.

(e) The masculine gender includes the feminine gender.

(f) Service of a document required to be served means either mailing the document by U.S. certified mail, return receipt requested, to the person to be served or service in the manner provided in Rule 4 of the N.C. Rules of Civil Procedure.

Rule 2. Petition for Hearing

(a) Notice to Judge. When the Commission, pursuant to its Rule 19, files with the Clerk a recommendation that a judge be censured or removed, the Clerk shall immediately transmit a copy of the recommendation by U.S. certified mail, return receipt requested, to the respondent named therein.

(b) Petition for Hearing. The respondent may petition the Court for a hearing upon the Commission's recommendation. The petition shall be signed by the judge or his counsel of record and specify the grounds upon which it is based. It must be filed with the Clerk within 10 days from the date shown on the return receipt as the time the respondent received the copy of the recommendation from the Clerk. At the time the petition is filed it shall be accompanied by a certificate showing service of a copy of the petition upon the Commission's attorney and its chairman or secretary. Upon the filing of his petition, the respondent becomes entitled under G.S. 7A–377 to file a brief and, upon filing a brief, to argue his case to the Court, in person and through counsel.

(c) Failure to File Petition. If a respondent fails to file a petition for hearing within the time prescribed, the Court will proceed to consider and act upon the recommendation on the record filed by the Commission. Failure to file a petition waives the right to file a brief and to be heard on oral argument.

(d) Briefs. Within 15 days after filing his petition, the respondent may file his brief with the Clerk. At the time the brief is filed the respondent shall also file a certificate showing service of a copy of the brief upon the Commission's attorney and its chairman or secretary. Within 15 days after the service of such brief upon him, the Commission's attorney may file a reply brief, together with a certificate of service upon the respondent and his attorney of record. The form and content of briefs shall be similar to briefs in appeals to the Court.

(e) Oral Argument. After the briefs are filed, and as soon as may be, the Court will set the case for argument on a day certain and notify the parties. Oral arguments shall conform as nearly as possible to the rules applicable to arguments on appeals to the

Court. A judge who has filed a brief may, if he desires, waive the oral argument. A judge who has filed a petition but who has not filed a brief will not be heard upon oral argument.

Rule 3. Decision by the Court

After considering the record, and the briefs and oral arguments if any, the Court will act upon the Commission's recommendation as required by G.S. 7A–377. The decision on a recommendation for removal shall be by a written opinion filed and published as any other opinion of the Court. Decision on a recommendation for censure shall be by a written order filed with the Clerk and published in the Advance Sheets and bound volumes of the Supreme Court Reports. (Amended April 14, 1976.)

Rule 4. Reproduction of Record and Briefs

As soon as the Commission files with the Clerk a recommendation of censure or removal and the transcript of the proceedings on which it is based, the Clerk will reproduce and distribute copies of the record as directed by the Court. When briefs are filed, one copy will suffice. The Clerk will also reproduce and distribute copies of the briefs as directed by the Court.

Rule 5. Costs

If the Court dismisses the Commission's recommendation the costs of the proceeding will be paid by the State; otherwise, by the judge. Reproduction and other costs in this Court will be taxed as in appeals to the Court, except there will be no filing fee.

RULES OF CONTINUING JUDICIAL EDUCATION

Adopted October 24, 1988

Table of Rules

Rule I. Coverage

These rules are applicable only to North Carolina District Court, Superior Court, and Court of Appeals Judges and to the Chief Justice and Associate Justices of the Supreme Court of North Carolina, including retired judges and justices qualified as emergency or recalled judges or justices.

Upon leaving judicial service, a judge or justice shall be bound by the rules of the Supreme Court of North Carolina for continuing legal education of members of the Bar.

Continuing legal education hours earned prior to entering judicial service and judicial education hours earned prior to leaving judicial service shall be recognized and accepted on a pro rata basis by the appropriate accrediting and reporting agency.

Rule II. Requirements

A. Every judge in the trial division shall, within the first year after appointment or election, attend a course of instruction or orientation for new judges provided by the Administrative Office of the Courts. Attendance will be counted as a part of the hours of instruction required for the biennium in which the instruction is received.

B. Each judge and justice of the trial and appellate division shall attend at least thirty (30) hours of instruction in one or more approved continuing legal or judicial education programs in each biennium, effective with the biennium beginning 1 July 1989 and ending 30 June 1991.

C. At least fifteen (15) of the thirty (30) hours required shall be continuing judicial education courses designed especially for judges and attended exclusively or primarily by judges. All Superior Court Judges are expected to attend the scheduled Superior Court Judges Conferences and the programs there presented. All District Court Judges are expected to attend the scheduled District Court Judges Conferences and the programs there presented.

For District Court Judges designated as Family Court Judges, at least twenty-four (24) of the thirty (30) hours shall be continuing judicial education courses designed especially for Family Court.

D. Judges participating as teachers, lecturers, discussion leaders, or panelists in an approved continuing judicial or legal education program shall receive five hours credit for each hour of actual presentation time. Presentation of the same material on subsequent occasions shall accrue credit for the actual time of presentation only.

E. Continuing judicial education hours shall be computed by the following formula:

$$\frac{\text{Sum of the Total Minutes of Actual Instruction}}{60} = \text{Total Hours}$$

The instruction may be in no less than fifteen (15) minute segments. Only actual instruction shall be included in computing the total hours of instruction. The following shall not be included: introductory remarks, breaks, business meetings, keynote speeches, and speeches in connection with meals.

Except as otherwise provided in this subsection E and the preceding subsection D, computation for credit of continuing legal education courses shall be computed in accordance with Regulation 5 of the Board of Continuing Legal Education of the North Carolina State Bar.

[Amended effective August 15, 2002. Amended effective Feb. 5, 2004.]

Rule III. Accredited Sponsors

A. Continuing legal education programs offered by the Conference of Superior Court Judges or the Conference of District Court Judges or others offered to judges by the Administrative Office of the Courts or the Institute of Government of the University of North Carolina at Chapel Hill are approved for credit as continuing judicial education under these rules.

B. All continuing legal education programs approved by the Board of Continuing Legal Education of the North Carolina State Bar are approved for credit as continuing legal education under these rules.

C. Programs offered for judges by any law school accredited by the American Bar Association and the following national providers of judicial education are approved for credit as continuing judicial education under these rules:

1. National Judicial College
2. American Academy of Judicial Education
3. National Council of Juvenile and Family Court Judges
4. American Bar Association
5. Institute for Court Management of the National Center for State Courts
6. Institute of Judicial Administration
7. National Institute of Justice
8. American Judges Association

D. Postgraduate law degree programs conducted by a law school accredited by the American Bar Association.

E. Any program not approved under A, B, C, or D above may be approved by the Chief Justice upon application by a judge who has attended or desires to attend the program. To be approved, a program must meet the following standards:

1. It must be an organized program of learning which contributes directly to the professional competency of a judge.

2. It must deal primarily with matters directly related to law or related fields or to the professional responsibility, administrative duties, or ethical obligations of a judge.

3. Instructors in the program must be qualified by practical or academic experience to teach in the topic or area of discipline covered by the course.

4. Thorough, high quality, written topic materials and/or outlines must be distributed to judges attending the program.

Rule IV. Reporting

A. The Administrative Office of the Courts is designated as the office in which all records, reports, and documents pertaining to continuing judicial education shall be filed and compiled.

B. Each judge must report in writing to the Administrative Office of the Courts, no later than July 31 following the end of each year of an educational biennium, the continuing education programs he has attended. Reports may be made sooner after attendance, and the Administrative Office of the Courts will maintain a cumulative record of such reports for the submitting judges. One year after the beginning of each educational biennium, the Administrative Office of the Courts shall notify all judges and justices subject to these rules that reports are required and that they are due by the following July 31. If a program is other than a continuing judicial education program offered by the Conference of Superior Court Judges, the Conference of District Court Judges, or the Administrative Office of the Courts or the Institute of Government, the judge must attach a copy of the program brochure or other material which outlines the program presentation and identifies the instructors, unless the program is certified as having previously received approval of the Chief Justice, pursuant to Section III.E. Forms for the report will be provided by the Administrative Office of the Courts.

C. As soon as practical after August 1 of the second year of each educational biennium, the Administrative Office of the Courts shall notify any judge or justice in writing of his or her delinquency. Any such delinquent judge or justice shall have sixty (60) days within which to comply with the requirements of these rules and notify the Administrative Office of the Courts of his or her compliance.

D. The Director of the Administrative Office of the Courts shall report to the Chief Justice the name of any judge or justice who does not meet the continuing judicial education requirements specified in these rules or who has not filed a timely report of his or her continuing judicial education activities, and the Chief Justice shall make such inquiry or investigation and take such action as he deems appropriate.

Rule V. Exemptions

The Chief Justice of the Supreme Court shall have the authority to relieve any judge or justice of the requirement of meeting the minimum hours required by these rules for undue hardship by reason of disability or other cause.

Rule VI. Expenses

The Administrative Office of the Courts shall fund the regular judicial conferences of the Judges of the Superior and District Court divisions and shall ensure that a sufficient number of hours of instructional material are provided to permit the judges of the trial division regularly attending the conferences to satisfy the requirements of this Order and shall provide reimbursement for expenses incurred in attending the conferences in accordance with its regular policies and practices.

For Judges and Justices of the Appellate Division, the Administrative Office of the Courts shall ensure the availability of a sufficient number of hours of instruction to satisfy the requirements of the Order either by providing and funding Appellate Court conferences or providing funding for alternative methods of satisfying such requirements in accordance with its regular policies and practices.

Judges and Justices attending continuing judicial education programs other than those presented at judicial conferences shall be reimbursed for their expenses in accordance with policies and practices established by the Administrative Office of the Courts, subject to the availability of funds.

Priority in allocation of funds by the Administrative Office of the Courts will be given to the regular judicial conferences of the Superior Court and District Court divisions and to other continuing judicial education programs sponsored or co-sponsored by the Administrative Office of the Courts.

NORTH CAROLINA STATE BAR RULES

Adopted December 8, 1994

Table of Sections

CHAPTER 1. RULES AND REGULATIONS OF THE NORTH CAROLINA STATE BAR

SUBCHAPTER A. ORGANIZATION OF THE NORTH CAROLINA STATE BAR

SECTION .0100 FUNCTIONS

.0101 Purpose

The North Carolina State Bar shall foster the following purposes, namely:

(1) to cultivate and advance the science of jurisprudence;

(2) to promote reform in the law and in judicial procedure;

(3) to facilitate the administration of justice;

(4) to uphold and elevate the standards of honor, integrity and courtesy in the legal profession;

(5) to encourage higher and better education for membership in the profession;

(6) to promote a spirit of cordiality and unity among the members of the Bar;

(7) to perform all duties imposed by law.

[History Note: Statutory Authority G.S. 84–23. Readopted effective December 8, 1994.]

.0102 Division of Work

(a) To facilitate the work for the accomplishment of the above enumerated purposes, the council may, from time to time, classify such work under appropriate sections and committees, either standing or special, of the North Carolina State Bar.

(b) The council shall determine the number of members, composition, method of appointment or election, functions, powers and duties, structure, authority to act, and other matters relating to each committee.

(c) Any committee may, at the discretion of the appointing or electing authority, be composed of council members or members of the North Carolina State Bar who are not members of the council or of lay persons or of any combination.

[History Note: Statutory Authority G.S. 84–22; G.S. 84–23. Readopted effective December 8, 1994.]

.0103 Cooperation With Local Bar Association Committees

The sections and committees so appointed may secure the cooperation of like sections and committees of the North Carolina Bar Association and all local bar associations of the state.

[History Note: Statutory Authority G.S. 84–23. Readopted effective December 8, 1994.]

.0104 Organization of Local Bar Associations

The council shall encourage and foster the organization of local bar associations.

[History Note: Statutory Authority G.S. 84–23. Readopted effective December 8, 1994.]

.0105 Annual Program

The council shall provide a suitable program for each annual meeting of the North Carolina State Bar.

[History Note: Statutory Authority G.S. 84–23. Readopted effective December 8, 1994.]

.0106 Reports Made to Annual Meeting

The annual reports of the several committees and boards shall be delivered to the secretary of the North Carolina State Bar before the annual meeting.

[History Note: Statutory Authority G.S. 84–23. Readopted effective December 8, 1994; amended December 10, 1999, effective February 3, 2000.]

SECTION .0200 MEMBERSHIP—ANNUAL MEMBERSHIP FEES

.0201 Classes of Membership

(a) Two Classes of Membership. Members of the North Carolina State Bar shall be divided into two classes: active members and inactive members.

(b) Active Member. The active members shall be all persons who have obtained licenses entitling them to practice law in North Carolina, including persons serving as justices or judges of any state or federal court in this state, unless classified as inactive members by the council. All active members must pay the annual membership fee.

(c) Inactive Members.

(1) The inactive members shall include:

(A) all persons who have been admitted to the practice of law in North Carolina but who the council has found are not engaged in the practice of law or holding themselves out as practicing attorneys and who do not occupy any public or private position in which they may be called upon to give legal advice or counsel or to examine the law or to pass upon the legal effect of any act, document, or law, and

(B) those persons granted emeritus pro bono status by the council and allowed to represent indigent clients on a pro bono basis under the supervision of active members working for nonprofit corporations organized pursuant to Chapter 55A of the General Statutes of North Carolina for the sole purpose of rendering legal services to indigents.

(2) Inactive members of the North Carolina State Bar may not practice law, except as provided in this rule for persons granted emeritus pro bono status, and are exempt from payment of membership dues during the period in which they are inactive members. For purposes of the State Bar's membership records, the category of inactive members shall be further divided into the following subcategories:

(A) Non-practicing. This subcategory includes those members who are not engaged in the practice of law or holding themselves out as practicing attorneys and who hold positions unrelated to the practice of law, or practice law in other jurisdictions.

(B) Retired. This subcategory includes those members who are retired from the practice of law and who no longer hold themselves out as practicing attorneys. A retired member must hold himself or herself out as a "Retired Member of the North Carolina State Bar" or by some similar designation, provided such designation clearly indicates that the attorney is "retired."

(C) Disability inactive status. This subcategory includes members who suffer from a mental or physical condition which significantly impairs the professional judgment, performance, or competence of an attorney, as determined by the courts, the council, or the Disciplinary Hearing Commission.

(D) Disciplinary suspensions/disbarments. This subcategory includes those members who have been suspended from the practice of law or who have been disbarred by the courts, the council, or the Disciplinary Hearing Commission for one or more violations of the Rules of Professional Conduct.

(E) Administrative suspensions. This subcategory includes those members who have been suspended from the practice of law, pursuant to the procedure set forth in Rule .0903 of subchapter 1D, for failure to fulfill the obligations of membership.

(F) Emeritus pro bono status. This subcategory includes those members who are permitted by the council to represent indigent persons under the supervision of active members who are employed by nonprofit corporations duly authorized to provide legal services to such persons. This status may be withdrawn by the council for good cause shown pursuant to the procedure set forth in Rule .0903 of subchapter 1D.

[History Note: Statutory Authority G.S. 84–16; G.S. 84–23. Readopted effective December 8, 1994. Amended effective March 6, 2008; March 6, 2014.]

.0202. Register of Members

(a) Initial Registration With State Bar. Every member shall register by completing and returning to the North Carolina State Bar a signed registration card containing the following information:

(1) name and address;

(2) date;

(3) date passed examination to practice in North Carolina;

(4) date and place sworn in as an attorney in North Carolina;

(5) date and place of birth;

(6) list of all other jurisdictions where the member has been admitted to the practice of law and date of admission;

(7) whether suspended or disbarred from the practice of law in any jurisdiction or court, and if so, when and where, and when readmitted.

(b) Membership Records of State Bar. The secretary shall keep a permanent register for the enrollment of members of the North Carolina State Bar. In appropriate places therein entries shall be made showing the address of each member, date of registration and class of membership, date of transfer from one class to another, if any, date and period of suspension, if any, and such other useful data which the council may from time to time require.

(c) Updating Membership Information. Each year before July 1, every member shall provide or verify the member's current name, mailing address, and e-mail address.

[History Note: Statutory Authority G.S. 84–23; G.S. 84–34. Readopted effective December 8, 1994. Amended effective October 7, 2010.]

.0203 Annual Membership Fees; When Due

(a) Amount and Due Date. The annual membership fee shall be in the amount as provided by law and shall be due and payable to the secretary of the North Carolina State Bar on January 1 of each year and the same shall become delinquent if not paid on or before July 1 of each year.

(b) Late Fee. Any attorney who fails to pay the entire annual membership fee in the amount provided bylaw and the annual Client Security Fund assessment approved by the North Carolina Supreme Court on or before July 1 of each year shall also pay a late fee of $30.00.

(c) Waiver of All or Part of Dues. No part of the annual membership fee or Client Security Fund assessment shall be prorated or apportioned to fractional parts of the year, and no part of the membership fee or Client Security Fund assessment shall be waived or rebated for any reason with the following exceptions:

(1) A person licensed to practice law in North Carolina for the first time by examination shall not be liable for dues or the Client Security Fund assessment during the year in which the person is admitted;

(2) A person licensed to practice law in North Carolina serving in the armed forces, whether in a legal or nonlegal capacity, will be exempt from payment of dues and Client Security Fund assessment for any year in which the member is on active duty in the military service;

(3) A person licensed to practice law in North Carolina who files a petition for inactive status on or before Dec. 31 of a given year shall not be liable for the membership fee or the Client Security Fund assessment for the following year if the petition is granted. A petition shall be deemed timely if it is postmarked on or before December 31.

[History Note: Statutory Authority G.S. 84–23; G.S. 84–34. Readopted effective December 8, 1994; amended effective September 7, 1995; December 7, 1995; March 7, 1996.]

.0204. "Good Standing" Definition and Certificates

(a) Definition. A lawyer who is an active member of the North Carolina State Bar and who is not subject to a pending administrative or disciplinary suspension or disbarment order or an order of suspension that has been stayed is in good standing with the North Carolina State Bar. An administrative or disciplinary suspension or disbarment order is "pending" if the order has been announced in open court by a state court of competent jurisdiction or by the Disciplinary Hearing Commission, or if the order has been entered by a state court of competent jurisdiction, by the Council or by the Disciplinary Hearing Commission but has not taken effect. "Good standing" makes no reference to delinquent membership obligations, prior discipline, or any disciplinary charges or grievances that may be pending.

(b) Certificate of Good Standing for Active Member. Upon application and payment of the prescribed fee, the Secretary of the North Carolina State Bar shall issue a certificate of good standing to any active member of the State Bar who is in good standing and who is current on all payments owed to the North Carolina State Bar. A certificate of good standing will not be issued unless the member pays any delinquency shown on the financial records of the North Carolina State Bar including outstanding judicial district bar dues. If the member contends that there is good cause for non-payment of some or all of the amount owed, the member may subsequently demonstrate good cause to the Administrative Committee pursuant to the procedure set forth in Rule .0903(e)(1) of subchapter 1D of these rules. If the member shows good cause, the contested amount shall be refunded to the member.

(c) Certificate of Good Standing for Inactive Member. Upon application, the Secretary of the North Carolina State Bar shall issue a certificate of good standing to any inactive member of the State Bar who was in good standing at the time that the member was granted inactive status and who is not subject to any disciplinary order or pending disciplinary order. The certificate shall state that the member is inactive and is ineligible to practice law in North Carolina.

[History Note: Statutory Authority G. S. 84–23. Adopted and effective October 1, 2003. Amended effective March 8, 2012.]

SECTION .0300 ELECTION AND SUCCESSION OF OFFICERS

.0301 Officers

(a) The officers of the North Carolina State Bar and the council shall consist of a president, a president-elect, a vice-president, and an immediate past president. These officers shall be deemed members of the council in all respects.

(b) There shall be a secretary who shall also have the title of executive director. The secretary shall not be a member of the council.

[History Note: Statutory Authority G.S. 84–22; G.S. 84–23. Readopted effective December 8, 1994.]

.0302 Eligibility for Office

The president, president-elect, and vice-president need not be members of the council at the time of their election.

[History Note: Statutory Authority G.S. 84–22; G.S. 84–23. Readopted effective December 8, 1994.]

.0303 Term of Office

(a) The term of each office shall be one year beginning at the conclusion of the annual meeting. Each officer will hold office until a successor is elected and qualified.

(b) The president shall assume the office of immediate past president at the conclusion of the term as president. The president-elect shall assume the office of president at the conclusion of the annual meeting following the term as president-elect.

[History Note: Statutory Authority G.S. 84–21; G.S. 84–22; G.S. 84–21. Readopted effective December 8, 1994.]

.0304 Elections

(a) A president-elect, vice-president and secretary shall be elected annually by the council at an election to take place at the council meeting held during the annual meeting of the North Carolina State Bar. All elections will be conducted by secret ballot.

(b) If there are more than two candidates for an office, then any candidate receiving a majority of the votes shall be elected. If no candidate receives a majority, then a run-off shall be held between the two candidates receiving the highest number of votes.

[History Note: Statutory Authority G.S. 84–22; G.S. 84–23. Readopted effective December 8, 1994.]

.0305 Nominating Committee

(a) There shall be a Nominating Committee appointed to nominate one or more candidates for each of the offices. The Nominating Committee shall be composed of the immediate past president and the five most recent living past presidents who are in good standing with the North Carolina State Bar. The Nominating Committee shall meet prior to the council meeting at which the election of officers will be held. The Nominating Committee shall submit its nominations in writing to the secretary at least 45 days prior to the election, and the secretary shall transmit the report by mail to the members of the council at least 30 days prior to the election.

(b) At the council meeting at which elections are held, the floor shall be open for additional nominations for each office at the time of the election.

[History Note: Statutory Authority G.S. 84–22; G.S. 84–23. Readopted effective December 8, 1994.]

.0306 Vacancies and Succession

(a) If the office of president becomes vacant for any reason, including resignation, death, disqualification, or permanent inability, the president-elect shall become president for the unexpired term and the next term. If the office of the president-elect becomes vacant because the president-elect must assume the presidency under the foregoing provision of this section, then the vice-president shall become the president-elect for the unexpired term and at the end of the unexpired term to which the vice-president ascended the office will become vacant and an election held in accordance with Rule .0304 of this subchapter; if the office of president-elect becomes vacant for any other reason, the vice-president shall become the president-elect for the unexpired term following which said officer shall assume the presidency as if elected president-elect. If the office of vice-president or secretary becomes vacant for any reason, including resignation, death, disqualification, or permanent inability, or if the office of president or president-elect becomes vacant without an available successor under these provisions then the office will be filled by election by the council at a special meeting of the council with such notice as required by Rule .0602 of this subchapter or at the next regularly scheduled meeting of the council.

(b) If the president is absent or unable to preside at any meeting of the North Carolina State Bar or the council, the president-elect shall preside, or if the president-elect is unavailable, then the vice-president shall preside. If none are available, then the council shall elect a member to preside during the meeting.

(c) If the president is absent from the state or for any reason is temporarily unable to perform the duties of office, the president-elect shall assume those duties until the president returns or becomes able to resume the duties. If the president-elect is unable to perform the duties, then the council may select one of its members to assume the duties for the period of inability.

[History Note: Statutory Authority G.S. 84–23. Readopted effective December 8, 1994.]

.0307 Removal From Office

The council may, upon giving due notice and an opportunity to be heard, remove from office any officer found by the council to have a disability or to have engaged in misconduct including misconduct not related to the office.

[History Note: Statutory Authority G.S. 84–21; 84–23. Readopted effective December 8, 1994; amended December 10, 1999, effective February 3, 2000.]

SECTION .0400 DUTIES OF OFFICERS

.0401 Compensation of Officers

The secretary shall receive a salary fixed by the council. All other officers shall serve without compensation except the per diem allowances fixed by statute for members of the council.

[History Note: Statutory Authority G.S. 84–23. Readopted effective December 8, 1994.]

.0402 President

The president shall preside over meetings of the North Carolina State Bar and the council. The president shall sign all resolutions and orders of the council in the capacity of president. The president shall execute, along with the secretary, all contracts ordered by the council. The president will perform all other duties prescribed for the office by the council.

[History Note: Statutory Authority G.S. 84–23. Readopted effective December 8, 1994.]

.0403 President–Elect, Vice–President, and Immediate Past President

The president-elect, vice-president, and immediate past president will perform all duties prescribed for the office by the council.

[History Note: Statutory Authority G.S. 84–23. Readopted effective December 8, 1994.]

.0404 Secretary

The secretary shall attend all meetings of the council and of the North Carolina State Bar, and shall record the proceedings of all such meetings. The secretary shall, with the president, president-elect or vice-president, execute all contracts ordered by the council. He or she shall have custody of the seal of the North Carolina State Bar, and shall affix it to all documents executed on behalf of the council or certified as emanating from the council. The secretary shall take charge of all funds paid into the North Carolina State Bar and deposit them in some bank selected by the council; he or she shall cause books of accounts to be kept, which shall be the property of the North Carolina State Bar and which shall be open to the inspection of any officer, committee or member of the North Carolina State Bar during usual business hours. At each January meeting of the council, the secretary shall make a full report of receipts and disbursements since the previous annual report, together with a list of all outstanding obligations of the North Carolina State Bar. The books of accounts shall be audited as of December 31 of each year and the secretary shall publish same in the annual reports as referred to above. He or she shall perform such other duties as may be imposed upon him or her, and shall give bond for the faithful performance of his or her duties in an amount to be fixed by the council with surety to be approved by the council.

[History Note: Statutory Authority G.S. 84–23. Readopted effective December 8, 1994.]

SECTION .0500 MEETINGS OF THE NORTH CAROLINA STATE BAR

.0501 Annual Meetings

The annual meeting of the North Carolina State Bar shall be held at such time and place within the state of North Carolina, after such notice (but not less than 30 days) as the council may determine.

[History Note: Statutory Authority G.S. 84–23. Readopted effective December 8, 1994.]

.0502 Special Meetings

(a) Special meetings of the North Carolina State Bar may be called upon 30 days' notice, as follows:

(1) by the secretary, upon direction of the council;

(2) by the secretary, upon the call addressed to the council, of not less than 25% of the active members of the North Carolina State Bar.

(b) At special meetings no subjects shall be dealt with other than those specified in the notice.

[History Note: Statutory Authority G.S. 84-23; G.S. 84-33. Readopted effective December 8, 1994.]

.0503 Notice of Meetings

Notice of all meetings shall be given by publication in such newspapers of general circulation as the council may select, or, in the discretion of the council, by mailing notice to the secretary of the several district bars or to the individual active members of the North Carolina State Bar.

[History Note: Statutory Authority G.S. 84-23; G.S. 84-33. Readopted effective December 8, 1994.]

.0504 Quorum

At all annual and special meetings of the North Carolina State Bar those active members of the North Carolina State Bar present shall constitute a quorum, and there shall be no voting by proxy.

[History Note: Statutory Authority G.S. 84-23; G.S. 84-33. Readopted effective December 8, 1994.]

.0505 Parliamentary Rules

Proceedings at any meeting of the North Carolina State Bar shall be governed by *Roberts' Rules of Order.*

[History Note: Statutory Authority G.S. 84-23. Readopted effective December 8, 1994.]

SECTION .0600 MEETINGS OF THE COUNCIL

.0601 Regular Meetings

Regular meetings of the council shall be held in each of the months of January, April and July, at such time and place after such notice (but not less than 30 days) as the council may determine; and on the day before the annual meeting of the North Carolina State Bar, at the location of said annual meeting. Any regular meeting may be adjourned from time to time as a majority of members present may determine.

[History Note: Statutory Authority G.S. 84-23. Readopted effective December 8, 1994; amended effective June 1, 1995.]

.0602 Special Meetings

The president in his or her discretion may call special meetings of the council. Upon written request of eight councilors, filed with the secretary requesting the president to call a special meeting of the council, the secretary shall, within five days thereafter, call such special meeting. The date fixed for such meeting shall not be less than five days nor more than 10 days from the date of such call.

[History Note: Statutory Authority G.S. 84-23. Readopted effective December 8, 1994.]

.0603 Notice of Called Special Meetings

Notice of called special meetings shall be signed by the secretary. The notice shall set forth the day and hour of the meeting and the place for holding the same. Any business may be presented for consideration at such special meeting. Such notice must be given to each councilor unless waived by him or her. A written waiver signed by any councilor shall be equivalent to notice as herein provided. Notice to councilors not waiving as aforesaid shall be in writing and may be communicated by telegraph, or by letter through the United States mail in the usual course, addressed to each of said councilors at his or her law office address. Notice by telegraph shall be filed with the telegraph carrier for transmission at least three days, and notice by mail shall be deposited in the United States post office at least five days, before the day fixed for the special meeting.

[History Note: Statutory Authority G.S. 84-23. Readopted effective December 8, 1994.]

.0604 Quorum at Meeting of Council

At meetings of the council the presence of 10 councilors shall constitute a quorum.

[History Note: Statutory Authority G.S. 84-23. Readopted effective December 8, 1994.]

SECTION .0700 STANDING COMMITTEES OF THE COUNCIL

.0701 Standing Committees and Boards

(a) Standing Committees. Promptly after his or her election, the president shall appoint members to the standing committees identified below to serve for one year beginning January 1 of the year succeeding his or her election. Members of the committees need not be councilors, except to the extent expressly required by these rules, and may include non-lawyers. Unless otherwise directed by resolution of the council, all members of a standing committee, whether councilors or non-councilors, shall be entitled to vote as members of the standing committee or any subcommittee or panel thereof.

(1) *Executive Committee.* It shall be the duty of the Executive Committee to receive reports and recommendations from standing committees, boards, and special committees; to nominate individuals for appointments made by the council; to make long range plans for the State Bar; and to perform such other duties and consider such other matters as the council or the president may designate.

(2) *Ethics Committee.* It shall be the duty of the Ethics Committee to study the rules of professional responsibility currently in effect; to make recommendations to the council for such amendments to the rules as the committee deems necessary or appropriate; to study and respond to questions that arise concerning the meaning and application of the rules of professional conduct; to issue opinions in response to questions of legal ethics in accordance with the provisions of Section .0100 of Subchapter 1D of these rules; to consider issues concerning the regulation of lawyers' trust accounts; and to perform such other duties and consider such other matters as the council or the president may designate.

(3) *Grievance Committee.* It shall be the duty of the Grievance Committee to exercise the disciplinary and disability functions and responsibilities set forth in Section .0100 of Subchapter 1B of these rules and to make recommendations to the council for such amendments to that section as the committee deems necessary or appropriate. The Grievance Committee shall sit in panels as assigned by the president. Each panel shall have at least ten members. Two members of each panel shall be non-lawyers, one member may be a lawyer who is not a member of the council, and the remaining members of each panel shall be councilors of the North Carolina State Bar. A quorum of a panel shall be five members serving at a particular time. Each panel shall exercise the powers and discharge the duties of the Grievance Committee with respect to the grievances and other matters referred to it by the chairperson of the Grievance Committee. Each panel member shall be furnished a brief description of all matters referred to other panels (and such other available information as he or she may request) and be given a reasonable opportunity to provide comments to such other panels. Each panel's decision respecting the grievances and other matters assigned to it will be deemed final action of the Grievance Committee, unless the full committee at its next meeting, by a majority vote of those present, elects to review a panel decision and upon further consideration decides to reverse or modify that decision. There will be no other right of appeal to the committee as a whole or to another panel. The president shall designate a vice-chairperson to preside over, and oversee the functions of, each panel. The vice-chairpersons shall have such other powers as may be delegated to them by the chairperson of the Grievance Committee. The Grievance Committee shall perform such other duties and consider such other matters as the council or the president may designate.

(4) *Authorized Practice Committee.* It shall be the duty of the Authorized Practice Committee to respond to or investigate inquiries and complaints about conduct that may constitute the unauthorized practice of law in accordance with the provisions of Section .0200 of Subchapter 1D of these rules; to study and advise the council on the appropriate and lawful use and regulation of legal assistants, paralegals and other lay persons in connection with the provision of law-related services; to study and advise the council on the regulation of professional organizations; and to perform such other duties and consider such other matters as the council or the president may designate.

(5) *Administrative Committee.* It shall be the duty of the Administrative Committee to study and make recommendations on policies concerning the administration of the State Bar, including the administration of the State Bar's facilities, automation, personnel, retirement plan, publications, and district bars; to oversee the membership functions of the State Bar, including the collection of dues, the suspension of members for failure to pay dues and other fees, and the transfer of members to active or inactive status in accordance with the provisions of Sections .0900 and .1000 of Subchapter 1D of these rules; and to perform such other duties and consider such other matters as the council or the president may designate. The committee may establish a Publications Board to oversee the regular publications of the State Bar.

(6) *Legal Assistance for Military Personnel (LAMP) Committee.* It shall be the duty of the LAMP Committee to serve as liaison for lawyers in the military service in this State; to improve legal services to military personnel and dependents stationed in this State; and to perform such other duties and consider such other matters as the council or the president may designate.

(7) *Finance and Audit Committee.* It shall be the duty of the Finance and Audit Committee to superin-

tend annually the preparation of the State Bar's operational budget and to make recommendations to the Executive Committee concerning that budget and the budgets for the boards listed in subsection (b) below; to make recommendations to the Executive Committee regarding the State Bar's financial policies; to examine the financial records of the State Bar at each regular meeting of the council and report its findings to the Executive Committee; to recommend to the Executive Committee annually the retention of an independent auditor; to direct the work of the independent auditor in accordance with the policies and procedures adopted by the council and the state auditor; and to review the results of the annual audit and make recommendations concerning the audit to the Executive Committee.

(b) Boards. The council of the State Bar shall make appointments to the following boards upon the recommendation of the Executive Committee. The boards are constituents of the North Carolina State Bar and, as standing committees of the State Bar, are subject to the authority of the council.

(1) *Interest on Lawyers' Trust Accounts (IOLTA) Board of Trustees.* The IOLTA Board shall be constituted in accordance with and shall carry out the provisions of the Plan for Disposition of Funds Received by the North Carolina State Bar from Interest on Trust Accounts set forth in Section .1300 of Subchapter 1D of these rules.

(2) *Board of Legal Specialization.* The Board of Legal Specialization shall be constituted in accordance with and shall carry out the provisions of the Plan of Legal Specialization set forth in Section .1700 of Subchapter 1D of these rules.

(3) *Client Security Fund Board of Trustees.* The Client Security Fund Board of Trustees shall be constituted in accordance with and shall carry out the provisions of the Rules Governing the Administration of the Client Security Fund of the North Carolina State Bar set forth in Section .1400 of Subchapter 1D of these rules.

(4) *Board of Continuing Legal Education (CLE).* The Board of Continuing Legal Education shall be constituted in accordance with and shall carry out the provisions of the Continuing Legal Education Rules and Regulations of the North Carolina State Bar set forth in Sections .1500 and .1600 of Subchapter 1D of these rules.

(5) *Lawyer Assistance Program Board.* The Lawyer Assistance Program Board shall be constituted in accordance with and shall carry out the provisions of the Rules Governing the Lawyer Assistance Program of the North Carolina State Bar set forth in Section .0600 of Subchapter 1D of these rules.

[History Note: Statutory Authority G.S. 84–22; G.S. 84–23. Readopted effective December 8, 1994; amended effective June 12, 1996; amended December 10, 1999, effective February 3, 2000; amended effective October 6, 2004; amended effective November 16, 2006; amended effective March 8, 2007; amended effective October 7, 2010.]

SECTION .0800 ELECTION AND APPOINTMENT OF STATE BAR COUNCILORS

.0801 Purpose

The purpose of these rules is to promulgate fair, open, and uniform procedures to elect and appoint North Carolina State Bar councilors in all judicial district bars. These rules should encourage a broader and more diverse participation and representation of all attorneys in the election and appointment of councilors.

[History Note: Statutory Authority G.S. 84–23. Readopted effective December 8, 1994.]

.0802. Election—When Held; Notice; Nominations

(a) Every judicial district bar, in any calendar year at the end of which the term of one or more of its councilors will expire, shall fill said vacancy or vacancies at an election to be held during that year.

(b) The officers of the district bar shall fix the time and place of such election and shall give to each active member (as defined in G.S. 84–16) of the district bar a written notice thereof directed to him or her at his or her address on file with the North Carolina State Bar, which notice shall be placed in the United States Mail, postage prepaid, at least 30 days prior to the date of the election.

(c) The district bar shall submit its written notice of the election to the North Carolina State Bar, at least six weeks before the date of the election.

(d) The North Carolina State Bar will, at its expense, mail these notices.

(e) The notice shall state the date, time, and place of the election, give the number of vacancies to be filled, identify how and to whom nominations may be made before the election, and advise that all elections must be by a majority of the votes cast. If the election will be held at a meeting of the bar, the notice will also advise that additional nominations may be made from the floor at the meeting itself.

In judicial districts that permit elections by mail or early voting, the notice to members shall advise that nominations may be made in writing directed to the president of the district bar and received prior to a date set out in the notice. Sufficient notice shall be provided to permit nominations received from district bar members to be included on the printed ballots.

[History Note: Statutory Authority G.S. 84–18; G.S. 84–23. Readopted effective December 8, 1994; amended effective November 5, 1999; amended effective August 27, 2013.]

.0803 Election—Voting Procedures

(a) All nominations made either before or at the meeting shall be voted on by secret ballot.

(b) Cumulative voting shall not be permitted.

(c) Nominees receiving a majority of the votes cast shall be declared elected.

[History Note: Statutory Authority G.S. 84–18; G.S. 84–23. Readopted effective December 8, 1994; amended effective November 5, 1999.]

.0804. Procedures Governing Elections by Mail

(a) Judicial district bars may adopt bylaws permitting elections by mail, in accordance with procedures approved by the N.C. State Bar Council and as set out in this section.

(b) Only active members of the judicial district bar may participate in elections conducted by mail.

(c) In districts which permit elections by mail, the notice sent to members referred to in Rule .0802(e) of this subchapter shall advise that the election will be held by mail.

(d) The judicial district bar shall mail a ballot to each active member of the judicial district bar at the member's address of record on file with the North Carolina State Bar. The ballot shall be accompanied by written instructions and shall state when and where the ballot should be returned.

(e) Each ballot shall be sequentially numbered with a red identifying numeral in the upper right hand corner of the ballot. The judicial district bar shall maintain appropriate records respecting how many ballots were mailed to prospective voters in each election, as well as how many ballots are returned.

(f) Only original ballots will be accepted. No photocopied or faxed ballots will be accepted.

[History Note: Statutory Authority G. S. 84–18; 84–23. Adopted effective November 5, 1999. Amended effective August 23, 2012.]

.0805. Procedures Governing Elections by Electronic Vote

(a) Judicial district bars may adopt bylaws permitting elections by electronic vote in accordance with procedures approved by the N.C. State Bar Council and as set out in this section.

(b) Only active members of the judicial district bar may participate in elections conducted by electronic vote.

(c) In districts which permit elections by electronic vote, the notice sent to members referred to in Rule .0802(e) of this subchapter shall advise that the election will be held by electronic vote and shall identify how and to whom nominations may be made before the election. The notice shall explain when the ballot will be available, how to access the ballot, and the method for voting online. The notice shall also list locations where computers will be available for active members to access the online ballot in the event they do not have personal online access.

(d) Write-in candidates shall be permitted and the instructions shall so state.

(e) Online balloting procedures must ensure that only one vote is cast per active member of the judicial district bar and that all members have access to a ballot.

[History Note: Statutory Authority G.S. 84-18. Adopted August 23, 2012.]

.0806. Procedures Governing Early Voting

(a) Judicial district bars may adopt bylaws permitting early voting for up to 10 business days prior to a councilor election, in accordance with procedures approved by the NC State Bar Council and as set out in this subchapter.

(b) Only active members of the judicial district bar may participate in early voting.

(c) In districts that permit early voting, the notice sent to members referred to in Rule .0802(e) of this subchapter shall advise that early voting will be permitted, and shall identify the locations, dates, and hours for early voting. The notice shall also advise that nominations may be made in writing directed to the president of the district bar and received prior to a date set out in the notice. Sufficient notice shall be provided to permit nominations received from district bar members to be included on the printed ballots.

(d) The notice sent to members referred to in Rule .0802(e) of this subchapter shall be placed in the United States Mail, postage prepaid, at least 30 days prior to the first day of the early voting period.

(e) Write-in candidates shall be permitted during the early voting period and at the election, and the instructions shall so state.

(f) Early voting locations and hours must be reasonably accessible to all active members of the judicial district.

[History Note: Adopted effective August 27, 2013.]

.0807. Vacancies

The unexpired term of any councilor whose office has become vacant because of resignation, death, or any cause other than the expiration of a term, shall be filled within 90 days of the occurrence of the vacancy by an election conducted in the same manner as above provided.

[History Note: Statutory Authority G.S. 84-18; 84-23. Readopted effective December 8, 1994; Former .0804 was amended and renumbered as .0805, effective November 5, 1999; Former .0805 was renumbered as .0806 effective August 23, 2012; Former .0806 was renumbered as .0807 effective August 27, 2013.]

.0808. Bylaws Providing for Geographical Rotation or Division of Representation

Nothing contained herein shall prohibit the district bar of any judicial district from adopting bylaws providing for the geographical rotation or division of its councilor representation.

[History Note: Statutory Authority G.S. 84-18; 84-23. Readopted effective December 8, 1994; Former .0805 was amended and renumbered as .0806, effective November 5, 1999; Former .0806 was renumbered as .0807 effective August 23, 2012; Former .0807 was renumbered as .0808 effective August 27, 2013.]

SECTION .0900 ORGANIZATION OF THE JUDICIAL DISTRICT BARS

.0901 Bylaws

(a) Each judicial district bar shall adopt bylaws for its governance subject to the approval of the council.

(b) Each judicial district bar shall submit its current bylaws to the secretary of the North Carolina State Bar for review by the council on or before June 1, 1996.

(c) Pending review by the council, any bylaws submitted to the secretary on behalf of a judicial district bar or which already exist in the files of the secretary shall be deemed official and authoritative.

(d) All amendments to the bylaws of any judicial district bar must be filed with the secretary within 30 days of adoption and shall have no force and effect until approved by the council.

(e) The secretary shall maintain an official record for each judicial district bar containing bylaws which have been approved by the council or for which approval is pending.

[History Note: Adopted effective March 7, 1996.]

.0902 Annual Membership Fee

If a judicial district bar elects to assess an annual membership fee from its active members pursuant to N.C.G.S. § 84–18.1(b), the following procedures shall apply:

(a) Notice to State Bar. The judicial district bar shall notify the North Carolina State Bar of its election to assess an annual membership fee each year at least thirty days prior to mailing to its members the first invoice therefore, specifying the amount of the annual membership fee, the date after which payment will be delinquent, and the amount of any late fee for delinquent payment.

(b) Accounting to State Bar. No later than thirty days after the end of the judicial district bar's fiscal year, the judicial district bar shall provide the North Carolina State Bar with an accounting of the annual membership fees it collected during such judicial district bar's fiscal year.

(c) Delinquency Date. The date upon which the annual membership fee shall be delinquent if not paid shall be not later than ninety days after, and not sooner than thirty days after, the date of the first invoice for the annual membership fee.

The delinquency date shall be stated on the invoice and the invoice shall advise each member that failure to pay the annual membership fee must be reported to the North Carolina State Bar and may result in suspension of the member's license to practice law.

(d) Late Fee. Each judicial district bar may impose, but shall not be required, to impose a late fee of any amount not to exceed fifteen dollars ($15.00) for non-payment of the annual membership fee on or before the stated delinquency date.

(e) Members Subject to Assessment. Only those lawyers who are active members of a judicial district bar may be assessed an annual membership fee.

(f) Members Exempt from Assessment.

(1) A person licensed to practice law in North Carolina for the first time by examination is not liable for judicial district bar membership fees during the year in which the person is admitted;

(2) A person licensed to practice law in North Carolina serving in the United States Armed Forces, whether in a legal or nonlegal capacity, is exempt from judicial district bar membership fees for any year in which the member serves some portion thereof on full-time active duty in military service;

(3) A lawyer who joins a judicial district bar after the beginning of its fiscal year is exempt from the obligation to pay the annual membership fee for that fiscal year only if the lawyer can demonstrate that he or she previously paid an annual membership fee to another judicial district bar with a fiscal year that runs coterminously, for a period of three (3) months or more, with the fiscal year of the lawyer's new judicial district bar.

(g) Hardship Waivers. A judicial district bar may not grant any waiver from the obligation to pay the judicial district bar's annual membership fee. A judicial district bar may waive the late fee upon a showing of good cause.

(h) Reporting Delinquent Members to State Bar. Twelve months after the date of the first invoice for the annual membership fee, the judicial district bar shall report to the North Carolina State Bar all of its members who have not paid the annual membership fee or any late fee.

[History Note: Statutory Authority G.S. 84-18.1; G.S. 84-23. Adopted effective December 20, 2000. Amended effective March 6, 2008; March 6, 2014.]

.0903. Fiscal Period

To avoid conflict with the assessment of the membership fees for the North Carolina State Bar, each judicial district bar that assesses a membership fee shall adopt a fiscal year that is not a calendar year. Any judicial district bar that assesses a mandatory membership fee for the first time after December 31, 2013, must adopt a fiscal year that begins July 1 and ends June 30.

[History Note: Statutory Authority G.S. 84-18; 84-23. Adopted effective December 20, 2000. Amended effective April 10, 2014.]

SECTION .1000 MODEL BYLAWS FOR USE BY JUDICIAL DISTRICT BARS

.1001 Name

The name of this District Bar shall be THE DISTRICT BAR OF THE __________ JUDICIAL DISTRICT, and shall be hereinafter referred to as the "District Bar".

[Adopted effective March 7, 1996.]

.1002 Authority and Purpose

The District Bar is formed pursuant to the provisions of Chapter 84 of the North Carolina General Statutes to promote the purposes therein set forth and to comply with the duties and obligations therein or thereunder imposed upon the Bar of this judicial district.

[Adopted effective March 7, 1996.]

.1003 Membership

The members of the District Bar shall consist of two classes: active and inactive.

(a) Active Members. The active members shall be all persons who, at the time of the adoption of these bylaws or any time thereafter

(1) are active members in good standing with the North Carolina State Bar and

(2) reside in the judicial district or

(3) practice in the judicial district and elect to belong to the District Bar as provided in G.S. 84–16.

(b) Inactive Members. The inactive members shall be all persons, who, at the time of the adoption of these bylaws or at any time thereafter

(1) have been granted voluntary inactive status by the North Carolina State Bar and

(2) reside in the judicial district and

(3) elect to participate, but not vote or hold office, in the District Bar by giving written notice to the Secretary of the District Bar.

[Adopted effective March 7, 1996.]

.1004 Officers

The officers of the District Bar shall be a President, a Vice President, and Secretary and/or Treasurer who shall be selected and shall serve for the terms set out herein.

(a) President. The President serving at the time these bylaws are effective shall continue to serve for a term ending at the next annual meeting following the adoption or effective date of these bylaws. The President for the following term shall be the then current Vice President. Thereafter, the duly elected Vice President shall automatically succeed to the office of the President for a term of one, two, or three years.

(b) Vice President. The Vice President serving at the time these bylaws are effective shall continue to serve for a term ending at the next annual meeting following the adoption or effective date of these bylaws, at which time said Vice President shall succeed to the office of the President. Thereafter, the Vice President shall be elected at the annual meeting as hereinafter provided for a term of one, two, or three years.

(c) Secretary and/or Treasurer. The Secretary and/or the Treasurer serving at the time these bylaws are effective shall each continue to serve in their respective offices until the expiration of the term of that office or until successors are appointed by the President (or be elected by the active members of the District Bar), whichever occurs later. In all other years, the Secretary and/or Treasurer shall be appointed by the President (or be elected by the active members of the District Bar) to serve for a term of one, two, or three years.

(d) Election. Before (or at) the annual meeting at which officers are to be elected, the Nominating Committee shall submit the names of its nominees for the office of Vice President to the Secretary. Nominations from the floor shall be permitted. If no candidate receives a majority of the votes cast, the candidate with the lowest number of votes shall be eliminated and a run-off election shall immediately be held among the remaining candidates. This procedure shall be repeated until a candidate receives a majority of the votes. [1]

[1] The procedure for voting for, and election of, councilors is set by statute and rules of the N.C. State Bar. District Bar voting procedure with regard to matters relating to District Bar dues is now statutorily prescribed in North Carolina General Statutes Section 84–18.1. The procedure, but not the manner or method of conducting the vote, to submit nominations to the Governor to fill vacancies on the District Court bench is set forth in North Carolina General Statutes Section 7A–142. It is suggested that, for voting upon, and elections for, other District Bar matters and issues, the District Bars be permitted to adopt bylaws providing for procedures as may seem appropriate for each District Bar. Such rules might address notice provisions, including how much notice is given and permissible methods of giving notice, what shall constitute a quorum (see footnote 2), and how any such election shall be conducted (including whether or not members must be present to vote, whether proxies will be permitted, whether or not absentee or some other form of mail ballot will be allowed and whether or not cumulative voting should be permitted when elections for multiple candidates or positions are being conducted).

(e) Duties. The duties of the officers shall be those usual and customary for such officers, including such duties as may be from time to time designated by resolution of the District Bar, the North Carolina State Bar Council or the laws of the State of North Carolina.

(f) Vacancies. If a vacancy in the office of the Vice President, Secretary–Treasurer occurs, the vacancy will be filled by the Board of Directors, if any, and if there is no Board of Directors, then by the vote of the active members at a special meeting of such members. The successor shall serve until the next annual meeting of the District Bar. If the office of the President becomes vacant, the Vice President shall succeed to the office of the President and the Board of Directors, if any, and if there is no Board of Directors, then by the vote of the active members at a special meeting of such members, will select a new Vice President, who shall serve until the next annual meeting.

(g) Notification. Within 10 days following the annual meeting, or the filling of a vacancy in any office, the President shall notify the Executive Director of the North Carolina State Bar of the names, addresses and telephone numbers of all officers of the District Bar.

(h) Record of Bylaws. The President shall ensure that a current copy of these bylaws is filed with the office of the Senior Resident Superior Court Judge with the ________________ Judicial District and with the Executive Director of the North Carolina State Bar.

(i) Removal From Office. The District Bar, by a two-thirds vote of its active members present at a duly called meeting, may, after due notice and an opportunity to be heard, remove from office any officer who has engaged in conduct which renders the officer unfit to serve, or who has become disabled, or for other good cause. The office of any officer who, during his or her term of office ceases to be an active member of the North Carolina State Bar shall immediately be deemed vacant and shall be filled as provided in Rule .1004(f) above.

[Adopted effective March 7, 1996.]

.1005 Councilor

The District Bar shall be represented in the State Bar Council by one or more duly elected councilors, the number of councilors being determined pursuant to G.S. 84–17. Any councilor serving at the time of the adoption of these bylaws shall complete the term of office to which he or she was previously elected. Thereafter, elections shall be held as necessary. Nominations shall be made and the election held as provided in G.S. 84–18 and in Section .0800 et seq. of Subchapter 1A of the Rules of the North Carolina State Bar (27 N.C.A.C. 1A .0800 et seq.). If more than one council seat is to be filled, separate elections shall be held for each vacant seat. A vacancy in the office of councilor shall be filled as provided by Rule.0804 of Subchapter 1A of the Rules of the North Carolina State Bar (27 N.C.A.C. 1A .0804).

[Adopted effective March 7, 1996. Amended effective November 5, 1999.]

.1006 Annual Membership Fee

(a) Each active member of the District Bar shall:

(1) Pay such annual membership fee, if any, as is prescribed by a majority vote of the active members of the District Bar present and voting at a duly called meeting of the District Bar, provided, however, that such fee may never exceed the amount of the annual membership fee currently imposed by the North Carolina State Bar. Each member shall pay the annual District Bar membership fee at the time and place set forth in the notice thereof mailed to the member by the Secretary–Treasurer; and

(2) Keep the Secretary–Treasurer notified of the member's current mailing address and telephone number.

(b) The annual membership fee shall be used to promote and maintain the administration, activities and programs of the District Bar.

[Adopted effective March 7, 1996.]

.1007 Meetings

(a) Annual Meetings. The District Bar shall meet each ________ at a time and place designated by the President. The President, Secretary or other Officer shall mail or deliver written notice of the annual meeting to each active member of the District Bar at the member's last known mailing address on file with the District Bar at least ten days before the date of the annual meeting and shall so certify in the official minutes of the meeting. Notice of the meeting mailed by the Executive Director of the North Carolina State Bar shall also satisfy the notice requirement. Failure to mail or deliver the notice as herein provided shall invalidate any action at the annual meeting.

(b) Special Meetings. Special meetings, if any, may be called at any time by the President or the Vice President. The President, Secretary or other Officer shall mail or deliver written notice of the special meeting to each active member of the District Bar at the member's last known mailing address on file with the District Bar at least ten days before the date of any special meeting. Such notice shall set forth the time and place for the special meeting and the purpose(s) thereof. Failure to mail or deliver the notice shall invalidate any action taken at a special meeting.

(c) Notice for meeting to vote on annual membership fee: Notwithstanding the notice periods set forth in paragraphs (a) and (b) above, the written notice for any meeting at which the active members will vote on whether to impose or increase an annual membership fee shall be mailed or delivered to each active member of the district bar at the member's last known mailing address on file with the North Carolina State Bar at least 30 days before the date of the meeting.

(d) Quorum. Twenty percent of the active members of the District Bar shall constitute a quorum, and a quorum shall be required to take official action on behalf of the District Bar.

[Adopted effective March 7, 1996. Amended effective Oct. 7, 2010.]

.1008 District Bar Finances

(a) Fiscal Year. The District Bar's fiscal year shall begin on ________ and shall end on ________.

(b) Duties of Treasurer. The Treasurer shall maintain the funds of the District Bar on deposit, initiate any necessary disbursements and keep appropriate financial records.

(c) Annual Financial Report. Each ________ before the annual meeting, the Treasurer shall prepare the District Bar's annual financial report for review by the Board of Directors, if any, and submission to the District Bar's annual meeting and the North Carolina State Bar.

(d) District Bar Checks. All checks written on district bar accounts (arising from the collection of mandatory dues) that exceed $500 must be signed by two of the following: (1) the treasurer, (2) any other officer, (3) another member of the board of directors, or (4) the executive secretary/director, if any.

(e) Fidelity Bond. If it is anticipated that receipts from membership fees will exceed $20,000 for any fiscal year, the District Bar shall purchase a fidelity bond at least equal in amount to the anticipated annual receipts to indemnify the District Bar for losses attributable to the malfeasance of the Treasurer or any other member having access to District Bar funds.

(f) Taxpayer Identification Number. The Treasurer shall be responsible for obtaining a federal taxpayer identification number for the District Bar.

[Adopted effective March 7, 1996. Amended effective July 22, 1999.]

.1009 Prohibited Activities

(a) Prohibited Expenditures. Mandatory District Bar dues, if any, shall not be used for the purchase of alcoholic beverages, gifts to public officials, including judges, charitable contributions, recreational activities or expenses of spouses of District Bar members or officers. However, such expenditures may be made from funds derived entirely from the voluntary contributions of District Bar members.

(b) Political Expenditures. The District Bar shall not make any expenditures to fund political and ideological activities.

(c) Political Activities. The District Bar shall not engage in any political or ideological conduct or activity, including the endorsement of candidates and the taking or advocation of positions on political issues, referendums, bond elections, and the like, however, the District Bar, and persons speaking on its behalf, may take positions on, or comment upon, issues relating to the regulation of the legal profession and issues or matters relating to the improvement of the quality and availability of legal services to the general public.

[Adopted effective March 7, 1996.]

.1010 Committees

(a) Standing committee(s): The standing committees shall be the Nominating Committee, Pro Bono Committee, Fee Dispute Resolution Committee, Grievance Committee, and Professionalism Committee provided that, with respect to the Fee Dispute Resolution Committee and the Grievance Committee, the district meets the State Bar guidelines relating thereto.

(b) Fee Dispute Resolution Committee:

(1) The Fee Dispute Resolution Committee shall consist of at least six but not more than eighteen persons appointed by the President to staggered three-year terms as provided in the District Bar's Fee Dispute Resolution Plan.

(2) The Fee Dispute Resolution Committee shall be responsible for implementing a Fee Dispute Resolution Plan approved by the Council of the North Carolina State Bar to resolve fee disputes efficiently, economically, and expeditiously without litigation.

(c) Grievance Committee.

(1) The Grievance Committee shall consist of at least five but not more than thirteen persons appointed by the President to staggered three year terms as provided by the Rules and Regulations of the North Carolina State Bar governing Judicial District Grievance Committees.

(2) The Grievance Committee shall assist the Grievance Committee of the North Carolina State Bar by receiving grievances, investigating grievances, evaluating grievances, informally mediating disputes, facilitating communication between lawyers and clients and referring members of the public to other appropriate committees or agencies for assistance.

(3) The Grievance Committee shall operate in strict accordance with the rules and policies of the North Carolina State Bar with respect to District Bar Grievance Committees.

(d) Special Committees. Special committees may be created and appointed by the President.

(e) Nominating Committee.

(1) The Nominating Committee shall be appointed by the officers (or the Board of Directors) of the District Bar and shall consist of at least three active members of the District Bar who are not officers or directors of the District Bar. [3]

(2) The Nominating Committee shall meet as necessary for the purpose of nominating active members of the District Bar as candidates for officers and councilor(s) and the Board of Directors, if any.

(3) The Nominating Committee members shall serve one-year terms beginning on _________ and ending on _________.

(4) Any active member whose name is submitted for consideration for nomination to any office or as a councilor must have indicated his or her willingness to serve if selected.

[3] The composition of the Nominating Committee set forth above is a suggestion only. The District Bars may choose to constitute their nominating committees in a different manner, as for example, letting the committee consist of the three most immediate past presidents of the District Bar who are still active members of the District Bar as defined herein. Smaller District Bars may choose to have no Nominating Committee and nominate and elect officers from the floor at the annual meeting of the District Bar.

(f) Pro Bono Committee.

(1) The Pro Bono Committee shall consist of at least five active members of the District Bar appointed by the President.

(2) The Pro Bono Committee shall meet at least once each quarter and shall have the duty of encouraging members of the District Bar to provide pro bono legal services. The Committee shall also develop programs whereby attorneys not involved in other volunteer legal service programs may provide pro bono legal service in their areas of concentration and practice.

(3) The members of the Pro Bono Committee shall serve one-year terms commencing on _________.

(g) Professionalism Committee:

(1) The Professionalism Committee shall consist of the three immediate past presidents of the district bar or such other members of the district bar as shall be appointed by the president.

(2) The purpose of the Professionalism Committee shall be the promotion of professionalism and thereby the bolstering of public confidence in the legal profession. The committee may further enhance professionalism through CLE programs and, when appropriate, through confidential peer intervention in association with the Professionalism Support Initiative (PSI) which is sponsored and supported by the Chief Justice's Commission on Professionalism. The PSI effort is to investigate and informally assist with client-lawyer, lawyer-lawyer, and lawyer-judge relationships to ameliorate disputes, improve communications, and repair relationships. The Professionalism Committee shall have no authority to discipline any lawyer or judge, or to force any lawyer or judge to take any action. The committee shall not investigate or attempt to resolve complaints of professional misconduct cognizable under the Rules of Professional Conduct and shall act in accordance with Rules 1.6(c) and 8.3 of the Rules of Professional Conduct. The committee shall consult and work with the Chief Justice's Commission on Professionalism when appropriate.

[Adopted effective March 7, 1996. Amended effective March 6, 2002; amended effective March 6, 2008.]

.1011 Board of Directors or Executive Committee

(a) Membership of Board. A Board of Directors consisting of at least _____ active members of the District Bar shall be elected. At all times, the Board of Directors shall include at least one director from each county in the Judicial District. The Board of Directors serving when these bylaws become effective shall continue to serve until the following annual meeting. Beginning on _________ immediately after the effective date of these bylaws, the President shall appoint an initial Board of Directors who shall serve three-year terms commencing on _________, except that the terms of the initial members of the Board shall be staggered at one-year intervals to ensure continuity and experience. To effect the staggered initial terms, the President will determine which of the initial members shall serve terms of less than three years.

The State Bar Councilor (or Councilors) from the judicial district shall be an ex officio member (or members) of the District Bar Board of Directors or Executive Committee.

(b) Terms of Directors. After the initial staggered terms of the Board of Directors expire, successors shall be elected by the active members at the annual District Bar meeting, as set out in Rule .1004(d) above, and Rule .1011(c) and (d) below. Following the completion of the initial staggered terms, the directors shall serve three-year terms beginning on __________ following their election.

(c) Designated and At–Large Seats in Multi–County Districts. In multi-county districts, one seat on the Board of Directors shall be set aside and designated for each county in the district. Only active members of the District Bar who reside or work in the designated county may be elected to a designated county seat. All other seats on the Board of Directors shall be at-large seats which may be filled by any active member of the District Bar.

(d) Elections. When one or more seats on the Board of Directors become vacant, an election shall be held at the annual meeting of the District Bar. Except as otherwise provided herein, the election shall be conducted as provided for in Rule .1004(d) above. The candidates receiving the highest number of votes cast will be elected, regardless of whether any of the candidates received a majority of the votes cast, provided that designated seats will be filled by the candidates receiving the highest number of votes who live or work in the designated county, regardless of whether any of the candidates received a majority of the votes cast.

(e) Vacancies. If a vacancy occurs on the Board of Directors, the President (or the Board of Directors) shall appoint a successor who shall serve until the next annual meeting of the District Bar. If the vacancy occurs in a designated seat for a particular county within the district, the successor will be selected from among the active members of the District Bar who live or work in the designated county.

(f) Duties of Board of Directors. The Board of Directors shall have the responsibilities described in Rules .1004(f) and .1007(c) above. The Board of Directors shall also consult with the officers regarding any matters of District Bar business or policy arising between meetings and may act for the District Bar on an emergency basis if necessary, provided that any such action shall be provisional pending its consideration by the District Bar at its next duly called meeting. The Board of Directors may not impose on its own authority any sort of fee upon the membership.

[Adopted effective March 7, 1996.]

.1012 Amendment of the Bylaws

The membership of the District Bar, by a __________ (majority, two-thirds, etc.) vote of the active members present at any duly called meeting at which there is a quorum present and voting throughout, may amend these bylaws in ways not inconsistent with the constitution of the United States, the policies and rules of the North Carolina State Bar and the laws of the United States and North Carolina.

[Adopted effective March 7, 1996.]

.1013 Selection of Nominees for District Court Judge

Unless otherwise required by law, the following procedures shall be used to determine the nominees to be recommended to the Governor pursuant to N.C. Gen. Stat. § 7A–142 for vacant district court judgeships in the judicial district.

(a) Meeting for Nominations: The nominees shall be selected by secret, written ballot of those members present at a meeting of the district bar called for this purpose. Fifteen (15) days notice of the meeting shall be given, by mail, to the last known address of each district bar member. Alternatively, if a bylaw permitting elections by mail is adopted by the district bar, the procedures set forth in the bylaw and in Rule .0804 of Subchapter 1A of the Rules of the North Carolina State Bar (27 N.C.A.C. 1A, .0804), shall be followed.

(b) Candidates: Persons who want to be considered for the vacancy shall notify the President in writing five (5) days prior to the meeting at which the election will be conducted or, if the election is by mail, five (5) days prior to the mailing of the ballots.

(c) Voting: Each district bar member eligible to vote pursuant to N.C. Gen. Stat. § 7A–142 may vote for up to five candidates. Cumulative voting is prohibited. Proxy voting is prohibited.

(d) Submission to Governor: The five candidates receiving the highest number of votes shall be the nominees to fill the vacancy on the district court and their names, and vote totals, shall be transmitted to the governor. In the event of a tie for fifth place, the names of those candidates involved in the tie shall be transmitted to the governor together with the names of the four candidates receiving the highest number of votes.

[History Note: Statutory Authority G.S. 84–18.1; G.S. 84–23; 7A–142. Adopted effective February 27, 2003. Amended effective March 6, 2014.]

SECTION .1100 OFFICE OF THE NORTH CAROLINA STATE BAR

.1101 Office

Until otherwise ordered by the council, the office of the North Carolina State Bar shall be maintained in the city of Raleigh at such place as may be designated by the council.

[History Note: Statutory Authority G.S. 84-23. Readopted effective December 8, 1994.]

SECTION .1200 FILING PAPERS WITH AND SERVING THE NORTH CAROLINA STATE BAR

.1201 When Papers Are Filed Under These Rules and Regulations

Whenever in these rules and regulations there is a requirement that petitions, notices or other documents be filed with or served on the North Carolina State Bar, or the council, the same shall be filed with or served on the secretary of the North Carolina State Bar.

[History Note: Statutory Authority G.S. 84-23. Readopted effective December 8, 1994.]

SECTION .1300 SEAL

.1301 Form and Custody of Seal

The North Carolina State Bar shall have a seal round in shape and having the words and figures, "The North Carolina State Bar July 1, 1933," with the word "Seal" in the center. The seal shall remain in the custody of the secretary at the office of the North Carolina State Bar, unless otherwise ordered by the council.

[History Note: Statutory Authority G.S. 84-23. Readopted effective December 8, 1994.]

SECTION .1400 RULEMAKING PROCEDURES

.1401 Publication for Comment

(a) As a condition precedent to adoption, a proposed rule or amendment to a rule must be published for comment as provided in subsection (c).

(b) A proposed rule or amendment to a rule must be presented to the Executive Committee and the council prior to publication for comment, and specifically approved for publication by both.

(c) A proposed rule or amendment to a rule must be published for comment in an official printed publication of the North Carolina State Bar that is mailed to the membership at least 30 days in advance of its final consideration by the council. The publication of any such proposal must be accompanied by a prominent statement inviting all interested parties to submit comment to the North Carolina State Bar at a specified postal or e-mail address prior to the next meeting of the Executive Committee, the date of which shall be set forth.

[History Note: Adopted effective August 23, 2007.]

.1402 Review by the Executive Committee

At its next meeting following the publication or republication of any proposed rule or amendment to a rule, the Executive Committee shall review the proposal and any comment that has been received concerning the proposal. The Executive Committee shall then:

(a) recommend the proposal's adoption by the council;

(b) recommend the proposal's adoption by the council with nonsubstantive modification;

(c) recommend to the council that the proposal be republished with substantive modification;

(d) defer consideration of the matter to its next regular business meeting;

(e) table the matter; or

(f) reject the proposal.

[History Note: Adopted effective August 23, 2007.]

.1403 Action by the Council and Review by the North Carolina Supreme Court

(a) Whenever the Executive Committee recommends adoption of any proposed rule or amendment to a rule in accordance with the procedure set forth in Rule .1402 above, the council at its next regular business meeting shall consider the proposal, the Executive Committee's recommendation, and any comment received from interested parties, and:

(1) decide whether to adopt the proposed rule or amendment, subject to the approval of the North Carolina Supreme Court as described in G.S. 84-21;

(2) reject the proposed rule or amendment; or

(3) refer the matter back to the Executive Committee for reconsideration.

(b) Any proposed rule or amendment to a rule adopted by the council shall be transmitted by the secretary to the North Carolina Supreme Court for its review on a schedule approved by the Court, but in no event later than 120 days following the council's adoption of the proposed rule or amendment.

(c) No proposed rule or amendment to a rule adopted by the council shall take effect unless and until it is approved by order of the North Carolina Supreme Court.

(d) The secretary shall promptly transmit the official text of any proposed rule or amendment to a rule adopted by the council and approved by the North Carolina Supreme Court to the Office of Administrative Hearings for publication in the North Carolina Administrative Code.

(e) Any action taken by the council or the North Carolina Supreme Court in regard to any proposed rule or amendment to a rule shall be reported in the next issue of the printed publication referenced in Rule .1401 above.

[History Note: Adopted effective August 23, 2007.]

SUBCHAPTER B. DISCIPLINE AND DISABILITY RULES

SECTION .0100 DISCIPLINE AND DISABILITY OF ATTORNEYS

.0101 General Provisions

Discipline for misconduct is not intended as punishment for wrongdoing but is for the protection of the public, the courts, and the legal profession. The fact that certain misconduct has remained unchallenged when done by others, or when done at other times, or that it has not been made the subject of earlier disciplinary proceedings, will not be a defense to any charge of misconduct by a member.

[History Note: Statutory Authority G.S. 84-23. Readopted effective December 8, 1994.]

.0102 Procedure for Discipline

(a) The procedure to discipline members of the bar of this state will be in accordance with the provisions hereinafter set forth.

(b) District bars will not conduct separate proceedings to discipline members of the bar but will assist and cooperate with the North Carolina State Bar in reporting and investigating matters of alleged misconduct on the part of its members.

(c) Concurrent Jurisdiction of State Bar and Courts.

(1) The Council of the North Carolina State Bar is vested, as an agency of the state, with the control of the discipline, disbarment, and restoration of attorneys practicing law in this state.

(2) The courts of this state have inherent authority to take disciplinary action against attorneys practicing therein, even in relation to matters not pending in the court exercising disciplinary authority.

(3) The authority of the North Carolina State Bar and the courts to discipline attorneys is separate and distinct, the North Carolina State Bar having derived its jurisdiction by legislative act and the courts from the inherent power of the courts themselves.

(4) Neither the North Carolina State Bar nor the courts are authorized or empowered to act for or in the name of the other, and the disciplinary action taken by either entity should be clearly delineated as to the source or basis for the action being taken.

(5) It is the position of the North Carolina State Bar that no trial court has the authority to preempt a North Carolina State Bar disciplinary proceeding with a pending civil or criminal court proceeding involving attorney conduct, or to dismiss a disciplinary proceeding pending before the North Carolina State Bar.

(6) Whenever the North Carolina State Bar learns that a court has initiated an inquiry or proceeding regarding alleged improper or unethical conduct of an attorney, the North Carolina State Bar may defer to the court and stay its own proceeding pending completion of the court's inquiry or proceeding. Upon request, the North Carolina State Bar will assist in the court's inquiry or proceeding.

(7) If the North Carolina State Bar finds probable cause and institutes disciplinary proceedings against an attorney for conduct which subsequently becomes an issue in a criminal or civil proceeding, the court may, in its discretion, defer its inquiry pending the completion of the North Carolina State Bar's proceedings.

(8) Upon the filing of a complaint by the North Carolina State Bar, the North Carolina State Bar will send a copy of the complaint to the chief resident superior court judge and to all superior court judges regularly assigned to the district in which the attorney maintains his or her law office. The North Carolina State Bar will send a copy of the complaint to the district attorney in the district in which the attorney

maintains a law office if the complaint alleges criminal activity by the attorney.

(9) The North Carolina State Bar will encourage judges to contact the North Carolina State Bar to determine the status of any relevant complaints filed against an attorney before the court takes disciplinary action against the attorney.

[History Note: Statutory Authority G.S. 84-23; G.S. 84-36. Readopted effective December 8, 1994.]

.0103 Definitions

Subject to additional definitions contained in other provisions of this subchapter, the following words and phrases, when used in this subchapter, will have, unless the context clearly indicates otherwise, the meanings given to them in this rule.

(1) Admonition—a written form of discipline imposed in cases in which an attorney has committed a minor violation of the Rules of Professional Conduct.

(2) Appellate division—the appellate division of the general court of justice.

(3) Board—the Board of Continuing Legal Education.

(4) Board of Continuing Legal Education—a standing committee of the council responsible for the administration of a program of mandatory continuing legal education and law practice assistance.

(5) Censure—a written form of discipline more serious than a reprimand issued in cases in which an attorney has violated one or more provisions of the Rules of Professional Conduct and has caused significant harm or potential significant harm to a client, the administration of justice, the profession, or a member of the public, but the misconduct does not require suspension of the attorney's license.

(6) Certificate of conviction—a certified copy of any judgment wherein a member of the North Carolina State Bar is convicted of a criminal offense.

(7) Chairperson of the Grievance Committee—councilor appointed to serve as chairperson of the Grievance Committee of the North Carolina State Bar.

(8) Commission—the Disciplinary Hearing Commission of the North Carolina State Bar.

(9) Commission chairperson—the chairperson of the Disciplinary Hearing Commission of the North Carolina State Bar.

(10) Complainant or complaining witness—any person who has complained of the conduct of any member of the North Carolina State Bar to the North Carolina State Bar.

(11) Complaint—a formal pleading filed in the name of the North Carolina State Bar with the commission against a member of the North Carolina State Bar after a finding of probable cause.

(12) Consolidation of cases—a hearing by a hearing panel of multiple charges, whether related or unrelated in substance, brought against one defendant.

(13) Council—the Council of the North Carolina State Bar.

(14) Councilor—a member of the Council of the North Carolina State Bar.

(15) Counsel—the counsel of the North Carolina State Bar appointed by the council.

(16) Court or courts of this state—a court authorized and established by the constitution or laws of the state of North Carolina.

(17) Criminal offense showing professional unfitness - the commission of, attempt to commit, conspiracy to commit, solicitation or subornation of any felony or any crime that involves false swearing, misrepresentation, deceit, extortion, theft, bribery, embezzlement, false pretenses, fraud, interference with the judicial or political process, larceny, misappropriation of funds, or property, overthrow of the government, perjury, willful failure to file a tax return, or any other offense involving moral turpitude or showing professional unfitness.

(18) Defendant—a member of the North Carolina State Bar against whom a finding of probable cause has been made.

(19) Disabled or disability—a mental or physical condition which significantly impairs the professional judgment, performance, or competence of an attorney.

(20) Grievance—alleged misconduct.

(21) Grievance Committee—the Grievance Committee of the North Carolina State Bar or any of its panels acting as the Grievance Committee respecting the grievances and other matters referred to it by the chairperson of the Grievance Committee.

(22) Hearing Committee—a hearing committee designated under Rule .0108(a)(2), .0114(d), .0114(x), .0118(b)(2), .0125(a)(6), .0125(b)(7) or .0125(c)(2) of this subchapter.

(23) Illicit drug—any controlled substance as defined in the North Carolina Controlled Substances Act, section 5, chapter 90, of the North Carolina General Statutes, or its successor, which is used or possessed without a prescription or in violation of the laws of this state or the United States.

(24) Incapacity or incapacitated—condition determined in a judicial proceeding under the laws of this or any other jurisdiction that an attorney is mentally defective, an inebriate, mentally disordered, or incompetent from want of understanding to manage his or her own affairs by reason of the excessive use of intoxicants, drugs, or other cause.

(25) Investigation—the gathering of information with respect to alleged misconduct, alleged disability, or a petition for reinstatement.

(26) Investigator—any person designated to assist in the investigation of alleged misconduct or facts pertinent to a petition for reinstatement.

(27) Lawyer Assistance Program Board—the Lawyer Assistance Program Board of the North Carolina State Bar.

(28) Letter of caution—communication from the Grievance Committee to an attorney stating that the past conduct of the attorney, while not the basis for discipline, is unprofessional or not in accord with accepted professional practice.

(29) Letter of notice—a communication to a respondent setting forth the substance of a grievance.

(30) Letter of warning—written communication from the Grievance Committee or the commission to an attorney stating that past conduct of the attorney, while not the basis for discipline, is an unintentional, minor, or technical violation of the Rules of Professional Conduct and may be the basis for discipline if continued or repeated.

(31) Member—a member of the North Carolina State Bar.

(32) Office of the Counsel—the office and staff maintained by the counsel of the North Carolina State Bar.

(33) Office of the Secretary—the office and staff maintained by the secretary-treasurer of the North Carolina State Bar.

(34) Party—after a complaint has been filed, the North Carolina State Bar as plaintiff or the member as defendant.

(35) Plaintiff—after a complaint has been filed, the North Carolina State Bar.

(36) Preliminary hearing—hearing by the Grievance Committee to determine whether probable cause exists.

(37) Probable cause—a finding by the Grievance Committee that there is reasonable cause to believe that a member of the North Carolina State Bar is guilty of misconduct justifying disciplinary action.

(38) Reprimand—a written form of discipline more serious than an admonition issued in cases in which a defendant has violated one or more provisions of the Rules of Professional Conduct and has caused harm or potential harm to a client, the administration of justice, the profession, or a member of the public, but the misconduct does not require a censure.

(39) Respondent—a member of the North Carolina State Bar who has been accused of misconduct or whose conduct is under investigation, but as to which conduct there has not yet been a determination of whether probable cause exists.

(40) Revised Rules of Professional Conduct - the Rules of Professional Conduct adopted by the Council of the North Carolina State Bar and approved by the North Carolina Supreme Court effective July 24, 1997.

(41) Rules of Professional Conduct - the Rules of Professional Conduct adopted by the Council of the North Carolina State Bar and approved by the North Carolina Supreme Court and which were in effect from Oct. 7, 1985 through July 23, 1997.

(42) Secretary—the secretary-treasurer of the North Carolina State Bar.

(43) Supreme Court—the Supreme Court of North Carolina.

(44) Will—when used in these rules, means a direction or order which is mandatory or obligatory.

[History Note: Statutory Authority G.S. 84-23. Readopted effective December 8, 1994; amended effective December 30, 1998; amended December 10, 1999, effective February 3, 2000 amended effective October 8, 2009.]

.0104 State Bar Council: Powers and Duties in Discipline and Disability Matters

The Council of the North Carolina State Bar will have the power and duty

(1) to supervise and conduct disciplinary proceedings in accordance with the provisions hereinafter set forth;

(2) to appoint members of the commission as provided by statute;

(3) to appoint a counsel. The counsel will serve at the pleasure of the council. The counsel will be a member of the North Carolina State Bar but will not be permitted to engage in the private practice of law;

(4) to order the transfer of a member to disability inactive status when such member has been judicially declared incompetent or has been involuntarily committed to institutional care because of incompetence or disability;

(5) to accept or reject the surrender of the license to practice law of any member of the North Carolina State Bar;

(6) to order the disbarment of any member whose resignation is accepted;

(7) to review the report of any hearing panel upon a petition for reinstatement of a disbarred attorney and to make final determination as to whether the license will be restored.

[History Note: Statutory Authority G.S. 84-23. Readopted effective December 8, 1994; amended effective September 7, 1995; October 8, 2009.]

.0105. Chairperson of the Grievance Committee: Powers and Duties

(a) The chairperson of the Grievance Committee will have the power and duty

(1) to supervise the activities of the counsel;

(2) to recommend to the Grievance Committee that an investigation be initiated;

(3) to recommend to the Grievance Committee that a grievance be dismissed;

(4) to direct a letter of notice to a respondent or direct the counsel to issue letters of notice in such cases or under such circumstances as the chairperson deems appropriate;

(5) to issue, at the direction and in the name of the Grievance Committee, a letter of caution, letter of warning, an admonition, a reprimand, or a censure to a member;

(6) to notify a respondent that a grievance has been dismissed, and to notify the complainant in accordance with Rule .0121 of this subchapter;

(7) to call meetings of the Grievance Committee.

(8) to issue subpoenas in the name of the North Carolina State Bar or direct the secretary to issue such subpoenas;

(9) to administer or direct the administration of oaths or affirmations to witnesses;

(10) to sign complaints and petitions in the name of the North Carolina State Bar;

(11) to determine whether proceedings should be instituted to activate a suspension which has been stayed;

(12) to enter orders of reciprocal discipline in the name of the Grievance Committee;

(13) to direct the counsel to institute proceedings in the appropriate forum to determine if an attorney is in violation of an order of the Grievance Committee, the commission, or the council;

(14) to rule on requests for reconsideration of decisions of the Grievance Committee regarding grievances;

(15) to tax costs of the disciplinary procedures against any defendant against whom the Grievance Committee imposes discipline, including a minimum administrative cost of $50;

(16) to dismiss a grievance upon request of the complainant, where it appears that there is no probable cause to believe that the respondent has violated the Rules of Professional Conduct and where counsel consents to the dismissal;

(17) to dismiss a grievance where it appears that the grievance has not been filed within the time period set out in Rule .0111(e).

(18) to dismiss a grievance where it appears that the complaint, even if true, fails to state a violation of the Rules of Professional Conduct and where counsel consents to the dismissal.

(19) to dismiss a grievance where it appears that there is no probable cause to believe that the respondent has violated the Rules of Professional Conduct and where counsel and a member of the Grievance Committee designated by the Committee consent to the dismissal.

(20) to appoint a subcommittee to make recommendations to the council for such amendments to the Discipline and Disability Rules as the subcommittee deems necessary or appropriate.

(b) The president, vice-chairperson, or a member of the Grievance Committee designated by the president or the chairperson or vice-chairperson of the committee may perform the functions, exercise the power, and discharge the duties of the chairperson or any vice-chairperson when the chairperson or a vice-chairperson is absent or disqualified.

(c) The chairperson may delegate his or her authority to the president, the vice chairperson of the committee, or a member of the Grievance Committee.

[History Note: Statutory Authority G.S. 84–23. Readopted effective December 8, 1994; amended effective February 20, 1995; March 6, 1997; October 2, 1997; December 30, 1998; March 3, 1999; February 3, 2000; March 10, 2011; August 23, 2012.]

.0106. Grievance Committee: Powers and Duties

The Grievance Committee will have the power and duty

(1) to direct the counsel to investigate any alleged misconduct or disability of a member of the North Carolina State Bar coming to its attention;

(2) to hold preliminary hearings, find probable cause and direct that complaints be filed;

(3) to dismiss grievances upon a finding of no probable cause;

(4) to issue a letter of caution to a respondent in cases wherein misconduct is not established but the activities of the respondent are unprofessional or not in accord with accepted professional practice. The letter of caution will recommend that the respondent be more professional in his or her practice in one or more ways which are to be specifically identified;

(5) to issue a letter of warning to a respondent in cases wherein no probable cause is found but it is determined by the Grievance Committee that the conduct of the respondent is an unintentional, minor, or technical violation of the Rules of Professional Conduct. The letter of warning will advise the attorney that he or she may be subject to discipline if such conduct is continued or repeated. The warning will specify in one or more ways the conduct or practice for which the respondent is being warned. A copy of the letter of warning will be maintained in the office of the counsel for three years subject to the confidentiality provisions of Rule .0129 of this subchapter;

(6) to issue an admonition in cases wherein the defendant has committed a minor violation of the Rules of Professional Conduct;

(7) to issue a reprimand wherein the defendant has violated one or more provisions of the Rules of Professional Conduct, and has caused harm or potential harm to a client, the administration of justice, the profession, or a member of the public, but the misconduct does not require a censure;

(8) to issue a censure in cases wherein the defendant has violated one or more provisions of the Rules of Professional Conduct and has caused significant harm or potential significant harm to a client, the administration of justice, the profession, or a member of the public, but the misconduct does not require suspension of the defendant's license;

(9) to direct that a petition be filed seeking a determination whether a member of the North Carolina State Bar is disabled;

(10) to include in any order of admonition, reprimand, or censure a provision requiring the defendant to complete a reasonable amount of continuing legal education in addition to the minimum amount required by the North Carolina Supreme Court;

(11) in its discretion, to refer grievances primarily attributable to unsound law office management to a program of law office management training approved by the State Bar in accordance with Rule .0112(i) of this subchapter.

(12) in its discretion, to refer grievances primarily attributable to the respondent's substance abuse or mental health problem to the Lawyer Assistance Program in accordance with Rule .0112(j) of this subchapter.

(13) in its discretion to refer grievances primarily attributable to the respondent's failure to employ sound trust accounting techniques to the trust account supervisory program in accordance with Rule .0112(k) of this subchapter.

[History Note: Statutory Authority G.S. 84–23. Readopted effective December 8, 1994; amended effective March 3, 1999; amended effective December 20, 2000; amended effective August 23, 2012.]

.0107 Counsel: Powers and Duties

The counsel will have the power and duty

(1) to initiate an investigation concerning alleged misconduct of a member;

(2) to direct a letter of notice to a respondent when authorized by the chairperson of the Grievance Committee;

(3) to investigate all matters involving alleged misconduct whether initiated by the filing of a grievance or otherwise;

(4) to recommend to the chairperson of the Grievance Committee that a matter be dismissed, that a letter of caution, or a letter of warning be issued, or that the grievance committee hold a preliminary hearing;

(5) to prosecute all disciplinary proceedings before the Grievance Committee, hearing panels, and the courts;

(6) to represent the North Carolina State Bar in any trial, hearing, or other proceeding concerning the alleged disability of a member;

(7) to appear on behalf of the North Carolina State Bar at hearings conducted by the Grievance Committee, hearing panels, or any other agency or court concerning any motion or other matter arising out of a disciplinary or disability proceeding;

(8) to appear at hearings conducted with respect to petitions for reinstatement of license by suspended or disbarred attorneys or by attorneys transferred to disability inactive status, to cross-examine witnesses testifying in support of such petitions, and to present evidence, if any, in opposition to such petitions;

(9) to employ such deputy counsel, investigators, and other administrative personnel in such numbers as the council may authorize;

(10) to maintain permanent records of all matters processed and of the disposition of such matters;

(11) to perform such other duties as the council may direct;

(12) after a finding of probable cause by the Grievance Committee, to designate the particular violations of the Rules of Professional Conduct to be alleged in a formal complaint filed with the commission;

(13) to file amendments to complaints and petitions arising out of the same transactions or occurrences as the allegations in the original complaints or petitions, in the name of the North Carolina State Bar, with the prior approval of the chairperson of the Grievance Committee;

(14) after a complaint is filed with the commission, to dismiss any or all claims in the complaint or to negotiate and recommend consent orders of discipline to the hearing panel.

[History Note: Statutory Authority G.S. 84–23; G.S. 84–31. Readopted effective December 8, 1994; amended effective March 3, 1999; amended effective October 8, 2009.]

.0108 Chairperson of the Hearing Commission: Powers and Duties

(a) The chairperson of the Disciplinary Hearing Commission of the North Carolina State Bar will have the power and duty

(1) to receive complaints alleging misconduct and petitions alleging the disability of a member filed by the counsel; petitions requesting reinstatement of license by members who have been involuntarily transferred to disability inactive status, suspended, or disbarred; motions seeking the activation of suspensions

which have been stayed; and proposed consent orders of disbarment;

(2) to assign three members of the commission, consisting of two members of the North Carolina State Bar and one nonlawyer to hear complaints, petitions, motions, and posthearing motions pursuant to Rule .0114(z)(2) of this subchapter. The chairperson will designate one of the attorney members as chairperson of the hearing panel. No panel member who hears a disciplinary matter may serve on the panel which hears the attorney's reinstatement petition. The chairperson of the commission may designate himself or herself to serve as one of the attorney members of any hearing panel and will be chairperson of any hearing panel on which he or she serves. Posthearing motions filed pursuant to Rule .0114(z)(2) of this subchapter will be considered by the same hearing panel assigned to the original trial proceeding. Hearing panel members who are ineligible or unable to serve for any reason will be replaced with members selected by the commission chairperson;

(3) to set the time and place for the hearing on each complaint or petition;

(4) to subpoena witnesses and compel their attendance and to compel the production of books, papers, and other documents deemed necessary or material to any hearing. The chairperson may designate the secretary to issue such subpoenas;

(5) to consolidate, in his or her discretion for hearing, two or more cases in which a subsequent complaint or complaints have been served upon a defendant within ninety days of the date of service of the first or a preceding complaint;

(6) to enter orders disbarring members by consent;

(7) to enter an order suspending a member pending disposition of a disciplinary proceeding when the member has been convicted of a serious crime or has pled no contest to a serious crime and the court has accepted the plea.

(b) The vice-chairperson of the disciplinary hearing commission may perform the function of the chairperson in any matter when the chairperson is absent or disqualified.

[History Note: Statutory Authority G.S. 84–23. Readopted effective December 8, 1994; amended effective September 7, 1995; amended effective October 8, 2009.]

.0109 Hearing Panel: Powers and Duties

Hearing panels of the Disciplinary Hearing Commission of the North Carolina State Bar will have the following powers and duties:

(1) to hold hearings on complaints alleging misconduct, petitions seeking a determinations of disability or reinstatement, or motions seeking the activation of suspensions which have been stayed, and to conduct proceedings to determine if persons or corporations should be held in contempt pursuant to G.S. § 84–28.1(b1);

(2) to enter orders regarding discovery and other procedures in connection with such hearings, including, in disability matters, the examination of a member by such qualified medical experts as the panel will designate;

(3) to subpoena witnesses and compel their attendance, and to compel the production of books, papers, and other documents deemed necessary or material to any hearing. Subpoenas will be issued by the chairperson of the hearing panel in the name of the commission. The chairperson may direct the secretary to issue such subpoenas;

(4) to administer or direct the administration of oaths or affirmations to witnesses at hearings;

(5) to make findings of fact and conclusions of law;

(6) to enter orders dismissing complaints in matters before the panel;

(7) to enter orders of discipline against or letters of warning to defendants in matters before the panel;

(8) to tax costs of the disciplinary proceedings against any defendant against whom discipline is imposed, provided, however, that such costs will not include the compensation of any member of the council, committees, or agencies of the North Carolina State Bar;

(9) to enter orders transferring a member to disability inactive status;

(10) to report to the council its findings of fact and recommendations after hearings on petitions for reinstatement of disbarred attorneys;

(11) to grant or deny petitions of attorneys seeking transfer from disability inactive status to active status;

(12) to enter orders reinstating suspended attorneys or denying reinstatement. An order denying reinstatement may include additional sanctions in the event violations of the petitioner's order of suspension are found;

(13) to enter orders activating suspensions which have been stayed or continuing the stays of such suspensions.

(14) to enter orders holding persons and corporations in contempt pursuant to G.S. § 84-28.1(b1) and imposing such sanctions allowed by law.

[History Note: Statutory Authority G.S. 84–23; G.S. 84–28; G.S. 84–28.1. Readopted effective December 8, 1994; amended effective March 3, 1999; amended effective October 8, 2009.]

.0110 Secretary: Powers and Duties in Discipline and Disability Matters

The secretary will have the following powers and duties in regard to discipline and disability procedures:

(1) to receive grievances for transmittal to the counsel, to receive complaints and petitions for transmittal to the commission chairperson, and to receive affidavits of surrender of license for transmittal to the council;

(2) to issue summonses and subpoenas when so directed by the president, the chairperson of the Grievance Committee, the chairperson of the commission, or the chairperson of any hearing panel;

(3) to maintain a record and file of all grievances not dismissed by the Grievance Committee;

(4) to perform all necessary ministerial acts normally performed by the clerk of the superior court in complaints filed before the commission;

(5) to enter orders of reinstatement where petitions for reinstatement of suspended attorneys are unopposed by the counsel;

(6) to dismiss reinstatement petitions based on the petitioner's failure to comply with the rules governing the provision and transmittal of the record of reinstatement proceedings;

(7) to determine the amount of costs assessed in disciplinary proceedings by the commission.

[History Note: Statutory Authority G.S. 84–22; G.S. 84–23; G.S. 84–32(c). Readopted effective December 8, 1994; amended effective October 8, 2009.]

.0111 Grievances—Form and Filing

(a) A grievance may be filed by any person against a member of the North Carolina State Bar. Such grievance may be written or oral, verified or unverified, and may be made initially to the counsel. The counsel may require that a grievance be reduced to writing in affidavit form and may prepare and distribute standard forms for this purpose.

(b) Upon the direction of the council or the Grievance Committee, the counsel will investigate such conduct of any member as may be specified by the council or Grievance Committee.

(c) The counsel may investigate any matter coming to the attention of the counsel involving alleged misconduct of a member upon receiving authorization from the chairperson of the Grievance Committee. If the counsel receives information that a member has used or is using illicit drugs, the counsel will follow the provisions of Rule .0130 of this subchapter.

(d) The N.C. State Bar may keep confidential the identity of an attorney or judge who reports alleged misconduct of another attorney pursuant to Rule 1.3 of the Rules of Professional Conduct and who requests to remain anonymous. Notwithstanding the foregoing, the N.C. State Bar will reveal the identity of a reporting attorney or judge to the respondent attorney where such disclosure is required by law, or by considerations of due process or where identification of the reporting attorney or judge is essential to preparation of the attorney's defense to the grievance and/or a formal disciplinary complaint.

(e) The counsel may decline to investigate the following allegations:

(i) that a member provided ineffective assistance of counsel in a criminal case, unless a court has granted a motion for appropriate relief based upon the member's conduct;

(ii) that a plea entered in a criminal case was not made voluntarily and knowingly, unless a court granted a motion for appropriate relief based upon the member's conduct;

(iii) that a member's advice or strategy in a civil or criminal matter was inadequate or ineffective.

(f) Limitation of Grievances.

(1) There is no time limitation for initiation of any grievance based upon a plea of guilty to a felony or upon conviction of a felony.

(2) There is no time limitation for initiation of any grievance based upon allegations of conduct that constitutes a felony, without regard to whether the lawyer is charged, prosecuted, or convicted of a crime for the conduct.

(3) There is no time limitation for initiation of any grievance based upon conduct that violates the Rules of Professional Conduct and has been found by a court to be intentional conduct by the lawyer. As used in this Rule, "court" means a state court of general jurisdiction of any state or of the District of Columbia or a federal court.

(4) All other grievances must be initiated within six years after the last act giving rise to the grievance.

[History Note: Statutory Authority G.S. 84-23. Readopted effective December 8, 1994; amended effective February 20, 1995; December 30, 1998; October 1, 2003; October 8, 2009.]

.0112. Investigations: Initial Determination; Notice and Response; Committee Referrals

(a) Investigation Authority. Subject to the policy supervision of the council and the control of the chair of the Grievance Committee, the counsel, or other personnel under the authority of the counsel, will investigate the grievance and submit to the chair a report detailing the findings of the investigation.

(b) Grievance Committee Action on Initial or Interim Reports. As soon as practicable after the receipt of the initial or any interim report of the counsel concerning any grievance, the chair of the Grievance Committee may

(1) treat the report as a final report;

(2) direct the counsel to conduct further investigation, including contacting the respondent in writing or otherwise; or

(3) direct the counsel to send a letter of notice to the respondent.

(c) Letter of Notice, Respondent's Response, and Request for Copy of Grievance. If the counsel serves a letter of notice upon the respondent, it will be served by certified mail and will direct that a response be provided within 15 days of service of the letter of notice upon the respondent. The response to the letter of notice shall include a full and fair disclosure of all facts and circumstances pertaining to the alleged misconduct. The response must be in writing and signed by the respondent. If the respondent requests it, the counsel will provide the respondent with a copy of the written grievance, unless the complainant requests anonymity pursuant to Rule .0111(d) of this subchapter.

(d) Request for Copy of Respondent's Response. The counsel may provide to the complainant a copy of the respondent's response to the letter of notice unless the respondent objects thereto in writing.

(e) Termination of Further Investigation. After the Grievance Committee receives the response to a letter of notice, the counsel may conduct further investigation or terminate the investigation, subject to the control of the chair of the Grievance Committee.

(f) Subpoenas. For reasonable cause, the chair of the Grievance Committee may issue subpoenas to compel the attendance of witnesses, including the respondent, for examination concerning the grievance and may compel the production of books, papers, and other documents or writings which the chair deems necessary or material to the inquiry. Each subpoena will be issued by the chair or by the secretary at the direction of the chair. The counsel, deputy counsel, investigator or any members of the Grievance Committee designated by the chair may examine any such witness under oath or otherwise.

(g) Grievance Committee Action on Final Reports. The Grievance Committee will consider the grievance as soon as practicable after it receives the final report of the counsel, except as otherwise provided in these rules.

(h) Failure of Complainant to Sign and Dismissal Upon Request of Complainant. The investigation into alleged misconduct of the respondent will not be abated by failure of the complainant to sign a grievance, by settlement or compromise of a dispute between the complainant and the respondent, or by the respondent's payment of restitution. The chair of the Grievance Committee may dismiss a grievance upon request of the complainant and with consent of the counsel where it appears that there is no probable cause to believe that the respondent violated the Rules of Professional Conduct.

(i) Referral to Law Office Management Training.

(1) If, at any time before a finding of probable cause, the Grievance Committee determines that the alleged misconduct is primarily attributable to the respondent's failure to employ sound law office management techniques and procedures, the committee may offer the respondent an opportunity to voluntarily participate in a law office management training program approved by the State Bar before the committee considers discipline.

If the respondent accepts the committee's offer to participate in the program, the respondent will then be required to complete a course of training in law office management prescribed by the chair which may include a comprehensive site audit of the respondent's records and procedures as well as attendance at continuing legal education seminars. If the respondent does not accept the committee's offer, the grievance will be returned to the committee's agenda for consideration of imposition of discipline.

(2) Completion of Law Office Management Training Program—If the respondent successfully completes the law office management training program, the committee may consider the respondent's successful completion of the law office management training program as a mitigating circumstance and may, but is not required to, dismiss the grievance for good cause shown. If the respondent fails to successfully complete the law office management training program as agreed, the grievance will be returned to the committee's agenda for consideration of imposition of discipline. The requirement that a respondent complete law office management training pursuant to this rule shall be in addition to the respondent's obligation to satisfy the minimum continuing legal education requirements contained in 27 N.C.A.C. 1D.1517.

(j) Referral to Lawyer Assistance Program.

(1) If, at any time before a finding of probable cause, the Grievance Committee determines that the alleged misconduct is primarily attributable to the respondent's substance abuse or mental health problem, the committee may offer the respondent an opportunity to voluntarily participate in a rehabilitation program under the supervision of the Lawyer Assistance Program Board before the committee considers discipline.

If the respondent accepts the committee's offer to participate in a rehabilitation program, the respondent must provide the committee with a written acknowledgement of the referral on a form approved by the chair. The acknowledgement of the referral must include the respondent's waiver of any right of confidentiality that might otherwise exist to permit the Lawyer Assistance Program to provide the committee with the information necessary for the committee to determine whether the respondent is in compliance with the rehabilitation program. If the respondent does not accept the committee's offer, the grievance will be returned to the committee's agenda for consideration of imposition of discipline.

(2) Completion of Rehabilitation Program—If the respondent successfully completes the rehabilitation program, the committee may consider successful completion of the program as a mitigating circumstance and may, but is not required to, dismiss the grievance for good cause shown. If the respondent fails to complete the rehabilitation program or fails to cooperate with the Lawyer Assistance Program Board, the Lawyer Assistance Program will report that failure to the counsel and the grievance will be returned to the committee's agenda for consideration of imposition of discipline.

(k) Referral to Trust Account Compliance Program

(1) If, at any time before a finding of probable cause, the Grievance Committee determines that the alleged misconduct is primarily attributable to the respondent's failure to employ sound trust accounting techniques, the committee may offer the respondent an opportunity to voluntarily participate in the State Bar's Trust Account Compliance Program for up to two years before the committee considers discipline.

If the respondent accepts the committee's offer to participate in the compliance program, the respondent must fully cooperate with the Trust Account Compliance Counsel and must provide to the Office of Counsel quarterly proof of compliance with all provisions of Rule 1.15 of the Rules of Professional Conduct. Such proof shall be in a form satisfactory to the Office of Counsel. If the respondent does not accept the committee's offer, the grievance will be returned to the committee's agenda for consideration of imposition of discipline.

(2) Completion of Trust Account Compliance Program— If the respondent successfully completes the program, the committee may consider successful completion of the program as a mitigating circumstance and may, but is not required to, dismiss the grievance for good cause shown. If the respondent does not fully cooperate with the Trust Account Compliance Counsel and/or does not successfully complete the program, the grievance will be returned to the committee's agenda for consideration of imposition of discipline.

(3) The committee will not refer to the program any case involving possible misappropriation of entrusted funds, criminal conduct, dishonesty, fraud, misrepresentation, or deceit, or any other case the committee deems inappropriate for referral. The committee will not refer to the program any respondent who has not cooperated fully and timely with the committee's investigation. If the Office of Counsel or the committee discovers evidence that a respondent who is participating in the program may have misappropriated entrusted funds, engaged in criminal conduct, or engaged in conduct involving dishonesty, fraud, misrepresentation, or deceit, the chair will terminate the respondent's participation in the program and the disciplinary process will proceed. Referral to the Trust Account Compliance Program is not a defense to allegations that a lawyer misappropriated entrusted funds, engaged in criminal conduct, or engaged in conduct involving dishonesty, fraud, misrepresentation, or deceit, and it does not immunize a lawyer from the disciplinary consequences of such conduct.

[History Note: Statutory Authority G.S. 84-23. Readopted effective December 8, 1994; amended effective February 20, 1995; March 6, 1997; December 30, 1998; December 20, 2000; March 6, 2002; March 10, 2010; March 10, 2011; August 25, 2011; August 23, 2012; March 5, 2015.]

.0113 Proceedings before the Grievance Committee

(a) The Grievance Committee or any of its panels acting as the Grievance Committee with respect to grievances referred to it by the chairperson of the Grievance Committee will determine whether there is probable cause to believe that a respondent is guilty of misconduct justifying disciplinary action. In its discretion, the Grievance Committee or a panel thereof may find probable cause regardless of whether the respondent has been served with a written letter of notice. The respondent may waive the necessity of a finding of probable cause with the consent of the counsel and the chairperson of the Grievance Committee. A decision of a panel of the committee may not be appealed to the Grievance Committee as a whole or to another panel (except as provided in 27 N.C.A.C. 1A, .0701(a)(3)).

(b) The chairperson of the Grievance Committee will have the power to administer oaths and affirmations.

(c) The chairperson will keep a record of the grievance committee's determination concerning each grievance and file the record with the secretary.

(d) The chairperson will have the power to subpoena witnesses, to compel their attendance, and compel the production of books, papers, and other documents deemed necessary or material to any preliminary hearing. The chairperson may designate the secretary to issue such subpoenas.

(e) The counsel and deputy counsel, the witness under examination, interpreters when needed, and, if deemed necessary, a stenographer or operator of a recording device may be present while the committee is in session and deliberating, but no persons other than members may be present while the committee is voting.

(f) The results of any deliberation by the Grievance Committee will be disclosed to the counsel and the secretary for use in the performance of their duties. Otherwise, a member of the committee, the staff of the North Carolina State Bar, any interpreter, stenographer, operator of a recording device, or any typist who transcribes recorded testimony may disclose matters occurring before the committee only when so directed by the committee or a court of record.

(g) At any preliminary hearing held by the Grievance Committee, a quorum of one-half of the members will be required to conduct any business. Affirmative vote of a majority of members present will be necessary to find that probable cause exists. The chairperson will not be counted for quorum purposes and will be eligible to vote regarding the disposition of any grievance only in case of a tie among the regular voting members.

(h) If probable cause is found and the committee determines that a hearing is necessary, the chairperson will direct the counsel to prepare and file a complaint against the respondent. If the committee finds probable cause but determines that no hearing is necessary, it will direct the counsel to prepare for the chairperson's signature an admonition, reprimand, or censure. If no probable cause is found, the grievance will be dismissed or dismissed with a letter of warning or a letter of caution.

(i) If no probable cause is found but it is determined by the Grievance Committee that the conduct of the respondent is unprofessional or not in accord with accepted professional practice, the committee may issue a letter of caution to the respondent recommending that the respondent be more professional in his or her practice in one or more ways which are to be specifically identified.

(j) Letters of Warning.

(1) If no probable cause is found but it is determined by the Grievance Committee that the conduct of the respondent is an unintentional, minor, or technical violation of the Rules of Professional Conduct, the committee may issue a letter of warning to the respondent. The letter of warning will advise the respondent that he or she may be subject to discipline if such conduct is continued or repeated. The letter will specify in one or more ways the conduct or practice for which the respondent is being warned. The letter of warning will not constitute discipline of the respondent.

(2) A copy of the letter of warning will be maintained in the office of the counsel for three years. If relevant, a copy of the letter of warning may be offered into evidence in any proceeding filed against the respondent before the commission within three years after the letter of warning is issued to the respondent. In every case filed against the respondent before the commission within three years after the letter of warning is issued to the respondent, the letter of warning may be introduced into evidence as an aggravating factor concerning the issue of what disciplinary sanction should be imposed. A copy of the letter of warning may be disclosed to the Grievance Committee if another grievance is filed against the respondent within three years after the letter of warning is issued to the respondent.

(3) A copy of the letter of warning will be served upon the respondent in person or by certified mail. A respondent who cannot, with due diligence, be served by certified mail or personal service shall be deemed served by the mailing of a copy of the letter of warning to the respondent's last known address on file with the N.C. State Bar. Service shall be deemed complete upon deposit of the letter of warning in a postpaid, properly addressed wrapper in a post office or official depository under the exclusive care and custody of the United States Postal Service. Within 15 days after service the respondent may refuse the letter of warning and request a hearing before the commission to determine whether a violation of the Rules of Professional Conduct has occurred. Such refusal and request will be in writing, addressed to the Grievance Committee, and served on the secretary by certified mail, return receipt requested. The refusal will state that the letter of warning is refused. If a refusal and request are not served within 15 days after service upon the respondent of the letter of warning, the letter of warning will be deemed accepted by the respondent. An extension of time may be granted by the chairperson of the Grievance Committee for good cause shown.

(4) In cases in which the respondent refuses the letter of warning, the counsel will prepare and file a complaint against the respondent for a hearing pursuant to Rule .0114 of this subchapter.

(k) Admonitions, Reprimands, and Censures.

(1) If probable cause is found but it is determined by the Grievance Committee that a complaint and hearing are not warranted, the committee shall issue an admonition in cases in which the respondent has committed a minor violation of the Rules of Professional Conduct, a reprimand in cases in which the respondent's conduct has violated one or more provisions of the Rules of Professional Conduct and caused harm or potential harm to a client, the administration of justice, the profession, or members of the public, or a censure in cases in which the respondent has violated one or more provisions of the Rules of Professional Conduct and the harm or potential harm caused by the respondent is significant and protection of the public requires more serious discipline. To determine whether more serious discipline is necessary to protect the public or whether the violation is minor and less senior discipline is sufficient to protect the public, the committee shall consider the factors delineated in subparagraphs (2) and (3) below.

(2) Factors that shall be considered in determining whether protection of the public requires a censure include, but are not limited to, the following:

(A) prior discipline for the same or similar conduct;

(B) prior notification by the North Carolina State Bar of the wrongfulness of the conduct;

(C) refusal to acknowledge wrongful nature of conduct;

(D) lack of indication of reformation;

(E) likelihood of repetition of misconduct;

(F) uncooperative attitude toward disciplinary process;

(G) pattern of similar conduct;

(H) violation of the Rules of Professional Conduct in more than one unrelated matter;

(I) lack of efforts to rectify consequences of conduct;

(J) imposition of lesser discipline would fail to acknowledge the seriousness of the misconduct and would send the wrong message to members of the Bar and the public regarding the conduct expected of members of the Bar;

(K) notification contemporaneous with the conduct at issue of the wrongful nature of the conduct and failure to take remedial action.

(3) factors that shall be considered in determining whether the violation of the Rules is minor and warrants issuance of an admonition include, but are not limited to, the following:

(A) lack of prior discipline for same or similar conduct;

(B) recognition of wrongful nature of conduct;

(C) indication of reformation;

(D) indication that repetition of misconduct not likely;

(E) isolated incident;

(F) violation of the Rules of Professional Conduct in only one matter;

(G) lack of harm or potential harm to client, administration of justice, profession, or members of the public;

(H) efforts to rectify consequences of conduct;

(I) inexperience in the practice of law;

(J) imposition of admonition appropriately acknowledges the minor nature of the violation(s) of the Revised Rules of Professional Conduct;

(K) notification contemporaneous with the conduct at issue of the wrongful nature of the conduct resulting in efforts to take remedial action;

(L) personal or emotional problems contributing to the conduct at issue;

(M) successful participation in and completion of contract with Lawyer's Assistance Program where mental health or substance abuse issues contributed to the conduct at issue.

(*l*) Procedures for Admonitions and Reprimands.

(1) A record of any admonition or reprimand issued by the Grievance Committee will be maintained in the office of the secretary.

(2) A copy of the admonition or reprimand will be served upon the respondent in person or by certified mail. A respondent who cannot, with due diligence, be served by certified mail or personal service shall be deemed served by the mailing of a copy of the admonition or reprimand to the respondent's last known address on file with the NC State Bar. Service shall be deemed complete upon deposit of the admonition or reprimand in a postpaid, properly addressed wrapper in a post office or official depository under the exclusive care and custody of the United States Postal Service.

(3) Within 15 days after service the respondent may refuse the admonition or reprimand and request a hearing before the commission. Such refusal and request will be in writing, addressed to the Grievance Committee, and served upon the secretary by certified mail, return receipt requested. The refusal will state that the admonition or reprimand is refused.

(4) In cases in which the respondent refuses an admonition or reprimand, the counsel will prepare and file a complaint against the respondent pursuant to Rule .0114 of this subchapter. If a refusal and request are not served upon the secretary within 15 days after service upon the respondent of the admonition or reprimand, the admonition or reprimand will be deemed accepted by the respondent. An extension of time may be granted by the chairperson of the Grievance Committee for good cause shown.

(m) Procedure for Censures.

(1) If the Grievance Committee determines that the imposition of a censure is appropriate,, the committee will issue a notice of proposed censure and a proposed censure to the respondent.

(2) A copy of the notice and the proposed censure will be served upon the respondent in person or by certified mail. A respondent who cannot, with due diligence, be served by certified mail or personal service shall be deemed served by the mailing of a copy of the notice and proposed censure to the respondent's last known address on file with the NC State Bar. Service shall be deemed complete upon deposit of the notice and proposed censure in a postpaid, properly addressed wrapper in a post office or official depository under the exclusive care and custody of the United States Postal Service. The respondent must be advised that he or she may accept the censure within 15 days after service upon him or her or a formal complaint will be filed before the commission.

(3) The respondent's acceptance must be in writing, addressed to the Grievance Committee, and served on the secretary by certified mail, return receipt requested. Once the censure is accepted by the respondent, the discipline becomes public and must be filed as provided by Rule .0123(a)(3) of this subchapter.

(4) If the respondent does not accept the censure, the counsel will file a complaint against the defendant pursuant to Rule .0114 of this subchapter.

(n) Formal complaints will be issued in the name of the North Carolina State Bar as plaintiff and signed by the chairperson of the Grievance Committee. Amendments to complaints may be signed by the counsel alone, with the approval of the chairperson of the Grievance Committee.

[History Note: Statutory Authority G.S. 84–23; G.S. 84–28. Readopted effective December 8, 1994; amended effective March 3, 1999; amended December 10, 1999, effective February 3, 2000; amended effective October 8, 2009.]

.0114 Formal Hearing

(a) Complaints will be filed with the secretary. The secretary will cause a summons and a copy of the complaint to be served upon the defendant and thereafter a copy of the complaint will be delivered to the chairperson of the commission, informing the chairperson of the date service on the defendant was effected.

(b) Service of complaints and summonses and other documents or papers will be accomplished as set forth in the North Carolina Rules of Civil Procedure.

(c) Complaints in disciplinary actions will allege the charges with sufficient precision to clearly apprise the defendant of the conduct which is the subject of the complaint.

(d) Within 20 days of the receipt of return of service of a complaint by the secretary, the chairperson of the commission will designate a hearing panel from among the commission members. The chairperson will notify the counsel and the defendant of the composition of the hearing panel. Such notice will also contain the time and place determined by the chairperson for the hearing to commence. The commencement of the hearing will be initially scheduled not less than 90 nor more than 150 days from the date of service of the complaint upon the defendant, unless one or more subsequent complaints have been served on the defendant within 90 days from the date of service of the first or a preceding complaint. When one or more subsequent complaints have been served on the defendant within 90 days from the date of service of the first or a preceding complaint, the chairperson of the commission may consolidate the cases for hearing, and the hearing will be initially scheduled not less than 90 nor more than 150 days from the date of service of the last complaint upon the defendant. By agreement between the parties and with the consent of the chair, the date for the initial setting of the hearing may be set less than 90 days after the date of service on the defendant.

(e) Within 20 days after the service of the complaint, unless further time is allowed by the chairperson of the hearing panel upon good cause shown, the defendant will file an answer to the complaint with the secretary and will serve a copy on the counsel.

(f) Failure to file an answer admitting, denying or explaining the complaint or asserting the grounds for failing to do so, within the time limited or extended, will be grounds for entry of the defendant's default and in such case the allegations contained in the complaint will be deemed admitted. The secretary will enter the defendant's default when the fact of default is made to appear by motion of the counsel or otherwise. The counsel may thereupon apply to the hearing panel for a default order imposing discipline, and the hearing panel will thereupon enter an order, make findings of fact and conclusions of law based on the admissions, and order the discipline deemed appropriate. The hearing panel may, in its discretion, hear such additional evidence as it deems necessary prior to entering the order of discipline. For good cause shown, the hearing panel may set aside the secretary's entry of default. After an order imposing discipline has been entered by the hearing panel upon the defendant's default, the hearing panel may set aside the order in accordance with Rule 60(b) of the North Carolina Rules of Civil Procedure.

(g) Discovery will be available to the parties in accordance with the North Carolina Rules of Civil Procedure. Any discovery undertaken must be completed before the date scheduled for commencement of the hearing unless the time for discovery is extended for good cause shown by the chairperson of the hearing panel. The chairperson of the hearing panel may thereupon reset the time for the hearing to commence to accommodate completion of reasonable discovery.

(h) The parties may meet by mutual consent prior to the hearing on the complaint to discuss the possibility of settlement of the case or the stipulation of any issues, facts, or matters of law. Any proposed settlement of the case will be subject to the approval of the hearing panel. If the panel rejects a proposed settlement, another hearing panel must be empaneled to try the case, unless all parties consent to proceed with the original committee. The parties may submit a proposed settlement to a second hearing panel, but the parties shall not have the right to request a third hearing panel if the settlement order is rejected by the second hearing panel. The second hearing panel shall either accept the settlement proposal or hear the disciplinary matter.

(i) At the discretion of the chairperson of the hearing panel, and upon five days' notice to the parties, a conference may be ordered before the date set for commencement of the hearing for the purpose of obtaining admissions or otherwise narrowing the issues presented by the pleadings. Such conference may be held before any member of the panel designated by its chairperson, who shall have the power to issue such orders as may be appropriate. At any conference which may be held to expedite the orderly conduct and disposition of any hearing, there may be considered in addition to any offers of settlement or proposals of adjustment, the following:

(1) the simplification of the issues;

(2) the exchange of exhibits proposed to be offered in evidence;

(3) the stipulation of facts not remaining in dispute or the authenticity of documents;

(4) the limitation of the number of witnesses:

(5) the discovery or production of data;

(6) such other matters as may properly be dealt with to aid in expediting the orderly conduct and disposition of the proceeding.

The chairperson may impose sanctions as set out in Rule 37(b) of the N.C. Rules of Civil Procedure against any party who willfully fails to comply with a prehearing order issued pursuant to this section.

(j) The chairperson of the hearing panel, without consulting the other panel members, may hear and dispose of all pretrial motions except motions the granting of which would result in dismissal of the charges or final judgment for either party. All motions which could result in dismissal of the charges or final judgment for either party will be decided by a majority of the members of the hearing panel. Any pretrial motion may be decided on the basis of the parties' written submissions. Oral argument may be allowed in the discretion of the chairperson of the hearing panel.

(k) The initial hearing date as set by the chairperson in accordance with Rule .0114(d) above may be reset by the chairperson, and said initial hearing or reset hearing may be continued by the chairperson of the hearing panel for good cause shown.

(*l*) After a hearing has commenced, no continuances other than an adjournment from day to day will be granted, except to await the filing of a controlling decision of an appellate court, by consent of all parties, or where extreme hardship would result in the absence of a continuance.

(m) The defendant will appear in person before the hearing panel at the time and place named by the chairperson. The hearing will be open to the public except that for good cause shown the chairperson of the hearing panel may exclude from the hearing room all persons except the parties, counsel, and those engaged in the hearing. No hearing will be closed to the public over the objection of the defendant. The defendant will, except as otherwise provided by law, be competent and compellable to give evidence for either of the parties. The defendant may be represented by counsel, who will enter an appearance.

(n) Pleadings and proceedings before a hearing panel will conform as nearly as practicable with requirements of the North Carolina Rules of Civil Procedure and for trials of nonjury civil causes in the superior courts except as otherwise provided herein.

(*o*) Pleadings or other documents in formal proceedings required or permitted to be filed under these rules must be received for filing by the secretary within the time limits, if any, for such filing. The date of receipt by the secretary, and not the date of deposit in the mails, is determinative.

(p) All papers presented to the commission for filing will be on letter size paper (8½ × 11 inches) with the exception of exhibits. The secretary will require a party to refile any paper that does not conform to this size.

(q) When a defendant appears in his or her own behalf in a proceeding, the defendant will file with the secretary, with proof of delivery of a copy to the counsel, an address at which any notice or other written communication required to be served upon the defendant may be sent, if such address differs from that last reported to the secretary by the defendant.

(r) When a defendant is represented by counsel in a proceeding, counsel will file with the secretary, with proof of delivery of a copy to the counsel, a written notice of such appearance which will state his or her name, address and telephone number, the name and address of the defendant on whose behalf he or she appears, and the caption and docket number of the proceeding. Any additional notice or other written communication required to be served on or furnished to a defendant during the pendency of the hearing may be sent to the counsel of record for such defendant at the stated address of the counsel in lieu of transmission to the defendant.

(s) The hearing panel will have the power to subpoena witnesses and compel their attendance, and to compel the production of books, papers, and other documents deemed necessary or material to any hearing. Such process will be issued in the name of the panel by its chairperson, or the chairperson may designate the secretary of the North Carolina State Bar to issue such process. Both parties have the right to invoke the powers of the committee with respect to compulsory process for witnesses and for the production of books, papers, and other writings and documents.

(t) In any hearing admissibility of evidence will be governed by the rules of evidence applicable in the superior court of the state at the time of the hearing. The chairperson of the hearing panel will rule on the admissibility of evidence, subject to the right of any member of the hearing panel to question the ruling. If a member of the hearing panel challenges a ruling relating to admissibility of evidence, the question will be decided by majority vote of the hearing panel.

(u) If the hearing panel finds that the charges of misconduct are not established by clear, cogent, and convincing evidence, it will enter an order dismissing the complaint. If the hearing panel finds that the charges of misconduct are established by clear, cogent, and convincing evidence, the hearing panel will enter an order of discipline. In either instance, the panel will file an order which will include the panel's findings of fact and conclusions of law.

(v) The secretary will ensure that a complete record is made of the evidence received during the course of all hearings before the commission as provided by G.S. 7A–95 for trials in the superior court. The secretary will preserve the record and the pleadings, exhibits, and briefs of the parties.

(w) If the charges of misconduct are established, the hearing panel will then consider any evidence relevant to the discipline to be imposed.

(1) Suspension or disbarment is appropriate where there is evidence that the defendant's actions resulted in significant harm or potential significant harm to the clients, the public, the administration of justice, or the legal profession, and lesser discipline is insufficient to adequately protect the public. The following factors shall be considered in imposing suspension or disbarment:

(A) intent of the defendant to cause the resulting harm or potential harm;

(B) intent of the defendant to commit acts where the harm or potential harm is foreseeable;

(C) circumstances reflecting the defendant's lack of honesty, trustworthiness, or integrity;

(D) elevation of the defendant's own interest above that of the client;

(E) negative impact of defendant's actions on client's or public's perception of the profession;

(F) negative impact of the defendant's actions on the administration of justice;

(G) impairment of the client's ability to achieve the goals of the representation;

(H) effect of defendant's conduct on third parties;

(I) acts of dishonesty, misrepresentation, deceit, or fabrication;

(J) multiple instances of failure to participate in the legal profession's self-regulation process.

(2) Disbarment shall be considered where the defendant is found to engage in:

(A) acts of dishonesty, misrepresentation, deceit, or fabrication;

(B) impulsive acts of dishonesty, misrepresentation, deceit, or fabrication without timely remedial efforts;

(C) misappropriation or conversion of assets of any kind to which the defendant or recipient is not entitled, whether from a client or any other source;

(D) commission of a felony.

(3) In all cases, any or all of the following factors shall be considered in imposing the appropriate discipline:

(A) prior disciplinary offenses in this state or any other jurisdiction, or the absence thereof;

(B) remoteness of prior offenses;

(C) dishonest or selfish motive, or the absence thereof;

(D) timely good faith efforts to make restitution or to rectify consequences of misconduct;

(E) indifference to making restitution;

(F) a pattern of misconduct;

(G) multiple offenses;

(H) effect of any personal or emotional problems on the conduct in question;

(I) effect of any physical or mental disability or impairment on the conduct in question;

(J) interim rehabilitation;

(K) full and free disclosure to the hearing panel or cooperative attitude toward the proceedings;

(L) delay in disciplinary proceedings through no fault of the defendant attorney;

(M) bad faith obstruction of the disciplinary proceedings by intentionally failing to comply with rules or orders of the disciplinary agency;

(N) submission of false evidence, false statements, or other deceptive practices during the disciplinary process;

(O) refusal to acknowledge wrongful nature of conduct;

(P) remorse;

(Q) character or reputation;

(R) vulnerability of victim;

(S) degree of experience in the practice of law;

(T) issuance of a letter of warning to the defendant within the three years immediately preceding the filing of the complaint;

(U) imposition of other penalties or sanctions;

(V) any other factors found to be pertinent to the consideration of the discipline to be imposed.

(x) In any case in which a period of suspension is stayed upon compliance by the defendant with conditions, the commission will retain jurisdiction of the matter until all conditions are satisfied. If, during the period the stay is in effect, the counsel receives information tending to show that a condition has been violated, the counsel may, with the consent of the chairperson of the Grievance Committee, file a motion in the cause with the secretary specifying the violation and seeking an order requiring the defendant to show cause why the stay should not be lifted and the suspension activated for violation of the condition. The counsel will also serve a copy of any such motion upon the defendant. The secretary will promptly transmit the motion to the chairperson of the commission who, if he or she enters an order to show cause, will appoint a hearing panel as provided in Rule

.0108(a)(2) of this subchapter, appointing the members of the hearing panel that originally heard the matter wherever practicable. The chairperson of the commission will also schedule a time and a place for a hearing and notify the counsel and the defendant of the composition of the hearing panel and the time and place for the hearing. After such a hearing, the hearing panel may enter an order lifting the stay and activating the suspension, or any portion thereof, and taxing the defendant with the costs, if it finds that the North Carolina State Bar has proven, by the greater weight of the evidence, that the defendant has violated a condition. If the hearing panel finds that the North Carolina State Bar has not carried its burden, then it will enter an order continuing the stay. In any event, the hearing panel will include in its order findings of fact and conclusions of law in support of its decision.

(y) All reports and orders of the hearing panel will be signed by the members of the panel, or by the chairperson of the panel on behalf of the panel, and will be filed with the secretary. The copy to the defendant will be served by certified mail, return receipt requested or personal service. A defendant who cannot, with due diligence, be served by certified mail or personal service shall be deemed served by the mailing of a copy of the order to the defendant's last known address on file with the N.C. State Bar. Service by mail shall be deemed complete upon deposit of the report or order enclosed in a postpaid, properly addressed wrapper in a post office or official depository under the exclusive care and custody of the United States Postal Service.

(z) Post Trial Motions.

(1) *Consent Orders After Trial.* At any time after a disciplinary hearing and prior to the execution of the panel's final order pursuant to Rule .0114(y) above, the panel may, with the consent of the parties, amend its decision regarding the findings of fact, conclusions of law, or the disciplinary sanction imposed.

(2) *New Trials and Amendment of Judgments.*

(A) As provided in Rule .0114(z)(2)(B) below, following a disciplinary hearing before the commission, either party may request a new trial or amendment of the hearing panel's final order, based on any of the grounds set out in Rule 59 of the North Carolina Rules of Civil Procedure.

(B) A motion for a new trial or amendment of judgment will be served, in writing, on the chairperson of the hearing panel which heard the disciplinary case no later than 20 days after service of the final order upon the defendant. Supporting affidavits, if any, and a memorandum setting forth the basis of the motion together with supporting authorities, will be filed with the motion.

(C) The opposing party will have 20 days from service of the motion to file a written response, any reply affidavits, and a memorandum with supporting authorities.

(D) The hearing panel may rule on the motion based on the parties' written submissions or may, in its discretion, permit the parties to present oral argument.

(3) *Relief From Judgment or Order.*

(A) Following a disciplinary proceeding before the commission, either party may file a motion for relief from the final judgment or order, based on any of the grounds set out in Rule 60 of the North Carolina Rules of Civil Procedure.

(B) Motions made under Rule .0114(z)(2)(B) above will be made no later than one year after the effective date of the order from which relief is sought. Motions pursuant to this section will be heard and decided in the same manner as motions submitted pursuant to Rule .0114(z)(2) above.

(4) *Effect of Filing Motion.* The filing of a motion under Rule .0114(z)(2) above or Rule .0114(z)(3) above will not automatically stay or otherwise affect the effective date of an order of the commission.

[History Note: Statutory Authority G.S. 84-23; G.S. 84-28; G.S. 84-28.1; G.S. 84-29; G.S. 84-30; G.S. 84-32(a). Readopted effective December 8, 1994; amended effective October 2, 1997; December 30, 1998; March 2, 2006; October 8, 2009.]

.0115 Effect of a Finding of Guilt in Any Criminal Case

(a) Any member who has been found guilty of or has tendered and has had accepted a plea of guilty or no contest to a criminal offense showing professional unfitness in any state or federal court, may be suspended from the practice of law as set out in Rule .0115(d) below.

(b) A certificate of the conviction of an attorney for any crime or a certificate of the judgment entered against an attorney where a plea of nolo contendere or no contest has been accepted by a court will be conclusive evidence of guilt of that crime in any disciplinary proceeding instituted against a member.

(c) Upon the receipt of a certified copy of a jury verdict showing a verdict of guilty, a certificate of the conviction of a member a criminal offense showing professional unfitness, or a certificate of the judgment entered against an attorney where a plea of nolo contendere or no contest has been accepted by a court, the Grievance Committee, at its next meeting following notification of the conviction, may authorize the filing of a complaint if one is not pending. In the hearing on such complaint, the sole issue to be determined will be the extent of the discipline to be imposed. The attorney may be disciplined based upon the conviction without awaiting the outcome of any appeals of the conviction or judgment, unless the attorney has obtained a stay of the disciplinary action as set out in G.S. § 84-28(d1). Such a stay shall not prevent the North Carolina State Bar from proceeding with a disciplinary proceeding against the attorney based upon the same underlying facts or events that were the subject of the criminal proceeding.

(d) Upon the receipt of a certificate of conviction of a member of a criminal offense showing professional unfitness, or a certified copy of a plea of guilty or no contest to such an offense, or a certified copy of a jury verdict showing a verdict of guilty to such an offense, the commission chairperson may, in the chairperson's discretion, enter an order suspending the member pending the disposition of the disciplinary proceeding against the member before the commission. The provisions of Rule .0124(c) of this subchapter will apply to the suspension.

(e) Upon the receipt of a certificate of conviction of a member of a criminal offense which does not show professional unfitness, or a certificate of judgment against a member upon a plea of no contest to such an offense, or a certified copy of a jury verdict showing a verdict of guilty to such an offense, the Grievance Committee will take whatever action, including authorizing the filing of a complaint, it may deem appropriate. In a hearing on any such complaint, the sole issue to be determined will be the extent of the discipline to be imposed. The attorney may be disciplined based upon the conviction without awaiting the outcome of any appeals of the conviction or judgment, unless the attorney has obtained a stay of the disciplinary action as set out in G.S. § 84-28(d1). Such a stay shall not prevent the North Carolina State Bar from proceeding with a disciplinary proceeding against the attorney based upon the same underlying facts or events that were the subject of the criminal proceeding.

[History Note: Statutory Authority G.S. 84-23; G.S. 84-28. Readopted effective December 8, 1994; amended effective November 7, 1996; amended effective March 6, 1997; December 30, 1998; amended effective February 3, 2000.]

.0116 Reciprocal Discipline and Disability Proceedings

(a) All members who have been disciplined in any state or federal court for a violation of the Rules of Professional Conduct in effect in such state or federal court or who have been transferred to disability inactive status or its equivalent by any state or federal court will inform the secretary of such action in writing no later than 30 days after entry of the order of discipline or transfer to disability inactive status. Failure to make the report required in this section may subject the member to professional discipline as set out in Rule 8.3 of the Revised Rules of Professional Conduct.

(b) Except as provided in subsection (c) below which applies to disciplinary proceedings in certain federal courts, reciprocal discipline and disability proceedings will be administered as follows:

(1) Upon receipt of a certified copy of an order demonstrating that a member has been disciplined or transferred to disability inactive status or its equivalent in another jurisdiction, state or federal, the Grievance Committee will forthwith issue a notice directed to the member containing a copy of the order from the other jurisdiction and an order directing that the member inform the committee within 30 days from service of the notice of any claim by the member that imposition of the identical discipline or an order transferring the member to disability inactive status in this state would be unwarranted and the reasons therefor. This notice is to be served on the member in accordance with the provisions of Rule 4 of the North Carolina Rules of Civil Procedure.

(2) If the discipline or transfer order imposed in the other jurisdiction has been stayed, any reciprocal discipline or transfer to disability inactive status imposed in this state will be deferred until such stay expires.

(3) Upon the expiration of 30 days from service of the notice issued pursuant to the provisions of Rule. 0116(b)(1) above, the chairperson of the Grievance Committee will impose the identical discipline or enter an order transferring the member to disability inactive status unless the Grievance Committee concludes

(A) that the procedure was so lacking in notice or opportunity to be heard as to constitute a deprivation of due process; or

(B) there was such an infirmity of proof establishing the misconduct as to give rise to the clear conviction that the Grievance Committee could not, consistent with its duty, accept as final the conclusion on that subject; or

(C) that the imposition of the same discipline would result in grave injustice; or

(D) that the misconduct established warrants substantially different discipline in this state; or

(E) that the reason for the original transfer to disability inactive status no longer exists.

(4) Where the Grievance Committee determines that any of the elements listed in Rule.0116(b)(3) above exist, the committee will dismiss the case or direct that a complaint be filed.

(5) If the elements listed in Rule.0116(b)(3) above are found not to exist, a final adjudication in another jurisdiction that an attorney has been guilty of misconduct or should be transferred to disability inactive status will establish the misconduct or disability for purposes of reciprocal discipline or disability proceedings in this state.

(c) Reciprocal discipline with certain federal courts will be administered as follows:

(1) Upon receipt of a certified copy of an order demonstrating that a member has been disciplined in a United States District Court in North Carolina, in the United States Fourth Circuit Court of Appeals, or in the United States Supreme Court, the chairperson of the Grievance Committee will forthwith issue a notice directed to the member. The notice will con-

tain a copy of the order from the court and an order directing the member to inform the committee within 10 days from service of the notice whether the member will accept reciprocal discipline which is substantially similar to that imposed by the federal court. This notice is to be served on the member in accordance with the provisions of Rule 4 of the North Carolina Rules of Civil Procedure. The member will have 30 days from service of the notice to file a written challenge with the committee on the grounds that the imposition of discipline by the North Carolina State Bar would be unwarranted because the facts found in the federal disciplinary proceeding do not involve conduct which violates the North Carolina Rules of Professional Conduct. If the member notifies the North Carolina State Bar within 10 days after service of the notice that he or she accepts reciprocal discipline which is substantially similar to that imposed by the federal court, substantially similar discipline will be ordered as provided in Rule .0116(c)(2) below and will run concurrently with the discipline ordered by the federal court.

(2) If the member notifies the North Carolina State Bar of his or her acceptance of reciprocal discipline as provided in Rule .0116(c)(1) above the chairperson of the Grievance Committee will execute an order of discipline which is of a type permitted by these rules and which is substantially similar to that ordered by the federal court and will cause said order to be served upon the member.

(3) If the discipline imposed by the federal court has been stayed, any reciprocal discipline imposed by the North Carolina State Bar will be deferred until such stay expires.

(4) Upon the expiration of 30 days from service of the notice issued pursuant to the provisions of Rule .0116(c)(1) above, the chairperson of the Grievance Committee will enter an order of reciprocal discipline imposing substantially similar discipline of a type permitted by these rules to be effective throughout North Carolina unless the member requests a hearing before the Grievance Committee and at such hearing

(A) the member demonstrates that the facts found in the federal disciplinary proceeding did not involve conduct which violates the North Carolina Rules of Professional Conduct, in which event the case will be dismissed; or

(B) the Grievance Committee determines that the discipline imposed by the federal court is not of a type described in Rule .0123(a) of this subchapter and, therefore, cannot be imposed by the North Carolina State Bar, in which event the Grievance Committee may dismiss the case or direct that a complaint be filed in the commission.

(5) All findings of fact in the federal disciplinary proceeding will be binding upon the North Carolina State Bar and the member.

(6) Discipline imposed by any other federal court will be administered as provided in Rule .0116(b) above.

(d) If the member fails to accept reciprocal discipline as provided in Rule .0116(c) above or if a hearing is held before the Grievance Committee under either Rule .0116(b) above or Rule .0116(c) above and the committee orders the imposition of reciprocal discipline, such discipline will run from the date of service of the final order of the chairperson of the Grievance Committee unless the committee expressly provides otherwise.

[History Note: Statutory Authority G.S. 84–23; G.S. 84–28. Readopted effective December 8, 1994; amended effective March 7, 1996; December 30, 1998.]

.0117 Surrender of License While Under Investigation

(a) A member who is the subject of an investigation into allegations of misconduct, but against whom no formal complaint has been filed before the commission may tender his or her license to practice by delivering to the secretary for transmittal to the council an affidavit stating that the member desires to resign and that

(1) the resignation is freely and voluntarily rendered, is not the result of coercion or duress, and the member is fully aware of the implications of submitting the resignation;

(2) the member is aware that there is presently pending an investigation or other proceedings regarding allegations that the member has been guilty of misconduct, the nature of which will specifically be set forth;

(3) the member acknowledges that the material facts upon which the grievance is predicated are true;

(4) the resignation is being submitted because the member knows that if charges were predicated upon the misconduct under investigation, the member could not successfully defend against them.

(b) The council may accept a member's resignation only if the affidavit required under Rule .0117(a) above satisfies the requirements stated therein and the member has provided to the North Carolina State Bar all documents and financial records required to be kept pursuant to the Rules of Professional Conduct and requested by the counsel. If the council accepts a member's resignation, it will enter an order disbarring the member. The order of disbarment is effective on the date the council accepts the member's resignation.

(c) The order disbarring the member and the affidavit required under Rule .0117(a) above are matters of public record.

(d) If a defendant against whom a formal complaint has been filed before the commission wishes to consent to disbarment, the defendant may do so by filing an affidavit with the chairperson of the commission. If the chairperson determines that the affidavit meets the requirements set out in .0117(a)(1), (2), (3), and (4) above, the chairperson will accept the surrender and issue an order of disbarment. The order of disbarment becomes effective upon entry of the order with the secretary. If the affidavit does not meet the requirements set out above, the consent to disbarment will not be accepted and the disciplinary complaint will be heard pursuant to Rule .0114 of this subchapter.

(e) After a member tenders his or her license or consents to disbarment under this section the member may not undertake any new legal matters. The member may complete any legal matters which were pending on the date of the tender of the affidavit or consent to disbarment which can be completed within 30 days of the tender or consent. The member has 30 days from the date on which the member tenders the affidavit of surrender or consent to disbarment in which to comply with all of the duties set out in Rule .0124 of this subchapter.

[History Note: Statutory Authority G.S. 84–23; G.S. 84–28; G.S. 84–32(b). Readopted effective December 8, 1994; amended effective March 2, 2006.]

.0118. Disability

(a) Transfer by Secretary Where Member Judicially Declared Incompetent—Where a member of the North Carolina State Bar has been judicially declared incapacitated, incompetent, or mentally ill by a North Carolina court or by a court of any other jurisdiction, the secretary, upon proper proof of such declaration, will enter an order transferring the member to disability inactive status effective immediately and for an indefinite period until further order of the Disciplinary Hearing Commission. A copy of the order transferring the member to disability inactive status will be served upon the member, the member's guardian, or the director of any institution to which the member is committed.

(b) Transfer to Disability Inactive Status by Consent—The chairperson of the Grievance Committee may transfer a member to disability inactive status upon consent of the member and the counsel.

(c) Initiation of Disability Proceeding.

(1) *Disability Proceeding Initiated by the North Carolina State Bar.*

(A) Evidence a Member has Become Disabled—When the North Carolina State Bar obtains evidence that a member has become disabled, the Grievance Committee will conduct an inquiry which substantially complies with the procedures set forth in Rule .0113 (a)–(h) of this subchapter. The Grievance Committee will determine whether there is probable cause to believe that the member is disabled within the meaning of Rule .0103(19) of this subchapter. If the Grievance Committee finds probable cause, the counsel will file with the commission a complaint in the name of the North Carolina State Bar, signed by the chairperson of the Grievance Committee, alleging disability. The chairperson of the commission shall appoint a hearing panel to determine whether the member is disabled.

(B) Disability Proceeding Initiated While Disciplinary Proceeding is Pending—If, during the pendency of a disciplinary proceeding, the counsel receives evidence constituting probable cause to believe the defendant is disabled within the meaning of Rule .0103(19) of this subchapter, the chairperson of the Grievance Committee may authorize the counsel to file a motion seeking a determination that the defendant is disabled and seeking the defendant's transfer to disability inactive status. The hearing panel appointed to hear the disciplinary proceeding will hear the disability proceeding.

(C) Pleading in the Alternative—When the Grievance Committee has found probable cause to believe a member has committed professional misconduct and the Grievance Committee or the chairperson of the Grievance Committee has found probable cause to believe the member is disabled, the State Bar may file a complaint seeking, in the alternative, the imposition of professional discipline for professional misconduct or a determination that the defendant is disabled.

(2) *Initiated by Hearing Panel During Disciplinary Proceeding*—If, during the pendency of a disciplinary proceeding, a majority of the members of the hearing panel find probable cause to believe that the defendant is disabled, the panel will, on its own motion, enter an order staying the disciplinary proceeding until the question of disability can be determined. The hearing panel will instruct the Office of Counsel of the State Bar to file a complaint alleging disability. The chairperson of the commission will appoint a new hearing panel to hear the disability proceeding. If the new panel does not find the defendant disabled, the disciplinary proceeding will resume before the original hearing panel.

(3) *Disability Proceeding where Defendant Alleges Disability in Disciplinary Proceeding*—If, during the course of a disciplinary proceeding, the defendant contends that he or she is disabled within the meaning of Rule .0103(19) of this subchapter, the defendant will be immediately transferred to disability inactive status pending conclusion of a disability hearing. The disciplinary proceeding will be stayed pending conclusion of the disability hearing. The hearing panel appointed to hear the disciplinary proceeding will hear the disability proceeding.

(d) Disability Hearings.

(1) *Burden of Proof.*

(A) In any disability proceeding initiated by the State Bar or by the commission, the State Bar bears the burden of proving the defendant's disability by clear, cogent, and convincing evidence.

(B) In any disability proceeding initiated by the defendant, the defendant bears the burden of proving the defendant's disability by clear, cogent, and convincing evidence.

(2) *Procedure*—The disability hearing will be conducted in the same manner as a disciplinary proceeding under Rule .0114 of this subchapter. The North Carolina Rules of Civil Procedure and the North Carolina Rules of Evidence apply, unless a different or more specific procedure is specified in these rules. The hearing will be open to the public.

(3) *Medical Examination*—The hearing panel may require the member to undergo psychiatric, physical, or other medical examination or testing by qualified medical experts selected or approved by the hearing panel.

(4) *Appointment of Counsel*—The hearing panel may appoint a lawyer to represent the defendant in a disability proceeding if the hearing panel concludes that justice so requires.

(5) *Order.*

(A) When Disability is Proven—If the hearing panel finds that the defendant is disabled, the panel will enter an order continuing the defendant's disability inactive status or transferring the defendant to disability inactive status. An order transferring the defendant to disability inactive status is effective when it is entered. A copy of the order shall be served upon the defendant or the defendant's guardian or lawyer of record.

(B) When Disability is Not Proven—When the hearing panel finds that it has not been proven by clear, cogent, and convincing evidence that the defendant is disabled, the hearing panel shall enter an order so finding. If the defendant had been transferred to disability inactive status pursuant to paragraph (c)(3) of this rule, the order shall also terminate the defendant's disability inactive status.

(e) Stay/Resumption of Pending Disciplinary Matters.

(1) *Stay or Abatement*—When a member is transferred to disability inactive status, any proceeding then pending before the Grievance Committee or the commission against the member shall be stayed or abated unless and until the member's disability inactive status is terminated.

(2) *Preservation of Evidence*—When a disciplinary proceeding against a member has been stayed because the member has been transferred to disability inactive status, the counsel may continue to investigate allegations of misconduct. The counsel may seek orders from the chairperson of the commission, or the chairperson of a hearing panel if one has been appointed, to preserve evidence of any alleged professional misconduct by the member, including orders which permit the taking of depositions. The chairperson of the commission, or the chairperson of a hearing panel if one has been appointed, may appoint counsel to represent the member when necessary to protect the interests of the member during the preservation of evidence.

(3) *Termination of Disability Inactive Status*—Upon termination of disability inactive status, all disciplinary proceedings pending against the member shall resume. The State Bar may immediately pursue any disciplinary proceedings that were pending when the member was transferred to disability inactive status and any allegations of professional misconduct that came to the State Bar's attention while the member was in disability inactive status. Any disciplinary proceeding pending before the commission that had been stayed shall be set for hearing by the chairperson of the commission.

(f) Fees and Costs—The hearing panel may direct the member to pay the costs of the disability proceeding, including the cost of any medical examination and the fees of any lawyer appointed to represent the member.

[History Note: Statutory Authority G.S. 84–23; G.S. 84–28(g); G.S. 84–28.1; G.S. 84–29; G.S. 84–30. Readopted effective December 8, 1994; amended effective March 5, 1998; amended effective March 6, 2002; amended effective October 8, 2009; amended effective March 8, 2013.]

.0119 Enforcement of Powers

In addition to the other powers contained herein, in proceedings before any subcommittee or panel of the Grievance Committee or the commission, if any person refuses to respond to a subpoena, refuses to take the oath or affirmation as a witness or thereafter refuses to be examined, refuses to obey any order in aid of discovery, or refuses to obey any lawful order of the panel contained in its decision rendered after hearing, the counsel or secretary may apply to the appropriate court for an order directing that person to comply by taking the requisite action.

[History Note: Statutory Authority G.S. 84–23; G.S. 84–28(i). Readopted effective December 8, 1994. Amended effective October 8, 2009.]

.0120 Notice to Member of Action and Dismissal

In every disciplinary case wherein the respondent has received a letter of notice and the grievance has been dismissed, the respondent will be notified of the dismissal by a letter by the chairperson of the Grievance Committee. The chairperson will have discretion to give similar notice to the respondent in cases wherein a letter of notice has not been issued but the chairperson deems such notice to be appropriate.

[History Note: Statutory Authority G.S. 84–23. Readopted effective December 8, 1994.]

.0121 Notice to Complainant

(a) If the Grievance Committee finds probable cause and imposes discipline, the chairperson of the Grievance Committee will notify the complainant of the action of the committee.

(b) If the Grievance Committee finds probable cause and refers the matter to the commission, the chairperson of the Grievance Committee will advise the complainant that the grievance has been received and considered and has been referred to the commission for hearing.

(c) If the Grievance Committee finds that there is no probable cause to believe that misconduct occurred and votes to dismiss a grievance, the chairperson of the Grievance Committee will advise the complainant that the committee did not find probable cause to justify imposing discipline and dismissed the grievance.

(d) If final action on a grievance is taken by the Grievance Committee in the form of a letter of caution or a letter of warning, the chairperson of the Grievance Committee will so advise the complainant. The communication to the complainant will explain that the letter of caution or letter of warning is not a form of discipline.

(e) If a grievance is referred to the Board of Continuing Legal Education, the chairperson of the Grievance Committee will advise the complainant of that fact and the reason for the referral. If the respondent successfully completes the prescribed training and the grievance is dismissed, the chairperson of the Grievance Committee will advise the complainant. If the respondent does not successfully complete the prescribed course of training, the chairperson of the Grievance Committee will advise the complainant that investigation of the original grievance has resumed.

[History Note: Statutory Authority G.S. 84–23. Readopted effective December 8, 1994; amended effective March 7, 1996.]

.0122 Appointment of Counsel to Protect Clients' Interests When Attorney Disappears, Dies, or Is Transferred to Disability Inactive Status

(a) Whenever a member of the North Carolina State Bar has been transferred to disability inactive status, disappears, or dies and no partner or other member of the North Carolina State Bar capable of protecting the interests of the attorney's clients is known to exist, the senior resident judge of the superior court in the district of the member's most recent address on file with the North Carolina State Bar, if it is in this state, will be requested by the secretary to appoint an attorney or attorneys to inventory the files of the member and to take action to protect the interests of the member and his or her clients.

(b) Any member so appointed will not be permitted to disclose any information contained in any files inventoried without the consent of the client to whom such files relate except as necessary to carry out the order of the court which appointed the attorney to make such inventory.

[History Note: Statutory Authority G.S. 84–23; G.S. 84–28(j). Readopted effective December 8, 1994.]

.0123 Imposition of Discipline; Findings of Incapacity or Disability; Notice to Courts

(a) Upon the final determination of a disciplinary proceeding wherein discipline is imposed, one of the following actions will be taken:

(1) *Admonition.* An admonition will be prepared by the chairperson of the Grievance Committee or the chairperson of the hearing panel depending upon the agency ordering the admonition. The admonition will be served upon the defendant. The admonition will not be recorded in the judgment docket of the North Carolina State Bar. Where the admonition is imposed by the Grievance Committee, the complainant will be notified that the defendant has been admonished, but will not be entitled to a copy of the admonition. An order of admonition imposed by the commission will be a public document.

(2) *Reprimand.* The chairperson of the Grievance Committee or chairperson of the hearing panel depending upon the body ordering the discipline, will file an order of reprimand with the secretary, who will record the order on the judgment docket of the North Carolina State Bar and will forward a copy to the complainant.

(3) *Censure, Suspension or Disbarment* The chairperson of the hearing panel will file the censure, order of suspension or disbarment with the secretary, who will record the order on the judgment docket of the North Carolina State Bar and will forward a copy to the complainant. The secretary will also cause a certified copy of the order to be entered upon the judgment docket of the superior court of the county of the defendant's last known address and of any county where the defendant maintains an office. A copy of the censure, order of suspension or disbarment will also be sent to the North Carolina Court of Appeals, the North Carolina Supreme Court, the United States District Courts in North Carolina, the Fourth Circuit Court of Appeals, and the United States Supreme Court. Censures imposed by the Grievance Committee will be filed by the panel chairperson with the secretary. Notice of the censure will be given to the

complainant and to the courts in the same manner as censures imposed by the commission.

(b) Upon the final determination of incapacity or disability, the chairperson of the hearing panel or the secretary, depending upon the agency entering the order, will file with the secretary a copy of the order transferring the member to disability inactive status. The secretary will cause a certified copy of the order to be entered upon the judgment docket of the superior court of the county of the disabled member's last address on file with the North Carolina State Bar and of any county where the disabled member maintains an office and will forward a copy of the order to the courts referred to in Rule .0123(a)(3) above.

[History Note: Statutory Authority G.S. 84–23; G.S. 84–32(a). Readopted effective December 8, 1994; amended effective November 7, 1996; amended effective October 8, 2009.]

.0124 Obligations of Disbarred or Suspended Attorneys

(a) A disbarred or suspended member of the North Carolina State Bar will promptly notify by certified mail, return receipt requested, all clients being represented in pending matters of the disbarment or suspension, the reasons for the disbarment or suspension, and consequent inability of the member to act as an attorney after the effective date of disbarment or suspension and will advise such clients to seek legal advice elsewhere. The written notice must be received by the client before a disbarred or suspended attorney enters into any agreement with or on behalf of any client to settle, compromise or resolve any claim, dispute or lawsuit of the client. The disbarred or suspended attorney will take reasonable steps to avoid foreseeable prejudice to the rights of his or her clients, including promptly delivering all file materials and property to which the clients are entitled to the clients or the clients' substituted attorney. No disbarred or suspended attorney will transfer active client files containing confidential information or property to another attorney, nor may another attorney receive such files or property, without prior written permission from the client.

(b) The disbarred or suspended member will withdraw from all pending administrative or litigation matters before the effective date of the suspension or disbarment and will follow all applicable laws and disciplinary rules regarding the manner of withdrawal.

(c) In cases not governed by Rule .0117 of this subchapter, orders imposing suspension or disbarment will be effective 30 days after being served upon the defendant. In such cases, after entry of the disbarment or suspension order, the disbarred or suspended attorney will not accept any new retainer or engage as attorney for another in any new case or legal matter of any nature. However, between the entry date of the order and its effective date, the member may complete, on behalf of any client, matters which were pending on the entry date and which can be completed before the effective date of the order.

(d) Within 10 days after the effective date of the disbarment or suspension order, the disbarred or suspended attorney will file with the secretary an affidavit showing that he or she has fully complied with the provisions of the order, with the provisions of this section, and with the provisions of all other state, federal, and administrative jurisdictions to which he or she is admitted to practice. The affidavit will also set forth the residence or other address of the disbarred or suspended member to which communications may thereafter be directed.

(e) The disbarred or suspended member will keep and maintain records of the various steps taken under this section so that, upon any subsequent proceeding, proof of compliance with this section and with the disbarment or suspension order will be available. Proof of compliance with this section will be a condition precedent to consideration of any petition for reinstatement.

(f) A suspended or disbarred attorney who fails to comply with Rules .0124(a)–(e) above may be subject to an action for contempt instituted by the appropriate authority. Failure to comply with the requirements of Rule .0124(a) above will be grounds for appointment of counsel pursuant to Rule .0122 of this subchapter.

[History Note: Statutory Authority G.S. 84–23. Readopted effective December 8, 1994; amended effective March 6, 1997.]

.0125. Reinstatement

(a) After Disbarment.

(1) *Reinstatement Procedure and Costs.* No person who has been disbarred may have his or her license restored but upon order of the council after the filing of a verified petition for reinstatement and the holding of a hearing before a hearing panel as provided herein. No such hearing will commence until security for the costs of such hearing has been deposited with the secretary in an amount not to exceed $500.00.

(2) *Time Limits.* No disbarred attorney may petition for reinstatement until the expiration of at least five years from the effective date of the disbarment.

(3) *Burden of Proof and Elements to be Proved.* The petitioner will have the burden of proving by clear, cogent and convincing evidence that

(A) not more than six months or less than 60 days before filing the petition for reinstatement, a notice of intent to seek reinstatement has been published by the petitioner in an official publication of the North Carolina State Bar. The notice will inform members of the Bar about the application for reinstatement and will request that all interested individuals file notice of their opposition or concurrence with the secretary within 60 days after the date of publication;

(B) not more than six months or less than 60 days before filing the petition for reinstatement, the petitioner has notified the complainant(s) in the disciplinary proceeding which led to the lawyer's disbarment of the notice of intent to seek reinstatement. The notice will specify that each complainant has 60 days from the date of publication in which to raise objections or support the lawyer's petition;

(C) the petitioner has reformed and presently possesses the moral qualifications required for admission to practice law in this state taking into account the gravity of the misconduct which resulted in the order of disbarment;

(D) permitting the petitioner to resume the practice of law within the state will not be detrimental to the integrity and standing of the bar, to the administration of justice, or to the public interest, taking into account the gravity of the misconduct which resulted in the order of disbarment;

(E) the petitioner's citizenship has been restored if the petitioner has been convicted of or sentenced for the commission of a felony;

(F) the petitioner has complied with Rule .0124 of this subchapter;

(G) the petitioner has complied with all applicable orders of the commission and the council;

(H) the petitioner has complied with the orders and judgments of any court relating to the matters resulting in the disbarment;

(I) the petitioner has not engaged in the unauthorized practice of law during the period of disbarment;

(J) the petitioner has not engaged in any conduct during the period of disbarment constituting grounds for discipline under G.S. 84–28(b);

(K) the petitioner understands the current Rules of Professional Conduct. Participation in continuing legal education programs in ethics and professional responsibility for each of the three years preceding the petition date may be considered on the issue of the petitioner's understanding of the Rules of Professional Conduct. Such evidence creates no presumption that the petitioner has met the burden of proof established by this section;

(L) the petitioner has reimbursed the Client Security Fund of the North Carolina State Bar for all sums, including costs other than overhead expenses, disbursed by the Client Security Fund as a result of the petitioner's misconduct. This section shall not be deemed to permit the petitioner to collaterally attack the decision of the Client Security Fund Board of Trustees regarding whether to reimburse losses occasioned by the misconduct of the petitioner. This provision shall apply to petitions for reinstatement submitted by attorneys who were disciplined after the effective date of this amendment;

(M) the petitioner has reimbursed all sums which the Disciplinary Hearing Commission found in the order of disbarment were misappropriated by the petitioner and which have not been reimbursed by the Client Security Fund.

(N) The petitioner paid all dues, Client Security Fund assessments, and late fees owed to the North Carolina State Bar as well as all attendee fees and late penalties due and owing to the Board of Continuing Legal Education at the time of disbarment.

(4) *Petitions filed less than seven years after disbarment*

(A) Proof of Competency and Learning. If less than seven years have elapsed between the effective date of the disbarment and the filing date of the petition for reinstatement, the also have the burden of proving by clear, cogent, and convincing evidence that the petitioner has the competency and learning in the law required to practice law in this state.

(B) Factors which may be considered in deciding the issue of competency include

(i) experience in the practice of law;

(ii) areas of expertise;

(iii) certification of expertise;

(iv) participation in continuing legal education programs in each of the three years immediately preceding the petition date;

(v) certification by three attorneys who are familiar with the petitioner's present knowledge of the law that the petitioner is competent to engage in the practice of law.

(C) The factors listed in Rule .0125(a)(4)(B) above are provided by way of example only. The petitioner's satisfaction of one or all of these factors creates no presumption that the petitioner has met the burden of proof established by this section.

(D) Passing Bar Exam as Conclusive Evidence. The attainment of a passing grade on a regularly scheduled written bar examination administered by the North Carolina Board of Law Examiners and taken voluntarily by the petitioner shall be conclusive evidence on the issue of the petitioner's competence to practice law.

(5) *Bar Exam Requirement for Petitions Filed More than Seven Years After Disbarment.* If seven years or more have elapsed between the effective date of disbarment and the filing of the petition for reinstatement, reinstatement will be conditioned upon the petitioner's attaining a passing grade on a regularly scheduled written bar examination administered by the North Carolina Board of Law Examiners.

(6) *Petition, Service and Hearing.* Verified petitions for reinstatement of disbarred attorneys will be filed with the secretary. Upon receipt of the petition,

the secretary will transmit the petition to the chairperson of the commission and serve a copy on the counsel. The chairperson will within 14 days appoint a hearing panel as provided in Rule .0108(a)(2) of this subchapter and schedule a time and place for a hearing to take place within 60 to 90 days after the filing of the petition with the secretary. The chairperson will notify the counsel and the petitioner of the composition of the hearing panel and the time and place of the hearing, which will be conducted in accordance with the North Carolina Rules of Civil Procedure for nonjury trials insofar as possible and the rules of evidence applicable in superior court.

(7) *Report of Findings.* As soon as possible after the conclusion of the hearing, the hearing panel will file a report containing its findings, conclusions, and recommendations with the secretary.

(8) *Appeal.* A petitioner in whose case the hearing panel recommends that reinstatement be denied may file notice of appeal to the council. Appeal from the report of the hearing panel must be taken within 30 days after service of the panel report upon the petitioner and shall be filed with the secretary. If no appeal is timely filed, the recommendation of the hearing panel to deny reinstatement will be deemed final. All cases in which the hearing panel recommends reinstatement of a disbarred attorney's license shall be heard by the council and no notice of appeal need be filed by the N.C. State Bar.

(9) *Transcript of Hearing Panel Proceedings.* The petitioner will have 60 days following the filing of the notice of appeal in which to produce a transcript of the trial proceedings before the hearing panel. The chairperson of the hearing panel, may, for good cause shown, extend the time to produce the record.

(10) *Record to the Council.*

(A) Composition of the Record. The petitioner will provide a record of the proceedings before the hearing panel, including a legible copy of the complete transcript, all exhibits introduced into evidence, and all pleadings, motions and orders, unless the petitioner and counsel agree in writing to shorten the record. The petitioner will provide the proposed record to the counsel not later than 90 days after the hearing before the hearing panel, unless an extension of time is granted by the secretary for good cause shown. Any agreement or order regarding the record will be in writing and will be included in the record transmitted to the council.

(B) Settlement of the Record.

(i) By agreement—at any time following service of the proposed record upon the counsel, the parties may by agreement entered in the record settle the record to the council.

(ii) By counsel's failure to object to the proposed record—within 20 days after service of the proposed record, the counsel may serve a written objection or a proposed alternative record upon the petitioner. If the counsel fails to serve a notice of approval or an objection or a proposed alternative record, the petitioner's proposed record will constitute the record to the council.

(iii) By judicial settlement—If the counsel raises a timely objection to the proposed record or serves a proposed alternative record upon the petitioner, either party may request the chairperson of the hearing panel which heard the reinstatement petition to settle the record. Such request shall be filed in writing with the hearing panel chairperson no later than 15 days after the counsel files an objection or proposed alternative record. Each party shall promptly provide to the chairperson a reference copy of the proposed record, amendments and objections filed by that party in the case. The chairperson of the hearing panel shall settle the record on appeal by order not more than 20 days after service of the request for judicial settlement upon the chairperson. The chairperson may allow oral argument by the parties or may settle the record based upon written submissions by the parties.

(C) Copy of Settled Record to Each Member. The petitioner will transmit a copy of the settled record to each member of the council and to the counsel no later than 30 days before the council meeting at which the petition is to be considered.

(D) Costs. The petitioner shall bear the costs of transcribing, copying, and transmitting the record to the council.

(E) Failure to Comply with Rule .0125(a)(8). If the petitioner fails to comply with any of the subsections of Rule .0125(a)(8) above, the counsel may petition the secretary to dismiss the petition.

(11) *Review by Council.* The council will review the report of the hearing panel and the record and determine whether, and upon what conditions, the petitioner will be reinstated.

(12) *Reapplication.* No person who has been disbarred and has unsuccessfully petitioned for reinstatement may reapply until the expiration of one year from the date of the last order denying reinstatement.

(b) After Suspension.

(1) *Restoration.* No attorney who has been suspended may have his or her license restored but upon order of the commission or the secretary after the filing of a verified petition as provided herein.

(2) *Suspension of 120 Days or Less.* No attorney who has been suspended for a period of 120 days or less is eligible for reinstatement until the expiration of the period of suspension and, in no event, until 10 days have elapsed from the date of filing the petition for reinstatement. No attorney whose license has been suspended for a period of more than 120 days is eligible for reinstatement until the expiration of the

period of suspension and, in no event, until 30 days have elapsed from the date of the filing of the petition for reinstatement.

(3) *Reinstatement Requirements.* Any suspended attorney seeking reinstatement must file a verified petition with the secretary, a copy of which the secretary will transmit to the counsel. The petitioner will have the burden of proving the following by clear, cogent, and convincing evidence:

(A) compliance with Rule .0124 of this subchapter;

(B) compliance with all applicable orders of the commission and the council;

(C) abstention from the unauthorized practice of law during the period of suspension;

(D) attainment of a passing grade on a regularly scheduled North Carolina bar examination, if the suspended attorney applies for reinstatement of his or her license more than seven years after the effective date of the suspension;

(E) abstention from conduct during the period of suspension constituting grounds for discipline under G.S. 84–28(b);

(F) Reimbursement of the Client Security Fund. Reimbursement of the Client Security Fund of the North Carolina State Bar for all sums, including costs other than overhead expenses, disbursed by the Client Security Fund as a result of the petitioner's misconduct. This section shall not be deemed to permit the petitioner to collaterally attack the decision of the Client Security Fund Board of Trustees regarding whether to reimburse losses occasioned by the misconduct of the petitioner. This provision shall apply to petitions for reinstatement submitted by attorneys who were disciplined after the effective date of this amendment;

(G) Reimbursement of Funds in DHC Order. Reimbursement of all sums which the Disciplinary Hearing Commission found in the order of suspension were misappropriated by the petitioner and which have not been reimbursed by the Client Security Fund.

(H) Satisfaction of Pre-Suspension CLE Requirements. Satisfaction of the minimum continuing legal education requirements, as set forth in Rule .1517 of Subchapter 1D of these rules, for the two calendar years immediately preceding the year in which the petitioner was suspended, which shall include the satisfaction of any deficit recorded in the petitioner's State Bar CLE transcript for such period; provided that the petitioner may attend CLE programs after the effective date of the suspension to make up any unsatisfied requirement. These requirements shall be in addition to any continuing legal education requirements imposed by the Disciplinary Hearing Commission;

(I) Satisfaction of Post-Suspension CLE Requirements. [effective for petitioners suspended on or after January 1, 1997] if two or more years have elapsed between the effective date of the suspension order and the date on which the reinstatement petition is filed with the secretary, the petitioner must, within one year prior to filing the petition, complete 15 hours of CLE approved by the Board of Continuing Legal Education pursuant to Subchapter 1D, Rule.1519 of these rules. Three hours of the 15 hours must be earned by attending courses of instruction devoted exclusively to professional responsibility and/or professionalism. These requirements shall be in addition to any continuing legal education requirements imposed by the Disciplinary Hearing Commission;

(J) Payment of Fees and Assessments—payment of all membership fees, Client Security Fund assessments, and late fees due and owing to the North Carolina State Bar, including any reinstatement fee due under Rule .0904 or Rule .1524 of subchapter 1D of these rules, as well as all attendee fees and late penalties due and owing to the Board of Continuing Legal Education at the time of suspension.

(4) *Investigation and Response.* The counsel will conduct any necessary investigation regarding the compliance of the petitioner with the requirements set forth in Rule .0125(b)(3) above, and the counsel may file a response to the petition with the secretary prior to the date the petitioner is first eligible for reinstatement. The counsel will serve a copy of any response filed upon the petitioner.

(5) *Failure of Counsel to File Response.* If the counsel does not file a response to the petition before the date the petitioner is first eligible for reinstatement, then the secretary will issue an order of reinstatement.

(6) *Specific Objections in Response.* If the counsel files a timely response to the petition, such response must set forth specific objections supported by factual allegations sufficient to put the petitioner on notice of the events at issue.

(7) *Reinstatement Hearing.* The secretary will, upon the filing of a response to the petition, refer the matter to the chairperson of the commission. The chairperson will within 14 days appoint a hearing panel as provided in Rule .0108(a)(2) of this subchapter, schedule a time and place for a hearing, and notify the counsel and the petitioner of the composition of the hearing panel and the time and place of the hearing. The hearing will be conducted in accordance with the North Carolina Rules of Civil Procedure for nonjury trials insofar as possible and the rules of evidence applicable in superior court.

(8) *Reinstatement Order.* The hearing panel will determine whether the petitioner's license should be reinstated and enter an appropriate order, which may include additional sanctions in the event violations of

the petitioner's order of suspension are found. In any event, the hearing panel must include in its order findings of fact and conclusions of law in support of its decision and tax such costs as it deems appropriate for the necessary expenses attributable to the investigation and processing of the petition against the petitioner.

(c) After Transfer to Disability Inactive Status.

(1) *Reinstatement.* No member of the North Carolina State Bar transferred to disability inactive status may resume active status until reinstated by order of the commission. Any member transferred to disability inactive status will be entitled to apply to the commission for reinstatement to active status once a year or at such shorter intervals as are stated in the order transferring the member to disability inactive status or any modification thereof.

(2) *Reinstatement Petition.* Petitions for reinstatement by members transferred to disability inactive status will be filed with the secretary. Upon receipt of the petition the secretary will refer the petition to the commission chairperson. The chairperson will appoint a hearing panel as provided in Rule .0108(a)(2) of this subchapter. A hearing will be conducted pursuant to the procedures set out in Rule .0114 of this subchapter.

(3) *Burden of Proof.* The member will have the burden of proving by clear, cogent, and convincing evidence that he or she is no longer disabled within the meaning of Rule .0103(19) of this subchapter and that he or she is fit to resume the practice of law.

(4) *Medical Records.* Within 10 days of filing the petition for reinstatement, the member will provide the secretary with a list of the name and address of every psychiatrist, psychologist, physician, hospital, and other health care provider by whom or in which the member has been examined or treated or sought treatment while disabled. At the same time, the member will also furnish to the secretary a written consent to release all information and records relating to the disability.

(5) *Judicial Findings.* Where a member has been transferred to disability inactive status based solely upon a judicial finding of incapacity, and thereafter a court of competent jurisdiction enters an order adjudicating that the member's incapacity has ended, the chairperson of the commission will enter an order returning the member to active status upon receipt of a certified copy of the court's order. Entry of the order will not preclude the North Carolina State Bar from bringing an action pursuant to Rule .0118 of this subchapter to determine whether the member is disabled.

(6) *Costs.* The hearing panel may direct the member to pay the costs of the reinstatement hearing, including the cost of any medical examination ordered by the panel.

(d) Conditions of Reinstatement. The hearing panel may impose reasonable conditions on a lawyer's reinstatement from disbarment, suspension or disability inactive status in any case in which the hearing panel concludes that such conditions are necessary for the protection of the public.

(e) After Entry of a Reciprocal Order of Suspension or Disbarment. After entry of a reciprocal order of suspension or disbarment: No member whose license to practice law has been suspended or who has been disbarred by any state or federal court and who is the subject of a reciprocal discipline order in North Carolina may seek reinstatement of his or her North Carolina law license until the member provides to the secretary a copy of an order reinstating the member to the active practice of law in the state or federal court which entered the original order of discipline.

[History Note: Statutory Authority G.S. 84-23; G.S. 84-28.1; G.S. 84-29; G.S. 84-30. Readopted effective December 8, 1994; amended effective February 20, 1995; March 6, 1997; October 2, 1997; December 30, 1998; July 22, 1999; August 24, 2000; March 6, 2002; February 27, 2003; October 8, 2009; March 10, 2011.]

.0126 Address of Record

Except where otherwise specified, any provision herein for notice to a respondent, member, petitioner, or a defendant will be deemed satisfied by appropriate correspondence addressed to that attorney by mail to the last address maintained by the North Carolina State Bar.

[History Note: Statutory Authority G.S. 84-23. Readopted effective December 8, 1994.]

.0127 Disqualification Due to Interest

No member of the council or hearing commission will participate in any disciplinary matter involving the member, any partner, or associate in the practice of law of the member, or in which the member has a personal interest.

[History Note: Statutory Authority G.S. 84-23. Readopted effective December 8, 1994.]

.0128 Trust Accounts; Audit

(a) For reasonable cause, the chairperson of the Grievance Committee is empowered to issue an investigative subpoena to a member compelling the production of any records required to be kept relative to the handling of client funds and property by the Rules of Professional Conduct for inspection, copying, or audit by the counsel or any auditor appointed by the counsel. For the purposes of this rule, circumstances that constitute reasonable cause, include, but are not limited to:

(1) any sworn statement of grievance received by the North Carolina State Bar alleging facts which, if true, would constitute misconduct in the handling of a client's funds or property;

(2) any facts coming to the attention of the North Carolina State Bar, whether through random review as contemplated by Rule .0128(b) below or otherwise, which if true, would constitute a probable violation of any provision of the Rules of Professional Conduct concerning the handling of client funds or property;

(3) two or more grievances received by the North Carolina State Bar over a twelve month period alleging facts which, if true, would indicate misconduct for neglect of a client matter or failure to communicate with a client;

(4) any failure to respond to any notices issued by the North Carolina State Bar with regard to a grievance or a fee dispute;

(5) any information received by the North Carolina State Bar which, if true, would constitute a failure to file any federal, state, or local tax return or pay an federal, state, or local tax obligation; or

(6) any finding of probable cause, indictment, or conviction relative to a criminal charge involving moral turpitude.

The grounds supporting the issuance of any such subpoena will be set forth upon the face of the subpoena.

(b) The chairperson of the Grievance Committee may randomly issue investigative subpoenas to members compelling the production of any records required to be kept relative to the handling of client funds or property by the Rules of Professional Conduct for inspection by the counsel or any auditor appointed by the counsel to determine compliance with the Rules of Professional Conduct. Any such subpoena will disclose upon its face its random character and contain a verification of the secretary that it was randomly issued. No member will be subject to random selection under this section more than once in three years. The auditor may report any violation of the Rules of Professional Conduct discovered during random audit to the Grievance Committee for investigation. The auditor may allow the attorney a reasonable amount of time to correct any procedural violation in lieu of reporting the matter to the Grievance Committee. The auditor shall have authority under the original subpoena for random audit to compel the production of any documents necessary to determine whether the attorney has corrected any violation identified during the audit.

(c) No subpoena issued pursuant to this rule may compel production within five days of service.

(d) The rules of evidence applicable in the superior courts of the state will govern the use of any material subpoenaed pursuant to this rule in any hearing before the commission.

(e) No assertion of attorney-client privilege or confidentiality will prevent an inspection or audit of a trust account as provided in this rule.

[History Note: Statutory Authority G.S. 84-23. Readopted effective December 8, 1994; amended effective November 16, 2006.]

.0129 Confidentiality

(a) Except as otherwise provided in this rule and G.S. 84-28(f), all proceedings involving allegations of misconduct by or alleged disability of a member will remain confidential until

(1) a complaint against a member has been filed with the secretary after a finding by the Grievance Committee that there is probable cause to believe that the member is guilty of misconduct justifying disciplinary action or is disabled;

(2) the member requests that the matter be made public prior to the filing of a complaint;

(3) the investigation is predicated upon conviction of the member of or sentencing for a crime;

(4) a petition or action is filed in the general courts of justice;

(5) the member files an affidavit of surrender of license; or

(6) a member is transferred to disability inactive status pursuant to Rule .0118(g). In such an instance, the order transferring the member shall be public. Any other materials, including the medical evidence supporting the order, shall be kept confidential unless and until the member petitions for reinstatement pursuant to Rule .0118(c), unless provided otherwise in the order.

(b) The previous issuance of a letter of warning, formerly known as a letter of admonition, or an admonition to a member may be revealed in any subsequent disciplinary proceeding.

(c) This provision will not be construed to prohibit the North Carolina State Bar from providing a copy of an attorney's response to a grievance to the complaining party where such attorney has not objected thereto in writing.

(d) This provision will not be construed to prohibit the North Carolina State Bar from providing information or evidence to any law enforcement or regulatory agency.

(e) This provision will not be construed to prevent the North Carolina State Bar, with the approval of the chairperson of the Grievance Committee, from notifying the Chief Justice's Commission on Professionalism of any allegation of unprofessional conduct by any member.

(f) This provision will not be construed to prevent the North Carolina State Bar from notifying the Lawyer Assistance Program of any circumstances that indicate a member may have a substance abuse or mental health issue.

(g) This provision will not be construed to prohibit the North Carolina State Bar, with the approval of the chairperson of the Grievance Committee, from providing information concerning the existence of a letter of caution, letter of warning, or admonition to any agency that regulates the legal profession in any other jurisdiction so long as the inquiring jurisdiction maintains the same level of confidentiality respecting the information as does the North Carolina State Bar.

(h) The secretary will transmit notice of all public discipline imposed and transfers to disability inactive status to the National Discipline Data Bank maintained by the American Bar Association.

(i) The secretary may also transmit any relevant information to the Client Security Fund Board of Trustees to assist the Client Security Fund Board in determining losses caused by dishonest conduct of members of the North Carolina State Bar.

[History Note: Statutory Authority G.S. 84–23. Readopted effective December 8, 1994; amended effective February 20, 1995; amended effective November 7, 1996; amended effective March 6, 2002; amended effective October 9, 2008.]

.0130 Disciplinary Amnesty in Illicit Drug Use Cases

(a) The North Carolina State Bar will not treat as a grievance information that a member has used or is using illicit drugs except as provided in Rules .0130(c), (d) and (e) below. The information will be provided to the director of the lawyer assistance program of the North Carolina State Bar.

(b) If the director of the lawyer assistance program concludes after investigation that a member has used or is using an illicit drug and the member participates and successfully complies with any course of treatment, prescribed by the lawyer assistance program, the member will not be disciplined by the North Carolina State Bar for illicit drug use occurring prior to the prescribed course of treatment.

(c) If a member under Rule .0130(b) above fails to cooperate with the Lawyer Assistance Program Board or fails to successfully complete any treatment prescribed for the member's illicit drug use, the director of the lawyer assistance program will report such failure to participate in or complete the prescribed treatment to the chairperson of the Grievance Committee. The chairperson of the Grievance Committee will then treat the information originally received as a grievance.

(d) A member charged with a crime relating to the use or possession of illicit drugs will not be entitled to amnesty from discipline by the North Carolina State Bar relating to the illicit drug use or possession.

(e) If the North Carolina State Bar receives information that a member has used or is using illicit drugs and that the member has violated some other provision of the Revised Rules of Professional Conduct, the information regarding the member's alleged illicit drug use will be referred to the director of the lawyer assistance program pursuant to Rule .0130(a) above. The information regarding the member's alleged additional misconduct will be reported to the chairperson of the Grievance Committee.

[History Note: Statutory Authority G.S. 84–23. Readopted effective December 8, 1994; amended December 10, 1999, effective February 3, 2000.]

SECTION .0200 RULES GOVERNING JUDICIAL DISTRICT GRIEVANCE COMMITTEES

.0201. Organization of Judicial District Grievance Committees

(a) Judicial Districts Eligible to Form District Grievance Committees.

(1) Any judicial district which has more than 100 licensed attorneys as determined by the North Carolina State Bar's records may establish a judicial district grievance committee (hereafter, "district grievance committee") pursuant to the rules and regulations set out herein. A judicial district with fewer than 100 licensed attorneys may establish a district grievance committee with consent of the Council of the North Carolina State Bar.

(2) One or more judicial districts, including those with fewer than 100 licensed attorneys, may also establish a multi-district grievance committee, as set out in Rule .0201(b)(2) below. Such multi-district grievance committees shall be subject to all of the rules and regulations set out herein and all references to district grievance committees in these rules shall also apply to multi-district grievance committees.

(b) Creation of District Grievance Committees.

(1) A judicial district may establish a district grievance committee at a duly called meeting of the judicial district bar, at which a quorum is present, upon the affirmative vote of a majority of the active members present. Within 30 days of the election, the president of the judicial district bar shall certify in writing the establishment of the district grievance committee to the secretary of the North Carolina State Bar.

(2) A multi-district grievance committee may be established by affirmative vote of a majority of the active members of each participating judicial district present at a duly called meeting of each participating judicial district bar, at which a quorum is present.

Within 30 days of the election, the chairperson of the multi-district grievance committee shall certify in writing the establishment of the district grievance committee to the secretary of the North Carolina State Bar. The active members of each participating judicial district may adopt a set of by-laws not inconsistent with these rules by majority vote of the active members of each participating judicial district present at a duly called meeting of each participating judicial district bar, at which a quorum is present. The chairperson of the multi-district grievance committee shall promptly provide a copy of any such bylaws to the secretary of the North Carolina State Bar.

(c) Appointment of District Grievance Committee Members.

(1) *Members of District Committees*—Each district grievance committee shall be composed of not fewer than five nor more than 21 members, all of whom shall be active members in good standing both of the judicial district bar to which they belong and of the North Carolina State Bar. In addition to the attorney members, each district grievance committee may also include one to five public members who have never been licensed to practice law in any jurisdiction. Public members shall not perform investigative functions regarding grievances but in all other respects shall have the same authority as the attorney members of the district grievance committee.

(2) The chairperson of the district grievance committee shall be selected by the president of the judicial district and shall serve at his or her pleasure. Alternatively, the chairperson may be selected and removed as provided in the district bar bylaws.

(3) The attorney and public members of the district grievance committee shall be selected by and serve at the pleasure of the president of the judicial district bar and the chairperson of the district grievance committee. Alternatively, the district grievance committee members may be selected and removed as provided in the district bar bylaws.

(4) The members of the district grievance committee, including the chairperson, shall be appointed for staggered three-year terms, except that the president and chairperson shall appoint some of the initial committee members to terms of less than three years, to effectuate the staggered terms. No member shall serve more than one term, without first having rotated off the committee for a period of at least one year between three-year terms. Any member who resigns or otherwise becomes ineligible to continue serving as a member shall be replaced by appointment by the president of the judicial district bar and the chairperson of the committee or as provided in the district bar bylaws as soon as practicable.

[History Note: Statutory Authority G.S. 84-23. Readopted effective December 8, 1994. Amended eff. October 7, 2010.]

.0202 Jurisdiction and Authority of District Grievance Committees

(a) District Grievance Committees Are Subject to the Rules of the North Carolina State Bar. The district grievance committee shall be subject to the rules and regulations adopted by the Council of the North Carolina State Bar.

(b) Grievances Filed With District Grievance Committee. A district grievance committee may investigate and consider grievances filed against attorneys who live or maintain offices within the judicial district and which are filed in the first instance with the chairperson of the district grievance committee. The chairperson of the district grievance committee will immediately refer to the State Bar any grievance filed locally in the first instance which

(1) alleges misconduct against a member of the district grievance committee;

(2) alleges that any attorney has embezzled or misapplied client funds; or

(3) alleges any other serious violation of the Rules of Professional Conduct which may be beyond the capacity of the district grievance committee to investigate.

(c) Grievances Referred to District Grievance Committee. The district grievance committee shall also investigate and consider such grievances as are referred to it for investigation by the counsel of the North Carolina State Bar.

(d) Grievances Involving Fee Disputes.

(1) *Notice to Complainant of Fee Dispute Resolution Program.* If a grievance filed initially with the district bar consists solely or in part of a fee dispute, the chairperson of the district grievance committee shall notify the complainant in writing within 10 working days of receipt of the grievance that the complainant may elect to participate in the North Carolina State Bar Fee Dispute Resolution Program. If the grievance consists solely of a fee dispute, the letter to the complainant shall follow the format set out in Rule .0208 of this subchapter. If the grievance consists in part of matters other than a fee dispute, the letter to the complainant shall follow the format set out in Rule .0209 of this subchapter. A respondent attorney shall not have the right to elect to participate in fee arbitration.

(2) *Handling Claims Not Involving Fee Dispute.* Where a grievance alleges multiple claims, the allegations not involving a fee dispute will be handled in the same manner as any other grievance filed with the district grievance committee.

(3) *Handling Claims Not Submitted to Fee Dispute Resolution by Complainant.* If the complainant elects not to participate in the State Bar's Fee Dispute Resolution Program, or fails to notify the chairperson that he or she elects to participate within 20

days following mailing of the notice referred to in Rule .0202(d)(1) above, the grievance will be handled in the same manner as any other grievance filed with the district grievance committee.

(4) *Referral to Fee Dispute Resolution Program.* Where a complainant timely elects to participate in fee dispute resolution, and the judicial district in which the respondent attorney maintains his or her principal office has a fee dispute resolution committee, the chairperson of the district grievance committee shall refer the portion of the grievance involving a fee dispute to the judicial district fee dispute resolution committee. If the judicial district in which the respondent attorney maintains his or her principal office does not have a fee dispute resolution committee, the chairperson of the district grievance committee shall refer the portion of the grievance involving a fee dispute to the State Bar Fee Dispute Resolution Program for resolution. If the grievance consists entirely of a fee dispute, and the complainant timely elects to participate in fee dispute resolution, no grievance file will be established.

(e) Authority of District Grievance Committees. The district grievance committee shall have authority to

(1) assist a complainant who requests assistance to reduce a grievance to writing;

(2) investigate complaints described in Rule .0202(b) and (c) above by interviewing the complainant, the attorney against whom the grievance was filed and any other persons who may have relevant information regarding the grievance and by requesting written materials from the complainant, respondent attorney, and other individuals;

(3) explain the procedures of the district grievance committee to complainants and respondent attorneys;

(4) find facts and recommend whether or not the State Bar's Grievance Committee should find that there is probable cause to believe that the respondent has violated one or more provisions of the Revised Rules of Professional Conduct. The district grievance committee may also make a recommendation to the State Bar regarding the appropriate disposition of the case, including referral to the Lawyer Assistance Program pursuant to Rule .0112(j) or to a program of law office management training approved by the State Bar;

(5) draft a written report stating the grounds for the recommended disposition of a grievance assigned to the district grievance committee;

(6) notify the complainant and the respondent attorney where the district grievance committee recommends that the State Bar find that there is no probable cause to believe that the respondent has violated the Rules of Professional Conduct. Where the district grievance committee recommends that the State Bar find that there is probable cause to believe that the respondent has violated one or more provisions of the Rules of Professional Conduct, the committee shall notify the respondent attorney of its recommendation and shall notify the complainant that the district grievance committee has concluded its investigation and has referred the matter to the State Bar for final resolution. Where the district grievance committee recommends a finding of no probable cause, the letter of notification to the respondent attorney and to the complainant shall follow the format set out in Rule .0210 of this subchapter. Where the district grievance committee recommends a finding of probable cause, the letter of notification to the respondent attorney shall follow the format set out in Rule .0211 of this subchapter. The letter of notification to the complainant shall follow the format set out in Rule .0212 of this subchapter;

(7) maintain records of grievances investigated by the district grievance committee for at least one year from the date on which the district grievance committee makes its final recommendation regarding a grievance to the State Bar.

[History Note: Statutory Authority G.S. 84–23. Readopted effective December 8, 1994; amended effective March 3, 1999; amended effective December 20, 2000; amended effective August 23, 2007.]

.0203 Meetings of the District Grievance Committees

(a) Notice of Meeting. The district grievance committee shall meet at the call of the chairperson upon reasonable notice, as often as is necessary to dispatch its business and not less than once every 60 days, provided the committee has grievances pending.

(b) Confidentiality. The district grievance committee shall meet in private. Discussions of the committee, its records and its actions shall be confidential. The names of the members of the committee shall not be confidential.

(c) Quorum. A simple majority of the district grievance committee must be present at any meeting in order to constitute a quorum. The committee may take no action unless a quorum is present. A majority vote in favor of a motion or any proposed action shall be required for the motion to pass or the action to be taken.

(d) Appearances by Complainants and Respondents. No complainant nor any attorney against whom a grievance has been filed may appear before the district grievance committee, present argument to or be present at the committee's deliberations.

[History Note: Statutory Authority G.S. 84–23. Readopted effective December 8, 1994.]

.0204 Procedure Upon Institution of a Grievance

(a) Receipt of Grievance. A grievance may be filed by any person against a member of the North

Carolina State Bar. Such grievance must be in writing and signed by the complaining person. A district grievance committee may, however, investigate matters which come to its attention during the investigation of a grievance, whether or not such matters are included in the original written grievance.

(b) Acknowledgment of Receipt of Grievance From State Bar. The chairperson of the district grievance committee shall send a letter to the complainant within 10 working days of receipt of the grievance from the State Bar, acknowledging that a grievance file has been set up. The acknowledgment letter shall include the name of the district grievance committee member assigned to investigate the matter and shall follow the format set out in Rule .0213 of this subchapter. A copy of the letter shall be sent contemporaneously to the office of counsel of the State Bar.

(c) Notice to State Bar of Locally Filed Grievances.

(1) Where a grievance is filed in the first instance with the district grievance committee, the chairperson of the district grievance committee shall notify the office of counsel of the State Bar of the name of the complainant, respondent attorney, file number and nature of the grievance within 10 working days of receipt of the grievance.

(2) The chairperson of the district grievance committee shall send a letter to the complainant within 10 working days of receipt of the grievance, acknowledging that a grievance file has been set up. The acknowledgment letter shall include the name of the district grievance committee member assigned to investigate the matter and shall follow the format set out in Rule .0213 of this subchapter.

(3) Grievances filed initially with the district grievance committee shall be assigned a local file number which shall be used to refer to the grievance. The first two digits of the file number shall indicate the year in which the grievance was filed, followed by the number of the judicial district, the letters GR, and ending with the number of the file. File numbers shall be assigned sequentially during the calendar year, beginning with the number 1. For example, the first locally filed grievance set up in the 10th judicial district in 1994 would bear the following number: 9410GR001.

(d) Assignment to Investigating Member. Within 10 working days after receipt of a grievance, the chairperson shall appoint a member of the district grievance committee to investigate the grievance and shall forward the relevant materials to the investigating member. The letter to the investigating member shall follow the format set out in Rule .0214 of this subchapter.

(e) Investigation of the Grievance.

(1) The investigating member shall attempt to contact the complainant as soon as possible but no later than 15 working days after receiving notice of the assignment. If the initial contact with the complainant is made in writing, the letter shall follow the format set out in Rule .0215 of this subchapter.

(2) The investigating member shall have the authority to contact other witnesses or individuals who may have information about the subject of the grievance, including the respondent.

(3) The failure of the complainant to cooperate shall not cause a grievance to be dismissed or abated. Once filed, grievances shall not be dismissed or abated upon the request of the complainant.

(f) Letter of Notice to Respondent Attorney and Responses.

(1) Within 10 working days after receipt of a grievance, the chairperson of the district grievance committee shall send a copy of the grievance and a letter of notice to the respondent attorney. The letter to the respondent attorney shall follow the form set out in Rule .0216 of this subchapter and shall be sent by U.S. Mail to the attorney's last known address on file with the State Bar. The letter of notice shall request the respondent to reply to the investigating attorney in writing within 15 days after receipt of the letter of notice.

(2) A substance of grievance will be provided to the district grievance committee by the State Bar at the time the file is assigned to the committee. The substance of grievance will summarize the nature of the complaint against the respondent attorney and cite the applicable provisions of the Rules of Professional Conduct, if any.

(3) The respondent attorney shall respond in writing to the letter of notice from the district grievance committee within 15 days of receipt of the letter. The chairperson of the district grievance committee may allow a longer period for response, for good cause shown.

(4) If the respondent attorney fails to respond in a timely manner to the letter of notice, the chairperson of the district grievance committee may seek the assistance of the State Bar to issue a subpoena or take other appropriate steps to ensure a proper and complete investigation of the grievance. District grievance committees do not have authority to issue a subpoena to a witness or respondent attorney.

(5) Unless necessary to complete its investigation, the district grievance committee should not release copies of the respondent attorney's response to the grievance to the complainant. The investigating attorney may summarize the response for the complainant orally or in writing.

(g) District Grievance Committee Deliberations.

(1) Upon completion of the investigation, the investigating member shall promptly report his or her findings and recommendations to the district grievance committee in writing.

(2) The district grievance committee shall consider the submissions of the parties, the information gathered by the investigating attorney and such other material as it deems relevant in reaching a recommendation. The district grievance committee may also make further inquiry as it deems appropriate, including investigating other facts and possible violations of the Rules of Professional Conduct discovered during its investigation.

(3) The district grievance committee shall make a determination as to whether or not it finds that there is probable cause to believe that the respondent violated one or more provisions of the Rules of Professional Conduct.

(h) Report of Committee's Decision.

(1) Upon making a decision in a case, the district grievance committee shall submit a written report to the office of counsel, including its recommendation and the basis for its decision. The original file and grievance materials of the investigating attorney shall be sent to the State Bar along with the report. The letter from the district bar grievance committee enclosing the report shall follow the format set out in Rule .0217 of this subchapter.

(2) The district grievance committee shall submit its written report to the office of counsel no later than 180 days after the grievance is initiated or received by the district committee. The State Bar may recall any grievance file which has not been investigated and considered by a district grievance committee within 180 days after the matter is assigned to the committee. The State Bar may also recall any grievance file for any reason.

(3) Within 10 working days of submitting the written report and returning the file to the office of counsel, the chairperson of the district grievance committee shall notify the respondent attorney and the complainant in writing of the district grievance committee's recommendation, as provided in Rule .0202(d)(6) of this subchapter.

[History Note: Statutory Authority G.S. 84–23. Readopted effective December 8, 1994.]

.0205 Record Keeping

The district grievance committee shall maintain records of all grievances referred to it by the State Bar and all grievances initially filed with the district grievance committee for at least one year. The district grievance committee shall provide such reports and information as are requested of it from time to time by the State Bar.

[History Note: Statutory Authority G.S. 84–23. Readopted effective December 8, 1994.]

.0206 Miscellaneous

(a) Assistance and Questions. The office of counsel, including the staff attorneys and the grievance coordinator, are available to answer questions and provide assistance regarding any matters before the district grievance committee.

(b) Missing Attorneys. Where a respondent attorney is missing or cannot be located, the district grievance committee shall promptly return the grievance file to the office of counsel for appropriate action.

[History Note: Statutory Authority G.S. 84–23. Readopted effective December 8, 1994.]

.0207 Conflicts of Interest

(a) No district grievance committee shall investigate or consider a grievance which alleges misconduct by any current member of the committee. If a file is referred to the committee by the State Bar or is initiated locally which alleges misconduct by a member of the district grievance committee, the file will be sent to the State Bar for investigation and handling within 10 working days after receipt of the grievance.

(b) A member of a district grievance committee shall not investigate or participate in deliberations concerning any of the following matters:

(1) alleged misconduct of an attorney who works in the same law firm or office with the committee member;

(2) alleged misconduct of a relative of the committee member;

(3) a grievance involving facts concerning which the committee member or a partner or associate in the committee member's law firm acted as an attorney.

[History Note: Statutory Authority G.S. 84–23. Readopted effective December 8, 1994.]

.0208 Letter to Complainant Where Local Grievance Alleges Fee Dispute Only

John Smith
Anywhere, N.C.

Re: Your complaint against Jane Doe

Dear Mr. Smith:

The [ ] district grievance committee has received your complaint against above-listed attorney. Based upon our initial review of the materials which you submitted, it appears that your complaint involves a fee dispute. Accordingly, I would like to take this opportunity to notify you of the North Carolina State Bar Fee Dispute Resolution Program. The program is designed to provide citizens with a means of resolving disputes over attorney fees at no cost to them and without going to court. A pamphlet which describes the program in greater detail is enclosed, along with an application form.

If you would like to participate in the fee dispute resolution program, please complete and return the form to me within 20 days of the date of this letter. If you decide to participate, no grievance file will be opened and the [ ] district bar grievance committee will take no other action against the attorney.

If you do not wish to participate in the fee dispute resolution program, you may elect to have your complaint investigated by the [ ] district grievance committee. If we do not hear from you within 20 days of the date of this letter, we will assume that you do not wish to participate in fee dispute resolution, and we will handle your complaint like any other grievance. However, the [ ] district grievance committee has no authority to attempt to resolve a fee dispute between an attorney and his or her client. Its sole function is to investigate your complaint and make a recommendation to the North Carolina State Bar regarding whether there is probable cause to believe that the attorney has violated one or more provisions of the Rules of Professional Conduct which govern attorneys in this state.

Thank you for your cooperation.

Sincerely yours,

[ ] Chairperson

[ ] District Bar Grievance Committee

cc: PERSONAL & CONFIDENTIAL
Director of Investigations
The N.C. State Bar

[History Note: Statutory Authority G.S. 84–23. Readopted effective December 8, 1994; amended effective August 23, 2007.]

.0209 Letter to Complainant Where Local Grievance Alleges Fee Dispute and Other Violations

John Smith
Anywhere, N.C.

Re: Your complaint against Jane Doe

Dear Mr. Smith:

The [ ] district grievance committee has received your complaint against above-listed attorney. Based upon our initial review of the materials which you submitted, it appears that your complaint involves a fee dispute as well as other possible violations of the rules of ethics. Accordingly, I would like to take this opportunity to notify you of the North Carolina State Bar Fee Dispute Resolution Program. The program is designed to provide citizens with a means of resolving disputes over attorney fees at no cost to them and without going to court. A pamphlet which describes the program in greater detail is enclosed, along with an application form.

If you would like to participate in the fee dispute resolution program, please complete and return the form to me within 20 days of the date of this letter. If you decide to participate, the fee dispute resolution committee will handle those portions of your complaint which involve an apparent fee dispute.

If you do not wish to participate in the fee dispute resolution program, you may elect to have your entire complaint investigated by the [ ] district grievance committee. If we do not hear from you within 20 days of the date of this letter, we will assume that you do not wish to participate in fee dispute resolution, and we will handle your entire complaint like any other grievance. However, the [ ] district grievance committee has no authority to attempt to resolve a fee dispute between an attorney and his or her client. Its sole function is to investigate your complaint and make a recommendation to the North Carolina State Bar regarding whether there is probable cause to believe that the attorney has violated one or more provisions of the Rules of Professional Conduct which govern attorneys in this state.

Thank you for your cooperation.

Sincerely yours,

[ ] Chairperson

[ ] District Bar Grievance Committee

cc: PERSONAL & CONFIDENTIAL
Director of Investigations
The N.C. State Bar

[History Note: Statutory Authority G.S. 84–23. Readopted effective December 8, 1994; amended effective August 23, 2007.]

.0210 Letter to Complainant/Respondent Where District Committee Recommends Finding of No Probable Cause

John Smith
Anywhere, N.C.

Re: Your complaint against Jane Doe

Our File No. [ ]

Dear Mr. Smith:

The [ ] district grievance committee has completed its investigation of your grievance. Based upon its investigation, the committee does not believe that there is probable cause to find that the attorney has violated any provisions of the Rules of Professional Conduct. The committee will forward a report with its recommendation to the North Carolina State Bar Grievance Committee. The final decision regarding your grievance will be made by the North Carolina State Bar Grievance Committee. You will be notified in writing of the State Bar's decision.

If you have any questions or wish to communicate further regarding your grievance, you may contact the North Carolina State Bar at the following address:

The North Carolina State Bar
Grievance Committee
P.O. Box 25908
Raleigh, N.C. 27611

Neither I nor any member of the [ ] district grievance committee can give you any advice regarding any legal rights you may have regarding the matters set out in your grievance. You may pursue any questions you have regarding your legal rights with an attorney of your choice.

Thank you very much for your cooperation.

Sincerely yours,

[ ] Chairperson

[ ] District Grievance Committee

cc: PERSONAL AND CONFIDENTIAL
[ ] Respondent Attorney

PERSONAL AND CONFIDENTIAL
Director of Investigations
The N.C. State Bar

[History Note: Statutory Authority G.S. 84–23. Readopted effective December 8, 1994.]

.0211 Letter to Respondent Where District Committee Recommends Finding of Probable Cause

Ms. Jane Doe
Anywhere, N.C.

Re: Grievance of John Smith

Our File No. [ ]

Dear Ms. Doe:

The [ ] district grievance committee has completed its investigation of Mr. Smith's grievance and has voted to recommend that the North Carolina State Bar Grievance Committee find probable cause to believe that you violated one or more provisions of the Rules of Professional Conduct. Specifically, the [ ] district grievance committee found that there is probable cause to believe that you may have violated [set out brief description of rule allegedly violated and pertinent facts].

The final decision in this matter will be made by the North Carolina State Bar Grievance Committee and you will be notified in writing of the State Bar's decision. The complainant has been notified that the [ ] district grievance committee has concluded its investigation and that the grievance has been sent to the North Carolina State Bar for final resolution, but has not been informed of the [ ] district committee's specific recommendation.

If you have any questions or wish to communicate further regarding this grievance, you may contact the North Carolina State Bar at the following address:

The North Carolina State Bar
Grievance Committee
P.O. Box 25908
Raleigh, N.C. 27611
Tel. 919–828–4620

Thank you very much for your cooperation.

Sincerely yours,

[ ] Chairperson

[ ] District Grievance Committee

cc: PERSONAL AND CONFIDENTIAL
Director of Investigations
The N.C. State Bar

[History Note: Statutory Authority G.S. 84–23. Readopted effective December 8, 1994.]

.0212 Letter to Complainant Where District Committee Recommends Finding of Probable Cause

John Smith
Anywhere, N.C.

Re: Your complaint against Jane Doe

Our File No. [ ]

Dear Mr. Smith:

The [ ] district grievance committee has completed its investigation of your grievance and has forwarded its file to the North Carolina State Bar Grievance Committee in Raleigh for final resolution. The final decision in this matter will be made by the North Carolina State Bar Grievance Committee and you will be notified in writing of the State Bar's decision.

If you have any questions or wish to communicate further regarding your grievance, you may contact the North Carolina State Bar at the following address:

The North Carolina State Bar
Grievance Committee
P.O. Box 25908
Raleigh, N.C. 27611

Neither I nor any member of the [ ] district grievance committee can give you any advice regarding any legal rights you may have regarding the matters set out in your grievance. You may pursue any questions you have regarding your legal rights with an attorney of your choice.

Thank you very much for your cooperation.

Sincerely yours,

[ ] Chairperson

[ ] District Grievance Committee

cc: PERSONAL AND CONFIDENTIAL
[ ] Respondent Attorney

PERSONAL AND CONFIDENTIAL
Director of Investigations
The N.C. State Bar

[History Note: Statutory Authority G.S. 84–23. Readopted effective December 8, 1994.]

.0213 Letter to Complainant Acknowledging Grievance

John Smith
Anywhere, N.C.

Re: Your complaint against Jane Doe

Our File No. [ ]

Dear Mr. Smith:

I am the chairperson of the [ ] district grievance committee. Your grievance against [respondent attorney] [was received in my office]/[has been forwarded to my office by the North Carolina State Bar] on [date]. I have assigned [investigator's name], a member of the [ ] district grievance committee, to investigate your grievance. [ ]'s name, address and telephone number are as follows: [ ].

Please be sure that you have provided all information and materials which relate to or support your complaint to the [ ] district grievance committee. If you have other information which you would like our committee to consider, or if you wish to discuss your complaint, please contact the investigating attorney by telephone or in writing as soon as possible.

After [ ]'s investigation is complete, the [ ] district grievance committee will make a recommendation to the North Carolina State Bar Grievance Committee regarding whether or not there is probable cause to believe that [respondent attorney] violated one or more provisions of the Rules of Professional Conduct. Your complaint and the results of our investigation will be sent to the North Carolina State Bar at that time. The [ ] district grievance committee's recommendation is not binding upon the North Carolina State Bar Grievance Committee, which will make the final determination. You will be notified in writing when the [ ] district grievance committee's investigation is concluded.

Neither the investigating attorney nor any member of the [ ] district grievance committee can give you any legal advice or represent you regarding any underlying legal matter in which you may be involved. You may pursue any questions you have about your legal rights with an attorney of your own choice.

Thank you very much for your cooperation.

Sincerely yours,

[ ] Chairperson

[ ] District Grievance Committee

cc: PERSONAL AND CONFIDENTIAL
Director of Investigations
The N.C. State Bar

[History Note: Statutory Authority G.S. 84–23. Readopted effective December 8, 1994.]

.0214 Letter to Investigating Attorney Assigning Grievance

James Roe
[ ] District Grievance Committee Member
Anywhere, N.C.

Re: Grievance of John Smith against Jane Doe
Our File No. [ ]

Dear Mr. Roe:

Enclosed you will find a copy of the grievance which I recently received regarding the above-captioned matter. Please investigate the complaint and provide a written report with your recommendations by [deadline].

Thank you very much.

Sincerely yours,

[ ] Chairperson

[ ] District Grievance Committee

cc: PERSONAL AND CONFIDENTIAL
Director of Investigations
The N.C. State Bar

[History Note: Statutory Authority G.S. 84–23. Readopted effective December 8, 1994.]

.0215 Letter to Complainant From Investigating Attorney

John Smith
Anywhere, N.C.

Re: Your complaint against Jane Doe
Our File No. [ ]

Dear Mr. Smith:

I am the member of the [ ] district grievance committee assigned to investigate your grievance against [respondent attorney]. It is part of my job to ensure that you have had a chance to explain your complaint and that the [ ] district grievance committee has copies of all of the documents which you believe relate to your complaint.

If you have other information or materials which you would like the [ ] district grievance committee to consider, or if you would like to discuss this matter, please contact me as soon as possible.

If you have already fully explained your complaint, you do not need to take any additional action regarding your grievance. The [ ] district grievance committee will notify you in writing when its investigation is complete. At that time, the matter will be forwarded to the North Carolina State Bar Grievance Committee in Raleigh for its final decision. You will be notified in writing of the North Carolina State Bar's decision.

Thank you very much for your cooperation.

Sincerely yours,

[ ] Investigating Member

[ ] District Grievance Committee

cc: PERSONAL AND CONFIDENTIAL
Chairperson, [ ] District Grievance Committee

[History Note: Statutory Authority G.S. 84–23. Readopted effective December 8, 1994.]

.0216 Letter of Notice to Respondent Attorney

Ms. Jane Doe
Anywhere, N.C.

Re: Grievance of John Smith

Our File No. [ ]

Dear Ms. Doe:

Enclosed you will find a copy of a grievance which has been filed against you by [complainant] and which was received in my office on [date]. As chairperson of the [ ] district grievance committee, I have asked [investigating attorney], a member of the committee, to investigate this grievance.

Please file a written response with [investigating attorney] within 15 days from receipt of this letter. Your response should provide a full and fair disclosure of all of the facts and circumstances relating to the matters set out in the grievance.

Thank you.

Sincerely yours,

[ ] Chairperson

[ ] District Grievance Committee

cc: PERSONAL AND CONFIDENTIAL
[ ] Investigating Member
[ ] District Grievance Committee

PERSONAL AND CONFIDENTIAL
Director of Investigations
N.C. State Bar

PERSONAL AND CONFIDENTIAL
[ ] Complainant

[History Note: Statutory Authority G.S. 84–23. Readopted effective December 8, 1994.]

.0217 Letter Transmitting Completed File to North Carolina State Bar

Director of Investigations
N.C. State Bar
P.O. Box 25908
Raleigh, N.C. 27611

Re: Grievance of John Smith

File No. [ ]

Dear Director:

The [ ] district grievance committee has completed its investigation in the above-listed matter. Based upon our investigation, the committee determined in its opinion that there is/is not probable cause to believe that the respondent violated one or more provisions of the Rules of Professional Conduct for the reasons set out in the enclosed report.

We are forwarding this matter for final determination by the North Carolina State Bar Grievance Committee along with the following materials:

1. The original grievance of [complainant].
2. A copy of the file of the investigating attorney.
3. The investigating attorney's report, which includes a summary of the facts and the reason(s) for the committee's decision.

Please let me know if you have any questions or if you need any additional information. Thank you.

Sincerely yours,

[ ] Chairperson

[ ] District Grievance Committee

[History Note: Statutory Authority G.S. 84–23. Readopted effective December 8, 1994.]

SUBCHAPTER C. RULES GOVERNING THE BOARD OF LAW EXAMINERS AND THE TRAINING OF LAW STUDENTS

SECTION. 0100 BOARD OF LAW EXAMINERS

.0101 Election

(a) At the first meeting of the council, it shall elect as members of the Board of Law Examiners, two members of the State Bar to serve for a term of one year from July 1, 1933; and two members of the State Bar to serve for a term of two years from July 1, 1933; and two members of the State Bar to serve for a term of three years from July 1, 1933.

The council, at its regular meeting, in April of each year, beginning in 1934, shall elect two members of the Board of Law Examiners to take office on the 1st day of July of the year in which they are elected, and such members shall serve for a term of three years or until their successors are elected and qualified.

Beginning with the year 1935 and every third year thereafter the council shall elect three members for a term of three years or until their successors are elected and qualified.

(b) No member of the council shall be a member of the Board of Law Examiners, and no member of the Board of Law Examiners shall be a member of the council.

[History Note: Statutory Authority G.S. 84–24. Readopted effective December 8, 1994.]

.0102 Examination of Applicants for License

All applicants for admission to the Bar shall first obtain a certificate or license from the Board of Law Examiners in accordance with the rules and regulations of that board.

[History Note: Statutory Authority G.S. 84–24. Readopted effective December 8, 1994.]

.0103 Admission to Practice

Upon receiving license to practice law from the Board of Law Examiners, the applicant shall be admitted to the practice thereof by taking the oath in the manner and form now provided by law.

[History Note: Statutory Authority G.S. 84–24. Readopted effective December 8, 1994.]

.0104 Approval of Rules and Regulations of Board of Law Examiners

The council shall, as soon as possible, after the presentation to it of rules and regulations for admission to the Bar, approve or disapprove such rules and regulations. The rules and regulations approved shall immediately be certified to the Supreme Court. Such rules and regulations as may not be approved by the council shall be the subject of further study and action, and for the purpose of study, the council and Board of Law Examiners may sit in joint session. No action, however, shall be taken by the joint meeting, but each shall act separately, and no rule or regulation shall be certified to the Supreme Court until approved by the council.

[History Note: Statutory Authority G.S. 84–24. Readopted effective December 8, 1994.]

.0105. Approval of Law Schools

Every applicant for admission to the North Carolina State Bar must meet the requirements set out in at least one of the numbered paragraphs below:

(1) The applicant holds an LL.B or J.D. degree from a law school that was approved by the American Bar Association at the time the degree was conferred; or

(2) Prior to August 1995, the applicant received an LL.B., J.D., LL.M., or S.J.D. degree from a law school that was approved by the council of the N.C. State Bar at the time the degree was conferred; or

(3) Prior to August 2004, the applicant received an LL.M or S.J.D. degree from a law school that was approved by the American Bar Association at the time the degree was conferred.

(4) The applicant holds an LL.B. or J.D. degree from a law school that was approved for licensure purposes in another state of the United States or the District of Columbia, was licensed in such state or district, and, at the time of the application for admission to the North Carolina State Bar, has been an active member in good standing of the bar in that state or district in each of the ten years immediately preceding application.

[History Note: Adopted effective March 3, 1999. Amended Feb. 27, 2003; March 5, 2015.]

SECTION .0200 RULES GOVERNING PRACTICAL TRAINING OF LAW STUDENTS

.0201 Purpose

The following rules are adopted to encourage law schools to provide their students with supervised practical training of varying kinds during the period of their formal legal education and to enable law students to obtain supervised practical training while serving as legal interns for government agencies.

[History Note: Statutory Authority G.S. 84–23. Readopted effective December 8, 1994; Amended effective June 7, 2001; amended effective March 5, 2008].

.0202 Definitions

The following definitions shall apply to the terms used in this section:

(1) Eligible persons—Persons who are unable financially to pay for the legal services of an attorney, as determined by a standard established by a judge of the General Court of Justice, a legal services corporation, or a law school legal aid clinic providing representation. "Eligible persons" includes non-profit organizations serving low-income communities.

(2) Government agencies—The federal or state government, any local government, or any agency, department, unit, or other entity of federal, state, or local government, specifically including a public defender's office or a district attorney's office.

(3) Law school—An ABA accredited law school or a law school actively seeking accreditation from the ABA and licensed by the Board of Governors of the University of North Carolina. If ABA accreditation is not obtained by a law school so licensed within three years of the commencement of classes, legal interns may not practice, pursuant to these rules, with any legal aid clinic of the law school.

(4) Legal aid clinic—A department, division, program, or course in a law school that operates under the supervision of an active member of the State Bar and renders legal services to eligible persons.

(5) Legal intern—A law student who is certified to provide supervised representation to clients or to appear on behalf of government agencies under the provisions of the rules of this Subchapter.

(6) Legal services corporation—A nonprofit North Carolina corporation organized exclusively to provide representation to eligible persons.

(7) Supervising attorney—An active member of the North Carolina State Bar who satisfies the requirements of Rule.0205 of this Subchapter and who supervises one or more legal interns.

[History Note: Statutory Authority G.S. 84–23. Readopted effective December 8, 1994; amended effective June 7, 2001; amended effective March 6, 2002; amended effective March 6, 2008.]

.0203 Eligibility

To engage in activities permitted by these rules, a law student must satisfy the following requirements:

(1) be enrolled in a law school approved by the Council of the North Carolina State Bar;

(2) have completed at least three semesters of the requirements for a professional degree in law (J.D. or its equivalent);

(3) be certified in writing by a representative of his or her law school, authorized by the dean of the law school to provide such certification, as being of good character with requisite legal ability and training to perform as a legal intern;

(4) be introduced to the court in which he or she is appearing by an attorney admitted to practice in that court;

(5) neither ask for nor receive any compensation or remuneration of any kind from any client for whom he or she renders services, but this shall not prevent an attorney, legal services corporation, law school, or government agency from paying compensation to the law student or charging or collecting a fee for legal services performed by such law student;

(6) certify in writing that he or she has read and is familiar with the North Carolina Rules of Professional Conduct and the opinions interpretive thereof.

[History Note: Statutory Authority G.S. 84–23. Readopted effective December 8, 1994; Amended effective June 7, 2001; amended effective March 6, 2008.]

.0204 Certification as Legal Intern

Upon receipt of the written materials required by Rule .0203(3) and (6) and Rule .0205(6), the North Carolina State Bar shall certify that the law student may serve as a legal intern. The certification shall be subject to the following limitations:

(a) Duration. The certification shall be effective for 18 months or until the announcement of the results of the first bar examination following the legal intern's graduation whichever is earlier. If the legal intern passes the bar examination, the certification shall remain in effect until the legal intern is sworn–in by a court and admitted to the bar.

(b) Withdrawal of Certification. The certification shall be withdrawn by the State Bar, without hearing or a showing of cause, upon receipt of

(1) notice from a representative of the legal intern's law school, authorized to act by the dean of the law

school, that the legal intern has not graduated but is no longer enrolled;

(2) notice from a representative of the legal intern's law school, authorized to act by the dean of the law school, that the legal intern is no longer in good standing at the law school;

(3) notice from a supervising attorney that the supervising attorney is no longer supervising the legal intern and that no other qualified attorney has assumed the supervision of the legal intern; or

(4) notice from a judge before whom the legal intern has appeared that the certification should be withdrawn.

[History Note: Statutory Authority G.S. 84–23. Readopted effective December 8, 1994; amended effective June 7, 2001.]

.0205 Supervision

(a) A supervising attorney shall

(1) be an active member of the North Carolina State Bar who has practiced law as a full-time occupation for at least two years;

(2) supervise no more than two legal interns concurrently, provided, however, there is no limit on the number of legal interns who may be supervised concurrently by an attorney who is a full-time member of a law school's faculty or staff whose primary responsibility is supervising legal interns in a legal aid clinic and, further provided, that an attorney who supervises legal interns through an externship or outplacement program of a law school legal aid clinic may supervise up to five legal interns;

(3) assume personal professional responsibility for any work undertaken by a legal intern while under his or her supervision;

(4) assist and counsel with a legal intern in the activities permitted by these rules and review such activities with the legal intern, all to the extent required for the proper practical training of the legal intern and the protection of the client;

(5) read, approve and personally sign any pleadings or other papers prepared by a legal intern prior to the filing thereof, and read and approve any documents prepared by a legal intern for execution by a client or third party prior to the execution thereof;

(6) prior to commencing the supervision, assume responsibility for supervising a legal intern by filing with the North Carolina State Bar a signed notice setting forth the period during which the supervising attorney expects to supervise the activities of an identified legal intern, and that the supervising attorney will adequately supervise the legal intern in accordance with these rules; and

(7) notify the North Carolina State Bar in writing promptly whenever the supervision of a legal intern ceases.

[History Note: Statutory Authority G.S. 84–23. Readopted effective December 8, 1994; amended effective June 7, 2001; amended effective March 6, 2002; amended effective March 6, 2008.]

.0206 Activities

(a) A properly certified legal intern may engage in the activities provided in this rule under the supervision of an attorney qualified and acting in accordance with the provisions of Rule .0205 of this subchapter.

(b) Without the presence of the supervising attorney, a legal intern may give advice to a client, including a government agency, on legal matters provided that the legal intern gives a clear prior explanation that the legal intern is not an attorney and the supervising attorney has given the legal intern permission to render legal advice in the subject area involved.

(c) A legal intern may represent an eligible person, the state in criminal prosecutions, a criminal defendant who is represented by the public defender, or a government agency in any proceeding before a federal, state, or local tribunal, including an administrative agency, if prior consent is obtained from the tribunal or agency upon application of the supervising attorney. Each appearance before the tribunal or agency shall be subject to any limitations imposed by the tribunal or agency including, but not limited to, the requirement that the supervising attorney physically accompany the legal intern.

(d) In all cases under this rule in which a legal intern makes an appearance before a tribunal or agency on behalf of a client who is an individual, the legal intern shall have the written consent in advance of the client. The client shall be given a clear explanation, prior to the giving of his or her consent, that the legal intern is not an attorney. This consent shall be filed with the tribunal and made a part of the record in the case. In all cases in which a legal intern makes an appearance before a tribunal or agency on behalf a government agency, the consent of the government agency shall be presumed if the legal intern is participating in an internship program of the government agency. A statement advising the court of the legal intern's participation in an internship program of the government agency shall be filed with the tribunal and made a part of the record in the case.

(e) In all cases under this rule in which a legal intern is permitted to make an appearance before a tribunal or agency, subject to any limitations imposed by the tribunal, the legal intern may engage in all activities appropriate to the representation of the client, including, without limitation, selection of and argument to the jury, examination and cross-examination of witnesses, motions and arguments thereon, and giving notices of appeal.

[History Note: Statutory Authority G.S. 84–23. Readopted effective December 8, 1994; Amended effective June 7, 2001; amended effective March 6, 2002; amended effective March 6, 2008.]

.0207 Use of Student's Name

(a) A legal intern's name may properly

(1) be printed or typed on briefs, pleadings, and other similar documents on which the legal intern has worked with or under the direction of the supervising attorney, provided the legal intern is clearly identified as a legal intern certified under these rules, and provided further that the legal intern shall not sign his or her name to such briefs, pleadings, or other similar documents;

(2) be signed to letters written on the letterhead of the supervising attorney, legal aid clinic, or government agency, provided there appears below the legal intern's signature a clear identification that the legal intern is certified under these rules. An appropriate designation is "Certified Legal Intern under the Supervision of [supervising attorney]."; and

(3) be printed on a business card, provided the name of the supervising attorney also appears on the business card and there appears below the legal intern's name a clear statement that the legal intern is certified under these rules. An appropriate designation is "Certified Legal Intern under the Supervision of [supervising attorney]."

(b) A student's name may not appear on the letterhead of a supervising attorney, legal aid clinic, or government agency.

[History Note: Statutory Authority G.S. 84–23. Readopted effective December 8, 1994; Amended effective June 7, 2001; amended effective March 6, 2008; amended effective October 7, 2010.]

SUBCHAPTER D. RULES OF THE STANDING COMMITTEES OF THE NORTH CAROLINA STATE BAR

SECTION .0100 PROCEDURES FOR RULING ON QUESTIONS OF LEGAL ETHICS

.0101 Definitions

(1) "Assistant executive director" shall mean the assistant executive director of the Bar.

(2) "Attorney" shall mean any active member of the Bar.

(3) "Bar" shall mean the North Carolina State Bar.

(4) "Chairperson" shall mean the chairperson or, in his or her absence, the vice-chairperson of the Ethics Committee of the Bar.

(5) "Committee" shall mean the Ethics Committee of the Bar.

(6) "Council" shall mean the council of the Bar.

(7) "Ethics advisory" shall mean a legal ethics opinion issued in writing by the executive director, the assistant executive director, or a designated member of the Bar's staff counsel. All ethics advisories shall be subsequently reviewed and approved, withdrawn or modified by the committee. Ethics advisories shall be designated by the letters "EA", numbered by year and order of issuance, and kept on file at the Bar.

(8) "Ethics decision" shall mean a written ethics opinion issued by the council in response to a request for an ethics opinion which, because of its special facts or for other reasons, does not warrant issuance of a formal ethics opinion. Ethics decisions shall be designated by the letters "ED", numbered by year and order of issuance, and kept on file at the Bar.

(9) "Executive director" shall mean the executive director of the Bar.

(10) "Formal ethics opinion" shall mean a published opinion issued by the council to provide ethical guidance for attorneys and to establish a principle of ethical conduct. A formal ethics opinion adopted under the Revised Rules of Professional Conduct (effective July 24, 1997, and as comprehensively revised in 2003) shall be designated as a "Formal Ethics Opinion" and numbered by year and order of issuance. Formal ethics opinions adopted under the repealed Rules of Professional Conduct (effective October 7, 1985 to July 23, 1997) are designated by the letters "RPC" and numbered serially. Formal ethics opinions adopted under the repealed Code of Professional Conduct (effective January 1, 1974 to October 6, 1985) are designated by the letters "CPR" and numbered serially. Formal ethics opinions adopted under the repealed Rules of Professional Conduct and the repealed Code of Professional Conduct are binding unless overruled by a provision of the Bar's current code of ethics, a revision of the rule of ethics upon which the opinion is based, or a subsequent formal ethics opinion on point.

(11) "Grievance Committee" shall mean the Grievance Committee of the Bar.

(12) "Informal ethics advisory" shall mean an informal ethics opinion communicated orally or via electronic mail by the executive director, the assistant executive director, or a designated member of the

Bar's legal staff counsel. A written record documenting the name of the inquiring attorney, the date of the informal ethics advisory, and the substance of the advice given shall be kept on file at the Bar. An informal ethics advisory is not binding upon the Bar in a subsequent disciplinary proceeding.

(13) "President" shall mean the president of the Bar or, in his or her absence, the presiding officer of the council.

(14) "Published" shall mean published for comment in the North Carolina State Bar *Newsletter* (prior to fall 1996), the North Carolina State Bar *Journal* (fall 1996 and thereafter) or other appropriate publication of the North Carolina State Bar.

(15) "Revised Rules of Professional Conduct" shall mean the code of ethics of the Bar effective July 24, 1997 and comprehensively revised effective March 1, 2003.

[History Note: Statutory Authority G.S. 84-23. Readopted effective December 8, 1994; amended effective March 5, 1998; amended effective February 5, 2004.]

.0102 General Provisions

(a) An attorney may ask the Bar to rule on actual or contemplated professional conduct of an attorney as provided in Section .0100 of this subchapter. In special circumstances, a ruling on the contemplated professional conduct of an attorney may be provided in response to the request of a person who is not a member of the Bar. The grant or denial of a request rests within the discretion of the executive director, assistant executive director, designated staff counsel, the chairperson, the committee, or the council, as appropriate.

(b) An attorney may request an informal ethics advisory by letter, electronic mail, telephone, or personal meeting with an appropriate member of the Bar staff. The executive director, assistant executive director, or designated staff counsel may provide an informal ethics advisory to guide the inquiring attorney's own prospective conduct if the inquiry is routine, the responsive advice is readily ascertained from the Revised Rules of Professional Conduct and formal ethics opinions, or the inquiry requires urgent action to protect some legal right, privilege, or interest.

(c) An attorney may request an ethics advisory or formal ethics opinion by sending a written inquiry to the Bar. The executive director, assistant executive director, or designated staff counsel may issue an ethics advisory to guide the inquiring attorney's own prospective conduct if the inquiry is routine, the responsive advice is readily ascertained from the Revised Rules of Professional Conduct and formal ethics opinions, or the inquiry requires urgent action to protect some legal right, privilege, or interest. An inquiry requesting an opinion about the professional conduct of another attorney, past conduct, or that presents a matter of first impression or of general interest to the Bar shall be referred to the committee for response by ethics decision or formal ethics opinion.

(d) All ethics inquiries, whether written or oral, shall present in detail all operative facts upon which the request is based. Inquiries should not disclose client confidences or other sensitive information not necessary to the resolution of the ethical question presented.

(e) Any attorney who requests an ethics opinion on the acts or contemplated professional conduct of another attorney, shall state, in the written inquiry, the name of the attorney and identify all persons whom the requesting attorney has reason to believe may be substantially affected by a response to the inquiry. The inquiry shall also provide evidence that the attorney whose conduct is at issue and all other identified interested persons have received copies of the inquiry from the requesting attorney.

(f) When a written ethics inquiry discloses conduct which may be actionable as a violation of the Revised Rules of Professional Conduct, the executive director, the assistant executive director, chairperson or the committee may refer the matter to the Grievance Committee for investigation.

(g) In general, no response shall be provided to an ethics inquiry that seeks an opinion on an issue of law.

(h) A decision not to issue a response to an ethics inquiry, whether by the executive director, assistant executive director, designated staff counsel, chairperson or the committee, shall not be appealable.

(i) Except as provided in Rule .0103(b) of this subchapter, the information contained in a request for an ethics opinion shall not be confidential.

[History Note: Statutory Authority G.S. 84-23. Readopted effective December 8, 1994; amended effective March 5, 1998.]

.0103 Informal Ethics Advisories and Ethics Advisories

(a) The executive director, assistant executive director, or designated staff counsel may honor or deny a request for an informal ethics advisory. Except as provided in Rule .0102(b), an attorney requesting an opinion concerning another attorney's professional conduct, past conduct, or matters of first impression shall be asked to submit a written inquiry for referral to the committee. An attorney requesting an opinion involving matters of widespread interest to the Bar or particularly complex factual circumstances may also be asked to submit a written inquiry for referral to the committee.

(b) The Bar's program for providing informal ethics advisories to inquiring attorneys is a designated lawyers' assistance program approved by the Bar and information received by the executive director, assistant executive director, or designated staff counsel from an attorney seeking an informal ethics advisory shall be confidential information pursuant to Rule 1.6(c) of the Revised Rules of Professional Conduct (2003); provided, however, such confidential information may be disclosed as allowed by Rule 1.6(b) and as necessary to respond to a false or misleading statement made about an informal ethics advisory. Further, if an attorney's response to a grievance proceeding relies in whole or in part upon the receipt of an informal ethics advisory, confidential information may be disclosed to Bar counsel, the Grievance Committee or other appropriate disciplinary authority.

(c) An ethics advisory issued by the executive director, assistant executive director, or designated staff counsel shall be promulgated under the authority of the committee and in accordance with such guidelines as the committee may establish and prescribe from time to time.

(d) An ethics advisory shall sanction or disapprove only the matter in issue, shall not otherwise serve as precedent and shall not be published.

(e) Ethics advisories shall be reviewed periodically by the committee. If, upon review, a majority of the committee present and voting decides that an ethics advisory should be withdrawn or modified, the requesting attorney shall be notified in writing of the committee's decision by the executive director or assistant executive director. Until such notification, the attorney shall be deemed to have acted ethically and in good faith if he or she acts pursuant to the ethics advisory which is later withdrawn or modified.

(f) If an inquiring attorney disagrees with the ethics advisory issued to him or her, the attorney may request reconsideration of the ethics advisory by writing to the committee prior to the next regularly scheduled meeting of the committee.

[History Note: Statutory Authority G.S. 84–23. Readopted effective December 8, 1994; amended effective March 5, 1998; amended effective February 5, 2004.]

.0104 Formal Ethics Opinions and Ethics Decisions

(a) Requests for formal ethics opinions or ethics decisions shall be made in writing and submitted to the executive director or assistant executive director who, after determining that a request is in compliance with Rule .0102 of this subchapter, shall transmit the request to the chairperson of the committee.

(b) If a formal ethics opinion or ethics decision is requested concerning contemplated or actual conduct of another attorney, that attorney shall be given an opportunity to be heard by the committee, along with the person who requested the opinion, under such guidelines as may be established by the committee. At the discretion of the chairperson and the committee, additional persons or groups shall be notified by the method deemed most appropriate by the chairperson and provided an opportunity to be heard by the committee.

(c) Upon initial consideration of the request, by vote of a majority of the members of the committee present at the meeting, the committee shall prepare a written proposed response to the inquiry and shall determine whether to issue the response as a proposed ethics decision or a proposed formal ethics opinion. Prior to the next regularly scheduled meeting of the committee, all proposed formal ethics opinions shall be published and all proposed ethics decisions shall be circulated to the members of the council.

(d) Prior to the next regularly scheduled meeting of the committee, any interested person or group may submit a written request to reconsider a proposed formal ethics opinion or a proposed ethics decision and may ask to be heard by the committee. The committee, under such guidelines as it may adopt, may allow or deny such request.

(e) Upon reconsideration of a proposed formal ethics opinion or proposed ethics decision, the committee may, by vote of not less than a majority of the duly appointed members of the committee, revise the proposed formal ethics opinion or proposed ethics decision. Prior to the next regularly scheduled meeting of the committee, all revised proposed formal ethics opinions shall be published and all revised proposed ethics decisions shall be circulated to the members of the council.

(f) Upon completion of the process, the committee shall determine, by a vote of not less than a majority of the duly appointed members of the committee, whether to transmit a proposed formal ethics opinion or proposed ethics decision to the council with a recommendation to adopt.

(g) Any interested person or group may request to be heard by the council prior to a vote on the adoption of a proposed formal ethics opinion or ethics decision. Whether permitted to appear before the council or not, the person or group has the right to file a written brief with the council under such rules as may be established by the council.

(h) The council's action on a proposed formal ethics opinion or ethics decision shall be determined by vote of the majority of the council present and voting. Notice of such action shall be provided to interested persons by the method deemed most appropriate by the chairperson.

(i) A formal ethics opinion or ethics decision may be reconsidered or withdrawn by the council pursuant to rules which it may establish from time to time.

(j) To vote, a member of the committee must be physically present at a meeting.

[History Note: Statutory Authority G.S. 84–23. Readopted effective December 8, 1994; amended effective March 5, 1998; amended effective February 5, 2004.]

SECTION .0200 PROCEDURES FOR THE AUTHORIZED PRACTICE COMMITTEE

.0201 General Provisions

The purpose of the committee on the authorized practice of law is to protect the public from being unlawfully advised and represented in legal matters by unqualified persons.

[History Note: Statutory Authority G.S. 84–37. Readopted effective December 8, 1994; amended December 10, 1999, effective February 3, 2000.]

.0202 Procedure

(a) The procedure to prevent and restrain the unauthorized practice of law shall be in accordance with the provisions hereinafter set forth.

(b) District bars shall not conduct separate proceedings into unauthorized practice of law matters but shall assist and cooperate with the North Carolina State Bar in reporting and investigating matters of alleged unauthorized practice of law.

[History Note: Statutory Authority G.S. 84–37. Readopted effective December 8, 1994.]

.0203 Definitions

Subject to additional definitions contained in other provisions of this subchapter, the following words and phrases, when used in this subchapter, have the meanings set forth in this rule, unless the context clearly indicates otherwise.

(1) Appellate division—the appellate division of the General Court of Justice.

(2) Chairperson of the Authorized Practice Committee—the councilor appointed to serve as chairperson of the Authorized Practice Committee of the State Bar.

(3) Complainant or the complaining witness—any person who has complained of the conduct of any person, firm or corporation as relates to alleged unauthorized practice of law.

(4) Complaint—a formal pleading filed in the name of the North Carolina State Bar in the superior court against a person, firm or corporation after a finding of probable cause.

(5) Council—the Council of the North Carolina State Bar.

(6) Councilor—a member of the Council of the North Carolina State Bar.

(7) Counsel—the counsel of the North Carolina State Bar appointed by the council.

(8) Court or courts of this state—a court authorized and established by the Constitution or laws of the state of North Carolina.

(9) Defendant—any person, firm or corporation against whom a complaint is filed after a finding of probable cause.

(10) Investigation—the gathering of information with respect to alleged unauthorized practice of law.

(11) Investigator—any person designated to assist in investigation of alleged unauthorized practice of law.

(12) Letter of notice—a communication to an accused individual or corporation setting forth the substance of alleged conduct involving unauthorized practice of law.

(13) Office of the counsel—the office and staff maintained by the Counsel of the North Carolina State Bar.

(14) Office of the Secretary—the office and staff maintained by the secretary of the North Carolina State Bar.

(15) Party—after a complaint has been filed, the North Carolina State Bar as plaintiff and the accused individual or corporation as defendant.

(16) Plaintiff—after a complaint has been filed, the North Carolina State Bar.

(17) Preliminary Hearing—hearing by the Authorized Practice Committee to determine whether probable cause exists.

(18) Probable Cause—a finding by the Authorized Practice Committee that there is reasonable cause to believe that a person or corporation has engaged in the unauthorized practice of law justifying legal action against such person or corporation.

(19) Secretary—the secretary of the North Carolina State Bar.

(20) Supreme Court—the Supreme Court of North Carolina.

[History Note: Statutory Authority G.S. 84–37. Readopted effective December 8, 1994; amended December 10, 1999, effective February 3, 2000; amended effective October 6, 2004.]

.0204 State Bar Council—Powers and Duties

The Council of the North Carolina State Bar shall have the power and duty

(1) to supervise the administration of the Authorized Practice Committee in accordance with the provisions of this subchapter;

(2) to appoint a counsel. The counsel shall serve at the pleasure of the council. The counsel shall be a

member of the North Carolina State Bar but shall not be permitted to engage in the private practice of law.

[History Note: Statutory Authority G.S. 84–37. Readopted effective December 8, 1994; amended December 10, 1999, effective February 3, 2000.]

.0205 Chairperson of the Authorized Practice Committee—Powers and Duties

(a) The chairperson of the Authorized Practice Committee shall have the power and duty

(1) to supervise the activities of the counsel;

(2) to recommend to the Authorized Practice Committee that an investigation be initiated;

(3) to recommend to the Authorized Practice Committee that a complaint be dismissed;

(4) to direct a letter of notice to an accused person or corporation or direct the counsel to issue letters of notice in such cases or under such circumstances as the chairperson deems appropriate;

(5) to notify the accused and any complainant that a complaint has been dismissed;

(6) to call meetings of the Authorized Practice Committee for the purpose of holding preliminary hearings;

(7) to issue subpoenas in the name of the North Carolina State Bar or direct to the secretary to issue such subpoenas;

(8) to administer oaths or affirmations to witnesses;

(9) to file and verify complaints and petitions in the name of the North Carolina State Bar.

(b) The president, vice-chairperson or senior council member of the Authorized Practice Committee shall perform the functions of the chairperson of the committee in any matter when the chairperson or vice-chairperson is absent or disqualified.

[History Note: Statutory Authority G.S. 84–37. Readopted effective December 8, 1994; amended December 10, 1999, effective February 3, 2000.]

.0206 Authorized Practice Committee—Powers and Duties

The Authorized Practice Committee shall have the power and duty

(1) to direct the counsel to investigate any alleged unauthorized practice of law by any person, firm, or corporation in this State;

(2) to hold preliminary hearings, find probable cause, and recommend to the Executive Committee that a complaint for injunction be filed in the name of the State Bar against the respondent;

(3) to dismiss allegations of the unauthorized practice of law upon a finding of no probable cause;

(4) to issue letters of caution, which may include a demand to cease and desist, to respondents in cases where the Committee concludes either that:

a. There is probable cause established to believe respondent has engaged in the unauthorized practice of law in North Carolina, but

(i) respondent has agreed to refrain from engaging in the conduct in the future;

(ii) respondent is unlikely to engage in the conduct again; or

(iii) either referral to a district attorney or complaint for injunction is not warranted under the circumstances; or

b. There is no probable cause established to believe respondent has engaged in the unauthorized practice of law in North Carolina, but

(i) the conduct of the respondent may be improper and may become the basis for injunctive relief if continued or repeated; or

(ii) the Committee otherwise finds it appropriate to caution the respondent.

(5) to direct counsel to stop an investigation and take no action;

(6) to refer a matter to another agency, including the district attorney for criminal prosecution and to other committees of the North Carolina State Bar; and

(7) to issue advisory opinions in accordance with procedures adopted by the council as to whether the actual or contemplated conduct of non-lawyers would constitute the unauthorized practice of law in North Carolina.

[History Note: Statutory Authority G.S. 84–37. Readopted effective December 8, 1994; amended effective February 20, 1995; amended December 10, 1999, effective February 3, 2000; amended effective October 6, 2004.]

.0207 Counsel—Powers and Duties

The counsel shall have the power and duty

(1) to initiate an investigation concerning the alleged unauthorized practice of law;

(2) to direct a letter of notice to a respondent when authorized by the chairperson of the Authorized Practice Committee;

(3) to investigate all matters involving alleged unauthorized practice of law whether initiated by the filing of a complaint or otherwise;

(4) to recommend to the chairperson of the Authorized Practice Committee that a matter be dismissed because the complaint is frivolous or falls outside the council's jurisdiction; that a letter of notice be issued; or that the matter be considered by the Authorized Practice Committee to determine whether probable cause exists;

(5) to prosecute all unauthorized practice of law proceedings before the Authorized Practice Committee and the courts;

(6) to represent the State Bar in any trial or other proceedings concerned with the alleged unauthorized practice of law.

(7) to employ assistant counsel, investigators, and other administrative personnel in such numbers as the council may from time to time authorize;

(8) to maintain permanent records of all matters processed and the disposition of such matters;

(9) to perform such other duties as the council may from time to time direct.

[History Note: Statutory Authority G.S. 84–37. Readopted effective December 8, 1994; amended December 10, 1999, effective February 3, 2000.]

.0208 Suing for Injunctive Relief

(a) Upon receiving a recommendation from the Authorized Practice Committee that a complaint seeking injunctive relief be filed, the Executive Committee shall review the matter at the same quarterly meeting and determine whether the recommended action is necessary to protect the public interest and ought to be prosecuted.

(b) If the Executive Committee decides to follow the Authorized Practice Committee's recommendation, it shall direct the counsel to prepare the necessary pleadings as soon as practical for signature by the chairperson and filing with the appropriate tribunal.

(c) If the Executive Committee decides not to follow the Authorized Practice Committee's recommendation, the matter shall go before the council at the same quarterly meeting to determine whether the recommended action is necessary to protect the public interest and ought to be prosecuted.

(d) If the council decides not to follow the Authorized Practice Committee's recommendation, the matter shall be referred back to the Authorized Practice Committee for alternative disposition.

(e) If probable cause exists to believe that a respondent is engaged in the unauthorized practice of law and action is needed to protect the public interest before the next quarterly meeting of the Authorized Practice Committee, the chairperson, with the approval of the president, may file and verify a complaint or petition in the name of the North Carolina State Bar.

[Adopted December 10, 1999, effective February 3, 2000.]

SECTION .0300 DISASTER RESPONSE PLAN

.0301 The Disaster Response Team

(a) The disaster response team should be composed of the following:

(1) the president of the State Bar, or if the president is unavailable, another officer of the State Bar;

(2) the counsel or his or her designee;

(3) the director of communications or his or her designee;

(4) the president of the Young Lawyers Division of the North Carolina Bar Association ("YLD") or his or her designee;

(5) the chairperson of the Client Assistance Committee; and

(6) other persons, such as the applicable local bar president(s), appointed by the president as necessary or appropriate for response in each individual situation.

(b) Implementation of the disaster response plan shall be the decision of the president or, if he or she is unavailable, the president-elect, vice-president or immediate past-president.

(c) The counsel, or his or her designee, shall be the coordinator of the disaster response team ("coordinator"). If the president or other officer is unavailable to decide whether to implement the disaster response plan for a particular event, then and only then shall the coordinator be authorized to make the decision to implement the disaster response plan.

(d) It shall be the responsibility of the coordinator to conduct periodic educational programs regarding the disaster response plan and to report regularly to the Client Assistance Committee.

[History Note: Statutory Authority G.S. 84–23. Readopted effective December 8, 1994; amended December 10, 1999, effective February 3, 2000.]

.0302 General Policy and Objectives

(a) Rapid Response.

(1) It is essential that the State Bar establish an awareness and sensitivity to disaster situations.

(2) The disaster response plan will be disseminated through the publications of the State Bar and continuing legal education programs.

(3) The disaster response team shall be properly trained to respond to initial inquiries and appear at the site.

(4) The disaster response team will provide victims and/or their families with written materials when requested.

(b) Effective Mobilization of Resources.

(1) An appropriate press release shall be prepared and disseminated.

(2) The coordinator shall confirm the individuals who will make up the disaster response team.

(3) Individual assignments of responsibilities shall be made to members of the team by the coordinator.

(4) The coordinator shall arrange for the State Bar to be represented at any victims' assistance center established at the disaster site. The coordinator will request the YLD to assist the State Bar by providing additional staffing.

(5) The coordinator shall contact the local district attorney(s) and request that he or she prosecute any persons engaging in the unauthorized practice of law (N.C.G.S. 84–2.1, 84–4, 84–7 and 84–8); improper solicitation (N.C.G.S. 84–38); division of fees (N.C.G.S. 84–38); and/or the common law crime of barratry (frequently stirring up suits and quarrels between persons).

(c) Publicity.

(1) It is important to focus on the fact that disaster response is a public service effort.

(2) The disaster response team shall ensure approval and dissemination of an even-handed press release.

(3) The director of communications will be utilized for press contacts.

(4) It is important to ensure that the press release indicates that the State Bar is a resource designed to assist victims, if requested.

(d) On-site Representation.

(1) It is normally desirable for the disaster response team to arrive at the site of the disaster as soon as possible.

(2) Only the president or president-elect or their designee will conduct press interviews on behalf of the State Bar.

(3) The availability of the State Bar at the site of the disaster should be made known to victims.

(4) The disaster response team shall establish a liaison with the State Emergency Management Division, Red Cross, Salvation Army, and other such organizations to provide assistance to victims and furnish written materials to these organizations.

(5) It is crucial that the State Bar not become identified with either side of any potential controversy.

(6) All members of the disaster response team must avoid making comments on the merits of claims that may arise from the disaster.

(e) Dissemination of Information to Affected Individuals.

(1) The team shall emphasize in all public statements that the State Bar's major and only legitimate concern is for those persons affected by the disaster and the public interest.

(2) The State Bar's role is limited to monitoring compliance with its disciplinary rules, to requesting reports of any violation needing investigation, and to informing victims of rules concerning client solicitation.

[History Note: Statutory Authority G.S. 84–23. Readopted effective December 8, 1994.]

.0303 Report on Results

(a) The coordinator will promptly convene a meeting of groups involved in the disaster to review the effectiveness of the plan in that particular disaster.

(b) The coordinator shall prepare a written report concerning significant matters relating to the disaster.

(c) The written report shall be submitted to the Client Assistance Committee as well as other involved organizations.

[History Note: Statutory Authority G.S. 84–23. Readopted effective December 8, 1994; amended December 10, 1999, effective February 3, 2000.]

SECTION .0400 [REPEALED]

SECTION .0500 [REPEALED]

SECTION. 0600 RULES GOVERNING THE LAWYER ASSISTANCE PROGRAM

.0601 Purpose

The purpose of the lawyer assistance program is to: (1) protect the public by assisting lawyers and judges who are professionally impaired by reason of substance abuse, addiction, or debilitating mental condition; (2) assist impaired lawyers and judges in recovery; and (3) educate lawyers and judges concerning the causes of and remedies for such impairment.

[History Note: Statutory Authority G.S. 84–22; G.S. 84–23. Readopted effective December 8, 1994; amended December 10, 1999, effective February 3, 2000.]

.0602 Authority

The council of the North Carolina State Bar hereby establishes the Lawyer Assistance Program Board (the board) as a standing committee of the council. The board has the authority to establish policies governing the State Bar's lawyer assistance program as needed to implement the purposes of this program. The authority conveyed is not limited by, but is fully coextensive with, the authority previously vested in State Bar's predecessor program, the Positive Action for Lawyers (PALS) program.

[History Note: Statutory Authority G.S. 84–22; G.S. 84–23. Readopted effective December 8, 1994; amended December 10, 1999, effective February 3, 2000.]

.0603 Operational Responsibility

The board shall be responsible for operating the lawyer assistance program subject to the statutes governing the practice of law, the authority of the council, and the rules of the board.

[History Note: Adopted December 10, 1999, effective February 3, 2000. Former .0603 was renumbered to .0613.]

.0604 Size of Board

The board shall have nine members. Three of the members shall be councilors of the North Carolina State Bar at the time of appointment; three of the members shall be non-lawyers or lawyers with experience and training in the fields of mental health, substance abuse or addiction; and three of the members shall be lawyers who are currently volunteers to the lawyer assistance program. In addition, the board may have the dean of a law school in North Carolina, or the dean's designee, appointed by the council as an ex officio member. No member of the Grievance Committee shall be a member of the board.

[History Note: Adopted December 10, 1999, effective February 3, 2000. Former .0604 was renumbered to .0614; amended effective November 16, 2006.]

.0605 Appointment of Members; When; Removal

The initial members of the board shall be appointed at the next meeting of the council following the creation of the board. Thereafter, members shall be appointed or reappointed, as the case may be, at the first quarterly meeting of the council each calendar year, provided that a vacancy occurring by reason of death, resignation, or removal shall be filled by appointment of the council at the next quarterly meeting following the event giving rise to the vacancy, and the person so appointed shall serve for the balance of the vacated term. Any member of the board may be removed at any time by an affirmative vote of a majority of the members of the council in session at a regularly called meeting.

[History Note: Adopted December 10, 1999, effective February 3, 2000. Former .0605 was renumbered to .0615.]

.0606 Term of Office and Succession

The members of the board shall be divided into three classes of equal size to serve in the first instance for terms expiring one, two and three years, respectively, after the first quarterly meeting of the council following creation of the board. Of the initial board, three members (one councilor, one mental health, substance abuse or addiction professional, and one lawyer-volunteer to the lawyer assistance program) shall be appointed to terms of one year; three members (one councilor, one mental health, substance abuse or addiction professional, and one lawyer-volunteer) shall be appointed to terms of two years; and three members (one councilor, one mental health, substance abuse or addiction professional, and one lawyer-volunteer) shall be appointed to terms of three years. Thereafter, the successors in each class of board members shall be appointed to serve for terms of three years. No member shall serve more than two consecutive three-year terms, in addition to service prior to the beginning of a full three-year term, without having been off the board for at least three years. Members of the board serving ex officio shall serve one-year terms and may serve up to three consecutive terms.

[History Note: Adopted December 10, 1999, effective February 3, 2000. Former .0606 was renumbered to .0616; amended effective November 16, 2006.]

.0607 Appointment of Chairperson

The chairperson of the board shall be appointed by the council annually at the time of its appointment of board members. The chairperson may be re-appointed for an unlimited number of one-year terms. The chairperson shall preside at all meetings of the board, shall prepare and present to the council the annual report of the board, and shall represent the board in its dealings with the public. A vacancy occurring by reason of death, resignation, or removal shall be filled by appointment of the council at the next quarterly meeting following the event giving rise to the vacancy, and the person so appointed shall serve for the balance of the vacated term.

[History Note: Adopted December 10, 1999, effective February 3, 2000. Former .0607 was renumbered to .0617.]

.0608 Appointment of Vice–Chairperson

The vice-chairperson of the board shall be appointed by the council annually at the time of its appointment of board members. The vice-chairperson may be re-appointed for an unlimited number of one-year terms. The vice-chairperson shall preside at and represent the board in the absence of the chairperson and shall perform such other duties as may be assigned to him or her by the chairperson or by the board. A vacancy occurring by reason of death, resignation, or removal shall be filled by appointment of the council at the next quarterly meeting following the event giving rise to the vacancy, and the person so appointed shall serve for the balance of the vacated term.

[History Note: Adopted December 10, 1999, effective February 3, 2000. Former .0608 was renumbered to .0618.]

.0609 Source of Funds

Funding for the program shall be provided from the general and appropriate special funds of the North Carolina State Bar and such other funds as may become available by grant or otherwise.

[History Note: Adopted December 10, 1999, effective February 3, 2000. Former .0609 was renumbered to .0619.]

.0610 Meetings

The annual meeting of the board shall be held in October of each year in connection with the annual meeting of the North Carolina State Bar. The board by resolution may set regular meeting dates and places. Special meetings of the board may be called at any time upon notice given by the chairperson, the vice-chairperson, or any two members of the board. Notice of meeting shall be given at least two days prior to the meeting by mail, telegram, facsimile transmission, electronic mail or telephone. A quorum of the board for conducting its official business shall be a majority of the members serving at a particular time.

[History Note: Adopted December 10, 1999, effective February 3, 2000. Former .0610 was renumbered to .0620.]

.0611 Annual Report

The board shall prepare at least annually a report of its activities and shall present the same at the annual meeting of the council.

[History Note: Adopted December 10, 1999, effective February 3, 2000.]

.0612 Powers and Duties of the Board

In addition to the powers and duties set forth elsewhere in these rules, the board shall have the following powers and duties:

(1) to exercise general supervisory authority over the administration of the lawyer assistance program consistent with these rules;

(2) to implement programs to investigate and evaluate reports that a lawyer's ability to practice law is impaired because of substance abuse, depression, or other debilitating mental condition; to confer with any lawyer who is the subject of such a report; and, if the report is verified, to provide referrals and assistance to the impaired lawyer;

(3) to adopt and amend regulations consistent with these rules with the approval of the council;

(4) to delegate authority to the staff of the lawyer assistance program subject to the review of the council;

(5) to delegate authority to investigate, evaluate, and intervene with impaired lawyers to committees composed of qualified volunteer lawyers and non-lawyers;

(6) to submit an annual budget for the lawyer assistance program to the council for approval and to ensure that expenses of the board do not exceed the annual budget approved by the council;

(7) to report annually on the activities and operations of the board to the council and make any recommendations for changes in the rules or methods of operation of the lawyer assistance program;

(8) to implement programs to investigate, evaluate, and intervene in cases referred to it by a disciplinary body, and to report the results of the investigation and evaluation to the referring body;

(9) to promote programs of education and awareness for lawyers, law students, and judges about the causes and remedies of lawyer impairment;

(10) to train volunteer lawyers to provide peer support, assistance and monitoring for impaired lawyers; and

(11) to administer the PALS revolving loan fund or other similar fund that may be established for the board's program to assist lawyers who are impaired because of a debilitating mental condition.

[History Note: Adopted December 10, 1999, effective February 3, 2000.]

.0613 Confidentiality

The lawyer assistance program is an approved lawyers' assistance program in accordance with the requirements of Rule 1.6(b) of the Revised Rules of Professional Conduct. Except as noted herein and otherwise required by law, information received during the course of investigating, evaluating, and assisting an impaired lawyer shall be privileged and held in the strictest confidence by the staff of the lawyer assistance program, the members of the board and the members of any committee of the board. If a report of impaired condition is made by members of a lawyer's family, and there is good cause shown, the board may, in its discretion, release information to appropriate members of the lawyer's family if the board or its duly authorized committee determines that such disclosure is in the best interest of the impaired lawyer.

[History Note: Statutory Authority G.S. 84–22; G.S. 84–23. Readopted effective December 8, 1994; renumbered from .0603 and amended December 10, 1999; effective February 3, 2000.]

.0614 Reserved

.0615 Regional Chapters

A committee may, under appropriate rules and regulations promulgated by the, board, establish regional chapters, composed of qualified volunteer lawyers and non-lawyers. A regional chapter may perform any or all of the duties and functions set forth in Section.0600 of this subchapter to the extent provided by the rules. of the board.

[History Note: Statutory Authority G.S. 84–22; G.S. 84–23. Readopted effective December 8, 1994; renumbered from .0605 and amended December 10, 1999, effective February 3, 2000.]

.0616 Suspension for Impairment, Reinstatement

If it appears that a lawyer's ability to practice law is impaired by substance abuse and/or chemical addiction, the board, or its duly authorized committee, may petition any superior court judge to issue an order, pursuant to the court's inherent authority, suspending the lawyer's license to practice law in this state for up to 180 days.

(a) The petition shall be supported by affidavits of at least two persons setting out the evidence of the lawyer's impairment.

(b) The petition shall be signed by the executive director of the lawyer assistance program and the executive director of the State Bar.

(c) The petition shall contain a request for a protective order sealing the petition and all proceedings respecting it.

(d) Except as set out in Rule .0606(j) below, the petition shall request the court to issue an order requiring the attorney to appear in not less than 10 days and show cause why the attorney should not be suspended from the practice of law. No order suspending an attorney's license shall be entered without notice and a hearing, except as provided in Rule .0606(j) below.

(e) The order to show cause shall be served upon the attorney, along with the State Bar's petition and supporting affidavits, as provided in Rule 4 of the North Carolina Rules of Civil Procedure.

(f) At the show cause hearing, the State Bar shall have the burden of proving by clear, cogent, and convincing evidence that the lawyer's ability to practice law is impaired.

(g) If the court finds that the attorney is impaired, the court may enter an order suspending the attorney from the practice of law for up to 180 days. The order shall specifically set forth the reasons for its issuance.

(h) At any time following entry of an order suspending an attorney, the attorney may petition the court for an order reinstating the attorney to the practice of law.

(i) A hearing on the reinstatement petition will be held no later than 10 days from the filing of the petition, unless the suspended lawyer agrees to a continuance. At the hearing, the suspended lawyer will have the burden of establishing by clear, cogent, and convincing evidence the following: (1) the lawyer's ability to practice law is no longer impaired; (2) the lawyer's debilitating condition is being treated and/or managed; (3) it is unlikely that the inability to practice law due to the impairment will recur; and (4) it is unlikely that the interest of the public will be unduly threatened by the reinstatement of the lawyer.

(j) No suspension of an attorney's license shall be allowed without notice and a hearing unless

(1) the State Bar files a petition with supporting affidavits, as provided in Rule .0606(a)–(c) above.

(2) the State Bar's petition and supporting affidavits demonstrate by clear, cogent, and convincing evidence that immediate and irreparable harm, injury, loss, or damage will result to the public, to the lawyer who is the subject of the petition, or to the administration of justice before notice can be given and a hearing had on the petition.

(3) the State Bar's petition specifically seeks the temporary emergency relief of suspending ex parte the attorney's license for up to 10 days or until notice be given and a hearing held, whichever is shorter, and the State Bar's petition requests the court to endorse an emergency order entered hereunder with the hour and date of its entry.

(4) the State Bar's petition requests that the emergency suspension order expire by its own terms 10 days from the date of entry, unless, prior to the expiration of the initial 10–day period, the court agrees to extend the order for an additional 10–day period for good cause shown or the respondent attorney agrees to an extension of the suspension period.

(k) The respondent attorney may apply to the court at any time for an order dissolving the emergency suspension order. The court may dissolve the emergency suspension order without notice to the State Bar or hearing, or may order a hearing on such notice as the court deems proper.

(*l*) The North Carolina State Bar shall not be required to provide security for payment of costs or damages prior to entry of a suspension order with or without notice to the respondent attorney.

(m) No damages shall be awarded against the State Bar in the event that a restraining order entered with or without notice and a hearing is dissolved.

[History Note: Statutory Authority G.S. 84–23; G.S. 84–28(i). Readopted effective December 8, 1994; amended effective September 7, 1995; renumbered from .0606 and amended December 10, 1999, effective February 3, 2000.]

.0617. Consensual Inactive Status

Notwithstanding the provisions of Rule .0616 of this subchapter, the court may enter an order transferring the lawyer to inactive status if the lawyer consents. The order may contain such other terms and provisions as the parties agree to and which are necessary for the protection of the public. A lawyer transferred to inactive status pursuant to this rule may not petition for reinstatement pursuant to Rule .0902 of this subchapter. The lawyer may apply to the court at any time for an order reinstating the lawyer to active status.

[History Note: Statutory Authority G.S. 84–23; G.S. 84–28(i). Readopted effective December 8, 1994; Renumbered from .0607 and Amended December 10, 1999, effective February 3, 2000. Amended effective March 8, 2013.]

.0618 Agents of the State Bar

All members of the board and its duly appointed committees shall be deemed to be acting as agents of the State Bar when performing the functions and duties set forth in this subchapter.

[History Note: Statutory Authority G.S. 84–22; G.S. 84–23. Readopted effective December 8, 1994; renumbered from .0608 and amended December 10, 1999, effective February 3, 2000.]

.0619 Judicial Committee

The Judicial Committee of the Lawyer Assistance Program Board shall implement a program of intervention for members of the judiciary with substance abuse problems affecting their professional conduct. The committee shall consist of at least two members of the state's judiciary. The committee will be governed by the rules of the Lawyer Assistance Program Board where applicable. Rules .0616 and .0617 of this subchapter are not applicable to the committee.

[History Note: Statutory Authority G.S. 84–22; G.S. 84–23. Readopted effective December 8, 1994; renumbered from .0609 and amended December 10, 1999, effective February 3, 2000.]

.0620 Rehabilitation Contracts for Lawyers Impaired by Substance Abuse

The board, or its duly authorized committee, has the authority to enter into rehabilitation contracts with lawyers suffering from substance abuse including contracts that provide for alcohol and/or drug testing. Such contracts may include the following conditions among others:

(a) that upon receipt of a report of a positive alcohol or drug test for a substance prohibited under the contract, the contract may be amended to include additional provisions considered to be in the best rehabilitative interest of the lawyer and the public; and

(b) that the lawyer stipulates to the admission of any alcohol and/or drug-testing results into evidence in any in camera proceeding brought under this section without the necessity of further authentication.

Adopted effective March 7, 1996; Renumbered from .610 and Amended December 10, 1999, effective February 3, 2000.]

.0621 Evaluations for Substance Abuse, Alcoholism and/or other Chemical Addictions

(a) Notice of Need for Evaluation. The Lawyer Assistance Program Board, or its duly authorized committee, may demand that a lawyer obtain a comprehensive evaluation of his or her condition by an approved addiction specialist if the lawyer's ability to practice law is apparently being impaired by substance abuse, alcoholism and/or other chemical addictions. This authority may be exercised upon recommendation of the director of the lawyer assistance program and the approval of at least three members of the board or appropriate committee, which shall include at least one person with professional expertise in chemical addiction. Written notice shall be provided to the lawyer informing the lawyer that the board has determined that an evaluation is necessary and demanding that the lawyer obtain the evaluation by a date set forth in the written notice.

(b) Failure to Comply. If the lawyer does not obtain an evaluation, the director of the lawyer assistance program shall obtain the approval of the chairperson of the board, or the chairperson of the appropriate committee of the board, to file a motion to compel an evaluation pursuant to the authority set forth in G.S. § 84–28(i) and (j) and in accordance with the procedure set forth in Rule 35 of the North Carolina Rules of Civil Procedure. All pleadings in such a proceeding shall be filed under seal and all hearings shall be held in camera. Written notice of the motion to compel an examination shall be served upon the lawyer in accordance with the North Carolina Rules of Civil Procedure at least ten days before the hearing on the matter.

[History Note: Adopted December 10, 1999, effective February 3, 2000.]

.0622 Grounds for Compelling an Evaluation

An order compelling the lawyer to obtain a comprehensive evaluation by an addiction specialist may be issued if the board establishes that the evaluation will assist the lawyer and the lawyer assistance program to assess the lawyer's condition and any risk that the condition may present to the public, and to determine an appropriate treatment for the lawyer.

[History Note: Adopted December 10, 1999, effective February 3, 2000.]

.0623 Failure to Comply with an Order Compelling an Evaluation

If a lawyer fails to comply with an order compelling a comprehensive evaluation by an addiction specialist, the board, or its duly authorized committee, may file a contempt proceeding to be held in camera. If the lawyer fails to comply with a contempt order, the lawyer shall be deemed to have waived confidentiality respecting communications made by the lawyer to the board or its committee. The board, or its duly authorized committee, may seek further relief and may file motions or proceedings in open court.

[History Note: Adopted December 10, 1999, effective February 3, 2000.]

SECTION .0700 PROCEDURES FOR FEE DISPUTE RESOLUTION

.0701 Purpose and Implementation

The purpose of the Fee Dispute Resolution Program shall be to assist lawyers and clients to settle disputes over fees. In doing so, the Fee Dispute Resolution Program shall assist the lawyers and clients in determining the appropriate fee for legal services rendered. The State Bar shall implement the Fee Dispute Resolution Program under the auspices of the Attorney Client Assistance Committee (the committee), which shall be offered to clients and their lawyers at no cost.

[History Note: Statutory Authority G.S. 84–23. Readopted effective December 8, 1994; amended December 10, 1999, effective February 3, 2000; amended effective May 4, 2000; amended effective March 8, 2007.]

.0702. Jurisdiction

(a) The committee has jurisdiction over a disagreement arising out of a client-lawyer relationship concerning the fees and expenses charged or incurred for legal services provided by a lawyer licensed to practice law in North Carolina.

(b) The committee does not have jurisdiction over the following:

1) disputes concerning fees or expenses established by a court, federal or state administrative agency, or federal or state official, or private arbitrator or arbitration panel;

2) disputes involving services that are the subject of a pending grievance complaint alleging the violation of the Revised Rules of Professional Conduct;

3) fee disputes that are or were the subject of litigation or arbitration unless;

(i) a court, arbitrator, or arbitration panel directs the matter to the State Bar for resolution or

(ii) both parties to the dispute agree to dismiss the litigation or arbitration without prejudice and pursue resolution through the State Bar's Fee Dispute Resolution program;

4) fee disputes between lawyers and service providers, such as court reporters and expert witnesses;

5) fee disputes between lawyers and individuals with whom the lawyer had no client-lawyer relationship, except in those case where the fee has been paid by a person other than the client; and

6) disputes concerning fees charged for ancillary services provided by the lawyer not involving the practice of law.

The committee shall encourage mediated settlement of fee disputes falling within its jurisdiction pursuant to Rule .0708 of this subchapter.

[History Note: Statutory Authority G.S. 84–23. Readopted effective December 8, 1994; amended effective May 4, 2000; March 11, 2010; August 23, 2012.]

.0703 Coordinator of Fee Dispute Resolution

The secretary-treasurer of the North Carolina State Bar shall designate a member of the staff to serve as coordinator of the Fee Dispute Resolution Program. The coordinator shall develop forms, maintain records, and provide statistics on the Fee Dispute Resolution Program. The coordinator shall also develop an annual report to the council.

[History Note: Statutory Authority G.S. 84–23. Readopted effective December 8, 1994; amended effective May 4, 2000; amended effective March 8, 2007.]

.0704 Reserved

.0705 Selection of Mediators

The State Bar will select a pool of qualified mediators. Selected mediators shall be certified by the North Carolina Dispute Resolution Commission or have a minimum of three (3) years experience as a mediator.

[History Note: Adopted effective May 4, 2000.]

.0706 Processing Requests for Fee Dispute Resolution

(a) Requests for fee dispute resolution shall be timely submitted in writing to the coordinator of fee dispute resolution addressed to the North Carolina State Bar, PO Box 25908, Raleigh, NC 27611. The attorney must allow at least 30 days after the client shall have received written notice of the fee dispute resolution program before filing a lawsuit. An attorney may file a lawsuit prior to expiration of the required 30–day notice period or after the petition is filed by the client if such is necessary to preserve a claim. However, the attorney must not take any further steps to pursue the litigation until he/she complies with the provision of the fee dispute resolution rules. Clients may request fee dispute resolution at any time prior to the filing of a lawsuit. No filing fee shall be required. The request should state with clarity and brevity the facts of the fee dispute and the names and addresses of the parties. It should also state that, prior to requesting fee dispute resolution, a reasonable attempt was made to resolve the dispute by agreement, the matter has not been adjudicated, and the matter is not presently the subject of litigation. All requests for resolution of a disputed fee must be filed before the statute of limitation has run or within three years of the ending of the client/attorney relationship, whichever comes last.

(b) The coordinator of fee dispute resolution or his/her designee shall investigate the request to determine its suitability for fee dispute resolution. If it is determined that the matter is not suitable for fee dispute resolution, the coordinator shall prepare a brief written report setting forth the facts and a recommendation for dismissal. Grounds for dismissal include, but are not limited to, the following:

(1) the request is frivolous or moot;

(2) the absence of jurisdiction; or

(3) the facts as stated support the conclusion that the fee was earned and is not excessive.

The report shall be forwarded to the chairperson of the committee. If the chairperson of the Attorney Client Assistance Committee of the State Bar concurs with the recommendation, the matter shall be dismissed and the parties notified.

(c) If the chairperson disagrees with the recommendation for dismissal, an attempt to resolve the dispute will be made pursuant to Rule .0707 below or the chair may recommend review by the full committee.

[History Note: Adopted effective May 4, 2000. Amended February 5, 2002; amended effective March 8, 2007.]

.0707 Mediation Proceedings

(a) The coordinator shall assign the case to a mediator who shall conduct a mediated settlement conference. The mediator shall be responsible for reserving a place and making arrangements for the conference at a time and place convenient to all parties.

(b) The attorney against whom a request for fee dispute resolution is filed must attend the mediated settlement conference in person and may not send another representative of his or her law firm. If a party fails to attend a mediated settlement conference without good cause, the mediator may either reschedule the conference or recommend dismissal.

(c) The mediator shall at all times be in control of the conference and the procedures to be followed. The mediator may communicate privately with any participant prior to and during the conference. Any private communication with a participant shall be disclosed to all other participants at the beginning of the conference. The mediator shall define and describe the following at the beginning of the conference:

(1) the process of mediation;

(2) the differences between mediation and other forms of conflict resolution;

(3) that the mediated settlement conference is not a trial, the mediator is not a judge, and the parties retain their right to trial if they do not reach settlement;

(4) The circumstances under which the mediator may meet and communicate privately with any of the parties or with any other person;

(5) Whether and under what conditions communications with the mediator will be held in confidence during the conference;

(6) The duties and responsibilities of the mediator and the participants; and

(7) That any agreement reached will be reached by mutual consent, reduced to writing and signed by all parties.

The mediator has a duty to be impartial and advise all participants of any circumstance bearing on possible bias, prejudice, or partiality. It is the duty of the mediator timely to determine and declare that an impasse exists and that the conference should end.

[History Note: Adopted effective May 4, 2000. Amended effective March 8, 2007.]

.0708 Finalizing the Agreement

If an agreement is reached in the conference, parties to the agreement shall reduce its terms to writing and sign it along with their counsel, if any, prior to leaving the conference.

[History Note: Adopted effective May 4, 2000.]

.0709 Record Keeping

The coordinator of fee dispute resolution shall keep a record of each request for fee dispute resolution. The record must contain the following information:

(1) the client's name;

(2) date of the request;

(3) the lawyer's name;

(4) the district in which the lawyer resides or maintains a place of business;

(5) how the dispute was resolved (dismissed for non-merit, mediated agreement, arbitration, etc.); and

(6) the time necessary to resolve the dispute.

[History Note: Adopted effective May 4, 2000.]

.0710 District Bar Fee Dispute Resolution

For the purpose of resolving disputes involving attorneys residing or doing business in the district, any district bar may adopt a fee dispute resolution program, subject to the approval of the council, which shall operate in lieu of the program described herein. Although such programs may be tailored to accommodate local conditions, they must be offered without cost, comply with the jurisdictional restrictions set forth in Rule .0702 of this subchapter, and be consistent with the provisions of Rules .0706 and .0707.

[History Note: Adopted effective May 4, 2000.]

SECTION .0800 [RESERVED]

SECTION .0900 PROCEDURES FOR ADMINISTRATIVE COMMITTEE

.0901 Transfer to Inactive Status

(a) Petition for Transfer to Inactive Status. Any member who desires to be transferred to inactive status shall file a petition with the secretary addressed to the council setting forth fully

(1) the member's name and current address;

(2) the date of the member's admission to the North Carolina State Bar;

(3) the reasons why the member desires transfer to inactive status;

(4) that at the time of filing the petition the member is in good standing having paid all membership fees, Client Security Fund assessments, late fees and costs assessed by the North Carolina State Bar, as well as all past due fees, fines and penalties owed to the Board of Continuing Legal Education and without any grievances or disciplinary complaints pending against him or her;

(5) any other matters pertinent to the petition.

(b) Conditions Upon Transfer. No member may be voluntarily transferred to disability-inactive status, retired/nonpracticing status, or emeritus pro bono status until:

(1) the member has paid all membership fees, Client Security Fund assessments, late fees, and costs assessed by the North Carolina State Bar or the Disciplinary Hearing Commission, as well as all past due fees, fines and penalties owed to the Board of Continuing Legal Education;

(2) the member acknowledges that the member continues to be subject to the Rules of Professional Conduct and to the disciplinary jurisdiction of the State Bar including jurisdiction in any pending matter before the Grievance Committee or the Disciplinary Hearing Commission; and,

(3) in the case of a member seeking emeritus pro bono status, it is determined by the Administrative Committee that the member is in good standing, is not the subject of any matter pending before the Grievance Committee or the Disciplinary Hearing Commission, and will be supervised by an active member employed by a nonprofit corporation qualified to render legal services pursuant to G.S. 84–5.1.

(c) Order Transferring Member to Inactive Status. Upon receipt of a petition which satisfies the provisions of Rule .0901(a) above, the council may, in its discretion, enter an order transferring the member to inactive status and, where appropriate, granting emeritus pro bono status. The order shall become effective immediately upon entry by the council. A copy of the order shall be mailed to the member.

[History Note: Statutory Authority G.S. 84–23. Readopted effective December 8, 1994. Amended effective March 7, 1996; February 3, 2000; March 6, 2008; March 6, 2014.]

.0902. Reinstatement from Inactive Status.

(a) Eligibility to Apply for Reinstatement. Any member who has been transferred to inactive status may petition the council for an order reinstating the member as an active member of the North Carolina State Bar.

(b) Definition of "Year." As used in this rule, a year is a 365 day period of time unless a calendar year is specified.

(c) Requirements for Reinstatement.

(1) *Completion of Petition.* The member must provide the information requested on a petition form prescribed by the council and must sign the petition under oath.

(2) *CLE Requirements for Calendar Year Before Inactive.* Unless the member was exempt from such requirements pursuant to Rule .1517 of this subchapter or is subject to the requirements in paragraph (c)(5) of this rule, the member must satisfy the minimum continuing legal education requirements, as set forth in Rule .1518 of this subchapter, for the calendar year immediately preceding the calendar year in which the member was transferred to inactive status, (the "subject year"), including any deficit from a prior

calendar year that was carried forward and recorded in the member's CLE record for the subject year.

(3) *Character and Fitness to Practice.* The member must have the moral qualifications, competency and learning in the law required for admission to practice law in the state of North Carolina, and must show that the member's resumption of the practice of law within this state will be neither detrimental to the integrity and standing of the Bar or the administration of justice nor subversive of the public interest.

(4) *Additional CLE Requirements.* If more than 1 year has elapsed between the date of the entry of the order transferring the member to inactive status and the date that the petition is filed, the member must complete 12 hours of approved CLE for each year that the member was inactive up to a maximum of 7 years. The CLE hours must be completed within 2 years prior to filing the petition. For each 12–hour increment, 6 hours may be taken online; 2 hours must be earned by attending courses in the areas of professional responsibility and/or professionalism; and 5 hours must be earned by attending courses determined to be practical skills courses by the Board of Continuing Legal Education or its designee. If during the period of inactivity the member complied with mandatory CLE requirements of another state where the member is licensed, those CLE credit hours may be applied to the requirements under this provision without regard to whether they were taken during the 2 years prior to filing the petition.

(5) *Bar Exam Requirement If Inactive 7 or More Years.* [Effective for all members who are transferred to inactive status on or after March 10, 2011.] If 7 years or more have elapsed between the date of the entry of the order transferring the member to inactive status and the date that the petition is filed, the member must obtain a passing grade on a regularly scheduled North Carolina bar examination. A member subject to this requirement does not have to satisfy the CLE requirements in paragraphs (c)(2) and (c)(4).

(A) Active Licensure in Another State. Each year of active licensure in another state during the period of inactive status shall offset one year of inactive status for the purpose of calculating the 7 years necessary to actuate this provision. If the member is not required to pass the bar examination as a consequence of offsetting, the member shall satisfy the CLE requirements set forth in paragraph (c)(4) for each year that the member was inactive up to a maximum of 7 years.

(B) Military Service. Each calendar year in which an inactive member served on full-time, active military duty, whether for the entire calendar year or some portion thereof, shall offset one year of inactive status for the purpose of calculating the 7 years necessary to actuate the requirement of this paragraph. If the member is not required to pass the bar examination as a consequence of offsetting, the member shall satisfy the CLE requirements set forth in paragraph (c)(4) for each year that the member was inactive up to a maximum of 7 years.

(6) *Payment of Fees, Assessments and Costs.* The member must pay all of the following:

(A) a $125.00 reinstatement fee;

(B) the membership fee and the Client Security Fund assessment for the year in which the application is filed;

(C) the annual membership fee, if any, of the member's district bar for the year in which the application is filed and any past due annual membership fees for any district bar with which the member was affiliated prior to transferring to inactive status;

(D) all attendee fees owed the Board of Continuing Legal Education for CLE courses taken to satisfy the requirements of paragraphs (c)(2), (4), and (5);

(E) any costs previously assessed against the member by the chairperson of the Grievance Committee, the Disciplinary Hearing Commission; and/or the secretary or council of the North Carolina State Bar; and

(F) all costs incurred by the North Carolina State Bar in investigating and processing the application for reinstatement.

(d) Service of Reinstatement Petition. The petitioner shall serve the petition on the secretary. The secretary shall transmit a copy of the petition to the members of the Administrative Committee and to the counsel.

(e) Investigation by Counsel. The counsel may conduct any necessary investigation regarding the petition and shall advise the members of the Administrative Committee of any findings from such investigation.

(f) Recommendation of Administrative Committee. After any investigation of the petition by the counsel is complete, the Administrative Committee will consider the petition at its next meeting and shall make a recommendation to the council regarding whether the petition should be granted. The chair of the Administrative Committee may appoint a panel composed of at least three members of the committee to consider any petition for reinstatement and, on behalf of the Administrative Committee, to make a recommendation to the council regarding whether the petition should be granted.

(1) *Conditions Precedent to Reinstatement.* Upon a determination that the petitioner has failed to demonstrate competence to return to the practice of law, the committee may require the petitioner to complete a specified number of hours of continuing legal education, which shall be in addition to the requirements set forth in Rule .0902(b)(2) and (4) above, as a

condition precedent to the committee's recommendation that the petition be granted,

(2) *Conditions Subsequent to Reinstatement.* Upon a determination that the petitioner is fit to return to the practice of law pursuant to the reasonable management of his or her substance abuse, addiction, or debilitating mental condition, the committee may recommend to the council that the reinstatement petition be granted with reasonable conditions to which the petitioner consents. Such conditions may include, but are not limited to, an evaluation by a mental health professional approved by the Lawyer Assistance Program (LAP), compliance with the treatment recommendations of the mental health professional, periodic submission of progress reports by the mental health professional to LAP, and waiver of confidentiality relative to diagnosis and treatment by the mental health professional.

(3) *Failure of Conditions Subsequent to Reinstatement.* In the event the petitioner fails to satisfy the conditions of the reinstatement order, the committee shall issue a notice directing the petitioner to show cause, in writing, why the petitioner should not be suspended from the practice of law. Notice shall be served and the right to request a hearing shall be as provided in Rule .0902(f) below. The hearing shall be conducted as provided in Section .1000 of this subchapter provided, however, the burden of proof shall be upon the petitioner to show by clear, cogent, and convincing evidence that he or she has satisfied the conditions of the reinstatement order.

(g) Hearing Upon Denial of Petition for Reinstatement.

(1) *Notice of Council Action and Request for Hearing.* If the council denies a petition for reinstatement, the petitioner shall be notified in writing within 14 days after such action. The notice shall be served upon the petitioner pursuant to Rule 4 of the N.C. Rules of Civil Procedure and may be served by a State Bar investigator or any other person authorized by Rule 4 of the N.C. Rules of Civil Procedure to serve process.

(2) The petitioner shall have 30 days from the date of service of the notice to file a written request for hearing upon the secretary. The request shall be served upon the secretary pursuant to Rule 4 of the N.C. Rules of Civil Procedure.

(3) *Hearing Procedure.* The procedure for the hearing shall be as provided in Section .1000 of this subchapter.

(h) Reinstatement by Secretary of the State Bar. Notwithstanding paragraph (e) of this rule, an inactive member may petition for reinstatement pursuant to paragraphs (a) and (b) of this rule and may be reinstated by the secretary of the State Bar upon a finding that the inactive member has complied with or fulfilled the conditions for reinstatement set forth in this rule; there are no issues relating to the inactive member's character or fitness; and the inactive member has paid all fees owed to the State Bar including the reinstatement fee. Reinstatement by the secretary is discretionary. If the secretary declines to reinstate a member, the member's petition shall be submitted to the Administrative Committee at its next meeting and the procedure for review of the reinstatement petition shall be as set forth in paragraph (e) of this rule.

(i) Denial of Petition. When a petition for reinstatement is denied by the council in a given calendar year, the member may not petition again until the following calendar year. The reinstatement fee, costs, and any fees paid pursuant to paragraph (c)(7) shall be retained. However, the State Bar membership fee, Client Security Fund assessment, and district bar membership fee assessed for the year in which the application is filed shall be refunded.

[History Note: Statutory Authority G.S. 84-23. Readopted effective December 8, 1994. Amended effective September 7, 1995; March 7, 1996; March 5, 1998; March 3, 1999; February 3, 2000; March 6, 2002; February 27, 2003; March 3, 2005; March 10, 2011; August 25, 2011; March 8, 2012; March 8, 2013; March 6, 2014; October 2, 2014.]

.0903. Suspension for Failure to Fulfill Obligations of Membership

(a) Procedure for Enforcement of Obligations of Membership. Whenever a member of the North Carolina State Bar fails to fulfill an obligation of membership in the State Bar, whether established by the administrative rules of the State Bar or by statute, the member shall be subject to administrative suspension from membership pursuant to the procedure set forth in this rule; provided, however, that the procedures for the investigation of and action upon alleged violations of the Rules of Professional Conduct by a member are set forth in subchapter 1B of these rules and that no aspect of any procedure set forth in this rule shall be applicable to the State Bar's investigation of or action upon alleged violations of the Rules of Professional Conduct by a member.

(1) The following are examples of obligations of membership that will be enforced by administrative suspension. This list is illustrative and not exclusive:

(A) Payment of the annual membership fee, including any associated late fee as set forth in G.S. 84-34;

(B) Payment of the annual Client Security Fund assessment;

(C) Payment of the costs of a disciplinary, disability, reinstatement, show cause, or other proceeding of the State Bar as ordered by the chair of the Grievance Committee, the Disciplinary Hearing Commission, the secretary, or the council;

(D) Filing of a pro hac vice registration statement as required in Rule .0101 of subchapter 1H of these rules; and

(E) Filing of an annual report form and attending continuing legal education activities as required by Sections .1500 and .1600 of subchapter 1D of these rules.

(b) Notice. Whenever it appears that a member has failed to comply, in a timely fashion, with an obligation of membership in the State Bar as established by the administrative rules of the State Bar or by statute, the secretary shall prepare a written notice directing the member to show cause, in writing, within 30 days of the date of service of the notice why he or she should not be suspended from the practice of law.

(c) Service of the Notice. The notice shall be served on the member by mailing a copy thereof by registered or certified mail or designated delivery service (such as Federal Express or UPS), return receipt requested, to the last known address of the member contained in the records of the North Carolina State Bar or such later address as may be known to the person attempting service. Service of the notice may also be accomplished by (i) personal service by a State Bar investigator or by any person authorized by Rule 4 of the North Carolina Rules of Civil Procedure to serve process, or (ii) email sent to the email address of the member contained in the records of the North Carolina State Bar if the member sends an email from that same email address to the State Bar acknowledging such service.

(d) Entry of Order of Suspension upon Failure to Respond to Notice to Show Cause. Whenever a member fails to show cause in writing within 30 days of the service of the notice to show cause upon the member, and it appears that the member has failed to comply with an obligation of membership in the State Bar as established by the administrative rules of the State Bar or by statute, the council may enter an order suspending the member from the practice of law. The order shall be effective 30 days after proof of service on the member. The order shall be served on the member by mailing a copy thereof by registered or certified mail or designated delivery service, return receipt requested, to the last-known address of the member contained in the records of the North Carolina State Bar or such later address as may be known to the person attempting service. Service of the order may also be accomplished by (i) personal service by a State Bar investigator or by any person authorized by Rule 4 of the North Carolina Rules of Civil Procedure to serve process, or (ii) email sent to the email address of the member contained in the records of the North Carolina State Bar if the member sends an email from that same email address to the State Bar acknowledging such service. A member who cannot, with due diligence, be served by registered or certified mail, designated delivery service, personal service, or email shall be deemed served by the mailing of a copy of the order to the member's last known address contained in the records of the North Carolina State Bar.

(e) Procedure upon Submission of a Timely Response to a Notice to Show Cause.

(1) *Consideration by Administrative Committee.* If a member submits a written response to a notice to show cause within 30 days of the service of the notice upon the member, the Administrative Committee shall consider the matter at its next regularly scheduled meeting. The member may personally appear at the meeting and be heard, may be represented by counsel, and may offer witnesses and documents. The counsel may appear at the meeting on behalf of the State Bar and be heard, and may offer witnesses and documents. The burden of proof shall be upon the member to show cause by clear, cogent, and convincing evidence why the member should not be suspended from the practice of law for the apparent failure to fulfill an obligation of membership in the State Bar as established by the administrative rules of the State Bar or by statute.

(2) *Recommendation of Administrative Committee.* The Administrative Committee shall determine whether the member has shown cause why the member should not be suspended. If the committee determines that the member has failed to show cause, the committee shall recommend to the council that the member be suspended.

(3) *Order of Suspension.* Upon the recommendation of the Administrative Committee, the council may enter an order suspending the member from the practice of law. The order shall be effective 30 days after proof of service on the member. The order shall be served on the member by mailing a copy thereof by registered or certified mail return receipt requested to the last-known address of the member according to the records of the North Carolina State Bar or such later address as may be known to the person effecting the service. Notice may also be by personal service by a State Bar investigator or any other person authorized by Rule 4 of the North Carolina Rules of Civil Procedure to serve process. Unless the member complies with or fulfills the obligation of membership within 30 days after service of the order, the obligations of a disbarred or suspended member to wind down the member's law practice within 30 days set forth in Rule .0124 of Subchapter 1B of these rules shall apply to the member upon the effective date of the order of suspension. If the member fails to fulfill the obligations set forth in Rule .0124 of Subchapter 1B within 30 days of the effective date of the order, the member shall be subject to professional discipline.

(f) Late Compliance. If a member fulfills the obligation of membership before a suspension order is entered by the council, no order of suspension will be entered.

(g) Administrative Suspension Pursuant to Statute. The provisions of this rule notwithstanding, if any section of the North Carolina General Statutes requires suspension of an occupational license, the procedure for suspension pursuant to such statute shall be as established by the statute. If no procedure is established by said statute, then the procedures specified in this rule shall be followed.

[History Note: Statutory Authority G.S. 84–23. Readopted effective December 8, 1994. Amended effective September 7, 1995; December 7, 1995; March 7, 1996; March 5, 1998; February 3, 2000; October 1, 2003; March 2, 2006; November 16, 2006; March 6, 2008; October 8, 2009; March 11, 2010; August 23, 2012; March 6, 2014.]

.0904. Reinstatement from Suspension

(a) Compliance Within 30 Days of Service of Suspension Order. A member who receives an order of suspension for failure to comply with an obligation of membership may preclude the order from becoming effective and shall not be required to file a formal reinstatement petition or pay the reinstatement fee if the member shows within 30 days after service of the suspension order that the member has done the following:

(1) fulfilled the obligations of membership set forth in the order;

(2) paid the administrative fees associated with the issuance of the suspension order, including the costs of service;

(3) paid any other delinquency shown on the financial records of the State Bar including outstanding judicial district bar dues;

(4) signed and filed CLE annual report forms as required by Rule .1522 of this subchapter;

(5) completed CLE hours as required by Rules .1518 and .1522 of this subchapter; and

(6) filed any IOLTA certification required by Rule .1319 of this subchapter.

(b) Reinstatement More than 30 Days after Service of Suspension Order. At any time more than 30 days after service of an order of suspension on a member, a member who has been suspended for failure to comply with an obligation of membership may petition the council for an order of reinstatement.

(c) Definition of "Year." As used in this rule, a year is a 365 day period of time unless a calendar year is specified.

(d) Requirements for Reinstatement.

(1) *Completion of Petition.* The member must provide the information requested on a petition form prescribed by the council and must sign the petition under oath.

(2) *CLE Requirements for Calendar Years Before Suspended.* Unless the member was exempt from such requirements pursuant to Rule .1517 of this subchapter or is subject to the requirements in paragraph (d)(4) of this rule, the member must satisfy the minimum continuing legal education (CLE) requirements, as set forth in Rule .1518 of this subchapter, for the calendar year immediately preceding the year in which the member was suspended (the "subject year"), including any deficit from a prior year that was carried forward and recorded in the member's CLE record for the subject year. The member shall also sign and file any delinquent CLE annual report form.

(3) *Additional CLE Requirements.* If more than 1 year has elapsed between the effective date of the suspension order and the date upon which the reinstatement petition is filed, the member must complete 12 hours of approved CLE for each year that the member was suspended up to a maximum of 7 years. The CLE must be completed within 2 years prior to filing the petition. For each 12–hour increment, 6 hours may be taken online; 2 hours must be earned by attending courses in the areas of professional responsibility and/or professionalism; and 5 hours must be earned by attending courses determined to be practical skills courses by the Board of Continuing Legal Education or its designee. If during the period of suspension the member complied with mandatory CLE requirements of another state where the member is licensed, those CLE credit hours may be applied to the requirements under this provision without regard to whether they were taken during the 2 years prior to filing the petition.

(4) *Bar Exam Requirement If Suspended 7 or More Years.* [Effective for all members who are administratively suspended on or after March 10, 2011.] If 7 years or more have elapsed between the effective date of the suspension order and the date that the petition is filed, the member must obtain a passing grade on a regularly scheduled North Carolina bar examination. A member subject to this requirement does not have to satisfy the CLE requirements in paragraphs (d)(2) and (d)(3).

(A) Active Licensure in Another State. Each year of active licensure in another state during the period of suspension shall offset one year of suspension for the purpose of calculating the 7 years necessary to actuate this provision. If the member is not required to pass the bar examination as a consequence of offsetting, the member shall satisfy the CLE requirements set forth in paragraph (d)(3) for each year that the member was suspended up to a maximum of 7 years.

(B) Military Service. Each calendar year in which a suspended member served on full-time, active military duty, whether for the entire calendar year or some portion thereof, shall offset one year of suspension for the purpose of calculating the 7 years necessary to actuate the requirement of this paragraph. If the member is not required to pass the bar examination as a consequence of offsetting, the member shall satisfy the CLE requirements set forth in paragraph (d)(3) for each year that the member was suspended up to a maximum of 7 years.

(5) *Character and Fitness to Practice.* The member must have the moral qualifications, competency and learning in the law required for admission to practice law in the state of North Carolina, and must show that the member's resumption of the practice of law will be neither detrimental to the integrity and standing of the Bar or the administration of justice nor subversive of the public interest.

(6) *Payment of Fees, Assessments and Costs.* The member must pay all of the following:

(A) a $125.00 reinstatement fee or $250.00 reinstatement fee if suspended for failure to comply with CLE requirements;

(B) all membership fees, Client Security Fund assessments, and late fees owed at the time of suspension and owed for the year in which the reinstatement petition is filed;

(C) all district bar annual membership fees owed at the time of suspension and owed for the year in which the reinstatement petition is filed;

(D) all attendee fees, fines and penalties owed the Board of Continuing Legal Education at the time of suspension and attendee fees for CLE courses taken to satisfy the requirements of paragraphs (d)(2) and (3) above;

(E) any costs assessed against the member by the chairperson of the Grievance Committee, the Disciplinary Hearing Commission, and/or the secretary or council of the North Carolina State Bar; and

(F) all costs incurred by the North Carolina State Bar in suspending the member, including the costs of service, and in investigating and processing the application for reinstatement.

(7) *Pro Hac Vice Registration Statements.* The member must file any overdue pro hac vice registration statement for which the member was responsible.

(8) *IOTLA Certification.* The member must complete any IOLTA certification required by Rule .1319 of this subchapter.

(9) *Wind Down of Law Practice During Suspension.* The member must demonstrate that the member fulfilled the obligations of a disbarred or suspended member set forth in Rule .0124 of Subchapter 1B during the 30 day period after the effective date of the order of suspension, or that such obligations do not apply to the member due to the nature of the member's legal employment.

(e) Procedure for Review of Reinstatement Petition. The procedure for review of the reinstatement petition shall be as set forth in Rule .0902(c)–(f) above.

(f) Reinstatement by Secretary of the State Bar. At any time during the year after the effective date of a suspension order, a suspended member may petition for reinstatement pursuant to paragraphs (b) and (c) of this rule and may be reinstated by the secretary of the State Bar upon a finding that the suspended member has complied with or fulfilled the obligations of membership set forth in the order; there are no issues relating to the suspended member's character or fitness; and the suspended member has paid the costs of the suspension and reinstatement procedure including the costs of service and the reinstatement fee. Reinstatement by the secretary is discretionary. If the secretary declines to reinstate a member, the member's petition shall be submitted to the Administrative Committee at its next meeting and the procedure for review of the reinstatement petition shall be as set forth in Rule .0902(c)–(f).

(g) Reinstatement from Disciplinary Suspension. Notwithstanding the procedure for reinstatement set forth in the preceding paragraphs of this Rule, if an order of reinstatement from disciplinary suspension is granted to a member pursuant to Rule .0125 of subchapter 1B of these rules, any outstanding order granting inactive status or suspending the same member for failure to fulfill the obligations of membership under this section shall be dissolved and the member shall be reinstated to active status.

(h) Denial of Petition. When a petition for reinstatement is denied by the council in a given calendar year, the member may not petition again until the following calendar year. The reinstatement fee, costs, and any fees paid pursuant to paragraph (d)(6) shall be retained. However, the State Bar membership fee, Client Security Fund assessment, and district bar membership fee assessed for the year in which the application is filed shall be refunded.

[History Note: Statutory Authority G.S. 84-23. Readopted effective December 8, 1994. Amended effective September 7, 1995; March 7, 1996; March 5, 1998; February 27, 2003; October 1, 2003; March 2, 2006; November 16, 2006; October 8, 2009; March 11, 2010; March 10, 2011; March 8, 2012; March 8, 2013; August 27, 2013; March 6, 2014; October 2, 2014.]

.0905. Pro Bono Practice by Out of State Lawyers

(a) A lawyer licensed to practice in another state but not North Carolina who desires to provide legal services free of charge to indigent persons may file a petition with the secretary addressed to the council setting forth:

(1) the petitioner's name and address;

(2) the state(s) in which the petitioner is or has been licensed and the date(s) when the petitioner was licensed;

(3) the name of a member who is employed by a nonprofit corporation qualified to render legal services

pursuant to G.S. 84–5.1 and has agreed to supervise the petitioner; and

(4) any other matters pertinent to the petition as determined by the council.

(b) Along with the petition, the petitioner shall provide in writing:

(1) a certificate of good standing from each jurisdiction in which the petitioner has been licensed;

(2) a record of any professional discipline ever imposed against the petitioner;

(3) a statement from the petitioner that the petitioner is submitting to the disciplinary jurisdiction of the North Carolina State Bar, and will be governed by the North Carolina Rules of Professional Conduct in regard to any law practice authorized by the council in consequence of the petition; and

(4) a statement from the member identified in the petition agreeing to supervise the petitioner in the provision of pro bono legal services exclusively for indigent persons.

(c) The petition shall be referred to the Administrative Committee for review. After reviewing the petition and other pertinent information, the committee shall make a recommendation to the council regarding whether the petition should be granted.

(d) Upon receipt of a petition and other information satisfying the provisions this rule, the council may, in its discretion, enter an order permitting the petitioner to provide legal services to indigent persons on a pro bono basis under the supervision of a member employed by a nonprofit corporation qualified to render legal services pursuant to G.S. 84–5.1. The order shall become effective immediately upon entry by the council. A copy or the order shall be mailed to the petitioner and to the supervising member. No person permitted to practice pursuant to such an order shall pay any membership fee to the North Carolina State Bar or any district bar or any other charge ordinarily imposed upon active members, nor shall any such person be required to attend continuing legal education courses.

(e) Permission to practice under this rule may be withdrawn by the council for good cause shown pursuant to the procedure set forth in Rule .0903 of this subchapter.

[History Note: Adopted effective March 6, 2008.]

SECTION .1000 RULES GOVERNING REINSTATEMENT HEARINGS BEFORE THE ADMINISTRATIVE COMMITTEE

.1001 Reinstatement Hearings

(a) Notice; Time and Place of Hearing.

(1) *Time and Place of Hearing.* The chairperson of the Administrative Committee (the committee) shall fix the time and place of the hearing within 30 days after the member's request for hearing is filed with the secretary. The hearing shall be held as soon as practicable after the request for hearing is filed but in no event more than 90 days after such request is filed unless otherwise agreed by the member and the chairperson of the committee.

(2) *Notice to Member.* The notice of the hearing shall include the date, time and place of the hearing and shall be served upon the member at least 10 days before the hearing date.

(b) Hearing Panel.

(1) *Appointment.* The chairperson of the committee shall appoint a hearing panel consisting of three members of the committee to consider the petition and make a recommendation to the council.

(2) *Presiding Panel Member.* The chairperson shall appoint one of the three members of the panel to serve as the presiding member. The presiding member shall rule on any question of procedure that may arise in the hearing; preside at the deliberations of the panel; sign the written determination of the panel; and report the panel's determination to the council.

(3) *Quorum.* A majority of the panel members is necessary to decide the matter.

(4) *Panel Recommendation.* Following the hearing on a contested reinstatement petition, the panel will make a written recommendation to the council on behalf of the committee regarding whether the member's license should be reinstated. The recommendation shall include appropriate findings of fact and conclusions of law.

(c) Burden of Proof.

(1) *Reinstatement From Inactive Status.* The burden of proof shall be upon the member to show by clear, cogent and convincing evidence that he or she has satisfied the requirements for reinstatement as set forth in Rule .0902(b) of this subchapter.

(2) *Reinstatement from Suspension for Nonpayment of Membership Fees, Late Fee, Client Security Fund Assessment, District Bar Membership Fees, or Assessed Costs.* The burden of proof shall be upon the member to show by clear, cogent and convincing evidence that he or she has satisfied the requirements for reinstatement as set forth in Rule .0904(c) of this subchapter.

(3) *Reinstatement From Suspension for Failure to Comply With the Rules Governing the Administration of the Continuing Legal Education Program.* The burden of proof shall be upon the member to

show by clear, cogent and convincing evidence that he or she has

(A) satisfied the requirements for reinstatement as set forth in Rule .0904(c) of this subchapter,

(B) cured any continuing legal education deficiency for which the member was suspended, and

(C) paid the reinstatement fee required by Rule .1512 and Rule .1609(a) of this subchapter.

(d) Conduct of Hearing.

(1) *Member's Rights.* The member shall have these rights at the hearing:

(A) to appear personally and be heard;

(B) to be represented by counsel;

(C) to call and examine witnesses;

(D) to offer exhibits; and

(E) to cross-examine witnesses.

(2) *State Bar Appears Through Counsel.* The counsel shall appear at the hearing on behalf of the State Bar and shall have the right

(A) to be heard;

(B) to call and examine witnesses;

(C) to offer exhibits; and

(D) to cross-examine witnesses.

(3) *Rules of Procedure and Evidence.* The hearing will be conducted in accordance with the North Carolina Rules of Civil Procedure for nonjury trials insofar as practicable and the Rules of Evidence applicable in superior court, unless otherwise provided by this subchapter or the parties agree to other rules.

(4) *Report of Hearing; Costs.* The hearing shall be reported by a certified court reporter. The member shall pay the costs associated with obtaining the court reporter's services for the hearing. The member shall pay the costs of the transcript and shall arrange for the preparation of the transcript with the court reporter. The member shall be taxed with all other costs of the hearing, but such costs shall not include any compensation to the members of the hearing panel.

(e) Hearing Panel Recommendation. The written recommendation of the hearing panel shall be served upon the member within seven days of the date of the hearing.

[Adopted effective March 7, 1996. Amended effective March 5, 1998; amended December 10, 1999, effective February 3, 2000.]

.1002 Review and Order of Council

(a) Review by Council of Recommendation of Hearing Panel.

(1) *Record to Council.*

(A) Compilation of Record

The member will compile a record of the proceedings before the hearing panel, including a legible copy of the complete transcript, all exhibits introduced into evidence and all pleadings, motions and orders, unless the member and counsel agree in writing to shorten the record. Any agreements regarding the record shall be included in the record transmitted to the council.

(B) Transmission of Record to Council

The member shall provide a copy of the record to the counsel not later than 90 days after the hearing unless an extension is granted by the president of the State Bar for good cause shown. The member will transmit a copy of the record to each member of the council no later than 30 days before the council meeting at which the petition is to be considered.

(C) Costs

The member shall bear all of the costs of transcribing, copying and transmitting the record to the members of the council.

(D) Dismissal for Failure to Comply

If the member fails to comply fully with any of the provisions of this rule, the counsel may file a motion with the secretary to dismiss the petition.

(2) *Oral or Written Argument.* In his or her discretion, the president of the State Bar may permit counsel for the State Bar and the member to present oral or written argument, but the council will not consider additional evidence not in the record transmitted from the hearing panel, absent a showing that the ends of justice so require or that undue hardship will result if the additional evidence is not presented.

(b) Order by Council. The council will review the recommendation of the hearing panel and the record and will determine whether and upon what conditions the member will be reinstated.

(c) Costs.

The council may tax the costs attributable to the proceeding against the member.

[Adopted effective March 7, 1996.]

SECTION .1100 [RESERVED]

SECTION .1200 [RESERVED]

SECTION .1300 RULES GOVERNING THE ADMINISTRATION OF THE PLAN FOR INTEREST ON LAWYERS' TRUST ACCOUNTS (IOLTA)

.1301. Purpose

The IOLTA Board of Trustees (board) shall carry out the provisions of the Plan for Interest on Lawyers' Trust Accounts and administer the IOLTA program (NC IOLTA). Any funds remitted to the North Carolina State Bar from banks by reason of interest earned on general trust accounts established by lawyers pursuant to Rule 1.15–2(b) of the Rules of Professional Conduct or interest earned on trust or escrow accounts maintained by settlement agents pursuant to N.C.G.S. 45A–9 shall be deposited by the North Carolina State Bar through the board in a special account or accounts which shall be segregated from other funds of whatever nature received by the State Bar.

The funds received, and any interest, dividends, or other proceeds earned on or with respect to these funds, net of banking charges described in section .1316(e)(1), shall be used for programs concerned with the improvement of the administration of justice, under the supervision and direction of the NC IOLTA Board. The board will award grants or non-interest bearing loans under the categories approved by the North Carolina Supreme Court being mindful of its tax exempt status and the IRS rulings that private interests of the legal profession are not to be funded with IOLTA funds.

The programs for which the funds may be awarded are:

(1) providing civil legal services for indigents;

(2) enhancement and improvement of grievance and disciplinary procedures to protect the public more fully from incompetent or unethical attorneys;

(3) development and maintenance of a fund for student loans to enable meritorious persons to obtain a legal education who would not otherwise have adequate funds for this purpose;

(4) such other programs designed to improve the administration of justice as may from time to time be proposed by the board and approved by the Supreme Court of North Carolina.

[History Note: Statutory Authority G.S. 84–23. Readopted effective December 8, 1994; amended effective April 3, 1996; amended effective March 6, 1997; amended effective March 6, 2008; amended effective March 8, 2012.]

.1302 Jurisdiction: Authority

The Board of Trustees of the North Carolina State Bar Plan for Interest on Lawyers' Trust Accounts (IOLTA) is created as a standing committee by the North Carolina State Bar Council pursuant to Chapter 84 of the North Carolina General Statutes for the disposition of funds received by the North Carolina State Bar from interest on trust accounts or from other sources intended for the provision of legal services to the indigent and the improvement of the administration of justice.

[History Note: Statutory Authority G.S. 84–23. Readopted effective December 8, 1994; amended effective March 8, 2007.]

.1303 Operational Responsibility

The responsibility for operating the program of the board rests with the governing body of the board, subject to the statutes governing the practice of law, the authority of the council and the rules of governance of the board.

[History Note: Statutory Authority G.S. 84–23. Readopted effective December 8, 1994.]

.1304 Size of Board

The board shall have nine members, at least six of whom must be attorneys in good standing and authorized to practice law in the state of North Carolina.

[History Note: Statutory Authority G.S. 84–23. Readopted effective December 8, 1994.]

.1305 Lay Participation

The board may have no more than three members who are not licensed attorneys.

[History Note: Statutory Authority G.S. 84–23. Readopted effective December 8, 1994.]

.1306 Appointment of Members; When; Removal

The members of the board shall be appointed by the Council of the North Carolina State Bar. The July quarterly meeting is when the appointments are made. Vacancies occurring by reason of death, resignation or removal shall be filled by appointment of the council at the next quarterly meeting following the event giving rise to the vacancy, and the person so appointed shall serve for the balance of the vacated term. Any member of the board may be removed at any time by an affirmative vote of a majority of the members of the council in session at a regularly called meeting.

[History Note: Statutory Authority G.S. 84-23. Readopted effective December 8, 1994.]

.1307 Term of Office

Each member who is appointed to the board shall serve for a term of three years beginning on September 1.

[History Note: Statutory Authority G.S. 84-23. Readopted effective December 8, 1994.]

.1308 Staggered Terms

It is intended that members of the board shall be elected to staggered terms such that three members are appointed in each year.

[History Note: Statutory Authority G.S. 84-23. Readopted effective December 8, 1994.]

.1309 Succession

Each member of the board shall be entitled to serve for two full three-year terms. No member shall serve more than two consecutive three-year terms, in addition to service prior to the beginning of a full three-year term, without having been off the board for at least three years.

[History Note: Statutory Authority G.S. 84-23. Readopted effective December 8, 1994.]

.1310 Appointment of Chairperson

The chairperson of the board shall be appointed from time to time as necessary by the council. The term of such individual as chairperson shall be for one year. The chairperson may be reappointed thereafter during his or her tenure on the board. The chairperson shall preside at all meetings of the board, shall prepare and present to the council the annual report of the board, and generally shall represent the board in its dealings with the public.

[History Note: Statutory Authority G.S. 84-23. Readopted effective December 8, 1994.]

.1311 Appointment of Vice-Chairperson

The vice chairperson of the board shall be appointed from time to time as necessary by the council. The term of such individual as vice chairperson shall be one year. The vice-chairperson may be reappointed thereafter during tenure on the board. The vice chairperson shall preside at and represent the board in the absence of the chairperson and shall perform such other duties as may be assigned to him or her by the chairperson or by the board.

[History Note: Statutory Authority G.S. 84-23. Readopted effective December 8, 1994.]

.1312. Source of Funds

Funding for the program carried out by the board shall come from funds remitted from depository institutions by reason of interest earned on trust accounts established by lawyers pursuant to Rule 1.15 of the Rules of Professional Conduct and Rule .1316 of this subchapter or interest earned on trust or escrow accounts maintained by settlement agents pursuant to N.C.G.S. 45A-9; voluntary contributions from lawyers; and interest, dividends, or other proceeds earned on the board's funds from investments or from other sources intended for the provision of legal services to the indigent and the improvement of the administration of justice.

[History Note: Statutory Authority G.S. 84-23. Readopted effective December 8, 1994; amended effective March 8, 2007; amended effective February 5, 2009; amended effective March 8, 2012.]

.1313 Fiscal Responsibility

All funds of the board shall be considered funds of the North Carolina State Bar, with the beneficial interest in those funds being vested in the board for grants to qualified applicants in the public interest, less administrative costs. These funds shall be administered and disbursed by the board in accordance with rules or policies developed by the North Carolina State Bar and approved by the North Carolina Supreme Court. The funds shall be used to pay the administrative costs of the IOLTA program and to fund grants approved by the board under the six categories approved by the North Carolina Supreme Court as outlined above.

(a) Maintenance of Accounts: Audit. The funds of the IOLTA program shall be maintained in a separate account from funds of the North Carolina State Bar such that the funds and expenditures therefrom can be readily identified. The accounts of the board shall be audited on an annual basis. The audit will be conducted after the books are closed at a time determined by the auditors, but not later than March 31 of the year following the year for which the audit is to be conducted.

(b) Investment Criteria. The funds of the board shall be handled, invested and reinvested in accordance with investment policies adopted by the Council of the North Carolina State Bar for handling of dues, rents, and other revenues received by the North Carolina State Bar in carrying out its official duties.

(c) Disbursements. Disbursement of funds of the board in the nature of grants to qualified applicants in the public interest, less administrative costs, shall be made by the board in accordance with policies developed by the North Carolina State Bar and approved by the North Carolina Supreme Court. The board shall adopt an annual operational budget and disbursements shall be made in accordance with the budget as adopted. The board shall determine the signatories on the IOLTA accounts.

[History Note: Statutory Authority G.S. 84-23. Readopted effective December 8, 1994.]

.1314 Meetings

The board by resolution may set regular meeting dates and places. Special meetings of the board may be called at any time upon notice given by the chairperson, the vice-chairperson or any two members of the board. Notice of meeting shall be given at least two days prior to the meeting by mail, telegram, facsimile transmission, or telephone. A quorum of the board for conducting its official business shall be a majority of the total membership of the board.

[History Note: Statutory Authority G.S. 84-23. Readopted effective December 8, 1994.]

.1315 Annual Report

The board shall prepare at least annually a report of its activities and shall present same to the council one month prior to its annual meeting.

[History Note: Statutory Authority G.S. 84-23. Readopted effective December 8, 1994.]

.1316 IOLTA Accounts

(a) IOLTA Account Defined. Pursuant to order of the North Carolina Supreme Court, every general trust account, as defined in the Rules of Professional Conduct, must be an interest or dividend-bearing account. (As used herein, "interest" shall refer to both interest and dividends.) Funds deposited in a general, interest-bearing trust account must be available for withdrawal upon request and without delay (subject to any notice period that the bank is required to reserve by law or regulation). Additionally, pursuant to N.C.G.S. 45A-9, a settlement agent who maintains a trust or escrow account for the purposes of receiving and disbursing closing funds and loan funds shall direct that any interest earned on funds held in that account be paid to the NC State Bar to be used for the purposes authorized under the Interest on Lawyers' Trust Account Program according to rule .1316(d) below. For the purposes of these rules, all such accounts shall be known as "IOLTA Accounts" (also referred to as "Accounts").

(b) Eligible Banks. Lawyers may maintain one or more IOLTA Account(s) only at banks and savings and loan associations chartered under North Carolina or federal law, as required by Rule 1.15 of the Rules of Professional Conduct, that offer and maintain IOLTA Accounts that comply with the requirements set forth in this subchapter (Eligible Banks). Settlement agents shall maintain any IOLTA Account as defined by N.C.G.S. 45A-9 and paragraph (a) above only at an Eligible Bank; however, a settlement agent that is not a lawyer may maintain an IOLTA Account at any bank that is insured by the Federal Deposit Insurance Corporation and has a certificate of authority to transact business from the North Carolina Secretary of State, provided the bank is approved by NC IOLTA. The determination of whether a bank is eligible shall be made by NC IOLTA, which shall maintain (i) a list of participating Eligible Banks available to all members of the State Bar and to all settlement agents, and (ii) a list of banks approved for non-lawyer settlement agent IOLTA Accounts available to non-lawyer settlement agents. A bank that fails to meet the requirements of this subchapter shall be subject only to termination of its eligible or approved status by NC IOLTA. A violation of this rule shall not be the basis for civil liability.

(c) Notice Upon Opening or Closing IOLTA Account. Every lawyer/, law firm, or settlement agent maintaining IOLTA Accounts shall advise NC IOLTA of the establishment or closing of each IOLTA Account. Such notice shall include (i) the name of the bank where the account is maintained, (ii) the name of the account, (iii) the account number, and (iv) the name and bar number of the lawyer(s) in the firm and/or the name(s) of any non-lawyer settlement agent(s) maintaining the account. The North Carolina State Bar shall furnish to each lawyer/, law firm, or settlement agent maintaining an IOLTA Accounts a suitable plaque explaining the program, which plaque shall be exhibited in the office of the lawyer/, law firm, or settlement agent.

(d) Directive to Bank. Every lawyer or law firm and every settlement agent maintaining a North Carolina IOLTA Account shall direct any bank in which an IOLTA Account is maintained to:

(1) remit interest, less any deduction for allowable reasonable bank service charges or fees, (as used herein, "service charges" shall include any charge or fee charged by a bank on an IOLTA Account) as defined in paragraph (e), at least quarterly to NC IOLTA;

(2) transmit with each remittance to NC IOLTA a statement showing for each account: (i) the name of the law firm/, lawyer, or settlement agent maintaining the account, (ii) the lawyer's/, law firm's, or settlement agent's IOLTA Account number, (iii) the earnings period, (iv) the average balance of the account for the earnings period, (v) the type of account, (vi) the rate of interest applied in computing the remittance, (vii) the amount of any service charges for the earnings period, and (viii) the net remittance for the earnings period; and

(3) transmit to the law firm/, lawyer, or settlement agent maintaining the account a report showing the

amount remitted to NC IOLTA, the earnings period, and the rate of interest applied in computing the remittance.

(e) Allowable Reasonable Service Charges. Eligible Banks may elect to waive any or all service charges on IOLTA Accounts. If a bank does not waive service charges on IOLTA Accounts, allowable reasonable service charges may be assessed but only against interest earned on the IOLTA Account or funds deposited by the lawyer/, law firm, or settlement agent in the IOLTA Account for the purpose of paying such charges. Allowable reasonable service charges may be deducted from interest on an IOLTA Account only at the rates and in accordance with the bank's standard practice for comparable non-IOLTA accounts. Allowable reasonable service charges for IOLTA Accounts are: (i) a reasonable Account maintenance fee, (ii) per check charges, (iii) per deposit charges, (iv) a fee in lieu of a minimum balance, (v) federal deposit insurance fees, and (vi) automated transfer (Sweep) fees. All service charges other than allowable reasonable service charges assessed against an IOLTA Account are the responsibility of and shall be paid by the lawyer or law firm. No service charges in excess of the interest earned on the Account for any month or quarter shall be deducted from interest earned on other IOLTA Accounts or from the principal of the Account.

[History Note: Statutory Authority G.S. 84–23. Readopted effective December 8, 1994; amended effective March 6, 2008; amended effective February 5, 2009; amended effective January 28, 2010; amended effective March 8, 2012; amended effective August 23, 2012.]

.1317 Comparability Requirements for IOLTA Accounts

This rule shall take effect on July 1, 2010.

(a) Comparability of Interest Rate. Eligible Banks that offer and maintain IOLTA Accounts must pay to an IOLTA Account the highest interest rate generally available from the bank to non-IOLTA Accounts (Comparable Rate) when the IOLTA Account meets or exceeds the same minimum balance or other account eligibility qualifications, if any. In determining the highest interest rate generally available from the bank to non-IOLTA accounts, an Eligible Bank may consider factors, in addition to the IOLTA account balance, customarily considered by the bank when setting interest rates for its customers, provided that such factors do not discriminate between IOLTA accounts and non-IOLTA accounts.

(b) Options for Satisfying Requirement. An Eligible Bank may satisfy the Comparable Rate requirement by electing one of the following options:

(1) use an account product that has a Comparable Rate;

(2) without actually changing the IOLTA Account to the bank's Comparable Rate product, pay the Comparable Rate on the IOLTA Account; or

(3) pay the benchmark rate (Benchmark), which shall be determined by NC IOLTA periodically, but not more frequently than every six months, to reflect the overall Comparable Rate for the NC IOLTA program. The Benchmark shall be a rate equal to the greater of: (i) 0.65% or (ii) 65% of the Federal Funds Target Rate as of the first business day of the IOLTA remitting period, and shall be net of allowable reasonable service charges. When applicable, NC IOLTA will express the Benchmark in relation to the Federal Funds Target Rate.

(c) Options for Account Types. An IOLTA Account may be established as:

(1) subject to paragraph (d), a business checking account with an automated investment feature (Sweep Account), such as an overnight investment in financial institution daily repurchase agreements or money market funds invested solely in or fully collateralized by US government securities, which are US Treasury obligations and obligations issued or guaranteed as to principal and interest by the United States or any agency or instrumentality thereof;

(2) a checking account paying preferred interest rates, such as market based or indexed rates;

(3) a public funds interest-bearing checking account, such as accounts used for governmental agencies and other non-profit organizations;

(4) an interest-bearing checking account such as a negotiable order of withdrawal (NOW) account, or business checking account with interest; or

(5) any other suitable interest-bearing deposit account offered by the bank to its non-IOLTA customers.

(d) Financial Requirements for Sweep Accounts. If a bank establishes an IOLTA Account as described in paragraph (c)(1), the following requirements must be satisfied: an overnight investment in a financial institution daily repurchase agreement shall be fully collateralized by United States government securities, as described in this Rule, and may be established only with an Eligible Bank that is "well capitalized" or "adequately capitalized" as those terms are defined by applicable federal statutes and regulations. A "money market fund" is an investment company registered under the Investment Company Act of 1940, as amended, that is qualified to hold itself out to investors as a money market fund under Rules and Regulations adopted by the Securities and Exchange Commission pursuant to said Act. A money market fund shall be invested solely in United States government securities or repurchase agreements fully collateralized by United States government securities, as described in this Rule, and, at the time of the investment, shall have total assets of at least two hundred fifty million dollars ($250,000,000.00).

(e) **Interest Calculation.** Interest shall be calculated in accordance with an Eligible Bank's standard practice for comparable non-IOLTA Accounts.

(f) **Higher Rates and Waiver of Service Charges Allowed.** Nothing in this rule shall preclude a participating bank from paying a higher interest rate than described above or electing to waive any service charges on IOLTA Accounts.

[Adopted Jan. 28, 2010, effective July 1, 2010.]

.1318 Confidentiality

(a) As used in this rule, "confidential information" means all information regarding IOLTA account(s) other than (1) a lawyer's or law firm's status as a participant, former participant, or non-participant in NC IOLTA, and (2) information regarding the policies and practices of any bank in respect of IOLTA trust accounts, including rates of interest paid, service charge policies, the number of IOLTA accounts at such bank, the total amount on deposit in all IOLTA accounts at such bank, the total amounts of interest paid to NC IOLTA, and the total amount of service charges imposed by such bank upon such accounts.

(b) Confidential information shall not be disclosed by the staff or trustees of NC IOLTA to any person or entity, except that confidential information may be disclosed (1) to any chairperson of the grievance committee, staff attorney, or investigator of the North Carolina State Bar upon his or her written request specifying the information requested and stating that the request is made in connection with a grievance complaint or investigation regarding one or more trust accounts of a lawyer or law firm; or (2) in response to a lawful order or other process issued by a court of competent jurisdiction, or a subpoena, investigative demand, or similar notice issued by a federal, state, or local law enforcement agency.

[Adopted effective March 6, 2008. Amended effective February 5, 2009; amended effective March 8, 2012.]

.1319 Certification

Every lawyer admitted to practice in North Carolina shall certify annually on or before June 30 to the North Carolina State Bar that all general trust accounts maintained by the lawyer or his or her law firm are established and maintained as IOLTA accounts as prescribed by Rule 1.15 of the Rules of Professional Conduct and Rule .1316 of this subchapter or that the lawyer is exempt from this provision because he or she does not maintain any general trust account(s) for North Carolina client funds. Any lawyer acting as a settlement agent who maintains a trust or escrow account used for the purpose of receiving and disbursing closing and loan funds shall certify annually on or before June 30 to the North Carolina State Bar that such accounts are established and maintained as IOLTA accounts as prescribed by N.C.G.S. 45A–9 and Rule .1316 of this subchapter.

[Adopted effective March 6, 2008. Amended effective Jan. 28, 2010; amended effective March 8, 2012.]

.1320 Noncompliance

Every lawyer must comply with all of the administrative requirements of this rule, including the certification required in Rule .1318 of this subchapter. A lawyer's failure to comply with the mandatory provisions of this subchapter shall be reported to the Administrative Committee which may initiate proceedings to suspend administratively the lawyer's active membership status and eligibility to practice law pursuant to Rule .0903 of this subchapter.

[Adopted effective March 6, 2008. Amended effective March 8, 2010.]

.1321 Severability

If any provision of this plan or the application thereof is held invalid, the invalidity does not affect other provisions or application of the plan which can be given effect without the invalid provision or application, and to this end the provisions of the plan are severable.

[Adopted effective March 6, 2008.]

SECTION .1400 RULES GOVERNING THE ADMINISTRATION OF THE CLIENT SECURITY FUND OF THE NORTH CAROLINA STATE BAR

.1401 Purpose; Definitions

(a) The Client Security Fund of the North Carolina State Bar was established by the Supreme Court of North Carolina pursuant to an order dated August 29, 1984. The fund is a standing committee of the North Carolina State Bar Council pursuant to an order of the Supreme Court dated October 10, 1984, as amended. Its purpose is to reimburse, in whole or in part in appropriate cases and subject to the provisions and limitations of the Supreme Court's orders and these rules, clients who have suffered financial loss as the result of dishonest conduct of lawyers engaged in the private practice of law in North Carolina, which conduct occurred on or after January 1, 1985.

(b) As used herein the following terms have the meaning indicated.

(1) "Applicant" shall mean a person who has suffered a reimbursable loss because of the dishonest

conduct of an attorney and has filed an application for reimbursement.

(2) "Attorney" shall mean an attorney who, at the time of alleged dishonest conduct, was licensed to practice law by the North Carolina State Bar. The fact that the alleged dishonest conduct took place outside the state of North Carolina does not necessarily mean that the attorney was not engaged in the practice of law in North Carolina.

(3) "Board" shall mean the Board of Trustees of the Client Security Fund.

(4) "Council" shall mean the North Carolina State Bar Council.

(5) "Dishonest conduct" shall mean wrongful acts committed by an attorney against an applicant in the nature of embezzlement from the applicant or the wrongful taking or conversion of monies or other property of the applicant, which monies or other property were entrusted to the attorney by the applicant by reason of an attorney-client relationship between the attorney and the applicant or by reason of a fiduciary relationship between the attorney and the applicant customary to the practice of law.

(6) "Fund" shall mean the Client Security Fund of the North Carolina State Bar.

(7) "Reimbursable losses" shall mean only those losses of money or other property which meet all of the following tests:

(A) the dishonest conduct which occasioned the loss occurred on or after January 1, 1985;

(B) the loss was caused by the dishonest conduct of an attorney acting either as an attorney for the applicant or in a fiduciary capacity for the benefit of the applicant customary to the private practice of law in the matter in which the loss arose;

(C) the applicant has exhausted all viable means to collect applicant's losses and has complied with these rules.

(8) The following shall not be deemed "reimbursable losses":

(A) losses of spouses, parents, grandparents, children and siblings (including foster and half relationships), partners, associates or employees of the attorney(s) causing the losses;

(B) losses covered by any bond, security agreement or insurance contract, to the extent covered thereby;

(C) losses incurred by any business entity with which the attorney or any person described in Rule .1401(b)(8)(A) above is an officer, director, shareholder, partner, joint venturer, promoter or employee;

(D) losses, reimbursement for which has been otherwise received from or paid by or on behalf of the attorney who committed the dishonest conduct;

(E) losses arising in investment transactions in which there was neither a contemporaneous attorney-client relationship between the attorney and the applicant nor a contemporaneous fiduciary relationship between the attorney and the applicant customary to the practice of law. By way of illustration but not limitation, for purposes of this rule (Rule .1401(b)(8)(E)), an attorney authorized or permitted by a person or entity other than the applicant as escrow or similar agent to hold funds deposited by the applicant for investment purposes shall not be deemed to have a fiduciary relationship with the applicant customary to the practice of law.

(9) "State Bar" shall mean the North Carolina State Bar.

(10) "Supreme Court" shall mean the North Carolina Supreme Court.

(11) "Supreme Court orders" shall mean the orders of the Supreme Court dated August 29, 1984, and October 10, 1984, as amended, authorizing the establishment of the Client Security Fund of the North Carolina State Bar and approving the rules of procedure of the Fund.

[History Note: Authority—Orders of the North Carolina Supreme Court, August 29, 1984, October 10, 1984. Readopted effective December 8, 1994.]

.1402 Jurisdiction: Authority

(a) Chapter 84 of the General Statutes vests in the State Bar authority to control the discipline, disbarment, and restoration of licenses of attorneys; to formulate and adopt rules of professional ethics and conduct; and to do all such things necessary in the furtherance of the purposes of the statutes governing the practice of the law as are not themselves prohibited by law. G.S. 84–22 authorizes the State Bar to establish such committees, standing or special, as from time to time the council deems appropriate for the proper discharge of its duties; and to determine the number of members, composition, method of appointment or election, functions, powers and duties, structure, authority to act, and other matters relating to such committees. The rules of the State Bar, as adopted and amended from time to time, are subject to approval by the Supreme Court under G.S. 84–21.

(b) The Supreme Court orders, entered in the exercise of the Supreme Court's inherent power to supervise and regulate attorney conduct, authorized the establishment of the Fund, as a standing committee of the council, to be administered by the State Bar under rules and regulations approved by the Supreme Court.

[History Note: Authority—Orders of the North Carolina Supreme Court, August 29, 1984, October 10, 1984. Readopted effective December 8, 1994.]

.1403 Operational Responsibility

The responsibility for operating the Fund and the program of the board rests with the board, subject to the Supreme Court orders, the statutes governing the practice of law, the authority of the council, and the rules of the board.

[History Note: Authority—Orders of the North Carolina Supreme Court, August 29, 1984, October 10, 1984. Readopted effective December 8, 1994.]

.1404 Size of Board

The board shall have five members, four of whom must be attorneys in good standing and authorized to practice law in the state of North Carolina.

[History Note: Authority—Orders of the North Carolina Supreme Court, August 29, 1984, October 10, 1984. Readopted effective December 8, 1994.]

.1405 Lay Participation

The board shall have one member who is not a licensed attorney.

[History Note: Authority—Orders of the North Carolina Supreme Court, August 29, 1984, October 10, 1984. Readopted effective December 8, 1994.]

.1406 Appointment of Members; When; Removal

The members of the board shall be appointed by the council. Any member of the board may be removed at any time by the affirmative vote of a majority of the members of the council at a regularly called meeting. Vacancies occurring by reason of death, disability, resignation, or removal of a member shall be filled by appointment of the president of the State Bar with the approval of the council at its next quarterly meeting following the event giving rise to the vacancy, and the person so appointed shall serve for the balance of the vacated term.

[History Note: Authority—Orders of the North Carolina Supreme Court, August 29, 1984, October 10, 1984. Readopted effective December 8, 1994.]

.1407 Term of Office

Each member who is appointed to the board, other than a member appointed to fill a vacancy created by the death, disability, removal or resignation of a member, shall serve for a term of five years beginning as of the first day of the month following the date upon which the appointment is made by the council. A member appointed to fill a vacancy shall serve the remainder of the vacated term.

[History Note: Authority—Orders of the North Carolina Supreme Court, August 29, 1984, October 10, 1984. Readopted effective December 8, 1994.]

.1408 Staggered Terms

It is intended that members of the board shall be elected to staggered terms such that one member is appointed in each year.

[History Note: Authority—Orders of the North Carolina Supreme Court, August 29, 1984, October 10, 1984. Readopted effective December 8, 1994.]

.1409 Succession

Each member of the board shall be entitled to serve for one full five-year term. A member appointed to fill a vacated term may be appointed to serve one full five-year term immediately following the expiration of the vacated term but shall not be entitled as of right to such appointment. No person shall be reappointed to the board until the expiration of three years following the last day of the previous term of such person on the board.

[History Note: Authority—Orders of the North Carolina Supreme Court, August 29, 1984, October 10, 1984. Readopted effective December 8, 1994.]

.1410 Appointment of Chairperson

The chairperson of the board shall be appointed from the members of the board annually by the council. The term of the chairperson shall be one year. The chairperson may be reappointed by the council thereafter during tenure on the board. The chairperson shall preside at all meetings of the board, shall prepare and present to the council the annual report of the board, and generally shall represent the board in its dealings with the public.

[History Note: Authority—Orders of the North Carolina Supreme Court, August 29, 1984, October 10, 1984. Readopted effective December 8, 1994.]

.1411 Appointment of Vice–Chairperson

The vice-chairperson of the board shall be appointed from the members of the board annually by the council. The term of the vice-chairperson shall be one year. The vice chairperson may be reappointed by the council thereafter during tenure on the board. The vice-chairperson shall preside at and represent the board in the absence of the chairperson and shall perform such other duties as may be assigned to him by the chairperson or by the board.

[History Note: Authority—Orders of the North Carolina Supreme Court, August 29, 1984, October 10, 1984. Readopted effective December 8, 1994.]

.1412 Source of Funds

Funds for the program carried out by the board shall come from assessments of members of the State Bar as ordered by the Supreme Court, from voluntary contributions, and as may otherwise be received by the Fund.

[History Note: Authority—Orders of the North Carolina Supreme Court, August 29, 1984, October 10, 1984. Readopted effective December 8, 1994.]

.1413 Fiscal Responsibility

All funds of the board shall be considered funds of the State Bar and shall be maintained, invested, and disbursed as follows:

(a) Maintenance of Accounts; Audit. The State Bar shall maintain a separate account for funds of the board such that such funds and expenditures therefrom can be readily identified. The accounts of the board shall be audited annually in connection with the audits of the State Bar.

(b) Investment Criteria. The funds of the board shall be kept, invested, and reinvested in accordance with investment policies adopted by the council for dues, rents, and other revenues received by the State Bar in carrying out its official duties. In no case shall the funds be invested or reinvested in investments other than such as are permitted to fiduciaries under the General Statutes of North Carolina.

(c) Disbursement. Disbursement of funds of the board shall be made by or under the direction of the secretary of the State Bar.

[History Note: Authority—Orders of the North Carolina Supreme Court, August 29, 1984, October 10, 1984. Readopted effective December 8, 1994.]

.1414 Meetings

The annual meeting of the board shall be held in October of each year in connection with the annual meeting of the State Bar. The board by resolution may set other regular meeting dates and places. Special meetings of the board may be called at any time upon notice given by the chairperson, the vice-chairperson, or any two members of the board. Notice of meeting shall be given at least two days prior to the meeting by mail, telegram, facsimile transmission or telephone. A quorum of the board for conducting its official business shall be a majority of the members serving at a particular time. Written minutes of all meetings shall be prepared and maintained.

[History Note: Authority—Orders of the North Carolina Supreme Court, August 29, 1984, October 10, 1984. Readopted effective December 8, 1994.]

.1415 Annual Report

The board shall prepare at least annually a report of its activities and shall present the same to the council at the annual meeting of the State Bar.

[History Note: Authority—Orders of the North Carolina Supreme Court, August 29, 1984, October 10, 1984. Readopted effective December 8, 1994.]

.1416 Appropriate Uses of the Client Security Fund

(a) The board may use or employ the Fund for any of the following purposes within the scope of the board's objectives as heretofore outlined:

(1) to make reimbursements on approved applications as herein provided;

(2) to purchase insurance to cover such losses in whole or in part as is deemed appropriate;

(3) to invest such portions of the Fund as may not be needed currently to reimburse losses, in such investments as are permitted to fiduciaries by the General Statutes of North Carolina;

(4) to pay the administrative expenses of the board, including employment of counsel to prosecute subrogation claims.

(b) The board with the authorization of the council shall, in the name of the North Carolina State Bar, enforce any claims which the board may have for restitution, subrogation, or otherwise, and may employ and compensate consultants, agents, legal counsel, and such other employees as it deems necessary and appropriate.

[History Note: Authority—Orders of the North Carolina Supreme Court, August 29, 1984, October 10, 1984. Readopted effective December 8, 1994.]

.1417 Applications for Reimbursement

(a) The board shall prepare a form of application for reimbursement which shall require the following minimum information, and such other information as the board may from time to time specify:

(1) the name and address of the applicant;

(2) the name and address of the attorney who is alleged to have engaged in dishonest conduct;

(3) the amount of the alleged loss for which application is made;

(4) the date on or period of time during which the alleged loss occurred;

(5) a general statement of facts relative to the application;

(6) a description of any relationship between the applicant and the attorney of the kinds described in Rules .1401(b)(8)(A) and (C) of this subchapter;

(7) verification by the applicant;

(8) all supporting documents, including

(A) copies of any court proceedings against the attorney;

(B) copies of all documents showing any reimbursement or receipt of funds in payment of any portion of the loss.

(b) The application shall contain the following statement in boldface type:

"IN ESTABLISHING THE CLIENT SECURITY FUND PURSUANT TO ORDER OF THE SUPREME COURT OF NORTH CAROLINA, THE NORTH CAROLINA STATE BAR DID NOT CREATE OR ACKNOWLEDGE ANY LEGAL RESPONSIBILITY FOR THE ACTS OF INDIVIDUAL ATTORNEYS IN THE PRACTICE OF LAW. ALL REIMBURSEMENTS OF LOSSES FROM THE CLIENT SECURITY FUND SHALL BE A MATTER OF GRACE IN THE SOLE DISCRETION OF THE BOARD ADMINISTERING THE FUND AND NOT A MATTER OF RIGHT. NO APPLICANT OR MEMBER OF THE PUBLIC SHALL HAVE ANY RIGHT IN THE CLIENT SECURITY FUND AS A THIRD PARTY BENEFICIARY OR OTHERWISE."

(c) The application shall be filed in the office of the State Bar in Raleigh, North Carolina, attention Client Security Fund Board, and a copy shall be transmitted by such office to the chairperson of the board.

[History Note: Authority—Orders of the North Carolina Supreme Court, August 29, 1984, October 10, 1984. Readopted effective December 8, 1994.]

.1418 Processing Applications

(a) The board shall cause an investigation of all applications filed with the State Bar to determine whether the application is for a reimbursable loss and the extent, if any, to which the application should be paid from the Fund.

(b) The chairperson of the board shall assign each application to a member of the board for review and report. Wherever possible, the member to whom such application is referred shall practice in the county wherein the attorney practices or practiced.

(c) A copy of the application shall be served upon or sent by registered mail to the last known address of the attorney who it is alleged committed an act of dishonest conduct.

(d) After considering a report of investigation as to an application, any board member may request that testimony be presented concerning the application. In all cases, the alleged defalcating attorney or his or her representative will be given an opportunity to be heard by the board if the attorney so requests.

(e) The board shall operate the Fund so that, taking into account assessments ordered by the Supreme Court but not yet received and anticipated investment earnings, a principal balance of approximately $1,000,000 is maintained. Subject to the foregoing, the board shall, in its discretion, determine the amount of loss, if any, for which each applicant should be reimbursed from the Fund. In making such determination, the board shall consider, inter alia, the following:

(1) the negligence, if any, of the applicant which contributed to the loss;

(2) the comparative hardship which the applicant suffered because of the loss;

(3) the total amount of reimbursable losses of applicants on account of any one attorney or firm or association of attorneys;

(4) the total amount of reimbursable losses in previous years for which total reimbursement has not been made and the total assets of the Fund;

(5) the total amount of insurance or other source of funds available to compensate the applicant for any reimbursable loss.

(f) The board may, in its discretion, allow further reimbursement in any year of a reimbursable loss reimbursed in part by it in prior years.

(g) Provided, however, and the foregoing notwithstanding, in no case shall the Fund reimburse the otherwise reimbursable losses sustained by any one applicant as a result of the dishonest conduct of one attorney in an amount in excess of $100,000.

(h) No reimbursement shall be made to any applicant unless reimbursement is approved by a majority vote of the entire board at a duly held meeting at which a quorum is present.

(i) No attorney shall be compensated by the board for prosecuting an application before it.

(j) An applicant may be advised of the status of the board's consideration of the application and shall be advised of the final determination of the board.

(k) All applications, proceedings, investigations, and reports involving applicants for reimbursement shall be kept confidential until and unless the board authorizes reimbursement to the applicant, or the attorney alleged to have engaged in dishonest conduct requests that the matter be made public. All participants involved in an application, investigation, or proceeding (including the applicant) shall conduct themselves so as to maintain the confidentiality of the application, investigation or proceeding. This provision shall not be construed to deny relevant information to be provided by the board to disciplinary committees or to anyone else to whom the council authorizes release of information.

(*l*) The board may, in its discretion, for newly discovered evidence or other compelling reason, grant a request to reconsider any application which the board has denied in whole or in part; otherwise, such denial is final and no further consideration shall be given by the board to such application or another application upon the same alleged facts.

[History Note: Authority—Orders of the North Carolina Supreme Court, August 29, 1984, October 10, 1984. Readopted effective December 8, 1994; amended effective March 6, 1997.]

.1419 Subrogation for Reimbursement

(a) In the event reimbursement is made to an applicant, the State Bar shall be subrogated to the amount reimbursed and may bring an action against the attorney or the attorney's estate either in the name of the applicant or in the name of the State Bar. As a condition of reimbursement, the applicant may be required to execute a "subrogation agreement" to such effect. Filing of an application constitutes an agreement by the applicant that the North Carolina State Bar shall be subrogated to the rights of the applicant to the extent of any reimbursement. Upon commencement of an action by the State Bar pursuant to its subrogation rights, it shall advise the reimbursed applicant at his or her last known address. A reimbursed applicant may then join in such action to recover any loss in excess of the amount reimbursed by the Fund. Any amounts recovered from the attorney by the board in excess of the amount to which the Fund is subrogated, less the board's actual costs of such recovery, shall be paid to or retained by the applicant as the case may be.

(b) Before receiving a payment from the Fund, the person who is to receive such payment or his or her legal representative shall execute and deliver to the board a written agreement stating that in the event the reimbursed applicant or his or her estate should ever receive any restitution from the attorney or his or her estate, the reimbursed applicant agrees that the Fund shall be repaid up to the amount of the reimbursement from the Fund plus expenses.

[History Note: Authority—Orders of the North Carolina Supreme Court, August 29, 1984, October 10, 1984. Readopted effective December 8, 1994.]

.1420 Authority Reserved by the Supreme Court

The Fund may be modified or abolished by the Supreme Court. In the event of abolition, all assets of the Fund shall be disbursed by order of the Supreme Court.

[History Note: Authority—Orders of the North Carolina Supreme Court, August 29, 1984, October 10, 1984. Readopted effective December 8, 1994.]

SECTION .1500 RULES GOVERNING THE ADMINISTRATION OF THE CONTINUING LEGAL EDUCATION PROGRAM

.1501 Scope, Purpose and Definitions

(a) Scope. Except as provided herein, these rules shall apply to every active member of the North Carolina State Bar.

(b) Purpose. The purpose of these continuing legal education rules is to assist lawyers licensed to practice and practicing law in North Carolina in achieving and maintaining professional competence for the benefit of the public whom they serve. The North Carolina State Bar, under Chapter 84 of the General Statutes of North Carolina, is charged with the responsibility of providing rules of professional conduct and with disciplining attorneys who do not comply with such rules. The Rules of Professional Conduct adopted by the North Carolina State Bar and approved by the Supreme Court of North Carolina require that lawyers adhere to important ethical standards, including that of rendering competent legal services in the representation of their clients.

At a time when all aspects of life and society are changing rapidly or becoming subject to pressures brought about by change, laws and legal principles are also in transition (through additions to the body of law, modifications and amendments) and are increasing in complexity. One cannot render competent legal services without continuous education and training.

The same changes and complexities, as well as the economic orientation of society, result in confusion about the ethical requirements concerning the practice of law and the relationships it creates. The data accumulated in the discipline program of the North Carolina State Bar argue persuasively for the establishment of a formal program for continuing and intensive training in professional responsibility and legal ethics.

It has also become clear that in order to render legal services in a professionally responsible manner, a lawyer must be able to manage his or her law practice competently. Sound management practices enable lawyers to concentrate on their clients' affairs while avoiding the ethical problems which can be caused by disorganization.

It is in response to such considerations that the North Carolina State Bar has adopted these minimum continuing legal education requirements. The purpose of these minimum continuing legal education requirements is the same as the purpose of the Rules of Professional Conduct themselves—to ensure that the public at large is served by lawyers who are competent and maintain high ethical standards.

(c) Definitions.

(1) "Accredited sponsor" shall mean an organization whose entire continuing legal education program has been accredited by the Board of Continuing Legal Education.

(2) "Active member" shall include any person who is licensed to practice law in the state of North Carolina and who is an active member of the North Carolina State Bar.

(3) "Administrative Committee" shall mean the Administrative Committee of the North Carolina State Bar.

(4) "Approved activity" shall mean a specific, individual legal education activity presented by an accredited sponsor or presented by other than an accredited sponsor if such activity is approved as a legal education activity under these rules by the Board of Continuing Legal Education.

(5) "Board" means the Board of Continuing Legal Education created by these rules.

(6) "Continuing legal education" or "CLE" is any legal, judicial or other educational activity accredited by the board. Generally, CLE will include educational activities designed principally to maintain or advance the professional competence of lawyers and/or to expand an appreciation and understanding of the professional responsibilities of lawyers.

(7) "Council" shall mean the North Carolina State Bar Council.

(8) "Credit hour" means an increment of time of 60 minutes which may be divided into segments of 30 minutes or 15 minutes, but no smaller.

(9) "Inactive member" shall mean a member of the North Carolina State Bar who is on inactive status.

(10) "In-house continuing legal education" shall mean courses or programs offered or conducted by law firms, either individually or in connection with other law firms, corporate legal departments, or similar entities primarily for the education of their members. The board may exempt from this definition those programs which it finds

(a) to be conducted by public or quasi-public organizations or associations for the education of their employees or members;

(b) to be concerned with areas of legal education not generally offered by sponsors of programs attended by lawyers engaged in the private practice of law.

(11) A "newly admitted active member" is one who becomes an active member of the North Carolina State Bar for the first time, has been reinstated, or has changed from inactive to active status.

(12) "Participatory CLE" shall mean courses or segments of courses that encourage the participation of attendees in the educational experience through, for example, the analysis of hypothetical situations, role playing, mock trials, roundtable discussions, or debates.

(13) "Professional responsibility" shall mean those courses or segments of courses devoted to a) the substance, underlying rationale, and practical application of the Rules of Professional Conduct; b) the professional obligations of the lawyer to the client, the court, the public, and other lawyers; c) moral philosophy and ethical decision-making in the context of the practice of law; and d) the effects of stress, substance abuse, and chemical dependency, or debilitating mental conditions on a lawyer's professional responsibilities and the prevention, detection, treatment, and etiology of stress, substance abuse, chemical dependency, and debilitating mental conditions. This definition shall be interpreted consistent with the provisions of Rule .1501(c)(4) or (6) above.

(14) "Professionalism" courses are courses or segments of courses devoted to the identification and examination of, and the encouragement of adherence to, non-mandatory aspirational standards of professional conduct which transcend the requirements of the Rules of Professional Conduct. Such courses address principles of competence and dedication to the service of clients, civility, improvement of the justice system, diversity of the legal profession and clients, advancement of the rule of law, service to the community, and service to the disadvantaged and those unable to pay for legal services.

(15) "Rules" shall mean the provisions of the continuing legal education rules established by the Supreme Court of North Carolina (Section.1500 of this subchapter).

(16) "Sponsor" is any person or entity presenting or offering to present one or more continuing legal education programs, whether or not an accredited sponsor.

(17) "Year" shall mean calendar year.

[History Note: Authority—Order of the North Carolina Supreme Court, October 7, 1987, 318 N.C. 711. Readopted effective December 8, 1994; amended effective March 6, 1997; December 30, 1998; March 3, 1999; amended effective June 7, 2001; amended effective March 3, 2005; amended effective March 8, 2007; amended effective October 9, 2008; amended effective August 25, 2011.]

.1502 Jurisdiction: Authority

The Council of the North Carolina State Bar hereby establishes the Board of Continuing Legal Education (board) as a standing committee of the council, which board shall have authority to establish regulations governing a continuing legal education program and a law practice assistance program for attorneys licensed to practice law in this state.

[History Note: Authority—Order of the North Carolina Supreme Court, October 7, 1987, 318 N.C. 711. Readopted effective December 8, 1994.]

.1503 Operational Responsibility

The responsibility for operating the continuing legal education program and the law practice assistance program shall rest with the board, subject to the statutes governing the practice of law, the authority of the council, and the rules of governance of the board.

[History Note: Authority—Order of the North Carolina Supreme Court, October 7, 1987, 318 N.C. 711. Readopted effective December 8, 1994.]

.1504 Size of Board

The board shall have nine members, all of whom must be attorneys in good standing and authorized to practice in the state of North Carolina.

[History Note: Authority—Order of the North Carolina Supreme Court, October 7, 1987, 318 N.C. 711. Readopted effective December 8, 1994.]

.1505 Lay Participation

The board shall have no members who are not licensed attorneys.

[History Note: Authority—Order of the North Carolina Supreme Court, October 7, 1987, 318 N.C. 711. Readopted effective December 8, 1994.]

.1506 Appointment of Members; When; Removal

The members of the board shall be appointed by the council. The first members of the board shall be appointed as of the quarterly meeting of the council following the creation of the board. Thereafter, members shall be appointed annually as of the same quarterly meeting. Vacancies occurring by reason of death, resignation, or removal shall be filled by appointment of the council at the next quarterly meeting following the event giving rise to the vacancy, and the person so appointed shall serve for the balance of the vacated term. Any member of the board may be removed at any time by an affirmative vote of a majority of the members of the council in session at a regularly called meeting.

[History Note: Authority—Order of the North Carolina Supreme Court, October 7, 1987, 318 N.C. 711. Readopted effective December 8, 1994.]

.1507 Term of Office

Each member who is appointed to the board shall serve for a term of three years beginning as of the first day of the month following the date on which the appointment is made by the council. See, however, Rule .1508 of this subchapter.

[History Note: Authority—Order of the North Carolina Supreme Court, October 7, 1987, 318 N.C. 711. Readopted effective December 8, 1994.]

.1508 Staggered Terms

It is intended that members of the board shall be elected to staggered terms such that three members are appointed in each year. Of the initial board, three members shall be elected to terms of one year, three members shall be elected to terms of two years, and three members shall be elected to terms of three years. Thereafter, three members shall be elected each year.

[History Note: Authority—Order of the North Carolina Supreme Court, October 7, 1987, 318 N.C. 711. Readopted effective December 8, 1994.]

.1509 Succession

Each member of the board shall be entitled to serve for one full three-year term and to succeed himself or herself for one additional three-year term. Thereafter, no person may be reappointed without having been off the board for at least three years.

[History Note: Authority—Order of the North Carolina Supreme Court, October 7, 1987, 318 N.C. 711. Readopted effective December 8, 1994.]

.1510 Appointment of Chairperson

The chairperson of the board shall be appointed from time to time as necessary by the council. The term of such individual as chairperson shall be one year. The chairperson may be reappointed thereafter during his or her tenure on the board. The chairperson shall preside at all meetings of the board, shall prepare and present to the council the annual report of the board, and generally shall represent the board in its dealings with the public.

[History Note: Authority—Order of the North Carolina Supreme Court, October 7, 1987, 318 N.C. 711. Readopted effective December 8, 1994.]

.1511 Appointment of Vice-Chairperson

The vice-chairperson of the board shall be appointed from time to time as necessary by the council. The term of such individual as vice-chairperson shall be one year. The vice-chairperson may be reappointed thereafter during tenure on the board. The vice-chairperson shall preside at and represent the board in the absence of the chairperson and shall perform such other duties as may be assigned to him or her by the chairperson or by the board.

[History Note: Authority—Order of the North Carolina Supreme Court, October 7, 1987, 318 N.C. 711. Readopted effective December 8, 1994.]

.1512 Source of Funds

(a) Funding for the program carried out by the board shall come from sponsor's fees and attendee's fees as provided below, as well as from duly assessed penalties for noncompliance and from reinstatement fees.

(1) Accredited sponsors located in North Carolina (for courses offered within or outside North Carolina), or accredited sponsors not located in North Carolina (for courses given in North Carolina), or unaccredited sponsors located within or outside of North Carolina

(for accredited courses within North Carolina) shall, as a condition of conducting an approved activity, agree to remit a list of North Carolina attendees and to pay a fee for each active member of the North Carolina State Bar who attends the program for CLE credit. The sponsor's fee shall be based on each credit hour of attendance, with a proportional fee for portions of a program lasting less than an hour. The fee shall be set by the board upon approval of the council. Any sponsor, including an accredited sponsor, which conducts an approved activity which is offered without charge to attendees shall not be required to remit the fee under this section. Attendees who wish to receive credit for attending such an approved activity shall comply with Rule .1512(a)(2) below.

(2) The board shall fix a reasonably comparable fee to be paid by individual attorneys who attend for CLE credit approved continuing legal education activities for which the sponsor does not submit a fee under Rule .1512(a)(1) above. Such fee shall accompany the member's annual affidavit. The fee shall be set by the board upon approval of the council.

(b) Funding for a law practice assistance program shall be from user fees set by the board upon approval of the council and from such other funds as the council may provide.

[History Note: Authority—Order of the North Carolina Supreme Court, October 7, 1987, 318 N.C. 711. Readopted effective December 8, 1994.]

.1513 Fiscal Responsibility

All funds of the board shall be considered funds of the North Carolina State Bar and shall be administered and disbursed accordingly.

(a) Maintenance of Accounts: Audit. The North Carolina State Bar shall maintain a separate account for funds of the board such that such funds and expenditures therefrom can be readily identified. The accounts of the board shall be audited on an annual basis in connection with the audits of the North Carolina State Bar.

(b) Investment Criteria. The funds of the board shall be handled, invested and reinvested in accordance with investment policies adopted by the council for the handling of dues, rents, and other revenues received by the North Carolina State Bar in carrying out its official duties.

(c) Disbursement. Disbursement of funds of the board shall be made by or under the direction of the secretary-treasurer of the North Carolina State Bar pursuant to authority of the council. The members of the board shall serve on a voluntary basis without compensation, but may be reimbursed for the reasonable expenses incurred in attending meetings of the board or its committees.

(d) All revenues resulting from the CLE program, including fees received from attendees and sponsors, late filing penalties, late compliance fees, reinstatement fees, and interest on a reserve fund shall be applied first to the expense of the CLE program including an adequate reserve fund; provided, however, that a portion of each sponsor or attendee fee, in an amount to be determined by the council but not to exceed $1.00 for each credit hour, shall be paid to the Chief Justice's Commission on Professionalism for administration of the activities of the commission. Excess funds may be expended by the council on lawyer competency programs approved by the council.

[History Note: Authority—Order of the North Carolina Supreme Court, October 7, 1987, 318 N.C. 711. Readopted effective December 8, 1994; amended effective December 30, 1998.]

.1514 Meetings

The annual meeting of the board shall be held in October of each year in connection with the annual meeting of the North Carolina State Bar. The board by resolution may set regular meeting dates and places. Special meetings of the board may be called at any time upon notice given by the chairperson, the vice-chairperson, or any two members of the board. Notice of meeting shall be given at least two days prior to the meeting by mail, telegram, facsimile transmission or telephone. A quorum of the board for conducting its official business shall be a majority of the members serving at a particular time.

[History Note: Authority—Order of the North Carolina Supreme Court, October 7, 1987, 318 N.C. 711. Readopted effective December 8, 1994.]

.1515 Annual Report

The board shall prepare at least annually a report of its activities and shall present the same to the council one month prior to its annual meeting.

[History Note: Authority—Order of the North Carolina Supreme Court, October 7, 1987, 318 N.C. 711. Readopted effective December 8, 1994.]

.1516 Powers, Duties, and Organization of the Board

(a) The board shall have the following powers and duties:

(1) to exercise general supervisory authority over the administration of these rules;

(2) to adopt and amend regulations consistent with these rules with the approval of the council;

(3) to establish an office or offices and to employ such persons as the board deems necessary for the proper administration of these rules, and to delegate

to them appropriate authority, subject to the review of the council;

(4) to report annually on the activities and operations of the board to the council and make any recommendations for changes in the rules or methods of operation of the continuing legal education program;

(5) to submit an annual budget to the council for approval and to ensure that expenses of the board do not exceed the annual budget approved by the council;

(6) to administer a law office assistance program for the benefit of lawyers who request or are required to obtain training in the area of law office management.

(b) The board shall be organized as follows:

(1) Quorum – Five members shall constitute a quorum of the board.

(2) The Executive Committee – The executive committee of the board shall be comprised of the chairperson, a vice-chairperson elected by the members of the board, and a member to be appointed by the chairperson. Its purpose is to conduct all necessary business of the board that may arise between meetings of the full board. In such matters it shall have complete authority to act for the board.

(3) Other Committees – The chairperson may appoint committees as established by the board for the purpose of considering and deciding matters submitted to them by the board.

(c) Appeals–Except as otherwise provided, the board is the final authority on all matters entrusted to it under Section .1500 and Section .1600 of this subchapter. Therefore, any decision by a committee of the board pursuant to a delegation of authority may be appealed to the full board and will be heard by the board at its next scheduled meeting. A decision made by the staff pursuant to a delegation of authority may also be reviewed by the full board but should first be appealed to any committee of the board having jurisdiction on the subject involved. All appeals shall be in writing. The board has the discretion to, but is not obligated to, grant a hearing in connection with any appeal regarding the accreditation of a program.

[History Note: Authority—Order of the North Carolina Supreme Court, October 7, 1987, 318 N.C. 711. Readopted effective December 8, 1994; amended effective March 3, 2005.]

.1517. Exemptions

(a) Notification of Board. To qualify for an exemption for a particular calendar year, a member shall notify the board of the exemption in the annual report for that calendar year sent to the member pursuant to Rule .1522 of this subchapter. All active members who are exempt are encouraged to attend and participate in legal education programs.

(b) Government Officials and Members of Armed Forces. The governor, the lieutenant governor, and all members of the council of state, members of the United States Senate, members of the United States House of Representatives, members of the North Carolina General Assembly and members of the United States Armed Forces on full-time active duty are exempt from the requirements of these rules for any calendar year in which they serve some portion thereof in such capacity.

(c) Judiciary and Clerks. Members of the state judiciary who are required by virtue of their judicial offices to take an average of twelve (12) or more hours of continuing judicial or other legal education annually and all members of the federal judiciary are exempt from the requirements of these rules for any calendar year in which they serve some portion thereof in such judicial capacities. A full-time law clerk for a member of the federal or state judiciary is exempt from the requirements of these rules for any calendar year in which the clerk serves some portion thereof in such capacity, provided, however, that the exemption shall not exceed two consecutive calendar years and, further provided, that the clerkship begins within one year after the clerk graduates from law school or passes the bar examination for admission to the North Carolina State Bar whichever occurs later.

(d) Nonresidents. Any active member residing outside of North Carolina who does not practice in North Carolina for at least six (6) consecutive months and does not represent North Carolina clients on matters governed by North Carolina law shall be exempt from the requirements of these rules.

(e) Law Teachers. An exemption from the requirements of these rules shall be given to any active member who does not practice in North Carolina or represent North Carolina clients on matters governed by North Carolina law and who is:

(1) A full-time teacher at the School of Government (formerly the Institute of Government) of the University of North Carolina;

(2) A full-time teacher at a law school in North Carolina that is accredited by the American Bar Association; or

(3) A full-time teacher of law-related courses at a professional school accredited by its respective professional accrediting agency.

(f) Special Circumstances Exemptions. The board may exempt an active member from the continuing legal education requirements for a period of not more than one year at a time upon a finding by the board of special circumstances unique to that member constituting undue hardship or other reasonable basis for exemption, or for a longer period upon a finding of a permanent disability.

(g) Pro Hac Vice Admissions. Nonresident attorneys from other jurisdictions who are temporarily admitted to practice in a particular case or proceeding pursuant to the provisions of G.S. 84–4.1 shall not be subject to the requirements of these rules.

(h) Senior Status Exemption. The board may exempt an active member from the continuing legal education requirements if

(1) the member is sixty-five years of age or older and

(2) the member does not render legal advice to or represent a client unless the member associates another active member who assumes responsibility for the advice or representation.

(i) CLE Record During Exemption Period. During a calendar year in which the records of the board indicate that an active member is exempt from the requirements of these rules, the board shall not maintain a record of such member's attendance at accredited continuing legal education activities. Upon the termination of the member's exemption, the member may request carry over credit up to a maximum of twelve (12) credits for any accredited continuing legal education activity attended during the calendar year immediately preceding the year of the termination of the exemption. Appropriate documentation of attendance at such activities will be required by the board.

(j) Permanent Disability. Attorneys who have a permanent disability that makes attendance at CLE programs inordinately difficult may file a request for a permanent substitute program in lieu of attendance and shall therein set out continuing legal education plans tailored to their specific interests and physical abilities. The board shall review and approve or disapprove such plans on an individual basis and without delay.

(k) Application for Substitute Compliance and Exemptions. Other requests for substitute compliance, partial waivers, and other exemptions for hardship or extenuating circumstances may be granted by the board on a yearly basis upon written application of the attorney.

(*l*) Bar Examiners. Credit is earned through service as a bar examiner of the North Carolina Board of Law Examiners. The board will award 12 hours of CLE credit for the preparation and grading of a bar examination by a member of the North Carolina Board of Law Examiners.

[History Note: Authority—Order of the North Carolina Supreme Court, October 7, 1987, 318 N.C. 711. Readopted effective December 8, 1994; amended effective February 12, 1997; amended effective October 1, 2003; amended effective March 3, 2005; amended effective October 7, 2010; amended effective October 2, 2014.]

.1518. Continuing Legal Education Program

(a) Annual Requirement. Each active member subject to these rules shall complete 12 hours of approved continuing legal education during each calendar year beginning January 1, 1988, as provided by these rules and the regulations adopted thereunder. Of the 12 hours:

(1) at least 2 hours shall be devoted to the areas of professional responsibility or professionalism or any combination thereof; and

(2) effective January 1, 2002, at least once every three calendar years, each member shall complete an hour of continuing legal education instruction on substance abuse and debilitating mental conditions as defined in Rule .1602 (a). This hour shall be credited to the annual 12–hour requirement but shall be in addition to the annual professional responsibility/professionalism requirement. To satisfy the requirement, a member must attend an accredited program on substance abuse and debilitating mental conditions that is at least one hour long.

(b) Carryover. Members may carry over up to 12 credit hours earned in one calendar year to the next calendar year, which may include those hours required by paragraph (a)(1) above. Additionally, a newly admitted active member may include as credit hours which may be carried over to the next succeeding year any approved CLE hours earned after that member's graduation from law school.

(c) Professionalism Requirement for New Members. Except as provided in paragraph (d)(1), each active member admitted to the North Carolina State Bar after January 1, 2011, must complete the North Carolina State Bar Professionalism for New Attorneys Program (PNA Program) in the year the member is first required to meet the continuing legal education requirements as set forth in Rule .1526(b) and (c) of this subchapter. CLE credit for the PNA Program shall be applied to the annual mandatory continuing legal education requirements set forth in paragraph (a) above.

(1) *Content and Accreditation.* The State Bar PNA Program shall consist of 12 hours of training in subjects designated by the State Bar including, but not limited to, professional responsibility, professionalism, and law office management. The chairs of the Ethics and Grievance Committees, in consultation with the chief counsel to those committees, shall annually establish the content of the program and shall publish the required content on or before January 1 of each year. To be approved as a PNA Program, a sponsor must satisfy the annual content requirements. At least 45 days prior to the presentation of a PNA Program, a sponsor must submit a detailed description of the program to the board for approval. Accredited sponsors shall not be exempt from the prior submission requirement and may not advertise a PNA Program until approved by the board. PNA Programs shall be specially designated by the board and no course that is not so designated shall satisfy the PNA Program requirement for new members.

(2) *Evaluation.* To receive CLE credit for attending a PNA Program, the participant must complete a

written evaluation of the program which shall contain questions specified by the State Bar. Sponsors shall collate the information on the completed evaluation forms and shall send a report showing the collated information, together with the original forms, to the State Bar when reporting attendance pursuant to Rule .1601(e)(1) of this subchapter.

(3) *Timetable and Partial Credit.* The PNA Program shall be presented in two six-hour blocks (with appropriate breaks) over two days. The six-hour blocks do not have to be attended on consecutive days or taken from the same provider; however, no partial credit shall be awarded for attending less than an entire six-hour block unless a special circumstances exemption is granted by the board. The board may approve an alternative timetable for a PNA program upon demonstration by the provider that the alternative timetable will provide an enhanced learning experience or for other good cause; however, no partial credit shall be awarded for attending less than the entire 12–hour program unless a special circumstances exemption is granted by the board.

(4) *Online and Prerecorded Programs.* The PNA Program may be distributed over the Internet by live web streaming (webcasting) but no part of the program may be taken online (via the Internet) on demand.

(d) Exemptions from Professionalism Requirement for New Members.

(1) *Licensed in Another Jurisdiction.* A member who is licensed by a United States jurisdiction other than North Carolina for five or more years prior to admission to practice in North Carolina is exempt from the PNA Program requirement and must notify the board of the exemption in the first annual report sent to the member pursuant to Rule .1522 of this subchapter.

(2) *Inactive Status.* A newly admitted member who is transferred to inactive status in the year of admission to the State Bar is exempt from the PNA Program requirement but, upon the entry of an order transferring the member back to active status, must complete the PNA Program in the year that the member is subject to the requirements set forth in paragraph (a) above unless the member qualifies for the exemption under paragraph (d)(1) of this rule.

(3) *Exemptions Under Rule .1517.* A newly admitted active member who qualifies for an exemption under Rule .1517 of this subchapter shall be exempt from the PNA Program requirement during the period of the Rule .1517 exemption. The member shall notify the board of the exemption in the first annual report sent to the member pursuant to Rule .1522 of this subchapter. The member must complete the PNA Program in the year the member no longer qualifies for the Rule .1517 exemption or the next calendar year unless the member qualifies for the exemption under paragraph (d)(1) of this rule.

(e) The board shall determine the process by which credit hours are allocated to lawyers' records to satisfy deficits. The allocation shall be applied uniformly to the records of all affected lawyers and may not be appealed by an affected lawyer.

[History Note: Authority—Order of the North Carolina Supreme Court, October 7, 1987, 318 N.C. 711. Readopted effective December 8, 1994. Amended February 12, 1997; December 30, 1998, March 3, 1999; November 6, 2001; October 1, 2003; March 11, 2010; August 25, 2011; March 6, 2014; March 5, 2015.]

.1519 Accreditation Standards

The board shall approve continuing legal education activities which meet the following standards and provisions.

(a) They shall have significant intellectual or practical content and the primary objective shall be to increase the participant's professional competence and proficiency as a lawyer.

(b) They shall constitute an organized program of learning dealing with matters directly related to the practice of law, professional responsibility, professionalism, or ethical obligations of lawyers.

(c) Credit may be given for continuing legal education activities where live instruction is used or mechanically or electronically recorded or reproduced material is used, including videotape or satellite transmitted programs. Subject to the limitations set forth in Rule .1611 of this subchapter, credit may also be given for continuing legal education activities on CD–ROM and on a computer website accessed via the Internet.

(d) Continuing legal education materials are to be prepared, and activities conducted, by an individual or group qualified by practical or academic experience.. Credit shall not be given for any continuing legal education activity taught or presented by a disbarred lawyer except a course on professional responsibility (including a course or program on the effects of substance abuse and chemical dependency, or debilitating mental conditions on a lawyer's professional responsibilities). The advertising for the activity shall disclose the lawyer's disbarment.

(e) Continuing legal education activities shall be conducted in a setting physically suitable to the educational activity of the program and, when appropriate, equipped with suitable writing surfaces or sufficient space for taking notes.

(f) Thorough, high quality, and carefully prepared written materials should be distributed to all attendees at or before the time the course is presented. These may include written materials printed from a computer presentation, computer website or CD–ROM. A written agenda or outline for a presentation satisfies this requirement when written materials are not suitable or readily available for a particular subject. The absence of written materials for distribution should, however, be the exception and not the rule.

(g) Any accredited sponsor must remit fees as required and keep and maintain attendance records of each continuing legal education program sponsored by it, which shall be furnished to the board in accordance with regulations.

(h) Except as provided in Rule .1611 of this subchapter, in-house continuing legal education and self-study shall not be approved or accredited for the purpose of complying with Rule .1518 of this subchapter.

(i) Programs that cross academic lines, such as accounting-tax seminars, may be considered for approval by the board. However, the board must be satisfied that the content of the activity would enhance legal skills or the ability to practice law.

[History Note: Authority—Order of the North Carolina Supreme Court, October 7, 1987, 318 N.C. 711. Readopted effective December 8, 1994. Amended effective December 30, 1998; October 1, 2003; February 5, 2009.]

.1520 Accreditation of Sponsors and Programs

(a) Accreditation of Sponsors. An organization desiring accreditation as an accredited sponsor of courses, programs, or other continuing legal education activities may apply for accredited sponsor status to the board. The board shall approve a sponsor as an accredited sponsor if it is satisfied that the sponsor's programs have met the standards set forth in Rule .1519 of this subchapter and regulations established by the board.

(b) Program Approval for Accredited Sponsors.

(1) Once an organization is approved as an accredited sponsor, the continuing legal education programs sponsored by that organization are presumptively approved for credit; however, no application must be made to the board for approval. At least 50 days prior to the presentation of a program, an accredited sponsor shall file an application, on a form prescribed by the board, notifying the board of the dates and locations of presentations of the program and the sponsor's calculation of the CLE credit hours for the program.

(2) The board may at any time revoke the accreditation of an accredited sponsor for failure to satisfy the requirements of Rule .1512 and Rule .1519 of this subchapter, and for failure to satisfy the Regulations Governing the Administration of the Continuing Legal Education Program set forth in Section .1600 of this subchapter.

(3) The board shall evaluate a program presented by an accredited sponsor and, upon a determination that the program does not satisfy the requirements of Rule .1519, notify the accredited sponsor that the program is not approved for credit. Such notice shall be sent by the board to the accredited sponsor within 45 days after the receipt of the application. If notice is not sent to the accredited sponsor within the 45-day period, the program shall be presumed to be approved. The accredited sponsor may request reconsideration of an unfavorable accreditation decision by submitting a letter of appeal to the board within 15 days of receipt of the notice of disapproval. The decision by the board on an appeal is final.

(c) Unaccredited Sponsor Request for Program Approval.

(1) Any organization not accredited as an accredited sponsor that desires approval of a course or program shall apply to the board. The board shall adopt regulations to administer the accreditation of such programs consistent with the provisions of Rule .1519 of this subchapter. Applicants denied approval of a program may request reconsideration of such a decision by submitting a letter of appeal to the board within 15 days of receipt of the notice of disapproval. The decision by the board on an appeal is final.

(2) The board may at any time decline to accredit CLE programs offered by a non-accredited sponsor for a specified period of time, as determined by the board, for failure to comply with the requirements of Rule .1512, Rule .1519 and Section .1600 of this subchapter.

(d) Member Request for Program Approval. An active member desiring approval of a course or program that has not otherwise been approved shall apply to the board. The board that shall adopt regulations to administer approval requests consistent with the requirements Rule .1519 of this subchapter. Applicants denied approval of a program may request reconsideration of such a decision by submitting a letter of appeal to the board within 15 days of the receipt of the notice of disapproval. The decision by the board on an appeal is final.

(e) Records. The board may provide by regulation for the accredited sponsor, unaccredited sponsor, or active member for whom a continuing legal education program has been approved to maintain and provide such records as required by the board.

[History Note: Authority—Order of the North Carolina Supreme Court, October 7, 1987, 318 N.C. 711. Readopted effective December 8, 1994. Amended effective February 27, 2003; March 3, 2005; October 7, 2010; March 6, 2014.]

.1521 Credit Hours

The board may designate by regulation the number of credit hours to be earned by participation, including, but not limited to, teaching, in continuing legal education activities approved by the board.

[History Note: Authority—Order of the North Carolina Supreme Court, October 7, 1987, 318 N.C. 711. Readopted effective December 8, 1994.]

.1522 Annual Report and Compliance Period

(a) Annual Written Report. Commencing in 1989, each active member of the North Carolina State Bar shall provide an annual written report to the North Carolina State Bar in such form as the board shall prescribe by regulation concerning compliance with the continuing legal education program for the preceding year or declaring an exemption under Rule .1517 of this subchapter. The annual report form shall be corrected, if necessary, signed by the member, and promptly returned to the State Bar. Upon receipt of a signed annual report form, appropriate adjustments shall be made to the member's continuing legal education record with the State Bar. No further adjustments shall thereafter be made to the member's continuing legal education record unless, on or before July 31 of the year in which the report form is mailed to members, the member shows good cause for adjusting the member's continuing legal education record for the preceding year.

(b) Compliance Period. The period for complying with the requirements of Rule .1518 of this subchapter is January 1 to December 31. A member may complete the requirements for the year on or by the last day of February of the succeeding year provided, however, that this additional time shall be considered a grace period and no extensions of this grace period shall be granted. All members are encouraged to complete the requirements within the appropriate calendar year.

(c) Report. Prior to January 31 of each year, the prescribed report form concerning compliance with the continuing legal education program for the preceding year shall be mailed to all active members of the North Carolina State Bar.

(d) Late Filing Penalty. Any attorney who, for whatever reasons, files the report showing compliance or declaring an exemption after the due date of the last day of February shall pay a $75.00 late filing penalty. This penalty shall be submitted with the report. A report that is either received by the board or postmarked on or before the due date shall be considered timely filed. An attorney who is issued a notice to show cause pursuant to Rule .1523(b) shall pay a late compliance fee of $125.00 pursuant to Rule.1523(e) of this subchapter. The board may waive the late filing penalty or the late compliance fee upon a showing of hardship or serious extenuating circumstances or other good cause.

[History Note: Authority—Order of the North Carolina Supreme Court, October 7, 1987, 318 N.C. 711. Readopted effective December 8, 1994; amended effective October 1, 2003; amended effective March 3, 2005; amended effective March 2, 2006; amended effective October 9, 2008.]

.1523 Noncompliance

(a) Failure to Comply With Rules May Result in Suspension. A member who is required to file a report of CLE credits and does not do so or who fails to meet the minimum requirements of these rules, including the payment of duly assessed penalties and attendee fees, may be suspended from the practice of law in the state of North Carolina.

(b) Notice of Failure to Comply. The board shall notify a member who appears to have failed to meet the requirements of these rules that the member will be suspended from the practice of law in this state, unless the member shows good cause in writing why the suspension should not be made or the member shows in writing that he or she has complied with the requirements within the 30–day period after service of the notice. Notice shall be served on the member by mailing a copy thereof by registered or certified mail or designated delivery service (such as Federal Express or UPS), return receipt requested, to the last known address of the member according to the records of the North Carolina State Bar or such later address as may be known to the person attempting service. Service of the notice may also be accomplished by (i) personal service by a State Bar investigator or by any person authorized by Rule 4 of the North Carolina Rules of Civil Procedure to serve process, or (ii) email sent to the email address of the member contained in the records of the North Carolina State Bar if the member sends an email from that same email address to the State Bar acknowledging such service.

(c) Entry of Order of Suspension Upon Failure to Respond to Notice to Show Cause. If a written response attempting to show good cause is not postmarked or received by the board by the last day of the 30–day period after the member was served with the notice to show cause, upon the recommendation of the board and the Administrative Committee, the council may enter an order suspending the member from the practice of law. The order shall be entered and served as set forth in Rule.0903(c) of this subchapter.

(d) Procedure Upon Submission of a Timely Response to a Notice to Show Cause

(1) *Consideration by the Board* If the member files a timely written response to the notice, the board shall consider the matter at its next regularly scheduled meeting or may delegate consideration of the matter to a duly appointed committee of the board. If the matter is delegated to a committee of the board and the committee determines that good cause has not been shown, the member may file an appeal to the board. The appeal must be filed within 30 calendar days of the date of the letter notifying the member of the decision of the committee. The board shall review all evidence presented by the member to determine whether good cause has been shown or to determine whether the member has complied with the require-

ments of these rules within the 30–day period after service of the notice to show cause.

(2) *Recommendation of the Board* The board shall determine whether the member has shown good cause why the member should not be suspended. If the board determines that good cause has not been shown or that the member has not shown compliance with these rules within the 30–day period after service of the notice to show cause, then the board shall refer the matter to the Administrative Committee for hearing together with a written recommendation to the Administrative Committee that the member be suspended.

(3) *Consideration by and Recommendation of the Administrative Committee.* The Administrative Committee shall consider the matter at its next regularly scheduled meeting. The burden of proof shall be upon the member to show cause by clear, cogent and convincing evidence why the member should not be suspended from the practice of law for the apparent failure to comply with the rules governing the continuing legal education program. Except as set forth above, the procedure for such hearing shall be as set forth in Rule .0903(d)(1) and (2) of this subchapter.

(4) *Order of Suspension.* Upon the recommendation of the Administrative Committee, the council may determine that the member has not complied with these rules and may enter an order suspending the member from the practice of law. The order shall be entered and served as set forth in Rule .0903(d)(3) of this subchapter.

(e) Late Compliance Fee. Any member to whom a notice to show cause is issued pursuant to paragraph (b) above shall pay a late compliance fee as set forth in Rule.1522(d) of this subchapter; provided, however, upon a showing of good cause as determined by the board as described in paragraph (d)(2) above, the fee may be waived.

[History Note: Authority—Order of the North Carolina Supreme Court, October 7, 1987, 318 N.C. 711. Readopted effective December 8, 1994; amended effective March 7, 1996; amended effective March 6, 1997; amended December 10,1999, effective February 3, 2000; amended effective October 1, 2003; amended effective October 9, 2008; amended effective August 23, 2012.]

.1524 Reinstatement

(a) Reinstatement Within 30 Days of Service of Suspension Order. A member who is suspended for noncompliance with the rules governing the continuing legal education program may petition the secretary for an order of reinstatement of the member's license at any time up to 30 days after the service of the suspension order upon the member. The secretary shall enter an order reinstating the member to active status upon receipt of a timely written request and satisfactory showing by the member that the member has cured the continuing legal education deficiency for which the member was suspended. Such member shall not be required to file a formal reinstatement petition or pay a $250 reinstatement fee.

(b) Procedure for Reinstatement More that 30 Days After Service of the Order of Suspension. Except as noted below, the procedure for reinstatement more than 30 days after service of the order of suspension shall be as set forth in Rule .0904(c) and (d) of this subchapter, and shall be administered by the Administrative Committee.

(c) Reinstatement Petition. At any time more than 30 days after service of an order of suspension on a member, a member who has been suspended for noncompliance with the rules governing the continuing legal education program may seek reinstatement by filing a reinstatement petition with the secretary. The secretary shall transmit a copy of the petition to each member of the board. The reinstatement petition shall contain the information and be in the form required by Rule .0904(c) of this subchapter. If not otherwise set forth in the petition, the member shall attach a statement to the petition in which the member shall state with particularity the accredited legal education courses which the member has attended and the number of credit hours obtained in order to cure any continuing legal education deficiency for which the member was suspended.

(d) Reinstatement Fee. In lieu of the $125.00 reinstatement fee required by Rule .0904(c)(4)(A), the petition shall be accompanied by a reinstatement fee payable to the board, in the amount of $250.00.

(e) Determination of Board; Transmission to Administrative Committee. Within 30 days of the filing of the petition for reinstatement with the secretary, the board shall determine whether the deficiency has been cured. The board's written determination and the reinstatement petition shall be transmitted to the secretary within five days of the determination by the board. The secretary shall transmit a copy of the petition and the board's recommendation to each member of the Administrative Committee.

(f) Consideration by Administrative Committee. The Administrative Committee shall consider the reinstatement petition, together with the board's determination, pursuant to the requirements of Rule .0902(c)–(f) of this subchapter.

(g) Hearing Upon Denial of Petition for Reinstatement. The procedure for hearing upon the denial by the Administrative Committee of a petition for reinstatement shall be as provided in Section .1000 of this subchapter.

[History Note: Authority—Order of the North Carolina Supreme Court, October 7, 1987, 318 N.C. 711. Readopted effective December 8, 1994; amended effective March 7, 1996; amended effective March 6, 1997; amended December 10, 1999, effective February 3, 2000; amended effective March 3, 2005.]

.1525 [Reserved]

.1526 Effective Date

(a) The effective date of these rules shall be January 1, 1988.

(b) Active members licensed prior to July 1 of any calendar year shall meet the continuing legal education requirements of these rules for such year.

(c) Active members licensed after June 30 of any calendar year must meet the continuing legal education requirements of these rules for the next calendar year.

[History Note: Authority—Order of the North Carolina Supreme Court, October 7, 1987, 318 N.C. 711. Readopted effective December 8, 1994.]

.1527 Regulations

The following regulations (Section .1600 of the Rules of the North Carolina State Bar) for the continuing legal education program are hereby adopted and shall remain in effect until revised or amended by the board with the approval of the council. The board may adopt other regulations to implement the continuing legal education program with the approval of the council.

[History Note: Authority—Order of the North Carolina Supreme Court, October 7, 1987, 318 N.C. 711. Readopted effective December 8, 1994.]

SECTION .1600 REGULATIONS CONCERNING THE ADMINISTRATION OF THE CONTINUING LEGAL EDUCATION PROGRAM

.1601 General Requirements for Course Approval

(a) Approval. CLE activities may be approved upon the written application of a sponsor, other than an accredited sponsor, or of an active member on an individual program basis. An application for such CLE course approval shall meet the following requirements:

(1) If advance approval is requested by a sponsor, the application and supporting documentation, including one substantially complete set of the written materials to be distributed at the course or program, shall be submitted at least 50 days prior to the date on which the course or program is scheduled. If advance approval is requested by an active member, the application need not include a complete set of written materials.

(2) In all other cases, the application and supporting documentation shall be submitted by the sponsor not later than 50 days after the date the course or program was presented or prior to the end of the calendar year in which the course or program was presented, whichever is earlier. Active members requesting credit must submit the application and supporting documentation within 50 days after the date the course or program was presented or, if the 50 days have elapsed, as soon as practicable after receiving notice from the board that the course accreditation request was not submitted by the sponsor.

(3) The application shall be submitted on a form furnished by the board.

(4) The application shall contain all information requested on the form.

(5) The application shall be accompanied by a course outline or brochure that describes the content, identifies the teachers, lists the time devoted to each topic, and shows each date and location at which the program will be offered.

(6) The application shall include a detailed calculation of the total CLE hours and hours of professional responsibility.

(b) Course Quality and Materials. The application and materials provided shall reflect that the program to be offered meets the requirements of Rule .1519 of this subchapter. Sponsors, including accredited sponsors, and active members seeking credit for an approved activity shall furnish, upon request of the board, a copy of all materials presented and distributed at a CLE course or program. Written materials consisting merely of an outline without citation or explanatory notations generally will not be sufficient for approval. Any sponsor, including an accredited sponsor, who expects to conduct a CLE activity for which suitable written materials will not be made available to all attendees may obtain approval for that activity only by application to the board at least 50 days in advance of the presentation showing why written materials are not suitable or readily available for such a program.

(c) Facilities. Sponsors must provide a facility conductive to learning with sufficient space for taking notes.

(d) Computer-Based CLE: Verification of Attendance. The sponsor of an on-line course must have a reliable method for recording and verifying attendance. The sponsor of a CD-ROM course must demonstrate that there is a reliable method for the user or the sponsor to record and verify participation in the course. A participant may periodically log on and off of a computer-based CLE course provided the total time spent participating in the course is equal to or exceeds the credit hours assigned to the program. A copy of the record of attendance must be forwarded to the board within 30 days after a member completes his or her participation in the course.

(e) **Records.** Sponsors, including accredited sponsors, shall within 30 days after the course is concluded

(1) furnish to the board a list in alphabetical order, in an electronic format if available, of the names of all North Carolina attendees and their North Carolina State Bar membership numbers;

(2) remit to the board the appropriate sponsor fee; and, if payment is not received by the board within 30 days after the course is concluded, interest at the legal rate shall be incurred; provided, however, the board may waive such interest upon a showing of good cause by a sponsor; and

(3) furnish to the board a complete set of all written materials distributed to attendees at the course or program.

(f) **Announcement.** Accredited sponsors and sponsors who have advance approval for courses may include in their brochures or other course descriptions the information contained in the following illustration:

> This course [or seminar or program] has been approved by the Board of Continuing Legal Education of the North Carolina State Bar for continuing legal education credit in the amount of ___ hours, of which ___ hours will also apply in the area of professional responsibility. This course is not sponsored by the board.

(g) **Notice.** Sponsors not having advanced approval shall make no representation concerning the approval of the course for CLE credit by the board. The board will mail a notice of its decision on CLE activity approval requests within (45) days of their receipt when the request for approval is submitted before the program and within (45) days when the request is submitted after the program. Approval thereof will be deemed if the notice is not timely mailed. This automatic approval will not operate if the sponsor contributes to the delay by failing to provide the complete information requested by the board or if the board timely notifies the sponsor that the matter has been tabled and the reason therefor.

[History Note: Authority—Order of the North Carolina Supreme Court, October 7, 1987, 318 N.C. 711. Readopted effective December 8, 1994; amended effective October 1, 2003; amended effective March 3, 2005; amended effective March 6, 2008; amended effective October 7, 2010.]

.1602 Course Content Requirements

(a) **Professional Responsibility Courses on Stress, Substance Abuse, Chemical Dependency, and Debilitating Mental Conditions.** Accredited professional responsibility courses on stress, substance abuse, chemical dependency, and debilitating mental conditions shall concentrate on the relationship between stress, substance abuse, chemical dependency, debilitating mental conditions, and a lawyer's professional responsibilities. Such courses may also include (1) education on the prevention, detection, treatment and etiology of stress, substance abuse, chemical dependency, and debilitating mental conditions, and (2) information about assistance for chemically dependent or mentally impaired lawyers available through lawyers' professional organizations. No more than three hours of continuing education credit will be granted to any one such course or segment of a course.

(b) **Law School Courses.** Courses offered by an ABA accredited law school with respect to which academic credit may be earned may be approved activities. Computation of CLE credit for such courses shall be as prescribed in Rule .1605(a) of this subchapter. No more than 12 CLE hours in any year may be earned by such courses. No credit is available for law school courses attended prior to becoming an active member of the North Carolina State Bar.

(c) **Law Practice Management Courses.** A CLE accredited course on law practice management must satisfy the accreditation standards set forth in Rule .1519 of this subchapter with the primary objective of increasing the participant's professional competence and proficiency as a lawyer. The subject matter presented in an accredited course on law practice management shall bear a direct relationship to either substantive legal issues in managing a law practice or a lawyer's professional responsibilities, including avoidance of conflicts of interest, protecting confidential client information, supervising subordinate lawyers and nonlawyers, fee arrangements, managing a trust account, ethical legal advertising, and malpractice avoidance. The following are illustrative, non-exclusive examples of subject matter that may earn CLE credit: employment law relating to lawyers and law practice; business law relating to the formation and operation of a law firm; calendars, dockets and tickler systems; conflict screening and avoidance systems; law office disaster planning; handling of client files; communicating with clients; and trust accounting. If appropriate, a law practice management course may qualify for professional responsibility (ethics) CLE credit. The following are illustrative, non-exclusive examples of subject matter that will NOT receive CLE credit: marketing; networking/rainmaking; client cultivation; increasing productivity; developing a business plan; improving the profitability of a law practice; selling a law practice; and purchasing office equipment (including computer and accounting systems).

(d) **Skills and Training Courses.** A course that teaches a skill specific to the practice of law may be accredited for CLE if it satisfies the accreditation standards set forth in Rule .1519 of this subchapter with the primary objective of increasing the participant's professional competence and proficiency as a lawyer. The following are illustrative, non-exclusive examples of subject matter that may earn CLE credit:

legal writing; oral argument; courtroom presentation; and legal research. A course that provides general instruction in non-legal skills shall NOT be accredited. The following are illustrative, non-exclusive examples of subject matter that will NOT receive CLE credit: learning to use software for an application that is not specific to the practice of law (e.g. word processing); learning to use office equipment (except as permitted by paragraph (e) of this rule); public speaking; speed reading; efficiency training; personal money management or investing; career building; marketing; and general office management techniques.

(e) **Technology Courses.** A course on a specific information technology product, device, platform, application, or other technology solution (IT solution) may be accredited for CLE if the course satisfies the accreditation standards in Rule .1519 of this subchapter; specifically, the primary objective of the course must be to increase the participant's professional competence and proficiency as a lawyer. The following are illustrative, nonexclusive examples of courses that may earn CLE credit: electronic discovery software for litigation; document automation/assembly software; document management software; practice management software; digital forensics for litigation; and digital security. A course on the selection of an IT solution or the use of an IT solution to enhance a lawyer's proficiency as a lawyer or to improve law office management may be accredited if the requirements of paragraphs (c) and (d) of this rule are satisfied. A course that provides general instruction on an IT solution but does not include instruction on the practical application of the IT solution to the practice of law shall not be accredited. The following are illustrative, non-exclusive examples of subject matter that will NOT receive CLE credit: generic education on how to use a tablet computer, laptop computer, or smart phone; training courses on Microsoft Office, Excel, Access, Word, Adobe, etc. programs; and instruction in the use of a particular desktop or mobile operating system. No credit will be given to a course that is sponsored by a manufacturer, distributor, broker, or merchandiser of the IT solution. A sponsor may not accept compensation from a manufacturer, distributor, broker, or merchandiser of an IT solution in return for presenting a CLE program about the IT solution. Presenters may include representatives of a manufacturer, distributor, broker, or merchandiser of the IT solution but they may not be the only presenters at the course and they may not determine the content of the course.

(f) Activities That Shall Not Be Accredited. CLE credit will not be given for general and personal educational activities. The following are illustrative, non-exclusive examples of subject matter that will NOT receive CLE credit:

(1) courses within the normal college curriculum such as English, history, social studies, and psychology;

(2) courses that deal with the individual lawyer's human development, such as stress reduction, quality of life, or substance abuse unless a course on substance abuse or mental health satisfies the requirements of Rule .1602(c);

(3) courses designed primarily to sell services or products or to generate greater revenue, such as marketing or advertising (as distinguished from courses dealing with development of law office procedures and management designed to raise the level of service provided to clients).

(g) **Service to the Profession Training.** A course or segment of a course presented by a bar organization may be granted up to three hours of credit if the bar organization's course trains volunteer attorneys in service to the profession, and if such course or course segment meets the requirements of Rule .1519(2)–(7) and Rule .1601(b), (c), and (g) of this subchapter; if appropriate, up to three hours of professional responsibility credit may be granted for such course or course segment.

(h) **In–House CLE and Self–Study.** No approval will be provided for in-house CLE or self-study by attorneys, except those programs exempted by the board under Rule .1501(c)(10) of this subchapter or as provided in Rule .1604(e) of this subchapter.

(i) **Bar Review/Refresher Course.** Courses designed to review or refresh recent law school graduates or attorneys in preparation for any bar exam shall not be approved for CLE credit.

[History Note: Authority—Order of the North Carolina Supreme Court, October 7, 1987, 318 N.C. 711. Readopted effective December 8, 1994. Amended March 6, 1997; March 5, 1998; March 3, 1999; June 7, 2001; March 3, 2005; March 2, 2006; March 8, 2007; October 9, 2008; March 6, 2014.]

.1603 Accredited Sponsors

In order to receive designation as an "accredited sponsor" of courses, programs or other continuing legal education activities under Rule .1520(a) of this subchapter, the application of the sponsor must meet the following requirements:

(1) The application for accredited sponsor status shall be submitted on a form furnished by the board.

(2) The application shall contain all information requested on the form.

(3) The application shall be accompanied by course outlines or brochures that describe the content, identify the instructors, list the time devoted to each topic, show each date and location at which three programs have been sponsored in each of the last three consecutive years, and enclose the actual course materials.

(4) The application shall include a detailed calculation of the total CLE hours specified in each of the programs sponsored by the organization.

(5) The application shall reflect that the previous programs offered by the organization in continuing legal education have been of consistently high quality and would otherwise meet the standards set forth in Rule .1519 of this subchapter.

(6) Notwithstanding the provisions of Rule .1603(3), (4) and (5) above, any law school which has been approved by the North Carolina State Bar for purposes of qualifying its graduates for the North Carolina bar examination, may become an accredited sponsor upon application to the board.

[History Note: Authority—Order of the North Carolina Supreme Court, October 7, 1987, 318 N.C. 711. Readopted effective December 8, 1994.]

.1604 Accreditation of Prerecorded Simultaneous Broadcast, and Computer–Based Programs

(a) Presentation Including Prerecorded Material. An active member may receive credit for attendance at, or participation in, a presentation where prerecorded material is used. Prerecorded material may be either in a video or an audio format.

(b) Simultaneous Broadcast. An active member may receive credit for participation in a live presentation which is simultaneously broadcast by telephone, satellite, live web streaming (webcasting), or video conferencing equipment. The member may participate in the presentation by listening to or viewing the broadcast from a location that is remote from the origin of the broadcast. The broadcast may include prerecorded material provided it also includes a live question and answer session with the presenter.

(c) Accreditation Requirements. A member attending a prerecorded presentation is entitled to credit hours if

(1) the live presentation or the presentation from which the program is recorded would, if attended by an active member, be an accredited course; and

(2) all other conditions imposed by the rules in Section .1600 of this subchapter, or by the board in advance, are met.

(d) Minimum Registration and Verification of Attendance. A minimum of three active members must register for the presentation of a prerecorded program. This requirement does not apply to the presentation of a live broadcast by telephone, satellite, or video conferencing equipment. Attendance at a prerecorded or simultaneously broadcast (by telephone, satellite, or video conferencing) program must be verified by (1) the sponsor's report of attendance or (2) the execution of an affidavit of attendance by the participant.

(e) Computer–Based CLE. Effective January 1, 2014, a member may receive up to six hours of credit annually for participation in a course on CD–ROM or on-line. A CD–ROM course is an educational seminar on a compact disk that is accessed through the CD–ROM drive of the user's personal computer. An on-line course is an educational seminar available on a provider's website reached via the Internet.

(1) A member may apply up to six credit hours of computer-based CLE to a CLE deficit from a preceding calendar year. Any computer-based CLE credit hours applied to a deficit from a preceding year will be included in calculating the maximum of six hours of computer-based CLE allowed in the preceding calendar year. A member may carry over to the next calendar year no more than six credit hours of computer-based CLE pursuant to Rule .1518(b) of this subchapter. Any credit hours carried-over pursuant to Rule .1518(b) of this subchapter will be included in calculating the six hours of computer-based CLE allowed in any one calendar year.

(2) To be accredited, a computer-based CLE course must meet all of the conditions imposed by the rules in Section .1600 of this subchapter, or by the board in advance, except where otherwise noted, and be interactive, permitting the participant to communicate, via telephone, electronic mail, or a website bulletin board, with the presenter and/or other participants.

[History Note: Authority—Order of the North Carolina Supreme Court, October 7, 1987, 318 N.C. 711. Readopted effective December 8, 1994. Amended effective March 6, 1997; March 3, 2005; May 4, 2005; March 2, 2006; March 6, 2008; March 6, 2014.]

.1605 Computation of Credit

(a) Computation Formula. CLE and professional responsibility hours shall be computed by the following formula:

$$\frac{\text{Sum of the Total Minutes of Actual Instruction}}{60} = \text{Total Hours}$$

For example, actual instruction totaling 195 minutes would equal 3.25 hours toward CLE.

(b) Actual Instruction. Only actual education shall be included in computing the total hours of actual instruction. The following shall not be included:

(1) introductory remarks;

(2) breaks;

(3) business meetings;

(4) speeches in connection with banquets or other events which are primarily social in nature;

(5) question and answer sessions at a ratio in excess of 15 minutes per CLE hour and programs less than 30 minutes in length provided, however, that the limitation on question and answer sessions shall not limit the length of time that may be devoted to participatory CLE.

(c) Teaching. As a contribution to professionalism, credit may be earned for teaching in an approved continuing legal education activity or a continuing paralegal education activity held in North Carolina and approved pursuant to Section .0200 of Subchapter G of these rules. Presentations accompanied by thorough, high quality, readable, and carefully prepared written materials will qualify for CLE credit on the basis of three hours of credit for each thirty minutes of presentation. Repeat presentations qualify for one-half of the credits available for the initial presentation. For example, an initial presentation of 45 minutes would qualify for 4.5 hours of credit.

(d) Teaching Law Courses

(1) *Law School Courses.* If a member is not a full-time teacher at a law school in North Carolina who is eligible for the exemption in Rule .1517(b) of this subchapter, the member may earn CLE credit for teaching a course or a class in a quarter or semester-long course at an ABA accredited law school. A member may also earn CLE credit by teaching a course or a class at a law school licensed by the Board of Governors of the University of North Carolina, provided the law school is actively seeking accreditation from the ABA. If ABA accreditation is not obtained by a law school so licensed within three years of the commencement of classes, CLE credit will no longer be granted for teaching courses at the school.

(2) *Graduate School Courses.* Effective January 1, 2012, a member may earn CLE credit by teaching a course on substantive law or a class on substantive law in a quarter or semester-long course at a graduate school of an accredited university.

(3) *Courses at Paralegal Schools or Programs.* Effective January 1, 2006, a member may earn CLE credit by teaching a paralegal or substantive law course or a class in a quarter or semester-long course at an ABA approved paralegal school or program.

(4) *Credit Hours.* Credit for teaching activities described in Rule .1605(d)(1) - (3) above may be earned without regard to whether the course is taught online or in a classroom. Credit will be calculated according to the following formula:

(A) Teaching a Course. 3.5 Hours of CLE credit for every quarter hour of credit assigned to the course by the educational institution, or 5.0 Hours of CLE credit for every semester hour of credit assigned to the course by the educational institution. (For example: a 3–semester hour course will qualify for 15 hours of CLE credit).

(B) Teaching a Class. 1.0 Hour of CLE credit for every 50—60 minutes of teaching.

(5) *Other Requirements.* The member shall also complete the requirements set forth in Rule .1518(b) of this subchapter.

[History Note: Authority—Order of the North Carolina Supreme Court, October 7, 1987, 318 N.C. 711. Readopted effective December 8, 1994; amended effective March 3, 1999; amended effective October 1, 2003; amended effective November 16, 2006; amended effective August 23, 2012.]

.1606 Fees

(a) Sponsor Fee—The sponsor fee, a charge paid directly by the sponsor, shall be paid by all sponsors of approved activities presented in North Carolina and by accredited sponsors located in North Carolina for approved activities wherever presented, except that no sponsor fee is required where approved activities are offered without charge to attendees. In any other instance, payment of the fee by the sponsor is optional. The amount of the fee, per approved CLE hour per active member of the North Carolina State Bar in attendance, is $3.00. This amount shall be allocated as follows: $1.25 to the Board of Continuing Legal Education to administer the CLE program; $1.00 to the Chief Justice's Commission on Professionalism ; $.050 to the North Carolina Equal Access to Justice Commission; and $0.25 to the State Bar to administer the funds distributed to the commissions. The fee is computed as shown in the following formula and example which assumes a 6–hour course attended by 100 North Carolina lawyers seeking CLE credit :

Fee: $3.00 × Total Approved CLE Hours (6) × Number of NC Attendees (100) = Total Sponsor Fee($1800)

(b) Attendee Fee—The attendee fee is paid by the North Carolina attorney who requests credit for a program for which no sponsor fee was paid. An attorney will be invoiced for any attendees fees owed following the submission of the attorney's annual report form pursuant to Rule .1522(a) of this subchapter. Payment shall be remitted within 30 (thirty) days of the date of the invoice. The amount of the fee, per approved CLE hour for which the attorney claims credit, is $3.00. This amount shall be allocated as follows: $1.25 to the Board of Continuing Legal Education to administer the CLE program; $1.00 to the Chief Justice's Commission on Professionalism ; $.050 to the North Carolina Equal Access to Justice Commission; and $0.25 to the State Bar to administer the funds distributed to the commissions. It is computed as shown in the following formula and example which assumes that the attorney attended an activity approved for 3 hours of CLE credit :

Fee: $3.00 × Total Approved CLE hours (3.0) = Total Attendee Fee ($9.00)

(c) Fee Review—The board will review the level of the fee at least annually and adjust it as necessary to maintain adequate finances for prudent operation of the board in a nonprofit manner. The council shall annually review the assessments for the Chief Justice's Commission on Professionalism and the North Carolina Equal Access to Justice Commission and adjust them as necessary to maintain adequate finances for the operation of the commissions.

(d) Uniform Application and Financial Responsibility—The fee shall be applied uniformly without exceptions or other preferential treatment for a sponsor or attendee. The board shall make reasonable efforts to collect the sponsor fee from the sponsor of a CLE program when appropriate under Rule .1606(a) above. However, whenever a sponsor fee is not paid by the sponsor of a program, regardless of the reason, the lawyer requesting CLE credit for the program shall be financially responsible for the fee.

[History Note: Authority—Order of the North Carolina Supreme Court, October 7, 1987, 318 N.C. 711. Readopted effective December 8, 1994; amended effective December 30, 1998; amended effective October 1, 2003; amended effective February 5, 2009; amended effective October 8, 2009.]

.1607 [Reserved]

.1608 [Reserved]

.1609 [Reserved]

.1610 [Reserved]

.1611 [Reserved]

SECTION .1700 THE PLAN OF LEGAL SPECIALIZATION

.1701 Purpose

The purpose of this plan of certified legal specialization is to assist in the delivery of legal services to the public by identifying to the public those lawyers who have demonstrated special knowledge, skill, and proficiency in a specific field, so that the public can more closely match its needs with available services; and to improve the competency of the bar by establishing an additional incentive for lawyers to participate in continuing legal education and meet the other requirements of specialization.

[History Note: Statutory Authority G.S. 84–23. Readopted effective December 8, 1994.]

.1702 Jurisdiction: Authority

The Council of the North Carolina State Bar (the council) with the approval of the Supreme Court of North Carolina hereby establishes the Board of Legal Specialization (board) as a standing committee of the council, which board shall be the authority having jurisdiction under state law over the subject of specialization of lawyers.

[History Note: Statutory Authority G.S. 84–23. Readopted effective December 8, 1994.]

.1703 Operational Responsibility

The responsibility for operating the specialization program rests with the board, subject to the statutes governing the practice of law, the authority of the council and the rules of governance of the board.

[History Note: Statutory Authority G.S. 84–23. Readopted effective December 8, 1994.]

.1704 Size of Board

The board shall have nine members, six of whom must be attorneys in good standing and authorized to practice law in the state of North Carolina. The lawyer members of the board shall be representative of the legal profession and shall include lawyers who are in general practice as well as those who specialize.

[History Note: Statutory Authority G.S. 84–23. Readopted effective December 8, 1994.]

.1705 Lay Participation

The board shall have three members who are not licensed attorneys.

[History Note: Statutory Authority G.S. 84–23. Readopted effective December 8, 1994.]

.1706 Appointment of Members; When; Removal

The members of the board shall be appointed by the council. The first members of the board shall be appointed as of the quarterly meeting of the council following the creation of the board. Thereafter, members shall be appointed annually as of the same quarterly meeting. Vacancies occurring by reason of death, resignation, or removal shall be filled by appointment of the council at the next quarterly meeting following the event giving rise to the vacancy, and the person so appointed shall serve for the balance of the vacated term. Any member of the board may be removed at any time by an affirmative vote of a majority of the members of the council in session at a regularly called meeting.

[History Note: Statutory Authority G.S. 84–23. Readopted effective December 8, 1994.]

.1707 Term of Office

Each member who is appointed to the board shall serve for a term of three years beginning as of the first day of the month following the date on which the appointment is made by the council. See, however, Rule .1708 of this subchapter.

[History Note: Statutory Authority G.S. 84–23. Readopted effective December 8, 1994.]

.1708 Staggered Terms

It is intended that members of the board shall be elected to staggered terms such that three members are appointed in each year. Of the initial board, three members (two lawyers and one nonlawyer) shall be elected to terms of one year; three members (two lawyers and one nonlawyer) shall be elected to terms of two years; and three members (two lawyers and one nonlawyer) shall be elected to terms of three years. Thereafter, three members (two lawyers and one nonlawyer) shall be elected in each year.

[History Note: Statutory Authority G.S. 84–23. Readopted effective December 8, 1994.]

.1709. Succession

Each member of the board shall be entitled to serve for one full three-year term and to succeed himself or herself for one additional three-year term. Thereafter, no person may be reappointed without having been off of the board for at least three years: provided, however, that any member who is designated chairperson at the time that the member's second three-year term expires may serve one additional year on the board in the capacity of chair.

[History Note: Statutory Authority G.S. 84–23. Readopted effective December 8, 1994; amended effective October 9, 2008; March 5, 2015.]

.1710 Appointment of Chairperson

The chairperson of the board shall be appointed from time to time as necessary by the council from among the lawyer members of the board. The term of such individual as chairperson shall be one year. The chairperson may be reappointed thereafter during his or her tenure on the board. The chairperson shall preside at all meetings of the board, shall prepare and present to the council the annual report of the board, and generally shall represent the board in its dealings with the public.

[History Note: Statutory Authority G.S. 84–23. Readopted effective December 8, 1994.]

.1711 Appointment of Vice-Chairperson

The vice-chairperson of the board shall be appointed from time to time as necessary by the council from among the lawyer members of the board. The term of such individual as vice-chairperson shall be one year. The vice-chairperson may be reappointed thereafter during his or her tenure on the board. The vice-chairperson shall preside at and represent the board in the absence of the chairperson and shall perform such other duties as may be assigned to him or her by the chairperson or by the board.

[History Note: Statutory Authority G.S. 84–23. Readopted effective December 8, 1994.]

.1712 Source of Funds

Funding for the program carried out by the board shall come from such application fees, examination fees, course accreditation fees, annual fees or recertification fees as the board, with the approval of the council, may establish.

[History Note: Statutory Authority G.S. 84–23. Readopted effective December 8, 1994.]

.1713 Fiscal Responsibility

All funds of the board shall be considered funds of the North Carolina State Bar and shall be administered and disbursed accordingly.

(a) Maintenance of Accounts: Audit. The North Carolina State Bar shall maintain a separate account for funds of the board such that such funds and expenditure therefrom can be readily identified. The accounts of the board shall be audited on an annual basis in connection with the audits of the North Carolina State Bar.

(b) Investment Criteria. The funds of the board shall be handled, invested and reinvested in accordance with investment policies adopted by the council for the handling of dues, rents and other revenues received by the North Carolina State Bar in carrying out its official duties.

(c) Disbursement. Disbursement of funds of the board shall be made by or under the direction of the secretary-treasurer of the North Carolina State Bar.

[History Note: Statutory Authority G.S. 84–23. Readopted effective December 8, 1994.]

.1714 Meetings

The annual meeting of the board shall be held in October of each year in connection with the annual meeting of the North Carolina State Bar. The board by resolution may set regular meeting dates and places. Special meetings of the board may be called at any time upon notice given by the chairperson, the vice-chairperson or any two members of the board. Notice of meeting shall be given at least two days prior to the meeting by mail, telegram, facsimile transmission, or telephone. A quorum of the board for conducting its official business shall be four or more of the members serving at the time of the meeting.

[History Note: Statutory Authority G.S. 84–23. Readopted effective December 8, 1994.]

.1715 Annual Report

The board shall prepare at least annually a report of its activities and shall present same to the council one month prior to its annual meeting.

[History Note: Statutory Authority G.S. 84–23. Readopted effective December 8, 1994.]

.1716 Powers and Duties of the Board

Subject to the general jurisdiction of the council and the North Carolina Supreme Court, the board shall have jurisdiction of all matters pertaining to regulation of certification of specialists in the practice of law and shall have the power and duty

(1) to administer the plan;

(2) subject to the approval of the council and the Supreme Court, to designate areas in which certificates of specialty may be granted and define the scope and limits of such specialities and to provide procedures for the achievement of these purposes;

(3) to appoint, supervise, act on the recommendations of and consult with specialty committees as hereinafter identified;

(4) to make and publish standards for the certification of specialists, upon the board's own initiative or upon consideration of recommendations made by the specialty committees, such standards to be designed to produce a uniform level of competence among the various specialties in accordance with the nature of the specialties;

(5) to certify specialists or deny, suspend or revoke the certification of specialists upon the board's own initiative, upon recommendations made by the specialty committees or upon requests for review of recommendations made by the specialty committees;

(6) to establish and publish procedures, rules, regulations, and bylaws to implement this plan;

(7) to propose and request the council to make amendments to this plan whenever appropriate;

(8) to cooperate with other boards or agencies in enforcing standards of professional conduct and to report apparent violations of the Rules of Professional Conduct to the appropriate disciplinary authority;

(9) to evaluate and approve, or disapprove, any and all continuing legal education courses, or educational alternatives, for the purpose of meeting the continuing legal education requirements established by the board for the certification of specialists and in connection therewith to determine the specialties for which credit shall be given and the number of hours of credit to be given in cooperation with the providers of continuing legal education; to determine whether and what credit is to be allowed for educational alternatives, including other methods of legal education, teaching, writing and the like; to issue rules and regulations for obtaining approval of continuing legal education courses and educational alternatives; to publish or cooperate with others in publishing current lists of approved continuing legal education courses and educational alternatives; and to encourage and assist law schools, organizations providing continuing legal education, local bar associations and other groups engaged in continuing legal education to offer and maintain programs of continuing legal education designed to develop, enhance and maintain the skill and competence of legal specialists;

(10) to cooperate with other organizations, boards, and agencies engaged in the recognition of legal specialists or concerned with the topic of legal specialization including, but not limited to, utilizing appropriate and qualified organizations that are ABA accredited, to prepare and administer the written specialty examinations for specialties based predominantly on federal law;

(11) notwithstanding any conflicting provision of the certification standards for any area of specialty, to direct any of the specialty committees not to administer a specialty examination if, in the judgment of the board, there are insufficient applicants or such would otherwise not be in the best interest of the specialization program.

[History Note: Statutory Authority G.S. 84–23. Readopted effective December 8, 1994; amended effective November 16, 2006.]

.1717 Retained Jurisdiction of the Council

The council retains jurisdiction with respect to the following matters:

(1) upon recommendation of the board, establishing areas in which certificates of specialty may be granted;

(2) amending this plan;

(3) hearing appeals taken from actions of the board;

(4) establishing or approving fees to be charged in connection with the plan;

(5) regulating attorney advertisements of specialization under the Rules of Professional Conduct.

[History Note: Statutory Authority G.S. 84–23. Readopted effective December 8, 1994.]

.1718 Privileges Conferred and Limitations Imposed

The board in the implementation of this plan shall not alter the following privileges and responsibilities of certified specialists and other lawyers.

(1) No standard shall be approved which shall in any way limit the right of a certified specialist to practice in all fields of law. Subject to Canon 6 of the Rules of Professional Conduct, any lawyer, alone or in association with any other lawyer, shall have the right to practice in all fields of law, even though he or she is certified as a specialist in a particular field of law.

(2) No lawyer shall be required to be certified as a specialist in order to practice in the field of law covered by that specialty. Subject to Canon 6 of the North Carolina Rules of Professional Conduct, any lawyer, alone or in association with any other lawyer, shall have the right to practice in any field of law, or

advertise his or her availability to practice in any field of law consistent with Canon 2 of the Rules of Professional Conduct, even though he or she is not certified as a specialist in that field.

(3) All requirements for and all benefits to be derived from certification as a specialist are individual and may not be fulfilled by nor attributed to the law firm of which the specialist may be a member.

(4) Participation in the program shall be on a completely voluntary basis.

(5) A lawyer may be certified as a specialist in no more than two fields of law.

(6) When a client is referred by another lawyer to a lawyer who is a recognized specialist under this plan on a matter within the specialist's field of law, such specialist shall not take advantage of the referral to enlarge the scope of his or her representation and, consonant with any requirements of the Rules of Professional Conduct, such specialist shall not enlarge the scope of representation of a referred client outside the area of the specialty field.

(7) Any lawyer certified as a specialist under this plan shall be entitled to advertise that he or she is a "Board Certified Specialist" in his or her specialty to the extent permitted by the Rules of Professional Conduct.

[History Note: Statutory Authority G.S. 84-23. Readopted effective December 8, 1994.]

.1719 Specialty Committees

(a) The board shall establish a separate specialty committee for each specialty in which specialists are to be certified. Each specialty committee shall be composed of seven members appointed by the board, one of whom shall be designated annually by the chairperson of the board as chairperson of the specialty committee. Members of each specialty committee shall be lawyers licensed and currently in good standing to practice law in this state who, in the judgment of the board, are competent in the field of law to be covered by the specialty. Members shall hold office for three years, except those members initially appointed who shall serve as hereinafter designated. Members shall be appointed by the board to staggered terms of office and the initial appointees shall serve as follows: two shall serve for one year after appointment; two shall serve for two years after appointment; and three shall serve for three years after appointment. Appointment by the board to a vacancy shall be for the remaining term of the member leaving the specialty committee. All members shall be eligible for reappointment to not more than one additional three-year term after having served one full three-year term, provided, however, that the board may reappoint the chairperson of a committee to a third three-year term if the board determines that the reappointment is in the best interest of the specialization program. Meetings of the specialty committee shall be held at regular intervals at such times, places and upon such notices as the specialty committee may from time to time prescribe or upon direction of the board.

(b) Each specialty committee shall advise and assist the board in carrying out the board's objectives and in the implementation and regulation of this plan in that specialty. Each specialty committee shall advise and make recommendations to the board as to standards for the specialty and the certification of individual specialists in that specialty. Each specialty committee shall be charged with actively administering the plan in its specialty and with respect to that specialty shall

(1) recommend to the board reasonable and nondiscriminatory standards applicable to that specialty;

(2) make recommendations to the board for certification, continued certification, denial, suspension, or revocation of certification of specialists and for procedures with respect thereto;

(3) administer procedures established by the board for applications for certification and continued certification as a specialist and for denial, suspension, or revocation of such certification;

(4) administer examinations and other testing procedures, if applicable, investigate references of applicants and, if deemed advisable, seek additional information regarding applicants for certification or continued certification as specialists;

(5) make recommendations to the board concerning the approval of and credit to be allowed for continuing legal education courses, or educational alternatives, in the specialty;

(6) perform such other duties and make such other recommendations as may be delegated to or requested of the specialty committee by the board.

(c) The board may appoint advisory members to a specialty committee to assist with the development, administration, and grading of the examination, the drafting of standards for a subspecialty, and any other activity set forth in paragraph (b) of this rule. Advisory members shall be non-voting except as to any specific activity delegated to the advisory members by the board or by the chair of the specialty committee, including the evaluation of applications for certification. No more than five advisory members may be appointed to a specialty committee. Advisory members shall be lawyers licensed and currently in good standing to practice law in this state who, in the judgment of the board, are competent in the field of law to be covered by the specialty. Advisory members shall hold office for an initial term of three years and shall thereafter serve at the discretion of the board for not more than two additional three-year terms. Appointment by the board to a vacancy shall be for the remaining term, if any, of the advisory member being replaced.

[History Note: Statutory Authority G.S. 84-23. Readopted effective December 8, 1994; amended effective November 7, 1996; amended effective March 10, 2011.]

.1720 Minimum Standards for Certification of Specialists

(a) To qualify for certification as a specialist, a lawyer applicant must pay any required fee, comply with the following minimum standards, and meet any other standards established by the board for the particular area of specialty.

(1) The applicant must be licensed in a jurisdiction of the United States for at least five years immediately preceding his or her application and must be licensed in North Carolina for at least three years immediately preceding his or her application. The applicant must be currently in good standing to practice law in this state and the applicant's disciplinary record with the courts, the North Carolina State Bar, and any other government licensing agency must support qualification in the specialty.

(2) The applicant must make a satisfactory showing according to objective and verifiable standards, as determined by the board after advice from the appropriate specialty committee, of substantial involvement in the specialty during the five calendar years immediately preceding the calendar year of application. Such substantial involvement shall be defined as to each specialty from a consideration of its nature, complexity, and differences from other fields and from consideration of the kind and extent of effort and experience necessary to demonstrate competence in that specialty. It is a measurement of actual experience within the particular specialty according to any of several standards. It may be measured by the time spent on legal work within the areas of the specialty, the number or type of matters handled within a certain period of time, or any combination of these or other appropriate factors. However, within each specialty, experience requirements should be measured by objective standards. In no event should they be either so restrictive as to unduly limit certification of lawyers as specialists or so lax as to make the requirement of substantial involvement meaningless as a criterion of competence. Substantial involvement may vary from specialty to specialty, but, if measured on a time-spent basis, in no event shall the time spent in practice in the specialty be less than 25 percent of the total practice of a lawyer engaged in a normal full-time practice. Reasonable and uniform practice equivalents may be established including, but not limited to, successful pursuit of an advance educational degree, teaching, judicial, government, or corporate legal experience.

(3) The applicant must make a satisfactory showing, as determined by the board after advice from the appropriate specialty committee, of continuing legal education in the specialty accredited by the board for the specialty, the minimum being an average of 12 hours of credit for continuing legal education, or its equivalent, for each of the three calendar years immediately preceding application. Upon establishment of a new specialty, this standard may be satisfied in such manner as the board, upon advice from the appropriate specialty committee, may prescribe or may be waived if, and to the extent, accreditable continuing legal education courses have not been available during the three years immediately preceding establishment of the specialty.

(4) The applicant must make a satisfactory showing, as determined by the board after advice from the appropriate specialty committee, of qualification in the specialty through peer review. The applicant must provide, as references, the names of at least ten lawyers, all of whom are licensed and currently in good standing to practice law in this state, or in any state, or judges, who are familiar with the competence and qualification of the applicant as a specialist. None of the references may be persons related to the applicant or, at the time of application, a partner of or otherwise associated with the applicant in the practice of law. The applicant by his or her application consents to confidential inquiry by the board or appropriate disciplinary body and other persons regarding the applicant's competence and qualifications to be certified as a specialist. An applicant must receive a minimum of five favorable peer reviews to be considered by the board for compliance with this standard.

(A) Each specialty committee shall evaluate the information provided by an applicant's references to make a recommendation to the board as to the applicant's qualification in the specialty through peer review. The evaluation shall include a determination of the weight to be given to each peer review and shall take into consideration a reference's years of practice, primary practice areas and experience in the specialty, and the context in which a reference knows the applicant.

(5) The applicant must achieve a satisfactory score on a written examination designed to test the applicant's knowledge and ability in the specialty for which certification is applied. The examination must be applied uniformly to all applicants within each specialty area. The board shall assure that the contents and grading of the examination are designed to produce a uniform level of competence among the various specialties.

(b) All matters concerning the qualification of an applicant for certification, including, but not limited to, applications, references, tests and test scores, files, reports, investigations, hearings, findings, recommendations, and adverse determinations shall be confidential so far as is consistent with the effective administration of this plan, fairness to the applicant and due process of law.

(c) The board may adopt uniform rules waiving the requirements of Rules .1720(a)(4) and (5) above for members of a specialty committee, including advisory members, at the time that the initial written examination for that specialty or any subspecialty of the specialty is given, and permitting said members to file applications to become a board certified specialist in that specialty upon compliance with all other required minimum standards for certification of specialists.

(d) Upon written request of the applicant and with the recommendation of the appropriate specialty committee, the board may for good cause shown waive strict compliance with the criteria relating to substantial involvement, continuing legal education, or peer review, as those requirements are set forth in the standards for certification for specialization. However, there shall be no waiver of the requirements that the applicant pass a written examination and be licensed to practice law in North Carolina for five years preceding the application.

[History Note: Statutory Authority G.S. 84–23. Readopted effective December 8, 1994; amended effective March 3, 2005; March 10, 2011; March 8, 2012; August 23, 2012; August 27, 2013.]

.1721 Minimum Standards for Continued Certification of Specialists

(a) The period of certification as a specialist shall be five years. During such period the board or appropriate specialty committee may require evidence from the specialist of his or her continued qualification for certification as a specialist, and the specialist must consent to inquiry by the board, or appropriate specialty committee of lawyers and judges, the appropriate disciplinary body, or others in the community regarding the specialist's continued competence and qualification to be certified as a specialist. Application for and approval of continued certification as a specialist shall be required prior to the end of each five-year period. To qualify for continued certification as a specialist, a lawyer applicant must pay any required fee, must demonstrate to the board with respect to the specialty both continued knowledge of the law of this state and continued competence and must comply with the following minimum standards.

(1) The specialist's disciplinary record with the courts, the North Carolina State Bar, and any other government licensing agency supports qualification in the specialty.

(2) The specialist must make a satisfactory showing, as determined by the board after advice from the appropriate specialty committee, of substantial involvement in the specialty during the entire period of certification as a specialist. Substantial involvement for continued certification shall be determined in accordance with the principles set forth in Rule .1720(a)(2) of this subchapter and the specific standards for each specialty. In addition, unless prohibited or limited by the standards for a particular specialty, the following judicial service may be substituted for the equivalent years of practice experience if the applicant's judicial service included presiding over cases in the specialty: service as a full-time state or federal trial, appellate, or bankruptcy judge (including service as a federal magistrate judge); service as a judge for the courts of a federally recognized Indian tribe; service as an administrative law judge for the Social Security Administration; and service as a commissioner or deputy commissioner of the Industrial Commission.

(3) The specialist must make a satisfactory showing, as determined by the board after advice from the appropriate specialty committee, of continuing legal education accredited by the board for the specialty during the period of certification as a specialist, the minimum being an average of 12 hours of credit for continuing legal education, or its equivalent, for each year during the entire period of certification as a specialist.

(4) The specialist must comply with the requirements set forth in Rules .1720(a)(1) and (4) of this subchapter.

(b) Upon written request of the applicant and with the recommendation of the appropriate specialty committee, the board may for good cause shown waive strict compliance with the criteria relating to substantial involvement, continuing legal education, or peer review, as those requirements are set forth in the standards for continued certification. Before or after taking a continuing legal education course that is not in the specialty or a related field, a specialist may petition the board to approve the program as satisfying the continuing legal education criteria for recertification. The petition shall show the relevancy of the program to the specialist's proficiency as a specialist, and be referred to the specialty committee for its recommendation prior to a decision by the board.

(c) After the period of initial certification, a specialist may request, in advance and in writing, approval from the board for a waiver of one year of the substantial involvement necessary to satisfy the standards for the specialist's next recertification. The specialist may request a waiver of one year of substantial involvement for every five years that the specialist has met the substantial involvement standard beginning with the period of initial certification. However, none of the years for which a waiver is requested may be consecutive. When a waiver of the substantial involvement requirement is granted, the specialist must satisfy all of the other requirements for recertification.

[History Note: Statutory Authority G.S. 84–23. Readopted effective December 8, 1994; amended effective March 6, 2002; February 5, 2009; March 8, 2012; August 27, 2013.]

.1722 Establishment of Additional Standards

The board may establish, on its own initiative or upon the specialty committee's recommendation, additional or more stringent standards for certification than those provided in Rules .1720 and .1721 of this subchapter. Additional standards or requirements established under this rule need not be the same for initial certification and continued certification as a specialist. It is the intent of the plan that all requirements for certification or recertification in any area of specialty shall be no more or less stringent than the requirements in any other area of specialty.

[History Note: Statutory Authority G.S. 84–23. Readopted effective December 8, 1994.]

.1723 Revocation or Suspension of Certification as a Specialist

(a) Automatic Revocation. The board shall revoke its certification of a lawyer as a specialist if the lawyer is disbarred or receives a disciplinary suspension from the North Carolina State Bar, a North Carolina court of law, or, if the lawyer is licensed in another jurisdiction in the United States, from a court of law or the regulatory authority of that jurisdiction. Revocation shall be automatic without regard for any stay of the suspension period granted by the disciplinary authority. This provision shall apply to discipline received on or after the effective date of this provision.

(b) Discretionary Revocation or Suspension. The board may revoke its certification of a lawyer as a specialist if the specialty is terminated or may suspend or revoke such certification if it is determined, upon the board's own initiative or upon recommendation of the appropriate specialty committee and after hearing before the board as provided in Rule .1802 and Rule .1803, that

(1) the certification of the lawyer as a specialist was made contrary to the rules and regulations of the board;

(2) the lawyer certified as a specialist made a false representation, omission or misstatement of material fact to the board or appropriate specialty committee;

(3) the lawyer certified as a specialist has failed to abide by all rules and regulations promulgated by the board;

(4) the lawyer certified as a specialist has failed to pay the fees required;

(5) the lawyer certified as a specialist no longer meets the standards established by the board for the certification of specialists;

(6) the lawyer certified as a specialist received public discipline from the North Carolina State Bar on or after the effective date of this provision, other than suspension or disbarment from practice, and the board finds that the conduct for which the professional discipline was received reflects adversely on the specialization program and the lawyer's qualification as a specialist; or

(7) the lawyer certified as a specialist was sanctioned or received public discipline on or after the effective date of this provision from any state or federal court or, if the lawyer is licensed in another jurisdiction, from the regulatory authority of that jurisdiction in the United States, and the board finds that the conduct for which the sanctions or professional discipline was received reflects adversely on the specialization program and the lawyer's qualification as a specialist.

(c) Report to Board. A lawyer certified as a specialist has a duty to inform the board promptly of any fact or circumstance described in Rules .1723(a) and (b) above.

(d) Reinstatement. If the board revokes its certification of a lawyer as a specialist, the lawyer cannot again be certified as a specialist unless he or she so qualifies upon application made as if for initial certification as a specialist and upon such other conditions as the board may prescribe. If the board suspends certification of a lawyer as a specialist, such certification cannot be reinstated except upon the lawyer's application therefore and compliance with such conditions and requirements as the board may prescribe.

[History Note: Statutory Authority G.S. 84–23. Readopted effective December 8, 1994; amended effective February 5, 2004.]

.1724 Right to Hearing and Appeal to Council

A lawyer who is denied certification or continued certification as a specialist or whose certification is suspended or revoked shall have the right to a hearing before the board and, thereafter, the right to appeal the ruling made thereon by the board to the council under such rules and regulations as the board and council may prescribe. (See Section .1800 of this subchapter.)

[History Note: Statutory Authority G.S. 84–23. Readopted effective December 8, 1994.]

.1725 Areas of Specialty

There are hereby recognized the following specialties:

(a) bankruptcy law

(1) consumer bankruptcy law

(2) business bankruptcy law

(b) estate planning and probate law

(c) real property law

(1) real property—residential

(2) real property—business, commercial, and industrial

(d) family law

(e) criminal law

(1) state criminal law

(2) juvenile delinquency law

(f) immigration law

(g) workers' compensation

(h) Social Security disability law

(i) elder law

(j) appellate practice

(k) trademark law

[History Note: Statutory Authority G.S. 84–23. Readopted effective December 8, 1994. Amended effective July 29, 1998; February 27, 2003; February 5, 2009; March 8, 2012; March 6, 2014.]

.1726 Certification Standards of the Specialties of Bankruptcy Law, Estate Planning and Probate Law, Real Property Law, Family Law, and Criminal Law

Previous decisions approving the certification standards for the areas of specialty listed above are hereby reaffirmed.

[History Note: Statutory Authority G.S. 84–23. Readopted effective December 8, 1994.]

SECTION .1800 HEARING AND APPEAL RULES OF THE BOARD OF LEGAL SPECIALIZATION

.1801 Reconsideration of Applications, Failure of Written Examinations and Appeals

(a) Applications Incomplete and/or Applicants Not in Compliance With Standards for Certification.

(1) *Incomplete Applications.* The executive director of the North Carolina State Bar Board of Legal Specialization (the board) will review every application to determine if the application is complete. The applicant will be notified of the incompleteness of his or her application. The applicant must submit the completed application within 21 days of the date of mailing of the notice. If the applicant fails to provide the required information for the application during the requisite time period, the executive director will refer the application to the specialty committee for review.

(2) *Applicant Not in Compliance.* The executive director shall refer to the specialty committee for review any application which appears complete on its face but which does not satisfactorily demonstrate compliance with the standards for certification in the specialty area for which certification is sought.

(3) *Specialty Committee Action.* The specialty committee shall review the incomplete applications and the applications not in compliance with the standards for certification. After reviewing the applications, the specialty committee shall recommend to the board the acceptance or rejection of the applications. The specialty committee shall notify the board of its recommendations in writing and the reason for any negative recommendation must be specified. The specialty committee must complete the above process within 14 days of receiving the applications.

(4) *Notification to Applicant of the Specialty Committee's Action.* The executive director shall promptly notify the applicant in writing of the specialty committee's recommendation of rejection of the application. The notification must specify the reason for the recommendation of rejection of the application. In addition, the notification shall inform the applicant of his or her right to petition the board for review of the application or request a hearing before the board.

(5) *Petition for Review by the Board.* Within 21 days of the mailing of the notice from the executive director that an application has been recommended for rejection by the specialty committee, the applicant may petition the board for review. The petition may be informal (e.g., by letter), but should include the date on which notice of the recommendation of rejection was received and the reasons for which the applicant believes the specialty committee's recommendation of rejection should not be accepted.

(6) *Review of Petition by the Board.* A three-member panel of the board, to be appointed by the chairperson of the board, shall review and take action by a majority of the panel upon the petition and notify the applicant of the board's decision. The notification shall inform the applicant of his or her right to appeal the decision to the North Carolina State Bar Council (the council) if the board's action is unfavorable to the applicant.

(7) *Request for Hearing.* In lieu of a petition for review, an applicant may request a hearing before the board. The applicant shall notify the board through its executive director in writing of such request for a hearing within 21 days of the mailing of the notice regarding the specialty committee's recommendation of rejection of the application. The applicant shall set forth the grounds for the hearing before the board. In such a request, the applicant shall list the names of prospective witnesses and identify documentation and other evidence to be introduced at the hearing before the board. The applicant shall be notified of the

board's decision, and if the board's decision is unfavorable to the applicant, the applicant will be notified of his or her right to appeal the board's decision to the council.

(8) *Hearing Procedures.*

(A) Notice: Time and Place of Hearing—The chairperson of the board shall fix the time and place of the hearing as soon as practicable after the applicant's request for hearing is received. The applicant shall be notified of the hearing date. Such notice shall be given to the applicant at least 10 days prior to the time fixed for the hearing.

(B) Quorum—A panel of three members of the board, as appointed by the chairperson, shall be necessary to conduct the hearing with the majority of those in attendance necessary to decide upon the matter.

(C) Representation by Counsel and Witnesses—The applicant may be represented by counsel or represent himself or herself at such hearing. The applicant may offer witnesses and documents and may cross-examine any witness.

(D) Written Briefs—The applicant is urged to submit a written brief (in quadruplicate) 10 days prior to the hearing to the executive director for distribution to the panel in support of his or her position. However, written briefs are not required.

(E) Depositions—Should the applicant or executive director desire to take a deposition prior to the board hearing of any voluntary witness who cannot attend the board hearing, such intention to take, and request to take, the deposition of a witness may be applied for in writing to the chairperson of the board together with a written consent signed by the potential witness that he or she will give a deposition for one party and a statement to the effect that the witness cannot attend the hearing along with the reason for such unavailability. The party seeking to take the deposition of a witness shall state in detail as to what the witness is expected to testify. If the chairperson is satisfied that such deposition from a possible witness will be relevant to the issue in question before the board, then the chairperson will authorize said taking of the deposition. The chairperson will also designate the executive director or a member of the specialty committee to be present at the deposition. The deposition may be taken orally or by video. Any refusal of the taking of the deposition by the chairperson shall be reviewed by the board at the request of the applicant. The cost connected with taking the deposition shall be borne by the party requesting the deposition.

(F) Continuances—Motions for continuance of the hearing should be made to the chairperson of the board and such motions will be granted or denied by the chairperson of the board.

(G) Burden of Proof: Preponderance of the Evidence—The panel of the board shall apply the preponderance of the evidence rule in determining whether or not to accept the application for certification. The burden of proof is upon the applicant.

(H) Conduct of Hearings: Rights of Parties

(i) Hearings shall be reported by a certified court reporter. The applicant shall pay the costs associated with obtaining the court reporter's services for the hearing. The applicant shall pay the costs of the transcript and shall arrange for the preparation of the transcript with the court reporter. The applicant shall be taxed with all other costs of the hearing, but such costs shall not include any compensation to the members of the board before whom the hearing is conducted. The board in its discretion may refund to the applicant all or some portion of the necessary costs incurred as a result of the hearing.

(ii) The applicant may retain counsel at all stages of the investigation and at all meetings. The applicant and his or her counsel shall have the right to attend all hearings.

(iii) Oral evidence at hearings shall be taken only on oath or affirmation. The applicant shall have the right to testify unless he or she specifically waives such right or fails to appear at the hearing. If the applicant does not testify on his or her behalf, the applicant may be called and examined by the panel of the board, the executive director, and any member of the specialty committee. The applicant's failure to appear at the hearing ordered by the board, after receipt of written notice, shall constitute a waiver of the applicant's right to a hearing before the board.

(iv) At any hearing, the panel of the board, the executive director, any member of the appropriate specialty committee, and the applicant shall have these rights: (a) to call and examine witnesses; (b) to offer exhibits; (c) to cross-examine witnesses on any matter relevant to the issues even though that matter was not covered in the direct examination; and (d) to impeach any witness regardless of who first called such witness to testify and to rebut any evidence.

(v) Hearings need not be conducted according to technical rules relating to evidence and witnesses. Any relevant evidence shall be admitted if it is the sort of evidence on which responsible persons are accustomed to rely in the conduct of serious affairs, regardless of any common law or statutory rule which might make improper the admission of such evidence over objection in civil actions.

(vi) Any hearing may be recessed or adjourned from time to time at the discretion of the panel.

(9) *Failure of Applicant to Petition the Board for Review or Request a Hearing Before the Board Within the Time Allowed by These Rules.* If the applicant does not petition the board for review or request a

hearing before the board regarding the specialty committee's recommendation of rejection of the application within the time allowed by these rules, the board shall act on the matter at its next board meeting.

(b) Failure of a Written Examination Prepared and Administered by a Certification Committee

(1) *Review of Examination*—Within 30 days of the mailing of the notice from the board's executive director that the applicant has failed the written examination, the applicant may review his or her examination at the office of the board at a time designated by the executive director. The applicant will be given the applicant's scores for each question on the examination. The applicant shall not remove the examination from the board's office.

(2) *Petition for Grade Review*—If, after reviewing the examination, the applicant feels an error or errors were made in the grading, the applicant may file with the executive director a petition for grade review. The petition must be filed within 45 days of the mailing of the notice of failure and should set out in detail the examination questions and answers which, in the opinion of the applicant, have been incorrectly graded. Supporting information may be filed to substantiate the applicant's claim.

(3) *Review Procedure*—The applicant's examination and petition shall be submitted to a panel consisting of a minimum of at least three members of the specialty committee (the review committee of the specialty committee). All information will be submitted in blind form, the staff being responsible for deleting any identifying information on the examination or the petition. The review committee of the specialty committee shall review the petition of the applicant and determine whether the grade of the examination should remain the same or be changed. The review committee shall make a written report to the board setting forth its recommendation relative to the grade on the applicant's examination and an explanation of its recommendation.

(4) *Decision of the Board*—The board shall consider the petition and the report and recommendation of the review committee and shall certify the applicant if it determines that the applicant has satisfied all of the standards for certification.

(c) Failure of a Written Examination Prepared and Administered by a Testing Organization on Behalf of the Board.

The applicant shall comply with the review and appeal procedures of any testing organization retained by the board to prepare and administer the certification examination.

[History Note: Statutory Authority G.S. 84–23. Readopted effective December 8, 1994; amended effective June 1, 1995; amended effective November 16, 2006; amended effective February 5, 2009.]

.1802 Denial, Revocation or Suspension of Continued Certification as a Specialist

(a) Denial of Continued Certification. The board, upon its initiative or upon recommendation of the appropriate specialty committee, may deny continued certification of a specialist, if the applicant does not meet the requirements as found in Rule .1721(a) of this subchapter.

(b) Revocation and Suspension of Certification as a Specialist. The board shall revoke the certification of a lawyer as provided in Rule .1723(a) of this subchapter and may revoke or suspend the certification of a lawyer as provided in Rule .1723(b) of this subchapter.

(c) Notification of Board Action. The executive director shall notify the lawyer of the board's action to grant or deny continued certification as a specialist upon application for continued certification pursuant to Rule .1721(a) of this subchapter, or to revoke or suspend continued certification pursuant to Rule .1723(a) or (b) of this subchapter. The lawyer will also be notified of his or her right to a hearing if a hearing is allowed by these rules.

(d) Request for Hearing. Within 21 days of the mailing of notice from the executive director of the board that the lawyer has been denied continued certification pursuant to Rule .1721(a) or that certification has been revoked or suspended pursuant to Rule .1723(b), the lawyer must request a hearing before the board in writing. There is no right to a hearing upon automatic revocation pursuant to Rule .1723(a).

(e) Hearing Procedure. Except as set forth in Rule .1802(f) below, the rules set forth in Rule .1801(a)(8) of this subchapter shall be followed when a lawyer requests a hearing regarding the denial of continued certification pursuant to Rule .1721(a) or the revocation or suspension of certification under Rule .1723(b).

(f) Burden of Proof: Preponderance of the Evidence. A three-member panel of the board shall apply the preponderance of the evidence rule in determining whether the lawyer's certification should be continued, revoked or suspended. In cases of denial of an application for continued certification under Rule .1721(a), the burden of proof is upon the lawyer. In cases of revocation or suspension under Rule .1723(b), the burden of proof is upon the board.

(g) Notification of Board's Decision. After the hearing, the board shall timely notify the lawyer of its decision to regarding continued certification as a specialist.

[History Note: Statutory Authority G.S. 84–23. Readopted effective December 8, 1994; amended effective February 5, 2004.]

.1803 Reconsideration of Failed Examination

(a) Review of Examination. Within 30 days of the date of the notice from the board's executive director that the applicant has failed the written examination, the applicant may review his or her examination at the office of the board at a time designated by the executive director. The applicant will be given the applicant's scores for each question on the examination. The applicant shall not copy, transcribe, or remove the examination from the board's office (or any other location established by the board for the review of the examination) and shall be subject to such other restrictions as the board deems necessary to protect the content of the examination.

(b) Petition for Grade Review. If, after reviewing the examination, the applicant feels an error or errors were made in the grading, the applicant may file with the executive director a petition for grade review. The petition must be filed within 45 days of the date of the notice of failure and should set out in detail the examination questions and answers which, in the opinion of the applicant, have been incorrectly graded. Supporting information may be filed to substantiate the applicant's claim.

(c) Denial of Petition by Chair. The director of the specialization program shall review the petition and determine whether, if all grading objections of the petitioner are decided in the petitioner's favor, the petitioner's grade on the examination would be changed to a passing grade. If the director determines that the petitioner's grade would not be changed to passing, the director shall notify the chair who may deny the petition on this basis.

(d) Review Procedure. The applicant's examination and petition shall be submitted to a panel consisting of three members of the specialty committee (the grade review panel). All identifying information shall be redacted from the examination and petition prior to submission to the grade review panel. The grade review panel shall review the petition of the applicant and determine whether the grade of the examination should be changed. The grade review panel shall make a written report to the board setting forth its recommendation relative to the grade on the applicant's examination and an explanation of its recommendation.

(e) Decision of the Board. The board shall consider the petition and the report of the grade review panel and shall certify the applicant if it determines by majority vote that the applicant has satisfied all of the standards for certification.

(f) Failure of Examination Prepared and Administered by a Testing Organization on Behalf of the Board. Notwithstanding paragraphs (a)—(d) of this rule, if the board is utilizing a qualified organization to prepare and administer the certification examination for a specialty pursuant to Rule .1716(10) of this subchapter, an applicant for such specialty shall only be entitled to the review and appeal procedures of the organization.

[History Note: Statutory Authority G.S. 84–23. Adopted effective March 11, 2010. Amended effective March 6, 2014.]

.1804 Appeal to the Council

(a) Appealable Decisions. An appeal may be taken to the council from a decision of the board which denies an applicant certification (i.e., when an applicant's application has been rejected because it is incomplete and/or not in compliance with the standards for certification or when an applicant fails the written specialty examination), denies an applicant continued certification as a specialist, or suspends or revokes a specialist's certification. (Persons who appeal the board's decision are referred to herein as appellants.)

(b) Filing the Appeal. An appeal from a decision of the board as described in Rule .1804(a) above may be taken by filing with the executive director of the North Carolina State Bar (the State Bar) a written notice of appeal not later than 21 days after the mailing of the board's decision to the applicant who is denied certification or continued certification or to a lawyer whose certification is suspended or revoked.

(c) Time and Place of Hearing. The appeal will be scheduled for hearing at a time set by the council. The executive director of the State Bar shall notify the appellant and the board of the time and place of the hearing before the council.

(d) Record on Appeal to the Council.

(1) The record on appeal to the council shall consist of all the evidence offered at the hearing before the board. The executive director of the board shall assemble the record and certify it to the executive director of the State Bar and notify the appellant of such action.

(2) The appellant shall make prompt arrangement with the court reporter to obtain and have filed with the executive director of the State Bar a complete transcript of the hearing. Failure of the appellant to make such arrangements and pay the costs shall be grounds for dismissal of the appeal.

(e) Parties Appearing Before the Council. The appellant may request to appear, with or without counsel, before the council and make oral argument. The board may appear on its own behalf or by counsel.

(f) Appeal Procedure. The council shall consider the appeal en banc. The council shall consider only the record on appeal, briefs, and oral arguments. The decision of the council shall be by a majority of those members voting. All council members present at the meeting may participate in the discussion and deliberation of the appeal. Members of the board who also serve on the council are recused from voting on the appeal.

(g) Notice of the Council's Decision. The appellant shall receive written notice of the council's decision.

[History Note: Statutory Authority G.S. 84–23. Readopted effective December 8, 1994.]

.1805 Judicial Review

(a) Appeals. The appellant or the board may appeal from an adverse ruling by the council.

(b) Wake County Superior Court. All appeals from the council shall lie to the Wake County Superior Court. (See *N.C. State Bar v. Du Mont,* 304 N.C. 627, 286 S.E.2d 89 (1982).)

(c) Judicial Review Procedures. Article 4 of G.S. 150–B shall be complied with by all parties relative to the procedures for judicial review of the council's decision.

[History Note: Statutory Authority G.S. 84–23. Readopted effective December 8, 1994.]

.1806 Additional Rules Pertaining to Hearings and Appeals

(a) Notices. Every notice required by these rules shall be mailed to the applicant.

(b) Expenses Related to Hearings and Appeals. In its discretion, the board may direct that the necessary expenses incurred in any investigation, processing, and hearing of any matter to the board or appeal to the council be paid by the board. However, all expenses related to travel to any hearing or appeal for the applicant, his or her attorney, and witnesses called by the applicant shall be borne by the applicant and shall not be paid by the board.

[History Note: Statutory Authority G.S. 84–23. Readopted effective December 8, 1994.]

SECTION .1900 RULES CONCERNING THE ACCREDITATION OF CONTINUING LEGAL EDUCATION FOR THE PURPOSES OF THE BOARD OF LEGAL SPECIALIZATION

.1901 General Provisions

(a) An applicant for certification in a specialty field must make a satisfactory showing of the requisite number of hours of continuing legal education (CLE) in the specialty field for each of the last three years prior to application in accord with the standards adopted by the board in the field. In no event will the number of hours be less than an average of twelve hours per year. The average number of hours is computed by adding all hours of continuing legal education credits in the field for three years and dividing by three.

(b) An applicant for continued certification must make a satisfactory showing of the requisite number of hours of continuing legal education (CLE) in the specialty field for each of the five years of certification in accord with the standards adopted by the board in the field. In no event will the number of hours be less than an average of twelve hours per year. The average number of hours is computed by adding all hours of continuing legal education credits in the field for the five years and dividing by five.

[History Note: Statutory Authority G.S. 84–23. Readopted effective December 8, 1994.]

.1902 Definitions

(1) Applicant. The person applying for certification or continued certification of specialization.

(2) Board. The North Carolina State Bar Board of Legal Specialization.

(3) Committee. The specialty committee appointed by the board in the applicant's specialty field.

(4) Sponsor. An organization offering continuing legal education courses for attendance by attorneys.

(5) Accredited Sponsor. A sponsor which has demonstrated to the satisfaction of the board that the continuing legal education programs offered by it meet the accreditation standards on a continuing basis warranting a presumption of accreditation.

(6) Accreditation. A determination by the board that the continuing legal education activities further the professional competence of the applicant and a certain number of hours of continuing legal education credit should be awarded for participation in the continuing legal education activity.

(7) Continuing Legal Education (CLE). Attendance at lecture-type instruction meeting the standards in Rule .1903 of this subchapter or participation in alternative activities described in Rule .1905 of this subchapter.

(8) Specialty Field. An area of the law as defined by the board in which the board certifies specialists.

[History Note: Statutory Authority G.S. 84–23. Readopted effective December 8, 1994.]

.1903 Accreditation Standards for Lecture–Type CLE Activities

(a) The CLE activity shall have significant intellectual or practical content and the primary objective shall be to increase the participant's professional competence in the applicant's specialty field.

(b) The CLE activity shall constitute an organized program of learning dealing with matters directly related to the practice of law, professional responsibility, or ethical obligations of lawyers in the applicant's specialty field.

(c) The CLE activity may be presented by either live instruction or mechanical or electronically recorded or reproduced material. If electronic transmission is used, an instructor should be present for comment or to answer questions. The board may reduce the hours of credit for electronic transmission when no instructor is present.

(d) Continuing legal education materials are to be prepared and activities conducted by an individual or group qualified by practical or academic experience in a setting suitable to the educational activity of the program.

(e) Except when not suitable or readily available because of the topic or the nature of the lecture, thorough, high quality, and carefully prepared written materials shall be provided to all attendees prior to or at the time the instruction is presented. Absence of materials should be the exception and not the rule.

[History Note: Statutory Authority G.S. 84–23. Readopted effective December 8, 1994.]

.1904 Computation of Hours of Instruction

(a) Hours of CLE will be computed by adding the number of minutes of actual instruction, dividing by 60 and rounding the results to the nearest one-tenth of an hour.

(b) Only actual instruction will be included in computing the total hours of actual instruction. The following will be excluded:

(1) introductory remarks;

(2) breaks;

(3) business meetings;

(4) keynote speeches or speeches in connection with meals;

(5) question and answer sessions in excess of fifteen minutes per hour of instruction;

(6) programs of less than 60 minutes in length.

[History Note: Statutory Authority G.S. 84–23. Readopted effective December 8, 1994.]

.1905 Alternatives to Lecture–Type CLE Course Instruction

(a) Teaching. Preparation and presentation of written materials at an accredited CLE course will qualify for CLE credit at the rate of six hours of credit for each hour of presentation as computed under Rule .1904 of this subchapter. In the case of joint preparation and/or presentation, each preparer and presenter will receive a proportionate share of the total credit available. Repeat presentations of substantially the same materials will qualify for one-half the credit available for the initial presentation. Instruction at an academic institution will qualify for three hours of CLE credit per semester hour taught in the specialty field.

(b) Publication. Publication of a scholarly article in the applicant's specialty field will qualify for CLE credit in the discretion of the specialty committee, subject to board approval, based on a review of the article, its content, and its quality. No more than ten hours of credit will be given for a single article.

(c) Self-Study. An individual may review video or audio tapes or manuscripts of lectures from qualified CLE courses, which lectures would meet the accreditation standards in Rule .1903 of this subchapter and receive credit according to the computation of hours in Rule .1904 of this subchapter provided that no more than two hours per year of self-study shall qualify to meet the CLE requirements for certification or recertification.

(d) Advanced Degrees. Attendance at courses of instruction at a law school which can be credited toward the earning of an advanced degree in the specialty field of the applicant will qualify for one hour of CLE credit per semester hour taken if attained in the required period prior to application for certification or recertification.

[History Note: Statutory Authority G.S. 84–23. Readopted effective December 8, 1994; amended effective March 7, 1996; amended effective February 5, 2009.]

.1906 Accreditation of Courses

(a) All courses offered by an accredited sponsor which relate to the specialty field as defined by the board shall be accredited and credit for attendance shall be given for the hours of instruction related to the specialty field of the applicant as determined by the board.

(b) The applicant shall make a showing that any course for which the applicant desires CLE credit offered by a sponsor not on the accredited sponsor list meets the accreditation standards of Rule .1903 of this subchapter. The board will then determine the number of hours of credit based upon the standards of Rule .1904 of this subchapter.

(c) An accredited sponsor may not represent or advertise that a CLE course is approved or that the attendees will be given CLE credit by the board unless such sponsor provides a brochure or other appropriate information describing the topics, hours of instruction, and instructors for its CLE offerings in a specialty field at least thirty days in advance of the date of the course.

(d) An unaccredited sponsor desiring advance accreditation of a course and the right to designate its accreditation for the appropriate number of CLE credits in its solicitations shall submit a brochure or other appropriate information describing the topics, hours of instruction, location, and instructors for its CLE offerings at least sixty days prior to the date of the course.

[History Note: Statutory Authority G.S. 84-23. Readopted effective December 8, 1994; amended effective October 1, 2003.]

.1907 Accreditation of Sponsor

(a) The following is the list of accredited sponsors:

(1) North Carolina Bar Foundation

(2) North Carolina Academy of Trial Lawyers

(3) Wake Forest University Continuing Legal Education

(4) University of North Carolina at Chapel Hill Continuing Legal Education

(5) Duke University School of Law Continuing Legal Education

(6) Norman Adrian Wiggins School of Law Continuing Legal Education

(7) Middle District Bankruptcy Seminar

(8) UCB Estate Planning and Taxation Seminar

(9) any member of the Association of Continuing Legal Education Administrators

(10) University of Miami School of Law

(11) any of the following groups: American Bar Association, American College of Probate Counsel, American College of Trial Counsel, American Patent Law Association, Association of American Law Schools, Association of Life Insurance Counsel, Conference of Chief Justices, Council on Legal Education for Professional Responsibility, Inc., Federal Bar Association, Federal Communications Bar Association, Judge Advocates Association, Maritime Law Association of the United States, National Association of Attorneys General, National Association of Bar Executives, National Association of Bar Presidents, National Association of Bar Counsel, National Association of Women Lawyers, National Bar Association, National Conference of Bar Examiners, National Conference of Commissioners on Uniform State Laws, National Conference of Judicial Councils, National District Attorneys Association, and National Legal Aid and Defender Association.

(b) Any sponsor not listed in Rule .1907(a) above desiring to attain accredited sponsor status must submit to the board a description of the courses offered for the two years prior to application to the board for accredited sponsor status. The board may request copies of any course materials used in any of the offered courses. If, in the judgment of the board, the sponsor has met the accreditation standards of Rule .1903 of this subchapter for each of the courses offered, the board will designate the sponsor as an accredited sponsor.

[History Note: Statutory Authority G.S. 84-23. Readopted effective December 8, 1994.]

.1908 Showing by Applicants

Every applicant will list each type of CLE activity under each of the following categories:

(1) attendance at CLE instruction offered by an accredited sponsor. The course name, sponsor, and number of hours of CLE shall be listed by the applicant;

(2) attendance at CLE instruction offered by a sponsor not on the accredited sponsor list or not given advanced approval by the board under Rule .1906 of this subchapter. A fee of $5.00 per course will be charged for accrediting each course listed by the applicant offered by a sponsor not on the accredited sponsor list or not given advanced approval under Rule .1906(d) of this subchapter. The course name, sponsor, and number of hours of CLE shall be listed by the applicant;

(3) participation as an instructor at a CLE course. The course name, sponsor, and number of hours of instruction or preparation shall be stated by the applicant;

(4) publication of a scholarly article. A copy of the publication shall accompany the application;

(5) self-study. A description of the materials used, the dates of use, the number of hours claimed, and the source from which they were obtained shall accompany the application.

[History Note: Statutory Authority G.S. 84-23. Readopted effective December 8, 1994.]

SECTION .2000 RULES OF THE BOARD OF LEGAL SPECIALIZATION FOR APPROVAL OF INDEPENDENT CERTIFYING ORGANIZATIONS

.2001 Policy Statement

These guidelines for reviewing independent organizations which certify lawyers as specialists are designed to thoroughly evaluate the purpose and function of such certifying organizations and the procedures they use in their certification processes.

These guidelines are not meant to be exclusive, but to provide a framework in which certifying organizations can be evaluated. The aim of this evaluation is to provide consumers of legal services a means of access to lawyers who are qualified in particular fields of law.

[History Note: Statutory Authority G.S. 84–23. Readopted effective December 8, 1994.]

.2002 General Procedure

As contemplated in Rule 2.5 of the North Carolina Rules of Professional Conduct, the North Carolina State Bar, through its Board of Legal Specialization (the board), shall, upon the filing of a completed application and the payment of any required fee, review the standards and procedures of any organization which certifies lawyers as specialists and desires the approval of the North Carolina State Bar. The board shall prepare an application form to be used by certifying organizations and shall administer the application process.

[History Note: Statutory Authority G.S. 84–23. Readopted effective December 8, 1994.]

.2003 Factors to Be Considered in Reviewing Certifying Organizations

(a) Purpose of the Organization. The stated purposes for the original formation of the organization and any subsequent changes in those purposes shall be examined to determine whether the organization is dedicated to the maintenance of professional competence.

(b) Background of the Organization. The length of time the organization has been in existence, whether the organization is a successor of another, the requirements for membership in the organization, the number of members which the organization has, the business structure under which the organization operates, and the professional qualifications of the individuals who direct the policies and operations of the organization shall be examined to determine whether the organization is a bona fide certifying organization.

[History Note: Statutory Authority G.S. 84–23. Readopted effective December 8, 1994.]

.2004 Standards for Approval of Certifying Organizations

The following standards are to be considered by the board in evaluating an application for approval of a certifying organization.

(1) Uniform Applicability of Certification Standards. In general, the standards for certification in any specialty field must be understandable and easily applied to individual applicants. Certification by the organization must be available to any attorney who meets the standards, and the organization must not certify an attorney who has not demonstrably met each standard. The organization must agree to promptly inform the board of any material changes in its standards, definitions of specialty fields or certifying procedures and must further agree to respond promptly to any reasonable requests for information from the board.

(2) Definitions of Specialty Fields. Every field of law in which certification is offered must be susceptible of meaningful definition and be an area in which North Carolina lawyers regularly practice.

(3) Decision Making by Recognized Experts. The persons in a certifying organization making decisions regarding applicants shall include lawyers who, in the judgment of the board, are experts in the subject areas of practice and who each have extensive practice or involvement in those areas of practice.

(4) Certification Standards. A certifying organization's standards for certification of specialists must include, as a minimum, the standards required for certification set out in the North Carolina Plan of Legal Specialization (Section .1700 of this subchapter) and in the rules, regulations and standards adopted by the board from time to time. Such standards shall not unlawfully discriminate against any lawyer properly qualified for certification as a specialist, but shall provide a reasonable basis for a determination that an applicant possesses special competence in a particular field of law, as demonstrated by the following means:

(a) *Substantial Involvement.* Substantial involvement in the area of specialty during the five-year period immediately preceding application to the certifying agency. Substantial involvement is generally measured by the amount of time spent practicing in the area of specialty. In no event may the time spent in practicing the specialty be less than 25 percent of the total practice of a lawyer engaged in a normal full-time practice;

(b) *Peer Review.* Peer recommendations from attorneys or judges who are familiar with the competence of the applicant in the area of specialty, none of whom are related to, engaged in legal practice with, or involved in continuing commercial relationships with the lawyer;

(c) *Written Examination.* Objective evaluation of the applicant's knowledge of the substantive and procedural law in the area of specialty as determined by written examination;

(d) *Continuing Legal Education.* At least 36 hours of approved continuing legal education credit in the area of specialty during the three years immediately preceding application to the certifying organization.

(5) Applications and Procedures. Application forms used by the certifying organization must be submitted to the board for review to determine that the requirements specified above are being met by applicants. Additionally, the certifying organization must submit a description of the process it uses to review applications.

(6) Requirements for Recertification. The standards used by a certifying organization must provide for certification for a limited period of time, which shall not exceed five years, after which time persons who have been certified must apply for recertification. Requirements for recertification must include continued substantial involvement in the area of specialty, continuing legal education, and appropriate peer review.

(7) Revocation of Certification. The standards used by a certifying organization shall include a procedure for revocation of certification. A certification shall be revoked upon a finding that the certificate holder has been disbarred or suspended from the practice of law. The standards shall require a certificate holder to report his or her disbarment or suspension from the practice of law to the certifying organization.

(8) Waiver. The standards used by a certifying organization may provide for waiver of the peer review and written examination requirements set forth in Rules .2004(4)(b) and (c) above for an applicant who was responsible for formulating and grading the organization's initial written examination in his or her area of specialty.

[History Note: Statutory Authority G.S. 84–23. Readopted effective December 8, 1994.]

.2005 Application Procedure

(a) The organization may file an application seeking approval of the organization by the board. Applications shall be on forms available from and approved by the board. The application fee shall be $1,000.

(b) The organization which has been approved shall provide its standards, definitions and/or certifying procedures to the board in January of each year and must pay an annual administrative fee of $100 to maintain its approved status.

(c) When the board determines that an approved certifying organization has ceased to exist, has ceased to operate its certification program in the manner described in its application, or has failed to comply with the requirements of Rule .2005(b) above, its approved status shall be revoked. After such a revocation, no North Carolina lawyer may publicize a certification from the organization in question.

(d) The appeal procedures of the board shall apply to any application by an organization for approval as a certifying organization and any decision to revoke a certifying organization's approved status.

[History Note: Statutory Authority G.S. 84–23. Readopted effective December 8, 1994.]

.2006 Effect of Approval of a Certifying Organization by the Board of Legal Specialization

When an organization is approved as a certifying organization by the board, any North Carolina lawyer certified as a specialist by that organization may publicize that certification.

[History Note: Statutory Authority G.S. 84–23. Readopted effective December 8, 1994.]

SECTION .2100 CERTIFICATION STANDARDS FOR THE REAL PROPERTY LAW SPECIALTY

.2101 Establishment of Specialty Field

The North Carolina State Bar Board of Legal Specialization (the board) hereby designates real property law, including the subspecialties of real property-residential transactions and real property-business, commercial, and industrial transactions as a field of law for which certification of specialists under the North Carolina Plan of Legal Specialization (see Section .1700 of this subchapter) is permitted.

[History Note: Statutory Authority G.S. 84–23. Readopted effective December 8, 1994.]

.2102 Definition of Specialty

The specialty of real property law is the practice of law dealing with real property transactions, including title examination, property transfers, financing, leases, and determination of property rights. Subspecialties in the field are identified and defined as follows:

(a) Real Property Law-Residential Transactions. The practice of law dealing with the acquisition, ownership, leasing, financing, use, transfer and disposition, of residential real property by individuals;

(b) Real Property Law-Business, Commercial, and Industrial Transactions. The practice of law dealing with the acquisition, ownership, leasing, management, financing, development, use, transfer, and disposition of residential, business, commercial, and industrial real property.

[History Note: Statutory Authority G.S. 84–23. Readopted effective December 8, 1994.]

.2103 Recognition as a Specialist in Real Property Law

A lawyer may qualify as a specialist by meeting the standards set for one or both of the subspecialties. If a lawyer qualifies as a specialist in real property law by meeting the standards set for the real property law-residential transactions subspecialty, the lawyer shall be entitled to represent that he or she is a "Board Certified Specialist in Real Property Law–Residential Transactions." If a lawyer qualifies as a specialist in real property law by meeting the standards set for the real property law-business, commercial, and industrial transactions, the lawyer shall be entitled to represent that he or she is a "Board Certified Specialist in Real Property Law–Business, Commercial, and Industrial Transactions." If a lawyer qualifies as a specialist in real property law by meeting the standards set for both the real property law-residential transactions subspecialty and the real property law-business, commercial, and industrial transactions subspecialty, the lawyer shall be entitled to represent that he or she is a "Board Certified Specialist in Real Property Law–Residential, Business, Commercial and Industrial Transactions."

[History Note: Statutory Authority G.S. 84–23. Readopted effective December 8, 1994.]

.2104 Applicability of Provisions of the North Carolina Plan of Legal Specialization

Certification and continued certification of specialists in real property law shall be governed by the provisions of the North Carolina Plan of Legal Specialization (see Section .1700 of this subchapter) as supplemented by these standards for certification.

[History Note: Statutory Authority G.S. 84–23. Readopted effective December 8, 1994.]

.2105 Standards for Certification as a Specialist in Real Property Law

Each applicant for certification as a specialist in real property law shall meet the minimum standards set forth in Rule .1720 of this subchapter. In addition, each applicant shall meet the following standards for certification in real property law:

(a) Licensure and Practice. An applicant shall be licensed and in good standing to practice law in North Carolina as of the date of application. An applicant shall continue to be licensed and in good standing to practice law in North Carolina during the period of certification.

(b) Substantial Involvement. An applicant shall affirm to the board that the applicant has experience through substantial involvement in the practice of real property law.

(1) Substantial involvement shall mean during the five years preceding the application, the applicant has devoted an average of at least 500 hours a year to the practice of real property law, but not less than 400 hours in any one year.

(2) Practice shall mean substantive legal work done primarily for the purpose of legal advice or representation, or a practice equivalent.

(3) Practice equivalent means service as a law professor concentrating in the teaching of real property law. Teaching may be substituted for one year of experience to meet the five-year requirement.

(c) Continuing Legal Education. An applicant must have earned no less than 36 hours of accredited continuing legal education (CLE) credits in real property law during the three years preceding application with not less than six credits in any one year. Of the 36 hours of CLE, at least 30 hours shall be in real property law and the balance may be in the related areas of environmental law, taxation, business organizations, estate planning and probate law, and elder law.

(d) Peer Review. An applicant must make a satisfactory showing of qualification through peer review. An applicant must provide the names of ten lawyers or judges who are familiar with the competence and qualification of the applicant in the specialty field. Written peer reference forms will be sent by the board or the specialty committee to each of the references. Completed peer reference forms must be received from at least five of the references. All references must be licensed and in good standing to practice in North Carolina. An applicant consents to the confidential inquiry by the board or the specialty committee of the submitted references and other persons concerning the applicant's competence and qualification.

(1) A reference may not be related by blood or marriage to the applicant nor may the reference be a partner or associate of the applicant at the time of the application.

(2) The references shall be given on standardized forms provided by the board with the application for certification in the specialty field. These forms shall be returned directly to the specialty committee.

(e) Examination. The applicant must pass a written examination designed to test the applicant's knowledge and ability in real property law.

(1) *Terms.* The examination(s) shall be in written form and shall be given annually. The examination(s) shall be administered and graded uniformly by the specialty committee.

(2) *Subject Matter.* The examination shall cover the applicant's knowledge in the following topics in real property law or in the subspecialty or subspecialties that the applicant has elected:

(A) title examinations, property transfers, financing, leases, and determination of property rights;

(B) the acquisition, ownership, leasing, financing, use, transfer, and disposition of residential real property by individuals;

(C) the acquisition, ownership, leasing, management, financing, development, use, transfer, and disposition of residential, business, commercial, and industrial real property.

[History Note: Statutory Authority G.S. 84–23. Readopted effective December 8, 1994; amended effective October 9, 2008.]

.2106 Standards for Continued Certification as a Specialist

The period of certification is five years. Prior to the expiration of the certification period, a certified specialist who desires continued certification must apply for continued certification within the time limit described in Rule .2106(d) below. No examination will be required for continued certification. However, each applicant for continued certification as a specialist shall comply with the specific requirements set forth below in addition to any general standards required by the board of all applicants for continued certification.

(a) Substantial Involvement. The specialist must demonstrate that, for each of the five years preceding application, he or she has had substantial involvement in the specialty as defined in Rule .2105(b) of this subchapter.

(b) Continuing Legal Education. The specialist must have earned no less than 60 hours of accredited continuing legal education credits in real property law as accredited by the board with not less than six credits earned in any one year. Of the 60 hours of CLE, at least 50 hours shall be in real property law and the balance may be in the related areas of environmental law, taxation, business organizations, estate planning and probate law, and elder law.

(c) Peer Review. The specialist must comply with the requirements of Rule .2105(d) of this subchapter.

(d) Time for Application. Application for continued certification shall be made not more than one hundred eighty (180) days nor less than ninety days prior to the expiration of the prior period of certification.

(e) Lapse of Certification. Failure of a specialist to apply for continued certification in a timely fashion will result in a lapse of certification. Following such lapse, recertification will require compliance with all requirements of Rule .2105 of this subchapter, including the examination.

(f) Suspension or Revocation of Certification. If an applicant's certification has been suspended or revoked during the period of certification, then the application shall be treated as if it were for initial certification under Rule .2105 of this subchapter.

[History Note: Statutory Authority G.S. 84–23. Readopted effective December 8, 1994; amended effective October 9, 2008.]

.2107 Applicability of Other Requirements

The specific standards set forth herein for certification of specialists in real property law are subject to any general requirement, standard, or procedure adopted by the board applicable to all applicants for certification or continued certification.

[History Note: Statutory Authority G.S. 84–23. Readopted effective December 8, 1994.]

SECTION .2200 CERTIFICATION STANDARDS FOR THE BANKRUPTCY LAW SPECIALTY

.2201 Establishment of Specialty Field

The North Carolina State Bar Board of Legal Specialization (the board) hereby designates bankruptcy law, including the subspecialties of consumer bankruptcy law and business bankruptcy law, as a field of law for which certification of specialists under the Plan of Legal Specialization (see Section .1700 of this subchapter) is permitted.

[History Note: Statutory Authority G.S. 84–23. Readopted effective December 8, 1994.]

.2202 Definition of Specialty

The specialty of bankruptcy law is the practice of law dealing with all laws and procedures involving the rights, obligations, and remedies between debtors and creditors in potential or pending federal bankruptcy cases and state insolvency actions. Subspecialties in the field are identified and defined as follows:

(a) Consumer Bankruptcy Law. The practice of law dealing with consumer bankruptcy and the representation of interested parties in contested matters or adversary proceedings in individual filings of Chapter 7, Chapter 12, or Chapter 13;

(b) Business Bankruptcy Law. The practice of law dealing with business bankruptcy and the representation of interested parties in contested matters or adversary proceedings in bankruptcy cases filed on behalf of debtors who are or have been engaged in business prior to an entity filing Chapter 7, Chapter 9, Chapter 11, or Chapter 12.

[History Note: Statutory Authority G.S. 84–23. Readopted effective December 8, 1994.]

.2203 Recognition as a Specialist in Bankruptcy Law

A lawyer may qualify as a specialist by meeting the standards set for one or both of the subspecialties. If a lawyer qualifies as a specialist in bankruptcy law by meeting the standards set for the consumer bankruptcy law subspecialty, the lawyer shall be entitled to represent that he or she is a "Board Certified Specialist in Consumer Bankruptcy Law." If a lawyer qualifies as a specialist in bankruptcy law by meeting the standards set for the business bankruptcy law subspecialty, the lawyer shall be entitled to represent that he or she is a "Board Certified Specialist in Business Bankruptcy Law." If a lawyer qualifies as a specialist in bankruptcy law by meeting the standards set for both the consumer bankruptcy law and the business bankruptcy law subspecialties, the lawyer shall be entitled to represent that he or she is a "Board Certified Specialist in Business and Consumer Bankruptcy Law."

[History Note: Statutory Authority G.S. 84–23. Readopted effective December 8, 1994.]

.2204 Applicability of Provisions of the North Carolina Plan of Legal Specialization

Certification and continued certification of specialists in bankruptcy law shall be governed by the provisions of the Plan of Legal Specialization (see Section .1700 of this subchapter) as supplemented by these standards for certification.

[History Note: Statutory Authority G.S. 84–23. Readopted effective December 8, 1994.]

.2205 Standards for Certification as a Specialist in Bankruptcy Law

Each applicant for certification as a specialist in bankruptcy law shall meet the minimum standards set forth in Rule .1720 of this subchapter. In addition, each applicant shall meet the following standards for certification as a specialist in bankruptcy law:

(a) Licensure and Practice. An applicant shall be licensed and in good standing to practice law in North Carolina as of the date of application. An applicant shall continue to be licensed and in good standing to practice law in North Carolina during the period of certification.

(b) Substantial Involvement. An applicant shall affirm to the board that the applicant has experience through substantial involvement in the practice of bankruptcy law.

(1) Substantial involvement shall mean during the five years preceding the application, the applicant has devoted an average of at least 500 hours a year to the practice of bankruptcy law, but not less than 400 hours in any one year.

(2) Practice shall mean substantive legal work done primarily for the purpose of legal advice or representation, or a practice equivalent.

(3) Practice equivalent shall mean, after admission to the bar of any state, District of Columbia, or a U.S. territorial possession

(A) service as a judge of any bankruptcy court, service as a clerk of any bankruptcy court, or service as a standing trustee;

(B) corporate or government service, including military service, after admission to the bar of any state, the District of Columbia, or any U.S. territorial possession, but only if the bankruptcy work done was legal advice or representation of the corporation, governmental unit, or individuals connected therewith;

(C) service as a deputy or assistant clerk of any bankruptcy court, as a research assistant to a bankruptcy judge, or as a law professor teaching bankruptcy and/or debtor-creditor related courses may be substituted for one year of experience to meet the five-year requirement.

(c) Continuing Legal Education. An applicant must have earned no less than 36 hours of accredited continuing legal education (CLE) credits in bankruptcy law, during the three years preceding application with not less than 6 credits in any one year.

(d) Peer Review. An applicant must make a satisfactory showing of qualification through peer review. An applicant must provide the names of ten lawyers or judges who are familiar with the competence and qualification of the applicant in the specialty field. Written peer reference forms will be sent by the board or the specialty committee to each of the references. Completed peer reference forms must be received from at least five of the references. All references must be licensed and in good standing to practice in North Carolina. An applicant consents to the confidential inquiry by the board or the specialty committee of the submitted references and other persons concerning the applicant's competence and qualification.

(1) A reference may not be a judge of any bankruptcy court.

(2) A reference may not be related by blood or marriage to the applicant nor may the reference be a partner or associate of the applicant at the time of the application.

(3) The references shall be given on standardized forms provided by the board with the application for certification in the specialty field. These forms shall be returned directly to the specialty committee.

(e) Examination. The applicant must pass a written examination designed to test the applicant's knowledge and ability in bankruptcy law.

[History Note: Statutory Authority G.S. 84–23. Readopted effective December 8, 1994; amended effective November 16, 2006.]

.2206 Standards for Continued Certification as a Specialist

The period of certification is five years. Prior to the expiration of the certification period, a certified specialist who desires continued certification must apply for continued certification within the time limit described in Rule .2206(d) below. No examination will be required for continued certification. However, each applicant for continued certification as a specialist shall comply with the specific requirements set forth below in addition to any general standards required by the board of all applicants for continued certification.

(a) Substantial Involvement. The specialist must demonstrate that, for each of the five years preceding application, he or she has had substantial involvement in the specialty as defined in Rule .2205(b) of this subchapter.

(b) Continuing Legal Education. Since last certified, a specialist must have earned no less than 60 hours of accredited continued legal education credits in bankruptcy law with not less than 6 credits earned in any one year.

(c) Peer Review. The specialist must comply with the requirements of Rule .2205(d) of this subchapter.

(d) Application for continued certification shall be made not more than 180 days nor less than 90 days prior to the expiration of the prior period of certification.

(e) Lapse of Certification. Failure of a specialist to apply for continued certification in a timely fashion will result in a lapse of certification. Following such lapse, recertification will require compliance with all requirements of Rule .2205 of this subchapter, including the examination.

(f) Suspension or Revocation of Certification. If an applicant's certification has been suspended or revoked during the period of certification, then the application shall be treated as if it were for initial certification under Rule .2205 of this subchapter.

[History Note: Statutory Authority G.S. 84–23. Readopted effective December 8, 1994.]

.2207 Applicability of Other Requirements

The specific standards set forth herein for certification of specialists in bankruptcy law are subject to any general requirement, standard, or procedure adopted by the board applicable to all applicants for certification or continued certification.

[History Note: Statutory Authority G.S. 84–23. Readopted effective December 8, 1994.]

SECTION .2300 CERTIFICATION STANDARDS FOR THE ESTATE PLANNING AND PROBATE LAW SPECIALTY

.2301 Establishment of Specialty Field

The North Carolina State Bar Board of Legal Specialization (the board) hereby designates estate planning and probate law as a field of law for which certification of specialists under the Plan of Legal Specialization (see Section .1700 of this subchapter) is permitted.

[History Note: Statutory Authority G.S. 84–23. Readopted effective December 8, 1994.]

.2302 Definition of Specialty

The specialty of estate planning and probate law is the practice of law dealing with planning for conservation and disposition of estates, including consideration of federal and state tax consequences; preparation of legal instruments to effectuate estate plans; and probate of wills and administration of estates, including federal and state tax matters.

[History Note: Statutory Authority G.S. 84–23. Readopted effective December 8, 1994.]

.2303 Recognition as a Specialist in Estate Planning and Probate Law

If a lawyer qualifies as a specialist in estate planning and probate law by meeting the standards set for the specialty, the lawyer shall be entitled to represent that he or she is a "Board Certified Specialist in Estate Planning and Probate Law."

[History Note: Statutory Authority G.S. 84–23. Readopted effective December 8, 1994.]

.2304 Applicability of Provisions of the North Carolina Plan of Legal Specialization

Certification and continued certification of specialists in estate planning and probate law shall be governed by the provisions of the Plan of Legal Specialization (see Section .1700 of this subchapter) as supplemented by these standards for certification.

[History Note: Statutory Authority G.S. 84–23. Readopted effective December 8, 1994.]

.2305 Standards for Certification as a Specialist in Estate Planning and Probate Law

Each applicant for certification as a specialist in estate planning and probate law shall meet the minimum standards set forth in Rule .1720 of this subchapter. In addition, each applicant shall meet the following standards for certification as a specialist in estate planning and probate law:

(a) Licensure and Practice. An applicant shall be licensed and in good standing to practice law in North Carolina as of the date of application. An applicant shall continue to be licensed and in good standing to practice law in North Carolina during the period of certification.

(b) Substantial Involvement. The applicant shall affirm to the board that the applicant has experience through substantial involvement in the practice of estate planning and probate law.

(1) Substantial involvement shall be measured as follows:

(A) Time Spent—During the five years preceding the application, the applicant has devoted an average of at least 500 hours a year to the practice of estate planning and probate law, but not less than 400 hours in any one year;

(B) Experience Gained—During the five years immediately preceding application, the applicant shall have had continuing involvement in a substantial portion of the activities described in each of the following paragraphs:

(i) counseled persons in estate planning, including giving advice with respect to gifts, life insurance, wills, trusts, business arrangements and agreements, and other estate planning matters;

(ii) prepared or supervised the preparation of (1) estate planning instruments, such as simple and complex wills (including provisions for testamentary trusts, marital deductions and elections), revocable and irrevocable inter vivos trusts (including short-term and minor's trusts), business planning agreements (including buy-sell agreements and employment contracts), powers of attorney and other estate planning instruments; and (2) federal and state gift tax returns, including representation before the Internal Revenue Service and the North Carolina Department of Revenue in connection with gift tax returns;

(iii) handled or advised with respect to the probate of wills and the administration of decedents' estates, including representation of the personal representative before the clerk of superior court, guardianship, will contest, and declaratory judgment actions;

(iv) prepared, reviewed or supervised the preparation of federal estate tax returns, North Carolina inheritance tax returns, and federal and state fiduciary income tax returns, including representation before the Internal Revenue Service and the North Carolina Department of Revenue in connection with such tax returns and related controversies.

(2) Practice shall mean substantive legal work done primarily for the purpose of legal advice or representation, or a practice equivalent.

(3) Practice equivalent shall mean

(A) receipt of an LL.M. degree in taxation or estate planning and probate law (or such other related fields approved by the specialty committee and the board from an approved law school) may be substituted for one year of experience to meet the five-year requirement;

(B) service as a trust officer with a corporate fiduciary having duties primarily in the area of estate and trust administration, may be substituted for one year of experience to meet the five-year requirement;

(C) service as a law professor concentrating in the teaching of taxation or estate planning and probate law (or such other related fields approved by the specialty committee and the board). Such service may be substituted for one year of experience to meet the five-year requirement.

(c) Continuing Legal Education. An applicant must have earned no less than 72 hours of accredited continuing legal education (CLE) credits in estate planning and probate law during the three years preceding application. Of the 72 hours of CLE, at least 45 hours shall be in estate planning and probate law (provided, however, that eight of the 45 hours may be in the related areas of elder law, Medicaid planning, and guardianship), and the balance may be in the related areas of taxation, business organizations, real property, family law, elder law, Medicaid planning, and guardianship.

(d) Peer Review. An applicant must make a satisfactory showing of qualification through peer review. An applicant must provide the names of ten lawyers or judges, all of whom are familiar with the competence and qualification of the applicant in the specialty field. Written peer reference forms will be sent by the board or the specialty committee to each of the references. Completed peer reference forms must be received from at least five of the references. All references must be licensed and in good standing to practice in North Carolina. An applicant consents to the confidential inquiry by the board or the specialty committee of the submitted references and other persons concerning the applicant's competence and qualification.

(1) A reference may not be related by blood or marriage to the applicant nor may the reference be a partner or associate of the applicant at the time of the application.

(2) The references shall be given on standardized forms provided by the board with the application for certification in the specialty field. These forms shall be returned directly to the specialty committee.

(e) Examination. The applicant must pass a written examination designed to test the applicant's knowledge and ability in estate planning and probate law.

(1) *Terms.* The examination shall be in written form and shall be given annually. The examination shall be administered and graded uniformly by the specialty committee.

(2) *Subject Matter.* The examination shall cover the applicant's knowledge and application of the law in the following topics:

(A) federal and North Carolina gift taxes;

(B) federal estate tax;

(C) North Carolina inheritance tax;

(D) federal and North Carolina fiduciary income taxes;

(E) federal and North Carolina income taxes as they apply to the final returns of the decedent and his or her surviving spouse;

(F) North Carolina law of wills and trusts;

(G) North Carolina probate law, including fiduciary accounting;

(H) federal and North Carolina income and gift tax laws as they apply to revocable and irrevocable inter vivos trusts;

(I) North Carolina law of business organizations, family law, and property law as they may be applicable to estate planning transactions;

(J) federal and North Carolina tax law applicable to partnerships and corporations (including S corporations) which may be encountered in estate planning and administration.

[History Note: Statutory Authority G.S. 84–23. Readopted effective December 8, 1994; amended effective October 9, 2008.]

.2306 Standards for Continued Certification as a Specialist

The period of certification is five years. Prior to the expiration of the certification period, a certified specialist who desires continued certification must apply for continued certification within the time limit described in Rule .2306(d) below. No examination will be required for continued certification. However, each applicant for continued certification as a specialist shall comply with the specific requirements set forth below in addition to any general standards required by the board of all applicants for continued certification.

(a) Substantial Involvement. The specialist must demonstrate that, for each of the five years preceding application, he or she has had substantial involvement in the specialty as defined in Rule .2305(b) of this subchapter.

(b) Continuing Legal Education. Since last certified, a specialist must have earned no less than 120 hours of accredited continuing legal education credits in estate planning and probate law. Of the 120 hours of CLE at least 75 hours shall be in estate planning and probate law (provided, however, that 15 of the 75 hours may be in the related areas of elder law, Medicaid planning, and guardianship), and the balance may be in the related areas of taxation, business organizations, real property, family law, elder law, Medicaid planning, and guardianship.

(c) Peer Review. The specialist must comply with the requirements of Rule .2305(d) of this subchapter.

(d) Time for Application. Application for continued certification shall be made not more than 180 days nor less than 90 days prior to the expiration of the prior period of certification.

(e) Lapse of Certification. Failure of a specialist to apply for continued certification in a timely fashion will result in a lapse of certification. Following such lapse, recertification will require compliance with all requirements of Rule .2305 of this subchapter, including the examination.

(f) Suspension or Revocation of Certification. If an applicant's certification has been suspended or revoked during the period of certification, then the application shall be treated as if it were for initial certification under Rule .2305 of this subchapter.

[History Note: Statutory Authority G.S. 84–23. Readopted effective December 8, 1994; amended effective October 9, 2008.]

.2307 Applicability of Other Requirements

The specific standards set forth herein for certification of specialists in estate planning and probate law are subject to any general requirement, standard, or procedure adopted by the board applicable to all applicants for certification or continued certification.

[History Note: Statutory Authority G.S. 84–23. Readopted effective December 8, 1994.]

SECTION .2400 CERTIFICATION STANDARDS FOR THE FAMILY LAW SPECIALTY

.2401 Establishment of Specialty Field

The North Carolina State Bar Board of Legal Specialization (the board) hereby designates family law as a field of law for which certification of specialists under the North Carolina Plan of Legal Specialization (see Section .1700 of this subchapter) is permitted.

[History Note: Statutory Authority G.S. 84–23. Readopted effective December 8, 1994.]

.2402 Definition of Specialty

The specialty of family law is the practice of law relating to marriage, divorce, alimony, child custody and support, equitable distribution, enforcement of support, domestic violence, bastardy, and adoption.

[History Note: Statutory Authority G.S. 84–23. Readopted effective December 8, 1994.]

.2403 Recognition as a Specialist in Family Law

If a lawyer qualifies as a specialist in family law by meeting the standards set for the specialty, the lawyer shall be entitled to represent that he or she is a "Board Certified Specialist in Family Law."

[History Note: Statutory Authority G.S. 84–23. Readopted effective December 8, 1994.]

.2404 Applicability of Provisions of the North Carolina Plan of Legal Specialization

Certification and continued certification of specialists in family law shall be governed by the provisions of the North Carolina Plan of Legal Specialization (see Section .1700 of this subchapter) as supplemented by these standards for certification.

[History Note: Statutory Authority G.S. 84–23. Readopted effective December 8, 1994.]

.2405 Standards for Certification as a Specialist in Family Law

Each applicant for certification as a specialist in family law shall meet the minimum standards set forth in Rule .1720 of this subchapter. In addition, each applicant shall meet the following standards for certification as a specialist in family law:

(a) Licensure and Practice. An applicant shall be licensed and in good standing to practice law in North Carolina as of the date of application. An applicant shall continue to be licensed and in good standing to practice law in North Carolina during the period of certification.

(b) Substantial Involvement. An applicant shall affirm to the board that the applicant has experience through substantial involvement in the practice of family law.

(1) Substantial involvement shall mean during the five years preceding the application, the applicant has devoted an average of at least 600 hours a year to the practice of family law, and not less than 400 hours during any one year.

(2) Practice shall mean substantive legal work done primarily for the purpose of legal advice or representation, or a practice equivalent.

(3) Practice equivalent shall mean

(A) service as a law professor concentrating in the teaching of family law. Such service may be substituted for one year of experience to meet the five-year requirement.

(B) service as a district court judge in North Carolina, hearing a substantial number of family law cases. Such service may be substituted for one year of experience to meet the five-year requirement.

(c) Continuing Legal Education. During the three calendar years prior to the year of application and the portion of the calendar year immediately prior to application, an applicant must have earned no less than 45 hours of accredited continuing legal education (CLE) credits in family law, nine of which may be in related fields. Related fields shall include taxation, trial advocacy, evidence, negotiation (including training in mediation, arbitration, and collaborative law), juvenile law, real property, estate planning and probate law, business organizations, employee benefits, bankruptcy, elder law, and immigration law. Only nine hours of CLE credit will be recognized for attendance at an extended negotiation or mediation training course. Parenting coordinator training will not qualify for family law or related field hours. At least 9 hours of CLE in family law or related fields must be taken during each of the three calendar years preceding application.

(d) Peer Review. An applicant must make a satisfactory showing of qualification through peer review. An applicant must provide the names of ten lawyers or judges who are familiar with the competence and qualification of the applicant in the specialty field. Written peer reference forms will be sent by the board or the specialty committee to each of the references. Completed peer reference forms must be received from at least five of the references. All references must be licensed and in good standing to practice in North Carolina. An applicant consents to the confidential inquiry by the board or the specialty committee of the submitted references and other persons concerning the applicant's competence and qualification.

(1) A reference may not be related by blood or marriage to the applicant nor may the reference be a partner or associate of the applicant at the time of the application.

(2) The references shall be given on standardized forms provided by the board with the application for certification in the specialty field. These forms shall be returned directly to the specialty committee.

(e) Examination. The applicant must pass a written examination designed to test the applicant's knowledge and ability in family law.

(1) *Terms.* The examination shall be in written form and shall be given annually. The examination shall be administered and graded uniformly by the specialty committee.

(2) *Subject Matter.* The examination shall cover the applicant's knowledge and application of the law relating to marriage, divorce, alimony, child custody and support, equitable distribution, enforcement of support, domestic violence, bastardy, and adoption including, but not limited to, the following:

(A) contempt (Chapter 5A of the North Carolina General Statutes);

(B) adoptions (Chapter 48);

(C) bastardy (Chapter 49);

(D) divorce and alimony (Chapter 50);

(E) Uniform Child Custody Jurisdiction and Enforcement Act (Chapter 50A);

(F) domestic violence (Chapter 50B);

(G) marriage (Chapter 51);

(H) powers and liabilities of married persons (Chapter 52);

(I) Uniform Interstate Family Support Act (Chapter 52C);

(J) Uniform Premarital Agreement Act (Chapter 52B);

(K) termination of parental rights, as relating to adoption and termination for failure to provide support (Chapter 7B, Article 11);

(L) garnishment and enforcement of child support obligations (Chapter 110, Article 9);

(M) Parental Kidnapping Prevention Act (28 U.S.C. §1738A);

(N) Internal Revenue Code § 71 (Alimony), 215 (Alimony Deduction), 121 (Exclusion of Gain from the Sale of Principal Residence), 151 and 152 (Dependency Exemptions), 1041 (Transfer of Property Incidental to Divorce), 2043 and 2516 (Gift Tax Exception), 414(p) (Defining QDRO Requirements), 408 (d)(6) (IRA Transfer Requirements for Non-Taxable Event), and regulations interpretive of these Code sections; and

(O) Federal Wiretap Law.

[History Note: Statutory Authority G.S. 84–23. Readopted effective December 8, 1994; amended February 5, 2002; Feb. 27, 2003; amended effective October 9, 2008.]

.2406 Standards for Continued Certification as a Specialist

The period of certification is five years. Prior to the expiration of the certification period, a certified specialist who desires continued certification must apply for continued certification within the time limit described in Rule .2406(d) below. No examination will be required for continued certification. However, each applicant for continued certification as a specialist shall comply with the specific requirements set forth below in addition to any general standards required by the board of all applicants for continued certification.

(a) Substantial Involvement. The specialist must demonstrate that, for each of the five years preceding application, he or she has had substantial involvement in the specialty as defined in Rule .2405(b) of this subchapter.

(b) Continuing Legal Education. Since last certified, a specialist must have earned no less than 60 hours of accredited continuing legal education credits in family law or related fields. Not less than nine credits may be earned in any one year, and no more than twelve credits may be in related fields. Related fields shall include taxation, trial advocacy, evidence, negotiations (including training in mediation, arbitration, and collaborative law), juvenile law, real property, estate planning and probate law, business organizations, employee benefits, bankruptcy, elder law, and immigration law. Only nine hours of CLE credit will be recognized for attendance at an extended negotiation or mediation training course. Parenting coordinator training will not qualify for family law or related field hours.

(c) Peer Review. The specialist must comply with the requirements of Rule .2405(d) of this subchapter.

(d) Time for Application. Application for continued certification shall be made not more than 180 days nor less than 90 days prior to the expiration of the prior period of certification.

(e) Lapse of Certification. Failure of a specialist to apply for continued certification in a timely fashion will result in a lapse of certification. Following such lapse, recertification will require compliance with all requirements of Rule .2405 of this subchapter, including the examination.

(f) Suspension or Revocation of Certification. If an applicant's certification has been suspended or revoked during the period of certification, then the application shall be treated as if it were for initial certification under Rule .2405 of this subchapter.

[History Note: Statutory Authority G.S. 84–23. Readopted effective December 8, 1994. Amended Feb. 27, 2003; amended effective October 9, 2008.]

.2407 Applicability of Other Requirements

The specific standards set forth herein for certification of specialists in family law are subject to any general requirement, standards, or procedure adopted by the board applicable to all applicants for certification or continued certification.

[History Note: Statutory Authority G.S. 84–23. Readopted effective December 8, 1994.]

SECTION .2500 CERTIFICATION STANDARDS FOR THE CRIMINAL LAW SPECIALTY

.2501 Establishment of Specialty Field

The North Carolina State Bar Board of Legal Specialization (the board) hereby designates criminal law, including the subspecialty of state criminal law, as a field of law for which certification of specialists under the North Carolina Plan of Legal Specialization (*see* Section .1700 of this subchapter) is permitted.

[History Note: Statutory Authority G.S. 84–23. Readopted effective December 8, 1994. Amended effective March 10, 2011.]

.2502 Definition of Specialty

The specialty of criminal law is the practice of law dealing with the defense or prosecution of those charged with misdemeanor and felony crimes in state and federal trial courts. The subspecialty in the field is identified and defined as follows:

State Criminal Law—The practice of criminal law in state trial and appellate courts.

[History Note: Statutory Authority G.S. 84–23. Readopted effective December 8, 1994. Amended effective March 10, 2011.]

.2503 Recognition as a Specialist in Criminal Law

A lawyer may qualify as a specialist by meeting the standards set for criminal law or the subspecialty of state criminal law. If a lawyer qualifies as a specialist by meeting the standards set for the criminal law specialty, the lawyer shall be entitled to represent that he or she is a "Board Certified Specialist in Criminal Law." If a lawyer qualifies as a specialist by meeting the standards set for the subspecialty of state criminal law, the lawyer shall be entitled to represent that he or she is a "Board Certified Specialist in State Criminal Law."

[History Note: Statutory Authority G.S. 84–23. Readopted effective December 8, 1994. Amended effective March 10, 2011.]

.2504 Applicability of Provisions of the North Carolina Plan of Legal Specialization

Certification and continued certification of specialists in criminal law shall be governed by the provisions of the North Carolina Plan of Legal Specialization (see Section .1700 of this subchapter) as supplemented by these standards for certification.

[History Note: Statutory Authority G.S. 84–23. Readopted effective December 8, 1994.]

.2505 Standards for Certification as a Specialist

Each applicant for certification as a specialist in criminal law or the subspecialty of state criminal law, shall meet the minimum standards set forth in Rule .1720 of this subchapter. In addition, each applicant shall meet the following standards for certification:

(a) Licensure and Practice. An applicant shall be licensed and in good standing to practice law in North Carolina as of the date of the application. During the period of certification an applicant shall continue to be licensed and in good standing to practice law in North Carolina.

(b) Substantial Involvement—An applicant shall affirm to the board that the applicant has experience through substantial involvement in the practice of criminal law.

(1) Substantial involvement shall mean during the five years immediately preceding the application, the applicant devoted an average of at least 500 hours a year to the practice of criminal law, but not less than 400 hours in any one year. "Practice" shall mean substantive legal work, specifically including representation in criminal jury trials, done primarily for the purpose of providing legal advice or representation, or a practice equivalent.

(2) "Practice equivalent" shall mean:

(A) Service as a law professor concentrating in the teaching of criminal law for one year or more, which may be substituted for one year of experience to meet the five-year requirement set forth in Rule .2505(b)(1) above;

(B) Service as a federal, state or tribal court judge for one year or more, which may be substituted for one year of experience to meet the five-year requirement set forth in Rule .2505(b)(1) above;

(3) For the specialty of criminal law and the subspecialty of state criminal law, the board shall require an applicant to show substantial involvement by providing information that demonstrates the applicant's significant criminal trial experience such as:

(A) representation during the applicant's entire legal career in criminal trials concluded by jury verdict;

(B) representation as principal counsel of record in federal felony cases or state felony cases (Class G or higher);

(C) court appearances in other substantive criminal proceedings in criminal courts of any jurisdiction; and

(D) representation in appeals of decisions to the North Carolina Court of Appeals, the North Carolina Supreme Court, or any federal appellate court.

(c) Continuing Legal Education

In the specialty of criminal law and the state criminal law subspecialty, an applicant must have earned no less than 40 hours of accredited continuing legal education credits in criminal law during the three years preceding the application, which 40 hours must include the following:

(1) at least 34 hours in skills pertaining to criminal law, such as evidence, substantive criminal law, criminal procedure, criminal trial advocacy and criminal trial tactics;

(2) at least 6 hours in the area of ethics and criminal law.

(d) Peer Review.

(1) Each applicant for certification as a specialist in criminal law and the subspecialty of state criminal law, must make a satisfactory showing of qualification through peer review.

(2) All references must be licensed and in good standing to practice in North Carolina and must be familiar with the competence and qualifications of the applicant in the specialty field. The applicant consents to the confidential inquiry by the board or the specialty committee of the submitted references and other persons concerning the applicant's competence and qualifications.

(3) Written peer reference forms will be sent by the board or the specialty committee to the references. Completed peer reference forms must be received from at least five of the references. The board or the specialty committee may contact in person or by telephone any reference listed by an applicant.

(4) Each applicant must provide for reference and independent inquiry the names and addresses of the following: (i) ten lawyers and judges who practice in the field of criminal law and who are familiar with the applicant's practice, and (ii) opposing counsel and the judge in last eight serious (Class G or higher) felony cases tried by the applicant.

(5) A reference may not be related by blood or marriage to the applicant nor may the reference be a partner or associate of the applicant at the time of the application.

(e) Examination. The applicant must pass a written examination designed to test the applicant's knowledge and ability.

(1) *Terms.* The examination(s) shall be in written form and shall be given at such times as the board deems appropriate. The examination(s) shall be administered and graded uniformly by the specialty committee.

(2) *Subject Matter.*

The examination shall cover the applicant's knowledge in the following topics in criminal law, and/or in the subspecialty of state criminal law, as the applicant has elected:

(A) the North Carolina and Federal Rules of Evidence;

(B) state and federal criminal procedure and state and federal laws affecting criminal procedure;

(C) constitutional law;

(D) appellate procedure and tactics;

(E) trial procedure and trial tactics;

(F) criminal substantive law;

(3) *Required Examination Components.*

(A) Criminal Law Specialty.

An applicant for certification in the specialty of criminal law must pass part I of the examination on general topics in criminal law and part II of the examination on federal and state criminal law.

(B) State Criminal Law Subspecialty.

An applicant for certification in the subspecialty of state criminal law must pass part I of the examination on general topics in criminal law and part III of the examination on state criminal law.

[History Note: Statutory Authority G.S. 84–23. Readopted effective December 8, 1994; amended effective February 5, 2004; amended effective October 6, 2004; amended effective August 23, 2007; amended effective March 10, 2011; amended effective March 8, 2013; amended effective October 2, 2014.]

.2506 Standards for Continued Certification as a Specialist

The period of certification is five years. A certified specialist who desires continued certification must apply for continued certification within the time limit described in Rule .2506(d) below. No examination will be required for continued certification. However, each applicant for continued certification as a specialist shall comply with the specific requirements set forth below in addition to any general standards required by the board of all applicants for continued certification.

(a) Substantial Involvement. The specialist must demonstrate that for the five years preceding reapplication he or she has had substantial involvement in the specialty or subspecialty as defined in Rule .2505(b).

(b) Continuing Legal Education. The specialist must have earned no less than 65 hours of accredited continuing legal education credits in criminal law with not less than 6 credits earned in any one year.

(c) Peer Review. The specialist must comply with the requirements of Rule .2505(d) of this subchapter.

(d) Time for Application. Application for continuing certification shall be made not more than 180 days nor less than 90 days prior to the expiration of the prior period of certification.

(e) Lapse of Certification. Failure of a specialist to apply for continued certification in a timely fashion will result in a lapse of certification. Following such lapse, recertification will require compliance with all requirements of Rule .2505 of this subchapter, including the examination.

(f) Suspension or Revocation of Certification. If an applicant's certification has been suspended or revoked during the period of certification, then the application shall be treated as if it were for initial certification under Rule .2505 of this subchapter.

[History Note: Statutory Authority G.S. 84-23. Readopted effective December 8, 1994; amended effective February 5, 2004.]

.2507 Applicability of Other Requirements

The specific standards set forth herein for certification of specialists in criminal law and the subspecialty of state criminal law are subject to any general requirement, standard, or procedure adopted by the board applicable to all applicants for certification or continued certification.

[History Note: Statutory Authority G.S. 84-23. Readopted effective December 8, 1994. Amended effective March 10, 2011.]

.2508. Standards for Certification as a Specialist in Juvenile Delinquency Law

Each applicant for certification as a specialist in juvenile delinquency law shall meet the minimum standards set forth in Rule .1720 of this subchapter. In addition, each applicant shall meet the following standards for certification:

(a) Licensure and Practice—An applicant shall be licensed and in good standing to practice law in North Carolina as of the date of the application. During the period of certification an applicant shall continue to be licensed and in good standing to practice law in North Carolina.

(b) Substantial Involvement—An applicant shall affirm to the board that the applicant has experience through substantial involvement in the practice of juvenile delinquency law.

(1) Substantial involvement shall mean during the five years immediately preceding the application, the applicant devoted an average of at least 500 hours a year to the practice of juvenile delinquency law, but not less than 400 hours in any one year. "Practice" shall mean substantive legal work, specifically including representation of juveniles or the state in juvenile delinquency court, done primarily for the purpose of providing legal advice or representation, or a practice equivalent.

(2) "Practice equivalent" shall mean:

(A) Service for one year or more as a state district court judge responsible for presiding over juvenile delinquency court for 250 hours each year may be substituted for one year of experience to meet the five-year requirement set forth in Rule .2508(b)(1) above;

(B) Service on or participation in the activities of local, state, or national civic, professional or government organizations that promote juvenile justice may be used to meet the requirement set forth in Rule .2508(b)(1) but not to exceed 100 hours for any year during the five years.

(C) Service as a law professor in a juvenile delinquency legal clinic at an accredited law school may be used to meet the requirement set forth in Rule .2508(b)(1).

(D) The practice of state criminal law may be used to meet the requirement set forth in Rule .2508(b)(1) but not to exceed 100 hours for any year during the five years. "Practice of state criminal law" shall mean substantive legal work representing adults or the state in the state's criminal district and superior courts.

(3) An applicant shall also demonstrate substantial involvement during the five years prior to application unless otherwise noted by providing information that demonstrates the applicant's significant juvenile delinquency court experience such as:

(A) Representation of juveniles or the state during the applicant's entire legal career in juvenile delinquency hearings concluded by disposition;

(B) Representation of juveniles or the state in juvenile delinquency felony cases;

(C) Court appearances in other substantive juvenile delinquency proceedings in juvenile court;

(D) Representation of juveniles or the state through transfer to adult court; and

(E) Representation of juveniles or the state in appeals of juvenile delinquency decisions.

(c) Continuing Legal Education—An applicant must have earned no less than 40 hours of accredited continuing legal education (CLE) credits in criminal and juvenile delinquency law during the three years preceding application. Of the 40 hours of CLE, at least 12 hours shall be in juvenile delinquency law, and the balance may be in the following related fields: substantive criminal law, criminal procedure, trial advocacy, and evidence.

(d) Peer Review—

(1) Each applicant for certification as a specialist in juvenile delinquency law must make a satisfactory showing of qualification through peer review.

(2) All references must be licensed and in good standing to practice in North Carolina and must be familiar with the competence and qualifications of the applicant in the specialty field. The applicant consents to the confidential inquiry by the board or the specialty committee of the submitted references and other persons concerning the applicant's competence and qualifications.

(3) Written peer reference forms will be sent by the board or the specialty committee to the references. Completed peer reference forms must be received from at least five of the references. The board or the specialty committee may contact in person or by telephone any reference listed by an applicant.

(4) Each applicant must provide for reference and independent inquiry the names and addresses of ten lawyers and judges who practice in the field of juvenile delinquency law or criminal law or preside over juvenile delinquency or criminal law proceedings and who are familiar with the applicant's practice.

(5) A reference may not be related by blood or marriage to the applicant nor may the reference be a partner or associate of the applicant at the time of the application.

(e) Examination—An applicant must pass a written examination designed to demonstrate sufficient knowledge, skills, and proficiency in the field of juvenile delinquency law to justify the representation of special competence to the legal profession and the public.

(1) *Terms*—The examination shall be given annually in written form and shall be administered and graded uniformly by the specialty committee.

(2) *Subject Matter*—The examination shall cover the applicant's knowledge in the following topics:

(A) North Carolina Rules of Evidence;

(B) State criminal substantive law;

(C) Constitutional law as it relates to criminal procedure and juvenile delinquency law;

(D) State criminal procedure;

(E) North Carolina Juvenile Code, Subchapters II and III, and related case law; and

(F) North Carolina caselaw as it relates to juvenile delinquency law.

(3) *Examination Components*—An applicant for certification in the subspecialty of juvenile delinquency law must pass part I of the criminal law examination on general topics in criminal law and part IV of the examination on juvenile delinquency law.

[History Note: Statutory Authority G.S. 84–23. Adopted effective August 25, 2011. Amended effective March 5, 2015.]

SECTION .2600 CERTIFICATION STANDARDS FOR THE IMMIGRATION LAW SPECIALTY

.2601 Establishment of Specialty Field

The North Carolina State Bar Board of Legal Specialization (the board) hereby designates immigration law as a field of law for which certification of specialists under the North Carolina Plan of Legal Specialization (see Section .1700 of this subchapter) is permitted.

[History Note: Adopted effective March 6, 1997.]

.2602 Definition of Specialty

The specialty of immigration law is the practice of law dealing with obtaining and retaining permission to enter and remain in the United States including, but not limited to, such matters as visas, changes of status, deportation and exclusion, naturalization, appearances before courts and governmental agencies, and protection of constitutional rights.

[History Note: Adopted effective March 6, 1997.]

.2603 Recognition as a Specialist in Immigration Law

If a lawyer qualifies as a specialist in immigration law by meeting the standards set for the specialty, the lawyer shall be entitled to represent that he or she is a "Board Certified Specialist in Immigration Law."

[History Note: Adopted effective March 6, 1997.]

.2604 Applicability of Provisions of the North Carolina Plan of Legal Specialization

Certification and continued certification of specialists in immigration law shall be governed by the provisions of the North Carolina Plan of Legal Specialization (see Section .1700 of this subchapter) as supplemented by these standards for certification.

[History Note: Adopted effective March 6, 1997.]

.2605 Standards for Certification as a Specialist in Immigration Law

Each applicant for certification as a specialist in immigration law shall meet the minimum standards set forth in Rule .1720 of this subchapter. In addition, each applicant shall meet the following standards for certification in immigration law:

(a) Licensure and Practice. An applicant shall be licensed and in good standing to practice law in North Carolina as of the date of application. An applicant shall continue to be licensed and in good standing to practice law in North Carolina during the period of certification.

(b) Substantial Involvement. An applicant shall affirm to the board that the applicant has experience through substantial involvement in the practice of immigration law.

(1) An applicant shall affirm that during the five years immediately preceding the application, the applicant devoted an average of at least 700 hours a year to the practice of immigration law, but not less than 400 hours in any one year. Service as a law professor concentrating in the teaching of immigration law may be substituted for one year of experience to meet the five-year requirement.

(2) An applicant shall show substantial involvement in immigration law for the required period by providing such information as may be required by the board regarding the applicant's participation in at least five of the seven categories of activities listed below during the five years immediately preceding the date of application:

(A) Family Immigration. Representation of clients before the U.S. Immigration and Naturalization Service and the State Department in the filing of petitions and applications.

(B) Employment Related Immigration. Representation of employers and/or aliens before at least one of the following: the N.C. Employment Security Commission, U.S. Department of Labor, U.S. Immigration and Naturalization Service, U.S. Department of State or U.S. Information Agency.

(C) Naturalization. Representation of clients before the U.S. Immigration and Naturalization Service and judicial courts in naturalization matters.

(D) Administrative Hearings and Appeals. Representation of clients before Immigration Judges in deportation, exclusion, bond redetermination, and other administrative matters; and the representation of clients in appeals taken before the Board of Immigration Appeals, Administrative Appeals Unit, Board of Alien Labor Certification Appeals, Regional Commissioners, Commissioner, Attorney General, Department of State Board of Appellate Review, and Office of Special Counsel for Immigration Related Unfair Employment Practices (OCAHO).

(E) Administrative Proceedings and Review in Judicial Courts. Representation of clients in judicial matters such as applications for habeas corpus, mandamus and declaratory judgments; criminal matters involving the immigration law; petitions for review in judicial courts; and ancillary proceedings in judicial courts.

(F) Asylum and Refugee Status. Representation of clients in these matters.

(G) Employer Verification, Sanctions, Document Fraud, Bond and Custody, Rescission, Registry, and Fine Proceedings. Representation of clients in these matters.

(c) Continuing Legal Education. An applicant must earn no less than 48 hours of accredited continuing legal education (CLE) credits in topics relating to immigration law during the four years preceding application. At least 20 of the 48 CLE credit hours must be earned during the first and second year preceding application and at least 20 of the CLE hours must be earned during the third and fourth years preceding application. Of the 48 hours, at least 42 must be in immigration law; the balance may be in the related areas of federal administrative procedure, trial advocacy, evidence, taxation, family law, employment law, and criminal law and procedure.

(d) Peer Review. An applicant must make a satisfactory showing of qualification through peer review. An applicant must provide the names of ten lawyers or judges who are familiar with the competence and qualification of the applicant in the specialty field. Written peer reference forms will be sent by the board or the specialty committee to each of the references. Completed peer reference forms must be received from at least five of the references. All references must be licensed and in good standing to practice in North Carolina. At least four of the completed peer reference forms received by the board must be from lawyers or judges who have substantial practice or judicial experience in immigration law. An applicant consents to the confidential inquiry by the board or the specialty committee of the submitted references and other persons concerning the applicant's competence and qualification.

(1) A reference may not be related by blood or marriage to the applicant nor may the reference be a partner or associate of the applicant at the time of the application.

(2) The references shall be given on standardized forms provided by the board with the application for certification in the specialty field. These forms shall be returned directly to the specialty committee.

(e) Examination. The applicant must pass a written examination designed to test the applicant's knowledge, skills, and proficiency in immigration law. The examination shall be in written form and shall be given annually. The examination shall be administered and graded uniformly by the specialty committee.

[History Note: Adopted effective March 6, 1997. Amended effective October 2, 2014.]

.2606 Standards for Continued Certification as a Specialist

The period of certification is five years. Prior to the expiration of the certification period, a certified specialist who desires continued certification must apply for continued certification within the time limit described in Rule .2606(d) below. No examination will be required for continued certification. However, each applicant for continued certification as a specialist shall comply with the specific requirements set forth below in addition to any general standards required by the board of all applicants for continued certification.

(a) Substantial Involvement. The specialist must demonstrate that, for each of the five years preceding application, he or she has had substantial involvement in the specialty as defined in Rule .2605(b) of this subchapter.

(b) Continuing Legal Education. The specialist must have earned no less than 60 hours of accredited continuing legal education credits in topics relating to immigration law as accredited by the board. At least 30 of the 60 CLE credit hours must be earned during the first three years after certification or recertification, as applicable. Of the 60 hours, at least 52 must be in immigration law; the balance may be in the related areas of federal administrative procedure, trial advocacy, evidence, taxation, family law, employment law, and criminal law and procedure.

(c) Peer Review. The specialist must comply with the requirements of Rule .2605(d) of this subchapter.

(d) Time for Application. Application for continued certification shall be made not more than one hundred eighty (180) days nor less than ninety days prior to the expiration of the prior period of certification.

(e) Lapse of Certification. Failure of a specialist to apply for continued certification in a timely fashion will result in a lapse of certification. Following such lapse, recertification will require compliance with all requirements of Rule .2605 of this subchapter, including the examination.

(f) Suspension or Revocation of Certification. If an applicant's certification has been suspended or revoked during the period of certification, then the application shall be treated as if it were for initial certification under Rule .2605 of this subchapter.

[History Note: Adopted effective March 6, 1997. Amended effective October 2, 2014.]

.2607 Applicability of Other Requirements

The specific standards set forth herein for certification of specialists in immigration law are subject to any general requirement, standard, or procedure adopted by the board applicable to all applicants for certification or continued certification.

[History Note: Adopted effective March 6, 1997.]

SECTION .2700 CERTIFICATION STANDARDS FOR THE WORKERS' COMPENSATION LAW SPECIALTY

.2701 Establishment of Specialty Field

The North Carolina State Bar Board of Legal Specialization (the board) hereby designates workers' compensation as a field of law for which certification of specialists under the North Carolina Plan of Legal Specialization (see Section .1700 of this subchapter) is permitted.

[History Note: Adopted effective May 4, 2000.]

.2702 Definition of Specialty

The specialty of workers' compensation is the practice of law involving the analysis of problems or controversies arising under the North Carolina Workers' Compensation Act (Chapter 97, North Carolina General Statutes) and the litigation of those matters before the North Carolina Industrial Commission.

[History Note: Adopted effective May 4, 2000.]

.2703 Recognition as a Specialist in Workers' Compensation Law

If a lawyer qualifies as a specialist in workers' compensation law by meeting the standards set for the specialty, the lawyer shall be entitled to represent that he or she is a "Board Certified Specialist in Workers' Compensation Law."

[History Note: Adopted effective May 4, 2000.]

.2704 Applicability of Provisions of the North Carolina Plan of Legal Specialization

Certification and continued certification of specialists in workers' compensation law shall be governed by the provisions of the North Carolina Plan of Legal Specialization (see Section .1700 of this subchapter) as supplemented by these standards for certification.

[History Note: Adopted effective May 4, 2000.]

.2705 Standards for Certification as a Specialist in Workers' Compensation Law

Each applicant for certification as a specialist in workers' compensation law shall meet the minimum standards set forth in Rule .1720 of this subchapter. In addition, each applicant shall meet the following standards for certification in workers' compensation law:

(a) Licensure and Practice—An applicant shall be licensed and in good standing to practice law in North Carolina as of the date of application. An applicant shall continue to be licensed and in good standing to practice law in North Carolina during the period of certification.

(b) Substantial Involvement—An applicant shall affirm to the board that the applicant has experience through substantial involvement in the practice of workers' compensation law.

(1) Substantial involvement shall mean during the five years immediately preceding the application, the applicant devoted an average of at least 500 hours a year to the practice of workers' compensation law, but not less than 400 hours in any one year. "Practice" shall mean substantive legal work done primarily for the purpose of providing legal advice or representation, or a practice equivalent.

(2) "Practice equivalent" shall mean:

(A) Service as a law professor concentrating in the teaching of workers' compensation law for one year or more may be substituted for one year of experience to meet the five-year requirement set forth in Rule .2705(b)(1) above;

(B) Service as a mediator of workers' compensation cases may be included in the hours necessary to satisfy the requirement set forth in Rule .2705(b)(1) above;

(C) Service as a deputy commissioner or commissioner of the North Carolina Industrial Commission may be substituted for the substantial involvement requirements in Rule .2705(b)(1) above provided

(i) the applicant was a full time deputy commissioner or commissioner throughout the five years prior to application, or

(ii) the applicant was engaged in the private representation of clients for at least one year during the five years immediately preceding the application; and, during this year, the applicant devoted not less than 400 hours to the practice of workers' compensation law. During the remaining four years, the applicant was either engaged in the private representation of clients and devoted an average of at least 500 hours a year to the practice of workers' compensation law, but not less than 400 hours in any one year, or served as a full time deputy commissioner or commissioner of the North Carolina Industrial Commission.

(3) The board may require an applicant to show substantial involvement in workers' compensation law by providing information regarding the applicant's participation, during the five years immediately preceding the date of the application, in activities such as those listed below:

(i) representation as principal counsel of record in complex cases tried to an opinion and award of the North Carolina Industrial Commission;

(ii) representation in occupational disease cases tried to an opinion and award of the North Carolina Industrial Commission; and

(iii) representation in appeals of decisions to the North Carolina Court of Appeals or the North Carolina Supreme Court.

(c) Continuing Legal Education—An applicant must earn no less than 36 hours of accredited continuing legal education (CLE) credits in workers' compensation law and related fields during the three years preceding application, with not less than six credits earned in courses on workers' compensation law in any one year. The remaining 18 hours may be earned in courses on workers' compensation law or any of the following related fields: civil trial practice and procedure; evidence; insurance; mediation; medical injuries, medicine, or anatomy; labor and employment law; Social Security disability law; and the law relating to long-term disability or Medicaid/Medicare claims.

(d) Peer Review—An applicant must make a satisfactory showing of qualification through peer review. An applicant must provide the names of ten lawyers, commissioners or deputy commissioners of the North Carolina Industrial Commission, or judges who are familiar with the competence and qualification of the applicant in the specialty field. Written peer reference forms will be sent by the board or the specialty committee to each of the references. Completed peer reference forms must be received from at least five of the references. All references must be licensed and in good standing to practice in North Carolina and have substantial practice or judicial experience in workers' compensation law. An applicant consents to the confidential inquiry by the board or the specialty committee of the submitted references and other persons concerning the applicant's competence and qualification.

(1) A reference may not be related by blood or marriage to the applicant nor may the reference be a partner or associate of the applicant at the time of the application.

(2) The references shall be given on standardized forms mailed by the board to each reference. These forms shall be returned directly to the specialty committee.

(e) Examination—An applicant must pass a written examination designed to demonstrate sufficient knowledge, skills, and proficiency in the field of workers' compensation law to justify the representation of special competence to the legal profession and the public. The examination shall be given annually in written form and shall be administered and graded uniformly by the specialty committee.

[History Note: Adopted effective May 4, 2000. Amended effective March 10, 2011; March 5, 2015.]

.2706 Standards for Continued Certification as a Specialist

The period of certification is five years. Prior to the expiration of the certification period, a certified specialist who desires continued certification must apply for continued certification within the time limit described in Rule .2706(d) below. No examination will be required for continued certification. However, each applicant for continued certification as a specialist shall comply with the specific requirements set forth below in addition to any general standards required by the board of all applicants for continued certification.

(a) Substantial Involvement—The specialist must demonstrate that, for each of the five years preceding application, he or she has had substantial involvement in the specialty as defined in Rule .2705(b) of this subchapter, provided, however, that a specialist who served on the Industrial Commission as a full time commissioner or deputy commissioner during the five years preceding application may substitute each year of service on the Industrial Commission for one year of practice.

(b) Continuing Legal Education—The specialist must earn no less than 60 hours of accredited continuing legal education (CLE) credits in workers' compensation law and related fields during the five years preceding application. Not less than six credits may be earned in any one year. Of the 60 hours of CLE, at least 30 hours shall be in workers' compensation law, and the balance may be in the following related fields: civil trial practice and procedure; evidence; insurance; mediation; medical injuries, medicine, or anatomy; labor and employment law; and Social Security disability law; and the law relating to long-term disability or Medicaid/Medicare claims. Effective March 10, 2011, the specialist must earn not less than six credits in courses on workers' compensation law each year and the balance of credits may be earned in courses on workers' compensation law or any of the related fields previously listed.

(c) Peer Review—The specialist must comply with the requirements of Rule .2705(d) of this subchapter.

(d) Time for Application—Application for continued certification shall be made not more than 180 days nor less than ninety days prior to the expiration of the prior period of certification.

(e) Lapse of Certification—Failure of a specialist to apply for continued certification in a timely fashion will result in a lapse of certification. Following such lapse, recertification will require compliance with all requirements of Rule .2705 of this subchapter, including the examination.

(f) Suspension or Revocation of Certification—If an applicant's certification has been suspended or revoked during the period of certification, then the application shall be treated as if it were for initial certification under Rule .2705 of this subchapter.

[History Note: Adopted effective May 4, 2000. Amended effective March 10, 2011; March 5, 2015.]

.2707 Applicability of Other Requirements

The specific standards set forth herein for certification of specialists in workers' compensation law are subject to any general requirement, standard, or procedure adopted by the board applicable to all applicants for certification or continued certification.

[History Note: Adopted effective May 4, 2000.]

SECTION .2800 CERTIFICATION STANDARDS FOR THE SOCIAL SECURITY DISABILITY LAW SPECIALTY

.2801 Establishment of Specialty Field

The North Carolina State Bar Board of Legal Specialization (the board) hereby designates Social Security disability law as a field of law for which certification of specialists under the North Carolina Plan of Legal Specialization (see Section.1700 of this subchapter) is permitted.

[History Note: Adopted effective March 2, 2006.]

.2802 Definition of Specialty

The specialty of Social Security disability law is the practice of law relating to the analysis of claims and controversies arising under Title II and Title XVI of the Social Security Act and the representation of claimants in those matters before the Social Security Administration and/or the federal courts.

[History Note: Adopted effective March 2, 2006.]

.2803 Recognition as a Specialist in Social Security Disability Law

If a lawyer qualifies as a specialist in Social Security disability law by meeting the standards set for the specialty, the lawyer shall be entitled to represent that he or she is a "Board Certified Specialist in Social Security Disability Law."

[History Note: Adopted effective March 2, 2006.]

.2804 Applicability of Provisions of the North Carolina Plan of Legal Specialization

Certification and continued certification of specialists in Social Security disability law shall be governed by the provisions of the North Carolina Plan of Legal Specialization (see Section .1700 of this subchapter) as supplemented by these standards for certification.

[History Note: Adopted effective March 2, 2006.]

.2805 Standards for Certification as a Specialist in Social Security Disability Law

Each applicant for certification as a specialist in Social Security disability law shall meet the minimum standards set forth in Rule .1720 of this subchapter. In addition, each applicant shall meet the following standards for certification in Social Security disability law:

(a) Licensure and Practice – An applicant shall be licensed and in good standing to practice law in North Carolina as of the date of application. An applicant shall continue to be licensed and in good standing to practice law in North Carolina during the period of certification.

(b) Substantial Involvement – An applicant shall affirm to the board that the applicant has experience through substantial involvement in the practice of Social Security disability law.

(1) "Substantial involvement" shall mean during the five years immediately preceding the application, the applicant devoted an average of at least 600 hours a year to the practice of Social Security disability law, but not less than 500 hours in any one year. "Practice" shall mean substantive legal work done primarily for the purpose of providing legal advice or representation, or a practice equivalent.

(2) "Practice equivalent" shall mean:

(A) Service as a law professor concentrating in the teaching of Social Security disability law for one year or more may be substituted for one year of experience to meet the five-year requirement set forth in Rule .2805(b)(1) above;

(B) Service as a Social Security administrative law judge, Social Security staff lawyer, or assistant United States attorney involved in cases arising under Title II and Title XVI may be substituted for three of the five years necessary to satisfy the requirement set forth in Rule .2805(b)(1) above;

(3) The board may require an applicant to show substantial involvement in Social Security disability law by providing information regarding the applicant's participation, during his or her legal career, as primary counsel of record in the following:

(A) Proceedings before an administrative law judge;

(B) Cases appealed to the appeals council of the Social Security Administration; and

(C) Cases appealed to federal district court.

(c) Continuing Legal Education—An applicant must earn no less than 36 hours of accredited continuing legal education (CLE) credits in Social Security disability law and related fields during the three years preceding application, with not less than six credits earned in any one year. Of the 36 hours of CLE, at least 18 hours shall be in Social Security disability law, and the balance may be in the following related fields: trial skills and advocacy; practice management; medical injuries, medicine, or anatomy; ERISA; labor and employment law; elder law; workers' compensation law; veterans' disability law; and the law relating to long term disability or Medicaid/Medicare claims.

(d) Peer Review – An applicant must make a satisfactory showing of qualification through peer review. An applicant must provide the names of ten lawyers or judges who are familiar with the competence and qualification of the applicant in the specialty field. Written peer reference forms will be sent by the board or the specialty committee to each of the references. Completed peer reference forms must be received from at least five of the references. All references must be licensed and in good standing to practice law in a jurisdiction in the United States and have substantial practice or judicial experience in Social Security disability law. An applicant consents to the confidential inquiry by the board or the specialty committee of the submitted references and other persons concerning the applicant's competence and qualification.

(1) A reference may not be related by blood or marriage to the applicant nor may the reference be a partner or associate of the applicant at the time of the application.

(2) The references shall be given on standardized forms mailed by the board to each reference. These forms shall be returned directly to the specialty committee.

(e) Examination – An applicant must pass a written examination designed to demonstrate sufficient knowledge, skills, and proficiency in the field of Social

Security disability law to justify the representation of special competence to the legal profession and the public. The examination shall be given annually in written form and shall be administered and graded uniformly by the specialty committee.

(1) *Subject Matter* – The examination shall cover the applicant's knowledge and application of the law relating to the following:

(A) Title II and Title XVI of the Social Security Act;

(B) Federal practice and procedure in Social Security disability cases;

(C) Medical proof of disability;

(D) Vocational aspects of disability;

(E) Workers' compensation offset;

(F) Eligibility for Medicare and Medicaid;

(G) Eligibility for Social Security retirement and survivors benefits;

(H) Interaction of Social Security benefits with employee benefits (e.g., long term disability and back pay);

(I) Equal Access to Justice Act; and

(J) Fee collection and other ethical issues in Social Security practice.

[History Note: Adopted effective March 2, 2006. Amended effective March 10, 2011.]

.2806 Standards for Continued Certification as a Specialist

The period of certification is five years. Prior to the expiration of the certification period, a certified specialist who desires continued certification must apply for continued certification within the time limit described in Rule .2806(d) below. No examination will be required for continued certification. However, each applicant for continued certification as a specialist shall comply with the specific requirements set forth below in addition to any general standards required by the board of all applicants for continued certification.

(a) Substantial Involvement. The specialist must demonstrate that, for each of the five years preceding application, he or she has had substantial involvement in the specialty as defined in Rule .2805(b) of this subchapter.

(b) Continuing Legal Education—The specialist must earn no less than 60 hours of accredited continuing legal education credits in Social Security disability law and related fields during the five years preceding application. Not less than six of the credits may be earned in any one year. Of the 60 hours of CLE, at least 20 hours shall be in Social Security disability law, and the balance may be in the following related fields: trial skills and advocacy; practice management; medical injuries, medicine, or anatomy; ERISA; labor and employment law; elder law; workers' compensation law; veterans' disability law; and the law relating to long term disability or Medicaid/Medicare claims.

(c) Peer Review. The specialist must comply with the requirements of Rule .2805(d) of this subchapter.

(d) Time for Application. Application for continued certification shall be made not more than 180 days nor less than 80 days prior to the expiration of the prior period of certification.

(e) Lapse of Certification. Failure of a specialist to apply for continued certification in a timely fashion will result in a lapse of certification. Following such lapse, recertification will require compliance with all requirements of Rule .2805 of this subchapter, including the examination.

(f) Suspension or Revocation of Certification. If an applicant's certification has been suspended or revoked during the period of certification, then the application shall be treated as if it were for initial certification under Rule .2805 of this subchapter.

[History Note: Adopted effective March 2, 2006. Amended effective March 10, 2011.]

.2807 Applicability of Other Requirements

The specific standards set forth herein for certification of specialists in Social Security disability law are subject to any general requirement, standard, or procedure adopted by the board applicable to all applicants for certification or continued certification.

[History Note: Adopted effective March 2, 2006.]

SECTION .2900 CERTIFICATION STANDARDS FOR THE ELDER LAW SPECIALTY

.2901 Establishment of Specialty Field

The North Carolina State Bar Board of Legal Specialization (the board) hereby designates elder law as a field of law for which certification of specialists under the North Carolina Plan of Legal Specialization (see Section .1700 of this subchapter) is permitted.

Adopted effective February 5, 2009.

.2902 Definition of Specialty

The specialty of elder law is the practice of law involving the counseling and representation of older persons and their representatives relative to the legal aspects of health and long term care planning; public benefits; surrogate decision-making, legal capacity; the conservation, disposition, and administration of the estates of older persons; and the implementation of decisions of older persons and their representatives relative to the foregoing with due consideration to the applicable tax consequences of an action, or the need for more sophisticated tax expertise.

Lawyers certified in elder law must be capable of recognizing issues that arise during counseling and representation of older persons, or their representatives, with respect to abuse, neglect, or exploitation of the older person, insurance, housing, long term care, employment, and retirement. The elder law specialist must also be familiar with professional and non-legal resources and services publicly and privately available to meet the needs of the older persons, and be capable of recognizing the professional conduct and ethical issues that arise during representation.

Adopted effective February 5, 2009.

.2903 Recognition as a Specialist in Elder Law

If a lawyer qualifies as a specialist in elder law by meeting the standards set for the specialty, the lawyer shall be entitled to represent that he or she is a "Board Certified Specialist in Elder Law."

Adopted effective February 5, 2009.

.2904 Applicability of Provisions of the North Carolina Plan of Legal Specialization

Certification and continued certification of specialists in elder law shall be governed by the provisions of the North Carolina Plan of Legal Specialization (see Section .1700 of this subchapter) as supplemented by these standards for certification.

Adopted effective February 5, 2009.

.2905 Standards for Certification as a Specialist in Elder Law

Each applicant for certification as a specialist in elder law shall meet the minimum standards set forth in Rule .1720 of this subchapter. In addition, each applicant shall meet the following standards for certification in elder law:

(a) Licensure and Practice—An applicant shall be licensed and in good standing to practice law in North Carolina as of the date of application. An applicant shall continue to be licensed and in good standing to practice law in North Carolina during the period of certification.

(b) Substantial Involvement—An applicant shall affirm to the board that the applicant has experience through substantial involvement in the practice of elder law.

(1) Substantial involvement shall mean during the five years immediately preceding the application, the applicant devoted an average of at least 700 hours a year to the practice of elder law, but not less than 400 hours in any one year. Practice shall mean substantive legal work done primarily for the purpose of providing legal advice or representation, or a practice equivalent.

(2) Practice equivalent shall mean service as a law professor concentrating in the teaching of elder law (or such other related fields as approved by the specialty committee and the board) for one year or more. Such service may be substituted for one year of experience to meet the five-year requirement set forth in Rule .2905(b)(1) above.

(c) Substantial Involvement Experience Requirements—In addition to the showing required by Rule .2905(b), an applicant shall show substantial involvement in elder law by providing information regarding the applicant's participation, during the five years immediately preceding the date of the application, in at least sixty (60) elder law matters in the categories set forth in Rule .2905(c)(3) below.

(1) As used in this section, an applicant will be considered to have participated in an elder law matter if the applicant:

(A) provided advice (written or oral, but if oral, supported by substantial documentation in the client's file) tailored to and based on facts and circumstances specific to a particular client;

(B) drafted legal documents such as, but not limited to, wills, trusts, or health care directives, provided that those legal documents were tailored to and based on facts and circumstances specific to the particular client;

(C) prepared legal documents and took other steps necessary for the administration of a previously prepared legal directive such as, but not limited to, a will or trust; or

(D) provided representation to a party in contested litigation or administrative matters concerning an elder law issue.

(2) Of the 60 elder law matters:

(A) forty (40) must be in the experience categories listed in Rule .2905(c)(3)(A) through (E) with at least five matters in each category;

(B) ten (10) must be in experience categories listed in Rule .2905(c)(3)(F) through (M), with no more than five in any one category; and

(C) the remaining ten (10) may be in any category listed in Rule .2905(c)(3), and are not subject to the limitations set forth in Rule .2905(c)(2)(B) or (C).

(3) *Experience Categories*:

(A) health and Personal Care Planning including giving advice regarding, and preparing, advance medical directives (medical powers of attorney, living wills, and health care declarations) and counseling older persons, attorneys-in-fact, and families about medical and life-sustaining choices, and related personal life choices.

(B) pre-Mortem Legal Planning including giving advice and preparing documents regarding wills, trusts, durable general or financial powers of attorney, real estate, gifting, and the financial and tax implications of any proposed action.

(C) fiduciary Representation including seeking the appointment of, giving advice to, representing, or serving as executor, personal representative, attorney-in-fact, trustee, guardian, conservator, representative payee, or other formal or informal fiduciary.

(D) legal Capacity Counseling including advising how capacity is determined and the level of capacity required for various legal activities, and representing those who are or may be the subject of guardianship/conservatorship proceedings or other protective arrangements.

(E) public Benefits Advice including planning for and assisting in obtaining Medicaid, supplemental security income, and veterans benefits.

(F) advice on Insurance Matters including analyzing and explaining the types of insurance available, such as health, life, long term care, home care, COBRA, medigap, long term disability, dread disease, and burial/funeral policies.

(G) resident Rights Advocacy including advising patients and residents of hospitals, nursing facilities, continuing care retirement communities, assisted living facilities, adult care facilities, and those cared for in their homes of their rights and appropriate remedies in matters such as admission, transfer and discharge policies, quality of care, and related issues.

(H) housing Counseling including reviewing the options available and the financing of those options such as: mortgage alternatives, renovation loan programs, life care contracts, and home equity conversion.

(I) employment and Retirement Advice including pensions, retiree health benefits, unemployment benefits, and other benefits.

(J) income, Estate, and Gift Tax Advice, including consequences of plans made and advice offered.

(K) public Benefits Advice, including planning for and assisting in obtaining Medicare, social security, and food stamps.

(L) counseling with regard to age and/or disability discrimination in employment and housing.

(M) litigation and Administrative Advocacy in connection with any of the above matters, including will contests, contested capacity issues, elder abuse (including financial or consumer fraud), fiduciary administration, public benefits, nursing home torts, and discrimination.

(d) Continuing Legal Education—An applicant must earn forty-five (45) hours of accredited continuing legal education (CLE) credits in elder law and related fields, as specified in this rule, during the three full calendar years preceding application and the year of application, with not less than nine (9) credits earned in any of the three calendar years. Of the forty-five CLE credits, at least ten (10) credits must be earned attending elder law-specific CLE programs. Related fields shall include the following: estate planning and administration, trust law, health and long term care planning, public benefits, veterans' benefits, surrogate decision-making, older persons' legal capacity, social security disability, Medicaid/Medicare claims, special needs planning and taxation. No more than twenty (20) credits may be earned in the related fields of estate taxation or estate administration

(e) Peer Review—An applicant must make a satisfactory showing of qualification through peer review. An applicant must provide the names of ten lawyers or judges who are familiar with the competence and qualification of the applicant in the specialty field. Written peer reference forms will be sent by the board or the specialty committee to each of the references. Completed peer reference forms must be received from at least five of the references. All references must be licensed and in good standing to practice in North Carolina and have substantial practice or judicial experience in elder law or in a related field as set forth in Rule .2905(d). An applicant consents to the confidential inquiry by the board or the specialty committee of the submitted references and other persons concerning the applicant's competence and qualification.

(1) A reference may not be related by blood or marriage to the applicant nor may the reference be a partner or associate of the applicant at the time of the application.

(2) The references shall be given on standardized forms mailed by the board to each reference. These forms shall be returned directly to the specialty committee.

(f) Examination—An applicant must pass a written examination designed to demonstrate sufficient knowledge, skills, and proficiency in the field of elder law to justify the representation of special competence to the legal profession and the public. The examination shall be given annually in written form and shall be administered and graded uniformly by the specialty committee or by any ABA accredited elder law certification organization with which the board contracts pursuant to Rule .1716(10) of this subchapter.

[Adopted effective February 5, 2009. Amended eff. March 11, 2010; March 10, 2011; March 8, 2012.]

.2906 Standards for Continued Certification as a Specialist

The period of certification is five years. Prior to the expiration of the certification period, a certified specialist who desires continued certification must apply for continued certification within the time limit described in Rule .2906(d) below. No examination will be required for continued certification. However, each applicant for continued certification as a specialist shall comply with the specific requirements set forth below in addition to any general standards required by the board of all applicants for continued certification.

(a) Substantial Involvement—The specialist must demonstrate that, for each of the five years preceding application, he or she has had substantial involvement in the specialty as defined in Rule .2905(b) of this subchapter.

(b) Continuing Legal Education—The specialist must earn seventy-five (75) hours of accredited continuing legal education (CLE) credits in elder law or related fields during the five calendar years preceding application, with not less than ten (10) credits earned in any calendar year. Related fields shall include the following: estate planning and administration, trust law, health and long term care planning, public benefits, surrogate decision-making, older persons' legal capacity, social security disability, Medicaid/Medicare claims and taxation. No more than forty (40) credits may be earned in the related fields of estate taxation or estate administration.

(c) Peer Review—The specialist must comply with the requirements of Rule .2905(e) of this subchapter.

(d) Time for Application—Application for continued certification shall be made not more than 180 days nor less than 90 days prior to the expiration of the prior period of certification.

(e) Lapse of Certification—Failure of a specialist to apply for continued certification in a timely fashion will result in a lapse of certification. Following such lapse, recertification will require compliance with all requirements of Rule .2905 of this subchapter, including the examination.

(f) Suspension or Revocation of Certification—If an applicant's certification has been suspended or revoked during the period of certification, then the application shall be treated as if it were for initial certification under Rule .2905 of this subchapter.

Adopted effective February 5, 2009.

.2907 Applicability of Other Requirements

The specific standards set forth herein for certification of specialists in elder law are subject to any general requirement, standard, or procedure adopted by the board applicable to all applicants for certification or continued certification.

Adopted effective February 5, 2009.

SECTION .3000 CERTIFICATION STANDARD FOR THE APPELLATE PRACTICE SPECIALTY

.3001 Establishment of Specialty Field

The North Carolina State Bar Board of Legal Specialization (the board) hereby designates appellate practice as a field of law for which certification of specialists under the North Carolina Plan of Legal Specialization (*see* Section .1700 of this subchapter) is permitted.

[Adopted effective March 10, 2011.]

.3002 Definition of Specialty

The specialty of appellate practice is the practice of law relating to appeals to the Appellate Division of the North Carolina General Courts of Justice, as well as appeals to appellate-level courts of any state or territory of the United States, the Supreme Court of the United States, the United States Courts of Appeals, the United States Court of Appeals for the Armed Forces and the United States Courts of Criminal Appeals for the armed forces, and any tribal appellate court for a federally recognized Indian tribe (hereafter referred to as a "state or federal appellate court" or collectively as "state and federal appellate courts").

[Adopted effective March 10, 2011.]

.3003 Recognition as a Specialist in Appellate Practice

If a lawyer qualifies as a specialist in appellate practice by meeting the standards for the specialty, the lawyer shall be entitled to represent that he or she is a "Board Certified Specialist in Appellate Practice." Any lawyer who is entitled to represent that he or she is a "Board Certified Specialist in Criminal Appellate Practice" (having been certified as such under the standards set forth in Section .2500 of this subchapter) at the time of the adoption of these standards shall also be entitled to represent that he or she is a "Board Certified Specialist in Appellate Practice" and shall thereafter meet the standards for continued certification under Rule .3006 of this section in lieu of the standards for continued certification under Rule .2506 of Section .2500 of this subchapter.

[Adopted effective March 10, 2011.]

.3004 Applicability of Provisions of the North Carolina Plan of Legal Specialization

Certification and continued certification of specialists in appellate practice shall be governed by the provisions of the North Carolina Plan of Legal Specialization (*see* Section .1700 of this subchapter) as supplemented by these standards for certification.

[Adopted effective March 10, 2011.]

.3005 Standards for Certification as a Specialist in Appellate Practice

Each applicant for certification as a specialist in appellate practice shall meet the minimum standards set forth in Rule .1720 of this subchapter. In addition, each applicant shall meet the following standards for certification in appellate practice:

(a) Licensure and Practice. An applicant shall be licensed and in good standing to practice law in North Carolina as of the date of application. An applicant shall continue to be licensed and in good standing to practice law in North Carolina during the period of certification.

Substantial Involvement—An applicant shall affirm to the board that the applicant has experience through substantial involvement in appellate practice.

(1) Substantial involvement shall mean that during the five years immediately preceding the application, the applicant devoted an average of at least 400 hours a year, and not less than 100 hours in any one year, to appellate practice. "Practice" shall mean substantive legal work done primarily for the purpose of providing legal advice or representation including activities described in paragraph (2) below, or a practice equivalent as described in paragraph (3) below.

(2) Substantive legal work in appellate practice includes, but is not limited to, the following: preparation of a record on appeal or joint appendix for filing in any state or federal appellate court; researching, drafting, or editing of a legal brief, motion, petition, or response for filing in any state or federal appellate court; participation in or preparation for oral argument before any state or federal appellate court; appellate mediation, either as the representative of a party or as a mediator, in any state or federal appellate court; consultation on issues of appellate practice including consultation with trial counsel for the purpose of preserving a record for appeal; service on a committee or commission whose principal focus is the study or revision of the rules of appellate procedure of the North Carolina or federal courts; authoring a treatise, text, law review article, or other scholarly work relating to appellate practice; teaching appellate advocacy at an ABA accredited law school; and coaching in appellate moot court programs.

(3) "Practice equivalent" shall include the following activities:

(A) Service as a trial judge for any North Carolina General Court of Justice, United States Bankruptcy Court, or United States District Court, including-service as a magistrate judge, for one year or more may be substituted for one year of experience toward the five-year requirement set forth in Rule .3005(b)(1).

(B) Service as a full-time, compensated law clerk for any North Carolina or federal appellate court for one year or more may be substituted for one year of experience toward the five-year requirement set forth in Rule .3005(b)(1).

(C) Service as an appellate judge for any North Carolina or federal appellate court may be substituted for the equivalent years of experience toward the five-year requirement set forth in Rule .3005(b)(1) as long as the applicant's experience, before the applicant took the bench, included substantial involvement in appellate practice (as defined in paragraph (b)(1)) for two years before the applicant's service as an appellate judge.

(4) An applicant must also demonstrate substantial involvement in appellate practice by providing information regarding the applicant's participation during his or her legal career in the following:

(A) Five (5) oral arguments to any state or federal appellate court; and

(B) Principal authorship of ten (10) briefs submitted to any state or federal appellate court.

(c) Continuing Legal Education. An applicant must earn no fewer than 36 hours of accredited continuing legal education (CLE) credits in appellate practice and related fields during the three years preceding application, with no less than six credits to be earned in any one year. Of the 36 hours of CLE, at least 18 hours shall be in appellate practice, and the balance may be in the following related fields: trial advocacy; civil trial practice and procedure; criminal trial practice and procedure; evidence; legal writing; legal research; and mediation. An applicant may ask the specialty committee to recognize an additional field as related to appellate practice for the purpose of meeting the CLE standard. An applicant who uses authorship of a treatise, text, law review article, or other scholarly work relating to appellate practice or the teaching of appellate advocacy at an ABA-accredited law school to satisfy the substantial involvement requirement in paragraph (b) of this rule may not use the same experience to satisfy the CLE requirements of this paragraph (c).

(d) Peer Review. An applicant must make a satisfactory showing of qualification through peer review. An applicant must provide the names of ten lawyers or judges who are familiar with the competence and qualification of the applicant in the specialty field. Written peer reference forms will be sent by the board or the specialty committee to each of the references. Completed peer reference forms must be received from at least five of the references. All references must be licensed and in good standing to practice law and must have significant legal or judicial experience in appellate practice. An applicant consents to confidential inquiry by the board or the specialty committee to the submitted references and other persons concerning the applicant's competence and qualification.

(1) A reference may not be related by blood or marriage to the applicant nor may the reference be a colleague at the applicant's place of employment at the time of the application.

(2) The references shall be given on standardized forms mailed by the board to each reference. These forms shall be returned to the board and forwarded by the board to the specialty committee.

(e) Examination. An applicant must pass an examination designed to allow the applicant to demonstrate sufficient knowledge, skills, and proficiency in the field of appellate practice to justify the representation of special competence to the legal profession and the public. The examination shall be given annually and shall be administered and graded uniformly by the specialty committee. The exam shall include a written component which may be take-home and may include an oral argument before a moot court.

(1) *Subject Matter*—The examination shall cover the applicant's knowledge and application of the following:

(A) The North Carolina Rules of Appellate Procedure;

(B) North Carolina General Statutes relating to appeals;

(C) The Federal Rules of Appellate Procedure;

(D) Federal statutes relating to appeals;

(E) The Local Rules and Internal Operating Procedures of the United States Court of Appeals for the Fourth Circuit;

(F) The Rules of the United States Supreme Court;

(G) Brief writing;

(H) Oral argument; and

(I) Principles of appellate jurisdiction.

[Adopted effective March 10, 2011.]

.3006 Standards for Continued Certification as a Specialist

The period of certification is five years. Prior to the expiration of the certification period, a certified specialist who desires continued certification must apply for continued certification within the time limit described in Rule .3006(d) below. No examination will be required for continued certification. However, each applicant for continued certification as a specialist shall comply with the specific requirements set forth below in addition to any general standards required by the board of all applicants for continued certification.

(a) Substantial Involvement. The specialist must demonstrate that, for each of the five years preceding application for continuing certification, he or she has had substantial involvement in the specialty as defined in Rule .3005(b) of this subchapter.

(b) Continuing Legal Education. The specialist must earn no less than 60 hours of accredited CLE credits in appellate practice and related fields during the five years preceding application for continuing certification. No less than six of the credits may be earned in any one year. Of the 60 hours of CLE, at least 20 hours shall be in appellate practice, and the balance may be in the related fields set forth in Rule .3005(c).

(c) Peer Review. The specialist must comply with the requirements of Rule .3005(d) of this subchapter.

(d) Time for Application. Application for continued certification shall be made not more than 180 days, nor less than 90 days, prior to the expiration of the prior period of certification.

(e) Lapse of Certification. Failure of a specialist to apply for continued certification in a timely fashion will result in a lapse of certification. Following such a lapse, recertification will require compliance with all requirements of Rule .3005 of this subchapter, including the examination.

(f) Suspension or Revocation of Certification. If an applicant's certification has been suspended or revoked during the period of certification, the application shall be treated as if it were for initial certification under Rule .3005 of this subchapter.

[Adopted effective March 10, 2011.]

.3007 Applicability of Other Requirements

The specific standards set forth herein for certification of specialists in appellate practice are subject to any general requirement, standard, or procedure, adopted by the board, that applies to all applicants for certification or continued certification.

[Adopted effective March 10, 2011.]

.3008 Advisory Members of the Appellate Practice Specialty Committee

The board may appoint former chief justices of the North Carolina Supreme Court to serve as advisory members of the Appellate Practice Specialty Committee. Notwithstanding any other provision in The Plan of Legal Specialization (Section .1700 of this subchapter) or this Section .3000, the board may waive the requirements of Rule .3005(d) and (e) above if an advisory committee member has served at least one year on the North Carolina Supreme Court and may permit the advisory member to file an application to become a board certified specialist in appellate practice upon compliance with all other required standards for certification in the specialty. Advisory members shall hold office for an initial term of three years and shall thereafter serve at the discretion of the board.

[Adopted effective March 10, 2011.]

SECTION .3100 CERTIFICATION STANDARD FOR THE TRADEMARK LAW SPECIALTY

.3101 Establishment of Specialty Field

The North Carolina State Bar Board of Legal Specialization (the board) hereby designates trademark law as a specialty for which certification of specialists under the North Carolina Plan of Legal Specialization (see Section .1700 of this subchapter) is permitted.

[Adopted effective March 8, 2013.]

.3102 Definition of Specialty

The specialty of trademark law is the practice of law devoted to commercial symbols, and typically includes the following: advising clients regarding creating and selecting trademarks; conducting and/or analyzing trademark searches; prosecuting trademark applications; enforcing and protecting trademark rights; and counseling clients on matters involving trademarks. Practitioners regularly practice before the United States Patent and Trademark Office (USPTO), the Trademark Trial and Appeal Board (TTAB), the Trademark Division of the NC Secretary of State's Office, and the North Carolina and/or federal courts.

[Adopted effective March 8, 2013.]

.3103 Recognition as a Specialist in Trademark Law

If a lawyer qualifies as a specialist in trademark law by meeting the standards set for the specialty, the lawyer shall be entitled to represent that he or she is a "Board Certified Specialist in Trademark Law."

[Adopted effective March 8, 2013.]

.3104 Applicability of Provisions of the North Carolina Plan of Legal Specialization

Certification and continued certification of specialists in trademark law shall be governed by the provisions of the North Carolina Plan of Legal Specialization (see Section .1700 of this subchapter) as supplemented by these standards for certification.

[Adopted effective March 8, 2013.]

.3105 Standards for Certification as a Specialist in Trademark Law

Each applicant for certification as a specialist in trademark law shall meet the minimum standards set forth in Rule .1720 of this subchapter. In addition, each applicant shall meet following standards for certification in trademark law:

(a) Licensure and Practice. An applicant shall be licensed and in good standing to practice law in North Carolina as of the date of application. An applicant shall continue to be licensed and in good standing to practice law in North Carolina during the period of certification.

(b) Substantial Involvement. An applicant shall affirm to the board that the applicant has experience through substantial involvement in trademark law.

(1) Substantial involvement shall mean that during the five years immediately preceding the application, the applicant devoted an average of at least 500 hours a year to the practice of trademark law, but not less than 400 hours in any one year.

(2) Practice shall mean substantive legal work in trademark law done primarily for the purpose of legal advice or representation or a practice equivalent.

(3) "Practice equivalent" shall mean:

(A) Service as a law professor concentrating in the teaching of trademark law which may be substituted for up to two years of experience to meet the five-year requirement set forth in Rule 3105(b)(1).

(B) Service as a trademark examiner at the USPTO or a functionally equivalent trademark office for any state or foreign government which may be substituted for up to two years of experience to meet the five-year requirement set forth in Rule .3105(b)(1).

(C) Service as an administrative law judge for the TTAB which may be substituted for up to three years of experience to meet the five-year requirement set forth in Rule .3105(b)(1).

(4) The board may, in its discretion, require an applicant to provide additional information as evidence of substantial involvement in trademark law, including information regarding the applicant's participation, during his or her legal career, in the following: portfolio management, prosecution of trademark applications, search and clearance of trademarks, licensing,

due diligence, domain name selection and dispute resolution, TTAB litigation, state court trademark litigation, federal court trademark litigation, trademark dispute resolution, and international trademark law.

(c) Continuing Legal Education. To be certified as a specialist in trademark law, an applicant must have earned no less than 36 hours of accredited continuing legal education credits in trademark law during the three years preceding application. The 36 hours must include at least 20 hours in trademark law and the remaining 16 hours in related courses including: business transactions, copyright, franchise law, internet law, sports and entertainment law, trade secrets, and unfair competition.

(d) Peer Review. An applicant must make a satisfactory showing of qualification through peer review. An applicant must provide the names of ten lawyers or judges who are familiar with the competence and qualification of the applicant in the specialty field. Written peer reference forms will be sent by the board or the specialty committee to each of the references. Completed peer reference forms must be received from at least five of the references. All references must be licensed and in good standing to practice law and must have significant legal or judicial experience in trademark law. An applicant consents to confidential inquiry by the board or the specialty committee to the submitted references and other persons concerning the applicant's competence and qualification.

(1) A reference may not be related by blood or marriage to the applicant nor may the reference be a colleague at the applicant's place of employment at the time of the application.

(2) The references shall be given on standardized forms mailed by the board to each reference. These forms shall be returned to the board and forwarded by the board to the specialty committee.

(e) Examination. An applicant must pass a written examination designed to demonstrate sufficient knowledge, skills, and proficiency in the field of trademark law to justify the representation of special competence to the legal profession and the public.

(1) *Terms*—The examination shall be given annually in written form and shall be administered and graded uniformly by the specialty committee.

(2) *Subject Matter*—The examination shall cover the applicant's knowledge and application of trademark law and rules of practice, and may include the following statutes and related case law:

(A) The Lanham Act (15 USC § 1501 et seq.)

(B) Trademark Regulations (37 CFR Part 2)

(C) Trademark Manual of Examining Procedure (TMEP)

(D) Trademark Trial and Appeal Board Manual of Procedure (TBMP)

(E) The Trademark Counterfeiting Act of 1984 (18 USC § 2320 et seq.)

(F) North Carolina Trademark Act (N.C. Gen. Stat Chap. 80).

[Adopted effective March 8, 2013.]

.3106 Standards for Continued Certification as a Specialist

The period of certification is five years. Prior to the expiration of the certification period, a certified specialist who desires continued certification must apply for continued certification within the time limit described in Rule .3106(d). No examination will be required for continued certification. However, each applicant for continued certification as a specialist shall comply with the specific requirements set forth below in addition to any general standards required by the board of all applicants for continued certification.

(a) Substantial Involvement. The specialist must demonstrate that, for each of the five years preceding application for continuing certification, he or she has had substantial involvement in the specialty as defined in Rule .3105(b) of this subchapter.

(b) Continuing Legal Education. The specialist must earn no less than 60 hours of accredited CLE credits in trademark law and related fields during the five years preceding application for continuing certification. No less than six of the credits may be earned in any one year. Of the 60 hours of CLE, at least 34 hours shall be in trademark law, and the balance of 26 hours may be in the related fields set forth in Rule .3105(c). of this subchapter.

(c) Peer Review. The specialist must comply with the requirements of Rule .3105(d) of this subchapter.

(d) Time for Application. Application for continued certification shall be made not more than 180 days, nor less than 90 days, prior to the expiration of the prior period of certification.

(e) Lapse of Certification. Failure of a specialist to apply for continued certification in a timely fashion will result in a lapse of certification. Following such a lapse, recertification will require compliance with all requirements of Rule .3105 of this subchapter, including the examination.

(f) Suspension or Revocation of Certification. If an applicant's certification has been suspended or revoked during the period of certification, the application shall be treated as if it were for initial certification under Rule .3105 of this subchapter.

[Adopted effective March 8, 2013.]

.3107 Applicability of Other Requirements

The specific standards set forth herein for certification of specialists in trademark law are subject to any general requirement, standard, or procedure adopted by the board applicable to all applicants for certification or continued certification.

[Adopted effective March 8, 2013.]

SUBCHAPTER E. REGULATIONS FOR ORGANIZATIONS PRACTICING LAW

SECTION .0100 REGULATIONS FOR PROFESSIONAL CORPORATIONS AND PROFESSIONAL LIMITED LIABILITY COMPANIES PRACTICING LAW

.0101 Authority, Scope, and Definitions

(a) Authority. Chapter 55B of the General Statutes of North Carolina, being "the Professional Corporation Act," particularly Section 55B–12, and Chapter 57C, being the "North Carolina Limited Liability Company Act," particularly Section 57C–2–01(c), authorizes the Council of the North Carolina State Bar (the council) to adopt regulations for professional corporations and professional limited liability companies practicing law. These regulations are adopted by the council pursuant to that authority.

(b) Statutory Law. These regulations only supplement the basic statutory law governing professional corporations (Chapter 55B) and professional limited liability companies (Chapter 57C) and shall be interpreted in harmony with those statutes and with other statutes and laws governing corporations and limited liability companies generally.

(c) Definitions. All terms used in these regulations shall have the meanings set forth below or shall be as defined in the Professional Corporation Act or the North Carolina Limited Liability Company Act as appropriate.

(1) "Council" shall mean the Council of the North Carolina State Bar.

(2) "Licensee" shall mean any natural person who is duly licensed to practice law in North Carolina.

(3) "Professional limited liability company or companies" shall mean any professional limited liability company or companies organized for the purpose of practicing law in North Carolina.

(4) "Professional corporations" shall mean any professional corporation or corporations organized for the purpose of practicing law in North Carolina.

(5) "Secretary" shall mean the secretary of the North Carolina State Bar.

[History Note: Statutory Authority G.S. 84–23. Readopted effective December 8, 1994.]

.0102 Name of Professional Corporation or Professional Limited Liability Company

(a) Name of Professional Corporation. The name of every professional corporation shall contain the surname of one or more of its shareholders or of one or more persons who were associated with its immediate corporate, individual, partnership, or professional limited liability company predecessor in the practice of law and shall not contain any other name, word, or character (other than punctuation marks and conjunctions) except as required or permitted by Rules .0102(a)(1), (2) and (5) below. The following additional requirements shall apply to the name of a professional corporation:

(1) *Corporate Designation.* The name of a professional corporation shall end with the following words:

(A) "Professional Association" or the abbreviation "P.A."; or

(B) "Professional Corporation" or the abbreviation "P.C."

(2) *Deceased or Retired Shareholder.* The surname of any shareholder of a professional corporation may be retained in the corporate name after such person's death, retirement or inactivity due to age or disability, even though such person may have disposed of his or her shares of stock in the professional corporation;

(3) *Disqualified Shareholder.* If a shareholder in a professional corporation whose surname appears in the corporate name becomes legally disqualified to render professional services in North Carolina or, if the shareholder is not licensed in North Carolina, in any other jurisdiction in which the shareholder is licensed, the name of the professional corporation shall be promptly changed to eliminate the name of such shareholder, and such shareholder shall promptly dispose of his or her shares of stock in the corporation;

(4) *Shareholder Becomes Judge or Official.* If a shareholder in a professional corporation whose surname appears in the corporate name becomes a judge or other adjudicatory officer or holds any other office which disqualifies such shareholder to practice law, the name of the professional corporation shall be promptly changed to eliminate the name of such shareholder and such person shall promptly dispose of his or her shares of stock in the corporation;

(5) *Trade Name Allowed.* A professional corporation shall not use any name other than its corporate

name, except to the extent a trade name or other name is required or permitted by statute, rule of court or the Rules of Professional Conduct.

(b) Name of Professional Limited Liability Company. The name of every professional limited liability company shall contain the surname of one or more of its members or one or more persons who were associated with its immediate corporate, individual, partnership, or professional limited liability company predecessor in the practice of law and shall not contain any other name, word or character (other than punctuation marks and conjunctions) except as required or permitted by Rules .0102(b)(1), (2) and (5) below. The following requirements shall apply to the name of a professional limited liability company:

(1) *Professional Limited Liability Company Designation.* The name of a professional limited liability company shall end with the words "Professional Limited Liability Company" or the abbreviations "P.L.L.C." or "PLLC";

(2) *Deceased or Retired Member.* The surname of any member of a professional limited liability company may be retained in the limited liability company name after such person's death, retirement, or inactivity due to age or disability, even though such person may have disposed of his or her interest in the professional limited liability company;

(3) *Disqualified Member.* If a member of a professional limited liability company whose surname appears in the name of such professional limited liability company becomes legally disqualified to render professional services in North Carolina or, if the member is not licensed in North Carolina, in any other jurisdiction in which the member is licensed, the name of the professional limited liability company shall be promptly changed to eliminate the name of such member, and such member shall promptly dispose of his or her interest in the professional limited liability company;

(4) *Member Becomes Judge or Official.* If a member of a professional limited liability company whose surname appears in the professional limited liability company name becomes a judge or other adjudicatory official or holds any other office which disqualifies such person to practice law, the name of the professional limited liability company shall be promptly changed to eliminate the name of such member and such person shall promptly dispose of his or her interest in the professional limited liability company;

(5) *Trade Name Allowed.* A professional limited liability company shall not use any name other than its limited liability company name, except to the extent a trade name or other name is required or permitted by statute, rule of court, or the Rules of Professional Conduct.

[History Note: Statutory Authority G.S. 84-23. Readopted effective December 8, 1994; amended effective March 6, 1997.]

.0103 Registration With the North Carolina State Bar

(a) Registration of Professional Corporation. At least one of the incorporators of a professional corporation shall be an attorney at law duly licensed to practice in North Carolina. The incorporators shall comply with the following requirements for registration of a professional corporation with the North Carolina State Bar:

(1) *Filing with State Bar.* Prior to filing the articles of incorporation with the secretary of state, the incorporators of a professional corporation shall file the following with the secretary of the North Carolina State Bar:

(A) the original articles of incorporation;

(B) an additional executed copy of the articles of incorporation;

(C) a conformed copy of the articles of incorporation;

(D) a registration fee of fifty dollars;

(E) an application for certificate of registration for a professional corporation (Form DC-1; see Section .0106(a) of this subchapter) verified by all incorporators, setting forth (i) the name and address of each person who will be an original shareholder or an employee who will practice law for the corporation in North Carolina; (ii) the name and address of at least one person who is an incorporator; (iii) the name and address of at least one person who will be an original director; and (iv) the name and address of at least one person who will be an original officer, and stating that all such persons are duly licensed to practice law in North Carolina. The application shall also (i) set forth the name, address, and license information of each original shareholder who is not licensed to practice law in North Carolina but who shall perform services on behalf of the corporation in another jurisdiction in which the corporation maintains an office; and (ii) certify that all such persons are duly licensed to practice law in the appropriate jurisdiction. The application shall include a representation that the corporation will be conducted in compliance with the Professional Corporation Act and these regulations; and

(F) a certification for professional corporation by the Council of the North Carolina State Bar (Form PC-2; see Rule .0106(b) of this subchapter), a copy of which shall be attached to the original, the executed copy, and the conformed copy of the articles of incorporation, to be executed by the secretary in accordance with Rule .0103(a)(2) below.

(2) *Certificates Issued by Secretary and Council.* The secretary shall review the articles of incorporation for compliance with the laws relating to professional corporations and these regulations. If the secretary determines that all persons who will be original

shareholders are active members in good standing with the North Carolina State Bar, or duly licensed to practice law in another jurisdiction in which the corporation shall maintain an office, and that the articles of incorporation conform with the laws relating to professional corporations and these regulations, the secretary shall take the following actions:

(A) execute the certification for professional corporation by the Council of the North Carolina State Bar (Form PC–2; see Rule .0106(b) of this subchapter) attached to the original, the executed copy, and the conformed copy of the articles of incorporation and return the original and the conformed copies of the articles of incorporation, together with the attached certificates, to the incorporators for filing with the secretary of state;

(B) retain the executed copy of the articles of incorporation together with the application (Form PC–1) and the certification of council (Form PC–2) in the office of the North Carolina State Bar as a permanent record;

(C) issue a certificate of registration for a professional corporation (Form PC–3; see Rule .0106(c) of this subchapter) to the professional corporation to become effective upon the effective date of the articles of incorporation after said articles are filed with the secretary of state.

(b) Registration of a Professional Limited Liability Company. At least one of the persons executing the articles of organization of a professional limited liability company shall be an attorney at law duly licensed to practice law in North Carolina. The persons executing the articles of organization shall comply with the following requirements for registration with the North Carolina State Bar:

(1) *Filing with State Bar.* Prior to filing the articles of organization with the secretary of state, the persons executing the articles of organization of a professional limited liability company shall file the following with the secretary of the North Carolina State Bar:

(A) the original articles of organization;

(B) an additional executed copy of the articles of organization;

(C) a conformed copy of the articles of organization;

(D) a registration fee of $50;

(E) an application for certificate of registration for a professional limited liability company (Form PLLC–1; see Rule .0106(f) of this subchapter) verified by all of the persons executing the articles of organization, setting forth (i) the name and address of each original member or employee who will practice law for the professional limited liability company in North Carolina; (ii) the name and address of at least one person executing the articles of organization; and (iii) the name and address of at least one person who will be an original manager, and stating that all such persons are duly licensed to practice law in North Carolina. The application shall also (i) set forth the name, address, and license information of each original member who is not licensed to practice law in North Carolina but who shall perform services on behalf of the professional limited liability company in another jurisdiction in which the professional limited liability company maintains an office; and (ii) certify that all such persons are duly licensed to practice law in the appropriate jurisdiction. The application shall include a representation that the professional limited liability company will be conducted in compliance with the North Carolina Limited Liability Company Act and these regulations;

(F) a certification for professional limited liability company by the Council of the North Carolina State Bar, (Form PLLC–2; see Rule .0106(g) of this subchapter), a copy of which shall be attached to the original, the executed copy, and the conformed copy of the articles of organization, to be executed by the secretary in accordance with Rule .0103(b)(2) below.

(2) *Certificates Issued by the Secretary.* The secretary shall review the articles of organization for compliance with the laws relating to professional limited liability companies and these regulations. If the secretary determines that all of the persons who will be original members are active members in good standing with the North Carolina State Bar, or duly licensed in another jurisdiction in which the professional limited liability company shall maintain an office, and the articles of organization conform with the laws relating to professional limited liability companies and these regulations, the secretary shall take the following actions:

(A) execute the certification for professional limited liability company by the Council of the North Carolina State Bar (Form PLLC–2) attached to the original, the executed copy and the conformed copy of the articles of organization and return the original and the conformed copy of the articles of organization, together with the attached certificates, to the persons executing the articles of organization for filing with the secretary of state;

(B) retain the executed copy of the articles of organization together with the application (Form PLLC–1) and the certification (Form PLLC–2) in the office of the North Carolina State Bar as a permanent record;

(C) issue a certificate of registration for a professional limited liability company (Form PLLC–3; see Rule .0106(h) of this subchapter) to the professional limited liability company to become effective upon the effective date of the articles of organization after said articles are filed with the secretary of state.

(c) Refund of Registration Fee. If the secretary is unable to make the findings required by Rules .0103(a)(2) or .0103(b)(2) above, the secretary shall refund the $50 registration fee.

(d) Expiration of Certificate of Registration. The initial certificate of registration for either a professional corporation or a professional limited liability company shall remain effective through June 30 following the date of registration.

(e) Renewal of Certificate of Registration. The certificate of registration for either a professional corporation or a professional limited liability company shall be renewed on or before July 1 of each year upon the following conditions:

(1) *Renewal of Certificate of Registration for Professional Corporation.* A professional corporation shall submit an application for renewal of certificate of registration for a professional corporation (Form PC-4; see Rule .0106(d) of this subchapter) to the secretary listing the names and addresses of all of the shareholders and employees of the corporation who practice law for the professional corporation in North Carolina and the name and address of at least one officer and one director of the professional corporation, and certifying that all such persons are duly licensed to practice law in the state of North Carolina and representing that the corporation has complied with these regulations and the provisions of the Professional Corporation Act. Such application shall also (i) set forth the name, address, and license information of each shareholder who is not licensed to practice law in North Carolina but who performs services on behalf of the corporation in another jurisdiction in which the corporation maintains an office; and (ii) certify that all such persons are duly licensed to practice law in the appropriate jurisdiction. Upon a finding by the secretary that all shareholders are active members in good standing with the North Carolina State Bar, or are duly licensed to practice law in another jurisdiction in which the corporation maintains an office, the secretary shall renew the certificate of registration by making a notation in the records of the North Carolina State Bar;

(2) *Renewal of Certificate of Registration for a Professional Limited Liability Company.* A professional limited liability company shall submit an application for renewal of certificate of registration for a professional limited liability company (Form PLLC-4; see Rule .0106(i) of this subchapter) to the secretary listing the names and addresses of all of the members and employees of the professional limited liability company who practice law in North Carolina, and the name and address of at least one manager, and certifying that all such persons are duly licensed to practice law in the state of North Carolina, and representing that the professional limited liability company has complied with these regulations and the provisions of the North Carolina Limited Liability Company Act. Such application shall also (i) set forth the name, address, and license information of each member who is not licensed to practice law in North Carolina but who performs services on behalf of the professional limited liability company in another jurisdiction in which the professional limited liability company maintains an office; and (ii) certify that all such persons are duly licensed to practice law in the appropriate jurisdiction. Upon a finding by the secretary that all members are active members in good standing with the North Carolina State Bar, or are duly licensed to practice law in another jurisdiction in which the professional limited liability company maintains an office, the secretary shall renew the certificate of registration by making a notation in the records of the North Carolina State Bar;

(3) *Renewal Fee.* An application for renewal of a certificate of registration for either a professional corporation or a professional limited liability company shall be accompanied by a renewal fee of $25;

(4) *Refund of Renewal Fee.* If the secretary is unable to make the findings required by Rules .0103(e)(1) or .0103(e)(2) above, the secretary shall refund the $25 registration fee;

(5) *Failure to Apply for Renewal of Certificate of Registration.* In the event a professional corporation or a professional limited liability company shall fail to submit the appropriate application for renewal of certificate of registration, together with the renewal fee, to the North Carolina State Bar within 30 days following the expiration date of its certificate of registration, the secretary shall send a notice to show cause letter to the professional corporation or the professional limited liability company advising said professional corporation or professional limited liability company of the delinquency and requiring said professional corporation or professional limited liability company to either submit the appropriate application for renewal of certificate of registration, together with the renewal fee and a late fee of $10, to the North Carolina State Bar within 30 days or to show cause for failure to do so. Failure to submit the application and the renewal fee within said thirty days, or to show cause within said time period, shall result in the suspension of the certificate of registration for the delinquent professional corporation or professional limited liability company and the issuance of a notification to the secretary of state of the suspension of said certificate of registration;

(6) *Reinstatement of Suspended Certificate of Registration.* Upon (a) the submission to the North Carolina State Bar of the appropriate application for renewal of certificate of registration, together with all past due renewal fees and late fees; and (b) a finding by the secretary that the representations in the application are correct, a suspended certificate of registration of a professional corporation or professional limited liability company shall be reinstated by the secretary by making a notation in the records of the North Carolina State Bar.

(7) *Inactive Status Pending Dissolution*—If a professional corporation or professional limited liability company notifies the State Bar in writing or, in response to a notice to show cause issued pursuant to Rule .0103(e)(5) of this subchapter, a delinquent professional corporation or professional limited liability company shows that the organization is no longer practicing law and is winding down the operations and financial activities of the organization, no renewal fee or late fee shall be owed and the organization shall be moved to inactive status for a period of not more than one year. If, at the end of that period, a copy of the articles of dissolution has not been filed with the State Bar, the secretary of the State Bar shall send a notice to show cause letter and shall pursue suspension of the certificate of registration as set forth in Rule. .0103(e)(5) of this subchapter.

[History Note: Statutory Authority G.S. 84-23. Readopted effective December 8, 1994; amended effective March 6, 1997; amended effective October 1, 2003.]

.0104 Management and Financial Matters

(a) Management. At least one director and one officer of a professional corporation and at least one manager of a professional limited liability company shall be active members in good standing with the North Carolina State Bar.

(b) Authority Over Professional Matters. No person affiliated with a professional corporation or a professional limited liability company, other than a licensee, shall exercise any authority whatsoever over the rendering of professional services in North Carolina or in matters of North Carolina law.

(c) No Income to Disqualified Person. The income of a professional corporation or of a professional limited liability company attributable to the practice of law during the time that a shareholder of the professional corporation or a member of a professional limited liability company is legally disqualified to render professional services in North Carolina or, if the shareholder or member is not licensed in North Carolina, in any other jurisdiction in which the shareholder or member is licensed or after a shareholder or a member becomes a judge, other adjudicatory officer, or the holder of any other office, as specified in Rules .0102(a)(4) or .0102(b)(4) of this subchapter, shall not in any manner accrue to the benefit of such shareholder, or his or her shares, or to such member.

(d) Stock of a Professional Corporation. A professional corporation may acquire and hold its own stock.

(e) Acquisition of Shares of Deceased or Disqualified Shareholder. Subject to the provisions of G.S. 55B-7, a professional corporation may make such agreement with its shareholders or its shareholders may make such agreement between themselves as they may deem just for the acquisition of the shares of a deceased or retiring shareholder or a shareholder who becomes disqualified to own shares under the Professional Corporation Act or under these regulations.

(f) Stock Certificate Legend. There shall be prominently displayed on the face of all certificates of stock in a professional corporation a legend that any transfer of the shares represented by such certificate is subject to the provisions of the Professional Corporation Act and these regulations.

(g) Transfer of Stock of Professional Corporation. When stock of a professional corporation is transferred to a licensee, the professional corporation shall request that the secretary issue a stock transfer certificate (Form PC-5; see Rule .0106(e) of this subchapter) as required by G.S. 55B-6. The secretary is authorized to issue the certificate which shall be permanently attached to the stub of the transferee's stock certificate in the stock register of the professional corporation. The fee for such certificate shall be two dollars for each transferee listed on the stock transfer certificate.

(h) Stock Register of Professional Corporation. The stock register of a professional corporation shall be kept at the principal office of the corporation and shall be subject to inspection by the secretary or his or her delegate during business hours at the principal office of the corporation.

[History Note: Statutory Authority G.S. 84-23. Readopted effective December 8, 1994; amended effective March 6, 1997.]

.0105 General and Administrative Provisions

(a) Administration of Regulations. These regulations shall be administered by the secretary, subject to the review and supervision of the council. The council may from time to time appoint such standing or special committees as it may deem proper to deal with any matter affecting the administration of these regulations. It shall be the duty of the secretary to bring to the attention of the council or its appropriate committee any violation of the law or of these regulations.

(b) Appeal to Council. If the secretary shall decline to execute any certificate required by Rule .0103(a)(2), Rule .0103(b)(2), or Rule .0104(g) of this subchapter, or to renew the same when properly requested, or shall refuse to take any other action requested in writing by a professional corporation or a professional limited liability company, the aggrieved party may request in writing that the council review such action. Upon receipt of such a request, the council shall provide a formal hearing for the aggrieved party through a committee of its members.

(c) Articles of Amendment, Merger, and Dissolution. A copy of the following documents, duly certified by the secretary of state, shall be filed with the secretary within 10 days after filing with the secretary of state:

(1) all amendments to the articles of incorporation of a professional corporation or to the articles of organization of a professional limited liability company;

(2) all articles of merger to which a professional corporation or a professional limited liability company is a party;

(3) all articles of dissolution dissolving a professional corporation or a professional limited liability company;

(4) any other documents filed with the secretary of state changing the corporate structure of a professional corporation or the organizational structure of a professional limited liability company.

(d) Filing Fee. Except as otherwise provided in these regulations, all reports or papers required by law or by these regulations to be filed with the secretary shall be accompanied by a filing fee of two dollars.

(e) Accounting for Filing Fees. All fees provided for in these regulations shall be the property of the North Carolina State Bar and shall be deposited by the secretary to its account, and such account shall be separately stated on all financial reports made by the secretary to the council and on all financial reports made by the council.

(f) Records of State Bar. The secretary shall keep a file for each professional corporation and each professional limited liability company which shall contain the executed articles of incorporation or organization, all amendments thereto, and all other documents relating to the affairs of the corporation or professional limited liability company.

(g) Additional Information. A professional corporation or a professional limited liability corporation shall furnish to the secretary such information and documents relating to the administration of these regulations as the secretary or the council may reasonably request.

[History Note: Statutory Authority G.S. 84–23. Readopted effective December 8, 1994.]

.0106 Forms

(a) Form PC–1:

Application for Certificate of Registration
for a Professional Corporation

The undersigned, being all of the incorporators of ________, a professional corporation to be incorporated under the laws of the state of North Carolina for the purpose of practicing law, hereby certify to the Council of the North Carolina State Bar:

1. At least one person who is an incorporator, at least one person who will be an original officer, and at least one person who will be an original director, and all persons who, to the best knowledge and belief of the undersigned, will be original shareholders and employees who will practice law for said professional corporation in North Carolina are duly licensed to practice law in the state of North Carolina. The names and addresses of such persons are:

Name and Position (incorporator, officer, director, shareholder, employee)	Address
____________	____________
____________	____________
____________	____________

2. Each original shareholder who is not licensed to practice law in North Carolina but who will perform services on behalf of the corporation in another jurisdiction in which the corporation maintains an office is duly licensed to practice law in that jurisdiction. The name, address, and license information of each such person are:

Name, Address, Jurisdiction of Licensure, License Number

____

____

3. The jurisdictions other than North Carolina in which the corporation will maintain an office are:

Name of Jurisdiction and Address of Office(s)

____

____

4. The undersigned represent that the professional corporation will be conducted in compliance with the Professional Corporations Act and with the North Carolina State Bar's Regulations for Professional Corporations and Professional Limited Liability Companies Practicing Law.

5. Application is hereby made for a Certificate of Registration to be effective upon the effective date of the professional corporation's articles of incorporation after said articles are filed with the secretary of state.

6. Attached hereto is the registration fee of $50.

This the ________ day of ________, 19____.

________________________ Incorporator

________________________ Incorporator

________________________ Incorporator

[Signatures of all incorporators.]

NORTH CAROLINA ____________ COUNTY

I hereby certify that ________, ________, ________, and ________, being all of the incorporators of ____________, a professional corporation, personally appeared before me this day and stated that they have read the foregoing Application for Certificate of Registration for a Professional Corporation and that the statements contained therein are true.

Witness my hand and notarial seal, this ___ day of __________, 19___.

______________________________ Notary Public

My commission expires: ______________

(b) Form PC–2:

Certification for Professional Corporation by Council of the North Carolina State Bar

The incorporators of ______________, a professional corporation, have certified to the Council of the North Carolina State Bar the names and addresses of all persons who will be original owners of said professional corporation's shares.

Based upon that certification and my examination of the roll of attorneys licensed to practice law in the state of North Carolina, I hereby certify that the ownership of the shares of stock is in compliance with the requirements of G.S. 55B–4(2) and G.S. 55B–6.

This certificate is executed under the authority of the Council of the North Carolina State Bar, this ___ day of _____, 19___.

____

Secretary of the North Carolina State Bar

[This certificate is required by G.S. 55B–4(4) and must be attached to the original articles of incorporation when filed with the secretary of state. See Rule .0103(a)(2) of this subchapter.]

(c) Form PC–3:

Certificate of Registration for a Professional Corporation

It appears that ______________, a professional corporation, has met all of the requirements of G.S. 55B–4, G.S. 55B–6 and the Regulations for Professional Corporations and Professional Limited Liability Companies Practicing Law of the North Carolina State Bar.

By the authority of the Council of the North Carolina State Bar, I hereby issue this Certificate of Registration for a Professional Corporation pursuant to the provisions of G.S. 55B–10 and the North Carolina State Bar's Regulations for Professional Corporations and Professional Limited Liability Companies Practicing Law.

This registration is effective upon the effective date of the articles of incorporation of said professional corporation, after said articles are filed with the secretary of state, and expires on June 30, 19___.

This the ___ day of _____, 19___.

____

Secretary of the North Carolina State Bar

(d) Form PC–4:

Application for Renewal of Certificate of Registration for Professional Corporation

Application is hereby made for renewal of the Certificate of Registration for Professional Corporation of ______________, a professional corporation.

In support of this application, the undersigned hereby certify to the Council of the North Carolina State Bar:

1. At least one of the officers and one of the directors, and all of the shareholders and employees of said professional corporation who practice law for said professional corporation in North Carolina are duly licensed to practice law in the state of North Carolina. The names and addresses of such persons are:

Name and Position (officer, director, shareholder, employee)	Address
______________	______________
______________	______________
______________	______________
______________	______________

2. Each shareholder who is not licensed to practice law in North Carolina but who performs services on behalf of the corporation in another jurisdiction in which the corporation maintains an office is duly licensed to practice law in that jurisdiction. The name, address, and license information of each such person are:

Name, Address, Jurisdiction of Licensure, License Number

____

____

3. The jurisdictions other than North Carolina in which the corporation maintains an office are:

Name of Jurisdiction and Address of Office(s)

____

____

____

4. At all times since the issuance of its Certificate of Registration for Professional Corporation, said professional corporation has complied with the North Carolina State Bar's Regulations for Professional Corporations and Professional Limited Liability Companies Practicing Law and with the Professional Corporations Act.

5. Attached hereto is the renewal fee of $25.

This the ___ day of _____, 19___.

____

(Professional Corporation)

By ______________________________

President (or Chief Executive)

NORTH CAROLINA _________ COUNTY

I hereby certify that ______________, being the __________ of ______________, a professional corporation, personally appeared before me this day and stated that he/she has read the foregoing Application for Renewal of Certificate of Registration for Professional Corporation and that the statements contained therein are true.

Witness my hand and notarial seal, this ___ day of _____, 19___.

______________________________ Notary Public

My commission expires: ______________

(e) **Form PC-5:**

North Carolina State Bar Stock Transfer Certificate

I hereby certify that ________ (transferee) is duly licensed to practice law in the State of North Carolina and as of this date may be a transferee of shares of stock in a professional corporation formed to practice law in the state of North Carolina.

This certificate is executed under the authority of the Council of the North Carolina State Bar, this ___ day of _____, 19___.

____

Secretary of the North Carolina State Bar

[This certificate is required by G.S. 55B-6 and must be attached to the transferee's stock certificate. See Rule .0104(g) of this subchapter.]

(f) **Form PLLC-1:**

Application for Certificate of Registration for a Professional Limited Liability Company

The undersigned, being all of the persons executing the articles of organization of ______________, a professional limited liability company to be organized under the laws of the state of North Carolina for the purpose of practicing law, hereby certify to the Council of the North Carolina State Bar:

1. At least one person executing the articles of organization, at least one person who will be an original manager, and all persons who, to the best knowledge and belief of the undersigned, will be original members and employees who will practice law for said professional limited liability company in North Carolina are duly licensed to practice law in the state of North Carolina. The names and addresses of all such persons are:

Name and Position (signer of articles, manager, member, employee)	Address
______________	______________
______________	______________
______________	______________

2. Each original member who is not licensed to practice law in North Carolina but who will perform services on behalf of the professional limited liability company in another jurisdiction in which the professional limited liability company maintains an office is duly licensed to practice law in that jurisdiction. The names, addresses, and license information of each such person are:

Name, Address, Jurisdiction Where Licensed, License Number

____

____

3. The jurisdictions other than North Carolina in which the professional limited liability company will maintain an office are:

Name of Jurisdiction and Address of Office(s)

____

____

____

4. The undersigned represent that the professional limited liability company will be conducted in compliance with the North Carolina Limited Liability Company Act and with the North Carolina State Bar's Regulations for Professional Corporations and Professional Limited Liability Companies Practicing Law.

5. Application is hereby made for a Certificate of Registration to be effective upon the effective date of the professional limited liability company's articles of organization after said articles are filed with the secretary of state.

6. Attached hereto is the registration fee of $50.

This the ___ day of _____, 19___.

____

____

____

[Signatures of all persons executing articles of organization.]

NORTH CAROLINA ______________ COUNTY

I hereby certify that __________, __________, __________, and __________, being all of the persons executing the articles of organization of ______________, a professional limited liability company, personally appeared before me this day and stated that they have read the foregoing Application for Certificate of Registration for a Professional Limited Liability Company and that the statements contained therein are true.

Witness my hand and notarial seal, this ___ day of _____, 19___.

______________________________ Notary Public

My commission expires: ______________

(g) **Form PLLC-2:**

Certification for Professional Limited Liability Company by Council of the North Carolina State Bar

All of the persons executing the articles of organization of ______________________, a professional limited liability company, have certified to the Council of the North Carolina State Bar the names and addresses of all persons who will be original members of said professional limited liability company.

Based upon that certification and my examination of the roll of attorneys licensed to practice law in the state of North Carolina, I hereby certify that the membership interest is in compliance with the requirements of G.S. 55C–2–01(c), and, by reference, G.S. 55B–4(2) and G.S. 55B–6.

This certificate is executed under the authority of the Council of the North Carolina State Bar, this ___ day of _____, 19___.

____

Secretary of the North Carolina State Bar

[This certificate is required by G.S. 55B–4(4) and G.S. 57C–2–01 and must be attached to the original articles of organization when filed with the secretary of state. See Rule .103(b)(2) of this subchapter.]

(h) Form PLLC–3:

Certificate of Registration for a Professional Limited Liability Company

It appears that ______________________, a professional limited liability company, has met all of the requirements of G.S. 57C–2–01 and the North Carolina State Bar's Regulations for Professional Corporations and Professional Limited Liability Companies Practicing Law.

By the authority of the Council of the North Carolina State Bar, I hereby issue this Certificate of Registration for a Professional Limited Liability Company pursuant to the provisions of G.S. 55B–10, G.S. 57C–2–01 and the North Carolina State Bar's Regulations for Professional Corporations and Professional Limited Liability Companies Practicing Law.

This registration is effective upon the effective date of the articles of organization of said professional limited liability company, after said articles are filed with the secretary of state, and expires on June 30, 19___.

This the ___ day of _____, 19___.

____

Secretary of the North Carolina State Bar

(i) Form PLLC–4:

Application for Renewal of Certificate of Registration for Professional Limited Liability Company

Application is hereby made for renewal of the Certificate of Registration for Professional Limited Liability Company of ______________________, a professional limited liability company.

In support of this application, the undersigned hereby certify to the Council of the North Carolina State Bar:

1. At least one of the managers, and all of the members and employees of said professional limited liability company who practice law for said professional limited liability company in North Carolina are duly licensed to practice law in the State of North Carolina. The names and addresses of all such persons are:

Name and Position (manager, member, employee)	Address
______________	______________
______________	______________
______________	______________
______________	______________

2. Each member who is not licensed to practice law in North Carolina but who performs services on behalf of the professional limited liability company in another jurisdiction in which the professional limited liability company maintains an office is duly licensed to practice law in that jurisdiction. The names, addresses, and license information of each such person are:

Name, Address, Jurisdiction Where Licensed, License Number

____

____

3. The jurisdictions other than North Carolina in which the professional limited liability company maintains an office are:

Name of Jurisdiction and Address of Office(s)

____

____

____

4. At all times since the issuance of its Certificate of Registration for Professional Limited Liability Company, said professional limited liability company has complied with the North Carolina State Bar's Regulations for Professional Corporations and Professional Limited Liability Companies Practicing Law and with the provisions of the North Carolina Limited Liability Company Act.

5. Attached hereto is the renewal fee of $25.

This the ___ day of _____, 19___.

____

(Professional Limited Liability Company)

By ______________________ Manager

NORTH CAROLINA __________ COUNTY

I hereby certify that ______, being a manager of ______, a professional limited liability company, personally appeared before me this day and stated that he/she has read the foregoing Application for Renewal of Certificate of Registration for Professional Limited Liability Company and that the statements contained therein are true.

Witness my hand and notarial seal, this ___ day of _____, 19___.

______________________ Notary Public

My commission expires: ______________

[History Note: Amended effective March 6, 1997.]

SECTION .0200 REGISTRATION OF INTERSTATE AND INTERNATIONAL LAW FIRMS

.0201 Registration Requirement

No law firm or professional organization that (1) maintains offices in North Carolina and one or more other jurisdictions, or (2) files for a certificate of authority to transact business in North Carolina from the North Carolina Secretary of State, may do business in North Carolina without first obtaining a certificate of registration from the North Carolina State Bar provided, however, that no law firm or professional organization shall be required to obtain a certificate of registration if all attorneys associated with the law firm or professional organization, or any law firm or professional organization that is in partnership with said law firm or professional organization, are licensed to practice law in North Carolina.

[History Note: Statutory Authority G.S. 84–23. Readopted effective December 8, 1994. Amended effective March 5, 1998; March 6, 2014.]

.0202 Conditions of Registration

The secretary of the North Carolina State Bar shall issue such a certificate of registration upon satisfaction of the following conditions:

(1) There shall be filed with the secretary of the North Carolina State Bar a registration statement disclosing:

(a) all names used to identify the filing law firm or professional organization;

(b) addresses of all offices maintained by the filing law firm or professional organization;

(c) the name and address of any law firm or professional organization with which the filing law firm or professional organization is in partnership and the name and address of such partnership;

(d) the name and address of each attorney who is a partner, shareholder, member or employee of the filing law firm or professional organization or who is a partner, shareholder, member or employee of a law firm or professional organization with which the filing law firm or professional organization is in partnership;

(e) the relationship of each attorney identified in Rule .0202(1)(d) above to the filing law firm or professional organization;

(f) the jurisdictions to which each attorney identified in Rule .0202(1)(d) above is admitted to practice law.

(2) There shall be filed with the registration statement a notarized statement of the filing law firm or professional organization executed by a responsible attorney associated with the filing law firm or professional organization who is licensed in North Carolina certifying that each attorney identified in Rule. 0202(1)(d) above who is not licensed to practice law in North Carolina is a member in good standing of the bar of each jurisdiction to which the attorney has been admitted.

(3) There shall be filed with the registration statement a notarized statement of the filing law firm or professional organization executed by a responsible attorney associated with the filing law firm or professional organization who is licensed in North Carolina affirming that each attorney identified in Rule. 0202(1)(d) above who is not licensed to practice law in North Carolina will govern his or her professional conduct with respect to legal matters arising from North Carolina in accordance with the Revised Rules of Professional Conduct of the North Carolina State Bar.

[History Note: Statutory Authority G.S. 84–23. Readopted effective December 8, 1994; amended effective March 5, 1998.]

.0203 Registration Fee

There shall be submitted with each registration statement and supporting documentation a registration fee of $500.00 as administrative cost.

[History Note: Statutory Authority G.S. 84–23. Readopted effective December 8, 1994.]

.0204 Certificate of Registration

A certificate of registration shall remain effective until January 1 following the date of filing and may be renewed annually by the secretary of the North Carolina State Bar upon the filing of an updated registration statement which satisfies the requirements set forth above and the submission of the registration fee.

[History Note: Statutory Authority G.S. 84–23. Readopted effective December 8, 1994.]

.0205 Effect of Registration

This rule shall not be construed to confer the right to practice law in North Carolina upon any lawyer not licensed to practice law in North Carolina.

[History Note: Statutory Authority G.S. 84–16; G.S. 84–23. Readopted effective December 8, 1994.]

.0206 Non-renewal of Registration

If a law firm or professional organization registered under these rules no longer meets the criteria for registration, it shall notify the State Bar in writing. If such written notice is not received by the State Bar on or before December 31 of the year in which registration is no longer required, the registration fee for the next calendar year, as set forth in Rule .0203 of this subchapter, shall be owed

[History Note: Adopted and effective October 1, 2003.]

SECTION .0300 RULES CONCERNING PREPAID LEGAL SERVICES PLANS

.0301 State Bar May Not Approve or Disapprove Plans

The North Carolina State Bar shall not approve or disapprove any prepaid legal services plan or render any legal opinion regarding any plan. The registration of any plan under these rules shall not be construed to indicate approval or disapproval of the plan.

[History Note: Statutory Authority G.S. 84–23; G.S. 84–23.1. Adopted effective December 8, 1994; amended effective August 23, 2007.]

.0302 Registration Requirement

A prepaid legal services plan ("plan") must be registered with the North Carolina State Bar before its implementation or operation in North Carolina. No licensed North Carolina attorney shall participate in a prepaid legal services plan in this state unless the plan has registered with the North Carolina State Bar and has complied with the rules set forth below. No prepaid legal services plan may operate in North Carolina unless at least one licensed North Carolina attorney has agreed to provide the legal services offered under the plan at all times during the operation of the plan. No prepaid legal services plan may operate in any manner that constitutes the unauthorized practice of law. No plan may operate until its registration has been accepted by the North Carolina State Bar in accordance with these rules.

[History Note: Statutory Authority G.S. 84–23; G.S. 84–23.1. Adopted effective December 8, 1994; amended effective February 5, 2004; amended effective August 23, 2007.]

.0303 Definition of Prepaid Plan

A prepaid legal services plan or a group legal services plan ("a plan") is any arrangement by which a person, firm or corporation, not otherwise authorized to engage in the practice of law, in exchange for any valuable consideration, offers to provide or arranges the provision of specified legal services that are paid for in advance of any immediate need for the specified legal services ("covered services"). In addition to covered services, a plan may provide specified legal services at fees that are less than what a non-member of the plan would normally pay. The North Carolina legal services offered by a plan must be provided by a North Carolina licensed lawyer who is not an employee, director, or owner of the plan. A prepaid legal services plan does not include the sale of an identified, limited legal service, such as drafting a will, for a fixed, one-time fee. [This definition is also found in Rule 7.3(d) of the Revised Rules of Professional Conduct.]

[History Note: Statutory Authority G.S. 84–23; G.S. 84–23.1. Adopted Effective December 8, 1994; amended effective August 23, 2007.]

.0304 Registration Procedures

To register with the North Carolina State Bar, a prepaid legal services plan must comply with all of the following procedures for initial registration:

(a) A prepaid legal services plan seeking to operate in North Carolina must file an initial registration statement form with the secretary of the North Carolina State Bar, using a form promulgated by the State Bar, requesting registration.

(b) The owner or sponsor of the prepaid legal services plan must fully disclose in its initial registration statement form filed with the secretary at least the following information: the name of the plan, the name of the owner or sponsor of the plan, a principal address for the plan in North Carolina, a designated plan representative to whom communications with the State Bar will be directed, all persons or entities with ownership interest in the plan and the extent of their interests, all terms and conditions of the plan, all services provided under the plan and a schedule of benefits and fees or charges for the plan, a copy of all plan documents, a copy of all plan marketing and advertising materials, a copy of all plan contracts with its customers, a copy of all plan contracts with plan attorneys, and a list of all North Carolina attorneys who have agreed to participate in the plan. Additionally, the owner or sponsor will provide a detailed statement explaining how the plan meets the definition of a prepaid legal services plan in North Carolina. The owner or sponsor of the prepaid legal services plan will certify or acknowledge the veracity of the information contained in the registration statement, an understanding of the rules applicable to prepaid legal services plans, and an understanding of the law on unauthorized practice.

(c) The Authorized Practice Committee ("committee"), as a duly authorized standing committee of the North Carolina State Bar Council, shall oversee the registration of prepaid legal services plans in accordance with these rules. The committee shall also establish any deadlines by when registrations may be submitted for review and any additional, necessary rules and procedures regarding the initial and annual registrations, and the revocation of registrations, of prepaid legal services plans.

[History Note: Statutory Authority G.S. 84–23; G.S. 84–23.1. Adopted Effective December 8, 1994; amended February 5, 2002; amended effective August 23, 2007; amended effective October 7, 2010.]

.0305 Registration

Counsel will review the plan's initial registration statement to determine whether the registration statement is complete and the plan, as described in the registration statement, meets the definition of a prepaid legal services plan and otherwise satisfies the requirements for registration provided by Rule .0304. If, in the opinion of counsel, the plan clearly meets the definition and the registration statement otherwise satisfies the requirements for registration, the secretary will issue a certificate of registration to the plan's sponsor. If, in the opinion of counsel, the plan does not meet the definition or otherwise fails to satisfy the requirements for registration, counsel will inform the plan's sponsor that the registration is not accepted and explain any deficiencies. Upon notice that the plan's registration has not been accepted, the plan sponsor may resubmit an amended plan registration form or request a hearing before the committee pursuant to Rule .0313 below. Counsel will provide a report to the committee each quarter identifying the plans submitted and the registration decisions made by counsel.

[History Note: Statutory Authority G.S. 84–23; G.S. 84–23.1. Adopted effective December 8, 1994; amended effective August 23, 2007; amended effective October 7, 2010.]

.0306 Requirement to File Amendments

Amendments to prepaid legal services plans and to other documents required to be filed upon registration of such plans shall be filed in the office of the North Carolina State Bar no later than 30 days after the adoption of such amendments. Plan amendments must be submitted in the same manner as the initial registration and may not be implemented until the amended plan is registered in accordance with Rule .0305.

[History Note: Statutory Authority G.S. 84–23; G.S. 84–23.1. Adopted effective December 8, 1994; amended effective August 23, 2007.]

.0307 Annual Registration

After its initial registration, a prepaid legal services plan may continue to operate so long as it is operated as registered and it renews its registration annually on or before January 31 by filing a registration renewal form with the secretary and paying the annual registration fee.

[History Note: Statutory Authority G.S. 84–23; G.S. 84–23.1. Adopted effective December 8, 1994; amended effective August 23, 2007.]

.0308 Registration Fee

The initial and annual registration fees for each prepaid legal services plan shall be $100. The fee is nonrefundable.

[History Note: Statutory Authority G.S. 84–23; G.S. 84–23.1. Adopted effective December 8, 1994; amended effective August 23, 2007; March 8, 2012.]

.0309 Index of Registered Plans

The North Carolina State Bar shall maintain an index of the prepaid legal services plans registered pursuant to these rules. All documents filed in compliance with this rule are considered public documents and shall be available for public inspection during normal business hours.

[History Note: Statutory Authority G.S. 84–23; G.S. 84–23.1. Adopted effective December 8, 1994; amended effective August 23, 2007.]

.0310 Advertising of State Bar Approval Prohibited

Any plan that advertises or otherwise represents that it is registered with the North Carolina State Bar shall include a clear and conspicuous statement within the advertisement or communication that registration with the North Carolina State Bar does not constitute approval of the plan by the State Bar.

[History Note: Statutory Authority G.S. 84–23; G.S. 84–23,1. Readopted effective December 8, 1994; amended effective February 5, 2002; amended effective August 23, 2007.]

.0311 State Bar Jurisdiction

The North Carolina State Bar retains jurisdiction of North Carolina licensed attorneys who participate in prepaid legal services plans and North Carolina licensed attorneys are subject to the rules and regulations of the North Carolina State Bar.

[History Note: Statutory Authority G.S. 84-23; G.S. 84-23.1. Readopted effective December 8, 1994; amended effective August 23, 2007.]

.0312 Revocation of Registration

Whenever it appears that a plan no longer meets the definition of a prepaid legal services plan; is marketed or operates in a manner that is not consistent with the representations made in the initial or amended registration statement and accompanying documents upon which the State Bar relied in registering the plan; is marketed or operates in a manner that would constitute the unauthorized practice of law; is marketed or operates in a manner that violates state or federal laws or regulations, including the rules and regulations of the North Carolina State Bar; or has failed to pay the annual registration fee, the committee may instruct the secretary to serve upon the plan's sponsor a notice to show cause why the plan's registration should not be revoked. The notice shall specify the plan's apparent deficiency and allow the plan's sponsor to file a written response within 30 days of service by sending the same to the secretary. If the sponsor fails to file a timely written response, the secretary shall issue an order revoking the plan's registration and shall serve the order upon the plan's sponsor. If a timely written response is filed, the secretary shall schedule a hearing, in accordance with Rule .0313 below, before the Authorized Practice Committee at its next regularly scheduled meeting and shall so notify the plan sponsor. All notices to show cause and orders required to be served herein may be served by certified mail to the last address provided for the plan sponsor on its most current registration statement or in accordance with Rule 4 of the North Carolina Rules of Civil Procedure and may be served by a State Bar investigator or any other person authorized by Rule 4 of the North Carolina Rules of Civil Procedure to serve process. The State Bar will not renew the annual registration of any plan that has received a notice to show cause under this section, but the plan may continue to operate under the prior registration until resolution of the show cause notice by the council.

[History Note: Statutory Authority G.S. 84-23; G.S. 84-23.1. Readopted effective December 8, 1994; amended effective August 23, 2007.]

.0313 Hearing before the Authorized Practice Committee

At any hearing concerning the registration of a prepaid legal services plan, the committee chair will preside to ensure that the hearing is conducted in accordance with these rules. The committee chair shall cause a record of the proceedings to be made. Strict compliance with the Rules of Evidence is not required, but may be used to guide the committee in the conduct of an orderly hearing. The plan sponsor may appear and be heard, be represented by counsel, offer witnesses and documents in support of its position and cross-examine any adverse witnesses. The counsel may appear on behalf of the State Bar and be heard, and may offer witnesses and documents. The burden of proof shall be upon the sponsor to establish the plan meets the definition of a prepaid legal services plan, that all registration fees have been paid, and that the plan has operated in a manner consistent with all material representations made in its then current registration statement, the law, and these rules. If the sponsor carries its burden of proof, the plan's registration shall be accepted or continued. If the sponsor fails to carry its burden of proof, the committee shall recommend to the council that the plan's registration be denied or revoked.

[History Note: Statutory Authority G.S. 84-23; 84-23.1. Readopted effective December 8, 1994; amended effective August 23, 2007.]

.0314 Action by the Council

Upon the recommendation of the committee, the council may enter an order denying or revoking the registration of the plan. The order shall be effective when entered by the council. A copy of the order shall be served upon the plan's sponsor as prescribed in Rule .0312 above.

[History Note: Statutory Authority G.S. 84-23; 84-23.1. Readopted effective December 8, 1994; amended effective August 23, 2007.]

SECTION .0400 RULES FOR ARBITRATION OF INTERNAL LAW FIRM DISPUTES

.0401 Purpose

Subject to these rules, the North Carolina State Bar will administer a voluntary binding arbitration program for resolution of disputed issues between lawyers arising out of the dissolution of law firms or disputes within law firms. The purpose of this arbitration procedure is to provide a mechanism for resolving economic disputes between lawyers arising out of the operation or dissolution of law firms.

[History Note: Statutory Authority G.S. 84-23. Readopted effective December 8, 1994.]

.0402 Submission to Arbitration

The program is voluntary. The procedure shall be instituted by a written submission to arbitration agreement, executed by all the parties to the dispute, in a form and manner as provided by the executive director of the North Carolina State Bar.

[History Note: Statutory Authority G.S. 84–23. Readopted effective December 8, 1994.]

.0403 Jurisdiction

The procedure may be used for the resolution of any dispute if all of the following conditions are met:

(a) the disputed issues submitted to arbitration hereunder shall be solely between or among lawyers who are members of the same law firm;

(b) the dispute arises out of an economic relationship between or among lawyers concerning the operation, dissolution, or proposed dissolution of the law firm of which they are members;

(c) at least one of the parties to such dispute resides or maintains an office for the practice of law in the state of North Carolina and is a member of the North Carolina State Bar;

(d) all parties agree in a written submission to arbitration agreement to submit the issues in dispute to binding arbitration under these rules and procedures.

[History Note: Statutory Authority G.S. 84–23. Readopted effective December 8, 1994.]

.0404 Administration

The North Carolina State Bar is the administrator of the arbitration program, through its executive director and his designees, to carry out all administrative functions, including those specified in Rules .0406 through .0410 of this subchapter.

[History Note: Statutory Authority G.S. 84–23. Readopted effective December 8, 1994.]

.0405 Uniform Arbitration Act

Except as modified herein, all arbitration procedures will be governed by Article 45A of Chapter 1 of the General Statutes of North Carolina (Uniform Arbitration Act). Said Uniform Arbitration Act and any amendments thereto are hereby incorporated by reference and constitute a part of these rules.

[History Note: Statutory Authority G.S. 84–23. Readopted effective December 8, 1994.]

.0406 List of Arbitrators

The North Carolina State Bar shall establish a list of arbitrators, consisting of attorneys or retired judges, who have been members of the North Carolina State Bar for at least ten years and who have indicated a willingness to serve. The parties shall, in their submission to arbitration agreement, elect to have one or three arbitrators. The administrator shall thereafter provide each party with the list of arbitrators.

[History Note: Statutory Authority G.S. 84–23. Readopted effective December 8, 1994.]

.0407 Selection of Arbitrators

If three arbitrators are to be selected, then

(a) each party to the dispute shall, within ten days after receipt of notice from the administrator, select one arbitrator on the approved list who shall be contacted by the administrator concerning his or her ability to serve and dates of availability. The two arbitrators so chosen shall execute an oath and appointment of arbitrator certificate provided by the administrator. Within fifteen days after certification, the two arbitrators shall choose a third from the administrator's approved list, who shall also execute an oath and appointment certificate. Failure of the two arbitrators to choose a third within the allotted time shall constitute a consent to have the third arbitrator chosen by the administrator;

(b) if the opposing parties cannot, because of the number of parties involved, settle upon two arbitrators who are to choose the third as set forth above, then the administrator shall notify the parties and appoint all three arbitrators from the approved list.

[History Note: Statutory Authority G.S. 84–23. Readopted effective December 8, 1994.]

.0408 Fees and Expenses

All expenses and the arbitrator(s') fees shall be paid by the parties. Arbitrator(s') compensation shall be at the same rate paid to retired judges who are assigned to temporary active service as provided in G.S. 7A–52 or any successor statutory provision. The administrator may require from each party an escrow deposit covering anticipated fees and expenses.

[History Note: Statutory Authority G.S. 84–23. Readopted effective December 8, 1994.]

.0409 Confidentiality

It is the policy of the North Carolina State Bar to protect the confidentiality of all arbitration proceedings. The parties, the arbitrators, and the North Carolina State Bar shall keep all proceedings confidential, except that any final award shall be enforceable under Chapter 1, Article 45A.

[History Note: Statutory Authority G.S. 84–23. Readopted effective December 8, 1994.]

.0410 Authority to Adopt Amendments and Regulations

The North Carolina State Bar may, from time to time, adopt and amend procedures and regulations consistent with these rules and amend or supplement these rules or otherwise regulate the arbitration procedure.

[History Note: Statutory Authority G.S. 84–23. Readopted effective December 8, 1994.]

SUBCHAPTER F. FOREIGN LEGAL CONSULTANTS

SECTION .0100 FOREIGN LEGAL CONSULTANTS

.0101 Applications

All applications for certification as a foreign legal consultant must be made on forms supplied by the North Carolina State Bar and must be complete in every detail. Every supporting document required by the application form must be submitted with each application. The application form may be obtained by writing or by telephoning the Bar's offices.

[Adopted effective March 7, 1996.]

.0102 Application Form

(a) The application for certification as a foreign legal consultant form requires an applicant to supply full and complete information under oath relating to the applicant's background, including family history, past and current residences, education, military service, past and present employment, citizenship, credit status, involvement in disciplinary, civil, or criminal proceedings, substance abuse, mental treatment and bar admission and discipline history.

(b) Every applicant must submit as part of the application:

(1) A certificate from the authority that has final jurisdiction regarding matters of professional discipline in the foreign country or jurisdiction in which the applicant is admitted to practice law, or the equivalent thereof. This certificate must be signed by a responsible official or one of the members of the executive body of the authority, imprinted with the official seal of the authority, if any, and must certify:

(A) The authority's jurisdiction in such matters;

(B) The applicant's admission to practice law, or the equivalent thereof, in the foreign country, the date of admission and the applicant's standing as an attorney or the equivalent thereof; and

(C) Whether any charge or complaint has ever been filed with the authority against the applicant and if so, the substance of and adjudication or resolution of each charge or complaint.

(2) A letter of recommendation from one of the members of the executive body of this authority or from one of the judges of the highest law court or court of general original jurisdiction of the foreign country, certifying the applicant's professional qualifications, and a certificate from the clerk of this authority or the clerk of the highest law court or court of general original jurisdiction, attesting to the genuineness of the applicant's signature;

(3) A letter of recommendation from at least two attorneys, or the equivalent thereof, admitted in and practicing law in the foreign country, stating the length of time, when, and under what circumstances they have known the applicant and their appraisal of the applicant's moral character;

(4) Two sets of clear fingerprints;

(5) Two executed informational Authorization and Release forms;

(6) A birth certificate;

(7) Copies of all applications to take a bar examination or an attorney's examination or for admission to the practice of law that the applicant has filed in any state or territory of the U.S., or the District of Columbia or in any foreign country;

(8) Certified copies of any legal proceedings in which the applicant has been a party;

(9) Two recent 2–inch by 3–inch photographs of the applicant showing a front view of the applicant's head and shoulders; and

(10) Any other relevant documents or information as may be required by the North Carolina State Bar.

(c) The Application Must Be Filed in Duplicate. The duplicate may be a photocopy of the original.

(d) The application and all required attachments shall be in English or accompanied by duly authenticated English translations.

[Adopted effective March 7, 1996.]

.0103 Requirements for Applicants

As a prerequisite to being certified as a foreign legal consultant, an applicant shall:

(a) Possess the qualifications of character and general fitness requisite for an attorney and counselor at law and be of good moral character and entitled to the high regard and confidence of the public and have satisfied the requirements of Section .0104 of this Chapter at the time the certificate is issued;

(b) Have been admitted to practice as an attorney, or the equivalent thereof, in a foreign country for at least five years as of the date of application for a certificate of registration;

(c) Certify in writing that he or she intends to practice in the State as a foreign legal consultant and intends to maintain an office in the State for this practice;

(d) Be at least 21 years of age;

(e) Have been actively and substantially engaged in the practice of law or a profession or occupation that requires admission to the practice of law, or the equivalent thereof, in the foreign country in which the applicant holds a license for at least five of the seven years immediately preceding the date of application for a certificate of registration and is in good standing as an attorney, or the equivalent thereof, in that country;

(f) Have filed an application as prescribed in section .0102 above;

(g) Be at all times in good professional standing and entitled to practice in every state or territory of the U.S. or in the District of Columbia, in which the applicant has been licensed to practice law, and in every foreign country in which the applicant is admitted to the practice of law or the equivalent thereof and is not under any pending charges of misconduct. The applicant may be inactive and in good standing in any foreign country or in any state or territory of the U.S. or in the District of Columbia; and

(h) Satisfy the Bar that the foreign country in which the applicant is licensed will admit North Carolina attorneys to practice as foreign legal consultants or the equivalent thereof.

[Adopted effective March 7, 1996.]

.0104 Burden of Proving Moral Character and General Fitness

Every applicant shall have the burden of proving that the applicant possesses the qualifications of character and general fitness requisite for an attorney and counselor-at-law and is possessed of good moral character and is entitled to the high regard and confidence of the public.

[Adopted effective March 7, 1996.]

.0105 Failure to Disclose

No one shall be issued a certificate of registration as a foreign legal consultant in this state:

(a) Who fails to disclose fully to the Bar, whether requested to do so or not, the facts relating to any disciplinary proceedings or charges as to the applicant's professional conduct, whether same have been terminated or not, in this or any other state, or any federal court or other jurisdiction or foreign country, or

(b) Who fails to disclose fully to the Bar, whether requested to do so or not, any and all facts relating to any civil or criminal proceedings, charges or investigations involving the applicant, whether the same have been terminated or not in this or any other state, or any federal court or other jurisdiction or foreign country.

[Adopted effective March 7, 1996.]

.0106 Investigation by Counsel

The counsel will conduct any necessary investigation regarding the application and will advise the Administrative Committee of the North Carolina State Bar (the committee) of the findings of any such investigation.

[Adopted effective March 7, 1996. Amended December 10, 1999, effective February 3, 2000.]

.0107 Recommendation of Administrative Committee

(a) Upon receipt of all completed application forms, attachments, filing fees and information required by the Bar, and completion of the Bar's investigation, the committee shall make a written recommendation to the council respecting whether an applicant for certification as a foreign legal consultant has met the requirements of G.S. § 84A–1 and these rules. Prior to making a written recommendation, the Committee may request further information from the applicant or other sources and may require the applicant to appear before it upon reasonable notice. The Committee's written recommendation shall include a statement of the reason(s) for the Committee's decision.

(b) A copy of the Committee's recommendation shall be served upon the applicant pursuant to Rule 4 of the N.C. Rules of Civil Procedure.

[Adopted effective March 7, 1996. Amended December 10, 1999, effective February 3, 2000.]

.0108 Appeal From Committee Decision

(a) The applicant will have 30 days from the date of service of the committee's recommendation in which to serve a written request for a hearing upon the secretary pursuant to Rule 4 of the N.C. Rules of Civil Procedure.

(b) If the applicant does not request a hearing in a timely fashion, the committee will forward its recommendation to the council. The council will consider the application and the recommendation of the committee and will make a final written recommendation to the

N.C. Supreme Court, as set out in Section .0110(f) below.

[Adopted effective March 7, 1996. Amended December 10, 1999, effective February 3, 2000.]

.0109 Hearing Procedure

(a) Notice, Time & Place of Hearing.

(1) The chair of the committee shall fix the time and place of hearing within 30 days after the applicant's request for a hearing is served upon the secretary. The hearing shall be held as soon as practicable after the request is filed.

(2) The notice of the hearing shall include the date, time and place of the hearing and shall be served upon the applicant at least 10 days before the hearing date.

(b) Hearing Panel.

(1) The chair of the committee shall appoint a hearing panel composed of three members of the committee to consider the application and make a written recommendation to the council.

(2) The chair shall appoint one of the three members of the panel to serve as the presiding member. The presiding member shall rule on any question of procedure which arises during the hearing; preside at the deliberations of the panel, sign the written determinations of the panel and report the panel's determination to the council.

(c) Proceedings before the Hearing Panel.

(1) A majority of the panel members is necessary to decide the application.

(2) Following the hearing on the contested application, the panel will make a written recommendation to the council on behalf of the committee regarding whether the application should be granted. The recommendation shall include appropriate findings of fact and conclusions of law.

(3) The applicant will have the burden of proving that he or she has met all the requirements of sections .0102–.0104 above.

(4) At the hearing, the applicant and State Bar counsel will have the right

(A) to appear personally and be heard

(B) to call and examine witnesses

(C) to offer exhibits

(D) to cross-examine witnesses.

(5) In addition the applicant will have the right to be represented by counsel.

(6) The hearing will be conducted in accordance with the North Carolina Rules of Civil Procedure for nonjury trials insofar as practicable and by the Rules of Evidence applicable in superior court, unless otherwise provided by this subchapter or the parties agree otherwise.

(7) The hearing shall be reported by a certified court reporter. The applicant will pay the costs associated with obtaining the court reporter's services for the hearing. The applicant shall pay the costs of the transcript and shall arrange for the preparation of the transcript with the court reporter. The applicant may also be taxed with all other costs of the hearing, but the costs shall not include any compensation to the members of the hearing panel.

(8) The written recommendation of the hearing panel shall be served upon the member and the counsel within 14 days of the date of the hearing.

[Adopted effective March 7, 1996. Amended December 10, 1999, effective February 3, 2000.]

.0110 Review and Order of Council

(a) Review by Council. The applicant shall compile a record of the proceedings before the hearing panel, including a legible copy of the complete transcript, all exhibits introduced into evidence at the hearing, all pleadings and all motions and orders, unless the applicant and counsel agree in writing to shorten the record. Any agreement regarding the record shall be included in the record transmitted to the council.

(b) Transmission of Record to Council. The applicant shall provide a copy of the record to the counsel not later than 90 days after the hearing unless an extension is granted by the president of the N.C. State Bar for good cause shown. The applicant shall transmit a copy of the record to each member of the council, at the applicant's expense, no later than 30 days before the council meeting at which the application is to be considered.

(c) Costs. The applicant shall bear all of the costs of transcribing, copying, and transmitting the record to the members of the council.

(d) Dismissal for Failure to Apply. If the applicant fails to comply fully with any provisions of this rule, the counsel may file a motion with the secretary to dismiss the application.

(e) Appearance Before the Council. In his or her discretion, the president of the State Bar may permit the counsel for the State Bar and the applicant to present oral or written argument but the council will not consider additional evidence not in the record transmitted from the hearing panel absent a showing that the ends of justice so require or that undue hardship will result if the additional evidence is not presented.

(f) Order by Council. The council will review the recommendation of the hearing panel and the record and will determine whether the applicant has met all of the requirements of sections .0102–.0104 above. The council will make a written recommendation to the N.C. Supreme Court regarding whether the application should be granted. The council's recommendation will contain a statement of the reasons for the recommendation and shall attach to it the application.

(g) Costs. The council may tax the costs attributable to the proceeding against the applicant.

[Adopted effective March 7, 1996.]

.0111 Application Fees; Refunds; Returned Checks

(a) Every application and every reapplication for certification as a foreign legal consultant shall be accompanied by a fee of $200 paid in U.S. currency.

(b) No part of the fee will be refunded.

(c) Failure to pay the application fees required by these rules shall cause the application to be deemed not filed. If the check payable for the application fee is not honored upon presentment for any reason other than error of the bank, the application will be deemed not filed. All checks presented to the Bar for any fees which are not honored upon presentment will be returned to the applicant, who shall pay the Bar in cash, cashier's check, certified check or money order any fees payable to the Bar, along with a $20 additional fee for processing the dishonored check.

[Adopted effective March 7, 1996.]

.0112 Permanent Record

All information furnished to the Bar by an applicant shall be deemed material, and all such information shall be and become a permanent record of the Bar. Records, papers and other documents containing information collected or compiled by the North Carolina State Bar and its members or employees as a result of any investigation, application, inquiry or interview conducted in connection with an application for certificate of registration are not public records within the meaning of Chapter 132 of the General Statutes.

[Adopted effective March 7, 1996.]

.0113 Denial; Re-application

No new application or petition for reconsideration of a previous application from an applicant who has been denied a certificate of registration as a foreign legal consultant shall be considered by the Bar within a period of three (3) years next after the date of such denial unless, for good cause shown, permission for reapplication or petition for a reconsideration is granted by the Bar.

[Adopted effective March 7, 1996.]

SUBCHAPTER G. THE PLAN FOR CERTIFICATION OF PARALEGALS

SECTION .0100 THE PLAN FOR CERTIFICATION OF PARALEGALS

.0101 Purpose

The purpose of this plan for certification of paralegals (plan) is to assist in the delivery of legal services to the public by identifying individuals who are qualified by education and training and have demonstrated knowledge, skill, and proficiency to perform substantive legal work under the direction and supervision of a licensed lawyer, and including any individual who may be otherwise authorized by applicable state or federal law to provide legal services directly to the public; and to improve the competency of those individuals by establishing mandatory continuing legal education and other requirements of certification.

[Adopted effective October 6, 2004.]

.0102 Jurisdiction: Authority

The Council of the North Carolina State Bar (the council) with the approval of the Supreme Court of North Carolina hereby establishes the Board of Paralegal Certification (board), which board shall have jurisdiction over the certification of paralegals in North Carolina.

[Adopted effective October 6, 2004.]

.0103 Operational Responsibility

The responsibility for operating the paralegal certification program rests with the board, subject to the statutes governing the practice of law, the authority of the council and the rules of governance of the board.

[Adopted effective October 6, 2004.]

.0104 Size and Composition of Board

The board shall have nine members, five of whom must be lawyers in good standing and authorized to practice law in the state of North Carolina. One of the members who is a lawyer shall be a program director at a qualified paralegal studies program. Four members of the board shall be paralegals certified under the plan provided, however, that the paralegals appointed to the inaugural board shall be exempt from this requirement during their initial and successive terms but each such member shall be eligible, during the shorter of such initial term or the alternative qualification period, for certification by the board upon the board's determination that the member meets the requirements for certification in Rule .0119(b).

[Adopted effective October 6, 2004. Amended effective March 2, 2006.]

.0105 Appointment of Members; When; Removal

(a) Appointment. The council shall appoint the members of the board, provided, however, after the appointment of the initial members of the board, each paralegal member appointed for an initial term shall be selected by the council from two nominees determined by a vote by mail or online of all active certified paralegals in an election conducted by the board.

(b) Procedure for Nomination of Candidates for Paralegal Members.

(1) *Composition of Nominating Committee.* At least 60 days prior to a meeting of the council at which one or more paralegal members of the board are subject to appointment for a full three year term, the board shall appoint a nominating committee comprised of certified paralegals as follows:

(i) A representative selected by the North Carolina Paralegal Association;

(ii) A representative selected by the North Carolina Bar Association Paralegal Division;

(iii) A representative selected by the North Carolina Advocates for Justice Legal Assistants Division;

(iv) Three representatives from three local or regional paralegal organizations to be selected by the board; and

(v) An independent paralegal (not employed by a law firm, government entity, or legal department) to be selected by the board.

(2) *Selection of Candidates.* The nominating committee shall meet within 30 days of its appointment to select five (5) certified paralegals as candidates for each paralegal member vacancy on the board for inclusion on the ballot to be mailed to all active certified paralegals.

(3) *Vote of Certified Paralegals.* At least 30 days prior to the meeting of the council at which a paralegal member appointment to the board will be made, a ballot shall be mailed or a notice of online voting shall be emailed or mailed to all active certified paralegals at each certified paralegal's physical or email address of record on file with the North Carolina State Bar. The ballot or notice shall be accompanied by written instructions, and shall state how many paralegal member positions on the board are subject to appointment, the names of the candidates selected by the nominating committee for each such position, and when and where the ballot should be returned. If balloting will be online, the notice shall explain how to access the ballot on the State Bar's paralegal website and the method for voting online. Write–in candidates shall be permitted and the instructions shall so state. Each ballot sent by mail shall be sequentially numbered with a red identifying numeral in the upper right hand corner of the ballot. Online balloting shall be by secure log-in to the State Bar's paralegal website using the certified paralegal's identification number and personal password. Any certified paralegal who does not have an email address on file with the State Bar shall be mailed a ballot. The board shall maintain appropriate records respecting how many ballots or notices are sent to prospective voters in each election as well as how many ballots are returned. Only original ballots will be accepted by mail. Ballots received after the deadline stated on the ballot or the email notice will not be counted. The names of the two candidates receiving the most votes for each open paralegal member position shall be the nominees submitted to the council.

(c) Time of Appointment. The first members of the board shall be appointed as of the quarterly meeting of the council following the creation of the board. Thereafter, members shall be appointed annually at the quarterly meeting of the council occurring on the anniversary of the appointment of the initial board.

(d) Vacancies. Vacancies occurring by reason of death, resignation, or removal shall be filled by appointment of the council, subject to the requirements of Rule .0105(a)1, at the next quarterly meeting following the event giving rise to the vacancy, and the person so appointed shall serve for the balance of the vacated term.

(e) Removal. Any member of the board may be removed at any time by an affirmative vote of a majority of the members of the council in session at a regularly called meeting.

[History Note: Statutory Authority G.S. 84–23. Adopted effective October 6, 2004. Amended effective March 8, 2007; March 11, 2010; August 25, 2011; March 6, 2014.]

.0106 Term of Office

Subject to Rule .0107 of this subchapter, each member of the board shall serve for a term of three years beginning as of the first day of the month following the date on which the council appoints the member.

[Adopted Effective October 6, 2004.]

.0107 Staggered Terms

The members of the board shall be appointed to staggered terms such that three members are appointed in each year. Of the initial board, three members (one lawyer and two paralegals) shall be appointed to terms of one year; three members (two lawyers and one paralegal) shall be appointed to terms of two years; and three members (two lawyers and one paralegal) shall be appointed to terms of three years. Thereafter, three members (lawyers or paralegals as necessary to fill expired terms) shall be appointed in each year for full three year terms.

[Adopted Effective October 6, 2004.]

.0108 Succession

Each member of the board shall be entitled to serve for one full three-year term and to succeed himself or herself for one additional three-year term. Each certified paralegal member shall be eligible for reappointment by the council at the end of his or her term without appointment of a nominating committee or vote of all active paralegals as would be otherwise required by Rule .0105 of this subchapter. Thereafter, no person may be reappointed without having been off of the board for at least three years.

[History Note: Statutory Authority G.S. 84–23. Adopted effective October 6, 2004. Amended effective March 6, 2014.]

.0109 Appointment of Chairperson

The council shall appoint the chairperson of the board from among the lawyer members of the board. The term of the chairperson shall be one year. The chairperson may be reappointed thereafter during his or her tenure on the board. The chairperson shall preside at all meetings of the board, shall prepare and present to the council the annual report of the board, and generally shall represent the board in its dealings with the public.

[Adopted Effective October 6, 2004.]

.0110 Appointment of Vice–Chairperson

The council shall appoint the vice-chairperson of the board from among the members of the board. The term of the vice-chairperson shall be one year. The vice-chairperson may be reappointed thereafter during his or her tenure on the board. The vice-chairperson shall preside at and represent the board in the absence of the chairperson and shall perform such other duties as may be assigned to him or her by the chairperson or by the board.

[Adopted Effective October 6, 2004.]

.0111 Source of Funds

Funding for the program carried out by the board shall come from such application fees, examination fees, annual fees or recertification fees as the board, with the approval of the council, may establish.

[Adopted Effective October 6, 2004.]

.0112 Fiscal Responsibility

All funds of the board shall be considered funds of the North Carolina State Bar and shall be administered and disbursed accordingly.

(a) Maintenance of Accounts: Audit – The North Carolina State Bar shall maintain a separate account for funds of the board such that such funds and expenditures there from can be readily identified. The accounts of the board shall be audited on an annual basis in connection with the audits of the North Carolina State Bar.

(b) Investment Criteria – The funds of the board shall be handled, invested and reinvested in accordance with investment policies adopted by the council for the handling of dues, rents and other revenues received by the North Carolina State Bar in carrying out its official duties.

(c) Disbursement – Disbursement of funds of the board shall be made by or under the direction of the secretary-treasurer of the North Carolina State Bar.

[Adopted Effective October 6, 2004.]

.0113 Meetings

The board by resolution may set regular meeting dates and places. Special meetings of the board may be called at any time upon notice given by the chairperson. Notice of meeting shall be given at least one day prior to the meeting by mail, electronic mail, telegram, facsimile transmission, or telephone. A quorum of the board for conducting its official business shall be five or more of the members serving at the time of the meeting.

[Adopted Effective October 6, 2004.]

.0114 Annual Report

The board shall prepare a report of its activities for the preceding year and shall present the same at the annual meeting of the council.

[Adopted Effective October 6, 2004.]

.0115 Powers and Duties of the Board

Subject to the general jurisdiction of the council and the North Carolina Supreme Court, the board shall have jurisdiction of all matters pertaining to certification of paralegals and shall have the power and duty

(1) to administer the plan of certification for paralegals;

(2) to appoint, supervise, act on the recommendations of, and consult with committees as appointed by the board or the chairperson;

(3) to certify paralegals or deny, suspend or revoke the certification of paralegals;

(4) to establish and publish procedures, rules, regulations, and bylaws to implement this plan;

(5) to propose and request the council to make amendments to this plan whenever appropriate;

(6) to cooperate with other boards or agencies in enforcing standards of professional conduct;

(7) to evaluate and approve continuing legal education courses for the purpose of meeting the continu-

ing legal education requirements established by the board for the certification of paralegals;

(8) to cooperate with other organizations, boards, and agencies engaged in the recognition, education, or regulation of paralegals; and

(9) to set fees, with the approval of the council, and to, in appropriate circumstances, waive such fees.

[Adopted Effective October 6, 2004. Amended effective March 2, 2006.]

.0116 Retained Jurisdiction of the Council

The council retains jurisdiction with respect to the following matters:

(1) amending this plan;

(2) hearing appeals taken from actions of the board;

(3) establishing or approving fees to be charged in connection with the plan;

(4) regulating the conduct of lawyers in the supervision of paralegals; and

(5) determining whether to pursue injunctive relief as authorized by G. S. 84–37 against persons acting in violation of this plan.

[Adopted Effective October 6, 2004.]

.0117 Privileges Conferred and Limitations Imposed

The board in the implementation of this plan shall not alter the following privileges and responsibilities of lawyers and their non-lawyer assistants.

(1) No rule shall be adopted which shall in any way limit the right of a lawyer to delegate tasks to a non-lawyer assistant or to employ any person to assist him or her in the practice of law.

(2) No person shall be required to be certified as a paralegal to be employed by a lawyer to assist the lawyer in the practice of law.

(3) All requirements for and all benefits to be derived from certification as a paralegal are individual and may not be fulfilled by nor attributed to the law firm or other organization or entity employing the paralegal.

(4) Any person certified as a paralegal under this plan shall be entitled to represent that he or she is a "North Carolina Certified Paralegal (NCCP)", a "North Carolina State Bar Certified Paralegal (NCSB/CP)" or a "Paralegal Certified by the North Carolina State Bar Board of Paralegal Certification."

[Adopted Effective October 6, 2004.]

.0118 Certification Committee

(a) **The board shall establish a separate certification committee.** The certification committee shall be composed of seven members appointed by the board, one of whom shall be designated annually by the chairperson of the board as chairperson of the certification committee. At least two members of the committee shall be lawyers, licensed and currently in good standing to practice law in this state, and two members of the committee shall be certified paralegals. The remaining members of the committee shall be either lawyers, licensed and currently in good standing to practice law in this state, or certified paralegals. The paralegals appointed to the inaugural committee shall be exempt from the certification requirement during their initial term but each such member shall be eligible, during the shorter of such initial term or the alternative qualification period, for certification by the board upon the board's determination that the committee member meets the requirements for certification in Rule .0119(b).

(b) Members shall hold office for three years, except those members initially appointed who shall serve as hereinafter designated. Members shall be appointed by the board to staggered terms and the initial appointees shall serve as follows: two shall serve for one year after appointment; two shall serve for two years after appointment; and three shall serve for three years after appointment. Appointment by the board to a vacancy shall be for the remaining term of the member leaving the committee. All members shall be eligible for reappointment to not more than one additional three-year term after having served one full three-year term, provided, however, that the board may reappoint the chairperson of the committee to a third three-year term if the board determines that the reappointment is in the best interest of the program. Meetings of the certification committee shall be held at regular intervals at such times, places and upon such notices as the committee may from time to time prescribe or upon direction of the board.

(c) The committee shall advise and assist the board in carrying out the board's objectives and in the implementation and regulation of this plan by advising the board as to standards for certification of individuals as paralegals. The committee shall be charged with actively administering the plan as follows:

(1) upon request of the board, make recommendations to the board for certification, continued certification, denial, suspension, or revocation of certification of paralegals and for procedures with respect thereto;

(2) draft and regularly revise the certification examination; and

(3) perform such other duties and make such other recommendations as may be delegated to or requested by the board.

[History Note: Statutory Authority G.S. 84–23. Adopted effective October 6, 2004. Amended effective March 2, 2006; March 6, 2014.]

.0119 Standards for Certification of Paralegals

(a) To qualify for certification as a paralegal, an applicant must pay any required fee, and comply with the following standards:

(1) *Education.* The applicant must have earned one of the following:

(A) an associate's, bachelor's, or master's degree from a qualified paralegal studies program;

(B) a certificate from a qualified paralegal studies program and an associate's or bachelor's degree in any discipline from any institution of post-secondary education that is accredited by an accrediting body recognized by the United States Department of Education (an accredited US institution) or an equivalent degree from a foreign educational institution if the degree is determined to be equivalent to a degree from an accredited US institution by an organization that is a member of the National Association of Credential Evaluation Services (NACES) or the Association of International Credentials Evaluators (AICE); or

(C) a juris doctorate degree from a law school accredited by the American Bar Association.

(2) *Examination.* The applicant must achieve a satisfactory score on a written examination designed to test the applicant's knowledge and ability. The board shall assure that the contents and grading of the examinations are designed to produce a uniform minimum level of competence among the certified paralegals.

(b) Alternative Qualification Period. For a period not to exceed two years after the date that applications for certification are first accepted by the board, an applicant may qualify by satisfying one of the following:

(1) earned a high school diploma, or its equivalent, worked as a paralegal and/or a paralegal educator in North Carolina for not less than 5000 hours during the five years prior to application, and, during the 12 months prior to application, completed three hours of continuing legal education in professional responsibility, as approved by the board;

(2) obtained and maintained at all times prior to application the designation Certified Legal Assistant (CLA)/Certified Paralegal (CP), PACE–Registered Paralegal (RP), or other national paralegal credential approved by the board and worked as a paralegal and /or a paralegal educator in North Carolina for not less than 2000 hours during the two years prior to application; or

(3) worked as a paralegal and/or a paralegal educator in North Carolina for not less than 2000 hours during the two years prior to application and fulfilled one of the following educational requirements:

(A) as set forth in Rule .0119(a)(1), or

(B) earned an associate's or bachelor's degree in any discipline from any institution of post-secondary education that is accredited by an accrediting body recognized by the United States Department of Education and successfully completed at least the equivalent of 18 semester credits at a qualified paralegal studies program, any portion of which credits may also satisfy the requirements for the associate's or bachelor's degree.

(c) Notwithstanding an applicant's satisfaction of the standards set forth in Rule .0119(a) or (b), no individual may be certified as a paralegal if:

(1) the individual's certification or license as a paralegal in any state is under suspension or revocation;

(2) the individual's license to practice law in any state is under suspension or revocation;

(3) the individual has been convicted of a criminal act that reflects adversely on the individual's honesty, trustworthiness, or fitness as a paralegal, or has engaged in conduct involving dishonesty, fraud, deceit, or misrepresentation, provided, however, the board may certify an applicant if, after consideration of mitigating factors, including remorse, reformation of character, and the passage of time, the board determines that the individual is honest, trustworthy, and fit to be a certified paralegal; or

(4) the individual is not a legal resident of the United States.

(d) All matters concerning the qualification of an applicant for certification, including, but not limited to, applications, examinations and examination scores, files, reports, investigations, hearings, findings, recommendations, and adverse determinations shall be confidential so far as is consistent with the effective administration of this plan, fairness to the applicant and due process of law.

(e) Qualified Paralegal Studies Program. A qualified paralegal studies program is a program of paralegal or legal assistant studies that is an institutional member of the Southern Association of Colleges and Schools or other regional or national accrediting agency recognized by the United States Department of Education, and is either

(1) approved by the American Bar Association;

(2) an institutional member of the American Association for Paralegal Education; or

(3) offers at least the equivalent of 18 semester credits of coursework in paralegal studies as prescribed by the American Bar Association Guidelines for the Approval of Paralegal Education.

(f) Designation as a Qualified Paralegal Studies Program. The board shall determine whether a paralegal studies program is a qualified paralegal studies program upon submission by the program of an application to the board provided, however, a paralegal studies program is not required to submit an application for qualification as long as the program satisfies the requirements of Rule .0119(e)(1) or (2).

(1) A program designated by the board as a qualified paralegal studies program shall renew its application for designation every five years.

(2) An applicant for certification who lists on a certification application a paralegal studies program that does not satisfy the requirements of Rule .0119(e)(1) or (2) or that has not been designated by the board as a qualified paralegal studies program shall be responsible for obtaining a completed application for designation from the program or shall submit the information required on the application for determination that the program is a qualified paralegal studies program.

(3) Designation of a paralegal studies program as a qualified paralegal studies program under this section does not constitute an approval or an endorsement of the program by the board or the North Carolina State Bar.

[History Note: Statutory Authority G.S. 84–23. Adopted effective October 6, 2004. Amended effective March 2, 2006; March 8, 2007; February 5, 2009; March 11, 2010; March 6, 2014; March 5, 2015.]

.0120 Standards for Continued Certification of Paralegals

(a) The period of certification as a paralegal shall be one (1) year. During such period the board may require evidence from the paralegal of his or her continued qualification for certification as a paralegal, and the paralegal must consent to inquiry by the board regarding the paralegal's continued competence and qualification to be certified. Application for and approval of continued certification shall be required annually prior to the end of each certification period. To qualify for continued certification as a paralegal, an applicant must demonstrate participation in not less than 6 hours of credit in board approved continuing legal education, or its equivalent, during the year within which the application for continued certification is made.

(b) Upon written request of the paralegal, the board may for good cause shown waive strict compliance by such paralegal with the criteria relating to continuing legal education, as those requirements are set forth in Rule .0120(a).

(c) A late fee of $25.00 will be charged to any certified paralegal who fails to file the renewal application within forty-five (45) days of the due date; provided, however, a renewal application will not be accepted more than ninety (90) days after the due date. Failure to renew shall result in lapse of certification.

[Adopted Effective October 6, 2004. Amended effective October 8, 2009.]

.0121 Lapse, Suspension or Revocation of Certification

(a) The board may suspend or revoke its certification of a paralegal, after hearing before the board on appropriate notice, upon a finding that

(1) the certification was made contrary to the rules and regulations of the board;

(2) the individual certified as a paralegal made a false representation, omission, or misstatement of material fact to the board;

(3) the individual certified as a paralegal failed to abide by all rules and regulations promulgated by the board;

(4) the individual certified as a paralegal failed to pay the fees required;

(5) the individual certified as a paralegal no longer meets the standards established by the board for the certification of paralegals;

(6) the individual is not eligible for certification on account of one or more of the grounds set forth in Rule.0019(c); or

(7) the individual violated the confidentiality agreement relative to the questions on the certification examination.

(b) An individual certified as a paralegal has a duty to inform the board promptly of any fact or circumstance described in Rule .0121(a).

(c) If an individual's certification lapses, or if the board revokes a certification, the individual cannot again be certified as a paralegal unless he or she so qualifies upon application made as if for initial certification and upon such other conditions as the board may prescribe. If the board suspends certification of an individual as a paralegal, such certification cannot be reinstated except upon the individual's application and compliance with such conditions and requirements as the board may prescribe.

[Adopted Effective October 6, 2004. Amended effective March 6, 2008.]

.0122. Right to Review and Appeal to Council

(a) Lapsed Certification. An individual whose certification has lapsed pursuant to Rule .0120(c) of this subchapter for failure to complete all of the requirements for renewal within the prescribed time limit shall have the right to request reinstatement for good cause shown. A request for reinstatement shall be in writing, must state the personal circumstances prohibiting or substantially impeding satisfaction of the requirements for renewal within the prescribed time limit, and must be made within 90 days of the date notice of lapse is mailed to the individual. The request for reinstatement shall be reviewed on the written record and ruled upon by the board. There shall be no other right to review by the board or appeal to the council under this rule.

(b) Denial of Certification or Continued Certification. An individual who is denied certification or continued certification as a paralegal or whose certification is suspended or revoked shall have the right to a review before the board pursuant to the procedures set forth below and, thereafter, the right to appeal the board's ruling thereon to the council under such rules and regulations as the council may prescribe.

(1) Notification of the Decision of the Board. Following the meeting at which the board denies certification for failure to meet the standards for certification, including failing the examination, denies continued certification, or suspends or revokes certification, the executive director shall promptly notify the individual in writing of the decision of the board. The notification shall specify the reason for the decision of the board and shall inform the individual of his or her right to request a review before the board.

(2) Request for Review by the Board. Except as provided in paragraph (e) of this rule, within 30 days of the mailing of the notice from the executive director described in paragraph (b) of this rule, the individual may request review by the board. The request shall be in writing and state the reasons for which the individual believes the prior decision of the board should be reconsidered and withdrawn. The request shall state whether the board's review shall be on the written record or at a hearing.

(3) Review by the Board. A three-member panel of the board shall be appointed by the chair of the board to reconsider the board's decision and take action by a majority of the panel. At least one member of the panel shall be a lawyer member of the board and at least one member of the panel shall be a paralegal member of the board. The decision of the panel shall constitute the final decision of the board.

(A) *Review on the Record.* If requested, the panel shall review the entire written record including the individual's application, all supporting documentation, and any written materials submitted by the individual within 30 days of mailing the request for review. The panel shall make its decision within sixty (60) days of receipt of the written request for review from the individual.

(B) *Review Hearing.* If requested, the panel shall hold a hearing at a time and location that is convenient for the panel members and the individual provided the hearing occurs within sixty (60) days of receipt of the written request for review from the individual. The hearing shall be informal. The Rules of Evidence and the Rules of Civil Procedure shall not apply. The individual may be represented by lawyer at the hearing, may offer witnesses and exhibits, and may question witnesses for the board. The panel may ask witnesses to appear and may consider exhibits on its own request. Witnesses shall not be sworn. The hearing shall not be reported unless the applicant pays the costs of the transcript and arranges for the preparation of the transcript with the court reporter.

(C) *Decision of the Panel.* The individual shall be notified in writing of the decision of the panel and, if unfavorable, the right to appeal the decision to the council under such rules and regulations as the council may prescribe. To exercise this right, the individual must file an appeal to the council in writing within 30 days of the mailing of the notice of the decision of the panel.

(c) Failure of Written Examination. Within 30 days of the mailing of the notice from the board's executive director that an individual has failed the written examination, the individual may review his or her examination upon the condition that the individual will not take the examination again until such time as the entire content of the examination has been replaced. Review of the examination shall be at the office of the board at a time designated by the executive director. The individual shall be allowed not more than three hours for such review and shall not remove the examination from the board's office or make photocopies of any part of the examination.

(1) Request for Review by the Board. Within 30 days of individual's review of his or her examination, the individual may request review by the board pursuant to the procedures set forth in paragraph (c) of this rule. The request should set out in detail the area or areas which, in the opinion of the individual, have been incorrectly graded. Supporting information may be filed to substantiate the individual's claim.

[Adopted Effective October 6, 2004. Amended effective March 8, 2007; February 5, 2009; March 8, 2013; August 27, 2013.]

.0123 Inactive Status Upon Demonstration of Hardship

(a) Inactive Status. The board shall transfer a certified paralegal to inactive status upon receipt of a petition, on a form approved by the board, demonstrating hardship as defined in paragraph (b) of this rule and upon payment of any fees owed to the board at the time of the petition unless waived by the board.

(1) The period of inactive status shall be one year from the designated renewal date.

(2) On or before the expiration of inactive status, a paralegal on inactive status must file a petition for (continued) inactive status or seek reinstatement to active status by filing a renewal application pursuant to Rule .0120 of this subchapter. Failure to petition for continued inactive status or renewal shall result in lapse of certification.

(3) A paralegal may be inactive for not more than a total of five consecutive years.

(4) During a period of inactive status, a paralegal is not required to pay the renewal fee or to complete continuing legal education.

(5) During a period of inactive status, a paralegal shall not be entitled to represent that he or she is a North Carolina certified paralegal or to use any of the designations set forth in Rule .0117(4) of this subchapter.

(b) **Hardship.** The following conditions shall qualify as hardship justifying a transfer to inactive status:

(1) Financial inability to pay the annual renewal fee and to pay for continuing legal education courses due to unemployment or underemployment of the paralegal for a period of three months or more;

(2) Disability or serious illness for a period of three months or more;

(3) Active military service; and

(4) Transfer of the paralegal's active duty military spouse to a location outside of North Carolina.

(c) **Reinstatement before Expiration of Inactive Status.** To be reinstated as a certified paralegal, the paralegal must petition the board for reinstatement by filing a renewal application prior to the expiration of the inactive status period and must pay the annual renewal fee. If the paralegal was inactive for a period of two consecutive calendar years or more during the year prior to the filing of the petition, the paralegal must complete 12 hours of credit in board-approved continuing paralegal education, or its equivalent. Of the 12 hours, at least 2 hours shall be devoted to the areas of professional responsibility or professionalism, or any combination thereof.

(d) **Certification after Expiration of Inactive Status Period.** If the inactive status period expires before the paralegal petitions for reinstatement, certification shall lapse, and the paralegal cannot again be certified unless the paralegal qualifies upon application made as if for initial certification.

[Adopted effective August 23, 2012.]

SECTION .0200 RULES GOVERNING CONTINUING PARALEGAL EDUCATION

.0201 Continuing Paralegal Education (CPE)

(a) Each active certified paralegal subject to these rules shall complete 6 hours of approved continuing education during each year of certification.

(b) Of the 6 hours, at least 1 hour shall be devoted to the areas of professional responsibility or professionalism or any combination thereof.

(1) A professional responsibility course or segment of a course shall be devoted to (1) the substance, the underlying rationale, and the practical application of the Rules of Professional Conduct; (2) the professional obligations of the lawyer to the client, the court, the public, and other lawyers, and the paralegal's role in assisting the lawyer to fulfill those obligations; (3) the effects of substance abuse and chemical dependency, or debilitating mental condition on a lawyer's or a paralegal's professional responsibilities; or (4) the effects of stress on a paralegal's professional responsibilities.

(2) A professionalism course or segment of a course shall be devoted to the identification and examination of, and the encouragement of adherence to, non-mandatory aspirational standards of professional conduct that transcend the requirements of the Rules of Professional Conduct. Such courses address principles of competence and dedication to the service of clients, civility, improvement of the justice system, advancement of the rule of law, and service to the community.

[History Note: Statutory Authority G.S. 84–23. Adopted effective August 18, 2005. Amended effective March 6, 2014.]

.0202 Accreditation Standards

The Board of Paralegal Certification shall approve continuing education activities in compliance with the following standards and provisions.

(a) An approved activity shall have significant intellectual or practical content and the primary objective of increasing the participant's professional competence and proficiency as a paralegal.

(b) An approved activity shall constitute an organized program of learning dealing with matters directly related to the practice of law, professional responsibility, professionalism, or ethical obligations of paralegals.

(c) A certified paralegal may receive credit for continuing education activities in which live instruction or recorded material is used. Recorded material includes videotaped or satellite transmitted programs, and programs on CD-ROM, DVD, or other similar electronic or digital replay formats. A minimum of three certified paralegals must register to attend the presentation of a prerecorded program. This requirement does not apply to participation from a remote location in the presentation of a live broadcast by telephone, satellite, or video conferencing equipment.

(d) A certified paralegal may receive credit for participation in a course on-line. An on-line course is an educational seminar available on a provider's website reached via the internet. To be accredited, a computer-based CLE course must be interactive, permitting the participant to communicate, via telephone, electronic mail, or a website bulletin board, with the presenter and/or other participants.

(e) Continuing education materials are to be prepared, and activities conducted, by an individual or group qualified by practical or academic experience in a setting physically suitable to the educational activity of the program and, when appropriate, equipped with suitable writing surfaces or sufficient space for taking notes.

(f) Thorough, high quality, and carefully prepared written materials should be distributed to all attendees at or before the time the course is presented. These may include written materials printed from a computer presentation, computer website, or CD-ROM. A written agenda or outline for a presentation satisfies this requirement when written materials are not suitable or readily available for a particular subject. The absence of written materials for distribution should, however, be the exception and not the rule.

(g) Any continuing legal education activity approved for lawyers by the North Carolina State Bar's Board of Continuing Legal Education meets these standards.

(h) In-house continuing legal education and self-study shall not qualify for continuing paralegal education (CPE) credit.

(i) A certified paralegal may receive credit for completion of a course offered by an ABA accredited law school with respect to which academic credit may be earned. No more than 6 CPE hours in any year may be earned by attending such courses. Credit shall be awarded as follows: 3.5 hours of CPE credit for every Quarter hour of credit assigned to the course by the educational institution, or 5.0 hours of CPE credit for every semester hour of credit assigned to the course by the educational institution.

[Adopted Effective August 18, 2005. Amended effective March 2, 2006; March 11, 2010; March 8, 2013.]

.0203 General Course Approval

(a) Approval—Continuing education activities, not otherwise approved or accredited by the North Carolina State Bar Board of Continuing Legal Education, may be approved upon the written application of a sponsor, or of a certified paralegal on an individual program basis. An application for continuing paralegal education (CPE) approval shall meet the following requirements:

(1) If advance approval is requested by a sponsor, the application and supporting documentation (*i.e.*, the agenda with timeline, speaker information and a description of the written materials) shall be submitted at least 45 days prior to the date on which the course or program is scheduled. If advance approval is requested by a certified paralegal, the application need not include a complete set of supporting documentation.

(2) If more than five certified paralegals request approval of a particular program, either in advance of the date on which the course or program is scheduled or subsequent to that date, the program will not be accredited unless the sponsor applies for approval of the program and pays the accreditation fee set forth in Rule .0204.

(3) In all other cases, the application and supporting documentation shall be submitted not later than 45 days after the date the course or program was presented.

(4) The application shall be submitted on a form furnished by the Board of Paralegal Certification.

(5) The application shall contain all information requested on the form.

(6) The application shall be accompanied by a course outline or brochure that describes the content, identifies the teachers, lists the time devoted to each topic and shows each date and location at which the program will be offered.

(7) The application shall include a detailed calculation of the total continuing paralegal education (CPE) hours and the hours of professional responsibility for the program.

(8) If the sponsor has not received notice of accreditation within 15 days prior to the scheduled date of the program, the sponsor should contact the Board of Paralegal Certification via telephone or e-mail.

(b) Announcement—Sponsors who have advance approval for courses from the Board of Paralegal Certification may include in their brochures or other course descriptions the information contained in the following illustration:

> This course [or seminar or program] has been approved by the North Carolina State Bar Board of Paralegal Certification for continuing paralegal education credit in the amount of ___ hours, of which ___ hours will also apply in the area of professional responsibility. This course is not sponsored by the Board of Paralegal Certification.

[Adopted effective August 18, 2005. Amended effective August 27, 2013.]

.0204 Fees

Accredited Program Fee—Sponsors seeking accreditation for a particular program (whether or not the sponsor itself is accredited by the North Carolina State Bar Board of Continuing Legal Education), that has not already been approved or accredited by the North Carolina State Bar Board of Continuing Legal Education, shall pay a non-refundable fee of $75.00. The program must be approved in accordance with Rule .0203(1). An accredited program may be advertised by the sponsor in accordance with Rule .0203(2).

[Adopted Effective August 18, 2005.]

.0205 Computation of Hours of Instruction

(1) Hours of continuing paralegal education (CPE) will be computed by adding the number of minutes of actual instruction, dividing by 60 and rounding the results to the nearest one-tenth of an hour.

(2) Only actual instruction will be included in computing the total hours. The following will be excluded:

(a) introductory remarks;

(b) breaks;

(c) business meetings.

(3) Teaching—Continuing paralegal education (CPE) credit may be earned for teaching an approved continuing education activity. Three CPE credits will be awarded for each thirty (30) minutes of presentation. Repeat live presentations will qualify for one-half of the credit available for the initial presentation. No credit will be awarded for video replays.

(4) Teaching at a Qualified Paralegal Studies Program—Continuing paralegal education (CPE) credit may be earned for teaching a course at a qualified paralegal studies program, which program shall be qualified pursuant to Rule .0119(a) of this subchapter. Two CPE credits will be awarded for each semester credit (or its equivalent) awarded to the course.

[Adopted Effective August 18, 2005.]

SUBCHAPTER H. REGISTRATION OF ATTORNEYS APPEARING *PRO HAC VICE*

SECTION .0100 REGISTRATION PROCEDURE

.0101 Registration

(a) Whenever an out-of-state attorney (the admittee) is admitted to practice *pro hac vice* pursuant to G.S. 84–4.1, it shall be the responsibility of the member of the North Carolina State Bar who is associated in the matter (the responsible attorney) to file with the secretary a complete registration statement verified by the admittee. This registration statement must be submitted within 30 days of the court's order admitting the admittee upon a form approved by the Council of the North Carolina State Bar.

(b) Failure of the responsible attorney to file the registration statement in a timely fashion shall be grounds for administrative suspension from the practice of law in North Carolina pursuant to the procedures set forth in Rule .0903 of subchapter D of these rules.

(c) Whenever it appears that a registration statement required by paragraph (a) above has not been filed in a timely fashion, notice of such apparent failure shall be sent by the secretary to the court in which the admittee was admitted *pro hac vice* for such action as the court deems appropriate.

[Adopted Effective March 2, 2006.]

CHAPTER 2. THE REVISED RULES OF PROFESSIONAL CONDUCT OF THE NORTH CAROLINA STATE BAR

PREAMBLE AND SCOPE

Rule 0.1 Preamble: A Lawyer's Professional Responsibilities

[1] A lawyer, as a member of the legal profession, is a representative of clients, an officer of the legal system, and a public citizen having special responsibility for the quality of justice.

[2] As a representative of clients, a lawyer performs various functions. As advisor, a lawyer provides a client with an informed understanding of the client's legal rights and obligations and explains their practical implications. As advocate, a lawyer zealously asserts the client's position under the rules of the adversary system. As negotiator, a lawyer seeks a result advantageous to the client but consistent with requirements of honest dealing with others. A As an evaluator, a lawyer acts by examining a client's legal affairs and reporting about them to the client or to others.

[3] In addition to these representational functions, a lawyer may serve as a third-party neutral, a nonrepresentational role helping the parties to resolve a dispute or other matter. Some of these Rules apply directly to lawyers who are or have served as third-party neutrals. See, e.g., Rules 1.12 and 2.4. In addition, there are Rules that apply to lawyers who are not active in the practice of law or to practicing lawyers even when they are acting in a nonprofessional capacity. For example, a lawyer who commits fraud in the conduct of a business is subject to discipline for engaging in conduct involving dishonesty, fraud, deceit or misrepresentation. See Rule 8.4

[4] In all professional functions a lawyer should be competent, prompt, and diligent. A lawyer should maintain communication with a client concerning the representation. A lawyer should keep in confidence information relating to representation of a client except so far as disclosure is required or permitted by the Rules of Professional Conduct or other law.

[5] A lawyer's conduct should conform to the requirements of the law, both in professional service to clients and in the lawyer's business and personal affairs. A lawyer should use the law's procedures only for legitimate purposes and not to harass or intimidate others. A lawyer should demonstrate respect for the legal system and for those who serve it, including judges, other lawyers, and public officials. While it is a lawyer's duty, when necessary, to challenge the rectitude of official action, it is also a lawyer's duty to uphold legal process.

[6] As a public citizen, a lawyer should seek improvement of the law, access to the legal system, the administration of justice, and the quality of service rendered by the legal profession. As a member of a learned profession, a lawyer should cultivate knowledge of the law beyond its use for clients, employ that knowledge in reform of the law, and work to strengthen legal education. In addition, a lawyer should further the public's understanding of and confidence in the rule of law and the justice system because legal institutions in a constitutional democracy depend on popular participation and support to maintain their authority. A lawyer should be mindful of deficiencies in the administration of justice and of the fact that the poor, and sometimes persons who are not poor, cannot afford adequate legal assistance. Therefore, all lawyers should devote professional time and resources and use civic influence to ensure equal access to our system of justice for all those who because of economic or social barriers cannot afford or secure adequate legal counsel. A lawyer should aid the legal profession in pursuing these objectives and should help the bar regulate itself in the public interest.

[7] A lawyer should render public interest legal service and provide civic leadership. A lawyer may discharge this responsibility by providing professional services at no fee or a reduced fee to persons of limited means or to public service or charitable groups or organizations, by service in activities for improving the law, society, the legal system or the legal profession, and by financial support for organizations that provide legal services to persons of limited means.

[8] The legal profession is a group of people united in a learned calling for the public good. At their best, lawyers assure the availability of legal services to all, regardless of ability to pay, and as leaders of their communities, states, and nation, lawyers use their education and experience to improve society. It is the basic responsibility of each lawyer to provide community service, community leadership, and public interest legal services without fee, or at a substantially reduced fee, in such areas as poverty law, civil rights, public rights law, charitable organization representation, and the administration of justice.

[9] The basic responsibility for providing legal services for those unable to pay ultimately rests upon the individual lawyer. Personal involvement in the problems of the disadvantaged can be one of the most rewarding experiences in the life of a lawyer. Every lawyer, regardless of professional prominence or professional workload, should find time to participate in, or otherwise support, the provision of legal services to the disadvantaged. The provision of free legal services to those unable to pay reasonable fees continues to be an obligation of each lawyer as well as the

profession generally, but the efforts of individual lawyers are often not enough to meet the need. Thus the profession and government instituted additional programs to provide legal services. Accordingly, legal aid offices, lawyer referral services, and other related programs were developed, and programs will be developed by the profession and the government. Every lawyer should support all proper efforts to meet this need for legal services.

[10] Many of a lawyer's professional responsibilities are prescribed in the Rules of Professional Conduct, as well as substantive and procedural law. However, a lawyer is also guided by personal conscience and the approbation of professional peers. A lawyer should strive to attain the highest level of skill, to improve the law and the legal profession, and to exemplify the legal profession's ideals of public service.

[11] A lawyer's responsibilities as a representative of clients, an officer of the legal system, and a public citizen are usually harmonious. Thus, when an opposing party is well represented, a lawyer can be a zealous advocate on behalf of a client and, at the same time, assume that justice is being done. So also, a lawyer can be sure that preserving client confidences ordinarily serves the public interest because people are more likely to seek legal advice, and thereby heed their legal obligations, when they know their communications will be private.

[12] In the nature of law practice, however, conflicting responsibilities are encountered. Virtually all difficult ethical problems arise from conflict between a lawyer's responsibilities to clients, to the legal system, and to the lawyer's own interest in remaining an ethical person while earning a satisfactory living. The Rules of Professional Conduct often prescribe terms for resolving such conflicts. Within the framework of these Rules, however, many difficult issues of professional discretion can arise. Such issues must be resolved through the exercise of sensitive professional and moral judgment guided by the basic principles underlying the Rules. These principles include the lawyer's obligation zealously to protect and pursue a client's legitimate interests, within the bounds of the law, while maintaining a professional, courteous and civil attitude toward all persons involved in the legal system.

[13] Although a matter is hotly contested by the parties, a lawyer should treat opposing counsel with courtesy and respect. The legal dispute of the client must never become the lawyer's personal dispute with opposing counsel. A lawyer, moreover, should provide zealous but honorable representation without resorting to unfair or offensive tactics. The legal system provides a civilized mechanism for resolving disputes, but only if the lawyers themselves behave with dignity. A lawyer's word to another lawyer should be the lawyer's bond. As professional colleagues, lawyers should encourage and counsel new lawyers by providing advice and mentoring; foster civility among members of the bar by acceding to reasonable requests that do not prejudice the interests of the client; and counsel and assist peers who fail to fulfill their professional duties because of substance abuse, depression, or other personal difficulties.

[14] The legal profession is largely self-governing. Although other professions also have been granted powers of self-government, the legal profession is unique in this respect because of the close relationship between the profession and the processes of government and law enforcement. This connection is manifested in the fact that ultimate authority over the legal profession is vested largely in the courts.

[15] To the extent that lawyers meet the obligations of their professional calling, the occasion for government regulation is obviated. Self-regulation also helps maintain the legal profession's independence from government domination. An independent legal profession is an important force in preserving government under law, for the abuse of legal authority is more readily challenged by a self-regulated profession.

[16] The legal profession's relative autonomy carries with it a responsibility to assure that its regulations are conceived in the public interest and not in furtherance of parochial or self-interested concerns of the bar. Every lawyer is responsible for observance of the Rules of Professional Conduct. A lawyer should also aid in securing their observance by other lawyers. Neglect of these responsibilities compromises the independence of the profession and the public interest which it serves.

[17] Lawyers play a vital role in the preservation of society. The fulfillment of this role requires an understanding by lawyers of their relationship to our legal system. The Rules of Professional Conduct, when properly applied, serve to define that relationship.

[Effective July 24, 1997. Amended effective February 27, 2003; amended effective November 16, 2006.]

Rule 0.2 Scope

[1] The Rules of Professional Conduct are rules of reason. They should be interpreted with reference to the purposes of legal representation and of the law itself. Some of the rules are imperatives, cast in the terms "shall" or "shall not." These define proper conduct for purposes of professional discipline. Others, generally cast in the term "may," are permissive and define areas under the Rules in which the lawyer has discretion to exercise professional judgment. No disciplinary action should be taken when the lawyer chooses not to act, or acts within the bounds of such discretion. Other Rules define the nature of relationships between the lawyer and others. The Rules are thus partly obligatory and disciplinary, and partly constitutive and descriptive in that they define a law-

yer's professional role. Many of the Comments use the term "should." Comments do not add obligations to the Rules but provide guidance for practicing in compliance with the Rules.

[2] The Rules presuppose a larger legal context shaping the lawyer's role. That context includes court rules and statutes relating to matters of licensure, laws defining specific obligations of lawyers, and substantive and procedural law in general. The Comments are sometimes used to alert lawyers to their responsibilities under such other law.

[3] Compliance with the Rules, as with all law in an open society, depends primarily upon understanding and voluntary compliance, secondarily upon reinforcement by peer and public opinion, and finally, when necessary, upon enforcement through disciplinary proceedings. The Rules do not, however, exhaust the moral and ethical considerations that should inform a lawyer, for no worthwhile human activity can be completely defined by legal rules. The Rules simply provide a framework for the ethical practice of law.

[4] Furthermore, for purposes of determining the lawyer's authority and responsibility, principles of substantive law external to these Rules determine whether a client-lawyer relationship exists. Most of the duties flowing from the client-lawyer relationship attach only after the client has requested the lawyer to render legal services and the lawyer has agreed to do so. But there are some duties, such as that of confidentiality under Rule 1.6, that attach when the lawyer agrees to consider whether a client-lawyer relationship shall be established. Rule 1.18. Whether a client-lawyer relationship exists for any specific purpose can depend on the circumstances and may be a question of fact.

[5] Under various legal provisions, including constitutional, statutory, and common law, the responsibilities of government lawyers may include authority concerning legal matters that ordinarily reposes in the client in private client-lawyer relationships. For example, a lawyer for a government agency may have authority on behalf of the government to decide upon settlement or whether to appeal from an adverse judgment. Such authority in various respects is generally vested in the attorney general and the state's attorney in state government, and their federal counterparts, and the same may be true of other government law officers. Also, lawyers under the supervision of these officers may be authorized to represent several government agencies in intragovernmental legal controversies in circumstances where a private lawyer could not represent multiple private clients. These rules do not abrogate any such authority.

[6] Failure to comply with an obligation or prohibition imposed by a Rule is a basis for invoking the disciplinary process. The Rules presuppose that disciplinary assessment of a lawyer's conduct will be made on the basis of the facts and circumstances as they existed at the time of the conduct in question and in recognition of the fact that a lawyer often has to act upon uncertain or incomplete evidence of the situation. Moreover, the Rules presuppose that whether or not discipline should be imposed for a violation, and the severity of a sanction, depend on all the circumstances, such as the willfulness and seriousness of the violation, extenuating factors, and whether there have been previous violations.

[7] Violation of a Rule should not give rise itself to a cause of action against a lawyer nor should it create any presumption in such a case that a legal duty has been breached. In addition, violation of a Rule does not necessarily warrant any other nondisciplinary remedy, such as disqualification of a lawyer in pending litigation. The rules are designed to provide guidance to lawyers and to provide a structure for regulating conduct through disciplinary agencies. They are not designed to be a basis for civil liability. Furthermore, the purpose of the Rules can be subverted when they are invoked by opposing parties as procedural weapons. The fact that a Rule is a just basis for a lawyer's self-assessment, or for sanctioning a lawyer under the administration of a disciplinary authority, does not imply that an antagonist in a collateral proceeding or transaction has standing to seek enforcement of the Rule. Accordingly, nothing in the Rules should be deemed to augment any substantive legal duty of lawyers or the extra-disciplinary consequences of violating such a Rule.

[8] The Comment accompanying each Rule explains and illustrates the meaning and purpose of the Rule. The Preamble and this note on Scope provide general orientation. The Comments are intended as guides to interpretation, but the text of each Rule is authoritative. Research notes were prepared to compare counterparts in the original Rules of Professional Conduct (adopted 1985, as amended) and to provide selected references to other authorities. The notes have not been adopted, do not constitute part of the Rules, and are not intended to affect the application or interpretation of the Rules and Comments.

[Effective July 24, 1997. Amended effective February 27, 2003; amended effective February 5, 2004.]

TERMINOLOGY

Rule 1.0 Terminology

(a) "Belief" or "believes" denotes that the person involved actually supposed the fact in question to be true. A person's belief may be inferred from circumstances.

(b) "Confidential information" denotes information described in Rule 1.6.

(c) "Confirmed in writing," when used in reference to the informed consent of a person, denotes informed consent that is given in writing by the person or a writing that a lawyer promptly transmits to the person confirming an oral informed consent. See paragraph (f) for the definition of "informed consent." If it is not feasible to obtain or transmit the writing at the time the person gives informed consent, then the lawyer must obtain or transmit it within a reasonable time thereafter.

(d) "Firm" or "law firm" denotes a lawyer or lawyers in a law partnership, professional corporation, sole proprietorship or other association authorized to practice law; or lawyers employed in a legal services organization or the legal department of a corporation, government entity, or other organization.

(e) "Fraud" or "fraudulent" denotes conduct that is fraudulent under the substantive or procedural law of North Carolina and has a purpose to deceive.

(f) "Informed consent" denotes the agreement by a person to a proposed course of conduct after the lawyer has communicated adequate information and explanation appropriate to the circumstances.

(g) "Knowingly," "known," or "knows" denotes actual knowledge of the fact in question. A person's knowledge may be inferred from circumstances.

(h) "Partner" denotes a member of a partnership, a shareholder in a law firm organized as a professional corporation, or a member of an association authorized to practice law.

(i) "Reasonable" or "reasonably" when used in relation to conduct by a lawyer denotes the conduct of a reasonably prudent and competent lawyer.

(j) "Reasonable belief" or "reasonably believes" when used in reference to a lawyer denotes that the lawyer believes the matter in question and that the circumstances are such that the belief is reasonable.

(k) "Reasonably should know" when used in reference to a lawyer denotes that a lawyer of reasonable prudence and competence would ascertain the matter in question.

(*l*) "Screened" denotes the isolation of a lawyer from any participation in a professional matter through the timely imposition of procedures within a firm that are reasonably adequate under the circumstances to protect information that the isolated lawyer is obligated to protect under these Rules or other law.

(m) "Substantial" when used in reference to degree or extent denotes a material matter of clear and weighty importance.

(n) "Tribunal" denotes a court, an arbitrator in a binding arbitration proceeding, or a legislative body, administrative agency, or other body acting in an adjudicative capacity. The term encompasses any proceeding conducted in the course of a trial or litigation, or conducted pursuant to the tribunal's rules of civil or criminal procedure or other relevant rules of the tribunal, such as a deposition, arbitration, or mediation. A legislative body, administrative agency or other body acts in an adjudicative capacity when a neutral official, after the presentation of evidence or legal argument by a party or parties, may render a binding legal judgment directly affecting a party's interests in a particular matter.

(*o*) "Writing" or "written" denotes a tangible or electronic record of a communication or representation, and any data embedded therein (commonly referred to as metadata), including handwriting, typewriting, printing, photostating, photography, audio or video recording, and electronic communications. A "signed" writing includes an electronic sound, symbol or process attached to or logically associated with a writing and executed or adopted by a person with the intent to sign the writing.

[Adopted July 24, 1997. Amended February 27, 2003; October 2, 2014; March 5, 2015.]

Comment

Confirmed in Writing

[1] If it is not feasible to obtain or transmit a written confirmation at the time the client gives informed consent, then the lawyer must obtain or transmit it within a reasonable time thereafter. If a lawyer has obtained a client's informed consent, the lawyer may act in reliance on that consent so long as it is confirmed in writing within a reasonable time thereafter.

Firm

[2] Whether two or more lawyers constitute a firm within paragraph (d) can depend on the specific facts. For example, two practitioners who share office space and occasionally consult or assist each other ordinarily would not be regarded as constituting a firm. However, if they present themselves to the public in a way that suggests that they are a firm or conduct themselves as a firm, they should be regarded as a firm for purposes of the Rules. The terms of any formal agreement between associated lawyers are relevant in determining whether they are a firm, as is the fact that they have mutual access to information concerning the clients they serve. Furthermore, it is relevant in doubtful cases to consider the underlying purpose of the Rule that is involved. A group of lawyers could be regarded as a firm for purposes of the Rule that the same lawyer should not represent opposing parties in litigation, while it might not be so regarded for purposes of the Rule that information acquired by one lawyer is attributed to another.

[3] With respect to the law department of an organization, including the government, there is ordinarily no question that the members of the department constitute a firm within the meaning of the Rules of Professional Conduct. There can be uncertainty, however, as to the identity of the client. For example, it may not be clear whether the law department of a corporation represents a subsidiary or an affiliated corporation, as well as the corporation by which the members of the department are directly employed. A similar question can arise concerning an unincorporated association and its local affiliates.

[4] Similar questions can also arise with respect to lawyers in legal aid and legal services organizations. Depending upon the structure of the organization, the entire organization or different components of it may constitute a firm or firms for purposes of these Rules.

Fraud

[5] When used in these Rules, the terms "fraud" or "fraudulent" refer to conduct that is characterized as such under the substantive or procedural law of North Carolina and has a purpose to deceive. This does not include merely negligent misrepresentation or negligent failure to apprise another of relevant information. For purposes of these Rules, it is not necessary that anyone has suffered damages or relied on the misrepresentation or failure to inform.

Informed Consent

[6] Many of the Rules of Professional Conduct require the lawyer to obtain the informed consent of a client or other person (e.g., a former client or, under certain circumstances, a prospective client) before accepting or continuing representation or pursuing a course of conduct. See, e.g. , Rules 1.6(a) and 1.7(b). The communication necessary to obtain such consent will vary according to the Rule involved and the circumstances giving rise to the need to obtain informed consent. The lawyer must make reasonable efforts to ensure that the client or other person possesses information reasonably adequate to make an informed decision. Ordinarily, this will require communication that includes a disclosure of the facts and circumstances giving rise to the situation, any explanation reasonably necessary to inform the client or other person of the material advantages and disadvantages of the proposed course of conduct and a discussion of the client's or other person's options and alternatives. In some circumstances it may be appropriate for a lawyer to advise a client or other person to seek the advice of other counsel. A lawyer need not inform a client or other person of facts or implications already known to the client or other person; nevertheless, a lawyer who does not personally inform the client or other person assumes the risk that the client or other person is inadequately informed and the consent is invalid. In determining whether the information and explanation provided are reasonably adequate, relevant factors include whether the client or other person is experienced in legal matters generally and in making decisions of the type involved, and whether the client or other person is independently represented by other counsel in giving the consent. Normally, such persons need less information and explanation than others, and generally a client or other person who is independently represented by other counsel in giving the consent should be assumed to have given informed consent.

[7] Obtaining informed consent will usually require an affirmative response by the client or other person. In general, a lawyer may not assume consent from a client's or other person's silence. Consent may be inferred, however, from the conduct of a client or other person who has reasonably adequate information about the matter. A number of Rules require that a person's consent be confirmed in writing. See Rules 1.7(b) and 1.9(a). For a definition of "writing" and "confirmed in writing," see paragraphs (*o*) and (c). Other Rules require that a client's consent be obtained in a writing signed by the client. See, e.g., Rules 1.8(a) and (g). For a definition of "signed," see paragraph (*o*).

Screened

[8] This definition applies to situations where screening of a personally disqualified lawyer is permitted to remove imputation of a conflict of interest under Rules 1.10, 1.11, 1.12 or 1.18.

[9] The purpose of screening is to assure the affected parties that confidential information known by the personally disqualified lawyer remains protected. The personally disqualified lawyer should acknowledge the obligation not to communicate with any of the other lawyers in the firm with respect to the matter. Similarly, other lawyers in the firm who are working on the matter should be informed that the screening is in place and that they may not communicate with the personally disqualified lawyer with respect to the matter. Additional screening measures that are appropriate for the particular matter will depend on the circumstances. To implement, reinforce, and remind all affected lawyers of the presence of the screening, it may be appropriate for the firm to undertake such procedures as a written undertaking by the screened lawyer to avoid any communication with other firm personnel and any contact with any firm files or other information, including information in electronic form, relating to the matter, written notice and instructions to all other firm personnel forbidding any communication with the screened lawyer relating to the matter, denial of access by the screened lawyer to firm files or other information, including information in electronic form, relating to the matter and periodic reminders of the screen to the screened lawyer and all other firm personnel.

[10] In order to be effective, screening measures must be implemented as soon as practical after a lawyer or law firm knows or reasonably should know that there is a need for screening.

CLIENT–LAWYER RELATIONSHIP

Rule 1.1 Competence

A lawyer shall not handle a legal matter that the lawyer knows or should know he or she is not competent to handle without associating with a lawyer who is competent to handle the matter. Competent representation requires the legal knowledge, skill, thoroughness, and preparation reasonably necessary for the representation.

[Adopted July 24, 1997. Amended February 27, 2003; October 2, 2014.]

Comment

Legal Knowledge and Skill

[1] In determining whether a lawyer employs the requisite knowledge and skill in a particular matter, relevant factors include the relative complexity and specialized nature of the matter, the lawyer's general experience, the lawyer's training and experience in the field in question, the preparation and study the lawyer is able to give the matter, and whether it is feasible to refer the matter to, or associate or consult with, a lawyer of established competence in the field in question. In many instances, the required proficiency is that of a general

practitioner. Expertise in a particular field of law may be required in some circumstances.

[2] A lawyer need not necessarily have special training or prior experience to handle legal problems of a type with which the lawyer is unfamiliar. A newly admitted lawyer can be as competent as a practitioner with long experience. Some important legal skills, such as the analysis of precedent, the evaluation of evidence, and legal drafting, are required in all legal problems. Perhaps the most fundamental legal skill consists of determining what kind of legal problems a situation may involve, a skill that necessarily transcends any particular specialized knowledge. A lawyer can provide adequate representation in a wholly novel field through necessary study. Competent representation can also be provided through the association of a lawyer of established competence in the field in question.

[3] In an emergency, a lawyer may give advice or assistance in a matter in which the lawyer does not have the skill ordinarily required where referral to, or consultation or association with, another lawyer would be impractical. Even in an emergency, however, assistance should be limited to that which is reasonably necessary under the circumstances, for ill-considered action under emergency conditions can jeopardize the client's interest.

[4] A lawyer may accept representation where the requisite level of competence can be achieved by reasonable preparation. This applies as well to a lawyer who is appointed as counsel for an unrepresented person.

Thoroughness and Preparation

[5] Competent handling of a particular matter includes inquiry into, and analysis of, the factual and legal elements of the problem, and use of methods and procedures meeting the standards of competent practitioners. It also includes adequate preparation. The required attention and preparation are determined, in part, by what is at stake; major litigation and complex transactions ordinarily require more extensive treatment than matters of lesser complexity consequence. An agreement between the lawyer and the client regarding the scope of the representation may limit the matters for which the lawyer is responsible. See Rule 1.2(c).

Retaining or Contracting with Other Lawyers

[6] Before a lawyer retains or contracts with other lawyers outside the lawyer's own firm to provide or assist in the provision of legal services to a client, the lawyer should ordinarily obtain informed consent from the client and must reasonably believe that the other lawyers' services will contribute to the competent and ethical representation of the client. *See also* Rules 1.2 (allocation of authority), 1.4 (communication with client), 1.5(e) (fee division), 1.6 (confidentiality), and 5.5(a) (unauthorized practice of law). The reasonableness of the decision to retain or contract with other lawyers outside the lawyer's own firm will depend upon the circumstances, including the education, experience, and reputation of the nonfirm lawyers; the nature of the services assigned to the nonfirm lawyers; and the legal protections, professional conduct rules, and ethical environments of the jurisdictions in which the services will be performed, particularly relating to confidential information.

[7] When lawyers from more than one law firm are providing legal services to the client on a particular matter, the lawyers ordinarily should consult with each other and the client about the scope of their respective representations and the allocation of responsibility among them. *See* Rule 1.2. When making allocations of responsibility in a matter pending before a tribunal, lawyers and parties may have additional obligations that are a matter of law beyond the scope of these Rules.

Maintaining Competence

[8] To maintain the requisite knowledge and skill, a lawyer should keep abreast of changes in the law and its practice, including the benefits and risks associated with the technology relevant to the lawyer's practice, engage in continuing study and education, and comply with all continuing legal education requirements to which the lawyer is subject.

Distinguishing Professional Negligence

[9] An error by a lawyer may constitute professional malpractice under the applicable standard of care and subject the lawyer to civil liability. However, conduct that constitutes a breach of the civil standard of care owed to a client giving rise to liability for professional malpractice does not necessarily constitute a violation of the ethical duty to represent a client competently. A lawyer who makes a good-faith effort to be prepared and to be thorough will not generally be subject to professional discipline, although he or she may be subject to a claim for malpractice. For example, a single error or omission made in good faith, absent aggravating circumstances, such as an error while performing a public records search, is not usually indicative of a violation of the duty to represent a client competently.

[10] Repeated failure to perform legal services competently is a violation of this rule. A pattern of incompetent behavior demonstrates that a lawyer cannot or will not acquire the knowledge and skills necessary for minimally competent practice. For example, a lawyer who repeatedly provides legal services that are inadequate or who repeatedly provides legal services that are unnecessary is not fulfilling his or her duty to be competent. This pattern of behavior does not have to be the result of a dishonest or sinister motive, nor does it have to result in damages to a client giving rise to a civil claim for malpractice in order to cast doubt on the lawyer's ability to fulfill his or her professional responsibilities.

Rule 1.2 Scope of Representation and Allocation of Authority between Client and Lawyer

(a) Subject to paragraphs (c) and (d), a lawyer shall abide by a client's decisions concerning the objectives of representation and, as required by Rule 1.4, shall consult with the client as to the means by which they are to be pursued. A lawyer may take such action on behalf of the client as is impliedly authorized to carry out the representation.

(1) A lawyer shall abide by a client's decision whether to settle a matter. In a criminal case, the lawyer shall abide by the client's decision, after consultation with the lawyer, as to a plea to be entered, whether to waive jury trial and whether the client will testify.

(2) A lawyer does not violate this rule by acceding to reasonable requests of opposing counsel that do not prejudice the rights of a client, or by being punctual in fulfilling all professional commitments, by avoiding

offensive tactics, or by treating with courtesy and consideration all persons involved in the legal process.

(3) In the representation of a client, a lawyer may exercise his or her professional judgment to waive or fail to assert a right or position of the client.

(b) A lawyer's representation of a client, including representation by appointment, does not constitute an endorsement of the client's political, economic, social or moral views or activities.

(c) A lawyer may limit the scope of the representation if the limitation is reasonable under the circumstances.

(d) A lawyer shall not counsel a client to engage, or assist a client, in conduct that the lawyer knows is criminal or fraudulent, but a lawyer may discuss the legal consequences of any proposed course of conduct with a client and may counsel or assist a client to make a good faith effort to determine the validity, scope, meaning or application of the law.

[Adopted July 24, 1997. Amended February 27, 2003.]

Comment

Scope of Representation Allocation of Authority between Client and Lawyer

[1] Paragraph (a) confers upon the client the ultimate authority to determine the purposes to be served by legal representation, within the limits imposed by law and the lawyer's professional obligations. The decisions specified in paragraph (a), such as whether to settle a civil matter, must also be made by the client. See Rule 1.4(a)(1) for the lawyer's duty to communicate with the client about such decisions. With respect to the means by which the client's objectives are to be pursued, the lawyer shall consult with the client as required by Rule 1.4(a)(2) and may take such action as is impliedly authorized to carry out the representation. Lawyers are encouraged to treat opposing counsel with courtesy and to cooperate with opposing counsel when it will not prevent or unduly hinder the pursuit of the objective of the representation. To this end, a lawyer may waive a right or fail to assert a position of a client without first obtaining the client's consent. For example, a lawyer may consent to an extension of time for the opposing party to file pleadings or discovery without obtaining the client's consent.

[2] On occasion, however, a lawyer and a client may disagree about the means to be used to accomplish the client's objectives. Clients normally defer to the special knowledge and skill of their lawyer with respect to the means to be used to accomplish their objectives, particularly with respect to technical, legal and tactical matters. Conversely, lawyers usually defer to the client regarding such questions as the expense to be incurred and concern for third persons who might be adversely affected. Because of the varied nature of the matters about which a lawyer and client might disagree and because the actions in question may implicate the interests of a tribunal or other persons, this Rule does not prescribe how such disagreements are to be resolved. Other law, however, may be applicable and should be consulted by the lawyer. The lawyer should also consult with the client and seek a mutually acceptable resolution of the disagreement. If such efforts are unavailing and the lawyer has a fundamental disagreement with the client, the lawyer may withdraw from the representation. See Rule 1.16(b)(4). Conversely, the client may resolve the disagreement by discharging the lawyer. See Rule 1.16(a)(3).

[3] At the outset of a representation, the client may authorize the lawyer to take specific action on the client's behalf without further consultation. Absent a material change in circumstances and subject to Rule 1.4, a lawyer may rely on such an advance authorization. The client may, however, revoke such authority at any time.

[4] In a case in which the client appears to be suffering diminished capacity, the lawyer's duty to abide by the client's decisions is to be guided by reference to Rule 1.14.

Independence from Client's Views or Activities

[5] Legal representation should not be denied to people who are unable to afford legal services, or whose cause is controversial or the subject of popular disapproval. By the same token, representing a client does not constitute approval of the client's views or activities.

Agreements Limiting Scope of Representation

[6] The scope of services to be provided by a lawyer may be limited by agreement with the client or by the terms under which the lawyer's services are made available to the client. When a lawyer has been retained by an insurer to represent an insured, for example, the representation may be limited to matters related to the insurance coverage. A limited representation may be appropriate because the client has limited objectives for the representation. In addition, the terms upon which representation is undertaken may exclude specific means that might otherwise be used to accomplish the client's objectives. Such limitations may exclude actions that the client thinks are too costly or that the lawyer regards as repugnant or imprudent.

[7] Although this Rule affords the lawyer and client substantial latitude to limit the representation, the limitation must be reasonable under the circumstances. If, for example, a client's objective is limited to securing general information about the law the client needs in order to handle a common and typically uncomplicated legal problem, the lawyer and client may agree that the lawyer's services will be limited to a brief telephone consultation. Such a limitation, however, would not be reasonable if the time allotted was not sufficient to yield advice upon which the client could rely. Although an agreement for a limited representation does not exempt a lawyer from the duty to provide competent representation, the limitation is a factor to be considered when determining the legal knowledge, skill, thoroughness and preparation reasonably necessary for the representation. See Rule 1.1.

[8] Although paragraph (c) does not require that the client's informed consent to a limited representation be in writing, a specification of the scope of representation will normally be a necessary part of any written communication of the rate or basis of the lawyer's fee. See Rule 1.0(e) for the definition of "informed consent."

[9] All agreements concerning a lawyer's representation of a client must accord with the Rules of Professional Conduct and other law. See, e.g., Rules 1.1, 1.8 and 5.6.

Criminal, Fraudulent and Prohibited Transactions

[10] Paragraph (d) prohibits a lawyer from knowingly counseling or assisting a client to commit a crime or fraud. This prohibition, however, does not preclude the lawyer from giving an honest opinion about the actual consequences that appear likely to result from a client's conduct. Nor does the

fact that a client uses advice in a course of action that is criminal or fraudulent of itself make a lawyer a party to the course of action. There is a critical distinction between presenting an analysis of legal aspects of questionable conduct and recommending the means by which a crime or fraud might be committed with impunity. There is also a distinction between giving a client legitimate advice about asset protection and assisting in the illegal or fraudulent conveyance of assets.

[11] When the client's course of action has already begun and is continuing, the lawyer's responsibility is especially delicate. The lawyer is required to avoid assisting the client, for example, by drafting or delivering documents that the lawyer knows are fraudulent or by suggesting how the wrongdoing might be concealed. A lawyer may not continue assisting a client in conduct that the lawyer originally supposed was legally proper but then discovers is criminal or fraudulent. The lawyer must, therefore, withdraw from the representation of the client in the matter. See Rule 1.16(a). In some cases, withdrawal alone might be insufficient. It may be necessary for the lawyer to give notice of the fact of withdrawal and to disaffirm any opinion, document, affirmation or the like. In extreme cases, substantive law may require a lawyer to disclose information relating to the representation to avoid being deemed to have assisted the client's crime or fraud. See Rule 4.1.

[12] Where the client is a fiduciary, the lawyer may be charged with special obligations in dealings with a beneficiary.

[13] Paragraph (d) applies whether or not the defrauded party is a party to the transaction. Hence, a lawyer must not participate in a transaction to effectuate criminal or fraudulent avoidance of tax liability. Paragraph (d) does not preclude undertaking a criminal defense incident to a general retainer for legal services to a lawful enterprise. The last clause of paragraph (d) recognizes that determining the validity or interpretation of a statute or regulation may require a course of action involving disobedience of the statute or regulation or of the interpretation placed upon it by governmental authorities.

[14] If a lawyer comes to know or reasonably should know that a client expects assistance not permitted by the Rules of Professional Conduct or other law or if the lawyer intends to act contrary to the client's instructions, the lawyer must consult with the client regarding the limitations on the lawyer's conduct. See Rule 1.4(a)(5).

Rule 1.3 Diligence

A lawyer shall act with reasonable diligence and promptness in representing a client.

[Adopted July 24, 1997. Amended February 27, 2003.]

Comment

[1] A lawyer should pursue a matter on behalf of a client despite opposition, obstruction or personal inconvenience to the lawyer, and take whatever lawful and ethical measures are required to vindicate a client's cause or endeavor. A lawyer must also act with commitment and dedication to the interests of the client and with zeal in advocacy upon the client's behalf. A lawyer is not bound, however, to press for every advantage that might be realized for a client. For example, a lawyer may have authority to exercise professional discretion in determining the means by which a matter should be pursued. See Rule 1.2. The lawyer's duty to act with reasonable diligence does not require the use of offensive tactics or preclude the treating of all persons involved in the legal process with courtesy and respect.

[2] A lawyer's work load must be controlled so that each matter can be handled competently.

[3] Perhaps no professional shortcoming is more widely resented than procrastination. A client's interests often can be adversely affected by the passage of time or the change of conditions; in extreme instances, as when a lawyer overlooks a statute of limitations, the client's legal position may be destroyed. Even when the client's interests are not affected in substance, however, unreasonable delay can cause a client needless anxiety and undermine confidence in the lawyer's trustworthiness. A lawyer's duty to act with reasonable promptness, however, does not preclude the lawyer from agreeing to a reasonable request for a postponement that will not prejudice the lawyer's client.

[4] Unless the relationship is terminated as provided in Rule 1.16, a lawyer should carry through to conclusion all matters undertaken for a client. If a lawyer's employment is limited to a specific matter, the relationship terminates when the matter has been resolved. If a lawyer has served a client over a substantial period in a variety of matters, the client sometimes may assume that the lawyer will continue to serve on a continuing basis unless the lawyer gives notice of withdrawal. Doubt about whether a client-lawyer relationship still exists should be clarified by the lawyer, preferably in writing, so that the client will not mistakenly suppose the lawyer is looking after the client's affairs when the lawyer has ceased to do so. For example, if a lawyer has handled a judicial or administrative proceeding that produced a result adverse to the client and the lawyer and the client have not agreed that the lawyer will handle the matter on appeal, the lawyer must consult with the client about the possibility of appeal before relinquishing responsibility for the matter. See Rule 1.4(a)(2). Whether the lawyer is obligated to prosecute the appeal for the client depends on the scope of the representation the lawyer has agreed to provide to the client. See Rule 1.2.

[5] To prevent neglect of client matters in the event of a sole practitioner's death or disability, the duty of diligence may require that each sole practitioner prepare a plan, in conformity with applicable rules, that designates another competent lawyer to review client files, notify each client of the lawyer's death or disability, and determine whether there is a need for immediate protective action. Cf. Rule .0122 of Subchapter 1B of the Rules of the North Carolina State Bar (providing for court appointment of a lawyer to inventory files and take other protective action to protect the interests of the clients of a lawyer who has disappeared or is deceased or disabled).

Distinguishing Professional Negligence

[6] Conduct that may constitute professional malpractice does not necessarily constitute a violation of the ethical duty to represent a client diligently. Generally speaking, a single instance of unaggravated negligence does not warrant discipline. For example, missing a statute of limitations may form the basis for a claim of professional malpractice. However, where the failure to file the complaint in a timely manner is due to inadvertence or a simple mistake such as mislaying the papers or miscalculating the date upon which the statute of limitations will run, absent some other aggravating factor, such an incident will not generally constitute a violation of this rule.

[7] Conduct sufficient to warrant the imposition of professional discipline is typically characterized by the element of intent or scienter manifested when a lawyer knowingly or recklessly disregards his or her obligations. Breach of the duty of diligence sufficient to warrant professional discipline occurs when a lawyer consistently fails to carry out the obligations that the lawyer has assumed for his or her clients. A pattern of delay, procrastination, carelessness, and forgetfulness regarding client matters indicates a knowing or reckless disregard for the lawyer's professional duties. For example, a lawyer who habitually misses filing deadlines and court dates is not taking his or her professional responsibilities seriously. A pattern of negligent conduct is not excused by a burdensome case load or inadequate office procedures.

Rule 1.4. Communication

(a) A lawyer shall:

(1) promptly inform the client of any decision or circumstance with respect to which the client's informed consent, as defined in Rule 1.0(f), is required by these Rules;

(2) reasonably consult with the client about the means by which the client's objectives are to be accomplished;

(3) keep the client reasonably informed about the status of the matter;

(4) promptly comply with reasonable requests for information; and

(5) consult with the client about any relevant limitation on the lawyer's conduct when the lawyer knows that the client expects assistance not permitted by the Rules of Professional Conduct or other law.

(b) A lawyer shall explain a matter to the extent reasonably necessary to permit the client to make informed decisions regarding the representation.

[Adopted July 24, 1997. Amended February 27, 2003; October 2, 2014.]

Comment

[1] Reasonable communication between the lawyer and the client is necessary for the client effectively to participate in the representation.

Communicating with Client

[2] If these Rules require that a particular decision about the representation be made by the client, paragraph (a)(1) requires that the lawyer promptly consult with and secure the client's consent prior to taking action unless prior discussions with the client have resolved what action the client wants the lawyer to take. For example, a lawyer who receives from opposing counsel an offer of settlement in a civil controversy or a proffered plea bargain in a criminal case must promptly inform the client of its substance unless the client has previously indicated that the proposal will be acceptable or unacceptable or has authorized the lawyer to accept or to reject the offer. See Rule 1.2(a).

[3] Paragraph (a)(2) requires the lawyer to consult with the client about the means to be used to accomplish the client's objectives. In some situations—depending on both the importance of the action under consideration and the feasibility of consulting with the client—this duty will require consultation prior to taking action. In other circumstances, such as during a trial when an immediate decision must be made, the exigency of the situation may require the lawyer to act without prior consultation. In such cases the lawyer must nonetheless act reasonably to inform the client of actions the lawyer has taken on the client's behalf. Additionally, paragraph (a)(3) requires that the lawyer keep the client reasonably informed about the status of the matter, such as significant developments affecting the timing or the substance of the representation.

Communicating with Client

[4] A lawyer's regular communication with clients will minimize the occasions on which a client will need to request information concerning the representation. When a client makes a reasonable request for information, however, paragraph (a)(4) requires prompt compliance with the request, or if a prompt response is not feasible, that the lawyer, or a member of the lawyer's staff, acknowledge receipt of the request and advise the client when a response may be expected. A lawyer should address with the client how the lawyer and the client will communicate, and should respond to or acknowledge client communications in a reasonable and timely manner.

Explaining Matters

[5] The client should have sufficient information to participate intelligently in decisions concerning the objectives of the representation and the means by which they are to be pursued, to the extent the client is willing and able to do so. Adequacy of communication depends in part on the kind of advice or assistance that is involved. For example, when there is time to explain a proposal made in a negotiation, the lawyer should review all important provisions with the client before proceeding to an agreement. In litigation a lawyer should explain the general strategy and prospects of success and ordinarily should consult the client on tactics that are likely to result in significant expense or to injure or coerce others. On the other hand, a lawyer ordinarily will not be expected to describe trial or negotiation strategy in detail. The guiding principle is that the lawyer should fulfill reasonable client expectations for information consistent with the duty to act in the client's best interests, and the client's overall requirements as to the character of representation. In certain circumstances, such as when a lawyer asks a client to consent to a representation affected by a conflict of interest, the client must give informed consent, as defined in Rule 1.0(e).

[6] Ordinarily, the information to be provided is that appropriate for a client who is a comprehending and responsible adult. However, fully informing the client according to this standard may be impracticable, for example, where the client is a child or suffers from diminished capacity. See Rule 1.14. When the client is an organization or group, it is often impossible or inappropriate to inform every one of its members about its legal affairs; ordinarily, the lawyer should address communications to the appropriate officials of the organization. See Rule 1.13. Where many routine matters are involved, a system of limited or occasional reporting may be arranged with the client.

Withholding Information

[7] In some circumstances, a lawyer may be justified in delaying transmission of information when the client would be likely to react imprudently to an immediate communica-

tion. Thus, a lawyer might withhold a psychiatric diagnosis of a client when the examining psychiatrist indicates that disclosure would harm the client. A lawyer may not withhold information to serve the lawyer's own interest or convenience or the interests or convenience of another person. Rules or court orders governing litigation may provide that information supplied to a lawyer may not be disclosed to the client. Rule 3.4(c) directs compliance with such rules or orders.

Rule 1.5 Fees

(a) A lawyer shall not make an agreement for, charge, or collect an illegal or clearly excessive fee or charge or collect a clearly excessive amount for expenses. The factors to be considered in determining whether a fee is clearly excessive include the following:

(1) the time and labor required, the novelty and difficulty of the questions involved, and the skill requisite to perform the legal service properly;

(2) the likelihood, if apparent to the client, that the acceptance of the particular employment will preclude other employment by the lawyer;

(3) the fee customarily charged in the locality for similar legal services;

(4) the amount involved and the results obtained;

(5) the time limitations imposed by the client or by the circumstances;

(6) the nature and length of the professional relationship with the client;

(7) the experience, reputation, and ability of the lawyer or lawyers performing the services; and

(8) whether the fee is fixed or contingent.

(b) When the lawyer has not regularly represented the client, the scope of the representation and the basis or rate of the fee and expenses for which the client will be responsible shall be communicated to the client, preferably in writing, before or within a reasonable time after commencing the representation.

(c) A fee may be contingent on the outcome of the matter for which the service is rendered, except in a matter in which a contingent fee is prohibited by paragraph (d) or other law. A contingent fee agreement shall be in a writing signed by the client and shall state the method by which the fee is to be determined, including the percentage or percentages that shall accrue to the lawyer in the event of settlement, trial or appeal; litigation and other expenses to be deducted from the recovery; and whether such expenses are to be deducted before or after the contingent fee is calculated. The agreement must clearly notify the client of any expenses for which the client will be liable whether or not the client is the prevailing party. Upon conclusion of a contingent fee matter, the lawyer shall provide the client with a written statement stating the outcome of the matter and, if there is a recovery, showing the remittance to the client and the method of its determination.

(d) A lawyer shall not enter into an arrangement for, charge, or collect:

(1) a contingent fee for representing a defendant in a criminal case; however, a lawyer may charge and collect a contingent fee for representation in a criminal or civil asset forfeiture proceeding if not otherwise prohibited by law; or

(2) a contingent fee in a civil case in which such a fee is prohibited by law.

(e) A division of a fee between lawyers who are not in the same firm may be made only if:

(1) the division is in proportion to the services performed by each lawyer or each lawyer assumes joint responsibility for the representation;

(2) the client agrees to the arrangement, including the share each lawyer will receive, and the agreement is confirmed in writing; and

(3) the total fee is reasonable.

(f) Any lawyer having a dispute with a client regarding a fee for legal services must:

(1) make reasonable efforts to advise his or her client of the existence of the North Carolina State Bar's program of fee dispute resolution at least 30 days prior to initiating legal proceedings to collect the disputed fee; and

(2) participate in good faith in the fee dispute resolution process if the client submits a proper request.

[Adopted July 24, 1997. Amended February 27, 2003.]

Comment

Appropriate Fees and Expenses

[1] Paragraph (a) requires that lawyers charge fees that are not clearly excessive under the circumstances. The factors specified in (1) through (8) are not exclusive. Nor will each factor be relevant in each instance. Paragraph (a) also requires that expenses for which the client will be charged must not be clearly excessive. A lawyer may seek reimbursement for expenses for in-house services, such as copying, or for other expenses incurred in-house, such as telephone charges, either by charging a reasonable amount to which the client has agreed in advance or by charging an amount that reasonably reflects the cost incurred by the lawyer.

Basis or Rate of Fee

[2] When the lawyer has regularly represented a client, an understanding will have ordinarily evolved concerning the basis or rate of the fee and the expenses for which the client will be responsible. In a new client-lawyer relationship, however, a written understanding as to fees and expenses should be promptly established. Generally, furnishing the client with a simple memorandum or copy of the lawyer's customary fee arrangements will suffice, provided that the writing states the general nature of the legal services to be provided, the basis, rate or total amount of the fee and whether and to what extent the client will be responsible for any costs, expenses or disbursements in the course of the

representation. A written statement concerning the terms of the engagement reduces the possibility of misunderstanding.

[3] Contingent fees, like any other fees, are subject to the standard of paragraph (a) of this Rule. In determining whether a particular contingent fee is clearly excessive, or whether it is reasonable to charge any form of contingent fee, a lawyer must consider the factors that are relevant under the circumstances. Applicable law may impose limitations on contingent fees, such as a ceiling on the percentage allowable, or may require a lawyer to offer clients an alternative basis for the fee. Applicable law also may apply to situations other than a contingent fee, for example, government regulations regarding fees in certain tax matters.

Terms of Payment

[4] A lawyer may require advance payment of a fee, but is obliged to return any unearned portion. See Rule 1.16(d). This does not apply when the advance payment is a true retainer to reserve services rather than an advance to secure the payment of fees yet to be earned. A lawyer may accept property in payment for services, such as an ownership interest in an enterprise, provided this does not involve acquisition of a proprietary interest in the cause of action or subject matter of the litigation contrary to Rule 1.8(i). However, a fee paid in property instead of money may be subject to the requirements of Rule 1.8(a) because such fees often have the essential qualities of a business transaction with the client.

[5] Once a fee agreement has been reached between attorney and client, the attorney has an ethical obligation to fulfill the contract and represent the client's best interests regardless of whether the lawyer has struck an unfavorable bargain. An attorney may seek to renegotiate the fee agreement in light of changed circumstances or for other good cause, but the attorney may not abandon or threaten to abandon the client to cut the attorney's losses or to coerce an additional or higher fee. Any fee contract made or remade during the existence of the attorney-client relationship must be reasonable and freely and fairly made by the client having full knowledge of all material circumstances incident to the agreement. If a dispute later arises concerning the fee, the burden of proving reasonableness and fairness will be upon the lawyer.

[6] An agreement may not be made whose terms might induce the lawyer improperly to curtail services for the client or perform them in a way contrary to the client's interest. For example, a lawyer should not enter into an agreement whereby services are to be provided only up to a stated amount when it is foreseeable that more extensive services probably will be required, unless the situation is adequately explained to the client. Otherwise, the client might have to bargain for further assistance in the midst of a proceeding or transaction. However, it is proper to define the extent of services in light of the client's ability to pay. A lawyer should not exploit a fee arrangement based primarily on hourly charges by using wasteful procedures.

Prohibited Contingent Fees

[7] Paragraph (d) prohibits a lawyer from charging a contingent fee in a domestic relations matter when payment is contingent upon the securing of a divorce or upon the amount of alimony or support to be obtained. This provision does not preclude a contract for a contingent fee for legal representation in connection with the recovery of post-judgment balances due under support alimony or other financial orders because such contracts do not implicate the same policy concerns.

Division of Fee

[8] A division of fee is a single billing to a client covering the fee of two or more lawyers who are not in the same firm. A division of fee facilitates association of more than one lawyer in a matter in which neither alone could serve the client as well, and most often is used when the fee is contingent and the division is between a referring lawyer and a trial specialist. Paragraph (e) permits the lawyers to divide a fee either on the basis of the proportion of services they render or if each lawyer assumes responsibility for the representation as a whole, in addition, the client must agree to the arrangement, including the share that each lawyer is to receive, and the agreement must be confirmed in writing. A lawyer may divide a fee with an out-of-state lawyer who refers a matter to the lawyer if the conditions of paragraph (e) are satisfied. Contingent fee agreements must be in a writing signed by the client and must otherwise comply with paragraph (c) of this Rule. Joint responsibility for the representation entails financial and ethical responsibility for the representation as if the lawyers were associated in a partnership. A lawyer should only refer a matter to a lawyer whom the referring lawyer reasonably believes is competent to handle the matter. See Rule 1.1.

[9] Paragraph (e) does not prohibit or regulate division of fees to be received in the future for work done when lawyers were previously associated in a law firm.

Disputes over Fees

[10] Participation in the fee dispute resolution program of the North Carolina State Bar is mandatory when a client requests resolution of a disputed fee. Before filing an action to collect a disputed fee, the client must be advised of the fee dispute resolution program. Notification must occur not only when there is a specific issue in dispute, but also when the client simply fails to pay. However, when the client expressly acknowledges liability for the specific amount of the bill and states that he or she cannot presently pay the bill, the fee is not disputed and notification of the client is not required. In making reasonable efforts to advise the client of the existence of the fee dispute resolution program, it is preferable to address a written communication to the client at the client's last known address. If the address of the client is unknown, the lawyer should use reasonable efforts to acquire the current address of the client. Notification is not required in those instances where the State Bar does not have jurisdiction over the fee dispute as set forth in 27 N.C.A.C. 1D, .0702.

[11] If fee dispute resolution is requested by a client, the lawyer must participate in the resolution process in good faith. The State Bar program of fee dispute resolution uses mediation to resolve fee disputes as an alternative to litigation. The lawyer must cooperate with the person who is charged with investigating the dispute and with the person(s) appointed to mediate the dispute. Further information on the fee dispute resolution program can be found at 27 N.C.A.C. 1D, .0700, et. seq. The lawyer should fully set forth his or her position and support that position by appropriate documentation.

[12] A lawyer may petition a tribunal for a legal fee if allowed by applicable law or, subject to the requirements for fee dispute resolution set forth in Rule 1.5(f), may bring an action against a client to collect a fee. The tribunal's determination of the merit of the petition or the claim is reached

by an application of law to fact and not by the application of this Rule. Therefore, a tribunal's reduction or denial of a petition or claim for a fee is not evidence that the fee request violates this Rule and is not admissible in a disciplinary proceeding brought under this Rule.

Rule 1.6 Confidentiality

(a) A lawyer shall not reveal information acquired during the professional relationship with a client unless the client gives informed consent, the disclosure is impliedly authorized in order to carry out the representation or the disclosure is permitted by paragraph (b).

(b) A lawyer may reveal information protected from disclosure by paragraph (a) to the extent the lawyer reasonably believes necessary:

(1) to comply with the Rules of Professional Conduct, the law or court order;

(2) to prevent the commission of a crime by the client;

(3) to prevent reasonably certain death or bodily harm;

(4) to prevent, mitigate, or rectify the consequences of a client's criminal or fraudulent act in the commission of which the lawyer's services were used;

(5) to secure legal advice about the lawyer's compliance with these Rules;

(6) to establish a claim or defense on behalf of the lawyer in a controversy between the lawyer and the client; to establish a defense to a criminal charge or civil claim against the lawyer based upon conduct in which the client was involved; or to respond to allegations in any proceeding concerning the lawyer's representation of the client;

(7) to comply with the rules of a lawyers' or judges' assistance program approved by the North Carolina State Bar or the North Carolina Supreme Court; or

(8) to detect and resolve conflicts of interest arising from the lawyer's change of employment or from changes in the composition or ownership of a firm, but only if the revealed information would not compromise the attorney-client privilege or otherwise prejudice the client.

(c) A lawyer shall make reasonable efforts to prevent the inadvertent or unauthorized disclosure of, or unauthorized access to, information relating to the representation of a client.

(d) The duty of confidentiality described in this Rule encompasses information received by a lawyer then acting as an agent of a lawyers' or judges' assistance program approved by the North Carolina State Bar or the North Carolina Supreme Court regarding another lawyer or judge seeking assistance or to whom assistance is being offered. For the purposes of this Rule, "client" refers to lawyers seeking assistance from lawyers' or judges' assistance programs approved by the North Carolina State Bar or the North Carolina Supreme Court.

[Adopted July 24, 1997. Amended February 27, 2003; October 2, 2014.]

Comment

[1] This Rule governs the disclosure by a lawyer of information relating to the representation of a client acquired during the lawyer's representation of the client. See Rule 1.18 for the lawyer's duties with respect to information provided to the lawyer by a prospective client, Rule 1.9(c)(2) for the lawyer's duty not to reveal information acquired during a lawyer's prior representation of a former client and Rules 1.8(b) and 1.9(c)(1) for the lawyer's duties with respect to the use of such information to the disadvantage of clients and former clients.

[2] A fundamental principle in the client-lawyer relationship is that, in the absence of the client's informed consent, the lawyer must not reveal information acquired during the representation. See Rule 1.0(e) for the definition of informed consent. This contributes to the trust that is the hallmark of the client-lawyer relationship. The client is thereby encouraged to seek legal assistance and to communicate fully and frankly with the lawyer even as to embarrassing or legally damaging subject matter. The lawyer needs this information to represent the client effectively and, if necessary, to advise the client to refrain from wrongful conduct. Almost without exception, clients come to lawyers in order to determine their rights and what is, in the complex of laws and regulations, deemed to be legal and correct. Based upon experience, lawyers know that almost all clients follow the advice given, and the law is upheld.

[3] The principle of client-lawyer confidentiality is given effect by related bodies of law: the attorney-client privilege, the work product doctrine and the rule of confidentiality established in professional ethics. The attorney-client privilege and work-product doctrine apply in judicial and other proceedings in which a lawyer may be called as a witness or otherwise required to produce evidence concerning a client. The rule of client-lawyer confidentiality applies in situations other than those where evidence is sought from the lawyer through compulsion of law. The confidentiality rule, for example, applies not only to matters communicated in confidence by the client but also to all information acquired during the representation, whatever its source. A lawyer may not disclose such information except as authorized or required by the Rules of Professional Conduct or other law. See also Scope.

[4] Paragraph (a) prohibits a lawyer from revealing information acquired during the representation of a client. This prohibition also applies to disclosures by a lawyer that do not in themselves reveal protected information but could reasonably lead to the discovery of such information by a third person. A lawyer's use of a hypothetical to discuss issues relating to the representation is permissible so long as there is no reasonable likelihood that the listener will be able to ascertain the identity of the client or the situation involved.

Authorized Disclosure

[5] Except to the extent that the client's instructions or special circumstances limit that authority, a lawyer is impliedly authorized to make disclosures about a client when appropriate in carrying out the representation. In some situations, for example, a lawyer may be impliedly authorized to admit a fact that cannot property be disputed or to make a

disclosure that facilitates a satisfactory conclusion to a matter. Lawyers in a firm may, in the course of the firm's practice, disclose to each other information relating to a client of the firm, unless the client has instructed that particular information be confined to specified lawyers.

Disclosure Adverse to Client

[6] Although the public interest is usually best served by a strict rule requiring lawyers to preserve the confidentiality of information acquired during the representation of their clients, the confidentiality rule is subject to limited exceptions. In becoming privy to information about a client, a lawyer may foresee that the client intends to commit a crime. Paragraph (b)(2) recognizes that a lawyer should be allowed to make a disclosure to avoid sacrificing the interests of the potential victim in favor of preserving the client's confidences when the client's purpose is wrongful. Similarly, paragraph (b)(3) recognizes the overriding value of life and physical integrity and permits disclosure reasonably necessary to prevent reasonably certain death or substantial bodily harm. Such harm is reasonably certain to occur if it will be suffered imminently or if there is a present and substantial threat that a person will suffer such harm at a later date if the lawyer fails to take action necessary to eliminate the threat. Thus, a lawyer who knows that a client has accidentally discharged toxic waste into a town's water supply may reveal this information to the authorities if there is a present and substantial risk that a person who drinks the water will contract a life-threatening or debilitating disease and the lawyer's disclosure is necessary to eliminate the threat or reduce the number of victims.

[7] A lawyer may have been innocently involved in past conduct by a client that was criminal or fraudulent. Even if the involvement was innocent, however, the fact remains that the lawyer's professional services were made the instrument of the client's crime or fraud. The lawyer, therefore, has a legitimate interest in being able to rectify the consequences of such conduct, and has the professional right, although not a professional duty, to rectify the situation. Exercising that right may require revealing information acquired during the representation. Paragraph (b)(4) gives the lawyer professional discretion to reveal such information to the extent necessary to accomplish rectification.

[8] Although paragraph (b)(2) does not require the lawyer to reveal the client's anticipated misconduct, the lawyer may not counsel or assist the client in conduct the lawyer knows is criminal or fraudulent. See Rule 1.2(d). See also Rule 1.16 with respect to the lawyer's obligation or right to withdraw from the representation of the client in such circumstances. Where the client is an organization, the lawyer may be in doubt whether contemplated conduct will actually be carried out by the organization. Where necessary to guide conduct in connection with this Rule, the lawyer may make inquiry within the organization as indicated in Rule 1.13(b).

[9] Paragraph (b)(4) addresses the situation in which the lawyer does not learn of the client's crime or fraud until after it has been consummated. Although the client no longer has the option of preventing disclosure by refraining from the wrongful conduct, there will be situations in which the loss suffered by the affected person can be prevented, rectified or mitigated. In such situations, the lawyer may disclose information acquired during the representation to the extent necessary to enable the affected persons to prevent or mitigate reasonably certain losses or to attempt to recoup their losses. Paragraph (b)(4) does not apply when a person who has committed a crime or fraud thereafter employs a lawyer for representation concerning that offense.

[10] A lawyer's confidentiality obligations do not preclude a lawyer from securing confidential legal advice about the lawyer's personal responsibility to comply with these Rules. In most situations, disclosing information to secure such advice will be impliedly authorized for the lawyer to carry out the representation. Even when the disclosure is not impliedly authorized, paragraph (b)(5) permits such disclosure because of the importance of a lawyer's compliance with the Rules of Professional Conduct.

[11] Where a legal claim or disciplinary charge alleges complicity of the lawyer in a client's conduct or other misconduct of the lawyer involving representation of the client, the lawyer may respond to the extent the lawyer reasonably believes necessary to establish a defense. The same is true with respect to a claim involving the conduct or representation of a former client. Such a charge can arise in a civil, criminal, disciplinary or other proceeding and can be based on a wrong allegedly committed by the lawyer against the client or on a wrong alleged by a third person, for example, a person claiming to have been defrauded by the lawyer and client acting together. The lawyer's right to respond arises when an assertion of such complicity has been made. Paragraph (b)(6) does not require the lawyer to await the commencement of an action or proceeding that charges such complicity, so that the defense may be established by responding directly to a third party who has made such an assertion. The right to defend also applies, of course, where a proceeding has been commenced.

[12] A lawyer entitled to a fee is permitted by paragraph (b)(6) to prove the services rendered in an action to collect it. This aspect of the rule expresses the principle that the beneficiary of a fiduciary relationship may not exploit it to the detriment of the fiduciary.

[13] Other law may require that a lawyer disclose information about a client. Whether such a law supersedes Rule 1.6 is a question of law beyond the scope of these Rules. When disclosure of information acquired during the representation appears to be required by other law, the lawyer must discuss the matter with the client to the extent required by Rule 1.4. If, however, the other law supersedes this Rule and requires disclosure, paragraph (b)(1) permits the lawyer to make such disclosures as are necessary to comply with the law.

[14] Paragraph (b)(1) also permits compliance with a court order requiring a lawyer to disclose information relating to a client's representation. If a lawyer is called as a witness to give testimony concerning a client or is otherwise ordered to reveal information relating to the client's representation, however, the lawyer must, absent informed consent of the client to do otherwise, assert on behalf of the client all nonfrivolous claims that the information sought is protected against disclosure by the attorney-client privilege or other applicable law. In the event of an adverse ruling, the lawyer must consult with the client about the possibility of appeal. See Rule 1.4. Unless review is sought, however, paragraph (b)(1) permits the lawyer to comply with the court's order.

[15] Paragraph (b) permits disclosure only to the extent the lawyer reasonably believes the disclosure is necessary to accomplish one of the purposes specified. Where practicable, the lawyer should first seek to persuade the client to take suitable action to obviate the need for disclosure. In any case, a disclosure adverse to the client's interest should be no greater than the lawyer reasonably believes necessary to accomplish the purpose. If the disclosure will be made in

connection with a judicial proceeding, the disclosure should be made in a manner that limits access to the information to the tribunal or other persons having a need to know it and appropriate protective orders or other arrangements should be sought by the lawyer to the fullest extent practicable.

[16] Paragraph (b) permits but does not require the disclosure of information acquired during a client's representation to accomplish the purposes specified in paragraphs (b)(1) through (b)(7). In exercising the discretion conferred by this Rule, the lawyer may consider such factors as the nature of the lawyer's relationship with the client and with those who might be injured by the client, the lawyer's own involvement in the transaction and factors that may extenuate the conduct in question. When practical, the lawyer should first seek to persuade the client to take suitable action, making it unnecessary for the lawyer to make any disclosure. A lawyer's decision not to disclose as permitted by paragraph (b) does not violate this Rule. Disclosure may be required, however, by other Rules. Some Rules require disclosure only if such disclosure would be permitted by paragraph (b). See Rules 1.2(d), 4.1(b), 8.1 and 8.3. Rule 3.3, on the other hand, requires disclosure in some circumstances regardless of whether such disclosure is permitted by this Rule. See Rule 3.3(c).

Detection of Conflicts of Interest

[17] Paragraph (b)(8) recognizes that lawyers in different firms may need to disclose limited information to each other to detect and resolve conflicts of interest, such as when a lawyer is considering an association with another firm, two or more firms are considering a merger, or a lawyer is considering the purchase of a law practice. *See* Rule 1.17, Comment [8]. Under these circumstances, lawyers and law firms are permitted to disclose limited information, but only once substantive discussions regarding the new relationship have occurred. Any such disclosure should ordinarily include no more than the identity of the persons and entities involved in a matter, a brief summary of the general issues involved, and information about whether the matter has terminated. Even this limited information, however, should be disclosed only to the extent reasonably necessary to detect and resolve conflicts of interest that might arise from the possible new relationship. Moreover, the disclosure of any information is prohibited if it would compromise the attorney-client privilege or otherwise prejudice the client (e.g., the fact that a corporate client is seeking advice on a corporate takeover that has not been publicly announced; that a person has consulted a lawyer about the possibility of divorce before the person's intentions are known to the person's spouse; or that a person has consulted a lawyer about a criminal investigation that has not led to a public charge). Under those circumstances, paragraph (a) prohibits disclosure unless the client or former client gives informed consent. A lawyer's fiduciary duty to the lawyer's firm may also govern a lawyer's conduct when exploring an association with another firm and is beyond the scope of these Rules.

[18] Any information disclosed pursuant to paragraph (b)(8) may be used or further disclosed only to the extent necessary to detect and resolve conflicts of interest. Paragraph (b)(8) does not restrict the use of information acquired by means independent of any disclosure pursuant to paragraph (b)(8). Paragraph (b)(8) also does not affect the disclosure of information within a law firm when the disclosure is otherwise authorized, such as when a lawyer in a firm discloses information to another lawyer in the same firm to detect and resolve conflicts of interest that could arise in connection with undertaking a new representation. *See* Comment [5].

Acting Competently to Preserve Confidentiality

[19] Paragraph (c) requires a lawyer to act competently to safeguard information acquired during the representation of a client against unauthorized access by third parties and against inadvertent or unauthorized disclosure by the lawyer or other persons who are participating in the representation of the client or who are subject to the lawyer's supervision. *See* Rules 1.1, 5.1, and 5.3. The unauthorized access to, or the inadvertent or unauthorized disclosure of, information acquired during the professional relationship with a client does not constitute a violation of paragraph (c) if the lawyer has made reasonable efforts to prevent the access or disclosure. Factors to be considered in determining the reasonableness of the lawyer's efforts include, but are not limited to, the sensitivity of the information, the likelihood of disclosure if additional safeguards are not employed, the cost of employing additional safeguards, the difficulty of implementing the safeguards, and the extent to which the safeguards adversely affect the lawyer's ability to represent clients (e.g., by making a device or important piece of software excessively difficult to use). A client may require the lawyer to implement special security measures not required by this Rule, or may give informed consent to forgo security measures that would otherwise be required by this Rule. Whether a lawyer may be required to take additional steps to safeguard a client's information to comply with other law—such as state and federal laws that govern data privacy, or that impose notification requirements upon the loss of, or unauthorized access to, electronic information—is beyond the scope of these Rules. For a lawyer's duties when sharing information with nonlawyers outside the lawyer's own firm, see Rule 5.3, Comments [3]–[4].

[20] When transmitting a communication that includes information acquired during the representation of a client, the lawyer must take reasonable precautions to prevent the information from coming into the hands of unintended recipients. This duty, however, does not require that the lawyer use special security measures if the method of communication affords a reasonable expectation of privacy. Special circumstances, however, may warrant special precautions. Factors to be considered in determining the reasonableness of the client's expectation of confidentiality include the sensitivity of the information and the extent to which the privacy of the communication is protected by law or by a confidentiality agreement. A client may require the lawyer to implement special security measures not required by this Rule or may give informed consent to the use of a means of communication that would otherwise be prohibited by this Rule. Whether a lawyer may be required to take additional steps to comply with other law, such as state and federal laws that govern data privacy, is beyond the scope of these Rules.

Former Client

[21] The duty of confidentiality continues after the client-lawyer relationship has terminated. See Rule 1.9(c)(2). See Rule 1.9(c)(1) for the prohibition against using such information to the disadvantage of the former client.

Lawyer's Assistance Program

[22] Information about a lawyer's or judge's misconduct or fitness may be received by a lawyer in the course of that lawyer's participation in an approved lawyers' or judges' assistance program. In that circumstance, providing for the confidentiality of such information encourages lawyers and

judges to seek help through such programs. Conversely, without such confidentiality, lawyers and judges may hesitate to seek assistance, which may then result in harm to their professional careers and injury to their clients and the public. The rule, therefore, requires that any information received by a lawyer on behalf of an approved lawyers' or judges' assistance program be regarded as confidential and protected from disclosure to the same extent as information received by a lawyer in any conventional client-lawyer relationship.

Rule 1.7 Conflict of Interest: Current Clients

(a) Except as provided in paragraph (b), a lawyer shall not represent a client if the representation involves a concurrent conflict of interest. A concurrent conflict of interest exists if:

(1) the representation of one client will be directly adverse to another client; or

(2) the representation of one or more clients may be materially limited by the lawyer's responsibilities to another client, a former client, or a third person, or by a personal interest of the lawyer.

(b) Notwithstanding the existence of a concurrent conflict of interest under paragraph (a), a lawyer may represent a client if:

(1) the lawyer reasonably believes that the lawyer will be able to provide competent and diligent representation to each affected client;

(2) the representation is not prohibited by law;

(3) the representation does not involve the assertion of a claim by one client against another client represented by the lawyer in the same litigation or other proceeding before a tribunal; and

(4) each affected client gives informed consent, confirmed in writing.

[Adopted July 24, 1997. Amended February 27, 2003.]

Comment

General Principles

[1] Loyalty and independent judgment are essential elements in the lawyer's relationship to a client. Concurrent conflicts of interest can arise from the lawyer's responsibilities to another client, a former client or a third person or from the lawyer's own interests. For specific Rules regarding certain concurrent conflicts of interest, see Rule 1.8. For former client conflicts of interest, see Rule 1.9. For conflicts of interest involving prospective clients, see Rule 1.18. For definitions of "informed consent" and "confirmed in writing," see Rule 1.0(f) and (c).

[2] Resolution of a conflict of interest problem under this Rule requires the lawyer to: 1) clearly identify the client or clients; 2) determine whether a conflict of interest exists; 3) decide whether the representation may be undertaken despite the existence of a conflict, i.e., whether the conflict is consentable; and 4) if so, consult with the clients affected under paragraph (a) and obtain their informed consent, confirmed in writing. The clients affected under paragraph (a) include both of the clients referred to in paragraph (a)(1) and the one or more clients whose representation might be materially limited under paragraph (a)(2).

[3] A conflict of interest may exist before representation is undertaken, in which event the representation must be declined, unless the lawyer obtains the informed consent of each client under the conditions of paragraph (b). To determine whether a conflict of interest exists, a lawyer should adopt reasonable procedures, appropriate for the size and type of firm and practice, to determine in both litigation and non-litigation matters the persons and issues involved. See also Comment to Rule 5.1, Ignorance caused by a failure to institute such procedures will not excuse a lawyer's violation of this Rule. As to whether a client-lawyer relationship exists or, having once been established, is continuing, see Comment to Rule 1.3 and Scope.

[4] If a conflict arises after representation has been undertaken, the lawyer ordinarily must withdraw from the representation, unless the lawyer has obtained the informed consent of the client under the conditions of paragraph (b). See Rule 1.16. Where more than one client is involved, whether the lawyer may continue to represent any of the clients is determined both by the lawyer's ability to comply with duties owed to the former client and by the lawyer's ability to represent adequately the remaining client or clients, given the lawyer's duties to the former client. See Rule 1.9. See also Comments [5] and [29].

[5] Unforeseeable developments, such as changes in corporate and other organizational affiliations or the addition or realignment of parties in litigation, might create conflicts in the midst of a representation, as when a company sued by the lawyer on behalf of one client is bought by another client represented by the lawyer in an unrelated matter. Depending on the circumstances, the lawyer may have the option to withdraw from one of the representations in order to avoid the conflict. The lawyer must seek court approval where necessary and take steps to minimize harm to the clients. See Rule 1.16. The lawyer must continue to protect the confidences of the client from whose representation the lawyer has withdrawn. See Rule 1.9(c).

Identifying Conflicts of Interest: Directly Adverse

[6] Loyalty to a current client prohibits undertaking representation directly adverse to that client without that client's informed consent. Thus, absent consent, a lawyer may not act as an advocate in one matter against a person the lawyer represents in some other matter, even when the matters are wholly unrelated. The client as to whom the representation is directly adverse is likely to feel betrayed, and the resulting damage to the client-lawyer relationship is likely to impair the lawyer's ability to represent the client effectively. In addition, the client on whose behalf the adverse representation is undertaken reasonably may fear that the lawyer will pursue that client's case less effectively out of deference to the other client, i.e., that the representation may be materially limited by the lawyer's interest in retaining the current client. Similarly, a directly adverse conflict may arise when a lawyer is required to cross-examine a client who appears as a witness in a lawsuit involving another client, as when the testimony will be damaging to the client who is represented in the lawsuit. On the other hand, simultaneous representation in unrelated matters of clients whose interests are only economically adverse, such as representation of competing economic enterprises in unrelated litigation, does not ordinarily constitute a conflict of

interest and thus may not require consent of the respective clients.

[7] Directly adverse conflicts can also arise in transactional matters. For example, if a lawyer is asked to represent the seller of a business in negotiations with a buyer represented by the lawyer, not in the same transaction but in another, unrelated matter, the lawyer could not undertake the representation without the informed consent of each client.

Identifying Conflicts of Interest: Material Limitation

[8] Even where there is no direct adverseness, a conflict of interest exists if a lawyer's ability to consider, recommend or carry out an appropriate course of action for the client may be materially limited as a result of the lawyer's other responsibilities or interests. For example, a lawyer asked to represent a seller of commercial real estate, a real estate developer and a commercial lender is likely to be materially limited in the lawyer's ability to recommend or advocate all possible positions that each might take because of the lawyer's duty of loyalty to the others. The conflict in effect forecloses alternatives that would otherwise be available to the client. The mere possibility of subsequent harm does not itself preclude the representation or require disclosure and consent. The critical questions are the likelihood that a difference in interests will eventuate and, if it does, whether it will materially interfere with the lawyer's independent professional judgment in considering alternatives or foreclose courses of action that reasonably should be pursued on behalf of the client.

Lawyer's Responsibilities to Former Clients and Other Third Persons

[9] In addition to conflicts with other current clients, a lawyer's duties of loyalty and independence may be materially limited by responsibilities to former clients under Rule 1.9 or by the lawyer's responsibilities to other persons, such as fiduciary duties arising from a lawyer's service as a trustee, executor or corporate director.

Personal Interest Conflicts

[10] The lawyer's own interest should not be permitted to have an adverse effect on representation of a client. For example, if the probity of a lawyer's own conduct in a transaction is in serious question, it may be difficult or impossible for the lawyer to give a client detached advice. Similarly, when a lawyer has discussions concerning possible employment with an opponent of the lawyer's client, or with a law firm representing the opponent, such discussions could materially limit the lawyer's representation of the client. In addition, a lawyer may not allow related business interests to affect representation, for example, by referring clients to an enterprise in which the lawyer has an undisclosed financial interest. See Rule 1.8 for specific Rules pertaining to a number of personal interest conflicts, including business transactions with clients. See also Rule 1.10 (personal interest conflicts under Rule 1.7 ordinarily are not imputed to other lawyers in a law firm).

[11] When lawyers representing different clients in the same matter or in substantially related matters are closely related by blood or marriage, there may be a significant risk that client confidences will be revealed and that the lawyer's family relationship will interfere with both loyalty and independent professional judgment. As a result, each client is entitled to know of the existence and implications of the relationship between the lawyers before the lawyer agrees to undertake the representation. Thus, a lawyer related to another lawyer, e.g., as parent, child, sibling or spouse, ordinarily may not represent a client in a matter where that lawyer is representing another party, unless each client gives informed consent. The disqualification arising from a close family relationship is personal and ordinarily is not imputed to members of firms with whom the lawyers are associated. See Rule 1.10.

[12] A lawyer is prohibited from engaging in sexual relationships with a client unless the sexual relationship predates the formation of the client-lawyer relationship. See Rule 1.19.

Interest of Person Paying for a Lawyer's Service

[13] A lawyer may be paid from a source other than the client, including a co-client, if the client is informed of that fact and consents and the arrangement does not compromise the lawyer's duty of loyalty or independent judgment to the client. See Rule 1.8(f). If acceptance of the payment from any other source presents a significant risk that the lawyer's representation of the client will be materially limited by the lawyer's own interest in accommodating the person paying the lawyer's fee or by the lawyer's responsibilities to a payer who is also a co-client, then the lawyer must comply with the requirements of paragraph (b) before accepting the representation, including determining whether the conflict is consentable and, if so, that the client has adequate information about the material risks of the representation.

Prohibited Representations

[14] Ordinarily, clients may consent to representation notwithstanding a conflict. However, as indicated in paragraph (b), some conflicts are nonconsentable, meaning that the lawyer involved cannot properly ask for such agreement or provide representation on the basis of the client's consent. When the lawyer is representing more than one client, the question of consentability must be resolved as to each client.

[15] Consentability is typically determined by considering whether the interests of the clients will be adequately protected if the clients are permitted to give their informed consent to representation burdened by a conflict of interest. Thus, under paragraph (b)(1), representation is prohibited if in the circumstances the lawyer cannot reasonably conclude that the lawyer will be able to provide competent and diligent representation. See Rule 1.1 (competence) and Rule 1.3 (diligence).

[16] Paragraph (b)(2) describes conflicts that are nonconsentable because the representation is prohibited by applicable law. For example, in some states substantive law provides that the same lawyer may not represent more than one defendant in a capital case, even with the consent of the clients, and under federal criminal statutes certain representations by a former government lawyer are prohibited, despite the informed consent of the former client. In addition, decisional law in some states limits the ability of a governmental client, such as a municipality, to consent to a conflict of interest.

[17] Paragraph (b)(3) describes conflicts that are nonconsentable because of the institutional interest in vigorous development of each client's position when the clients are aligned directly against each other in the same litigation or other proceeding before a tribunal. Whether clients are aligned directly against each other within the meaning of this paragraph requires examination of the context of the proceeding. Although this paragraph does not preclude a lawyer's multiple representation of adverse parties to a me-

diation (because mediation is not a proceeding before a "tribunal" under Rule 1.0(m)), such representation may be precluded by paragraph (b)(1).

Informed Consent

[18] Informed consent requires that each affected client be aware of the relevant circumstances and of the material and reasonably foreseeable ways that the conflict could have adverse effects on the interests of that client. See Rule 1.0(e) (informed consent). The information required depends on the nature of the conflict and the nature of the risks involved. When representation of multiple clients in a single matter is undertaken, the information must include the implications of the common representation, including possible effects on loyalty, confidentiality and the attorney-client privilege and the advantages and risks involved. See Comments [30] and [31] (effect of common representation on confidentiality).

[19] Under some circumstances it may be impossible to make the disclosure necessary to obtain consent. For example, when the lawyer represents different clients in related matters and one of the clients refuses to consent to the disclosure necessary to permit the other client to make an informed decision, the lawyer cannot properly ask the latter to consent. In some cases the alternative to common representation can be that each party may have to obtain separate representation with the possibility of incurring additional costs. These costs, along with the benefits of securing separate representation, are factors that may be considered by the affected client in determining whether common representation is in the client's interests.

Consent Confirmed in Writing

[20] Paragraph (b) requires the lawyer to obtain the informed consent of the client, confirmed in writing. Such a writing may consist of a document executed by the client or one that the lawyer promptly records and transmits to the client following an oral consent. See Rule 1.0(b). See also Rule 1.0(n) (writing includes electronic transmission). If it is not feasible to obtain or transmit the writing at the time the client gives informed consent, then the lawyer must obtain or transmit it within a reasonable time thereafter. See Rule 1.0(b). The requirement of a writing does not supplant the need in most cases for the lawyer to talk with the client, to explain the risks and advantages, if any, of representation burdened with a conflict of interest, as well as reasonably available alternatives, and to afford the client a reasonable opportunity to consider the risks and alternatives and to raise questions and concerns. Rather, the writing is required in order to impress upon clients the seriousness of the decision the client is being asked to make and to avoid disputes or ambiguities that might later occur in the absence of a writing.

Revoking Consent

[21] A client who has given consent to a conflict may revoke the consent and, like any other client, may terminate the lawyer's representation at any time. Whether revoking consent to the client's own representation precludes the lawyer from continuing to represent other clients depends on the circumstances, including the nature of the conflict, whether the client revoked consent because of a material change in circumstances, the reasonable expectations of the other client and whether material detriment to the other clients or the lawyer would result.

Consent to Future Conflict

[22] Whether a lawyer may properly request a client to waive conflicts that might arise in the future is subject to the test of paragraph (b). The effectiveness of such waivers is generally determined by the extent to which the client reasonably understands the material risks that the waiver entails. The more comprehensive the explanation of the types of future representations that might arise and the actual and reasonably foreseeable adverse consequences of those representations, the greater the likelihood that the client will have the requisite understanding. Thus, if the client agrees to consent to a particular type of conflict with which the client is already familiar, then the consent ordinarily will be effective with regard to that type of conflict. If the consent is general and open-ended, then the consent ordinarily will be ineffective, because it is not reasonably likely that the client will have understood the material risks involved. On the other hand, if the client is an experienced user of the legal services involved and is reasonably informed regarding the risk that a conflict may arise, such consent is more likely to be effective, particularly if, e.g., the client is independently represented by other counsel in giving consent and the consent is limited to future conflicts unrelated to the subject of the representation. In any case, advance consent cannot be effective if the circumstances that materialize in the future are such as would make the conflict nonconsentable under paragraph (b).

Conflicts in Litigation

[23] Paragraph (b)(3) prohibits representation of opposing parties in the same litigation, regardless of the clients' consent. On the other hand, simultaneous representation of parties whose interests in litigation may conflict, such as coplaintiffs or codefendants, is governed by paragraph (a)(2). A conflict may exist by reason of substantial discrepancy in the parties' testimony, incompatibility in positions in relation to an opposing party or the fact that there are substantially different possibilities of settlement of the claims or liabilities in question. Such conflicts can arise in criminal cases as well as civil. The potential for conflict of interest in representing multiple defendants in a criminal case is so grave that ordinarily a lawyer should decline to represent more than one codefendant. On the other hand, common representation of persons having similar interests in civil litigation is proper if the requirements of paragraph (b) are met.

[24] Ordinarily a lawyer may take inconsistent legal positions in different tribunals at different times on behalf of different clients. The mere fact that advocating a legal position on behalf of one client might create precedent adverse to the interests of a client represented by the lawyer in an unrelated matter does not create a conflict of interest. A conflict of interest exists, however, if there is a significant risk that a lawyer's action on behalf of one client will materially limit the lawyer's effectiveness in representing another client in a different case; for example, when a decision favoring one client will create a precedent likely to seriously weaken the position taken on behalf of the other client. Factors relevant in determining whether the clients need to be advised of the risk include; where the cases are pending, whether the issue is substantive or procedural, the temporal relationship between the matters, the significance of the issue to the immediate and long-term interests of the clients involved and the clients' reasonable expectations in retaining the lawyer. If there is significant risk of material limitation, then absent informed consent of the affected clients, the lawyer must refuse one of the representations or withdraw from one or both matters.

[25] When a lawyer represents or seeks to represent a class of plaintiffs or defendants in a class-action lawsuit, unnamed members of the class are ordinarily not considered to be clients of the lawyer for purposes of applying paragraph (a)(1) of this Rule. Thus, the lawyer does not typically need to get the consent of such a person before representing a client suing the person in an unrelated matter. Similarly, a lawyer seeking to represent an opponent in a class action does not typically need the consent of an unnamed member of the class whom the lawyer represents in an unrelated matter.

Nonlitigation Conflicts

[26] Conflicts of interest under paragraphs (a)(1) and (a)(2) arise in contexts other than litigation. For a discussion of directly adverse conflicts in transactional matters, see Comment [7]. Relevant factors in determining whether there is significant potential for material limitation include the duration and intimacy of the lawyer's relationship with the client or clients involved, the functions being performed by the lawyer, the likelihood that disagreements will arise and the likely prejudice to the client from the conflict. The question is often one of proximity and degree. See Comment [8].

[27] For example, conflict questions may arise in estate planning and estate administration. A lawyer may be called upon to prepare wills for several family members, such as husband and wife, and, depending upon the circumstances, a conflict of interest may be present. In estate administration the identity of the client may be unclear under the law of a particular jurisdiction. Under one view, the client is the fiduciary; under another view the client is the estate or trust, including its beneficiaries. In order to comply with conflict of interest rules, the lawyer should make clear the lawyer's relationship to the parties involved.

[28] Whether a conflict is consentable depends on the circumstances. See Comment [15]. For example, a lawyer may not represent multiple parties to a negotiation whose interests are fundamentally antagonistic to each other, but common representation is permissible where the clients are generally aligned in interest even though there is some difference in interest among them. Thus, a lawyer may seek to establish or adjust a relationship between clients on an amicable and mutually advantageous basis; for example, in helping to organize a business in which two or more clients are entrepreneurs, working out the financial reorganization of an enterprise in which two or more clients have an interest or arranging a property distribution in settlement of an estate. The lawyer seeks to resolve potentially adverse interests by developing the parties' mutual interests. Otherwise, each party might have to obtain separate representation, with the possibility of incurring additional cost, complication or even litigation. Given these and other relevant factors, the clients may prefer that the lawyer act for all of them.

Special Considerations in Common Representation

[29] In considering whether to represent multiple clients in the same matter, a lawyer should be mindful that if the common representation fails because the potentially adverse interests cannot be reconciled, the result can be additional cost, embarrassment and recrimination. Ordinarily, the lawyer will be forced to withdraw from representing all of the clients if the common representation fails. In some situations, the risk of failure is so great that multiple representation is plainly impossible. For example, a lawyer cannot undertake common representation of clients where contentious litigation or negotiations between them are imminent or contemplated. Moreover, because the lawyer is required to be impartial between commonly represented clients, representation of multiple clients is improper when it is unlikely that impartiality can be maintained. Generally, if the relationship between the parties has already assumed antagonism, the possibility that the clients' interests can be adequately served by common representation is not very good. Other relevant factors are whether the lawyer subsequently will represent both parties on a continuing basis and whether the situation involves creating or terminating a relationship between the parties.

[30] A particularly important factor in determining the appropriateness of common representation is the effect on client-lawyer confidentiality and the attorney-client privilege. With regard to the attorney-client privilege, the prevailing rule is that, as between commonly represented clients, the privilege does not attach. Hence, it must be assumed that if litigation eventuates between the clients, the privilege will not protect any such communications, and the clients should be so advised.

[31] As to the duty of confidentiality, continued common representation will almost certainly be inadequate if one client asks the lawyer not to disclose to the other client information relevant to the common representation. This is so because the lawyer has an equal duty of loyalty to each client, and each client has the right to be informed of anything bearing on the representation that might affect that client's interests and the right to expect that the lawyer will use that information to that client's benefit. See Rule 1.4. The lawyer should, at the outset of the common representation and as part of the process of obtaining each client's informed consent, advise each client that information will be shared and that the lawyer will have to withdraw if one client decides that some matter material to the representation should be kept from the other. In limited circumstances, it may be appropriate for the lawyer to proceed with the representation when the clients have agreed, after being properly informed, that the lawyer will keep certain information confidential. For example, the lawyer may reasonably conclude that failure to disclose one client's trade secrets to another client will not adversely affect representation involving a joint venture between the clients and agree to keep that information confidential with the informed consent of both clients.

[32] When seeking to establish or adjust a relationship between clients, the lawyer should make clear that the lawyer's role is not that of partisanship normally expected in other circumstances and, thus, that the clients may be required to assume greater responsibility for decisions than when each client is separately represented. Any limitations on the scope of the representation made necessary as a result of the common representation should be fully explained to the clients at the outset of the representation. See Rule 1.2(c).

[33] Subject to the above limitations, each client in the common representation has the right to loyal and diligent representation and the protection of Rule 1.9 concerning the obligations to a former client. The client also has the right to discharge the lawyer as stated in Rule 1.16.

Organizational Clients

[34] A lawyer who represents a corporation or other organization does not, by virtue of that representation, necessarily represent any constituent or affiliated organization,

such as a parent or subsidiary. See Rule 1.13(a). Thus, the lawyer for an organization is not barred from accepting representation adverse to an affiliate in an unrelated matter, unless the circumstances are such that the affiliate should also be considered a client of the lawyer, there is an understanding between the lawyer and the organizational client that the lawyer will avoid representation adverse to the client's affiliates, or the lawyer's obligations to either the organizational client or the new client are likely to limit materially the lawyer's representation of the other client.

[35] A lawyer for a corporation or other organization who is also a member of its board of directors should determine whether the responsibilities of the two roles may conflict. The lawyer may be called on to advise the corporation in matters involving actions of the directors. Consideration should be given to the frequency with which such situations may arise, the potential intensity of the conflict, the effect of the lawyer's resignation from the board and the possibility of the corporation's obtaining legal advice from another lawyer in such situations. If there is material risk that the dual role will compromise the lawyer's independence of professional judgment, the lawyer should not serve as a director or should cease to act as the corporation's lawyer when conflicts of interest arise. The lawyer should advise the other members of the board that in some circumstances matters discussed at board meetings while the lawyer is present in the capacity of director might not be protected by the attorney-client privilege and that conflict of interest considerations might require the lawyer's recusal as a director or might require the lawyer and the lawyer's firm to decline representation of the corporation in a matter.

Rule 1.8 Conflict of Interest: Current Clients: Specific Rules

(a) A lawyer shall not enter into a business transaction with a client or knowingly acquire an ownership, possessory, security or other pecuniary interest directly adverse to a client unless:

(1) the transaction and terms on which the lawyer acquires the interest are fair and reasonable to the client and are fully disclosed and transmitted in writing in a manner that can be reasonably understood by the client;

(2) the client is advised in writing of the desirability of seeking and is given a reasonable opportunity to seek the advice of independent legal counsel on the transaction; and

(3) the client gives informed consent, in a writing signed by the client, to the essential terms of the transaction and the lawyer's role in the transaction, including whether the lawyer is representing the client in the transaction.

(b) A lawyer shall not use information relating to representation of a client to the disadvantage of the client unless the client gives informed consent, except as permitted or required by these Rules.

(c) A lawyer shall not solicit any substantial gift from a client, including a testamentary gift, or prepare on behalf of a client an instrument giving the lawyer or a person related to the lawyer any substantial gift unless the lawyer or other recipient of the gift is related to the client. For purposes of this paragraph, related persons include a spouse, child, grandchild, parent, grandparent or other relative or individual with whom the lawyer or the client maintains a close, familial relationship.

(d) Prior to the conclusion of representation of a client, a lawyer shall not make or negotiate an agreement giving the lawyer literary or media rights to a portrayal or account based in substantial part on information relating to the representation.

(e) A lawyer shall not provide financial assistance to a client in connection with pending or contemplated litigation, except that:

(1) a lawyer may advance court costs and expenses of litigation, the repayment of which may be contingent on the outcome of the matter, and

(2) a lawyer representing an indigent client may pay court costs and expenses of litigation on behalf of the client.

(f) A lawyer shall not accept compensation for representing a client from one other than the client unless:

(1) the client gives informed consent;

(2) there is no interference with the lawyer's independence of professional judgment or with the client-lawyer relationship; and

(3) information relating to representation of a client is protected as required by Rule 1.6.

(g) A lawyer who represents two or more clients shall not participate in making an aggregate settlement of the claims of or against the clients, or in a criminal case an aggregated agreement as to guilty or nolo contendere pleas, unless each client gives informed consent, in a writing signed by the client. The lawyer's disclosure shall include the existence and nature of all the claims or pleas involved and of the participation of each person in the settlement.

(h) A lawyer shall not;

(1) make an agreement prospectively limiting the lawyer's liability to a client for malpractice unless the client is independently represented in making the agreement; or

(2) settle a claim or potential claim for such liability with an unrepresented client or former client unless that person is advised in writing of the desirability of seeking and is given a reasonable opportunity to seek the advice of independent legal counsel in connection therewith.

(i) A lawyer shall not acquire a proprietary Interest in the cause of action or subject matter of litigation the lawyer is conducting for a client, except that the lawyer may:

(1) acquire a lien authorized by law to secure the lawyer's fee or expenses, provided the requirements of Rule 1.8(a) are satisfied; and

(2) contract with a client for a reasonable contingent fee in a civil case, except as prohibited by Rule 1.5.

(j) While lawyers are associated in a firm, a prohibition in the foregoing paragraphs (a) through (*l*), that applies to any one of them shall apply to all of them.

[Adopted June 24, 1997. Amended February 27, 2003.]

Comment

Note: See Rule 1.19 for the prohibition on client-lawyer sexual relationships.

Business Transactions Between Client and Lawyer

[1] A lawyer's legal skill and training, together with the relationship of trust and confidence between lawyer and client, create the possibility of overreaching when the lawyer participates in a business, property or financial transaction with a client, for example, a loan or sales transaction or a lawyer investment on behalf of a client. The requirements of paragraph (a) must be met even when the transaction is not closely related to the subject matter of the representation, as when a lawyer drafting a will for a client learns that the client needs money for unrelated expenses and offers to make a loan to the client. See Rule 5.7. It also applies to lawyers purchasing property from estates they represent. It does not apply to ordinary fee arrangements between client and lawyer, which are governed by Rule 1.5, although its requirements must be met when the lawyer accepts an interest in the client's business or other nonmonetary property as payment of all or part of a fee. In addition, the Rule does not apply to standard commercial transactions between the lawyer and the client for products or services that the client generally markets to others, for example, banking or brokerage services, medical services, products manufactured or distributed by the client, and utilities' services. In such transactions, the lawyer has no advantage in dealing with the client, and the restrictions in paragraph (a) are unnecessary and impracticable.

[2] Paragraph (a)(1) requires that the transaction itself be fair to the client and that its essential terms be communicated to the client, in writing, in a manner that can be reasonably understood. Paragraph (a)(2) requires that the client also be advised, in writing, of the desirability of seeking the advice of independent legal counsel. It also requires that the client be given a reasonable opportunity to obtain such advice. Paragraph (a)(3) requires that the lawyer obtain the client's informed consent, in a writing signed by the client, both to the essential terms of the transaction and to the lawyer's role. When necessary, the lawyer should discuss both the material risks of the proposed transaction, including any risk presented by the lawyer's involvement, and the existence of reasonably available alternatives and should explain why the advice of independent legal counsel is desirable. See Rule 1.0(e) (definition of informed consent).

[3] The risk to a client is greatest when the client expects the lawyer to represent the client in the transaction itself or when the lawyer's financial interest otherwise poses a significant risk that the lawyer's representation of the client will be materially limited by the lawyer's financial interest in the transaction. Here the lawyer's role requires that the lawyer must comply, not only with the requirements of paragraph (a), but also with the requirements of Rule 1.7. Under that Rule, the lawyer must disclose the risks associated with the lawyer's dual role as both legal adviser and participant in the transaction, such as the risk that the lawyer will structure the transaction or give legal advice in a way that favors the lawyer's interests at the expense of the client. Moreover, the lawyer must obtain the client's informed consent. In some cases, the lawyer's interest may be such that Rule 1.7 will preclude the lawyer from seeking the client's consent to the transaction.

[4] If the client is independently represented in the transaction, paragraph (a)(2) of this Rule is inapplicable, and the paragraph (a)(1) requirement for full disclosure is satisfied either by a written disclosure by the lawyer involved in the transaction or by the client's independent counsel. The fact that the client was independently represented in the transaction is relevant in determining whether the agreement was fair and reasonable to the client as paragraph (a)(1) further requires.

Use of Information Related to Representation

[5] Use of information relating to the representation to the disadvantage of the client violates the lawyer's duty of loyalty. Paragraph (b) applies when the information is used to benefit either the lawyer or a third person, such as another client or business associate of the lawyer. For example, if a lawyer learns that a client intends to purchase and develop several parcels of land, the lawyer may not use that information to purchase one of the parcels in competition with the client or to recommend that another client make such a purchase. The Rule does not prohibit uses that do not disadvantage the client. For example, a lawyer who learns a government agency's interpretation of trade legislation during the representation of one client may properly use that information to benefit other clients. Paragraph (b) prohibits disadvantageous use of client information unless the client gives informed consent, except as permitted or required by these Rules. See Rules 1.2(d), 1.6, 1.9(c), 3.3, 4.1, 8.1 and 8.3.

Gifts to Lawyers

[6] A lawyer may accept a gift from a client, if the transaction meets general standards of fairness. For example, a simple gift such as a present given at a holiday or as a token of appreciation is permitted. If a client offers the lawyer a more substantial gift, paragraph (c) does not prohibit the lawyer from accepting it, although such a gift may be voidable by the client under the doctrine of undue influence, which treats client gifts as presumptively fraudulent. In any event, due to concerns about overreaching and imposition on clients, a lawyer may not suggest that a substantial gift be made to the lawyer or for the lawyer's benefit, except where the lawyer is related to the client as set forth in paragraph (c).

[7] If effectuation of a substantial gift requires preparing a legal instrument such as a will or conveyance, the client should have the detached advice that another lawyer can provide. The sole exception to this Rule is where the client is a relative of the donee.

[8] This Rule does not prohibit a lawyer from seeking to have the lawyer or a partner or associate of the lawyer named as executor of the client's estate or to another potentially lucrative fiduciary position. Nevertheless, such appointments will be subject to the general conflict of interest provision in Rule 1.7 when there is a significant risk that the lawyer's interest in obtaining the appointment will materially limit the lawyer's independent professional judgment in advising the client concerning the choice of an executor or other fiduciary. In obtaining the client's informed consent to the conflict, the lawyer should advise the client concerning

the nature and extent of the lawyer's financial interest in the appointment as well as the availability of alternative candidates for the position.

Literary Rights

[9] An agreement by which a lawyer acquires literary or media rights concerning the conduct of the representation creates a conflict between the interests of the client and the personal interests of the lawyer. Measures suitable in the representation of the client may detract from the publication value of an account of the representation. Paragraph (d) does not prohibit a lawyer representing a client in a transaction concerning literary property from agreeing that the lawyer's fee shall consist of a share in ownership in the property, if the arrangement conforms to Rule 1.5 and paragraphs (a) and (*l*).

Financial Assistance

[10] Lawyers may not subsidize lawsuits or administrative proceedings brought on behalf of their clients, including making or guaranteeing loans to their clients for living expenses, because to do so would encourage clients to pursue lawsuits that might not otherwise be brought and because such assistance gives lawyers too great a financial stake in the litigation. These dangers do not warrant a prohibition on a lawyer lending a client court costs and litigation expenses, including the expenses of medical examination and the costs of obtaining and presenting evidence, because these advances are virtually indistinguishable from contingent fees and help ensure access to the courts. Similarly, an exception allowing lawyers representing indigent clients to pay court costs and litigation expenses regardless of whether these funds will be repaid is warranted.

Person Paying for a Lawyer's Services

[11] Lawyers are frequently asked to represent a client under circumstances in which a third person will compensate the lawyer, in whole or in part. The third person might be a relative or friend, an indemnitor (such as a liability insurance company) or a co-client (such as a corporation sued along with one or more of its employees). Because third-party payers frequently have interests that differ from those of the client, including interests in minimizing the amount spent on the representation and in learning how the representation is progressing, lawyers are prohibited from accepting or continuing such representations unless the lawyer determines that there will be no interference with the lawyer's independent professional judgment and there is informed consent from the client. See also Rule 5.4(c) (prohibiting interference with a lawyer's professional judgment by one who recommends, employs or pays the lawyer to render legal services for another).

[12] Sometimes, it will be sufficient for the lawyer to obtain the client's informed consent regarding the fact of the payment and the identify of the third-party payer. If, however, the fee arrangement creates a conflict of interest for the lawyer, then the lawyer must comply with Rule, 1.7. The lawyer must also conform to the requirements of Rule 1.6 concerning confidentiality. Under Rule 1.7(a), a conflict of interest exists if there is significant risk that the lawyer's representation of the client will be materially limited by the lawyer's own interest in the fee arrangement or by the lawyer's responsibilities to the third-party payer (for example, when the third-party payer is a co–client). Under Rule 1.7(b), the lawyer may accept or continue the representation with the informed consent of each affected client, unless the conflict is nonconsentable under that paragraph. Under Rule 1.7(b), the informed consent must be confirmed in writing.

Aggregate Settlements

[13] Differences in willingness to make or accept an offer of settlement are among the risks of common representation of multiple clients by a single lawyer. Under Rule 1.7, this is one of the risks that should be discussed before undertaking the representation, as part of the process of obtaining the clients' informed consent. In addition, Rule 1.2(a) protects each client's right to have the final say in deciding whether to accept or reject an offer of settlement and in deciding whether to enter a guilty or nolo contendere plea in a criminal case. The rule stated in this paragraph is a corollary of both these Rules and provides that, before any settlement offer or plea bargain is made or accepted on behalf of multiple clients, the lawyer must inform each of them about all the material terms of the settlement, including what the other clients will receive or pay if the settlement or plea offer is accepted. See also Rule 1.0(e) (definition of informed consent). Lawyers representing a class of plaintiffs or defendants, or those proceeding derivatively, may not have a full client-lawyer relationship with each member of the class; nevertheless, such lawyers must comply with applicable rules regulating notification of class members and other procedural requirements designed to ensure adequate protection of the entire class.

Limiting Liability and Settling Malpractice Claims

[14] Agreements prospectively limiting a lawyer's liability for malpractice are prohibited unless the client is independently represented in making the agreement because they are likely to undermine competent and diligent representation. Also, many clients are unable to evaluate the desirability of making such an agreement before a dispute has arisen, particularly if they are then represented by the lawyer seeking the agreement. This paragraph does not, however, prohibit a lawyer from entering into an agreement with the client to arbitrate legal malpractice claims, provided such agreements are enforceable and the client is fully informed of the scope and effect of the agreement. Nor does this paragraph limit the ability of lawyers to practice in the form of a limited-liability entity, where permitted by law, provided that each lawyer remains personally liable to the client for his or her own conduct and the firm complies with any conditions required by law, such as provisions requiring client notification or maintenance of adequate liability insurance. Nor does it prohibit an agreement in accordance with Rule 1.2 that defines the scope of the representation, although a definition of scope that makes the obligations of representation illusory will amount to an attempt to limit liability.

[15] Agreements settling a claim or a potential claim for malpractice are not prohibited by this Rule. Nevertheless, in view of the danger that a lawyer will take unfair advantage of an unrepresented client or former client, the lawyer must first advise such a person in writing of the appropriateness of independent representation in connection with such a settlement. In addition, the lawyer must give the client or former client a reasonable opportunity to find and consult independent counsel.

Acquiring Proprietary interest in Litigation

[16] Paragraph (i) states the traditional general rule that lawyers are prohibited from acquiring a proprietary interest in litigation. Like paragraph (e), the general rule, has its basis in common law champerty and maintenance, and is

designed to avoid giving the lawyer too great an interest in the representation. In addition, when the lawyer acquires an ownership interest in the subject of the representation, it will be more difficult for a client to discharge the lawyer if the client so desires. The Rule also permits a lawyer to acquire a lien to secure the lawyer's fee or expenses provided the requirements of Rule 1.7 are satisfied. Specifically, the lawyer must reasonably believe that the representation will not be adversely affected after taking into account the possibility that the acquisition of a proprietary interest in the client's cause of action or any res involved therein may cloud the lawyer's judgment and impair the lawyer's ability to function as an advocate. The lawyer must also disclose the risks involved prior to obtaining the client's consent. Prior to initiating a foreclosure on property subject to a lien securing a legal fee, the lawyer must notify the client of the right to require the lawyer to participate in the mandatory fee dispute resolution program. See Rule 1.5(f).

[17] The Rule is subject to specific exceptions developed in decisional law and continued in these Rules. The exception for certain advances of the costs of litigation is set forth in paragraph (e). In addition, paragraph (*l*) sets forth exceptions for liens authorized by law to secure the lawyer's fees or expenses and contracts for reasonable contingent fees. The law of each jurisdiction determines which liens are authorized by law. These may include liens granted by statute, liens originating in common law and liens acquired by contract with the client. When a lawyer acquires by contract a security interest in property other than that recovered through the lawyer's efforts in the litigation, such an acquisition is a business or financial transaction with a client and is governed by the requirements of paragraph (a). Contracts for contingent fees in civil cases are governed by Rule 1.5.

Imputation of Prohibitions

[18] Under paragraph (i), a prohibition on conduct by an individual lawyer in paragraphs (a) through (i) also applies to all lawyers associated in a firm with the personally prohibited lawyer. For example, one lawyer in a firm may not enter into a business transaction with a client of another member of the firm without complying with paragraph (a), even if the first lawyer is not personally involved in the representation of the client.

Rule 1.9 Duties to Former Clients

(a) A lawyer who has formerly represented a client in a matter shall not thereafter represent another person in the same or a substantially related matter in which that person's interests are materially adverse to the interests of the former client unless the former client gives informed consent, confirmed in writing.

(b) A lawyer shall not knowingly represent a person in the same or a substantially related matter in which a firm with which the lawyer formerly was associated had previously represented a client

(1) whose interests are materially adverse to that person; and

(2) about whom the lawyer had acquired information protected by Rules 1.6 and 1.9(c) that is material to the matter; unless the former client gives informed consent, confirmed in writing.

(c) A lawyer who has formerly represented a client in a matter or whose present or former firm has formerly represented a client in a matter shall not thereafter:

(1) use information relating to the representation to the disadvantage of the former client except as these Rules would permit or require with respect to a client, or when the information has become generally known; or

(2) reveal information relating to the representation except as these Rules would permit or require with respect to a client.

[Adopted July 24, 1997. Amended February 27, 2003.]

Comment

[1] After termination of a client-lawyer relationship, a lawyer has certain continuing duties with respect to confidentiality and conflicts of interest and thus may not represent another client except in conformity with this Rule. Under this Rule, for example, a lawyer could not properly seek to rescind on behalf of a new client a contract drafted on behalf of the former client. So also a lawyer who has prosecuted an accused person could not properly represent the accused in a subsequent civil action against the government concerning the same transaction. Nor could a lawyer who has represented multiple clients in a matter represent one or more of the clients in the same or a substantially related matter after a dispute arose among the clients in that matter, unless all affected clients give informed consent or the continued representation of the client(s) is not materially adverse to the interests of the former clients. See Comment [9]. Current and former government lawyers must comply with this Rule to the extent required by Rule 1.11.

[2] The scope of a "matter" for purposes of this Rule depends on the facts of a particular situation or transaction. The lawyer's involvement in a matter can also be a question of degree. When a lawyer has been directly involved in a specific transaction, subsequent representation of other clients with materially adverse interests in that transaction clearly is prohibited. The underlying question is whether the lawyer was so involved in the matter that the subsequent representation can be justly regarded as a changing of sides in the matter in question.

[3] Matters are "substantially related" for purposes of this Rule if they involve the same transaction or legal dispute or if there otherwise is a substantial risk that information as would normally have been obtained in the prior representation would materially advance the client's position in the subsequent matter. For example, a lawyer who has represented a businessperson and learned extensive private financial information about that person may not then represent that person's spouse in seeking a divorce, Similarly, a lawyer who has previously represented a client in securing environmental permits to build a shopping center would be precluded from representing neighbors seeking to oppose rezoning of the property on the basis of environmental considerations; however, the lawyer would not be precluded, on the grounds of substantial relationship, from defending a tenant of the completed shopping center in resisting eviction for nonpayment of rent. Information that has been disclosed to the public or to other parties adverse to the former client ordinarily will not be disqualifying. Information acquired in a prior representation may have been rendered obsolete by

the passage of time, a circumstance that may be relevant in determining whether two representations are substantially related. In the case of an organizational client, general knowledge of the client's policies and practices ordinarily will not preclude a subsequent representation; on the other hand, knowledge of specific facts gained in a prior representation that are relevant to the matter in question ordinarily will preclude such a representation. A former client is not required to reveal the information learned by the lawyer to establish a substantial risk that the lawyer has information to use in the subsequent matter. A conclusion about the possession of such information may be based on the nature of the services the lawyer provided the former client and information that would in ordinary practice be learned by a lawyer providing such services.

Lawyers Moving Between Firms

[4] When lawyers have been associated within a firm but then end their association, the question of whether a lawyer should undertake representation is more complicated. There are several competing considerations. First, the client previously represented by the former firm must be reasonably assured that the principle of loyalty to the client is not compromised. Second, the rule should not be so broadly cast as to preclude other persons from having reasonable choice of legal counsel. Third, the rule should not unreasonably hamper lawyers from forming new associations and taking on new clients after having left a previous association. In this connection, it should be recognized that today many lawyers practice in firms, that many lawyers to some degree limit their practice to one field or another, and that many move from one association to another several times in their careers. If the concept of imputation were applied with unqualified rigor, the result would be radical curtailment of the opportunity of lawyers to move from one practice setting to another and of the opportunity of clients to change counsel.

[5] Paragraph (b) operates to disqualify the lawyer only when the lawyer involved has actual knowledge of information protected by Rules 1. 6 and 1.9(c). Thus, if a lawyer while with one firm acquired no knowledge or information relating to a particular client of the firm, and that lawyer later joined another firm, neither the lawyer individually nor the second firm is disqualified from representing another client in the same or a related matter even though the interests of the two clients conflict. See Rule 1.10(b) for the restrictions on a firm once a lawyer has terminated association with the firm.

[6] Application of paragraph (b) depends on a situation's particular facts, aided by inferences, deductions or working presumptions that reasonably may be made about the way in which lawyers work together. A lawyer may have general access to files of all clients of a law firm and may regularly participate in discussions of their affairs; It should be inferred that such a lawyer in fact is privy to all information about all the firm's clients. In contrast, another lawyer may have access to the files of only a limited number of clients and participate in discussions of the affairs of no other clients; in the absence of information to the contrary, it should be inferred that such a lawyer in fact is privy to information about the clients actually served but not those of other clients, In such an inquiry, the burden of proof should rest upon the firm whose disqualification is sought.

[7] Independent of the question of disqualification of a firm, a lawyer changing professional association has a continuing duty to preserve confidentiality of information about a client formerly represented. See Rules 1.6 and 1.9(c).

[8] Paragraph (c) provides that information acquired by the lawyer in the course of representing a client may not subsequently be used or revealed by the lawyer to the disadvantage of the client. However, the fact that a lawyer has once served a client does not preclude the lawyer from using generally known information about that client when later representing another client. Whether information is "generally known" depends in part upon how the information was obtained and in part upon the former client's reasonable expectations. The mere fact that information is accessible through the public record or has become known to some other persons, does not necessarily deprive the information of its confidential nature. If the information is known or readily available to a relevant sector of the public, such as the parties involved in the matter, then the information is probably considered "generally known." See Restatement (Third) of The Law of Governing Lawyers, 111 cmt. d.

[9] The provisions of this Rule are for the protection of former clients and can be waived if the client gives informed consent, which consent must be confirmed in writing under paragraphs (a) and (b). See Rule 1.0(e). With regard to the effectiveness of an advance waiver, see Comment [22] to Rule 1.7. With regard to disqualification of a firm with which a lawyer is or was formerly associated, see Rule 1.10.

Rule 1.10 Imputation of Conflicts of Interest: General Rule

(a) While lawyers are associated in a firm, none of them shall knowingly represent a client when any one of them practicing alone would be prohibited from doing so by Rules 1.7 or 1.9. , unless the prohibition is based on a personal interest of the prohibited lawyer, including a prohibition under Rule 6.6, and does not present a significant risk of materially limiting the representation of the client by the remaining lawyers in the firm.

(b) When a lawyer has terminated an association with a firm, the firm is not prohibited from thereafter representing a person with interests materially adverse to those of a client represented by the formerly associated lawyer and not currently represented by the firm, unless:

(1) the matter is the same or substantially related to that in which the formerly associated lawyer represented the client; and

(2) any lawyer remaining in the firm has information protected by Rules 1. 6 and 1.9(c) that is material to the matter.

(c) When a lawyer becomes associated with a firm, no lawyer associated in the firm shall knowingly represent a person in a matter in which that lawyer is disqualified under Rule 1.9 unless:

(1) the personally disqualified lawyer is timely screened from any participation in the matter; and

(2) written notice is promptly given to any affected former client to enable it to ascertain compliance with the provisions of this Rule.

(d) A disqualification prescribed by this rule may be waived by the affected client under the conditions stated in Rule 1.7.

(e) The disqualification of lawyers associated in a firm with former or current government lawyers is governed by Rule 1.11.

[Adopted July 24, 1997. Amended February 27, 2003.]

Comment

Definition of "Firm"

[1] For purposes of the Rules of Professional Conduct, the term "firm" denotes lawyers in a law partnership, professional corporation, sole proprietorship or other association authorized to practice law; or lawyers employed in a legal services organization or the legal department of a corporation or other organization. See Rule 1.0(c). Whether two or more lawyers constitute a firm within this definition can depend on the specific facts. See Rule 1.0—Comments [2]–[4].

Principles of Imputed Disqualification.

[2] The rule of imputed disqualification stated in paragraph (a) gives effect to the principle of loyalty to the client as it applies to lawyers who practice in a law firm. Such situations can be considered from the premise that a firm of lawyers is essentially one lawyer for purposes of the rules governing loyalty to the client, or from the premise that each lawyer is vicariously bound by the obligation of loyalty owed by each lawyer with whom the lawyer is associated. Paragraph (a) operates only among the lawyers currently associated in a firm. When a lawyer moves from one firm to another, the situation is governed by Rules 1.9(b) and 1.10(b).

[3] The rule in paragraph (a) does not prohibit representation where neither questions of client loyalty nor protection of confidential information are presented. Where one lawyer in a firm could not effectively represent a given client because of strong political beliefs, for example, but that lawyer will do no work on the case and the personal beliefs of the lawyer will not materially limit the representation by others in the firm, the firm should not be disqualified. On the other hand, if an opposing party in a case were owned by a lawyer in the law firm, and others in the firm would be materially limited in pursuing the matter because of loyalty to that lawyer, the personal disqualification of the lawyer would be imputed to all others in the firm.

[4] The rule in paragraph (a) also does not prohibit representation by others in the law firm where the person prohibited from involvement in a matter is a nonlawyer, such as a paralegal or legal secretary. Nor does paragraph (a) prohibit representation if the lawyer is prohibited from acting because of events before the person became a lawyer, for example, work that the person did while a law student. Such persons, however, ordinarily must be screened from any personal participation in the matter to avoid communication to others in the firm of confidential information that both the nonlawyers and the firm have a legal duty to protect. See Rules 1.0(k) and 5.3.

[5] Rule 1.10(b) operates to permit a law firm, under certain circumstances, to represent a person with interests directly adverse to those of a client represented by a lawyer who formerly was associated with the firm. The Rule applies regardless of when the formerly associated lawyer represented the client. However, the law firm may not represent a person with interests adverse to those of a present client of the firm, which would violate Rule 1.7. Moreover, the firm may not represent the person where the matter is the same or substantially related to that in which the formerly associated lawyer represented the client and any other lawyer currently in the firm has material information protected by Rules 1.6 and 1.9(c).

[6] Where the conditions of paragraph (c) are met, imputation is removed, and consent to the new representation is not required. Lawyers should be aware, however, that courts may impose more stringent obligations in ruling upon motions to disqualify a lawyer from pending litigation.

[7] Requirements for screening procedures are stated in Rule 1.0(k). Paragraph (c)(2) does not prohibit the screened lawyer from receiving a salary or partnership share established by prior independent agreement, nor does it specifically prohibit the receipt of a part of the fee from the screened matter. However, Rule 8.4(c) prohibits the screened lawyer from participating in the fee if such participation was impliedly or explicitly offered as an inducement to the lawyer to become associated with the firm.

[8] Notice, including a description of the screened lawyer's prior representation and of the screening procedures employed, generally should be given as soon as practicable after the need for screening becomes apparent.

[9] Rule 1.10(d) removes imputation with the informed consent of the affected client or former client under the conditions stated in Rule 1.7. The conditions stated in Rule 1.7 require the lawyer to determine that the representation is not prohibited by Rule 1.7(b) and that each affected client or former client has given informed consent to the representation, confirmed in writing. In some cases, the risk may be so severe that the conflict may not be cured by client consent. For a discussion of the effectiveness of client waivers of conflicts that might arise in the future, see Rule 1.7, Comment [22]. For a definition of informed consent, see Rule 1.0(e).

[10] Where a lawyer has joined a private firm after having represented the government, imputation is governed by Rule 1.11 (b) and (c), not this Rule. Under Rule 1.11(d), where a lawyer represents the government after having served clients in private practice, nongovernmental employment or in another government agency, former-client conflicts are not imputed to government lawyers associated with the individually disqualified lawyer.

[11] Where a lawyer is prohibited from engaging in certain transactions under Rule 1.8, paragraph (i) of that Rule, and not this Rule, determines whether that prohibition also applies to other lawyers associated in a firm with the personally prohibited lawyer.

Rule 1.11 Special Conflicts of Interest for Former and Current Government Officers and Employees

(a) Except as law may otherwise expressly permit, a lawyer who has formerly served as a public officer or employee of the government:

(1) is subject to Rule 1.9(c); and

(2) shall not otherwise represent a client in connection with a matter in which the lawyer participated personally and substantially as a public officer or employee, unless the appropriate government agency

gives its informed consent, confirmed in writing, to the representation.

(b) When a lawyer is disqualified from representation under paragraph (a), no lawyer in a firm with which that lawyer is associated may knowingly undertake or continue representation in such a matter unless:

(1) the disqualified lawyer is timely screened from any participation in the matter; and

(2) written notice is promptly given to the appropriate government agency to enable it to ascertain compliance with the provisions of this rule.

(c) Except as law may otherwise expressly permit, a lawyer having information that the lawyer knows is confidential government information about a person acquired when the lawyer was a public officer or employee, may not represent a private client whose interests are adverse to that person in a matter in which the information could be used to the material disadvantage of that person. As used in this Rule, the term "confidential government information" means information that has been obtained under governmental authority and which, at the time this Rule is applied, the government is prohibited by law from disclosing to the public or has a legal privilege not to disclose and which is not otherwise available to the public. A firm with which that lawyer is associated may undertake or continue representation in the matter only if the disqualified lawyer is timely screened from any participation in the matter.

(d) Except as law may otherwise expressly permit, a lawyer currently serving as a public officer or employee:

(1) is subject to Rules 1.7 and 1.9; and

(2) shall not:

(A) participate in a matter in which the lawyer participated personally and substantially while in private practice or nongovernmental employment, unless the appropriate government agency gives its informed consent, confirmed in writing; or

(B) negotiate for private employment with any person who is involved as a party or as lawyer for a party in a matter in which the lawyer is participating personally and substantially, except that a lawyer serving as a law clerk to a judge, other adjudicative officer or arbitrator may negotiate for private employment as permitted by Rule 1.12(b) and subject to the conditions stated in Rule 1.12(b).

(e) As used in this Rule, the term "matter" includes:

(1) any judicial or other proceeding, application, request for a ruling or other determination, contract, claim, controversy, investigation, charge, accusation, arrest or other particular matter involving a specific party or parties, and

(2) any other matter covered by the conflict of interest rules of the appropriate government agency.

[Adopted July 24, 1997. Amended February 27, 2003; amended effective October 6, 2004.]

Comment

[1] A lawyer who has served or is currently serving as a public officer or employee is personally subject to the Rules of Professional Conduct, including the prohibition against concurrent conflicts of interest stated in Rule 1.7 . In addition, such a lawyer is may be subject to statutes and government regulations regarding conflict of interest. Such statutes and regulations may circumscribe the extent to which the government agency may give consent under this Rule. See Rule 1.0(e) for the definition of informed consent.

[2] Paragraphs (a)(1), (a)(2) and (d)(1) restate the obligations of an individual lawyer who has served or is currently serving as an officer or employee of the government toward a former government or private client. Rule 1.10, however, is not applicable to the conflicts of interest addressed by this Rule. Rather, paragraph (b) sets forth a special imputation rule for former government lawyers that provides for screening and notice. Because of the special problems raised by imputation within a government agency, paragraph (d) does not impute the conflicts of a lawyer currently serving as an officer or employee of the government to other associated government officers or employees, although ordinarily it will be prudent to screen such lawyers.

[3] Paragraphs (a)(2) and (d)(2) impose additional obligations on a lawyer who has served or is currently serving as an officer or employee of the government. They apply in situations where a lawyer is not adverse to a former client and are designed to prevent a lawyer from exploiting public office for the advantage of another client. For example, a lawyer who has pursued a claim on behalf of the government may not pursue the same claim on behalf of a later private client after the lawyer has left government service, except when authorized to do so by the government agency under paragraph (a). Similarly, a lawyer who has pursued a claim on behalf of a private client may not pursue the claim on behalf of the government, except when authorized to do so by paragraph (d). As with paragraphs (a)(1) and (d)(1), Rule 1.10 is not applicable to the conflicts of interest addressed by these paragraphs.

[4] This Rule represents a balancing of interests. On the one hand, where the successive clients are a government agency and another client, public or private, the risk exists that power or discretion vested in that agency might be used for the special benefit of a the other client. A lawyer should not be in a position where benefit to the other client might affect performance of the lawyer's professional functions on behalf of the government. Also, unfair advantage could accrue to the other client by reason of access to confidential government information about the client's adversary obtainable only through the lawyer's government service. On the other hand, the rules governing lawyers presently or formerly employed by a government agency should not be so restrictive as to inhibit transfer of employment to and from the government. The government has a legitimate need to attract qualified lawyers as well as to maintain high ethical standards. The provisions for screening and waiver in paragraph (b) are necessary to prevent the disqualification rule from imposing too severe a deterrent against entering public service. The limitation of disqualification in paragraphs (a)(2) and (d)(2) to matters involving a specific party or

parties, rather than extending disqualification to all substantive issues on which the lawyer worked, serves a similar function.

[5] When a lawyer has been employed by one government agency and then moves to a second government agency, it may be appropriate to treat that second agency as another client for purposes of this Rule, as when a lawyer is employed by a city and subsequently is employed by a federal agency. However, because the conflict of interest is governed by paragraph (d), the latter agency is not required to screen the lawyer as paragraph (b) requires a law firm to do. The question of whether two government agencies should be regarded as the same or different clients for conflict of interest purposes is beyond the scope of these Rules. See Rule 1.13 Comment [6].

[6] Paragraphs (b) and (c) contemplate a screening arrangement. See Rule 1.0(k) (requirements for screening procedures). These paragraphs do not prohibit a lawyer from receiving a salary or partnership share established by prior independent agreement. nor do they specifically prohibit the receipt of a part of the fee from the screened matter. However, Rule 8.4(c) prohibits the screened lawyer from participating in the fee if such participation was impliedly or explicitly offered as an inducement to the lawyer to become associated with the firm.

[7] Notice, including a description of the screened lawyer's prior representation and of the screening procedures employed, generally should be given as soon as practicable after the need for screening becomes apparent. When disclosure is likely significantly to injure the client, a reasonable delay may be justified.

[8] Paragraph (c) operates only when the lawyer in question has knowledge of the information, which means actual knowledge; it does not operate with respect to information that merely could be imputed to the lawyer.

[9] Paragraph (a) and (d) do not prohibit a lawyer from jointly representing a private party and a government agency when doing so is permitted by Rule 1.7 and is not otherwise prohibited by law.

Rule 1.12 Former Judge, Arbitrator, Mediator, or Other Third–Party Neutral

(a) Except as stated in paragraph (d), a lawyer shall not represent anyone in connection with a matter in which the lawyer participated personally and substantially as a judge or other adjudicative officer or law clerk to such a person or as an arbitrator, mediator or other third-party neutral, unless all parties to the proceeding give informed consent, confirmed in writing.

(b) A lawyer shall not negotiate for employment with any person who is involved as a party or as lawyer for a party in a matter in which the lawyer is participating personally and substantially as a judge or other adjudicative officer or as an arbitrator, mediator or other third-party neutral. A lawyer serving as a law clerk to a judge or other adjudicative officer may negotiate for employment with a party or lawyer involved in a matter in which the clerk is participating personally and substantially, but only after the lawyer has notified the judge or other adjudicative officer.

(c) If a lawyer is disqualified by paragraph (a), no lawyer in a firm with which that lawyer is associated may knowingly undertake or continue representation in the matter unless:

(1) the disqualified lawyer is timely screened from any participation in the matter; and

(2) written notice is promptly given to the parties and any appropriate tribunal to enable them to ascertain compliance with the provisions of this rule.

(d) An arbitrator selected as a partisan of a party in a multimember arbitration panel is not prohibited from subsequently representing that party.

[Adopted July 24, 1997. Amended February 27, 2003.]

Comment

[1] This Rule generally parallels Rule 1.11. The term "personally and substantially" signifies that a judge who was a member of a multimember court, and thereafter left judicial office to practice law, is not prohibited from representing a client in a matter pending in the court, but in which the former judge did not participate. So also the fact that a former judge exercised administrative responsibility in a court does not prevent the former judge from acting as a lawyer in a matter where the judge had previously exercised remote or incidental administrative responsibility that did not affect the merits. Compare the Comment to Rule 1.11. The term "adjudicative officer" includes such officials as judges pro tempore, referees, special masters, hearing officers and other parajudicial officers, and also lawyers who serve as part-time judges.

[2] Like former judges, lawyers who have served as arbitrators, mediators or other third-party neutrals may be asked to represent a client in a matter in which the lawyer participated personally and substantially. This Rule forbids such representation unless all of the parties to the proceedings give their informed consent, confirmed in writing. See Rule 1.0(e) and (b). Other law or codes of ethics governing third-party neutrals may impose more stringent standards of personal or imputed disqualification. See Rule 2.4.

[3] Although lawyers who serve as third-party neutrals do not have information concerning the parties that is protected under Rule 1.6, they typically owe the parties an obligation of confidentiality under law or codes of ethics governing third-party neutrals. Thus, paragraph (c) provides that conflicts of the personally disqualified lawyer will be imputed to other lawyers in a law firm unless the conditions of this paragraph are met.

[4] Requirements for screening procedures are stated in Rule 1.0(k). Paragraph (c)(1) does not prohibit the screened lawyer from receiving a salary or partnership share established by prior independent agreement, nor does it specifically prohibit the receipt of a part of the fee from the screened matter. However, Rule 8.4(c) prohibits the screened lawyer from participating in the fee if such participation was impliedly or explicitly offered as an inducement to the lawyer to become associated with the firm.

[5] Notice, including a description of the screened lawyer's prior representation and of the screening procedures employed, generally should be given as soon as practicable after the need for screening becomes apparent. When disclosure

is likely to significantly injure the client, a reasonable delay may be justified.

Rule 1.13 Organization as Client

(a) A lawyer employed or retained by an organization represents the organization acting through its duly authorized constituents.

(b) If a lawyer for an organization knows that an officer, employee. or other person associated with the organization is engaged in action, intends to act or refuses to act in a matter related to the representation that is a violation of a legal obligation to the organization, or a violation of law which reasonably might be imputed to the organization, and is likely to result in substantial injury to the organization, then the lawyer shall proceed as is reasonably necessary in the best interest of the organization. Unless the lawyer reasonably believes that it is not necessary in the best interest of the organization to do so, the lawyer shall refer the matter to higher authority in the organization, including, if warranted by the circumstances, to the highest authority that can act on behalf of the organization as determined by applicable law.

(c) If, despite the lawyer's efforts in accordance with paragraph (b), the highest authority that can act on behalf of the organization insists upon action, or a refusal to act, that is clearly a violation of law and is likely to result in substantial injury to the organization, the lawyer may reveal such information outside the organization to the extent permitted by Rule 1.6 and may resign in accordance with Rule 1.16.

(d) Paragraph (c) shall not apply with respect to information relating to a lawyer's representation of an organization to investigate an alleged violation of law, or to defend the organization or an officer, employee, or other constituent associated with the organization against a claim arising out of an alleged violation of law.

(e) A lawyer who reasonably believes that he or she has been discharged because of the lawyer's actions taken pursuant to paragraphs (b) or (c), or who withdraws under circumstances that require or permit the lawyer to take action under these Rules, shall proceed as the lawyer reasonably believes necessary to assure that the organization's highest authority is informed of the lawyer's discharge or withdrawal.

(f) In dealing with an organization's directors, officers, employees, members, shareholders, or other constituents, a lawyer shall explain the identity of the client when the lawyer knows or reasonably should know that the organization's interests are adverse to those of the constituents with whom the lawyer is dealing.

(g) A lawyer representing an organization may also represent any of its directors, officers, employees, members, shareholders, or other constituents, subject to the provisions of Rule 1.7. If the organization's consent to the dual representation is required by Rule 1.7, the consent shall be given by an appropriate official of the organization other than the individual who is to be represented, or by the shareholders.

[Adopted July 24, 1997. Amended February 27, 2003; amended effective March 2, 2006.]

Comment

The Entity as the Client

[1] An organizational client is a legal entity, but it cannot act except through its officers, directors, employees, shareholders and other constituents. Officers, directors, employees and shareholders are the constituents of the corporate organizational client. The duties defined in this Comment apply equally to unincorporated associations. "Other constituents" as used in this Comment means the positions equivalent to officers, directors, employees and shareholders held by persons acting for organizational clients that are not corporations.

[2] When one of the constituents of an organizational client communicates with the organization's lawyer in that person's organizational capacity, the communication is protected by Rule 1.6. Thus, by way of example, if an organizational client requests its lawyer to investigate allegations of wrongdoing, interviews made in the course of that investigation between the lawyer and the client's employees or other constituents are covered by Rule 1.6. This does not mean, however, that constituents of an organizational client are the clients of the lawyer. The lawyer may not disclose to such constituents information relating to the representation except for disclosures explicitly or impliedly authorized by the organizational client in order to carry out the representation or as otherwise permitted by Rule 1.6.

[3] When constituents of the organization make decisions for it, the decisions ordinarily must be accepted by the lawyer even if their utility or prudence is doubtful. Decisions concerning policy and operations, including ones entailing serious risk, are not as such in the lawyer's province. Paragraph (b) makes clear, however, that when the lawyer knows that the organization may be substantially injured by action of an officer or other constituent that violates a legal obligation to the organization or is a violation of the law that might be imputed to the organization, the lawyer must proceed as is reasonably necessary in the best interest of the organization. As defined in Rule 1.0(g), knowledge can be inferred from circumstances, and a lawyer cannot ignore the obvious.

[4] In determining how to proceed under paragraph (b), the lawyer should give due consideration to the seriousness of the violation and its consequences, the responsibility in the organization and the apparent motivation of the person involved, the policies of the organization concerning such matters, and any other relevant considerations. Ordinarily, referral to a higher authority would be necessary. In some circumstances, however, it may be appropriate for the lawyer to ask the constituent to reconsider the matter; for example, if the circumstances involve a constituent's innocent misunderstanding of law and subsequent acceptance of the lawyer's advice, the lawyer may reasonably conclude that the best interest of the organization does not require that the matter be referred to higher authority. If a constituent persists in conduct contrary to the lawyer's advice, it will be necessary for the lawyer to take steps to have the matter reviewed by a higher authority in the organization. If the matter is of

sufficient seriousness and importance or urgency to the organization, referral to higher authority in the organization may be necessary even if the lawyer has not communicated with the constituent. Any measures taken should, to the extent practicable, minimize the risk of revealing information relating to the representation to persons outside the organization. Even in circumstances where a lawyer is not obligated by Rule 1.13 to proceed, a lawyer may bring to the attention of an organizational client, including its highest authority, matters that the lawyer reasonably believes to be of sufficient importance to warrant doing so in the best interest of the organization.

[5] Paragraph (b) also makes clear that when it is reasonably necessary to enable the organization to address the matter in a timely and appropriate manner, the lawyer must refer the matter to higher authority, including, if warranted by the circumstances, the highest authority that can act on behalf of the organization under applicable law. The organization's highest authority to whom a matter may be referred ordinarily will be the board of directors or similar governing body. However, applicable law may prescribe that under certain conditions the highest authority reposes elsewhere, for example, in the independent directors of a corporation.

Relation to Other Rules

[6] The authority and responsibility provided in this Rule are concurrent with the authority and responsibility provided in other Rules. In particular, this Rule does not limit or expand the lawyer's responsibility under Rule 1.6, 1.8, 1.16, 3.3, or 4.1. If the lawyer reasonably believes that disclosure of information protected by Rule 1.6 is necessary to prevent the commission of a crime by an organizational client, for example, disclosure is permitted by Rule 1.6(b)(2).

If the lawyer's services are being or have been used by an organizational client to further a crime or fraud by the organization, Rule 1.6(b)(4) permits the lawyer to disclose confidential information to prevent, mitigate, or rectify the consequences of such conduct. In such circumstances, Rule 1.2(d) may be applicable, in which event, withdrawal from the representation under Rule 1.16(a)(1) may be required.

[7] Paragraph (d) makes clear that the authority of a lawyer to disclose information relating to a representation in circumstances described in paragraph (c) does not apply with respect to information relating to a lawyer's engagement by an organization to investigate an alleged violation of law or to defend the organization or an officer, employee, or other person associated with the organization against a claim arising out of an alleged violation of law. This is necessary in order to enable organizational clients to enjoy the full benefits of legal counsel in conducting an investigation or defending against a claim.

[8] A lawyer who reasonably believes that he or she has been discharged because of the lawyer's actions taken pursuant to paragraphs (b) and (c), or who withdraws in circumstances that require or permit the lawyer to take action under these Rules, must proceed as the lawyer reasonably believes necessary to assure that the organization's highest authority is informed of the lawyer's discharge or withdrawal.

Government Agency

[9] The duty defined in this Rule applies to governmental organizations. Defining precisely the identity of the client and prescribing the resulting obligations of such lawyers may be more difficult in the government context and is a matter beyond the scope of these Rules. See Scope [18]. Although in some circumstances the client may be a specific agency, it may also be a branch of government, such as the executive branch, or the government as a whole. For example, if the action or failure to act involves the head of a bureau, either the department of which the bureau is a part or the relevant branch of government may be the client for purposes of this Rule. Moreover, in a matter involving the conduct of government officials, a government lawyer may have authority under applicable law to question such conduct more extensively than that of a lawyer for a private organization in similar circumstances. Thus, when the client is a governmental organization, a different balance may be appropriate between maintaining confidentiality and assuring that the wrongful act is prevented or rectified, for public business is involved. In addition, duties of lawyers employed by the government or lawyers in military service may be defined by statutes and regulation. This Rule does not limit that authority. See Scope.

Clarifying the Lawyer's Role

[10] There are times when the organization's interest may be or become adverse to those of one or more of its constituents. In such circumstances the lawyer should advise any constituent, whose interest the lawyer finds adverse to that of the organization of the conflict or potential conflict of interest, that the lawyer cannot represent such constituent, and that such person may wish to obtain independent representation. Care must be taken to assure that the individual understands that, when there is such adversity of interest, the lawyer for the organization cannot provide legal representation for that constituent individual, and that discussions between the lawyer for the organization and the individual may not be privileged.

[11] Whether such a warning should be given by the lawyer for the organization to any constituent individual may turn on the facts of each case.

Dual Representation

[12] Paragraph (g) recognizes that a lawyer for an organization may also represent a principal officer or major shareholder, director, employee, member, or other constituent.

Derivative Actions

[13] Under generally prevailing law, the shareholders or members of a corporation may bring suit to compel the directors to perform their legal obligations in the supervision of the organization. Members of unincorporated associations have essentially the same right. Such an action may be brought nominally by the organization, but usually is, in fact, a legal controversy over management of the organization.

[14] The question can arise whether counsel for the organization may defend such an action. The proposition that the organization is the lawyer's client does not alone resolve the issue. Most derivative actions are a normal incident of an organization's affairs, to be defended by the organization's lawyer like any other suit. However, if the claim involves serious charges of wrongdoing by those in control of the organization, a conflict may arise between the lawyer's duty to the organization and the lawyer's relationship with the board. In those circumstances, Rule 1.7 governs who should represent the directors and the organization.

Rule 1.14 Client With Diminished Capacity

(a) When a client's capacity to make adequately considered decisions in connection with a representa-

tion is diminished, whether because of minority, mental impairment or for some other reason, the lawyer shall, as far as reasonably possible, maintain a normal client-lawyer relationship with the client.

(b) When the lawyer reasonably believes that the client has diminished capacity, is at risk of substantial physical, financial or other harm unless action is taken and cannot adequately act in the client's own interest, the lawyer may take reasonably necessary protective action, including consulting with individuals or entities that have the ability to take action to protect the client and, in appropriate cases, seeking the appointment of a guardian ad litem or guardian.

(c) Information relating to the representation of a client with diminished capacity is protected by Rule 1.6. When taking protective action pursuant to paragraph (b), the lawyer is impliedly authorized under Rule 1.6(a) to reveal information about the client, but only to the extent reasonably necessary to protect the client's interests.

[Adopted July 24, 1997. Amended February 27, 2003.]

Comment

[1] The normal client-lawyer relationship is based on the assumption that the client, when properly advised and assisted, is capable of making decisions about important matters. When the client is a minor or suffers from a diminished mental capacity, however, maintaining the ordinary client-lawyer relationship may not be possible in all respects. In particular, a severely incapacitated person may have no power to make legally binding decisions. Nevertheless, a client with diminished capacity often has the ability to understand, deliberate upon, and reach conclusions about matters affecting the client's own well-being. For example, children as young as five or six years of age, and certainly those of ten or twelve, are regarded as having opinions that are entitled to weight in legal proceedings concerning their custody. So also, it is recognized that some persons of advanced age can be quite capable of handling routine financial matters while needing special legal protection concerning major transactions.

[2] The fact that a client suffers a disability does not diminish the lawyer's obligation to treat the client with attention and respect. Even if the person has a legal representative, the lawyer should as far as possible accord the represented person the status of client, particularly in maintaining communication.

[3] The client may wish to have family members or other persons participate in discussions with the lawyer. When necessary to assist in the representation, the presence of such persons generally does not affect the applicability of the attorney-client evidentiary privilege. Nevertheless, the lawyer must keep the client's interests foremost and, except for protective action authorized under paragraph (b), must to look to the client, and not family members, to make decisions on the client's behalf.

[4] If a legal representative has already been appointed for the client, the lawyer should ordinarily look to the representative for decisions on behalf of the client. In matters involving a minor, whether the lawyer should look to the parents as natural guardians may depend on the type of proceeding or matter in which the lawyer is representing the minor. [4] If the lawyer represents the guardian as distinct from the ward, and is aware that the guardian is acting adversely to the ward's interest, the lawyer may have an obligation to prevent or rectify the guardian's misconduct. See Rule 1.2(d).

Taking Protective Action

[5] If a lawyer reasonably believes that a client is at risk of substantial physical, financial or other harm unless action is taken, and that a normal client-lawyer relationship cannot be maintained as provided in paragraph (a) because the client lacks sufficient capacity to communicate or to make adequately considered decisions in connection with the representation, then paragraph (b) permits the lawyer to take protective measures deemed necessary. Such measures could include; consulting with family members, using a reconsideration period to permit clarification or improvement of circumstances, using voluntary surrogate decisionmaking tools such as durable powers of attorney or consulting with support groups, professional services, adult-protective agencies or other individuals or entities that have the ability to protect the client. In taking any protective action, the lawyer should be guided by such factors as the wishes and values of the client to the extent known, the client's best interests and the goals of intruding into the client's decisionmaking autonomy to the least extent feasible, maximizing client capacities and respecting the client's family and social connections.

[6] In determining the extent of the client's diminished capacity, the lawyer should consider and balance such factors as; the client's ability to articulate reasoning leading to a decision, variability of state of mind and ability to appreciate consequences of a decision; the substantive fairness of a decision; and the consistency of a decision with the known long-term commitments and values of the client. In appropriate circumstances, the lawyer may seek guidance from an appropriate diagnostician.

[7] If a legal representative has not been appointed, the lawyer should consider whether appointment of a guardian ad litem or guardian is necessary to protect the client's interests. Thus, if a client with diminished capacity has substantial property that should be sold for the client's benefit, effective completion of the transaction may require appointment of a legal representative. In addition, rules of procedure in litigation sometimes provide that minors or persons with diminished capacity must be represented by a guardian or next friend if they do not have a general guardian. In many circumstances, however, appointment of a legal representative may be more expensive or traumatic for the client than circumstances in fact require. Evaluation of such circumstances is a matter entrusted to the professional judgment of the lawyer. In considering alternatives, however, the lawyer should be aware of any law that requires the lawyer to advocate the least restrictive action on behalf of the client.

Disclosure of the Client's Condition

[8] Disclosure of the client's diminished capacity could adversely affect the client's interests. For example, raising the question of diminished capacity could, in some circumstances, lead to proceedings for involuntary commitment. Information relating to the representation is protected by Rule 1.6. Therefore, unless authorized to do so, the lawyer may not disclose such information. When taking protective action pursuant to paragraph (b), the lawyer is impliedly authorized to make the necessary disclosures, even when the

client directs the lawyer to the contrary. Nevertheless, given the risks of disclosure, paragraph (c) limits what the lawyer may disclose in consulting with other individuals or entitles or seeking the appointment of a legal representative. At the very least, the lawyer should determine whether it is likely that the person or entity consulted with will act adversely to the client's interests before discussing matters related to the client. The lawyer's position in such cases is an unavoidably difficult one.

Emergency Legal Assistance

[9] In an emergency where the health, safety or a financial interest of a person with seriously diminished capacity is threatened with imminent and irreparable harm, a lawyer may take legal action on behalf of such a person even though the person is unable to establish a client-lawyer relationship or to make or express considered judgments about the matter, when the person or another acting in good faith on that person's behalf has consulted with the lawyer. Even in such an emergency, however, the lawyer should not act unless the lawyer reasonably believes that the person has no other lawyer, agent or other representative available. The lawyer should take legal action on behalf of the person only to the extent reasonably necessary to maintain the status quo or otherwise avoid imminent and irreparable harm. A lawyer who undertakes to represent a person in such an exigent situation has the same duties under these Rules as the lawyer would with respect to a client.

[10] A lawyer who acts on behalf of a person with seriously diminished capacity in an emergency should keep the confidences of the person as if dealing with a client, disclosing them only to the extent necessary to accomplish the intended protective action. The lawyer should disclose to any tribunal involved and to any other counsel involved the nature of his or her relationship with the person. The lawyer should take steps to regularize the relationship or implement other protective solutions as soon as possible.

Rule 1.15 Safekeeping Property

This rule has three subparts, Rule 1.15–1, Definitions; Rule 1.15–2, General Rules; and Rule 1.15–3, Records and Accountings The subparts set forth the requirements for preserving client property, including the requirements for preserving client property in a lawyer's trust account. The comment for all three subparts as well as the annotations appear after the text for Rule 1.15–3.

[Amended effective February 5, 2009.]

Rule 1.15–1. Definitions

For purposes of this Rule 1.15, the following definitions apply:

(a) "Bank" denotes a bank or savings and loan association chartered under North Carolina or federal law.

(b) "Client" denotes a person, firm, or other entity for whom a lawyer performs, or is engaged to perform, any legal services.

(c) "Dedicated trust account" denotes a trust account that is maintained for the sole benefit of a single client or with respect to a single transaction or series of integrated transactions.

(d) "Demand deposit" denotes any account from which deposited funds can be withdrawn at any time without notice to the depository institution.

(e) "Entrusted property" denotes trust funds, fiduciary funds and other property belonging to someone other than the lawyer which is in the lawyer's possession or control in connection with the performance of legal services or professional fiduciary services.

(f) "Fiduciary account" denotes an account, designated as such, maintained by a lawyer solely for the deposit of fiduciary funds or other entrusted property of a particular person or entity.

(g) "Fiduciary funds" denotes funds belonging to someone other than the lawyer that are received by or placed under the control of the lawyer in connection with the performance of professional fiduciary services.

(h) "Funds" denotes any form of money, including cash, payment instruments such as checks, money orders, or sales drafts, and receipts from electronic fund transfers.

(i) "General trust account" denotes any trust account other than a dedicated trust account.

(j) "Item" denotes any means or method by which funds are credited to or debited from an account; for example: a check, substitute check, remotely created check, draft, withdrawal order, automated clearinghouse (ACH) or electronic transfer, electronic or wire funds transfer, electronic image of an item and/or information in electronic form describing an item, or instructions given in person or by telephone, mail, or computer.

(k) "Legal services" denotes services rendered by a lawyer in a client-lawyer relationship.

(*l*) "Professional fiduciary services" denotes compensated services (other than legal services) rendered by a lawyer as a trustee, guardian, personal representative of an estate, attorney-in-fact, or escrow agent, or in any other fiduciary role customary to the practice of law.

(m) "Trust account" denotes an account, designated as such, maintained by a lawyer for the deposit of trust funds.

(n) "Trust funds" denotes funds belonging to someone other than the lawyer that are received by or placed under the control of the lawyer in connection with the performance of legal services.

[Adopted July 24, 1997. Amended effective March 6, 2008; amended effective October 8, 2009; amended effective August 23, 2012.]

Rule 1.15–2. General Rules

(a) Entrusted Property. All entrusted property shall be identified, held, and maintained separate from the property of the lawyer, and shall be deposited, disbursed, and distributed only in accordance with this Rule 1,15.

(b) Deposit of Trust Funds. All trust funds received by or placed under the control of a lawyer shall be promptly deposited in either a general trust account or a dedicated trust account of the lawyer. Trust funds placed in a general account are those which, in the lawyer's good faith judgment, are nominal or short-term. General trust accounts are to be administered in accordance with the Rules of Professional Conduct and the provisions of 27 NCAC Chapter 1, Subchapter D, Section.1300.

(c) Deposit of Fiduciary Funds. All fiduciary funds received by or placed under the control of a lawyer shall be promptly deposited in a fiduciary account or a general trust account of the lawyer.

(d) Safekeeping of Other Entrusted Property. A lawyer may also hold entrusted property other than fiduciary funds (such as securities) in a fiduciary account. All entrusted property received by a lawyer that is not deposited in a trust account or fiduciary account (such as a stock certificate) shall be promptly identified, labeled as property of the person or entity for whom it is to be held, and placed in a safe deposit box or other suitable place of safekeeping. The lawyer shall disclose the location of the property to the client or other person for whom it is held. Any safe deposit box or other place of safekeeping shall be located in this state, unless the lawyer has been otherwise authorized in writing by the client or other person for whom it is held.

(e) Location of Accounts. All trust accounts shall be maintained at a bank in North Carolina or a bank with branch offices in North Carolina except that, with the written consent of the client, a dedicated trust account may be maintained at a bank that does not have offices in North Carolina or at a financial institution other than a bank in or outside of North Carolina. A lawyer may maintain a fiduciary account at any bank or other financial institution in or outside of North Carolina selected by the lawyer in the exercise of the lawyer's fiduciary responsibility.

(f) Segregation of Lawyer's Funds. No funds belonging to a lawyer shall be deposited in a trust account or fiduciary account of the lawyer except:

(1) funds sufficient to open or maintain an account, pay any bank service charges, or pay any tax levied on the account; or

(2) funds belonging in part to a client or other third party and in currently or conditionally to the lawyer.

(g) Mixed Funds Deposited Intact. When funds belonging to the lawyer are received in combination with funds belonging to the client or other persons, all of the funds shall be deposited intact. The amounts currently or conditionally belonging to the lawyer shall be identified on the deposit slip or other record. After the deposit has been finally credited to the account, the lawyer may withdraw the amounts to which the lawyer is or becomes entitled. If the lawyer's entitlement is disputed, the disputed amounts shall remain in the trust account or fiduciary account until the dispute is resolved.

(h) Items Payable to Lawyer. Any item drawn on a trust account or fiduciary account for the payment of the lawyer's fees or expenses shall be made payable to the lawyer and shall indicate on the item the client balance on which the item is drawn. Any item that does not capture this information may not be used to withdraw funds from a trust account or a fiduciary account for payment of the lawyer's fees or expenses.

(i) No Bearer Items. No item shall be drawn on a trust account or fiduciary account made payable to cash or bearer and no cash shall be withdrawn from a trust account or fiduciary account by means of a debit card.

(j) No Personal Benefit. A lawyer shall not use or pledge any entrusted property to obtain credit or other personal benefit for the lawyer or any person other than the legal or beneficial owner of that property.

(k) Bank Directive. Every lawyer maintaining a trust account or fiduciary account with demand deposit at a bank or other financial institution shall file with the bank or other financial institution a written directive requiring the bank or other financial institution to report to the executive director of the North Carolina State Bar when an instrument drawn on the account is presented for payment against insufficient funds. No trust account or fiduciary account shall be maintained in a bank or other financial institution that does not agree to make such reports.

(*l*) Notification of Receipt. A lawyer shall promptly notify his or her client of the receipt of any entrusted property belonging in whole or in part to the client.

(m) Delivery of Client Property. A lawyer shall promptly pay or deliver to the client, or to third persons as directed by the client, any entrusted property belonging to the client and to which the client is currently entitled.

(n) Property Received as Security. Any entrusted property or document of title delivered to a lawyer as security for the payment of a fee or other obligation to the lawyer shall be held in trust in accordance with this Rule 1.15 and shall be clearly identified as property held as security and not as a completed transfer of beneficial ownership to the lawyer. This provision does not apply to property received by a lawyer on account of fees or other amounts owed to the lawyer at the time of receipt; however, such transfers are subject to the rules governing legal fees or business transactions between a lawyer and client.

(o) Duty to Report Misappropriation. A lawyer who discovers or reasonably believes that entrusted property has been misappropriated or misapplied shall promptly inform the North Carolina State Bar.

(p) Interest on Deposited Funds. Under no circumstances shall the lawyer be entitled to any interest earned on funds deposited in a trust account or fiduciary account. Except as authorized by Rule .1316 of subchapter 1D of the Rules and Regulations of the North Carolina State Bar, any interest earned on a trust account or fiduciary account, less any amounts deducted for bank service charges and taxes, shall belong to the client or other person or entity entitled to the corresponding principal amount.

(q) Abandoned Property. If entrusted property is unclaimed, the lawyer shall make due inquiry of his or her personnel, records and other sources of information in an effort to determine the identity and location of the owner of the property. If that effort is successful, the entrusted property shall be promptly transferred to the person or entity to whom it belongs. If the effort is unsuccessful and the provisions of G.S. 116B–18 are satisfied, the property shall be deemed abandoned, and the lawyer shall comply with the requirements of Chapter 116B of the General Statutes concerning the escheat of abandoned property.

[Adopted July 24, 1997. Amended effective March 6, 2008; amended effective February 5, 2009; amended effective August 23, 2012.]

Rule 1.15–3 Records and Accountings

(a) Check Format. All general trust accounts, dedicated trust accounts, and fiduciary accounts must use business-size checks that contain an Auxiliary On-Us field in the MICR line of the check.

(b) Minimum Records for Accounts at Banks. The minimum records required for general trust accounts, dedicated trust accounts, and fiduciary accounts maintained at a bank shall consist of the following:

(1) all records listing the source and date of receipt of any funds deposited in the account including, but not limited to, bank receipts, deposit slips and wire and electronic transfer confirmations, and, in the case of a general trust account, all records also listing the name of the client or other person to whom the funds belong;

(2) all canceled checks or other items drawn on the account, or printed digital images thereof furnished by the bank, showing the amount, date, and recipient of the disbursement, and, in the case of a general trust account, the client balance against which each item is drawn, provided, that:

(A) digital images must be legible reproductions of the front and back of the original items with no more than six images per page and no images smaller than 1–3/16 × 3 inches; and

(B) the bank must maintain, for at least six years, the capacity to reproduce electronically additional or enlarged images of the original items or records related thereto upon request within a reasonable time;

(3) all instructions or authorizations to transfer, disburse, or withdraw funds from the trust account (including electronic transfers or debits), or a written or electronic record of any such transfer, disbursement, or withdrawal showing the amount, date, and recipient of the transfer or disbursement, and, in the case of a general trust account, also showing the name of the client or other person to whom the funds belong;

(4) all bank statements and other documents received from the bank with respect to the trust account, including, but not limited to notices of return or dishonor of any item drawn on the account against insufficient funds;

(5) in the case of a general trust account, a ledger containing a record of receipts and disbursements for each person or entity from whom and for whom funds are received and showing the current balance of funds held in the trust account for each such person or entity; and

(6) any other records required by law to be maintained for the trust account.

(c) Minimum Records for Accounts at Other Financial Institutions. The minimum records required for dedicated trust accounts and fiduciary accounts at financial institutions other than a bank shall consist of the following:

(1) all records listing the source and date of receipt of all funds deposited in the account including, but not limited to, depository receipts, deposit slips, and wire and electronic transfer confirmations;

(2) a copy of all checks or other items drawn on the account, or printed digital images thereof furnished by the depository, showing the amount, date, and recipient of the disbursement, provided, that the images satisfy the requirements set forth in Rule 1.15–3(b)(2);

(3) all instructions or authorizations to transfer, disburse, or withdraw funds from the account (including electronic transfers or debits) or a written or electronic record of any such transfer, disbursement, or withdrawal showing the amount, date, and recipient of the transfer or disbursement;

(4) all statements and other documents received from the depository with respect to the account, including, but not limited to notices of return or dishonor of any item drawn on the account for insufficient funds; and

(5) any other records required by law to be maintained for the account.

(d) Reconciliations of General Trust Accounts.

(1) *Quarterly Reconciliations.* At least quarterly, the individual client balances shown on the ledger of a

general trust account must be totaled and reconciled with the current bank statement balance for the trust account as a whole.

(2) *Monthly Reconciliations.* Each month, the balance of the trust account as shown on the lawyer's records shall be reconciled with the current bank statement balance for the trust account.

(3) The lawyer shall retain a record of the reconciliations of the general trust account for a period of six years in accordance with Rule 1.15–3(g).

(e) Accountings for Trust Funds. The lawyer shall render to the client a written accounting of the receipts and disbursements of all trust funds (i) upon the complete disbursement of the trust funds, (ii) at such other times as may be reasonably requested by the client, and (iii) at least annually if the funds are retained for a period of more than one year.

(f) Accountings for Fiduciary Property. Inventories and accountings of fiduciary funds and other entrusted property received in connection with professional fiduciary services shall be rendered to judicial officials or other persons as required by law. If an annual or more frequent accounting is not required by law, a written accounting of all transactions concerning the fiduciary funds and other entrusted property shall be rendered to the beneficial owners, or their representatives, at least annually and upon the termination of the lawyer's professional fiduciary services.

(g) Minimum Record Keeping Period. A lawyer shall maintain, in accordance with this Rule 1.15, complete and accurate records of all entrusted property received by the lawyer, which records shall be maintained for at least the six (6) year period immediately preceding the lawyer's most recent fiscal year end .

(h) Audit by State Bar. The financial records required by this Rule 1.15 shall be subject to audit for cause and to random audit by the North Carolina State Bar; and such records shall be produced for inspection and copying in North Carolina upon request by the State Bar.

[Effective May 4, 2000. Amended February 27, 2003; amended effective October 6, 2004; amended effective March 6, 2008.]

Comment

[1] The purpose of a lawyer's trust account or fiduciary account is to segregate the funds belonging to others from those belonging to the lawyer. Money received by a lawyer while providing legal services or otherwise serving as a fiduciary should never be used for personal purposes. Failure to place the funds of others in a trust or fiduciary account can subject the funds to claims of the lawyer's creditors or place the funds in the lawyer's estate in the event of the lawyer's death or disability.

Property Subject to these Rules

[2] Any property belonging to a client or other person or entity that is received by or placed under the control of a lawyer in connection with the lawyer's furnishing of legal services or professional fiduciary services must be handled and maintained in accordance with this Rule 1.15. The minimum records to be maintained for accounts in banks differ from the minimum records to be maintained for accounts in other financial institutions (where permitted), to accommodate brokerage accounts and other accounts with differing reporting practices.

Client Property

[3] Every lawyer who receives funds belonging to a client must maintain a trust account. The general rule is that every receipt of money from a client or for a client, which will be used or delivered on the client's behalf, is held in trust and should be placed in the trust account. All client money received by a lawyer, except that to which the lawyer is immediately entitled, must be deposited in a trust account, including funds for payment of future fees and expenses. Client funds must be promptly deposited into the trust account. Client funds must be deposited in a general trust account if there is no duty to invest on behalf of the client. Generally speaking, if a reasonably prudent person would conclude that the funds in question, either because they are nominal in amount or are to be held for a short time, could probably not earn sufficient interest to justify the cost of investing, the funds should be deposited in the general trust account. In determining whether there is a duty to invest, a lawyer shall exercise his or her professional judgment in good faith and shall consider the following:

a) The amount of the funds to be deposited;

b) The expected duration of the deposit, including the likelihood of delay in the matter for which the funds are held;

c) The rates of interest or yield at financial institutions where the funds are to be deposited;

d) The cost of establishing and administering dedicated accounts for the client's benefit, including the service charges, the costs of the lawyer's services, and the costs of preparing any tax reports required for income accruing to the client's benefit;

e) The capability of financial institutions, lawyers, or law firms to calculate and pay income to individual clients;

f) Any other circumstances that affect the ability of the client's funds to earn a net return for the client.

When regularly reviewing the trust accounts, the lawyer shall determine whether changed circumstances require further action with respect to the funds of any client. The determination of whether a client's funds are nominal or short-term shall rest in the sound judgment of the lawyer or law firm. No lawyer shall be charged with an ethical impropriety or breach of professional conduct based on the good faith exercise of such judgment. A law firm with offices in another state may send a North Carolina client's funds to a firm office in another state for centralized processing provided, however, the funds are promptly deposited into a trust account with a bank that has branch offices in North Carolina, and further provided, the funds are transported and held in a safe place until deposited into the trust account. If this procedure is followed, client consent to the transfer of the funds to an out-of-state office of the firm is not required. However, all such client funds are subject to the requirement of these rules. Funds delivered to the lawyer by the client for payment of future fees or expenses should never be used by the lawyer for personal purposes or subjected to the potential claims of the lawyer's creditors.

[4] This rule does not prohibit a lawyer who receives an instrument belonging wholly to a client or a third party from delivering the instrument to the appropriate recipient without first depositing the instrument in the lawyer's trust account.

Property from Professional Fiduciary Service

[5] The phrase "professional fiduciary service," as used in this rule, is service by a lawyer in any one of the various fiduciary roles undertaken by a lawyer that is not, of itself, the practice of law, but is frequently undertaken in conjunction with the practice of law. This includes service as a trustee, guardian, personal representative of an estate, attorney-in-fact, and escrow agent, as well as service in other fiduciary roles "customary to the practice of law."

[6] Property held by a lawyer performing a professional fiduciary service must also be segregated from the lawyer's personal property, properly labeled, and maintained in accordance with the applicable provisions of this rule.

[7] When property is entrusted to a lawyer in connection with a lawyer's representation of a client, this rule applies whether or not the lawyer is compensated for the representation. However, the rule does not apply to property received in connection with a lawyer's uncompensated service as a fiduciary such as a trustee or personal representative of an estate. (Of course, the lawyer's conduct may be governed by the law applicable to fiduciary obligations in general, including a fiduciary's obligation to keep the principal's funds or property separate from the fiduciary's personal funds or property, to avoid self-dealing, and to account for the funds or property accurately and promptly).

[8] Compensation distinguishes professional fiduciary service from a fiduciary role that a lawyer undertakes as a family responsibility, as a courtesy to friends, or for charitable, religious or civic purposes. As used in this rule, "compensated services" means services for which the lawyer obtains or expects to obtain money or any other valuable consideration. The term does not refer to or include reimbursement for actual out-of-pocket expenses.

Property Excluded from Coverage of Rules

[9] This rule also does not apply when a lawyer is handling money for a business or for a religious, civic, or charitable organization as an officer, employee, or other official regardless of whether the lawyer is compensated for this service. Handling funds while serving in one of these roles does not constitute "professional fiduciary service," and such service is not "customary to the practice of law."

Burden of Proof

[10] When a lawyer is entrusted with property belonging to others and does not comply with these rules, the burden of proof is on the lawyer to establish the capacity in which the lawyer holds the funds and to demonstrate why these rules should not apply.

Prepaid Legal Fees

[11] Whether a fee that is prepaid by the client should be placed in the trust account depends upon the fee arrangement with the client. A retainer fee in its truest sense is a payment by the client for the reservation of the exclusive services of the lawyer, which is not used to pay for the legal services provided by the lawyer and, by agreement of the parties, is nonrefundable upon discharge of the lawyer. It is a payment to which the lawyer is immediately entitled and, therefore, should not be placed in the trust account. A "retainer," which is actually a deposit by the client of an advance payment of a fee to be billed on an hourly or some other basis, is not a payment to which the lawyer is immediately entitled. This is really a security deposit and should be placed in the trust account. As the lawyer earns the fee or bills against the deposit, the funds should be withdrawn from the account. Rule 1.16(d) requires the refund to the client of any part of a fee that is not earned by the lawyer at the time that the representation is terminated.

Abandoned Property

[12] Should a lawyer need technical assistance concerning the escheat of property to the State of North Carolina, the lawyer should contact the escheat officer at the Office of the North Carolina State Treasurer in Raleigh, North Carolina.

Disputed Funds

[13] A lawyer is not required to remit to the client funds that the lawyer reasonably believes represent fees owed. However, a lawyer may not hold funds to coerce a client into accepting the lawyers's contention. The disputed portion of the funds must be kept in a trust account and the lawyer should suggest means for prompt resolution of the dispute, such as the State Bar's program for fee dispute resolution. See Rule 1.5(f). The undisputed portion of the funds shall be promptly distributed.

[14] Third parties may have lawful claims against specific funds or other property in a lawyer's custody, such as a client's creditor who has a lien on funds recovered in a personal injury action. A lawyer may have a duty under applicable law to protect such third-party claims against wrongful interference by the client. In such cases, when the third-party claim is not frivolous under applicable law, the lawyer must refuse to surrender the property to the client until the claim is resolved. A lawyer should not unilaterally assume to arbitrate a dispute between the client and the third party, but, when there are substantial grounds for dispute as to the person entitled to the funds, the lawyer may file an action to have a court resolve the dispute.

Responsibility for Form of Checks, Records and Accountings

[15] It is the lawyer's responsibility to assure that complete and accurate records of the receipt and disbursement of entrusted property are maintained in accordance with this rule. The required record retention period of six years set forth in this rule does not preclude the State Bar from seeking records for a period prior to the retention period and, if obtained, from pursuing a disciplinary action based thereon if such action is not prohibited by law or other rules of the State Bar.

[16] Many businesses are now converting paper checks to automated clearinghouse (ACH) debits to decrease costs and increase operating efficiencies. When a check is converted, the check is taken either at the point-of-sale or through the mail for payment, the account information is captured from the check, and an electronic transaction is created for payment through the ACH system. The original physical check is typically destroyed by the converting entity (although an image of the check may be stored for a certain period of time). If a check drawn on a trust account is converted to ACH, the lawyer will not receive either the physical check or a check image. The transaction will appear on the lawyer's trust account statement as an ACH debit with limited information about the payment (e.g., dollar amount, date processed, originator of the ACH debit).

[17] To prevent conversion of a check to ACH without authorization, a lawyer is required to use checks with an "Auxiliary On–Us field." A check will not be eligible for conversion to ACH if it contains an Auxiliary On–Us field, which is an additional field that appears in the left-most position of the MICR (magnetic ink character recognition) line on a business size check. The lawyer should confirm with the lawyer's financial institution that the Auxiliary On-Us field is included on the lawyer's trust account checks. Including an Auxiliary On–Us field on the check will require using checks that are longer than six inches. As with the other information in the MICR line of a check, the routing, account and payment numbers, the financial institution issuing the check determines the content of the Auxiliary On–Us field.

[18] Authorized ACH debits that are electronic transfers of funds (in which no checks are involved) are allowed provided the lawyer maintains a record of the transaction as required by Rule 1.15–3(b)(3) and (c)(3). The record, whether consisting of the instructions or authorization to debit the account, a record or receipt from the register of deeds or a financial institution, or the lawyer's independent record of the transaction, must show the amount, date, and recipient of the transfer or disbursement, and, in the case of a general trust account, also show the name of the client or other person to whom the funds belong.

[19] The lawyer is responsible for keeping a client, or any other person to whom the lawyer is accountable, advised of the status of entrusted property held by the lawyer. In addition, the lawyer must take steps to discover any unauthorized transactions involving trust funds as soon as possible. Therefore, it is essential that the lawyer regularly reconcile a general trust account. This means that, at least once a month, the lawyer must reconcile the current bank statement balance with the balance shown for the entire account in the lawyer's records, such as a check register or its equivalent, as of the date of the bank statement. At least once a quarter, the lawyer must reconcile the individual client balances shown on the lawyer's ledger with the current bank statement balance. Monthly reconciliation will help to uncover unauthorized ACH transactions promptly. The current bank balance is the balance obtained when subtracting outstanding checks and other withdrawals from the bank statement balance and adding outstanding deposits to the bank statement balance. With regard to trust funds held in any trust account, there is also an affirmative duty to produce a written accounting for the client and to deliver it to the client, either at the conclusion of the transaction or periodically if funds are held for an appreciable period. Such accountings must be made at least annually or at more frequent intervals if reasonably requested by the client.

Bank Notice of Overdrafts

[20] A properly maintained trust account should not have any items presented against insufficient funds. However, even the best-maintained accounts are subject to inadvertent errors by the bank or the lawyer, which may be easily explained. The reporting requirement should not be burdensome and may help avoid a more serious problem.

Rule 1.15–4 [Reserved]

[Former Rule 1.15–4 rescinded March 6, 2008.]

Rule 1.16 Declining or Terminating Representation

(a) Except as stated in paragraph (c), a lawyer shall not represent a client or, where representation has commenced, shall withdraw from the representation of a client if:

(1) the representation will result in violation of law or the Rules of Professional Conduct;

(2) the lawyer's physical or mental condition materially impairs the lawyer's ability to represent the client; or

(3) the lawyer is discharged.

(b) Except as stated in paragraph (c), a lawyer may withdraw from representing a client if:

(1) withdrawal can be accomplished without material adverse effect on the interests of the client; or

(2) the client knowingly and freely assents to the termination of the representation; or

(3) the client persists in a course of action involving the lawyer's services that the lawyer reasonably believes is criminal or fraudulent; or

(4) the client insists upon taking action that the lawyer considers repugnant, imprudent,-or contrary to the advice and judgment of the lawyer, or with which the lawyer has a fundamental disagreement; or

(5) the client has used the lawyer's services to perpetrate a crime or fraud; or

(6) the client fails substantially to fulfill an obligation to the lawyer regarding the lawyer's services and has been given reasonable warning that the lawyer will withdraw unless the obligation is fulfilled; or

(7) the representation will result in an unreasonable financial burden on the lawyer or has been rendered unreasonably difficult by the client; or

(8) the client insists upon presenting a claim or defense that is not warranted under existing law and cannot be supported by good faith argument for an extension, modification, or reversal of existing law; or

(9) other good cause for withdrawal exists.

(c) A lawyer must comply with applicable law requiring notice to or permission of a tribunal when terminating a representation. When ordered to do so by a tribunal, a lawyer shall continue representation notwithstanding good cause for terminating the representation.

(d) Upon termination of representation, a lawyer shall take steps to the extent reasonably practicable to protect a client's interests, such as giving reasonable notice to the client, allowing time for employment of other counsel, surrendering papers and property to which the client is entitled and refunding any advance payment of fee or expense that has not been earned or

incurred. The lawyer may retain papers relating to the client to the extent permitted by other law.

[Adopted July 27, 1997. Amended February 27, 2003.]

Comment

[1] A lawyer should not accept representation in a matter unless it can be performed competently, promptly, without improper conflict of interest and to completion. Ordinarily, a representation in a matter is completed when the agreed-upon assistance has been concluded. See Rules 1.2(c) and 6.5. See also Rule 1.3. Comment [4].

Mandatory Withdrawal

[2] A lawyer ordinarily must decline or withdraw from representation if the client demands that the lawyer engage in conduct that is illegal or violates the Rules of Professional Conduct or other law. The lawyer is not obliged to decline or withdraw simply because the client suggests such a course of conduct; a client may make such a suggestion in the hope that a lawyer will not be constrained by a professional obligation.

[3] When a lawyer has been appointed to represent a client, withdrawal ordinarily requires approval of the appointing authority. Similarly, court approval or notice to the court is often required by applicable law before a lawyer withdraws from pending litigation. Difficulty may be encountered if withdrawal is based on the client's demand that the lawyer engage in unprofessional conduct. The court may request an explanation for the withdrawal, while the lawyer may be bound to keep confidential the facts that would constitute such an explanation. The lawyer's statement that professional considerations require termination of the representation ordinarily should be accepted as sufficient. Lawyers should be mindful of their obligations to both clients and the court under Rules 1.6 and 3.3.

Discharge

[4] A client has a right to discharge a lawyer at any time, with or without cause, subject to liability for payment for the lawyer's services. Where future dispute about the withdrawal may be anticipated, it may be advisable to prepare a written statement reciting the circumstances.

[5] Whether a client can discharge appointed counsel may depend on applicable law. A client seeking to do so should be given a full explanation of the consequences. These consequences may include a decision by the appointing authority that appointment of successor counsel is unjustified, thus requiring self-representation by the client.

[6] If the client has severely diminished capacity, the client may lack the legal capacity to discharge the lawyer, and in any event the discharge may be seriously adverse to the client's interests. The lawyer should make special effort to help the client consider the consequences and may take reasonably necessary protective action as provided in Rule 1.14.

Optional Withdrawal

[7] A lawyer may withdraw from representation in some circumstances. The lawyer has the option to withdraw if it can be accomplished without material adverse effect on the client's interests. Forfeiture by the client of a substantial financial investment in the representation may have such effect on the client's interests. Withdrawal is also justified if the client persists in a course of action that the lawyer reasonably believes is criminal or fraudulent, for a lawyer is not required to be associated with such conduct even if the lawyer does not further it. Withdrawal is also permitted if the lawyer's services were misused in the past even if that would materially prejudice the client. The lawyer may also withdraw where the client insists on a taking action that the lawyer considers repugnant or imprudent or with which the lawyer has a fundamental disagreement.

[8] A lawyer may withdraw if the client refuses to abide by the terms of an agreement relating to the representation, such as an agreement concerning fees or court costs or an agreement limiting the objectives of the representation.

Assisting the Client upon Withdrawal

[9] Even if the lawyer has been unfairly discharged by the client, a lawyer must take all reasonable steps to mitigate the consequences to the client.

[10] The lawyer may never retain papers to secure a fee. Generally, anything in the file that would be helpful to successor counsel should be turned over. This includes papers and other things delivered to the discharged lawyer by the client such as original instruments, correspondence, and canceled checks. Copies of all correspondence received and generated by the withdrawing or discharged lawyer should be released as well as legal instruments, pleadings, and briefs submitted by either side or prepared and ready for submission. The lawyer's personal notes and incomplete work product need not be released.

[11] A lawyer who represented an indigent on an appeal which has been concluded and who obtained a trial transcript furnished by the state for use in preparing the appeal, must turn over the transcript to the former client upon request, the transcript being property to which the former client is entitled.

Rule 1.17. Sale of a Law Practice

A lawyer or a law firm may sell or purchase a law practice, or an area of law practice, including good will, if the following conditions are satisfied:

(a) The seller ceases to engage in the private practice of law, or in the area of practice that has been sold, from an office that is within a one-hundred (100) mile radius of the purchased law practice, except the seller may continue to practice law with the purchaser and may provide legal representation at no charge to indigent persons or to members of the seller's family;

(b) The entire practice, or the entire area of practice, is sold to one or more lawyers or law firms;

(c) Written notice is sent to each of the seller's clients regarding:

(1) the proposed sale, including the identity of the purchaser;

(2) the client's right to retain other counsel and to take possession of the client's files prior to the sale or at any time thereafter; and

(3) the fact that the client's consent to the transfer of the client's files and legal representation to the purchaser will be presumed if the client does not take any action or does not otherwise object within thirty (30) days of receipt of the notice.

(d) If the seller or the purchaser identifies a conflict of interest that prohibits the purchaser from representing the client, the seller's notice to the client shall advise the client to retain substitute counsel.

(e) If a client cannot be given notice, the representation of that client may be transferred to the purchaser only upon entry of an order so authorizing by a court having jurisdiction. The seller may disclose to the court in camera information relating to the representation only to the extent necessary to obtain an order authorizing the transfer of a file. In the event the court fails to grant a substitution of counsel in a matter, that matter shall not be included in the sale and the sale otherwise shall be unaffected.

(f) The fees charged clients shall not be increased by reason of the sale.

(g) The seller and purchaser may agree that the purchaser does not have to pay the entire sales price for the seller's law practice in one lump sum. The seller and purchaser may enter into reasonable arrangements to finance the purchaser's acquisition of the seller's law practice without violating Rules 1.5(e) and 5.4(a). The seller, however, shall have no say regarding the purchaser's conduct of the law practice.

[Adopted July 24, 1997. Amended February 27, 2003; November 16, 2006; October 2, 2014.]

Comment

[1] The practice of law is a profession, not merely a business. Clients are not commodities that can be purchased and sold at will. Pursuant to this Rule, when a lawyer or an entire firm ceases to practice and other lawyers or firms take over the representation, the selling lawyer or firm may obtain compensation for the reasonable value of the practice as may withdrawing partners of law firms. See Rules 5.4 and 5.6.

Termination of Practice by the Seller

[2] The requirement that all of the private practice be sold is satisfied if the seller in good faith makes the entire practice available for sale to the purchasers. The fact that a number of the seller's clients decide not to be represented by the purchasers but take their matters elsewhere, therefore, does not result in a violation. Return to private practice as a result of an unanticipated change in circumstances does not necessarily result in a violation. For example, a lawyer who has sold the practice to accept an appointment to judicial office does not violate the requirement that the sale be attendant to cessation of practice if the lawyer later resumes private practice upon being defeated in a contested or a retention election for the office.

[3] The requirement that the seller cease to engage in the private practice of law does not prohibit employment as an independent contract lawyer or an employee for the practice. Permitting the seller to continue to work for the practice will assist in the smooth transition of cases and will provide mentoring to new lawyers. The requirement that the seller cease private practice also does not prohibit employment as a lawyer on the staff of a public agency or a legal services entity that provides legal services to the poor, or as in-house counsel to a business. Similarly, the Rule allows the seller to provide *pro bono* representation to indigent persons on his own initiative and to provide legal representation to family members without charge. *See also* 98 Formal Ethics Opinion 6 (1998)(requirements in rule relative to sale of law practice to lawyer who is stranger to the firm do not apply to the sale of law practice to lawyer who is a current employee of firm).

[4] The Rule permits a sale attendant upon discontinuing the private practice of law from an office that is within a one-hundred (100) mile radius of the purchased practice. Its provisions, therefore, accommodate the lawyer who sells the practice upon the occasion of moving to another part of North Carolina or to another state.

Sale of Entire Practice or Entire Area of Practice

[5] The Rule requires that the seller's entire practice, or an entire area of practice, be sold. The prohibition against sale of a less than the entire practice area protects those clients whose matters are less lucrative and who might find it difficult to secure other counsel if a sale could be limited to substantial fee-generating matters. The purchasers are required to undertake all client matters in the practice or practice area, subject to client consent. This requirement is satisfied, however, even if a purchaser is unable to undertake a particular client matter because of a conflict of interest.

Client Confidences, Consent and Notice

[6] Written notice of the proposed sale must be sent to all clients who are currently represented by the seller and to all former clients whose files will be transferred to the purchaser. Although it is not required by this rule, the placement of a notice of the proposed sale in a local newspaper of general circulation would supplement the effort to provide notice to clients as required by paragraph (c) of the rule.

[7] A lawyer or law firm ceasing to practice cannot be required to remain in practice because some clients cannot be given actual notice of the proposed purchase. Since these clients cannot themselves consent to the purchase or direct any other disposition of their files, the Rule requires an order from a court having jurisdiction authorizing their transfer or other disposition. The Court can be expected to determine whether reasonable efforts to locate the client have been exhausted, and whether the absent client's legitimate interests will be served by authorizing the transfer of the file so that the purchaser may continue the representation. Preservation of client confidences requires that the petition for a court order be considered in camera.

[8] Negotiations between seller and prospective purchaser prior to disclosure of information relating to a specific representation of an identifiable client no more violate the confidentiality provisions of Rule 1.6 than do preliminary discussions concerning the possible association of another lawyer or mergers between firms, with respect to which client consent is not required. *See* Rule 1.6(b)(8). Providing the purchaser access to detailed information relating to the representation, such as the client's file, however, requires client consent. The Rule provides that before such information can be disclosed by the seller to the purchaser the client must be given actual written notice of the contemplated sale, including the identity of the purchaser, and must be told that the decision to consent or make other arrangements must be made within 30 days. If nothing is heard from the client within that time, consent to the sale is presumed.

[9] All the elements of client autonomy, including the client's absolute right to discharge a lawyer and transfer the representation to another, survive the sale of the practice. The notice to clients must advise clients that they have a

right to retain a lawyer other than the purchaser. In addition, the notice must inform clients that their right to counsel of their choice continues after the sale even though they consent to the transfer of the representation to the purchaser.

Fee Arrangements Between Client and Purchaser

[10] The sale may not be financed by increases in fees charged the clients of the practice. Existing agreements between the seller and the client as to fees and the scope of the work must be honored by the purchaser.

Other Applicable Ethical Standards

[11] Lawyers participating in the sale of a law practice are subject to the ethical standards applicable to involving another lawyer in the representation of a client. These include, for example, the seller's obligation to exercise competence in identifying a purchaser qualified to assume the practice and the purchaser's obligation to undertake the representation competently (see Rule 1.1); the obligation to avoid disqualifying conflicts, and to secure the client's informed consent for those conflicts that can be agreed to (see Rule 1.7 regarding conflicts and Rule 1.0(e) for the definition of informed consent); and the obligation to protect information relating to the representation (see Rules 1.6 and 1.9).

[12] If approval of the substitution of the purchasing lawyer for the selling lawyer is required by the rules of any tribunal in which a matter is pending, such approval must be obtained before the matter can be included in the sale (see Rule 1.16).

[13] After purchase, the law practice may retain the same name subject to the requirements of Rule 7.5. The seller's retirement or discontinuation of affiliation with the law practice must be indicated on letterhead and other communications as necessary to avoid misleading the public as to the seller's relationship to the law practice. If the seller becomes an independent contract lawyer or employee of the practice, the letterhead and other communications must indicate that the seller is no longer the owner of the firm; an "of counsel" designation would be sufficient to do so.

Applicability of the Rule

[14] This Rule applies to the sale of a law practice by representatives of a deceased, disabled or disappeared lawyer. Thus, the seller may be represented by a non-lawyer representative not subject to these Rules. Since, however, no lawyer may participate in a sale of a law practice which does not conform to the requirements of this Rule, the representatives of the seller as well as the purchasing lawyer can be expected to see to it that they are met.

[15] Admission to or retirement from a law partnership or professional association, retirement plans and similar arrangements, and a sale of tangible assets of a law practice, do not constitute a sale or purchase governed by this Rule.

[16] This Rule does not apply to the transfers of legal representation between lawyers when such transfers are unrelated to the sale of a practice.

Rule 1.18. Duties to Prospective Client

(a) A person who consults with a lawyer about the possibility of forming a client-lawyer relationship with respect to a matter is a prospective client.

(b) Even when no client-lawyer relationship ensues, a lawyer who has learned information from a prospective client shall not use or reveal that information, except as Rule 1.9 would permit with respect to information of a former client.

(c) A lawyer subject to paragraph (b) shall not represent a client with interests materially adverse to those of a prospective client in the same or a substantially related matter if the lawyer received information from the prospective client that could be significantly harmful to that person in the matter, except as provided in paragraph (d). If a lawyer is disqualified from representation under this paragraph, no lawyer in a firm with which that lawyer is associated may knowingly undertake or continue representation in such a matter, except as provided in paragraph (d).

(d) Representation is permissible if both the affected client and the prospective client have given informed consent, confirmed in writing, or:

(1) the disqualified lawyer is timely screened from any participation in the matter; and

(2) written notice is promptly given to the prospective client.

[Adopted February 27, 2003. Amended October 2, 2014.]

Comment

[1] Prospective clients, like clients, may disclose information to a lawyer, place documents or other property in the lawyer's custody, or rely on the lawyer's advice. A lawyer's consultations with a prospective client usually are limited in time and depth and leave both the prospective client and the lawyer free (and sometimes required) to proceed no further. Hence, prospective clients should receive some but not all of the protection afforded clients.

[2] A person becomes a prospective client by consulting with a lawyer about the possibility of forming a client-lawyer relationship with respect to a matter. Whether communications, including written, oral, or electronic communications, constitute a consultation depends on the circumstances. For example, a consultation is likely to have occurred if a lawyer, either in person or through the lawyer's advertising in any medium, specifically requests or invites the submission of information about a potential representation without clear and reasonably understandable warnings and cautionary statements that limit the lawyer's obligations, and a person provides information in response. In such a situation, to avoid the creation of a duty to the person under this Rule, a lawyer has an affirmative obligation to warn the person that a communication with the lawyer will not create a client-lawyer relationship and information conveyed to the lawyer will not be confidential or privileged. *See also* Comment [4]. In contrast, a consultation does not occur if a person provides information to a lawyer in response to advertising that merely describes the lawyer's education, experience, areas of practice, and contact information, or provides legal information of general interest. Such a person is communicating information unilaterally to a lawyer, without any reasonable expectation that the lawyer is willing to discuss the possibility of forming a client-lawyer relationship, and is thus not a "prospective client". Moreover, a person who communicates with a lawyer for the purpose of disqualifying the lawyer is not a "prospective client."

[3] It is often necessary for a prospective client to reveal information to the lawyer during an initial consultation prior to the decision about formation of a client-lawyer relationship. The lawyer often must learn such information to determine whether there is a conflict of interest with an existing client and whether the matter is one that the lawyer is willing to undertake. Paragraph (b) prohibits the lawyer from using or revealing that information, except as permitted by Rule 1.9, even if the client or lawyer decides not to proceed with the representation. The duty exists regardless of how brief the initial conference may be.

[4] In order to avoid acquiring disqualifying information from a prospective client, a lawyer considering whether or not to undertake a new matter should limit the initial consultation to only such information as reasonably appears necessary for that purpose. Where the information indicates that a conflict of interest or other reason for non-representation exists, the lawyer should so inform the prospective client or decline the representation. If the prospective client wishes to retain the lawyer, and if consent is possible under Rule 1.7, then consent from all affected present or former clients must be obtained before accepting the representation.

[5] A lawyer may condition a consultation with a prospective client on the person's informed consent that no information disclosed during the consultation will prohibit the lawyer from representing a different client in the matter. *See* Rule 1.0(f) for the definition of informed consent. If the agreement expressly so provides, the prospective client may also consent to the lawyer's subsequent use of information received from the prospective client.

[6] Even in the absence of an agreement, under paragraph (c), the lawyer is not prohibited from representing a client with interests adverse to those of the prospective client in the same or a substantially related matter unless the lawyer has received from the prospective client information that could be significantly harmful if used in the matter.

[7] Under paragraph (c), the prohibition in this Rule is imputed to other lawyers as provided in Rule 1.10, but, under paragraph (d), imputation may be avoided if the lawyer obtains the informed consent, confirmed in writing, of both the prospective and affected clients. In the alternative, imputation may be avoided if all disqualified lawyers are timely screened and written notice is promptly given to the prospective client. See Rule 1.0(k) (requirements for screening procedures). Paragraph (d)(1) does not prohibit the screened lawyer from receiving a salary or partnership share established by prior independent agreement, nor does it specifically prohibit the receipt of a part of the fee from the screened matter. However, Rule 8.4(c) prohibits the screened lawyer from participating in the fee if such participation was impliedly or explicitly offered as an inducement to the lawyer to become associated with the firm.

[8] Notice, including a description of the screened lawyer's prior representation and of the screening procedures employed, generally should be given as soon as practicable after the need for screening becomes apparent. When disclosure is likely to significantly injure the client, a reasonable delay may be justified.

[9] For the duty of competence of a lawyer who gives assistance on the merits of a matter to a prospective client, see Rule 1.1. For a lawyer's duties when a prospective client entrusts valuables or papers to the lawyer's care, see Rule 1.15. For the special considerations when a prospective client has diminished capacity, see Rule 1.14.

Rule 1.19 Sexual Relations with Clients Prohibited

(a) A lawyer shall not have sexual relations with a current client of the lawyer.

(b) Paragraph (a) shall not apply if a consensual sexual relationship existed between the lawyer and the client before the legal representation commenced.

(c) A lawyer shall not require or demand sexual relations with a client incident to or as a condition of any professional representation.

(d) For purposes of this rule, "sexual relations" means:

(1) Sexual intercourse; or

(2) Any touching of the sexual or other intimate parts of a person or causing such person to touch the sexual or other intimate parts of the lawyer for the purpose of arousing or gratifying the sexual desire of either party.

(e) For purposes of this rule, "lawyer" means any lawyer who assists in the representation of the client but does not include other lawyers in a firm who provide no such assistance.

[Adopted July 24, 1997. Amended February 27, 2003.]

Comment

[1] Rule 1.17, the general rule on conflict of interest, has always prohibited a lawyer from representing a client when the lawyer's ability to competently represent the client may be impaired by the lawyer's other personal or professional commitments. Under the general rule on conflicts and the rule on prohibited transactions (Rule 1.8), relationships with clients, whether personal or financial, that affect a lawyer's ability to exercise his or her independent professional judgment on behalf of a client are closely scrutinized. The rules on conflict of interest have always prohibited the representation of a client if a sexual relationship with the client presents a significant danger to the lawyer's ability to represent the client adequately. The present rule clarifies that a sexual relationship with a client is damaging to the lawyer-client relationship and creates an impermissible conflict of interest which cannot be ameliorated by the consent of the client.

Exploitation of the Lawyer's Fiduciary Position

[2] The relationship between a lawyer and client is a fiduciary relationship in which the lawyer occupies the highest position of trust and confidence. The relationship is also inherently unequal. The client comes to a lawyer with a problem and puts his or her faith in the lawyer's special knowledge, skills, and ability to solve the client's problem. The same factors that lead the client to place his or her trust and reliance in the lawyer also have the potential to place the lawyer in a position of dominance and the client in a position of vulnerability.

[3] A sexual relationship between a lawyer and a client may involve unfair exploitation of the lawyer's fiduciary position. Because of the dependence that so often characterizes the attorney-client relationship, there is a significant possibility that a sexual relationship with a client resulted from the exploitation of the lawyer's dominant position and

influence. Moreover, if a lawyer permits the otherwise benign and even recommended client reliance and trust to become the catalyst for a sexual relationship with a client, the lawyer violates one of the most basic ethical obligations, i.e., not to use the trust of the client to the client's disadvantage. This same principle underlies the rules prohibiting the use of client confidences to the disadvantage of the client and the rules that seek to ensure that lawyers do not take financial advantage of their clients. (See Rule 1.6 and Rule 1.8.)

Impairment of the Ability to Represent the Client Competently

[4] A lawyer must maintain his or her ability to represent a client dispassionately and without impairment to the exercise of independent professional judgment on behalf of the client. The existence of a sexual relationship between lawyer and client under the circumstances proscribed by this rule presents a significant danger that the lawyer's ability to represent the client competently may be adversely affected because of the lawyer's emotional involvement. This emotional involvement has the potential to undercut the objective detachment that is demanded for adequate representation. A sexual relationship also creates the risk that the lawyer will be subject to a conflict of interest. For example, a lawyer who is sexually involved with his or her client risks becoming an adverse witness to his or her own client in a divorce action where there are issues of adultery and child custody to resolve. Finally, a blurred line between the professional and personal relationship may make it difficult to predict to what extent client confidences will be protected by the attorney-client privilege in the law of evidence since client confidences are protected by privilege only when they are imparted in the context of the attorney-client relationship.

No Prejudice to Client

[5] The prohibition upon representing a client with whom a sexual relationship develops applies regardless of the absence of a showing of prejudice to the client and regardless of whether the relationship is consensual.

Prior Consensual Relationship

[6] Sexual relationships that predate the lawyer-client relationship are not prohibited. Issues relating to the exploitation of the fiduciary relationship and client dependency are not present when the sexual relationship exists prior to the commencement of the lawyer-client relationship. However, before proceeding with the representation in these circumstances, the lawyer should be confident that his or her ability to represent the client competently will not be impaired.

No Imputed Disqualification

[7] The other lawyers in a firm are not disqualified from representing a client with whom the lawyer has become intimate. The potential impairment of the lawyer's ability to exercise independent professional judgment on behalf of the client with whom he or she is having a sexual relationship is specific to that lawyer's representation of the client and is unlikely to affect the ability of other members of the firm to competently and dispassionately represent the client.

COUNSELOR

Rule 2.1 Advisor

In representing a client, a lawyer shall exercise independent, professional judgment and render candid advice. In rendering advice, a lawyer may refer not only to law, but also to other considerations such as moral, economic, social, and political factors that may be relevant to the client's situation.

[Adopted July 24, 1997. Amended February 27, 2003.]

Comment

Scope of Advice

[1] A client is entitled to straightforward advice expressing the lawyer's honest assessment. Legal advice often involves unpleasant facts and alternatives that a client may be disinclined to confront. In presenting advice, a lawyer endeavors to sustain the client's morale and may put advice in as acceptable a form as honesty permits. However, a lawyer should not be deterred from giving candid advice by the prospect that the advice will be unpalatable to the client.

[2] Advice couched in narrow legal terms may be of little value to a client, especially where practical considerations such as cost or effects on other people are predominant. Purely technical legal advice, therefore, can sometimes be inadequate. It is proper for a lawyer to refer to relevant moral and ethical considerations in giving advice. Although a lawyer is not a moral advisor as such, moral and ethical considerations impinge upon most legal questions and may decisively influence how the law will be applied.

[3] A client may expressly or impliedly ask the lawyer for purely technical advice. When such a request is made by a client experienced in legal matters, the lawyer may accept it at face value. When such a request is made by a client inexperienced in legal matters, however, the lawyer's responsibility as advisor may include indicating that more may be involved than strictly legal considerations.

[4] Matters that go beyond strictly legal questions may also be in the domain of another profession. Family matters can involve problems within the professional competence of psychiatry, clinical psychology, or social work; business matters can involve problems within the competence of the accounting profession or of financial specialists. Where consultation with a professional in another field is itself something a competent lawyer would recommend, the lawyer should make such a recommendation. At the same time, a lawyer's advice at its best often consists of recommending a course of action in the face of conflicting recommendations of experts.

Offering Advice

[5] In general, a lawyer is not expected to give advice until asked by the client. However, when a lawyer knows that a client proposes a course of action that is likely to result in substantial adverse legal consequences to the client, the lawyer's duty to the client under Rule 1.4 may require that the lawyer offer advice if the client's course of action is related to the representation. Similarly, when a matter is likely to involve litigation, it may be necessary under Rule 1.4 to inform the client of forms of dispute resolution that might constitute reasonable alternatives to litigation. A

lawyer ordinarily has no duty to initiate investigation of a client's affairs or to give advice that the client has indicated is unwanted, but a lawyer may initiate advice to a client when doing so appears to be in the client's interest.

Rule 2.2 [Reserved]

[Former Rule 2.2 rescinded February 27, 2003.]

Rule 2.3 Evaluation for Use by Third Persons

(a) A lawyer may undertake an evaluation of a matter affecting a client for the use of someone other than the client if:

(1) the lawyer reasonably believes that making the evaluation is compatible with other aspects of the lawyer's relationship with the client; and

(2) the client so requests or the client consents after consultation

(b) Except as disclosure is required in connection with a report of an evaluation, information relating to the evaluation is otherwise protected by Rule 1.6.

[Adopted July 24, 1997. Amended February 17, 2003.]

Comment

Definition

[1] An evaluation may be performed at the client's direction but for the primary purpose of establishing information for the benefit of third parties; for example, an opinion concerning the title of property rendered at the behest of a vendor for the information of a prospective purchaser, or at the behest of a borrower for the information of a prospective lender. In some situations, the evaluation may be required by a government agency; for example, an opinion concerning the legality of the securities registered for sale under the securities laws. In other instances, the evaluation may be required by a third person, such as a purchaser of a business.

[2] A legal evaluation should be distinguished from an investigation of a person with whom the lawyer does not have a client-lawyer relationship. For example, a lawyer retained by a purchaser to analyze a vendor's title to property does not have a client-lawyer relationship with the vendor. So also, an investigation into a person's affairs by a government lawyer, or by special counsel by a government lawyer, or by special counsel employed by the government, is not an evaluation as that term is used in this Rule. The question is whether the lawyer is retained by the person whose affairs are being examined. When the lawyer is retained by that person, the general rules concerning loyalty to client and preservation of confidences apply, which is not the case if the lawyer is retained by someone else. For this reason, it is essential to identify the person by whom the lawyer is retained. This should be made clear not only to the person under examination, but also to others to whom the results are to be made available.

Duty to Third Person

[3] When the evaluation is intended for the information or use of a third person, a legal duty to that person may or may not arise. That legal question is beyond the scope of this Rule. However, since such an evaluation involves a departure from the normal client-lawyer relationship, careful analysis of the situation is required. The lawyer must be satisfied as a matter of professional judgment that making the evaluation is compatible with other functions undertaken in behalf of the client. For example, if the lawyer is acting as advocate in defending the client against charges of fraud, it would normally be incompatible with that responsibility for the lawyer to perform an evaluation for others concerning the same or a related transaction. Assuming no such impediment is apparent, however, the lawyer should advise the client of the implications of the evaluation, particularly the lawyer's responsibilities to third persons and the duty to disseminate the findings.

Access to and Disclosure of Information

[4] The quality of an evaluation depends on the freedom and extent of the investigation upon which it is based. Ordinarily a lawyer should have whatever latitude of investigation seems necessary as a matter of professional judgment. Under some circumstances, however, the terms of the evaluation may be limited. For example, certain issues or sources may be categorically excluded, or the scope of search may be limited by time constraints or the noncooperation of persons having relevant information. Any such limitations that are material to the evaluation should be described in the report. If after a lawyer has commenced an evaluation, the client refuses to comply with the terms upon which it was understood the evaluation was to have been made, the lawyer's obligations are determined by law, having reference to the terms of the client's agreement and the surrounding circumstances.

Financial Auditors' Requests for Information

[5] When a question concerning the legal situation of a client arises at the instance of the client's financial auditor and the question is referred to the lawyer, the lawyer's response may be made in accordance with procedures recognized in the legal profession. Such a procedure is set forth in the American Bar Association Statement of Policy Regarding Lawyers' Responses to Auditors' Requests for Information, adopted in 1975.

Rule 2.4 Lawyer Serving as Third-Party Neutral

(a) A lawyer serves as a third-party neutral when the lawyer assists two or more persons who are not clients of the lawyer to reach a resolution of a dispute or other matter that has arisen between them. Service as a third-party neutral may include service as an arbitrator, a mediator or in such other capacity as will enable the lawyer to assist the parties to resolve the matter.

(b) A lawyer serving as a third-party neutral shall inform unrepresented parties that the lawyer is not representing them. When the lawyer knows or reasonably should know that a party does not understand the lawyer's role in the matter, the lawyer shall explain the difference between the lawyer's role as a third-party neutral and a lawyer's role as one who represents a client.

[Adopted February 27, 2003.]

Comment

[1] Alternative dispute resolution has become a substantial part of the civil justice system. Aside from representing clients in dispute-resolution processes, lawyers often serve as third-party neutrals. A third-party neutral is a person, such as a mediator, arbitrator, conciliator or evaluator, who assists the parties, represented or unrepresented, in the resolution of a dispute or in the arrangement of a transaction. Whether a third-party neutral serves primarily as a facilitator, evaluator or decisionmaker depends on the particular process that is either selected by the parties or mandated by a court.

[2] The role of a third-party neutral is not unique to lawyers, although, in some court-connected contexts, only lawyers are allowed to serve in this role or to handle certain types of cases. In performing this role, the lawyer may be subject to court rules or other law that apply either to third-party neutrals generally or to lawyers serving as third-party neutrals. Lawyer–neutrals may also be subject to various codes of ethics, such as the Rules of the North Carolina Supreme Court for the Dispute Resolution Commission and the North Carolina Canons of Ethics for Arbitrators.

[3] Unlike nonlawyers who serve as third-party neutrals, lawyers serving in this role may experience unique problems as a result of differences between the role of a third-party neutral and a lawyer's service as a client representative. The potential for confusion is significant when the parties are unrepresented in the process. Thus, paragraph (b) requires a lawyer-neutral to inform unrepresented parties that the lawyer is not representing them. For some parties, particularly parties who frequently use dispute-resolution processes, this information will be sufficient. For others, particularly those who are using the process for the first time, more information will be required. Where appropriate, the lawyer should inform unrepresented parties of the important differences between the lawyer's role as third-party neutral and a lawyer's role as a client representative, including the inapplicability of the attorney-client evidentiary privilege. The extent of disclosure required under this paragraph will depend on the particular parties involved and the subject matter of the proceeding, as well as the particular features of the dispute-resolution process selected.

[4] A lawyer who serves as a third-party neutral subsequently may be asked to serve as a lawyer representing a client in the same matter. The conflicts of interest that arise for both the individual lawyer and the lawyer's law firm are addressed in Rule 1.12.

[5] Lawyers who represent clients in alternative dispute-resolution processes are governed by the Rules of Professional Conduct. When the dispute-resolution process takes place before a tribunal, as in binding arbitration (see Rule 1.0(m)), the lawyer's duty of candor is governed by Rule 3.3. Otherwise, the lawyer's duty of candor toward both the third-party neutral and other parties is governed by Rule 4.1.

ADVOCATE

Rule 3.1 Meritorious Claims and Contentions

A lawyer shall not bring or defend a proceeding, or assert or controvert an issue therein, unless there is a basis in law and fact for doing so that is not frivolous, which includes a good faith argument for an extension, modification or reversal of existing law. A lawyer for the defendant in a criminal proceeding, or the respondent in a proceeding that could result in incarceration, may nevertheless so defend the proceeding as to require that every element of the case be established.

[Adopted July 24, 1997. Amended February 27, 2003.]

Comment

[1] The advocate has a duty to use legal procedure for the fullest benefit of the client's cause, but also a duty not to abuse legal procedure. The law, both procedural and substantive, establishes the limits within which an advocate may proceed. However, the law is not always clear and never is static. Accordingly, in determining the proper scope of advocacy, account must be taken of the law's ambiguities and potential for change.

[2] The filing of an action or defense or similar action taken for a client is not frivolous merely because the facts have not first been fully substantiated or because the lawyer expects to develop vital evidence only by discovery. What is required of lawyers, however, is that they inform themselves about the facts of their clients' cases and the applicable law and determine that they can make good faith arguments in support of their clients' positions. Such action is not frivolous even though the lawyer believes that the client's position ultimately will not prevail. The action is frivolous, however, if the lawyer is unable either to make a good faith argument on the merits of the action taken or to support the action taken by a good faith argument for an extension, modification or reversal of existing law.

[3] The lawyer's obligations under this Rule are subordinate to federal or state constitutional law that entitles a defendant in a criminal matter to the assistance of counsel in presenting a claim that otherwise would be prohibited by this Rule.

Rule 3.2 Expediting Litigation

A lawyer shall make reasonable efforts to expedite litigation consistent with the interests of the client.

[Adopted July 24, 1997. Amended February 27, 2003.]

Comment

[1] Dilatory practices bring the administration of justice into disrepute. Although there will be occasions when a lawyer may properly seek a postponement for personal reasons, it is not proper for a lawyer to routinely fail to expedite litigation solely for the convenience of the advocates. Nor will a failure to expedite be reasonable if done for the purpose of frustrating an opposing party's attempt to obtain rightful redress or repose. It is not a justification that similar conduct is often tolerated by the bench and bar. The question is whether a competent lawyer acting in good faith would regard the course of action as having some substantial purpose other than delay. Realizing financial or other benefit from otherwise improper delay in litigation is not a legitimate interest of the client.

Rule 3.3 Candor Toward the Tribunal

(a) A lawyer shall not knowingly:

(1) make a false statement of material fact or law to a tribunal or fail to correct a false statement of material fact or law previously made to the tribunal by the lawyer;

(2) fail to disclose to the tribunal legal authority in the controlling jurisdiction known to the lawyer to be directly adverse to the position of the client and not disclosed by opposing counsel; or

(3) offer evidence that the lawyer knows to be false. If a lawyer, the lawyer's client, or a witness called by the lawyer, has offered material evidence and the lawyer comes to know of its falsity, the lawyer shall take reasonable remedial measures, including, if necessary, disclosure to the tribunal. A lawyer may refuse to offer evidence, other than the testimony of a defendant in a criminal matter, that the lawyer reasonably believes is false.

(b) A lawyer who represents a client in an adjudicative proceeding and who knows that a person intends to engage, is engaging or has engaged in criminal or fraudulent conduct related to the proceeding shall take reasonable remedial measures, including, if necessary, disclosure to the tribunal.

(c) The duties stated in paragraphs (a) and (b) continue to the conclusion of the proceeding, and apply even if compliance requires disclosure of information otherwise protected by Rule 1.6.

(d) In an ex parte proceeding, a lawyer shall inform the tribunal of all material facts known to the lawyer that will enable the tribunal to make an informed decision, whether or not the facts are adverse.

[Adopted July 24, 1997. Amended February 27, 2003.]

Comment

[1] This Rule governs the conduct of a lawyer who is representing a client in the proceedings of a tribunal. See Rule 1.0(m) for the definition of "tribunal." It also applies when the lawyer is representing a client in an ancillary proceeding conducted pursuant to the tribunal's adjudicative authority, such as a deposition. Thus, for example, paragraph (a)(3) requires a lawyer to take reasonable remedial measures if the lawyer comes to know that a client who is testifying in a deposition has offered evidence that is false.

[2] This Rule sets forth the special duties of lawyers as officers of the court to avoid conduct that undermines the integrity of the adjudicative process. A lawyer acting as an advocate in an adjudicative proceeding has an obligation to present the client's case with persuasive force. Performance of that duty while maintaining confidences of the client, however, is qualified by the advocate's duty of candor to the tribunal. Consequently, although a lawyer in an adjudicative proceeding is not required to present an impartial exposition of the law or to vouch for the evidence submitted in a cause, the lawyer must not allow the tribunal to be misled by false statements of material fact or law or evidence that the lawyer knows to be false.

Representations by a Lawyer

[3] An advocate is responsible for pleadings and other documents prepared for litigation, but is usually not required to have personal knowledge of matters asserted therein, for litigation documents ordinarily present assertions by the client, or by someone on the client's behalf, and not assertions by the lawyer. Compare Rule 3.1. However, an assertion purporting to be on the lawyer's own knowledge, as in an affidavit by the lawyer or in a statement in open court, may properly be made only when the lawyer knows the assertion is true or believes it to be true on the basis of a reasonably diligent inquiry. There are circumstances where failure to make a disclosure is the equivalent of an affirmative misrepresentation. The obligation prescribed in Rule 1.2(d) not to counsel a client to commit or assist the client in committing a fraud applies in litigation. Regarding compliance with Rule 1.2(d), see the Comment to that Rule. See also the Comment to Rule 8.4(b).

Legal Argument

[4] Legal argument based on a knowingly false representation of law constitutes dishonesty toward the tribunal. A lawyer is not required to make a disinterested exposition of the law, but must recognize the existence of pertinent legal authorities. Furthermore, as stated in paragraph (a)(2), an advocate has a duty to disclose directly adverse authority in the controlling jurisdiction that has not been disclosed by the opposing party. The underlying concept is that legal argument is a discussion seeking to determine the legal premises properly applicable to the case.

Offering Evidence

[5] Paragraph (a)(3) requires that the lawyer refuse to offer evidence that the lawyer knows to be false, regardless of the client's wishes. This duty is premised on the lawyer's obligation as an officer of the court to prevent the trier of fact from being misled by false evidence. A lawyer does not violate this Rule if the lawyer offers the evidence for the purpose of establishing its falsity.

[6] If a lawyer knows that the client intends to testify falsely or wants the lawyer to introduce false evidence, the lawyer should seek to persuade the client that the evidence should not be offered. If the persuasion is ineffective and the lawyer continues to represent the client, the lawyer must refuse to offer the false evidence. If only a portion of a witness's testimony will be false, the lawyer may call the witness to testify but may not elicit or otherwise permit the witness to present the testimony that the lawyer knows is false.

[7] The duties stated in paragraphs (a) and (b) apply to all lawyers, including defense counsel in criminal cases. See Comment [9].

[8] The prohibition against offering false evidence only applies if the lawyer knows that the evidence is false. A lawyer's reasonable belief that evidence is false does not preclude its presentation to the trier of fact. A lawyer's knowledge that evidence is false, however, can be inferred from the circumstances. See Rule 1.0(f). Thus, although a lawyer should resolve doubts about the veracity of testimony or other evidence in favor of the client, the lawyer cannot ignore an obvious falsehood.

[9] Although paragraph (a)(3) only prohibits a lawyer from offering evidence the lawyer knows to be false, it permits the lawyer to refuse to offer testimony or other proof that the lawyer reasonably believes is false. Offering such proof may reflect adversely on the lawyer's ability to discriminate in the quality of evidence and thus impair the lawyer's effectiveness

as an advocate. Because of the special protections historically provided criminal defendants, however, this Rule does not permit a lawyer to refuse to offer the testimony of such a client where the lawyer reasonably believes but does not know that the testimony will be false. Unless the lawyer knows the testimony will be false, the lawyer must honor the client's decision to testify. See also Comment [7].

Remedial Measures

[10] Having offered material evidence in the belief that it was true, a lawyer may subsequently come to know that the evidence is false. Or, a lawyer may be surprised when the lawyer's client, or another witness called by the lawyer, offers testimony the lawyer knows to be false, either during the lawyer's direct examination or in response to cross-examination by the opposing lawyer. In such situations or if the lawyer knows of the falsity of testimony elicited from the client during a deposition, the lawyer must take reasonable remedial measures. The lawyer's action must also be seasonable: depending upon the circumstances, reasonable remedial measures do not have to be undertaken immediately, however, the lawyer must act before a third party relies to his or her detriment upon the false testimony or evidence. The advocate's proper course is to remonstrate with the client confidentially, advise the client of the lawyer's duty of candor to the tribunal and seek the client's cooperation with respect to the withdrawal or correction of the false statements or evidence. If that fails, the advocate should seek to withdraw if that will remedy the situation. If withdrawal from the representation is not permitted or will not undo the effect of the false evidence, the advocate's only option may be to make such disclosure to the tribunal as is reasonably necessary to remedy the situation, even if doing so requires the lawyer to reveal information that otherwise would be protected by Rule 1.6. It is for the tribunal then to determine what should be done — making a statement about the matter to the trier of fact, ordering a mistrial or perhaps nothing.

[11] The disclosure of a client's false testimony can result in grave consequences to the client, including not only a sense of betrayal but also loss of the case and perhaps a prosecution for perjury. But the alternative is that the lawyer cooperate in deceiving the court, thereby subverting the truth-finding process which the adversary system is designed to implement. See Rule 1.2(d). Furthermore, unless it is clearly understood that the lawyer will act upon the duty to disclose the existence of false evidence, the client can simply reject the lawyer's advice to reveal the false evidence and insist that the lawyer keep silent. Thus the client could in effect coerce the lawyer into being a party to fraud on the court.

Preserving Integrity of Adjudicative Process

[12] Lawyers have a special obligation to protect a tribunal against criminal or fraudulent conduct that undermines the integrity of the adjudicative process, such as bribing, intimidating or otherwise unlawfully communicating with a witness, juror, court official or other participant in the proceeding, unlawfully destroying or concealing documents or other evidence or failing to disclose information to the tribunal when required by law to do so. Thus, paragraph (b) requires a lawyer to take reasonable remedial measures, including disclosure if necessary, whenever the lawyer knows that a person, including the lawyer's client, intends to engage, is engaging or has engaged in criminal or fraudulent conduct related to the proceeding.

Constitutional Requirements

[13] The general rule that an advocate must reveal the existence of perjury with respect to a material fact—even that of a client—applies to defense counsel in criminal cases, as well as in other instances. However, the definition of the lawyer's ethical duty in such a situation may be qualified by constitutional provisions for due process and the right to counsel in criminal cases. These provisions have been construed to require that counsel present an accused as a witness if the accused wishes to testify, even if counsel knows the testimony will be false. The obligation of the advocate under these Rules is subordinate to such a constitutional requirement.

Duration of Obligation

[14] A practical time limit on the obligation to rectify false evidence or false statements of material fact or law has to be established. The conclusion of the proceeding is a reasonably definite point for the termination of the obligation. A proceeding has concluded within the meaning of this Rule when no matters in the proceeding are still pending before the tribunal or the proceeding has concluded pursuant to the rules of the tribunal such as when a final judgment in the proceeding is affirmed on appeal, a bankruptcy case is closed, or the time for review has passed.

Ex Parte Proceedings

[15] Ordinarily, an advocate has the limited responsibility of presenting one side of the matters that a tribunal should consider in reaching a decision; the conflicting position is expected to be presented by the opposing party. However, in any ex parte proceeding, such as an application for a temporary restraining order, there is no balance of presentation by opposing advocates. The object of an ex parte proceeding is nevertheless to yield a substantially just result. The judge has an affirmative responsibility to accord the absent party just consideration. The lawyer for the represented party has the correlative duty to make disclosures of material facts known to the lawyer and that the lawyer reasonably believes are necessary to an informed decision.

Withdrawal

[16] Normally, a lawyer's compliance with the duty of candor imposed by this Rule does not require that the lawyer withdraw from the representation of a client whose interests will be or have been adversely affected by the lawyer's disclosure. The lawyer may, however, be required by Rule 1.16(a) to seek permission of the tribunal to withdraw if the lawyer's compliance with this Rule's duty of candor results in such an extreme deterioration of the client-lawyer relationship that the lawyer can no longer competently represent the client. Also see Rule 1.16(b) for the circumstances in which a lawyer will be permitted to seek a tribunal's permission to withdraw. In connection with a request for permission to withdraw that is premised on a client's misconduct, a lawyer may reveal information relating to the representation only to the extent reasonably necessary to comply with this Rule or as otherwise permitted by Rule 1.6.

Rule 3.4 Fairness to Opposing Party and Counsel

A lawyer shall not:

(a) unlawfully obstruct another party's access to evidence or unlawfully alter, destroy or conceal a document or other material having potential evidentiary value. A lawyer shall not counsel or assist another person to do any such act;

(b) falsify evidence, counsel or assist a witness to testify falsely, counsel or assist a witness to hide or leave the jurisdiction for the purpose of being unavailable as a witness, or offer an inducement to a witness that is prohibited by law;

(c) knowingly disobey or advise a client or any other person to disobey an obligation under the rules of a tribunal, except a lawyer acting in good faith may take appropriate steps to test the validity of such a an obligation;

(d) in pretrial procedure,

(1) make a frivolous discovery request,

(2) fail to make a reasonably diligent effort to comply with a legally proper discovery request by an opposing party or

(3) fail to disclose evidence or information that the lawyer knew, or reasonably should have known, was subject to disclosure under applicable law, rules of procedure or evidence, or court opinions;

(e) in trial, allude to any matter that the lawyer does not reasonably believe is relevant or that will not be supported by admissible evidence, assert personal knowledge of facts in issue except when testifying as a witness, ask an irrelevant question that is intended to degrade a witness, or state a personal opinion as to the justness of a cause, the credibility of a witness, the culpability of a civil litigant, or the guilt or innocence of an accused; or

(f) request a person other than a client to refrain from voluntarily giving relevant information to another party unless:

(1) the person is a relative or a managerial employee or other agent of a client; and

(2) the lawyer reasonably believes that the person's interests will not be adversely affected by refraining from giving such information.

[Adopted July 24, 1997. Amended February 27, 2003; amended effective October 1, 2003; amended effective November 16, 2006.]

Comment

[1] The procedure of the adversary system contemplates that the evidence in a case is to be marshalled competitively by the contending parties. Fair competition in the adversary system is secured by prohibitions against destruction or concealment of evidence, improperly influencing witnesses, obstructive tactics in discovery procedure, and the like.

[2] Documents and other items of evidence are often essential to establish a claim or defense. Subject to evidentiary privileges, the right of an opposing party, including the government, to obtain evidence through discovery or subpoena is an important procedural right. The exercise of that right can be frustrated if relevant material is altered, concealed or destroyed. Applicable law in many jurisdictions makes it an offense to destroy material for purpose of impairing its availability in a pending proceeding or one whose commencement can be foreseen. Falsifying evidence is also generally a criminal offense. Paragraph (a) applies to evidentiary material generally, including computerized information. Applicable law may permit a lawyer to take temporary possession of physical evidence of client crimes for the purpose of conducting a limited examination that will not alter or destroy material characteristics of the evidence. In such a case, applicable law may require the lawyer to turn the evidence over to the police or other prosecuting authority, depending on the circumstances.

[3] With regard to paragraph (b), it is not improper to pay a witness's expenses, including lost income, or to compensate an expert witness on terms permitted by law. The common law rule in most jurisdictions is that it is improper to pay an occurrence witness any fee for testifying and that it is improper to pay an expert witness a contingent fee.

[4] Rules of evidence and procedure are designed to lead to just decisions and are part of the framework of the law. Paragraph (c) permits a lawyer to take steps in good faith and within the framework of the law to test the validity of rules; however, the lawyer is not justified in consciously violating such rules and the lawyer should be diligent in the effort to guard against the unintentional violation of them. As examples, a lawyer should subscribe to or verify only those pleadings that the lawyer believes are in compliance with applicable law and rules; a lawyer should not make any prefatory statement before a tribunal in regard to the purported facts of the case on trial unless the lawyer believes that the statement will be supported by admissible evidence; a lawyer should not ask a witness a question solely for the purpose of harassing or embarrassing the witness; and a lawyer should not, by subterfuge, put before a jury matters which it cannot properly consider.

[5] Paragraph (d) makes it clear that a lawyer must be reasonably diligent in making inquiry of the client, or third party, about information or documents responsive to discovery requests or disclosure requirements arising from statutory law, rules of procedure, or caselaw. "Reasonably" is defined in Rule 0.1, *Terminology*, as meaning "conduct of a reasonably prudent and competent lawyer." Rule 0.1(i). When responding to a discovery request or disclosure requirement, a lawyer must act in good faith. The lawyer should impress upon the client the importance of making a thorough search of the client's records and responding honestly. If the lawyer has reason to believe that a client has not been forthcoming, the lawyer may not rely solely upon the client's assertion that the response is truthful or complete.

[6] To bring about just and informed decisions, evidentiary and procedural rules have been established by tribunals to permit the inclusion of relevant evidence and argument and the exclusion of all other considerations. The expression by a lawyer of a personal opinion as to the justness of a cause, as to the credibility of a witness, as to the culpability of a civil litigant, and as to the guilt or innocence of an accused is not a proper subject for argument to the trier of fact and is prohibited by paragraph (e). However, a lawyer may argue, on an analysis of the evidence, for any position or conclusion with respect to any of the foregoing matters.

[7] Paragraph (f) permits a lawyer to advise managerial employees of a client to refrain from giving information to another party because the statements of employees with managerial responsibility may be imputed to the client. See also Rule 4.2.

Rule 3.5. Impartiality and Decorum of the Tribunal

(a) A lawyer shall not:

(1) seek to influence a judge, juror, prospective juror, or other official by means prohibited by law;

(2) communicate *ex parte* with a juror or prospective juror except as permitted by law;

(3) communicate *ex parte* with a judge or other official except:

(A) in the course of official proceedings;

(B) in writing, if a copy of the writing is furnished simultaneously to the opposing party;

(C) orally, upon adequate notice to opposing party; or

(D) as otherwise permitted by law;

(4) engage in conduct intended to disrupt a tribunal, including:

(A) failing to comply with known local customs of courtesy or practice of the bar or a particular tribunal without giving opposing counsel timely notice of the intent not to comply;

(B) engaging in undignified or discourteous conduct that is degrading to a tribunal; or

(C) intentionally or habitually violating any established rule of procedure or evidence; or

(5) communicate with a juror or prospective juror after discharge of the jury if:

(A) the communication is prohibited by law or court order;

(B) the juror has made known to the lawyer a desire not to communicate; or

(C) the communication involves misrepresentation, coercion, duress or harassment.

(b) All restrictions imposed by this rule also apply to communications with, or investigations of, members of the family of a a juror or a prospective juror.

(c) A lawyer shall reveal promptly to the court improper conduct by a juror or a prospective juror, or by another toward a juror, a prospective juror or a member of a juror or a prospective juror's family.

[Adopted July 24, 1997. Amended February 27, 2003; March 5, 2015.]

Comment

[1] Many forms of improper influence upon a tribunal are proscribed by criminal law. Others are specified in the North Carolina Code of Judicial Conduct, with which an advocate should be familiar. A lawyer is required to avoid contributing to a violation of provisions. This rule also prohibits gifts of substantial value to judges or other officials of a tribunal and stating or implying an ability to influence improperly a public official.

[2] To safeguard the impartiality that is essential to the judicial process, jurors and prospective jurors should be protected against extraneous influences. When impartiality is present, public confidence in the judicial system is enhanced. There should be no extrajudicial communication with prospective jurors prior to trial or with jurors during trial by or on behalf of a lawyer connected with the case. Furthermore, a lawyer who is not connected with the case should not communicate with a juror or a prospective juror about the case.

[3] After the jury has been discharged, a lawyer may communicate with a juror unless the communication is prohibited by law or court order. The lawyer must refrains from asking questions or making comments that tend to harass or embarrass the juror or to influence actions of the juror in future cases, and must respect the desire of the juror not to talk with the lawyer. The lawyer may not engage in improper conduct during the communication.

[4] Vexatious or harassing investigations of jurors or prospective jurors seriously impair the effectiveness of our jury system. For this reason, a lawyer or anyone on the lawyer's behalf who conducts an investigation of jurors or prospective jurors should act with circumspection and restraint.

[5] Communications with, or investigations of, members of families of jurors or prospective jurors by a lawyer or by anyone on the lawyer's behalf are subject to the restrictions imposed upon the lawyer with respect to the lawyer's communications with, or investigations of, jurors or prospective jurors.

[6] Because of the duty to aid in preserving the integrity of the jury system, a lawyer who learns of improper conduct by or towards a juror, a prospective juror, or a member of the family of either should make a prompt report to the court regarding such conduct.

[7] The impartiality of a public servant in our legal system may be impaired by the receipt of gifts or loans. A lawyer, therefore, is never justified in making a gift or a loan to a judge, a hearing officer, or an official or employee of a tribunal.

[8] All litigants and lawyers should have access to tribunals on an equal basis. Generally, in adversary proceedings, a lawyer should not communicate with a judge relative to a matter pending before, or which is to be brought before, a tribunal over which the judge presides in circumstances which might have the effect or give the appearance of granting undue advantage to one party. For example, a lawyer should not communicate with a tribunal by a writing unless a copy thereof is promptly delivered to opposing counsel or to the adverse party if unrepresented. Ordinarily, an oral communication by a lawyer with a judge or hearing officer should be made only upon adequate notice to opposing counsel or, if there is none, to the opposing party. A lawyer should not condone or lend himself or herself to private importunities by another with a judge or hearing officer on behalf of the lawyer or the client.

[9] The advocate's function is to present evidence and argument so that the cause may be decided according to law. Refraining from abusive or obstreperous conduct is a corollary of the advocate's right to speak on behalf of litigants. A lawyer may stand firm against abuse by a judge but should avoid reciprocation; the judge's default is no justification for similar dereliction by an advocate. An advocate can present the cause, protect the record for subsequent review, and preserve professional integrity by patient firmness no less effectively than by belligerence or theatrics.

[10] As professionals, lawyers are expected to avoid disruptive, undignified, discourteous, and abusive behavior. Therefore, the prohibition against conduct intended to disrupt a tribunal applies to conduct that does not serve a legitimate goal of advocacy or a requirement of a procedural rule and includes angry outbursts, insults, slurs, personal attacks, and unfounded personal accusations as well as to threats, bullying, and other attempts to intimidate or humiliate judges, opposing counsel, litigants, witnesses, or court personnel. Zealous advocacy does not rely upon such tactics and is never a justification for such conduct. This conduct is prohibited both in open court and in ancillary proceedings conducted pursuant to the authority of the tribunal (e.g., depositions). *See* comment [11], Rule 1.0(n). Similarly, insults, slurs, threats, personal attacks, and groundless personal accusations made in documents filed with the tribunal are also prohibited by this Rule. "Conduct of this type breeds disrespect for the courts and for the legal profession. Dignity, decorum, and respect are essential ingredients in the proper conduct of a courtroom, and therefore in the proper administration of justice." *Atty. Grievance Comm'n v. Alison*, 565 A.2d 60, 666 (Md. 1989). *See also* Rule 4.4(a) (prohibiting conduct that serves no substantial purpose other than to embarrass, delay, or burden a third person) and Rule 8.4(d) (prohibiting conduct prejudicial to the administration of justice).

[11] The duty to refrain from disruptive conduct applies to any proceeding of a tribunal, including a deposition or mediation. *See* Rule 1.0(n).

Rule 3.6 Trial Publicity

(a) A lawyer who is participating or has participated in the investigation or litigation of a matter shall not make an extrajudicial statement that the lawyer knows or reasonably should know will be disseminated by means of public communication and will have a substantial likelihood of materially prejudicing an adjudicative proceeding in the matter.

(b) Notwithstanding paragraph (a), a lawyer may state :

(1) the claim, offense or defense involved and, except when prohibited by law, the identity of the persons involved;

(2) the information contained in a public record;

(3) that an investigation of a matter is in progress;

(4) the scheduling or result of any step in litigation;

(5) a request for assistance in obtaining evidence and information necessary thereto;

(6) a warning of danger concerning the behavior of a person involved, when there is reason to believe that there exists the likelihood of substantial harm to an individual or to the public interest; and

(7) in a criminal case, in addition to subparagraphs (1) through (6):

(A) the identity, residence, occupation and family status of the accused;

(B) if the accused has not been apprehended, information necessary to aid in apprehension of that person;

(C) the fact, time and place of arrest; and

(D) the identity of investigating and arresting officers or agencies and the length of the investigation.

(c) Notwithstanding paragraph (a), a lawyer may make a statement that a reasonable lawyer would believe is required to protect a client from the substantial undue prejudicial effect of recent publicity not initiated by the lawyer or the lawyer's client. A statement made pursuant to this paragraph shall be limited to such information as is reasonably necessary to mitigate the recent adverse publicity.

(d) No lawyer associated in a firm or government agency with a lawyer subject to paragraph (a) shall make a statement prohibited by paragraph (a).

(e) The foregoing provisions of Rule 3.6 do not preclude a lawyer from replying to charges of misconduct publicly made against the lawyer or from participating in the proceedings of legislative, administrative, or other investigative bodies.

[Adopted July 24, 1997. Amended February 27, 2003; amended effective October 9, 2008.]

Comment

[1] It is difficult to strike a balance between protecting the right to a fair trial and safeguarding the right of free expression. Preserving the right to a fair trial necessarily entails some curtailment of the information that may be disseminated about a party prior to trial, particularly where trial by jury is involved. If there were no such limits, the result would be the practical nullification of the protective effect of the rules of forensic decorum and the exclusionary rules of evidence. On the other hand, there are vital social interests served by the free dissemination of information about events having legal consequences and about legal proceedings themselves. The public has a right to know about threats to its safety and measures aimed at assuring its security. It also has a legitimate interest in the conduct of judicial proceedings, particularly in matters of general public concern. Furthermore, the subject matter of legal proceedings is often of direct significance in debate and deliberation over questions of public policy.

[2] Special rules of confidentiality may validly govern proceedings in juvenile, domestic relations and mental disability proceedings, and perhaps other types of litigation. Rule 3.4(c) requires compliance with such rules.

[3] The Rule sets forth a basic general prohibition against a lawyer's making statements that the lawyer knows or should know will have a substantial likelihood of materially prejudicing an adjudicative proceeding. Recognizing that the public value of informed commentary is great and the likelihood of prejudice to a proceeding by the commentary of a lawyer who is not involved in the proceeding is small, the rule applies only to lawyers who are, or who have been involved in the investigation or litigation of a case, and their associates. A lawyer who is subject to the rule must take reasonable measures to insure the compliance of nonlawyer assistants and may not employ agents to make statements the lawyer is prohibited from making. Rule 5.3 and Rule 8.4(a); see, e.g., Rule 3.8(f)(prosecutor's duty to exercise reasonable care to prevent persons assisting prosecutor or

associated with prosecutor from making improper extrajudicial statements).

[4] Paragraph (b) identifies specific matters about which a lawyer's statements would not ordinarily be considered to present a substantial likelihood of material prejudice, and should not in any event be considered prohibited by the general prohibition of paragraph (a). Paragraph (b) is not intended to be an exhaustive listing of the subjects upon which a lawyer may make a statement, but statements on other matters may be subject to paragraph (a). Although paragraph (b)(2) allows extrajudicial statements about information in a public record, a lawyer may not use this safe harbor to justify, by means of filing pleadings or other public records, statements prohibited by paragraph (a). *See also* Rule 3.1.

[5] There are, on the other hand, certain subjects that are more likely than not to have a material prejudicial effect on a proceeding, particularly when they refer to a civil matter triable to a jury, a criminal matter, or any other proceeding that could result in incarceration. These subjects relate to:

(1) the character, credibility, reputation or criminal record of a party, suspect in a criminal investigation or witness, or the identity of a witness, or the expected testimony of a party or witness;

(2) in a criminal case or proceeding that could result in incarceration, the possibility of a plea of guilty to the offense or the existence or contents of any confession, admission, or statement given by a defendant or suspect or that person's refusal or failure to make a statement;

(3) the performance or results of any examination or test or the refusal or failure of a person to submit to an examination or test, or the identity or nature of physical evidence expected to be presented;

(4) any opinion as to the guilt or innocence of a defendant or suspect in a criminal case or proceeding that could result in incarceration;

(5) information that the lawyer knows or reasonably should know is likely to be inadmissible as evidence in a trial and that would, if disclosed, create a substantial risk of prejudicing an impartial trial; or

(6) the fact that a defendant has been charged with a crime, unless there is included therein a statement explaining that the charge is merely an accusation and that the defendant is presumed innocent until and unless proven guilty.

[6] Another relevant factor in determining prejudice is the nature of the proceeding involved. Criminal jury trials will be most sensitive to extrajudicial speech. Civil trials may be less sensitive. Non-jury hearings and arbitration proceedings may be even less affected. The Rule will still place limitations on prejudicial comments in these cases, but the likelihood of prejudice may be different depending on the type of proceeding.

[7] Finally, extrajudicial statements that might otherwise raise a question under this Rule may be permissible when they are made in response to statements made publicly by another party, another party's lawyer, or third persons, where a reasonable lawyer would believe a public response is required in order to avoid prejudice to the lawyer's client. When prejudicial statements have been publicly made by others, responsive statements may have the salutary effect of lessening any resulting adverse impact on the adjudicative proceeding. Such responsive statements should be limited to contain only such information as is necessary to mitigate undue prejudice created by the statements made by others. Moreover, when there is sufficient prior notice, a lawyer is encouraged to seek judicial intervention to prevent improper extrajudicial statements that may be prejudicial to the client and thereby avoid the necessity of a public response.

[8] See Rule 3.8(f) for additional duties of prosecutors in connection with extrajudicial statements about criminal proceedings.

Rule 3.7 Lawyer as Witness

(a) A lawyer shall not act as advocate at a trial in which the lawyer is likely to be a necessary witness unless:

(1) the testimony relates to an uncontested issue;

(2) the testimony relates to the nature and value of legal services rendered in the case; or

(3) disqualification of the lawyer would work substantial hardship on the client.

(b) A lawyer may act as advocate in a trial in which another lawyer in the lawyer's firm is likely to be called as a witness unless precluded from doing so by Rule 1.7 or Rule 1.9.

[Adopted July 24, 1997. Amended February 27, 2003.]

Comment

[1] Combining the roles of advocate and witness can prejudice the tribunal and the opposing party and can also involve a conflict of interest between the lawyer and client.

Advocate–Witness Rule

[2] The tribunal has proper objection when the trier of fact may be confused or misled by a lawyer serving as both advocate and witness. The opposing party has proper objection where the combination of roles may prejudice that party's rights in the litigation. A witness is required to testify on the basis of personal knowledge, while an advocate is expected to explain and comment on evidence given by others. It may not be clear whether a statement by an advocate-witness should be taken as proof or as an analysis of the proof.

[3] To protect the tribunal, paragraph (a) prohibits a lawyer from simultaneously serving as advocate and necessary witness except in those circumstances specified in paragraphs (a)(1) through (a)(3). Paragraph (a)(1) recognizes that if the testimony will be uncontested, the ambiguities in the dual role are purely theoretical. Paragraph (a)(2) recognizes that where the testimony concerns the extent and value of legal services rendered in the action in which the testimony is offered, permitting the lawyers to testify avoids the need for a second trial with new counsel to resolve that issue. Moreover, in such a situation the judge has firsthand knowledge of the matter in issue; hence, there is less dependence on the adversary process to test the credibility of the testimony.

[4] Apart from these two exceptions, paragraph (a)(3) recognizes that a balancing is required between the interests of the client and those of the tribunal and the opposing party. Whether the tribunal is likely to be misled or the opposing party is likely to suffer prejudice depends on the nature of the case, the importance and probable tenor of the lawyer's testimony, and the probability that the lawyer's testimony

will conflict with that of other witnesses. Even if there is risk of such prejudice, in determining whether the lawyer should be disqualified, due regard must be given to the effect of disqualification on the lawyer's client. It is relevant that one or both parties could reasonably foresee that the lawyer would probably be a witness. The conflict of interest principles stated in Rules 1.7, 1.9 and 1.10 have no application to this aspect of the problem.

[5] Because the tribunal is not likely to be misled when a lawyer acts as advocate in a trial in which another lawyer in the lawyer's firm will testify as a necessary witness, paragraph (b) permits the lawyer to do so except in situations involving a conflict of interest.

Conflict of Interest

[6] In determining if it is permissible to act as advocate in a trial in which the lawyer will be a necessary witness, the lawyer must also consider that the dual role may give rise to a conflict of interest that will require compliance with Rules 1.7 or 1.9. For example, if there is likely to be substantial conflict between the testimony of the client and that of the lawyer, the representation involves a conflict of interest that requires compliance with Rule 1.7. This would be true even though the lawyer might not be prohibited by paragraph (a) from simultaneously serving as advocate and witness because the lawyer's disqualification would work a substantial hardship on the client. Similarly, a lawyer who might be permitted to simultaneously serve as an advocate and a witness by paragraph (a)(3) might be precluded from doing so by Rule 1.9. The problem can arise whether the lawyer is called as a witness on behalf of the client or is called by the opposing party. Determining whether or not such a conflict exists is primarily the responsibility of the lawyer involved. If there is a conflict of interest, the lawyer must secure the client's informed consent, confirmed in writing. In some cases, the lawyer will be precluded from seeking the client's consent. See Rule 1.7. See Rule 1.0(b) for the definition of "confirmed in writing" and Rule 1.0(e) for the definition of "informed consent."

[7] Paragraph (b) provides that a lawyer is not disqualified from serving as an advocate because a lawyer with whom the lawyer is associated in a firm is precluded from doing so by paragraph (a). If, however, the testifying lawyer would also be disqualified by Rule 1.7 or Rule 1.9 from representing the client in the matter, other lawyers in the firm will be precluded from representing the client by Rule 1.10 unless the client gives informed consent under the conditions stated in Rule 1.7.

Rule 3.8 Special Responsibilities of a Prosecutor

The prosecutor in a criminal case shall:

(a) refrain from prosecuting a charge that the prosecutor knows is not supported by probable cause;

(b) make reasonable efforts to assure that the accused has been advised of the right to, and the procedure for obtaining, counsel and has been given reasonable opportunity to obtain counsel;

(c) not seek to obtain from an unrepresented accused a waiver of important pretrial rights, such as the right to a preliminary hearing;

(d) after reasonably diligent inquiry, make timely disclosure to the defense of all evidence or information required to be disclosed by applicable law, rules of procedure, or court opinions including all evidence or information known to the prosecutor that tends to negate the guilt of the accused or mitigates the offense, and, in connection with sentencing, disclose to the defense and to the tribunal all unprivileged mitigating information known to the prosecutor, except when the prosecutor is relieved of this responsibility by a protective order of the tribunal;

(e) not subpoena a lawyer in a grand jury or other criminal proceeding to present evidence about a past or present client, or participate in the application for the issuance of a search warrant to a lawyer for the seizure of information of a past or present client in connection with an investigation of someone other than the lawyer, unless:

(1) the information sought is not protected from disclosure by any applicable privilege;

(2) the evidence sought is essential to the successful completion of an ongoing investigation or prosecution; and

(3) there is no other feasible alternative to obtain the information;

(f) except for statements that are necessary to inform the public of the nature and extent of the prosecutor's action and that serve a legitimate law enforcement purpose, refrain from making extrajudicial comments that have a substantial likelihood of heightening public condemnation of the accused and exercise reasonable care to prevent investigators, law enforcement personnel, employees or other persons assisting or associated with the prosecutor in a criminal case from making an extrajudicial statement that the prosecutor would be prohibited from making under Rule 3.6 or this Rule.

[Adopted July 24, 1997. Amended February 27, 2003; amended effective November 16, 2006.]

Comment

[1] A prosecutor has the responsibility of a minister of justice and not simply that of an advocate; the prosecutor's duty is to seek justice, not merely to convict. This responsibility carries with it specific obligations to see that the defendant is accorded procedural justice and that guilt is decided upon the basis of sufficient evidence. Precisely how far the prosecutor is required to go in this direction is a matter of debate and varies in different jurisdictions. *See* the ABA Standards of Criminal Justice Relating to the Prosecution Function. A systematic abuse of prosecutorial discretion could constitute a violation of Rule 8.4.

[2] The prosecutor represents the sovereign and, therefore, should use restraint in the discretionary exercise of government powers, such as in the selection of cases to prosecute. During trial, the prosecutor is not only an advocate, but he or she also may make decisions normally made by an individual client, and those affecting the public interest should be fair to all. In our system of criminal justice, the accused is to be given the benefit of all reasonable doubt.

With respect to evidence and witnesses, the prosecutor has responsibilities different from those of a lawyer in private practice; the prosecutor should make timely disclosure to the defense of available evidence known to him or her that tends to negate the guilt of the accused, mitigate the degree of the offense, or reduce the punishment. Further, a prosecutor should not intentionally avoid pursuit of evidence merely because he or she believes it will damage the prosecutor's case or aid the accused.

[3] Paragraph (c) does not apply, however, to an accused appearing *pro se* with the approval of the tribunal. Nor does it forbid the lawful questioning of a an uncharged suspect who has knowingly waived the rights to counsel and silence.

[4] Every prosecutor should be aware of the discovery requirements established by statutory law and case law. *See, e.g.*, N.C. Gen. Stat. § 15A–903 et. seq, *Brady v. Maryland*, 373 U.S. 83 (1963); *Giglio v. U.S.*, 405 U.S. 150 (1972); *Kyles v. Whitley*, 514 U.S. 419 (1995). The exception in paragraph (d) recognizes that a prosecutor may seek an appropriate protective order from the tribunal if disclosure of information to the defense could result in substantial harm to an individual or to the public interest.

[5] Paragraph (e) is intended to limit the issuance of lawyer subpoenas in grand jury and other criminal proceedings, and search warrants for client information, to those situations in which there is a genuine need to intrude into the client-lawyer relationship. The provision applies only when someone other than the lawyer is the target of a criminal investigation.

[6] Paragraph (f) supplements Rule 3.6, which prohibits extrajudicial statements that have a substantial likelihood of prejudicing an adjudicatory proceeding. In the context of a criminal prosecution, a prosecutor's extrajudicial statement can create the additional problem of increasing public condemnation of the accused. Although the announcement of an indictment, for example, will necessarily have severe consequences for the accused, a prosecutor can, and should, avoid comments which have no legitimate law enforcement purpose and have a substantial likelihood of increasing public opprobrium of the accused. Nothing in this Comment is intended to restrict the statements which a prosecutor may make which comply with Rule 3.6(b) or 3.6(c).

[7] Like other lawyers, prosecutors are subject to Rules 5.1 and 5.3, which relate to responsibilities regarding lawyers and nonlawyers who work for or are associated with the lawyer's office. Paragraph (f) reminds the prosecutor of the importance of these obligations in connection with the unique dangers of improper extrajudicial statements in a criminal case. In addition, paragraph (f) requires a prosecutor to exercise reasonable care to prevent persons assisting or associated with the prosecutor from making improper extrajudicial statements, even when such persons are not under the direct supervision of the prosecutor. Ordinarily, the reasonable care standard will be satisfied if the prosecutor issues the appropriate cautions to law- enforcement personnel and other relevant individuals.

TRANSACTIONS WITH PERSON OTHER THAN CLIENTS

Rule 4.1 Truthfulness in Statements to Others

In the course of representing a client a lawyer shall not knowingly make a false statement of material fact or law to a third person.

[Adopted July 24, 1997. Amended February 27, 2003.]

Comment

Misrepresentation

[1] A lawyer is required to be truthful when dealing with others on a client's behalf, but generally has no affirmative duty to inform an opposing party of relevant facts. A misrepresentation can occur if the lawyer incorporates or affirms a statement of another person that the lawyer knows is false. Misrepresentations can also occur by partially true but misleading statements or omissions that are the equivalent of affirmative false statements. For dishonest conduct that does not amount to a false statement or for misrepresentations by a lawyer other than in the course of representing a client, see Rule 8.4.

Statements of Fact

[2] This Rule refers to statements of fact. Whether a particular statement should be regarded as one of fact can depend on the circumstances. Under generally accepted conventions in negotiation, certain types of statements ordinarily are not taken as statements of material fact. Estimates of price or value placed on the subject of a transaction and a party's intentions as to an acceptable settlement of a claim are ordinarily in this category, and so is the existence of an undisclosed principal except where nondisclosure of the principal would constitute fraud. Lawyers should be mindful of their obligations under applicable law to avoid criminal and tortious misrepresentation.

Crime or Fraud by Client

[3] Under Rule 1.2(d), a lawyer is prohibited from counseling or assisting a client in conduct that the lawyer knows is criminal or fraudulent. Ordinarily, a lawyer can avoid assisting a client's crime or fraud by withdrawing from the representation. Sometimes it may be necessary for the lawyer to give notice of the fact of withdrawal and to disaffirm an opinion, document, affirmation or the like. In extreme cases, substantive law may require a lawyer to disclose information relating to the representation to avoid being deemed to have assisted the client's crime or fraud. Rule 1.6(b)(1) permits a lawyer to disclose information when required by law. Similarly, Rule 1.6(b)(4) permits a lawyer to disclose information when necessary to prevent, mitigate, or rectify the consequences of a client's criminal or fraudulent act in the commission of which the lawyer's services were used.

Rule 4.2 Communication With Person Represented by Counsel

(a) During the representation of a client, a lawyer shall not communicate about the subject of the representation with a person the lawyer knows to be represented by another lawyer in the matter, unless the lawyer has the consent of the other lawyer or is authorized to do so by law or a court order. It is not a violation of this rule for a lawyer to encourage his or

her client to discuss the subject of the representation with the opposing party in a good-faith attempt to resolve the controversy.

(b) Notwithstanding section (a) above, in representing a client who has a dispute with a government agency or body, a lawyer may communicate about the subject of the representation with the elected officials who have authority over such government agency or body even if the lawyer knows that the government agency or body is represented by another lawyer in the matter, but such communications may only occur under the following circumstances:

(1) In writing, if a copy of the writing is promptly delivered to opposing counsel;

(2) orally, upon adequate notice to opposing counsel; or

(3) in the course of official proceedings.

[Adopted July 24, 1997. Amended February 27, 2003.]

Comment

[1] This Rule contributes to the proper functioning of the legal system by protecting a person who has chosen to be represented by a lawyer in a matter against possible overreaching by other lawyers who are participating in the matter, interference by those lawyers with the client-lawyer relationship and the uncounselled disclosure of information relating to the representation.

[2] This Rule does not prohibit a lawyer who does not have a client relative to a particular matter from consulting with a person or entity who, though represented concerning the matter, seeks another opinion as to his or her legal situation. A lawyer from whom such an opinion is sought should, but is not required to, inform the first lawyer of his or her participation and advice.

[3] This Rule does not prohibit communication with a represented person, or an employee or agent of such a person, concerning matters outside the representation. For example, the existence of a controversy between a government agency and a private party, or between two organizations, does not prohibit a lawyer for either from communicating with nonlawyer representatives of the other regarding a separate matter. Also, a lawyer having independent justification or legal authorization for communicating with a represented person is permitted to do so.

[4] A lawyer may not make a communication prohibited by this Rule through the acts of another. See Rule 8.4(a). However, parties to a matter may communicate directly with each other, and a lawyer is not prohibited from advising a client or, in the case of a government lawyer, investigatory personnel, concerning a communication that the client, or such investigatory personnel, is legally entitled to make. The Rule is not intended to discourage good faith efforts by individual parties to resolve their differences. Nor does the Rule prohibit a lawyer from encouraging a client to communicate with the opposing party with a view toward the resolution of the dispute.

[5] Communications authorized by law may include communications by a lawyer on behalf of a client who is exercising a constitutional or other legal right to communicate with the government. When a government agency or body is represented with regard to a particular matter, a lawyer may communicate with the elected government officials who have authority over that agency under the circumstances set forth in paragraph (b).

[6] Communications authorized by law may also include investigative activities of lawyers representing governmental entities, directly or through investigative agents, prior to the commencement of criminal or civil enforcement proceedings. When communicating with the accused in a criminal matter, a government lawyer must comply with this Rule in addition to honoring the constitutional rights of the accused. The fact that a communication does not violate a state or federal constitutional right is insufficient to establish that the communication is permissible under this Rule.

[7] A lawyer who is uncertain whether a communication with a represented person is permissible may seek a court order. A lawyer may also seek a court order in exceptional circumstances to authorize a communication that would otherwise be prohibited by this Rule, for example, where communication with a person represented by counsel is necessary to avoid reasonably certain injury.

[8] This Rule applies to communications with any person, whether or not a party to a formal adjudicative proceeding, contract or negotiation, who is represented by counsel concerning the matter to which the communication relates. The Rule applies even though the represented person initiates or consents to the communication. A lawyer must immediately terminate communication with a person if, after commencing communication, the lawyer learns that the person is one with whom communication is not permitted by this Rule.

[9] In the case of a represented organization, this Rule prohibits communications with a constituent of the organization who supervises, directs or consults with the organization's lawyer concerning the matter or has authority to obligate the organization with respect to the matter or whose act or omission in connection with the matter may be imputed to the organization for purposes of civil or criminal liability . It also prohibits communications with any constituent of the organization, regardless of position or level of authority, who is participating or participated substantially in the legal representation of the organization in a particular matter. Consent of the organization's lawyer is not required for communication with a former constituent unless the former constituent participated substantially in the legal representation of the organization in the matter. If an employee or agent of the organization is represented in the matter by his or her own counsel, the consent by that counsel to a communication would be sufficient for purposes of this Rule. Compare Rule 3.4(f). In communicating with a current or former constituent of an organization, a lawyer must not use methods of obtaining evidence that violate the legal rights of the organization. See Rule 4.4, Comment [2].

[10] The prohibition on communications with a represented person only applies in circumstances where the lawyer knows that the person is in fact represented in the matter to be discussed. This means that the lawyer has actual knowledge of the fact of the representation; but such actual knowledge may be inferred from the circumstances. See Rule 1.0(f). Thus, the lawyer cannot evade the requirement of obtaining the consent of counsel by closing eyes to the obvious.

[11] In the event the person with whom the lawyer communicates is not known to be represented by counsel in the matter, the lawyer's communications are subject to Rule 4.3.

Rule 4.3 Dealing With Unrepresented Person

In dealing on behalf of a client with a person who is not represented by counsel, a lawyer shall not:

(a) give legal advice to the person, other than the advice to secure counsel, if the lawyer knows or reasonably should know that the interests of such person are or have a reasonable possibility of being in conflict with the interests of the client; and

(b) state or imply that the lawyer is disinterested. When the lawyer knows or reasonably should know that the unrepresented person misunderstands the lawyer's role in the matter, the lawyer shall make reasonable efforts to correct the misunderstanding.

[Adopted July 24, 1997. Amended February 27, 2003.]

Comment

[1] An unrepresented person, particularly one not experienced in dealing with legal matters, might assume that a lawyer is disinterested in loyalties or is a disinterested authority on the law even when the lawyer represents a client. To avoid a misunderstanding, a lawyer will typically need to identify the lawyer's client and, where necessary, explain that the client has interests opposed to those of the unrepresented person. For misunderstandings that sometimes arise when a lawyer for an organization deals with an unrepresented constituent, see Rule 1.13(d).

[2] The Rule distinguishes between situations involving unrepresented persons whose interests may be adverse to those of the lawyer's client and those in which the person's interests are not in conflict with the client's. In the 'former situation', the possibility that the lawyer will compromise the unrepresented person's interests is so great that the Rule prohibits the giving of any advice, apart from the advice to obtain counsel. This Rule does not prohibit a lawyer from negotiating the terms of a transaction or settling a dispute with an unrepresented person. So long as the lawyer has explained that the lawyer represents an adverse party and is not representing the person, the lawyer may inform the person of the terms on which the lawyer's client will enter into an agreement or settle a matter, prepare documents that require the person's signature and explain the lawyer's own view of the meaning of the document or the lawyer's view of the underlying legal obligations.

Rule 4.4. Respect for Rights of Third Persons

(a) In representing a client, a lawyer shall not use means that have no substantial purpose other than to embarrass, delay, or burden a third person, or use methods of obtaining evidence that violate the legal rights of such a person.

(b) A lawyer who receives a writing relating to the representation of the lawyer's client and knows or reasonably should know that the writing was inadvertently sent shall promptly notify the sender.

[Adopted July 24, 1997. Amended February 27, 2003; August 18, 2005; October 2, 2014; March 5, 2015.]

Comment

[1] Responsibility to a client requires a lawyer to subordinate the interests of others to those of the client, but that responsibility does not imply that a lawyer may disregard the rights of third persons. It is impractical to catalogue all such rights, but they include legal restrictions on methods of obtaining evidence from third persons and unwarranted intrusions into privileged relationships, such as the client-lawyer relationship.

[2] Threats, bullying, harassment, insults, slurs, personal attacks, unfounded personal accusations generally serve no substantial purpose other than to embarrass, delay, or burden others and violate this rule. Conduct that serves no substantial purpose other than to intimidate, humiliate, or embarrass lawyers, litigants, witnesses, or other persons with whom a lawyer interacts while representing a client also violates this rule. *See also* Rule 3.5(a) (prohibiting conduct intended to disrupt a tribunal) and Rule 8.4(d) (prohibiting conduct prejudicial to the administration of justice).

[3] Paragraph (b) recognizes that lawyers sometimes receive writings that were mistakenly sent or produced by opposing parties or their lawyers. See Rule 1.0(*o*) for the definition of "writing," which includes electronic communications and metadata. A writing is inadvertently sent when it is accidentally transmitted, such as when an electronic communication or letter is misaddressed or a document or electronically stored information is accidentally included with information that was intentionally transmitted. If a lawyer knows or reasonably should know that such a writing was sent inadvertently, then this rule requires the lawyer promptly to notify the sender in order to permit that person to take protective measures. This duty is imputed to all lawyers in a firm. Whether the lawyer who receives the writing is required to take additional steps, such as returning the writing, is a matter of law beyond the scope of these rules, as is the question of whether the privileged status of a writing has been waived. Similarly, this Rule does not address the legal duties of a lawyer who receives a writing that the lawyer knows or reasonably should know may have been inappropriately obtained by the sending person. Metadata in electronic documents creates an obligation under this Rule only if the receiving lawyer knows or reasonably should know that the metadata was inadvertently sent to the receiving lawyer. A lawyer who receives an electronic communication from the opposing party or the opposing party's lawyer must refrain from searching for or using confidential information found in the metadata embedded in the communication. See 2009 Formal Ethics Opinion 1.

[4] Some lawyers may choose to return a writing or delete electronically stored information unread, for example, when the lawyer learns before receiving the writing that it was inadvertently sent. Whether the lawyer is required to do so is a matter of law. When return of the writing is not required by law, the decision voluntarily to return such a writing or delete electronically stored information is a matter of professional judgment ordinarily reserved to the lawyer. See Rules 1.2 and 1.4.

LAW FIRMS AND ASSOCIATIONS

Rule 5.1 Responsibilities of Partners, Managers, and Supervisory Lawyers

(a) A partner in a law firm, and a lawyer who individually or together with other lawyers possesses comparable managerial authority, shall make reasonable efforts to ensure that the firm or the organization has in effect measures giving reasonable assurance that all lawyers in the firm or the organization conform to the Rules of Professional Conduct.

(b) A lawyer having direct supervisory authority over another lawyer shall make reasonable efforts to ensure that the other lawyer conforms to the Rules of Professional Conduct.

(c) A lawyer shall be responsible for another lawyer's violation of the Rules of Professional Conduct if:

(1) the lawyer orders or, with knowledge of the specific conduct, ratifies the conduct involved; or

(2) the lawyer is a partner or has comparable managerial authority in the law firm in which the other lawyer practices, or has direct supervisory authority over the other lawyer, and knows of the conduct at a time when its consequences can be avoided or mitigated but fails to take reasonable remedial action to avoid the consequences.

[Adopted July 24, 1997. Amended February 27, 2003.]

Comment

[1] Paragraph (a) applies to lawyers who have managerial authority over the professional work of a firm or legal-department of an organization. See Rule 1.0(c). This includes members of a partnership, the shareholders in a law firm organized as a professional corporation, and members of other associations authorized to practice law; lawyers having comparable managerial authority in a legal services organization or a law department of an enterprise or government agency; and lawyers who have intermediate managerial responsibilities in a firm. Paragraph (b) applies to lawyers who have supervisory authority over the work of other lawyers in a firm or organization.

[2] Paragraph (a) requires lawyers with managerial authority within a firm or organization to make reasonable efforts to establish internal policies and procedures designed to provide reasonable assurance that all lawyers in the firm or organization will conform to the Rules of Professional Conduct. Such policies and procedures include those designed to detect and resolve conflicts of interest, identify dates by which actions must be taken in pending matters, account for client funds and property and ensure that inexperienced lawyers are properly supervised.

[3] Other measures that may be required to fulfill the responsibility prescribed in paragraph (a) can depend on the firm's or organization's structure and the nature of its practice. In a small firm of experienced lawyers, informal supervision and periodic review of compliance with the required systems ordinarily will suffice. In a large firm or organization, or in practice situations in which difficult ethical problems frequently arise, more elaborate measures may be necessary. Some firms, for example, have a procedure whereby junior lawyers can make confidential referral of ethical problems directly to a designated senior partner or special committee. See Rule 5.2. Firms and organizations, whether large or small, may also rely on continuing legal education in professional ethics. In any event, the ethical atmosphere of a firm or organization can influence the conduct of all its members and the partners and managing lawyers may not assume that all lawyers associated with the firm or organization will inevitably conform to the Rules.

[4] Paragraph (c) expresses a general principle of personal responsibility for acts of another. See also Rule 8.4(a).

[5] Paragraph (c)(2) defines the duty of a partner or other lawyer having comparable managerial authority in a law firm, as well as a lawyer who has direct supervisory authority over performance of specific legal work by another lawyer. Whether a lawyer has such supervisory authority in particular circumstances is a question of fact. Partners and lawyers with comparable authority have at least indirect responsibility for all work being done by the firm, while a partner or manager in charge of a particular matter ordinarily also has supervisory responsibility for the work of other firm lawyers engaged in the matter. Appropriate remedial action by a partner or managing lawyer would depend on the immediacy of that lawyer's involvement and the seriousness of the misconduct. A supervisor is required to intervene to prevent avoidable consequences of misconduct if the supervisor knows that the misconduct occurred. Thus, if a supervising lawyer knows that a subordinate misrepresented a matter to an opposing party in negotiation, the supervisor as well as the subordinate has a duty to correct the resulting misapprehension.

[6] Professional misconduct by a lawyer under supervision could reveal a violation of paragraph (b) on the part of the supervisory lawyer even though it does not entail a violation of paragraph (c) because there was no direction, ratification or knowledge of the violation.

[7] Apart from this Rule and Rule 8.4(a), a lawyer does not have disciplinary liability for the conduct of a partner, associate or subordinate. Moreover, this Rule is not intended to establish a standard for vicarious criminal or civil liability for the acts of another lawyer. Whether a lawyer may be liable civilly or criminally for another lawyer's conduct is a question of law beyond the scope of these Rules.

[8] The duties imposed by this Rule on managing and supervising lawyers do not alter the personal duty of each lawyer in a firm to abide by the Rules of Professional Conduct. See Rule 5.2(a).

Rule 5.2 Responsibilities of a Subordinate Lawyer

(a) A lawyer is bound by the Rules of Professional Conduct notwithstanding that the lawyer acted at the direction of another person.

(b) A subordinate lawyer does not violate the Rules of Professional Conduct if that lawyer acts in accordance with a supervisory lawyer's reasonable resolution of an arguable question of professional duty.

[Adopted July 24, 1997. Amended February 27, 2003.]

Comment

[1] Although a lawyer is not relieved of responsibility for a violation by the fact that the lawyer acted at the direction of a supervisor, that fact may be relevant in determining whether a lawyer had the knowledge required to render conduct a violation of the Rules. For example, if a subordinate filed a frivolous pleading at the direction of a supervisor, the subordinate would not be guilty of a professional violation unless the subordinate knew of the document's frivolous character.

[2] When lawyers in a supervisor-subordinate relationship encounter a matter involving professional judgment as to ethical duty, the supervisor may assume responsibility for making the judgment. Otherwise a consistent course of action or position could not be taken. If the question can reasonably be answered only one way, the duty of both lawyers is clear and they are equally responsible for fulfilling it. However, if the question is reasonably arguable, someone has to decide upon the course of action. That authority ordinarily reposes in the supervisor, and a subordinate may be guided accordingly. For example, if a question arises whether the interests of two clients conflict under Rule 1.7, the supervisor's reasonable resolution of the question should protect the subordinate professionally if the resolution is subsequently challenged.

Rule 5.3. Responsibilities Regarding Nonlawyer Assistants

With respect to a nonlawyer employed or retained by or associated with a lawyer:

(a) a partner, and a lawyer who individually or together with other lawyers possesses comparable managerial authority in a law firm or organization shall make reasonable efforts to ensure that the firm or organization has in effect measures giving reasonable assurance that the nonlawyer's conduct is compatible with the professional obligations of the lawyer;

(b) a lawyer having direct supervisory authority over the nonlawyer shall make reasonable efforts to ensure that the nonlawyer's conduct is compatible with the professional obligations of the lawyer; and

(c) a lawyer shall be responsible for conduct of such a nonlawyer that would be a violation of the Rules of Professional Conduct if engaged in by a lawyer if:

(1) the lawyer orders or, with the knowledge of the specific conduct, ratifies the conduct involved; or

(2) the lawyer is a partner or has comparable managerial authority in the law firm or organization in which the person is employed, or has direct supervisory authority over the nonlawyer, and knows of the conduct at a time when its consequences can be avoided or mitigated but fails to take reasonable remedial action to avoid the consequences.

[Adopted July 24, 1997. Amended February 27, 2003; October 2, 2014.]

Comment

[1] Paragraph (a) requires lawyers with managerial authority within a law firm or organization to make reasonable efforts to ensure that the firm has in effect measures giving reasonable assurance that nonlawyers in the firm and nonlawyers outside the firm who work on firm matters act in a way compatible with the professional obligations of the lawyer. *See* Comment [6] to Rule 1.1 (retaining lawyers outside the firm) and Comment [1] to Rule 5.1 (responsibilities with respect to lawyers within a firm). Paragraph (b) applies to lawyers who have supervisory authority over such nonlawyers within or outside the firm. Paragraph (c) specifies the circumstances in which a lawyer is responsible for the conduct of such nonlawyers within or outside the firm that would be a violation of the Rules of Professional Conduct if engaged in by a lawyer.

[2] Lawyers generally employ assistants in their practice, including secretaries, investigators, law student interns, and paraprofessionals. Such assistants, whether employees or independent contractors, act for the lawyer in rendition of the lawyer's professional services. A lawyer must give such assistants appropriate instruction and supervision concerning the ethical aspects of their employment, particularly regarding the obligation not to disclose information relating to representation of the client, and should be responsible for their work product. The measures employed in supervising nonlawyers should take account of the fact that they do not have legal training and are not subject to professional discipline.

Nonlawyers Outside the Firm

[3] A lawyer may use nonlawyers outside the firm to assist the lawyer in rendering legal services to the client. Examples include the retention of an investigative or paraprofessional service, hiring a document management company to create and maintain a database for complex litigation, sending client documents to a third party for printing or scanning, and using an Internet-based service to store client information. When using such services outside the firm, a lawyer must make reasonable efforts to ensure that the services are provided in a manner that is compatible with the lawyer's professional obligations and, depending upon the risk of unauthorized disclosure of confidential client information, should consider whether client consent is required. *See* Rule 1.1, cmt. [7]. The extent of this obligation will depend upon the circumstances, including the education, experience, and reputation of the nonlawyer; the nature of the services involved; the terms of any arrangements concerning the protection of client information; and the legal and ethical environments of the jurisdictions in which the services will be performed, particularly with regard to confidentiality. *See also* Rules 1.1 (competence), 1.2 (allocation of authority), 1.4 (communication with client), 1.6 (confidentiality), 5.4(a) (professional independence of the lawyer), and 5.5(a) (unauthorized practice of law). When retaining or directing a nonlawyer outside the firm, a lawyer should communicate directions appropriate under the circumstances to give reasonable assurance that the nonlawyer's conduct is compatible with the professional obligations of the lawyer.

[4] Where the client directs the selection of a particular nonlawyer service provider outside the firm, the lawyer ordinarily should agree with the client concerning the allocation of responsibility for monitoring as between the client and the lawyer. *See* Rule 1.2. When making such an allocation in a matter pending before a tribunal, lawyers and

parties may have additional obligations that are a matter of law beyond the scope of these Rules.

[5] A lawyer who discovers that a nonlawyer has wrongfully misappropriated money from the lawyer's trust account must inform the North Carolina State Bar pursuant to Rule 1.15–2(*o*)

Rule 5.4 Professional Independence of a Lawyer

(a) A lawyer or law firm shall not share legal fees with a nonlawyer, except that:

(1) an agreement by a lawyer with the lawyer's firm, partner, or associate may provide for the payment of money, over a reasonable period of time after the lawyer's death, to the lawyer's estate or to one or more specified persons;

(2) a lawyer who purchases the practice of a deceased, disabled, or disappeared lawyer may, pursuant to the provisions of Rule 1.17, pay to the estate or other representative of that lawyer the agreed-upon purchase price;

(3) a lawyer who undertakes to complete unfinished legal business of a deceased lawyer or a disbarred lawyer may pay to the estate of the deceased lawyer or to the disbarred lawyer that portion of the total compensation that fairly represents the services rendered by the deceased lawyer or the disbarred lawyer;

(4) a lawyer or law firm may include nonlawyer employees in a compensation or retirement plan even though the plan is based in whole or in part on a profit-sharing arrangement; and

(5) a lawyer may share court-awarded legal fees with a nonprofit organization that employed, retained or recommended employment of the lawyer in the matter.

(b) A lawyer shall not form a partnership with a nonlawyer if any of the activities of the partnership consist of the practice of law.

(c) A lawyer shall not permit a person who recommends,, engages, or pays the lawyer to render legal services for another to direct or regulate the lawyer's professional judgment in rendering such legal services.

(d) A lawyer shall not practice with or in the form of a professional corporation or association authorized to practice law for a profit, if:

(1) a nonlawyer owns any interest therein, except that a fiduciary representative of the estate of a lawyer may hold the stock or interest of the lawyer for a reasonable time during administration; or

(2) a nonlawyer has the right to direct or control the professional judgment of a lawyer.

[Adopted July 24, 1997. Amended February 27, 2003.]

Comment

[1] The provisions of this Rule express traditional limitations on sharing fees. These limitations are to protect the lawyer's professional independence of judgment. Where someone other than the client pays the lawyer's fee or salary, or recommends employment of the lawyer, that arrangement does not modify the lawyer's obligation to the client. As stated in paragraph (c), such arrangements should not interfere with the lawyer's professional judgment.

[2] This Rule also expresses traditional limitations on permitting a third party to direct or regulate the lawyer's professional judgment in rendering legal services to another. See also Rule 1.8(f) (lawyer may accept compensation from a third party as long as there is no interference with the lawyer's independent professional judgment and the client gives informed consent).

[3] Although a nonlawyer may serve as a director or officer of a professional corporation organized to practice law if permitted by law, such a nonlawyer director or officer may not have the authority to direct or control the conduct of the lawyers who practice with the firm.

Rule 5.5. Unauthorized Practice of Law

(a) A lawyer shall not practice law in a jurisdiction where doing so violates the regulation of the legal profession in that jurisdiction.

(b) A lawyer who is not admitted to practice in this jurisdiction shall not:

(1) except as authorized by these Rules or other law, establish an office or other systematic and continuous presence in this jurisdiction for the practice of law; or

(2) hold out to the public or otherwise represent that the lawyer is admitted to practice law in this jurisdiction.

(c) A lawyer admitted to practice in another United States jurisdiction, and not disbarred or suspended from practice in any jurisdiction, does not engage in the unauthorized practice of law in this jurisdiction if the lawyer's conduct is in accordance with these Rules and:

(1) the lawyer is authorized by law or order to appear before a tribunal or administrative agency in this jurisdiction or is preparing for a potential proceeding or hearing in which the lawyer reasonably expects to be so authorized;

(2) the lawyer acts with respect to a matter that arises out of or is otherwise reasonably related to the lawyer's representation of a client in a jurisdiction in which the lawyer is admitted to practice and the lawyer's services are not services for which pro hac vice admission is required;

(3) the lawyer acts with respect to a matter that is in or is reasonably related to a pending or potential arbitration, mediation, or other alternative dispute resolution proceeding in this or another jurisdiction, if the lawyer's services arise out of or are reasonably related to the lawyer's representation of a client in a

jurisdiction in which the lawyer is admitted to practice and are not services for which pro hac vice admission is required; or

(4) the lawyer is associated in the matter with a lawyer admitted to practice in this jurisdiction who actively participates in the representation and the lawyer is admitted pro hac vice or the lawyer's services are not services for which pro hac vice admission is required.

(d) A lawyer admitted to practice in another United States jurisdiction or in a foreign jurisdiction, and not disbarred or suspended from practice in any jurisdiction, or the equivalent thereof, does not engage in the unauthorized practice of law in this jurisdiction and may establish an office or other systematic and continuous presence in this jurisdiction for the practice of law if the lawyer's conduct is in accordance with these Rules and:

(1) the lawyer provides legal services to the lawyer's employer or its organizational affiliates; the services are not services for which pro hac vice admission is required; and, when the services are performed by a foreign lawyer and require advice on the law of this or another US jurisdiction or of the United States, such advice is based upon the advice of a lawyer who is duly licensed and authorized by the jurisdiction to provide such advice; or

(2) the lawyer is providing services limited to federal law, international law, the law of a foreign jurisdiction or the law of the jurisdiction in which the lawyer is admitted to practice, or the lawyer is providing services that the lawyer is authorized by federal or other law or rule to provide in this jurisdiction.

(e) A lawyer admitted to practice in another United States jurisdiction, and not disbarred or suspended from practice in any jurisdiction, does not engage in the unauthorized practice of law in this jurisdiction and may establish an office or other systematic and continuous presence in this jurisdiction for the practice of law if the lawyer's conduct is in accordance with these Rules, the lawyer is the subject of a pending application for admission to the North Carolina State Bar by comity, having never previously been denied admission to the North Carolina State Bar for any reason, and the lawyer satisfies the following conditions:

(1) is licensed to practice law in a state with which North Carolina has comity in regard to admission to practice law;

(2) is a member in good standing in every jurisdiction in which the lawyer is licensed to practice law;

(3) has satisfied the educational and experiential requirements prerequisite to comity admission to the North Carolina State Bar;

(4) is domiciled in North Carolina;

(5) has established a professional relationship with a North Carolina law firm and is actively supervised by at least one licensed North Carolina attorney affiliated with that law firm; and

(6) gives written notice to the secretary of the North Carolina State Bar that the lawyer intends to begin the practice of law pursuant to this provision, provides the secretary with a copy of the lawyer's application for admission to the State Bar, and agrees that the lawyer is subject to these rules and the disciplinary jurisdiction of the North Carolina State Bar. A lawyer acting pursuant to this provision may not provide services for which pro hac vice admission is required, and shall be ineligible to practice law in this jurisdiction immediately upon being advised that the lawyer's application for comity admission has been denied.

(f) A lawyer shall not assist another person in the unauthorized practice of law.

(g) A lawyer or law firm shall not employ a disbarred or suspended lawyer as a law clerk or legal assistant if that individual was associated with such lawyer or law firm at any time on or after the date of the acts which resulted in disbarment or suspension through and including the effective date of disbarment or suspension.

(h) A lawyer or law firm employing a disbarred or suspended lawyer as a law clerk or legal assistant shall not represent any client represented by the disbarred or suspended lawyer or by any lawyer with whom the disbarred or suspended lawyer practiced during the period on or after the date of the acts which resulted in disbarment or suspension through and including the effective date of disbarment or suspension.

(i) For the purposes of paragraph (d), the foreign lawyer must be a member in good standing of a recognized legal profession in a foreign jurisdiction, the members of which are admitted to practice as lawyers or counselors at law or the equivalent, and are subject to effective regulation and discipline by a duly constituted professional body or a public authority.

[Adopted July 24, 1997. Amended February 27, 2003; November 16, 2006; October 2, 2014.]

Comment

[1] A lawyer may practice law only in a jurisdiction in which the lawyer is authorized to practice. The practice of law in violation of lawyer-licensing standards of another jurisdiction constitutes a violation of these Rules. This Rule does not restrict the ability of lawyers authorized by federal statute or other federal law to represent the interests of the United States or other persons in any jurisdiction.

[2] There are occasions in which lawyers admitted to practice in another United States jurisdiction, but not in North Carolina, and not disbarred or suspended from practice in any jurisdiction, may provide legal services on a temporary basis North Carolina under circumstances that do not create significant an unreasonable risk to the interests of their clients, the courts, or the public. Paragraphs (c), (d), and (e) identify seven situations in which the lawyer may engage in such conduct without fear of violating this Rule.

All such conduct is subject to the duty of competent representation. See Rule 1.1. Rule 5.5 does not address the question of whether other conduct constitutes the unauthorized practice of law. The fact that conduct is not included or described in this Rule is not intended to imply that such conduct is the unauthorized practice of law. With the exception of paragraphs (d) and (e), this Rule does not authorize a US or foreign lawyer to establish an office or other systematic and continuous presence in North Carolina without being admitted to practice here. Presence may be systematic and continuous even if the lawyer is not physically present in this jurisdiction. A lawyer not admitted to practice in North Carolina must not hold out to the public or otherwise represent that the lawyer is admitted to practice law in North Carolina. *See also* Rules 7.1(a) and 7.5(b). However, a lawyer admitted to practice in another jurisdiction who is partner, shareholder, or employee of an interstate or international law firm that is registered with the North Carolina State Bar pursuant to 27 N.C.A.C. 1E, Section .0200, may practice, subject to the limitations of this Rule, in the North Carolina offices of such law firm.

[3] Paragraphs (c), (d), and (e) apply to lawyers who are admitted to practice law in any United States jurisdiction, which includes the District of Columbia and any state, territory, or commonwealth of the United States and, where noted, any foreign jurisdiction. The word "admitted" in paragraphs (c), (d)(2), and (e) contemplates that the lawyer is authorized to practice in the jurisdiction in which the lawyer is admitted and excludes a lawyer who while technically admitted is not authorized to practice because, for example, the lawyer is on inactive status.

[4] Paragraphs (c), (d), and (e) do not authorize communications advertising legal services in North Carolina by lawyers who are admitted to practice in other jurisdictions. Nothing in these paragraphs authorizes a lawyer not licensed in this jurisdiction to solicit clients in North Carolina. Whether and how lawyers may communicate the availability of their services in this jurisdiction are governed by Rules 7.1–7.5.

[5] Lawyers not admitted to practice generally in North Carolina may be authorized by law or order of a tribunal or an administrative agency to appear before the tribunal or agency. Such authority may be granted pursuant to formal rules or law governing admission pro hac vice or pursuant to informal practice of the tribunal or agency. Under paragraph (c)(1), a lawyer does not violate this Rule when the lawyer appears before such a tribunal or agency. Nor does a lawyer violate this Rule when the lawyer engages in conduct in anticipation of a proceeding or hearing, such as factual investigations and discovery conducted in connection with a litigation or administrative proceeding, in which an out-of-state lawyer has been admitted or in which the lawyer reasonably expects to be admitted.

[6] Paragraph (c)(2) recognizes that the complexity of many matters requires that a lawyer whose representation of a client consists primarily of conduct in a jurisdiction in which the lawyer is admitted to practice, also be permitted to act on the client's behalf in other jurisdictions in matters arising out of or otherwise reasonably related to the lawyer's representation of the client. This conduct may involve negotiations with private parties, as well as negotiations with government officers or employees, and participation in alternative dispute-resolution procedures. This provision also applies when a lawyer is conducting witness interviews or other activities in this jurisdiction in preparation for a litigation or other proceeding that will occur in another jurisdiction where the lawyer is either admitted generally or expects to be admitted pro hac vice.

[7] Paragraph (c)(3) permits a lawyer admitted to practice law in another jurisdiction to perform services on a temporary basis in North Carolina if those services are in or reasonably related to a pending or potential arbitration, mediation, or other alternative dispute resolution proceeding in this or another jurisdiction, and if the services arise out of or are reasonably related to the lawyer's practice in a jurisdiction in which the lawyer is admitted to practice. The lawyer, however, must obtain admission pro hac vice in the case of a court-annexed arbitration or mediation or otherwise if court rules or law so require.

[8] Paragraph (c)(4) recognizes that association with a lawyer licensed to practice in North Carolina is likely to protect the interests of both clients and the public. The lawyer admitted to practice in North Carolina, however, may not serve merely as a conduit for an out-of-state lawyer but must actively participate in and share actual responsibility for the representation of the client. If the admitted lawyer's involvement is merely pro forma, then both lawyers are subject to discipline under this Rule.

[9] Paragraphs (d) and (e) identify three circumstances in which a lawyer who is admitted to practice in another jurisdiction, or a foreign jurisdiction, and is not disbarred or suspended from practice in any jurisdiction or the equivalent thereof, may establish an office or other systematic and continuous presence in North Carolina for the practice of law. Except as provided in these paragraphs, a lawyer who is admitted to practice law in another jurisdiction and who desires to establish an office or other systematic or continuous presence in North Carolina must be admitted to practice law generally in North Carolina.

[10] Paragraph (d)(1) applies to a lawyer who is employed by a client to provide legal services to the client or its organizational affiliates, i.e., entities that control, are controlled by, or are under common control with the employer. This paragraph does not authorize the provision of personal legal services to the employer's officers or employees. The paragraph applies to in-house corporate lawyers, government lawyers, and others who are employed to render legal services to the employer. The lawyer's ability to represent the employer outside the jurisdiction in which the lawyer is licensed generally serves the interests of the employer and does not create an unreasonable risk to the client and others because the employer is well situated to assess the lawyer's qualifications and the quality of the lawyer's work.

[11] Paragraph (d)(2) recognizes that a lawyer may provide legal services in a jurisdiction in which the lawyer is not licensed when authorized to do so by federal or other law, which includes statute, court rule, executive regulation, or judicial precedent.

[12] Paragraph (e) permits a lawyer who is awaiting admission by comity to practice on a provisional and limited basis if certain requirements are met. As used in this paragraph, the term "professional relationship" refers to an employment or partnership arrangement.

[13] The definition of the practice of law is established by N.C.G.S. § 84-2.1. Limiting the practice of law to members of the bar protects the public against rendition of legal services by unqualified persons. Paragraph (d) does not prohibit a lawyer from employing the services of paraprofessionals and delegating functions to them, so long as the lawyer supervis-

es the delegated work and retains responsibility for their work. *See* Rule 5.3

[14] Lawyers may also provide professional advice and instruction to nonlawyers whose employment requires knowledge of law; for example, claims adjusters, employees of financial or commercial institutions, social workers, accountants, and persons employed in government agencies. In addition, a lawyer may counsel nonlawyers who wish to proceed *pro se.* However, a lawyer may not assist a person in practicing law in violation of the rules governing professional conduct in that person's jurisdiction.

[15] Paragraphs (g) and (h) clarify the limitations on employment of a disbarred or suspended lawyer. In the absence of statutory prohibitions or specific conditions placed on a disbarred or suspended lawyer in the order revoking or suspending the license, such individual may be hired to perform the services of a law clerk or legal assistant by a law firm with which he or she was not affiliated at the time of or after the acts resulting in discipline. Such employment is, however, subject to certain restrictions. A licensed lawyer in the firm must take full responsibility for, and employ independent judgment in, adopting any research, investigative results, briefs, pleadings, or other documents or instruments drafted by such individual. The individual may not directly advise clients or communicate in person or in writing in such a way as to imply that he or she is acting as a lawyer or in any way in which he or she seems to assume responsibility for a client's legal matters. The disbarred or suspended lawyer should have no communications or dealings with, or on behalf of, clients represented by such disbarred or suspended lawyer or by any individual or group of individuals with whom he or she practiced during the period on or after the date of the acts which resulted in discipline through and including the effective date of the discipline. Further, the employing lawyer or law firm should perform no services for clients represented by the disbarred or suspended lawyer during such period. Care should be taken to ensure that clients fully understand that the disbarred or suspended lawyer is not acting as a lawyer, but merely as a law clerk or lay employee. Under some circumstances, as where the individual may be known to clients or in the community, it may be necessary to make an affirmative statement or disclosure concerning the disbarred or suspended lawyer's status with the law firm. Additionally, a disbarred or suspended lawyer should be paid on some fixed basis, such as a straight salary or hourly rate, rather than on the basis of fees generated or received in connection with particular matters on which he or she works. Under these circumstances, a law firm employing a disbarred or suspended lawyer would not be acting unethically and would not be assisting a nonlawyer in the unauthorized practice of law.

[16] A lawyer or law firm should not employ a disbarred or suspended lawyer who was associated with such lawyer or firm at any time on or after the date of the acts which resulted in the disbarment or suspension through and including the time of the disbarment or suspension. Such employment would show disrespect for the court or body which disbarred or suspended the lawyer. Such employment would also be likely to be prejudicial to the administration of justice and would create an appearance of impropriety. It would also be practically impossible for the disciplined lawyer to confine himself or herself to activities not involving the actual practice of law if he or she were employed in his or her former office setting and obliged to deal with the same staff and clientele.

Rule 5.6 Restrictions on Right to Practice

A lawyer shall not participate in offering or making:

(a) a partnership, shareholders, operating, employment, or other similar type of agreement that restricts the right of a lawyer to practice after termination of the relationship, except an agreement concerning benefits upon retirement; or

(b) an agreement in which a restriction on the lawyer's right to practice is part of the settlement of a controversy between private parties.

[Adopted July 24, 1997. Amended February 24, 2003.]

Comment

[1] An agreement restricting the right of lawyers to practice after leaving a firm not only limits their professional autonomy but also limits the freedom of clients to choose a lawyer. Paragraph (a) prohibits such agreements except for restrictions incident to provisions concerning retirement benefits for service with the firm.

[2] Paragraph (b) prohibits a lawyer from agreeing not to represent other persons in connection with setting a claim on behalf of a client.

[3] This Rule does not prohibit restrictions that may be included in the terms of the sale of a law practice pursuant to Rule 1.17.

Rule 5.7 Responsibilities Regarding Law–Related Services

(a) A lawyer shall be subject to the Rules of Professional Conduct with respect to the provision of law-related services, as defined in paragraph (b), if the law-related services are provided:

(1) by the lawyer in circumstances that are not distinct from the lawyer's provision of legal services to clients; or

(2) by a separate entity controlled by the lawyer individually or with others if the lawyer fails to take reasonable measures to assure that a person obtaining the law-related services knows that the services of the separate entity are not legal services and that the protections of the client-lawyer relationship do not exist.

(b) The term "law-related services" denotes services that might reasonably be performed in conjunction with and in substance are related to the provision of legal services, and that are not prohibited as unauthorized practice of law when provided by a nonlawyer.

[Adopted February 27, 2003.]

Comment

[1] A broad range of economic and other interests of clients may be served by lawyers' engaging in the delivery of law-related services. Examples of law-related services include providing financial planning, accounting, trust services, real estate counseling, legislative lobbying, economic analysis,

social work, psychological counseling, tax preparation, and patent, medical or environmental consulting.

[2] When a lawyer performs law-related services or controls an organization that does so, there exists the potential for ethical problems. Principal among these is the possibility that the person for whom the law-related services are performed fails to understand that the services may not carry with them the protections normally afforded as part of the client-lawyer relationship. The recipient of the law-related services may expect, for example, that the protection of client confidences, prohibitions against representation of persons with conflicting interests, and obligations of a lawyer to maintain professional independence apply to the provision of law-related services when that may not be the case.

[3] Rule 5.7 applies to the provision of law-related services by a lawyer even when the lawyer does not provide any legal services to the person for whom the law-related services are performed. The Rule identifies the circumstances in which all of the Rules of Professional Conduct apply to the provision of law-related services. Even when those circumstances do not exist, however, the conduct of a lawyer involved in the provision of law-related services is subject to those Rules that apply generally to lawyer conduct, regardless of whether the conduct involves the provision of legal services. See, e.g., Rule 8.4.

[4] When law-related services are provided by a lawyer under circumstances that are not distinct from the lawyer's provision of legal services to clients, the lawyer in providing the law-related services must adhere to the requirements of the Rules of Professional Conduct as provided in Rule 5.7(a)(1).

[5] Law–related services also may be provided through an entity that is distinct from that through which the lawyer provides legal services. If the lawyer individually or with others has control of such an entity's operations, the Rule requires the lawyer to take reasonable measures to assure that each person using the services of the entity knows that the services provided by the entity are not legal services and that the Rules of Professional Conduct that relate to the client-lawyer relationship do not apply. A lawyer's control of an entity extends to the ability to direct its operation. Whether a lawyer has such control will depend upon the circumstances of the particular case.

[6] When a client-lawyer relationship exists with a person who is referred by a lawyer to a separate law-related service entity controlled by the lawyer, individually or with others, the lawyer must comply with Rule 1.8(a).

[7] In taking the reasonable measures referred to in paragraph (a)(2) to assure that a person using law-related services understands the practical effect or significance of the inapplicability of the Rules of Professional Conduct, the lawyer should communicate to the person receiving the law-related services, in a manner sufficient to assure that the person understands the significance of the fact, that the relationship of the person to the business entity will not be a client-lawyer relationship. The communication should be made before entering into an agreement for provision of or providing law-related services, and preferably should be in writing.

[8] The burden is upon the lawyer to show that the lawyer has taken reasonable measures under the circumstances to communicate the desired understanding. For instance, a sophisticated user of law-related services, such as a publicly held corporation, may require a lesser explanation than someone unaccustomed to making distinctions between legal services and law-related services, such as an individual seeking tax advice from a lawyer-accountant or investigative services in connection with a lawsuit.

[9] Regardless of the sophistication of potential recipients of law-related services, a lawyer should take special care to keep separate the provision of law-related and legal services in order to minimize the risk that the recipient will assume that the law-related services are legal services. The risk of such confusion is especially acute when the lawyer renders both types of services with respect to the same matter. Under some circumstances the legal and law-related services may be so closely entwined that they cannot be distinguished from each other, and the requirement of disclosure and consultation imposed by paragraph (a)(2) of the Rule cannot be met. In such a case a lawyer will be responsible for assuring that both the lawyer's conduct and, to the extent required by Rule 5.3, that of nonlawyer employees in the distinct entity that the lawyer controls complies in all respects with the Rules of Professional Conduct.

[10] When a lawyer is obliged to accord the recipients of such services the protections of those Rules that apply to the client-lawyer relationship, the lawyer must take special care to heed the proscriptions of the Rules addressing conflict of interest (Rules 1.7 through 1.11, especially Rules 1.7(a)(2) and 1.8(a), (b) and (f)), and scrupulously to adhere to the requirements of Rule 1.6 relating to disclosure of confidential information. The promotion of the law-related services must also in all respects comply with Rules 7.1 through 7.3, dealing with advertising and solicitation.

[11] When the full protections of all of the Rules of Professional Conduct do not apply to the provision of law-related services, principles of law external to the Rules, for example, the law of principal and agent, govern the legal duties owed to those receiving the services. Those other legal principles may establish a different degree of protection for the recipient with respect to confidentiality of information, conflicts of interest and permissible business relationships with clients. See also Rule 8.4 (Misconduct).

PUBLIC SERVICE

Rule 6.1. Voluntary Pro Bono Publico Service

Every lawyer has a professional responsibility to provide legal services to those unable to pay. A lawyer should aspire to render at least (50) hours of pro bono publico legal services per year. In fulfilling this responsibility, the lawyer should:

(a) provide a substantial majority of the (50) hours of legal services without fee or expectation of fee to:

(1) persons of limited means;

(2) charitable, religious, civic, community, governmental and educational organizations in matters that are designed primarily to address the needs of persons of limited means; or

(3) individuals, groups or organizations seeking to secure or protect civil rights, civil liberties or public rights, or charitable, religious, civic, community, governmental and educational organizations in matters in furtherance of their organizational purposes, where the payment of standard legal fees would significantly deplete the organization's economic resources or would be otherwise inappropriate

(b) provide any additional services through:

(1) the delivery of legal services described in paragraph (a) at a substantially reduced fee; or

(2) participation in activities for improving the law, the legal system or the legal profession.

In addition, a lawyer should voluntarily contribute financial support to organizations that provide legal services to persons of limited means.

[Adopted effective January 28, 2010.]

COMMENT

[1] Every lawyer, regardless of professional prominence or professional work load, has a responsibility to provide legal services to those unable to pay, and personal involvement in the problems of the disadvantaged can be one of the most rewarding experiences in the life of a lawyer. The North Carolina State Bar urges all lawyers to provide a minimum of 50 hours of pro bono services annually. It is recognized that in some years a lawyer may render greater or fewer hours than the annual standard specified, but during the course of his or her legal career, each lawyer should render on average per year the number of hours set forth in this Rule. Services can be performed in civil matters or in criminal or quasi-criminal matters for which there is no government obligation to provide funds for legal representation, such as post-conviction death penalty appeal cases.

[2] The critical need for legal services among persons of limited means is recognized in paragraphs (a)(1) and (2) of the Rule. Legal services to persons of limited means consists of a full range of activities, including individual and class representation, the provision of legal advice, legislative lobbying, administrative rule making and the provision of free training or mentoring to those who represent persons of limited means. The variety of these activities should facilitate participation by government lawyers, even when restrictions exist on their engaging in the outside practice of law.

[3] Persons eligible for legal services under paragraphs (a)(1) and (2) are those who qualify for participation in programs funded by the Legal Services Corporation and those whose incomes and financial resources are slightly above the guidelines utilized by such programs but, nevertheless, cannot afford counsel. Legal services can be rendered to individuals or to organizations such as homeless shelters, battered women's centers and food pantries that serve those of limited means. The term "governmental organizations" includes, but is not limited to, public protection programs and sections of governmental or public sector agencies.

[4] Because service must be provided without fee or expectation of fee, the intent of the lawyer to render free legal services is essential for the work performed to fall within the meaning of paragraph (a). Accordingly, services rendered cannot be considered pro bono if an anticipated fee is uncollected, but the award of statutory attorneys' fees in a case originally accepted as pro bono would not disqualify such services from inclusion under this section. Lawyers who do receive fees in such cases are encouraged to contribute an appropriate portion of such fees to organizations described in paragraphs (a)(2) and (3).

[5] Constitutional, statutory or regulatory restrictions may prohibit or impede government and public sector lawyers and judges from performing the pro bono services outlined in paragraphs (a)(1), (2), and (3), and (b) (1). Accordingly, where those restrictions apply, government and public sector lawyers and judges may fulfill their pro bono responsibility by performing services outlined in paragraph (b)(2). Such lawyers and judges are not expected to undertake the reporting outlined in paragraph twelve of this Comment.

[6] Paragraph (a)(3) includes the provision of certain types of legal services to those whose incomes and financial resources place them above limited means. Examples of the types of issues that may be addressed under this paragraph include First Amendment claims, Title VII claims and environmental protection claims. Additionally, a wide range of organizations may be represented, including social service, medical research, cultural and religious groups.

[7] Paragraph (b)(1) covers instances in which lawyers agree to and receive a modest fee for furnishing legal services to persons of limited means. Participation in judicare programs and acceptance of court appointments in which the fee is substantially below a lawyer's usual rate are encouraged under this section.

[8] Paragraph (b)(2) recognizes the value of lawyers engaging in activities that improve the law, the legal system or the legal profession. Serving on bar association committees; serving on boards of pro bono or legal services programs; taking part in Law Day activities; acting as a continuing legal education instructor, a mediator or an arbitrator; and engaging in legislative lobbying to improve the law, the legal system or the profession are a few examples of the many activities that fall within this paragraph.

[9] Because the efforts of individual lawyers are not enough to meet the need for free legal services that exists among persons of limited means, the government and the profession have instituted additional programs to provide those services. Every lawyer should financially support such programs, in addition to either providing direct pro bono services or making financial contributions when pro bono service is not feasible.

[10] Law firms should act reasonably to enable and encourage all lawyers in the firm to provide the pro bono legal services called for by this Rule.

[11] The responsibility set forth in this Rule is not intended to be enforced through disciplinary process.

[12] Lawyers are encouraged to report pro bono legal services to Legal Aid of North Carolina, the North Carolina Equal Access to Justice Commission, or other similar agency as appropriate in order that such service might be recognized and serve as an inspiration to others.

Rule 6.2 [Reserved]

Rule 6.3 Membership in Legal Services Organization

A lawyer may serve as a director, officer or member of a legal services organization, apart from the law firm in which the lawyer practices, notwithstanding that the organization serves persons having interests adverse to a client of the lawyer. The lawyer shall not knowingly participate in a decision or action of the organization:

(a) if participating in the decision or action would be incompatible with the lawyer's obligations to a client under Rule 1.7; or

(b) where the decision or action could have a material adverse effect on the representation of a client of the organization whose interests are adverse to a client of the lawyer.

[Adopted July 24, 1997. Amended February 27, 2003.]

Comment

[1] Lawyers should be encouraged to support and participate in legal service organizations. A lawyer who is an officer or a member of such an organization does not thereby have a client-lawyer relationship with persons served by the organization. However, there is potential conflict between the interests of such persons and the interests of the lawyer's clients. If the possibility of such conflict disqualified a lawyer from serving on the board of a legal services organization, the profession's involvement in such organizations would be severely curtailed.

[2] It may be necessary in appropriate cases to reassure a client of the organization that the representation will not be affected by conflicting loyalties of a member of the board. Established written policies in this respect can enhance the credibility of such assurances.

Rule 6.4 Law Reform Activities Affecting Client Interests

A lawyer may serve as a director, officer or member of an organization involved in reform of the law or its administration notwithstanding that the reform may affect the interests of a client of the lawyer. When the lawyer knows that the interests of a client may be materially benefited by a decision in which the lawyer participates, the lawyer shall disclose that fact but need not identify the client.

[Adopted July 24, 1997. Amended February 27, 2003.]

Comment

[1] Lawyers involved in organizations seeking law reform generally do not have a client-lawyer relationship with the organization. Otherwise, it might follow that a lawyer could not be involved in a bar association law reform program that might indirectly affect a client. See also Rule 1.2(b). For example, a lawyer concentrating in antitrust litigation might be regarded as disqualified from participating in drafting revisions of rules governing that subject. In determining the nature and scope of participation in such activities, a lawyer should be mindful of obligations to clients under other Rules, particularly Rule 1.7. A lawyer is professionally obligated to protect the integrity of the program by making an appropriate disclosure within the organization when the lawyer knows a private client might be materially benefited.

Rule 6.5 Limited Legal Services Programs

(a) A lawyer who, under the auspices of a program sponsored by a nonprofit organization or court, provides short-term limited legal services to a client without expectation by either the lawyer or the client that the lawyer will provide continuing representation in the matter:

(1) is subject to Rules 1.7 and 1.9(a) only if the lawyer knows that the representation of the client involves a conflict of interest; and

(2) is subject to Rule 1.10 only if the lawyer knows that another lawyer associated with the lawyer in a law firm is disqualified by Rule 1.7 or 1.9(a) with respect to the matter.

(b) Except as provided in paragraph (a)(2), Rule 1.10 is inapplicable to a representation governed by this Rule.

[Adopted February 27, 2003.]

Comment

[1] Legal services organizations, courts and various nonprofit organizations have established programs through which lawyers provide short-term limited legal services — such as advice or the completion of legal forms—that will assist persons to address their legal problems without further representation by a lawyer, in these programs, such as legal-advice hotlines, advice-only clinics or pro se counseling programs, a client-lawyer relationship is established, but there is no expectation that the lawyer's representation of the client will continue beyond the limited consultation. Such programs are normally operated under circumstances in which it is not feasible for a lawyer to systematically screen for conflicts of interest as is generally required before undertaking a representation. See, e.g., Rules 1.7, 1.9 and 1.10.

[2] A lawyer who provides short-term limited legal services pursuant to this Rule must secure the client's informed consent to the limited scope of the representation. See Rule 1.2(c). If a short-term limited representation would not be reasonable under the circumstances, the lawyer may offer advice to the client but must also advise the client of the need for further assistance of counsel. Except as provided in this Rule, the Rules of Professional Conduct, including Rules 1.6 and 1.9(c), are applicable to the limited representation.

[3] Because a lawyer who is representing a client in the circumstances addressed by this Rule ordinarily is not able to check systematically for conflicts of interest, paragraph (a) requires compliance with Rules 1.7 or 1. 9(a) only if the lawyer knows that the representation presents a conflict of interest for the lawyer, and with Rule 1.10 only if the lawyer knows that another lawyer in the lawyer's firm is disqualified by Rules 1.7 or 1.9(a) in the matter.

[4] Because the limited nature of the services significantly reduces the risk of conflicts of interest with other matters being handled by the lawyer's firm, paragraph (b) provides that Rule 1.10 is inapplicable to a representation governed by this Rule except as provided by paragraph (a)(2). Paragraph (a)(2) requires the participating lawyer to comply with Rule 1.10 when the lawyer knows that the lawyer's firm is disqualified by Rules 1.7 or 1.9(a). By virtue of paragraph (b),

however, a lawyer's participation in a short-term limited legal services program will not preclude the lawyer's firm from undertaking or continuing the representation of a client with interests adverse to a client being represented under the program's auspices. Nor will the personal disqualification of a lawyer participating in the program be imputed to other lawyers participating in the program.

[5] If, after commencing a short-term limited representation in accordance with this Rule, a lawyer undertakes to represent the client in the matter on an ongoing basis, Rules 1.7, 1.9(a) and 1.10 become applicable.

Rule 6.6 Action as a Public Official

A lawyer who holds public office shall not

(a) use his or her public position to obtain, or attempt to obtain, a special advantage in legislative matters for himself or herself, or for a client under circumstances where the lawyer knows or it is obvious that such action is not in the public interest;

(b) use his or her public position to influence, or attempt to influence, a tribunal to act in favor of himself or herself or his or her client;

(c) accept anything of value from any person when the lawyer knows or it is obvious that the offer is for the purpose of influencing the lawyer's action as a public official.

[Adopted July 24, 1997. Amended February 27, 2003.]

Comment

[1] Lawyers often serve as legislators or as holders of other public offices. This is highly desirable, as lawyers are uniquely qualified to make significant contributions to the improvement of the legal system. A lawyer who is a public officer, whether full or part time, should not engage in activities in which the lawyer's personal or professional interests are or foreseeably may be in conflict with his or her official duties.

INFORMATION ABOUT LEGAL SERVICES

Rule 7.1 Communications Concerning a Lawyer's Services

(a) A lawyer shall not make a false or misleading communication about the lawyer or the lawyer's services. A communication is false or misleading if it:

(1) contains a material misrepresentation of fact or law, or omits a fact necessary to make the statement considered as a whole not materially misleading;

(2) is likely to create an unjustified expectation about results the lawyer can achieve, or states or implies that the lawyer can achieve results by means that violate the Rules of Professional Conduct or other law; or

(3) compares the lawyer's services with other lawyers' services, unless the comparison can be factually substantiated.

(b) A communication by a lawyer that contains a dramatization depicting a fictional situation is misleading unless it complies with paragraph (a) above and contains a conspicuous written or oral statement, at the beginning and the end of the communication, explaining that the communication contains a dramatization and does not depict actual events or real persons.

[Adopted July 24, 1997. Amended February 27, 2003; October 2, 2014.]

Comment

[1] This Rule governs all communications about a lawyer's services, including advertising permitted by Rule 7.2. Whatever means are used to make known a lawyer's services, statements about them must be truthful.

[2] Truthful statements that are misleading are also prohibited by this Rule. A truthful statement is misleading if it omits a fact necessary to make the lawyer's communication considered as a whole not materially misleading. A truthful statement is also misleading if there is a substantial likelihood that it will lead a reasonable person to formulate a specific conclusion about the lawyer or the lawyer's services for which there is no reasonable factual foundation.

[3] An advertisement that truthfully reports a lawyer's achievements on behalf of clients or former clients may be misleading if presented so as to lead a reasonable person to form an unjustified expectation that the same results could be obtained for other clients in similar matters without reference to the specific factual and legal circumstances of each client's case. Similarly, an unsubstantiated comparison of the lawyer's services or fees with the services or fees of other lawyers may be misleading if presented with such specificity as would lead a reasonable person to conclude that the comparison can be substantiated. The inclusion of an appropriate disclaimer or qualifying language may preclude a finding that a statement is likely to create unjustified expectations or otherwise mislead the public.

[4] See also Rule 8.4(e) for the prohibition against stating or implying an ability to influence improperly a government agency or official or to achieve results by means that violate the Rules of Professional Conduct or other law.

Rule 7.2. Advertising

(a) Subject to the requirements of Rules 7.1 and 7.3, a lawyer may advertise services through written, recorded, or electronic communication, including public media.

(b) A lawyer shall not give anything of value to a person for recommending the lawyer's services except that a lawyer may

(1) pay the reasonable costs of advertisements or communications permitted by this Rule;

(2) pay the usual charges of a not-for-profit lawyer referral service that complies with Rule 7.2(d), or a

prepaid or group legal services plan that complies with Rule 7.3(d); and

(3) pay for a law practice in accordance with Rule 1.17.

(c) Any communication made pursuant to this rule, other than that of a lawyer referral service as described in paragraph (d), shall include the name and office address of at least one lawyer or law firm responsible for its content.

(d) A lawyer may participate in a lawyer referral service subject to the following conditions:

(1) the lawyer is professionally responsible for its operation including the use of a false, deceptive, or misleading name by the referral service;

(2) the referral service is not operated for a profit;

(3) the lawyer may pay to the lawyer referral service only a reasonable sum which represents a proportionate share of the referral service's administrative and advertising costs;

(4) the lawyer does not directly or indirectly receive anything of value other than legal fees earned from representation of clients referred by the service;

(5) employees of the referral service do not initiate contact with prospective clients and do not engage in live telephone or in-person solicitation of clients;

(6) the referral service does not collect any sums from clients or potential clients for use of the service; and

(7) all advertisements by the lawyer referral service shall:

(A) state that a list of all participating lawyers will be mailed free of charge to members of the public upon request and state where such information may be obtained; and

(B) explain the method by which the needs of the prospective client are matched with the qualifications of the recommended lawyer.

[Adopted July 24, 1997. Amended February 27, 2003; October 2, 2014.]

Comment

[1] To assist the public in learning about and obtaining legal services, lawyers are permitted to make known their services not only through reputation, but also through organized information campaigns in the form of advertising. Advertising involves an active quest for clients, contrary to the tradition that a lawyer should not seek clientele. However, the public's need to know about legal services can be fulfilled in part through advertising. This need is particularly acute in the case of persons of moderate means who have not made extensive use of legal services. The interest in expanding public information about legal services ought to prevail over considerations of tradition. Nevertheless, advertising by lawyers may entail the risk of practices that are misleading or overreaching.

[2] This Rule permits public dissemination of information concerning a lawyer's name or firm name, address, email address, website, and telephone number; the kinds of services the lawyer will undertake; the basis on which the lawyer's fees are determined, including prices for specific services and payment and credit arrangements; a lawyer's foreign language ability; names of references and, with their consent, names of clients regularly represented; and other information that might invite the attention of those seeking legal assistance.

[3] Questions of effectiveness and taste in advertising are matters of speculation and subjective judgment. Television, the Internet, and other forms of electronic communication are now among the most powerful media for getting information to the public, particularly persons of low and moderate income; prohibiting television, Internet, and other forms of electronic advertising, therefore, would impede the flow of information about legal services to many sectors of the public. Limiting the information that may be advertised has a similar effect and assumes that the bar can accurately forecast the kind of information that the public would regard as relevant. But see Rule 7.1(b) for the disclaimer required in any advertisement that contains a dramatization and see Rule 7.3(a) for the prohibition against a solicitation through a real-time electronic exchange initiated by the lawyer.

[4] Neither this Rule nor Rule 7.3 prohibits communications authorized by law, such as notice to members of a class in class action litigation.

Paying Others to Recommend a Lawyer

[5] Except as permitted under paragraphs (b)(1)–(b)(3), lawyers are not permitted to pay others for recommending the lawyer's services or for channeling professional work in a manner that violates Rule 7.3. A communication contains a recommendation if it endorses or vouches for a lawyer's credentials, abilities, competence, character, or other professional qualities. Paragraph (b)(1), however, allows a lawyer to pay for advertising and communications permitted by this Rule, including the costs of print directory listings, on-line directory listings, newspaper ads, television and radio airtime, domain-name registrations, sponsorship fees, Internet-based advertisements, and group advertising. A lawyer may compensate employees, agents, and vendors who are engaged to provide marketing or client-development services, such as publicists, public-relations personnel, business-development staff, and website designers. Moreover, a lawyer may pay others for generating client leads, such as Internet-based client leads, as long as the lead generator does not recommend the lawyer, any payment to the lead generator is consistent with Rule 1.5(e) (division of fees) and 5.4 (professional independence of the lawyer), and the lead generator's communications are consistent with Rule 7.1 (communications concerning a lawyer's service). To comply with Rule 7.1, a lawyer must not pay a lead generator if the lead generator states, implies, or creates an impression that it is recommending the lawyer, is making the referral without payment from the lawyer, or has analyzed a person's legal problems when determining which lawyer should receive the referral. *See* also Rule 5.3 (duties of lawyers and law firms with respect to the conduct of nonlawyers); Rule 8.4(a) (duty to avoid violating the Rules through the acts of another).

[6] A lawyer may pay the usual charges of a prepaid or group legal services plan or a not-for-profit lawyer referral service. A legal services plan is defined in Rule 7.3(d). Such a plan assists people who seek to secure legal representation. A lawyer referral service, on the other hand, is any organization that holds itself out to the public as a lawyer referral service. Such referral services are understood by the public to be consumer-oriented organizations that provide unbiased

referrals to lawyers with appropriate experience in the subject matter of the representation and afford other client protections, such as complaint procedures or malpractice insurance requirements. Consequently, this Rule only permits a lawyer to pay the usual charges of a not-for-profit lawyer referral service.

[7] A lawyer who accepts assignments or referrals from a prepaid or group legal service plan or referrals from a lawyer referral service must act reasonably to assure that the activities of the plan or service are compatible with the lawyer's professional obligations. See Rule 5.3. Any lawyer who participates in a legal services plan or lawyer referral service is professionally responsible for the operation of the service in accordance with these rules regardless of the lawyer's knowledge, or lack of knowledge, of the activities of the service. Legal service plans and lawyer referral services may communicate with the public, but such communication must be in conformity with these Rules. Thus, advertising must not be false or misleading, as would be the case if the communications of a group advertising program or a group legal services plan would mislead prospective clients to think that it was a lawyer referral service sponsored by a state agency or bar association. The term "referral" implies that some attempt is made to match the needs of the prospective client with the qualifications of the recommended lawyer. To avoid misrepresentation, paragraph (d)(7)(B) requires that every advertisement for the service must include an explanation of the method by which a prospective client is matched with the lawyer to whom he or she is referred. In addition, the lawyer may not allow in-person, telephonic, or real-time contacts that would violate Rule 7.3.

Rule 7.3. Direct Contact with Potential Clients

(a) A lawyer shall not by in-person, live telephone, or real-time electronic contact solicit professional employment when a significant motive for the lawyer's doing so is the lawyer's pecuniary gain, unless the person contacted:

(1) is a lawyer; or

(2) has a family, close personal, or prior professional relationship with the lawyer.

(b) A lawyer shall not solicit professional employment from a potential client by written, recorded or electronic communication or by in-person, telephone or real-time electronic contact even when not otherwise prohibited by paragraph (a), if:

(1) the target of the solicitation has made known to the lawyer a desire not to be solicited by the lawyer; or

(2) the solicitation involves coercion, duress, harassment, compulsion, intimidation, or threats.

(c) Targeted Communications. Unless the recipient of the communication is a person specified in paragraphs (a)(1) or (a)(2), every written, recorded, or electronic communication from a lawyer soliciting professional employment from anyone known to be in need of legal services in a particular matter shall include the statement, in capital letters, "THIS IS AN ADVERTISEMENT FOR LEGAL SERVICES" (the advertising notice), which shall be conspicuous and subject to the following requirements:

(1) *Written Communications.* Written communications shall be mailed in an envelope. The advertising notice shall be printed on the front of the envelope, in a font that is as large as any other printing on the front or the back of the envelope. If more than one color or type of font is used on the front or the back of the envelope, the font used for the advertising notice shall match in color, type, and size the largest and widest of the fonts. The front of the envelope shall contain no printing other than the name of the lawyer or law firm and return address, the name and address of the recipient, and the advertising notice. The advertising notice shall also be printed at the beginning of the body of the enclosed written communication in a font as large as or larger than any other printing contained in the enclosed written communication. If more than one color or type of font is used on the enclosed written communication, then the font of the advertising notice shall match in color, type, and size the largest and widest of the fonts. Nothing on the envelope or the enclosed written communication shall be more conspicuous than the advertising notice.

(2) *Electronic Communications.* The advertising notice shall appear in the "in reference" or subject box of the address or header section of the communication. No other statement shall appear in this block. The advertising notice shall also appear, at the beginning and ending of the electronic communication, in a font as large as or larger than any other printing in the body of the communication or in any masthead on the communication. If more than one color or type of font is used in the electronic communication, then the font of the advertising notice shall match in color, type, and size the largest and widest of the fonts. Nothing in the electronic communication shall be more conspicuous than the advertising notice.

(3) *Recorded Communications.* The advertising notice shall be clearly articulated at the beginning and ending of the recorded communication.

(d) Notwithstanding the prohibitions in paragraph (a), a lawyer may participate with a prepaid or group legal service plan subject to the following:

(1) *Definition.* A prepaid legal services plan or a group legal services plan ("a plan") is any arrangement by which a person, firm, or corporation, not otherwise authorized to engage in the practice of law, in exchange for any valuable consideration, offers to provide or arranges the provision of legal services that are paid for in advance of any immediate need for the specified legal service ("covered services"). In addition to covered services, a plan may provide specified legal services at fees that are less than what a non-member of the plan would normally pay. The North Carolina legal services offered by a plan must be provided by a licensed lawyer who is not an employee, director or owner of the plan. A prepaid legal services plan does not include the sale of an identified,

limited legal service, such as drafting a will, for a fixed, one-time fee.

(2) *Conditions for Participation.*

(A) The plan must be operated by an organization that is not owned or directed by the lawyer;

(B) The plan must be registered with the North Carolina State Bar and comply with all applicable rules regarding such plans;

(C) The lawyer must notify the State Bar in writing before participating in a plan and must notify the State Bar no later than 30 days after the lawyer discontinues participation in the plan;

(D) After reasonable investigation, the lawyer must have a good faith belief that the plan is being operated in compliance with the Revised Rules of Professional Conduct and other pertinent rules of the State Bar;

(E) All advertisements by the plan representing that it is registered with the State Bar shall also explain that registration does not constitute approval by the State Bar; and

(F) Notwithstanding the prohibitions in paragraph (a), the plan may use in-person or telephone contact to solicit memberships or subscriptions provided:

(i) The solicited person is not known to need legal services in a particular matter covered by the plan; and

(ii) The contact does not involve coercion, duress, or harassment and the communication with the solicited person is not false, deceptive or misleading.

[Adopted July 24, 1997. Amended February 27, 2003; October 6, 2004; November 16, 2006; August 23, 2007; August 25, 2011; October 2, 2014.]

Comment

[1] A solicitation is a communication initiated by the lawyer that is directed to a specific person and that offers to provide, or can reasonably be understood as offering to provide, legal services. In contrast, a lawyer's communication typically does not constitute a solicitation if it is directed to the general public, such as through a billboard, an Internet banner advertisement, a website or a television commercial, or if it is in response to a request for information or is automatically generated in response to Internet searches.

[2] There is a potential for abuse when a solicitation involves direct in-person, live telephone, or real-time electronic contact by a lawyer with someone a known to need legal services. These forms of contact subject a person to the private importuning of the trained advocate in a direct interpersonal encounter. The person, who may already feel overwhelmed by the circumstances giving rise to the need for legal services, may find it difficult fully to evaluate all available alternatives with reasoned judgment and appropriate self-interest in the face of the lawyer's presence and insistence upon being retained immediately. The situation is fraught with the possibility of undue influence, intimidation, and over-reaching.

[3] This potential for abuse inherent in direct in-person, live telephone, or real-time electronic solicitation justifies its prohibition, particularly because lawyers have alternative means of conveying necessary information to those who may be in need of legal services. In particular, communications can be mailed or transmitted by email or other electronic means that do not involve real-time contact and do not violate other laws governing solicitations. These forms of communications and solicitations make it possible for the public to be informed about the need for legal services, and about the qualifications of available lawyers and law firms, without subjecting the public to direct in-person, telephone or real-time electronic persuasion that may overwhelm a person's judgment.

[4] The use of general advertising and written, recorded or electronic communications to transmit information from lawyer to the public, rather than direct in-person, live telephone or real-time electronic contact, will help to assure that the information flows cleanly as well as freely. The contents of advertisements and communications permitted under Rule 7.2 can be permanently recorded so that they cannot be disputed and may be shared with others who know the lawyer. This potential for informal review is itself likely to help guard against statements and claims that might constitute false and misleading communications, in violation of Rule 7.1. The contents of direct in-person, live telephone, or real-time electronic contact can be disputed and may not be subject to third-party scrutiny. Consequently, they are much more likely to approach (and occasionally cross) the dividing line between accurate representations and those that are false and misleading.

[5] There is far less likelihood that a lawyer would engage in abusive practices against a former client, or a person with whom the lawyer has a close personal or family relationship, or in situations in which the lawyer is motivated by considerations other than the lawyer's pecuniary gain. Nor is there a serious potential for abuse when the person contacted is a lawyer. Consequently, the general prohibition in Rule 7.3(a) and the requirements of Rule 7.3(c) are not applicable in those situations. Also, paragraph (a) is not intended to prohibit a lawyer from participating in constitutionally protected activities of public or charitable legal-service organizations or bona fide political, social, civic, fraternal, employee or trade organizations whose purposes include providing or recommending legal services to its members or beneficiaries.

[6] But even permitted forms of solicitation can be abused. Thus, any solicitation which contains information which is false or misleading within the meaning of Rule 7.1, which involves coercion, duress, harassment, compulsion, intimidation, or threats within the meaning of Rule 7.3(b)(2), or which involves contact with someone who has made known to the lawyer a desire not to be solicited by the lawyer within the meaning of Rule 7.3(b)(1) is prohibited. Moreover, if after sending a letter or other communication as permitted by Rule 7.2 the lawyer receives no response, any further effort to communicate with the recipient of the communication may violate the provisions of Rule 7.3(b).

[7] This Rule is not intended to prohibit a lawyer from contacting representatives of organizations or groups that may be interested in establishing a group or prepaid legal plan for their members, insureds, beneficiaries, or other third parties for the purpose of informing such entities of the availability of and details concerning the plan or arrangement which the lawyer or lawyer's firm is willing to offer. This form of communication is not directed to people who are

seeking legal services for themselves. Rather, it is usually addressed to an individual acting in a fiduciary capacity seeking a supplier of legal services for others who may, if they choose, become potential clients of the lawyer. Under these circumstances, the activity which the lawyer undertakes in communicating with such representatives and the type of information transmitted to the individual are functionally similar to and serve the same purpose as advertising permitted under Rule 7.2.

[8] Paragraph (c) of this rule requires that all targeted mail solicitations of potential clients must be mailed in an envelope on which the statement, "This is an advertisement for legal services," appears in capital letters in a font at least as large as any other printing on the front or the back of the envelope. The statement must appear on the front of the envelope with no other distracting extraneous written statements other than the name and address of the recipient and the name and return address of the lawyer or firm. Postcards may not be used for targeted mail solicitations. No embarrassing personal information about the recipient may appear on the back of the envelope. The advertising notice must also appear in the "in reference" or subject box of an electronic communication (email) and at the beginning of any paper or electronic communication in a font that is at least as large as the font used for any other printing in the paper or electronic communication. On any paper or electronic communication required by this rule to contain the advertising notice, the notice must be conspicuous and should not be obscured by other objects or printing or by manipulating fonts. For example, inclusion of a large photograph or graphic image on the communication may diminish the prominence of the advertising notice. Similarly, a font that is narrow or faint may render the advertising notice inconspicuous if the fonts used elsewhere in the communication are chubby or flamboyant. The font size requirement does not apply to a brochure enclosed with the written communication if the written communication contains the required notice. As explained in 2007 Formal Ethics Opinion 15, the font size requirement does not apply to an insignia or border used in connection with a law firm's name if the insignia or border is used consistently by the firm in official communications on behalf of the firm. Nevertheless, any such insignia or border cannot be so large that it detracts from the conspicuousness of the advertising notice. The requirement that certain communications be marked, "This is an advertisement for legal services," does not apply to communications sent in response to requests of potential clients or their spokespersons or sponsors. General announcements by lawyers, including changes in personnel or office location, do not constitute communications soliciting professional employment from a client known to be in need of legal services within the meaning of this Rule.

[9] Paragraph (d) of this Rule permits a lawyer to participate with an organization which uses personal contact to solicit members for its group or prepaid legal service plan, provided that the personal contact is not undertaken by any lawyer who would be a provider of legal services through the plan. The organization must not be owned by or directed (whether as manager or otherwise) by any lawyer or law firm that participates in the plan. For example, paragraph (d) would not permit a lawyer to create an organization controlled directly or indirectly by the lawyer and use the organization for the in-person or telephone solicitation of legal employment of the lawyer through memberships in the plan or otherwise. The communication permitted by these organizations also must not be directed to a person known to need legal services in a particular matter, but is to be designed to inform potential plan members generally of another means of affordable legal services. Lawyers who participate in a legal service plan must reasonably assure that the plan sponsors are in compliance with Rule 7.3(d) as well as Rules 7.1, 7.2 and 7.3(b). See 8.4(a).

Rule 7.4 Communication of Fields of Practice

(a) A lawyer may communicate the fact that the lawyer does or does not practice in particular fields of law.

(b) A lawyer shall not state or imply that the lawyer is certified as a specialist in a field of practice unless:

(1) the certification was granted by the North Carolina State Bar;

(2) the certification was granted by an organization that is accredited by the North Carolina State Bar; or

(3) the certification was granted by an organization that is accredited by the American Bar Association under procedures and criteria endorsed by the North Carolina State Bar; and

(4) the name of the certifying organization is clearly identified in the communication.

[Adopted July 24, 1997. Amended February 27, 2003.]

Comment

[1] The use of the word "specialize" in any of its variant forms connotes to the public a particular expertise often subject to recognition by the state. Indeed, the North Carolina State Bar has instituted programs providing for official certification of specialists in certain areas of practice. Certification signifies that an objective entity has recognized an advanced degree of knowledge and experience in the specialty area greater than is suggested by general licensure to practice law. Certifying organizations are expected to apply standards of experience, knowledge and proficiency to insure that a lawyer's recognition as a specialist is meaningful and reliable. To avoid misrepresentation and deception, a lawyer may not communicate that the lawyer has been recognized or certified as a specialist in a particular field of law, except as provided by this rule. The rule requires that a representation of specialty may be made only if the certifying organization is the North Carolina State Bar, an organization accredited by the North Carolina State Bar, or an organization accredited by the American Bar Association under procedures approved by the North Carolina State Bar. To insure that consumers can obtain access to useful information about an organization granting certification, the name of the certifying organization or agency must be included in any communication regarding the certification.

[2] A lawyer may, however, describe his or her practice without using the term "specialize" in any manner which is truthful and not misleading. This rule specifically permits a lawyer to indicate areas of practice in communications about the lawyer's services. If a lawyer practices only in certain fields, or will not accept matters except in a specified field or fields, the lawyer is permitted to so indicate. The lawyer

may, for instance, indicate a "concentration" or an "interest" or a "limitation."

[3] Recognition of expertise in patent matters is a matter of long-established policy of the Patent and Trademark Office. A lawyer admitted to engage in patent practice before the United States Patent and Trademark Office may use the designation "Patent Attorney" or a substantially similar designation.

Rule 7.5 Firm Names and Letterheads

(a) A lawyer shall not use a firm name, letterhead, or other professional designation that violates Rule 7.1. A trade name may be used by a lawyer in private practice if it does not imply a connection with a government agency or with a public or charitable legal services organization and is not false or misleading in violation of Rule 7.1. Every trade name used by a law firm shall be registered with the North Carolina State Bar for a determination of whether the name is misleading.

(b) A law firm with offices in more than one jurisdiction may use the same name or other professional designation in each jurisdiction, but identification of the lawyers in an office of the firm shall indicate the jurisdictional limitations on those not licensed to practice in the jurisdiction where the office is located.

(c) A law firm maintaining offices only in North Carolina may not list any person not licensed to practice law in North Carolina as a lawyer affiliated with the firm unless the listing properly identifies the jurisdiction in which the lawyer is licensed and states that the lawyer is not licensed in North Carolina.

(d) The name of a lawyer holding a public office shall not be used in the name of a law firm, or in communications on its behalf, during any substantial period in which the lawyer is not actively and regularly practicing with the firm, whether or not the lawyer is precluded from practicing law.

(e) Lawyers may state or imply that they practice in a partnership or other professional organization only when that is the fact.

[Adopted July 24, 1997. Amended February 27, 2003.]

Comment

[1] A firm may be designated by the names of all or some of its members, by the names of deceased or retired members where there has been a continuing succession in the firm's identity, or by a trade name such as the "ABC Legal Clinic." A lawyer or law firm may also be designated by a distinctive website address or comparable professional designation. Use of trade names in law practice is acceptable so long as they are not misleading and are otherwise in conformance with the rules and regulations of the State Bar. If a private firm uses a trade name that includes a geographical name such as "Springfield Legal Clinic," an express disclaimer that it is a public legal aid agency may be required to avoid a misleading implication, A firm name that includes the surname of a deceased or retired partner is, strictly speaking, a trade name. However, the use of such names, as well as designations such as "Law Offices of John Doe." "Smith and Associates." and "Jones Law Firm" a are useful means of identification and are permissible without registration with the State Bar. However, it is misleading to use the surname of a lawyer not associated with the firm or a predecessor of the firm. It is also misleading to use a designation such as "Smith and Associates" for a solo practice. The name of a retired partner may be used in the name of a law firm only if the partner has ceased the practice of law.

[2] This rule does not prohibit the employment by a law firm of a lawyer who is licensed to practice in another jurisdiction, but not in North Carolina, provided the lawyer's practice is limited to areas that do not require a North Carolina law license such as immigration law, federal tort claims, military law, and the like. The lawyer's name may be included in the firm letterhead, provided all communications by such lawyer on behalf of the firm indicate the jurisdiction in which the lawyer is licensed as well as the fact that the lawyer is not licensed in North Carolina. If law offices are maintained in another jurisdiction, the law firm is an interstate law firm and must register with the North Carolina State Bar as required by 27 N.C.A.C. 1E, Section .0200.

[3] Nothing in these rules shall be construed to confer the right to practice North Carolina law upon any lawyer not licensed to practice law in North Carolina.

[4] With regard to paragraph (d), lawyers sharing office facilities, but who are not in fact associated with each other in a law firm, may not denominate themselves as, for example, "Smith and Jones," for that title suggests that they are practicing law together in a firm.

Rule 7.6 [Reserved]

MAINTAINING THE INTEGRITY OF THE PROFESSION

Rule 8.1 Bar Admission and Disciplinary Matters

An applicant for admission to the bar, or a lawyer in connection with a bar admission application or in connection with a disciplinary matter, shall not:

(a) knowingly make a false statement of material fact; or

(b) fail to disclose a fact necessary to correct a misapprehension known by the person to have arisen in the matter, or knowingly fail to respond to a lawful demand for information from an admissions or disciplinary authority, except that this rule does not require disclosure of information otherwise protected by Rule 1.6.

[Adopted July 24, 1997. Amended February 27, 2003.]

Comment

[1] The duty imposed by this Rule extends to persons seeking admission to the bar as well as to lawyers. Hence, if a person makes a material false statement in connection with

an application for admission, it may be the basis for subsequent disciplinary action if the person is admitted, and in any event may be relevant in a subsequent admission application. The duty imposed by this Rule applies to a lawyer's own admission or discipline as well as that of others. Thus, it is a separate professional offense for a lawyer to knowingly make a misrepresentation or omission in connection with a disciplinary investigation of the lawyer's own conduct. Paragraph (b) of this Rule also requires correction of any prior misstatement in the matter that the applicant or lawyer may have made and affirmative clarification of any misunderstanding on the part of the admissions or disciplinary authority of which the person involved becomes aware. It should also be noted that G.S. Sect. 84-28(b)(3) defines failure to answer a formal inquiry of the North Carolina State Bar as misconduct for which discipline is appropriate.

[2] This Rule is subject to the provisions of the fifth amendment of the United States Constitution and corresponding provisions of the North Carolina Constitution. A person relying on such a provision in response to a question, however, should do so openly and not use the right of nondisclosure as a justification for failure to comply with this Rule.

[3] A lawyer representing an applicant for admission to the bar, or representing a lawyer who is the subject of a disciplinary inquiry or proceeding, is governed by the rules applicable to the client-lawyer relationship, including Rule 1.6 and, in some cases, Rule 3.3.

Rule 8.2 Judicial and Legal Officials

(a) A lawyer shall not make a statement that the lawyer knows to be false or with reckless disregard as to its truth or falsity concerning the qualifications or integrity of a judge, or other adjudicatory officer or of a candidate for election or appointment to judicial office.

(b) A lawyer who is a candidate for judicial office shall comply with the applicable provisions of the Code of Judicial Conduct.

[Adopted July 24, 1997. Amended February 27, 2003.]

Comment

[1] Assessments by lawyers are relied on in evaluating the professional or personal fitness of persons being considered for election or appointment to judicial office. Expressing honest and candid opinions on such matters contributes to improving the administration of justice. Conversely, false statements by a lawyer can unfairly undermine public confidence in the administration of justice.

[2] When a lawyer seeks judicial office, the lawyer should be bound by applicable limitations on political activity.

[3] To maintain the fair and independent administration of justice, lawyers are encouraged to continue traditional efforts to defend judges and courts unjustly criticized. Adjudicatory officials, not being wholly free to defend themselves, are entitled to receive the support of the bar against such unjust criticism.

[4] While a lawyer as a citizen has a right to criticize such officials publicly, the lawyer should be certain of the merit of the complaint, use appropriate language, and avoid petty criticisms, for unrestrained and intemperate statements tend to lessen public confidence in our legal system. Criticisms motivated by reasons other than a desire to improve the legal system are not justified.

Rule 8.3. Reporting Professional Misconduct

(a) A lawyer who knows that another lawyer has committed a violation of the Rules of Professional Conduct that raises a substantial question as to that lawyer's honesty, trustworthiness, or fitness as a lawyer in other respects, shall inform the North Carolina State Bar or the court having jurisdiction over the matter.

(b) A lawyer who knows that a judge has committed a violation of applicable rules of judicial conduct that raises a substantial question as to the judge's fitness for office shall inform the North Carolina Judicial Standards Commission or other appropriate authority.

(c) This Rule does not require disclosure of information otherwise protected by Rule 1.6.

(d) A lawyer who is disciplined in any state or federal court for a violation of the Rules of Professional Conduct in effect in such state or federal court shall inform the secretary of the North Carolina State Bar of such action in writing no later than 30 days after entry of the order of discipline.

(e) A lawyer who is serving as a mediator and who is subject to the North Carolina Supreme Court Standards of Professional Conduct for Mediators (the Standards) is not required to disclose information learned during a mediation if the Standards do not allow disclosure. If disclosure is allowed by the Standards, the lawyer is required to report professional misconduct consistent with the duty to report set forth in paragraph (a).

[Adopted July 24, 1997. Amended February 27, 2003; amended effective October 7, 2010.]

Comment

[1] Self-regulation of the legal profession requires that members of the profession initiate disciplinary investigation when they know of a violation of the Rules of Professional Conduct. Lawyers have a similar obligation with respect to judicial misconduct. An apparently isolated violation may indicate a pattern of misconduct that only a disciplinary investigation can uncover. Reporting a violation is especially important where the victim is unlikely to discover the offense.

[2] Although the North Carolina State Bar is always an appropriate place to report a violation of the Rules of Professional Conduct, the courts of North Carolina have concurrent jurisdiction over the conduct of the lawyers who appear before them. Therefore, a lawyer's duty to report may be satisfied by reporting to the presiding judge the misconduct of any lawyer who is representing a client before the court. The court's authority to impose discipline on a lawyer found to have engaged in misconduct extends beyond the usual sanctions imposed in an order entered pursuant to Rule 11 of the North Carolina Rules of Civil Procedure.

[3] A report about misconduct is not required where it would involve violation of Rule 1.6. However, a lawyer should encourage a client to consent to disclosure where prosecution would not substantially prejudice the client's interests.

[4] If a lawyer were obliged to report every violation of the Rules, the failure to report any violation would itself be a professional offense. Such a requirement existed in many jurisdictions but proved to be unenforceable. This Rule limits the reporting obligation to those offenses that a self-regulating profession must vigorously endeavor to prevent. A measure of judgment is, therefore, required in complying with the provisions of this Rule. The term "substantial" refers to the seriousness of the possible offense and not the quantum of evidence of which the lawyer is aware. A report should be made to the North Carolina State Bar unless some other agency or court is more appropriate in the circumstances. Similar considerations apply to the reporting of judicial misconduct.

[5] The duty to report professional misconduct does not apply to a lawyer retained to represent a lawyer whose professional conduct is in question. Such a situation is governed by the Rules applicable to the client-lawyer relationship.

[6] Information about a lawyer's or judge's misconduct or fitness may be received by a lawyer in the course of that lawyer's participation in an approved lawyers' or judges' assistance program. In that circumstance, providing for an exception to the reporting requirements of paragraphs (a) and (b) of this Rule encourages lawyers and judges to seek treatment through such a program. Conversely, without such an exception, lawyers and judges may hesitate to seek assistance from these programs, which may then result in additional harm to their professional careers and additional injury to the welfare of clients and the public. For this reason, Rule 1.6 (c) includes in the definition of confidential information any information regarding a lawyer or judge seeking assistance that is received by a lawyer acting as an agent of a lawyers' or judges' assistance program approved by the North Carolina State Bar or the North Carolina Supreme Court. Because such information is protected from disclosure by Rule 1.6, a lawyer is exempt from the reporting requirements of paragraphs (a) and (b) with respect to such information. On the other hand, a lawyer who receives such information would nevertheless be required to comply with the Rule 8.3 reporting provisions to report misconduct if the impaired lawyer or judge indicates an intent to engage in illegal activity; for example, conversion of client funds to his or her use.

[7] The North Carolina Supreme Court has adopted Standards of Professional Conduct for Mediators (the Standards) to regulate the conduct of certified mediators and mediators in court-ordered mediations. Mediators governed by the Standards are required to keep confidential the statements and conduct of the parties and other participants in the mediation, with limited exceptions, to encourage the candor that is critical to the successful resolution of legal disputes. Paragraph (e) recognizes the concurrent regulatory function of the Standards and protects the confidentiality of the mediation process. Nevertheless, if the Standards allow disclosure, a lawyer serving as a mediator who learns of or observes conduct by a lawyer that is a violation of the Rules of Professional Conduct is required to report consistent with the duty set forth in paragraph (a) of this Rule. In the event a lawyer serving as a mediator is confronted with professional misconduct by a lawyer participating in a mediation that may not be disclosed pursuant to the Standards, the lawyer/mediator should consider withdrawing from the mediation or taking such other action as may be required by the Standards. See, e.g., N.C. Dispute Resolution Commission Advisory Opinion 10–16 (February 26, 2010).

Rule 8.4 Misconduct

It is professional misconduct for a lawyer to:

(a) violate or attempt to violate the Rules of Professional Conduct, knowingly assist or induce another to do so, or do so through the acts of another;

(b) commit a criminal act that reflects adversely on the lawyer's honesty, trustworthiness or fitness as a lawyer in other respects;

(c) engage in conduct involving dishonesty, fraud, deceit or misrepresentation;

(d) engage in conduct that is prejudicial to the administration of justice;

(e) state or imply an ability to influence improperly a government agency or official;

(f) knowingly assist a judge or judicial officer in conduct that is a violation of applicable rules of judicial conduct or other law; or

(g) intentionally prejudice or damage his or her client during the course of the professional relationship, except as may be required by Rule 3.3.

[Adopted July 24, 1997. Amended February 27, 2003; March 5, 2015.]

Comment

[1] Lawyers are subject to discipline when they violate or attempt to violate the Rules of Professional Conduct, knowingly assist or induce another to do so or do so through the acts of another, as when they request or instruct an agent to do so on the lawyer behalf. Paragraph (a), however, does not prohibit a lawyer from advising a client or, in the case of a government lawyer, investigatory personnel, of action the client, or such investigatory personnel, is lawfully entitled to take.

[2] Many kinds of illegal conduct reflect adversely on a lawyer's fitness to practice law, such as offenses involving fraud and the offense of willful failure to file an income tax return. However, some kinds of offenses carry no such implication. Although a lawyer is personally answerable to the entire criminal law, a lawyer should be professionally answerable only for offenses that indicate lack of those characteristics relevant to law practice. Offenses involving violence, dishonesty, breach of trust, or serious interference with the administration of justice are in that category. A pattern of repeated offenses, even ones of minor significance when considered separately, can indicate indifference to legal obligation. A lawyer's dishonesty, fraud, deceit, or misrepresentation is not mitigated by virtue of the fact that the victim may be the lawyer's partner or law firm. A lawyer who steals funds, for instance, is guilty of the most serious disciplinary violation regardless of whether the victim is the lawyer's employer, partner, law firm, client, or a third party.

[3] The purpose of professional discipline for misconduct is not punishment, but to protect the public, the courts, and the legal profession. Lawyer discipline affects only the lawyer's license to practice law. It does not result in incarceration. For this reason, to establish a violation of paragraph (b), the burden of proof is the same as for any other violation of the Rules of Professional Conduct: it must be shown by clear, cogent, and convincing evidence that the lawyer committed a criminal act that reflects adversely on the lawyer's honesty, trustworthiness, or fitness as a lawyer. Conviction of a crime is conclusive evidence that the lawyer committed a criminal act although, to establish a violation of paragraph (b), it must be shown that the criminal act reflects adversely on the lawyer's honesty, trustworthiness, or fitness as a lawyer. If it is established by clear, cogent, and convincing evidence that a lawyer committed a criminal act that reflects adversely on the lawyer's honesty, trustworthiness, or fitness as a lawyer, the lawyer may be disciplined for a violation of paragraph (b) although the lawyer is never prosecuted or is acquitted or pardoned for the underlying criminal act.

[4] A showing of actual prejudice to the administration of justice is not required to establish a violation of paragraph (d). Rather, it must only be shown that the act had a reasonable likelihood of prejudicing the administration of justice. For example, in *State Bar v. DuMont*, 52 N.C. App. 1, 277 S.E.2d 827 (1981), *modified on other grounds*, 304 N.C. 627, 286 S.E.2d 89 (1982), the defendant was disciplined for advising a witness to give false testimony in a deposition even though the witness corrected his statement prior to trial. The phrase "conduct prejudicial to the administration of justice" in paragraph (d) should be read broadly to proscribe a wide variety of conduct, including conduct that occurs outside the scope of judicial proceedings. In *State Bar v. Jerry Wilson*, 82 DHC 1, for example, a lawyer was disciplined for conduct prejudicial to the administration of justice after forging another individual's name to a guarantee agreement, inducing his wife to notarize the forged agreement, and using the agreement to obtain funds.

[5] Threats, bullying, harassment, and other conduct serving no substantial purpose other than to intimidate, humiliate, or embarrass anyone associated with the judicial process including judges, opposing counsel, litigants, witnesses, or court personnel violate the prohibition on conduct prejudicial to the administration of justice. When directed to opposing counsel, such conduct tends to impede opposing counsel's ability to represent his or her client effectively. Comments "by one lawyer tending to disparage the personality or performance of another tend to reduce public trust and confidence in our courts and, in more extreme cases, directly interfere with the truth-finding function by distracting judges and juries from the serious business at hand." *State v. Rivera*, 350 N.C. 285, 291, 514 S.E.2d 720, 723 (1999). *See* Rule 3.5, cmt. [10] and Rule 4.4, cmt. [2].

[6] A lawyer may refuse to comply with an obligation imposed by law upon a good faith belief that no valid obligation exists. The provisions of Rule 1.2(d) concerning a good faith challenge to the validity, scope, meaning or application of the law apply to challenges of legal regulation of the practice of law.

[7] Lawyers holding public office assume legal responsibilities going beyond those of other citizens. A lawyer's abuse of public office can suggest an inability to fulfill the professional role of lawyers. The same is true of abuse of positions of private trust such as trustee, executor, administrator, guardian, agent and officer, director or manager of a corporation or other organization.

Rule 8.5. Disciplinary Authority; Choice of Law

(a) Disciplinary Authority. A lawyer admitted to practice in North Carolina is subject to the disciplinary authority of North Carolina, regardless of where the lawyer's conduct occurs. A lawyer not admitted in North Carolina is also subject to the disciplinary authority of North Carolina if the lawyer renders or offers to render any legal services in North Carolina. A lawyer may be subject to the disciplinary authority of both North Carolina and another jurisdiction for the same conduct.

(b) Choice of Law. In any exercise of the disciplinary authority of North Carolina, the rules of professional conduct to be applied shall be as follows:

(1) for conduct in connection with a matter pending before a tribunal, the rules of the jurisdiction in which the tribunal sits, unless the rules of the tribunal provide otherwise; and

(2) for any other conduct, the rules of the jurisdiction in which the lawyer's conduct occurred, or, if the predominant effect of the conduct is in a different jurisdiction, the rules of that jurisdiction shall be applied to the conduct. A lawyer is not subject to discipline if the lawyer's conduct conforms to the rules of a jurisdiction in which the lawyer reasonably believes the predominant effect of the lawyer's conduct will occur.

[Adopted July 24, 1997. Amended February 27, 2003; October 2, 2014.]

Comment

Disciplinary Authority

[1] It is longstanding law that conduct of a lawyer admitted to practice in North Carolina is subject to the disciplinary authority of North Carolina. Extension of the disciplinary authority of North Carolina to other lawyers who render or offer to render legal services in North Carolina is for the protection of the citizens of North Carolina.

Choice of Law

[2] A lawyer may be potentially subject to more than one set of rules of professional conduct which impose different obligations. The lawyer may be licensed to practice in more than one jurisdiction with differing rules, or may be admitted to practice before a particular court with rules that differ from those of the jurisdiction or jurisdictions in which the lawyer is licensed to practice. Additionally, the lawyer's conduct might involve significant contacts with more than one jurisdiction.

[3] Paragraph (b) seeks to resolve such potential conflicts. Its premise is that minimizing conflicts between rules, as well as uncertainty about which rules are applicable, is in the best interest of both clients and the profession (as well as the bodies having authority to regulate the profession). Accordingly, it takes the approach of (i) providing that any particular conduct of a lawyer shall be subject to only one set of

rules of professional conduct, (ii) making the determination of which set of rules applies to particular conduct as straightforward as possible, consistent with recognition of appropriate regulatory interests of relevant jurisdictions, and (iii) providing a safe harbor for lawyers who act reasonably in the face of uncertainty.

[4] Paragraph (b)(1) provides that as to a lawyer's conduct relating to a proceeding pending before a tribunal, the lawyer shall be subject only to the rules of the jurisdiction in which the tribunal sits unless the rules of the tribunal, including its choice of law rule, provide otherwise. As to all other conduct, including conduct in anticipation of a proceeding not yet pending before a tribunal, paragraph (b)(2) provides that a lawyer shall be subject to the rules of the jurisdiction in which the lawyer's conduct occurred, or, if the predominant effect of the conduct is in another jurisdiction, the rules of that jurisdiction shall be applied to the conduct. In the case of conduct in anticipation of a proceeding that is likely to be before a tribunal, the predominant effect of such conduct could be where the conduct occurred, where the tribunal sits or in another jurisdiction.

[5] When a lawyer's conduct involves significant contacts with more than one jurisdiction, it may not be clear whether the predominant effect of the lawyer's conduct will occur in a jurisdiction other than the one in which the conduct occurred. So long as the lawyer's conduct conforms to the rules of a jurisdiction in which the lawyer reasonably believes the predominant effect will occur, the lawyer is not subject to discipline under this Rule. With respect to conflicts of interest, in determining a lawyer's reasonable belief under paragraph (b)(2), a written agreement between the lawyer and client that reasonably specifies a particular jurisdiction as within the scope of that paragraph may be considered if the agreement was obtained with the client's informed consent confirmed in the agreement.

[6] If North Carolina and another admitting jurisdictions were to proceed against a lawyer for the same conduct, they should, applying this rule, identify the same governing ethics rules. They should take all appropriate steps to see that they do apply the same rule to the same conduct, and in all events should avoid proceeding against a lawyer on the basis of two inconsistent rules.

[7] The choice of law provision applies to lawyers engaged in transnational practice, unless international law, treaties or other agreements between competent regulatory authorities in the affected jurisdictions provide otherwise.

RULES GOVERNING ADMISSION TO THE PRACTICE OF LAW IN THE STATE OF NORTH CAROLINA

Effective February 1, 1976

Table of Rules

SECTION .0100 ORGANIZATION

.0101. Address

The offices of the Board of Law Examiners of the State of North Carolina are located at 5510 Six Forks Road, Suite 300, Raleigh, NC 27609. The mailing address is 5510 Six Forks Road, Suite 300, Raleigh, NC 27609. The Offices are open from 8:30 a.m. to 5:00 p.m. Monday through Friday, excepts holidays.

[Amended August 23, 1979; February 5, 2002; March 5, 2015.]

.0102 Purpose

The Board of Law Examiners of the State of North Carolina was created for the purpose of examining applicants and providing rules and regulations for admission to the bar, including the issuance of licenses therefor.

.0103 Membership

The Board of Law Examiners of the State of North Carolina consists of eleven members of the N.C. Bar elected by the Council of the North Carolina State Bar. One member of said board is elected by the board to serve as chairman for such period as the board may determine. The board also employs an executive director to enable the board to perform its duties promptly and properly. The executive director, in addition to performing the administrative functions of the positions, may act as attorney for the board.

[Amended August 14, 1991.]

SECTION .0200 GENERAL PROVISIONS

.0201 Compliance Provisions

No person shall be admitted to the practice of law in North Carolina unless that person has complied with these rules and the laws of the state.

[Amended February 3, 1988.]

.0202 Definitions

(1) The term "board" as used in this chapter refers to the "Board of Law Examiners of the State of North Carolina." A majority of the members of the board shall constitute a quorum, and the action of a majority of a quorum, present and voting, shall constitute the action of the board.

(2) The term "secretary" as used in this chapter refers to the "Executive Director of the Board of Law Examiners of the State of North Carolina."

(3) As used in these rules, the word "filing" or "filed" shall mean received in the office of the Board of Law Examiners. Except that applications placed in the United States mail properly addressed to the Board of Law Examiners and bearing sufficient first class postage and postmarked by the United States Postal Service on or before a deadline date will be considered as having been timely filed if all required fees are included in the mailing. Mailings which are postmarked after a deadline or which if postmarked on or before a deadline and do not include required fees or which include a check in payment of required fees which is not honored due to insufficient funds will not be considered as timely filed. Applications which are not properly signed and notarized; or which do not include the properly executed Authorization and Release forms; or which are illegible; or which answers to the questions are not complete will not be considered filed and will be returned.

(4) As used in these rules, the word "Chapter" refers to the "Rules Governing Admission to the Practice of Law in the State of North Carolina."

[Amended February 3, 1988; August 14, 1991; July 29, 1998.]

.0203 Applicants

For the purpose of these rules, applicants are classified either as "general applicants" or as "comity applicants." To be classified as a "general applicant" and certified as such for admission to practice law, an applicant must satisfy the requirements of Rule .0501 of this Chapter. To be classified as a "comity applicant" and certified as such for admission to practice law, a person shall satisfy the requirements of Rule .0502 of this Chapter.

.0204 List

As soon as possible after each filing deadline for applications, the secretary shall prepare and maintain a list of general applicants for the ensuing examination.

[Amended February 25, 1980.]

.0205 Hearings

Every applicant may be required to appear before the board to be examined about any matters pertaining to the applicant's moral character and general fitness, educational background or any other matters set out in Section .0500 of this Chapter.

[Amendment approved February 3, 1988.]

.0206 Nonpayment of Fees

Failure to pay the application fees required by these rules shall cause the application not to be deemed filed. If the check payable for the application fee is not honored upon presentment for any reason other than error of the bank the application will be deemed not timely filed and will have to be refiled. All checks payable to the Board for any fees which are not honored upon presentment shall be returned to the applicant who shall pay to the Board in cash, cashier's check, certified check or money order any fees payable to the Board including a fee for processing that check.

[Amended February 3, 1988; August 14, 1991; September 3, 1992.]

SECTION .0300 [RESERVED]

[Repealed February 3, 1988.]

SECTION .0400 APPLICATIONS OF GENERAL APPLICANTS

.0401 How to Apply

Applications for admission to an examination must be made upon forms supplied by the board and must be complete in every detail. Every supporting document required by the application form must be submitted with each application. The application form may be obtained by writing or downloading from the Board's website www.ncble.org.

[Amended February 3, 1988; February 5, 2002.]

.0402 Application Form

(1) The Application For Admission to Take the North Carolina Bar Examination form requires an applicant to supply full and complete information relating to the applicant's background, including family history, past and current residences, education, military service, past and present employment, credit status, involvement in disciplinary, civil or criminal proceedings, substance abuse, mental treatment and bar admission and discipline history. Applicants must list references and submit as part of the application:

—Four Certificates of Moral Character from individuals who know the applicant;

—A recent photograph;

—One set of clear fingerprints;

—Two executed informational Authorization and Release forms;

—A birth certificate;

—Transcripts from the applicant's undergraduate schools;

—A copy of all applications to take a bar examination or an attorney's examination or for admission to the practice of law that the applicant has filed with any state, territory, or the District of Columbia;

—A certificate from the proper court or agency of every state in which the applicant is or has been licensed, that the applicant is in good standing and not under pending charges of misconduct;

—Copies of any legal proceedings in which the applicant has been a party.

The application must be filed in duplicate. The duplicate may be a photocopy of the original.

(2) An applicant who has aptly filed a complete Application For Admission to Take the North Carolina Bar Examination for a particular bar examination may file a Supplemental Application on forms supplied by the Board, along with the applicable fees for the next subsequent bar examination. An applicant who has filed a Supplemental Application as provided by this rule immediately preceding the filing deadline specified in Rule .0403 of this Chapter may file a subsequent Supplemental Application along with the applicable fees for the next examination. The Supplemental Application will update the information previously submitted to the Board by the applicant. Said Supplemental Application must be filed by the deadline set out in Rule .0403 of this Chapter.

[Amended February 25, 1980; May 5, 1981; February 3, 1988; May 5, 1994; January 28, 2010.]

.0403 Filing Deadlines

(1) Applications shall be filed and received by the secretary at the offices of the board on or before the first Tuesday in January immediately preceding the date of the July written bar examination and on or before the first Tuesday in October immediately preceding the date of the February written bar examination.

(2) Upon payment of a late filing fee of $250 (in addition to all other fees required by these rules), an applicant may file a late application with the board on or before the first Tuesday in March immediately preceding the July written bar examination and on or

before the first Tuesday in November immediately preceding the February written bar examination.

(3) Applicants who fail to timely file their application will not be allowed to take the Bar Examination designated on the application.

(4) Any applicant who has aptly filed an application to stand the February written bar examination may make application to take the immediately following July bar examination by filing a Supplemental Application with the secretary of the board at the offices of the board on or before the first Tuesday in May immediately preceding the July written bar examination.

[Amended February 5, 1979; February 25, 1980; August 14, 1991; July 29, 1998; February 5, 2002.]

.0404 Fees

Every application by an applicant who:

(1) is not a licensed attorney in any other jurisdiction shall be accompanied by a fee of $700.00.

(2) is or has been a licensed attorney in any other jurisdiction shall be accompanied by a fee of $1500.00.

(3) is filing to take the North Carolina Bar Examination using a Supplemental Application shall be accompanied by a fee of $400.00.

(4) is filing after the deadline set out in Rule .0403(1) shall be accompanied by a late fee of $250.00 in addition to all other fees required by these rules.

[Amended February 25, 1980; May 4, 1982; August 28, 1984; February 3, 1988; July 26, 1990; May 5, 1994; November 2, 1995; February 5, 2002; January 28, 2010.]

.0405 Refund of Fees

No part of the fee required by Rule .0404(1)(2)(3) of this Chapter shall be refunded to the applicant unless the applicant shall file with the secretary a written request to withdraw as an applicant, not later than the 15th day of June preceding the July written bar examination and not later than the 15th day of January preceding the February written bar examination in which event not more than one-half of the fee may be refunded to the applicant in the discretion of the board. No portion of any late fee will be refunded.

[Amended February 25, 1980; February 3, 1988; September 3, 1992.]

SECTION .0500 REQUIREMENTS FOR APPLICANTS

.0501 Requirements for General Applicants

As a prerequisite to being licensed by the board to practice law in the State of North Carolina, a general applicant shall:

(1) possess the qualifications of character and general fitness requisite for an attorney and counselor-at-law, and be of good moral character and entitled to the high regard and confidence of the public and have satisfied the requirements of Section .0600 of this Chapter both at the time the license is issued and at the time of standing and passing a written bar examination as prescribed in Section .0900 of this Chapter.

(2) possess the legal educational qualifications as prescribed in Section .0700 of this Chapter;

(3) be of the age of at least eighteen (18) years;

(4) have filed formal application as a general applicant in accordance with Section .0400 of this Chapter;

(5) stand and pass a written bar examination as prescribed in Section .0900 of this Chapter;

(6) have stood and passed the Multistate Professional Responsibility Examination approved by the Board within the twenty-four (24) month period next preceding the beginning day of the written bar examination prescribed by Section .0900 of this Chapter which the applicant applies to take, or shall take and pass the Multistate Professional Responsibility Examination within the twelve (12) month period thereafter. The time limits are tolled for a period not exceeding four (4) years for any applicant who is a servicemember as defined in the Servicemembers Civil Relief Act, 50 U.S.C. Appx. § 511, while engaged in active service as defined in 10 U.S.C. § 101, and who provides a letter or other communication from the servicemember's commanding officer stating that the servicemember's current military duty prevents attendance for the examination, stating that military leave is not authorized for the servicemember at the time of the letter, and stating when the servicemember would be authorized military leave to take the examination.

(7) if the applicant is or has been a licensed attorney, then the applicant be in good standing in every jurisdiction within each state, territory of the United States, or the District of Columbia, in which the applicant is or has been licensed to practice law and not under any charges of misconduct while the application is pending before the Board.

(a) For purposes of this rule, an applicant is "in good standing" in a jurisdiction if:

(i) the applicant is an active or inactive member of the bar of the jurisdiction and the jurisdiction issues a certificate attesting to the applicant's good standing therein; or

(ii) the applicant was formerly a member of the bar of the jurisdiction and the jurisdiction certifies the applicant was in good standing at the time that the applicant ceased to be a member.

(b) if the jurisdiction in which the applicant is inactive or was formerly a member will not certify the applicant's good standing solely because of the nonpayment of dues, the Board, in its discretion, may waive such certification from that jurisdiction.

[Amended August 23, 1979; February 25, 1980; June 8, 1983; August 28, 1984; September 19, 1985; February 3, 1988; May 5, 1994; amended effective March 6, 1997; amended effective February 20, 2004; amended effective July 18, 2008; amended effective August 26, 2008.]

.0502 Requirements for Comity Applicants

Any attorney at law duly admitted to practice in another state, or territory of the United States, or the District of Columbia, upon written application may, in the discretion of the Board, be licensed to practice law in the State of North Carolina without written examination provided each such applicant shall:

(1) File with the Secretary, upon such forms as may be supplied by the Board, a typed application in duplicate which will be considered by the board after at least six (6) months from the date of filing; the application requires:

(a) That an applicant supply full and complete information in regard to his background, including family, past residences, education, military, employment, credit status, whether he has been a party to any disciplinary or legal proceedings, mental illness, references, the nature of the applicant's practice of law, and familiarity with the Code of Professional Responsibility as Promulgated by the North Carolina State Bar;

(b) That the applicant furnish the following documentation:

i. Certificates of Moral Character from four (4) individuals who know the applicant;

ii. A recent photograph;

iii. Two (2) sets of clear fingerprints;

iv. A certification of the Court of Last Resort from the jurisdiction from which the applicant is applying;

v. Transcripts from the applicant's undergraduate and graduate schools;

vi. A copy of all applications for admission to the practice of law that he has filed with any state, territory, or the District of Columbia;

vii. A certificate of his admission to the bar of any state, territory, or the District of Columbia;

viii. A certificate from the proper court or body of every state in which the applicant is licensed therein that he is in good standing and not under pending charges of misconduct;

(2) Pay to the Board with each typewritten application, a fee of $ $2000.00, no part of which may be refunded to the applicant whose application is denied;

(3) Prove to the satisfaction of the Board that the applicant is duly licensed to practice law in a state, or territory of the United States, or the District of Columbia, having comity with North Carolina and, except as otherwise provided in this subsection 3, that in such state, or territory of the United States, or the District of Columbia, while so licensed therein, the applicant has been for a least four out of the last six years, immediately preceding the filing of this application with the Secretary, actively and substantially engaged in the full-time practice of law. Practice of law for the purposes of this rule when conducted pursuant to a license granted by another jurisdiction shall include:

(a) The practice of law as defined by G.S. 84–2.1; or

(b) Activities which would constitute the practice of law if done for the general public; or

(c) Legal service as a corporate counsel; or

(d) Judicial service in a court of record or other legal service with any local or state government or with the federal government; or

(e) Service as a member of a Judge Advocate General's Department of one of the military branches of the United States, whether or not such service is in the jurisdiction in which the applicant is duly licensed; or

(f) A full time faculty member in a law school approved by the Council of the North Carolina State Bar.

Employment in North Carolina, when conducted pursuant to a license granted by another jurisdiction, to meet the requirement of this rule is limited to:

(a) Employment as house counsel by a person, firm, association, or corporation engaged in business in this state which business does not include the selling or furnishing of legal advice or services to others; or

(b) Employment as a full time faculty member of a law school approved by the Council of the North Carolina State Bar; or

(c) Employment as a full time member of the faculty of the Institute of Government of the University of North Carolina at Chapel Hill; or

(d) Service as a member of a Judge Advocate General's Department of one of the military branches of the United States; or

(e) Service as a United States Attorney for a federal judicial district in North Carolina, or as an Assistant United States Attorney in the office of a United States Attorney for a federal judicial district in North Carolina; or

(f) Service in North Carolina as an attorney in a federal public defender's office or a federal community defender's office for a federal judicial district in North Carolina.

(4) Satisfy the board that the state, or territory of the United States, or the District of Columbia in which the applicant is licensed and from which he seeks comity will admit North Carolina attorneys to

the practice of law in such state, or territory of the United States, or the District of Columbia without written examination, other than the Multistate Professional Responsibility Examination;

(5) Be in good standing in every jurisdiction within each state, territory of the United States, or the District of Columbia, in which the applicant is or has been licensed to practice law and not under any charges of misconduct while the application is pending before the Board.

(a) For purposes of this rule, an applicant is "in good standing" in a jurisdiction if:

(i) the applicant is an active or inactive member of the bar of the jurisdiction and the jurisdiction issues a certificate attesting to the applicant's good standing therein; or

(ii) the applicant was formerly a member of the jurisdiction and the jurisdiction certifies the applicant was in good standing at the time that the applicant ceased to be a member.

(b) if the jurisdiction in which the applicant is inactive or was formerly a member will not certify the applicant's good standing solely because of the non-payment of dues, the Board, in its discretion, may waive such certification from that jurisdiction.

The applicant must not only be in good standing but also must be an active member of each jurisdiction on which the applicant relies for admission by comity.

(6) Be of good moral character and have satisfied the requirements of Section .0600 of this Chapter;

(7) Meet the educational requirements of Section .0700 of this Chapter as hereinafter set out if first licensed to practice law after August, 1971;

(8) Not have taken and failed the written North Carolina Bar Examination within ten (10) years prior to the date of filing the applicant's comity application;

(9) Have stood and passed the Multistate Professional Responsibility Examination approved by the Board.

[Amended August 23, 1979; February 25, 1980; May 4, 1982; November 10, 1982; June 8, 1983; August 28, 1984; September 19, 1985; February 3, 1988; August 14, 1991; May 5, 1994; November 2, 1995; July 29, 1998; amended effective February 20, 2004.]

.0503. Requirements for Military Spouse Comity Applicants

A Military Spouse Comity Applicant, upon written application may, in the discretion of the Board, be granted a license to practice law in the State of North Carolina without written examination provided that:

(1) The Applicant fulfills all of the requirements of Rule .0502, except that;

(a) in lieu of the requirements of paragraph (3) of Rule .0502, a Military Spouse Comity Applicant shall prove to the satisfaction of the Board that the Military Spouse Comity Applicant is duly licensed to practice law in a state or territory of the United States, or the District of Columbia, and that the Military Spouse Comity Applicant has been for at least four out of the last eight years immediately preceding the filing of this application with the Secretary, actively and substantially engaged in the full-time practice of law. Practice of law for the purposes of this rule shall be defined as it would be defined for any other comity applicant; and

(b) Paragraph (4) of Rule .0502 shall not apply to a Military Spouse Comity Applicant.

(2) **Military Spouse Comity Applicant defined.** A Military Spouse Comity Applicant is any person who is;

(a) An attorney at law duly admitted to practice in another state or territory of the United States, or the District of Columbia; and

(b) Identified by the Department of Defense (or, for the Coast Guard when it is not operating as a service in the Navy, by the Department of Homeland Security) as the spouse of a service member of the United States Uniformed Services; and

(c) Is residing, or intends within the next six months to be residing, in North Carolina due to the service member's orders for a permanent change of station to the State of North Carolina.

(3) **Procedure.** In addition to the documentation required by paragraph (1) of Rule .0502, a Military Spouse Comity Applicant must file with the Board the following:

(a) A copy of the service member's military orders reflecting a permanent change of station to a military installation in North Carolina; and

(b) A military identification card which lists the Military Spouse Comity Applicant as the spouse of the service member.

(4) **Fee.** A Military Spouse Comity Applicant shall pay a fee of $1,500 in lieu of the fee required in paragraph (2) of Rule .0502. This fee shall be non-refundable.

[Adopted effective March 8, 2013.]

SECTION .0600 MORAL CHARACTER AND GENERAL FITNESS

.0601 Burden of Proof

Every applicant shall have the burden of proving that the applicant possesses the qualifications of character and general fitness requisite for an attorney and counselor-at-law and is possessed of good moral character and is entitled to the high regard and confidence of the public.

[Amended February 3, 1988.]

.0602 Permanent Record

All information furnished to the board by an applicant shall be deemed material, and all such information shall be and become a permanent record of the board.

.0603 Failure to Disclose

No one shall be licensed to practice law by examination or comity or be allowed to take the bar examination in this state:

(1) who fails to disclose fully to the Board, whether requested to do so or not, the facts relating to any disciplinary proceedings or charges as to the applicant's professional conduct, whether same have been terminated or not, in this or any other state, or any federal court or other jurisdiction, or

(2) who fails to disclose fully to the board, whether requested to do so or not, any and all facts relating to any civil or criminal proceedings, charges or investigations involving the applicant, whether the same have been terminated or not in this or any other state or in any of the federal courts or other jurisdictions.

[Amended February 3, 1988.]

.0604 Bar Candidate Committee

Every applicant shall appear before a bar candidate committee, appointed by the chairman of the board, in the judicial district in which the applicant resides, or in such other judicial district as the board in its sole discretion may designate to the applicant, to be examined about any matter pertaining to the applicant's moral character and general fitness to practice law. An applicant who has appeared before a bar candidate committee may, in the board's discretion, be excused from making a subsequent appearance before a bar candidate committee. The applicant shall give such information as may be required on such forms provided by the board. A bar candidate committee may require the applicant to make more than one appearance before the committee and to furnish to the committee such information and documents as it may reasonably require pertaining to the moral character and general fitness of the applicant to be licensed to practice law in North Carolina. Each applicant will be advised when to appear before the bar candidate committee. There can be no changes once the initial assignment is made.

[Amended February 25, 1980; February 3, 1988.]

.0605 Denial; Re-application

No new application or petition for reconsideration of a previous application from an applicant who has either been denied permission to take the bar examination or has been denied a license to practice law on the grounds set forth in Section .0600 shall be considered by the board within a period of three (3) years next after the date of such denial unless, for good cause shown, permission for re-application or petition for a reconsideration is granted by the board.

[Amended February 3, 1988.]

SECTION .0700 EDUCATIONAL REQUIREMENTS

.0701 General Education

Each applicant must have satisfactorily completed the academic work required for admission to a law school approved by the Council of the North Carolina State Bar.

[Amended February 3, 1988.]

POLICY FOR APPROVAL OF LAW SCHOOLS FOR GRADUATES TO TAKE THE NORTH CAROLINA BAR EXAMINATION

BE IT RESOLVED that the policy of the North Carolina State Bar in approving law schools for purposes of its graduates to be eligible to sit for the North Carolina Bar examination is as follows:

(a) Such law schools located in the State of North Carolina as are approved by the Council of the North Carolina State Bar.

(b) With respect to law schools located outside North Carolina, but within the United States and Canada and which have been accredited by the American Bar Association, those graduates who have received an LLB, JD, LLM, or SJD are eligible to apply for admission to practice law in the State of North Carolina. This rule shall take effect for students currently enrolled in U. S. law schools on July 14, 1992, and the current policy for approval shall continue until such date as to U. S. law schools. As to persons currently enrolled in Canadian law schools, this policy shall be effective from and after July 14, 1989.

(c) The existing policies with respect to approval of law schools outside the United States and Canada are rescinded as of July 14, 1989, and from and after such date, no person shall be permitted to apply for admission to practice law in this state unless he or she meets the requirements of (a) or (b) above.

[Adopted by the State Bar Council July 14, 1989.]

.0702 Legal Education

Every applicant applying for admission to practice law in the State of North Carolina, before being granted a license to practice law, shall prove to the satisfaction of the board that said applicant has graduated from a law school approved by the Council of the North Carolina State Bar or that said applicant will graduate within thirty (30) days after the date of the written bar examination from a law school approved by the Council of the North Carolina State Bar. There shall be filed with the secretary a certificate of the dean, or other proper official of said law school, certifying the date of the applicant's graduation. A list of the approved law schools is available in the office of the secretary.

[Amended February 25, 1980; February 3, 1988.]

SECTION .0800 PROTEST

.0801 Nature of Protest

Any person may protest the application of any applicant to be admitted to the practice of law either by examination or by comity.

.0802 Format

A protest shall be made in writing, signed by the person making the protest and bearing the person's home and business address, and shall be filed with the secretary prior to the date on which the applicant is to be examined.

[Amended February 3, 1988.]

.0803 Notification; Right to Withdraw

The secretary shall notify immediately the applicant of the protest and of the charges therein made; and the applicant thereupon may file with the secretary a written withdrawal as a candidate for admission to the practice of law at that examination.

.0804 Hearing

In case the applicant does not withdraw as a candidate for admission to the practice of law at that examination, the person or persons making the protest and the applicant in question shall appear before the board at a time and place to be designated by the board. In the event time will not permit a hearing on the protest prior to the examination, the applicant may take the written examination, and the results will be sealed until final disposition of the protest in favor of the applicant.

[Amended February 3, 1988.]

.0805 Refusal to License

Nothing herein contained shall prevent the board on its own motion from refusing to issue a license to practice law until the board has been fully satisfied as to the moral character and general fitness of the applicant as provided by Section .0600 of this Chapter.

[Amended August 23, 1979; February 3, 1988.]

SECTION .0900 EXAMINATIONS

.0901 Written Examination

Two written bar examinations shall be held each year for those applying to be admitted to the practice of law in North Carolina.

[Amended February 25, 1980; February 3, 1988.]

.0902 Dates

The written bar examinations shall be held in the City of Raleigh, Wake County or adjoining counties in the months of February and July on such dates as the board may set from year to year.

[Amended February 25, 1980. Amended effective October 6, 2004.]

.0903 Subject Matter

The examination may deal with the following subjects: Business Associations (including agency, corporations, and partnerships), Civil Procedure, Constitutional Law, Contracts, Criminal Law and Procedure, Evidence, Family Law, Legal Ethics, Real Property, Secured Transactions including The Uniform Commercial Code, Taxation, Torts, Trusts, Wills, Decedents' Estates and Equity.

[Amended August 23, 1979; September 19, 1985.]

.0904 Passing Score

The board shall determine what shall constitute the passing of an examination.

SECTION .1000 REVIEW OF WRITTEN BAR EXAMINATION

.1001 Review

An unsuccessful applicant to the bar examination may examine the test booklets containing the applicant's essay examination along with such answers to the examination as the Board determines will be of assistance to the applicants and the essay examination in the Board's offices.

[Amended February 3, 1988. Amended effective November 8, 2007.]

.1002 Fees

The Board will furnish an unsuccessful applicant a copy of the applicant's essay examination at a cost to be determined by the Secretary, not to exceed $20.00. No copies of the Board's grading guide will be made or furnished to the applicant.

[Amended February 3, 1988. Amended effective November 8, 2007.]

.1003 Multistate Bar Examination

There is no provision for review of the Multistate Bar Examination.

.1004 Scores

(1) Upon written request the board will release to an unsuccessful applicant the applicant's scores on the bar examination.

(2) Upon written request of an applicant, the board will furnish the Multistate Bar Examination score of said applicant to another board of bar examiners, or like organization that administers the admission of attorneys into that jurisdiction.

[Amended February 25, 1980; August 24, 1981; February 3, 1988.]

.1005 Board Representative

The secretary of the board serves as the representative of the board during this review of the written bar examination by an unsuccessful applicant. The secretary is not authorized to discuss any specific questions and answers on the bar examination.

SECTION .1100 RULEMAKING PROCEDURES [REPEALED]

[Repealed August 23, 1977.]

SECTION .1200 BOARD HEARINGS

.1201 Nature of Hearings

(1) All general applicants may be required to appear before the board or a panel at a hearing to answer inquiry about any matter under these rules.

(2) Each comity applicant shall appear before the board or panel to satisfy the board that he or she has met all the requirements of Rule .0502.

[Amended August 23, 1979.]

.1202 Notice of Hearing

The chairman will schedule the hearings before the board or panel and such hearings will be scheduled by the issuance of a notice of hearing mailed to the applicant or the applicant's attorney within a reasonable time before the date of the hearing.

[Amended August 23, 1979; February 3, 1988.]

.1203. Conduct of Hearings

(1) All hearings shall be heard by the Board except that the Chairman may designate two or more members or Emeritus Members as that term is defined in the Policy of the North Carolina State Bar Council creating Emeritus Members to serve as a Panel to conduct the hearings.

(2) The Panel will make a determination as to the applicant's eligibility to stand the written bar examination or to be licensed by comity. The panel may grant the application, deny the application, or refer it to the Board for a de novo hearing. The applicant will be notified in writing of the Panel's determination. In the event of an adverse determination by the Panel, the applicant may request a hearing de novo before the Board by giving written notice to the secretary at the offices of the Board within ten (10) days following receipt of the Panel's determination. Failure to file such notice in the manner and within the time stated shall operate as a waiver of the right of the applicant to request a hearing de novo before the Board and shall result in the determination of the Panel becoming final.

(3) The Board or a Panel of the Board may require an applicant to make more than one appearance before the Board or Panel, to furnish information and documents as it may reasonably require, and to submit to reasonable physical or mental examinations, all

at the applicant's expense, pertaining to the moral character or general fitness of the applicant to be licensed to practice law in North Carolina.

(4) The Board or a Panel of the Board may allow an applicant to take the bar examination but seal the results of that examination until the Board or a Panel has made a final determination that the applicant possesses the qualifications of character and general fitness requisite for an attorney and counsellor at law and is possessed of good moral character and is entitled to the high regard and confidence of the public.

[Amended August 23, 1979; February 25, 1980; June 8, 1983; February 3, 1988; September 3, 1992; July 29, 1998; August 25, 2011.]

.1204 Continuances; Motions for

Continuances, adjournments and like dispositions will be granted to a party only in compelling circumstances, especially when one such disposition has been previously requested by and granted to that party. Motions for continuance should be made to the secretary of the board and will be granted or denied by the chairman of the board.

.1205 Subpoenas

(1) The board shall have the power to subpoena and to summon and examine witnesses under oath and to compel their attendance and the production of books, papers and other documents and writings deemed by it to be necessary or material to the hearing as set forth in G.S. 84–24.

(2) The secretary of the board is delegated the power to issue subpoenas in the board's name.

.1206 Depositions and Discovery

(1) A deposition may be used in evidence when taken in compliance with the N.C. Rules of Civil Procedure, G.S. 1A–1. The board may also allow the use of depositions or written interrogatories for the purpose of discovery or for the use as evidence in the hearing or for both purposes pursuant to the N.C. Rules of Civil Procedure.

(2) Any party or the board may submit sworn affidavits as evidence to be considered by the board in a board hearing. The board will take under consideration sworn affidavits presented to the board by persons desiring to protest an applicant's admission to the North Carolina Bar.

[Amended August 23, 1979.]

.1207 Reopening of a Case

After a final decision has been reached by the board in any matter, a party may petition the board to reopen or reconsider a case. Petitions will not be granted except when petitioner can show that the reasons for reopening or reconsidering the case are to introduce newly discovered evidence which was not presented at the initial hearing because of some justifiable, excusable or unavoidable circumstances and that fairness and justice require reopening or reconsidering the case. The petition shall be made within a reasonable time and not more than ninety days after the decision of the Board has been entered.

[Amended February 3, 1988; September 3, 1992.]

SECTION .1300 LICENSES

.1301 Interim Permit for Comity Applicants [Deleted]

[Deleted by amendment approved August 14, 1991.]

.1302 Licenses for General Applicants

Upon compliance with the rules of the board, and all orders of the board, the secretary, upon order of the board, shall issue a license to practice law in North Carolina to each applicant as may be designated by the board in the form and manner as may be prescribed by the board, and at such times as prescribed by the board.

SECTION .1400 JUDICIAL REVIEW

.1401 Appeals

A general applicant may appeal from an adverse ruling or determination by the board as to the applicant's eligibility to take the written examination. After a general applicant has successfully passed the written examination, the applicant may appeal from any adverse ruling or determination withholding the applicant's license to practice law. A comity applicant may appeal from an adverse ruling of the Board of Law Examiners denying the applicant's application to the North Carolina Bar by comity for failure to meet any of the requirements of Rule .0502 of this Chapter.

[Amended February 3, 1988.]

.1402 Notice of Appeal

Notice of appeal shall be given, in writing, within twenty (20) days after notice of such ruling or determination and written exceptions to the ruling or determination filed with the secretary, which exceptions shall state the grounds of objection to such ruling or determination. Failure to file such notice of appeal in the manner and within the time stated shall operate as a waiver of the right to appeal and shall result in the decision of the board becoming final.

.1403 Record to Be Filed

Within sixty days after receipt of the notice of appeal, and after the applicant has paid the cost of preparing the record, the Secretary shall prepare, certify, and file with the clerk of the Superior Court of Wake County the record of the case, comprising:

(1) the application and supporting documents or papers filed by the applicant with the board;

(2) a complete transcription of the testimony when taken at the hearing;

(3) copies of all pertinent documents and other written evidence introduced at the hearing;

(4) a copy of the decision of the board; and

(5) a copy of the notice of appeal containing the exceptions filed to the decision.

With the permission of the court, the record may be shortened by stipulation of all parties to the review proceedings. Any party unreasonably refusing to stipulate to limit the record may be taxed by the court for such additional costs as may be occasioned by the refusal. The court may require or permit subsequent corrections or additions to the record when deemed desirable.

[Amended February 3, 1988.]

.1404 Wake County Superior Court

Such appeal shall lie to the Superior Court of Wake County and shall be heard by the presiding judge or resident judge, without a jury, who may hear oral arguments and receive written briefs, but no evidence not offered at the hearing shall be taken except that in cases of alleged omissions or errors in the record. Testimony thereon may be taken by the court. The findings of fact by the board, when supported by competent evidence, shall be conclusive and binding upon the court. The court may affirm, reverse or remand the case for further proceedings. If the court reverses or remands for further proceedings the decision of the board, the judge shall set out in writing, which writing shall become a part of the record, the reasons for such reversal or remand.

.1405 North Carolina Supreme Court

Any party to the review proceeding, including the board, may appeal to the Supreme Court from the decision of the superior court. No appeal bond shall be required of the board.

SUPREME COURT LIBRARY RULES

Adopted December 20, 1967

Table of Rules

GENERAL PROVISIONS

Rule 1. Short Title

The following rules and regulations shall be known and may be cited as North Carolina Supreme Court Library Rules.

Rule 2. Definitions

Subject to additional definitions contained in subsequent sections and applicable to specific parts of these Rules, and unless the context otherwise requires, the following definitions shall apply for purposes of these Rules:

(a) "Assistant Librarian" means the Assistant Librarian of the Supreme Court Library.

(a1) "User" means:

i. justice, judge, employee, or volunteer of the Appellate Division of the General Court of Justice;

ii. employee of the State of North Carolina in the discharge of official duties; and

iii. practicing attorney licensed in the State of North Carolina.

(a2) "Authorized visitor" means:

i. employee of a user possessing permission on standard from issued by a member of the Library staff to visit the facility; and

ii. person possessing permission on standard form issued by the Librarian to visit the facility.

(b) "Librarian" means the Librarian of the Supreme Court Library.

(c) "Library" means the North Carolina Supreme Court Library.

(d) "Library Committee" means that committee appointed and acting pursuant to Section 7A–13 of the General Statutes of North Carolina.

(e) "Library material" means any book, paper, document, map, magazine, pamphlet, newspaper, manuscript, film, periodical, or other item or material, regardless of physical form or characteristics, that is a part of the collection or holdings of the Library.

(f) "Official Register" means that list of positions of the State of North Carolina that is appended to these Rules as Appendix I.

(g) "Rules" means any rules or regulations contained in the North Carolina Supreme Court Library Rules.

(h) "Staff" means any assistants or other persons or employees appointed by or working under the supervision of the Librarian of the Supreme Court Library.

[Amended November 28, 1972; amended effective March 1, 2005.]

HOURS AND USE OF LIBRARY

Rule 3. Hours

Except on State Holidays or when the Library Committee authorizes that it be closed, the Library shall be open to users and authorized visitors on Monday through Friday from eight-thirty o'clock in the morning until four-thirty o'clock in the afternoon.

[Amended July 24, 1980; amended effective January 1, 1984; amended effective March 1, 2004; amended effective March 1, 2005.]

Rule 4. Use During Regular Hours

Any user or authorized visitor who acts in a quiet, orderly, and lawful manner and who abides by the Rules and the reasonable requests of the staff may visit the Library and reasonably use its material to such extent, in such manner, and for such duration as in the discretion of the Librarian reasonably does not or will not interfere with the performance of the Library's primary function of serving the Appellate Division of the General Court of Justice.

[Amended effective March 1, 2005.]

Rule 5. Use After Hours

Only members and employees of the Supreme Court and the Court of Appeals may enter the Library or use the material or facilities of the Library when the Library is not open for public use.

[Amended April 14, 1975; July 24, 1980; amended effective September 1, 1982.]

Rule 6. Entrance and Exits

All visitors and users of the Library shall enter and leave the Library through an elevator except in emergency situations and times when an elevator is not in operation.

Rule 7. Conduct

Smoking, consumption of food or beverages other than from water fountains in the Library, loud talking, boisterous or disorderly conduct, and the use of dictating equipment shall not be permitted in the Library.

USE OF MATERIAL

Rule 8. Clearing of Tables

At the end of each day the staff shall clear all tables and reshelve all unshelved books in the reading area of the Library; however, provided that no books shall be left on tables for more than two consecutive nights, the staff may leave material on tables overnight when the person using the material leaves on it a signed and dated request that it not be reshelved.

Rule 9. Abuse of Material

No person shall damage or abuse any Library material or equipment in any respect. Marking, writing upon, cutting, tearing, defacing, disfiguring, soiling, obliterating, or breaking such material or equipment, or folding pages, closing a book with a writing instrument or other object within it, tearing out or removing any page or pocket part without authority, or stacking other books or heavy objects on an open book are included within this prohibition.

Rule 10. Replacement of Lost Materials

Any person who unintentionally or inadvertently shall lose or misplace any Library material and for that reason fail to return it within the time that it is due to be returned shall, within thirty (30) days from such due date, make such replacement as will be acceptable to the Librarian in his discretion, or pay to the Library the fair value of the material as determined by the Librarian.

SERVICES

Rule 11. Copy Service

(a) All copies made by members and employees of the Supreme Court and the Court of Appeals shall be furnished without charge.

(b) Provided that the number of copies made in any one month does not exceed three hundred (300) pages, or with the permission of the Librarian regardless of the number of pages, such copies as made by persons holding positions listed in the Official Register if used in the discharge of their official duties shall be made without charge.

(c) Except as provided for in sections (a) and (b) of this Rule, patrons may make photocopies for ten cents ($.10) per page.

[Amended July 24, 1980; amended effective November 2, 2004.]

Rule 12. Research Service

No member of the Library staff shall do law research for or give legal advice or counsel to any person except as requested by a member of the Supreme Court or the Court of Appeals for his own use, or as authorized by the Librarian.

BORROWING AND REMOVING MATERIAL

Rule 13. Who May Borrow Material

The following persons only may borrow and remove material from the Library:

(a) Members and employees of the Supreme Court and the Court of Appeals, in person or upon his or her signed memorandum.

(b) The Attorney General and members of his staff who are members of the North Carolina State Bar, Inc., in person or upon his or her signed memorandum.

(c) The Governor and members of the Council of State, in person or upon his or her signed memorandum.

(d) The President of the Senate, the Speaker of the House of Representatives, and the respective chairmen of the committees of the General Assembly, in person or upon his or her signed memorandum.

(e) The heads or duly constituted representatives of established agencies or institutions that offer reciprocal services to the Library and that are engaged in what the Librarian in his discretion deems to be worthy educational, historical, library, archival, or bibliographical activity for which they have a legitimate need to borrow the material requested.

(f) The Secretary-Treasurer of the North Carolina State Bar, Inc.

[Amended July 24, 1980.]

Rule 14. Return of Borrowed Material

Material borrowed from the Library shall be returned to the Library within the time provided below:

(a) Members of the Supreme Court and the Court of Appeals shall return borrowed material as early as possible, but in no event shall any item be retained for more than one week from the time of borrowing.

(b) Borrowers who are not members of the Supreme Court or the Court of Appeals shall return borrowed material before the closing of the Library on the day that the item is borrowed except when upon the borrower's written request stating good reason the Librarian or the Assistant Librarian in his or her respective discretion authorizes that any specific item be retained by the borrower until a later time as set by the Librarian or the Assistant Librarian.

Rule 15. Receipts for Borrowed Material

Each person who borrows material from the Library shall give a receipt therefor on a form prescribed for that purpose by the Librarian and available in the Library.

Rule 16. Borrowing Proscriptions and Limitations

The Librarian in his discretion may limit or proscribe the borrowing of old books, rare books, digests, indexes, general reference materials, looseleaf services, encyclopedias, advance sheets, and other materials that because of their particular value, nature, or frequent use should remain in the Library at all times or have only limited circulation.

Rule 17. Removal From the Justice Building

No borrower, except a Judge of the Court of Appeals upon his written request, may remove any Library material from the Justice Building except when each of the following conditions exists:

(a) It is not reasonably possible for the person desiring to use the material to do so within the Justice Building.

(b) It is impracticable to copy the material by use of the facilities available in the Justice Building, or such copies reasonably would not serve the purpose of the person desiring to borrow the material.

(c) Material that is identical or substantially the same may not be borrowed and removed from the North Carolina State Library or any other public library in Raleigh.

(d) The material is not out of print and it reasonably could be replaced.

(e) The Library has more than one copy of the material.

Rule 18. Transportation of Material

Library materials may not be sent through State Interoffice Mail or transported by or through any other person, agency, or means that the Librarian in his discretion deems unsafe.

INTERNAL RULES

Rule 19. Policies and Procedures

The Librarian shall be responsible for the general administration of the Library, and he shall execute the policies established by the Library Committee.

PENALTY

Rule 20. Contempt of Court

Any person who intentionally and wilfully violates any North Carolina Supreme Court Library Rule shall, upon formal complaint filed in the Supreme Court by the Librarian, be subject to being adjudged in contempt of the Supreme Court.

RECORDS AND ANNUAL REPORT

Rule 21. Records and Annual Report

The Librarian shall keep Library records in a form acceptable to the Library Committee, and on or before September 1 of each year he shall make to the Supreme Court a summary report of Library activities for the fiscal year that ended on the preceding June 30.

APPENDIX I. OFFICIAL REGISTER STATE OF NORTH CAROLINA

(1) The Senators, Representatives, Legislative Services Officer, Director of Legislative Drafting and Director of Research for the General Assembly.

(2) The Governor, Lieutenant Governor, Secretary of State, Auditor, Treasurer, Superintendent of Public Instruction, Attorney General, Commissioner of Agriculture, Commissioner of Labor, and Commissioner of Insurance.

(3) The Secretary of the Department of Administration, Secretary of the Department of Commerce, Secretary of the Department of Correction, Secretary of the Department of Crime Control and Public Safety, Secretary of the Department of Cultural Resources, Secretary of the Department of Human Resources, Secretary of the Department of Natural Resources and Community Development, Secretary of the Department of Revenue, and Secretary of the Department of Transportation.

(4) The Judges of the Superior Court and the Judges of the District Court.

(5) The District Attorneys and the Public Defenders.

(6) The State Librarian.

(7) The Director of the Division of Archives and History.

(8) The Director, Assistant Director, and Counsel of the Administrative Office of the Courts.

(9) The Chairman of the Judicial Standards Commission.

(10) The Secretary-Treasurer of the North Carolina State Bar, Inc.

(11) The State President of the Department of Community Colleges.

(12) The Director of the Office of Administrative Hearings.

(13) The Chairman of the Administrative Review Commission.

[Adopted November 28, 1972, amended July 24, 1980; amended effective June 21, 1984; March 18, 1986; September 12, 1988.]

MEDICO–LEGAL GUIDELINES OF NORTH CAROLINA

Adopted 1991; Revised 2001; Revised 2005; Revised 2008

Table of Contents

Preamble to Medico–Legal Guidelines

History Leading to the Proposed Revision of the N.C. Medico–Legal Code

Since the adoption of the original Medico–Legal Code by the North Carolina Bar Association and North Carolina Medical Society in 1956, the environment in which the physician and attorney interact has changed radically. With the introduction of standard rules of civil procedure and evidence, the broad bounds of contact between attorney, witnesses, and parties were defined. Adoption and subsequent revision of Rules of Professional Conduct further defined the attorney's ethical conduct and served as a guide in contact with physicians. Physicians, largely unfamiliar with these legal rules and guides, reacted only within the boundaries of professional respect, dignity, decorum, and the ethical principles of their health care profession. With the rise in importance and frequency of medical litigation, the professions have scrutinized attorney and physician conduct and have reached a consensus that there is a need to revise their inter-professional code. The Code was previously revised in 1972, 1986, and 1991 in attempts to update the original 1956 Code. The 1991 version was called "The Medico–Legal Guidelines of North Carolina" (the term "Guidelines" as used hereafter refers to all such versions as well as this document).

Recent Revisions

In 1997, the Joint Committee of the North Carolina Medical Society and North Carolina Bar Association decided the Guidelines should be updated given various changes in the law and because the Guidelines had not been effective in resolving certain recurring disputes between physicians and attorneys.[1] Significant revisions were made, and finally, in 2000, the Medical

Society and the Bar Association adopted the 2000 Medico–Legal Guidelines.

In 2005, the Medico–Legal Liaison Committee updated the Guidelines to incorporate HIPAA privacy regulations and update other cited authorities. In 2008, Medico–Legal Guidelines were revised to include information concerning appropriate handling of mental health, substance abuse, and psychotherapy records. In 2014, the Medico–Legal Guidelines were revised again to reflect changes in applicable laws, the HITECH Act, the evolving use of electronic medical records, as well as the Medico–Legal Liaison Committee's recognition that the Medico–Legal Guidelines could be more user-friendly.

Physician Complaints

The Guidelines cannot recite all of the complaints that Physicians may have when dealing with attorneys, but common complaints include attorneys' use and sometimes misuse of subpoena power, including the failure to give physicians adequate notice of legal proceedings and the failure to pay fees of fact medical witnesses and retained medical witnesses.[2]

Physicians complain that they are uncertain of their legal duties in certain areas. Physicians are frequently confused about the duties attendant to their release of confidential medical information. They are not certain as to when they may, may not, and when they must release confidential medical records or speak with an attorney about a patient. They are often unsure about what services to bill for, whom to bill, and how to ensure payment resulting from services rendered in legal cases involving medical issues. They complain that they receive conflicting responses from attorneys regarding their duties and rights.[3]

Treating physicians, who may be potential defendants in professional liability litigation, complain that attorneys investigating those claims mislead them. The climate of inter-professional mistrust created in the professional liability context invades all areas of litigation.

Attorney Complaints

Likewise, the Guidelines cannot recite all of the complaints attorneys have about physicians. Common attorney complaints are that physicians fail to comply with subpoenas for their records or presence as a witness, that they fail to provide complete medical records, and that they bill excessively for medical records, consultation and testimony. Attorneys also complain that treating physicians refuse or are reluctant to consult with their patient's attorney or to provide live testimony on behalf of their patient. These areas of conflict cause problems for patients and attorneys, who of necessity rely on medical evidence in cases involving medical factual issues.

Scope

Throughout its history, the scope of various versions of the Guidelines has been limited to physician-attorney interactions. The Guidelines still purposefully do not apply to other health care professionals. However, there is no reason that the Guidelines cannot be considered by attorneys and other health care providers in their interactions with each other. While the more recently adopted Guidelines, including the current version, have more specifically addressed certain areas such as workers' compensation, testimony regarding patient capacity/competency and cases involving drug and alcohol abuse medical records, the continual changes in various areas, including significant rule making changes in the area of workers' compensation make it difficult to incorporate all current rules and regulations into the Guidelines. Thus, the Guidelines are not intended to be, and should not be viewed as an exhaustive recitation of all applicable rules and regulations at any given time.

Professional Liability

Historically, the Guidelines have not addressed the interaction between attorneys and physicians who are defendants in professional liability actions. This relationship is governed by mandatory statutes, rules of ethics, and rules of procedure, and is not appropriately a subject of these Guidelines. However, these Guidelines do discuss situations where a physician may be a potential defendant in a professional liability case and also address situations where the physician is not a party-defendant but the legal action is based on claim of professional negligence asserted by a patient whom the physician treated or evaluated.[4] The Guidelines address some of the recurring concerns in this difficult area.

Treating Versus Non–Treating Witnesses

In earlier editions, the Guidelines did not always distinguish between physicians who were retained expert medical opinion witnesses and those medical witnesses who were fact witnesses by virtue of treating the attorney's client as a patient. The relationship between a physician who is a retained expert and an attorney is voluntary and reciprocal, and fee arrangements between them are business agreements restricted only by prevailing law and any ethical guidelines or requirements applicable to the attorney and/or physician. By contrast, interactions between treating physicians and patient's attorneys are not chosen, arising instead from their respective connections and duties to their mutual patient/client. The Guidelines, recognizing this distinction, preclude retained experts and attorneys from invoking the assistance of the Medico–Legal Liaison Committee in fee disputes arising between them. Nevertheless, some effort has been made in the more recent versions of the Guidelines to address matters related to "retained medical witnesses" and "fact medical witnesses" and to distinguish between the two types of witnesses where appropriate.

[Revised 2008. Amended eff. July 1, 2014.]

1Despite the presence of the Guidelines, recurring disputes persist between physicians and attorneys in the litigation context. Some of these disputes have been addressed to the Joint Committee of the North Carolina Medical Society and North Carolina Bar Association for dispute resolution. Other disputes have been explored by the North Carolina Bar Association Medico–Legal Liaison Committee, which conducted public hearings prior to preparing a new draft version of the North Carolina Medico–Legal Guidelines. The Committee invited speakers to the hearings who had experienced difficulty with the implementation of the Guidelines, and believed that the Guidelines needed change.

2See Definitions of "Fact Medical Witnesses" and "Retained Medical Witnesses" in Section III, H. 1 and 2, as well as discussion of fees in Section V.

3This occurs, in part, because the law is unclear in certain areas and uncertain in others, as reflected in these Guidelines. There also continue to be changes in the laws and rules that govern the interaction between physicians and attorneys, and thus at any given time it may be difficult to be aware of all of the changes in the law affecting those interactions.

4In such latter situations, the physician may be required to provide testimony affecting defendant(s), including those for example who are co-workers, entities at which the physician or other health care provider works, colleagues, or persons or entities with whom a referral relationship exists.

Guideline I. Introduction

The North Carolina Medico–Legal Guidelines are the product of collaboration between the North Carolina Medical Society and North Carolina Bar Association. The Guidelines are the end-product of decades of cooperation between physicians and attorneys aimed at improving their inter-professional interactions in medical litigation. The Guidelines are not intended to and do not expand or limit any obligations of physicians or attorneys under existing federal or state laws or regulations.

The relationship between a physician and an attorney should be based upon mutual respect, courtesy, and understanding. Medical testimony is generally indispensable in legal cases to prove or disprove the nature or extent of injuries or other legally relevant medical conditions. Therefore, when accepting a patient, a physician also accepts the incidental obligation to cooperate in any legal proceedings in which the patient may become involved.[5] When attorneys make inappropriate or inconsiderate demands on physicians, they cause animosity between the professions. Without mutual cooperation by physicians and attorneys, their patients/clients become the unfortunate victim of professional ill will.

To promote inter-professional cooperation and courtesy, the particular responsibilities and expectations of physicians and attorneys should be more clearly defined. These Guidelines set out these responsibilities and expectations, citing legal and/or medical authority where applicable. These Guidelines are not exclusive, nor do they cover all situations or seek to define the outer limits of professional interrelationships. The Guidelines establish minimum aspirational standards for those relationships and encourage civility between the professions.

The Guidelines use a definition of "medical records" that was agreed upon by the North Carolina Medical Society and the North Carolina Bar Association. Other than in the Guidelines, this specific definition likely does not appear elsewhere unless it was borrowed from the Guidelines. As reflected in the definitions sections of the Guidelines, as well as in Appendix A–1 and A–2 to the Guidelines, there are numerous statutes and regulations, both Federal and State, which give a definition of the term "medical records" or of the type of information contained in a patient's medical records. The North Carolina Medical Board also has position statements related specifically to medical records.[6] The statutory definitions and Medical Board position statements are not completely consistent with one another and thus defining what constitutes a patient's "medical records" that a physician must produce in response to a release or subpoena seeking the production of all of the patient's medical records has been and continues to be a source of confusion between physicians and attorneys. This confusion has the potential to, and has in fact, caused problems for both physicians and attorneys when a complete set of medical records is not produced in response to a medical records release or a subpoena. Unfortunately, given all of the potential documents (in hard copy and in electronic form), as well as various machines that now store patient data, determining everything that may constitute the complete medical records of a patient is very difficult, even when the patient or attorney seeking medical records is very specific about what is sought. When a patient or attorney generically requests "medical records," this difficulty is increased. The Guidelines attempt to create a common framework for the production of medical information maintained by physicians with respect to their patients and to further discussion between physicians and attorneys regarding the information sought and to be produced pursuant to a medical records release or a subpoena. Generally, it is the goal of these Guidelines to encourage attorneys to be as specific as possible when requesting information in the custody or control of a physician that may constitute patient "medical records" and for physicians and their staff responding to medical records requests and subpoenas to consider all of the potential sources of patient information.

[Revised 2008. Amended eff. July 1, 2014.]

[5]See AMA Code of Medical Ethics, § 9.07 "Medical Testimony," Noting that "physicians have an obligation to assist in the administration of justice."

[6]See N.C. Medical Board Position Statements: "Access to medical records," "Medical record documentation" and "Retention of medical records."

Guideline II. Specific Regulations

These Guidelines do not and are not intended to supplant any mandatory rules, laws or regulations. Mandatory rules (for example the Rules of Professional Conduct governing attorney behavior, the North Carolina Rules of Civil Procedure governing court procedure, the North Carolina Rules of Evidence governing the admissibility of evidence in court proceedings and the Rules of the North Carolina Industrial Commission governing workers' compensation cases), other rules, statutes, and regulations (including but not limited to HIPAA and the HITECH Act) take precedence over these Guidelines, and are always subject to change. Some relevant citation to applicable rules, laws, professional codes and position statements, and/or regulations are contained in the text of these Guidelines.

DEFINITIONS

The following definitions apply throughout these Guidelines:

A. "Physician" Defined: A physician is a person licensed to practice medicine by the North Carolina Medical Board as that term has historically been understood, i.e., medical and osteopathic physicians.[7]

B. "Attorney" Defined: An attorney is a person licensed to practice law in North Carolina by the North Carolina State Bar, or otherwise authorized to practice by North Carolina law.[8]

C. "Health information" Defined: Health Information means any information, whether oral or recorded in any form or medium, that: (1) Is created or received by a health care provider, health plan, public health authority, employer, life insurer, school or university, or health care clearinghouse; and (2) Related to the past, present, or future physical or mental health or condition of an individual; the provision of health care to an individual; or the past, present, or future payment for the provision of health care to an individual.[9]

D. "Designated Record Set" Defined. Designated record set means (1) a group of records maintained by or for a covered entity that is: (i) The medical records and billing records about individuals maintained by or for a covered health care provider; (ii) The enrollment, payment, claims adjudication, and case or medical management record systems maintained by or for a health plan; or (iii) Used, in whole or in part, by or for the covered entity to make decisions about individuals. (2) For purposes of this definition, the term "record" means any item, collection or grouping of information that includes protected health information and is maintained, collected, used, or disseminated by or for a covered entity.[10]

E. "Medical Records" Defined:[11] Medical records are a collection of Health Information and the Designated Record Set for a particular individual whether created by a physician or other health care provider,[12] as well as received from a physician or other health care provider. If they contain information covered by the prohibitions against redisclosure found in 42 C.F.R. Part 2, in N.C.G.S. Sections 8–53.3, 53.4, 53.5, 53.7, or 53.8, in N.C.G.S. Chapter 122C, or in any other provision of federal or state law, the physician may produce the balance of the record, redacting the portion that may not be redisclosed, along with a statement that "the redacted records may not be released without either patient consent or a court order in accordance with applicable laws and regulations."[13] Medical records contain information that may be or are inherently sensitive and personal, and contain information that relates to an individual's physical or mental condition, medical history, medical diagnosis, or medical treatment, as well as demographic and other information that identifies or has the potential to identify the individual (e.g., patient name, address, social security number, unique identifier, etc.).[14]

F. "Medical Report" Defined: A medical report is a report generated by a physician at the request of an attorney in order to assist the attorney in preparing for litigation which involves a patient's medical condition, treatment, or prognosis. A medical report may be a narrative summary of the medical record, or it may be a response to requests for expert opinions regarding the patient's condition, treatment, or prognosis not contained in the medical record. The preparation of a medical report may, in some instances, require the physician to obtain a current evaluation of the patient.[15]

G. "Independent Medical Examination" Defined: An independent medical examination is a medical examination in which a person is required or agrees to submit to a medical examination by a physician selected or approved by a court, administrative agency or other adjudicatory body or by the mutual agreement of the parties.[16]

H. "Medical Witness" Defined: A medical witness is a physician or other healthcare provider who provides testimony concerning one or more medical issues involved in a lawsuit or claim. Three types of medical witnesses are recognized by the N.C. Medico–Legal Guidelines.[17] They are:

1. *"Retained Medical Witness" Defined:* A retained medical witness is a physician or other healthcare provider who has been retained by one of the parties to litigation to provide expert opinion testimony or evidence concerning one or more medical issues involved in the lawsuit or claim.[18]

2. *"Fact Medical Witness" Defined:* A fact medical witness is a physician or other healthcare provider who is called upon to testify or provide evidence because they have treated a patient who is a party or witness in a lawsuit or claim.[19]

3. *"Independent Medical Witness" Defined:* An independent medical witness is a physician or other healthcare provider who has been selected or approved by a court, administrative agency or other adjudicatory body or by the mutual agreement of the parties to perform an independent medical examination.

[Revised 2008. Amended eff. July 1, 2014.]

7 N.C. Gen. Stat. Ch. 90, Art. 1 governs the licensure of medical and osteopathic physicians in North Carolina. A physician should expect any non-physician practitioners working under their supervision to follow the Guidelines as well. Other health care providers not working under the supervision of a physician also are encouraged to follow the Guidelines but are not required to do so unless otherwise instructed by their regulatory Board.

8 An attorney should expect any non-attorney personnel working under their supervision to follow the Guidelines as well.

9 45 C.F.R. § 160.103

10 45 C.F.R. § 164.501

11 As indicated in the "Introduction," other definitions of "medical records" appear in North Carolina and Federal statutes and regulations. See Appendix A–2.

12 N.C. Medical Board "Access to medical records" (Position Statement adopted 11/93, amended 5/96, 5/97, 3/02, 8/03 and 9/10) ("Each licensee has a duty on the request of a patient or the patient's representative to release a copy of the record in a timely manner to the patient or the patient's representative, unless the licensee believes that such release would endanger the patient's life or cause harm to another person. This includes medical records received from other licensee offices or health care facilities.")

13 Production of a "privilege log" or similar document describing the information that is redacted would violate several of these provisions, as a description of the type of medical care sought would itself be confidential.

14 See AMA Code of Medical Ethics Sec. 5.07, "Confidentiality: Computers" and Sec. 5.075 Confidentiality: Disclosure of Records to Data Collection Companies" (regarding confidentiality and computerized data bases). N.C. Gen, Stat. § 132–1.10(d) prohibits anyone who is preparing or filing a document to be recorded or filed with the court to include social security numbers and other personal confidential information.

15 See N.C. Gen. Stat. 90–411 (regarding reasonable fees for the preparation of medical reports). See also N.C. Rule of Civil Procedure 35.

16 Independent medical examinations occur in a number of contexts. For civil actions in North Carolina's state courts, see N.C. Rule of Civil Procedure 35. In workers' compensation cases, independent medical examinations can occur upon agreement of the parties, order of the Industrial Commission, or pursuant to N.C. Gen. Stat. § 97–27. Reference should be made to any Rules adopted by the Industrial Commission for guidance regarding communications with independent medical witnesses in workers' compensation cases. http://www.ic.nc.gov/ncic/pages/comprule.htm With regard to social security disability claims, see 20 C.F.R. §§ 404.1517 and 416.917, which discuss when the Social Security Administration will purchase a consultative examination of a disability claimant. The reports generated from these examinations are kept in the claimant's file and are available for review by the claimant and/or the claimant's representative by going to the office that has the file. The reports are not automatically sent to the claimant or the claimant's representative. The claimant may direct the Social Security Administration to release the report to his or her own doctor. See also 20 C.F.R. §§ 404.1519 to 404.1519t, 416.919 to 404.1519t, 409.1512, and 416.927 (regarding Social Security Administration Medical Advisors).

17 The obligations of medical witnesses under the Guidelines may differ, depending upon which type of medical witness they are and/or testimony they are providing. See also *Turner v. Duke University*, 325 N.C. 152, 381 S.E.2d 706 (1989) for a discussion about the differences between the first two types of medical witnesses identified.

18 See AMA Code of Medical Ethics, Sec. 9.07, "Medical Testimony" ("When physicians choose to provide expert testimony, they should have recent and substantive experience or knowledge in the area in which they testify, and be committed to evaluating cases objectively and to providing an independent opinion. Their testimony should reflect current scientific thought and standards of care that have gained acceptance among peers in the relevant field. If a medical witness knowingly provides testimony based on a theory not widely accepted in the profession, the witness should characterize the theory as such. Also, testimony pertinent to a standard of care must consider standards that prevailed at the time the event under review

occurred.") See also Rule 702(b)—(e), (h) of the North Carolina Rules of Evidence.

19See AMA Code of Medical Ethics, Sec. 9.07, "Medical Testimony" ("Physicians who serve as fact witnesses must deliver honest testimony. This requires that they engage in continuous self-examination to ensure that their testimony represents the facts of the case. When treating physicians are called upon to testify in matters that could adversely impact their patients' medical interests, they should decline to testify unless the patient consents or unless ordered to do so by legally constituted authority. If, as a result of legal proceedings, the patient and the physician are placed in adversarial positions it may be appropriate for a treating physician to transfer the care of the patient to another physician.")

Guideline III. Specific Situations

A. Medical Records

1. *Ownership of Medical Records*

Usually, records made or collected by or at the direction of a physician in connection with the treatment and evaluation of a patient are maintained and retained by the physician, hospital or other individual or institutional care giver. The original record is deemed to be the property of the physician, hospital, or other individual or institutional care giver. The patient has a qualified right to say who may receive information contained in the record.[20]

2. *The Patient's Right to Seek an Amendment to the Designated Record Set*

Under HIPAA, a patient has a right to have a covered entity amend protected health information or a record about the individual in a designated record set for as long as the protected health information is maintained in the designated record set. A covered entity may deny an individual's request for amendment, if it determines that the protected health information or record that is the subject of the request: (i) was not created by the covered entity, unless the individual provides a reasonable basis to believe that the originator of protected health information is no longer available to act on the requested amendment; (ii) is not part of the designated record set; (iii) would not be available for inspection under 45 C.F.R. § 164.524; or (iv) is accurate and complete.[21]

3. *Inspection and Copying of Medical Records*

a. Required Authorization

An original of the medical records or any part thereof should not be removed from the possession of a physician, hospital, or other individual or institutional care giver except upon court order, but the original should be available for inspection or copying with proper authorization.[22] A patient may give verbal authorization for the production of medical records, but a physician has the right to require that any request for medical records be in writing,[23] and if the patient is directing that the medical records be provided to anyone other than the patient, the request must be in writing.[24] Proper written authorization can be provided by the patient, an individual empowered by law to act on the patient's behalf regarding disclosure of medical records, or by order of a court or administrative agency having jurisdiction and authority to mandate such disclosure. Specifically in workers' compensation cases, there is a statutory policy "to protect the employee's right to a confidential physician-patient relationship while allowing the parties to have reasonable access to all relevant medical information, including medical records, reports, and information necessary to the fair and swift administration and resolution of workers' compensation claims, while limiting unnecessary communications with and administrative requests to health care providers."[25]

b. What Should be Produced in Response to Appropriate Authorization.

Under HIPAA, an individual has a right of access to inspect and obtain a copy of protected health information about the individual in a designated record set, for as long as the protected health information is maintained in the designated record set, except for: (i) psychotherapy notes; (ii) information compiled in reasonable anticipation of, or for use in, a civil, criminal, or administrative action or proceeding; and (iii) protected health information maintained by a covered entity that is:(A) subject to the Clinical Laboratory Improvements Amendments of 1988, 42 U.S.C. 263a, to the extent the provision of access to the individual would be prohibited by law; or (B) exempt from the Clinical Laboratory Improvements Amendments of 1988, pursuant to 42 CFR 493.3(a)(2).[26] Although attorneys are encouraged to be as specific as possible, when a request for "medical records" is made, all documents meeting the definition of "medical records" set forth in the Guidelines should be produced unless a smaller subset of records is requested.

c. Permissible Charges for Copying Medical Records and Format in which Records are Provided.

In personal injury liability and social security disability cases, permissible charges for copies of medical records are governed by N.C. Gen. Stat. 90–411. Further, in personal injury liability cases, a physician may not charge for copies of medical records requested by a patient's attorney if they wish to preserve a lien for their medical services against the patient's recovery of monetary damages for personal injury from a third party.[27] In cases other than those involving personal injury liability or social security disability, "a reasonable cost-based fee" that includes only the cost of "copying, including the cost of supplies and labor of copying" as well as the cost of postage if the copy is sent by mail, can be charged.[28] Under HIPAA, a covered entity must produce the records in the form or format requested by the individual, if it is readily producible in such form or format.[29] If records are maintained electronically, and cannot be produced in the format requested by the patient, a copy must be provided in a "readable electronic form" rather than a hard copy.[30] HIPAA provides that if access can be provided in electronic format, and that format is requested by an individual, then the patient should be allowed to receive it by paying a reasonable fee associated with reproducing the records electronically, but under the HITECH Act, the cost of producing records maintained in an electronic health record cannot exceed the labor and supply costs of reproducing the same.[31] In workers' compensation cases, permissible charges for copies of medical records are governed by N.C. Gen. Stat. § 97–26.1.[32] In social security disability cases, see 20 C.F.R. §§ 404.1514 and 416.914, and N.C. Gen Stat. § 90–411.

d. Withholding Records where Patient Account for Medical Services Not Paid

A physician may not refuse to provide copies of medical records (including the bill for services provided to the patient) on the ground that the patient has not paid the amount due on his account for medical and other services.[33]

2. *Requesting Medical Records or a Medical Report From a Treating Physician*

a. Notice

An attorney should give a patient's treating physician reasonable notice of the need for inspection and copying of medical records, or of the need for preparation of a medical report. The notice should clearly specify the information and documents requested. Notice may be provided by written correspondence, or by a subpoena, and should be accompanied by appropriate authorization to release the information requested.

b. Authorization

Proper authorization is necessary before a physician can release medical information. No attorney should request and no physician should furnish any medical information concerning the history, physical or mental examination, condition, diagnosis or prognosis of a patient except with the written consent of the patient, the patient's authorized representative, an appropriate judicial or administrative order, or in conformity with other applicable legal authority.[34] A physician may disclose to a family member or other person(s) identified by a patient prior to his or her death who was involved in the individual's care or payment for health care prior to the individual's death, protected health information of the individual that is relevant to such person's involvement, unless doing so is inconsistent with any prior expressed preference of the individual that is known to the physician.[35] The scope of the authorization determines the scope of the inspection, release, copying or report. If the requesting attorney wants information beyond what is authorized to be released, the attorney must obtain additional authorization. A subpoena signed by an attorney, without more, is insufficient to allow a physician to produce any patient medical information.

c. Promptness

The physician, with proper authorization from the patient or the patient's authorized representative, should promptly furnish the attorney with a complete medical record or medical report. HIPAA requires that records be produced within 30 days of a request or within 60 days if the requested records are kept off-site.[36] Delay in providing the medical record or medical information may prejudice the opportunity of the patient to settle their claim or lawsuit, may delay the trial of a case, or may cause additional expense or the loss of important testimony.[37]

3. *Special Considerations for Substance Abuse Diagnosis and Treatment Records and for Psychotherapy Notes*

Under federal and state law, information about an individual's substance abuse or mental health diagnosis or treatment can be a trap for the unwary litigator seeking this information as well as for the physician or health care facility holding the information. Protected information includes any information about an individual, whether or not the information is in writing or recorded in some other form, and includes the patient's identity, address, medical or treatment information, and all communications by the patient to program staff.[38] The facility is prohibited from even acknowledging whether the individual is or ever was a patient at the facility absent the patient's written consent or an appropriate court order.[39] Disclosure—and subsequent re-disclosure—of records generated at a federally-assisted drug or alcohol abuse facility is strictly prohibited by complex federal rules, with criminal penalties for violation.[40] See Appendices G–1 and G–2 for an authorization form that complies with all federal and state laws and rules regarding release of substance abuse and mental health records.

a. Substance Abuse Records: (Mental health information that is part of a substance abuse record is treated in the same manner as described herein.)

A subpoena alone, even one signed by a judge, is never sufficient to compel disclosure of certain types of these records; the party seeking disclosure must provide either highly specific written consent from the patient that meets the requirements of the rules, or a court order framed in precise accord with the rules along with a subpoena.[41] There are separate federal rules governing procedures and criteria for issuance of court orders authorizing disclosure of substance abuse records for noncriminal and criminal purposes,[42] although exemptions do exist for reporting incidents of suspected child abuse and neglect to appropriate State or local authorities.[43] A court order allowing disclosure of substance abuse records must:

1. Limit disclosure to those parts of the patient record essential to fulfill the objective of the order.

2. Limit disclosure to those persons whose need for the information is the basis for the order.

3. Include necessary measures to limit disclosure for the protection of the patient, physician-patient relationship and treatment services, i.e. sealing the case record.

Disclosure of substance abuse records may only occur if other ways of obtaining the information are not available or would not be effective and the public interest and need for disclosure outweigh the potential injury to the patient, physician-patient relationship and treatment services.[44]

Attorneys seeking court orders for the production of substance abuse documents should make sure that the order they obtain contains the appropriate language to allow a physician to disclose such records and be in compliance with 42 CFR Part 2.

b. Mental Health Records:

The Mental Health, Developmental Disabilities, and Substance Abuse Act of 1985 has specific rules regarding the disclosure of information by physicians at facilities whose primary purpose is to provide services for the care, treatment, habilitation, or rehabilitation of the mentally ill, the developmentally disabled, or substance abusers.[4546]

c. Psychotherapy Notes:

HIPAA provides extra protections for psychotherapy notes.[47] A specific authorization separate from any other authorizations must be obtained for any use or disclosure of psychotherapy notes. For more information see 45 C.F.R. § 164.508(a)(2).[48]

d. Communicable Diseases

Physicians are required to keep strictly confidential all information and records, whether publicly or privately maintained, that identify a person who has AIDS virus infection or who has or may have certain other communicable diseases.[49] In certain circumstances enumerated in N.C. Gen. Stat. § 130A–143, such information may be disclosed.

B. Guidance to Physicians about Capacity or Competency

Physicians may be asked on behalf of a patient to testify as to the capacity of the patient to take certain actions, serve in certain roles or their competency generally. While the guidelines cannot serve as an exhaustive list of all of the questions a physician may be asked about their patients, the following opinions are those that an attorney may routinely ask a physician to give about their patient, along with the standards upon which the physician will be asked to opine:

1. *Opinions of Incompetency for Incompetency Procedures.*

"Incompetent adult" means an adult or emancipated minor who lacks sufficient capacity to manage the adult's own affairs or to make or communicate important decisions concerning the adult's person, family, or property whether the lack of capacity is due to mental illness, mental retardation, epilepsy, cerebral palsy, autism, inebriety, senility, disease, injury, or similar cause or condition.[50]

2. *Opinions of Capacity/Incapacity to Serve as Fiduciary*

Individuals may be appointed to serve as a fiduciary in many roles, including any one or more of the following: Personal Representative (Executor or Administrator of a decedent's estate). Trustee of an inter vivos or testamentary trust, Agent (Attorney–in–Fact) under a General Power of Attorney, or Health Care Agent under a Health Care Power of Attorney. The North Carolina Uniform Fiduciaries Act does not provide any method or standard for determining incapacity of a fiduciary. Some documents, particularly trusts, may provide for a mechanism or procedure for determining the incapacity of a fiduciary. If an individual fits the definition of "incompetent adult" as described above, the individual is not fit to serve as a fiduciary. Given the high level of responsibility and good faith, and the potential consequences to the person or property of others, the level of capacity for a fiduciary should be higher than for an individual simply acting for himself.

3. *Opinions on Testamentary Capacity or Lack Thereof.*

A testator has testamentary capacity if he comprehends the natural objects of his bounty; understands the kind, nature and extent of his property; knows the manner in which he desires his act to take effect; and realizes the effect his act will have upon his estate.[51] The capacity required to create, amend, revoke, or add property to a revocable trust is the same as the capacity required to make a will.[52]

4. *Opinions on Contractual Capacity or Lack Thereof.*

A higher level of mental capacity is necessary to enter into a contract than is required for testamentary capacity. In North Carolina, courts have said the measure of capacity is the ability to understand the nature of the contract, its scope and effect, or its nature and consequences. It is not that the person should be able to act wisely or discreetly, nor to drive a good bargain, but that he should be in such possession of his faculties as to enable him to know at least what he is doing and to contract understandingly.[53]

C. Consultation and Testimony

1. *Consultations*

It is professional courtesy for physicians and attorneys to cooperate with one another and to abide by applicable statutes and rules so that the medical questions involved in controversies are fairly and adequately explored and presented. Where appropriate, a frank discussion between the patient's physician and the patient's attorney is helpful to give each a complete understanding of the medical and legal issues involved. When such a discussion occurs, their mutual patient/client benefits: time is saved, confusion is minimized (making settlement more likely), and interprofessional understanding is enhanced. To that end, the patient's physician(s) and attorney(s) should attempt, when appropriate, to discuss the medical questions prior to mediation, deposition, or trial. The patient's physician and the attorney should agree up front regarding the charges, if any, by the physician for consulting with the attorney at the various stages of litigation so as to avoid any later dispute.

However, patients' physicians may not communicate with an attorney or any other person about a patient's treatment, evaluation, or condition without the written authorization of the patient or the patient's authorized representative, or a court order, or other lawful authority. In workers' compensation cases, there may be circumstances under which the employer or its representative may communicate with physicians.[54] When in doubt, a physician should contact the N.C. Industrial Commission to ascertain the current status of the law on this issue.

A physician has an obligation to consult with a patient's attorney if the patient has given them written consent to do so. If a patient who has a legal claim requests a physician's assistance, the physician should furnish medical evidence, with the patient's consent, in order to secure the patient's legal rights.[55] However, this obligation to consult may be limited if the patient has, or may have, a potential malpractice claim against the physician.[56] If a physician is unclear whether the obligation to consult with a patient's attorney may be limited, the physician is encouraged to ask the advice of their professional liability insurer, consult with legal counsel for the North Carolina Medical Society, and/or consult with their own attorney.

An attorney investigating a potential professional liability claim should avoid misleading the physician regarding the physician's potential malpractice liability. Where the patient's attorney is investigating a specific physician's potential professional liability or reasonably foresees that the physician's actions may be the basis of a claim, the attorney has an obligation to so advise that physician.[57]

2. *Physician Deposition Testimony*

Deposition testimony of a physician is sometimes necessary and is preferably arranged at a scheduled time at a convenient place that can reasonably accommodate a deposition. If the physician can provide reasonable accommodations at his/her office, the attorney should agree to do the deposition there.[58] Depositions are necessary for one or more reasons. A deposition is a discovery tool which allows one side of a lawsuit to discover the information known to witnesses for the other side. Typically, the attorney opposing the patient's claim is prohibited from communicating with the patient's physician prior to trial except at a deposition.[59] The opposing attorney is frequently in need of the physician's deposition testimony in order to defend against the patient's claim. The deposition is usually that attorney's only opportunity to discern the physician's opinion regarding the patient's medical condition. A deposition may also be necessary to perpetuate testimony[60] or for later use instead of the physician's appearance at trial in order to accommodate the physician's schedule, even though a physician's appearance in court is usually the most effective way to present testimony. A deposition may be a preferable alternative to trial testimony, however, when the attorney believes the physician's testimony is of secondary importance. Physicians should agree to videotaped depositions when requested as this is usually being done to accommodate the physician's schedule. North Carolina Rules of Evidence and of Civil Procedure sometimes prohibit an attorney from using a deposition in state civil court. In those instances, the physician must appear in court to testify.[61]

[Revised 2008. Amended eff. July 1, 2014.]

[20]In workers' compensation cases, see N.C. Gen. Stat. § 97–25.6 and rights of employer to receive information even absent consent of employee. See also AMA Code of Medical Ethics, Sec. 10.1 "Fundamental Elements of the Patient–Physician Relationship" ("The patient has the right to receive information from physicians Patients are also entitled to obtain copies or summaries of their medical records [and] to have their questions answered "); See also footnote 12. Complex rules govern the disclosure of medical information about an individual's substance abuse, diagnosis or treatment, and the disclosure of such information is not exhaustively addressed in these Guidelines. See Part IV(A)(4), infra, and N.C. Gen. Stat. § 122C–3(9). HIPAA citation regarding personal representatives can be found at 45 C.F.R. 164.502(g).

[21]45 C.F.R. 164.526(a)

[22]HIPAA mandates that a valid authorization must contain, at a minimum: (1) a description of the information to be used or disclosed; (2) the name(s) of those authorized to make the requested use or disclosure; (3) the name of the person(s) to whom the covered entity may make the requested use or disclosure; (4) the purpose of the use or disclosure; (5) an expiration date or event (e.g., end of research study); and (6) the signature of the individual and date (if the authorization is signed by a personal representative of the individual, a description of such representative's authority). 45 C.F.R. § 164.508(c) (1)(i–vi). Also, § 164.508(c)(2) requires that the authorization contain statements adequate to place the individual on notice that the individual has the right to revoke the authorization, the ability or inability to condition treatment, payment, enrollment or eligibility for benefits on whether the individual signs the authorization, and the potential for information to be disclosed pursuant to the authorization to be subject to redisclosure.

[23]45 C.F.R. § 164.524(b)(*l*)

[24]45 C.F.R. § 164.524(b)(3)(ii)

[25]N.C. Gen. Stat. § 97–25.6(a). N.C. Gen. Stat. § 97–25.6(c)(1) provides that "an employer is entitled, without the express authorization of the employee, to obtain the employee's medical records containing relevant medical information from the employee's health care providers.". N.C. Gen. Stat. § 97–25.6(b) defines "relevant medical information" is defined as any medical record, report, or information that is any of the following: (1) Restricted to the particular evaluation, diagnosis, or treatment of the injury or disease for which compensation, including medical compensation, is sought; (2) Reasonably related to the injury or disease for which the employee claims compensation; and/or (3) Related to an assessment of the employee's ability to return to work as a result of the particular injury or disease. Reference should be made to the Rules of the Industrial Commission or contact made with the Industrial Commission regarding the right of the employer or others acting on its behalf to obtain medical records without the express authorization of the employee. HIPAA permits such disclosure under an exemption that reads: "A covered entity may disclose protected health information as authorized by and to the extent necessary to comply with laws relating to workers' compensation " 45 C.F.R. § 164.512(*l*). See also AMA Code of Medical Ethics, Sec. 5.09 "Confidentiality: Industry–Employed Physicians and Independent Medical Examiners," ("When a physician renders treatment to an employee with a work-related illness or injury, the release of medical information to the employer as to the treatment provided may be subject to the provisions of worker's compensation laws. The physician must comply with the requirements of such laws, if applicable. However, the physician may not otherwise discuss the employee's health condition with the employer without the employee's consent or, in the event of the employee's incapacity, the appropriate proxy's consent.")

[26]45 C.F.R. § 164.524(*l*)

[27]See N.C. Gen. Stat. §§ 44–49 and 44–50. See also N.C. Rule of Professional Conduct 1.15–1 and N.C. RPC 69, ("Payment of Client Funds to Medical Provider") and N.C. RPC 125 ("Disbursement of Settlement Proceeds") (requiring attorney to obey client's instruction not to pay medical providers from the proceeds of settlement in the absence of a valid physician's lien).

[28]45 C.F.R. § 164.524(c)(4)

[29]45 C.F.R. § 164.524(c)(2)

[30]78 Fed. Reg. at 5.702

[31]45 C.F.R. § 164.524(c)(2); HITECH Act; North Carolina currently has no statute setting forth the costs of producing records electronically, and thus the HIPAA standard in 45 C.F.R. § 164.524(c)(4) should apply.

[32]North Carolina Industrial Commission Minutes, January 12, 1995. See Appendix E for additional information.

[33]See N.C. Medical Board, "Access to medical records" (Position Statement, adopted 11/93, amended 5/96, 9/97, 3/02, 8/03 and 9/10) ("Medical records should not be withheld because an account is overdue or a bill is owed.") An attorney may not pay client bills for treatment, although they may advance medical litigation expenses on behalf of a client. See N.C. Rule of Professional Conduct 1.8(e), RPC 80, "Lending Money to a Client," and CPR 157 (attorney may advance cost of medical examination if same is litigation expense).

[34]See N.C. Gen. Stat. §§ 8–53 and 8–44.1; N.C. Rule of Civil Procedure 45(c); the Rules of the Industrial Commission. See RPC 162, "Communications with Opposing Party's Physicians" (prohibiting attorney from communicating with opposing party's non-party treating physicians unless the opposing party consents, in non-workers' compensation setting); RPC 180 "Communications with Opposing Party's Physicians" (extending that prohibition to passive listening); RPC 224 (extending prohibition to employer's attorney in workers' compensation setting). See also RPC 184 "Communications with Physicians Performing Autopsy" (allowing opposing counsel to communicate with pathologist performing autopsy without decedent's personal representative's consent). Compare AMA Code of Medical Ethics §§ 5.05 "Confidentiality," ("The physician should not reveal confidential information without the express consent of the patient, subject to certain exceptions which are ethically justified because of overriding considerations."); See also Sec. 5.055 "Confidential Care for Minors," and Sec. 5.06 "Confidentiality: Attorney–Physician Relation"

[35]45 C.F.R. § 164.510(b)(5)

[36]45 C.F.R. § 164.524(b)(2)(i) and (ii)

[37]N.C. Medical Board "Medical record documentation" (Position Statement, adopted 5/94, amended 5/96, 5/09 and 5/13) (medical record "provides a legal document to verify the delivery of care").

[38]42 C.F.R. § 2.11

[39]42 C.F.R. § 2.13

[40]See 42 U.S.C. 290dd–3; 42 C.F.R. § 2.1 et seq. Examples of federal assistance triggering coverage of the rules include tax exemption and participation in Medicare or Medicaid. 42 C.F.R. § 2.12(B). Also, see N.C. Gen. Stat. §§ 122C–51 et seq.

[41]See 42 C.F.R. §§ 2.31, 2.33 (written consent); 42 C.F.R. § 2.61 et seq. (court orders).

[42]See 42 C.F.R. §§ 2.64, 2.65

[43]See 42 U.S.C. §§ 290dd–2 and N.C. Gen. Stat. § 122C–52 through 55.

[44]42 CFR § 2.64

[45]See N.C. Gen. Stat. §§ 122C–52 through 56.

[46]See Appendices G–1, G–2 and I for sample releases and a court order satisfying requirements for disclosure of substance abuse and mental health records.

[47]See Appendix A–1 for the definition of *psychotherapy notes*.

[48]See Appendices G–3 and G–4 for a sample authorization form satisfying HIPAA requirements for release of psychotherapy notes.

[49]N.C. Gen. Stat. § 130A–143.

[50]N.C. Gen. Stat. § 35A–1101(7)

[51]In re Estate of Whitaker, 144 N.C. App. 245, 547 S.E.2d 853 (2001)

[52] N.C. Gen. Stat. § 36C–6–601

[53]Matthews v. James, 88 N.C. App. 32, 362 S.E.2d 594 (1987)

[54]See N.C. Gen. Stat. § 97–25.6 and footnote 25.

[55]See AMA Code of Medical Ethics § 9.07, "Medical Testimony," ("As citizens and as professionals with specialized knowledge and experience, physicians have an obligation to assist in the administration of justice. When a legal claim pertains to a patient the physician has treated, the physician must hold the patient's medical interests paramount, including the confidentiality of the patient's health information, unless the physician is authorized or legally compelled to disclose the information. Physicians who serve as fact witnesses must deliver honest testimony. This requires that they engage in continuous self-examination to ensure that their testimony represents the facts of the case. When treating physicians are called upon to testify in matters that could adversely impact their patients' medical interests, they should decline to testify unless the patient consents or unless ordered to do so by legally constituted authority. If, as a

result of legal proceedings, the patient and the physician are placed in adversarial positions it may be appropriate for a treating physician to transfer the care of the patient to another physician.")

[56]Compare § 9.07, "Medical Testimony and § 8.12, "Patient Information" (requiring physicians to be honest and open in their dealings with patients even in situations where "a patient suffers significant medical complications that may have resulted from the physician's mistake or judgment. In these situations, the physician is ethically required to inform the patient of all the facts necessary to ensure understanding of what has occurred. Concern regarding legal liability which might result following truthful disclosure should not affect the physician's honesty with a patient.").

[57]See Rule 4.3 of the North Carolina Revised Rules of Professional Conduct.

[58]In criminal cases in North Carolina state courts, medical witnesses usually testify at the trial because medical testimony is rarely taken by deposition.

[59]Crist v. Moffatt, 326 N.C. 326, 389 S.E.2d 41 (1990); RPC 162.

[60]This occurs when the witness may be legally unavailable at the time of a subsequent trial.

[61]For example, absent the consent of the opposing party, witness depositions may not be used in lieu of live testimony unless an exception applies. N.C. R. Civ. P. 32(a)(4). See also N.C. Gen. Stat. § 8–83(11).

Guideline IV. Trial Situations

A. Subpoenas.

1. *Witness Subpoenas*

a. North Carolina State Courts

Under North Carolina law, physicians, acting as medical witnesses[62] are required to be subpoenaed before the Court may award them an expert witness fee after they have testified at a deposition or trial.[63] Physicians should not attempt to avoid service of subpoenas.

In issuing trial subpoenas to physicians, attorneys must consider and be mindful of the physician's patient scheduling needs. For that reason, the attorney should notify the physician of the intent to subpoena the physician to trial. The trial subpoena itself should be issued as soon as practical, but in no event should a subpoena be issued later than seven days before trial. Only a rare emergency calls for later issuance of the subpoena.[64] Where appropriate, the subpoena for attendance at the trial as a witness should reflect the actual time for the physician to appear and/or "will call when needed" or "on standby," if the actual time is uncertain. If the actual time is uncertain, the attorney or someone in the attorney's office should keep the physician informed on a daily basis as to the status of the trial. An attorney has little or no control over scheduling a case.[65] Accordingly, physicians should not necessarily alter the office schedule but should bear in mind the possibility of being called to court. At the same time, the attorney or someone in the attorney's office should keep the physician informed on a daily basis as to the status of the calendar. When a case is postponed or not reached during a court session, the attorney should immediately notify the physician. Physicians have continuing and often unpredictable responsibilities to their patients and, insofar as they are able, attorneys should make arrangements with a minimum of inconvenience or delay.

Court calendaring systems vary between judicial districts[66] in North Carolina. Under court calendaring rules in some judicial districts, a case will automatically reappear on a trial calendar if it has previously been postponed or not reached. The new trial session, and the case's position on the trial calendar, if known, should be relayed to the physician by letter as soon as possible. If for some reason the new trial week is inconvenient for the physician, they should notify the attorney immediately and in no event later than one week after notice of the new trial date.[67]

b. Workers' Compensation Cases

The Workers Compensation Rules of the North Carolina Industrial Commission and Chapter 97 of the North Carolina General Statutes should be consulted regarding the testimony of physicians. A party to a workers' compensation case must obtain permission from the Industrial Commission before taking and offering the deposition of a medical witness.[68] In those rare instances when physicians are subpoenaed to testify at a hearing, they will be on telephone standby until notified.

2. *Subpoenas for Medical Records*

Often parties to a lawsuit will subpoena medical records to a trial without requesting the presence of the physician who made them. As in the case of trial subpoenas to physicians (see Section V.A.1. above), subpoenas for medical records should be issued as soon as possible, but in no event should a subpoena be issued later than seven days before trial. Only a rare emergency calls for later issuance of the subpoena.[69] A physician's options in responding to a subpoena for medical records depend in part on who is subpoenaing the records, and on what authorization that person has to view the records. Subpoenas for medical records containing substance abuse and psychiatric information require special attention. See IV A. 4. above.

a. Records Subpoenaed With Authorization and/or Pursuant to Court Order or Other Authority

If the party subpoenaing the medical record has the written consent of the patient or the patient's personal representative to inspect the records, or if the subpoena is accompanied by a judicial or administrative order, or is issued in conformity with other applicable legal authority the subpoena may be complied with in one of several ways. The custodian of the records may bring them to court and testify to their authenticity and completeness, or the records may be mailed to the presiding judge or their designee accompanied by an affidavit authenticating them signed by the medical record custodian.[70] Only those medical records expressly authorized by the order should be released in accordance with the order.[71]

b. Records Subpoenaed Without Authorization and Without Court Order or Other Authority

Medical records are often subpoenaed to North Carolina state courts by parties without authorization to inspect the records and without a court order requiring their disclosure.[72] This happens often in personal injury cases, where defense attorneys routinely subpoena plaintiffs' medical records for a variety of legitimate reasons.[73] A party may properly subpoena medical records they lack authorization to inspect by stating in writing on the subpoena that the records are being subpoenaed by one without legal authority to inspect them, and who will not inspect them absent the written consent of the patient or the patient's personal representative or judicial or administrative order, or in conformity with other applicable legal authority.[74]

Prior to the release of medical records subpoenaed without authorization and without court order or other authority, it is imperative to make sure that the release of such information is permitted under HIPAA. HIPAA will not allow health care providers to release health information pursuant to a subpoena that is not accompanied by an order of court or administrative tribunal, unless the health care provider receives "satisfactory assurance" from the requesting party that reasonable efforts have been made to (1) provide notice to the person whose records are being requested or (2) secure a qualified protective order for the records. Each of these alternatives must meet the requirements enumerated in the HIPAA rules. In the absence of such "satisfactory assurances" from outside sources, the health care provider must make a reasonable effort to provide the notice or seek a qualified protective order sufficient to meet the requirements of the rule.

Also, before releasing medical records subpoenaed without authorization and without court order or other authority, a physician should receive one of the following:

1. The patient's written authorization to release the information requested;

2. A court order to release the requested information;

3. A qualified protective order meeting the requirements of Section 164.512 (e);

4. Evidence demonstrating that reasonable efforts have been made to provide written notice to the individual whose records are being requested, in accordance with the requirements of Section 164.512 (e)(1)(iii); or

5. Evidence demonstrating that reasonable efforts have been made to secure a qualified protective order for the requested records, in accordance with the requirements of Section 164.512 (e)(1)(iv).[75]

Absent one of the above, a written objection to the subpoena may be made on the grounds that compliance would be in violation of HIPAA, specifically Section 164.512(e). The objection must be (1) in writing, (2) delivered to the party or attorney designated in the subpoena and (3) made within 10 days after service of the subpoena or before the time specified for compliance if the time is less than 10 days after service.[76]

In the event of an objection or a question about compliance, records subpoenaed without authority may be placed in a sealed envelope addressed to the Judge presiding at the session of court to which the records have been subpoenaed, and marked: "To remain sealed until otherwise ordered by the presiding Judge."[77]

B. Notice for Trial.

1. *Initial Trial Settings*

It is imperative both from the standpoint of the efficient administration of justice and the physician's scheduling needs that medical witnesses receive as much notice as possible in the setting of a particular case for trial. Under present calendaring procedures in North Carolina state court civil actions, only the week for trial can be designated specifically. There can be no assurances as to when or if the case will be reached that particular week.

2. *Medical Witness Availability*

Once an attorney has first received notification that a trial is to be scheduled, they should contact their medical witnesses regarding availability for trial. At that time, each medical witness should inform the attorney of those weeks when they will not be available to testify. Once the case has received a definite trial setting, the attorney should immediately confirm the medical witness' availability for that particular week by letter.

3. *Final Trial Calendar*

When a case appears on the final trial calendar for a particular week, the attorney should notify the medical witness regarding the calendaring of the case, its status on the calendar, and an estimate as to the day when the case will be reached. This should be confirmed in writing to the medical witness. If the medical witness has not already been subpoenaed, that should be done at this time.

4. *Court Appearance*

The business of the courts cannot be governed by the convenience of witnesses, whoever they may be. However, court appearances interrupt medical witness' professional schedule and attorneys should make every reasonable effort to minimize that interruption. The attorney should not require medical witnesses to come in court and sit for long periods of time waiting to be put on the witness stand. The attorney should give the medical witness as much advance notice as is reasonably possible, so that their patient schedule may be rearranged with a minimum of disruption. The medical witness should be alerted by telephone a reasonable time before he or she is actually needed in court.

Medical witnesses are obligated to be in court at the time requested, and should notify the attorney of their arrival. Timing is important not only for the orderly presentation of the case, but also for the convenience of everyone involved in the proceedings. Physicians have ongoing and often unpredictable responsibilities to patients. In such instances, the attorney should request that the medical witnesses be allowed to testify out of order or at another time. When a medical emergency arises, attorneys should be notified immediately in order to make alternative arrangements and, if appropriate, to seek the court's release of the medical witness or postponement of the medical witness' appearance until the emergency has passed.

C. Fact Medical Witnesses and Retained Medical Witnesses.

1. *Generally*

a. Expert Status

As a fact medical witness, the physician's role is to provide information, not to advocate a position. The attorneys serve as the advocates. The fact medical witnesses, the court, and the attorneys should show mutual respect and consideration to each other. A retained medical witness will be expected to advocate on behalf of the party who retained them.

In general, in a court of law, there are two types of witnesses—fact and expert. Expert witnesses, because they possess knowledge not generally known to the jury, are allowed to express opinions. In order to be an expert, it is necessary to know more than the jury knows and to have an opinion about the subject under inquiry. In cases of alleged medical negligence, more stringent requirements apply. The presiding judge at trial may make an initial inquiry into the qualifications of an expert witness to testify and either permit or limit the testimony.

Because medical witnesses virtually always testify as experts, even when they may also be fact witnesses, the Guidelines treat all medical witnesses as expert witnesses, and differentiate between the types of expert medical witnesses.[78] In order to be accepted as an expert in a trial in North Carolina state courts, the presiding judge must find that the witness has expertise.[79]

Treating physicians, as fact medical witnesses, typically testify as hybrid fact-expert witnesses, because of their training and knowledge and by virtue of their treatment of a patient whose medical condition is at issue. They may testify about medical observations,[80] or to observations of facts unrelated to their medical expertise. They may also testify about their expert opinions within the scope of their medical expertise. These witnesses are referred to as fact medical witnesses in the Guidelines.

It is not necessary that a medical witness have treated or examined a patient in order to testify as an expert. Expert medical testimony may be based upon a review of the medical chart or a hypothetical set of facts. Witnesses who testify in this fashion typically have been retained by one of the parties for the purpose of providing expert opinion testimony, and do not have a physician-patient relationship with the party whose medical condition is at issue. These witnesses are referred to as retained medical witnesses in the Guidelines.

b. Preparation

Proper preparation for conferences, depositions, and trial testimony includes a review of the relevant medical records. The physician's office staff should cooperate in scheduling preparatory conferences and depositions at a mutually convenient time, when they are least likely to be interrupted by patient problems, other appointments or operating times. Attorneys should go to the physician's offices for such conferences unless the physician desires to meet elsewhere.

c. Independent Medical Examinations

Attorneys should provide independent medical witnesses with the ground rules of the independent medical examination submitted to them in writing, including who is to get a report, where copies should be sent, who is to pay for the examination, and the purpose and extent of the examination. Where the examination has been ordered selected or approved by a court, administrative agency or other adjudicatory body, attorneys should also provide the independent medical witness with a copy of the order approving or selecting them.

2. *Fees*

a. General Considerations

Medical witness charges for assisting attorneys in legal matters should be reasonable, reflecting the physician's experience, the level of specialization, the environment in which the physician practices, and the demand for his or her services. While an agreement on the fees charged by a retained medical witness will usually be negotiated at the beginning of the relationship, an attempt should also be made to discuss and agree upon the fees to be charged by the fact medical witness prior to the fact medical witness undertaking any specific task. It is generally accepted practice in North Carolina state court civil cases that fact medical witnesses are entitled to reasonable compensation for time spent in conferences, preparation of medical reports, depositions, time spent out of the office for court or other appearances, and for travel costs. The fact medical witness may require payment for depositions, conferences, and consultations at the time of the service.

The recommended fee for a fact medical witness' court appearance should be measured from the time the fact medical witness leaves their office to go to court until they return to their office from court, and should also include compensation for time spent preparing to testify, even though a successful patient at trial is only allowed to recover from the opposing party the time actually spent at the trial testifying.[81] Under certain circumstances, the presiding judge will set a fee for the medical witness.[82]

An attorney is ethically prohibited from having an economic interest in a client's claim. Therefore, while an attorney may advance fees which are incurred in pursuing claims,[83] all such fees are ultimately the responsibility of the patient/client.[84]

An attorney should not place an undue burden on fact medical witnesses for services rendered at an attorney's request on behalf of a patient/client. No attorney should request a fact medical witness to consult with them or prepare a medical report for them where the client is unable to pay for the same, unless they are willing to advance the cost of such litigation expenses or they have informed the fact medical witness that the client is unable to pay for their services. If the client is unwilling to ultimately pay for the same, the attorney should not request such services.

For some patients and clients, prepayment is not feasible and alternative methods of payment must be considered. The fact medical witness, attorney, and the patient may agree to any lawful method of payment.

b. Fees in Workers' Compensation Cases

In workers' compensation cases, all expert witness fees, which include fees for fact medical witnesses and retained medical witnesses, may be subject to approval by the NC Industrial Commission. Regardless of the fees that such witnesses may charge, those fees may be limited by maximum amounts set by the Industrial Commission. Failure to promptly pay an expert witness following entry of an order to do so will result in the assessment of a 10% penalty. Medical witnesses and attorneys should seek an understanding as to the terms of payment for an expert witness fee, to the extent possible, prior to obtaining expert witness testimony in workers' compensation cases.[85]

c. Prohibition Against Contingent Fees

Attorneys are prohibited from offering and physicians are prohibited from accepting fees wholly or partially contingent upon the outcome of the matter in which medical testimony is offered.[86] A fee shall not be deemed contingent for the reason that the patient's financial condition may render collection difficult in the event that the patient does not prevail in a legal action.

d. Fees for Retained Medical Witnesses

All services and fees of retained medical witnesses are subject to negotiation between the physician and the contracting party. Also, unless agreed to between the parties, any such service rendered does not create a physician/patient relationship.

Retained medical witnesses are permitted to charge a reasonable fee if their court appearance is canceled without sufficient time for the physician to reschedule patients, surgery, and consultations. However, retained medical witnesses should make a reasonable effort to profitably reschedule their time in order to minimize expense or loss.

e. Fees for Independent Medical Witnesses

Independent medical witness fees may either be established by the court, administrative agency or other adjudicatory body selecting or approving them, or by the party seeking their appointment, or by the parties by agreement. Independent medical witnesses should determine how they will be paid, and by whom, prior to conducting the independent medical examination.

f. Pro Bono/Criminal Cases

When an attorney stipulates in writing that they are handling a client's case without charge or expectation of payment from any recovery, then a treating physician should consider providing medical reports and testimony free of charge. Should an attorney be awarded payment unexpectedly, the treating physician should be notified promptly by the attorney so that a charge may be made by the physician if appropriate.

If the patient is a victim in a criminal prosecution case, then the treating physician should provide a medical report to the investigating law enforcement agency free of charge.

[Revised 2008. Amended eff. July 1, 2014.]

62See Section III(E) above defining the types of medical witnesses recognized under the Guidelines. Where the Guidelines refer to a physician as a 'medical witness' the statement refers to all types of medical witnesses defined therein.

63N.C. Gen. Stat. § 7A–305(d)(11) allows a Court the discretion in a civil case to award "reasonable and necessary fees of expert witnesses solely for actual time spent providing testimony at trial, deposition, or other proceedings." N.C. Gen. Stat. § 7A–314(d) addresses the compensation of an expert witness in both criminal and civil cases, noting that the expert witness "shall receive such compensation and allowances as the court, or the Judicial Standards Commission, in its discretion, may authorize." Each allows the Court in its discretion to authorize payment of expert witness fees and allowances, but only when the witness has testified (either at trial or deposition) after having been served with a subpoena. State v. Johnson, 282 N.C. 1, 191 S.E.2d 641 (1972); Town of Chapel Hill v. Fox, 120 N.C. App. 630, 463 S.E.2d 421 (1995). Neither section compels parties to seek a judicial determination of expert witness fees or who is to pay them. N.C. Gen. Stat. § 7A–454 addresses under what circumstances a court may order payment of expert witnesses who testify on behalf of indigent criminal defendants. N.C. Rule of Evidence 706 governs who shall pay, and what amount, shall be paid to expert witnesses appointed by the Court in civil and criminal actions. N.C. Gen. Stat. § 15–7 governs the payment of physicians appointed to conduct post-mortem examinations of homicide victims. In cases before the Industrial Commission, expert witness fees are set by the Commissioner or Deputy Commissioner hearing the case. See N.C. Gen. Stat. §§ 97–90(c) and 97–26.1.

64A specific example of a "rare emergency" arises pursuant to the statutory provisions of N.C. Gen. Stat. § 50B–2, which permits a party alleging acts of domestic violence to seek a hearing on an ex parte or expedited basis.

65Each time a case is scheduled for trial, an attorney must prepare the case fully and subpoena all the witnesses. Many times cases are scheduled for trial several times before they are actually called for trial by the Court.

66Judicial Districts in North Carolina include one or more counties, depending upon whether the district is primarily urban or rural.

67This is because attorneys do not have power to postpone scheduled trials and must apply to a Judge for a continuance. The later the application for a continuance, the less likely it is that the Court will grant the requested postponement.

68See N.C. Gen. Stat. § 97–80 (d) and (e).

69As noted in Section V.A.1.a., a "rare emergency" may arise pursuant to the statutory provisions of N.C. Gen. Stat. § 50B–2, which permits a party alleging acts of domestic violence to seek a hearing on an ex parte or expedited basis.

70See N.C. Rule of Civil Procedure 45(c). Although Rule 45(c) specifically authorizes the "custodian of hospital medical records" to respond to a subpoena for "hospital medical records as defined in N.C. Gen. Stat. § 8–44.1" by certified mailing of the records, it has become common practice in North Carolina state courts for all types of medical records to be sent by certified mail unless an issue arises as to the authorization of the subpoenaing party to inspect the records. N.C. Gen. Stat. § 8–44.1 broadly defines "hospital medical records." A physician should not assume it is sufficient to send an affidavit in lieu of the personal appearance of the records custodian and should confirm with the patient's attorney that an affidavit will be acceptable.

7145 C.F.R. § 164.512(e).

72N.C. Gen. Stat. § 8–53 authorizes a resident or presiding judge, in the trial division where the case is pending, or the Industrial Commission pursuant to law, to order the disclosure of the records without authorization at or before trial where to do so is necessary to a proper administration of justice. A person responding to such a subpoena where no authorization appears should only send the subpoena to the court where the action is pending.

73Defense counsel may subpoena to a court proceeding the records of current and/or prior treating physicians they have no authority to inspect. In this situation, the attorneys involved expect that, if the patient's attorney objects to disclosure of the records to the defense counsel, the presiding judge at the trial of the action will examine the records in camera (privately) to determine whether the records should be ordered released for the inspection of the subpoenaing party. See N.C. Rule of Professional Conduct 1.2(c) and RPC 236 "Misuse of Subpoena Process" (prohibiting abuse of the subpoena process by subpoenaing medical records to an attorney's office where no legal proceeding is occurring).

74See Appendix C, Sample Subpoena for Medical Records without Authorization and without Court Order or Other Authority to Inspect.

7545 C.F.R. § 164.512(e).

76N.C. Rule of Civil Procedure, Rule 45(c).

77See Appendix C, Sample Letter to Accompany Records sent to Court in Response to Sample Subpoena for Medical Records without Authorization and without Court Order or Other Authority to Inspect.

78See II (E) above for definition of the three types of expert medical witnesses.

79If a medical witness is not tendered to and accepted by the presiding judge as an expert, they may not express expert medical opinions and the judge will not have authority to award them an expert witness fee.

80Medical observations will often be based on medical expertise and therefore be based on expert opinion. For example, when testifying to their medical diagnosis of a patient, the fact medical witness is expressing an expert medical opinion.

81N.C. Gen. Stat. § 7A–305(d)(11).

82This only occurs on motion of the party prevailing in a matter, if they have called the medical witness, the medical witness has testified pursuant to subpoena, and has been received by the court as an expert witness. In this instance, the prevailing party seeks to have the fee set and taxed against the losing party as a court cost. See N.C. Gen. Stat. § 7A–314. This fee may not necessarily represent the entire fee owed a retained or fact medical witness by virtue of their contractual relationship with the attorney and/or their patient or client. Nothing compels a party to move for expert witness fees to be taxed as costs. See also N.C. Gen. Stat. §§ 6–20 and 7A–305.

83Such fees are called 'litigation expenses' and are to be distinguished from charges for treatment, which may not be ethically advanced by attorneys. See footnote 33.

84Where the attorney incurring the fee does not represent the patient, the fee is nonetheless a litigation expense to be borne by his or her client. This typically happens when the defense attorney takes the deposition of a fact medical witness, and is responsible for their fees for testifying.

85See N. C. Gen. Stat. §§ 97–25.6(i) and 97–26.1(iii) and NC Industrial Commission Rule 610(3).

86See AMA Code of Medical Ethics §§ 9.07 "Medical Testimony" ("Physician testimony must not be influenced by financial compensation; for example, it is unethical for a physician to accept compensation that is contingent upon the outcome of litigation.") and 8.10 "Lien Laws" (allowing liens only where "the fee is fixed in amount and not contingent on the amount of settlement of the patient's claim against a third party). See also Rule 702(f) of the North Carolina Rules of Evidence. Cf. N.C. Gen. Stat. §§ 44–49 through 44–51 (N.C. lien laws allocating fees based on pro rata share of percentage of recovery).

Guideline V. N.C. Bar Association Medico–Legal Liaison Committee

The N.C. Bar Association Medico–Legal Liaison Committee is composed of attorneys whose professional practice includes working with individuals and businesses who regularly represent or serve as legal counsel for patients, hospitals and related entities, insurance carriers, physicians, and other licensed and non-licensed health care providers, or otherwise have reason to interact with health care providers as a part of their practice. Its purpose is to create a better understanding, a closer relationship, and unity between the medical and legal professions, so that each may better serve the other and the public. In order to fulfill that purpose, the Medico–Legal Liaison Committee shall meet at least annually to:

- Promulgate revisions to these Guidelines as necessary to keep them legally current and effective;
- Report as necessary to the N.C. Medical Society and N.C. Bar Association about the work of the Committee and make any appropriate recommendations; and
- Accept and mediate reported complaints of attorneys and physicians who experience problems related to a failure to comply with these Guidelines[87] and, where appropriate, forward such reports to the proper disciplinary authorities.

[Revised 2008. Amended eff. July 1, 2014.]

87However, the Medico–Legal Liaison Committee will not mediate fee disputes between retained expert witnesses and attorneys, or between independent medical witnesses and attorneys.

Appendix A-1. Relevant HIPAA Definitions

45 C.F.R. 160.103 Definitions.

Health information means any information, whether oral or recorded in any form or medium, that:

1. Is created or received by a health care provider, health plan, public health authority, employer, life insurer, school or university, or health care clearinghouse; and

2. Related to the past, present, or future physical or mental health or condition of an individual; the provision of health care to an individual; or the past, present, or future payment for the provision of health care to an individual.

Individually identifiable health information is information that is a subset of health information, including demographic information collected from an individual, and:

1. Is created or received by a health care provider, health plan, employer, or health care clearinghouse; and

2. Relates to the past, present, or future physical or mental health or condition of an individual; the provision of health care to an individual; or the past, present, or future payment for the provision of health care to an individual; and

(i) That identifies the individual; or

(ii) With respect to which there is a reasonable basis to believe the information can be used to identify the individual.

45 C.F.R. 164.501 Definitions.

Designated record set means:

1. A group of records maintained by or for a covered entity that is:

(i) The medical records and billing records about individuals maintained by or for a covered health care provider;

(ii) The enrollment, payment, claims adjudication, and case or medical management record systems maintained by or for a health plan; or

(iii) Used, in whole or in part, by or for the covered entity to make decision about individuals.

2. For purposes of the paragraph, the term records means any item, collection, or grouping of information that includes protected health information and is maintained, collected, used, or disseminated by or for a covered entity.

Protected health information means individually identifiable health information:

1. Except as provided in paragraph (2) of this definition, that is:

(i) Transmitted by electronic media;

(ii) Maintained in any medium described in the definition of electronic media at § 162.103 of this subchapter; or

(iii) Transmitted or maintained in any other form or medium.

2. *Protected health information* excludes individually identifiable health information in:

(i) Education records covered by the Family Educational Right and Privacy Act, as amended, 20 U.S.C. 1232g;

(ii) Records described at 20 U.S.C. 1232g(a)(4)(B)(iv); and

(iii) Employment records held by a covered entity in its role as employer.

Psychotherapy notes means notes records (in any medium) by a health care provider who is a mental health professional documenting or analyzing the contents of conversation during a private counseling session or a group, joint, or family counseling session and that are separated from the rest of the individual's medical record.

Psychotherapy notes excludes medication prescription and monitoring, counseling session start and stop times, the modalities and frequencies of treatment furnished, results of clinical tests, and any summary of the following items: Diagnosis, functional status, the treatment plan, symptoms, prognosis, and progress to date.

Appendix A–2. Pertinent North Carolina Statutes and Regulations Regarding Medical Records

"Medical records" are defined by the following North Carolina statutory or regulatory provisions:

- N.C. Gen. Stat. § 8-44.1 (2005) [1]
- N.C. Gen. Stat. § 90-410(2) (2005) [2]
- N.C. Gen. Stat. § 58-39-15(18) (2005) [3]
- N.C. Gen. Stat. § 130A-372 (2005) [4]
- 10A N.C. Admin. Code § 14J.0101 (2005) [5]
- 10A N.C. Admin. Code § 14J.1701 (2005) [6]

Other provisions of North Carolina law refer to information about patients' medical services using terms other than "medical record":

- Individuals receiving services for mental health, substance abuse, or mental retardation are referred to as "clients," and information about their treatment is called "confidential information," defined in N.C. Gen. Stat. § 122C-3(9) (2005) [7]. Compilations of such information are sometimes called the "client record." [8] Note that substance abuse information also is likely to be subject to the strict provisions of the federal drug and alcohol abuse facility law.
- Both § 130A-45.8 (2005), [9] concerning patient information held by public health authorities, and § 131E-97 (2005), [10] addressing patient information held by "health care facilities," draw a distinction between the patient's medical records and financial records.
- N.C. Gen. Stat. § 131E-14.1 (2005) defines both "patient data" and "patient identifying information". [11]
- Medical information governed by the Division of Aging and the Division of Social Services is considered "client information." [12]
- 10A N.C. Admin. Code 47B.0102(6) (2005) defines "identifying information" with respect to cancer patients. [13]

[1] "Hospital medical records" are defined as "records made in connection with the diagnosis, care and treatment of any patient or the charges for such services except that records covered by N. C. Gen. Stat. § 122–8.1, N. C. Gen. Stat. § 90–109.1 and federal statutory or regulatory provisions regarding alcohol and drug abuse, are subject to the requirements of said statutes." (Please note that N.C. Gen. Stat. § 122–8.1 and N.C. Gen. Stat. § 90–109.1 have been repealed).

[2] Medical records are defined as "personal information that relates to an individual's physical or mental condition, medical history, or medical treatment, excluding X-rays and fetal monitor records."

[3] Information about patients is subject to three definitions under N.C. Gen. Stat. § 58-39-15 of the North Carolina insurance statutes:

(18) "Medical-record information" means personal information that:

a. Relates to an individual's physical or mental condition, medical history, or medical treatment; and

b. Is obtained from a medical professional or medical-care institution, from the individual or from the individual's spouse, parent, or legal guardian.

(19) "Personal information" means any individually identifiable information gathered in connection with an insurance transaction from which judgements can be made about an individual's character, habits, avocations, finances, occupation, general reputation, credit, health, or any other personal characteristics. "Personal information" includes an individual's name and address and medical record information, but does not include privileged information.

(22) "Privileged information" means any individually identifiable information that (i) relates to a claim for insurance benefits or a civil or criminal proceeding involving an individual, and (ii) is collected in connection with or in reasonable anticipation of a claim for insurance benefits or civil or criminal proceedings involving an individual: Provided, however, information otherwise meeting the requirements of this subsection shall nevertheless be considered personal information under this Article if it is disclosed in violation of N.C. Gen. Stat. § 58–39–75 (2005).

[4] Medical records are defined as "health data relating to the diagnosis or treatment of physical or mental ailments of individuals."

[5] The medical record of an inmate of a local confinement facility is defined as "a record of medical problems, examinations, diagnoses and treatments."

[6] The definition in footnote 4 also applies to inmates in municipal lock-up facilities.

[7] "Confidential information" is defined in § 122C–3(9) as:

... any information, whether recorded or not, relating to an individual served by a facility that was received in connection with the performance of any function of the facility. 'Confidential information' does not include statistical information from reports and records or information regarding treatment or services which is shared for training, treatment, habilitation, or monitoring purposes that does not identify clients either directly or by reference to publicly known or available information.

10A N.C. Admin. Code 26B.0103(b)(3) (2005) further provides that confidential information as defined in Section 122C–3 "includes but is not limited to photographs, videotapes, audiotapes, client records, reimbursement records, verbal information relative to clients served, client information stored in automated files, and clinical staff member client files."

[8] The Administrative Code has several slightly differing definitions for this information. 10A N.C. Admin. Code 26B.0103(b)(1) (2005) defines "client record" as "any documentation made of confidential information." 10A N.C. Admin. Code 26D.0103(8) (2005) defines "client record" as "a written account of all mental health and mental retardation services provided to an inmate the time of acceptance of the inmate as the client until termination of services. This information is documented on standard forms which are filed in a standard order in an identifiable folder." 10A N.C. Admin. Code 27G.0103(b)(12) (2005) defines "client record" as "a documented account of all services provided to a client." 10A N.C. Admin. Code 21A.0201(22) (2005) contains this definition: "'client information' or 'client record' means any information, including information stored in computer data banks or computer files relating to a client that was received in connection with the performance of any function of the agency." 10A N.C. Admin. Code 28A.0102(b)(6) (2005) defines

"client record" as "any record made of confidential information."

9 N.C.G.S. § 130A-45.8 (2004) provides:

(a) Medical records compiled and maintained by public health authorities in connection with the admission, treatment, and discharge of individual patients are not public records as defined by Chapter 132 of the General Statutes.

(b) Charges, accounts, credit histories, and other personal financial records compiled and maintained by public health authorities in connection with the admission, treatment and discharge of individual patients are not public records as defined by Chapter 132 of the General Statutes.

10 Section 131E-97 (2005) provides:

(a) Medical records compiled and maintained by health care facilities in connection with the admission, treatment, and discharge of individual patients are not public records as defined by Chapter 132 of the General Statutes.

(b) Charges, accounts, credit histories, and other personal financial records compiled and maintained by health care facilities in connection with the admission, treatment, and discharge of individual patients are not public records as defined by Chapter 132 of the General Statutes.

11 Section 131E-214.1, concerning statewide data processing of certain information about patients, includes the following definitions:

(4) "Patient data" means data that includes a patient's age, sex, zip code, third-party coverage, principal and other diagnosis, date of admission, procedure and discharge date, principal and other procedures, total charges and components of the total charges, attending physician identification number, and hospital or freestanding ambulatory surgical facility identification number.

(5) "Patient identifying information" means the name, address, social security number, or similar information by which the identity of a patient can be determined with reasonable accuracy and speed either directly or by reference to other publicly available information. The term does not include a number assigned to a patient by a health care provider if that number does not consist of or contain numbers, including social security or drivers license numbers, that could be used to identify a patient with reasonable accuracy and speed from sources external to the health care provider.

12 Both 10A N.C. Admin. Code 5J.0101(3) (2005) and 10A N.C. Admin. Code 69.0101(3) (2005) provide that "'client information' or 'client record' means any information, whether recorded or not, including information stored in computer data banks or files, relating to a client which was received in connection with the performance of any function of the agency."

13 The pertinent regulation defines "identifying information" as "any portion of any abstract or incidence report that might reveal the personal identity of a cancer patient." All health care facilities and providers that detect, diagnose, or treat cancer shall report to the central cancer registry each diagnosis of cancer in any person who is screened, diagnosed or treated.

Appendix B. Sample Subpoena for Medical Records Without Authorization and Without Court Order or Other Authority to Inspect

STATE OF NORTH CAROLINA

File No.

______________________ County

In The General Court Of Justice
☐ District ☐ Superior Court Division

Additional File Numbers

VERSUS

SUBPOENA

G.S. 1A-1, Rule 45

Party Requesting Subpoena
☐ State/Plaintiff ☐ Defendant

NOTE TO PARTIES NOT REPRESENTED BY COUNSEL: *Subpoenas may be produced at your request, but must be signed and issued by the office of the Clerk of Superior Court, or by a magistrate or judge.*

TO

Name And Address Of Person Subpoenaed

Alternate Address

Telephone No.

Telephone No.

YOU ARE COMMANDED TO: *(check all that apply):*

☐ appear and testify, in the above entitled action, before the court at the place, date and time indicated below.

☐ appear and testify, in the above entitled action, at a deposition at the place, date and time indicated below.

☐ produce and permit inspection and copying of the following items, at the place, date and time indicated below.

☐ See attached list. *(List here if space sufficient)*

Name And Location Of Court/Place Of Deposition/Place To Produce

Date To Appear/Produce

Time To Appear/Produce
☐ AM ☐ PM

Name And Address Of Applicant Or Applicant's Attorney

Date

Signature

Telephone No.

☐ Deputy CSC ☐ Assistant CSC ☐ Clerk Of Superior Court ☐ Superior Court Judge
☐ Magistrate ☐ Attorney/DA ☐ District Court Judge

RETURN OF SERVICE

I certify this subpoena was received and served on the person subpoenaed as follows:

By ☐ personal delivery.
☐ registered or certified mail, receipt requested and attached.
☐ telephone communication *(For use only by the sheriff's office for witness subpoenaed to appear and testify.)*
☐ I was unable to serve this subpoena.

Service Fee		Date Served	Signature of Authorized Server	Title
$	☐ Paid ☐ Due			

NOTE TO PERSON REQUESTING SUBPOENA: *A copy of this subpoena must be delivered, mailed or faxed to the attorney for each party in this case. If a party is not represented by an attorney, the copy must be mailed or delivered to the party. This does not apply in criminal cases.*

AOC-G-100, Rev. 10/03
2003 Administrative Office of the Courts

(Please See Reverse Side)

NOTE: Rule 45, North Carolina Rules of Civil Procedure, Parts (c) and (d).

(c) Protection Of Persons Subject To Subpoena

(1) Avoid undue burden or expense. - A party or an attorney responsible for the issuance and service of a subpoena shall take reasonable steps to avoid imposing an undue burden or expense on a person subject to the subpoena. The court shall enforce this subdivision and impose upon the party or attorney in violation of this requirement an appropriate sanction that may include compensating the person unduly burdened for lost earnings and for reasonable attorney's fees.

(2) For production of public records or hospital medical records. - Where the subpoena commands any custodian of public records or any custodian of hospital medical records, as defined in G.S. 8-44.1, to appear for the sole purpose of producing certain records in the custodian's custody, the custodian subpoenaed may, in lieu of personal appearance, tender to the court in which the action is pending by registered or certified mail or by personal delivery, on or before the time specified in the subpoena, certified copies of the records requested together with a copy of the subpoena and an affidavit by the custodian testifying that the copies are true and correct copies and that the records were made and kept in the regular course of business, or if no such records are in the custodian's custody, an affidavit to that effect. When the copies of records are personally delivered under this subdivision, a receipt shall be obtained from the person receiving the records. Any original or certified copy of records or an affidavit delivered according to the provisions of this subdivision, unless otherwise objectionable, shall be admissible in any action or proceeding without further certification or authentication. Copies of hospital medical records tendered under this subdivision shall not be open to inspection or copied by any person, except to the parties to the case or proceedings and their attorneys in depositions, until ordered published by the judge at the time of the hearing or trial. Nothing contained herein shall be construed to waive the physician-patient privilege or to require any privileged communication under law to be disclosed.

(3) Written objection to subpoena. - Subject to subsection (d) of this rule, a person commanded to appear at a deposition or to produce and permit the inspection and copying of records may, within 10 days after service of the subpoena or before the time specified for compliance if the time is less than 10 days after service, serve upon the party or the attorney designated in the subpoena written objection to the subpoena, setting forth the specific grounds for the objection. The written objection shall comply with the requirements of Rule 11. Each of the following grounds may be sufficient for objecting to a subpoena:

a. The subpoena fails to allow reasonable time for compliance.
b. The subpoena requires disclosure of privileged or other protected matter and no exception or waiver applies to the privilege or protection.
c. The subpoena subjects a person to an undue burden.
d. The subpoena is otherwise unreasonable or oppressive.
e. The subpoena is procedurally defective.

(4) Order of court required to override objection. - If objection is made under subdivision (3) of this subsection, the party serving the subpoena shall not be entitled to compel the subpoenaed person's appearance at a deposition or to inspect and copy materials to which an objection has been made except pursuant to an order of the court. If objection is made, the party serving the subpoena may, upon notice to the subpoenaed person, move at any time for an order to compel the subpoenaed person's appearance at the deposition or the production of the materials designated in the subpoena. The motion shall be filed in the court in the county in which the deposition or production of materials is to occur.

(5) Motion to quash or modify subpoena. - A person commanded to appear at a trial, hearing, deposition, or to produce and permit the inspection and copying of records, books, papers, documents, or other tangible things, within 10 days after service of the subpoena or before the time specified for compliance if the time is less than 10 days after service, may file a motion to quash or modify the subpoena. The court shall quash or modify the subpoena if the subpoenaed person demonstrates the existence of any of the reasons set forth in subdivision (3) of this subsection. The motion shall be filed in the court in the county in which the trial, hearing, deposition, or production of materials is to occur.

(6) Order to compel; expenses to comply with subpoena. - When a court enters an order compelling a deposition or the production of records, books, papers, documents, or other tangible things, the order shall protect any person who is not a party or an agent of a party from significant expense resulting from complying with the subpoena. The court may order that the person to whom the subpoena is addressed will be reasonably compensated for the cost of producing the records, books, papers, documents, or tangible things specified in the subpoena.

(7) Trade secrets, confidential information. - When a subpoena requires disclosure of a trade secret or other confidential research, development, or commercial information, a court may, to protect a person subject to or affected by the subpoena, quash or modify the subpoena, or when the party on whose behalf the subpoena is issued shows a substantial need for the testimony or material that cannot otherwise be met without undue hardship, the court may order a person to make an appearance or produce the materials only on specified conditions stated in the order.

(8) Order to quash; expenses. - When a court enters an order quashing or modifying the subpoena, the court may order the party on whose behalf the subpoena is issued to pay all or part of the subpoenaed person's reasonable expenses including attorney's fees.

(d) Duties In Responding To Subpoena

(1) Form of response. - A person responding to a subpoena to produce documents shall produce them as they are kept in the usual course of business or shall organize and label the documents to correspond with the categories in the request.

(2) Specificity of objection. - When information subject to a subpoena is withheld on the objection that is is subject to protection as trial preparation materials, or that it is otherwise privileged, the objection shall be made with specificity and shall be supported by a description of the nature of the communications, records, books, papers, documents, or other tangible things not produced, sufficient for the requesting party to contest the objection.

INFORMATION FOR WITNESS

NOTE: *If you have any questions about being subpoenaed as a witness, you should contact the person named on the other side of this Subpoena in the box labeled "Name And Address Of Applicant Or Applicant's Attorney.*

DUTIES OF A WITNESS

- Unless otherwise directed by the presiding judge, you must answer all questions asked when you are on the stand giving testimony.
- In answering questions, speak clearly and loudly enough to be heard.
- Your answers to questions must be truthful.
- If you are commanded to produce any items, you must bring them with you to court or to the deposition.
- You must continue to attend court until released by the court. You must continue to attend a deposition until the deposition is completed.

BRIBING OR THREATENING A WITNESS

It is a violation of State law for anyone to attempt to bribe, threaten, harass, or intimidate a witness. If anyone attempts to do any of these things concerning your involvement as a witness in a case, you should promptly report that to the district attorney or the presiding judge.

WITNESS FEE

A witness under subpoena and that appears in court to testify, is entitled to a small daily fee, and to travel expense reimbursement, if it is necessary to travel outside the county in order to testify. (The fee for an "expert witness" will be set by the presiding judge.) After you have been discharged as a witness, if you desire to collect the statutory fee, you should immediately contact the Clerk's office and certify to your attendance as a witness so that you will be paid any amount due you.

AOC-G-100, Side Two, Rev. 10/03
2003 Administrative Office of the Courts

Appendix C. Sample Letter to Accompany Records Sent to Court in Response to Sample Subpoena for Medical Records Without Authorization and Without Court Order or Other Authority to Inspect

Instructions:

- Place the subpoenaed records and an affidavit certifying their authenticity in a sealed envelope. Mark the outside of the sealed envelope: "To remain sealed until otherwise ordered by the presiding Judge at the trial (or hearing) of [Case name and file number]".
- Attach the following letter to the exterior of the sealed envelope containing the records and the authenticating affidavit.
- Place the sealed envelope and attached letter in a separate envelope addressed to 'Presiding Judge' in care of the Clerk of Superior Court for the County in which the action is pending.

Date

Superior or District Court Judge Presiding over Trial (or Hearing)

Clerk of Superior Court, Civil or Criminal Division

Address

Re: Case Caption

Name of Patient:

Dear Presiding Judge:

The records of our patient, (name), have been subpoenaed to the trial (or hearing) above-captioned by, (name of subpoenaing, attorney or party), who has not presented us with evidence of legal authority or authorization to inspect, copy, or disclose these records. Therefore, we are sending these records to you sealed and marked "To remain sealed until otherwise ordered by the presiding Judge at the trial (or hearing) above-captioned." We ask that these records remain sealed from inspection until it is judicially determined that the subpoenaing party may lawfully unseal and inspect them. Thank you for your attention to this request.

Sincerely yours,

Medical Records Custodian

Enclosure (sealed records)

Appendix D. Affidavit of Medical Record Custodian

STATE OF NORTH CAROLINA	IN THE GENERAL COURT OF JUSTICE [SUPERIOR or DISTRICT] COURT DIVISION
COUNTY OF ________	FILE NO.: _____

(NAME OF PLAINTIFF))
)
Plaintiff;)
vs.) **AFFIDAVIT OF MEDICAL RECORD CUSTODIAN**
(NAME OF DEFENDANT))
)
Defendant.)

__________, being first duly sworn, deposes and says that I am a custodian of records for NAME OF FACILITY and the attached records are:

1. A true and accurate copy of the medical records incurred for the medical treatment of NAME OF PATIENT;

2. These records were made and kept in the regular course of business at or near the time of the acts, conditions, or events recorded; and

3. They were made by persons having knowledge of the information set forth in those records.

____
AFFIANT

Subscribed and sworn to before me, this_____ day of __________, 20_____.

____
NOTARY PUBLIC
My commission expires:__________
NOTARY SEAL

Appendix E. Sample Letter Requesting Medical Records

Date

Health Care Provider or Facility Name and Address

Attn.: Medical Records Custodian

RE: Names: ≪John Patient≫

DOB:

SS#:

Dear Medical Records Custodian:

Please be advised that this law firm has been authorized to obtain the medical records of ≪John Patient≫. Enclosed is an authorization for the release of medical records.[1]

[Optional] If the case involves a personal injury liability claim, the letter must so indicate and should reference the statutory charges at the time:

These records are sought with regard to a personal injury liability claim. **N.C. Gen. Stat § 90–411 (2005) sets the maximum charges permissible for medical records requested in personal injury liability claims as follows:** "The maximum fee for each request shall be seventy-five (75) cents per page for the first 25 pages, fifty (50) cents per page for pages 26 through 100, and twenty-five (25) cents for each page in excess of 100 pages, provided that the health care provider may impose a minimum fee of up to ten dollars ($10.00), inclusive of copying costs."

Please forward to the office of the undersigned counsel the following items:

1. A complete copy of all medical records, as defined in the *2005 Medico–Legal Guidelines*,[2] including laboratory reports, interpretations of all diagnostic images and studies, and all other information in your possession regarding ≪John Patient≫;

2. All billing information, including ledger cards, insurance claim forms, etc., whether stored on paper or in electronic format, as the same pertains to medical services rendered to ≪John Patient≫. (For additional information, see Appendix A–1); and

3. All correspondence, whether stored on paper or in electronic format, to and from any other person or entity concerning ≪John Patient≫.

[Optional] Our firm's check will be forwarded to you upon receipt of your bill for any copying costs consistent with fees set out in North Carolina General Statute § 90–411, a copy of which is attached for your information.

[Optional] Please note that, in the event that you wish to preserve a provider's lien created by N.C.G.S. §§ 44–49 and 44–50, you must provide, without charge, a copy of the records and billing information requested above.

Thank you for your assistance.

Law & Jones, PLLC

1 Lawyers Drive

Anytown, North Carolina

PLEASE NOTE FOR WORKERS' COMPENSATION CASES SPECIAL RULES APPLY: This form is suggested for personal injury cases pending in the Courts. Special rules apply to Workers' Compensation cases. When a health care provider bills an employer's compensation insurance carrier or third-party administrator (adjusting agency), one free copy of medical records associated with the services must be provided, unless arrangements have been made to provide the free copy to a rehabilitation nurse. Fees for additional copies to these or other parties are set by the N.C. Industrial Commission (as an exception to N.C. Gen. Stat. § 90–411, codified at § 97–26.1) at a maximum of $.50 per page for the first 40 pages, and $.20 per page for additional pages, with an allowable minimum fee of $10.00 (inclusive of per page charges). (See January 12, 1995, *Minutes* of the N.C. Industrial Commission.) Industrial Commission Rule 607 provides that, if requested, parties must provide each other with copies of medical and rehabilitation records in their possession within 30 days, and with copies of additional records they obtain thereafter within 15 days after they come into the party's possession.

[1] See N.C. Gen. Stat. § 8-53 to determine who should execute authorizations regarding decedents.

[2] **"Medical Record" Defined**: The medical record is a collection of protected health information for a particular individual, that: is created or received by a physician or other health care provider; relates to the past, present, or future physical or mental health or condition of the individual; and includes information about the provision of health care to that individual and the past, present, or future payments by or on behalf of that individual for the provision of health care. Medical records are inherently sensitive and personal and contain information that relates to an individual's physical or mental condition, medical history, medical diagnosis, or medical treatment as well as demographic and other information that identifies or has the potential to identify the individual (e.g., patient name, address, social security number, unique identifier, etc.).

Appendix F. Selected Statements of the North Carolina Medical Board

- The Physician–Patient Relationship
- Medical Record Documentation
- Access to Medical Records
- Retention of Medical Records

THE PHYSICIAN–PATIENT RELATIONSHIP

The North Carolina Medical Board recognizes the movement toward restructuring the delivery of health care and the significant needs that motivate that movement. The resulting changes are providing a wider range and variety of health care delivery options to the public. Notwithstanding these developments in health care delivery, the duty of the physician remains the same: to provide competent, compassionate, and economically prudent care to all his or her patients. Whatever the health care setting, the Board holds that the physician's fundamental relationship is always with the patient, just as the Board's relationship is always with the individual physician. Having assumed care of a patient, the physician may not neglect that patient nor fail for any reason to prescribe the full care that patient requires in accord with the standards of acceptable medical practice. Further, it is the Board's position that it is unethical for a physician to allow financial incentives or contractual ties of any kind to adversely affect his or her medical judgment or patient care.

Therefore, it is the position of the North Carolina Medical Board that any act by a physician that violates or may violate the trust a patient places in the physician places the relationship between physician and patient at risk. This is true whether such an act is entirely self-determined or the result of the physician's contractual relationship with a health care entity. The Board believes the interests and health of the people of North Carolina are best served when the physician-patient relationship remains inviolate. The physician who puts the physician-patient relationship at risk also puts his or her relationship with the Board in jeopardy.

Elements of the Physician–Patient Relationship

The North Carolina Medical Board licenses physicians as a part of regulating the practice of medicine in this state. Receiving a license to practice medicine grants the physician privileges and imposes great responsibilities. The people of North Carolina expect a licensed physician to be competent and worthy of their trust. As patients, they come to the physician in a vulnerable condition, believing the physician has knowledge and skill that will be used for their benefit.

Patient trust is fundamental to the relationship thus established. It requires that:

- There be adequate communication between the physician and the patient;
- The physician report all significant findings to the patient or the patient's legally designated surrogate/guardian/personal representative;
- There be no conflict of interest between the patient and the physician or third parties;
- personal details of the patient's life shared with the physician be held in confidence;
- The physician maintain professional knowledge and skills;
- There be respect for the patient's autonomy;
- The physician be compassionate;
- The physician respect the patient's right to request further restrictions on medical information disclosure and to request alternative communications;
- The physician be an advocate for needed medical care, even at the expense of the physician's personal interests; and
- The physician provide neither more nor less than the medical problem requires.

The Board believes the interests and health of the people of North Carolina are best served when the physician–patient relationship, founded on patient trust, is considered sacred, and when the elements crucial to that relationship and to that trust—communication, patient primacy, confidentiality, competence, patient autonomy, compassion, selflessness, appropriate care—are foremost in the hearts, minds, and actions of the physicians licensed by the Board.

This same fundamental physician–patient relationship also applies to mid-level health care providers such as physician assistants and nurse practitioners in all practice settings.

Termination of the Physician–Patient Relationship

The Board recognizes the physician's right to choose patients and to terminate the professional relationship with them when he or she believes it is best to do so. That being understood, the Board maintains that termination of the physician-patient relationship must be done in compliance with the physician's obligation to support continuity of care for the patient.

The decision to terminate the relationship must be made by the physician personally. Further, termination must be accompanied by appropriate written notice given by the physician to the patient or the patient's representative sufficiently far in advance (at least 30 days) to allow other medical care to be secured. Should the physician be a member of a group, the notice of termination must state clearly whether the termination involves only the individual physician or includes other members of the group. In the latter case, those members of the group joining in the termination must be designated. It is advisable that the notice of termination also include instructions for transfer of or access to the patient's medical records.

(Adopted July 1995)

(Amended July 1998, January 2000; March 2002, August 2003)

MEDICAL RECORD DOCUMENTATION

North Carolina Medical Board takes the position that physicians and physician extenders should maintain accurate patient care records of history, physical findings, assessments of findings, and the plan for treatment. The Board recommends the Problem Oriented Medical Record method known as SOAP (developed by Lawrence Weed).

SOAP charting is a schematic recording of facts and information. The S refers to "subjective information" (patient history and testimony about feelings). The O refers to objective material and measurable data (height, weight, respiration rate, temperature, and all examination findings). The A is the assessment of the subjective and objective material that can be the diagnosis but is always the total impression formed by the care provided after review of all materials gathered. And finally, the P is the treatment plan presented in sufficient detail to allow another care provider to follow the plan to completion. The plan should include a follow-up schedule.

Such a chronological document

- records pertinent facts about an individual's health and wellness;
- enables the treating care provider to plan and evaluate treatments or interventions;

- enhances communication between professionals, assuring the patient optimum continuity of care;
- assists both patient and physician to communicate to third party participants;
- allows the physician to develop an ongoing quality assurance program;
- provides a legal document to verify the delivery of care; and
- is available as a source of clinical data for research and education.

Certain items should appear in the medical record as a matter of course:

- The purpose of the patient encounter;
- The assessment of patient condition;
- The services delivered—in full detail;
- The rationale for the requirement of any support services;
- The results of therapies or treatments;
- The plan for continued care;
- whether or not informed consent was obtained; and, finally,
- that the delivered services were appropriate for the condition of the patient.

The record should be legible. When the care giver will not write legibly, notes should be dictated, transcribed, reviewed, and signed within reasonable time. Signature, date, and time should also be legible. All therapies should be documented as to indications, method of delivery, and response of the patient. Special instructions given to other care givers or the patient should be documented: Who received the instructions and did they appear to understand them?

All drug therapies should be named, with dosage instructions and indication of refill limits. All medications a patient receives from all sources should be inventoried and listed to include the method by which the patient understands they are to be taken. Any refill prescription by phone should be recorded in full detail.

The physician needs and the patient deserves clear and complete documentation.

(Adopted 5/94)

(Amended 5/96)

ACCESS TO MEDICAL RECORDS

A physician's policies and practices relating to medical records under their control should be designed to benefit the health and welfare of patients, whether current or past, and should facilitate the transfer of clear and reliable information about a patient's care. Such policies and practices should conform to applicable federal and state laws governing health information.

It is the position of the North Carolina Medical Board that notes made by a physician in the course of diagnosing and treating patients are primarily for the physician's use and to promote continuity of care. Patients, however, have a substantial right of access to their medical records and a qualified right to amend their records pursuant to the HIPAA privacy regulations.

Medical records are confidential documents and should only be released when permitted by law or with proper written authorization of the patient. Physicians are responsible for safeguarding and protecting the medical record and for providing adequate security measures.

Each physician has a duty on the request of a patient or the patient's representative to release a copy of the record in a timely manner to the patient or the patient's representative, unless the physician believes that such release would endanger the patient's life or cause harm to another person. This includes medical records received from other physician offices or health care facilities. A summary may be provided in lieu of providing access to or copies of medical records only if the patient agrees in advance to such a summary and to any fees imposed for its production.

Physicians may charge a reasonable fee for the preparation and/or the photocopying of medical and other records. To assist in avoiding misunderstandings, and for a reasonable fee, the physician should be willing to review the medical records with the patient at the patient's request. Medical records should not be withheld because an account is overdue or a bill is owed (including charges for copies or summaries of medical records).

Should it be the physician's policy to complete insurance or other forms for established patients, it is the position of the Board that the physician should complete those forms in a timely manner. If a form is simple, the physician should perform this task for no fee. If a form is complex, the physician may charge a reasonable fee.

To prevent misunderstandings, the physician's policies about providing copies or summaries of medical records and about completing forms should be made available in writing to patients when the physician-patient relationship begins.

Physicians should not relinquish control over their patients' medical records to third parties unless there is an enforceable agreement that includes adequate provisions to protect patient confidentiality and to ensure access to those records.[1]

When responding to subpoenas for medical records, unless there is a court or administrative order, physicians should follow the applicable federal regulations.

(Adopted November 1993)

(Amended May 1996, September 1997, March 2002, August 2003)

RETENTION OF MEDICAL RECORDS

The North Carolina Medical Board supports and adopts the following language of Section 7.05 of the American Medical Association's current *Code of Medical Ethics* regarding the retention of medical records by physicians.

7.05: Retention of Medical Records

Physicians have an obligation to retain patient records which may reasonably be of value to a patient. The following guidelines are offered to assist physicians in meeting their ethical and legal obligations:

1. Medical considerations are the primary basis for deciding how long to retain medical records, For example, operative notes and chemotherapy records should always be part of the patient's chart. In deciding whether to keep certain parts of the record, an appropriate criterion is whether a physician would want the information if he or she were seeing the patient for the first time.

2. If a particular record no longer needs to be kept for medical reasons, the physician should check state laws to see if there is a requirement that records be kept for a minimum length of time. Most states will not have such a provision. If they do, it will be part of the statutory code or state licensing board.

3. In all cases, medical records should be kept for at least as long as the length of time of the statute of limitations for medical malpractice claims. The statute of limitations may be three or more years, depending on the state law. State medical associations and insurance carriers are the best resources for this information.

4. Whatever the statute of limitations, a physician should measure time from the last professional contact with the patient.

5. If a patient is a minor, the statute of limitations for medical malpractice claims may not apply until the patient reaches the age of majority.

6. Immunization records always must be kept.

7. The record of any patient covered by Medicare or Medicaid must be kept at least five years.

8. In order to preserve confidentiality when discarding old records, all documents should be destroyed.

9. Before discarding old records, patients should be given an opportunity to claim the records or have them sent to another physician, if it is feasible to give them the opportunity.

Please Note:

(a.) North Carolina has no statute relating specifically to the retention of medical records.

(b.) Several North Carolina statutes relate to time limitations for the filing of malpractice actions. Legal advice should be sought regarding such limitations.

(Adopted 5/98)

1. See also Position Statement on Departures from or Closings of Medical Practices.

Appendix G–1. Sample Authorization Form to Use and Disclose Health Information

(Meets federal and North Carolina state law requirements for disclosure of mental health and substance abuse records)

Individual's name: **Date of Birth:** ______________

____

Individual's address: **Individual's ID#:** ______________

____

____

I hereby voluntarily authorize the use and disclosure of my protected health information as described below:

1. Specific description of the information to be used or disclosed:

____

____

The above information will be called "authorized information" throughout the rest of this form.

2. Person (or class of persons) authorized to make the use or disclosure of authorized information:

____

____

3. Person (or class of persons) to whom the use or disclosure of authorized information may be made:

____

____

4. Authorized information will be used and/or disclosed for the following purpose(s):

____

____

5. This authorization expires (must be no longer than reasonable to accomplish purposes in Paragraph 4):

____

6. Furthermore, by signing below, I understand that:

- my personal information will be released to the person or class of persons listed above;
- this information may include information regarding mental health, drugs & alcohol, HIV/AIDS and other communicable diseases, and/or genetic testing (unless specifically excluded above);
- I may revoke this authorization at any time by a written notification of my desire to revoke it to the medical provider named in number 2 above;
- any action already taken in reliance on this authorization cannot be reversed, and my revocation will not affect those actions;
- the medical provider named in number 2 above may not condition its treatment of me on whether or not I sign this authorization; and
- information released may no longer be protected by federal privacy regulations except information concerning substance abuse is subject to the following requirements:

- This information has been disclosed from records protected by Federal confidentiality rules (42 CFR Part 2). The Federal rules prohibit making any further disclosure of this information unless further disclosure is expressly permitted by the written consent of the person to whom it pertains or as otherwise permitted by 42 CFR Part 2. A general authorization for the release of medical or other information is NOT sufficient for this purpose.

Individual's Signature ____________________ **Date:** ______________________

[Revised 2008.]

Appendix G–2. Authorization Form to Use and Disclose Protected Health Information

(By Authorized Personal Representative)

(Meets federal and North Carolina state law requirements for disclosure of mental health and substance abuse records)

Patient's name: _______________ **Date of birth:** _______________

Representative's name and address: _____ **Relationship:** _______________

____

______________________________ **Patient's ID #:** _______________

____

On behalf of _______________, I hereby voluntarily authorize the use and
(patient name)
disclosure of his/her protected health information:

1. Specific description of the information to be used or disclosed:

____

____

The above information will be called "authorized information" throughout the rest of this form.

2. Person (or class of persons) authorized to make the use or disclosure of authorized information:

____

____

3. Person (or class of persons) to whom the use or disclosure of authorized information may be made:

____

____

4. Authorized information will be used and/or disclosed for the following purpose(s):

____

____

5. This authorization expires (must be no longer than reasonable to accomplish purposes in Paragraph 4):

____

6. Furthermore, by signing below, I understand that:

- the personal information will be released to the person or persons listed in number 3 above;
- this information may include information regarding mental health, drugs & alcohol, HIV/AIDS and other communicable diseases, and/or genetic testing (unless specifically excluded above);
- I may revoke this authorization at any time by a written notification of my desire to revoke it to the medical provider named in number 2 above;
- any action already taken in reliance on this authorization cannot be reversed, and my revocation will not affect those actions;
- the medical provider named in number 2 above may not condition treatment of _______________ on whether or not I sign this
(patient name)
authorization; and

- information released may no longer be protected by federal privacy regulations except information concerning substance abuse treatment is subject to the following requirements:
  - This information has been disclosed from records protected by Federal confidentiality rules (42 CFR Part 2). The Federal rules prohibit making any further disclosure of this information unless further disclosure is expressly permitted by the written consent of the person to whom it pertains or as otherwise permitted by 42 CFR Part 2. A general authorization for the release of medical or other information is NOT sufficient for this purpose.

Personal Representative's signature __________________ Date: __________

[Revised 2008.]

Appendix G-3. Sample Authorization Form to Use and Disclose Health Information Regarding Psychotherapy Notes

Individual's name: ________________ **Date of birth:** ________________

____

Individual's address: ________________ **Individual's ID#:** ________________

____

____

I hereby voluntarily authorize the use and disclosure of my protected health information regarding psychotherapy notes defined in 45 CFR 164.501 as follows and as described below:

"Psychotherapy notes means notes records (in any medium) by a health care provider who is a mental health professional documenting or analyzing the contents of conversation during a private counseling session or a group, joint, or family counseling session and that are separated from the rest of the individual's medical record.

Psychotherapy notes excludes medication prescription and monitoring, counseling session start and stop times, the modalities and frequencies of treatment furnished, results of clinical tests, and any summary of the following items: Diagnosis, functional status, the treatment plan, symptoms, prognosis, and progress to date."

1. Specific description of the information to be used or disclosed:

____

____

____

The above information will be called "authorized information" throughout the rest of this form.

2. Person (or class of persons) authorized to make the use or disclosure of authorized information:

____

____

____

3. Person (or class of persons) to whom the use or disclosure of authorized information may be made:

____

____

____

4. Authorized information will be used and/or disclosed for the following purpose(s):

____

____

____

5. This authorization expires: ________________

6. Furthermore, by signing below, I understand that:

- my personal information will be released to the person or class of persons listed above;

- this information includes information regarding psychotherapy notes as defined above;
- I may revoke this authorization by a written notification of my desire to revoke it to the medical provider named in number 2 above;
- any action already taken in reliance on this authorization cannot be reversed, and my revocation will not affect those actions;
- the medical provider named in number 2 above may not condition its treatment of me on whether or not I sign this authorization; and
- information released may no longer be protected by federal privacy regulations.

Individual's Signature ______ Date: ______

[Added 2008.]

Appendix G–4. Authorization Form to Use and Disclose Protected Health Information Regarding Psychotherapy Notes

(By Authorized Personal Representative)

Patient's name: ______________ **Date of birth:** ______________

Representative's name and address: ______ **Relationship:** ______________

____

______________ **Patient's ID #:** ______________

On behalf of ______________, I hereby voluntarily authorize the use and
(patient name)
disclosure of his/her protected health information regarding psychotherapy notes defined in 45 CFR 164.501 as follows and as described below:

"Psychotherapy notes means notes records (in any medium) by a health care provider who is a mental health professional documenting or analyzing the contents of conversation during a private counseling session or a group, joint, or family counseling session and that are separated from the rest of the individual's medical record.

Psychotherapy notes excludes medication prescription and monitoring, counseling session start and stop times, the modalities and frequencies of treatment furnished, results of clinical tests, and any summary of the following items: Diagnosis, functional status, the treatment plan."

1. Specific description of the information to be used or disclosed:

____

____

____

The above information will be called "authorized information" throughout the rest of this form.

2. Person (or class of persons) authorized to make the use or disclosure of authorized information:

____

____

____

3. Person (or class of persons) to whom the use or disclosure of authorized information may be made:

____

____

____

4. Authorized information will be used and/or disclosed for the following purpose(s):

____

____

____

5. This authorization expires: ______________

6. Furthermore, by signing below, I understand that:

- the personal information will be released to the person or persons listed in number 3 above;
- this information includes information regarding psychotherapy notes as defined above;

- I may revoke this authorization by a written notification of my desire to revoke it to the medical provider named in number 2 above;
- any action already taken in reliance on this authorization cannot be reversed, and my revocation will not affect those actions;
- the medical provider named in number 2 above may not condition treatment of ______________ on whether or not I sign this
(patient name)
authorization; and
- information released may no longer be protected by federal privacy regulations.

Personal Representative's signature ______________ Date: ________

[Added 2008.]

Appendix H. North Carolina Laws Addressing Licensed Professionals and Other Designated Officials Authorization To Disclose Confidential Information or Protected Health Information

NCGS § 7B–302 Confidential information disclosed by a director of the department of social services to any federal, State, or local governmental entity, or its agent pursuant to mandated responsibilities shall not be redisclosed except for purposes connected with carrying out their mandated responsibilities.

NCGS § 7B–601 Guardian ad litem may obtain confidential information or reports regarding abused or neglected juvenile

NCGS § 8–53.3 Psychologist shall not disclose confidential information obtained in the course of rendering professional services unless compelled by court order or statutory duty to report suspected abuse or neglect

NCGS § 8–53.4 School counselor shall not disclose confidential information obtained in the course of rendering professional services unless compelled by court order or student waives privilege

NCGS § 8–53.5 Licensed marital and family therapists, or any of the person's employees or associates, shall not disclose confidential information obtained in the course of rendering professional services unless compelled by court order

NCGS § 8–53.7 Social worker shall not disclose confidential information obtained in the course of rendering professional services unless compelled by court order

NCGS § 8–53.8 Counselor shall not disclose confidential information obtained in the course of rendering professional services unless compelled by court order

NCGS § 8–53.9 Optometrist shall not disclose confidential information obtained the course of rendering professional services unless compelled by court order

NCGS § 8–53.10 Peer support group counselor privilege shall not be grounds for the failure to report suspected child abuse or neglect to the appropriate county department of social services, or for failure to report a disabled adult suspected to be in need of protective services to the appropriate county department of social services by the law enforcement officer or civilian employee of a law enforcement agency who also services in the capacity of a peer support group counselor

NCGS § 8–53.13 Nurse shall not disclose confidential information obtained in the course of rendering professional nursing services unless compelled by court order

[Added 2008.]

Appendix I. Sample Court Order Allowing Release of Mental Health, Substance Abuse, and/or Psychotherapy Records Including Protected Health Information Pursuant to 42 CFR 2.64

____

Plaintiff

vs.

____

Defendant

This cause coming on to be heard upon motion of (Petitioner) for release of mental health or substance abuse records including protected health information; and this Court having considered the pleadings and the arguments of counsel; this Court makes the following:

FINDINGS OF FACT

1. (Petitioner) seeks substance records including protected health information because (state reason).

2. The patient and person from whom disclosure is sought has been given adequate notice in a manner which will not disclose patient identifying information to other persons and an opportunity to file a written response to the application, or to appear in person, for the limited purpose of providing evidence on the statutory and regulatory criteria for the issuance of the court order.

Based upon the foregoing Findings of Fact, this Court makes the following:

CONCLUSIONS OF LAW

1. Disclosure of the requested mental health or substance abuse protected health information sought is not otherwise available or would not be effective.

2. The public interest and need for the disclosure of the requested mental health or substance abuse protected health information outweigh the potential injury to the patient, the physician-patient relationship and the treatment services.

Based upon the foregoing Conclusions of Law, it is therefore Ordered that:

ORDER

1. The person from whom disclosure is sought provide the requested mental health or substance abuse protected health information to (petitioner) limiting disclosure to those parts of the patient's record which are essential to fulfill the objective of the order.

2. The requested mental health or substance abuse protected health information be provided limiting disclosure to those persons whose need for information is the basis for the order.

3. The requested mental health or substance abuse protected health information disclosed to (petitioner) pursuant to this court order included in the records of this proceeding shall be sealed. (optional)

This the ___ day of __________, ___.

____

Judge's Signature

[Added 2008.]

The North Carolina Industrial Commission rules have been moved to be part of the North Carolina Administrative Code. They are now published in Title 4, Chapter 10, of the North Carolina Administrative Code. See below for subchapters.

Subchapter A: Workers' Compensation Rules

Subchapter B: Tort Claims Rules

Subchapter C: Rules for Utilization of Rehabilitation Professionals in Workers' Compensation Claims

Subchapter D: Workers' Compensation for Managed Care Organizations

Subchapter E: Administrative Rules of the Industrial Commission

Subchapter F: Electronic Billing Rules

Subchapter G: Rules for Mediated Settlement and Neutral Evaluation Conferences

Subchapter H: Rules of the Industrial Commission Relating to the Law-Enforcement Officers', Firemen's, Rescue Squad Workers' and Civil Air Patrol Members' Death Benefits Act

Subchapter I: Childhood Vaccine-Related Injury Rules of the North Carolina Industrial Commission

Subchapter J: Fees for Medical Compensation

Subchapter K: Rules for the Eugenics Asexualization and Sterilization Compensation Program

Subchapter I: Industrial Commission Forms

GUIDELINES FOR RESOLVING SCHEDULING CONFLICTS

IN ORDER TO PROVIDE A UNIFORM STANDARD FOR THE RESOLUTION OF SCHEDULING CONFLICTS BETWEEN AND AMONG THE STATE AND FEDERAL TRIAL AND APPELLATE COURTS OF NORTH CAROLINA THE FOLLOWING GUIDELINES ARE HEREBY ESTABLISHED:

1. It shall be the duty of counsel, other than solo practitioners, to have another member of the firm reasonably well acquainted with the case to the end that, where practicable, substitution of counsel may be made in order to avoid conflict.

2. In resolving scheduling conflicts the following priorities should ordinarily prevail:

a. Appellate cases should prevail over trial cases;

b. The case in which the trial date has been first set (by published calendar, order or notice) should take precedence;

c. Criminal felony trials should prevail over civil trials;

d. Trials should prevail over motion hearings.

e. In resolving conflicts between the several divisions of the North Carolina General Court of Justice, the provisions of Rule 3, General Rules of Practice for the Superior and District Courts, shall control.

3. In addition to the above priorities, consideration should be given to the comparative age of the cases, their complexity, the estimated trial time, the number of attorneys and parties involved, whether the trial involves a jury, and the difficulty or ease of rescheduling.

4. It shall be the duty of an attorney promptly upon learning of a scheduling conflict to give written notice to opposing counsel, the clerk of all courts and the presiding judges, if known, in all cases, stating therein the circumstances relevant to a resolution of the conflict under these guidelines.

5. The judges of the courts involved in a scheduling conflict shall promptly confer, resolve the conflict, and notify counsel of the resolution.

6. If the judges of the courts involved are unable to resolve the conflict they shall so notify the chairman of the State-Federal Judicial Council of North Carolina. The chairman and vice-chairman of the State-Federal Judicial Council of North Carolina shall then resolve the conflict.

7. Nothing in these guidelines is intended to prevent courts from voluntarily yielding a favorable scheduling position, and judges of all courts are urged to communicate with each other in an effort to lessen the impact of conflicts and continuances on all courts.

ADOPTED by the State-Federal Judicial Council of North Carolina on this the 20th day of June 1985.

J. RICH LEONARD
Secretary

Approved by the respective courts on the dates indicated.

THE UNITED STATES COURT OF APPEALS FOR THE FOURTH CIRCUIT

July 8, 1985 — HARRISON L. WINTER, Chief Judge

THE SUPREME COURT OF NORTH CAROLINA

July 26, 1985 — JOSEPH BRANCH, Chief Justice

THE UNITED STATES DISTRICT COURT FOR THE EASTERN DISTRICT OF NORTH CAROLINA

June 27, 1985 — W. EARL BRITT, Chief Judge

THE UNITED STATES DISTRICT COURT FOR THE MIDDLE DISTRICT OF NORTH CAROLINA

July 16, 1985 — HIRAM H. WARD, Chief Judge

THE UNITED STATES DISTRICT COURT FOR THE WESTERN DISTRICT OF NORTH CAROLINA

July 17, 1985 — ROBERT D. POTTER, Chief Judge